RESEARCH HANDBOOK ON ENVIRONMENT, HEALTH AND THE WTO

RESEARCH HANDBOOKS ON THE WTO

This timely series of *Research Handbooks* analyses the interface between international economic law and other disciplines at the centre of current debate about the role and impact of the WTO. Each volume is edited by a prominent expert at the heart of this debate and brings together original contributions from an internationally recognisable cast of leading scholars and practitioners.

These *Handbooks* will be essential reference tools for academic researchers and doctoral students as well as for policymakers and practicing lawyers.

Titles in this series include:

Research Handbook on the Protection of Intellectual Property under WTO Rules
Intellectual Property in the WTO, Volume I
Edited by Carlos M. Correa

Research Handbook on the Interpretation and Enforcement of Intellectual Property under WTO Rules
Intellectual Property in the WTO, Volume II
Edited by Carlos M. Correa

Research Handbook on the WTO Agriculture Agreement
New and Emerging Issues in International Agricultural Trade Law
Edited by Joseph A. McMahon and Melaku Genboye Desta

Research Handbook on Environment, Health and the WTO
Edited by Geert Van Calster and Denise Prévost

Research Handbook on Environment, Health and the WTO

Edited by

Geert Van Calster

KU Leuven, Belgium

and

Denise Prévost

Maastricht University, The Netherlands

RESEARCH HANDBOOKS ON THE WTO

Edward Elgar
Cheltenham, UK • Northampton, MA, USA

Published by
Edward Elgar Publishing Limited
The Lypiatts
15 Lansdown Road
Cheltenham
Glos GL50 2JA
UK

Edward Elgar Publishing, Inc.
William Pratt House
9 Dewey Court
Northampton
Massachusetts 01060
USA

A catalogue record for this book
is available from the British Library

Library of Congress Control Number: 2009941097

This book is available electronically in the ElgarOnline.com Law Subject Collection, E-ISBN 978 1 78100 614 6

ISBN 978 1 84720 897 2 (cased)

Typeset by Servis Filmsetting Ltd, Stockport, Cheshire
Printed by MPG PRINTGROUP, UK

Contents

PART III   ENVIRONMENTAL REGULATION AND TRADE
           LAW

Section 1   Climate Change Mitigation

Section 2   Other Than Climate Change

Contributors

Alberto Alemanno is Associate Professor of Law at HEC Paris where he holds a Jean Monnet Chair in EU and Risk Regulation as well as Adjunct Professor at Georgetown Law where he teaches Global Risk Regulation. Formerly *Référendaire* (clerk) at the Court of Justice of the European Union and Teaching Assistant at the College of Europe in Bruges. He has published widely in the areas of EU law, international economic law and risk regulation, including the books *Trade in Food – Regulatory and Judicial Approaches in the EU and the WTO* (Cameron May, 2007), *Governing Disasters – The Challenges of Emergency Risk Regulation* (Edward Elgar, 2011) and *Better Business Regulation in a Risk Society* (Springer, 2012). His latest edited volume is *New Directions in European Food Law – The First Ten Years of the European Food Safety Authority* (Ashgate, 2013).

He is the founder and editor of the *European Journal of Risk Regulation* as well as the scientific director of the Summer Academy in Global Food Law & Policy. Originally from Italy, Alemanno earned a law degree cum laude from the Università degli Studi di Torino, LL.M. degrees from Harvard Law School and the College of Europe, and a Ph.D. in International Law and Economics from Bocconi University. For more information see: www.albertoalemanno.eu.

Alessandra Arcuri is Associate Professor of Law and Economics and of International Economic Law at the Erasmus School of Law. Her research focuses on risk law, international economic law and law and economics. Previous research positions and awards include: Jean Monnet Fellow at the European University Institute (EUI), Florence (project on the regulation of organic products); Global Fellow at NYU Law School (project on the precautionary principle); Marie Curie Fellow at Hamburg University (project on the role of Coase's theory in environmental law); EUR Fellowship at Erasmus University (project on multi-level risk regulation and the WTO). Dr. Arcuri has taught courses in several universities in the world, including Lund University, African Universities in Lomè, Luiss Guido Carli University, in Rome, and the University of Siena. She holds a law degree from La Sapienza University, Rome, an LL.M. from Utrecht University and a Ph.D. from the Erasmus School of Law.

Jeffery Atik is Professor of Law at Loyola Law School in Los Angeles. He writes on international trade, international intellectual property and regulatory competition issues. Prior to joining the Loyola faculty in 2001, he was Professor of Law at Suffolk University Law School in Boston. He has also taught at Berkeley, Boston College, Indiana-Bloomington, UCLA, Washington-St. Louis and The Fletcher School of Law and Diplomacy. Professor Atik has served on three NAFTA binational panels reviewing antidumping cases, including the review in *Softwood Lumber from Canada*. He practiced law with Shearman & Sterling (New York); Testa Hurwitz (Boston); and Brown & Dobson (Milan). He is a member of the New York, Connecticut, Massachusetts and Missouri bars.

Heike Baumüller is a Ph.D. researcher with the Centre for Development Research at the University of Bonn where she examines the role of mobile phones in raising agricultural productivity among smallholder farmers. From 2008–2009, she was a Senior Research Fellow with the Energy, Environment and Development Programme at Chatham House, focusing on the environmental and socio-economic dimensions of trade in natural resources. Prior to joining Chatham House, Ms. Baumüller worked as an independent consultant in Cambodia (2007–2008) where she conducted research on the impacts of trade and investment policies on sustainable development. From 2000 to 2006, she coordinated the Environment and Natural Resources Programme and led the implementation of projects on fisheries and biotechnology at the International Centre for Trade and Sustainable Development (ICTSD) in Geneva. She holds a Master of Environmental Studies from Macquarie University, Sydney.

Javier de Cendra de Larragán is Dean of the IE Law School and Professor of EU law. He is also honorary senior research fellow at University College London, visiting professor at KU Leuven (until 2011), visiting professor at the University of Malta, legal expert at the Malta Forum on Legal Issues of Adaptation to Climate Change, and member of the international advisory board of CEID Colombia. Javier's fields of expertise span across environmental and energy law, with a particular focus on climate change. Javier has engaged intensively in research and consultancy on climate change and energy law.

Thomas Cottier is Managing Director of the World Trade Institute and the Institute of European and International Economic Law and Professor of European and International Economic Law at the University of Bern, Switzerland. He is the managing director of the World Trade Institute and directs the national research programme on trade law and policy (NCCR Trade Regulation: From Fragmentation to Coherence) located at the WTI. He was educated at the University of Bern, University of Michigan Law School, and was a visiting fellow at Cambridge University, UK. He taught at the University of St. Gallen, Neuchatel and the Geneva Graduate Institute in Geneva and also regularly teaches at the Europa Institut Saarbrücken, Germany, Paris I (Sorbonne), Turin University, Italy and Wuhan University, China. He was a member of the Swiss National Research Council from 1997 to 2004 and served on the board of the International Plant Genetic Resources Institute (IPGRI), Rome, during the same period. He served the Baker & McKenzie law firm as Of Counsel from 1998 to 2005. Professor Cottier has a long-standing involvement in GATT/WTO activities. He served on the Swiss negotiating team of the Uruguay Round from 1986 to 1993, first as Chief negotiator on dispute settlement and subsidies for Switzerland and subsequently as Chief negotiator on TRIPs. He was the Deputy-Director General of the Swiss Intellectual Property Office and served as a member or chair of several GATT and WTO panels. Professor Cottier has written and published on a wide range of trade, European law and international law issues. His main research interests are in constitutional theory of multi-level governance and theory of international law, external relations of the EU, intellectual property, innovation and the challenges of climate change in international economic law.

Kasturi Das is an economist and policy analyst presently based in New Delhi, India. Her current areas of research include trade policy and WTO-related issues, climate change policy, trade-climate interface, and technology transfer. She has published extensively in several peer-reviewed journals of repute and edited volumes. Dr. Das is presently working with the Research and Information System for Developing Countries (RIS), New Delhi as a Consultant in the rank of Associate Professor. She is also a visiting faculty at The Energy and Resources Institute (TERI) University; Foreign Service Institute (Ministry of External Affairs, Govt. of India); and Indian Society of International Law. She serves as a referee for several reputed journals, including the *World Development* and *Journal of World Intellectual Property*. Dr. Das was the 'Governance of Clean Development Visiting Fellow 2011' at the University of East Anglia, UK.

Panagiotis Delimatsis is Associate Professor of Law and Co-Director of the Tilburg Law and Economics Center (TILEC) at Tilburg University, the Netherlands. Dr. Delimatsis' research focuses on regulatory diversity, domestic regulatory reform, good governance and institutional design, and the effects of unduly burdensome domestic regulations on factor mobility. He has published extensively on international trade and European law issues in top refereed journals, including the *European*

Journal of International Law, the *Journal of International Economic Law*, the *Common Market Law Review*, the *Journal of World Trade* and the *World Trade Review*. He is the author of *International Trade in Services and Domestic Regulations – Necessity, Transparency, and Regulatory Diversity* (International Economic Law Series, Oxford University Press, 2007). Dr. Delimatsis also co-edited two collective volumes, the first on *The Prospects of International Trade Regulation* (Cambridge University Press, 2011) and the second on *Financial Services at the Crossroads – Implications for Supervision, Institutional Design and Trade* (Kluwer Law International, 2011).

Marsha A. Echols is the Director of The World Food Law Institute and a Professor at Howard University School of Law in Washington, D.C. She is the author of *Food Safety and the WTO: The Interplay of Culture, Science and Technology* and *Geographical Indications for Food Products: International Legal and Regulatory Perspectives* (both published by Kluwer Law International) and of several journal articles about international food regulation. Her research often assesses the international trade and regulatory consequences of differing national food cultures. Professor Echols is often involved in international dispute resolution, having served as a Panelist in a WTO dispute, as a Member of the United Nations Administrative Tribunal, and as Vice-Chair of the International Dispute Resolution Committee of the D.C. Bar. She is a member of the US Department of Agriculture's Agricultural Policy Advisory Committee (APAC), the Council on Foreign Relations and the Secretary of State's Advisory Committee on Private International Law. She is Liaison to UNIDROIT for the ABA Section of International Law. She is a member of the Board of Directors of the Woodstock Theological Center at Georgetown University and of the Friends of the National Arboretum, among others. A graduate of Howard University, she holds advanced degrees from Georgetown University Law Center (J.D.), the Free University of Brussels (LL.M.) and Columbia University Law School (LL.M., J.S.D.).

Tracey Epps is senior trade law adviser in the Legal Division of the New Zealand Ministry of Foreign Affairs and Trade. She is also a part-time Senior Lecturer on the Faculty of Law at the University of Otago. Tracey holds a B.A/LL.B.(Hons) from the University of Auckland and an LL.M. and S.J.D. from the University of Toronto. She is the author of *International Trade and Health Protection: A Critical Analysis of the WTO's Agreement on the Application of Sanitary and Phytosanitary Measures* (Edward Elgar, 2008) and is co-author (together with Andrew Green) of *Reconciling Trade and Climate Change: How the WTO Can Help Address Climate Change* (Edward Elgar, 2010).

Lukasz Gruszczynski is Assistant professor at the Institute of Legal Studies, Polish Academy of Sciences (Warsaw, Poland) and a guest lecturer in public international and European law at the Kozminski Academy. Dr. Gruszczynski is also a managing editor of the *Polish Yearbook of International Law* and a correspondent editor of the *European Journal of Risk Regulation*. His current research focuses on the use of science and scientific expertise in international law (in particular WTO law), international risk regulation and problems posed by technical barriers to trade. In 2010 he published a book with Oxford University Press (*Regulating Health and Environmental Risks under WTO Law. A Critical Analysis of the SPS Agreement*).

Alexia Herwig is Assistant Professor in the area of Subsidiarity and Multilevel Governance at the Faculty of Law of the University of Antwerp. Previously, she was an FWO post-doc fellow at the Centre for Law and Cosmopolitan Values at the University of Antwerp and a research fellow at the Collaborative Research Centre 'Transformations of the State' at the University of Bremen in the project on social regulation and world trade. She has researched and published widely on transnational food safety governance and WTO law. Her publications have appeared or are due to appear with *Global Policy*, the *Leiden Journal of International Law*, Hart and Brill.

Christian Joerges was a Professor of Economic Law at the European University Institute until 2007 and is since then Research Professor at the University of Bremen and Co-Director of the Centre for European Law and Politics. In the context of the Bremen Collaborative Research Centre on 'Transformations of the State', he is directing, together with Josef Falke, a project on the tensions between trade liberalisation and social regulation. From February 2013 onwards he will also hold a part-time senior professorship at the Hertie School of Governance in Berlin. His most noted book is *Darker Legacies of Law in Europe: The Shadow of National Socialism and Fascism over Europe and its Legal Traditions*, ed. with Navraj S. Galeigh (Hart Publishing, 2003). Recent publications include: *Constitutionalism Multilevel Trade Governance and International Economic law*, ed. with Ernst-Ulrich Petersmann (Hart Publishing, 2006, 2nd ed. 2011), *Karl Polanyi, Globalisation and the Potential of Law in Transnational Markets* edited with Josef Falke (Hart Publishing, 2011). 'Unity in Diversity as Europe's Vocation and Conflicts Law as Europe's Constitutional Form' in *The Changing Role of Law in the Age of Supra- and Transnational Governance*, ed. by Rainer Nickel and Andrea Greppi (Nomos, 2013), 99–133.

Bryan Mercurio is Professor of Law and Associate Dean (Research) at The Chinese University of Hong Kong. He is a specialist in international economic law, with particular expertise in WTO law, free trade agreements and the intersection between international trade and intellectual property law. He previously worked in the public and private sector as well as at the University of New South Wales (UNSW), where he was the Director of the International Trade and Development Project at the Gilbert + Tobin Centre of Public Law. He is currently a Professorial Visiting Fellow at UNSW, founding member and on the Executive Board of the Society of International Economic Law, founding member of the Asian International Economic Law Network and member of the Asian World Trade Organization Research Network.

Peter Morrison is presently senior legal counsellor in the WTO Trade in Services Division. He has provided legal advice to dispute settlement panels, the negotiators of the General Agreement on Trade in Services (GATS), and the judges of the WTO Appellate Body. He was educated at McGill University and the University of Paris, and previously worked in Canada's foreign ministry on economic and trade law issues. During his career, he has headed the World Trade Group of a UK-based international law firm, and taught part-time at the University of London.

Laura Nielsen holds her Ph.D. from the University of Copenhagen and her LL.M in International Trade Law from Roger's College of Law, University of Arizona. She is currently an Associate Professor of WTO Law at the Faculty of Law, University of Copenhagen. Her main research areas are trade and environment, animal welfare and climate change – but she also publishes on agricultural subsidies as well as her newest research topic: local content measures. She was formerly with the Danish Mission to the WTO in 2002, and a visiting scholar in the WTO in 2006.

Joost Pauwelyn is Professor of International Law at the Graduate Institute of International and Development Studies (IHEID) in Geneva, Switzerland and Co-Director of the Institute's Centre for Trade and Economic Integration (CTEI). He is also Senior Advisor with the law firm of King & Spalding LLC. His area of expertise is international economic law, in particular, the law of international trade and investment. Before joining the Graduate Institute in 2007, he was a tenured professor at Duke Law School, USA. He also served as legal officer at the WTO from 1996 to 2002 and practiced law at a major Brussels law firm. He received degrees from the Universities of Namur and Leuven, Belgium as well as Oxford University and holds a doctorate from the University of Neuchâtel. He is the author of, amongst other works, *International Trade Law* (2nd ed., 2012, with A. Guzman), *Conflict of Norms in Public International Law* (2003, winner of the Guggenheim Prize), *The Transformation of World Trade* (Michigan Law Review, 2005) and *Optimal Protection of International Law: Navigating between European Absolutism and American Voluntarism* (2008). He also edited books on *The Law, Economics and Politics of Retaliation in WTO Dispute Settlement* (2010, with C. Bown) and *Global Challenges at the Intersection of Trade, Energy and the Environment* (2010). During the academic year 2012–2013, Professor Pauwelyn will be on a sabbatical leave from the Graduate Institute and be a Visiting Professor at Stanford Law School (fall term) and Harvard Law School (spring term).

Jacqueline Peel is a Professor at the University of Melbourne Law School specializing in the areas of international environmental law, trade and environment, and risk regulation. Professor Peel is the author of numerous publications in these fields, including *Principles of International Environmental Law* (Cambridge University Press, 3rd ed., 2012, co-authored with Philippe Sands), *Science and Risk Regulation in International Law* (Cambridge University Press, 2010) and *The Precautionary Principle in Practice* (Federation Press, 2005). During 2012–2013 she is a Visiting Scholar at Berkeley Law School and the Stanford Woods Institute for the Environment in California, USA.

Donald H. Regan is the William W. Bishop, Jr. Collegiate Professor of Law and Professor of Philosophy in the University of Michigan. His writing on WTO law has focused primarily on the relationship between trade liberalization and national regulatory autonomy.

Luca Rubini is Reader (Associate Professor) in International Economic Law and deputy director of the Institute of European Law at Birmingham Law School. He served as law clerk of Advocate General Jacobs at the European Court of Justice. Dr. Rubini had held visiting positions at the European University Institute (Florence), the Institute of International Economic Law (Georgetown), the World Trade Institute (University of Berne) and Bocconi University, Milan. He is fellow of the Centre of European Law, King's College London, and visiting professor at ASERI (Catholic University, Milan). Dr. Rubini's main research interest lies in subsidy law and policy, and he is presently extending his focus to the analysis of the various linkages between energy, trade and climate change. He is the author of *The Definition of Subsidy and State Aid – WTO Law and EC Law in Comparative Perspective* (Oxford University Press, 2009). Dr. Rubini is currently working on a new project on the governance of legitimate subsidies in the WTO which will be published by Cambridge University Press.

Dalindyebo Shabalala is Assistant Professor, International Economic Law (Intellectual Property) at Maastricht University, as of 15 August 2009. He is Academic Coordinator for Project Acquisition of IGIR. He was appointed with additional funding from the India Institute of Maastricht University and his activities include research on and capacity building in India. His research focuses on climate change and intellectual property issues on one hand and on IP and development issues on the other. Previously, he was the managing attorney of CIEL's Geneva office, and Director of CIEL's Intellectual Property and Sustainable Development Project. He focused on issues at the intersection of intellectual property and climate change, human health, biodiversity and food security, as well as addressing systemic reform of the international intellectual property system. Mr. Shabalala was a Research Fellow in the Innovation, Access to Knowledge, and Intellectual Property Programme at the South Centre (2005–2006), an intergovernmental organization of developing countries in Geneva, Switzerland. Before this, he worked as an intern at the South Centre with Dr. Carlos Correa in the Intellectual Property Policy Research and Development Project, researching patent policy in developing countries.

Nashina Shariff is currently completing her Masters in Climate Sciences with a specialization in Economics at the University of Bern. She is a member of a research team focussing on the inter-linkages between trade regulation and climate at the World Trade Institute (NCCR Trade Regulation). Nashina holds a Bachelor of Science (Honours) in Physics from Queen's University in Canada. Prior to coming to Bern, Ms. Shariff spent eight years as Associate Director of the Toxics Watch Society of Alberta, an influential environmental NGO in Canada. During this time she was involved in the development of climate change and air pollution policy at the federal, provincial and international levels, including contributing to several publications on these subjects.

Tania Voon is Professor and Associate Dean (Research) at Melbourne Law School. She is a former Legal Officer of the Appellate Body Secretariat of the WTO and has previously practised law with Mallesons Stephen Jaques and the Australian Government Solicitor, and taught law at Georgetown University, the University of Western Ontario, the Australian National University, Monash University, and Bond University. Professor Voon undertook her Master of Laws at Harvard Law School and her Ph.D. in Law at the University of Cambridge. She has published widely in the areas of public international law and international economic law. She is the author of *Cultural Products and the World Trade Organization* (Cambridge University Press, 2007) and a member of the Indicative List of Governmental and Non-Governmental Panelists for resolving WTO disputes. She is also a member of the editorial boards of the *Journal of International Economic Law* and the *Indian Journal of International Economic Law*, coordinator of *ASIL Reports on International Organizations*, and editor (international economic law) of *ASIL Insights*. She has provided expert advice and training to entities such as Telstra, the Australian Department of Foreign Affairs and Trade, the European Parliament, the WTO, and the WHO, and NGOs such as the McCabe Centre for Law and Cancer and the Canadian International Development Agency.

David A. Wirth is Professor of Law at Boston College Law School in Newton, Massachusetts, where he teaches primarily in the field of public international law, with a specialty in international environmental law. Prior to entering academia, Professor Wirth was Senior Attorney and Co-Director of the International Program at the Washington, D.C. office of the Natural Resources Defense Council (NRDC), a nonprofit public interest law firm specializing in environmental issues. Professor Wirth has also been Attorney-Adviser for Oceans and International Environmental and Scientific Affairs in the Office of the Legal Adviser of the US Department of State in Washington, D.C., where he had principal responsibility for all international environmental issues. Professor Wirth is a 1981 graduate of the Yale Law School and served as law clerk to Judge William H. Timbers of US Court of Appeals for the Second Circuit in New York for a year thereafter. He holds undergraduate and graduate degrees in chemistry from, respectively, Princeton and Harvard Universities.

ZhongXiang Zhang is a distinguished professor at School of Economics, Fudan University, Shanghai, China. He is officially awarded as a 'Shanghai distinguished expert' through the Shanghai 1000-talent scheme. He is also a distinguished professor at the Chinese Academy of Sciences, Beijing; an adjunct senior fellow at East-West Center, USA; and an adjunct professor at the Chinese Academy of Social Sciences, Peking University and University of Hawaii at Manoa. He is co-editor of both *Environmental Economics and Policy Studies* and *International Journal of Ecological Economics & Statistics*, and is serving on the editorial boards of ten other leading international journals including *Climate Policy, Energy Policy, Energy and Environment, Environmental Science and Policy*, and *International Environmental Agreements: Politics, Law and Economics*. As a balanced economist undertaking both academic and policy-oriented work, he authors about 200 journal articles, book chapters and other publications, and authors/edits 18 books and special issues of international journals (*Energy Economics, Energy Policy, International Economics and Economic Policy, International Environmental Agreements: Politics, Law and Economics, Journal of Policy Modeling*, and *Mineral Economics*). He is among the most cited authors by the *IPCC Climate Change 2001* and *2007*, and by *Trade and Climate Change: WTO-UNEP Report*, and is among Social Science Research Network Top 200 Economics Authors. He is also among IDEAS/RePEc list of both the leading energy economists and the leading environmental economists in the world. Based on the number of author-weighted journal pages, he is among the Top 1000 Economists in the worldwide ranking. He was involved in a variety of activities with chief climate negotiators from a dozen key countries; served as an expert to many national and international organizations, including UNCTAD, UNEP, UNDP, European Commission, North American Commission for Environmental Cooperation, ADB, OECD, IEA, the World Bank, and IPCC; organized high-profile international conferences in Asia, Europe (including the conference at the European Commission); and frequently keynotes major international conferences in Asia, Europe and North America including three-time plenary address at the International Association for Energy Economics international conferences.

Preface

The 'domestic regulatory autonomy' debate in world trade law pitches the freedom of a sovereign State to pursue important 'regulatory' interests (such as environment, public health, consumer protection and animal welfare) against the free trade commitments which the same State has voluntarily committed to. At multilateral level, these trade commitments are found in the agreements of the World Trade Organization (WTO).

Free trade agreements, including those making up the body of WTO law, are not oblivious to the continuing desire of participating States to regulate to promote the societal interests referred to above. Consequently they provide, to varying degrees, room for 'domestic regulatory autonomy', subject of course to the checks and balances provided by the legal disciplines in the relevant agreement. These disciplines aim to limit the impact of national regulations on liberalised trade, both by preventing disguised protectionism and by reducing the trade restrictive effect of legitimate regulation. This fragile balance between free trade and regulatory autonomy is particularly crucial in the sensitive areas of health and the environment, as shown through the discussions in this volume. Its contours have been sketched through the interpretation of key WTO provisions in considerable case law, initially under the GATT 1947, and increasingly under the WTO agreements.

The analysis of GATT 1947 Panels focused on two main issues. First, the *like product analysis* within GATT non-discrimination rules circumscribed the possibilities for regulatory distinctions. GATT Panels reviewed this issue inter alia in the *US – Tuna/Dolphin* Cases, in *US – Malt Beverages*, and in *US – Taxes on Automobiles*. The 1970 Working Party Report on Border Tax Adjustments inadvertently served as the principal lead in the discussion on like products and product distinctions made on the basis of non-product-related processes and production methods.

Second, the 'balancing' role of the *exceptions* of GATT Article XX, and the extent to which health and environment objectives could be pursued in otherwise GATT-inconsistent regulation, received useful clarification. In particular GATT Article XX(b) and (g), and the 'chapeau' of Article XX were relevantly applied in *US – Tuna/Dolphin*, and in *Thailand – Cigarettes*.

With the establishment of the WTO came increased attention to the importance of achieving an appropriate balance between free trade and regulatory autonomy in the area of health and the environment, in keeping with growing national attention to these concerns. Consequently, case law addressing these issues reflected greater sensitivity to the complexities involved. First, case law on the GATT regulatory disciplines reached new levels of sophistication, including through the rejection of the consideration of the 'aim-and-effect' of a measure in the determination of likeness of products. Second, domestic regulatory measures became subject to a much wider plethora of agreements, with detailed disciplines going beyond non-discrimination rules. The GATT is no longer singlehandedly relevant. The TBT and SPS Agreements in particular (both building upon pre-WTO codes), now may catch domestic regulatory measures affecting trade in goods, including in the field of health and the environment, and discipline their trade restrictive effects even if they are non-discriminatory. In addition, with GATS, regulations to pursue health objectives in the area of trade in services may now also come within the ambit of WTO obligations, albeit providing States with more say in the applicability of some of these and leaving greater elbow room for regulation. WTO case law was therefore immediately relevant to trade and health/environment discussions. This is seen with the very first WTO case, *US – Gasoline*, and subsequently with later benchmark decisions such as *US – Shrimp/Turtle*, *EC – Asbestos* (where the demarcation between GATT and TBT was raised as an issue for the first time), *EC – Hormones* and *Brazil – Tyres*.

This volume groups analysis of a dream team of international academics and practitioners. The topics which they review reflect the most relevant anchor points for the interaction between trade, health and environmental concerns. Not only do these contributions present the state of the art on a number of topics of continuing relevance for the delicate balance between trade and health/environment regulation, such as the scope for precautionary measures, the relevance of regulatory purpose and the choice of an appropriate level of protection; but they also cover emerging issues of great importance for this balance, including the scope in WTO law for measures to address the challenges of climate change, non-communicable diseases, animal welfare and public health services.

A current series of dispute settlement reports in the WTO is further refining the debate, in particular the very recent Appellate Body decisions in *US – Clove Cigarettes*, *US – Tuna II* and *China – Raw Materials*, new discussions on export restrictions in the *China – Rare Earths* dispute, and the pending litigation in *EC – Seal Products, Canada – Renewable Energy* and *Australia – Plain Packaging of Tobacco*. Given the speed of development, the delay between writing, editing and publication may mean that not all the detail of the most recent reports has been included in the various chapters. However the conceptual analysis in which these reports play out, has.

The issues addressed in this volume touch upon the lives and well-being of many. 'Trade' here is reflected in health and welfare opportunities gained and lost, not in mere export and import statistics.

Geert Van Calster
Denise Prévost

PART I

GENERAL ISSUES

1. The precautionary principle in conflicts law perspectives*

Alexia Herwig and Christian Joerges

I. INTRODUCTION

In this contribution, we pursue two objectives. The first is to explore a new potential of the conflicts law approach which has first been developed at the European University Institute in Florence[1] and in the context of two interdisciplinary projects[2] and proffered as the appropriate constitutional form for transnational law.[3] The second is to discuss in an exemplary way instances of a conflicts law approach or a lack thereof in the jurisprudence

---

*   We are indebted to our editors for many helpful comments. We would also like to acknowledge the intense discussion of our paper in Bremen at the Centre of European Law and Politics with Henning Deters, Josef Falke, Carola Glinski and Ulf Uetzmann and the comments by Lars Viellechner on the passages on Nico Krisch's theory of legal pluralism. Special thanks, last but not least, to Monika Hobbie for her editorial assistance. The usual disclaimer applies.

[1] The first systematic presentation of the idea was in Joerges, C. (2005), *Rethinking European Law's Supremacy*, with Comments by D. Chalmers, R. Nickel, F. Rödl and R. Wai, EUI Working Paper Law 2/2005, San Domenico di Fiesole: European University Institute, http://cadmus.eui.eu/bitstream/handle/1814/3332/?sequence=1.

[2] Namely the Bremen project on 'Transformations of the State' in which Alexia Herwig was involved until 2008 (see for a description http://www.sfb597.uni-bremen.de) and the European Project on 'Reconstituting Democracy in Europe' which was organised by ARENA, University of Oslo (see for a description http://www.reconproject.eu/), both accessed 1 December 2011.

[3] For detailed recent presentations of the argument see Joerges, C. (2010), 'Integration through Conflicts Law: On the Defence of the European Project by means of alternative conceptualisation of legal constitutionalisation', in R. Nickel (ed.), *Conflict of Laws and Laws of Conflict in Europe and Beyond – Patterns of Supranational and Transnational Juridification*, Antwerp: Intersentia, 377–400; Joerges, C., and F. Rödl (2011), 'Reconceptualising the Constitution of Europe's Post-national Constellation – by Dint of Conflict of Laws', in I. Lianos and O. Odudu (eds), *Regulating Trade in Services in the EU and the WTO. Trust, Distrust and Economic Integration,* Cambridge: Cambridge University Press, 762–780. For a critical discussion see Joerges, C., P.F. Kjaer and T. Ralli (eds) (2011), *Transnational Legal Theory*, Special Issue on 'Conflicts Law as Constitutional Form in the Postnational Constellation', **2**, 153–165.

of World Trade Organization (WTO) dispute settlement bodies and in European law dealing with the precautionary principle or with legal norms reflective of precautionary thinking. We do not aim to give an exhaustive overview of how the relevant laws and tribunals deal or have dealt with the precautionary principle or norms based on it. This, however, does not mean that the cases were selected at random. The cases we discuss are of exemplary systemic relevance for how the balance between trade and non-trade (health and environmental) concerns was struck in the legal texts under consideration.

Our contribution proceeds as follows: we first develop the main tenets of the conflicts law approach and demarcate it from rivalling approaches. We believe that this critical contrast will not only help to illuminate the specifics of our approach but also shed new light on the competing projects. We argue that 'global legal pluralism' as defended by Nico Krisch has affinities with conflicts law but remains amorphous and fails to realise that precisely the discrepancies between different types of orders can be reconstructed in conflicts law perspectives. Supranational decision-making as advocated in the work of Giandomenico Majone[4] overlaps with our thinking in important respects and can even – certainly to Majone's surprise – be reconstructed in conflicts law terms; we argue, however, that Majone's distinction between a supranational commitment to efficiency and regulatory policies which require democratic legitimacy cannot be upheld.[5] This leads us to propose conflicts law as a 'third way' in which law addresses the political at all, and between all, levels of governance. Our approach is not, however, meant to offer ready-made answers to the broad variety of European and WTO conflict constellations. It presupposes instead a procedural notion of law which seeks to promote a deliberative mode of conflict resolution.

Next, we submit that the precautionary principle can be understood as a conflicts law device and we show the emergence of the principle in European law as a way to manage diversity. In the final part of this chapter, we turn to the examination of pertinent, exemplary jurisprudence. We discuss the WTO Panel report in *EC – Biotech,* the *Continued*

---

[4]   See his seminal *Regulating Europe* (1996), London, New York: Routledge.
[5]   The notion of 'technocracy' is widely used in the characterisation of Giandomenico Majone's work on Europe. That is not wrong as long as one remains aware of what he explained on p. 1 of his seminal *Regulating Europe*: 'At the end of the period of reconstruction of the national economies shattered by the war income redistribution and discretionary macroeconomic management emerged as the top policy priorities of most Western European governments . . .'

Suspension reports and the *Temelín* judgment of the European Court of Justice (ECJ).

II. CONFLICTS LAW AS CONSTITUTIONAL FORM

Conflicts law has a reconstructive and a prescriptive dimension. We claim that legal controversies over the justification of regulatory limitations on free movement rights and Community prerogatives can be understood in conflicts law perspectives, namely as conflicts over diverging policies which are claiming recognition. Contrary to the typical constellation of private international law cases, however, jurisdictional authority in the EU is not located within a single territorial framework. Contradictory policies and interests collide within a 'multi-level' framework; they are often not resolved by prioritising one legal system but by compromise solutions which reconcile national concerns with European commitments. We suggest that legal conflicts over the justification of regulatory policies under WTO law can be interpreted in the same manner.

In EU law, the principle of mutual recognition provides an illustration of one type of these conflicts. According to the principle of mutual recognition, products lawfully marketed in one EU Member State are entitled to free circulation in other Member States into which they are imported unless restrictions can be justified under one of the exceptions from the free trade principle explicitly named in Article 36 TFEU (the Treaty on the Functioning of the European Union) or for overriding reasons related to the public interest as they have been recognised since *Cassis de Dijon*.[6] In that case, Germany sought to prohibit the sale of the French liqueur Cassis de Dijon as 'Likör' in Germany since its alcohol content was lower than that which German regulations prescribed for beverages of the type 'Likör'. Germany argued on grounds of consumer protection (legitimate consumer expectations) that the French product should not bear the name 'Likör' as this could confuse consumers. Now, this legal conflict can be

---

[6] Case 120/78, ECR [1979] 649 – *Cassis de Dijon*. The provision in Article 36 is an exception to the prohibition on quantitative restrictions on exports and imports and measures having equivalent effect in Articles 34 and 35 TFEU. It is similar to GATT Article XX in that it contains a limited list of policy objectives, namely public morals, public policy or public security; the protection of health and life of humans, animals or plants; the protection of national treasures possessing artistic, historic or archaeological value; or the protection of industrial and commercial property and includes some form of proportionality review.

understood as a horizontal conflict between two EU Member States over differing regulatory policies and over which one of the two should be allowed to exercise its jurisdiction to prescribe in respect of the naming of an imported product. In its judgment the ECJ did not question in principle Germany's concern with consumer protection but insisted on a mode of protection which was in line with Community concerns. In WTO law, a dispute over whether or not a Member's regulation falling under Articles III or XI of the GATT (General Agreement on Tariffs and Trade)[7] can be justified under Article XX of the GATT[8] can likewise be understood as such a horizontal conflict over regulatory policies between im- and exporting WTO Members.

Diagonal conflicts exist where there are divergent EU and national political orientations that span two different levels of governance.[9] Typical examples of this in EU law are conflicts over EU secondary legislation pursuing the economic aim of harmonisation and diverging national regulations adopted on grounds such as consumer or environmental protection. Vertical conflicts are conflicts over the supremacy of EU law.[10]

Three arguments militate for conflicts law mechanisms as an appropriate constitutional model for supra- and transnational governance.

The first is an argument from the perspective of democracy. Under conditions of globalisation and Europeanisation, nation states are increasingly unable to guarantee the inclusion of all those affected by their poli-

---

[7]   Articles XI and III of the GATT cover market access through the elimination of quantitative restrictions and non-discriminatory treatment behind the border respectively. Quantitative restrictions on import and export are prohibited, subject to some listed exceptions. Article III applies to internal taxes and charges and to laws, regulations and requirements affecting the internal sale, offering for sale, purchase, transportation, distribution or use applied to products that are like or in a relationship of direct competition and substitution. Very generally, changes in the competitive relationship between these products through the measures mentioned must be avoided.

[8]   Article XX ('General Exceptions') describes and delimits the measure which the contracting parties may adopt.

[9]   See Joerges, C. (1997), 'The Impact of European Integration on Private Law: Reductionist Perceptions, True Conflicts and a New Constitutional Perspective', *European Law Journal*, **3**, 378; Schmid, C. (2008), 'Diagonal Competence Conflicts between European Competition Law and National Law. The Example of Book Price Fixing', *European Review of Private Law*, **8**, 155.

[10]   See for a recent particularly controversial example on the impact of the Posted Workers Directive (Directive 96/71/EC, OJ L18/1996, 1) in Sweden Case C-341/05, *Laval un Partneri Ltd v Svenska Byggnadsarbetareförbundet*, [2007] ECR I-11767.

cies in decision-making.[11] Their policies produce extraterritorial impacts, yet foreign affected interests are typically not represented in national legislative processes. However, the notion of self-legislation postulates that the addressees of a law must at the same time be their authors and would thus demand the inclusion of the other.[12] It should be noted that such transboundary impacts are on the cards twice: on the one hand, there is the importing state which seeks to regulate production of the imported product that occurred in another state. On the other hand, there is the exporting state which seeks to introduce its products with its risk into the importing state. The conflicts law approach should hence not be misread as some reactionary effort to 'bring the nation state back in'. Quite to the contrary, our approach departs from nation states failures and seeks to legitimate EU and also WTO law through their potential to compensate for these deficits by obliging states to be accountable to outside affected interests and to move towards cooperative problem-solving where one-sided national problem-solving has become inconceivable. In this way, EU and WTO law can strengthen democracy without having to establish themselves as democratic federal states.[13]

The second argument is an argument from the viewpoint of diversity. Supra- and transnational law cannot replace national legal systems.

---

[11]   This argument gets, albeit in different versions, increasing recognition; see, e.g., Howse, R., and K. Nicolaïdis (2008), 'Democracy without Sovereignty: The Global Vocation of Political Ethics', in T. Broude and Y. Shany (eds), *The Shifting Allocation of Authority in International Law. Considering Sovereignty, Supremacy and Subsidiarity*, Oxford: Hart Publishing, 163; they state at 167: '[Our] horizontal reading of subsidiarity and supremacy follows directly from the limits of the notion of sovereignty in a world where laws and actions within a polity increasingly have external effects. Supremacy and subsidiarity therefore can be defined in a dialectic way as complementary principles to deal with the fundamental conundrum of transnational democracy. Supremacy serves as a meta-norm of conflict of laws between Member States such as to enhance the representation of foreigners inside the jurisdiction of every Member State, and to ask when and to what extent these interests should trump the domestic social contract.'

[12]   Jürgen Habermas deserves to be cited literally: 'Nation-states . . . encumber each other with the external effects of decisions that impinge on third parties who had no say in the decision-making process. Hence, states cannot escape the need for regulation and coordination in the expanding horizon of a world society that is increasingly self-programming, even at the cultural level. . . .'; such in his 'Does the Contitutionalization of International Law Still Have a Chance?' (translated by Cirian Cronin), in Habermas, J. (2007), *The Divided West*, Cambridge: Polity Press, 113, 176.

[13]   For a recent elaboration of this dimension see Roedel, F. (2011), 'Democratic Juridification Without Statisation: Law of Conflict of Laws Instead of a World State', *Transnational Legal Theory*, **2**, 215.

Competences are limited and shared with states, with the latter disposing of far greater administrative resources than the EU or WTO. This is why the institutionalisation of supra- and transnational regimes remains dependent upon the cooperation of states and intra-state institutions for the implementation of their prescriptions. In addition to this empirical argument, there are normative reasons for the respect of regulatory diversity. For instance, in some political systems social conditions allow for participatory legislative processes, which confer legitimacy qua procedure on legislative acts. In others, such as Belgium, significant counter-majoritarian elements are necessary to legitimate legislative acts. In a conflict between two such states over a regulatory policy, supra- and transnational law could not pronounce itself – even indirectly – on which political system is right and must accordingly content itself with managing this diversity in a manner both states can accept, albeit possibly on different grounds. With the deepening socio-economic diversity in the EU especially after enlargement this argument seems ever more irrefutable: 'one size does *not* fit all' simply because political preferences and priorities are not formed in a vacuum.

The third argument is an institutional and constitutional one. It builds upon the highly contested leader of the American 'conflict of laws revolution' of the 1960s.[14] Currie has suggested that controversies over the application of foreign law need to be traced back to the policies underlying the rules at issue and reconstructed as controversies over the 'governmental interests' of the concerned jurisdictions. Often such conflicts are 'false' or can be avoided through moderate and restrained constructions of legal provisions; where this is not the case (in 'true conflicts'), Currie insisted that the forum state applied its own law. True conflicts are of a political nature, he argued, which courts are not legitimated to resolve in favour of a foreign sovereign.[15] We disagree – precisely because we advocate transnational compensation of nation state failures. In particular in the European Union with its commitment to open economies and a rich institutional machinery of conflicts resolution Currie's suggestion is simply inadequate. His *monitum* as to the 'political' dimensions of conflicts,

---

[14]   Currie's work is collected in Currie, B. (1963), *Selected Essays on the Conflict of Laws*, Durham, NC: Duke University Press.

[15]   Currie, B. (1963), 'The Constitution and the Choice of Law: Governmental Interests and the Judicial Function' in Currie, note 14, 188, at 272: '[The c]hoice between the competing interests of co-ordinated states is a political function of a high order, which ought not, in a democracy, to be committed to the judiciary: . . . the court is not equipped to perform such a function; and the Constitution specifically confers that function upon Congress.'

however, needs to be taken seriously. This *monitum* does not justify parochialism, but prudence and eventually judicial restraint. Such caution is all
the more required in the case of WTO panels and the Appellate Body. The
weighing and balancing approach to the necessity analysis first articulated
in *Korea – Beef* and used in *Brazil – Tyres* in a way that allowed the panel
to evaluate the importance of social regulatory objectives itself in a proactive manner reveals that the interpretation and application of Article XX
GATT *can* lead to the second-guessing of national regulatory policies.[16]
According to our conflicts law approach, these bodies should rather seek
to identify norms and principles that mediate the conflicts but give due
recognition to the political nature of regulatory concerns.

Premises 1–3 together lead to the conclusion that supra- and transnational law must find a way to organise and manage diversity and pay
genuine respect to the reasons for diversity, notably by finding rules that
deserve recognition in the respective Member States or WTO members.[17]
We have already indicated in our remarks on the principle of mutual recognition that the conflicts law approach does not, like private international
law, insist on the application of the law of one concerned jurisdiction.
The kind of conflicts solution we advocate seeks to ensure accountability
beyond the national borders to outside affected interests – without thereby
negating the political nature of social regulation of economic activities. It
is often more adequate to develop a 'substantive' response which both of
the involved jurisdictions can accept. To take up the example of *Cassis
de Dijon*[18] again: The ECJ's holding allowed Cassis de Dijon to be sold
as 'Likör' in Germany but with an indication of its – surprisingly low –
alcohol percentage; the ECJ's labelling requirement provided sufficient
protection of consumer expectations in Germany while allowing for the
free circulation of Cassis as marketed and regulated in France. *Cassis* is an

---

[16] Appellate Body Report, *Measures Affecting Imports of Fresh, Chilled and
Frozen Beef*, WT/DS/AB161, 169/R, adopted 10 January 2001, para. 162. *Brazil –
Tyres* concerned environmental protection objectives. This report provides the first
clear evidence that panels actually assess the importance of the interest concerned
because the environmental protection objectives at issue were classified as merely
'important' whereas in all previous cases, the panel or Appellate Body classified
the interests at stake as 'very important'. See Panel Report, *Brazil – Measures
Affecting Imports of Retreaded Tyres*, WT/DS332//R. adopted 17 December
2007, para. 7.112, Appellate Body Report, *Brazil – Measures Affecting Imports of
Retreaded Tyres*, WT/DS332/AB/R, adopted 17 December 2007, para. 179.

[17] Premises 1–3 make up the prescriptive dimension of conflicts law, while the
distinctions between different types of conflict constellations are a reconstructive
exercise.

[18] See note 6 above and accompanying text.

easy case which legal systems are well equipped to deal with ('first order conflicts', in our parlance).[19] Contemporary regulatory techniques are typically more demanding, in particular in the field of social regulation. They tend to require cooperative regulatory policy-making ('second order

---

[19]   In the WTO, naming and labelling requirements have been challenged in several disputes, notably the recent *US – Tuna II* report. We cannot enter into a detailed discussion of this report. We do wish to point out, however, that the WTO panel report in *US – Tuna* may have required a more careful solution than the one the panel adopted. This TBT dispute concerned US measures allowing only the DPCIA dolphin-friendly label with stricter requirements of protection measures than the rivalling AIDCP dolphin label. In essence, the panel found the US restriction to one label unnecessary because both types of labels could be allowed on the market without compromising the US's protection objective. Neither of the two labels protected dolphins perfectly against mortality, which led the panel to consider them to be alternatives. Notwithstanding the burden of proof being on the complainant, the panel assumed that the imperfections were equivalent. If they are not equivalent, however, allowing both labels on the market misinforms consumers as they are unlikely to be aware of and unable to understand the differing dolphin protection requirements and their effectiveness. The comparison with the issue of alcohol content in *Cassis de Dijon* teaches one thing: labels are a conflicts law solution only if the information conveyed by a naming or labelling scheme is not too complex. In *Cassis de Dijon* the relevant information was readily ascertainable on the bottle and easily understandable, in *US – Tuna* it is not. The Appellate Body reversed the panel's findings on the ground that it had improperly compared dolphin protection requirements outside the Eastern Tropical Pacific with those inside it for the two labels. See Appellate Report, *US – Measures Concerning the Importation, Marketing and Sale of Tuna and Tuna Products*, WT/DS381/AB/R, adopted 13 June 2012, paras 330–331 and Panel Report, *US – Tuna*, WT/DS/381/R, paras 7.571–7.574, 7.599, 7.620–7.621. Alessandra Arcuri also questions the panel's assumption of equal effectiveness. See Arcuri, A. (2012), 'Back to the Future: US – Tuna II and the New Environment-Trade Debate', *European Journal of Risk Regulation* 3 (2), 177–189. The report is also interesting from the perspective of precaution. As Arcuri mentions, the panel acknowledged that data on the impact of fishing techniques was imperfect but notwithstanding the complainant's burden of proof concluded that Mexico had been successful in showing that a less restrictive alternative was reasonably available. We would make the case that formal rules on the allocation of the burden of proof are not satisfactory for resolving controversies over social regulatory policies. For an conflicts law analysis of the Appellate Body's jurisprudence on the term 'international standards' see Glinksi, C. (2012), 'Private Norms as International Standards? – Regime Collisions in Tuna-Dolphin II', *European Journal of Risk Regulation,* 3 (4), 545–560 and *idem* (2011), *General Clauses and Private Regulation – Regime Collisions in Tuna-Dolphin III*, paper presented at the workshop 'The Conflicts-Law Approach on Trial, Seminar at the Evangelische Akademie Loccum, Germany, October 2011 (on file with authors) and a case note on the *US – Tuna* Appellate Body decision, see Gruszczynski, L. (2012), 'Retuning Tuna? Appellate Body Report in *US – Tuna II*', *European Journal of Risk Regulation*, 3 (3), 430–436.

conflicts'). In the EU, the paradigm example of such efforts is comitology. 'Cooperative problem solving' is a functional necessity here. What is functionally necessary should not be declared to be legitimate without further ado. The conflicts law approach strives for a 'constitutionalisation' of transnational regulatory politics – an issue which we cannot take up here.[20] Last but not least, the law must be expected to acknowledge the involvement of non-governmental actors in regulatory policy-making – but also supervise the ensuing governance arrangements and para-legal norms generated by self-regulatory organisations so as to ensure that such practices 'deserve recognition'('third order conflicts').[21]

We would like to underline that we understand the conflicts law approach as a reconstructive exercise, an effort to re-conceptualise the law's operation within the framework of the existing systems of multilevel governance and social regulation.[22] These existing systems, we suggest, are proto-legitimate inasmuch as they have the potential to become transnational accountability mechanisms of nation states and their regulatory policies so as to mediate between regulatory concerns and commitments to trade liberalisation. Conflicts law deals with discrete problems of fine-tuning, which, we argue, have political dimensions which the law cannot substitute; what law can and should instead accomplish is to provide norms for the accountability of political decision-makers. In this sense, conflicts laws is concerned with 'Recht-fertigung' – a notion whose literal and non-literal meaning translate into law-making *and* justification in English. Conflicts law is not concerned with the development of a comprehensive constitutional project for the international order. This should also make clear that our defence of respect for diversity in multilevel governance systems of liberalised trade is not a call for unprincipled pluralism.

---

[20] See Joerges, C., and J. Neyer (1997), 'From Intergovernmental Bargaining to Deliberative Political Processes: The Constitutionalisation of Comitology', *European Law Journal*, **3**, 273, and the contribution in Joerges, C. and E. Vos (1999), *EU Committees: Social Regulation, Law and Politics*, Oxford: Hart Publishing.

[21] For an early exemplary discussion see Joerges, C., H. Schepel and E. Vos (1999), *The Law's Problems with the Involvement of Non-Governmental Actors in Europe's Legislative Processes: The Case of Standardisation under the "New Approach"*, EUI Working Paper LAW No. 99/9, San Domenico di Fiesole: European University Institute.

[22] According to Krisch, N. (2010), *Beyond Constitutionalism: The Pluralist Structure of Postnational Law*, Oxford: OUP, 76, 77, this is a key difference with his pluralist account. Conflict law seeks *legal* responses where pluralists give up; these responses are generated within existing institutional frameworks and respect the commitments to European integration and post-national cooperation.

III.   PRECAUTION AS CONFLICTS LAW IN THE REALMS OF RISK REGULATION

The precautionary principle has been called 'one of the most significant principles of the contemporary era'.[23] Its success is indeed remarkable.[24] In the EU, the principle has gained quasi-constitutional status in Article 191 TFEU with defined contours and broad application to the field of risk regulation. It is nevertheless by no means uniformly understood and far from being universally accepted.[25] We are interested here in the principle's career as a response to the insights into the limits of science and its way to deal with uncertainty where scientific certainty ends. The resort to science as a meta-rule for the adjudication of conflicts was the precursor of precaution in the EU. We review the European development briefly before turning to WTO law.

A.   Science in the Light of Conflicts Law

1.   The turn to science in EU law
Once the ECJ had expanded the reach of the free movement provisions in what was then Article 30 EC Treaty (now 34 TFEU) through its *Dassonville* decision,[26] it was faced with a large number of disputes over EU Member States' regulatory policies and forced to decide whether or not to give priority to the free circulation of products or to the protection objectives of the importing Member States. Initially, in the *Cassis de*

---

[23]   Thus the preface to Fisher, E., J.S. Jones and R. von Schomberg (eds), (2006), *Implementing the Precautionary Principle*, Cheltenham: Edward Elgar Publishing, 11.

[24]   For condensed summaries of an abundant multidisciplinary and transnational discussion see Herwig, A. (2006), 'The Precautionary Principle in Support of Practical Reason: an Argument Against Formalistic Interpretations of the Precautionary Principle', in C. Joerges and E.-U. Petersmann (eds), *Constitutionalism, Multilevel Trade Governance and Social Regulation*, Oxford: Hart Publishing, 301; Weimer, M. (2010), 'Applying Precaution in Community Authorisation of Genetically Modified Products – Challenges and Suggestions for Reform', *European Law Journal*, **16** (5), 624–657.

[25]   Various multilateral environmental agreements make references to the precautionary principle as well but the principle has not been much developed through further legislation or adjudication nor has it found comprehensive application to the field of risk regulation.

[26]   According to *Dassonville*, facially-neutral measures could nevertheless be considered as measures having an equivalent effect to a restriction if they hindered or impeded market access of products from other Member States. Case C-8/74 *Procureur du Roi v. Benoît and Gustave Dassonville* [1974] ECR 837 at 852, para. 5.

Dijon decision, Member States were in principle entitled to pursue their regulatory concerns (in casu with consumer protection) without interference from the European Community as to the goal to be pursued. Alas, such elegant solutions to conflicts were not always at hand and it became clear that giving free reign to the regulatory concerns of the EU Member States could endanger the creation of the common market. In this situation, the ECJ turned to science in order to manage conflicts of jurisdiction in the Community. EU Member States had to be able to muster scientific evidence in support of their regulatory concerns if they wished to justify risk regulations that impeded the free circulation of intra-Community trade.[27] Similarly, in disputes over the legal treaty base for EU secondary legislation and legislation delegated to the Commission, the ECJ examined scientific arguments.[28]

This turn to science was as promising as it was problematic. Through linking up with science, Community law was able to acquire a new basis for validity and avoid political disputes over its competences. Science, by virtue of being a language with a universal grammar (there is no such thing as 'German physics' or 'European mathematics') helps national legal systems to overcome their parochialism and particularism and become accountable to outside affected interests. Moreover, where Member States seek to regulate on the grounds of an empirically existing or potential danger, a requirement to substantiate their concerns with evidence is a reasonable corollary. Science, in other words, furnished supranational criteria for differentiating between the legitimate and illegitimate regulatory concerns of Member States.

Nevertheless, with a turn to science, there is also the danger of camouflaging the political nature of decisions on risk regulation through scientific empiricism. For instance, the ECJ restricted the regulatory discretion of Member States by requiring them to respect the findings of the international and European scientific research community.[29] It still left some

---

[27] See, for instance, Case C-17/93 *Van der Veldt* [1994] ECR 1227 at 1274.

[28] See the case law discussed in Joerges, C. (1997), 'Scientific Expertise in Social Regulation and the European Court of Justice: Legal Frameworks for Denationalized Governance Structures', in C. Joerges, K-H. Ladeur and E. Vos (eds), *Integrating Scientific Expertise into Regulatory Decision-Making. National Traditions and European Innovations*, Baden-Baden: Nomos, 306; Joerges, C., and C. Godt (2005), 'Free Trade with Hazardous Products? The Erosion of National and the Birth of Transnational Governance', in S. Leibfried and M. Zürn (eds), *Transformation of the State*, Cambridge: Cambridge University Press, 93. The following remarks draw on these articles.

[29] E.g. Case 178/84 *Commission v. Germany* [1987] ECR 1227 at 1274 – *Reinheitsgebot* (purity of beer).

space for the political to influence decision-making on risk by recognizing the concept of *per se* dangerous substances. Although the Court recognised in principle that Member States were free to decide how to react to uncertainties in the absence of harmonisation,[30] it also limited Member States' discretion on this matter through some qualifiers:[31] Member States were entitled to react to uncertainties if these were also encountered by other countries or international organisations and were required to give mutual recognition to scientific tests carried out in other Member States if these were the same as those they would have required.[32] In one case, the ECJ left Member States with the discretion to pursue their own regulatory philosophy, in another case it forced upon Germany a horizontal rather than product-compositional approach to food additives.[33] In a preliminary reference, the Court classified a product as a cosmetic rather than a medicinal product[34] – and then restricted the discretion of Member States stating that it is required by 'the nature of things and apart from any provision laid down to that effect' to seek the assistance of 'experts on scientific and technical issues'.[35]

2.   The turn to science in WTO law

With the entry into force of the Agreement on Sanitary and Phytosanitary Measures (SPS Agreement) in 1995 WTO law had in place a set of rules that called on WTO Members to justify their regulation of SPS risks with scientific evidence.[36] Article 2.2 of the SPS Agreement provides that SPS measures have to be maintained with sufficient scientific evidence and be based on scientific principles. The obligation pertaining to sufficient scientific evidence is concretised by Articles 5.1 and 5.2, which call on Members

---

[30]   Case 174/82 *Officier van Justitie v. Sandoz* [1983] ECR 2445.

[31]   These do not require authorities to establish a 'danger' but they must review their levels of protection in light of new scientific findings; see Case 94/83 *Criminal Proceedings against Albert Heijn BV* [1984] ECR 3263.

[32]   Case 53/80 *Kaasfabriek Eyssen (Nisin)* [1981] ECR 409 at 422.

[33]   See for the former Case 188/84 *Woodworking Machines* [1986] ECR 419 and for the latter Case 178/84 (note 26 above) at 1274.

[34]   Case C-212/91 *Angelopharm GmbH v. Freie und Hansestadt Hamburg* [1994] ECR I-171.

[35]   At I-211 (para. 33).

[36]   The types of risks and measures to which the SPS Agreement applies are listed in Annex A1. These include certain food- and feedstuff risks and risks to animal, plant and human life and health from pests and zoonoses. According to the Panel in *EC – Biotech*, measures regulating indirect sources of these risks also fall under the SPS Agreement. The Panel also adopted an expansive interpretation of some of the enumerated risks, for instance the term 'pests' which it defined as anything that is unwarranted or a nuisance.

to base their SPS measures on risk assessments in accordance with internationally recognised methods. For pest and disease risks, an evaluation of the likelihood of the materialisation of the hazard has to be performed while for food- and feedstuff hazards risk assessments need only evaluate the potential of the materialisation of the hazard.[37] According to the Appellate Body, likelihood denotes probability while potential denotes possibility and implies a lower threshold of probability.[38] The Appellate Body has also characterised risk assessment as a rigorous, objective process of inquiry.[39]

As in EU law, panels and the Appellate Body have sometimes used the evidentiary requirements of the SPS Agreement carefully and have recognized the political nature of decisions about risk and at other times have interfered with the regulatory approaches of the Members. In its first SPS decision in *EC – Hormones,* the Appellate Body explained that the right of WTO Members to set their appropriate level of protection (ALOP) different from that of an international standard as set out in Article 3.3 was an autonomous right whose exercise would not automatically place the burden of proof on the regulating Member.[40] In that same case, the Appellate Body also rejected the notion that a risk assessment had to establish a minimum magnitude of risk or be only quantitative and it allowed Members to base themselves on minority scientific opinion from respected and qualified sources.[41] The Appellate Body also preserved regulatory discretion by accepting in principle politically motivated distinctions for the purpose of an Article 5.5 analysis which, as interpreted, requires Members to avoid arbitrary and unjustifiable differences between ALOPs in different yet comparable situations: In *EC – Hormones,* it found that there was a fundamental difference between naturally-occurring and added hormones and that the massive governmental intervention required to regulate the former rendered the comparison absurd.[42] Admittedly, this was not a difficult issue to decide. What is important to retain is that the Appellate Body accepted that the probability or possibility of the harm defined by Annex A1 of the SPS Agreement is not the only permissible ground upon which distinctions in ALOPs between different situations

---

[37] SPS Agreement, Annex A4.

[38] Appellate Body Report, *European Communities – Measures Concerning Meat and Meat Products (Hormones) ('EC – Hormones'),* WT/DS26/AB/R and WT/DS48/AB/R, adopted 13 February 1998, para. 184.

[39] Appellate Body Report, *EC – Hormones*, para. 187.

[40] Appellate Body Report, *EC – Hormones*, paras 104 and 172.

[41] WTO Appellate Body Report, *EC – Hormones,* paras. 186 and 194.

[42] *Ibid.*, at 221.

can be drawn. Indeed, the only way to understand the significance of natural as opposed to artificial exposures, we would like to suggest, is to see it as a political appreciation of qualitative differences between risks.

On the other hand, the Appellate Body has interpreted the concept of 'based on' in Article 5.1 as a requirement that the scientific evidence be specific to the actual exposure targeted by the measure and likened this to a causation analysis.[43] Prior to *Continued Suspension,* panels and the Appellate Body have also adopted an intrusive standard of review of the factual evidence presented by Members with a view to determining whether or not this evidence constitutes a risk assessment.[44] In another case, a Panel restricted the right of Members to determine their levels of protection autonomously by holding that there was a requirement of proportionality between the risk established and the risk management measure chosen. In this case, the Panel and experts had concluded that there was a negligible (but not non-existent) risk of fire blight transmission through contaminated apples but considered the risk management meas-

---

[43]   Appellate Body Report, *EC – Hormones*, para. 200, See also Panel Report, *EC – Hormones* (USA), WT/DS26/R, adopted 13 February 1998, para. 8.257; Panel Report, *EC – Hormones* (Canada), WT/DS48/R, adopted 13 February 1998, para. 8.260; Panel Report, *Australia – Measures Affecting Importation of Salmon* (*'Australia – Salmon'*), WT/DS18/R, adopted 6 November 1998, para. 8.74; Appellate Body Report, *Japan – Measures Affecting the Importation of Apples* (*'Japan – Apples'*), WT/DS245/AB/R, adopted 26 November 2003, para. 202; Panel Report, *Japan – Apples*, WT/DS245/R, adopted 26 November 2003, para. 8.271; Panel Report, *European Communities – Measures Affecting the Approval and Marketing of Biotech Products* (*'EC-Biotech'*), WT/DS291/R, WT/DS292/R, WT/DS293/R, paras 7.3099, 7.3147–7.3148; Panel Report, *United States – Certain Measures Affecting Imports of Poultry from China* (*'US – Poultry'*), WT/DS392/R, adopted 25 October 2010, para. 7.202; Panel Report, *Australia – Measures Affecting the Importation of Apples from New Zealand,* WT/DS367/R, adopted 17 December 2010, paras 7.537–7.542; 7.544–7.545, 7.564, 7.687. In *US/Canada – Continued Suspension,* the Appellate Body confirmed that a risk assessment must show a causal connection between the agent and the hazard but rejected the idea that the causal contribution of the agent had to be isolated from that of other exposures. Appellate Body Report, *United States – Continued Suspension of Obligations in the EC – Hormones Dispute* (*'US/Canada – Continued Suspension'*), WT/DS320/AB/R, adopted 10 November 2008, para. 562; Appellate Body Report, *Canada – Continued Suspension of Obligations in the EC – Hormones Dispute* (*'US/ Canada – Continued Suspension'*), WT/DS321/AB/R, adopted 10 November 2008, para. 562.

[44]   Ming Du, M. (2010), 'Standard of Review under the SPS Agreement after *EC – Hormones II*', *International and Comparative Law Quarterly*, **59**, 441, at 448–449, 450–451; Epps, T. (2008), 'Reconciling Public Opinion and WTO Rules under the SPS Agreement', *World Trade Review*, **7**, 359–383.

ures to be out of proportion to the magnitude of risk.[45] Finally, as regards the obligation in Article 5.5 a recent Panel considered that differences between comparable situations would not be arbitrary or unjustifiable only if there were differences in risk – thereby denying that the decision on the level of risk tolerance must always look at all the characteristics of the risk, such as the manner of its imposition, the benefits from taking the risk and others and conflicting with what was implied in *EC – Hormones*.[46]

3. The limits of the authority of science

Above, we suggested that requirements related to the provision of validated scientific evidence for risk regulation can in principle function as a conflicts law mechanism but this potential erodes where science is invoked to operate as the final arbiter and yardstick in the assessment and delimitation of legitimate and illegitimate regulation.

To use the law to substantiate the thresholds defining the epistemological validity of scientific evidence is to conflate two categorically different media. Science is not concerned with, and hence not able to resolve, the questions lawyers pose. This is because scientific research is in principle explorative. In legal perceptions, the scientific system generates paradoxes because the knowledge it produces is always a step towards further inquiries and amounts to the generation of new uncertainties.[47] Science only has a limited authority.[48] In cases where science is unable to provide the necessary specific and validated evidence in part or in whole, it is neither credible nor logical to reject regulations as being based on evidence that

---

[45]   Appellate Body Report, *Japan – Apples*, paras 162–163; Panel Report, *Japan – Apples*, para. 8.102. See also Arcuri, A. (2010), 'Food Safety at the WTO after "Continued Suspension": A Paradigm Shift?', Rotterdam Institute of Law and Economics (RILE) Working Paper Series www.rile.nl, No. 2010/04pls, accessed 26 January 2012, 13; also published in A. Antoniadis, R. Schütze and E. Spaventa (eds). (2010), *The European Union and Global Emergencies: A Law and Policy Analysis*, Oxford: Hart Publishing.

[46]   Panel Report, *US – Poultry*, para. 7.263.

[47]   See Luhmann, N. (1993), *Das Recht der Gesellschaft*, Frankfurt/M: Suhrkamp, 142. For more comprehensive discussion see Everson, M. 'Three Intimate Tales of Law and Science: Hope, Despair and Transcendence', in M. Everson and E. Vos (eds), *Uncertain Risks Regulated*, Oxford-New York: Routledge-Cavendish, 347–358; Wagner, M. (2011), 'Law Talk v. Science Talk: The Languages of Law and Science in WTO Proceedings', *Fordham International Law Journal*, **35** (1), 151–200.

[48]   We do not deny that there are clear cases where an absence of sufficiently validated and specific evidence indicates that no risk is present. What we wish to suggest is that there are cases where science is significantly less clear, where there are competing paradigms or other important uncertainties.

is too general or insufficiently scientifically validated. According to Sheila Jasanoff, the need to rely on evidentiary inferences and extrapolations is such a pervasive feature in risk regulation that subjecting this type of scientific evidence to the same evidentiary standards as used for 'research science' means applying empirically inappropriate evidentiary standards.[49] This is echoed by other commentators who maintain that an absence of evidence should not be equated with an absence of risk.[50] There is another epistemological problem of importance: sometimes, competing scientific studies can be based on different paradigms of interpretation, analysis or method and have reached different stages of corroboration. However, because they depart from different paradigms, the one with greater corroboration does not negate the other study or studies and it would be illogical to prefer it simply because it reached higher stages of corroboration.

The other problematic aspects revolve around political legitimacy. Commentators have expressed the criticism that the requirement of specificity of a risk assessment may make the regulation of certain 'real world' risks difficult if not impossible.[51] Because it can be difficult to provide adequate evidence for very low-dose, chronic exposures, exposures to complex risks or combined exposure, requirements of specificity disfavour the regulation of these types of risk. If the authority of science is limited in cases with elements of uncertainty, inferences or competing paradigms, as we suggest above, it becomes implausible to reject regulations exclusively on empirical or epistemological grounds in close-call cases where the evidence is of different epistemological validity. Science, we are told, cannot prove the absence of risk (the negative), it can only prove the positive (that a risk exists). As

---

[49]   Jasanoff, S. (1990), *The Fifth Branch: Science Advisers as Policymakers*, Cambridge, Mass: Harvard University Press, 42, 77–9 (arguing that filling gaps in the knowledge base, knowledge synthesis, and prediction of uncertain events are key features of regulatory science that distinguish it from laboratory science and that the same evidentiary standards should not apply to both).

[50]   Weimer, note 24, at 628, citing Fisher, E. (2007), 'Precaution, Precaution Everywhere: Developing a "Common Understanding" of Precautionary Principle in the European Community', *Maastricht Journal of European and Comparative Law*, **9** (1), 7–28.

[51]   Sykes, A.O. (2005), 'Domestic Regulation, Sovereignty, and Scientific Evidence Requirements: A Pessimistic View', in P.C. Mavroidis and A.O. Sykes (eds), *The WTO and International Trade Law/Dispute Settlement,* Cheltenham, UK and Northampton, MA: Edward Elgar, 178, at 189; Gruszczynski, L. (2006) *The Role of Science in Risk Regulation under the SPS Agreement*, EUI Working Paper Law No. 2006/03, 2006, available at http://papers.ssrn.com/sol3/papers. cfm?abstract_id=891114, at 25–6 (with further references) at 17.

a result, science cannot and should not be the ultimate yardstick for the illegality of regulations in such difficult cases.[52] To use it as such gives rise to an accountability problem because scientists would not and could not assume responsibility for the decision on whether or not to regulate yet the regulator refers to the expert evidence as the reason for (non-)regulation.[53] Instead, the quantum of proof has to be adjusted depending on the nature of the hazard, further ensuing consequences, the cost of hazard mitigation, modes of risk imposition and risk distribution, in short, a political appreciation of all relevant characteristics of the hazard.[54] In other words, we question the standard picture of risk assessment as providing the empirical facts that political risk management *must* work with. Instead, the regulator should have *some* freedom to select on political grounds among evidence with different degrees of validation rather than being constrained to use the one with the highest degree of validation. The question of the sufficiency of evidence is then always a question of a mixed normative-factual nature but this does not mean that the regulator has complete discretion. In clear cases, we can very well use empirical criteria as the basis for a reasonable decision; in cases with more uncertainty, we can also use criteria of threshold empirical reasonableness and of fairness and procedural legitimacy as such basis but these will inevitably be specified in a different manner in the involved states.[55]

In the final analysis then, law and regulation being concerned with normative questions of what one ought to do cannot delegate decision-making

---

[52]   Peel, J. (2004), *Risk Regulation under the WTO/SPS Agreement: Science as an International Normative Yardstick*, New York University School of Law Jean Monnet Working Paper 02/04, New York NY: NYU School of Law, available at http://www.jeanmonnetprogram.org/papers/04/040201.pdf, accessed 26 January 2012, 95–97.

[53]   Herwig, A. (2008), 'Whither Science in WTO Dispute Settlement?', *Leiden Journal of International Law*, **21** (4), 1–24, at 19, and Herwig, note 24, at 306.

[54]   *Ibid.* See also Forster, C. (2008), 'Public Opinion and the Interpretation of the World Trade Organisation's Agreement on Sanitary and Phytosanitary Measures', *Journal of International Economic Law*, **11** (2), 427–458.

[55]   For a clarification of the reason for the mixed factual-normative nature of evidentiary questions for law-making purposes from the perspective of theories of equality see Herwig, A. (forthcoming), 'How and Why does Expert Involvement Contribute to the Legitimacy of Policy-making? Some Reflections on Equality in the Context of WTO and CAC Policy on SPS Matters', in M. Ambrus et al., *The Role of Experts in International Decision-making: Decision-makers, Advisors or Irrelevant*, Cambridge: CUP. For a more applied analysis reaching similar conclusions about the necessarily open, normative content of precaution, see von Schomberg, R. (2012), 'The Precautionary Principle: Its Use within Hard and Soft Law', *European Journal of Risk Regulation*, **3** (2), 147–156.

authority to science, which is concerned with the empirical side only and committed to the logic of scientific discourses. It therefore becomes important for supra- and transnational law to acknowledge the important element of political choice and responsibility in risk regulation. Note, however, that acceptance of the political through the law calls into question the legitimacy of law itself – at least if it occurs as an unqualified surrender to politics. Does the law have anything to offer to preserve politics without succumbing completely to it? We return to this point in section C below.

B.   The Turn to Precaution

Precaution, we would like to suggest below, is an improvement over unrelenting scientific empiricism. It can be applied in a supra- or transnational fashion yet acknowledges the political–normative elements in regulatory decision-making. In other words, it can function as a conflicts law mechanism.

1.   Precaution in EU law
The precautionary principle can be found in international legal instruments. However, the EU is the legal system in which the principle has been developed significantly further and it has been elevated to constitutional status in Article 191 TFEU which stipulates that Union policy on the environment shall aim at a high level of protection and be based on the precautionary principle. The ECJ extended the applicability of the precautionary principle to the field of human health in the BSE case.[56]

The Commission also published a Communication on the Precautionary Principle that lays out further guidelines on the implementation of the precautionary principle in Union policy.[57] According to this Communication, there are empirical threshold criteria for the precautionary principle to become available (scientific evidence is insufficient or uncertain and there are reasonable grounds for concern) but the decision on whether or not to respond to these uncertainties and regulate based on precaution is identified as one of risk management and thus as belonging to politics.[58] The response

---

[56]   Case C-180/96 *UK v. Commission* [1998] ECR I-2265, para. 99. See also Weimer, note 24, at 630ff. with further references to case law.

[57]   Communication of the Commission on the Precautionary Principle ('Communication on the Precautionary Principle'), COM (2000) 1 of 02.02.2000, available at http://ec.europa.eu/dgs/health_consumer/library/pub/pub07_en.pdf, accessed 26 January 2012.

[58]   Communication on the Precautionary Principle, note 57, at 3; Weimer, note 24, at 5–6.

is also subject to requirements of proportionality, non-discrimination and cost-benefit analysis.[59] As Weimer astutely observes, there is a tension between these standards of rationality and the requirement for broad-based participatory processes in precautionary governance.[60] The Communication considers the precautionary principle to be a general principle of law, applicable to environmental protection and human, animal and plant life or health.[61] This has subsequently been confirmed by the General Court.[62] The consequence of this legal status, Weimer notes, is that the precautionary principle is relevant for the interpretation of EU law, constitutes a benchmark for the assessment of the validity of secondary legislation and is binding on Community institutions when they take risk regulatory decisions.[63] The General Court has also endorsed some of the substantive provisions of the Communication by accepting the risk assessment/risk management divide and the requirement for empirical thresholds for the precautionary principle set forth in the Communication.[64] In the preliminary reference in *Gowan* the ECJ considered that the same findings justify recourse to the precautionary principle as identified in the Communication.[65] In particular, the ECJ found the absence of a scientific method for the analysis of endocrine disruptors coupled with some general evidence of the disrupting effects on the endocrine system of certain substances sufficient for the Commission to take precautionary action. However, its review of the other elements of precautionary policies as set forth in the Communication is rather cursory. Noting the wide discretion the Commission enjoys, the ECJ does not find that the proportionality principle has been infringed.[66] The reasons the Court gives are that the Commission attempted to balance conflicting interests, that renewal of the authorisation was possible after 18 months, that new uses could in principle be authorised and that the restrictions imposed on the use of fenarimol do not appear to be unsuitable for the protection of health given the concerns with disruption of the endocrine system of fenarimol and the

---

[59]   Communication on the Precautionary Principle, note 57, at 10.

[60]   Weimer, note 24, at 630.

[61]   Communication on the Precautionary Principle, note 57, at 10.

[62]   Case T-13/99 *Pfizer Animal Health SA v. Council* [2002] ECR II-3305, Case T-70/99 *Alpharma v. Council* [2002] ECR II-3495, Cases T-74, 76, 93-85, 132, 137 and 141/00 *Artedogan GmbH v. Commission* [2002] ECR II-4945.

[63]   Weimer, note 24, at 632. See also Case C-236/01 *Monsanto v. Italy*, [2003] ECR I-8105.

[64]   Weimer, note 24, at 632 with reference to the CFI decision in *Pfizer*.

[65]   Case C-77/09 *Gowan Comércio Internacional e Serviços Lda*, Judgment of 22 December 2010, nyr, para. 76.

[66]   *Ibid.*, at 86.

level of uncertainty.[67] There is no review of whether an adequate cost-benefit analysis was performed and the level of protection and restrictions imposed are consistent with those in similar situations.

2.   Precaution in WTO law

There is no explicit legal principle of precaution in the SPS Agreement. The Appellate Body found it imprudent to take a decision on whether or not the precautionary principle had become customary international law or a general principle of law that should have been used in the interpretation of the SPS Agreement in accordance with Article 31.3(c) of the Vienna Convention on the Law of Treaties (VCLT).[68] Be that as it may, it noted that the precautionary principle could not relieve panels of the task of interpreting the provisions of the SPS Agreement pursuant to the normal rules of treaty interpretation and has not been written into the SPS Agreement as a separate ground of exception.[69] The *EC – Biotech* Panel took an even more restrictive approach. It *de facto* rejected any independent, interpretative weight of the precautionary principle enshrined in multilateral environmental agreements (MEAs) through its interpretation of Article 31.3(c) VCLT as requiring that membership of an MEA must at least encompass all WTO members before it can be used in a contextual interpretation of WTO law.[70]

Even if there is no formal legal principle of precaution, the principle possibly exerts an indirect influence. It could in particular be enshrined in the international standards WTO members are called on to use as a basis for their municipal measures absent the required scientific justification and whose close transposition into national law entitles them to a presumption of SPS and GATT 1994 consistency.[71] The international

---

[67]   *Ibid.*, at 83–85.

[68]   Appellate Body Report, *EC – Hormones,* para. 123.

[69]   *Ibid.* Unless the Appellate Body implicitly took the same restrictive view as to the interpretation of the term 'applicable in the relation between the parties' in Article 31.3(c) VCLT as the Panel in *EC – Biotech*, one wonders how the AB could arrive at this conclusion without having first undertaken an interpretation of the SPS Agreement in accordance with Article 31.3(c) VCLT in which it accepted for the purposes of the interpretation that the precautionary principle had indeed become a relevant rule of law applicable in the relation between the parties.

[70]   The Panel did concede, however, that formulations of the precautionary principle in MEAs could be used to confirm a textual interpretation of WTO law. Panel Report, *EC–Biotech*, note 43, at paras.7.68 and 7.92. For a critique of this finding, see Herwig, A. (2008), 'Whither Science in WTO Dispute Settlement?', note 53, at 18 *et seq.*

[71]   SPS Agreement, Articles 3.1, 3.2 and 3.3.

standardisation organisations have recognised that the precautionary principle matters in international standard-setting but have not been able to agree on substantive guidelines for its use.[72] Second, the Appellate Body considered that the precautionary principle found reflection in provisions of the SPS Agreement: especially in Article 5.7, which deals with situations of insufficient scientific evidence but also in Article 5.1 where irreversible risks are concerned.[73] As we show below, some of the dispute settlement decisions on Articles 5.7, 2.2 and 5.1 can be understood to have applied precautionary thinking in the sense of conflicts law.

C.   Precaution in Conflicts Law Perspectives

We would like to argue that the precautionary principle can be understood as a supranational conflicts law mechanism if it is interpreted in a way that keeps the principle open for empirical (scientific) and normative (political) elements. Although the formulation of the precautionary principle is not identical in all legal texts, the common denominator is that it allows for taking regulatory action when there are threats of a hazard but a lack of full scientific certainty.[74] At the same time, the precautionary principle leaves open which factors can justify a decision to take regulatory action.

In the case of many international formulations of the principle, the precautionary principle is a reason-blocking device that affirms that the lack of full scientific certainty shall not be used as a reason not to take regulatory action.[75] Note that this formulation makes it possible that other empirical (scientific) or political (normative) considerations can be used as a reason for or against the taking of regulatory action.

---

[72]   Codex Alimentarius Commission (2011), *Working Principles for Risk Analysis For Application in the Framework of the Codex Alimentarius Commission in Procedural Manual*, 20th ed., 105–111, at 106 para. 11.

[73]   Appellate Body Report, *EC – Hormones*, para. 123.

[74]   E.g. EC Communication on the Precautionary Principle, para. 4 preamble and para. 5.1; Principle 15 Rio Declaration on Environment and Development: 'Where there are threats of serious or irreversible damage, lack of full scientific certainty shall not be used as a reason for postponing cost-effective measures to prevent environmental degradation.'

[75]   Principle 15 of the Rio Declaration on Environment and Development, available at http://www.unep.org/Documents.multilingual/Default.asp?Documen tID=78&ArticleID=1163, accessed 31 January 2012, states as follows: 'In order to protect the environment, the precautionary approach shall be widely applied by States according to their capabilities. Where there are threats of serious or irreversible damage, lack of full scientific certainty shall not be used as a reason for postponing cost-effective measures to prevent environmental degradation.'

In contrast to this, the EU Commission's Communication on the Precautionary Principle is more detailed. It affirms repeatedly that the decision on whether or not to act in the face of suspected hazards is an 'eminently political decision' or an 'eminently political responsibility', and 'a function of the risk level that is "acceptable" to the society on which the risk is imposed'.[76] The Preamble of the Commission Communication then affirms that the unacceptability of risk, the scientific uncertainty and public concerns all have to be taken into account by decision-makers.[77] In addition, the Communication states that regulatory action based on the precautionary principle has to be proportionate, non-discriminatory, consistent with similar measures taken, subject to cost-benefit analysis of action and non-action, reviewable in light of new scientific data and capable of assigning responsibility for producing such data.[78]

The Commission Communication therefore makes it clear that empirical and normative reasons and public concerns all have to be considered in decisions based on the precautionary principle. Through this guideline and the standards applicable to precautionary measures, a reasoning process is pre-structured through some supranational and legally verifiable elements (e.g. proportionality, non-discrimination, extent of uncertainty and quality of the preliminary evidence) but because of the imminently political and broad nature of some of these elements and the fact that their relative weights cannot be pre-defined in detail by the law, the law must confine itself to setting up robust procedures with reflexive elements, *inter alia* for assessing the acceptability of risk, carrying out and defining what the costs and benefits are, assessing public concerns and collecting new evidence.

This, we would like to suggest, is consistent with the idea of conflicts law: the need for supra- and transnational law to set up structures of accountability that allow risk-averse and risk-tolerant societies to work out their differences in a space legally defined through meta-rules acceptable to both of them. Now, the need for some empirical corroboration of precautionary policies (albeit of lesser weight than 'full scientific certainty') requires the risk-averse state to explain its precautionary policy in terms of evidence that is scientific and thus acceptable as a regulatory 'grammar' for the more risk-tolerant state. Inasmuch as the risk-averse state claims to regulate on grounds of protection against danger, the requirement for some minimally

---

[76]   Communication on the Precautionary Principle, note 57, at para. 5.2.1 and preamble para. 5.
[77]   Communication on the Precautionary Principle, note 57, preamble para. 5.
[78]   Communication on the Precautionary Principle, note 57, preamble para. 6 and para. 6.2.

objective empirical scientific support that the precautionary principle imposes is a requirement of consistency that is therefore acceptable also to the risk-averse state and one that the law can verify. The precautionary principle neither precludes nor requires explicitly that normative factors have a role to play in the decision on whether or not to take precautionary action. It confers freedom on the regulating state to evaluate whether the less corroborated empirical evidence creates sufficient concern to warrant regulatory action based on the nature of the suspected hazard. This should motivate the exporting state whose products are subject to the foreign regulation at issue to engage with the importing state's policy reasons for regulation, e.g. because these concerns can be addressed in different ways or the balance of benefits and costs is different than that which the importing state has determined. Here again are some supranational elements that the law can verify – albeit only at the margins. The law can verify whether a very rough relation of inverse proportionality is respected, such that suspected hazards that are qualitatively not very serious require evidence of a relatively higher degree of corroboration to warrant precautionary measures compared to more serious hazards where the evidentiary requirements can be further relaxed. Note that the precautionary principle does not necessarily define the respective weights of empirical and normative considerations beyond some minimal threshold. Precisely because of its relative indeterminacy, the precautionary principle opens up a space for a cooperative search for a politically sensitive and legally sensible solution to a complex conflict constellation. It encourages the importing and exporting state to give reasons in the light of the concerns of the respective other state. This is an excellent illustration of what a conflicts law perspective argues for: that European and transnational law derive their legitimacy from their ability to set up legal structures that require the inclusion of the other in the assessment of conflict constellations. This potential of the precautionary principle's indeterminacy comes close to the principle of *comitas* in private international law: the duty of the forum state to give sympathetic and genuine consideration to the possible application of foreign law out of concern for the equality of other states before the forum state's courts thereby instituting a civility of nations without, however, requiring them to apply foreign law if it is inconsistent with the public policy of the forum state.[79] As one of us has observed previously:

---

[79]   Joel Paul traces the evolution of the *comitas* principle in private international law and describes how the principle aimed at fostering good foreign relations by giving equal treatment to foreign law in the forum state's courts but always leaving open the possibility of not applying foreign law. Paul, J.R. (2008),

Comitas would suggest a search for a middle ground between law and politics by advising the latter to take the expertise of the former seriously, and by advising the former to be aware of the limited legitimacy of law that did not originate in a democratic process. What we find worth remembering, however, is that *comitas* was used, and continues to be used, when courts have arrived at the borderlines of adjudication. Where they are not empowered with the assessment of policies and economic interests, they may still function as *fora* or as instigator of fair and workable compromises.[80]

With this understanding of the precautionary principle, the principle respects the three prescriptive premises of conflicts law: it requires states to take seriously the extraterritorial effects they produce and to reconsider them in light of the concerns of the affected jurisdictions but it tolerates diversity and limits judicial review to a marginal one.

D. Rival Approaches: Global Legal Pluralism and Limited Supranationalism

In this section, we discuss two competing theories on the legitimacy of supra- and transnational regulation with the aim of substantiating the specifics of the conflicts law approach further. 'Limited supranationalism' is the notion we use to characterise the work of Giandomenico Majone on the EU. Majone does not advocate a transformation of the EU into a democratic polity. To him, the absence of democracy as we know it from the constitutional nation state is not a problem but an advantage when it comes to specific regulatory objectives in particular in the spheres of social regulation. He argues that Europe could ensure the acceptance of its involvement in problem-solving if carried out by non-majoritarian institutions in an objective and expertise-based fashion, subject to reason-giving requirements and judicial review and limited to the policy areas in which regulation is concerned with the establishment of markets and the correction of market failures.[81] These are notably characterised by being about

---

'The Transformation of International Comity', *Law and Contemporary Problems*, **71** (3), 19–38, at 33.

[80]   Joerges, C., and J. Neyer (2003), 'Politics, Risk Management, WTO Governance and the Limits of Legalisation', *Science and Public Policy*, **30** (3), 219–225, at 225.

[81]   This implies, however, that Europe should stay out of contested distributional and welfare state policies. For his earlier position, see Majone, G. (1989), 'Regulating Europe: Problems and Prospects', *Jahrbuch zur Staats- und Verwaltungswissenschaft*, **3**, 159–177; *idem* (1994), 'The European Commmunity as a Regulatory State', 1994-V/1 *Collected Course of the Academy of European Law*, Den Haag, Boston, MA, London: Martinus Nijhoff, 321–419; and more

aggregate efficiency gains or pareto-optimality and not redistribution.[82] According to Majone, redistribution involves worsening the position of some for the benefit of others and requires majoritarian legitimation and a sufficient degree of homogeneity.[83] Efficiency-based policies allow for a net gain of everyone and are claimed to be capable of legitimation by non-majoritarian institutions.[84]

Now, we agree that expertise sometimes possesses such normative authority in virtue of its clear epistemological authority and that it is useful for transnational accountability as a universal grammar. But often, science does not possess such clear authority: scientific findings will be contested, data missing, paradigms of inquiry will differ or methods be unavailable to assess complex problems. What is more, as soon as there is evidence of risk, science runs out: it can not tell us whether the risk is worth taking. Nor does an absence of evidence on risk imply that a product cannot be regulated on different grounds, such as consumer choice or a desire to maintain traditional forms of agriculture. In all these cases, an important political (or normative) element of decision-making remains: is the evidence sufficient or not for taking regulatory action, is it worthwhile taking a risk or possibly experiencing a hazard and are there other grounds for regulating or rejecting a product?

What the area of food safety risk regulation also shows is that relatively mundane risks, such as the use of hormones for growth promotion in beef or traditional but not perfectly safe ways of food-processing, can become politically contested and are not easily characterised as purely technical issues. The example of the politically highly contested nuclear energy and its potential cross-border effects viewed through the lens of conflicts laws also shows that Europe must address politically contentious matters and will need to find *sui generis* responses to generate legitimacy.

Our argument that the turn to science and with it to precaution can be understood as conflicts law is thus not an argument for using science to impose uniform regulatory solutions on countries or making national regulations perfectly rational. Rather, the argument is based on the recognition that scientific support for national regulations makes the state

---

recently his scepticism of European expansionism into contested policy areas *idem* (2010), *Europe as the Would-be World Power. The EU at Fifty*, Cambridge: CUP, 128 *et seq.*; *idem* (1998), 'Europe's Democracy Deficit: A Question of Standards', *European Law Journal*, **4** (1), 5–28.

[82] See Majone, G. (1998), 'Europe's Democracy Deficit: A Question of Standards', *European Law Journal*, **4** (1), 5–28, at 13–14, 28.

[83] *Ibid.*

[84] *Ibid.*, at 28.

accountable to outside affected interests in a minimal fashion in the sense of making them understandable without imposing unity: as soon as evidence is accepted by the scientific community it becomes available as a justification for national regulatory measures but states may rely on very different scientific findings or take different decisions on whether or not the risk is worth taking. At a minimum, they must have demonstrated a real engagement with the scientific evidence even if they ultimately regulate based on other grounds. To explore the simile from language again: Science provides for a grammar that makes utterances intelligible even though the speakers disagree on content; it is about syntax, not semantics. It may at first sight be surprising, if not paradoxical, but it seems to us that Majone's thoughtful critique of the use European authorities make of the precautionary principle[85] militates in fact in favour of our re-interpretation of that principle as a conflicts law device. As Majone convincingly argues, the ambiguities and uncertainties cannot be 'resolved';[86] it is nevertheless possible, as Majone points out in his references to the ECJ,[87] to channel the use of the principle by procedural standards. Majone's second objection concerns the controversies between in particular the US and the EU which the European departure from 'sound science' in favour of precaution has caused. In both respects we submit that our conflicts law approach provides orientation in the handling of these difficulties. There is no way to get rid of scientific uncertainties and there is no 'higher law' available which would provide us with legitimated 'solutions' of the trade conflicts between the US, the EU and developing countries. The complexity of the conflict constellations to which European and WTO law have to respond can only be constructively handled with the help of procedural criteria which further deliberative problem-solving and arguing as we have outlined in section III.C.

With global legal pluralism, exemplified in the work of Nico Krisch, conflicts law shares the recognition that supra- and transnational law must avoid hierarchy and substantive unification of the legal orders. Both also see conflicts as inevitable. However, one important difference between conflicts law as we propose it here and Nico Krisch's account is that the

---

[85]   Majone, G. (2002), 'What Price Safety? The Precautionary Principle and its Policy Implications', *Journal of Common Market Studies*, **40** (1), 89–109.

[86]   As he very lucidly puts it: The 'distinction between situations where scientific information is sufficient to permit a formal risk assessment, and those where "scientific information is insufficient, inconclusive or uncertain" [is artificial]. In reality, these are two points on a knowledge-ignorance continuum rather than two qualitatively distinct situations.' *Ibid.* at 104.

[87]   *Ibid.*, at 98.

latter allows a legal regime to define through its institutions 'the terms on which it interacts with others. Different polities may then come to conflicting terms'.[88] This allows for a multiplicity of responses, from constructive engagement, accommodation or compromise to greater withdrawal and isolation.[89] However, a regime is entitled to respect only inasmuch as its practices foster public autonomy.[90] Nico Krisch endorses a Habermasian concept of public autonomy in which the equal autonomy of all must be reciprocally respected.[91] Thus, the deliberative pedigree, inclusiveness or the strength of arguments for furthering particular goals confer public autonomy credentials.[92] But the demands of universality (at least potentially) are to be counterbalanced by the right to self-determination and particularism.[93] The latter could be seen as making concessions to voluntarism or facts because Krisch argues that people's felt allegiances also matter.[94] Although Krisch characterises respect for the equal autonomy of all as a moral duty, it can become positivised in legal interface

---

[88]   Krisch, note 22, at 103.

[89]   This is of course not what conflicts law endorses.

[90]   Krisch, note 22, at 100–103, and for theoretical background see 91–96.

[91]   *Ibid.*, at 99–100.

[92]   *Ibid.*, at 101.

[93]   *Ibid.*, at 100–101.

[94]   *Ibid.*, at 87–88, 95, 102. Note, though, that Krisch does not explain fully and convincingly why the fact of allegiance matters. Is it because allegiances or associations are morally relevant because, as he suggests on p. 93, the question of public autonomy or democracy comprises the prior moral question of whom to associate with and whom not to associate with? But this criterion itself cannot settle the issue of whether one should opt for the larger, more-inclusive or the smaller, less-inclusive polity because it does not offer us any yardstick for deciding adverse claims of inclusion. Or does he work back towards principles of social justice from the fact of a pluralism of associations as pp. 96 and 98 would suggest? But why should the fact of felt allegiance (or of the good) be prior to the right? Indeed, on p. 97 he concedes as much. Or is he of the view that full democratic inclusion is contingent upon but regulative of certain facts as pp. 99–100 suggest, such as non-radical moral disagreement? It seems doubtful that the fragmentation of the global order into different spheres or law and governance reaches such radical levels of disagreement in most cases and across all issues. And even if one concedes that democracy is contingent upon a thicker sense of community and shared values as provided by nation states, towns, internet communities, professional associations or the like, there still is the question of why proxies for full democratic inclusion enshrined in public rules do not work for structuring the relationship between various communities. Or are our felt allegiances merely an empirical obstacle on the way to realising fully inclusive universal social practices? But this does not square with his fundamental critique of constitutionalism. And finally, is it always possible to balance universalism with particularism or are there sometimes hard conflicts? We return to this point below in the Epilogue.

norms.[95] These are the gateway of openness, closure, friendliness or hostility of the various legalities and are various ways of conditional recognition or taking account of other legal materials.[96]

This is not the place to engage in an intensive discussion of Krisch's account, except to note that one is left puzzled. We agree with Lars Viellechner that Krisch's endorsement of public autonomy seems to recognise the central vantage point of a constitutionalist ordering.[97] But this raises the question of why autonomy-enhancing duties of reason-giving, transparency and conflicts law meta-norms cannot be inscribed in binding legal obligations. Moreover, if legal orders have to commit to the preservation of public autonomy, it seems their conflicts are shallow ones of misunderstanding or misinformation rather than deep ones, which a constitutionalist framework could handle easily by instituting norms of information exchange, reason-giving and other mechanisms that foster learning. Absent a legal commitment to autonomy preservation qua constitutionalisation, the problem with Krisch's interface norms is that they can remain just voluntaristic mechanisms of disengagement if used by the wrong kinds of regimes for the wrong kinds of reasons.

Nolens volens Krisch could therefore turn out to be an apologetic of closure, suppression of voices and power play.[98] And finally, while checks by neighbouring legal regimes can nudge the regimes being checked towards becoming more inclusive, absent a constitutional commitment to autonomy, these checks can only be as good as the surrounding legal regimes themselves are inclusive and representative of the broadest possible array of interests. With power and wealth asymmetries and fundamen-

---

[95]   *Ibid.*, at 296.

[96]   *Ibid.*, at 285–291.

[97]   For an insightful critique of Krisch's book, see Viellechner, L. (2012), 'Beyond Constitutionalism. The Pluralist Structure of Postnational Law. By Nico Krisch. Oxford: OUP, 2010, xxiv + 358 pp. Hb. £50.00.' *European Law Journal*, **18** (4), 595–598. Lars Viellechner also argues that conflicts law and Krisch's pluralism are both approaches seeking to combine constitutionalism and pluralism. See *idem* (forthcoming), 'Constitutionalism as a Cipher: On the Convergence of Constitutionalist and Pluralist Approaches to the Globalization of Law', *Goettingen Journal of International Law*. The key difference, as we see it, is that conflicts law seeks a constitutional commitment to legal responses for managing legal and political conflicts, whereas Krisch's pluralism seeks political responses.

[98]   As Koskeniemmi has observed: 'The problem of legal pluralism is the way it ceases to pose demands on the world. Its theorists are so enchanted by the complex interplay of regimes and a positivist search for an all inclusive vocabulary that they lose the critical point of their exercise.' Koskeniemmi, M. (2011), *The Politics of International Law*, Oxford: Hart Publishing, at 353.

tally undemocratic regimes one cannot be certain at all that the current global order reflects interests in a balanced way.[99]

Law, and supranational conflicts law in particular, as we see it, however, require the inclusion of 'the Other' and therefore openness and a constructive engagement of the legal orders and regimes with each other according to justiciable legal norms. The notion of Howse and Nicolaïdis of horizontal subsidiarity echoes this.[100] What they envision as the right model for the EU – the generation of processes rather than outcomes conducive to dialogue across polities and a normative and institutional framework that reflects a commitment to democracy, the rule of law and peaceful settlement of disputes sensitive to diversity, is strikingly similar to conflicts law.[101] Supra- and transnational law has to put in place procedures that enable reason-giving and accountability, procedures that one can specify and reason about. This, we hope to have shown, is different from Krisch's call for pluralism.

IV. ILLUSTRATION THROUGH CASES OF EXEMPLARY IMPORTANCE

The two WTO dispute settlement decisions we contrast in this section mark the demise and revival of precautionary thinking in the SPS Agreement and help us to draw out, through one negative and one positive example, what solutions conflicts law can bring to transnational disputes over risk regulation.

A. Precaution is Dead . . .

The *EC – Biotech* Panel report is the most explicit in its refusal of precautionary thinking, even if it is not the only one that took a restrictive stance

---

[99]   For this public choice problem and a discussion of global administrative law pluralism and other models, see Herwig, A. (2011), 'The Contribution of Global Administrative Law to the Legitimacy of the Codex Alimentarius Commission', in O. Dilling, M. Herberg and G. Winter (eds), *Transnational Administrative Rule-Making: Performance, Legal Effects, and Legitimacy*, Oxford: Hart, 171–212, at 200.

[100]   Howse, R. and K. Nicolaïdis (2002), 'This is my Eutopia . . . Narrative as Power', *Journal of Common Market Studies*, **40** (4), 767–792, at 784.

[101]   *Ibid.*, at 771, 782, 784, 785, 788; see also Howse, R. and K. Nicolaïdis (2008), 'Democracy without Sovereignty: The Global Vocation of Political Ethics', in T. Broude and Y. Shany (eds), *The Shifting Allocation of Authority in International Law: Considering Sovereignty, Supremacy and Subsidiarity*, Oxford: Hart Publishing, 163–191, at 164, 182, 191.

towards the precautionary principle. The case concerned three different types of measures: the general EU moratorium on the approval of GMOs, the product-specific moratorium and the safeguards that several EU Member States had taken against specific GM products that had received Community authorisation.

To situate the *EC – Biotech* report in its legal context, we first discuss briefly selected aspects of previous WTO dispute settlement decisions.[102] Even though *EC – Hormones* did not deal directly with Article 5.7 of the SPS Agreement, the Appellate Body displayed a certain sensitivity towards precautionary concerns that is very consistent with our understanding of conflicts law. The Appellate Body recognised that a risk assessment did not have to establish a minimum magnitude of risk and allowed WTO Members to base themselves on minority scientific opinion.[103] It also noted that panels charged with the task of assessing whether a measure was based on a risk assessment should bear in mind that responsible governments act from a standpoint of caution and prudence where irreversible and especially life-threatening risks are concerned.[104] This can certainly be understood as an acknowledgement that the question of whether or not evidence is sufficient to regulate is not one that can be delegated to science alone but must be based on a political decision. This statement seems to conflict with the Appellate Body's other finding that risk assessments had to be specific to the substance and form of exposure targeted by the measure in order for the measure to be based on a risk assessment in the sense of Article 5.1.[105] We would like to suggest that, by not deciding this issue in *EC – Hormones,* the Appellate Body displayed some prudent management of the dispute because it left it to the disputing parties to work out how to reconcile scientific and political rationality in risk regulation.

Subsequent dispute settlement panels and the Appellate Body abandoned this prudence. Already the Panel and Appellate Body report in *Japan – Apples* can be interpreted as limiting recourse to the precautionary principle qua Article 5.7 to situations where validated scientific risk assessments are unavailable or information is lacking, thus limiting the grounds for recourse to the precautionary principle to scientific ones.[106]

---

[102]   We do not discuss the *Japan – Agricultural Products* findings on Article 5.7, which, to us, follow directly from the legal text of the SPS Agreement.

[103]   Appellate Body Report, *EC – Hormones,* paras. 186, 194.

[104]   *Ibid.*, at para. 123.

[105]   *Ibid.*, at paras. 199–200.

[106]   Appellate Body Report, *Japan – Apples,* para. 185; Panel Report, *Japan – Apples,* para. 8.219. As the Appellate Body explained, when there is relevant scientific evidence, recourse to Article 5.7 of the SPS Agreement is possible only when

What remained implicit in *Japan – Apples*, the Panel in *EC – Biotech* made explicit. Thus, the Panel found that recourse to Article 5.7 was precluded when a risk assessment existed.[107] This decision suggests that risk assessments can simply be transposed from one political regulatory context to another, notwithstanding the politico-normative embedded-ness that must also play a role in determining which quantum of proof is acceptable for regulatory intervention.[108] In the end, the Panel upset the EU's constitutional settlement which recognised diversity as legitimate.[109] The Panel also imposed a very high evidentiary burden on the EC for it to be able to show that the evidence supporting the Member States' safe-guard measures were risk assessments. It rejected even very suggestive if not probative evidence and, because of its formalistic delineation of Articles 5.1 and 5.7, never bothered to investigate whether this evidence was enough to call into question the sufficiency of previous evidence as required by Article 5.7.[110] From the perspective of conflicts law, this deci-sion is misguided because it reduces the central question of whether or not regulatory intervention is justified to an empirical or scientific one and displays unjustified faith in the ability of science to answer key questions in risk regulation. What the Panel's decision in essence means is that once a risk assessment has been performed, legitimate reasons for regulatory diversity arising from different political choices for a higher or lower quantum of empirical proof of risk cease to exist.

The Panel's decision on the compatibility of the general and product-specific moratoria with Annex C of the SPS Agreement also reveals its scepticism towards the precautionary principle. Amidst intra-Community controversy over GMOs, the EC had come to stop approvals on GMOs until further evidence was available. The Panel found that this constituted undue delay and infringed Annex C without attaching weight to the fact

---

this evidence has not come to conclusive or reliable results. As one of us argued elsewhere, the reference to 'conclusive' and 'reliable' seems to refer to terms for establishing the validity of scientific findings. The reasons for this interpretation of the findings in *Japan – Apples* are given in Herwig, note 24, at 316–319.

[107]   The EC had acknowledged that the assessments of the relevant Community scientific committees constituted a risk assessment but made the case that notwith-standing this risk assessment, Member States had 1) undertaken a different risk assessment or 2) had found scientific evidence to be insufficient.

[108]   We have developed this argument in Section III.A.3 above.

[109]   Joerges, C. (2009), 'Judicialization and Transnational Governance: The Example of WTO Law and the GMO Dispute', in Bogdan Iancu (ed.), *The Law/Politics Distinction in Contemporary Public Law Adjudication,* Utrecht: Eleven International Publishing, 67–84.

[110]   For a detailed discussion, Herwig, note 53, at 11–15, 17.

that GMO approval was politically contested. Again, this diminishes the important element of political decision on risk that the precautionary principle and conflicts law want to safeguard and gives the interests of biotechnology companies seeking authorisation greater weight.[111]

As discussed above, the panel's findings on the relevance of Multilateral Environmental Agreements for the contextual interpretation of the SPS Agreement limit the potential impact of the precautionary principle as enshrined in non-WTO law on the SPS Agreement. The result was that the SPS Agreement's science-based rationality resulting from the *EC – Biotech* decision would trump international political resolutions of regulatory problems inspired by precautionary thinking.

We thus beg to differ with Nico Krisch's assessment of the *EC – Biotech* report. Krisch sees the unclear relationship between WTO law and the Biosafety Protocol and the Panel's refusal to give weight to MEAs in the interpretation of the SPS Agreement as an instance of systemic pluralism, as a contestation over the right constituency to take decisions on GMOs but points out that engagement remains possible. His overall assessment is positive.[112] He characterises the Panel's findings as narrow since it did not reject the European system of prior approvals outright and indicated to the EU that it could well have taken restrictive measures against GMOs if only its risk assessment had identified uncertainties or constraints.[113] We fail to see what is narrow or pluralistic about the Panel's findings. The case was – partly – about an intra-European disagreement about GMOs, with the Commission and several Member States in favour of their authorisation and the Member States taking the safeguard measures against. By finding that once a risk assessment existed, recourse to Article 5.7 was impossible, the Panel made such intra-European disagreement impossible and created a hierarchy in favour of the Community that was not there before.

B.   ... Long Live Precaution

In *Continued Suspension,* the Appellate Body resurrected precaution. The case was the second round of the growth hormones dispute. When the EC failed to implement the findings in the first hormones case, the complainants requested authorisation from the Dispute Settlement Body (DSB) to suspend concessions vis-à-vis the EC. After some time, the EC requested the establishment of a panel alleging that novel scientific evidence had

---

[111]   Joerges, note 109, 81.
[112]   See Krisch, note 22, at 206–207, 212, 215, 221.
[113]   *Ibid.*, at 214.

now brought it into compliance with the SPS Agreement. On appeal, the Appellate Body reversed several of the problematic findings of the Panel.

The first important reversal focused on the question of whether 'sufficiency' as the delineator between Articles 5.1 and 5.7 was to be determined according to scientific or political criteria or both. The Panel had found that the political aims (i.e. the degree of risk aversion and tolerance) of the regulator did not have any influence on whether or not scientific evidence was sufficient.[114] The Appellate Body rejected this finding and struck a middle ground: it considered that the political aims of the regulator justified framing the risk assessment by asking certain questions of scientists but that the issue of whether or not scientific evidence is sufficient would be determined according to scientific criteria.[115] In effect, this allows regulators to ask many questions of scientists, including ones science cannot answer,[116] and allows easier recourse to Article 5.7 of the SPS Agreement. The Appellate Body has prudently refrained from saying how it would look upon a situation where the regulator deliberately frames the risk assessment so as to make it difficult or impossible to carry it out. This indeterminacy is precisely what allows disputing parties to work out between themselves how to account for their regulatory choices and economic activities to each other through recourse to scientific and political argument.

Next, the Appellate Body was faced with the question of whether and under which circumstances Article 5.7 measures could be justified when there was pre-existing sufficient evidence and an international standard of the Codex Alimentarius Commission. The *Continued Suspension* Panel had found that the existence of a Codex standard on four of the five growth hormones at issue generally implied that there was a situation of sufficient scientific evidence.[117] The Appellate Body modified the Panel's approach and found instead that the existence of a Codex standard had probative but not dispositive weight.[118] On the question of what type of evidence could justify Article 5.7 measures when there was pre-existing sufficient evidence the Panel had opined that only a critical mass of new evidence calling into question fundamental precepts of previous

---

[114]   Panel Report, *US – Continued Suspension*, paras 7.609–7.612; Panel Report, *Canada – Continued Suspension*, paras. 7.587–7.590.

[115]   Appellate Body Report, *US/Canada – Continued Suspension,* paras 685–686.

[116]   For instance, regulators could ask scientists to research risks that are notoriously difficult to assess because no good methodology exists.

[117]   Panel Report, *US – Continued Suspension*, para. 7.644; Panel Report, *Canada – Continued Suspension*, para. 7.622.

[118]   Appellate Body Report, *US/Canada – Continued Suspension*, paras 694–697.

knowledge could justify recourse to Article 5.7.[119] The Appellate Body equated this with a requirement of a paradigm shift and considered this much too strict.[120] Instead, it ruled that the new evidence had to be of such a nature as to call into question previous findings so that one could no longer have reasonable confidence in them.[121] Through both findings the Appellate Body enabled precautionary regulation and protected regulatory diversity. Henceforth, it is possible for one WTO Member to accept products on the basis of a risk assessment while the hurdle for another WTO Member to regulate or ban the product temporarily on the basis of preliminary evidence is not too high. This is what conflicts law calls for.

V.   EPILOGUE: WHERE THE LAW ENDS . . .

Atomic energy, the notion used in the Euratom Treaty of 1957,[122] or nuclear energy, the concept preferred today, is the best conceivable case for the conflicts approach. The risks of this type of energy cannot be confined within the territory of one single state. This is why the decision to rely on this type of energy production reveals a democratic deficit of national decision-making. The example illustrates at the same time the need if not necessity to seek transnational cooperation, be it in the fundamental decisions on the use of that energy, be it in the control of its risks or in the search for renewable forms of energy which might pave the way towards a less risky future. Last but not least, decision-making in this field confirms the validity of Brainerd Currie's queries with judicial decision-making in cases of 'true conflicts':[123] What body could possibly be the final arbiter in controversies about the use or non-use of atomic energy?

It is the vocation of Europe, so we have argued, to compensate the structural deficits of nation state decision-making and to organise cooperative problem-solving where national solutions are inconceivable. Unfortunately, in the field of nuclear energy, European law is far from providing such frameworks. The 1957 Treaty emphasised in its preamble that 'nuclear energy is an indispensible aid for the development and invigoration of the market and for peaceful advance' and then underlined the determination 'to create the conditions for the establishment of a

---

[119]   Panel Report, *US – Continued Suspension*, paras 6.141, 7.648; Panel Report, *Canada – Continued Suspension*, paras 6.133, 7.626.
[120]   Appellate Body Report, *US/Canada – Continued Suspension*, para. 706.
[121]   *Ibid.*, at para. 725.
[122]   Consolidated version in OJ C 84, 1 of 30.3.2010.
[123]   See note 15 and accompanying text.

powerful nuclear energy industry'. The decision for or against the use of this form of energy was left to individual nation states. Back in 1957 this could be understood as deference to their political autonomy and should also be read in the context of the then prevailing optimistic consensus. By now, after quite bitter experiences with the risks of atomic energy and after decades of heated debates in a number of European countries, the premises of 1957 are technologically and politically outdated. The Treaty of Lisbon, however, has confirmed the old consensus, re-iterating in Article 194(2) TFEU that 'each member state has the right to determine the conditions for the use of its own energy resources, to choose between different energy resources and to determine the general structure for its energy provision'. This provision confirms also the so-called 'autonomy' of the Euratom Treaty with an implication of particular interest here: the principle of precaution is inapplicable under the Euratom Treaty.[124]

Is that state of the law sustainable even after Fukushima? This seems unpredictable. One pertinent encounter, however, has occurred and reached the ECJ's Grand Chamber:[125] The background to this case dispute between Austria and the Czech Republic has a long history stretching back to 1985.[126] The conflict was generated by Austrian concerns over the Temlín nuclear power plant. The plant had been duly authorised by the Czech Republic and had been running on a trial basis since 1985 and at full capacity since 2003 after a technological upgrading of Temelín's Soviet style equipment which was accomplished in bilateral bargaining and under the supervision of the European Commission. Austria felt more at ease, but would certainly have preferred a response respecting its principled rejection of atomic energy in a referendum of 1978 which was 'constitutionalised' by unanimous parliamentary vote in 1997.[127]

These irreconcilable positions reached the law through a back door.

---

[124]   This oddity has motivated Members of the European Convention, among them the late Neil MacCormick, to ask for the integration of the Euratom Treaty into the general European institutional framework (see their submission to the Convention: Conv 563/03 and for an overview http://www.eu-energy.com/euratom-reform.htm, accessed 15 October 2011. In the same vein the Editorial in 45 *CMLRev* (2007), 929, at 934. That motion remained unsuccessful.

[125]   C-115/08, *Land Oberösterreich v ČEZ*, judgment of 27.10.2009, nyr

[126]   For a comprehensive reconstruction see Hummer, W. (2008), 'Temelín: Das Kernkraftwerk an der Grenze', *Zeitschrift für öffentliches Recht*, **63**, 501–557, at 523–532.

[127]   Austria, after a referendum held in 1978, committed in its constitution to the rejection of atomic energy and confirmed its position by a unanimous parliamentary vote in 1997. See Pelinka, A. (1983), 'The Nuclear Power Referendum in Austria', *Electoral Studies*, **2** (3), 253–261.

Upper Austria, the owner of land located at a distance of just 60 km from Temelín, complained about ionizing radiation from that power station. Upper Austria based its claim on the *actio negatoria* of Paragraph 364(2) of the Austrian Civil Code.[128] There was thus a horizontal conflict in private international law between two EU Member States: on the one hand, Austria's claim in real property backed up by a constitutional rejection of nuclear energy; on the other hand, the freedom of the owner of the authorised power plant to use his land for nuclear power generation pursuant to the law of the Czech Republic that had issued the authorisation.

Pursuant to the Brussels Convention of 1968, the conflict came to the ECJ for adjudication.[129] AG Maduro in his opinion of 11 January 2006, and the ECJ in its judgment of 18 May 2006, discussed whether rights *in rem* were at issue so that the Austrian courts could invoke Article 16 of the Convention and claim exclusive jurisdiction. Or was this matter to be qualified as a tort in the sense of Article 5 III of the Brussels Convention and therefore governed by the *lex loci delicti?* Which characterisation was the proper one? Giving exclusive jurisdiction to Austrian courts would amount to authorising Austria to decide over the Czech Republic's energy policy. That seems beyond the authority of private international law – and this intuition was confirmed by the ECJ:

> ... it cannot be considered that an action such as that pending before the national court should in general be decided according to the rules of one State rather than the other and in conclusion: this is no case of exclusive Austrian *in rem* jurisidiction.[130]

The flipside, however, of allowing the Czech Republic to operate the plant without regard for the Austrian concerns is equally unsatisfactory because it amounts to rejecting Austrian commitments. Is there a third way? The two countries agreed to cooperate over energy partnerships and safety measures – but this did not bring the dispute to an end.[131] Upper Austria continued to pursue its claim and obtained a judgment from

---

[128]   § 364(2) of the Austrian Civil Code provides: 'The owner of a land may prohibit his neighbour from producing effects, emanating from the latter's land, by effluent, smoke, gases, heat, odours, noise, vibration and the like, in so far as they exceed normal local levels and significantly interfere with the usual use of the land. Direct transmission, without a specific legal right, is unlawful in all circumstances.' [Translation from Case C-115/08, para. 36.]

[129]   The Brussels Convention provides private international law rules for conflicts of laws between EU Member States. The ECJ is given jurisdiction over disputes arising under the Convention.

[130]   Case C-343/04, para. 36.

[131]   See para. 1 *et seq.* of AG Maduro's Opinion in Case C-115/08.

Austria's *Oberster Gerichtshof* in which the court refused to recognise the Czech authorisation on the basis of exception from the *actio negatoria* in Paragraph 364a.[132] The *Oberster Gerichtshof* failed to see a good reason why Austrian law should restrict the property rights of Austrian landowners purely in the interests of protecting foreign policies and the fostering of economic and governmental interests.[133]

This Austrian view, understandable as it may seem domestically, is unacceptable in a European forum, however. Unsurprisingly, the principled refusal to recognise the Czech Republic's authorisation because of its 'foreign' origin was held to be irreconcilable with Austria's European commitments in the eyes of both the ECJ and its Advocate General. The grounds on which this conclusion was reached, however, were different – and this difference is enlightening.

The ECJ found the Austrian decision discriminatory.[134] In this holding the ECJ failed to give any normative weight to the democratic and constitutional credentials of the Austrian position; it also failed to discuss the lack of any European competence to authorise the construction and operation of nuclear installations.[135]

AG Poiares Maduro had operated on different grounds. In his analysis, the Temelín case was characterised by 'reciprocal externalities',[136] a finding which seems to be fully compatible with our 'external effects' theorem and its objective of

> making national authorities, insofar as is possible, attentive to the impact of their decisions on the interests of other Member States and their citizens since this goal can be said to be at the core of the project of European integration and to be embedded in its rules.[137]

The dilemma of the Temelín constellation, however, stems from the reciprocity of these externalities. In his assessment of this conflict AG Maduro

---

[132] This provision reads: 'However, if the interference is caused, in excess of that level, by a mining installation or an officially authorised installation on the neighbouring land, the landowner is entitled only to bring court proceedings for compensation for the damage caused, even where the damage is caused by circumstances which were not taken into account in the official authorisation process.' [Translation taken from Case C-115/08, para. 37.]

[133] See the report on this judgment in Case C-115/08, [2009] ECR I-10165, at para. 51.

[134] Case C-115/08, para. 86 *et seq.*

[135] Articles 30–31 Euratom Treaty only set forth procedures for the coordination of national standards for the protection of dangers from ionizing radiation; see paras 111 *et seq.* of Case C-115/08, [2009] ECR I-10265.

[136] See para. 1 of his Opinion in Case C-115/08.

[137] *Ibid.*

seems to take a step too far and too fast when arguing that the economic freedoms are not duly respected where

> the extraterritorial application of that [Austrian] State measure may affect economic activity in another Member State [the Czech Republic] or between other Member States. What is relevant is for the cross-border impact of the measure of one Member State to be liable to affect the enjoyment of the internal market advantages by economic operators established in other Member States.[138]

What the AG fails to explain is why European economic freedoms should trump Austria's constitutional provisions and the political rights of its citizens in a field where the Union is not empowered to govern. Austria's autonomy *not* to use atomic energy is subjected to the priorities of the Czech Republic when Austria is asked to

> take account of the fact that Community law specifically authorises the development of nuclear installations and the development of nuclear industries in general [and of] the fact that the authorisation granted to the Temelín facility by the Czech authorities was granted in accordance with the standards established by the relevant Community law.[139]

The principle of precaution has not been invoked in this conflict. We do not suggest that it provides a 'solution'. But we submit that it helps us to understand this 'true conflict': Austria's risk aversion and the Czech Republic's risk propensity contradict each other and must be reconciled somehow. This, however, cannot be done one-sidedly by one Member State nor by judicial fiat of the ECJ. The contradiction which the principle of precaution brings to the fore requires a European response, albeit one which is backed by democratic political processes. The deeper failure of European law in the present case is that it has institutionalised a structure which inhibits political contestation and democratic decision-making.[140]

---

[138]   *Ibid.*, para. 10.

[139]   *Ibid.*, para. 16.

[140]   Christian Joerges has defended, in a contribution to the Conference 'The European Citizens' Initiative: How to get it started', organized by The Green/European Free Alliance in the EP, the idea that this new instrument which was introduced by Article 11(4) TEU could be used to initiate such debates; see Joerges, C. (2011), 'The Timeliness of Direct Democracy in the EU – The Example of Nuclear Energy in the EU and the Institutionalisation of the European Citizens Initiative in the Lisbon Treaty', Contribution to the Conference 'The European Citizens' Initiative: How to get it started', Brussels, 29 June 2011, organised by The Green/European Free Alliance in the EP; the talk is available at http://www.greenmediabox.eu/archive/2011/06/29/eci/, accessed 15 October 2011; the written version is forthcoming in *Beijing Law Review*, **2** (3) and will be available at www.scirp.org/journal/blr.

2. Regulatory purpose in GATT Article III, TBT Article 2.1, the Subsidies Agreement, and elsewhere: *Hic et ubique*

Donald H. Regan

I. INTRODUCTION

There are many areas of WTO law where it seems clear that the legality of a challenged measure depends on whether it was motivated by some type of prohibited purpose. And yet the Appellate Body has been very loath to discuss the cases in those terms. GATT Article III (as applied to origin-neutral measures) is the paradigmatic example; but there are many other examples, including GATT Article I (as applied to origin-neutral measures), Article 5.5 of the Agreement on Sanitary and Phytosanitary Measures (SPS), and certain provisions of the Subsidies Agreement, such as Article 1.1(a)(1)(ii) (foregoing revenue "otherwise due") and Article 3.1(a) ("contingent . . . on export performance"). There are hopeful signs in the recent trilogy of cases on Article 2.1 of the Agreement on Technical Barriers to Trade (TBT). That is not because the Appellate Body talks explicitly about prohibited purpose as the core of a violation of TBT 2.1; it does not. Rather, it is because in these cases the Appellate Body is explicit and emphatic about the role of *justification by a legitimate regulatory purpose* in *preventing* the finding of a violation. If we cannot be candid about the role of prohibited purpose, then emphasizing justification by a legitimate purpose may be the next best thing. Indeed, the new cases raise important issues about the relationship between the presence of prohibited purpose and the absence of legitimate justification.

I shall not attempt an encyclopedic treatment of regulatory purpose in WTO law, nor in any corner of it. I shall look at the high spots, mixing discussion of the jurisprudence and of the theory of WTO law. In section II, I discuss GATT Article III – specifically *Japan – Alcohol,*[1] *Chile – Alcohol,*[2]

[1] *Japan – Taxes on Alcoholic Beverages,* WT/DS8&10&11/AB/R, adopted 1 November 1996.

[2] *Chile – Taxes on Alcoholic Beverages,* WT/DS87&110/AB/R, adopted 12 January 2000.

EC – Asbestos,[3] *Dominican Republic – Cigarettes,*[4] and *Philippines – Spirits.*[5] At the end of the section, I will say something about how we prove protectionist purpose. In section III, I consider the national treatment discussions in the three recent TBT cases: *United States – Clove Cigarettes,*[6] *United States – Tuna II,*[7] and *United States – COOL.*[8] The very brief section IV is about most-favored nation obligations under TBT 2.1 and GATT Article I. Section V is about the two provisions of the Subsidies Agreement that I mentioned above. Section VI draws together and organizes the conclusions of the preceding sections.

II.   GATT ARTICLE III

A.   Prehistory

Our story begins in the last years of the GATT, when original-neutral internal measures first received significant attention. The adopted report in *US – Malt Beverages*[9] clearly indicated that a crucial determinant of product likeness under GATT Article III (both III:2 and III:4) was the regulatory purpose. "[T]he purpose of Article III is not to prevent contracting parties from differentiating between different product categories for policy purposes unrelated to the protection of domestic production" (¶ 5.25). "Consequently, in determining whether two products subject to different treatment are like products, it is necessary to consider whether such product differentiation is being made 'so as to afford protection to domestic production'" (¶ 5.25). With regard to a provision the Panel held illegal, "the United States did not claim any public policy purpose for this Mississippi tax provision [which imposed a lower tax on wine made from

---

³   *European Communities – Measures Affecting Asbestos and Asbestos-Containing Products,* WT/DS135/AB/R, adopted 5 April 2001.

⁴   *Dominican Republic – Measures Affecting the Importation and Internal Sale of Cigarettes,* WT/DS302/AB/R, adopted 19 May 2005.

⁵   *Philippines – Taxes on Distilled Spirits,* WT/DS396&403/AB/R, adopted 20 January 2012.

⁶   *United States – Measures Affecting the Production and Sale of Clove Cigarettes,* WT/DS406/AB/R, adopted 24 April 2012.

⁷   *United States – Measures Concerning the Importation, Marketing and Sale of Tuna and Tuna Products,* WT/DS381/AB/R, adopted 13 June 2012.

⁸   *United States – Certain Country of Origin Labeling (COOL) Requirements,* WT/DS384&386/AB/R, adopted 23 July 2012.

⁹   *United States – Measures Affecting Alcoholic and Malt Beverages,* GATT Panel Report DS23/R, adopted 19 June 1992, BISD 39S/206.

a variety of grape grown in Mississippi] other than to subsidize small local producers" (¶ 5.26). Conversely, with respect to a different provision that the Panel upheld, "both the statements of the parties and the legislative history suggest that the alcohol content of beer has not been singled out as a means of favouring domestic producers over foreign producers" (¶ 5.74).

Then in *United States – Taxes on Automobiles*,[10] decided in the final months of the GATT, the Panel was even more explicit that "likeness" under Article III was determined by the "aims and effects" of the measure (e.g., ¶¶ 5.9, 5.10). But this report, which ruled in favor of the United States on many aspects (although not all) of its automobile fuel economy regulation, infuriated the losing complainant, the European Communities, which excoriated the so-called "aims and effects test" and prevented the adoption of the report. It is hard to believe that the reaction was really to the aims and effects test itself, since the Contracting Parties had adopted the *Malt Beverages* report (admittedly not quite so explicit, but surely clear enough) just two years before, and the European Communities itself was arguing for something very like the "aims and effects" test just a few years later. Even so, it seems likely that the Division of the brand new Appellate Body that decided *Japan – Alcohol* just two years later wanted to avoid any similar reaction, and the "aims and effects" test – or at least explicit allegiance to the aims and effects test – became collateral damage.[11]

B.   GATT Article III:2 – *Japan – Alcohol, Chile – Alcohol,* and *Philippines – Spirits*

In doctrinal discussions of GATT Article III, it is customary to begin with III:2, first sentence. Perhaps it seems proper to "begin at the beginning". But I shall begin with III:2, second sentence, which is much more revealing about the implicit structure of all three main branches of Article III (III:2, first sentence; III:2, second sentence; and III:4). In *Japan – Alcohol*, the Appellate Body established a three-element test for a violation of III:2, second sentence. The third element requires us to ask whether the measure is "applied . . . so as to afford protection to domestic production". This language comes, of course, from Article III:1, which the Appellate Body has told us informs not just III:2, second sentence, but also III:2, first

---

[10]   *United States – Taxes on Automobiles*, GATT Panel Report DS31/R, 11 October 1994, unadopted.

[11]   The story is told in Robert Hudec, "GATT/WTO Constraints on National Regulation: Requiem for an 'Aims and Effects' Test", *International Lawyer*, 32(3): 619–649 (1998).

sentence and III:4.[12] Hence, what we learn about the meaning of this language in our analysis of III:2, second sentence, should guide our interpretation of both III:2, first sentence, and III:4.[13]

In the part of the *Japan – Alcohol* report that discusses the "so as to afford protection" prong of III:2, second sentence, the Appellate Body famously said, "This is not an issue of intent" (§H.2(c)). They appeared to turn their back on at least the "aims" part of "aims and effects". They elaborated, and I would say implicitly qualified, this statement in the very next sentence: "It is not necessary for a panel to sort through the many reasons legislators and regulators often have for what they do and weigh the relative significance of those reasons to establish legislative or regulatory intent." At this point, what they seem to be denying specifically is the need to rummage around in the intentions of all the individual legislators or regulators. And the following sentences in the report, about not needing to find a desire to engage in protectionism, should be read with that in mind. But what has become famous is just the statement that "This is not an issue of intent" (and of course, the sentence about discerning "protective application" from "the design, the architecture, and the revealing structure of a measure", which we will return to) (§H.2(c)).

A few years later, the Appellate Body decided *Chile – Alcohol*, perhaps the most unaccountably ignored case in all the WTO jurisprudence. *Chile – Alcohol* says that the "so as to afford protection" issue under III:2, second sentence, *is* about regulatory purpose. But more than that – it also tells us that that was precisely the point of *Japan- Alcohol* itself.[14] It is worth quoting at length:

> We emphasized [in *Japan – Alcohol*] that . . . [t]he *subjective* intentions inhabiting the minds of individual legislators or regulators do not bear upon the inquiry, if only because they are not accessible to treaty interpreters. It does not follow, however, that the statutory purposes or objectives – that is, the purpose or objectives of a Member's legislature and government as a whole – to the extent that they are given *objective* expression in the statute itself, are not pertinent. To the contrary, . . . (¶ 62). [Emphases in the original.]

---

[12]   With regard to III:2, first sentence, see *Japan – Alcohol*, §H.1; with regard to Article III:4, see *EC – Asbestos*, ¶¶ 93, 98.

[13]   Notice there is no possibility of the "applied so as to afford protection" language meaning different things in Article III:1 and Article III:2, second sentence, since the language does not actually appear in III:2, second sentence (nor in the Note *Ad* III:2). It is incorporated there by reference to III:1.

[14]   Julio Lacarte-Muró, who was the Presiding Member of the Division in *Japan – Alcohol*, was also in the Division that decided *Chile – Alcohol*. (He was also the Chairman of the GATT Panel that decided *US – Malt Beverages*.) What *Chile* says about what *Japan* means ought to be reliable.

> We called [in *Japan – Alcohol*] for examination of the design, architecture and structure of a tax measure precisely to permit identification of a measure's objectives or purposes as revealed or objectified in the measure itself. Thus, we consider that a measure's purposes, objectively manifested in the design, architecture and structure of the measure, *are* intensely pertinent to the task of evaluating whether or not that measure is applied so as to afford protection to domestic production (¶ 71). [Emphasis in the original.]

Unfortunately, this is the only time the Appellate Body has been willing to admit openly that the central issue under Article III is regulatory purpose. And this part of the *Chile – Alcohol* report has disappeared from the general consciousness almost as completely as if it had never been written. In the "so as to afford protection" discussion in *Philippines – Spirits*, the most recent Article III case, the Appellate Body cites *Japan – Alcohol* for the proposition that the issue is not one of intent (¶250), and it never mentions *Chile – Alcohol* at all.

Can we find any explanation for why *Chile – Alcohol has* been so widely ignored, or perhaps just misunderstood? One feature of the opinion that may have occasioned misunderstanding is the statement that the relevant purpose must be "revealed or objectified in the measure itself", or that it must be "objectively manifested in the design, architecture and structure of the measure", or "given *objective* expression in the statute itself". These references to *objective* manifestation and expression might lead the reader to think that what the Appellate Body is proposing is not really a purpose test after all, since purpose is not "objective" in the way nice, solid, empirical *effects* are. But that ignores the fact that the Appellate Body talks about purpose, again and again. And the discussion surrounding the various references to "objective" purpose makes it clear that what the Appellate Body is rejecting (and what they say was rejected in *Japan – Alcohol* also) is an approach to the identification of the legislature's purpose that tries to ascertain the motives of all the *individual legislators* and then aggregate those individual motives into a collective purpose. Plainly, the *Chile – Alcohol* Appellate Body thinks the notion of the purpose of a collective body makes sense, but the collective purpose is not simply an aggregate of individual intentions.

Another way to misread the Appellate Body's assertions that the regulator's purpose must be "objectified" or "objectively manifested" in the measure is to think that somehow the tribunals must reach their conclusion just by intense empathic scrutiny of the terms of the measure itself. This, of course, is absurd. On any remotely plausible view, it will be necessary to think, for example, about the economic context of the measure, such as who actually competes with whom in what products. (I emphasize that this is an example, not the complete list of relevant considerations.)

All that is meant by the references to the purpose's being "objectified" in the measure is that the measure must actually be the result of protectionist political forces at work in the legislative or regulatory process. The fact that some individual legislators were motivated by protectionism will not invalidate the measure, if the adoption and design of the measure can be fully explained in non-protectionism terms. In such a case, the individual legislator's protectionist purpose was not given "objective expression" in the measure.[15]

We should emphasize that in *Chile – Alcohol*, the Appellate Body does not merely *say* that purpose is the crux of the matter. The regulator's purpose is what the argument before the Panel and the Appellate Body was centrally about. The Appellate Body endorses the Panel's inquiry into whether Chile's attempt to explain the "design, architecture and structure" of the measure by reference to putative non-protectionist purposes was persuasive: "[T]he Panel did no more than try to relate the observable structural features of the measure with its declared purposes, a task that is unavoidable in appraising the application of the measure as protective or not of domestic production" (¶72). And the Appellate Body endorses the Panel's conclusion that Chile's attempt was not persuasive: "The conclusion of protective application reached by the Panel becomes very difficult to resist, in the absence of countervailing explanations by Chile" (¶71). Now, the proffered "countervailing explanations", as we have noted, are explanations in terms of putative non-protectionist *purposes*. The only thing that these could plausibly be said to "countervail" is an explanation in terms of *protectionist purpose*, which is strongly suggested by the structure of the tax scheme. What becomes "difficult to resist", when these alternative purposive explanations are rejected, is precisely the explanation in terms of protectionist purpose. So even though the Appellate Body never says in so many words that the law was motivated by protectionism, protectionist *purpose* is what the code phrase "protective application" must refer to.[16]

---

[15]   Lest the reader imagine that the purpose objectified in the measure is the *measure's* purpose, but not the *legislature's* purpose, note that in the passage quoted above from ¶62, the Appellate Body *equates* the "statutory purposes or objectives" with "the purpose or objectives of a Member's legislature and government as a whole".

[16]   Henrik Horn & Petros Mavroidis, "Still Hazy After All These Years: The Interpretation of National Treatment in the GATT/WTO Case-Law on Tax Discrimination", *European J. Int'l Law*, 15(1): 39–69 (2004), suggest that the finding of bad purpose in *Chile – Alcohol* is wrong. Indeed, they appear to suggest that it is so obviously wrong that the Appellate Body could not actually have been applying a purpose test (p. 59). To my mind, the opinion makes it clear that the

This is no less true in *Japan – Alcohol* itself. That case tells us that a violation of III:2, second sentence, requires: (1) domestic and imported products that are "directly competitive or substitutable"; (2) that these products are "not similarly taxed"; and (3) that the measure be applied "so as to afford protection". The Appellate Body emphasizes that the third prong of this test is a required, distinct element, and that it is different from the second prong (§H.2(c)). But what can the third prong be about? The structure of the test makes one thing clear: the third prong is *not* just about finding a disparate impact on competitive conditions for domestic and foreign products. The first two prongs, taken together, guarantee that there will be such disparate impact. And yet, something more is required for a violation. There is some tendency in the trade-law community (happily less pronounced now than it used to be) to think that all measures with disparate impact should be sent to Article XX. So it is worth emphasizing that the Appellate Body *rejected* that view right at the beginning, in *Japan – Alcohol*.

Very well. Something more than disparate impact is needed for a violation of III:2, second sentence. What is the something more? The Appellate Body says that considering the design, architecture, and revealing structure of the measure will allow us to discern "protective application", but that is totally unhelpful. The phrase "protective application" is just a nominalization of the prohibition on measures that are "applied so as to afford protection". So looking for "protective application" is just looking for a violation; it does not tell us what a violation looks like. The Appellate Body sometimes says that the magnitude of the dissimilar taxation might establish a violation; so perhaps "protective application" is just a *very big* disparate impact on competitive conditions. But how big is very big? Or perhaps a measure manifests "protective application" just in case the Appellate Body disapproves of it? But the Appellate Body is not supposed to decide on its own whims. What we need to know is, what are appropriate *grounds* for the Appellate Body's approval or disapproval? In the end,

---

Appellate Body was thinking about purpose, even if they got the wrong result. And I am inclined to think they got the right result. The bizarre, kinked graph of *ad valorem* tax rate versus alcohol content seems almost impossible to explain except in terms of protectionist purpose. And the fact that even in the high-alcohol, high-tax bracket the majority of the spirits was Chilean is not inconsistent with protectionist purpose, if, for example, the high-alcohol Chilean spirits are still much cheaper than the imported spirits (so that they are less affected by the *ad valorem* tax), or if most of the high-alcohol Chilean spirits are made by the same producers who produce the low-alcohol spirits. The facts in the Panel report are consistent with these possibilities, and I think even suggest them, although it is not easy to pull out just the facts one would like.

the only way to give any content to the idea of "protective application" in the *Japan – Alcohol* analysis is to admit that the issue is protectionist purpose.[17]

Actually, there is one other possibility we should consider. We might suggest that there is "protective application" when (a) there is a disparate impact on the competitive conditions for domestic and imported products (protective *effect*), and (b) the measure is not fully justified by any plausible legitimate purpose. (Note that condition (b) will be satisfied *either* when the purpose is illegitimate *or* when the purpose is legitimate but it does not fully justify the measure.) Logically speaking, "protective application" in this sense is clearly distinct from protectionist purpose. Sometimes regulators adopt regulations that are not well-crafted to achieve their goals. They might, for example, quite innocently use unnecessarily trade-restrictive means to achieve some perfectly legitimate goal. Such a measure would *not* be fully justified by the legitimate purpose, and if the measure had protective effect, then it would come under our latest suggested definition of "protective application", even though there was no protectionist purpose.

Now, a measure that comes under this definition of "protective application" is inefficient, even if it has no protectionist purpose. So one might wonder why no tribunal has ever suggested this definition.[18] One possible reason is that there is a kind of incoherence in the definition. If what we are concerned about is just the inefficiency that is caused by unjustified measures, without regard to whether they reflect protectionist purpose, then there is actually no reason to require protective effect. Consider for example that under the "least restrictive alternative" obligations in TBT 2.2 and SPS 5.6, it is irrelevant whether the measure has protective effect. The truth is, there is no reason to care about protective effect *except as evidence of protectionist purpose*. Protective effect has no normative significance in itself; it is neither a cause nor even a significant indicator of inefficiency, since it will result from many efficient measures. But GATT

---

[17]   It might be suggested that the point of the word "applied" in III:1 is to focus our attention on effects, as opposed to purpose. But even if we think "applied" is meant to signal a contrast, I doubt that the contrast is the one between effects and purpose. Rather, it is between the application of the measure and the actual terms of the measure. Even-handed laws may be *applied* un-even-handedly; and the language of III:1 reminds us that in such a case, the un-even-handed *application* is what matters.

[18]   The Appellate Body in the recent TBT cases suggests something very like this as the test under TBT 2.1, but of course they do not call it "protective application", since that is a GATT III phrase; and the TBT is in any event a different agreement with a different logic, as we shall see in section III.

Article III requires protective effect as an element of a violation; that much is uncontroversial. And that only makes sense if GATT III is about protectionist purpose.

There is another reason why we should not adopt the suggested definition of "protective application" as protective effect plus non-justification. As we just said, many perfectly innocent and desirable measures have protective effect. So if the test is to guarantee appropriate scope for Members' regulatory autonomy, it is the "non-justification" element of the test that must do this. Now, with the test stated in terms of non-justification, tribunals will be called upon to decide whether the measure is justified or not, presumably under a normal "preponderance of the evidence" or "balance of the probabilities" standard. That effectively substitutes the tribunal's decision about justification for the regulator's decision. But in an ordinary GATT Article III case involving an original-neutral regulation, we should presume that the good-faith regulator is in a better position to make the required judgment about regulatory justification than the tribunal. This is especially so when there are issues about how to evaluate and balance various local benefits and costs (a matter on which the tribunal has no competence at all, except to judge the *plausibility* of the regulator's claims about what it values and how much); but it is also true even if the issue is just the *efficacy* of various measures in the local context (as it is, say, under the less restrictive alternative test).[19] So in an Article III case involving an origin-neutral regulation, the tribunal should not substitute its judgment about justification for the regulator's judgment, *unless* the evidence of non-justification (regarding either the efficacy of actual and alternative measures, or the plausibility of the asserted purposes) is so clear and convincing that, in conjunction with protective effect, it demonstrates bad faith – which in this context means protectionist purpose.

Of course, it will be more acceptable for the tribunal to rely directly on its own judgment about justification if there is some *a priori* reason in the case at hand to doubt the good faith of the regulator. This arguably explains why we send GATT cases involving origin-specific internal measures or border measures (excluding at-the-border application of origin-neutral internal measures) to Article XX. The choice of a border measure or an origin-specific internal measure already suggests protectionist purpose, because a non-protectionist purpose can normally be achieved

---

[19]   For explanation of the fact that the less restrictive alternative test does not require evaluation of the regulator's purposes, see Donald Regan, "The Meaning of 'Necessary' in GATT Article XX and GATS Article XIV: The Myth of Cost-Benefit Balancing", *World Trade Review*, 6: 347–369 (2007).

by an origin-neutral internal measure. Because we already suspect the regulator's good faith, we go to Article XX and put the burden on the regulator to prove justification – which in effect substitutes the tribunal's judgment for the regulator's judgment. But still, in an ordinary GATT Article III case involving an origin-neutral internal measure, the tribunal should not second-guess the regulator's judgment, unless the evidence of non-justification is so strong that, in conjunction with protective effect, it reveals protectionist purpose. Once again, "protective application" must refer to protectionist purpose.[20]

So much for III:2, second sentence. The next question is, does what we have learned about III:2, second sentence, tell us anything about III:2, *first sentence*, where there is no separate "so as to afford protection" inquiry? Yes, what we have learned is highly relevant. The *Japan – Alcohol* Appellate Body tells us that the reason there is no separate "so as to afford protection" step under III:2, first sentence, is just that the two steps of III:2, first sentence, already capture the "so as to afford protection" idea. But our discussion of III:2, second sentence, has revealed that the "so as to afford protection" inquiry is about protectionist purpose. It follows that we must interpret the elements of the test under III:2, *first sentence*, in such a way that only measures motivated by protectionist purpose fall foul of III:2, first sentence. In fact, there is clear internal evidence that the *Japan – Alcohol* Appellate Body satisfied this stricture. In the course of the discussion of "likeness" under III:2, first sentence, they say it would not have affected the outcome of the case if vodka and shochu were found unlike (§H.1(a)). But then the analysis would have proceeded under III:2, second sentence, and the "so as to afford protection" inquiry would have been a required separate step involving, as we have seen, an investigation into protectionist purpose. So, when the Appellate Body tells us the result would have been the same even under III:2, second sentence, that implies that they think the vodka/shochu distinction was motivated by protectionist purpose.

How is this requirement of protectionist purpose reflected in the *text* of III:2, first sentence? It is reflected in the flexibility of the term "like". It is often said (and correctly) that "like" is a narrower term than "directly competitive or substitutable". It is not so often noticed that, in ordinary usage, it is a *categorically different* concept. "Directly competitive or substitutable" is unambiguously an empirical, economic concept focusing on consumer behavior; it cannot be read to include any reference to

---

[20]   There may be a different reason for substituting the tribunal's judgment about justification for the regulator's judgment in some cases under the TBT and SPS Agreements. See section III below.

regulatory purpose, which is why, under III:2, second sentence, purpose must be considered in a separate step. In contrast, "like" is *not* unambiguously purely empirical. "Like" can be read to contain an implicit reference to regulatory purpose – which is just how the GATT Panel in *US – Malt Beverages* explicitly read it. And it must be that the *Japan – Alcohol* Appellate Body read it this way also, given their statement that the outcome would have been the same even if they had decided the vodka/shochu issue under III:2, second sentence. What the *Japan* Appellate Body really decided about vodka and shochu was that they were very closely competitive *and* there was no regulatory justification for taxing them differently that was plausible enough to overcome the appearance of protectionist purpose created by "the design, the architecture, and the revealing structure" of the measure. (Note the word "revealing", which in this context suggests the disclosure of something not just previously unknown, but *hidden*, as regulators try to hide protectionist purpose). The *Japan – Alcohol* Appellate Body felt obliged to try to make something of the different structure of III:2, first sentence, and III:2, second sentence; but we see that in the end the difference in structure reflects no difference in the *substance* of the inquiry under the two sentences, but only a difference in the format.[21]

C.   GATT Article III:4 – *EC – Asbestos* and *Dominican Republic – Cigarettes*

In *EC – Asbestos*, the Appellate Body says that the general principle of Article III:1 (the avoidance of measures that are "applied . . . so as to

---

[21]   The most recent word on Article III:2, first sentence, is in *Philippines – Spirits*. Influenced by *EC – Asbestos*, the Appellate Body says that "likeness" under III:2, first sentence, is purely a matter of the competitive relationship; and the only difference between "like" and "directly competitive or substitutable" is that the former requires near-perfect substitutability, while the latter is significantly broader (¶¶119 & n. 211, 148–149). This deprives "like" of the flexibility that we have seen in the text allows us to consider protectionist purpose. Of course, we can still consider protectionist purpose under the "taxed in excess" prong of III:2, first sentence, in the same way that *Dominican Republic – Cigarettes* considers protectionist purpose under the "less favorable treatment" prong in III:4. (See section II.C below.) But that would seem especially artificial here. Better to eliminate the need for it, by not importing the *Asbestos* approach to "likeness" into III:2, first sentence. (I shall argue in section II.C that the *Asbestos* definition of "likeness" was misguided even in *Asbestos* itself. And in section III, we shall see that there is a *different* potential objection to transplanting the *Asbestos* definition of "likeness" to TBT 2.1, as the Appellate Body has done in *US – Clove Cigarettes*. *Asbestos* created a cancer that is metastasizing through the body of WTO jurisprudence.)

afford protection to domestic production") informs Article III:4, just as it informs Article III:2 (¶93); and it says that the phrase "like products" in III:4 must be interpreted to "give proper scope and meaning" to the general principle of Article III:1 (¶98). From this the Appellate Body infers that "a determination of 'likeness' under Article III:4 is, fundamentally, a determination about the nature and extent of a competitive relationship between and among products" (¶99). This is a non sequitur. What *does* follow is that the existence of a competitive relationship is a *necessary* condition for likeness: a measure cannot be *protecting* domestic products against imports unless the domestic and imported goods compete with each other. But the Appellate Body treats competitive relationship as necessary *and sufficient* for "likeness". Their argument gives no warrant for that. We have seen that in Article III:2, first sentence, "likeness" is a matter of *both* competitive relationship *and* the non-existence of regulatory justification for the distinction(s) the measure makes between products. That is what allows III:2, first sentence, to embody the general anti-protectionism principle of III:1. As we shall see below, there is another possible way to make III:4, taken as a whole, reflect the principle of III:1, through the interpretation of "less favorable treatment". But that does not change the fact that the Appellate Body's argument for its interpretation of "likeness" is incomplete.[22] Nor does it change the fact that the interpretation does violence to the ordinary meaning in context of the phrase "like products". Surely, as the concurring Member of the Division in *Asbestos* points out, two products with very different health consequences (not just for the purchaser but for other people who may occupy or work in the space where materials containing the products are installed) are *unlike*, even if the actual purchasers treat the products as perfect substitutes (¶¶149–154).

Perhaps I should just stop here. The Appellate Body announces an interpretation of "likeness" that, insofar as it ignores regulatory purpose, is both implausible and unsupported. But I suspect that many people find the Appellate Body's interpretation of likeness appealing, because it holds

---

[22]   In *US – Clove Cigarettes*, the Appellate Body claims to find another argument in *Asbestos,* namely, that we must not interpret "like products" in such a way as to deprive the "less favorable treatment" inquiry of any purchase (that's right so far), and it is "products that are in a competitive relationship in the marketplace [that] could be affected through treatment of *imports* 'less favorable' than the treatment accorded to *domestic* products" (*Clove Cigarettes* ¶110, quoting *Asbestos* ¶99, emphasis in *Asbestos* and *Clove*). I shall explain in section III why this argument is unpersuasive. But the important point for present purposes is this: even if *Asbestos* offers this as a distinct argument, and even if it is a good argument, it still proves only that competitive relationship is *necessary* for likeness, not that it is *necessary and sufficient*. So it makes no difference to my criticism of *Asbestos* in the text.

out the possibility of deciding the issue of likeness by econometric studies. So it is worth continuing, to explain why even that possibility is a fantasy, at least if the concept of likeness is to do the work the Appellate Body seems to demand of it.

It is hard to know just how to discuss the *Asbestos* opinion, because there is a striking incongruence between the nominal ground of decision and the length and focus of the opinion. Technically, all the Appellate Body holds with regard to "like products" is that Canada failed to carry its burden of making a prima facie case. But if that were really their rationale, the opinion could have been much shorter. According to the Appellate Body, Canada introduced no evidence at all on consumer preferences and habits regarding asbestos and PCG fibers (¶¶139, 145). But then the opinion could have consisted of the Appellate Body's brief argument for the *necessity* of a competitive relationship, plus one more sentence about the failure to introduce any evidence on this topic. In fact, of course, there is a lengthy and detailed discussion of the health dangers of asbestos. The Appellate Body says this is relevant because the health dangers make it less likely that there is a market for asbestos (¶145), and they seem to suggest that that increases Canada's burden of proving the proposition that asbestos and PCG fibers compete. But the weight of Canada's burden does not matter, if Canada really offered no evidence at all. And the opinion reads as if the Appellate Body is trying to make a case for the *substantive* conclusion that asbestos and PCG really are unlike, because they do not compete. This seems remarkably implausible. France obviously thinks some non-negligible number of people would buy asbestos if it were not prohibited, else there would be no point to adopting the prohibition or defending it. And Canada obviously thinks some people would buy asbestos if it were not prohibited, else there would be no point to challenging the prohibition. So we are led to inquire whether the Appellate Body's notion of "competitive relationship" is somehow subtler than I have suggested. Is there some way to claim that asbestos and PCG fibers are not in a competitive relationship after all?

Two possibilities suggest themselves. First, the Appellate Body denies that just *any* competitive relationship is enough to establish likeness; rather, "likeness" depends on the "nature and extent" of the competitive relationship (¶99). So the Appellate Body does not have to deny that there is *any* competition. Unfortunately, they do not explain just what "nature and extent" of competition are necessary to establish likeness; nor even why the "nature and extent" of the competition matter. Remember that their argument for the relevance of competition was (apparently) that in the absence of competition, protectionism was logically impossible. That suggests that all that matters is the existence of *some* competition, since any degree of competition suffices to make protectionism logically possible. If the "nature and extent" of the competition are relevant, that must be because we are actually interested, not just in whether protectionism is logically possible, but in whether it is *plausible* or *likely* as the explanation of the measure under review. But while the nature and extent of the competition are certainly relevant to answering that question, there is a great deal else that is also relevant, such as the existence of health dangers, *whether or not those dangers have any effect on consumer behavior and hence on the competitive relationship.* The existence of health dangers makes it much more plausible that the regulator's purpose was innocent. In sum, the only obvious explanation of why we should be interested in the "nature and extent" of the competition explains at the same time why we should be interested in much more than the facts about competition. We are led ineluctably to a consideration of regulatory purpose.

Second, some people have found in the *Asbestos* opinion the suggestion that asbestos and PCG are not in competition *in the sense relevant to likeness*, because, given the dangers to health, no *fully informed and rational* consumer would buy asbestos. That *actual* consumers (or a significant number) are willing to buy asbestos is simply irrelevant. Now, even this claim about the behavior of informed and rational consumers seems doubtful, if we remember that rationality is generally thought to be compatible with different attitudes to risk and time. But I shall not pursue that, because there is a more important point for our present purposes. This "ideal consumer" approach would abandon entirely the idea that likeness is grounded in the actual, empirical market. Rather, the test for likeness would now be found in an *idealized* market. This would undercut the main ground of appeal of the "competitive relationship" approach, the idea that we can ascertain likeness by the use of econometric techniques. We cannot do econometric studies on a hypothetical ideal market.

Note also that if we say products are not "like" if they would not compete in an idealized market, then we are saying in effect that regulation is acceptable when it is designed to mimic an ideal market; we are saying that regulating to mimic an ideal market is not protectionist, even if it makes a foreign product that competes in the empirical market worse off. But of course, a *fully* ideal market requires not just informed and rational consumers, but also the internalization of any externalities caused by those consumers' choices. Which suggests that we should regard products as unlike not only when they would not compete in the choices of fully rational consumers, but also when one of them causes externalities that the other does not, which regulation is necessary to internalize. At this point, we are saying in effect that products are unlike whenever some legitimate regulatory purpose justifies distinguishing between them.

We have now considered two suggestions about how we might understand "competitive relationship" so as to support the claim that asbestos and PCG fibers do not compete and hence are unlike. Strikingly, but not really surprisingly, both suggestions (about the "nature and extent" of the competition, and about fully rational consumers) lead us directly to a consideration of regulatory purpose. If asbestos and PCG fibers are "unlike" – as of course they are – the reason is that there are good non-protectionist reasons for the regulator to treat them differently. The lesson is that there is no middle ground between a purely empirical competitive relationship test (which the Appellate Body implicitly rejected way back in *Japan – Alcohol*, when it required a distinct "so as to afford protection" inquiry under III:2, second sentence), and a test based on regulatory purpose.[23]

We turn now to the second element of an Article III:4 violation, "less favorable treatment". In *Asbestos*, after observing that their interpretation of "like products" is relatively broad, the Appellate Body reminds us that Article III:4 is violated only if "like" foreign products are subjected to "less favorable treatment" than domestic products. Then they say in ¶100: "[A] Member may draw distinctions between products which have been found to be 'like', without, for this reason alone, according to the group of 'like' *imported* products 'less favourable treatment' than that accorded to the group of 'like' *domestic* products." [Emphases in original.] Unfortunately, the Appellate Body does not discuss the matter further, since the Panel's findings on "less favorable treatment" were not appealed. This ¶100 is delphic, to say the least. Instead of canvassing the various things it might mean, I shall merely note that it is plainly offered as a *counterweight* to the Appellate Body's broad notion of likeness, and then pass on to *Dominican*

---

[23] I have to include at least a footnote on the topic of so-called "unincorporated PPM's" – taxes or regulations that distinguish between physically identical products on the basis of the way they were produced. Many people believe that the products distinguished by such a PPM are automatically "like". They are physically identical – how could they be more "like" than that? But Article III does not say the test of likeness is based exclusively in the physical constitution of the products any more than it says likeness is based exclusively in market competition. Sometimes there is a sound regulatory reason to distinguish between physically identical products that have been produced in different ways: conservation of species can provide one sort of example; climate change provides another. The basic analysis of likeness is the same, whether we are dealing with an unincorporated PPM or an "ordinary" regulation that distinguishes products on the basis of their own physical properties. See Robert Howse & Donald Regan, "The Product/Process Distinction – An Illusory Basis for Disciplining 'Unilateralism' in Trade Policy", *European J. Int'l Law*, 11(2): 249–289 (2000).

Republic – Cigarettes, which is now the leading case on "less favorable treatment" in GATT III:4.

One issue in *Dominican Republic – Cigarettes* was whether the requirement of a bond of RD$5 million (the same amount for any manufacturer or importer of cigarettes) constituted "less favorable treatment" of an importer of Honduran cigarettes because it had a lower market share in the Dominican market than two large Dominican manufacturers, and thus had a higher per-unit cost of the bond requirement. Both the Panel and the Appellate Body concluded that there was *not* less favorable treatment. Conceding the difference in per-unit costs of the bond requirement, the Appellate Body wrote: "However, the existence of a detrimental effect on a given imported product resulting from a measure does not necessarily imply that this measure accords less favorable treatment to imports if the detrimental effect is explained by factors or circumstances unrelated to the foreign origin of the product, such as the market share of the importer in this case" (¶96). And further on, "the difference between the per-unit costs of the bond requirement alleged by Honduras does not depend on the foreign origin of the imported cigarettes" (¶96). These excerpts, and the full paragraph in which they appear, are not a model of expository clarity. But plainly the crucial question is what the Appellate Body means when it raises the issue of whether the disparate impact of the measure on foreign products is "explained by" or "depends on" the foreign origin of the products. What sort of "explanation" or "dependence" does the Appellate Body have in mind?

It is helpful here to recall the facts of *Chile – Alcohol,* and to imagine that we are applying to those facts a legal analysis structured along the lines of Article III:4 instead of Article III:2, second sentence. If we focus just on the formal operation of the Chilean law, we might say the higher *ad valorem* tax on the group of imported spirits as compared to the group of domestic spirits is "explained" by the higher alcohol content (on average) of the imported products; and obviously their higher alcohol content is a different fact from their foreign origin. So if we read the references to "explanation" in *DR – Cigarettes* as concerned solely with the formal operation of the law, then an origin-neutral regulation will never accord "less favorable treatment", because there will always be a formal legal explanation for the different treatment other than the origin of the products. This approach would validate all origin-neutral regulation, which is obviously not what we want. To avoid this result, we must say that the different treatment is "explained" by the foreign origin if and only if the formally origin-neutral criterion was chosen as a proxy for foreign origin. This seems obviously right. But now "less favorable treatment" is a matter of regulatory purpose. Once again, of course, the Appellate Body avoids saying explicitly that the issue is protectionist purpose. But there is no other reading of this part of the opinion that makes nearly as good sense of it.

US – Clove Cigarettes, in a rather opaque footnote (¶179, n. 372), seems to reject this interpretation of *DR – Cigarettes*. The *Clove Cigarettes* Appellate Body say they disagree with the United States' suggestion that *DR – Cigarettes* requires a further inquiry into whether "the detrimental effect is unrelated to the foreign origin of the product". Their view seems to be that the real issue in *DR – Cigarettes* was whether the disparate impact was explained by the *measure*, and *not* whether it was explained by the foreign origin of the products. The Appellate Body does not quote the passages from *DR – Cigarettes* that we looked at above, which refer explicitly to the question whether the disparate impact is "explained by" the foreign origin, or "depends on" the foreign origin. Instead they quote a sentence that says, "the difference between the per-unit costs of the bond requirement alleged by Honduras is explained by the fact that the importer of Honduran cigarettes has a smaller market share than two domestic producers" (*DR – Cigarettes* ¶96). And they say this reveals that the reason *DR – Cigarettes* found no violation was that the disparate impact "was not attributable to the specific measure at issue but, rather, was a function of sales volume". There are two problems with this. First, it ignores the fact that the sentence the *Clove Cigarettes* Appellate Body quotes from *DR – Cigarettes*, which indeed does not mention "foreign origin", appears *between* the two sentences I quoted, which *do* talk about foreign origin. We need to make something of the references to foreign origin, which the *Clove – Cigarettes* opinion gives no account of. More important, the notion that the disparate impact in *DR – Cigarettes* was not attributable to the measure, but rather to the sales volume, makes no sense. It was attributable to *both* the measure (specifically, to the fact that the measure required the same bond regardless of sales volume) *and* the sales volume. The law and the facts worked together to produce the outcome, as they always do. The question in *DR – Cigarettes* was not whether the disparate impact was attributable to the measure (there is nothing in the *DR – Cigarettes* report to suggest the Appellate Body ever doubted that), but whether the measure itself was adopted in order to disadvantage foreign cigarettes. The *DR – Cigarettes* Appellate Body's unwillingness to talk openly about purpose means that they never say that explicitly; but as I have explained, it is the only sensible reading. The idea that the disparate impact was not attributable to the measure is not a sensible reading; and it does not account for the repeated references to foreign origin.[24]

---

[24]   Perhaps when the *Clove Cigarettes* Appellate Body suggests the disparate impact is not attributable to the measure, they are calling attention to the fact that

In support of the claim that the question is whether the disparate impact is attributable to the measure, *Clove Cigarettes* quotes from *Thailand – Cigarettes* the statement that "there must be in every case a genuine relationship between the measure at issue and its adverse impact on competitive opportunities".[25] But nobody has ever doubted that, in the abstract. The issue at this point in *Thailand – Cigarettes* was about what *probability* of adverse impact was required; and "genuine relationship" was the Appellate Body's answer to (and redirection of) that question. They were not saying the disparate impact had to be attributable to the measure as an *alternative* to saying the disparate impact had to be attributable to the foreign origin of the products. They were not saying anything inconsistent with the correct view, that there is a violation only when the disparate impact is attributable *both* to the measure (along with the facts, of course) *and* to the foreign origin, because the measure is motivated by a concern with the origin of the products. Finally, *Clove Cigarettes* says that in *Thailand – Cigarettes*, the Appellate Body "eschewed" an additional inquiry into whether the detrimental impact on foreign products was related to their foreign origin. But *Thailand – Cigarettes* "eschewed" such an inquiry only in the sense that they did not explicitly undertake it. They did not reject the relevance of the question. Rather, it was obvious that a specific inquiry into this question was unnecessary, because the measure at issue was origin-specific.[26] In sum, *Clove Cigarettes* provides no reason to reconsider our interpretation of *DR – Cigarettes*.

---

the bond requirement does not explicitly define two types of cigarette and specify different treatment for them (as the United States scheme in *Clove Cigarettes* does, or as the French asbestos regulation does for insulating materials). That is true. But the differential per unit cost of the bond depending on the sales volume in the Dominican Republic follows logically from the form of the law. The Appellate Body's point (or what I suggested might be their point) seems irrelevant, unless it is intended to suggest that the authors of the law may not have been *thinking* about the disparate impact, and so did not intend it. This is just another route to thinking about regulatory purpose. And I would say that the form of the law, rather than making it look more innocent, is actually a ground for suspicion. I am not at all certain *DR – Cigarettes* got the right result on the bond requirement. At least I wish the report in that case showed more awareness of the general discriminatory tendency of flat-rate financial impositions, for just the reasons the case illustrates.

25   *Thailand – Customs and Fiscal Measures on Cigarettes from the Philippines*, WT/DS371/AB/R, adopted 15 July 2011, ¶134.

26   It *might* be better to say the Appellate Body described and discussed the measure *as if* it were origin-specific, because there is a bare possibility of arguing that it was formally origin-neutral, which some readers may be conscious of. (It is not worth explaining why.) Note that if we take seriously this bare possibility, then by discussing the measure as if it were origin-specific, the Appellate Body *implicitly*

It should perhaps be noted that what *Clove Cigarettes* specifically rejects is a "further" inquiry into explanation by foreign origin, or an "additional" inquiry. Perhaps what they are saying is that whether the disparate impact is explained by the foreign origin of the products is relevant, but it is somehow adequately taken into account by looking at whether the *measure* explains the disparate impact. In that case, the *Clove Cigarettes* footnote is just another instance of the confusion caused by an unwillingness to talk, not just about protectionist purpose, but about anything that even makes it too clear that protectionist purpose is the issue.

D. Proving Protectionist Purpose

I think it is clear enough for present purposes what we mean by "protectionism" and "protectionist purpose". Roughly speaking, protectionism is legislation or regulation that is adopted to advantage domestic producers vis-à-vis their foreign competitors. And "protectionist purpose" is just the legislature's or regulator's purpose to advantage domestic producers. But given the doubts some readers will have about the notion of an institutional purpose, or about the provability of such a purpose, it is worth pausing briefly over the question of how we prove protectionist purpose.

First, remember a forgotten line from the Appellate Body Report in *Japan – Alcohol*. After the famous bit about "the design, the architecture, and the revealing structure" of the measure, the Appellate Body goes on to say: "Most often, there will be other factors to be considered as well. In conducting this inquiry, panels should give full consideration to all the relevant facts and all the relevant circumstances in any given case" (§H.2(c)). So, we are allowed, indeed adjured, to look at *all* relevant facts and circumstances. The range of "relevant facts and circumstances" includes, for example, Ministerial statements, as in *Canada – Periodicals.*[27] Ministerial statements are not just the assertions of ordinary individual legislators, but come rather from legislators or office-holders specifically charged to speak for the government as a whole. "Relevant facts and circumstances" includes the unexplained alteration of the recommendation in a government technical report, as in *Australia – Salmon.*[28] It even includes facts

---

decided that the superficially origin-neutral measure was motivated by the foreign origin of certain products. They did not eschew the inquiry.

[27] *Canada – Certain Measures Concerning Periodicals*, WT/DS31/AB/R, adopted 30 July 1997, §VI.B.3.

[28] *Australia – Measures Affecting Importation of Salmon*, WT/DS18/AB/R, adopted 6 November 1998, §V.C.3, paras. 12–15.

about the existence or absence of lobbying, as in *EC – Hormones*.[29] (I shall not devote a separate section of this chapter to Article 5.5 of the SPS Agreement, but notice that the Appellate Body's interest in such evidence as I have just mentioned in *Salmon* and *Hormones* indicates that protectionist purpose is the ultimate issue under that provision.) Despite what the Appellate Body has said about not presuming that a new regulation is protectionist just because an old one was,[30] it is surely a relevant fact or circumstance that a new regulation seems like nothing more than a transparent reformulation of one just invalidated, as in *US – FSC 21.5*.[31] Facts about timing are surely relevant, as, for example, if a new regulation with protective effect is adopted just when competition from a foreign source appears or becomes serious. A "relevant circumstance" is whether innocent (non-protectionist) explanations for the measure are available. And it is relevant whether less trade-restrictive measures that achieve the same putative goal are clearly available. Finally, sometimes the structure of the measure is so bizarre that in conjunction with disparate impact on competitive conditions, it is almost insurmountable evidence of protectionist intent all by itself, as in *Chile – Alcohol*. *Chile – Alcohol*, incidentally, illustrates why we cannot argue against a purpose test on the ground that it puts an impossible burden of proof on the complainant, to prove that there is no non-protectionist justification for the measure. Once the complainant has given the tribunal strong reason to think there is protectionist purpose, it will be incumbent on the respondent to offer other explanations – just as happened in *Chile – Alcohol*.[32]

I do not claim that there will always be enough evidence to allow us to decide with confidence whether there was protectionist purpose. But even the sceptic should concede that there will be many cases in which the answer is clear. Surely there was protectionist purpose in *Japan – Alcohol*; surely there was not in *Asbestos*. And we must keep in mind that *no* plausible test can be expected to give us a confident answer in every case. If pro-

---

[29]   *European Communities – Measures Concerning Meat and Meat Products (Hormones)*, WT/DS26&48/AB/R, adopted 13 February 1998, ¶244.

[30]   E.g., *Chile – Alcohol*, ¶74.

[31]   *United States – Tax Treatment for "Foreign Sales Corporations", Recourse to Article 21.5 of the DSU*, WT/DS108/AB/R, adopted 29 January 2002.

[32]   This is the same dynamic the Appellate Body has explicitly recognized in connection with "necessity" under certain provisions of GATT Article XX or GATS Article XIV: the burden is on the respondent to prove necessity, but once the respondent makes it plausible that the measure is necessary, it is incumbent on the complainant to suggest less restrictive alternative measures. E.g., *United States – Measures Affecting the Cross-Border Supply of Gambling and Betting Services*, WT/DS285/AB/R, adopted 20 April 2005, ¶¶309–311.

tectionist purpose is what we really care about (and under GATT Article III it is), then we can do well enough at identifying it to make it the test, instead of just repeating the empty phrase "protective application".

E.   Summing Up Section II

In the end, it does not matter whether we locate the purpose inquiry under one element of a violation or another – whether, for example, we consider purpose in connection with "likeness" or under "less favorable treatment" in GATT Article III:4. We can argue about which way of structuring the analysis under III:4 or III:2, first sentence, is most natural or most perspicuous; there are advantages to both possibilities.[33] It would be best if all three of the primary provisions of Article III were structured like III:2, second sentence, with a separate step for considering the issue of purpose. Since III:2, first sentence, and III:4 are not structured that way, the best approach might be to admit that *both* "like products" *and* "less favorable treatment of imports" or "imports taxed in excess" include implicit reference to protectionist purpose. The drafters of GATT Article III did not start out with clear and definite concepts of "like products", and "less favorable treatment", and the other terms they use, and then just happen to notice that by combining these terms they could describe conduct they wanted to forbid. Rather, they started out with the idea that they wanted to forbid protectionism by internal measures, and they tried to find a way to spell that out.[34] We should not expect too much from individual words and phrases. What matters in the end is that we consider protectionist purpose somewhere.

III.   NATIONAL TREATMENT AND REGULATORY PURPOSE IN THE TECHNICAL BARRIERS TO TRADE AGREEMENT: TBT 2.1

The Appellate Body has recently produced a trilogy of reports that discuss Article 2.1 of the TBT Agreement: *US – Clove Cigarettes, US – Tuna II,* and

---

[33]   For example, although I generally prefer thinking about purpose in connection with "like products" under GATT Article III, thinking about it under "less favorable treatment" avoids the stumbling block (for some people) that on my view even physically identical products may be unlike. See n. 23 above.

[34]   In case the reader objects to my speaking of "protectionism", when Article III:1 uses the word "protection", note that *Japan – Alcohol* says: "The broad and fundamental purpose of Article III is to avoid protectionism [in internal measures]" (§F).

US – COOL.[35] The most important for our purposes is *Clove Cigarettes*. It was the first of the three, and it sets out the general analytic framework most clearly, not least because it has the simplest facts. In what follows, I shall criticize certain aspects of the Appellate Body's analysis, so I want to emphasize at the outset that I agree wholeheartedly with the most important of the Appellate Body's holdings. The Appellate Body says repeatedly that a measure will *not* violate TBT 2.1 if any detrimental impact it has on the competitive opportunities of foreign products "stems exclusively from legitimate regulatory distinctions" (¶¶ 174, 175, *et passim*). They infer this from the "context, object, and purpose" of the TBT (¶ 181), especially the sixth recital in the Preamble, which asserts the Members' rights to protect various legitimate interests. This holding, that TBT 2.1 does not forbid disparate impact on foreign products that flows from legitimate regulatory distinctions, is exactly right. Indeed, although I shall suggest that the *Clove Cigarettes* analysis of "likeness" relies too heavily on GATT Article III (and specifically on *Asbestos*), I would be delighted to see the Appellate Body read this bottom line of *Clove Cigarettes* back into GATT Article III. There is no Article III report that says so bluntly that measures fully justified by legitimate purposes do not violate that Article.[36]

Perhaps my remaining criticisms are cavils, but I shall press on. My main objection to the *Clove Cigarettes* report is its adoption of the *Asbestos* analysis of likeness. TBT 2.1 is written in terms very similar to the terms of GATT III:4; in particular, the two elements of a violation of 2.1 (once we have made the threshold determination that the measure is a technical regulation) are "like products" and "less favorable treatment". Leaning on *Asbestos,* the Appellate Body in *Clove Cigarettes* concludes that under TBT 2.1, likeness is a matter of "the nature and extent of a competitive relationship between and among the products at issue" (¶120). In *Asbestos*, my objection to this definition of "likeness" was that it was

---

[35]   Full citations for these cases appear in notes 6–8 above.

[36]   The three new TBT reports are not terribly revealing on the question of just what counts as a "legitimate objective". In all three cases the Appellate Body accepts the objectives of the challenged measures as legitimate. The Appellate Body recognizes that the list of purposes in TBT 2.2 is *not* exclusive (E.g., *Tuna* ¶313). In the case that gives most attention to the issue of legitimacy, *US – COOL*, the Appellate Body emphasizes that the burden is on the complainant to show that the regulator's purpose is *not* legitimate (¶449), and they are notably cool to Canada's attempts to limit the range of legitimate purposes in various ways (¶¶434–453). All of this is consistent with, and even suggests, what I would regard as the correct view, that any purpose that is not positively forbidden is legitimate. The only examples of positively forbidden purposes that come immediately to mind are protectionism or other origin-based discrimination.

too broad. By treating a necessary condition for likeness under Article III (competitive relationship) as also a sufficient condition, and by ignoring distinctions between products that would justify legitimate regulation, this test sometimes found products like when they were not. But just as we can obviate any harm from this overbreadth in the "likeness" element of GATT Article III by finding a protectionist purpose requirement in the "less favorable treatment" element, so also the worry about overbreadth is obviated in the TBT 2.1 context by the Appellate Body's clear statement that TBT 2.1 is not violated by disparate impact that is explained by legitimate regulatory purposes. Perhaps paradoxically, my main objection to *Clove Cigarettes'* use of the *Asbestos* test is that *in the TBT context*, the competitive relationship test may be too *narrow*. It may sometimes find that products are *not* like, because they do not compete with each other, when they should be regarded as like for TBT purposes. Competitive relationship is indeed necessary for likeness under GATT Article III, but arguably it should not be necessary under TBT 2.1.

Before I answer the Appellate Body's specific arguments for importing the *Asbestos* test into TBT 2.1, let me give a hypothetical example where I think the *Asbestos* test leads us astray. Consider the facts of *Clove Cigarettes*, with one alteration: let us assume that clove cigarettes and menthol cigarettes do not compete at all. Perhaps because of a quirk in the genetics of taste, people who like the taste of clove cannot abide the taste of menthol, and vice versa, so that no one who smokes one sort of cigarette would ever smoke the other. In this case, on the Appellate Body's analysis, clove cigarettes and menthol cigarettes are unlike. But it seems to me that (for TBT 2.1 purposes) they are still plainly like. They both consist mostly of tobacco rolled up in small, light paper tubes, albeit with different flavorings added. They are both smoked, for purposes including stimulation, relaxation, easing social interaction, feeding a nicotine addiction, being "cool", and perhaps even in some cases enjoying the taste. They both pose grave dangers to health, because of the tobacco. There is controversy about whether chemicals in one or the other pose additional health risks, but there is little doubt that by far the biggest health risk is the one they share. They are both to some extent "starter cigarettes", smoked by young people who do not like unflavored "regular" cigarettes, although in time they may come to. As a result of all this, they are "like" *in the sense that* we would expect a rational regulator to treat them the same, or at least similarly. And thus, when the regulator does not treat them the same, we are led to suspect some distortion of the regulatory process. Of course, if the products do not compete, we do not have the same clear expectation about the nature of the distortion that we have when they do compete; we cannot be dealing with protectionism. And hence it may be that we should want a clearer case for "likeness" in the sense of regulatory indistinguish-ability when the products do not compete than when they do. But surely such a case can sometimes be made, even for goods that do not compete.

In fact, it is easy to imagine what could produce the political distor-tion in my hypothetical case: lobbying by the tobacco industry against banning menthol cigarettes. Indonesia claimed, plausibly, that the failure to ban menthol cigarettes in the actual case reflected lobbying by Philip Morris (although the Panel did not find it necessary to make a finding on this).[37] It seems probable that the lobbying effort would be virtually the same in the hypothetical case as in the actual case, despite the absence of competition between clove and menthol cigarettes. I have not tried to find details on Philip Morris's lobbying effort, but it would be surprising if they devoted significant effort, or any effort, to promoting the ban on clove cigarettes, as distinct from opposing a ban on menthol cigarettes. Even in the actual case, the competitive danger from clove cigarettes was slight; they had only a small market share,[38] and clove is not a common or specially popular flavor in the United States. To actively promote the ban on clove cigarettes would be to promote a law based on the proposi-tion that tobacco is dangerous, especially for young people, which is not a view the tobacco industry willingly promotes, even now. Finally, Philip Morris may actually benefit from the availability of clove cigarettes, despite the existence of some competition with its menthol cigarettes. If clove cigarettes are in fact a "starter" cigarette, from which young smokers often move on to regular cigarettes, then presumably some of those young smokers end up as smokers of Philip Morris's non-menthol brands. In sum, the lobbying and consequent political distortion in the actual case probably did not depend at all on the existence of competition between menthol and clove cigarettes. So why should we make that competition a prerequisite for a violation?

I am not suggesting that the TBT gives tribunals a roving commission to try to uncover and suppress all political distortions. But in my hypo-thetical case, we have a situation that seems to fall easily within TBT 2.1's definition of a national treatment violation: We have a domestic product and a foreign product that are "like" in a sense that seems much more natural than the *Asbestos* competitive relationship sense. (Remember that in the TBT, there is no equivalent of GATT III:1 to require a competitive

---

[37]   *United States – Measures Affecting the Production and Sale of Clove Cigarettes*, WT/DS406/R, adopted as modified 24 April 2012, ¶7.313 *et passim*.
[38]   Clove cigarettes accounted for 0.1% of the U.S. market between 2000 and 2009. *Ibid.*, ¶2.25.

relationship.) And the foreign product is treated less favorably in an ordinary sense. *Furthermore*, picking up on a theme from *Dominican Republic – Cigarettes*, there is an obvious way in which the worse treatment of the foreign product is *explained* by the fact that it is foreign: in general, domestic firms have much more leverage in the lobbying process than foreign firms or governments.

My hypothetical does not involve discriminatory purpose *in the sense of* a purpose that aims *specifically* at treating the domestic product and the imported product differently. A specific goal of differential treatment would make sense only if the products competed. But my hypothetical does involve what we might call "discrimination in respect of the regulatory purpose". The regulator has a purpose to spare menthol cigarettes from prohibition, even as it prohibits clove cigarettes, which seem indistinguishable on impartial regulatory grounds. And as I suggested, it is easy to see how this discrimination in respect of the regulatory purpose is explained by the facts about national origin. A national treatment violation in GATT Article III requires discriminatory purpose in the narrow sense above, but that is because GATT III:1 talks about protection, which requires competition. There is nothing in the general idea of "national treatment" that requires comparing the treatment of products that compete. (And of course the words "national treatment" do not appear in the TBT at all.) My hypothetical seems to involve a violation of TBT 2.1.

Time now to consider the reasons the Appellate Body gives in *Clove Cigarettes* for importing the *Asbestos* "competitive relationship" test into the TBT. In a prefatory discussion, the Appellate Body analogizes the fifth and sixth recitals of the TBT Preamble to GATT Articles III and XX (¶¶92–96). Both the TBT and the GATT address the question of the proper relationship between the desire for trade liberalization and a concern for Members' regulatory autonomy. And the Appellate Body says that the "the balance set out in the Preamble of the TBT Agreement . . . is not, in principle, different from the balance set out in the GATT 1994" (¶96). Fair enough. The GATT 1994 and the TBT are both WTO agreements adopted at the same time, and we should expect that at the *fundamental* level, they embody the same view about the role of trade liberalization. But it is also clear that at the *operational* level, they make different choices. In connection with technical regulations, TBT 2.2 imposes a freestanding obligation not to use unnecessarily trade-restrictive means, which the GATT does not. TBT 2.4 imposes an obligation to use international standards, provided they are not ineffective or inappropriate, which the GATT does not. So it seems perfectly possible that TBT 2.1 should create a more expansive "national treatment" obligation than GATT Article III, that it might forbid different treatment of like domestic and foreign products ("like" as menthol cigarettes and clove cigarettes are like) even in the absence of competition between them.

The Appellate Body's strongest argument, to my mind, is just the similarity in the language of TBT 2.1 and GATT III:4. But set against that is a hugely important difference in context. As the Appellate Body emphasized in *Asbestos*, GATT III:4 is informed by GATT III:1, which talks about "protection". In fact, GATT III:1 provided the *Asbestos* Appellate Body's primary argument for their "competitive relationship" interpretation of "likeness". But there is no comparable context for TBT 2.1. So the primary argument for that interpretation of "likeness" does not apply to TBT 2.1.

The Appellate Body in *Clove Cigarettes* implicitly recognizes that the primary argument in *Asbestos* cannot be transferred to the TBT context, but they claim to find in *Asbestos* another argument, namely, that it is "products that are in a competitive relationship in the marketplace [that] could be affected through treatment of *imports* 'less favorable' than the treatment accorded to *domestic* products" (*Clove Cigarettes* ¶110, quoting *Asbestos* ¶99, emphasis in *Asbestos* and *Clove*). The claim here seems to be that unless the imported product and the domestic product are in competition, we cannot say that the imported product is harmed by being treated less favorably than the domestic product. And then, since the concept of less favorable treatment "informs the determination of likeness", the fact that harm from less favorable treatment requires competition means that likeness requires competition (¶111). The problem with this is that it does not seem correct to claim that harm from less favorable treatment requires competition.

Consider again my hypothetical case, where menthol cigarettes and clove cigarettes do not compete. If we come to the case with a fresh eye, before we have any reason to think there is political distortion, we will assume that the treatment of the domestic product, menthol cigarettes, indicates how the United States thinks this product should be treated on the basis of the relevant regulatory considerations. And of course, we would expect that other products that are like menthol cigarettes in all respects relevant to a proper regulatory decision would be treated the same way. In other words, the treatment of menthol cigarettes provides a baseline for how all such products should be treated. If we now consider clove cigarettes, we see that even though they are like menthol cigarettes in all respects relevant to regulation, they are treated differently, and less favorably. They are worse off with the treatment they get than they would have been if they had been accorded the baseline treatment accorded menthol cigarettes. At this point, it seems completely natural to say that clove cigarettes are harmed by being treated less favorably than menthol cigarettes, even though they do not compete with each other.

It may be that what the Appellate Body really has in mind is some such claim as the following: giving the imported product less favorable treatment than the domestic product can only harm the imported product *specifically in its relation to the domestic product* if the products are in competition. That seems true enough; it is only if the products are in competition that we can understand the notion of harm to the imported product *specifically in its relation to the domestic product*. But introducing the requirement that the harm to the imported product from less favorable treatment must be harm "specifically in its relation to the domestic product" seems completely question-begging, once we have seen that we can give a perfectly natural sense to harm from less favorable treatment even in the absence of competition.[39]

The Appellate Body also says in the course of its discussion: "the concept of 'treatment no less favourable' links the products to the marketplace, because it is only in the marketplace that it can be determined how the measure treats like imported and domestic products" (¶111). Now, it is true that we are concerned with treatment that affects how the products fare in the market; and in that sense, the "treatment" is determined by the marketplace effects. But it simply does not follow that "less favorable treatment" requires market competition *between the products being compared*. In my hypothetical case, the harm to clove cigarettes is being excluded from the market for cigarettes *in general*. Clove cigarettes are treated less favorably than menthol cigarettes in that they are excluded from that market, while menthol cigarettes are allowed to operate in it. It is simply irrelevant to this market-based less favorable treatment that clove cigarettes and menthol cigarettes do not compete directly with each other. Indeed, we can use a standard formulation and say that clove cigarettes are denied "equality of competitive conditions" with menthol cigarettes – not equality of conditions in the competition between clove cigarettes and menthol cigarettes, which by hypothesis does not exist, but equality of competitive conditions in the larger market for cigarettes in general.

The Appellate Body suggests one final argument against making "likeness" depend on regulatory purpose. They suggest that products may be

---

[39]   If the Appellate Body were willing to admit the importance of discriminatory *purpose*, it might make the argument that there will be no *specific purpose to treat the products differently* in the absence of competition. True enough. But once again, it seems question-begging to insist on a specific purpose to discriminate, as opposed to what I have called above "discrimination in respect of the regulatory purpose".

"like" with respect to one relevant regulatory purpose and "unlike" with respect to another, and then the tribunal will be unable to choose (¶115). But the right question for the tribunal is whether, in light of the entire constellation of relevant purposes taken together, there is a plausible case for regulating the products differently. The existence of a relevant purpose that suggests different treatment will normally justify different treatment, even if there are other relevant purposes that would not justify different treatment. Only in the unusual case where there are regulatory purposes that *positively require* similar treatment, even in the face of independent reasons for different treatment, will there be any real problem; and except in rare cases, the regulator's appreciation of this sort of situation should control. Note further that the very question that the Appellate Body's approach purports to avoid under the "likeness" inquiry comes back in their "less favorable treatment" inquiry into whether the regulation is justified by legitimate regulatory purposes. I cannot see that anything is gained by putting the issue off. Indeed, I have been explaining why something may be lost, since the Appellate Body's approach to "likeness" means there will be no TBT 2.1 violation in cases like my hypothetical. I am not absolutely sure we should find a violation in my hypothetical, but the argument for doing so seems plausible, and the Appellate Body has given no persuasive reason why we should not.

Now, I have suggested that there can be a "national treatment" violation of TBT 2.1 even when the products whose treatment we compare do not compete with each other. And I have done so by explaining why prohibited discriminatory purpose (in a broad sense) need not depend on the existence of competition. But that still leaves a crucial question: what is the relation between the existence of discriminatory purpose and the absence of justification by legitimate regulatory purposes? The Appellate Body says repeatedly that there will not be a violation of TBT 2.1 if the measure is justified by legitimate regulatory purposes. (Again, I think they got that exactly right.) But they never say precisely what *does* constitute a violation (aside from "less favorable treatment of imported like products", which is just the language we are trying to interpret, and unrevealing references to "discrimination" and "even-handedness"). The opinions strongly suggest that competitive relationship, plus disparate impact, plus *non*-justification by legitimate regulatory purposes add up to a violation. But back in section II.B, I argued against this approach under GATT Article III. Is it any more satisfactory under TBT 2.1? Perhaps it is, a bit.

Taking a sideways step, consider that the TBT and SPS Agreements both include a free-standing less restrictive alternative obligation. (TBT 2.2, SPS 5.6) The burden of proof that there is an available less restrictive alternative is on the complainant, but it is just an ordinary "preponderance of the evidence" burden (perhaps with some extra "margin of appreciation" if the objective of the measure is a particularly sensitive one).[40] This means that we are in effect substituting the tribunal's judgment about the efficacy of various measures for the regulator's judgment, just as we do under GATT Article XX (as discussed in section II.B). But here the reason cannot be any *a priori* suspicion of the regulator's motives, such as we have under the GATT with border measures (other than at-the-border application of origin-neutral internal measures) or origin-specific internal measures. The only plausible explanation for relying on the tribunal's judgment in these SPS and TBT cases is that we think that *with regard to measures that fall under the SPS Agreement or measures that are technical regulations under the TBT Agreement*, the tribunal is as competent as the regulator to judge the efficacy of measures.[41] That does seem at least somewhat plausible, although perhaps more obviously so in the case of the SPS than in the case of the TBT. This idea would also explain why the SPS and the TBT Agreements supplement the GATT with new obligations *that operate only in specific kinds of cases* (that is, only in cases involving SPS measures or technical regulations). These are cases where we seem to think the nature of the available evidence will give the tribunal a leg up.[42]

What does this discussion of TBT 2.2 tell us about whether we should make "non-justification" a determinative issue under TBT 2.1? Doing this without any provisos would amount to substituting the tribunal's judgment about justification for the regulator's. The question about justification in a 2.1 case will often depend on a mix of more particular questions about the efficacy of measures and about the valuation of goals. Because

---

[40]   Note that the degree of sensitivity should be evaluated from the *regulator's* point of view, although of course the tribunal's view of what is plausible will inevitably effect how the tribunal responds to the regulator's claims.

[41]   Efficacy is the issue. The less restrictive alternative test, which merely asks whether the same amount of the objective can be achieved with less trade restriction, does not require any *valuation* of effects by the tribunal. (See note 19 above.) The tribunals should no more substitute their *evaluative* judgments for the regulator's under the TBT and SPS than under GATT. That is the point of saying, in both the TBT and the SPS, that the regulator gets to choose its own level of protection.

[42]   Notice that this also suggests a criterion that tribunals should consider in deciding what measures count as SPS measures or technical regulations (issues that were controversial in *European Communities – Measures Affecting the Approval and Marketing of Biotech Products*, WT/DS291&292&293/R, adopted 21 November 2006, and *US – Tuna II,* for example). It only makes sense to apply the stringent obligations of the SPS or the TBT in cases where there is reason to think the tribunals can make better judgments about efficacy than they can in the general range of GATT cases. It would take me too far afield to discuss what this criterion might mean for *Biotech* or *Tuna II.*

we are dealing with a technical regulation, we may well think the tribunal can do as well as the regulator at judgments of *efficacy*. But there is still no reason to substitute the tribunal's judgment for the regulator's on issues of *valuation*, especially in light of the statement in the sixth recital of the Preamble to the TBT that a Member is entitled to protect legitimate values "at the levels it considers appropriate". As under GATT Article III, the tribunal should reject the regulator's *evaluative* judgments only if the claims made by the regulator seem so implausible as to make us doubt the regulator's good faith.

Interestingly, if we now consider *Clove – Cigarettes*, there is a sense in which even the 2.1 analysis involves only an issue about efficacy. The essence of the Appellate Body's criticism of the United States regulation is that it acts against a danger from clove cigarettes and ignores an identical danger from menthol cigarettes. In order to make the judgment that there is an unjustified difference here, it is not necessary to decide how important it is to reduce the danger from smoking. It is only necessary to decide that clove cigarettes and menthol cigarettes create the same danger (per cigarette). If you like, this is a judgment that prohibiting menthol cigarettes would be equally efficacious with prohibiting clove cigarettes as a means of reducing the danger from smoking. So perhaps this is a case where the tribunal is straightforwardly justified in substituting its own judgment about justification for the judgment of the regulator.[43] Remember also that the Appellate Body's test requires not just non-justification, but also disparate impact (to say nothing of competitive relationship, which the Appellate Body requires, but which I would do away with). This certainly increases the tribunal's confidence (and ours), by giving us some reason to suspect the regulator's impartiality. In sum, prohibited purpose may not always play quite such an indispensable role in TBT 2.1 as it does in GATT Article III; but it is almost certain to figure in the mix. And it is just as true here as it was under GATT Article III that disparate impact (and likewise competitive relationship) is of no significance in itself; it is significant only because it suggests prohibited purpose and makes us less inclined to trust the regulator's decision.

---

[43]   One might worry that the Appellate Body dismissed too easily the United States' claim that they had not banned menthol cigarettes because they wanted to study the public health consequences, and the "black market" consequences, of banning at a stroke the preferred smoke of many millions of nicotine addicts. But the Appellate Body could not have accepted this argument, reminiscent of Article 5.7 of the SPS Agreement, without also inventing a 5.7-like obligation to pursue the research and act on it. Perhaps they should have, but I can understand their not wanting to get into this.

US –Tuna II and *US – COOL* we can deal with briefly. Both cases operate with the same basic analysis as *Clove Cigarettes* – and most particularly, both repeat that a measure will *not* violate TBT 2.1 if it is fully justified by legitimate regulatory purposes (*Tuna* ¶216; *COOL* ¶272). In both cases, as in *Clove Cigarettes*, there is much to discuss about how the Appellate Body *applies* that legitimate regulatory purpose test. In the end, of course, the significance of any test depends on how it is applied. But except for a few limited comments, I will leave that discussion for another time. With regard to *Tuna II*, the Appellate Body sees this case the same way they saw *Clove Cigarettes*. Their main complaint is that the United States acted against a danger to dolphins from tuna-fishing methods used by fleets supplying Mexican producers, while ignoring comparable dangers to dolphins from fishing methods used by the fleets that supplied American producers (¶292).

We cannot describe *US – COOL* the same way as *Clove Cigarettes* and *Tuna II*, not least because the meat labeling regulations are not really aimed at reducing a danger; they are designed to create a benefit, consumer information. But there is arguably a different way in which *US – COOL* seems to involve differential solicitude for the interests of domestic and foreign producers (quite aside from the fact that anything that encourages segregation of domestic and foreign products will tend to favor the domestic products, as in *Korea – Beef*).[44] The COOL regulations provide for completely informative labels on "all-American" meat products, but only for much less informative labels on foreign meat products; and this difference will very likely reinforce the natural preference of American consumers for American meat. Noticing this particular type of differential solicitude for foreign and domestic producers also reveals a connection between our analysis and the Appellate Body's complaint that the prescribed labels fail to exploit a lot of the information that the regulations effectively require to be collected. The differential treatment we have identified consists precisely in exploiting the information when doing so benefits domestic producers, and not otherwise.[45]

Two final points. First, in the new TBT trilogy, the Appellate Body

---

[44]   *Korea – Measures Affecting Imports of Fresh, Chilled and Frozen Beef*, WT/DS161&169/AB/R, adopted 10 January 2001.
[45]   The Appellate Body makes this complaint about the failure to fully exploit the information in ¶347. Another possibility, which is fun to imagine but not terribly plausible, is that with this complaint, the Appellate Body is creating a dual of the "least restrictive alternative" obligation: just as Members are required by TBT 2.2 to achieve any given amount of a legitimate objective by the least trade-restrictive means possible, so for any given level of trade-restrictiveness (in this

makes quite aggressive use of its "stems from legitimate regulatory distinctions" test. It is striking that the Appellate Body finds 2.1 violations in all three cases (in one instance overruling the Panel's refusal to find one); and they refuse to find 2.2 violations in either case where the issue was presented (in both instances overruling the Panel's finding of such a violation). The refusal to find 2.2 violations seems right. In neither of the cases was there good reason to think the United States could have achieved what they did achieve with less trade restriction. As to 2.1, there does seem to be differential attention to domestic and foreign sources of the dangers the regulations address in *Clove Cigarettes* and *Tuna II*; and as we have explained, we can find another sort of differential solicitude for the concerns of domestic and foreign producers in *COOL*. Neither *Tuna II* nor *COOL* is an open-and-shut case. But the judgments are more than defensible, if we regard the Appellate Body as free to substitute its own judgment for the regulator's judgment on empirical issues, especially in light of the disparate impact in both cases. Notice finally that none of this analysis depends on the existence of competition between the domestic and foreign products, even though there was such competition in all three cases, which may have made it somewhat easier to attribute prohibited motivation.

And the final point. In *Clove Cigarettes* the Appellate Body seems to suggest that *de jure* distinctions that disfavor foreign products are automatic violations of TBT 2.1 (¶¶182,215). That seems inconsistent with the idea that the TBT strikes the same fundamental balance between trade liberalization and Members' regulatory autonomy as does the GATT. After all, even *de jure* violations of GATT Article III are in principle justifiable under Article XX. And since there is no separate Article XX equivalent in the TBT, we need to be careful about creating automatic violations of TBT 2.1. The ultimate principle announced in *Clove Cigarettes* – that a measure does not violate TBT 2.1 if it flows exclusively from legitimate purposes – should apply across the board, to regulations that make *de jure* distinctions quite as much as to regulations that are origin-neutral. Against this, it might be argued that justification for *de jure* discrimination, rare in any event, will be even rarer in connection with technical regulations, so that in the TBT context a flat ban on *de jure* discrimination makes sense. But that argument needs to be made. We should not install such a flat ban by inadvertence.

---

case, from the costs of information-collection), the Members must achieve as much of the legitimate objective as possible.

IV.   THE MOST-FAVORED NATION PRINCIPLE IN GATT ARTICLE I AND TBT 2.1

The fundamental principle announced in *Clove Cigarettes* – that measures do not violate the national treatment obligation of TBT 2.1 if they are fully justified by legitimate regulatory purposes – should apply also to most-favored nation complaints, whether under TBT 2.1 or GATT Article I. Formally, the principle as announced in *Clove Cigarettes* is part of the "less favorable treatment" analysis, and since that phrase is part of both the national treatment aspect and the most-favored nation aspect of TBT 2.1, it should be clear that the principle applies to most-favored nation complaints under TBT 2.1. It would then be very odd if the principle did not apply to GATT Article I, even though the "less favorable treatment" language does not appear there. The TBT is in some respects more constraining of Members' technical regulations than the GATT; so far, there is no respect in which the TBT is *less* constraining (except in the basic limitation of its scope to technical regulations). Since it was adopted to deal with perceived weaknesses of the GATT, we would not expect it to be less constraining in any respect. But the TBT would create a weaker most-favored nation obligation than the GATT if the *Clove Cigarettes* principle applied to most-favored nation cases under TBT 2.1 but not under GATT Article I. In fact, the idea that measures are legal if they are fully justified by legitimate regulatory purposes is one that is required by the rationale of the entire WTO, and it should govern our reading of all the WTO agreements.

The most-favored nation principle is an anti-discrimination principle, like the national treatment principle. Our theoretical argument that GATT Article III is about protectionist *purpose* can be applied to show that GATT Article I is about discriminatory *purpose*. One adopted GATT Panel report said so explicitly.[46] But even that report was not able to tell us precisely what the objectionable purpose was, since some discrimination, to discourage free-riding in tariff negotiations, is plainly accepted. I shall not pursue this interesting question; but note that importing the *Clove Cigarettes* principle about regulatory justification into GATT Article I has the happy effect of making this question much less pressing. Note also that just as TBT 2.1 may be relevant to discrimination *even between like products that do not compete with each other*, there is no obvious reason why the same should not be true of GATT Article I. Just revise my hypothetical

---

[46] *Japan – Tariff on Import of Spruce-Pine-Fir (SPF) Dimension Lumber*, GATT Panel Report adopted 19 July 1989, BISD 36S/167, ¶5.10.

in which clove cigarettes and menthol cigarettes do not compete with each other by assuming that the menthol cigarettes sold in the United States are made in Thailand, for example.

V.   THE SUBSIDIES AGREEMENT: ARTICLE 1.1(a) (1)(ii) ("OTHERWISE DUE") AND ARTICLE 3.1(a) ("CONTINGENT IN FACT UPON EXPORT PERFORMANCE")

Finally, I want to look briefly at two provisions of the Subsidies Agreement that seem plainly to involve issues of prohibited regulatory purpose, but where again the Appellate Body has been unwilling to say so. First, consider the *US – FSC 21.5* decision,[47] on the issue of whether the exclusion from taxation of extraterritorial income attributable to export sales (roughly speaking) was a financial contribution under Article 1.1(a)(1)(ii) in the form of foregoing revenue that is "otherwise due". The Appellate Body says that Members get to choose their own approach to what to tax, and that the test of whether revenue is "otherwise due" must be grounded in the commitments of the Member's own tax system (¶89). Having said this, the Appellate Body obviously will not be able to find that revenue that is foregone is "otherwise due" without finding some kind of internal inconsistency in the Member's tax system. In a striking echo of GATT Article III, they say that Panels must "compar[e] the fiscal treatment of the income subject to the contested measure and the fiscal treatment of certain other income. In general terms, in this comparison, like will be compared with like" (¶90). Panels "should seek to compare the fiscal treatment of legitimately comparable income" (¶91). And again, "the normative benchmark for determining whether revenue foregone is otherwise due must allow a comparison of the fiscal treatment of comparable income, in the hands of taxpayers in similar situations" (¶98). So, revenue otherwise due is foregone when the fiscal rule treats comparable situations differently.

This is some progress, but it still does not solve the problem that the grounds for comparability or likeness must themselves be found in the Member's own tax system – it is the Member's own system that must tell us *both* that the cases are comparable and that they are treated differently. How can we distinguish a system that is internally inconsistent from one that is merely very complex? It is clear that the real question must be whether the Member is "fiddling" its tax rules to achieve some

---

[47]   A full citation appears in note 31 above.

problematic or prohibited objective. That is to say, the question is about purpose. So what is the prohibited purpose here? In the context of SCM 1.1(a)(1)(ii), the problematic or prohibited objective is specificity – giving the benefit of foregoing revenue only to a favored firm or group of firms who are not distinguished from other taxpayers by any general principles of the system.[48]

Of course the Appellate Body has never said the issue is purpose. But in *US – Aircraft (Boeing)*,[49] they say somewhat mysteriously: "[A] panel examining a claim under Article 1.1(a)(1)(ii) of the *SCM Agreement* should first identify the tax treatment that applies to the income of the alleged recipients. Identifying such tax treatment will entail consideration of the objective reasons behind that treatment and, where it involves a change in a Member's tax rules, an assessment of the reasons underlying that change" (¶812). It is not clear what "objective reasons behind that treatment" or "the reasons underlying [a] change" could refer to except the regulator's purpose. It might be said that we can normally identify the treatment without identifying the purpose; but by the same token, we can normally identify the treatment without identifying the "underlying reasons". We need to know the purpose, or the "reasons", to know what to *make* of the treatment, how to understand it. Further on the Appellate Body says: "the Panel record does not support the contention that Washington State implemented House Bill 2294 . . . to counteract the effects of pyramiding. House Bill 2294 was implemented in order to provide certain tax incentives to the aerospace industry" (¶830). That certainly sounds like a claim about purpose.

Another provision of the Subsidies Agreement that involves the search for prohibited purpose is Article 3.1(a), specifically the issue of when a measure is "contingent . . . in fact . . . upon export performance". Consider only the most recent case. In *EC – Aircraft (Airbus)* we encounter the sort of hemming and hawing that is familiar from the GATT Article III cases.[50] "The standard for determining whether the granting of a subsidy is 'in fact tied to . . . anticipated exportation' is an objective standard, to be established on the basis of the total configuration of facts constituting

---

[48]   A consequence of this analysis is that *when the type of subsidy is that defined by SCM 1.1(a)(1)(ii)*, we cannot separate the issue of the existence of the subsidy from the issue of specificity. We can separate these issues in connection with other types of subsidy, but not with this type.

[49]   *United States – Measures Affecting Trade in Large Civil Aircraft (Second Complaint)*, WT/DS353/AB/R, adopted 23 March 2012.

[50]   *European Communities and Certain Member States – Measures Affecting Trade in Large Civil Aircraft*, WT/DS316/AB/R, adopted 1 June 2011.

and surrounding the granting of the subsidy, including the design, structure, and modalities of operation of the measure granting the subsidy. . . .
We note, however, that while the standard for *de facto* export contingency
cannot be satisfied by the subjective motivation of the granting government, objectively reviewable expressions of a government's policy objectives for granting a subsidy may, however, constitute relevant evidence
in an inquiry into whether a subsidy is geared to induce the promotion
of future export performance by the recipient" (¶1050). "Similarly, the
standard does not require a panel to ascertain a government's reason(s)
for granting a subsidy. The government's reason for granting a subsidy
only explains *why* the subsidy is granted. It does not necessarily answer the
question as to *what* the government did, in terms of the design, structure,
and modalities of operation of the subsidy, in order to induce the promotion of future export performance by the recipient. Indeed, whether the
granting of a subsidy is conditional on future export performance must
be determined by assessing *the subsidy itself*, in the light of the relevant
factual circumstances, rather than by reference to the granting authority's reasons for the measure. This is not to say, however, that evidence
regarding the policy reasons of a subsidy is necessarily excluded from the
inquiry into whether a subsidy is geared to induce the promotion of future
export performance by the recipient" (¶1051). But why would "objectively
reviewable expressions of a government's policy objectives" or "evidence
regarding the policy reasons of a subsidy" be relevant at all, unless the
question was about the government's purpose, at least in part?

Both of the passages just quoted refer to the question whether the
subsidy is "geared to induce the promotion of future export performance".
This seems to be the Appellate Body's latest attempt to find a way to avoid
talking explicitly about purpose. To be sure, they offer a numerical analysis of the concept of "geared to". They say a subsidy is "geared to" induce
export performance if it could be expected, on the information available
to the regulator at the time of adoption, that the new production induced
by the subsidy would be devoted to export sales in a higher proportion
than previously existing production (¶¶1048–49). Tying the definition to
expectations based on the information available to the regulator suggests
an implicit concern with the regulator's purpose. But beyond that, if we
try to believe that "geared to" is *not* really about purpose, then it does
not seem to make sense. Why are export subsidies so strongly disfavored?
Presumably there is both a political explanation, that export subsidies are
regarded as a particularly blatant "attack" on other Members' markets,
and an economic explanation, that export subsidies can be strongly presumed to be inefficient, much more strongly than non-export subsidies.

But the *numerical* definition of "geared to" does not really capture either of these ideas.

If a country subsidizes an exporting industry (in some way that is not *de jure* contingent on export performance), and the reason for the subsidy is that the industry generates positive externalities, then even if this subsidy is "geared to" export performance in the Appellate Body's numerical sense (as it could perfectly well be), it does not seem to be specially objectionable politically, and it is not economically inefficient. Such a subsidy should not be prohibited, even though it is actionable. Conversely, a country that wants to improve its trade balance might well subsidize an exporting industry (again, in a way that is not *de jure* contingent on export performance) precisely in order to increase the country's exports, *even if the new production is not expected to be exported at a higher rate than existing production.* If this export-inflating purpose is clearly established, both of the reasons for specially disfavoring export subsidies seem to be implicated, even though the subsidy is *not* "geared to" export performance in the Appellate Body's sense (unless, perhaps, we consider "gearing" at the economy-wide level, a possibility the Appellate Body does not discuss). I would not conclude immediately that this should be a prohibited subsidy under the Subsidies Agreement; but whether it should be or not depends on what we think of this pure export-inflating purpose. The *numerical* sense of "geared to" does not seem to help us answer that question. Of course, it may be that what we really object to is just a purpose to promote exports *in a "geared" fashion.* That would explain why "gearing" is significant as *evidence* on the question of *de facto* export-contingency. But it means that purpose is still the ultimate issue.

VI. CONCLUSION

The provisions we have considered are all about discrimination. This is obvious in the case of GATT Articles I and III, and TBT 2.1. It is obvious in the case of SPS 5.5, where the third element of a violation is "discrimination or a disguised restriction on international trade". It may be less obvious in the two Subsidies Agreement provisions we have been considering, but 1.1(a)(1)(ii) is about discrimination between different domestic taxpayers (even though it is not any domestic taxpayer that we are ultimately concerned to protect), and 3.1(a) is about discrimination between domestic and foreign purchasers (even though it is neither of those that we are ultimately concerned to protect). Even with regard to the "core" anti-discrimination principles, concerning national treatment and most-favored nation treatment, I have suggested that the discrimination need not always be between *competitors*. It must be between competitors under GATT Article III, because of III:1. But it is not obvious that it must be between competitors under TBT 2.1, or even under GATT Article I.

Both case law and theory reveal that in all the provisions we have considered, with the possible partial exception of TBT 2.1, the ultimate concern is with discriminatory *purpose*, or at least with what I have called "discrimination in respect of the regulatory purpose". Even under TBT 2.1, disparate impact, by suggesting discrimination in respect of the regulatory purpose, gives us more confidence in substituting the tribunal's judgment about regulatory justification for the regulator's judgment. In the context of the provisions we have discussed, where our goal is to suppress certain inefficient regulation, neither *de jure* discrimination nor disparate impact (which incidentally includes numerically-defined "gearing") has any significance in itself. Both are relevant only as evidence of prohibited purpose. *De jure* discrimination is very strong evidence of prohibited purpose; disparate impact is vanishingly weak evidence, considered in isolation. *De jure* discrimination and disparate impact may of course be important in themselves in other sorts of discrimination law, like race or sex discrimination, where we are concerned with symbolism or we are trying to overcome a history of discrimination. But those are not our concerns in the WTO. So in the WTO, purpose is what matters.

3. Equivalence and risk regulation under the World Trade Organization's SPS Agreement

*Marsha A. Echols**

I. INTRODUCTION

It is recognized that there can be health and safety risks incident to imports of foods, plants, animals and plant or animal products. The Agreement on the Application of Sanitary and Phytosanitary Measures (SPS Agreement) is about the application of safety measures for humans, plants, animals and their products. It was written, in part, to ensure that safety measures are not used to restrict the trade in agriculture that was liberalized by the Agreement on Agriculture (AoA). The negotiators agreed that this goal would be achieved, inter alia, when a covered safety measure is 'applied only to the extent necessary to protect human, animal or plant life or health, is based on scientific principles and is not maintained without sufficient scientific evidence'.[1]

The SPS Agreement enshrines in international trade rules a new statement of the right of a World Trade Organization (WTO) Member to take certain sanitary and phytosanitary measures necessary for the protection of human, animal or plant life or health. Much of the SPS Agreement details the limitations on the right to take sanitary and phytosanitary measures. The limitations include the traditional trade disciplines in Article 2.3, the requirement in Article 2.2 that a measure be based on scientific principles and not be maintained without sufficient scientific evidence and the Article 5 requirement that a sanitary or phytosanitary[2] measure be based on a risk assessment.

Article 4 concerning equivalence is less well known. It is a tool for

* Professor Echols thanks her Research Assistant, Brandon Young, for his invaluable assistance.

[1] Agreement on the Application of Sanitary and Phytosanitary Measures (SPS Agreement), The Legal Texts: The Results of the Uruguay Round of Multilateral Trade Negotiations (Cambridge University Press 1994) at Art. 2.2.

[2] In this Chapter, 'SPS' will sometimes be employed instead of the full phraseology 'sanitary and phytosanitary'.

facilitating exports through following a recognition that the SPS safety measures or safety system of an exporting WTO Member, although different from those of the importing jurisdiction, are equivalent because they achieve the importing Member's appropriate level of sanitary or phytosanitary protection.

The recognition of equivalence is a risk management option[3] that facilitates trade by pre-approving certain exports as a group instead of shipment by shipment. The recognition occurs after the importing jurisdiction receives an assurance that safety risks or its other concerns are addressed through the regulatory measures of the exporting jurisdiction, which are different but which nevertheless provide equivalent protections. Each importing jurisdiction judges the level of the risk and the appropriate risk management option (the appropriate level of protection and the measure to apply).[4] In doing so, it makes determinations and choices that result in measures that might differ from the choices and measures of governments in other jurisdictions. A successful equivalence negotiation results in a bilateral agreement or an exchange of letters in which equivalence is recognized. The agreement relieves the exporter from having to prove the conformity of each imported product.[5]

The text of Article 4 is deceptively simple, but has proved to be so complex and costly to implement that there are few full equivalence agreements, in spite of years of bilateral and multilateral discussions and guidance documents from the WTO and the so-called Three Sisters. For an informed understanding of equivalence, it is essential to refer to develop-

---

[3]   The recognition of equivalence is exercised as part of a risk analysis, which is a multi-component approach to food, plant and animal safety. The basic components of risk analysis are typical elements of a regulatory response to a hazard, namely risk assessments, risk management and risk communication. The SPS Agreement refers explicitly only to risk assessment (Art. 5) but it implicitly recognizes risk management in its text about harmonization (Art. 3) and equivalence (Art. 4).

[4]   According to the World Organisation for Animal Health (OIE): 'It is now recognised that significantly different animal health and production systems can provide equivalent animal and human health protection for the purpose of international trade, with benefits to both the importing country and the exporting country.' OIE, *OIE Procedures Relevant to the Agreement on the Application of Sanitary and Phytosanitary Measures of the World Trade Organization*, Art. 5.3.2.

[5]   There is no requirement that the agreements be identical or reciprocal. 'Equivalence Agreements with USA, Canada, NZ, Chile, Switzerland are different in scope and ambition.' Delegation of the European Commission to the USA, European Union Rules for Food Imports and the Concept of Equivalence, 27/28 Aug. 2008, available at http://www.fsis.usda.gov/OPPDE/nacmpi/Aug2008/13-Maier.pdf (last visited 17 Mar. 2012).

ments at and documents from the three intergovernmental organizations that are named in Article 3 (Harmonization) of the SPS Agreement – the Codex Alimentarius Commission (Codex or Commission), the World Organisation for Animal Health[6] (OIE) (formerly the International Office of Epizootics), and the international and regional organizations operating within the framework of the International Plant Protection Convention (IPPC).[7] Both the OIE and the IPPC have observer status with the WTO's Committee on Sanitary and Phytosanitary Measures.[8] Also there are a few bilateral equivalence agreements – mainly concerning SPS safety measures, not SPS safety systems. The European Union (EU) and the United States (US) have concluded bilateral equivalence agreements with a select few of their trading partners and with each other.

The complexity of and demands during equivalence negotiations have led to disaffection with the possibilities of Article 4. Some countries say that the equivalence negotiation is so costly and time-consuming that it is often easier for the exporting jurisdiction to adopt and to apply the same measure as the importing country.[9] Developing countries complained at

---

[6]   The World Organisation for Animal Health (OIE) is a 178-member intergovernmental organization with its headquarters in Paris, France. The home page of the institution is http://www.oie.int. It is still often referred to by the acronym OIE in reference to its former name. The institution was created in 1924 by the International Agreement for the Creation of an Office International des Epizooties in Paris, available at http://www.oie.int/about-us/key-texts/basic-texts/interna tional-agreement-for-the-creation-of-an-office-international-des-epizooties/ (last visited 13 Dec. 2011). The 1924 Agreement was a follow-up to the Resolution adopted by the International Conference for the Study of Epizootics on 27 May 1921, Id.

[7]   The International Plant Protection Convention (IPPC) is an agreement among 177 signatories to protect the health of plants and plant products. Its purpose is 'securing common and effective action to prevent the spread and introduction of pests of plants and plant products, and to promote appropriate measures for their control. . . ." Art. I.1, IPPC. The contracting parties are to adopt specified legislative, technical and administrative measures. Id. https://www.ippc. int. (last visited 13 Dec. 2011) The Food and Agriculture Organization (FAO) provides the Rome-based Secretariat for the IPPC.

[8]   See the list of observers at http://www.wto.org/english/thewto_e/igo_obs_e. htm (last visited 13 Dec. 2011). The OIE also has observer status with the Committee on Technical Barriers to Trade. Id.

[9]   See, Kasturi Das, *Coping with SPS Challenges in South Asia*, South Asian Yearbook of Trade and Development 105, 153 (2009). The US Food and Drug Administration took a similar position: 'FDA officials now report that the costs of developing such [seafood equivalence] agreements may outweigh the food safety benefits and, therefore, these assessments are no longer an FDA priority.' General Accounting Office, Food Safety: FDA's Imported Seafood Safety Program Shows

SPS Committee meetings about the costs and time involved in equivalence discussions and that importing jurisdictions often push demands of recognition of equivalence so far that they result in a de facto request for 'duplication' or 'sameness' of measures and do not adequately explain the required level[10] of protection. This negates the notion of equivalence as a trade facilitation tool. And it has led to rarely voiced questions about whether some specific demands by the importing authorities are a disguised restriction on international trade (Art. 2.3) or are necessary (Art. 2.1). As a consequence of the difficulty in concluding equivalence agreements, some WTO Members have begun to discuss simpler approaches, with 'comparability' being an option under consideration. In addition to the poultry disputes, the EU–US negotiations regarding the equivalence of their measures concerning the safety of certain shellfish illustrate these difficulties. In the future these Article 4.2 type agreements, mutual recognition arrangements and as-yet-undefined market access tools, might fill the void left by Article 4.1's unworkable complexity. Unless the options include a tool that facilitates exports by developing countries, the market access opportunity envisioned by the drafters of Article 4 will be incomplete.

II.   THE MEANING OF EQUIVALENCE

The SPS Agreement, in Article 4.1, states:

> Members shall accept the sanitary or phytosanitary measures of other Members as equivalent, even if these measures differ from their own or from those used by other Members trading in the same product, if the exporting Member objectively demonstrates to the importing Member that its measures achieve the importing Member's appropriate level of sanitary or phytosanitary protection.

Article 4 is a directive to WTO Members about a risk regulation option, which must be chosen by an importing government when certain cond-

---

Some Progress, but Further Improvements Are Needed, p. 4, Jan. 2004, available at http://www.gao.gov/new.items/d04246.pdf.

See the list of observers at http://www.wto.org/english/thewto_e/igo_obs_e.htm. The OIE also has observer status with the Committee on Technical Barriers to Trade. Id. (last visited 17 Mar. 2012).

[10]   WTO Secretariat, *China/FAO Citrus Symposium, Sanitary and Phytosanitary issues and the SPS Agreement* Beijing, 14–17 May 2001 (*China Citrus*), http://www.fao.org/docrep/003/x6732e/x6732e13.htm#5 (last visited 18 Dec. 2011).

itions are met ('shall accept the sanitary or phytosanitary measures of other Members as equivalent. . .').[11]

The text does not define the word equivalence. Perhaps as a consequence, the SPS Committee, Codex, OIE and IPPC focus instead on the procedure that leads to the recognition of equivalence. The definition of equivalence[12] for SPS Agreement purposes has been less of an issue than the procedure for the recognition of equivalence, but the differences in the definitions indicate different emphases and, perhaps, regulatory goals. The WTO Secretariat focuses on the outcome – the recognition. It defines equivalence as 'when governments recognize other countries' measures as acceptable even if they are different from their own, so long as an equivalent level of protection is provided'.[13] The definitions followed by Codex and the EU present other meanings for the word. The Codex Alimentarius defines equivalence so as to emphasize that it is the 'state' (circumstance) in which the exporting jurisdiction's measures, although different, achieve the importing jurisdiction's appropriate level of sanitary protection.[14] The EU distinguishes between equivalence (the word in the title of Article 4) and equivalent (the word in the text of Article 4). For the EU equivalence

---

[11]   SPS Agreement, note 1, Art. 8 and Annex C, In contrast the Agreement on Technical Barriers to Trade (TBT Agreement) presents the recognition of equivalence in Art. 2.7 as a more flexible risk management option ('give positive consideration to accepting as equivalent technical regulations of other Members'). The Legal Texts: The Results of the Uruguay Round of Multilateral Trade Negotiations (Cambridge University Press 1994). Both agreements contain rules about the more detailed procedures of control, inspection and approval. *See,* SPS Agreement, note 1, Art. 8 and Annex C. *And see* TBT Agreement, Arts 5–9 and Annex 3. This chapter concerns equivalence in the context of the SPS Agreement. It will refer to the rules of the TBT Agreement and the approaches of other standard setting bodies by way of comparison or to make clear the rule of the SPS Agreement.

[12]   Safety equivalence differs from several other notions of equivalence, like the economics, mathematics and physics concepts. It also is unlike substantial equivalence, a term used in the regulation of genetically modified foods. See, e.g., David A. Devernoe, *Substantial Equivalence: A Valid International Sanitary and Phytosanitary Risk Assessment Objective for Genetically Modified Foods,* 51 Case W. Res. Law Rev 257 (2000).

[13]   WTO, *Current issues in SPS,* available at http://www.wto.org/english/ tratop_e/sps_e/sps_issues_e.htm (last visited 24 Mar. 2012).

[14]   Equivalence is 'the state wherein sanitary measures applied in an importing country, though different from the measures applied in an importing country, achieve, as demonstrated by the exporting country, the importing country's appropriate level of sanitary protection'. Codex Alimentarius, *Guidelines for the Judgment of Equivalence of Sanitary Measures Associated with Food Inspection and Certification Measures (Equivalence Guidelines),* § 3, CAC/GL 53-2003.

means the capability (possibility) of a different system or measure to meet the 'same' objectives as those of the importing jurisdiction, while equivalent means that the different systems are capable of meeting (do meet) the same objectives.

A pivotal issue for understanding the meaning of Article 4 and the attendant obligations is determining what must be 'equivalent' and what must be the 'same'. The text of Article 4 refers to the 'same' product but never mentions the 'same' level of protection, although its wording ('achieve the . . . appropriate level of sanitary or phytosanitary protection') is interpreted to mean the same level of protection. The introductory language of the SPS Committee's Decision (not its text) refers to both equivalence and same. It says 'This decision . . . outlines steps designed to make it easier for all WTO Members to make use of the "equivalence" provisions of the SPS Agreement, i.e. Article 4. This involves governments accepting different measures which provide the same level of health protection for food, animals and plants.' Another point often discussed is whether, in spite of the SPS text, the importing jurisdiction can require, in fact or *de facto*, that the measures be the same rather than equivalent. As stated in the Preamble to the 2001 SPS Committee Decision, '. . .equivalence of sanitary or phytosanitary measures does not require duplication or sameness of measures, but the acceptance of alternative measures that meet an importing Member's appropriate level of sanitary or phytosanitary protection'.[15]

According to this wording, the measures may differ but the level of protection they provide must be the same. Thus the same 'level' of protection must be achieved, although the means (measures) to reach it are different. This conclusion results in a major complexity in equivalence negotiations. The importing authority must explain its level of protection, which is somewhat conceptual and difficult to explain (in contrast, for example, to a quantifiable pesticide minimum residue level). The exporting authority must understand that level of protection, then must determine and, if true, prove that its measures achieve the same level of protection.

Another issue was whether the equivalence obligation concerns an SPS measure (e.g., a test method) or an SPS system. Article 4.1 uses the word 'measures', so did not answer the question. After much discussion, both were accepted and reflected in the guidelines described below. Testing, controls, audits and verification, certification and approved certifiers and

---

[15]   SPS Committee, *Decision on the Implementation of Article 4 of the Agreement on the Application of Sanitary and Phytosanitary Measures (Equivalence Decision)*, G/SPS/19 http://www.wto.org/english/tratop_e/sps_e/equivalence2001_e.htm (last visited 10 Oct. 2011).

traceability are among the many aspects of equivalence discussions and are themselves measures.

Another significant issue is whether the importing jurisdiction has properly chosen its appropriate level of protection.[16] In several articles of the SPS Agreement the text recognizes the right of a WTO Member to apply the level of protection that it determines is appropriate to the risk at issue.[17] However that right is circumscribed by conditions. The WTO Member must avoid arbitrary and unjustifiable restrictions in the levels it considers appropriate in different situations and must ensure that the measure is not more trade restrictive than required to achieve the appropriate level of protection. It should minimize negative trade effects. The WTO Appellate Body report in *Beef Hormones* addressed the first of these conditions. It agreed with the panel about one comparison but disagreed about another. It decided that the difference in the EC levels of protection in respect of the natural and synthetic hormones when used for growth promotion, on the one hand, and carbadox and olaquindox (anti-microbial agents or compounds), on the other, is 'unjustifiable'.[18] In *Salmon* the Appellate Body also concluded that there had been discrimination but it broadened its conclusion beyond Article 5.5 by referring to Article 2.2.[19]

According to the Appellate Body,

> It is well to bear in mind that, after all, the difference in levels of protection that is characterizable as arbitrary or unjustifiable is only an element of (indirect) proof that a Member may actually be applying an SPS measure in a manner that discriminates between Members or constitutes a disguised restriction on international trade, prohibited by the basic obligations set out in Article 2.3 of the SPS Agreement.[20]

Regarding equivalence, the SPS Committee linked it with risk by requiring that, after a request for the recognition of equivalence by an exporting

---

[16]   It is the 'level of protection deemed appropriate by the Member establishing a . . .measure'. SPS Agreement, note 1, Annex A, para. 5.

[17]   In addition to Art. 4 of the SPS Agreement, see, its Arts. 5.3–5.6. Id.

[18]   *EC – Measures Concerning Meat and Meat Products (Beef Hormones)*, ¶ 235, WT/DS26/AB/R and WT/DS48/AB/R (1998),

[19]   The Appellate Body found that there were arbitrary or unjustifiable distinctions in the levels of sanitary protection it considers to be appropriate in different situations (on the one hand, the salmon products at issue from adult, wild, ocean-caught Pacific salmon and, on the other hand, whole, frozen herring for use as bait and live ornamental finfish), which result in discrimination or a disguised restriction on international trade, *Australia – Measures Affecting Importation of Salmon (Salmon)* WT/DS18/AB/R (1998).

[20]   *Beef Hormones*, note 18, at ¶ 241.

WTO Member, the importing government should explain the objective and rationale of its sanitary or phytosanitary measure, the risks that the relevant measure is intended to address and its appropriate level of protection 'accompanied by a copy of the risk assessment on which the sanitary or phytosanitary measure is based or a technical justification based on a relevant international standard, guideline or recommendation'.[21]

The equivalence language of the SPS Agreement is mandatory ('Members shall accept. . .'). However, the mandate applies only when it is shown that the 'measures' of the exporting jurisdiction meet the 'appropriate level of protection' chosen by the importing WTO member. The technical negotiations often center around 'objectively demonstrating' that the measures in the exporting jurisdiction meet the appropriate level of protection of the importing Member, as well as the differences (if any) between 'measures' and 'system'. The Equivalence Decision refers to 'science-based and technical information to support its objective demonstration'.[22]

While there is a required foundation for a safety measure, each jurisdiction is free to apply its 'appropriate level of protection', which may be higher (more demanding) than the international standard or the standard of its trading partners. However, a WTO Member should, when determining its appropriate level of sanitary or phytosanitary protection, 'take into account the objective of minimizing negative trade effects'.[23]

Whether the importing jurisdiction should judge a covered safety *measure* related to a *system* is a recurring issue. The SPS Committee recognized the debate and admitted that either a measure or a system could be considered. But it did not develop clear and specific guidelines in its 2005 Decision. The IPPC Secretariat seems to include all possibilities in its Guidelines.[24]

The SPS Committee decided,

> Equivalence can be accepted for a specific measure or measures related to a certain product or categories of products, or on a systems-wide basis. Members shall, when so requested, seek to accept the equivalence of a measure related to

---

[21]   Implementation Decision, note 15, at ¶ 2.
[22]   Id. at Preamble.
[23]   SPS Agreement, note 1, at Art. 5.4.
[24]   'Equivalence determinations are based on the specified pest risk and equivalence may apply to individual measures, a combination of measures, or integrated measures in a systems approach.' IPPC Guidelines, Outline of Requirements. In its Principles of Plant Quarantine as Related to International Trade, the IPPC Guidelines state that countries should recognize as equivalent measures that are 'not identical but which have the same effect'. International Standards for Phytosanitary Measures No. 1, Principle 7 (Feb. 1995).

a certain product or category of products. . . . The acceptance of the equivalence of a measure related to a single product may not require the development of a systems-wide equivalence agreement.[25]

III. EQUIVALENCE AND THE RISK ANALYSIS PROCESS

The determination by the importing country that it is willing to permit imports is a risk management decision.[26] When regulators in the importing country determine there is a hazard[27] that presents a risk,[28] they then

---

[25] Implementation Decision, note 15, at ¶ 1.

[26] Risk management is the 'process of weighing policy alternatives in the light of the results of risk assessment and, if required, selecting and implementing appropriate control options, including regulatory measures'. There are four elements of risk management: risk evaluation, risk management option assessment, implementation of management decision, and monitoring and review. FAO, *Risk management and food safety*: Food and Nutrition Paper 65 at p. 4 (1997), available at http://www.fao.org/docrep/w4982e/w4982e00.htm (last visited 24 Apr. 2012). The EU uses a different definition, which clearly takes into account a broader range of considerations and gives regulators room for more options. Its basic food safety regulation defines risk management as 'weighing policy alternatives in consultation with interested parties, considering risk assessment and other legitimate factors, and, if need be, selecting appropriate prevention and control options'. §3.12, *Reg. (EC) No 178/2002 of the European Parliament and of the Council of 28 January 2002 laying down the general principles and requirements of food law, establishing the European Food Safety Authority and laying down procedures in matters of food safety*, OJ L 31, p. 1, 1 Feb. 2002.

[27] The SPS Agreement does not define a hazard. The Codex Alimentarius does, describing a hazard as a 'biological, chemical or physical agent in, or condition of, food with the *potential* to cause an adverse health effect'. *Hazard Analysis and Critical Control Point (HACCP) System and Guidelines for Its Application,* Annex to CAC/RCP 1-1969, Rev. 3 (1997). Such a measure is within the scope of the SPS Agreement, which defined as covering any 'measure applied: (a) to protect animal or plant life or health within the territory of the Member from risks arising from the entry, establishment or spread of pests, diseases, disease-carrying organisms or disease-causing organisms; (b) to protect human or animal life or health within the territory of the Member from risks arising from additives, contaminants, toxins or disease-causing organisms in foods, beverages or feedstuffs; (c) to protect human life or health within the territory of the Member from risks arising from diseases carried by animals, plants or products thereof, or from the entry, establishment or spread of pests; or (d) to prevent or limit other damage within the territory of the Member from the entry, establishment or spread of pests'. SPS Agreement, note 1, at Annex A.1.

[28] A risk is a 'function of the probability of an adverse health effect and the severity of that effect, consequential to a hazard(s) in food'. Codex Alimentarius,

conduct a risk analysis – a process that involves risk assessment, risk management and risk communication.[29]

According to the Codex Alimentarius a risk assessment is a 'scientifically based process' that includes (i) hazard identification, (ii) hazard characterization, (iii) exposure assessment, and (iv) risk characterization.[30] The definition in the SPS Agreement is more complex. The WTO defines a risk assessment as an 'evaluation of the likelihood of entry, establishment or spread of a pest or disease within the territory of an importing Member according to the sanitary or phytosanitary measures which might be applied, . . . or the evaluation of the potential for adverse effects on human or animal health . . . arising from the presence of additives, contaminants, toxins or disease-causing organisms in food, beverages or feedstuffs'.[31] The next task is to decide a response that establishes the appropriate level of protection. Usually the regulators choose among various risk management options. The available options could range from a ban on imports to unrestricted commerce. The option selected is likely to involve a more nuanced approach than either of the above two options. Obviously, the WTO implications of the choices would vary, as would the effect on the bilateral (or perhaps international) flow of trade.

Under the SPS Agreement, to reduce the barriers to trade, a country that has conducted a risk assessment and chosen its domestic risk management option 'shall' respond positively to the request of an exporting jurisdiction to discuss an equivalence agreement. The exporting jurisdiction would be asked to prove that its standards, measures or system (three very different criteria) are 'equivalent' and so offer the level of protection required by the importing jurisdiction. Audits might be conducted by both

---

Definitions for the Purposes of the Codex Alimentarius http://www.fao.org/DOC REP/005/Y2200E/y2200e07.htm

[29]   Id.

[30]   Id. Cf. Art. 5.1 of the SPS Agreement, which focuses on risks and risk assessment techniques: 'Members shall ensure that their sanitary or phytosanitary measures are based on an assessment, as appropriate to the circumstances, of the risks to human, animal or plant life or health, taking into account risk assessment techniques developed by the relevant international organizations.'

[31]   The full definition in Annex A.4 of the SPS Agreement states that a risk assessment is an 'evaluation of the likelihood of entry, establishment or spread of a pest or disease within the territory of an importing Member according to the sanitary or phytosanitary measures which might be applied, and of the associated potential biological and economic consequences; or the evaluation of the potential for adverse effects on human or animal health arising from the presence of additives, contaminants, toxins or disease-causing organisms in food, beverages or feedstuffs'.

countries, with a required certification of conformity by an authority in the exporter's jurisdiction. As previously noted, the procedure for proving equivalence is a lengthy, technical and costly process of ensuring and certifying that the two measures or systems are equivalent.

IV.   THE 'THREE SISTERS' AND EQUIVALENCE

Article 3 of the SPS Agreement (Harmonization) expressly recognizes a role for 'international standards, guidelines or recommendations'. It urges WTO Members to participate in relevant international organizations, but mentions specifically Codex, OIE and IPPC. The goal is to promote within the organizations the development and review of international standards, guidelines or recommendations concerning all aspects of SPS measures.[32]

This goal has been achieved in broad terms with regard to the development and periodic review of documents concerning equivalence. The SPS Committee, established by Article 12 of the SPS Agreement, played an early and major role in promoting an understanding of Article 4. The SPS Committee has served as a coordinator and catalyst for the work of the Three Sisters on this topic. In addition, the Codex, OIE and IPPC have developed guidelines and procedures about equivalence. In their approaches, each has directly or indirectly combined equivalence and one or more components of risk analysis. Their published guidelines or procedures regarding equivalence form the basis for a harmonized approach to equivalence for foods, plants and animals. Each document provides details about the institution's view of the equivalence process.

A.   Codex Alimentarius Commission

The Codex Alimentarius Commission has jurisdiction over issues related to trade in foods, including food safety and food quality. It published *Guidelines for the Development of Equivalence Agreements regarding Food Import and Export Inspection and Certification Systems* and *Guidelines on the Judgment of Equivalence of Sanitary Measures Associated with Food Inspection and Certification Systems.*[33] The CAC Guidelines address general principles for the determination of equivalence, the context of an equivalence determination, objective basis of comparison, procedure for

---

[32]   SPS Agreement, note 1 at §3.4.
[33]   Equivalence Guidelines, note 14.

the determination of equivalence and, in an appendix, additional guidance for equivalence determinations, among other provisions of the Guidelines. The development of the Guidelines required years of discussions in committees, working groups and at the Commission. Developing countries attempted to influence the creation of Codex guidelines that would facilitate access by their products to developed country markets. In spite of the involvement of dozens of delegations, the resulting Codex documents are rarely if ever relied on.

B.   World Organisation for Animal Health

The OIE is responsible for promoting and protecting animal health. It created the *OIE Procedures Relevant to the Agreement on the Application of Sanitary and Phytosanitary Measures of the World Trade Organization*.[34] The procedures are intended to assist OIE members to determine whether a sanitary measure from a different system may provide the same level of health protection. The OIE Guidelines include general considerations on the judgment of equivalence of sanitary measures, prerequisite considerations in a judgment of equivalence, principles for the judgment of equivalence, and the sequence of steps in the judgment of equivalence.

C.   International Plant Protection Convention Organizations

The IPPC brings together organizations whose goal is to protect cultivated and wild plants by preventing the introduction and spread of pests. It published *Guidelines for the Determination and Recognition of Equivalence of Phytosanitary Measures*[35] (IPPC Guidelines). The IPPC Guidelines address specifically non-discrimination, information exchange, technical assistance, timeliness, factors considered in determining equivalence, non-disruption of trade and, in an annex, recommendations for a procedure for the determination of equivalence.

These documents of Codex, the OIE and the IPPC are harmonized international guidelines and recommendations, as contemplated by

---

[34]   OIE Procedures Relevant to the Agreement on the Application of Sanitary and Phytosanitary Measures of the World Trade Organization (OIE Guidelines) at Art. 5.3.2, available at www.oie.int/fileadmin/Home/eng/Health.../en_chapitre_1.5.3.pdf (last visited 25 Apr. 2012). Note that the OIE refers to a system instead of to a measure, and to 'same' instead of 'equivalent'.

[35]   IPPC, International Standards for Phytosanitary Measures, Pub. No. 24 (2005), (IPPC Equivalence Guidelines), available at www.furs.si/law/FAO/ZVR/ENG/ISPM_24.pdf (last visited 25 Apr. 2012).

Article 3.1 of the SPS Agreement.[36] Either qualifies as an international standard[37] and allows the recognition that follows it to benefit from two important presumptions. A domestic measure that conforms to an international standard is 'deemed to be necessary'[38] to protect human, animal or plant life or health. It also benefits from a presumption of conformity with the SPS Agreement and the GATT 1994.[39] This should mean that the conforming measure meets the 'necessary' tests of Articles 2.1 and 2.2. In spite of these benefits, many importing governments decide to require a higher level of protection than that offered by the relevant international standard.[40]

The consequence of these provisions is that an exporting country whose safety measure conforms to an international standard is not guaranteed that an importing jurisdiction will recognize the exporter's measure as equivalent and grant market access. This difficulty might occur if the importing jurisdiction demands a level of protection that is higher than the international standard.

V. THE SPS COMMITTEE AND ITS DECISION ON EQUIVALENCE

The SPS Committee has played a pivotal role in promoting the understanding of equivalence, in addressing the concerns of developing countries and

---

[36] The language of Art. 3.1 refers to 'international standards, guidelines or recommendations'. For WTO purposes, the three have the same effect. According to Art. 3.1, 'To harmonize sanitary and phytosanitary measures on as wide a basis as possible, Members shall base their sanitary or phytosanitary measures on international standards, guidelines or recommendations, where they exist', unless a higher level of protection is chosen and justified. A safety measure that is based on a harmonized text meets the necessity test in Art. 2.2.

[37] In this chapter, the term 'international standard' refers to the three types of documents.

[38] 'Sanitary or phytosanitary measures which conform to international standards, guidelines or recommendations shall be deemed to be necessary to protect human, animal or plant life or health,. . . .' SPS Agreement, note 1, at Art. 3.2.

[39] 'Sanitary or phytosanitary measures which conform to international standards, guidelines or recommendations shall be . . .presumed to be consistent with the relevant provisions of this Agreement and of GATT 1994.' Id.

[40] Governments may introduce or maintain sanitary or phytosanitary measures that result in a higher level of sanitary or phytosanitary protection than would be achieved by measures based on the relevant international standard, if there is a scientific justification for the choice or, after a risk assessment, the higher level must be determined to be appropriate. SPS Agreement, note 1, at Art. 3.3.

in improving equivalence procedures.[41] It was established to 'provide a regular forum for consultations'[42] (which it has done), to carry out the functions necessary to implement the SPS Agreement and to further its objectives. It must encourage and facilitate *ad hoc* consultations or negotiations among Members on specific sanitary or phytosanitary issues.[43]

The SPS Committee's Equivalence Decision was the first indication of the vital role the SPS Committee would play regarding equivalence. Its work on equivalence was requested by the WTO's General Council and was designed largely to address questions and concerns of developing countries. 'The concept appears rather straightforward and is indeed frequently applied at the level of specific measures. . . . But it is one of the significant stumbling blocks in the implementation of the SPS Agreement.'[44] The WTO General Council had requested the SPS Committee 'to examine

---

[41]   'In the First Review of the Agreement, the Committee recognized the need for further efforts to facilitate the practical application of Art. 4, including the recognition of equivalence of measures applied by developing country Members. In response to the conclusions of the First Review, the Committee held a first informal meeting to discuss the issue of equivalence and the implementation of Art. 4 in June 2000. The importance of these deliberations was emphasized by the General Council when it requested, during a Special Session on 18 October 2000, that the SPS Committee '. . . examine the concerns of developing countries regarding the equivalence of SPS measures and to come up with concrete options as to how to deal with them . . .' Discussions by the Committee in a series of informal meetings and Special Meetings led to the adoption of a formal Decision on equivalence. In adopting this Decision, several Members noted the need to clarify certain provisions of the Decision. SPS Committee, *Review of the Operation and Implementation of the Agreement on the Application of SPS Measures*, at ¶.18 (G/SPS/36), 11 July 2005. Early documents issued by the Committee are available at Major Decisions and Documents, Summer 2008, available at http://www.wto.org/english/res_e/booksp_e/sps_major_decisions08_e.pdf.

[42]   SPS Agreement, note 1, at Art. 12.1.

[43]   Id. The TBT Agreement contains language that by implication addresses equivalence and makes a more direct link between equivalence and conformity assessment than does the text of the SPS Agreement. 'Members shall give positive consideration to accepting as equivalent technical regulations of other Members, even if those regulations differ from their own, provided they are satisfied that these regulations adequately fulfill the objectives of their own regulations.' TBT Agreement, note 11 at Art. 2.7. The TBT Agreement's instructions to WTO Members about the recognition of equivalence are not mandatory. Members need only give 'positive consideration' to accepting as equivalent the mandatory regulations of other WTO Members and only when they 'adequately fulfill' the 'objectives' of the importing jurisdiction. Equivalence agreements concerning trade in organic food products fall within this category. The TBT Committee has been less involved in developing the rules of equivalence for technical barriers to trade.

[44]   *China Citrus*, note 10.

the concerns of developing countries regarding the equivalence of SPS measures and to come up with concrete options as to how to deal with them'.[45] Nevertheless, the impact of the Equivalence Decision that resulted from the discussions within the Committee is useful for and applicable to all WTO Members.

The 2001 WTO Ministerial Conference recognized the Committee's work on equivalence and instructed the Committee to develop a specific implementation plan.[46]

The SPS Committee did not explain the legal effect of the Equivalence Decision in a WTO dispute. It would be reasonable to think that, at the least, it could be used in a dispute settlement proceeding, as provided in Article 2 of the Understanding on Rules and Procedures Governing the Settlement of Disputes[47] (DSU) and could lead to the use of experts as provided in Article 11.2 of the SPS Agreement.

The Equivalence Decision could be used to 'clarify the existing provisions of those agreements [including the SPS Agreement] in accordance with customary rules of interpretation of public international law'. According to the customary international law stated in Article 31of the Vienna Convention on the Law of Treaties,[48] ordinary meaning, context and object and purpose aid in interpreting a treaty. So does 'any subsequent agreement between the parties regarding the interpretation of the treaty or the application of its provisions'.[49] The Equivalence Decision meets this last provision. The title of the Equivalence Decision details its specific purpose. It is a 'Decision on the Implementation of Article 4 of the Agreement on the Application of Sanitary and Phytosanitary Measures'. Its provisions, which apply to all WTO Members, interpret Article 4

---

[45]   Implementation Decision, note 15.

[46]   Id. at ¶ 3.3. *See* the plan of the SPS Committee at Equivalence – Programme for Further Work, G/SPS/20 (21 Mar. 2002).

[47]   'The dispute settlement system of the WTO is a central element in providing security and predictability to the multilateral trading system. The Members recognize that it serves to preserve the rights and obligations of Members under the covered agreements, and to clarify the existing provisions of those agreements in accordance with customary rules of interpretation of public international law. Recommendations and rulings of the DSB cannot add to or diminish the rights and obligations provided in the covered agreements.' WTO, Understanding on Rules and Procedures Governing the Settlement of Disputes, Art. 2, The Legal Texts: The Results of the Uruguay Round of Multilateral Trade Negotiations (Cambridge University Press 1994).

[48]   Done at Vienna on 23 May 1969. Entered into force on 27 January 1980. U.N. Treaty Series, vol. 1155, p. 33, available at http://untreaty.un.org/ilc/texts/instruments/english/conventions/1_1_1969.pdf.

[49]   Id. at Art. 31.3(a).

by stating how it is to be implemented. In its Preamble the Equivalence Decision notes that it is to 'make operational the provisions of Article 4; and that 'Members have faced difficulties applying the provisions of Article 4'. There is a second means for using the Equivalence Decision in a WTO dispute concerning Article 4. A panel could use Article 11.2 of the SPS Agreement[50] to obtain the advice of experts about technical aspects of equivalence and the Equivalence Decision. It could also seek input from international organizations, such as the Codex Alimentarius Commission.

It is less clear that the Equivalence Decision could be treated as binding. The Panel in China Poultry stated its view that the Equivalence Decision 'is not binding and does not determine the scope of Article 4'.[51] A challenge to an importing jurisdiction's appropriate level of protection would more likely be raised under Articles 4 and 5 and paragraph 5 of annex A, all of which refer to the appropriate level of protection. The Equivalence Decision says that the importing Member 'should indicate' its appropriate level of protection[52] but the exporting Member 'shall provide' information to support its request.[53] Any binding obligation in this regard under the Decision falls only on the exporting Member. In contrast Article 4.1 imposes the obligation on the importing Member to 'accept the sanitary or phytosanitary measures of other Members as equivalent', if the exporting Member objectively demonstrates that its measures achieve the appropriate level of protection. If the dispute concerned the sufficiency of the demonstration of equivalence, again the exporting Member probably would consider Article 4.1 binding but not the parallel provisions of the Equivalence Decision. Perhaps a preliminary answer to the question whether the Decision would be considered a binding document in a WTO dispute is to refer to the text of the DSU, which refers to claims

---

[50]   According to Art. 11.2, in a 'dispute under this Agreement involving scientific or technical issues, a panel should seek advice from experts chosen by the panel in consultation with the parties to the dispute. To this end, the panel may, when it deems it appropriate, establish an advisory technical experts group, or consult the relevant international organizations, at the request of either party to the dispute or on its own initiative.' SPS Agreement, note 1.

[51]   *US – Certain Measures Affecting Imports of Poultry from China*, ¶¶ 2.5–2.16, WT/DS392/R (2010) (*China Poultry*) at ¶ 7.136. The Panel discussed the Decision in ¶¶ 7.133–7.137 of its Report, although Art. 4 was not within its terms of reference.

[52]   Equivalence Decision, note 15, at Art. 2.

[53]   Id. at Art. 4. It 'shall provide appropriate science-based and technical information to support its objective demonstration that its measure achieves the appropriate level of protection. . .'.

based only on 'covered Agreements'.[54] The Decision is not a covered Agreement.

The Equivalence Decision builds on the skeletal but mandatory language of the SPS Agreement's Article 4.1, which obliges WTO Members to 'accept' an exporting jurisdiction's different measures as equivalent, if the measures 'achieve' the importing jurisdiction's appropriate level of sanitary or phytosanitary protection. The implementation of the Article 4.1 directive was found to be complex, time consuming, costly and uncertain. Developing country exporters believed that they were especially adversely affected. The SPS Committee's Decision gives some guidance to both exporting and importing jurisdictions. Subsequent to its 2001 Equivalence Decision, the SPS Committee continued over several years its efforts to clarify guiding principles regarding the recognition of equivalence. A decision clarifying paragraphs 5 and 6 of the 2001 Decision was issued in 2002 and other clarifications followed.[55] Detailed directions about domestic procedures were included in the documents of Codex, OIE and the IPPC, which have been cited.

Section 1 of the Equivalence Decision begins by characterizing the types of measures referred to in Article 4.1 of the SPS Agreement. The Equivalence Decision describes the possibilities as a 'specific measure or measures related to a certain product or categories of products, or on a systems-wide basis'. The SPS Committee Members agreed that equivalence may take many different forms, ranging from the acceptance of the equivalence of particular sanitary and phytosanitary measures to protect against specific risks in a specific product, to formal systems-wide or broad-ranging agreements on equivalence, but warned that the more broad-ranging the equivalence agreement, the more difficult it might be to conclude.[56] Test methods, microbiological criteria, product characteristics and production processes are among the measures used to determine the safety of a product and against which imported products and systems are measured. For example, to protect against the risks of certain fruit fly species, a regulatory authority might choose heat treatment, cold treatment, chemical treatments or irradiation.[57] The measures used may vary by product and by country.

---

[54]   *See, e.g.*, DSU, note 48, at Art. 3.1.

[55]   Implementation Decision, note 15. *See*, Revisions including clarifications adopted by the Committee (G/SPS/19/Rev.1), the 2004 revision herein referred to as the Implementation Decision (G/SPS/19/Rev.2), and earlier Addenda to the Decision (G/SPS/19/Add.1, Add. 2 and Add. 3)

[56]   *China Citrus*, note 10.

[57]   Id.

The test methods themselves are often the subject of equivalence requests. Such a request requires a less comprehensive approach than when a safety system or even multiple product categories are involved in the request. For example, Brazil requested and was granted an equivalence determination from the United States for a laboratory analytical screening *method* to detect E coli 0157:H7. Canada's request for an equivalence determination for its control *program* for *Listeria monocytogenes* also was granted by the US. In contrast the request from Japan for the use of private laboratories to perform residue testing was denied because of insufficient government oversight. The tests and repeated tests can become financially and administratively costly, especially for developing countries.

The on-going EU–US discussions about live, bivalve mollusks[58] illustrates a system-wide approach to equivalence and the role of testing and inspection methods in negotiations about the recognition of equivalence.[59] The two jurisdictions use different measures to achieve the safety of these products. The safety issue and the different responses of the EU's microbiology focus and the US's environmental focus can be understood from a comment by the United Kingdom's Food Safety Agency.[60] The US tests the water in which bivalve molluscs are reared for coliforms.[61] According to the US the 'goal . . . is to control the safety of shellfish for human consumption by preventing harvest from contaminated growing waters'.[62]

---

[58]   The Harmonized System uses the spelling mollusc. Harmonized System 0307. Oysters, mussels, clams, cockles and scallops are molluscs.

[59]   The dispute also illustrates a difficulty in the use of process standards. For example, under a hazard analysis critical control point (HAACP) system, the comparison between the results of two systems can be difficult for determining whether the appropriate level of protection has been met and whether the process standards are necessary,

[60]   'Since these species are either filter feeders or feed exclusively on filter feeders they are susceptible to picking up and accumulating toxins or bacteriological contaminants from their environment. If these products are contaminated and eaten there could be a risk to human health. Therefore these species can only be commercially harvested from approved production areas, which are monitored to ensure they meet the toxin and microbiological criteria' Food Safety Agency, *Importing fishery products or bivalve molluscs*, available at http://www.food.gov.uk/foodindustry/imports/want_to_import/fisheryproducts/ (last visited 18 Dec. 2011).

[61]   'A person shall not offer for transportation, or transport, in interstate traffic any molluscan shellfish handled or stored in such an insanitary manner, or grown in an area so contaminated, as to render such molluscan shellfish likely to become agents in, and their transportation likely to contribute to the spread of communicable disease from one State or possession to another.' 21 C.F.R. 1240.60 (a) (Molluscan shellfish).

[62]   FDA (National Shellfish Sanitation Program), NSSP 2009 Section IV .03, *Sanitary Survey and the Classification of Growing Waters*, (available at: http://

The EU tests the flesh of the bivalve molluscs for the pathogen *Escherichia coli*.[63] Imports of these products into the EU are permitted only when the area of production appears on a list.[64]

While the two approaches and the resulting measures are different, they could provide the level of protection chosen by each jurisdiction, i.e., be equivalent. The EU says that the two approaches, although different, achieve the same level of protection and are equivalent. The US FDA disagrees and has blocked imports of these EU products into the US. After years of discussions, the two could not reach an agreement about equivalence, with the consequence that the EU, in turn, eventually banned US exports.[65] No resolution of the differences appears imminent.

Australia and the US entered into a meat equivalence agreement in 2011

---

www.fda.gov/Food/FoodSafety/Product-SpecificInformation/Seafood/FederalSt atePrograms/NationalShellfishSanitationProgram/ucm053724.htm) (last visited 18 Dec. 2011).

[63] Commission *Reg. (EC) No 2073/2005 of 5 Nov. 2005 on microbiological criteria for foodstuffs*, OJ L338, p 1, updated by Commission *Reg. (EC) No 1441/2007 of 5 Dec. 2007,* OJ L 322, p. 12, 12 July 2007.

[64] The EU uses a series of regulations to address food safety. The basic law is *Reg. (EC) No 178/2002 of the European Parliament and of the Council of 28 January 2002 laying down the general principles and requirements of food law, establishing the European Food Safety Authority and laying down procedures in matters of food safety*, OJ L 31, p. 1, 1 Feb. 2002. The regulation applicable to food of animal origin is *Reg. (EC) No. 853/2004 of the European Parliament and of the Council of 29 April 2004 laying down specific hygiene rules for food of animal origin*, OJ L 139, p. 55, 30 April 2004. Art. 6(1)(b) of that Regulation requires that the country of export and the production area (Art. 12) be included on the lists for live bivalve molluscs (Art. 13) in *Reg. (EC) No. 854/2004 of the European Parliament and of the Council of 29 April 2004 laying down specific rules for the organization of official controls on products of animal origin*, OJ L 226, p. 83, 25 June 2004. '. . .live bivalve molluscs . . . shall be from production areas in third countries that appear on lists drawn up and updated' according to the Regulation. Id. at Art. 13(1)). The EU temporarily permitted US imports while equivalency talks continued and used the FDA EU Fish and Fishery Products Export Certification List to approve US seafood shipments into the EU. Then the EU created its Official List of approved establishments, as explained in this note.

[65] According to an unnamed US government official, the EU linked the discussions about the equivalence of the two systems (which require 'sufficient scientific evidence' to support a recognition of equivalence) to support US exports with a demand for an equivalence agreement concerning EU exports of these products to the US. The official believed that the EU's linking of its consideration of approving US exports with the negotiation of an equivalence agreement contravenes links being made by the EU.

that again focuses on the safety of a system.[66] The two countries renewed their equivalence agreement following changes in the Australian law and several years of (non-confrontational) discussions, as the US concluded that slaughter inspection in Australian approved establishments meets all requirements of US law for the import of the product to the United States[67] and provides the 'same' level of safety protection as US domestic slaughter inspection.[68] While the discussions and administrative procedure were lengthy (1996–1999), the authorities had a history of working together and of meat trade, which made the discussions somewhat easier. Still, the process was complex.

FSIS meat regulations illustrate the complexity of efforts to negotiate an equivalence agreement. They require that the other meat inspection system must impose 'equivalent' requirements about (1) ante-mortem and post-mortem inspection; (2) official controls by the national government over plant construction, facilities, and equipment; (3) direct and continuous supervision of slaughter activities and product preparation; (4) separation of establishments certified to export from those not certified; (5) maintenance of a single standard of inspection and sanitation throughout certified establishments; (6) requirements for sanitation at establishments certified to export and for sanitary handling of product; and (7) official controls over condemned product.[69] In addition, FSIS conducts a document review[70] and an on-site review. The foreign country provides a self-assessment of its national meat or poultry inspection system.[71] FSIS

---

[66]   Australia's Meat Safety Enhancement Program; Notice of Affirmation of Equivalence Decision: Notice of affirmation of equivalence decision, 76 Federal Register 11752, 3 Mar. 2011.

[67]   Under the Federal Meat Inspection Act, which is administered by the US Department of Agriculture, no carcasses, parts of carcasses, meat, or meat food products may be imported into the US unless the livestock from which they were produced was slaughtered and processed in accordance with all provisions and regulations applicable to such Arts in commerce within the US. 21 U.S.C. 620.

[68]   USDA (FSIS), http://www.federalregister.gov/Art.s/2011/03/03/2011-4902/australias-meat-safety-enhancement-program-notice-of-affirmation-of-equivalence-decision#h-11 (last visited 18 Dec. 2011).

[69]   9 C.F.R. § 327.2.

[70]   The document review evaluates the laws, regulations, and other implementing documentation used by the country to enact its inspection program.

[71]   The self-assessment is organized by six components: government oversight, statutory authority and food safety regulations, sanitation, Hazard Analysis and Critical Control Point (HACCP) systems, chemical residue testing programs, and microbiological testing programs. FSIS evaluates the information submitted in these self-assessment documents and conducts an on-site review to verify all

then evaluates the information in the self-assessment documents before conducting an on-site review (including review of laboratories and the government's oversight of the individual domestic establishments).[72]

In its first attempt to interpret Article 4, the SPS Committee leaned toward a simpler approach to equivalence. It said that an importing jurisdiction 'shall' seek to accept a product or product category approach (instead of a systems approach), when such is requested by the exporting jurisdiction. It also noted that, when the discussions concern a single product, a systems-wide equivalence agreement might not be necessary, but an evaluation of the 'product-related infrastructure and programmes' might be necessary.[73]

Another part of section 1 of the Equivalence Decision is related to Article 4.2 of the SPS Agreement, which obliges WTO Members, when requested, to enter into consultations to achieve bilateral or multilateral agreements about the recognition of the equivalence of specified sanitary or phytosanitary measures. The Decision is hardly more specific than Article 4.2, but it does reinforce the idea of 'more comprehensive and broad-ranging' agreements on equivalence 'where necessary and appropriate'. The equivalence documents developed in Codex, OIE and the IPPC seem to meet this goal.

Based on the text of this section 1, it is possible to review the remainder of the Decision for its directives regarding product-based equivalence, systems-based equivalence and for its instructions to exporting and to importing jurisdictions. Not mentioned in section 1, but essential to the Decision, are its texts about transparency and technical assistance.

The text of section 4 of the Equivalence Decision contains instructions to the exporting jurisdiction, which is the '*demandeur*'. The *demandeur* requests the recognition of its measure or system and provides supporting information. Since its measure relates to food, plant or animal safety, the measure must meet the requirements of Article 2.3 of the SPS Agreement, including that it be based on scientific principles and underpinned by sufficient scientific evidence. The Equivalence Decision refers to this information and to providing access to the exporting jurisdiction's territory

---

aspects of the country's inspection program, including laboratories and the foreign government's oversight of the individual establishments within the country.

[72]   Following this bilateral process, FSIS must follow US administrative procedures, that include public notice of FSIS plans to enter the equivalence agreement and a public comment period. 9 C.F.R. 327.2.

[73]   This wording about product-related infrastructure and programmes refers to testing, inspection and other relevant 'requirements specific to product safety'. Equivalence Decision, note 15.

for inspection, testing and other relevant procedures.[74] The exporting jurisdiction 'shall provide appropriate science-based and technical information to support its objective demonstration that its measure achieves the appropriate level of protection identified by the importing Member'. Relevant international standards (such as those of Codex, OIE and IPPC) or relevant risk assessments (of the exporting jurisdiction or another) are among the information to be provided. These documents will be analyzed by the importing jurisdiction to determine whether they achieve the level of protection sought.[75]

Sections 2–3 and 5–8 of the Equivalence Decision are addressed to the importing jurisdiction. Subsequent clarifications by the Committee, as noted above in note 55, developed the meaning of sections 5 and 6.

The starting point for the importing jurisdiction is that, when requested, the importing jurisdiction 'should' explain the objective and rationale of its sanitary measure, using a copy of the risk assessment or a technical justification based on an international standard on which it relied.[76] It should be timely in its response to a request for the consideration of the equivalence of its measures, acting 'normally with a six-month period'.[77] The Decision also notes that the importing jurisdiction should provide any additional information that may 'assist the exporting Member to provide an objective demonstration' of the equivalence of its own measure'.[78] It should 'identify clearly' the risks the relevant measure is intended to address.[79] And the importing jurisdiction should indicate the appropriate level of protection that its measure is designed to achieve.[80] The importing jurisdiction should accelerate its procedure for determining the equivalence of products that it has historically imported from the exporting jurisdiction.[81]

Paragraph 5 of the Decision reads: 'The importing Member should accelerate its procedure for determining equivalence in respect of those products which it has historically imported from the exporting Member.' Regarding the clarification of paragraph 5 of the Decision, the Committee noted the importance of the exporting jurisdiction's historic trade data and said that it should be taken into account in the recognition of meas-

---

[74]   Id. at § 4.
[75]   Id. at § 7.
[76]   Id. at § 2.
[77]   Id. at § 3.
[78]   Id. at § 2.
[79]   Id. at § 2.
[80]   Id. at § 2.
[81]   Id. at § 5.

ures proposed by it.[82] In a 2004 further explanation of paragraph 5 of the Decision, the Committee explained 'information and experience'.[83] Two of the three points in the explanation refer to 'experience', which can only exist if there has already been some interaction between authorities in the two countries. They are the historic knowledge and confidence that the importing jurisdiction's competent authority has about the competent authority in the exporting jurisdiction and the 'existence of an evaluation and recognition of the products-related system of inspection and certification' by the importing jurisdiction of the exporting one. The third point, about information, refers to 'available scientific information'. This point adds nothing substantive to the SPS Committee's initial Decision but does state the logical conclusion that the more relevant information and experience are available, the faster the procedure for recognition of equivalence should be. Addendum 3 also urges importing countries to consider the relevant information and experience that the sanitary and phytosanitary services already have about the measure(s) for which recognition of equivalence is requested[84] and asks the importing jurisdiction not to seek relevant information that is already available.[85] This suggestion and others made in the 2004 addendum were intended, in part, to hasten and lessen the costs of the negotiations.[86]

Paragraph 6 of the Decision aims to deter any disruption of trade, after a request for the recognition of equivalence. The paragraph says the request for recognition of equivalence 'shall not be in itself a reason to disrupt or suspend on-going imports from that Member of the product in question'. When the request concerns the recognition of the equivalence of measures related to a specific product, the request must not be used as a reason to disrupt or suspend on-going imports of the products at issue.[87] In its clarification of paragraph 6, the Committee repeated this idea but added that the importing jurisdiction could still act to

---

[82]   Id. at ¶¶ 1–3. The Committee noted that both the Codex Commission and OIE mentioned the use of historic data in their documents.

[83]   Id. at ¶ 1.

[84]   Id. at Add. 3.

[85]   Id. at ¶ 4.

[86]   Two of the clarifications in Addendum 3 are addressed to Members, rather than to importing Members. This indicates that officials in both the exporting and importing jurisdiction should consider the existence of useful information between competent authorities related to products other than the product at issue (¶ 2) and the risk of the product so that, when there is a low risk, requirements can be reduced and the procedure can be accelerated (¶ 3).

[87]   Equivalence Decision, note 15 at § 6.

achieve its appropriate level of protection, including in an emergency situation.[88]

The Decision also guides the importing jurisdiction concerning its technical data. The importing jurisdiction also must provide 'appropriate science-based and technical information' to support its 'objective demonstration' that its measure achieves the specific appropriate level of protection it has identified. Like for the exporting jurisdiction, the Decision mentions relevant international standards or relevant risk assessments undertaken by the importing Member or by another Member, as examples of this information.[89]

The Decision makes several references to the Three Sister organizations and their role in developing the understanding of the equivalence obligation in Article 4 of the SPS Agreement. For that purpose, the Committee urged its members to participate actively in the then ongoing Codex work and in the future work of the OIE and IPPC.[90] It encouraged Codex to complete its work and encouraged OIE and the IPPC body to elaborate equivalence guidelines on sanitary and phytosanitary measures and equivalence agreements in the animal health and plant protection areas.[91] The three institutions were invited to keep the Committee informed about their equivalence activities.[92] This request to the three institutions was a request that they contribute to international equivalence transparency.

The Committee was even more explicit in its instructions to WTO Members and to itself. Members should provide information regarding their 'experience' implementing Article 4 and to inform the Committee about any bilateral equivalence agreement or arrangement they conclude.[93] The Committee committed to provide for notification by Members when they conclude a bilateral equivalence agreement or arrangement,[94] to consider establishing a standing agenda item on equivalence[95] and to develop

---

[88]   Id. at Add.1, § 6.

[89]   Id. at § 4.

[90]   Id. at § 9. Members were asked to assist developing country Members to participate in the three institutions. Id.

[91]   Id. at § 10.

[92]   Id.

[93]   Id. at § 12.

[94]   Id. at § 12. In its 2002 addendum to the Decision, the Committee agreed a format and recommended procedures for the notification of determinations of the recognition of the equivalence of sanitary or phytosanitary measures. SPS Committee, *Notification of Determination of the Recognition of Equivalence of SPS Measures* (G/SPS/7/REV.2/ADD.1).

[95]   Implementation Decision, note 15, at § 12.

a specific implementation program for Article 4.[96] In 2007, at a meeting which heard the US describe the EU–US poultry dispute, the Committee said that equivalence continued to be a standing item on its agenda, although at times no WTO Member brought an issue to the attention of the Committee.

The required proof of compliance or conformity with the demands of the importing government usually requires documentation and understanding of technical and scientific data. Often smaller countries and developing countries have difficulty (or are unable) to meet those demands. The 2001 Equivalence Decision mentions meeting this need through technical assistance.[97] By focusing on the difficulties that meeting equivalence requirements posed for developing country exporters, the initial equivalence discussions within the SPS Committee also directly and by implication touched on Article 9 of the SPS Agreement (regarding technical assistance).[98] That assistance has been provided by some developed WTO Members and also by the WTO, FAO, the World Bank and other international organizations, among many others.

The covered safety measures of both the exporting and importing jurisdictions must be based on scientific principles and scientific evidence, whether developed domestically or by others, including the Three Sisters or a third party, as well as on other SPS Agreement disciplines.[99] The general interpretation of this language is that a risk assessment, as described in Article 5, meets those tests.

With regard to the scientific basis for a determination about the

---

[96] Id. at § 13. The program was to give particular consideration of problems encountered by developing countries. Id.

[97] 'This assistance may, inter alia, be to help an exporting Member identify and implement measures which can be recognized as equivalent, or to otherwise enhance market access opportunities. Such assistance may also be with regard to the development and provision of the appropriate science-based and technical information.' Id. at Equivalence Decision, at para.8.

[98] SPS Agreement, note 1 at Art. 9: '1. Members agree to facilitate the provision of technical assistance to other Members, especially developing country Members, either bilaterally or through the appropriate international organizations. Such assistance may be, inter alia, in the areas of processing technologies, research and infrastructure, including in the establishment of national regulatory bodies, and may take the form of advice, credits, donations and grants, including for the purpose of seeking technical expertise, training and equipment to allow such countries to adjust to, and comply with, sanitary or phytosanitary measures necessary to achieve the appropriate level of sanitary or phytosanitary protection in their export markets.'

[99] For example, among the other disciplines are risk assessment (Art. 5), regionalization (Art. 6), transparency (Art. 7) and nondiscrimination (Art. 2.3).

equivalence of a safety measure, the SPS Committee said, in section 7 of its Equivalence Decision: 'When considering a request for recognition of equivalence, the importing Member should analyze the science-based and technical information provided by the exporting Member on its sanitary or phytosanitary measures with a view to determining whether these measures achieve the level of protection provided by its own SPS measures.'

VI.   THE EQUIVALENCE PROCEDURE

There is no set equivalence determination procedure. Each importing jurisdiction creates its own process. Australia[100] and the European Union,[101] among others, have described generally their procedures. The US procedure for determining the equivalence of imported poultry products was described in one of the poultry disputes.[102] The Panel explained that the process starts by an applicant country making an equivalence request, after which USDA evaluates the equivalence of the applicant country's poultry inspection system including on-site visits and audits. If it is equivalent, the applicant country must certify establishments as fit to export. USDA conducts ongoing equivalence verifications. USDA divides the stages into equivalence determination, certification of establishments and ongoing equivalence verification.

By referring to the guidelines and procedures of the 'Three Sisters' and current practice, it is reasonable to foresee several likely scenarios. The World Organisation for Animal Health developed a Terrestrial

---

[100]   Australia describes a three stage process. The first stage involves information gathering and dialogue with representatives of the exporting jurisdiction. The second stage is probably the longest and most complex, because during it the food safety issues are identified and the scientific evidence is collected. The final stage is the documentation of the equivalence decision. Its guidelines include a Proposed diagram for the process of equivalence determination. Food Standards Australia New Zealand, *SANZ Guidelines Determining the Equivalence of Food Safety Measures*, available at http://www.foodstandards.gov.au/_srcfiles/Equivalence%20 Determination%20Guidelines_jan04.pdf. (last visited 23 Mar. 2012).

[101]   The EU compares objectives, legal basis, infrastructure and individual measures; emphasizes control system, to reliably guarantee compliance with rules of the exporting country; conducts a weight of evidence assessment of the overall performance, to compare the resulting level of protection rather than individual measures and conducts on-site visits to verify. Delegation of the European Union to the USA.

[102]   *China Poultry*, note 51, at paras 2.5–2.16. Eventually China withdrew its major claim because the challenged statute had expired. There was no appeal to the Appellate Body.

Animal Health Code, whose Chapter 5 addresses Procedures Relevant to the Agreement on the Application of Sanitary and Phytosanitary Measures (OIE Procedures), including determinations of equivalence to 'assist OIE Members to determine whether sanitary measures arising from different animal health and production systems may provide the same level of animal and human health protection'.[103] The Secretariat of the International Plant Protection Convention drafted *Guidelines for the Determination and Recognition of Equivalence of Phytosanitary Measures*[104] (IPPC Guidelines). According to the IPPC, equivalence 'generally applies to cases where phytosanitary measures already exist for a specific pest associated with trade in a commodity or commodity class'.[105] In addition there are the Codex Guidelines on Equivalence.

A. The Burden on the Exporting Jurisdiction

Article 4.1 of the SPS Agreement places the burden on the exporting jurisdiction to convince its trading partner of the equivalence of its measures. A recognition of equivalence is possible only 'if the exporting Member objectively demonstrates to the importing Member that its measures achieve the importing Member's appropriate level of sanitary or phytosanitary protection'. Technical and scientific data are essential to meet this burden, including, as stated by the SPS Committee, information such as 'reference to relevant international standards, or to relevant risk assessments undertaken by the importing Member or by another Member'.[106] The guidelines for risk assessments are spelled out in Article 5 of the SPS Agreement.[107] Several of the risk assessment factors listed in Article 5.2 are actually considered during equivalence negotiations. Among them are available scientific evidence; relevant processes and production methods;

---

[103] OIE Guidelines, note 34, at Art. 5.3.2.
[104] IPPC Guidelines, note 35.
[105] Id.
[106] Equivalence Decision, note 15, at ¶ 4.
[107] Art. 5 of the SPS Agreement provides (in part): '1. Members shall ensure that their sanitary or phytosanitary measures are based on an assessment, as appropriate to the circumstances, of the risks to human, animal or plant life or health, taking into account risk assessment techniques developed by the relevant international organizations.

2. In the assessment of risks, Members shall take into account available scientific evidence; relevant processes and production methods; relevant inspection, sampling and testing methods; prevalence of specific diseases or pests; existence of pest- or disease-free areas; relevant ecological and environmental conditions; and quarantine or other treatment.'

relevant inspection, sampling and testing methods; prevalence of specific diseases or pests; existence of pest- or disease-free areas; relevant ecological and environmental conditions; and quarantine or other treatment.

There are no fixed criteria and procedures for determining equivalence. The importing jurisdiction must offer information concerning its appropriate level of protection – its level of health protection. This is the 'target' that the exporter must meet in its system or measure. Among the many possibilities, it must specify 'as precisely as possible an objective basis for comparison of the sanitary measures proposed by the exporting country and its own measures'.[108] The IPPC Guidelines suggest that the negotiations might address the effect of the measure, as demonstrated in laboratory or field conditions, the examination of relevant literature on the effect of the measure, the results of experience in the practical application of the measure, and the factors affecting the implementation of the measure (e.g. the policies and procedures of the contracting party).[109]

The equivalence documents of the Three Sisters offer lists of considerations and graphics to illustrate a suggested equivalence procedure. The details of their guidelines and procedures differ, but their general frameworks are similar.

Testing for *E. coli* 0157:H7[110] and traceability are among the current pivotal issues, meaning that a government seeking an equivalence agreement regarding meat must be able to satisfy the importing government of the equivalence (perhaps verging on 'sameness') of its measures to prevent and test for this type of *E. coli* and to conduct product or animal tracing. To enter the US, producers in other countries might be required to test for *Pre-Harvest Management Controls and Intervention Options for Reducing Escherichia coli O157:H7 Shedding in Cattle*[111] and *E. coli Testing for Process Control Verification in Cattle and Swine Slaughter Establishments.*[112]

---

[108]   Equivalence Guidelines, note 14, at ¶ 6: Objective Basis of Comparison.

[109]   IPPC Guidelines, note 36, at § 3.5.

[110]   Escherichia coli O157:H7 is a pathogen and a hazard. It is usually found in the intestines and feces of animals. Risk assessments show that E. coli can cause gastroenteritis or more serious harm in humans. FDA, *Bad Bug Book: Foodborne Pathogenic Microorganisms and Natural Toxins HandbookEscherichia coli* O157:H7, http://www.fda.gov/food/foodsafety/foodborneillness/foodborneill nessfoodbornepathogensnaturaltoxins/badbugbook/ucm071284.htm (last visited 11 Oct. 2011).

[111]   FSIS/USDA,   http://www.fsis.usda.gov/PDF/Reducing_Ecoli_Shedding_ In_Cattle_0510.pdf (last visited 1 Oct. 2011).

[112]   FSIS/USDA, http://www.fsis.usda.gov/PDF/Guideline_for_Ecoli_Testing_ Cattle_Swine_Estab.pdf (last visited 11 Oct. 2011).

More stringent rules for product tracing are expected under recent US food safety legislation for foods (other than meat, eggs and poultry).[113] The current rules, developed as part of the 'Bioterrorism Act'[114] and amended in 2011,[115] require product tracing one step back and one step forward. The EU also has rules governing the tracing of any food, feed, food-producing animal or substance that will be used for consumption, through all stages of production, processing and distribution.[116] The details of the approaches differ, making it difficult for an exporter to comply with both regulations easily.

The US makes determinations of equivalence by evaluating whether foreign food regulatory systems attain the appropriate level of protection provided by the US domestic system.[117] FSIS evaluates foreign food regulatory systems for equivalence through document reviews, on-site audits and port-of-entry re-inspection of products at the time of importation. The document review is an evaluation of the country's laws, regulations and other written information. It focuses on six risk areas: Government Oversight, Statutory Authority and Food Safety Regulations, Sanitation, Hazard Analysis and Critical Control Point Systems, Chemical Residues and Microbiological Testing Programs.[118] The EU includes its equivalence arrangements both in broader

---

[113]   Under section 204 of the Food Safety Modernization Act, FDA and USDA should develop 'a product tracing system to receive information that improves the capacity of the Secretary to effectively and rapidly track and trace food that is in the United States or offered for import into the United States' 21 U.S.C. 2223.

[114]   Public Health Security and Bioterrorism Preparedness and Response Act of 2002, P.L. 107-188. Section 306(a) of the Act refers to recordkeeping that permits product tracing or traceability. The records must 'allow the Secretary to identify the immediate previous sources and the immediate subsequent recipients of food'. 21 U.S.C. 350c.

[115]   The amendment was made by section 204 of the Food Safety Modernization Act, P.L. 111-353. Section 204 (enhancing tracking and tracing of food and record-keeping) requires FDA to conduct pilot projects, then to develop a product tracing plan. The law also refers to more technical matters, such as 'methods for rapid and effective tracking and tracing of foods in a manner that is practicable for facilities of varying sizes, including small businesses' and appropriate technologies that enhance the tracking and tracing of food. 21 U.S.C. 2223.

[116]   EU Health and Consumer Protection Directorate-General, Food traceability, http://ec.europa.eu/food/food/foodlaw/traceability/factsheet_trace_2007_en.pdf (last visited 11 Oct. 2011).

[117]   http://www.fsis.usda.gov/regulations/Equivalence_Process_Overview/index.asp (last visited 6 Oct. 2011).

[118]   Id.

agreements[119] and in specific equivalence agreements, such as an exchange of letters with the US.[120]

According to the SPS Agreement, the exporting country must provide reasonable access to the importing country for inspection, testing and other relevant procedures for the recognition of equivalence, when requested.[121] The importing jurisdiction may require that certain tests be conducted in the exporting jurisdiction and may apply its own criteria regarding test results. Testing for the levels and results of heat treatment (e.g., high temperature forced air, vapor heat treatment, hot water dip) and cold treatment (e.g., cold storage, both in-transit and in country of origin); and chemical treatments (e.g., fumigants, dips, dustings, flood spraying); or irradiation are examples.

VII.   WTO ISSUES

There has not been an Appellate Body report and there have been no formal WTO disputes challenging a WTO Member's application of Article 4, in spite of recognized dissatisfaction with the Article's inability to foster market access.

WTO SPS dispute settlement reports offer most guidance about risk assessment and controls, but do not elaborate on Article 4. At times requests for consultations in SPS matters indirectly concern equivalence-related matters, including specific measures[122] (such as traceability) considered during equivalence negotiations, the 'necessary' requirements of Articles 2.1 and 2.2, and the prohibition on disguised restrictions on international trade rule in Article 2.3. For example, in its request for Consultations in *European Communities – Certain Measures Affecting Poultry Meat and Poultry Meat Products from the United States*, the US referred to SPS Agreement Articles 2.2 (basic rights and obligations), 5 (risk assessment) and 8 (control, inspection and approval procedures)

---

[119]   For links to several of these agreements, see, EU Commission, *International Affairs – Sanitary and Phytosanitary Agreements*, http://ec.europa.eu/food/international/trade/agreements_en.htm (last visited 12 Oct. 2011).

[120]   CRS Report to Congress, http://www.cnie.org/nle/crsreports/International/inter-13.cfm (last visited 12 Oct. 2011).

[121]   SPS Agreement, note 1, at Art. 4.1.

[122]   Art. 2.1 of the SPS Agreement uses the word 'measures', which is found also in Art. III.1 of the. General Agreement on Tariffs and Trade (1994). As the term has been interpreted and generally understood, 'measure' reaches almost every aspect of equivalence requirements – laws, regulations, requirements, methods of analysis, and testing protocols, among others.

and Annex C(1) (control, inspection and approval procedures) but not to Article 4.[123]

In 1997 the EU revised its regulations and, as a consequence refused imports of poultry from the US. The EU had determined that the US process of spin-chilling poultry with chlorinated water as a decontaminant at the end of the production process was not equivalent to the EU's approach that applied sanitary and other controls throughout the slaughter process. It therefore banned poultry imports from the US.[124] Years of discussions and negotiations followed without success in achieving a bilateral understanding.

The two WTO Members did enter into a Veterinary Equivalence Agreement through an exchange of letters. The agreement covers trade in red meat, dairy, fish products, specific interim conditions for egg products and the majority of US pet food exports – but not poultry. 'The objective of the EU–US veterinary equivalence agreement is to agree on the equivalence of our respective systems in order to facilitate trade in animals and animal products while maintaining an appropriate level of public and animal health protection.' A fundamental element of these agreements is the recognition that the EU's (or the US's) level of protection can be achieved by equivalent, not identical, measures. The two jurisdictions were unable to agree to include poultry in the Veterinary Equivalence Agreement so the lengthy disagreement continued, including in discussions at the Transatlantic Economic Council.

In 2002, the US again requested the European Commission to recognize as equivalent the use of certain slaughterhouse inspection practices and four sanitation treatments in poultry processing. The approvals were

---

[123] *European Communities – Certain Measures Affecting Poultry Meat and Poultry Meat Products from the United States, Request for Consultations by the United States*, WT/DS389/1, G/SPS/GEN/894, G/AG/GEN/81, G/TBT/D/35, G/L/881 (20 Jan. 2009) (*EC Poultry*).

[124] 'During the course of the negotiations, the United States was unable to conclude that the EU system for poultry and poultry products provides an equivalent level of protection to that afforded under the current U.S. system. Because the current list of EU poultry establishments eligible to ship to the United States was developed prior to the importation of HACCP requirements, and because the United States does not have the same level of experience with the EU system for poultry that it does for meat, the United States will not be able to accept imports of poultry from the EU until it is able to conduct appropriate inspections and confirm delivery of its appropriate level of protection.' US Dept. of Agriculture, United States – European Union Veterinary Equivalence Talks (30 Apr. 1997), available at http://www.usda.gov/news/releases/1997/05/0144; US Considers Retaliation Against EU Meat Exports, IDDA LEGIS-LETTER (April 1997), available at http://www.iddanet.org/0497leg.htm (last visited 6 Dec. 2011).

refused. Then in 2004 the EU imposed a ban on poultry imports from Texas because of avian influenza – another sanitary measure.[125] The US imposed its own ban on poultry imports from the EU, after which the EU initiated a WTO dispute settlement process,[126] as did the United States.

Since this poultry dispute was not resolved, in 2008, six years later, the US requested consultations at the WTO. The basis for the dispute was described, in part, as follows (with no mention of equivalence): 'The EC prohibits the import of poultry treated with any substance other than water unless that substance has been approved by the EC. Consequently, the EC prohibits the import of poultry that has been processed with chemical treatments ('pathogen reduction treatments' or PRTs) designed to reduce the amount of microbes on the meat, effectively prohibiting the shipment of virtually all US poultry to the EC.'[127] In its request for consultations, the US cited Articles 2.2, 5, and 8, and Annex C(1) of the SPS Agreement and Article 14 of the TBT Agreement (among others), but not the equivalence provisions of either agreement. This dispute was not continued to a conclusion, perhaps reflecting the view of the Congressional Research Service that a solution appears to be 'elusive'.[128] The other poultry dispute that is mentioned in conjunction with equivalence is a complaint filed by China against the United States.[129] Like the others, the Request for Consultations did not reference Article 4[130] of the SPS Agreement but it did cite Articles 3.1 and 3.3

---

[125]   EU, 'Commission suspends EU poultry imports from the USA after avian influenza outbreak in Texas' (24 Feb. 2004), available at http://europa.eu/rapid/pressReleasesAction.do?reference=IP/04/257&format=HTML&aged=0&language=EN&guiLanguage=en. Another dispute concerning poultry and avian influenza was initiated by the US in March 2012. *See, India – Measures Concerning the Importation of Certain Agricultural Products from the United States*, DS430, Request for Consultations by the United States, WT/DS430/1, G/SPS/GEN/1138, G/L/981 (8 March 2012). Again, Art. 4 of the SPS Agreement is not cited in the Request for Consultations.

[126]   *United States – Measures Affecting Imports of Poultry Products*, DS100 (1997).

[127]   *EC Poultry*, note 123.

[128]   'Even if the case advances to a dispute resolution panel, a solution appears to be elusive. The two sides maintain widely divergent views not only on the poultry issue but on some aspects of the basic approach to food safety regulation'; Congressional Research Service, US– EU Poultry Dispute, Dec. 2010, p. 4.

[129]   *China Poultry*, note 51. The Request for Consultations did refer to Art. 4.2 of the Agreement on Agriculture, by which China asserted that the US failure to allow poultry imports was a quantitative restriction, at ¶ 3.1(iii).

[130]   The Panel noted that Art. 4 was not within its terms of reference but nevertheless examined the US contention that Art. 4 was the applicable provision,

and makes a general reference to the provisions of the SPS Agreement. China complained that, because of US legislation, the Department of Agriculture (USDA) was prevented from implementing its importation program for poultry from China. That program involved an equivalence determination.[131]

Although these two disputes did not directly concern Article 4, in a dispute concerning equivalence, claims could be made against an importing Member under Article 4 and also under several of the sections of the SPS Agreement cited, specifically Articles 2.2, 3.3 and 5.[132] Article 3.3 could be relevant when the claim is that there is no scientific justification for an existing measure or that the importing Member failed to meet all the requirements of paragraphs 1–8 of Article 5 (relating to Assessment of Risk and Determination of the Appropriate Level of Sanitary or Phytosanitary Protection). This Article would be read in conjunction with the wording in Article 2.2 about scientific principles and sufficient scientific evidence. Paragraphs 4 and 5 might be most pertinent. Paragraph 4 of Article 5 says that Members 'should' take into account the objective of minimizing negative trade effects, when determining the appropriate level of protection. Paragraph 5 is stronger, because it says that the importing Member 'shall' avoid arbitrary or unjustifiable distinctions in the levels it considers to be appropriate in different situations Article 2 contains a 'necessary' rule under which a measure 'shall' be '*applied* only to the extent necessary' (emphasis added).

More recently, India contended at the SPS Committee that the new US food safety law fails to meet the equivalence (and harmonization) principles of the SPS Agreement.

---

rather than the SPS Agreement texts cited by China. Id. at ¶ 7.125. 'We recognize that China has made no claim with respect to the consistency of Section 727 with Article 4 and thus Article 4 is outside our terms of reference. Therefore, we are not going into an analysis of what is required to comply with the obligations in Article 4. Rather, our examination of this provision, simply concerns a determination of whether it is the only provision in the SPS Agreement that could apply to Section 727 [a funding provision].' At ¶ 7.132.

[131] *China Poultry* note 51, at ¶ 2.6.

[132] In *China Poultry*, China made claims under Art. 2.3 (arbitrarily and unjustifiably discriminates), Art. 5.5 (the higher level of sanitary protection applied to China is arbitrary and unjustifiable, resulting in discrimination), Arts 5.1 and 5.2 of the SPS Agreement, because it is not based on a risk assessment that takes into account the factors in Art. 5.2 and Art. 2.2 (not maintained based on scientific evidence). Id. at ¶ 3.1. (viii) Art. 5.6 of the SPS Agreement, because it is inconsistent with the obligation that SPS measures not be unduly trade-restrictive.

A.   'Equivalence', 'Comparability' and Ad Hoc Arrangements

Despite the Decision on Equivalence and its implementation, there remain questions and complaints about the process for the recognition of equivalence and about whether specific domestic procedures are compatible with the SPS Agreement or are too complex. Developing countries raised many questions about the implementation of Article 4, then about the SPS Committee's 2001 Decision. Developed countries present some of the same points. For example, the US told the SPS Committee that often an equivalence agreement is unnecessary and cumbersome to negotiate.[133] The questions persist. Recently, China, India and Japan have questioned the compatibility of the US FSMA with Article 4.[134]

Several alternatives to equivalence have been tried, including comparability, mutual recognition and ad hoc acceptance of specific measures, products or technical treatments. These are more limited than harmonized (common) standards.[135] Mutual recognition is a kind of reciprocity, in which the parties agree to recognize and accept one or more of each other's (different) regulatory measures.[136] Comparability appears to be the principal concept under consideration as an alternative to food safety equivalence agreements but ad hoc arrangements like an exchange of letters are more frequent. Either of these seems to be within the scope of Article 4.2, which contemplates bilateral and wider agreements that are short of harmonization.[137]

As explained by New Zealand, comparability is a less proscriptive approach than a detailed equivalence review. That country prepared draft guidelines for judging the comparability of meat hygiene systems and expected discussions with Australia, Canada, the EU and the US con-

---

[133]   SPS Committee, *Equivalence – Submission from the United States*, G/SPS/GEN/212, 7 Nov. 2000.

[134]   E.g., China's concerns are detailed in US Food Safety Modernization Act – concerns of China (299). *See*, Committee on Sanitary and Phytosanitary Measures, Meeting of 30–31 March 2011, Agenda Item 3(b)(iii).

[135]   The SPS Agreement defines harmonization as the 'establishment, recognition and application of common sanitary and phytosanitary measures by different Members'. Note 1 at Annex A, ¶ 2.

[136]   *See*, e.g., Trans-Atlantic Consumer Dialogue, TACD Briefing Paper on Mutual Recognition Agreements (MRAs), Mar. 2001, available at http://tacd.org/index2.php?option=com_docman&task=doc_view&gid=102&Itemid= (last visited 6 Dec. 2011).

[137]   'Members shall, upon request, enter into consultations with the aim of achieving bilateral and multilateral agreements on recognition of the equivalence of specified sanitary or phytosanitary measures.'

cerning mutual acceptance of their meat hygiene programs. New Zealand included comparability and mutual recognition in its strategic objectives at Codex, because of what it felt were limitations in the application of equivalence. According to one of those involved in the discussions, 'we should reduce the resources we put into checking things that don't make a difference. Instead, we should be saying to each other: "these are our expectations in terms of food safety and public health outcomes; how you achieve them is up to you"'. The document which described the New Zealand position referred to 'the development of guidelines for the comparability and mutual acceptance of food control systems'. A few countries (Australia, Canada, the EU, US) are at the early stages of informal discussions on comparability. They are interested in the concept but uncommitted concerning a generalizable outcome.[138] No developing country is involved in the discussions. Meanwhile the US and New Zealand entered into a comparability arrangement in 2012.

Although it does not use the word comparability, a release about the Canada–EU Veterinary Equivalence Accord refers to both equivalence and mutual recognition ('...following an EU–Canada agreement to mutually recognise production standards and food safety measures for these products. Such an equivalence agreement enables both sides to adopt simplified import certificates for these products, which should increase trade and reduce the costs of production, inspection and certification').

Mutual agreement is being raised again as a possible regulatory alternative to an equivalence agreement. Its use for food safety purposes could be bolstered by its use for other purposes. The US–EU High Level Regulatory Forum is discussing mutual recognition of compatible or

---

[138] The discussions were mentioned by Deputy Commissioner of FDA Michael Taylor and others at a public meeting in 2011. '[W]e've been working for some time to develop a comparability assessment tool and we piloted it with New Zealand ... And we're also in the midst of comparability assessments with the European Union on each other's shellfish oversight systems.' FDA, *FDA Public Hearing on Ensuring the Safety of Imported Foods and Animal Feed: Comparability of Food Safety Systems and Import Practices of Foreign Countries*, 30 Mar 2011, http://www.fda.gov/Food/NewsEvents/WorkshopsMeetingsConferences/ucm254816.htm (last visited 19 Dec. 2011). The system being applied for comparability discussions considers ten factors: Regulatory Foundation, Training Program, Inspection Program, Inspection Audit Program, Food-related Illness and Outbreaks and Food Defense Preparedness and Response, Compliance and Enforcement Program, Industry and Community Relations, Program Resources, Program Assessment, and Laboratory Support. FDA, *Manufactured Food Regulatory Program Standards*, May 2007, http://www.fda.gov/downloads/RegulatoryInformation/Guidances/UCM125448.pdf (last visited 20 Dec. 2011).

comparable regulatory regimes. Under this proposal, a mutual recognition agreement would commit the participants to accept the approval decisions of the other signatory. A refusal to accept would be based on 'reason' and could be followed by consultation and mediation.[139]

VIII.   CONCLUSIONS

Mandating the recognition of equivalence was one of the novel features of the SPS Agreement. Equivalence removes a barrier to international commerce.

However, the obligation exists only when the exporting authority can prove that its measures achieve the level of protection chosen by the importing jurisdiction. Since it is extremely difficult to present that proof, there are few equivalency arrangements. This failure to make Article 4 the trade facilitation tool for which many countries (especially developing countries) hoped is a major shortcoming of the SPS Agreement.

The skeleton of Article 4 has been fleshed out with the help of the SPS Committee's Decision, the Guidelines of the Codex Alimentarius Commission and the IPPC, the Procedures of the OIE and on-going activities, especially in the SPS Committee. There has been no specific case law from the WTO dispute settlement mechanism to enlarge these understandings.

While these developments were occurring at multilateral level, many governments were, and still are, negotiating limited bilateral equivalence arrangements. The negotiations center around the demands of the importing jurisdiction for assurances that the measures or system in the exporting jurisdiction could satisfy the importer's appropriate level of protection. Sometimes the demands appear closer to requiring the 'same' measures rather than equivalent ones and to focus on the system rather than the 'measure' mentioned by Article 4 of the SPS Agreement.

The length, technicality and complexity of the process have led to at least two developments – consideration of comparability agreements and of mutual recognition. It became apparent that the process of negotiating a bilateral equivalence agreement was beyond the administrative and financial capabilities of many developing and small countries. This situation was a stated reason for proposals to substitute comparability for equivalence. This idea might signal a transition from a detailed approach

---

[139]   John Morrall III, *Determining Compatible Regulatory Regimes between the U.S. and the EU*, p. 1 and ANNEX A (US Chamber of Commerce 2011).

to a simpler one, though most trading countries might be unable to meet the comparability criteria. The idea is to recognize a different approach to food safety that recognizes comparable systems and accepts the certifications of their competent authorities. Whether this approach will provide more market access than equivalence is unclear. Nor is it certain that SPS mutual recognition will be a notable trade facilitation tool. What seems likely is that some WTO Members will continue to develop approaches that improve on equivalence, but that years will pass before an agreed approach is reached. Since these tools might not benefit many developing countries, they should consider their own regional arrangements, while they push for more flexible developed country approaches.

These new approaches will be subject to the disciplines of the SPS Agreement and other WTO rules. Clearly, before requesting trade consultations, a potential complainant must consider the strong weight given to food safety. Under the SPS Agreement the logical points of discussion would be the compatibility of a measure with Articles 2.1 and 2.3. However, the absence of any request for consultations or dispute that directly questions a refusal to recognize equivalence or a delay in recognition might be evidence of the perceived fruitlessness of using the WTO dispute resolution process. As some have said, it might be easier to adopt the same measures as the importing jurisdiction, if that is possible.

4. On the efficiency of health measures and the 'appropriate level of protection'
Jeffery Atik*

I. THE APPROPRIATE LEVEL OF PROTECTION

The concept of 'appropriate level of protection' (ALOP) runs throughout the SPS Agreement.[1] ALOP reflects the considerable margin of appreciation retained by WTO Members in the application of health measures and a resigned acceptance of a permanent condition of heterogeneous (and hence conflicting) national regulatory approaches with their accompanying drag on international trade. By its terms, 'appropriate level of protection' emphasizes the continuing discretion WTO Members enjoy in determining their respective SPS policies. Generally speaking each country can mandate what level of protection is 'appropriate'; the operative presumption of the SPS Agreement is national autonomy in setting health and food safety targets. Of course the SPS Agreement meaningfully cabins these respective autonomies: not all is permitted. Addressing antisocial use of SPS measures in order to achieve otherwise prohibited commercial goals (so-called 'disguised restraints on trade') is the raison d'être of the SPS Agreement.

The SPS Agreement, by and large, does not set the levels of protection SPS measures are to obtain. That said, the Agreement does pressure WTO Members to adopt international standards, each of which will have a particular level of protection – that is effectiveness – associated with it. Setting an 'appropriate level of protection' has several operational consequences within the SPS Agreement, however. Importantly, a relevant 'appropriate level of protection' functions in a variety of specific tests provided by the SPS Agreement. Use of a particular 'appropriate level of protection' permits a more focused check as to whether national health measures

*   This chapter was developed for the American Society of International Law's International Economic Law Research Forum held on 5 December 2009 at the Chicago-Kent College of Law. I am grateful for the helpful comments of Joanne Scott and David Wirth and for the research assistance of Parham Rezvani.
[1]   WTO Agreement on the Application of Sanitary and Phytosanitary Measures (SPS Agreement), Apr. 15, 1994, 1867 U.N.T.S. 493.

are deemed to be violative of international trade obligations. The SPS Agreement defines the 'appropriate level of sanitary or phytosanitary protection' as '[t]he level of protection deemed appropriate by the Member establishing a sanitary or phytosanitary measure to protect human, animal or plant health or life within its territory'.[2] A note attached to this definition adds: 'Many Members otherwise refer to this concept as the "acceptable level of risk".'[3]

The note relating ALOP[4] to the notion of acceptable level of risk both aids and hinders our understanding of the definition. The concept of acceptable level of risk is not, despite what the note indicates, equivalent to ALOP: acceptable level of risk addresses residual SPS risk experienced in the territory of the WTO member (once an SPS measure is in place), whereas appropriate level of protection measures the protection an SPS measure provides. For example, an acceptable level of risk for defined exposure to a carcinogen may be expressed as 1 in 1,000,000. Exposure to any risk greater than this (e.g. 1 in 500,000) would not be 'acceptable' to the Member setting the level. The counterpart ALOP might be expressed as 99.9999; a 'higher' ALOP corresponds to a smaller acceptable level of risk.

SPS protection is related to residual risk – but as residual risk remains after a measure is in effect, it seems counterintuitive to describe this residual risk as the extent of an SPS measure's protection. A more intuitive reading of a measure's level of protection (LOP) is the reduction of risk – from risk in a measure's absence to the residual risk tolerated upon a measure's implementation. Yet the definition found in the Note to the SPS Agreement does not appear to be quite so nuanced. An SPS measure may be 'credited' with an effectiveness it does not earn. If the background level of risk (in the absence of a measure) is 1 in 100, an ineffective SPS measure might be described as 'providing' for a 99 percent level of protection! The scarecrow in the field may in fact have no effect on the presence or absence of crows; it is the credence of the farmer that imputes the scarecrow's effectiveness.

The definition of 'appropriate level of protection' contained in the SPS Agreement makes clear that the appropriateness of a particular level of SPS protection is to be 'deemed' by the WTO Member implementing the SPS measure of concern.[5] Neither the WTO, nor any particular WTO

---

[2]   SPS Agreement, Annex A, para. 5.
[3]   Note to paragraph 5, Annex A, SPS Agreement.
[4]   *Id.*
[5]   SPS Agreement, Annex A, para. 5.

Member, nor any other body is competent to determine the appropriateness of the level of protection for a WTO Member. The definition of ALOP stresses that the determination of an appropriate level of SPS protection is a unilateral, discretionary act by the WTO Member implementing an SPS measure.[6]

That said, the SPS Agreement does impose limits on the particular SPS measures that may be maintained by a WTO Member. The autonomy in setting a national 'appropriate level of protection' does not translate into a license to freely impose SPS measures of any form in disregard of their effects on trade. Yet many of the tests applied to challenged SPS measures explicitly call for consideration of the ALOP associated with the challenged measure.

The concept of 'appropriate level of sanitary or phytosanitary protection' builds on, and assumes the existence of, a workable notion of 'level of protection'. A level of protection can be associated with a particular measure – or with a series of measures operating in concert to address a particular SPS risk. The level of protection expresses the effectiveness of a measure within its broader context (including both physical context and legal context). The term presumes some regulatory effectiveness. That said, one can imagine a completely ineffective 'SPS' measure – as perhaps were many ancient laws aimed at controlling outbreaks of the Plague – or even SPS measures that are counterproductive (reducing the cat population which led to greater numbers of Plague-bearing rats) – increasing rather than decreasing the SPS risk of concern. Thus, in a very simple way, the very notion of a (positive) level of protection requires that a purported SPS measure be in fact effective in some perceptible degree. To require a level of protection is to require that there be a 'rational relationship' between an end (reduction of an SPS risk) and a means (the purported SPS measure).

While the term 'level of protection' is used throughout the SPS Agreement, the definition makes clear that this is shorthand for 'level of sanitary or phytosanitary protection'.[7] An SPS measure may provide social benefits beyond reducing SPS risks. For example, an SPS measure may redirect (or reduce) consumption in socially beneficial ways in addition to improving the public health. An SPS measure restricting the production or sale of hamburgers (at the farm, slaughterhouse and restaurant) to reduce E. coli contamination may indirectly raise prices, lower consumption and hence production and so (by limiting the emission of

---

[6]   SPS Agreement, Annex A.
[7]   SPS Agreement, Annex A.

methane from cattle) reduce greenhouse gas levels. Yet the relevant 'level of protection' associated with an SPS measure is its reduction in SPS risks. Other social benefits do not come into play.

'Level of protection' is most frequently associated with a challenged measure. At times, however, the level of protection of some regulatory alternative will be relevant; at times it is the level of protection of a measure adopted by the exporting country (for purposes of demonstrating equivalence). Finally, 'level of protection' may be associated with the general regulatory structure.

In some basic way, the SPS Agreement presumes a rational legislator who conducts a risk assessment (in the presence and absence of a considered measure) and then sets an appropriate level of protection the measure aims to achieve.

II.   SPS MEASURES AND GATT ARTICLE XX(B)

The SPS Agreement functions as a *lex specialis* within the WTO system. By its terms, it applies exclusively to SPS measures. It serves to provide legal grounds for challenging SPS measures, and for insulating such measures from challenge. For a challenged SPS measure to be upheld in dispute resolution (or rather, for it to be WTO-legal) it must survive a number of specific tests set forth in the SPS Agreement. While the ultimate determination is the compatibility of an SPS measure with the SPS Agreement (and hence GATT 1994),[8] the specific tests depend not so much on a direct examination of the measure but rather they depend on comparisons involving the appropriate level of protection associated with that measure. It is a measure's asserted (or divined) appropriate level of SPS protection that is the functional object of many of the major disciplines contained in the SPS Agreement.

The SPS Agreement provides a series of specific tests in response to the considerably more vague and unpredictable treatment of SPS measures under the pre-WTO era GATT. Prior to the Uruguay Round's reforms,

---

[8]   The requirements of the SPS Agreement differ markedly from those imposed by the GATT. However, Article 2.4 of the SPS Agreement provides that SPS measures 'which conform to the relevant portions of [the SPS Agreement] shall be presumed to be in accordance with the obligations of the Members under the provisions of GATT 1994 which related to the use of [SPS] measures, in particular the provisions of Article XX(b)'. Thus, an SPS measure that is compliant with the SPS Agreement enjoys substantial (though not complete) immunity from a GATT-based challenge in WTO dispute settlement.

SPS measures were subject to GATT rules. SPS measures were distinguished in their treatment under the GATT by the specific exception provided to them through operation of GATT Article XX(b). GATT Article XX(b) exempts from GATT coverage (and so presumably permits) any measure 'necessary to protect human, animal or plant life or health'.[9] There is no defined category of SPS measures under the GATT – and not all SPS measures (as now defined in the SPS Agreement) would qualify for the exception in GATT Article XX(b). The SPS Agreement's definition of SPS measure (found in Annex A) speaks of '[a]ny measure applied . . . to protect . . .', whereas the GATT Article XX(b) exception only applies to measures '*necessary* to protect . . .' [emphasis added]. A measure may be an SPS measure ('applied to protect'),[10] yet not be necessary to protect and so subject to a GATT challenge (as it would thereby fall out of the exceptions GATT Article XX(b) establishes). And of course even a measure meeting the requirements of GATT Article XX(b) would still be vulnerable to attack under the *chapeau* of GATT Article XX.

Still the GATT Article XX(b) exception does contain the requirement of a nexus of protection between a challenged measure and its health objective.[11] Broadly speaking, GATT Article XX (the general exception provision of the GATT) privileges certain categories of measures. Generally regulatory measures may be struck down under a number of GATT rules – most importantly the prohibition on discrimination in internal regulation provided by GATT Article III and the prohibition of quantitative restrictions provided by GATT Article XI. Absent an exception, many SPS measures would run afoul of either GATT Article III or GATT Article XI. What makes an SPS measure exceptional (and so legitimate) under GATT Article XX(b) is the presence of its specific *kind* of social benefit – its protection of human, animal or plant life or health.[12]

III. PROPORTIONALITY AND COST-BENEFIT ANALYSIS

As discussed below, the SPS Agreement sets out a series of tests that a challenged measure must meet, each test utilizing the notion of 'appropriate

---

[9]   General Agreement on Tariffs and Trade, Oct. 30, 1947, 55 U.N.T.S. 194; 61 Stat. pt. 5; T.I.A.S. No. 1700, Art. XX(b) (GATT).

[10]   SPS Agreement, Annex A.

[11]   GATT, Art. XX(b).

[12]   *Id.*, at Art. XX(b).

level of SPS protection'.[13] These SPS tests evolved from more basic legal tests found in administrative, constitutional and international law, such as proportionality and cost-benefit analysis, although the SPS Agreement formulations are both novel and distinctive. Proportionality considers the benefits and burdens of a particular measure in a relatively non-qualitative way. Cost benefit analysis is asserted to be more precise – the costs and benefits of a measure are more carefully gauged. A presumptive case for upholding a measure is made where the benefit exceeds the associated cost under a cost-benefit approach.

The unstated concept of an *achieved* level of protection replaces 'benefit' in the various calculations made under the SPS Agreement. As discussed above, the level of SPS protection may not reflect all the social benefits of an SPS measure. This implicit undercounting of the aggregate social benefit is distinct from the problem of 'externalities' – benefits that are realized outside the territory of the country imposing the SPS measure. One country's restriction of alcohol (through publicity campaigns, for example) may produce benefits in another. Any such positive spillovers are irrelevant to any WTO Member's attainment of its ALOP.

A particular measure may *achieve* a level of protection that equals or exceeds the level of protection the implementing WTO Member 'deems' appropriate – that is, some measures may constitute regulatory overkill. These measures, it will be seen, are particularly vulnerable to challenge in WTO dispute settlement.

The SPS Agreement provides various formulations for the 'cost' or 'burden' of an SPS measure for purposes of comparison with the measure's level of protection, such as 'negative trade effects',[14] 'discrimination or a disguised restriction on international trade'[15] or 'constraining . . . exports'.[16] These formulations grossly undercount the costs of an SPS measure, as only trade effects are considered. As a good deal of the burden from restricted imports fall on the frustrated exporting state, the 'cost' or 'burden' formulation inevitably internalizes concerns that would not otherwise be considered by an internally-focused legislator.

---

[13]   Tests involving ALOPs are found in SPS Agreement Articles 3.3, 4.1, 5.5 and 5.6.

[14]   SPS Agreement, Art. 5.4.

[15]   *Id.*, at Art. 5.5

[16]   *Id.*, at Art. 5.8

IV.   'APPROPRIATE LEVEL OF PROTECTION' AND THE SPS AGREEMENT'S TESTS

A.   Overview

As discussed below, various tests set out in the SPS Agreement depend on a calculation of a Member's 'appropriate level of protection'. Again, a Member's ALOP is that level of protection it deems appropriate. The SPS Agreement anticipates that ALOPs are set prior to the adoption of an SPS measure (much as it presumes – and effectively requires – that there be a risk assessment prior to the adoption of an SPS measure as well). Experience suggests that this is largely a fantasy – ordinarily legislation does not involve the setting of a particular health target and then an assessment of measures that attain this target. At the very least, legislators consider other factors in standard setting, including (principally) cost and enforceability.

The more common scenario encountered is that of an extant measure under WTO challenge with no clear articulation of the Member's determined ALOP that motivated the adoption of that measure. In these prototypical cases, the Member's ALOP is inferred, typically from the level of protection achieved by the very measure under challenge. Articulation of an ALOP is frequently ex post. Thus, there is a persistent (and pernicious) circularity present in many SPS cases – a measure is attacked, yet the LOP achieved by the measure is presumed to be the Member's ALOP and so enjoys the presumption of legislative correctness recognized by the SPS Agreement.

The four principal tests found in the SPS Agreement incorporating the notion of 'appropriate level of SPS protection' (discussed below) are:

- SPS Agreement, Article 3.3 – concerning departures from international standards
- SPS Agreement, Article 4.1 – concerning equivalency determinations
- SPS Agreement, Article 5.5 – consistency requirement
- SPS Agreement, Article 5.6 – 'not more trade restrictive than required' test

As will be developed, determining (for purposes of administering these tests) what a particular Member's 'appropriate level of SPS protection' is, is elusive. At times, the tests seem to conflate an idealized, ex ante 'appropriate level of protection' a rational legislator might set with an actual level of protection achieved by an extant measure. There is a certain conceptual sloppiness that runs through the SPS Agreement in this regard.

B. ALOPs and Departures from International Standards

Article 3.3 of the SPS Agreement permits a WTO Member to implement an SPS measure that results in a higher level of SPS protection than would be achieved by measures based on an international standard 'as a consequence of the level of [SPS] protection a Member determines to be appropriate . . .'.[17]

Article 3.3 seems to anticipate that the Member first determine an appropriate level of protection and then discover that such a level of protection cannot be achieved by a measure based on an international standard. Depending on the particular risk involved, this can be a fairly abstract undertaking. How does a Member discover that a measure based on an international standard simply is not good enough? Presumably the legislator runs a thought experiment, imagining a measure based on an international standard and then reckoning the level of protection that that measure in that context achieves.

Again, this is a much more difficult undertaking than a cursory reading of the test suggests. What is the level of protection that would be realized, were the international standard implemented? For many health measures, experience from other Members where the international standard prevails would not necessarily predict the level of protection achieved in the territory of the involved Member – the effectiveness of health measures is context specific. And even if the level of protection achievable in a Member's territory by an international standard were ascertainable, accounting for the rejection of the international standard (on the projection that it would not provide an appropriate level of protection) is not straightforward.

What Members actually do (at least in context of dispute settlement) is promulgate idiosyncratic measures and then ex post seek to justify them by telling a story of careful legislative deliberation (which likely never happened) in which (1) the international standard was rejected for failing to provide for an appropriate level of protection and (2) the idiosyncratic measure was selected as it does in fact achieve that level of protection. A first order check on the plausibility of such an account would be to simply compare the respective levels of protection of the idiosyncratic measure with that of a measure consistent with the international standard. The claim would clearly fail if the idiosyncratic measure does not achieve at least a marginally greater level of protection than does the measure based on the international standard.

---

[17] SPS Agreement, Art. 3.3.

C.   ALOP and Equivalency

Note that the equivalence requirement set out in Article 4.1 of the SPS Agreement is at best a soft one. There is no mechanism in dispute settlement – or otherwise – whereby an exporting Member may *insist* that its SPS product regulation is equivalent to that of the importing Member and on that basis that its goods must be admitted. Rather SPS Article 4.1 exhorts the importing Member to accord recognition of compliance to products that conform with the SPS measures of other Members when those measures 'achieve' the importing Member's ALOP.

Article 4.1 of the SPS Agreement provides:

> Members shall accept the sanitary or phytosanitary measures of other Members as equivalent, even if these measures differ from their own or from those used by other Members trading in the same product, if the exporting Member objectively demonstrates to the importing Member that its measures achieve the importing Member's appropriate level of sanitary or phytosanitary protection. For this purpose, reasonable access shall be given, upon request, to the importing Member for inspection, testing and other relevant procedures.

Article 4.1 does not anticipate the direct comparison of the relevant SPS measures adopted by the importing and exporting Members. Rather, it matches the SPS measure adopted by the exporting Member with the appropriate level of protection set by the importing Member.[18] The SPS Agreement leaves unstated how the appropriate level of protection of the importing Member is to be determined. There is no readily available 'level of protection' in sight. Rather, the importing Member's 'appropriate level of SPS protection' must be adduced, and here there are a variety of possible techniques. First, the comparable SPS measure adopted by the importing country as implemented in *its* regulatory context may be examined in order to calculate (or perhaps better describe) its *achieved* level of protection. An inference must then follow that the *achieved* level of protection of the measure adopted by the importing Member must equal *or exceed* its deemed 'appropriate level of protection'. Here, the achieved level of protection of the implemented measure serves as a *proxy* for what the terms of Article 4.1 call for – direct consideration of the assuredly 'equivalent' measure with the importing Member's appropriate level of protection. The effect of using the *achieved* level of protection derived from the importing country's measure (as opposed to the elusive 'appropriate level of protection' derived from the importing country's measure) to evaluate the

---

[18]   *Id.*

exporting country's measure approaches a direct comparison of these two measures – which does correspond to the simple notion of equivalence.

Alternatively, the appropriate level of protection might be determined by viewing other measures as indicating the importing Member's general policy of risk tolerance. Or one might simply examine legislative utterances (such as the US Delaney Clause's call for 'zero' risk exposure to carcinogens in foods)[19] as the 'appropriate level of protection'.

WTO dispute settlement at this point offers no answers – there are no decided cases involving SPS Article 4.1. There is, however, an equivalence case decided under the former US–Canada Free Trade Agreement.[20] The relevant provision to the US–Canada FTA did not employ the notion of level of protection, so the tribunal's analysis is of limited value. Rather, we can simply borrow the setting of *UHT Milk* to explore the exercise Article 4.1 of the SPS Agreement demands.

UHT Milk did not involve an ordinary discrepancy in regulation. Rather, the case centered on the unavailability of US milk inspectors in Canadian dairies. When Puerto Rico joined the National Conference on Interstate Milk Shipments, an organization of state milk control agencies, it adopted the Pasteurized Milk Ordinance. Puerto Rico then withdrew the authorization that had theretofore permitted a Quebec dairy concern to sell UHT milk in Puerto Rico. Section 11 of the Pasteurized Milk Ordinance would have authorized the entry of the UHT milk if it were shown that it was processed under regulations 'substantially equivalent' to those provided by the Ordinance:

> Milk and milk products from points beyond the limits of routine inspection of [Puerto Rico] or its jurisdiction, may be sold in [Puerto Rico] or its jurisdiction, provided they are produced and pasteurized, ultra-pasteurized or aseptically processed under regulations which are substantially equivalent to this Ordinance . . .

Both the dairy and Quebec insisted that Quebec's milk production standards were equivalent (in the sense of equivalent in substance) to the standards embodied in the Ordinance, and that Section 11 of the ordinance was satisfied. However, neither federal nor Puerto Rico officials were willing to engage in an equivalency exercise. While various solutions were proposed, Puerto Rico interpreted the Ordinance as requiring that qualified

---

[19] Federal Food, Drug, and Cosmetic Act of 1938, 21 U.S.C. 348.

[20] In the Matter of Puerto Rico Regulations on the Import, Distribution and Sale of U.H.T. Milk from Quebec, No. USA-93-1807-01, June 3, 1993, 16 ITRD. 1769.

US officials inspect the Quebec dairies in order to demonstrate that these production facilities were in fact compliant with Ordinance standards.

Had an equivalency process be undertaken, it may have revealed that the Quebec milk production regime was 'substantially equivalent' to the Ordinance. In such case, one would have expected the Puerto Rico import ban to be lifted. Under Article 4.1 of the SPS Agreement, the inquiry would not have involved a finding as to any particular degree of resemblance between the two milk production standards. Indeed, the Quebec milk regulations may have had an entirely different design, yet might still have been 'equivalent' in the sense of Article 4.1 of the SPS Agreement were Puerto Rico's ALOP determined to be achieved by the Quebec-origin UHT milk.

For equivalency purposes, the relevant level of protection to be achieved by the measure imposed by the exporting Member is the level advanced in the territory of the importing Member – which may differ considerably from the level of protection the same measure achieves in its native regulatory context (or in the territories of other WTO Members).

Level of protection is context-specific. A particular measure may alter a set level of protection in one country's territory yet fail miserably in another. Identical SPS measures differ in their effect in different settings. As such, it is of little relevance for demonstrating equivalency that the exporting Member's measure equals or even greatly exceeds the importing Member's 'appropriate level of protection' in the exporting Member's territory. Rather, the importing Member can rightly insist that Article 4.1 requires demonstrating that the imported product (which embodies its home standard) satisfies the importing Member's 'appropriate level of protection' when that product is *imported and consumed* in the latter Member's territory. This is frequently a speculative exercise, as equivalence cases prototypically involve import prohibitions – there is no direct experience with the excluded product to assess what level of protection its introduction would achieve.

D.   ALOP and Consistency

The SPS Agreement imposes a soft requirement that Members address SPS risks consistently across regulatory contexts. Article 5.5 of the SPS Agreement provides:

> With the objective of achieving consistency in the application of appropriate level of sanitary and phytosanitary protection against risks to human life or health, or to animal or plant life or health, each Member shall avoid arbitrary or unjustifiable distinctions in the levels it considers to be appropriate in differ-

ent situations, if such distinctions result in discrimination or a disguised restriction on international trade . . .[21]

Article 5.5 sets out a goal of consistency of ALOPs in its own right. It is not readily apparent why ALOPs need to be consistent – a rational legislator might prefer different levels of protection for different risks (due to, for example, differences in non-SPS social benefits or differences in regulatory burdens beyond restrictions to trade). Inconsistency in ALOPs is often suggestive, however, that the primary motive for a particular measure (the one that aims to achieve the relatively higher ALOP) is not a bona fide health concern, but rather protectionism.

The operative part of Article 5.5 calls on each Member to 'avoid arbitrary or unjustifiable distinctions' in ALOPs in 'different situations'.[22] Despite the softness of the phrase 'avoid', SPS Article 5.5 is justiciable – the WTO dispute settlement body considered and then rejected an Article 5.5 claim in *EC – Hormones*[23] and found valid an Article 5.5 claim in *Australia – Salmon*.[24] Mere distinctions in ALOPs are not sufficient – the differences must be arbitrary or unjustifiable. Thus, one line of inquiry in an Article 5.5 dispute (once a difference in ALOPs is demonstrated) is whether the difference is 'arbitrary or unjustifiable'. Presumably, there are situations (and perhaps many situations) where a difference in ALOP is not arbitrary or is justified.

Article 5.5 of the SPS Agreement speaks of distinctions in ALOPs in 'different situations'.[25] Despite what this phrase suggests, there need be a considerable commonality of facts between the two regulatory contexts in order to permit consideration of inconsistency of ALOPs between them. Perhaps Article 5.5 would have been better drafted referring to 'like situations' (akin to 'like products' in several important GATT disciplines), rather than 'different situations', to suggest the necessity of commonality. An ALOP for salmonella bears no meaningful relationship to an ALOP for mad-cow disease; these are 'different situations' in the ordinary sense

---

[21]   SPS Agreement, Art. 5.5.

[22]   *Id.*

[23]   Panel Report, *EC – Measures Affecting Meat and Meat Products*, WT/DS26/R/USA (Aug. 18, 1997) adopted Feb. 13, 1998, as modified by Appellate Body Report WT/DS26/AB/R, WT/DS48/AB/R; Panel Report, *EC – Measures Affecting Meat and Meat Products*, WT/DS48/R/CAN (Aug. 18, 1997) adopted Feb. 13, 1998, as modified by Appellate Body Report WT/DS26/AB/R, WT/DS48/AB/R.

[24]   Appellate Body Report, *Australia – Measures Affecting Importation of Salmon*, WT/DS18/AB/R (Oct. 20, 1998) (adopted Nov. 6, 1998).

[25]   SPS Agreement, Art. 5.5.

of these words, but would not be a basis for an Article 5.5 challenge due to the absence of commonality between them. Both decisional law (chiefly *EC – Hormones*[26] and *Australia – Salmon*) and the promulgated WTO Guidelines[27] make the requirement of commonality clear.

Common elements between the two 'different situations' may be 'the same type of substance or pathogen, and/or the same type of adverse health effect'.[28] In *Australia – Salmon*, both these elements of commonality were present between the challenged measure (import prohibition of salmon) and the non-control of the import of certain baits and ornamental fish. These baits and ornamental fish could also host the same exotic pathogens that Australia feared would be introduced by imported Canadian salmon. As the pathogens were the same, the result to the Australian salmon-farming industry would be the same as well.

Finally, Article 5.5 of the SPS Agreement requires that distinctions in ALOPs (in different situations) may not result in discrimination or a disguised restriction on trade. In imposing this limitation, Article 5.5 recalls and invokes the considerable acquis built around similar phrasing found in the *chapeau* of GATT Article XX. Yet there is a substantial difference in context. The *chapeau* of GATT Article XX withdraws the availability of the various exceptions provided by the subparagraphs of GATT Article XX where the application of a measure 'constitute[s]' discrimination or a disguised restraint on trade. The prohibited elements (discrimination or disguised restraint on trade) are to be found in the application of the measure, and not in the measure itself, in order to nullify an Article XX exception. In Article 5.5 of the SPS Agreement, the forbidden element (again, discrimination or disguised restraint on trade) is found neither in the measure, nor in its application, but rather in the 'result' of the identified distinctions in ALOPs. Note that the application of many SPS measures will result in some restriction on international trade, and some SPS measures may effect discrimination. The 'disguise' of a measure with an impact on trade results not so much from the application of the measure as

---

[26]   The Appellate Body stated in *EC – Hormones* at ¶ 217 that:

[t]he situations exhibiting differing levels of protection cannot, of course, be compared unless they are comparable, that is, unless they present some common element or elements sufficient to render them comparable. If the situations proposed to be examined are totally different from one another, they would not be rationally comparable and the differences in levels of protection cannot be examined for arbitrariness.

[27]   *Guidelines to Further the Practical Implementation of Article 5.5*, G/SPS/15, dated July 18, 2000.

[28]   *Id.* at ¶ A-2.

from the mala fides of its asserted object or motivation (the protection of health in SPS cases). Similarly, the setting of an inconsistent ALOP (particularly one that is more strict than others in comparable situations) may be effected in order to mask commercial motives. Distinctions in ALOPs may indicate a greater probability that improper (i.e. protectionist) motivations are at play.[29]

E. ALOP and 'Not More Trade Restrictive' Test

Article 5.6 of the SPS Agreement obligates a Member, when implementing SPS measures, to attain a determined appropriate level of protection, to ensure that these measures are 'not more trade restrictive than required' to achieve its ALOP.[30]

Article 5.6 provides:

> Without prejudice to [SPS Article 3(2)], when establishing or maintaining sanitary or phytosanitary measures to achieve the appropriate level of sanitary or phytosanitary protection, Members shall ensure that such measures are not more trade-restrictive than required to achieve their appropriate level of sanitary or phytosanitary protection, taking into account technical and economic feasibility.

The note to Article 5.6 makes clear that a measure will meet this test 'unless there is another measure that achieves' the ALOP and 'is significantly less restrictive to trade . . .'.[31] Thus, in order to challenge a Member's ALOP using Article 5.6, the complaining Member must put forward an alternative SPS measure that achieves the ALOP of the Member imposing the challenged measure. The proposed alternative measure need not be more effective than the challenged measure in addressing the relevant risk; indeed, it may be less effective, so long as it achieves the implementing Member's ALOP. However, where there is no regulatory alternative identified that achieves a Member's ALOP, Article 5.6 is not available to challenge a measure.

There are both substantive and procedural aspects of Article 5.6. Again, as a matter of substance, there must exist an alternative that achieves the relevant ALOP. But as a matter of procedure, the complaining Member must identify (or nominate) one or more alternative measures. This

---

[29] Jeffery Atik, 'The Weakest Link: Demonstrating the Inconsistency of "Appropriate Levels of Protection" in Australia-Salmon', 24 *Risk Analysis* 483 (2004).

[30] SPS Agreement, Art. 5.6.

[31] *Id.*, at Note 3.

requirement flows from the complainant's burden of proof. For example, in *Australia – Apples*, New Zealand identified a number of alternatives in its Article 5.6 challenge.[32] The Panel found only one alternative sufficiently developed by the complainant, and so 'discounted' the other alternatives presented.

Once the alternative measure is identified, it is then up to the panel to make the 'requisite comparison between the level of protection that would be achieved by the alternative measure and the importing Member's [ALOP]'.[33] This is a substantial challenge for a panel, involving a complex (and highly speculative) assessment, involving, among other considerations, substantial scientific expertise.

The negative implication of the note to Article 5.6 is that where there is an identified alternative measure that is 'significantly less restrictive to trade' and which also achieves the Member's ALOP, the challenged measure may fail Article 5.6. It is debatable whether or not Article 5.6 fully imposes the so-called 'least restrictive means' test, given the point of softness with respect to the degree of restrictiveness of the regulatory alternative.

In application, however, Article 5.6 does call for a hunt for a regulatory alternative that achieves the ALOP achieved by the actual measure. In order to challenge an SPS measure via Article 5.6 in situations where the ALOP has not been articulated by the regulating Member, presumably one first infers the ALOP from the measure itself. Once again, this exercise is fraught with difficulty. It is not clear, when the ALOP is derived from the proxy level of protection achieved from an implemented measure, that the ALOP is merely met or is in fact greatly exceeded.

An implemented SPS measure may meet, exceed or fail to achieve an ALOP if an ALOP may be determined independently of the challenged measure itself. For example, the Australian quarantine reviewed in *Australia – Salmon* was determined to fail to achieve Australia's ALOP. Where the ALOP is inferred from the challenged measure itself, it is hard to imagine how the ALOP could either fail to achieve or exceed the measure's effective level of protection. By bootstrapping, the ALOP *is* the challenged SPS measure's effective LOP. No liability under Article 5.6 can result.

Assume the ALOP with respect to a particular SPS risk (could it be known) is 97 percent effectiveness. A measure that provides for 99 percent effectiveness (however this is determined) would achieve this ALOP;

---

32   Panel Report, *Australia – Apples*, ¶¶ 7.1109–7.1118.
33   Appellate Body Report, *Australia – Apples*, ¶ 344.

indeed it would exceed it. The presence of a regulatory alternative that (1) if implemented would achieve 98 percent effectiveness (and which would thus also achieve the ALOP) and (2) that was significantly less restrictive to trade would support an Article 5.6 challenge. But once we can no longer independently stipulate the ALOP (as it typically is obscure) but can only divine it from the challenged measure itself, we obtain a different result. We inspect the existing measure, observe its 99 percent level of protection, and then surmise that the ALOP is also 99 percent. The regulatory alternative which provides a 98 percent level of protection no longer serves as a ground for challenge to the extant measure, notwithstanding it is significantly less trade restrictive, as it cannot achieve the ALOP *derived* from the challenged measure!

The obligation established by Article 5.6 is further softened by consideration of 'technical and economic feasibility'.[34] As a practical matter, WTO Members are likely to be accorded a broad margin of appreciation with respect to an asserted legitimate rejection of a proffered regulatory alternative due to considerations of 'technical and economic feasibility'.

V. 'APPROPRIATE LEVELS OF PROTECTION' AND THE LEGITIMACY OF SPS MEASURES

A. Overview

As this review has shown, the concept of 'appropriate level of protection' is used to scrutinize a particular aspect of a challenged measure. Yet each test asks something specific with respect to a disputed measure's achieved level of protection.

- Article 3.3 of the SPS Agreement asks whether an idiosyncratic measure achieves a higher appropriate level of protection in instances where that ALOP would not be achieved by a measure based on an international standard. Here there are two relevant comparisons: the first is made between the idiosyncratic measure's LOP and the implementing Member's asserted 'higher' ALOP; the second is between the implementing Member's ALOP and the LOP achieved (or achievable) by a measure based on an international standard.

---

[34] SPS Agreement, Art. 5.6.

- Article 4.1 of the SPS Agreement compares the LOP achievable by an imported good embodying a foreign standard and asks whether that LOP equals or exceeds the ALOP of the importing Member.
- Article 5.5 of the SPS Agreement asks whether the ALOP set by a Member in one context is consistent with the ALOP it sets in another.
- Article 5.6 of the SPS Agreement requires that a measure not be 'more trade restrictive than required' to achieve that Member's ALOP. Where an alternate measure exists, of which the LOP equals or exceeds the ALOP *and* that measure is significantly less trade restrictive than the challenged measure (that also exceeds the ALOP), the challenged measure will be found inconsistent.

Note the various calculations (for purposes of making comparisons) required:

1. A Member's ALOP must be determined with respect to a particular risk in order to carry out the Article 3.3, 4.1, 5.5 and 5.6 tests. As discussed above, knowing a Member's ALOP is not an easy task; often it is inferred from the achieved LOP of the challenged measure.
2. The achieved LOP of an idiosyncratic measure must be determined in order to carry out the test set out in Article 3.3.
3. The achieved LOP associated with the introduction of an imported good embodying a foreign standard must be determined in order to carry out the test set out in Article 4.1.
4. The ALOP of a Member in a 'different situation' must be determined in order to carry out the test set out in Article 5.5.
5. The achievable LOP of an alternative measure must be determined in order to carry out the test set out in Article 5.6. Note also that Article 5.6 anticipates a comparison of the trade restrictiveness of the alternate measure with that of the challenged measure.

B.   ALOP and Minimizing Negative Trade Effects

Article 5.4 of the SPS Agreement exhorts Members to 'take into account' the objective (set out in the Preamble) of minimizing negative trade effects when determining their appropriate levels of protection. The Panel in *EC – Hormones* determined that Article 5.4 was hortatory and did not establish a legal obligation. Notwithstanding this, the call of Article 5.4 to 'take into account' suggests that it is appropriate for Members to balance their health concerns (as expressed by their determination of appropriate levels of protection) with adverse trade effects.

The 'test' is a non sequitur – only measures, and not policy goals, can negatively affect trade. A particular level of protection deemed appropriate by a Member may be attained by a number of alternate measures with differing trade effects (or by a unique measure with a particular trade effect, or sadly perhaps by no measure at all, where the available technology constraint makes exposure to a risk unavoidable). Thus, a legislator's 'taking into account' presupposes the fixing of an appropriate level of protection associated with a unique, discrete measure. For the exhortation to have any meaning, it must anticipate instances where an otherwise attractive measure (from a policy perspective) is rejected. This may unrealistically require legislative altruism – as health protection (a largely internalized benefit) is to be sacrificed for the benefit of trade (which generates some important external benefits unlikely to be captured by legislators).

Article 5.3 of the SPS Agreement identifies factors to be considered in conducting risk assessment and in determining the ALOP. Note that Article 5.3 more precisely recognizes that these factors are associated with 'the measure to be applied for achieving an appropriate level of sanitary and phytosanitary protection' and not with the level per se.[35]

C.   ALOP and Indeterminacy

The notion of 'appropriate level of protection' underlies the central tests set out in the SPS Agreement. These tests, with their much greater specificity, represent a substantial advance over the 'necessary to protect human, animal or plant life or health' test set out in GATT Article XX(b).They also permit more science-based (or risk analysis-based) consideration of regulatory approaches.

'Appropriate level of protection', however, suffers from indeterminacy and incomparability challenges that often cannot be satisfied. As such, tests involving ALOP (and levels of protection generally) are only accidentally available and are of dubious reliability.

As observed earlier, the idea of a readily ascertainable 'appropriate level of protection' for a particular SPS risk is most often a fantasy. Where SPS measures exist, it is rarely clear that the enacting legislature considered a desired level of protection independently of its consideration of the measure itself. Thus, the notion that the determination of an 'appropriate' level of protection precedes design or identification of a particular measure is wishful thinking. It presumes a more rational legislative process

---

[35]   *Id.*, Art. 5.3.

(one that might be greatly desired by risk-analysis policy professionals) than likely exists anywhere.

There may in fact be some instances where the process is followed. Historically, risk analysis proceeded from exposure studies – where there may be a relatively continuous relationship of risk and exposure, as in the case of a known carcinogen. (The degree of continuity may not hold up to scientific challenge – though that is a debate for another place.) Where this is the case, a legislator can pick a particular level or risk as 'acceptable' and then read the particular exposure level associated with that level of risk. The resulting measure limits exposure to this 'revealed' exposure. A simple translation is made from this 'acceptable level of risk' to its corresponding 'appropriate level of protection'. Next, the legislator crafts a measure that limits exposure to that level corresponding to the ALOP. Note that there is no question of the measure's level of protection exceeding the ALOP. The measure is designed to effectively and efficiently achieve the ALOP – its LOP is equivalent to the ALOP associated with the particular risk. But continuous risk/exposure data are rare and somewhat unreliable – usually a particular risk/exposure relationship is an extrapolation from other risk/exposure levels. Often the data source involves very high exposure (and high risk) – whether a similar relationship between exposure and risk attains at much lower exposure levels is not clear.

Many other SPS risks – and SPS measures responding to these risks – do not resemble the simple exposure-based risk profile displayed by carcinogens. Even a legislator that conducts a serious risk assessment with respect to, say, Avian flu, is hard put to meaningfully set an 'appropriate level of protection' with respect to that risk – where risk encompasses elements of (1) introduction of Avian flu, (2) the extent of its subsequent spread and (3) its consequences. Even with respect to a particular measure under consideration (say, an import ban on poultry) it may be fanciful to speak of its level of protection (unless one presumes the LOP to be absolute!).

In most cases, there is unlikely to be clearly articulated desiderata of LOP independent of a particular measure. This is particularly true when there is no range of measures or where there are no feasible alternate measures. Measures are designed and adopted because they address risk, because they reduce risk in some meaningful way.

It is a significant challenge to identify the level of protection that results from an existing SPS measure. One can only observe the continuing occurrences of the risk addressed by the relevant measure – it is a speculation to attribute a reduction in these occurrences to the presence of the measure. One cannot easily know what the rate of occurrences would be in the absence of the measure – as in the case of protection provided by the proverbial scarecrow: one cannot presume effectiveness merely from the absence of crows. There may be data drawn from prior to the implementation of the measure that is suggestive of the measure's effectiveness, but there may be independent factors actually responsible for any observed reduction in risk.

The achieved level of protection of extant measures is sufficiently problematic. Far greater difficulty attaches to calculations of (1) the LOP that would be achieved were a measure implemented in a different Member's territory and (2) the LOP of a non-implemented or hypothetical measure.

It is an obvious error to assume that a measure 'borrowed' from another jurisdiction will result in the same LOP that it achieves in its native setting. Health measures are notoriously site specific in their effectiveness. Yet several of the SPS Agreement's tests seem to invite this error. Given the complexities of health risk, physical factors are likely to generate variances in effectiveness. Legal context is also likely to affect the LOP achieved by a borrowed measure. A discrete SPS regulation sits within a larger regulatory context – which includes measures that support, or at times obstruct, attainments of the desired ALOP. Enforcement (in its complete sense) is also likely to differ significantly between measures; the ultimate degree that enforcement efficiency contributes to a measure's effectiveness will certainly vary among WTO Members.

With 'borrowed' measures, there is some experience to draw on in estimating an eventual level of protection. Yet several of the SPS Agreement's tests permit consideration of measures that are hypothetical alternatives. Here there is very little data to generate a projected LOP.

D. ALOP and Incomparability

The various tests set out in the SPS Agreement involve comparisons of ALOPs with ALOPs, ALOPS with LOPs achieved by a particular measure, and finally LOPs of two different measures. The SPS Agreement presumes that these varieties of levels of protections can be readily determined and then meaningfully compared. Much as is the case with determinacy, there is little to inspire confidence in the reliability of inferences drawn from 'comparisons' of ALOPs. Here the uncertainties of determining the underlying relevant LOPs are necessarily magnified.

The uncertainties surrounding LOPs of protection suggest that a generous 'appreciation' of a Member's SPS measure likely operates. Relatively speaking, the achieved LOP of the challenged measure is more likely discernible. Thus, in comparisons of this value with LOPs of alternate measures (where estimation is more soft), the probabilistic variance of the compared LOP may straddle the LOP of the challenged measure. A legal heuristic may resolve these cases in favor of the challenged measure. This may not be an offensive result, as it is in keeping with the presumption of regulatory discretion the SPS Agreement is meant to concede. It does make challenges more unlikely, however, in the absence of a starkly greater LOP on behalf of the alternative measure.

Various SPS disciplines – including the critical requirement of the conduct of a risk assessment in connection with the implementation of an SPS measure that departs from an international standard – anticipate the setting of an ALOP. It remains unclear to what degree the Article 3.3 authorization can legitimate a long-standing measure – that is, a measure that pre-dates the SPS Agreement. It is difficult to imagine the SPS Agreement laying waste to the existing stock of SPS measures due to the absence of a conforming risk assessment (as was certainly the case for most aged SPS measures). The requirement of a risk assessment is understood to not be a formal prerequisite for the enactment of an SPS measure – which in turn suggests that an ex post risk assessment might serve to justify the continuance of an existing SPS measure upon challenge in WTO dispute settlement.

The same reasoning seems to apply to the setting of (and articulation of) a Member's ALOP – at least with respect to the maintenance of pre-WTO era SPS measures. A long-standing measure should not be vulnerable to WTO attack merely because the Member imposing the measure failed to express an ALOP in connection with the adoption of the measure. The articulation of an ALOP can be thought of as part of 'risk management' and not risk assessment; hence articulating an ALOP is not explicitly mandated by the SPS Agreement. That stated, the Appellate Body has found an 'implicit obligation' for a Member maintaining an SPS measure to establish and articulate an ALOP,[36] citing Articles 5.3 and 5.4. In *Australia – Apples*, the Appellate Body observed that '[o]therwise, and especially in assessing whether an SPS measure is consistent with Article 5.6, it would be impossible to examine whether alternative measures achieve the appropriate level of protection'.[37]

New measures may be treated more severely. In *Australia – Apples*, the Panel and the Appellate Body search for a statement of Australia's ALOP. And Australia provides an ALOP (along with what purports to be a conforming risk assessment). That said, the statement of the ALOP provided by Australia is so vague as to almost lack content: 'providing a high level

---

[36]   Appellate Body report, *Australia – Apples*, para. 343, citing Appellate Body report, *Australia – Salmon*, para. 206.

[37]   Appellate Body report, *Australia – Apples*, para. 343.

of sanitary or phytosanitary protection aimed at reducing risk to a very low level, but not to zero'.

To some degree, the expression suggests Australia is seeking the highest level of protection functionally available. To insist on zero risk with respect to imported apples would expose Australia to charges of inconsistency and discrimination – as some risk (though perhaps a very low level) is tolerated through the very presence of domestic cultivation. (Note however that France articulated a 'zero risk' tolerance in *EC – Asbestos* – a GATT-based dispute involving a mix of import and domestic prohibitions.)

The phrase 'very low level' is not particularly instructive. The Panel and the Appellate Body in *Australia – Apples* appear to indulge (without examination) the notion that the challenged measures do in fact achieve the ALOP as expressed by Australia; indeed the essence of New Zealand's complaint is that the Australian measures are unduly strict, not that they are ineffective.

ALOPs may be expressed either quantitatively or qualitatively. This of course introduces considerable flexibility in setting SPS standards. It is, however, very difficult to operationalize a vague 'qualitative' formulation such as 'very low level' in applying the various tests found in the SPS Agreement. A complainant must establish that an alternative measure also achieves the ALOP of the respondent Member – and it may be difficult if not impossible to meet this burden.

The Appellate Body reversed the panel's finding of an Article 5.6 violation in *Australia – Apples* (it found that panel to have improperly extended findings from its Article 5.1 determination to the Article 5.6 objection and to have failed to respect the independent determination Article 5.6 requires). When the Appellate Body inquires as to whether it may 'complete the analysis' of New Zealand's Article 5.6 complaint, it recalls Australia's statement of its ALOP. It then asks whether the alternate (and less trade restrictive) measure proposed by New Zealand would achieve Australia's ALOP – that is, whether it would reduce the particular risk to a 'very low level'. The Appellate Body finds the record insufficient to assess what the risk of New Zealand's measure might be. Lacking this, the Appellate Body is unable to reach the secondary conclusion as to whether such determined risk satisfies Australia's ALOP.

We could imagine other cases where a properly informed complainant (and a properly instructed panel) could have reached ultimate findings as to the level of protection to be achieved by a proposed alternate measure in an Article 5.6 challenge. Even so, difficulties persist. Imagine a panel to reach a quantitative finding as to the risk achievable by an alternate measure. What quantitative finding satisfies 'very low level'?

In the alternative, the panel could reach a finding that the proposed alternate measure would achieve a level of protection that can properly be expressed qualitatively. Here two outcomes suggest themselves. The first would be a qualitative formulation that corresponds to the ALOP: that is, a finding that the proposed alternative would achieve a 'very low level' of risk. Of course this is utterly conclusory. Or the panel could express the achievable level of risk using another formulation – which hardly increases the rigor and predictability of the test.

VI.   THE ILLUSIONS OF THE SPS AGREEMENT

The various tests incorporated in the SPS Agreement promise a more objective, more precise set of determinations to signal when a Member's SPS measure must give way to trade considerations. These tests appear technical on their face, involving simple comparisons along fairly discrete dimensions. As many of the more important of these rely on the identification (if not quantification) of the concept of 'appropriate level of protection', they may only be as effective (in the sense of objective, precise and predictable) as the very notion of ALOP admits. Examination of ALOP reveals significant challenges to these expectations. The contradictions and indeterminacies found within the idea of ALOP in turn renders resort to the various SPS Agreement tests problematic.

   At best, these tests, based on the apparent (though not real) substantiality of the notion of ALOP, permit the SPS Agreement to appear more exact and exacting than it in fact is. In the end, it is more doubtful that the SPS Agreement achieves, other than by accident, an appropriate balance between an appropriate deference to the independent and varied choices made by WTO members in their respective health policies and the maintenance of an open trade system.

5. The International Organization for Standardization: private voluntary standards as swords and shields
*David A. Wirth**

INTRODUCTION

Corporations may choose to "go green" for any number of reasons, and in any number of ways. Customers or consumers through the marketplace may signal a demand for environmentally friendly goods or services. Alternatively, businesses may consciously choose to cultivate an environmentally responsible image. Concern among the public in the neighborhood of a manufacturing plant may create pressure for greener policies. Firms may retool manufacturing processes in response to demands from workers exposed to hazardous materials. Investments in energy efficiency or reductions in the use of toxic substances may result in significant cost savings, benefiting the firm's bottom line. Government regulation, the possibility of enforcement, or potential tort liability may also act as incentive-creating mechanisms. Other drivers include the cultivation of environmentally responsible consumer markets and price premiums for environmentally friendly products.

Considerations such as these among a wide variety of firms and industries have led to coordinated approaches to addressing environmental concerns in the form of private voluntary standards. This chapter

*   This chapter is reproduced with permission of the publishers from Boston College Environmental Affairs Law Review, vol. 36, no. 1 page 79 (2009). © 2008 David A. Wirth. This chapter is based on a paper presented at the symposium, "The Greening of the Corporation" at Boston College Law School on October 25, 2007. From 1997 to 2001 the author was a member of the American National Standards Institute-Registrar Accreditation Board (ANSI-RAB) Management Committee for the Environmental Management System (EMS) component of the National Accreditation Program (NAP, now the ANSI-ASQ National Accreditation Board). This project was supported by a generous grant from the Boston College Law School Fund and draws on some of the author's previously published work. The author gratefully acknowledges Ira R. Feldman's helpful comments on an earlier draft and Mark Sullivan's editing of the references. The responsibility for all views expressed in this chapter, however, is the author's own.

discusses one example of these efforts: environmental undertakings in the International Organization for Standardization (ISO). After describing the structure and operation of ISO, the chapter evaluates both the benefits and limitations of ISO standards in the field of the environment. The utility of, and concerns about, ISO standards are particularly pronounced in international trade agreements such as the World Trade Organization (WTO) suite of agreements. Because of the structure of these agreements, ISO standards may operate either as a sword – a negative standard used to challenge a domestic regulatory action – or a shield – an internationally agreed reference point that bolsters the legitimacy of a national measure. The chapter examines the potential for ISO standards on eco-labeling to act as swords to attack domestic requirements, and those on life cycle analysis to serve as shields to insulate municipal actions from international challenge in areas such as climate protection.

I.   ISO'S ENVIRONMENTAL STANDARDS

The International Organization for Standardization (ISO), created immediately after World War II with headquarters in Geneva, is an international federation of standardizing bodies from 162 countries.[1] ISO is not an intergovernmental organization, such as the United Nations, constituted by multilateral agreement whose members are states represented by governmental authorities.[2] Although the ISO member from some countries is a governmental entity such as a national standardizing body, ISO is primarily a forum for coordinating standardizing efforts by private business.[3] The U.S. member of ISO is the American National Standards Institute (ANSI), a private entity.[4] For the United States, the primary, although not sole, participants in ISO processes are representatives of private industry.[5]

ISO's principal work product consists of voluntary standards adopted by consensus.[6] In contrast to some of the output of intergovernmental

---

[1]   *See About ISO*, http://www.iso.org/iso/about.htm (last visited Sept. 17, 2011).

[2]   The principal treatment of the ISO's environmental activities in a treatise is Ira R. Feldman and Douglas Weinfield, "Environmental Management Systems", *in* Michael Gerrard (editor), *Environmental Law Practice Guide: State and Federal Law* (New York: Mathew Bender, 2008), Volume 1, § 6A.

[3]   Gerrard, note 2 above, § 6A.01[2][a].

[4]   *See* ANSI: *Historical Overview*, http://www.ansi.org/about_ansi/introduc tion/history.aspx?menuid=1 (last visited Sept. 17, 2011).

[5]   Gerrard, note 2 above, § 6A.01[2][a].

[6]   The process for adopting ISO standards involves a complex procedure of drafts and commenting. "Consensus" is defined as "[g]eneral agreement, char-

organizations, ISO standards are strictly hortatory and are not binding under international law.[7] At least so far as the United States is concerned, ISO standards are both adopted by and addressed to private parties. Although ISO standards are voluntary, they often have considerable influence. Probably the best-known ISO standards are those adopted for film speeds. As a result of harmonization through ISO, film with standardized speeds of 100, 200, or 400, is compatible with virtually all cameras of whatever brand available throughout the world.

In the mid-1990s, ISO's Technical Committee (TC) 207 on environmental management began to issue its 14000 series of environmental management standards, a process which is still ongoing.[8] The centerpiece of the program is ISO 14001 on environmental management systems (EMS). Unlike product standards such as film speeds, EMS is a process-oriented approach designed to help an organization "to develop and implement its environmental policy and manage its environmental aspects," including "organizational structure, planning activities, responsibilities, practices, procedures, processes and resources."[9]

---

acterized by the absence of sustained opposition to substantial issues by any important part of the concerned interests and by a process that involves seeking to take into account the views of all parties concerned and to reconcile any conflicting arguments," qualified by a note observing that "[c]onsensus need not imply unanimity." *See Glossary of Terms and Abbreviations Used in ISO/TC Business Plans*, http://isotc.iso.org/livelink/livelink.exe/fetch/2000/2122/687806/Glossary. htm?nodeid=2778927&vernum=0 (last visited Sept. 17, 2011) [hereinafter ISO Glossary]. Publication of an ISO standard requires approval by 75 percent of the members casting a vote. Int'l Org. for Standardization [ISO], *Environmental Management Systems – Requirements with Guidance for Use* at iv, ISO 14001 (Nov. 15, 2004) (ISO 14000 Environmental Management CD-ROM, 2007).

[7]   Gerrard, note 2 above, § 6A.01[3][a].

[8]   *See* ISO, *About ISO/TC207*, http://www.tc207.org/About207.asp (last visited Sept. 17, 2011). *See generally* Joseph Cascio (editor), *The ISO 14000 Handbook* (Milwaukee: ASCQ Quality Press, 1996); Tom Tibor and Ira Feldman, *ISO 14000: A Guide to the New Environmental Management Standards* (Chicago: Irwin Professional Publishers, 1996); Christopher L. Bell, "ISO 14001: Application of International Environmental Management Systems Standards in the United States", 25 *Environmental Law Reporter* (1995) 10,678; David W. Case, "Changing Corporate Behavior Through Environmental Management Systems", 31 *William & Mary Environmental Law & Policy Review* (2008) 75; Paulette L. Stenzel, "Can the ISO 14000 Series Environmental Management Standards Provide a Viable Alternative to Government Regulation?", 37 *American Business Law Journal* (2000) 237.

[9]   *Environmental Management Systems – Requirements with Guidance for Use*, *supra* note 6, § 3.8 & n.2; *see also* ISO, *Environmental Management Systems – General Guidelines on Principles, Systems and Support Techniques*, ISO 14004 (Nov. 15, 2004).

Also included in the 14000 series are standards for environmental assessments,[10] product labeling and declarations,[11] life cycle assessment,[12] environmental communication,[13] and greenhouse gas emission reporting.[14]

Although the standard is intended to have societal benefits as well, the principal purpose of ISO 14001 is to assist businesses in developing and implementing their own environmental policies and programs. Apart from its voluntary character, the standard is strictly procedural in nature and does not specify particular outcomes. The program also includes a private third-party auditing and certification scheme to verify compliance and implementation.[15] The ISO 14000 series of standards is consequently

---

[10]   See ISO, *Environmental Management – Environmental Assessment of Sites and Organizations (EASO)*, ISO 14015 (Nov. 15, 2001).

[11]   See ISO, *Environmental Labels and Declarations – General Principles*, ISO 14020 (Sept. 15, 2000); ISO, *Environmental Labels and Declarations – Self-Declared Environmental Claims (Type II Environmental Labelling)*, ISO 14021 (Sept. 15, 1999); ISO, *Environmental Labels and Declarations – Type I Environmental Labelling – Principles and Procedures*, ISO 14024 (Apr. 1, 1999); ISO, *Environmental Labels and Declarations – Type III Environmental Declarations – Principles and Procedures*, ISO 14025 (July 1, 2006).

[12]   See ISO, *Environmental Management – Life Cycle Assessment – Principles and Framework*, ISO 14040 (July 1, 2006); ISO, *Environmental Management – Life Cycle Assessment – Requirements and Guidelines*, ISO 14044 (July 1, 2006); *see also* ISO, *Environmental Management – Life Cycle Impact Assessment – Examples of Application of ISO 14042*, ISO/TR 14047 (Oct. 1, 2003); ISO, *Environmental Management – Life Cycle Assessment – Data Documentation Format*, ISO/TS 14048 (Apr. 1, 2002); ISO, *Environmental Management – Life Cycle Assessment – Examples of Application of ISO 14041 to Goal and Scope Definition and Inventory Analysis*, ISO/TR 14049 (Mar. 15, 2000).

[13]   See ISO, *Environmental Management – Environmental Communication – Guidelines and Examples*, ISO 14063 (Aug. 1, 2006).

[14]   ISO, *Greenhouse Gases – Part 1: Specification with Guidance at the Organization Level for Quantification and Reporting of Greenhouse Gas Emissions and Removals*, ISO 14064-1 (Mar. 1, 2006); ISO, *Greenhouse Gases – Part 2: Specification with Guidance at the Project Level for Quantification, Monitoring and Reporting of Greenhouse Gas Emission Reductions or Removal Enhancements*, ISO 14064-2 (Mar. 1, 2006); ISO, *Greenhouse Gases – Part 3: Specification with Guidance for the Validation and Verification of Greenhouse Gas Assertions*, ISO 14064-3 (Mar. 1, 2006); ISO, *Greenhouse Gases – Requirements for Greenhouse Gas Validation and Verification Bodies for Use in Accreditation or Other Forms of Recognition*, ISO 14065 (Apr. 15, 2007).

[15]   See ISO, *Guidelines for Quality and/or Environmental Management Systems Auditing*, ISO 19011 (Oct. 1, 2002). These principles for auditing also apply to the ISO 9000 series of standards on quality management systems (QMS). Gerrard, note 2 above, § 6A.01[2][a]. The ISO 9000 series is similar in structure to ISO 14001 and served as a model for the subsequent development of ISO's environmental standards. Of the ISO 14000 series of standards,

fundamentally different in kind from mandatory governmentally adopted requirements such as effluent limitations adopted under the Clean Water Act.

In 2008, just over ten years after the issuance of ISO 14001, ISO undertook a process for reviewing and revising that standard.[16] In early 2011, TC 207 published a new standard in the series, ISO 14005, on the phased implementation of EMSs and the use of environmental performance evaluations.[17] Environmentally related efforts are also taking place in other technical committees besides TC 207.[18] As of this writing, for instance, there has been some activity underway in ISO with respect to liquid biofuels undertaken by TC 28 on petroleum products and lubricants, which in 2007 created a new subcommittee to work on this topic.[19] In 2010 ISO adopted a new standard 26000 addressing social responsibility, which also has an environmental component.

---

only 14001 on environmental management systems is subject to a certification process.

[16] *See* ISO, Technical Comm. 207 on Environmental Management, *Communiqué: 14th Annual Meeting of ISO Technical Committee 207 on Environmental Management*, ISO TC207 N840 (June 29, 2007), *available at* http://www.tc207.org/PDF/N932Communique_16_207PlenaryCairo.pdf   (last visited Sept. 17, 2011). See also ISO, Technical Comm. 207 on Environmental Management, Environmental Management, Resolutions of the 16th Plenary Meeting, ISO TC207 N931 (July 6, 2009), available at http://www.tc207.org/PDF/N931FinalResolutions16_TC207PlenaryCairo2009EF.pdf   (last   visited Sept. 17, 2011); ISO, Technical Comm. 207 on Environmental Management, Announcement of ISO/TC 207's 17th Plenary Meetings 2010, ISO TC207 N958 (Feb. 1, 2010), available at http://www.tc207.org/PDF/N958_N959_ISOTC2072010PlenaryMeetingsAnnouncemenSchedule.pdf (last visited Sept. 17, 2011).

[17] *See* Susan L.K. Briggs, "ISO 14000 Hits 10-Year Mark", *Quality Progress* (Aug. 2007) 67–68 (identifying need to address applicability of ISO 14001 to small- and mid-sized organizations; credibility of certificates; and compatibility with other management systems). See also New ISO standard on phased implementation of environmental management systems will benefit SMEs (ISO press release Feb. 7, 2011), available at http://www.iso.org/iso/pressrelease.htm?refid=Ref1398 (last visited Sept. 17, 2011).

[18] Briggs, note 17 above, 68.

[19] See TC208/SC7 homepage, http://www.iso.org/iso/iso_catalogue/catalogue_tc/catalogue_tc_browse.htm?commid=551957 (last visited Sept. 17, 2011). See also http://publicaa.ansi.org/sites/apdl/Documents/Meetings%20and%20Events/ANSI%20Biofuels%20Standards%20Panel/TC%2028%20Biofuels%20SC%20Proposal%20-%20Clean.pdf (proposal to create ISO/TC 28 Subcommittee on Liquid Biofuels) (last visited Sept. 17, 2011).

II.   BENEFITS OF ISO'S ENVIRONMENTAL STANDARDS

ISO standards, including the 14000 series, potentially have a global reach. A large proportion of the countries on the planet participate in ISO activities, and ISO standards have a high profile within multinational corporations. A number of beneficial consequences flow from these attributes.

One salient feature of ISO 14001, often cited, is the effect of elevating environmental issues within an enterprise. Because an EMS is addressed to the entirety of the production process, at least in principle the exercise of preparing and adopting an EMS engages the entire corporation, including top management.

Although EMS is a process-oriented approach that in principle is distinct from substantive, governmentally established regulatory requirements, the two are quite obviously interrelated. That is, an ISO-conforming EMS ought to assist a firm in meeting performance-based standards such as emissions limitations promulgated under the major environmental regulatory statutes. Among other benefits of ISO 14001 are "[r]educed environmental footprint in terms of environmental emissions, discharges and waste; [i]mproved internal communications and external partnerships; [and] [c]ontinual system improvements resulting from EMS objectives, targets, programs, periodic audits and management reviews."[20]

ISO standards set out uniform expectations from one country to another. To that extent, the meaning of an ISO-conforming environmental management system is similar or identical regardless of location. A corollary benefit of uniformity that is frequently identified is the salutary effect on international trade. Although this attribute is not necessarily immediately obvious in the case of ISO 14001, which adopts a process-oriented approach,[21] other standards in the ISO 14000 series demonstrate the utility of homogeneity. One of the motivations for standards on environmental labeling, for instance, is to assure consistency for environmental claims and to assure that environmental labels do not operate as disguised barriers to trade.[22] ISO standards on reporting greenhouse gas emissions or removals are designed to assure consistency

---

[20]   Briggs, note 17 above, 67.

[21]   *See ISO 14001*, note 6 above, Introduction.

[22]   *See ISO 14020*, note 11 above, § 4.3.1 ("Procedures and requirements for environmental labels and declarations shall not be prepared, adopted, or applied with a view to, or with the effect of, creating unnecessary obstacles to international trade.").

in metrics from one country to another so as to facilitate comparability of data.[23]

Although perhaps easily overlooked from a U.S. perspective, ISO standards are also effective in elevating environmental protection to an international plane. Although voluntary and adopted primarily by industry representatives for the benefit of industry, ISO standards nonetheless are, indeed, standards. If nothing else, the mere existence of ISO standards on the environment signals that this subject matter is an issue of transnational importance. The process of developing ISO standards, moreover, encourages an international dialogue that also helps to lift the topics addressed by the standards above the domestic level.

Some governments, particularly those of developing countries, may have limited or inadequate regulatory infrastructure. In such a setting, ISO standards can create a template for national laws and regulations. Because they are addressed directly to private parties, including multinational corporations, ISO standards in such a setting can also operate as something of a default safety net. In situations where governments may be less than effective in assuring environmental quality, ISO requirements may serve literally as a standard for governments and the public to hold private entities accountable.

One of the principal features of ISO 14001 is the availability of third-party certification. Although firms may utilize ISO standards without seeking certification, which like the standards themselves is voluntary, the availability of third-party certification is an additional factor that tends to encourage consistency. There may be additional benefits to certification in the form of market share and institutional reputation. Some customers may demand ISO 14001 certification from their suppliers.

ISO 14001 consequently is written so as to be "auditable" or verifiable. The third-party certification scheme is designed to increase public confidence in corporate accountability. In principle, if a corporation is ISO 14001 certified, then consumers and the public can have a certain level of confidence in purchasing goods or services from it. Certification is also a way to promote positive relationships with local communities, which may be concerned about the environmental performance of a nearby facility. Moreover, the prospect of certification creates incentives for industry to adopt environmental management systems. More than 21,000

---

[23] *See ISO 14064–1,* note 14 above, § 0.2 ("ISO 14064 is expected to benefit organizations, governments, project proponents and stakeholders worldwide by providing clarity and consistency for quantifying, monitoring, reporting and validating or verifying [greenhouse gas] inventories or projects.").

entities in North America have now received certification under ISO 14001.[24]

It is also possible for entities to self-declare or self-certify. The number of facilities that are implementing ISO 14001, as an indicator of the reach of the Standard, is consequently likely higher than the number of certifications. Although the obvious value of third-party certification is credibility, the Standard itself anticipates that this is not necessary to obtain the benefits of ISO 14001.[25] For instance, local governments or utilities may wish to improve their environmental performance by making use of ISO standards, but may feel that other forms of political accountability render certification redundant or unnecessary.

In the United States, ISO 14001 has had particular utility in the public sector, where it has served as a basis for the adoption of EMSs for public buildings and undertakings. The Clinton administration promulgated an executive order which specifically required the implementation of EMSs by federal agencies and facilities by the end of 2005.[26] While not mentioning ISO 14001 by name, the ISO Standard has been the typical model for implementation of the Executive Order, an important instrument for reducing the federal government's environmental footprint.

---

[24] Briggs, note 17 above, 67.

[25] *See ISO 14001*, note 6 above, § 1 (The Standard is "applicable to any organization that wishes to . . . demonstrate conformity with this International Standard by . . . making a self-determination and self-declaration . . . ."). ISO 14031 provides guidance intended to improve the efficacy of EMSs, but "is not intended for use as a specification standard for certification or registration purposes or for the establishment of any other environmental management system conformance requirements." ISO, *Environmental Management – Environmental Performance Evaluation – Guidelines*, ISO 14031, § 1 (Nov. 15, 1999). Rather, ISO 14031 "would appear to offer a cost effective methodology through which organizations can add real, tangible value, by focusing on critical areas of environmental performance." José Flávio Guerra Machado Coelho, "Sustainability Performance Evaluation: Management Systems Model for Individual Organizations and Supply Chains", 40 (Nov. 2005) (unpublished Ph.D. thesis, Central Queensland University) (on file with the Boston College Environmental Affairs Law Review), *abstract available at* http://library-resources.cqu.edu.au/thesis/adt-QCQU/uploads/approved/adt-QCQU20060720.094327/catalog-adt-QCQU20060720.094327.html (last visited Sept. 17, 2011).

[26] Executive Order No. 13,148, 65 *Federal Register* 24,595, 24,597–98 (Apr. 21, 2000). This Executive Order has been superseded by Executive. Order 13,423, 72 *Federal Register* 3919, 3920 (Jan. 24, 2007), which also requires EMSs for federal agencies and facilities. *See generally* Ann Rhodes, "Note, ISO Enters the Public Sector Through the United States Forest Service", 18 *Colorado Journal of International Environmental Law & Policy* (2007) 417.

Governmental entities at the state and local level have also successfully employed EMSs, including those that conform to ISO 14001.[27]

III.   CONCERNS ABOUT ISO'S ENVIRONMENTAL STANDARDS

In utilizing and evaluating ISO standards such as the 14000 series, one must be aware of their origins. ISO is an international consortium of national standardizing bodies, and the ISO process involves harmonization of potentially disparate national standards. ISO standards are voluntary and addressed directly to private parties – largely industry – and are adopted by a process that involves national delegations composed almost exclusively of industry representatives.

Although environmental organizations and academics have been invited to participate in the ISO process in the United States, it would be difficult to say that ISO as a forum reflects a balanced representation of stakeholders on environmental issues; the prevailing tone is still very much industry-oriented. Because of the voluntary nature of ISO standards, the perception of industry domination of the forum, the lengthy and complicated process for adoption of ISO standards, and the expense of attending frequent overseas meetings, few American non-profit environmental organizations have made a significant commitment to the ISO process.

Moreover, ISO standards are adopted by consensus, which is very carefully defined in the ISO universe.[28] Although there are different tests at different stages of the process, "consensus" generally means widespread acceptance after lengthy consultation. It is therefore unlikely that ISO standards will serve as a dynamic driver of improvements in environmental quality. To the contrary, concern about the potential for the ISO process to produce modest, least-common-denominator outputs is frequently expressed.

A.   Relationship to Public Regulation in the United States

To the extent that ISO processes are directed at selecting among essentially arbitrary choices of little societal impact but of great practical utility to

---

[27]   *See, e.g., ISO 14001 in Pennsylvania: EMS for Local Government*, http://www.dep.state.pa.us/dep/deputate/pollprev/iso14001/emslgo.htm   (last   visited Sept. 17, 2011) (state program supporting implementation of ISO 14001-like EMSs in local municipalities).

[28]   *See ISO Glossary*, note 6 above.

industry, such as standardizing film speeds, the Organization's institutional structure has been of little concern from the point of view of public policy. The specifications chosen for film speeds do not really matter so long as they are compatible with all cameras around the world. But by moving into the field of the environment, the ISO 14000 standards have entered an arena of public policy which, in the United States and many other countries, is already governed by a complex web of governmentally mandated standards. This feature is not necessarily undesirable from a normative point of view, but it suggests that the relationship between ISO standards and governmental regulatory requirements is, at least potentially, a delicate one.

One relatively obvious distinction is that ISO standards are responsive to a different constituency than is public regulation. Where environmental statutory and regulatory requirements, at least in principle, have an aura of democratic legitimacy, the principal audience for ISO standards can be expected to be motivated primarily by market-driven factors, such as profitability. The consensus requirement creates additional reservations about the potential for downward inertia originating from literally around the globe. In such a setting, objections to excessive stringency can be expected to dominate by comparison with initiatives that might push for greater rigor. The voluntary nature of ISO standards renders them fundamentally different in kind from most governmentally established environmental requirements. Last, unlike public enforcement processes, the principal means of implementation is through a private third-party auditing process, also voluntary in nature.

These sorts of concerns have led to an equivocal relationship between private voluntary processes and federal regulators in the United States. On the one hand, there is potentially some synergy between ISO standards and the goals of public regulation. An ISO-conforming EMS may help a firm meet regulatory requirements, and the third-party auditing process may identify compliance problems at an early stage. Participation of regulatory officials in the normative phase of these voluntary undertakings can be beneficial, and, on occasion, private voluntary standards may be appropriate alternatives to mandatory, governmental regulation. For example, a voluntary consensus standard may generate better data than the regulatory process, may be an efficacious vehicle for educating regulatory officials as to the practical needs of industry, and, if effective, may obviate the need for regulatory intervention altogether.[29] For these

---

[29]   For example, EMSs have been used as a component of injunctive relief in civil enforcement settlements. *See* U.S. Environmental Protection Agency,

reasons, a variety of federal authorities encourage federal officials to participate in the process of drafting, and to make use of the work product from, voluntary standard-setting efforts.[30]

On the other hand, it is equally clear that federal agencies must in all cases abide by the statutory standards that govern the agencies' activities. Whatever their policy merits, ISO standards domestically are private, voluntary undertakings. Consequently, federal agencies may use governmental standards adopted by a non-governmental entity, like ISO, regardless of the respect accorded such a body, only as hortatory guidance which must be reevaluated by reference to appropriate statutory standards.[31] This result is self-evident, as ISO, whose members are representatives of

---

Action Plan for Promoting the Use of Environmental Management Systems (EMS) (2001), *available at* http://www.epa.gov/ems/position/action.htm (follow "Goal 3" hyperlink) (last visited Sept. 17, 2011). EMSs are referenced in EPA's audit and self-disclosure policy. *See* "Incentives for Self-Policing: Discovery, Disclosure, Correction and Prevention of Violations", 65 *Federal Register* 19,618, 19,621 (Apr. 11, 2000). EMSs have featured prominently in a variety of EPA corporate excellence programs, the most recent version of which was the National Environmental Performance Track, terminated in 2009 by the Obama administration. *See* U.S. Environmental Protection Agency, Performance Track, available at http://www.epa.gov/performancetrack/ (last visited Sept. 17, 2011).

[30] *See e.g.*, National Technology Transfer and Advancement Act of 1995, 15 U.S.C. § 3701 nt. (2006) (specifying that "all Federal agencies and departments shall use technical standards that are developed or adopted by voluntary consensus standards bodies, using such technical standards as a means to carry out policy objectives or activities determined by the agencies and departments" and that "Federal agencies and departments shall consult with voluntary, private sector, consensus standards bodies and shall . . . participate with such bodies in the development of technical standards"); "OMB Circular No. A-119; Federal Participation in the Development and Use of Voluntary Consensus Standards and in Conformity Assessment Activities", 63 *Federal Register* 8546 (Feb. 19, 1998). Section 6 of the Circular specifies that "[a]ll federal agencies must use voluntary consensus standards in lieu of government-unique standards in their procurement and regulatory activities, except where inconsistent with law or otherwise impractical." 63 *Federal Register* 8546 (Feb. 19, 1998) at 8554. Section 7 states that "[a]gencies must consult with voluntary consensus standards bodies, both domestic and international, and must participate with such bodies in the development of voluntary consensus standards when consultation and participation is in the public interest and is compatible with their missions, authorities, priorities, and budget resources." 63 *Federal Register* 8546 (Feb. 19, 1998) at 8555–56.

[31] *See, e.g.*, "OMB Circular No. A-119; Federal Participation in the Development and Use of Voluntary Consensus Standards and in Conformity Assessment Activities", 63 *Federal Register* 8546 (Feb. 19, 1998) at 8555. ("This policy does not preempt or restrict agencies' authorities and responsibilities to make regulatory decisions authorized by statute. Such regulatory authorities and responsibilities include determining the level of acceptable risk; setting the level of

affected industries, does not necessarily represent the public interest more broadly. Indeed, it is not difficult to imagine a setting in which the array of interests that shape an industry-dominated, voluntary standard-setting process is expressly contrary to the well-being of the public in the United States and abroad. Even so, there is frequently a residual concern about a potentially hidden agenda to substitute ISO standards for federal regulation. Presumably for reasons such as these, federal officials tend to play a deferential role, and U.S. governmental input tends to be of limited importance in the process.[32]

B.   Procedural Character and Substantive Limitations

ISO 14001, unlike a product standard such as film speed, is fundamentally procedural in nature. With the benefit of hindsight, it is perhaps easy to see why this is so. The process of drafting ISO 14001 involved the reconciliation of competing approaches, including in particular the European Eco-Management and Audit Scheme (EMAS),[33] some of which continue to exist as alternatives or supplements to ISO 14001. To that extent, the utility to industry may be maximized and the overlap with regulatory requirements adopted through governmental processes reduced. In particular, an ISO 14001-conforming EMS is designed to help a company achieve its own environmental goals through an iterative process of "continual improvement."[34]

Even so, ISO 14001 has been criticized for its failure to engage with substantive regulatory requirements. Consistent with ISO 14001's systems – as opposed to a substantive – approach, a company may receive ISO

---

protection; and balancing risk, cost, and availability of technology in establishing regulatory standards.")

[32]   At least some knowledgeable observers feel that governmental entities, such as the National Institute of Standards and Technology, should play a more active role in ANSI and, through it, ISO, at least with respect to standard-setting activities like the ISO 14000 series that have public policy implications. Telephone Interview with Ira R. Feldman, President and Senior Counsel, Greentrack Strategies (Feb. 8, 2008).

[33]   *See* Regulation 761/2001/EC of the European Parliament and the Council of 19 March 2001. Allowing Voluntary Participation by Organisations in a Community Eco-Management and Audit Scheme (EMAS), OJ 2001 L114/1. *See generally EMAS: The Community Eco-Management and Audit Scheme*, http://ec.europa.eu/environment/emas/index_en.htm (last visited Sept. 17, 2011).

[34]   ISO 14001, note 6 above, § 3.2 (defining "continual improvement" as a "recurring process of enhancing the environmental management system in order to achieve improvements in overall environmental performance consistent with the organization's environmental policy").

14001 certification even with outstanding regulatory violations.[35] Not surprisingly, this attribute of the ISO standards has been the subject of serious criticism.[36] The public, being unfamiliar with the nuances of the standard and the meaning of ISO certification, may very well be misled into thinking that certification is an indication of superior substantive environmental performance.

Another attribute of ISO 14001 that has been the subject of considerable criticism is the lack of transparency in the process. As they are under development, ISO standards are generally not publicly available. Even the standards themselves are copyrighted and proprietary, and at least in principle must be purchased for use.[37]

The process of preparing an ISO 14001-conforming EMS does not necessarily involve any public participation, and the standard specifies little if any provision of environmentally related information to the public.[38] ISO 14001 calls for an enterprise to make its generic environmental policy available to the public.[39] As to the EMS itself, "[t]he organization shall decide whether to communicate externally about its significant environmental aspects."[40] Otherwise, the only requirement is to "establish, implement and maintain a procedure(s) for . . . receiving, documenting and responding to relevant communication from external interested parties,"[41] presumably including the public.[42]

ISO certification is also somewhat less effective than might appear at first blush. The ISO 14001 auditing and certification process is similar in concept to a financial audit. As demonstrated by recent public accounting scandals, there may be good cause for concern about the existence of a

---

[35] *See, e.g.*, Gerrard, note 2 above, § 6A.04[2].

[36] *E.g.*, Naomi Roht-Arriaza, "Shifting the Point of Regulation: The International Organization for Standardization and Global Lawmaking on Trade and the Environment", 22 *Ecology Law Quarterly* (1995) 479, at 534–38.

[37] Int'l Org. for Standardization & Int'l Electrotechnical Comm'n, Copyright, Standards and the Internet, *available at* http://www.iso.org/iso/copyright_infor mation_brochure.pdf (last visited Sept. 17, 2011).

[38] *See generally* ISO 14063, note 13 above. ISO 14063 addresses the transmittal of environmentally related information, including to the public. See ISO 14063, note 13 above, § 1. That standard, however, contains no substantive minimum standard for transparency, but instead describes good practice standards for environmental communication policies and approaches if an entity chooses to undertake such activities.

[39] ISO 14001, note 6 above, § 4.2(g).

[40] ISO 14001, note 6 above, § 4.4.3.

[41] ISO 14001, note 6 above, § 4.4.3, 4.4.3(b).

[42] *But see* note 38 above and accompanying text (ISO 14063 specifies form of, but not need for, environmental communication).

multiplicity of auditing and certifying entities competing with each other for business.[43] The disclosure of substantive regulatory violations that might be identified during an audit is a particularly sensitive issue. Such a situation can trigger a race-to-the-bottom dynamic, in which companies seeking certification may engage in "forum shopping" by choosing registrars (certifying bodies or auditors) that are perceived as likely to apply less rather than more rigorous approaches to the certification process.[44]

The certification process itself may give little reason for confidence, at least to third parties who might rely upon it as an indication of quality control. To facilitate external evaluation, the standards themselves must be "auditable" – meaning capable of unbiased verification.[45] While ostensibly facilitating objectivity, this feature can encourage a kind of checklist approach to the audit process based on items whose presence or absence can be impartially confirmed in a binary on/off mode.[46] In the evaluation of training courses provided by registrars to auditors, for instance, this may translate into factors such as whether the instructor spent the required minimum amount of time with students.[47] Consistent with the

---

[43]   In the United States, registrars are accredited to award ISO 14001 certification by the American National Standards Institute-American Society for Quality (ANSI-ASQ) National Accreditation Board (formerly the American National Standards Institute-Registrar Accreditation Board National Accreditation Program (ANSI-RAB NAP)). *See* ANAB, http://www.anab.org (last visited Sept. 17, 2011). As of this writing, the ANSI-ASQ National Accreditation Board has accredited about 25 registrars to perform ISO 14001 audits. *Id.* (follow "Directory" hyperlink; then search for standard "ISO 14001"). Some of those companies are headquartered abroad in countries such as Canada, the United Kingdom, Mexico, Korea and China. The potential for registrars (certification bodies or auditors) to be accredited by counterparts of the ANSI-RAB NAP in foreign countries in turn can trigger "forum shopping" at the next rung up the institutional ladder. *Id.* (follow "MCAA" hyperlink).

[44]   *See* Briggs, note 17 above, 67–68 (noting that "the underlying competitiveness of the certification industry can drive auditors to cut audit durations," and noting pressure on auditors to refrain from issuing nonconformances (NCRs)).

[45]   *See* ISO 19011, note 15 above. ("Guidelines for Quality and/or Environmental Management Systems Auditing.").

[46]   *See* Briggs, note 17 above, 67 ("[U]sers want verification that an EMS results in improved performance, not just conformance to requirements during a certification audit. Because there is inconsistency in results, users are questioning the value of accredited certification.").

[47]   *See generally* Registrar Accreditation Board and Quality Society of Australasia International (RABSQA), *Training Course Certification: Training Provider Administration Requirements* (2007), *available at* http://www.rabqsa.com/docs/downloads/TCD62.pdf (standards for certifying training providers) (last visited Sept. 17, 2011).

basic approach, qualitative criteria such as teaching effectiveness are not taken into account. The emphasis in the certification process consequently tends to be on rote satisfaction of objectively verifiable requirements rather than on exceeding or surpassing minimum standards.

IV. SWORDS, SHIELDS, AND TRADE AGREEMENTS

The motivation for the adoption of ISO standards, even those within the 14000 series, may be quite diverse. ISO standards on greenhouse gases do not require any particular substantive performance requirements. Instead, these standards address primarily the integrity of data reporting. Consequently, they would appear to be of limited application, primarily in settings such as the calculation of offsets and trading of emissions rights where a standard format for collecting and reporting data is required.

ISO standards on eco-labeling, by contrast, appear to have been motivated by a concern to rein in or discipline a proliferation of divergent approaches, which among other things could operate as trade barriers. While the biofuels initiative in TC 28 is at an early stage of development and little information is publicly available, the likely scope will include harmonization of standards and test methods.[48] This effort appears to have been commenced in response to a high current level of interest in public policy for biofuels and a variety of proposals for private voluntary certification and labeling schemes for them.

As demonstrated by these latter initiatives, ISO standards may well be intended to establish not only a floor, but also a ceiling. That is, part of the motivation for their adoption may be to encourage uniformity as a response to a proliferation of divergent approaches. From this point of view, the concern is that the effect of ISO standards may very well operate so as to impede the development of creative new approaches to environmental problems.

A. Transformative Effect of Trade Agreements

In the mid-1990s – probably not entirely by chance coinciding with the development of the ISO 14000 series – the public policy effect of ISO standards received considerable impetus in the form of the adoption of two new international trade agreements: the North American Free

---

[48] *See* note 19 above.

Trade Agreement (NAFTA),[49] and the Uruguay Round of Multilateral Negotiations in GATT,[50] which created the World Trade Organization (WTO). Chapter Nine of NAFTA addresses "technical barriers to trade," as does the WTO Agreement on Technical Barriers to Trade (TBT Agreement).[51] A wide variety of regulatory requirements that have environmental or public health implications, including specifications for consumer products and children's toys, appliance efficiency criteria, and vehicle fuel efficiency standards, are potentially covered by these requirements.[52]

International obligations or "disciplines" on trade are almost exclusively "negative," in the sense that they establish constraints on governmental action. A partial analogy can be found in the Dormant Commerce Clause of the U.S. Constitution,[53] which places similar limitations on state-level regulation even in the absence of congressional legislation. Trade agreements encourage liberalized or free trade through requirements that limit governmental intrusion into what otherwise would be a free market. From an environmental point of view, this phenomenon is the equivalent of deregulation – in the sense of reducing the level of governmental intervention in the market in the form of tariffs or other prescriptive requirements – and trade agreements by virtue of their negative obligations are inherently deregulatory. This momentum largely explains the phenomenon of globalization, at least as it has been defined for the past decade or so:

---

[49]   *E.g.*, North American Free Trade Agreement, U.S.-Can.-Mex., 17 December 1992, in force 1 January 1994, 32 *International Legal Materials* (1993) 289 [hereinafter NAFTA].

[50]   *See* Final Act Embodying the Results of the Uruguay Round of Multilateral Trade Negotiations, 15 April 1994, in force 1 January 1995, 1867 *United Nations Treaty Series* 14; Marrakesh Agreement Establishing the World Trade Organization, 15 April 1994, in force 1 January 1995, 1867 *United Nations Treaty Series* 154.

[51]   *See* NAFTA, note 49 above, ch. 9; Agreement on Technical Barriers to Trade, 15 April 1994, in force 1 January 1995, 1868 *United Nations Treaty Series* 120 [hereinafter TBT Agreement].

[52]   The TBT Agreement applies to all products in international trade and governs a "technical regulation," which is defined as an instrument which "lays down product characteristics or their related processes and production methods, including the applicable administrative provisions, with which compliance is mandatory. It may also include or deal exclusively with terminology, symbols, packaging, marking or labelling requirements as they apply to a product, process or production method." TBT Agreement, note 51 above, Annex 1, ¶ 1 ("Terms and their Definitions for the Purpose of This Agreement").

[53]   *See, e.g., City of Philadelphia v. New Jersey*, 437 U.S. 617, 622–23 (1978) (applying Dormant Commerce Clause to interstate trade in waste).

getting governments out of the business of impeding private interactions and transactions, thereby facilitating their global reach.

Environmental protection by contrast anticipates affirmative governmental intervention in the marketplace to offset market failures. That explains the clash between the two approaches: one operates to disable governmental action, while the other depends on invigorating government. Obligations in trade agreements *proscribe* certain governmental behaviors that impede trade, while environmental laws *prescribe* affirmative governmental actions to protect public health and ecosystems. In other words, free trade agreements do not contain any affirmative obligations to protect the environment or public health; rather, they establish constraints on the capacity of member states to implement domestic regulatory standards.[54] Like most international trade agreements, the WTO TBT Agreement is asymmetric, in that it contains no minimum standards of performance in the field of environment or in most other areas of social and regulatory policy.

Consistent with that approach, the WTO TBT Agreement defines "standards," as that term is used in that text, to include voluntary guidelines adopted by an "international standardizing body,"[55] a term which was expressly intended to include ISO.[56] Although standards adopted by ISO are non-binding instruments addressed directly to private entities, the TBT Agreement then goes on to require the utilization of "relevant international standards" where they exist in promulgating governmentally mandated regulatory requirements.[57] Governmental regulations that conform to the standards adopted by such an international standardizing

---

[54]   *See, e.g.*, Douglas J. Caldwell and David A. Wirth, "Trade and the Environment: Equilibrium or Imbalance?", 17 *Michigan Journal of International Law* (1996) 563, 586 (book review).

[55]   TBT Agreement, note 51 above, at Annex 1, ¶ 2 ("Terms and Their Definitions for the Purpose of This Agreement."). According to the TBT Agreement, a "standard" is a

> [d]ocument approved by a recognized body, that provides, for common and repeated use, rules, guidelines or characteristics for products or related processes and production methods, with which compliance is not mandatory. It may also include or deal exclusively with terminology, symbols, packaging, marking or labelling requirements as they apply to a product, process or production method.

[56]   *See* TBT Agreement, note 51 above, at Annex 1, ¶ 2 (expressly referencing "the sixth edition of the ISO/IEC Guide 2: 1991, General Terms and Their Definitions Concerning Standardization and Related Activities").

[57]   TBT Agreement, note 51 above, Art. 2.4.

body are entitled to a rebuttable presumption of validity.[58] To justify a departure from international standards, presumably because they are insufficiently rigorous, a WTO member would have to demonstrate that a harmonized international standard "would be an ineffective or inappropriate means for the fulfilment of the legitimate objectives pursued."[59] The WTO jurisprudence interpreting this provision suggests that the threshold for justifying a departure from international standards is high.[60]

Thanks to the structure of the TBT Agreement, those national regulatory requirements that are not based on the output, when it exists, of such a body are therefore particularly vulnerable to challenge as unnecessary obstacles to international trade. And the sorts of governmental requirements that are most likely to create impediments to international trade are those that are more rigorous than the international requirements, which may well be the product of a least-common-denominator consensus in an industry-dominated forum. The result is that, through a trade agreement, the expectations of what, at least from the point of view of the United States, is a *private* standardizing organization are transformed into an outer limit of rigor – a ceiling – for *public* regulation to protect health and environment domestically.

Initially, the requirements of the Uruguay Round TBT Agreement and other trade agreements may appear to be similar to those in the United States, such as OMB Circular A-119, which counsel reliance on ISO standards to the extent consistent with statutory mandates.[61] In actuality, however, the two situations are very different. While authorizing consistency where possible with ISO standards as non-binding advisory guidelines, the OMB Circular, as it must, reasserts the primacy of congressionally enacted legislative requirements.[62] By contrast, NAFTA and the WTO TBT Agreement adopt the *private* standard as a reference point and

---

[58]   TBT Agreement, note 51 above, Art. 2.5.

[59]   TBT Agreement, note 51 above, Art 2.4. The analogous passage in NAFTA sets out a similar approach. NAFTA, note 49 above, ch. 9, arts. 905 and 915 (defining "standard" as "a document, approved by a recognized body, that provides, for common and repeated use, rules, guidelines or characteristics . . . with which compliance is not mandatory").

[60]   *See, e.g.,* WTO Appellate Body Report, *European Communities – Trade Description of Sardines*, WT/DS231/AB/R (Sept. 26, 2002) (requiring application of non-binding standard promulgated by Codex Alimentarius Commission) [hereinafter *EC – Sardines*].

[61]   *See* "OMB Circular A–119; Federal Participation in the Development and Use of Voluntary Consensus Standards and in Conformity Assessment Activities", 63 *Federal Register* 8546, at 8554 (Feb. 19, 1998).

[62]   Note 61 above.

require *public* authorities to justify departures, especially those tending in the direction of more rigorous requirements, from those privately agreed expectations. This situation in effect bootstraps a non-governmental standard into one with binding significance for governmentally established regulatory requirements, at least as a matter of international law.

Departures from the benchmark standard by domestic regulatory authorities can then be challenged by foreign governments through the trade agreement dispute settlement process, among the more efficacious known in the international legal system.[63] In other words, operating through the TBT Agreement, non-binding ISO standards may acquire international legal significance, may be transformed from minimum standards of performance into regulatory ceilings from which governments must justify departure in terms of greater rigor, and, at least from the U.S. point of view, may metamorphose from strictly private, non-governmental instruments to standards with international legal significance.

On the domestic level, the results of WTO and NAFTA dispute settlement processes – the international equivalent of judicial opinions – do not have the force of law.[64] They do, however, create serious expectations on the international level, and are possibly binding as a matter of international law.[65] A finding by an international trade agreement dispute

---

[63] *See* Understanding on Rules and Procedures Governing the Settlement of Disputes, April 15, 1994, Marrakesh Agreement Establishing the World Trade Organization, note 50 above at Annex 2, Legal Instruments – Results of Uruguay Round (containing the "Understanding on Rules and Procedures Governing the Settlement of Disputes"). *See generally* David Palmeter and Petros C. Mavroidis, *Dispute Settlement in the World Trade Organization: Practice and Procedure* (Boston: Kluwer Law International, 1999) (providing analysis of WTO dispute settlement procedures).

[64] 19 U.S.C. § 3312 (2006) (relationship of NAFTA to federal and state law); 19 U.S.C. § 3512 (2006) (relationship of Uruguay Round agreements to federal and state law); cf. *Medellin v. Texas*, 552 U.S. 491, 510-514 (2008) (domestic effect of decisions of International Court of Justice).

[65] *See, e.g.*, John H. Jackson, "International Law Status of WTO Dispute Settlement Reports: Obligation to Comply or Option to 'Buy Out?'" 98 *American Journal of International Law* (2004) 109, 117–23 (results of WTO dispute settlement proceedings binding under international law). *But see* Judith Hippler Bello, "The WTO Dispute Settlement Understanding: Less Is More", 90 *American Journal of International Law* (1996) 416, 416–18 (results of WTO dispute settlement proceedings not binding under international law, but merely give rise to right to retaliate); Warren F. Schwartz and Alan O. Sykes, "The Economic Structure of Renegotiation and Dispute Resolution in the World Trade Organization", 31 *Journal of Legal Studies* (2002) S179, S181 (WTO dispute settlement system better understood as providing for "efficient breach").

settlement panel or the WTO's Appellate Body that the United States is not complying with its international obligations also engages serious separation of powers considerations, and the courts may be reluctant to impede implementation by the Executive Branch, the "sole organ" of the Nation in foreign affairs.[66] The back-impact of international trade agreement dispute settlement proceedings within the United States consequently may be considerable. The limited jurisprudence on the subject suggests that, although WTO panel and Appellate Body reports do not have the force of law, reviewing courts are inclined to give them considerable deference,[67] presumably so as to avoid interference with the Executive's prerogative in foreign affairs and to avoid the appearance of judicial management of the foreign relations of the United States.

B.   Eco-Labeling

ISO standards for "eco-labeling" illustrate this phenomenon well. Eco-labeling schemes, by communicating distinctions in similar products based on relative environmental impact, are designed to inform consumers of environmentally preferable product choices. Foreign eco-labels have been the subject of criticism from U.S. industry, which has asserted in particular that a governmentally sponsored, voluntary program currently implemented by the European Union discriminates against U.S. exports.[68]

Eco-labeling is a good example of the interaction between international trade agreements and private voluntary standards. Operating through the WTO TBT Agreement as standards adopted by an international standardizing body, eco-labeling criteria published by ISO may very well require governments to justify departures from those private, hortatory principles adopted primarily by industry.

ISO standards govern unilateral environmental claims made by manu-

---

[66]   *See United States v. Curtiss-Wright Exp. Corp.*, 299 U.S. 304, 319 (1936).

[67]   *E.g., George E. Warren Corp. v. EPA*, 159 F.3d 616, 623–24 (D.C. Cir. 1998) (judicial review of reformulated gasoline rule promulgated under Clean Air Act after successful WTO challenge and adverse WTO Appellate Body report). *See generally* Patrick C. Reed, "Relationship of WTO Obligations to U.S. International Trade Law: Internationalist Vision Meets Domestic Reality", 38 *Georgetown Journal of International Law* (2006) 209 (analyzing domestic effect of WTO dispute settlement proceedings in U.S. court proceedings).

[68]   *See* Regulation 1980/2000/EC of the European Parliament and of the Council of 17 July 2000 on a Revised Community Eco-label Award Scheme, OJ 2000 L 237/1. *See generally European Union Eco-label Home Page*, http://ec.europa.eu/environment/ecolabel/index_en.htm (last visited Sept. 17, 2011).

facturers, known as "type II" labels.[69] They also address governmentally or privately established schemes that include a single mark, such as the U.S. Government-sponsored, voluntary Energy Star logo for identifying energy-efficient personal computers.[70] These are known as "type I" labels.[71] "Type III" labels, also governed by an ISO standard,[72] transmit quantified information in a manner similar to the identification of fat, carbohydrates, and protein on nutrition labels in the United States.[73] During the drafting process that led to the adoption of ISO's eco-labeling standards, there was express concern for constraining or "disciplining" the potential abuse of environmental labeling schemes as unjustified barriers to international trade.

As a consequence, according to ISO standards, eco-labels must be "accurate, verifiable, relevant, not misleading,"[74] and "based on scientific methodology that is sufficiently thorough and comprehensive to support the claim."[75] Those requirements all sound more than reasonable in the abstract, but each must be understood as a negative discipline. That is, if a label is *not* "relevant," then the label violates the standard and potentially the TBT Agreement as well. These negative tests can be adjudicated by international trade agreement dispute settlement bodies.[76] When applied to a situation such as precautionary labeling, among the least intrusive of regulatory interventions, the situation becomes even more complex in areas such as the evaluation of policy-relevant science that by definition involve a measure of judgment.

---

[69]   ISO 14021, note 11 above, § 1. Among the claims potentially covered by this Standard are self-declared or self-certified conformance to ISO 14001. *See* text accompanying note 25 above.

[70]   *See History of Energy Star*, http://www.energystar.gov/index.cfm?c=about. ab_history (last visited Sept. 17, 2011).

[71]   ISO 14024, note 11 above, § 3.1.

[72]   ISO 14025, note 11 above, § 1.

[73]   *See generally* Center for Food Safety and Applied Nutrition, Department of Health and Human Services, *How to Understand and Use the Nutrition Facts Label 1–3* (2004), http://www.cfsan.fda.gov/~acrobat/foodlab.pdf (last visited Sept. 17, 2011).

[74]   ISO 14020, note 11 above, § 4.2.1.

[75]   ISO 14020, note 11 above, § 4.4.1.

[76]   *E.g. EC – Sardines*, note 60 above. *See generally* Palmeter and Mavroidis, note 63 above (detailing WTO dispute settlement procedures).

C.   Life Cycle Assessment

In contrast to the situation with eco-labeling, in which ISO standards act as a "sword" with which one state may challenge another's domestic regulation, this same structure may act as a "shield" in situations in which a state chooses to rely on international standards. A good example of this latter phenomenon is California's new Low-Carbon Fuel Standard (LCFS),[77] a requirement designed to reduce the carbon intensity – carbon emitted per unit of fuel consumed – of fuels in California by ten percent by the year 2020.[78]

Similar to the approach employed with automobile fuel efficiency requirements on the federal level, the LCFS applies an averaging approach, which means that each provider must meet the reduction target as measured against the totality of the fuels it sells on the California market (as opposed to, say, in each gallon). The LCFS specifies application of a life cycle analysis (LCA) so as to take into account emissions not only from combustion, but also production and transport, of fuels.[79] These factors include emissions associated with extraction, protection of sensitive lands and ecosystems, and a variety of other emissions which, in the case of imported fuels, are physically located in the country of export.[80]

One of the basic obligations found in international trade agreements is the "national treatment" discipline, specifying non-discriminatory treatment of imported products by comparison with their domestically produced counterparts.[81] Similarly, the "most-favored nation" discipline requires states

---

[77]   California Alternative and Renewable Fuel, Vehicle Technology, Clean Air, and Carbon Reduction Act of 2007, California Health and Safety Code §§ 44270–44274.5 (West Supp. 2010); 17 California Code of Regulations 95,481 (implementing regulation); *see* California Air Resources Board. And California Energy Commission, *State Alternative Fuels Plan 78–80* (2007), *available at* http://www.energy.ca.gov/2007publications/CEC-600-2007-011/CEC-600-2007-011-CM F.PDF (last visited Sept. 17, 2011).

[78]   David Crane and Brian Prusnek, Office of the Governor of the State of California, *The Role of a Low Carbon Fuel Standard in Reducing Greenhouse Gas Emissions and Protecting our Economy* 1 (Jan. 8, 2007), *available at* http://www. mnclimatechange.us/ewebeditpro/items/O3F14021.pdf (last visited Sept. 17, 2011).

[79]   *See generally* TIAX LLC, *Full Fuel Cycle Assessment: Well-to-Wheels Energy Inputs, Emissions, and Water Impacts* (2007), *available at* http://www. energy.ca.gov/2007publications/CEC-600-2007-004/CEC-600-2007-004-REV. PDF (providing a detailed life cycle analysis under various approaches) (last visited Sept. 17, 2011).

[80]   Note 79 above at 73–76.

[81]   General Agreement on Tariffs and Trade, Art. 3, 30 October 1947, in force 1 January 1948, 55 *United Nations Treaty Series* 194, *as incorporated into*

of import to refrain from discriminatory treatment among products on the basis of their national origin, as in preferential treatment for Mexican oil by comparison with Saudi oil.[82] As demonstrated by a well-known dispute involving the U.S. embargo of shrimp harvested in a manner that harms endangered sea turtles,[83] so-called "process and production methods" (PPMs) – which regulate how an imported product is produced as opposed to its content – may be suspect from a trade point of view.

ISO standards for life cycle assessment, like those for eco-labeling, are undoubtedly intended to discipline or constrain the potential for abuse. At the same time, the ISO methodology for conducting an LCA is remarkably malleable. In particular, a life cycle assessment that conforms to ISO standards "assesses, in a systematic way, the environmental aspects and impacts of product systems, from raw material acquisition to final disposal, in accordance with the stated goal and scope."[84] An ISO-conforming LCA is characterized by "flexibility,"[85] "addresses potential environmental impacts,"[86] and includes within its scope the "acquisition of raw materials; . . . distribution/transportation; [and] disposal of process wastes and products."[87] If ISO standards meet California's regulatory needs, and California chooses to rely upon them in performing the LCA called for by the program, then the same WTO TBT Agreement that transforms ISO standards for eco-labeling into a "sword" could very likely tend to shield California's Low-Carbon Fuel Standard from a trade-based challenge.

CONCLUSION

By adopting the 14000 series of standards on environmental management, the International Organization for Standardization (ISO) has decisively moved into a major public policy arena, not just in the United States but in other countries as well. ISO is an important forum for harmonizing private voluntary initiatives from around the world. The benefits of laying down international minimum standards through ISO are substantial,

---

Final Act Embodying the Results of the Uruguay Round of Multilateral Trade Negotiations, note 50 above.

[82] General Agreement on Tariffs and Trade, Art. I, note 81 above.

[83] WTO Panel Report, *United States – Sections 7.16 of the Import Prohibition of Certain Shrimp and Shrimp Products*, WT/DS58/R (May 15, 1998).

[84] ISO 14040, note 12 above, § 4.3(a).

[85] Note 12 above § 4.3(g).

[86] Note 12 above § 4.3(i).

[87] Note 12 above § 5.2.3.

although there are also significant concerns about the potential impacts of non-binding standards of the ISO variety on public regulation.

Simultaneously with the adoption of ISO's standards on the environment, major new trade agreements that created the World Trade Organization and encouraged the liberalization of trade in North America also addressed measures such as food safety standards and eco-labeling with new international disciplines. By expressly referencing ISO standards, these international trade agreements have created a new category of legal and policy questions. ISO's private voluntary standards can act as ceilings on the rigor of governmentally established requirements, as in the case of eco-labeling, which can be used as swords by one state to challenge the national measures of another. Through the same process, as in the case of life cycle analysis, ISO standards may act as a floor, which in turn can shield national measures from attack by reference to trade-based tests.

Private voluntary standards, such as those published by ISO, do not necessarily fall neatly into the categories of "swords" or "shields," but, indeed, can simultaneously operate as both. For example, ISO standards for life cycle assessment, as they operate through the TBT Agreement, are undoubtedly intended to discipline or constrain the potential for abuse. To that extent, ISO standards operate as a regulatory ceiling, which can be used as "swords" by one state to challenge the national measures of another. But they can equally well insulate life cycle analyses that conform to international standards from trade-based challenges emanating from abroad.

This phenomenon, not to mention its consequences, is seriously underappreciated by many constituencies, including legislators, regulators, agency officials, and the environmental community. As ISO quietly proceeds to move forward with yet another series of standards on social responsibility, we the public may discover only too late that important public policies are affected in a forum that receives little public scrutiny, that is largely inaccessible except to the business community, and that does not necessarily reflect the public interest. There is no doubt that efforts with significant public policy consequences will continue in ISO, and most likely will expand. What those undertakings mean for efforts to promote environmental sustainability is, however, indeterminate.

During the debate over NAFTA, George Will praised an agreement designed to "propel a free society into an exhilaratingly unknowable future."[88] Perhaps nowhere is the effect of international trade agreements

---

[88]   George Will, "Judicial Activism Aims at an Impossible Task", *Newsday*, July 8, 1993, 102.

more "unknowable" than in the effect of international, private, voluntary standards on domestic, mandatory, governmentally established regulation. Whether, a decade and a half after the entry into force of these agreements, this effect on balance is "exhilarating" or the opposite is still an open question.

6. Law and economics of the SPS Agreement: a critical perspective
*Alessandra Arcuri**

I. INTRODUCTION

In high-tech and globalized societies the realm of environment, health and safety regulation (hereinafter risk regulation) is unsurprisingly contentious. On one hand the development of new technologies lies at the very heart of contemporary economies; on the other hand citizens are becoming increasingly aware of the risks that these technologies entail. Some groups will profit from technology while other groups will likely bear the costs. The implementation of certain safety standards may be very costly for the industry, but at the same time the lack of such standards may cause outrage among citizens and widespread damage across society. This type of conflict commonly accompanies the decision-making process about risk within a jurisdiction.

To add fuel to the fire, the process of economic globalization driven by the World Trade Organization (WTO) challenges the current differences in risk governance among jurisdictions. WTO Members, in fact, are bound by the obligations established by the Agreement on Sanitary and Phytosanitary Standards (SPS). This Agreement carries with it the potential of (re-)designing the risk regulation policy at the global level, because it demands consideration of international standards and it establishes specific procedures that need to be followed by Members when designing their risk regulation measures. The enforcement of these rules has already shown the tensions underpinning this body of law. The WTO disputes between the European Union (EU) and the United States (US) over the use of hormones in beef for growth promotion purposes and over the marketing and approval of genetically modified organisms (GMOs) are icons of these inter-jurisdictional conflicts and differences in risk governance.

*   I am grateful to the editors of the volume as well as to Ellen Hey, Roger Van den Bergh, Michael Faure, Donatella Porrini, Alessio Pacces and Felice Simonelli for insightful comments on earlier drafts of this chapter. Thanks also to Susan A. Russell for the language editing and to Jamaal Mohuddy and Sascha Grievink for research assistance. All errors remain the sole responsibility of the author. This

This chapter uses Law and Economics theory to examine some of the issues raised by the implementation of the SPS Agreement. While Law and Economics has been little applied to the field of public international law and international economic law,[1] some scholars have already used economic analysis of law to shed light on the linkage between risk policies and international trade law.[2] Two interrelated questions have been explored by this scholarship. The first is whether it is desirable to harmonize risk regulation via the WTO. The second question studies the desirability of resorting to 'a universal scale for assessing the legitimacy of health and safety precautions by reference to an objective cost benefit analysis'.[3] The goal of this chapter is to critically discuss this body of research and, on this basis, provide an answer to the above questions.

The chapter is structured as follows. The next section (II) presents the basic legal architecture of the SPS Agreement, conceptualized in light of the harmonization debate. Section III provides an answer to the first question concerning the economic desirability of harmonizing risk regulation via the WTO. Building on previous Law and Economics literature, it is argued that striving for a WTO-driven harmonization of risk regulation is not welfare-enhancing. While full harmonization may not be desirable, it remains important for the WTO Panels and Appellate Body (AB) (hereinafter generally referred to as 'WTO Courts') to screen out protectionist SPS measures. Some scholars have argued that the best criterion to achieve this goal is to rely on cost-benefit analysis. In contrast to this scholarship, in section IV, it is contended that cost-benefit analysis should not be taken as the criterion to assess the legitimacy of SPS measures. The chapter concludes by setting forth a proposal for a regime that balances the WTO trade-related concerns with the interest of its Members in establishing their own risk policies.

---

research was supported by an EUR Fellowship granted by Erasmus University Rotterdam, which is gratefully acknowledged.

[1]   A number of important contributions in this field have been delivered during a Symposium organized to draw attention to the potential to apply Law and Economics to the field of public international law; see van Aaken, Engel and Ginsburg (2008); several essays on this topic are collected in an edited volume Posner (2010); for a seminal work in this field see, Bagwell, Mavroidis and Staiger (2002).

[2]   See, for instance, Guzman (2004); Trebilcock and Soloway (2002); Trebilcock, and Howse (1998); Tracthman (2007).

[3]   Collins (2009), 1071 (in abstract).

II.   THE SPS AGREEMENT: BETWEEN HARMONIZATION AND REGULATORY AUTONOMY

The obligations of the SPS Agreement include but are by no means confined to the principle of non-discrimination. In addition to the basic obligation of not using SPS measures to discriminate (Article 2.3), the SPS Agreement indicates three criteria that Members should respect when adopting a sanitary or phytosanitary measure. 'Members shall ensure that any sanitary or phytosanitary measure is applied only to the extent *necessary to protect human, animal or plant life or health*, is *based on scientific principles* and is *not maintained without sufficient scientific evidence*, except as provided for in paragraph 7 of Article 5' (Article 2.2, emphasis added). The Agreement further clarifies that measures conforming to international standards shall be deemed necessary to protect human, animal or plant life or health (Article 3.2). The new obligations created by the SPS Agreement well exemplify the 'post-discriminatory' dimension of WTO law.

The basic framework set up by the SPS Agreement can be described as two-tiered because two alternative courses of action are left open for WTO Members.[4] On one side, Members can align their SPS measures to international standards. This option is likely to be the safest because internationally harmonized measures are deemed necessary to protect human or animal health and in conformity with the whole SPS Agreement and the GATT (Article 3.2); consequently it would be very hard to challenge them before the WTO Courts. This Chapter defines this alternative as the *harmonization rule*. On the other side, Members can adopt SPS measures that diverge from international standards, but they should be able to justify their measures in relation to the three criteria listed by Article 2.2 read in conjunction with Articles 3.3 and 5. This alternative will be dubbed the *autonomy rule*. Under this second option, SPS measures are more prone to be challenged because of the ambiguities intrinsic to the criteria listed by Article 2.2. Table 6.1 illustrates this two-tiered framework.

This framework creates new boundaries for the health, safety and

---

[4]   This framework simplifies all the options available to Members. The Appellate Body in *EC-Hormones* has identified three alternatives: 'based on', 'conforming to' and 'deviating from' international standards. I treat the 'based on' and 'conforming to' alternatives together because the practical relevance of this distinction may be less salient than what it may appear at first sight. This issue is further discussed at the end of the next section (section II.A); Appellate Body Report, *EC Measures Concerning Meat and Meat Products (Hormones)*, WT/DS26/AB/R, WT/DS48/AB/R, adopted 16 January 1998, AB-1997-4 (*EC – Hormones*).

Table 6.1

Two-tiered SPS legal framework	Harmonization with international standards (Articles 3.1 and 3.2) (Harmonization rule)
	SPS measures diverging from international legal standards (Articles 2.2 and 3.3 read in conjunction with Article 5) (Autonomy rule)

environmental policies of WTO Members insofar as these policies should be based either on international standards or comply with the criteria established by Article 2.2. Considering the boundaries created by the outlined two-tiered framework and the wide membership of the WTO, it is not an overstatement to say that the SPS Agreement has the *potential* for (re-)defining worldwide risk policies. To assess the implications of the SPS Agreement for worldwide risk policy one needs to fully understand the possible interpretations of the abovementioned rules. To better unfold the various aspects of the SPS Agreement framework, the harmonization and the autonomy rules will be analyzed separately with an intermezzo, which outlines their relationship. The disputes that thus far have been adjudicated under the SPS Agreement will be used in the following discussion to delineate the contours of the harmonization rule, the autonomy rule and their relationship respectively.[5]

---

[5]   These include: *EC – Hormones*, note 4 above; Panel Report, *European Communities – Measures Affecting the Approval and Marketing of Biotech Products*, WT/DS291/R, WT/DS292/R, WT/DS293/R, adopted 29 September 2006, (*EC – Biotech*); Appellate Body Report, *Japan – Measures Affecting Agricultural Product*, WT/DS76/AB/R, adopted 19 March 1999, DSR 1999:I, 277, (*Japan – Agricultural Products II*); Appellate Body Report, *Japan – Measures Affecting the Importation of Apples,* WT/DS245/AB/R, adopted 10 December 2003, DSR 2003:IX, 4391, (*Japan – Apples*); Appellate Body Report, *Australia – Measures Affecting Importation of Salmon*, WT/DS18/AB/R, adopted 6 November 1998, DSR 1998:VIII, 3327 (*Australia – Salmon*); Panel Reports, *Canada/United States – Continued Suspension of Obligations in the EC – Hormones Disputes*, WT/DS320/R, WT/DS321/R, adopted 16 October 2008, AB-2008-5, (*US – Continued Suspension*); Panel Report, *Australia – Measures Affecting the Importation of Apples from New Zealand*, WT/DS367/R, adopted 9 August 2010; Appellate Body Report, *Australia – Measures Affecting the Importation of Apples from New Zealand*, WT/DS367/AB/R, adopted 29 November 2010, AB-2010-2 (*Australia – Imported Apples*). Note that by 2010, the SPS Agreement was invoked in 37 disputes; cfr. the database compiled by WorldTradeLaw.net, available at: http://www.worldtradelaw.net/dsc/database/agreementcount.asp.

A.   Harmonization with International Standards

The harmonization of SPS measures is one of the general goals listed in the Preamble of the SPS Agreement.[6] As previously mentioned, the most relevant provisions for harmonization are contained in Article 3 paragraphs 1 and 2 of the SPS Agreement, which provide that:

> (1) [t]o harmonize sanitary and phytosanitary measures . . . Members shall *base* their sanitary or phytosanitary measures *on* international standards, guidelines or recommendations, where they exist; . . .
> (2) Sanitary or phytosanitary measures which *conform to* international standards, guidelines or recommendations shall be deemed to be necessary to protect human, animal or plant life or health, and presumed to be consistent with the relevant provisions of this Agreement and of GATT 1994.[7]

Article 3.3 adds that Members may introduce SPS measures 'which result in a higher level of sanitary or phytosanitary protection than would be achieved by measures based on the relevant international standards'. The Article further specifies the conditions that should be respected if Members adopt standards resulting in higher levels of protection than international ones.

From a first reading of these provisions it can be inferred that Members are *not obliged* to harmonize; the SPS Agreement, in fact, does not contain any explicit provision in this respect. Even if not obliged, however, Members are encouraged to engage in a process of harmonization. In this sense, the harmonization rule may have a relevant influence on Members' risk policies. By creating a presumption of compliance for measures that *conform to* international standards (i.e. are identical to international standards, Article 3.2), incentives are given to Members towards a strong form of harmonization. The strength of these incentives will depend on the conditions imposed on Members by the autonomy rule, an issue discussed in more detail below. Here it can be noted that the stricter the standard of review applied under the autonomy rule, the higher the incentives for Members to adopt SPS measures that conform to international standards.

---

[6]   In the sixth preambular paragraph of the SPS Agreement we read: '*Desiring* to further the use of harmonized sanitary and phytosanitary measures between Members, on the basis of international standards, guidelines and recommendations developed by the relevant international organizations, including the Codex Alimentarius Commission, the International Office of Epizootics, and the relevant international and regional organizations operating within the framework of the International Plant Protection Convention, without requiring Members to change their appropriate level of protection of human, animal or plant life or health.'

[7]   Emphasis added.

The Appellate Body (AB) in one of the most influential rulings in this area, *EC–Hormones*, adopted a cautious approach in relation to the harmonization rule. Most notably, the Panel's finding that the meaning of the expressions 'based on' and 'conform to' is identical was reversed by the AB. The AB's interpretation of the wording of Articles 3.1 and 3.2 appears to leave a wider margin of discretion to Members that decide to engage in a process of harmonization; these countries shall *base* SPS measures *on* international standards. 'A measure . . . *based on* the same standard *might not conform* to that standard, as where only some, not all, of the elements of the standard are incorporated into the measure.'[8] In this way the AB tried to flesh out the harmonization rule. Even more,

> [i]t is clear to us that harmonization of SPS measures of Members on the basis of international standards is projected in the Agreement, as a *goal*, yet to be realized *in the future*. To read Article 3.1 as requiring Members to harmonize their SPS measures *by conforming those measures with international standards*, guidelines and recommendations, *in the here and now*, is, in effect, to vest such international standards, guidelines and recommendations (which are by the terms of the Codex *recommendatory* in form and nature) with *obligatory* force and effect.[9]

The practical relevance of this interpretation appears less far-reaching than the AB's wording seems to suggest. In practice, Members will benefit from a safe harbor only when their SPS measures conform to international standards, because only in this instance will the presumption of compliance provided for in Article 3.2 apply.[10] In other circumstances it may be difficult to show that measures, while not conforming to, are based on international standards.

From this brief analysis it can be preliminarily concluded that while Members are not required to harmonize, the SPS Agreement does encourage such a process. Moreover, whilst the AB has emphasized that the type of harmonization promoted by the SPS Agreement is not a full one, the incentives to harmonize set up by Article 3 remain rather strong.

B.   The Relationship between the Harmonization Mandate and the Autonomy Rule

To shed more light on the potential implications of the SPS Agreement in relation to worldwide risk policy, one needs to investigate the relationship

---

[8]   Appellate Body Report, *EC – Hormones*, note 4 above, para. 163, emphasis added.

[9]   *Ibid.* para. 165, emphasis in the original.

[10]   *Ibid.* para. 171.

between the harmonization mandate and the autonomy rule. Is one of the two alternatives to be preferred? Is there a rule-exception relationship between the two? The answer to the latter question specifies the hierarchical relationship between the two rules.

As is well known, in *EC–Hormones*, the Panel had identified a rule-exception relationship between the harmonization and the autonomy rule. In the words of the Panel 'Article 3.1 imposes an obligation on all Members to base their sanitary measures on international standards except as otherwise provided for in the SPS Agreement, and in particular in Article 3.3 thereof. In this sense, Article 3.3 provides an *exception* to the general obligation contained in Article 3.1.'[11] As a *sequitur*, the Panel placed the burden of proof in relation to the obligations created by Article 3.3 on the defending party. The Panel's interpretation of the relationship between the harmonization mandate and the autonomy rule has, however, been overturned by the AB which argued that all obligations under Article 3 have the same legal standing. Accordingly, the AB has ruled that the burden of proving a *prima facie* violation of SPS obligations under Article 3.1 as well as 3.3, 5.1 and 5.5 remains with the complaining party.[12] In the words of the AB, '[t]he right of a Member to determine its own appropriate level of sanitary protection is an important right' and therefore international regimes should not be granted any privileged status.[13]

At first glance, one may conclude that the AB, in recognition of the importance of the Members' autonomy in deciding their appropriate level of safety, has adopted a deferential stance; upon further scrutiny, however, the approach of the AB in *EC–Hormones* appears to some extent ambiguous and less deferential. In fact, after having established that the Panel erred in imposing the burden of proof on the European Communities, the AB

[11] Panel Report, *EC Measures Concerning Meat and Meat Products (Hormones), Complaint by the United States*, WT/DS26/R/USA, adopted 13 February 1998, modified by Appellate Body Report, WT/DS26/AB/R, WT/DS48/AB/R, DSR 1998:III, 699 and Panel Report, *EC Measures Concerning Meat and Meat Products (Hormones), Complaint by Canada*, WT/DS48/R/CAN, adopted 13 February 1998, modified by Appellate Body Report, WT/DS26/AB/R, WT/DS48/AB/R, DSR 1998:II, 235.

[12] Appellate Body Report, *EC – Hormones*, note 4 above, paras 102–04 and 169–72. In the wording of the AB, 'Article 3.3 recognizes the autonomous right of a Member to establish such higher level of protection.' For a discussion of the problematic implications of the use of this jargon, and more generally of the rule-exception distinction used by WTO jurisprudence see Broude (2007).

[13] This reading of the SPS Agreement has been reiterated in various cases and has been used as a template to interpret the relationship of other norms, such as the relationship between Articles 2.2/5.1 and 5.7 SPS in *EC – Biotech*, note 5 above.

quickly concluded that the US and Canada, without being requested to do so, did indeed bring sufficient evidence that the European measures were not in compliance with the obligations set up by the joint reading of Articles 3.3, 5.1 and 5.5. As some commentators have already noted, the AB has chosen to 'hide' its justification for the latter finding in a footnote;[14] for the reader of the one hundred-page ruling, such a choice is at best startling. In footnote 180 of the AB Report we read: 'After careful consideration of the panel record, we are satisfied that the United States and Canada, although not required to do so by the Panel, did, in fact, make this *prima facie* case that the SPS measures related to the hormones involved here, except MGA, are not based on a risk assessment.'[15] The justification offered by the AB remains too vague to be persuasive. This is not to say that the AB reached an incorrect conclusion; nevertheless the lack of an articulate motivation for its decision, for instance by indicating what pardicular evidence brought by US and Canada were decisive, displays a certain degree of judicial activism that conflicts with the deferential approach adopted in interpreting the relationship between the harmonization and the autonomy rules.

By recognizing that Articles 3.1, 3.2 and 5 are all on the same level, the AB has paid the highest respect to Members' freedom in shaping risk policies. From this perspective, harmonization is only 'weakly' promoted by the SPS Agreement. However, in *EC–Hormones* the AB sidestepped the hierarchy that it unequivocally defended by remaining silent on the question of how the burden of proof was met by the US and Canada, further adding ambiguity to the question of harmonization.

C. SPS Measures Diverging from International Standards

Probably the most salient provisions of the SPS Agreement are those relating to Members' freedom to set their own risk policies. In the following sections, these provisions and the interpretation thereof given by the WTO Courts are discussed.

1. Scientific justification or risk assessment?
Article 3.3 pins down the conditions that should be met by Members that introduce measures that diverge from international standards. Members

---

[14]   Quick and Bluthner (1999).

[15]   Appellate Body Report, *EC – Hormones,* note 4 above, footnote 180; the AB further specifies that 'it is also well to remember that a prima facie case is one which, in the absence of effective refutation by the defending party, requires a panel, as a matter of law, to rule in favour of the complaining party presenting the prima facie case'.

are allowed to adopt measures diverging from international standards 'if there is a scientific justification, or as a consequence of the level of sanitary or phytosanitary protection a Member determines to be appropriate in accordance with the relevant provisions of paragraphs 1 through 8 of Article 5'. This means that Members can establish different SPS measures if they have a scientific justification *or* if a risk assessment that justifies the measures has been performed (Articles 5.1 through 5.8). These two alternatives have been practically reduced to the same thing by the AB: Members should in any case carry out a risk assessment to justify SPS measures.[16] As one author has noted, such a reading might frustrate the principle of effective treaty interpretation, a principle recognized in previous WTO case law.[17]

2.   Defining risk assessment: value judgments in or out?

Whilst Article 3.3 has been interpreted restrictively by the AB, the concept of risk assessment has received a more generous interpretation.[18] In *EC –*

---

[16]   Cfr. Appellate Body Report, *EC – Hormones*, note 4 above, paras 175–77; this approach was reiterated by the AB in *Japan – Agricultural Products II*, note 5 above, para. 79.

[17]   Gruszczynski (2006), 12.

[18]   Article 5, paragraphs 1 through 4, of the SPS Agreement deals with the question of risk assessment and the determination of the level of safety:

Assessment of Risk and Determination of the Appropriate Level of Sanitary or Phytosanitary Protection

1.   Members shall ensure that their sanitary or phytosanitary measures are based on an assessment, as appropriate to the circumstances, of the risks to human, animal or plant life or health, taking into account risk assessment techniques developed by the relevant international organizations.

2.   In the assessment of risks, Members shall take into account available scientific evidence; relevant processes and production methods; relevant inspection, sampling and testing methods; prevalence of specific diseases or pests; existence of pest- or disease-free areas; relevant ecological and environmental conditions; and quarantine or other treatment.

3.   In assessing the risk to animal or plant life or health and determining the measure to be applied for achieving the appropriate level of sanitary or phytosanitary protection from such risk, Members shall take into account as relevant economic factors: the potential damage in terms of loss of production or sales in the event of the entry, establishment or spread of a pest or disease; the costs of control or eradication in the territory of the importing Member; and the relative cost-effectiveness of alternative approaches to limiting risks.

4.   Members should, when determining the appropriate level of sanitary or phytosanitary protection, take into account the objective of minimizing negative trade effects.

Hormones, the Panel, after distinguishing risk assessment from risk management, had ruled out any role for socio-political value judgments within risk assessment; accordingly, political considerations were not to enter the realm of risk assessment. The AB found this approach incorrect and thereafter the practice of risk assessment under the SPS Agreement framework can legitimately include socio-political issues.[19]

The acknowledgement that risk assessment includes value judgments is crucial to avoid the danger of vesting science with the role of 'neutral arbiter,' a myth dangerously latent in much risk regulation, as brilliantly illustrated by Vern Walker.[20] The recognition by the AB that risk assessment includes policy choices is therefore an invaluable contribution to the interpretation of the SPS Agreement. At the same time, the AB could have better clarified some important aspects of the risk assessment/risk management debate.

While a strict separation between risk assessment and risk management may outshine how policy and science unavoidably intermingle, a denial of the existence of different spheres in risk-based decisions may produce other types of confusion. In this respect the traditional distinction between risk assessment and risk management could be maintained to indicate that in addition to scientific studies, which *per se* cannot be entirely value free, considerations of cultural attitudes towards risk and other societal values are also part of the decision-making process. As a matter of analytical clarity and more generally of transparency, one should be able to distinguish the policy choices permeating the scientific field from the political choices made by the decision-maker when adopting a certain regulation. An example of the former is the degree of conservativism endorsed in risk assessments (for instance, the selection of a certain safety factor);[21] an example of the latter is the decision to employ certain technologies about which citizens are particularly anxious (e.g. biotechnology) for research purposes only, in order to build trust while the degree of uncertainty over the effects of the technology is reduced. The argument here is that an explicit recognition of these differences would enhance the transparency of disputes over risks.

Some light on this issue has been shed by the AB Report in *US – Continued Suspension*. The AB has clarified that the appropriate level of protection can have an influence on the 'scope' and 'methods' used for the

---

[19]   Appellate Body Report, *EC – Hormones*, note 4 above, paras 181, 186 and 187 respectively.

[20]   Walker (2003).

[21]   For an explanation of the concept of safety factor see Walker (2003), 219.

risk assessment.[22] For example, if a Member decides to set the appropriate level of protection at a higher level than the one that would be achieved by a measure based on an international standard, the parameters used to conduct a risk assessment may vary accordingly. Such an interpretation of 'risk assessment' seems to strengthen the regulatory autonomy of WTO Members.

3.   The specificity requirement

Another problem with the concept of risk assessment, as specified by the AB, is what has been termed the specificity requirement, i.e. the fact that scientific studies, to fall within the definition of risk assessment, should be very closely related to the substance, which is the object of the dispute. For instance in *EC – Hormones*, the prohibition of imports of meat and meat products derived from cattle treated with hormones concerned only six specific hormones: oestradiol-17β, progesterone, testosterone, trenbolone acetate, zeranol and melengestrol acetate. General studies on carcinogenic properties of estrogen were not considered to be sufficiently specific for the case, and thus failed to meet the specificity test.[23] The application of the specificity requirement may easily restrict the scope of Members' autonomy to shape their own risk policies. In this respect, it has been argued that 'if the extrapolation does not satisfy the specificity require-ment . . . , it may appear that in low-risk situations the appropriate level of protection is an illusory right'.[24]

4.   The ambiguity of a rationality test

As mentioned above, SPS measures should be based on risk assessment. But, what does 'based on' mean? The AB in *EC–Hormones* established that measures can be said to be based on a risk assessment when there is a 'rational relationship between the measure and the risk assessment'. The exact meaning of this rational relationship, however, remains vague. The 'rational relationship' concept was partly clarified in *Japan – Apples*, where an analytical approach resembling a proportionality test was

---

[22]   Appellate Body Reports, *US – Continued Suspension*, note 5 above, para. 685. For a more extended comment on this case, see Arcuri (2011); see also Arcuri, Gruszczynski and Herwig, (2010).

[23]   Appellate Body Report, *EC – Hormones*, note 4 above, paras 199–200. As noted by Joost Pawelyn, the Panel in *Australia – Salmon* (para. 8.58) has applied a somewhat more lax approach in considering which evidence can be used in the practice of risk assessment; see Pauwelyn (1999), footnote 27.

[24]   Gruszczynski (2006), 17.

adopted.[25] One commentator has noted that, while the *Japan – Apples* Panel used a jargon compatible with a proportionality test, the AB merely 'tolerated' such jargon.[26] *Japan – Apples* may then have opened the door to a proportionality test, but this test is far from crystallized in WTO jurisprudence. In this context, it should be noted that the proportionality test is the closest proxy to cost-benefit analysis. The AB, however, has never endorsed a cost-benefit test. On the contrary, in other cases the AB has accepted approaches manifestly conflicting with the cost-benefit analysis approach; for instance, in *Australia – Salmon* the AB has held that Members may set their appropriate level of protection at 'zero risk',[27] a criterion hardly reconcilable with the cost-benefit analysis approach.

5. Insufficiency of scientific evidence

Another crucial notion for assessing the legitimacy of SPS measures is the concept of 'insufficiency of relevant scientific evidence'. Members are allowed to adopt precautionary measures only if scientific evidence is insufficient to allow a risk assessment to be conducted. Interpreting this concept thus has implications for the autonomy rule. If insufficiency of scientific evidence is seen as an absolute criterion, the autonomy rule shrinks. An absolutist approach to the concept of insufficient scientific evidence means that Members could hardly question a national or international standard that is based on risk assessment. This clearly emerges from the way the concept has been interpreted by the Panel in *EC – Biotech*. Some European Member States found that the scientific evidence regarding the safety of certain GMOs was insufficient. The Panel argued that, given the fact that a risk assessment had already been performed at the European level, scientific evidence should be regarded as sufficient, despite the fact that some European Member States were unsatisfied with that assessment.[28] By avoiding judging more substantive issues, the Panel denied that there can be different standards in assessing uncertainty in the context of risk analysis. In other words, it has ruled out that there can be divergences among experts about the degree of uncertainty and, most importantly, it has rejected a 'relational' conceptualization of insufficiency of scientific evidence. Such a conceptualization posits that the in/-sufficiency of scientific evidence can be determined also on the basis of the chosen level of protection of Members.

---

[25] Cfr. AB Report, *Japan – Apples*, note 5 above, paras 144–47 and 162–63. In *EC – Biotech*, the Panel seems to have followed this approach.

[26] Foster (2006), at 316.

[27] AB Report, *Australia – Salmon*, note 5 above, para. 125.

[28] Panel Report, *EC – Biotech*, note 5 above, paras 73259–60.

The AB in *US – Continued Suspension* has clarified this issue and has indirectly overturned the approach endorsed by the Panel in *EC – Biotech*. While emphasizing that '[t]he determination as to whether available scientific evidence is sufficient to perform a risk assessment must remain . . . a rigorous and objective process,' the AB has also made clear that this determination cannot be divorced by the assessment of the appropriate level of protection.[29] This view allows the coexistence of different assessments of scientific evidence: a country setting a high level of protection can legitimately consider as insufficient the evidence deemed sufficient by another country. Such an interpretative turn implies the strengthening of the autonomy rule.

6.   In sum

From this analysis, the relationship between the harmonization and the autonomy rules emerges as still evolving. In theory, risk assessment can include value-laden judgments; it remains unclear however to what extent and for what reasons Members could adopt measures that are not a direct translation of scientific reports and to what extent Members may choose data among equally plausible studies. It is clear however that if the autonomy rule in the SPS Agreement endorses the myth of science as a neutral arbiter we would have worldwide harmonization of risk policies. It would be a form of indirect harmonization implemented by the WTO Courts that would judge each time whether the measures adopted conform to science. In light of the vast literature that has pinpointed the 'mythical' connotations of such a conception of science, it could be concluded that in such cases we would have an arbitrary form of harmonization shaped by the WTO Courts; institutions, it must be noted, that are not accountable to legislatures.[30] If some cases, especially the *EC – Biotech* Panel report, may have opened the door to such an arbitrary form of harmonization, the AB in *US – Continued Suspension* has taken a much more balanced approach. It remains to be seen how the criteria discussed will be interpreted in the future.

D.   An Afterthought: Global Risk Regulation or Global Deregulation?

Before turning to the economic analysis of the question of whether and to what extent harmonization is desirable, let me briefly investigate whether

---

[29]   Appellate Body Report, *US – Continued Suspension*, note 5 above, paras 685–86.

[30]   For a critical discussion of the lack of accountability of WTO Courts see Guzman (2004).

a hypothetical WTO-driven harmonization of health and safety standards leads in the direction of global deregulation.

It is well known that the WTO has no positive agenda in terms of transnational risk regulation. When creating inter-state risks (e.g. air pollution, risks of accident at nuclear power plants located at the border, etc.), no WTO Member could be held responsible for a violation of a WTO rule. Also, the standards immediately relevant to the SPS Agreement are not necessarily mandatory; for instance, the standards established by the Codex Alimentarius Commission need not be implemented by governments. Notwithstanding this lack of a positive agenda in the field of risk law, 'WTO rules may transubstantiate voluntary standards into mandatory ones'.[31] For this reason, the SPS Agreement is likely to influence Members' risk policies. To avoid being brought before the WTO Courts and possibly having to bear retaliatory measures Members may decide to repeal all safety measures that do not conform to international standards. From this perspective, the SPS Agreement could be seen as a mechanism for global risk de-regulation.[32]

However the picture is more complex. Oversimplifying somewhat, the effects of a strong harmonization mandate could go in *two opposite directions*: de-regulation or regulation of previously unregulated areas. On one hand, countries maintaining standards higher than those established by international standard setting organizations may decide to repeal or lower their own standards, i.e. they would undergo a process of deregulation. On the other hand, countries with standards lower than internationally established ones may have incentives to adopt the international standards because some of their exports could be blocked as a result of non-compliance with internationally accepted standards. Such countries accordingly would undergo a process of regulation.

Given the state of the art, it is difficult to assess whether one of these two scenarios is likely to occur. Much will depend on the future interpretation of the SPS Agreement and on the specific regulatory differences that create frictions to international trade as well as on the processes taking place within the SPS Committee.[33] However, it is important to point out that under a strongly harmonized regime both scenarios are plausible.

---

[31]   Charnovitz (2005), 30.

[32]   A similar consideration was reflected in Clarke and Barlow (1997), 81, quoted by Howse (1998), at 2330.

[33]   For an interesting analysis of the work of the SPS Committee see Lang and Scott (2009).

III. THE ECONOMICS OF WTO-PROMOTED GLOBALIZATION OF RISK POLICIES

This section focuses on the question of the desirability of worldwide harmonization of risk policies. Two sub-questions underlie this issue. Is it desirable to globally harmonize risk policy? And, is the WTO the best institution to promote such type of harmonization? The Law and Economics scholarship on environmental federalism in Europe and in the US offers some guidance to the present analysis and the relevant insights therein developed will be applied, *mutatis mutandis*, to the context of global risk policy.[34] From the outset it should be noted that while important analogies can be drawn from the analysis of regions such as the EU or federal states such as the US, one major difference characterizes the international arena: it lacks a single institution dealing with risk policies. Given these premises, this analysis will begin by briefly recalling the arguments in favor of decentralization and centralization of risk regulation.

Law and Economics scholars largely agree that when preferences are heterogeneous a decentralized system is superior to harmonization because more preferences can be satisfied.[35] Take as an example the safety laws regarding the production of cheese, where a tradeoff exists between safety and quality (e.g. think of the question of unpasteurized milk used in raw cheese). For instance, if in France people value good cheese more than safety while in the Netherlands people prefer a higher safety level to 'unsafe but tasty French cheese', two different rules will be able satisfy the preferences of both the French and the Dutch. Because the production of certain types of cheese may be possible only when low hygienic standards are enforced, the French rule would be 'cheese friendly' aiming at low safety whereas the Dutch rule would be 'safety oriented'. Going from a single rule that only satisfies the preferences of one group of people (either the Dutch or the French) to two rules, where both preferences are satisfied, is clearly efficient.[36] In addition, decentralized decision-making has the advantage of stimulating competition between different legal systems. The latter phenomenon is commonly referred to as 'regulatory compet-

---

[34]   In general see also Ogus (1999). For a discussion of the European situation: Van den Bergh (2000); see also De Búrca (1999), 24 and 32–38; Bermann (1994). For the US analysis see Revesz (1992), and Revesz (1996); Revesz (1997a); Revesz (1997b); Revesz (2000a); Revesz (2000b); Esty and Geradin (2000).

[35]   The seminal contribution is: Tiebout (1956).

[36]   In economic terms, this would be a Pareto improvement, which describes a situation where at least one person can be made better off without anybody else being made worse off.

ition' or 'competitive governments' and is widely recognized as promoting efficiency.[37] Finally, different geographical circumstances may justify different regulatory responses to risk.

Decentralization cannot always work efficiently, however. If the problem addressed has a transboundary character it will be difficult for local governments to adopt optimal rules. Economists explain the inefficiencies generated by this situation with the concept of 'transboundary externality'. Air or sea pollution, for instance, might have a transnational dimension. In these cases, isolated national responses are likely to be inadequate; governments, in fact, lack incentives to reduce this type of pollution because the negative effects of profitable activities are largely borne by other countries. In short, global pollution needs global governance. Next to transboundary externalities the risk of a race-to-the-bottom is mentioned as an argument in favor of centralization. However, some authors have argued that the risk of a race-to-the-bottom is often nonexistent and instead a race-to-the-top may be plausible.[38] Finally, harmonized rules may be necessary to facilitate trade. This last argument is the most relevant in the context of WTO law and is likely to be the one the negotiators had in mind when the SPS Agreement was drafted.

A.   The Strong Case for Decentralizing Risk Policy

If the outlined interpretative grid is used to analyze whether WTO-promoted world-wide harmonization of risk policies is appropriate, it appears that the case for harmonization is rather weak. First of all, risk preferences are plausibly heterogeneous.[39] A representative example where risk preferences diverge in different countries is in the area of biotechnology.[40] Several studies have shown that European consumers are more skeptical of genetically modified (GM) foods than US consumers.[41] For

---

[37]   For a general discussion of this argument see Breton (1996); Ogus (1999). For a discussion of this issue limited to the European context see Van den Bergh (2000).

[38]   In this respect David Vogel describes the 'California effect', by which he indicates 'the ratcheting upward of regulatory standards in competing political jurisdictions'; the author argues that this is a general phenomenon and therefore 'applies to many national regulations as well'. Vogel (1995), chapter 8, at 259.

[39]   Guzman argues that regulatory diversity in the field of health and safety should be justified by different risk preferences; Guzman (2004).

[40]   Another interesting example is the differences in risk perceptions and risk aversion towards beef food safety; for a study of this case, including a good review of literature, see Schroeder, Tonsor, Pennings and Mintert (2007), article 65.

[41]   For a review of this rich body of literature see Harrison, Boccaletti and House (2004).

instance, a survey of the European public's view of biotechnology by the International Research Group on Biotechnology and the Public found that the majority of Europeans consumers are opposed to GM foods.[42] By contrast a majority of US consumers were willing to purchase GM foods.[43] Differences also exist between European countries, as emerged from a study that compared the attitudes of consumers in Italy, Germany, the UK, France and Spain.[44]

More generally, differences in risk preferences can be explained by the fact that risk perceptions are influenced, among other things, by cultural and/or political values and by ethical concerns.[45] Different rules in the field of risk law might thus be necessary to satisfy more preferences. As risk law embraces various areas, one could further investigate whether in some sectors preferences are more or less heterogeneous than in others.

The argument of 'competitive governments' is also a salient one in the context of risk regulation. Governments have endorsed different approaches to risk regulation, where a 'rational-instrumental model' has often been juxtaposed to an 'administrative-constitutional one'.[46] These models are difficult to compare, if not incommensurable as argued by Elizabeth Fisher, because they are rooted in very different ways of conceptualizing risk. It is not inconceivable that these models will eventually merge; however, by leaving governments free to adhere to one approach over another means allowing a process of learning-by-doing that will plausibly lead to the selection of the best model.

In sum, absent transboundary externalities, in an international context, non-uniform risk rules appear superior for at least two reasons: (1) they allow for the satisfaction of more preferences; and (2) decentralization encourages a form of political competition, which is particularly important given the existing differences in approaching risk regulation.

---

[42]   Gaskell (2000); see also Gaskell, Bauer, Durant and Allum (1999) and Gaskell, Bauer and Durant (1998).

[43]   International Food Information Council Foundation, *More U.S. consumers see Potential Benefits to Food Biotechnology* (2001) as quoted in Harrison, Boccaletti and House (2004).

[44]   PABE Final Report, 'Public Perceptions of Agricultural Biotechnology in Europe', http://csec.lancs.ac.uk/pabe/docs/pabe_finalreport.pdf (2001), in particular 36–46.

[45]   Renn and Rohrmann (2000); Douglas and Wildavsky (1982); Kahan, Slovic, Braman, and Gastil (2006); Kane (1998).

[46]   In these two ideal models, risk is differently conceptualized and managed: in the rational-instrumental model, the nature of risk problems is perceived to be objective and quantifiable whereas in the deliberative-constitutional model 'complexity, uncertainty and socio-political ambiguity dominate'. Cfr. Fisher (2006), 17.

B.   Diversification of Risk Policies as a Risk Reduction Strategy: a Novel Argument Favoring Decentralization

Thus far the desirability of global risk policy has been appraised by applying a well-developed economic theoretical framework, commonly referred to as the economics of federalism. New insights for assessing the efficiency of the level of governance of risk policy are here introduced. In particular, the argument is made that decentralization may promote the efficiency of risk governance. The thrust of this argument is that different rules can perform a risk-reduction function.[47] The following example illustrates this point.

Consider the risk related to the introduction of a new species of fish into a lake; if the introduced species is a predator it could eventually destroy its host environment; this happened, for instance, in Lake Victoria with the introduction of the Nile perch.[48] If the fish is simultaneously introduced in many lakes the risk of loss of biodiversity is much greater than if the fish is introduced in one lake only.[49] Likewise, when regulators are uncertain about some risks, different rules may result in the spreading of risk.

This risk-reduction strategy is comparable to what investors do by diversifying their portfolios. As diversification can reduce risk only when risks are specific,[50] so can different rules reduce risk only when risks are local. In the presence of transboundary risks, different rules cannot reduce risks (as in presence of systemic risks diversification cannot limit risk). Thus, absent interstate externalities (as discussed below), non-harmonized regimes appear welfare superior to harmonization because of the risk-reduction function that such a regime would perform.

This analogy is particularly appropriate for the case studied; yet some important qualifiers should be applied. In this analogy, risk regulation can be seen as an investment; in practice, a lax or a stringent risk regulation can generate different outputs. However, while in the case of portfolio theory the costs and benefits go to a single investor, in the case under investigation the costs and benefits accrue to the *global community*.

---

[47]   For a more formal analysis of this issue see Arcuri and Dari-Mattiacci (2010).

[48]   Goldschmidt (1996).

[49]   Unfortunately, the ecosystem of Lake Victoria was quite unique; in fact, the varieties of cichlid fish species (now to a great extent extinguished) present in Lake Victoria cannot easily be found in other natural ecosystems.

[50]   Specific risk is defined as 'the risk which is unique to an individual asset. It represents the component of an asset's return which is uncorrelated with general market moves.' Available at http://www.riskglossary.com (last visited December 13, 2007).

While in the case of portfolio theory the investor is one, in the case of risk regulation, the actors are as many as the number of regulators. The most direct implication of this difference is that the process of diversification in global risk policy would be the consequence of an uncoordinated process. Moreover, decentralization cannot coincide with diversification. In fact, the possibility that under decentralization a harmonized regime would be reached cannot be ruled out. Nevertheless, it appears plausible to believe that under conditions of uncertainty decentralization will bring about different risk policies and in turn diversification of risk.

C.   Rethinking WTO-promoted Worldwide Harmonization of Risk Policies: the Weak Case for Harmonization

The strong presumption in favor of non-uniform rules that emerged from the previous analysis leaves us with the question of whether WTO-promoted harmonization of risk law can be nevertheless justified. Two arguments that could in principle justify harmonization of risk law are discussed here: 1) the presence of transboundary externalities and 2) the promotion of trade.

1.   Transboundary externalities

As noted above, transboundary externalities are generally considered a powerful rationale for the harmonization of rules.[51] For the case under analysis, however, this argument fails to be convincing. To better understand the weaknesses of this argument, two types of transboundary externalities should be distinguished: (1) trade-related and (2) non-trade-related. Trade-related externalities refer to externalities that come into being with the occurrence of trade. An example of this type of externality is the trade of goods posing a risk for the importing country, such as the trade of chemical substances, pesticides and the like. Non-trade related externalities exist independently from trade. An example of this second type of externality is a local activity, such as the operation of a nuclear power plant at the border, which entails risk for neighboring countries.

In the case of a trade-related externality an adequate solution would be the end of trade or the introduction of a standard which would restrict trade (either concerning the process and production methods (PPMs)[52] or

---

[51]   If Coasean bargaining is possible the reason for harmonization would cease to exist. This case is not discussed in this chapter.

[52]   For an analysis of the types of PPMs and the use of PPMs in international trade see Charnovitz (2002), 59–110. The author convincingly argues, among other things, that PPMs are not illegal under the WTO legal framework and he further

the product itself); not the harmonization of rules! Differently put, harmonization is not necessary to cure the market failures created by trade-related externalities; quite the contrary, allowing trade restrictions could be a way to solve the problems generated by trade-related transboundary externalities.

Only in the case of non-trade-related externalities harmonization of standards are likely to be necessary to internalize the externality. In the previous example, a common safety standard for the operation of nuclear power plants could be an adequate response. In the category of transboundary externalities, it could theoretically be possible to use also trade-restrictive measures (and not harmonization) for internalization purposes. Such strategies, as the example below shows, would be very difficult to implement however. For instance, the problem of air pollution contributing to climate change could be tackled by trade measures. If the amount of air pollution generated by the factories in State A is substantially contributing to climate change, other WTO Members could limit the imports of products produced by those factories.[53] This strategy is rather unattractive for at least two reasons. Firstly, it may be the case that not all products will be destined for export, and thus trade restrictions may be sub-optimal. Secondly, it would be very difficult to coordinate the actions of all WTO importing Members so as to achieve optimal deterrence. Thus, the uncoordinated actions of WTO Members will probably result in over- or underdeterrence. Because trade-restrictive measures are difficult to use with non-trade-related externalities, harmonization appears to be the best alternative left.

However, the WTO is poorly equipped to cope with this type of transboundary externality. The main problem is that the WTO lacks a positive mandate to regulate in the field of international risk law. As noted above, the WTO neither has a positive mandate to manage transboundary risks nor has the power to sanction governments imposing risks on other jurisdictions. In order to justify WTO-promoted harmonization aimed at the governance of transboundary risks, the WTO must radically change its goals by adding the protection of the environment, health and safety as one of its main goals, and should further incorporate tools to achieve this goal. At the moment such a metamorphosis is unlikely. The creation of

---

suggests different typologies of PPMs that can help illuminate what types of PPMs are more prone to be used as protectionist devices.

[53]   To a certain extent, some Multilateral Environmental Treaties (MEAs), such as the Montreal Protocol on Substances that Deplete the Ozone Layer, embody similar norms. For a discussion of the possible conflicts and compatibilities between MEAs and WTO law see Schoenbaum (1997). On the issue of border tax adjustments, see Pauwelyn (2007).

a Global Environmental Organization, as suggested by some scholars,[54] and/or the improvement of the World Health Organization and the Codex Alimentarius Commission could be a more effective institutional solution to achieve the goal of global environmental and human health protection.

In conclusion, the presence of transboundary externalities does not justify WTO-promoted harmonization of risk law. To the contrary, the WTO's (partial) solutions to the problem of transboundary externalities favor a decentralized system in which countries are allowed to use trade-restrictive measures, such as product standards or PPMs.

2.　The promotion of trade

Finally, the last and probably only legitimate reason to promote harmonization is the protection of open and competitive markets. The danger of concealing protectionist measures behind health and safety or environmental regulations is very concrete and harmonization may appear to be a legitimate strategy to counter protectionism. The costs of protectionism, or better eco-protectionism, are not disputed here and accordingly neither are the need of strategies to counter them. However, the question arises whether harmonization is the best tool to contain protectionism.

On one hand, harmonization will obviously decrease barriers to trade. On the other hand, harmonization in the context of risk policies has high costs: different preferences are trumped, government competition is blocked and the risk-reduction function of heterogeneous risk policies (diversification) is undermined. In comparing the costs and benefits of harmonization, it may be useful to recall that trade liberalization is not an end *per se* but rather a means to reach higher levels of welfare among trading partners.

Ricardo's theory of comparative advantage is often invoked as the conceptual justification for free trade. Yet, if it is true that comparative advantages are functions, among other things, of government policies, regulatory heterogeneity should be considered one of the conditions for the existence of comparative advantage.[55] Thus, liberalization of trade through

---

[54]　A major proponent of the creation of a Global Environmental Organization is Daniel Esty; see Esty, (2000); *contra* Juma (2000). For an alternative proposal see Guzman (2002).

[55]　As Michael Trebilcock and Robert Howse have clearly put it: '[T]he theory of comparative advantage is centrally predicated on nations exploiting their differences (not similarities) in international trade. Few international trade theorists believe any longer that comparative advantage is exclusively exogenously determined, but is significantly shaped by endogenous government policies (e.g. collective investments in infrastructure, education, law and order, healthcare, research and development). Exploiting differences in government policies is no less legitimate than exploiting differences in natural endowments.' Trebilcock and Howse (1998), 14.

harmonization may undermine its very reason for being, i.e. comparative advantages. In this respect Trebilcock and Howse have pointed out that:

> it would be a major and unfortunate irony if the price of adopting rules that are designed to remove constraints on and enhance competition in international goods and services markets is the adoption of rules or institutions that have the effect of monopolizing or cartelizing government policy-making i.e. enhanced competition in economic markets at the price of reduced competition in political markets.[56]

From the above we can conclude that harmonization as a means to achieve the goals of international trade has high costs and little justification. The conclusion that harmonization is not an optimal solution leaves us with the question of how to deal with protectionism and the relative increase of non-tariff barriers in the form of risk regulation.

Ideally, the WTO Courts would need a clear-cut criterion to judge the legitimacy of trade-restrictive risk regulatory measures. The Law and Economics scholarship has suggested that risk regulation can be greatly improved if cost-benefit analysis would be performed and its results followed.[57] Could then cost-benefit analysis become the criterion to assess the legitimacy of risk regulation at the WTO?

IV. COST-BENEFIT ANALYSIS AND THE LEGITIMACY OF RISK REGULATION[58]

In a 2009 article published in the *Journal of World Trade*, David Collins has argued that a test, closely resembling cost-benefit analysis, should be used to resolve disputes concerning trade and human health. The article focuses on a specific ratio, called the *J*-value, dealing only with the assessment of regulatory measures protecting human lives. The *J*-value can be considered a sub-set of cost-benefit analysis, or in the words of the author 'a sophisticated form of cost-benefit analysis'.[59] Collins' contribution is the most radical proposal for the use of an efficiency criterion to assess the legitimacy of risk regulation at the WTO. Yet, other scholars have argued

---

[56]   *Ibid.* 9.

[57]   See for instance Viscusi (1992); Zerbe Jr. and Dively (1994); Pildes and Sunstein (1995); Zerbe Jr. (1998); Arrow, Cropper, Eads, Hahn, Lave, Noll, Portney, Russell, Schmalensee, Smith and Stavins (1996); Morrall (1997), 71–87; Hahn and Sunstein (2002); Sunstein (2002a); Sunstein (2005); and Revesz and Livermore (2008).

[58]   Parts of this section draw Arcuri (forthcoming 2012).

[59]   Collins (2008), 1072.

that cost-benefit analysis can be considered one substantive benchmark to judge the consistency of risk regulatory measures with international trade law.[60] Since most Law and Economics scholars advocate for the use of cost-benefit analysis to increase the rationality of risk regulation, it is worth investigating whether this methodology could become a criterion for the assessment of the legitimacy of risk policies.

Let me first note that the practice of using cost-benefit analysis to shape national risk policy arguably has its origin in American legal history.[61] The use of cost-benefit analysis for assessing regulation was mainstreamed in the eighties, after Executive Order 12291 was issued in 1981 by President Ronald Reagan. The Order required that all major regulations by federal agencies should be accompanied by a Regulatory Impact Analysis (RIA), which includes the assessment of costs and benefits of regulation.[62] All subsequent administrations, from Clinton[63] to Obama have kept cost-benefit analysis as the central methodology for regulatory review.[64]

Several other OECD countries have followed suit and use cost-benefit analysis to assess the efficiency of regulation.[65] The US experience, however, remains one of the most significant across the globe both for its consolidated use in the practice of regulatory making and for the debate that it has spurred among academics and representatives of the civil society. The following analysis will accordingly draw on this debate.

A.   Cost-Benefit Analysis and its Discontents

If cost-benefit analysis has gained widespread acceptance in the policy-making realm, the group of cost-benefit analysis skeptics has also grown.[66]

---

[60]   See Bohanes (2002).

[61]   For a more extended discussion of the institutionalization of cost-benefit analysis see Arcuri (2012) and Morrall (1997).

[62]   The Order provided that 'Regulatory action shall not be undertaken unless the potential benefits to society from the regulation *outweigh* the potential costs to society'. Emphasis added; Cfr. Section 2(b), Executive Order 12291, 46 F.R. 13193, Feb. 17 1981.

[63]   See Clinton, Executive Orders 12866; for a more detailed account see Sunstein (2002), 11–12.

[64]   The commitment of President Barack Obama to cost-benefit analysis was further evidenced by the appointment of Professor Cass Sunstein as head of the Office of Information and Regulatory Affairs (OIRA), the central body for regulatory review.

[65]   For a recent overview of the EU practices see Renda (2010).

[66]   See for instance Kelman (1981); McGarity (1998); Ackerman and Heinzerling (2004); Driesen (2006); Parker (2006).

The critiques that have been raised can be grouped at least into two categories.[67] First, the methodologies currently used in cost-benefit analysis cannot deliver reliable numbers. Second, cost-benefit analysis has been used to deregulate rather than to enact 'better' regulation. In the following, I am going to review briefly these two sets of critiques.

1. Contested numbers

It is beyond the scope of this chapter to conduct a complete review of cost-benefit analysis methodologies. By focusing on a few representative issues (i.e. the value of human lives and the discount rate), this section aims at showing some of the problems inherent to the economic methodologies used to monetize the costs and benefits of regulation.

The promise of several health and safety regulations is to save human lives. Thus, if the efficiency of these regulatory measures is to be assessed using cost-benefit analysis, the calculation of the monetary value of human lives is inescapable. While economists seem to have reached some consensus on the basic methodology to assign a monetary value to human life, they still struggle on a few computational issues. The different approaches may lead to a difference of a couple of million dollars per statistical life.

The basic methodology on which consensus coalesced is the so-called value of a statistical life (VSL).[68] The VSL life reflects the tradeoffs people are willing to make between very small risks of death and money. The variables underlying the calculation of the VSL are the risk of death that one person is faced with (e.g. 1/10.000) and her willingness to pay to eliminate it (e.g. $500). The VSL is then calculated by dividing the first factor by the second (e.g. $500/0.0001). With the numerical example used above, we would have a VSL of $5 million. While the basic idea is agreed upon, the VSL remains far from uncontested.

As reported by an article published in *The New York Times* in 2011, '[a]gencies are allowed to set their own numbers. The E.P.A. and the Transportation Department use numbers that are $3 million apart.'[69] In

---

[67] Another important set of critiques not discussed in this chapter is those based on the concept of incommensurability. Those critiques consider the foundations of cost-benefit analysis flawed because its methodology relies on the monetization of incommensurable goods, such as human lives and the environment. Relevant scholarship in this area include Radin (1987); Sagoff (1981); Ackerman and Heinzerling (2004); and Sunstein (1994).

[68] The work of Professor William Kip Viscusi is one of the most important in this field; cfr. Viscusi (1992); Viscusi (1998); Viscusi (2008). For an overview of how this practice emerged see Arcuri (forthcoming 2012), p. 12.

[69] Appelbaum (2011).

its Circular A-4 of September 17, 2003, the OMB has set the VSL between $1 and $10 million. The EPA, in its 2010 Guidelines, suggests a VSL figure of approximately $7.4 million.[70] Notably these are different numbers used within the US. If we compare these numbers with those used in Europe (with an economy comparable to the US) the divergence increases. The Annexes on the 2009 Impact Assessment Guidelines by the European Commission proposed a value in the range of €1–2 million, far lower than the American one.[71]

The differences between these numbers can partly be ascribed to different methodologies and partly remain unexplained. As to the methodology, it suffices to mention that the statistical data are mostly derived from the blue-collar labor market. The differential paid to workers with risky jobs to compensate for the risk they bear has been used as basis for the value of the willingness to pay to avoid risk (so-called hedonic wage studies). Some scholars have criticized this method because it relies on a biased sample (those who take riskier jobs have lower-than-average incomes).[72] Moreover, the risks analyzed in hedonic wage studies are mostly voluntarily taken, whereas the health and safety risks addressed by regulation are often involuntarily taken. This distinction is relevant because people rate risk not only on the basis of annual numbers of deaths for the activity considered; they incorporate other considerations in their judgment of risk as evidenced by the so-called 'psychometric paradigm'.[73] This means that, *ceteris paribus*, some risks are judged as more serious than others. In very concrete terms, the VSL may have to be adjusted depending on the type of deaths to be averted.

While economists continue to fuel the discussion on the 'right' methodology to calculate the VSL, policymakers need to use some numbers. It remains problematic that they do use different numbers leading to different results, at times without even specifying the reason of their choice.[74]

---

[70]   Environmental Protection Agency (EPA) (2010).

[71]   European Commission, Impact Assessment Guidelines, 15 January 2009, SEC(2009) 92, in Annexes to Impact Assessment Guidelines, p. 43.

[72]   Revesz (1999).

[73]   A conspicuous number of studies, also called the 'psychometric paradigm', have shown that people often characterize risks on the basis of some of the following qualitative dimensions: risk is voluntarily or involuntarily taken; risk is chronic or catastrophic; it is common or dread; it is known or unknown to those exposed; it is known or unknown to science; it is old or new; it is controllable or uncontrollable by those exposed. A risk that is voluntarily taken is rated less dangerous than a risk that is involuntarily taken; a chronic risk is feared less than a catastrophic one, and so on. Johnson and Tversky (1984); Slovic (1987); Slovic (1991).

[74]   Similar problems emerge when the value of environmental goods, such as the preservation of landscape/biodiversity/animal species is considered. For an

Next to the VSL, other issues contribute to render the cost-benefit arithmetic fuzzy. The cost-benefit analyst has to compare costs and benefits occurring in different times. As with the VSL, economics provides us with a tool: the *discount rate*. As with the VSL, consensus exists on the basic idea. Costs and benefits occurring in the future need to be discounted to their present value and a rate can be used for this purpose.[75] As with the VSL, the devil is in the details and when it comes to agreeing on a number and on the underlying methodological issues, the profession is divided. The tragedy is that, 'the long term interest rate determines any project's fate'.[76]

As a matter of simple mathematics, the longer the time-frame under consideration, the larger the difference in final numbers. For example, the present value of a project leading to €1 billion benefits in 10 years, with a rate of 5 percent, is € 613,913,253.541, ca. 61 percent of the original value. The present value of the same project delivering the benefits in 75 years, with the same discount rate, is € 25,751,502.277, only 2.57 percent of the original €1 billion; if we further lengthen our temporal horizon, say to 150 years, we obtain a meager € 663,139.870, ca. the 0.07 percent of the original €1 billion. To better appreciate the impact of the rate, consider that the same value, applying a rate of 10 percent for a time-span of 150 years, would result in only € 618.155, the 0.0001 percent of the original value.

For short-term regulatory measures, agencies have suggested discount rates ranging from 3 to 7 percent.[77] For measures with inter-generational effects, the debate is rather on whether a discount rate should be used at all. In fact, any positive discount rate makes nearly all projects with benefits in a distant future fail a cost-benefit test. While some scholars have argued for a zero-discount rate in case of measures affecting future generations,[78] other scholars have argued just the opposite (i.e. that future generations should be disregarded).[79]

---

overview of economic methodologies used for these purposes see Garrod and Willis (1999).

[75]   The present value is commonly obtained by dividing the future value by a factor that is $1 + r$ at the power of the n years considered: $V_0 = V_1/(1+r)^n$.

[76]   Poem attributed to Kenneth Boulding; quoted in Heinzerling (1999), 44. The poem further reads: 'At two percent the case is clear; At three some sneaking doubts appear; At four it draws its final breadth; At five percent is certain death.'

[77]   Cfr. EPA (2010) and Office of Management and Budget (OMB) Circular A-94. Note, however that until 1984 the OMB was suggesting a discount rate as high as 10 percent.

[78]   Ramsey (1928); Revesz (1999).

[79]   Posner (2007).

While the list of disputed measuring techniques can go on,[80] it is time to draw a few conclusions. Economics provides a set of sophisticated tools to calculate costs and benefits. However, many controversies linger on these numbers and the methodologies used to produce them. Small variations in the assumptions may cause differences of millions of dollars and eventually determine the outcome of the analysis. In the view of many, the methodological problems underlying the practice of cost-benefit analysis constitute an argument sufficient to dismiss cost-benefit analysis as a meaningful tool to support the decision-maker in achieving better regulation.

2.   Cost-benefit analysis and the deregulatory agenda

Another contested aspect of cost-benefit analysis is its alleged neutrality. Several scholars have made the case that cost-benefit analysis has been used as a de-regulatory tool rather than a tool to rationalize regulatory policy. Bruce Ackerman, Lisa Heinzerling and Rachel Massey published a study in 2005 where they showed that, if cost-benefit analysis had been systematically used in the seventies, it would have led to the non-adoption of some very successful regulatory measures, such as the decision to remove lead from gasoline in the seventies or the regulation of workplace exposure to vinyl chloride in 1974.[81] By now we know that these rules have yielded substantial benefits; however, at the time of the regulations, information about the risk associated with these substances was uncertain, and accordingly the benefits of the regulation would have been grossly underestimated. Others have contended that the adoption of important environmental and safety regulation in the US, such as a ban on asbestos or the prohibition of hazardous pesticides, was thwarted by the use of cost-benefit analysis mandated by statutes, such as the Toxic Substances Control Act (TSCA) and the Federal Insecticide Fungicide and Rodenticide Act (FIFRA).[82]

Looking at the practice, a deregulatory philosophy has arguably accompanied the process of institutionalization of cost-benefit analysis into the law-making process. Besides the infamous 'quality of life' review program, where a first form of cost-benefit analysis was used to halt social and

---

[80]   Other thorny methodological issues include: the choice of the willingness to pay (WTP) or willingness to accept (WTA) measures; the question of how to deal with uncertainty (i.e. lack of accurate knowledge about the probability of certain events); the question of how to deal with redistributive issues. For an overview see Arcuri, forthcoming (2012).

[81]   Ackerman, Heinzerling and Massey (2005).

[82]   Driesen (2006), 347–48; McGarity (2002), 2343.

environmental regulation, cost-benefit analysis gained momentum under administrations that fully endorsed a deregulatory agenda (e.g. under President Reagan in the US and under Prime Minister Thatcher in the UK).[83] Empirical studies have shown that the second Bush Administration used cost-benefit analysis to weaken regulation.[84] One author has further contended that cost-benefit analysis has not only been used in practice as a tool to stir deregulation; it is the methodology itself that is intrinsically biased against regulation.[85] The association of cost-benefit analysis with deregulation has been brilliantly captured by one commentator, who has characterized the US Office of Information and Regulatory Affairs (the cost-benefit gatekeeper) as 'a black hole' of regulation: 'Regulations went in but never came out – or so it was perceived – and cost-benefit ratios were in large part responsible.'[86]

B. The Case Against Cost-Benefit Analysis at the WTO

The previous section has reviewed some important critiques raised against the paradigm of cost-benefit analysis. The debate on whether the arguments reviewed are sufficiently strong to reject cost-benefit analysis in the process of risk regulation is still open. Here it is contended that, at least for the purposes of applying the SPS Agreement, the case is clearly against cost-benefit analysis. It is important to distinguish two scenarios: under the first scenario, cost-benefit analysis is used as a substantive criterion to assess the rationality of SPS measures; under the second scenario, cost-benefit analysis is used as a procedural criterion. In the following sections the two scenarios are treated separately.

1. Cost-benefit analysis as a substantive criterion

When cost-benefit analysis is used as a substantive criterion, SPS measures with costs higher than benefits would be considered irrational and therefore should be found in violation of the SPS Agreement. For the sake of illustration, let us assume an improbable (but not impossible) dispute at the WTO. Say that a least-developed country decides to restrict the importation of products considered dangerous for human health (say GMOs or poultry contaminated with dioxin). Say that the US and/

---

[83]   It is interesting to note that cost-benefit analysis was introduced in the United Kingdom under the so-called Deregulation Initiative initiated by Margaret Thatcher in 1985.

[84]   Driesen (2006), 380, Lowenstein and Revesz (2004).

[85]   Driesen (2006), 385–399.

[86]   Pilkey (2008), 1423.

or Europe are major exporters of these products. The least developed country has based its trade-restrictive measure on a cost-benefit analysis. The complainant, to win the case, should prove that the measure does not pass a cost-benefit test. To do so, it can argue that some of the valuations performed by the governmental agency of the least-developed country were wrong. Imagine the types of arguments that could be brought before a WTO panel to contest this cost-benefit analysis: the 'VSL should have been much lower', as poor people should be valued less than rich people,[87] 'a very high discount rate should have been used' as for poor people the future is much less valuable, etc. The application of certain theories, such as a lower VSL for poor people,[88] by virtue of the very assumptions, may lead to a situation where developing countries would *de facto* be banned from adopting health and safety measures that would pass a cost-benefit test in developed countries. Such a scenario would exacerbate an already-existing imbalance of power between developed and developing countries in the WTO, lamented by many. More generally, in a dispute between a developed and a developing country, the danger is that we may be faced with a series of arguments that would transform the WTO into a grotesque and unfair institution in the eyes of the general public. Surely, a disservice to the image of the WTO.

The problems of using cost-benefit analysis as a substantive criterion is not confined to possible conflicts between developed and developing countries. Cost-benefit analysis is also unlikely to provide an objective and uncontroversial criterion to resolve disputes involving two developed Members, say the US and Europe. The existing different approaches to the methodologies that can be employed in cost-benefit analysis are likely to add fuel to the controversy, rather than mitigating it. Moreover, panels (or the Appellate Body) would have to decide on methodological issues, a task which is arguably well beyond their competence.

Another argument should be added to the case against cost-benefit as a substantive criterion in WTO law. Normally, the costs considered by cost-benefit analysis are intra-jurisdictional. Thus, the costs to foreign exporters are likely not to be included in the equation. This means that one of the main effects central to WTO disputes (trade-restrictive effects) may (legitimately) have been left out of the analysis.

Finally, it should be noted that governments already using (and gener-

---

[87]   Posner and Sunstein (2005), 567; Sunstein (2005), 144.
[88]   It is worth emphasizing that these theories have been defended by no less than Professor Sunstein, the current head of the US OIRA Cfr. Posner and Sunstein (2005), 567; Sunstein (2005), 144.

ally supporting) cost-benefit analysis are not bound by the results of cost-benefit analysis; this is because efficiency can hardly be considered as the ultimate normative value of several contemporary societies.[89] If the WTO would use cost-benefit analysis as a substantive criterion to judge the reasonableness of health and safety measures, it would impose on all its Members a rationalist regulatory philosophy that may conflict with deliberative modes of decision-making and, possibly, with their constitutions.[90]

2.   Cost-benefit analysis as a procedural criterion

A softer and arguably more acceptable way to use cost-benefit analysis would be to require Members to perform such an analysis as a prerequisite of good risk regulation; however, the WTO Courts would not be allowed to review the quality of the analysis. Jan Bohanes has defended the use of cost-benefit analysis as a procedural criterion arguing that, 'despite its flaws, . . . [cost-benefit analysis] can greatly enhance the quality of decision-making or at least clarify and put into perspective some of the trade-offs involved'.[91] Using cost-benefit analysis as a procedural criterion may then be seen as a good compromise.

Members can be required to perform a cost-benefit analysis before adopting health and safety trade-restrictive measures, but once they have complied with this requirement, panels should not enter into the merits of the analysis. The problem with a *purely procedural* criterion, however, is that nearly any Member could draft a document under the label of cost-benefit analysis without seriously engaging in studying the potential costs and benefits of regulation. This criterion may then be considered as little efficacious. One could further distinguish a *purely procedural* from a *semi-procedural* criterion. By contrast, under a semi-procedural criterion, panels may consider whether the analysis has been performed according to some objective criteria. While panels would not have to decide on eminently substantive issues (whether one methodology is better than another), they could assess whether the analysis has been conducted in

---

[89]   Even in the US, where the main regulatory approach is the maximization of net benefit, there is room for other regulatory approaches. See, for instance, Section 1 of the Executive Order 12866, which provides that 'agencies should select those approaches that maximize net benefits, . . . unless a statute requires another regulatory approach'. Executive Order 12866, 58 F.R. 51735, Sept. 30, 1993.

[90]   I have argued elsewhere that the WTO Courts in SPS cases have been juggling two different regulatory philosophies, one more oriented towards a quantitative-risk paradigm and the other towards an holistic-risk paradigm. After *US – Continued Suspension*, the AB seems to have shifted towards the holistic-risk paradigm, see Arcuri (2011), note 22 above.

[91]   Bohanes (2002), 369.

conformity with the methodology chosen by the government in official guidelines and documents. Assume that an official guideline suggests a VSL in the range of US $ 3–7 million, and the cost-benefit analysis used a VSL of US $20 million; in such a case, a panel may consider this choice as an indication of an arbitrary manner of conducting the analysis. Likewise, the fact that a regulatory agency performs a cost-benefit analysis using totally different criteria for two comparable policies, may be considered as an indication of arbitrariness.

Yet, one important argument, raised against cost-benefit analysis as a substantive criterion, is valid also against the endorsement of cost-benefit analysis as a procedural criterion. Requiring Members to conduct cost-benefit analysis would impose on them a rationalist regulatory philosophy that may conflict with their constitutive values. One could counter-argue that, given that the criterion is only procedural, there is no imposition on a Member of an obligation to endorse a certain regulatory philosophy, as the Member remains free not to follow the result of the cost-benefit analysis. However, such reasoning fails to appreciate the power of numbers. Numbers convey messages in a persuasive way. The ultimate result of cost-benefit analysis is a number expressing the net benefits in monetary terms; the 'ultimate numbers' are those used to defend or attack the desirability of a certain policy. Even if the duty to perform cost-benefit analysis does not entail a duty to follow its prescription, the risk that the numbers generated by that analysis will disproportionately influence policymaking is real.

Some scholars have identified several cases in which 'numbers' have been used in the policymaking debate as 'objective' arguments in favor of a certain policy, even when these numbers, and the assumptions made to generate them, were rather shaky.[92] A serious problem evidenced by

---

[92]   Hassenzahl, for instance, reviewed five studies containing rather precise numerical risk comparisons, all criticized for inaccuracies and false precision. Notwithstanding the critiques raised, the numbers produced by these studies have been widely cited in peer-reviewed literature and political debate to defend or attack certain risk regulatory policies, without mention of the critiques. See Hassenzahl (2006). One of the studies cited is by the legal scholar Lisa Heinzerling, who has investigated the use of the widely cited table drafted by the economist John Morrall, which lists the costs per life saved of various types of risk-reducing regulation. The table's numbers depended on a set of (questionable) assumptions. What is puzzling is that even authors who explicitly reject those assumptions have relied on the table's numbers to criticize regulation. In the case of Morrall's table, something as fundamental as the discount rate was overlooked, Heinzerling (1998). For a reply to Heinzerling see Morrall, (2003); and for a reply to Morrall's reply see Parker (2004).

these studies is that the process by which the numbers are generated and the value judgments on which these numbers depend are not debated or exposed to public scrutiny. Citizens are likely to be confronted only with the final numbers of cost-benefit analysis, not with the assumptions and methods used to reach these figures. The number-crunching underpinning the practice of cost-benefit analysis, rather than enhancing transparency, may thus obscure issues and be used to exclude the public from the debate.[93] In other words, cost-benefit analysis may bury eminently political debates in falsely precise numbers, endangering basic principles of deliberative democracies.[94] From this perspective, requiring Members to conduct cost-benefit analysis may conflict with deliberative and democratic modes of governance.

V.   A PROPOSAL

The previous analysis has shown that neither harmonization nor cost-benefit analysis provide a solution to the problems created by SPS

---

[93]   As brilliantly put by Douglas Kysar: 'In practice, the "game" of regulatory cost-benefit analysis is just that, a structured exercise in which competing interests pursue policy outcomes not through direct argument and suasion, but through use of alternative assumptions, valuation techniques, discount rates, and other seemingly technical trappings of the cost-benefit methodology. As a result, subjects of ordinary moral and political discourse become debated through a stylized cost-benefit vernacular', Kysar (2011), 47.

[94]   Some scholars, however, seem to purport the view that excluding the public from regulatory policy may indeed be desirable and reconcilable with democratic values. For instance, Professor Sunstein has argued that because of the cognitive limitations of the layman, insulated experts should decide risk matters: 'democratic governments should respond to people's values, not their blunders', Sunstein (2005), 126. However, what Sunstein characterizes as blunders, may simply be attitudes towards risks that are formed on the basis of parameters other than expected probabilities and magnitude of the harm; these attitudes have been largely studied by cognitive psychologists (Cfr. The explanation of the 'psychometric paradigm,' in note 73 above). Next to these considerations, it has been shown that risk preferences are formed on the basis of culture. For instance, individualist types perceive risks differently from egalitarians: environmental risks tend to be perceived as not very serious by individualists, whereas they are feared by egalitarians. Scholars engaged in such research have criticized the technocratic model underpinning cost-benefit analysis: 'the idea that expert cost-benefit analysis respects citizens' "values" but not their "blunders" is . . . misleading. When expert regulators reject as irrational public assessments of the risks associated with putatively dangerous activities . . . they are in fact overriding public *values*' (Kahan et al. (2006), 1105, emphasis in original).

protectionist measures. Let me emphasize that the above analysis is not meant to demonize harmonization. There is, however, a major difference between coerced and spontaneous (voluntary) harmonization. The process of spontaneous harmonization is reconcilable with competitive governments, where governments will decide to align their rules with what they deem to be superior rules. Further, by leaving jurisdictional units free to harmonize, one can plausibly assume that harmonization will occur only when inter-jurisdictional differences in preferences are reduced. Thus, the promotion of a form of spontaneous harmonization may produce some benefits. Article 3 of the SPS Agreement can then be (re-)read as promoting such a type of harmonization.

The autonomy rule (formed by the joint reading of Articles 2.2, 3.3 and 5) now has holes in it and quite a few interpretative issues are left to the discretion of the WTO Courts. This is a dangerous situation that could transform the spontaneous harmonization mandate of Article 3 into a form of coercive harmonization. The AB in *US – Continued Suspension* seems to have dispelled some of the existing ambiguities, reinforcing the autonomy rule. Notwithstanding this major improvement, the balance between preserving autonomy and controlling protectionism is not yet clear. In the following I suggest some interpretative canons to (re-)construe the autonomy rule in such a way that protectionist measures could be filtered out.

My proposal is to reinterpret the autonomy rule in light of the principle of non-discrimination. In other words, the primary role of non-discrimination should be re-established. This would indeed be consistent with the goals of the SPS Agreement as stated in its first and last preambular paragraphs, where it can be derived that the underlying *rationale* of the Agreement is still non-discrimination.[95] This proposal may be considered conflicting with the 'post-discriminatory' nature of several WTO Agreements, including the SPS Agreement. The term post-discriminatory,

---

[95]   The first and the last preambular paragraphs of the SPS Agreement read respectively: '*Reaffirming* that no Member should be prevented from adopting or enforcing measures necessary to protect human, animal or plant life or health, subject to the requirement that these measures are not applied in a manner which would constitute a means of arbitrary or unjustifiable discrimination between Members where the same conditions prevail or a disguised restriction on international trade;' and '*Desiring* therefore to elaborate rules for the application of the provisions of GATT 1994 which relate to the use of sanitary or phytosanitary measures, in particular the provisions of Article XX(b).' The last preambular paragraph is related to the principle of non-discrimination indirectly. In fact, art. XX, as discussed in section III, has been interpreted giving preponderant weight to its chapeau.

originally coined by Robert Hudec, refers to the fact that trade-restrictive measures can be non-discriminatory and yet result in violation of WTO law.[96] This was the case, for instance, in the *Hormones* dispute where EC rules, while being judged non-discriminatory, were nevertheless condemned and found in violation of WTO law.

Even though the SPS Agreement has undoubtedly opened the door to find non-discriminatory SPS measures illegal, it may be plausibly argued that the SPS post-discriminatory criteria have been drafted in the hope of establishing objective criteria to identify protectionist measures. Borrowing the words of Hudec, 'if you scrape off all that surface legal doctrine, you will find that most of these criteria . . . are really aimed at establishing whether or not there has been a discriminatory purpose to the measure in question'.[97] For this reason, it is here suggested to reinterpret the post-discriminatory criteria embodied in the autonomy rule as criteria targeting only those measures that in one way or another have a protectionist intent.

Thus, what needs to be defined is a set of criteria that can guide the WTO Courts to filter out protectionist measures. The above analysis has shown that cost-benefit analysis cannot work as a criterion to assess the legitimacy of SPS measures. What can be done, then, is to resort to the criteria established in the SPS Agreement, namely to look at the scientific basis of the measures, while respecting the regulatory autonomy of the WTO Members.

As discussed above, science should not be seen as a panacea or as a neutral arbiter. In fact, in the practice of risk assessment different methodological choices (e.g. which model should be used to extrapolate data, which risks should be studied, whether cumulative effects should be studied as well, etc.) that will lead to different results can all be plausible. One way to rethink the role of risk assessment is to adhere to a procedural interpretation of the autonomy rule.[98] This would imply that Members should show that they carried out a risk assessment (in whatever format). As argued by Walker '[w]hen there are two plausible scientific accounts and it is uncertain which will prove to be correct, then a Member should be entitled, without further explanation, to base its regulation on either account, as a matter of its own science policy'.[99] A procedural interpretation of this rule could avoid the second-guessing of the rationality of

---

[96]   Hudec (2003).

[97]   *Ibid.*, 189.

[98]   This solution, for different reasons, and in somewhat different ways, has also been suggested by other scholars: Guzman (2004); Bohanes (2002).

[99]   Walker (1998), 303.

measures by the WTO Courts and yet would expose Members to minimal duties for justifying their measures.[100] The procedural burdens, such as the duty to engage in risk assessment, expose states to scrutiny from citizens and firms.

At the same time a purely procedural interpretation of this rule has at least one downside: Members could still adopt protectionist measures whilst abiding with the procedure. Thus, while procedural burdens would render the adoption of protectionist measures more difficult because of increased transparency in the system,[101] the problem of protectionist measures could not be solved entirely. To reduce this problem, the procedural criterion could be coupled with a minimal substantive criterion according to which science can be used to identify and condemn those cases in which measures are based on manifestly implausible scientific theories.

---

[100]   In this context Guzman has noted: 'By exposing a country's policies and justifications to scrutiny, procedural requirements ensure that protectionism masquerading as an SPS concern will be exposed to both international and domestic political pressures, dramatically limiting the ability of states to use the SPS Agreement as cover for protectionism;' cfr. Guzman (2004), 6.

[101]   A pertinent critique to this 'risk-assessment procedural rule' is that it may suffer from the same problems of 'the cost-benefit analysis procedural rule'. Could the use of science really increase transparency of the policymaking process in the realm of risk regulation? It is true that the results of scientific studies can equally be mis-used in public debates and the general public may have difficulties in grasping the underlying assumptions. I believe, however, that the two cases are different, if not in kind at least in terms of degree for at least three reasons. First, the result of cost-benefit analysis is expressed in one number that subsumes different studies (e.g. choice of discount rate, valuation of human lives, valuation of environmental goods, which in turn depend on scientific assessments of certain facts); this implies that the number of assumptions to be understood require a much wider expertise than those required by risk assessment of specific substances. Second, the cost-benefit analysis final number has a normative dimension that is absent in scientific studies. In practice, the number resulting from a cost-benefit analysis tells us whether the project has passed the test or not; positive net benefits means that the cost-benefit test has been passed and *vice versa*. By contrast risk assessment delivers information only about the existence of a certain risk. Simplifying somewhat risk assessment does *not* tell us whether a substance is safe, rather it presents a probability that the substance is harmful to a group of people/a specific environment. Finally, scientific studies can be said to be falsifiable; economic science, and more specifically economic methodology used in cost-benefit analysis, much less so. Think, for example, of the controversies around the appropriate discount rate to be used; while a number of arguments underlying the different theories can be constructed and rationally discussed, it is hard to defend that these theories could be empirically tested. For a thorough discussion of methodology and 'falsification' in economic theory see Blaug (1980).

The rich scholarship in the field of risk analysis could help to build a taxonomy of risks that would indicate where more or less deference is required.[102] While developing such a taxonomy is an exercise outside the scope of this Chapter, an idea on possible manners to build a classification of risks that could be used in practice is briefly sketched out.[103] Risks could be grouped into categories similar to those proposed by Klinke and Renn.[104] These two authors, inspired by Greek mythology, have identified six typologies of risks and have matched each typology with a certain risk management strategy. In general, there seem to be good reasons to treat regulations relating to highly uncertain and contentious risks with more deference while regulation relating to risks that are familiar, known and controllable should pass a more severe scrutiny.

In the categories of risks for which more deference would be advised, the procedural dimension of the rule should prevail, and thus Members will simply be expected to conduct risk assessment. By contrast for the categories of risks where less deference is advised the substantive dimensions of the rule should be given more weight, as illustrated in Table 6.2. In the latter case, for instance, governments could be asked to provide sound motivations[105] for why they deviated from the results of most scientific studies. Such a taxonomy could assist the WTO Courts in the process of adjudicating SPS cases; it would bring more objectivity to the process and it would take into account the complexities underlying the risk regulation arena.

---

[102] Next to the literature on the psychometric paradigm, quoted in note 73 above, all the sociological literature and cultural studies provide rich insights into the field of risk analysis; cfr., for instance, Renn (1992); Slovic (1999); Kahan et al. (2006).

[103] The suggestion of this Chapter that such a taxonomy should be followed by the WTO Courts leaves open the legal question of whether the WTO Courts could follow such a taxonomy because it could be considered in line with the letter of the SPS Agreement or whether a separate document endorsing the taxonomy should be agreed upon by Members in order for the Courts to follow it. In order to answer this question one should analyze to what extent contemporary theoretical developments in risk analysis can/should affect the interpretation of the SPS Agreement.

[104] Klinke and Renn (2002).

[105] Motivations can be of different nature; they could include scientific reasons (e.g. a minority – but highly respected – scientific opinion) as well as issues related to consumer preferences and values or to ethical issues. For instance, empirical data showing that citizens are particularly averse towards a certain risk or that the risk would only be borne by poorest sections of the society could be considered a sound motivation to justify political choices that diverge from what would be suggested on the basis of the scientific studies.

Table 6.2   Spectrum of the relationship between a risk taxonomy and the procedural/substantive interpretation of the autonomy rule

Most familiar and acceptable risks		Highly uncertain and controversial risks
Minimum degree of deference	⟶	Maximum degree of deference
Eminently substantive interpretation		Eminently procedural interpretation

VI. CONCLUSIONS

Today, the variety of food available to (mostly western) consumers is substantially wider than what their local region could possibly offer. The food on sale in western capitals includes a wide range of disparate products: Italian pasta, Japanese sushi, Mexican wraps, Indonesian Leompia, French fries and many others. Likewise, in many restaurants in European, American and Japanese towns you can order excellent Italian, French, South African, Chilean and Californian wines as well as sake. These are the wonders of the global village, made partly possible by the WTO. But when it comes to risk the global village becomes divided.

This chapter has shown that worldwide harmonization of risk law is undesirable from a Law and Economics perspective. First of all, peoples have different preferences towards risk. Next, such harmonization would not allow for a diversification of risk that appears to be an efficient risk reduction strategy and, finally, competition among governments would be severely impaired.

Whether the WTO has engaged in a process of worldwide harmonization of risk law is still unclear. The jurisprudence relating to the SPS Agreement has been ambiguous. On one hand, the WTO Courts, most particularly its AB, have tried to respect the freedom of Members to design their own risk policies. On the other hand, much room has been left to discretionary decisions by these organs that could eventually lead to a form of coerced harmonization, guided by the WTO Courts, which are bodies unqualified to set worldwide risk policies. In particular, the 'rational relationship' criterion, established by the AB in the *Hormones* case, seems to fall short of its ambition to set the balance between harmonization and autonomy. In *US – Continued Suspension*, though, the AB's jurisprudence seems to have taken a new turn, reinforcing the autonomy rule.

Given the risks of protectionism due to an increased use of risk regulation that may function as powerful non-tariff barriers to trade, absolute and unconditional deference is not desirable either. The proposal advanced by some Law and Economics scholars to use cost-benefit analysis to assess the legitimacy of SPS measures should not be seen as the solution. The analysis in this Chapter has shown that, all in all, the view that cost-benefit analysis should become a criterion to determine the legitimacy of SPS measures, is at best naïve and at worse fundamentally illiberal and undemocratic.

The suggested solution articulated in this Chapter is to re-interpret the SPS Agreement, by giving more body to the autonomy rule. A procedural interpretation of the obligations contained in the autonomy rule may deter the use of regulation for protectionist purposes. This procedural canon can be complemented by a minimal substantive requirement that the scientific studies upon which decisions have been based are not manifestly implausible. In addition, a taxonomy of typologies of risk delineating which types of risks deserve more or less deference could be built and subsequently rules with a different balance in the procedural/substantive canons can be matched to each typology of risks.

The tensions between free trade and risk law are not likely to diminish in the near future. A re-interpretation of the SPS post-discriminatory criteria, as suggested in this Chapter, can arguably mitigate such tensions. More generally, as an important point of departure for the adjudication of future disputes, the welfare-enhancing effects of the decentralization of risk policies and the corresponding downsides of a WTO-promoted harmonization of risk law should be recognized.

BIBLIOGRAPHY

Aaken, Anne van, Christoph Engel and Tom Ginsburg, 'Public International Law and Economics: Symposium Introduction', 1 *University of Illinois Law Review* (2008), 1–4.

Ackerman, Frank and Lisa Heinzerling, *Priceless: On Knowing the Price of Everything and the Value of Nothing* (New York: The New Press, 2004).

Ackerman, Frank, Lisa Heinzerling and Rachel Massey, 'Applying Cost-Benefit to Past Decisions: Was Environmental Protection Ever a Good Idea?', 57 *Administrative Law Review* (2005), 155–92.

Appelbaum, Binyamin, 'As U.S. Agencies Put More Value on a Life, Businesses Fret', *New York Times*, February 17, 2011.

Arcuri, Alessandra, 'Food Safety at the WTO after "Continued Suspension": a Paradigm Shift?' in Antonis Antoniadis, Robert Schütze and Eleanor Spaventa (eds), *The European Union and Global Emergencies: A Law and Policy Analysis* (Oxford: Hart Publishing, 2011), 205–24, available as *RILE Working Paper No. 2010/04* at ssrn: http://ssrn.com/abstract=1633390.

Arcuri, Alessandra, 'Risk Regulation' in Alessio Pacces and Roger Van den Bergh (eds), *Encyclopedia of Law and Economics* (Edward Elgar Publishing, forthcoming 2012). Available at SSRN: http://ssrn.com/abstract=1931592.

Arcuri, Alessandra and Giuseppe Dari-Mattiacci, 'Centralization versus Decentralization as a Risk-Return Trade-off', 53 *Journal of Law and Economics* (2010), 359–78. Available as working paper at SSRN: http://ssrn.com/abstract=1013329

Arcuri, Alessandra, Lukasz Gruszczynski and Alexia Herwig, 'Independence of Experts and Standards for Evaluation of Scientific Evidence under the SPS Agreement – New Directions in the SPS Case Law', 1(2) *European Journal of Risk Regulation* (2010), 183–88.

Arrow, Kenneth J., Maureen L. Cropper, George C. Eads, Robert W. Hahn, Lester B. Lave, Roger G. Noll, Paul R. Portney, Milton Russell, Richard Schmalensee, V. Kerry Smith and Robert N. Stavins, 'Is there a Role for Cost-Benefit Analysis in Environmental, Health and Safety Regulation?', 272 *Science* (1996), 221–22.

Bagwell, Kyle, Petros C. Mavroidis and Robert W. Staiger, 'It's a Question of Market Access', 96 *American Journal of International Law* (2002), 56–76.

Bergh, Roger van den, 'Towards an Institutional Legal Framework for Regulatory Competition in Europe', 53(4) *Kiklos* (2000), 435–65.

Bermann, George A., 'Taking Subsidiarity Seriously: Federalism in the European Community and the United States', 94(2) *Columbia Law Review* (1994), 331–456.

Blaug, Mark, *The Methodology of Economics: or How Economists Explain* (Cambridge, UK: Cambridge University Press, 1980).

Bohanes, Jan, 'Risk Regulation in WTO Law – A Procedure-Based Approach to the Precautionary Principle', 40 *Columbia Journal of Transnational Law* (2002), 323–89.

Breton, Albert, *Competitive Governments* (Cambridge, UK: Cambridge University Press, 1996).

Broude, Tomer, 'Genetically Modified Rules: the Awkward Rule-Exception-Right Distinction in EC – Biotech', 6(2) *World Trade Review* (2007), 215–31.

Búrca, Gráinne de, 'Reappraising Subsidiarity's Significance after Amsterdam', 7/99 *Harvard Jean Monnet Working Paper* (1999), 1–42.

Charnovitz, Steve, 'The Law of Environmental "PPMs" in the WTO: Debunking the Myth of Illegality', 27 *Yale Journal of International Law* (2002), 59–110.

Charnovitz, Steve, 'International Standards and the WTO', No. 133 *GWU Law School, Legal Studies Research Paper* (2005), 1–31.

Clarke, Tony and Maude Barlow, *MAI: The Multilateral Agreement on Investment and the Threat to Canadian Sovereignty* (St. Paul, MN: Apex Print, 1997).

Collins, David, 'Health Protection at the WTO: The J-Value as a Universal Standard for Reasonableness of Regulatory Precautions', 43(5) *Journal of World Trade* (2009), 1071–91.

Douglas, Mary and Aaron Wildavsky, *Risk and Culture: An Essay on the Selection of Technical and Environmental Dangers* (Berkeley, CA: University of California Press, 1982).

Driesen, David M., 'Is Cost-Benefit Analysis Neutral?', 77 *University of Colorado Law Review* (2006), 335–405.

Durant, John, Martin W. Bauer and George Gaskell (eds), *Biotechnology in the Public Sphere: A European Sourcebook* (London, UK: Science Museum, 1998), 189–214.

Environmental Protection Agency, 'Guidelines for Preparing Economic Analyses', December 2010.

Esty, Daniel C., 'The Value of Creating a Global Environmental Organization', 6(12) *Environment Matters* (2000), 13–15.

Esty, Daniel C. and Damien Geradin, 'Regulatory Co-opetition', 3 *Journal of International Economic Law* (2000), 235–55.

European Commission, Impact Assessment Guidelines, 15 January 2009, SEC(2009) 92.

Fisher, Elizabeth C., 'Beyond the Science/Democracy Dichotomy: The World Trade Organisation Sanitary and Phytosanitary Agreement and Administrative Constitutionalism', in Christian Joerges and Ernst-Ulrich Petersmann (eds), *Constitutionalism, Multi-Level Trade Governance, and Social Regulation* (Oxford, UK: Hart Publishing, 2006).

Foster, Caroline E., 'Japan – Measures Affecting the Importation of Apples: Rotten to the Core?', 25 *Australian Year Book of International Law* (2006), 309–30.

Frey, Bruno S., *Not Just for The Money. An Economic Theory of Personal Motivation* (Cheltenham, UK: Edward Elgar Publishing, 1997).

Frey, Bruno S., 'Morality and Rationality in Environmental Policy', 22 *Journal of Consumer Policy* (1999), 395–417.

Frey, Bruno S., Felix Oberholzer-Gee and Reiner Eichenberger, 'The Old Lady Visits Your Backyard: A Tale of Morals And Markets', 104 *The Journal of Political Economy* (1996), 1297–313

Garrod, Guy and Kenneth G. Willis, *Economic Valuation of the Environment: Methods and Case Studies*, (Cheltenham, UK: Edward Elgar Publishing, 1999).

Gaskell, George, 'Agricultural Biotechnology and Public Attitudes in the European Union', 3(2–3) *AgBioForum* (2000), 87–96.

Gaskell, George, Martin W. Bauer, John Duran and Nicholas Allum, 'Worlds Apart? The Reception of Genetically Modified Foods in Europe and the U.S.', 285(5426) *Science* (1999), 384–88.

Goldschmidt, Tijs, *Darwin's Dreampond: Drama in Lake Victoria* (Cambridge, MA: MIT Press, 1996).

Gruszczynski, Lukasz 'The Role of Science in Risk Regulation under the SPS Agreement', No. 2006/03 *EUI Law Working Paper* (2006), 1–31.

Guzman, Andrew T., 'Global Governance and the WTO', No. 89 *UC Berkeley Public Law Research Paper* (2002), 1–84.

Guzman, Andrew T., 'Food Fears: Health and Safety at the WTO', 45 *Virginia Journal of International Law* (2004), 1–40.

Hahn, Robert W. and Cass R. Sunstein, 'A New Executive Order for Improving Federal Regulation? Deeper and Wider Cost-Benefit Analysis', 150 *John M. Olin Law and Economics Working Paper Series* (2002), 1–65.

Harrison, R. Wes, Stefano Boccaletti and Lisa House, 'Risk Perceptions of Urban Italian and United States Consumers for Genetically Modified Foods', 7(4) *AgBioForum* (2004), 195–201.

Hassenzahl, David M., 'Implications of Excessive Precision for Risk Comparisons: Lessons from the Past Four Decades', 26(1) *Risk Analysis* (2006), 265–76.

Heinzerling, Lisa, 'Regulatory Costs of Mythic Proportions', 107 *Yale Law Journal* (1998), 1981–2070.

Heinzerling, Lisa, 'Discounting Our Future', 34(1) *Wyoming Land and Water Law Review* (1999), 39–74.

Howse, Robert, 'Science, Democracy and Free Trade: Risk Regulation on Trial at the World Trade Organization', 98 *Michigan Law Review* (1998), 2329–57.

Hudec, Robert E., 'Science and "Post-Discriminatory" WTO Law', 26 *Boston College International and Comparative Law Review* (2003), 185–95.

Israel, Brian D., 'An Environmental Justice Critique of Risk Assessment', 3 *New York University Environmental Law Journal* (1995), 469–522.

Joerges, Christian and Ernst-Ulrich Petersmann (eds), *Constitutionalism, Multi-Level Trade Governance, and Social Regulation* (Oxford, UK: Hart Publishing, 2006).

Johnson, Eric J. and Amos Tversky, 'Representation of Perceptions of Risks', 113 *Journal of Experimental Psychology: General* (1984), 55–70.

Juma, Calestous, 'The Perils of Centralizing Global Environmental Governance', 6(12) *Environment Matters* (2000), 13–15.

Kahan, Dan M., Paul Slovic, Donald Braman and John Gastil, 'Fear of Democracy: A Cultural Evaluation of Sunstein on Risk', 119 *Harvard Law Review* (2006), 1071–109.

Kane, Pat, 'There's Method in the Magic', in Jane Franklin (ed.), *The Politics of Risk Society* (Cambridge, UK: Polity Press, 1998).

Kelman, Steven, 'Cost-Benefit Analysis: An Ethical Critique', January/February, *AEI Journal on Government and Society Regulation* (1981), 33–40.

Klinke, Andreas and Ortwin Renn, 'A New Approach to Risk Evaluation and Management: Risk-Based, Precaution-Based, and Discourse-Based Strategies', 22(6) *Risk Analysis* (2002), 1071–94.

Kysar, Douglas A., 'Politics by Other Meanings: A Comment on "Retaking Rationality Two Years Later"', 48(1) *Houston Law Review* (2011), 43–77.

Lang, Andrew and Joanne Scott, 'The Hidden World of WTO Governance', 20 *European Journal of International Law* (2009), 575–614.

Leitner, Kara and Lester Simon, 'WTO Dispute Settlement: 1995–2003 A Statistical Analysis', 7(1) *Journal of International Economic Law* (2004), 169–81.

Livermore, Michael A., 'A Brief Comment on "Humanizing Cost-Benefit Analysis"', 1 *European Journal of Risk Regulation* (2011), 13–17.

Lowenstein, Laura J. and Richard L. Revesz, 'Anti-Regulation Under the Guise of Rational Regulation: The Bush Administration's Approaches to Valuing Human Lives in Environmental Cost-Benefit Analysis', 34 *Environmental Law Reporter* (2004), 10954–74.

McGarity, Thomas O., 'A Cost-Benefit State', 50 *Administrative Law Review* (1998), 7–79.

McGarity, Thomas O., 'Professor Sunstein's Fuzzy Math', 90 *Georgetown Law Journal* (2002), 2341–79.

Morrall, John F., *An Assessment of the US Regulatory Impact Analysis Program*, in *OECD Regulatory Impact Analysis, Best Practices in OECD Countries* (Paris: OECD Publications, 1997), 71–87.

Morrall, John F., 'Saving Lives: A Review of the Record', 27 *Journal of Risk and Uncertainty* (2003), 221–37.

Ogus, Anthony, 'Competition between National Legal Systems: A Contribution of Economic Analysis to Comparative Law', 48(2) *The International and Comparative Law Quarterly* (1999), 405–18.

PABE Final Report, 'Public Perceptions of Agricultural Biotechnology in Europe', http:// csec.lancs.ac.uk/pabe/docs/pabe_finalreport.pdf (2001).

Parker, Richard W., 'Is Government Regulation Irrational?: A Reply to Morrall and Hahn', Paper 31 *University of Connecticut School of Law Articles and Working Papers*, (2004), 1–22.

Parker, Richard W., 'The Empirical Roots of the "Regulatory Reform" Movement: A Critical Appraisal', 58 *Administrative Law Review* (2006), 359–400.

Pauwelyn, Joost, 'The WTO Agreement on Sanitary and Phytosanitary Measures as Applied in the First Three SPS Disputes', 2(4) *Journal of International Economic Law* (1999), 641–64.

Pauwelyn, Joost, 'U.S. Federal Climate Policy and Competitiveness Concerns: The Limits and Options of International Trade Law', *Working Paper, Nicolas Institute for Environmental Policy Solutions, Duke University*, (2007).

Pildes, Richard H. and Cass R. Sunstein, 'Reinventing the Regulatory State', 62 *The University of Chicago Law Review* (1995), 1–129.

Pilkey, Orrin H., 'Reforming Cost-Benefit Calculations', 320(5882) *Science* (2008), 1423.

Posner, Eric A., 'Agencies Should Ignore Distant-Future Generations', 74 *University of Chicago Law Review* (2007), 139–43.

Posner, Eric A., *Economics of Public International Law*, (Cheltenham, UK: Edward Elgar Publishing, 2010).

Posner, Eric A. and Cass R. Sunstein, 'Dollars and Death', 72 *University of Chicago Law Review* (2005), 537–98.

Quick, Reinhard and Andreas Bluthner, 'Has the Appellate Body Erred? An Appraisal and Criticism of the Ruling in the WTO Hormones Case', 2(4) *Journal of International Economic Law* (1999), 603–39.

Radin, Margaret J., 'Market-Inalienability', 100 *Harvard Law Review* (1987), 1849–937.

Ramsey, Frank P., 'A Mathematical Theory of Saving', 38 *Economic Journal* (1928), 543–59.

Renda, Andrea, 'The development of RIA in the European Union: an overview,' paper presented at the World Bank Regulatory Reform Conference in Belgrade, Serbia, September 13– 14, 2010. Available at http://papers.ssrn.com/sol3/papers.cfm?abstract_id=1679764.

Renn, Ortwin, 'Concepts of Risk: A Classification', in Sheldon Krimsky and Dominic Godling (eds), *Social Theories of Risk* (Westport, CT: Praeger, 1992), 53–79.

Renn, Ortwin and Bernd Rohrmann (eds), *Cross-cultural Risk Perception – A Survey of Empirical Studies* (Dordrecht: Kluwer Academic Publisher, 2000).

Revesz, Richard L., 'Rehabilitating Interstate Competition: Rethinking the Race-to-the-

Bottom Rationale for Federal Environmental Regulation', 67 *New York University Law Review* (1992), 1210–54.

Revesz, Richard L., 'Federalism and Interstate Environmental Externalities', 144 *University of Pennsylvania Law Review* (1996), 2341–416.

Revesz, Richard L., 'Federalism and Environmental Regulation: Lessons for the European Union and the International Community', 83(7) *Virginia Law Review* (1997a), 1331–46.

Revesz, Richard L., 'The Race for the Bottom and Federal Environmental Regulation: A Response to Critics', 82 *Minnesota Law Review* (1997b), 535–64.

Revesz, Richard L., 'Environmental Regulation, Cost-Benefit Analysis and the Discounting of Human Lives', 99 *Columbia Law Review* (1999), 941–1017.

Revesz, Richard L., 'Federalism and Regulation: Extrapolating from the Analysis of Environmental Regulation in the United States', 3 *Journal of International Economic Law* (2000a), 219–33.

Revesz, Richard L., 'Environmental Regulation in Federal Systems', 1 *Yearbook of European Environmental Law* (2000b), 1–35.

Revesz, Richard L. and Michael A. Livermore, *Retaking Rationality: How Cost-Benefit Analysis Can Better Protect the Environment and Our Health* (New York: Oxford University Press, 2008).

Sagoff, Mark, 'Economic Theory and Environmental Law', 79 *Michigan Law Review* (1981), 1393–419.

Schoenbaum, Thomas J., 'International Trade and Protection of the Environment: The Continuing Search for Reconciliation', 91(2) *American Journal of International Law* (1997), 268–313.

Schroeder, Ted C., Glynn T. Tonsor, Joost M.E. Pennings and James Mintert, 'Consumer Food Safety Risk Perceptions and Attitudes: Impacts on Beef Consumption across Countries', 7(1) *The B.E. Journal of Economic Analysis & Policy* (2007), article 65.

Slovic, Paul, 'Perception of Risk', 236 *Science* (1987), 280–85.

Slovic, Paul, 'Beyond Numbers: A Broader Perspective on Risk Perception and Risk Communication', in D.G. Mayo and R.D. Hollander (eds), *Acceptable Evidence – Science and Value in Risk Management* (New York: Oxford University Press, 1991), 48–65.

Slovic, Paul, 'Trust, Emotion, Sex, Politics, and Science: Surveying the Risk-Assessment Battlefield', 19 *Risk Analysis* (1999), 689–701.

Sunstein, Cass R., 'Incommensurability and Valuation in Law', 92 *Michigan Law Review* (1994), 779–861.

Sunstein, Cass R., *The Cost-Benefit State: The Future of Regulatory Protection* (Chicago, IL: American Bar Association, 2002).

Sunstein, Cass R., *Laws of Fear: Beyond the Precautionary Principle* (Cambridge, UK: Cambridge University Press, 2005).

Sunstein, Cass R. and Richard H. Thaler, 'Libertarian Paternalism is Not an Oxymoron', 70(4) *University of Chicago Law Review* (2003), 1159–202.

Thomas, William A., 'Supreme Court Review of the OSHA Benzene Standard', 36(3) *The American Statistician, Part 2: Proceedings of the Sixth Symposium on Statistics and the Environment* (1982), 264–66.

Tiebout, Charles, 'A Pure Theory of Local Expenditures', 64(5) *Journal of Political Economy* (1956), 416–33.

Trachtman, Joel P., 'Regulatory Jurisdiction and the WTO', 10(3) *Journal of International Economic Law* (2007), 631–51.

Trebilcock, Michael J. and Robert Howse, 'Trade Liberalization and Regulatory Diversity: Reconciling Competitive Markets with Competitive Politics', 6 *European Journal of Law and Economics* (1998), 5–37.

Trebilcock, Michael J. and Julie Soloway, 'International Trade Policy and Domestic Food Safety Regulation: The Case for Substantial Deference by the WTO Dispute Settlement Body under the SPS Agreement' in Daniel M. Kennedy and James D. Southwick (eds), *The Political Economy of International Trade Law: Essays in Honour of Robert E. Hudec* (Cambridge, UK: Cambridge University Press, 2002), 537–74.

Viscusi, W. Kip, *Fatal Trade-off: Public and Private Responsibilities for Risk* (New York: Oxford University Press, 1992).

Viscusi, W. Kip, *Rational Risk Policy: The Arne Ryde Memorial Lectures* (Oxford, UK: Clarendon Press, 1998).

Viscusi, W. Kip, 'How to Value a Life', 32 *Journal of Economic Finance* (2008), 311–23.

Vogel, David, *Trading Up: Consumer and Environmental Regulation in a Global Economy* (Cambridge, MA: Harvard University Press, 1995).

Walker, Vern R., 'Keeping the WTO from Becoming the "World Trans-science Organization": Scientific Uncertainty, Science Policy, and Fact-finding in the Growth Hormones Dispute', 31 *Cornell International Law Journal* (1998), 251–320.

Walker, Vern, 'The Myth of Science as a "Neutral Arbiter" for Triggering Precautions', 26 *Boston College International and Comparative Law Review* (2003), 197–228.

Wiener, Jonathan B., 'Whose Precaution After All? A Comment on the Comparison and the Evolution of Risk Regulatory Systems', 13 *Duke Journal of Comparative and International Law* (2003), 207–62

Zerbe, Richard O. Jr. and Dwight D. Dively, *Benefit-Cost Analysis in Theory and in Practice* (New York: Harper Collins, 1994).

Zerbe, Richard O. Jr., 'Is Cost-Benefit Analysis Legal? Three Rules', 17 *Journal of Policy Analysis and Management* (1998), 419–56.

WTO CASES

Appellate Body Report, *EC Measures Concerning Meat and Meat Products (Hormones)*, WT/DS26/AB/R, WT/DS48/AB/R, adopted 16 January 1998, AB-1997-4 (*EC – Hormones*).

Appellate Body Report, *Australia – Measures Affecting Importation of Salmon*, WT/DS18/AB/R, adopted 6 November 1998, DSR 1998:VIII, 3327 (*Australia – Salmon*).

Appellate Body Report, *Japan – Measures Affecting Agricultural Product*, WT/DS76/AB/R, adopted 19 March 1999, DSR 1999:I, 277 (*Japan – Agricultural Products II*).

Appellate Body Report, *Japan – Measures Affecting the Importation of Apples*, WT/DS245/AB/R, adopted 10 December 2003, DSR 2003:IX, 4391 (*Japan – Apples*).

Panel Report, *European Communities – Measures Affecting the Approval and Marketing of Biotech Products*, WT/DS291/R, WT/DS292/R, WT/DS293/R, adopted 29 September 2006 (*EC – Biotech*).

Panel Reports, *Canada/United States – Continued Suspension of Obligations in the EC – Hormones Disputes*, WT/DS320/R, WT/DS321/R, adopted 16 October 2008, AB-2008-5 (*US – Continued Suspension*).

Panel Report, *Australia – Measures Affecting the Importation of Apples from New Zealand*, WT/DS367/R, adopted 9 August 2010, Appellate Body Report, *Australia – Measures Affecting the Importation of Apples from New Zealand*, WT/DS367/AB/R, adopted 29 November 2010, AB-2010-2 (*Australia – Apples*).

7. Trade, environment and animal welfare: conditioning trade in goods and services on conduct in another country?

Peter Morrison and Laura Nielsen

I. INTRODUCTION

A. Protection of the Environment or Animal Welfare in the Course of Trade

When States deem international protection of the environment or animal welfare insufficient, they may unilaterally seek to promote those interests through trade measures. States may, for example, prohibit the import of fur and skins derived from animals that are skinned alive, even though no fully global international or multilateral treaty outlaws these practices.[1] Such trade measures must be in conformity with WTO[2] law, which consists largely of negative obligations on how *not* to restrict trade, rather than positive rules that directly regulate the environment or animal welfare. Measures to protect the environment or animal welfare that impose trade restrictions may therefore violate a substantive obligation under WTO law and hence need to be justified in order to be WTO consistent.

The interface between trade and environment as well as trade and animal welfare is traditionally discussed in relation to trade in goods, and measures affecting trade in goods have been the subject of several GATT[3] and WTO cases, as well as much scholarly analysis. The innovative idea

---

[1]   Regional treaties may, however, outlaw some inhumane practices.

[2]   The World Trade Organization was established in 1995 by the founding act – Final Act Embodying the Results of the Uruguay Round of Multilateral Trade Negotiations, 15 April 1994, 1967 U.N.T.S. 14 (1994). The WTO Agreement establishes the WTO, and all other agreements are annexed to this agreement. See the Marrakesh Agreement Establishing the World Trade Organization, 15 April, 1994, 1967 U.N.T.S. 14 (1994), into force 1 January 1995 [hereinafter the WTO Agreement].

[3]   The reference to 'GATT' here means the de facto trade organization from 1948 to 1994, see the General Agreement on Tariffs and Trade, 30 October 1947, 55 U.N.T.S. 194.

in this chapter is to analyse *also* that interface in relation to trade in services.

In the trade in services area, a State may choose to regulate the behaviour of its own citizens when consuming services abroad (in WTO terminology 'consumption abroad' or 'mode 2') going far beyond what can be done with respect to trade in goods. In the services area, a State can prohibit its citizens from consuming services in relation to a broader range of environmental and animal welfare concerns than those purely related to trade in a specific good. An example of this difference between goods and services approaches concerns hunting for endangered species. Clearly, this practice does not necessarily lead to the *trade* of the dead endangered species or parts thereof, which is prohibited under CITES[4] and therefore also by most WTO Members. Where there is no trade in these species or parts thereof, a trade ban would obviously not have any effect on practices in a host State of an endangered species that allows it to be hunted. In such a case, however, a State can bar its citizens abroad from dealings with suppliers of services involving the hunting of endangered species.

This chapter seeks to clarify how far a State can go in seeking to avoid directly or indirectly 'sponsoring' unacceptable behaviour taking place outside its own territory, in relation to trade in both goods and services. Is it, for example, legal to prohibit firms or individuals from buying services abroad from a fur coat maker that engages in making, selling or servicing furs and skins from animals skinned alive? Or dining in a restaurant abroad that serves foie gras, or perhaps even monkeys' brains eaten directly from live and un-anaesthetized monkeys? Or is it legal to ban imports of cosmetics tested on animals in a foreign country? In answering those questions, we recall that all States under the notion of *pacta sunt servanda* must live up to all their international obligations, and all measures must of course be evaluated in relation to all relevant treaty or customary law obligations. In this chapter we focus primarily on whether States live up to their WTO obligations when protecting animals or the environment within another State's jurisdiction. However, we also reflect on whether certain types of trade measure violate other norms in *jus gentium* – for example whether sovereignty is infringed, or whether issues arise concerning extraterritorial jurisdiction.

---

[4]   See Convention on International Trade in Endangered Species of Wild Fauna and Flora, 3 March 1973, 993 U.N.T.S. 243, 12 I.L.M. 1085 (1973).

B.   Animal Welfare and the Environment

Animal welfare is often analysed alongside or even as a part of environmental issues, although this topic is not really an environmental one.[5] In this chapter, we do not wish to opine on whether it is desirable to treat animal welfare in connection with environmental discourses, or whether it would be preferable to treat the area as distinct from the environmental field. We do, however, wish to set out briefly what the primary differences are between animal welfare and environmental issues, and why we have chosen to include both areas in this chapter.

Animal welfare is the protection of individual specimens of animals, their welfare, and sometimes even whether they have a right to life.[6] It can also be argued that special protection of certain classes of animals, such as great apes and pets falls under the notion of animal welfare – even if this special protection is not directly connected with their welfare. Rather, some practices, such as wearing dog and cat fur, may be considered inappropriate in some societies – regardless of whether the cats and dogs were killed humanely. In this chapter, these public moral issues are treated as part of our definition of animal welfare. Environmental protection of animals is, on the other hand, the protection of the species with the aim to preserve biodiversity.[7] Environmental protection of animals is guided by science in how it establishes the number of specimens left in a species. If very few remain, the species is deemed endangered and thus protected by various multilateral environmental agreements (MEAs) covering the topic.[8] These MEAs do not, however, give an 'all-round' protection of the endangered species, meaning that States sometimes decide to protect the species through trade measures. An example of this practice arose when the US decided to protect endangered sea turtles from being drowned when fishermen harvested shrimp.[9] Animal welfare, on the other hand, is guided

---

[5]   See e.g., Patricia Birnie et al., *International Law & the Environment* (Oxford: Oxford University Press, 3rd ed., 2009), 596–7; Laura Nielsen, *The WTO, Animals and PPMs* (Leiden: Martinus Nijhoff Publishers, 2007), 16–17.

[6]   See e.g., Nielsen, above note 5, at 83–106. For the newest developments and analysis concerning the legal status of animals and whether they can be right-holders in national systems, see e.g., Richard L. Cupp, Jr., 'Moving Beyond Animal Rights: A Legal Contractualist Critique', 46 *San Diego L. Rev.* 27 (2009), available at http://papers.ssrn.com/sol3/papers.cfm?abstract_id=1411863 last visited on 7 September 2011.

[7]   See e.g., Nielsen, above note 5, at 41–81.

[8]   See ibid.

[9]   This is not covered by CITES that solely relates to trade in endangered species and the incidental taking of them, but this does nevertheless fall under the

by human judgment as to the degree of suffering an animal should endure – and this of course differs greatly from country to country.[10] Whereas biodiversity protection is established in several MEAs, no international agreements on animal welfare exist, although a few regional ones are in force.[11] Animal welfare concerns are therefore more likely than biodiversity worries to tempt governments to use unilateral trade measures – in particular because there are fewer hard law treaties on animal welfare issues, and less of a 'tradition' for negotiating them, and governments hence often will have no alternative option than to resort to unilateral measures.

Both animal welfare and environmental issues are included in this Chapter for two reasons. First, the two topics are often treated as if they were identical in the trade discourse, despite their very different characteristics and core 'motivations'. It is therefore important to illustrate how to distinguish between them. Second, the two areas, as well as human health and labour issues, are treated under the same legal provisions in the WTO agreements, and therefore – from a practical point of view – it makes sense to analyse them together. Human health protection in the course of trade in goods with the aim to ensure the safety of food and animal feed is, however, not included in this Chapter as it generally falls within a *lex specialis* agreement under the WTO.[12] Neither the environment nor

---

Bonn Convention, see Convention on the Conservation of Migratory Species of Wild Animals, Jan. 1980, 19 I.L.M. 15 (1980) [hereinafter the Bonn Convention], but the US is not a party to that treaty, see http://www.cms.int last visited on 7 September 2011.

[10]   In Germany, animals are now included in the Constitution, see Cupp, above note 6, at 29, citing to John Hooper, 'German Parliament Votes to Give Animals Constitutional Rights', *The Guardian* (18 May 2002).

[11]   See e.g., See European Convention for the Protection of Animals During International Transport, Paris, 13 December 1968, European Treaty Series, No. 65, 103, 193 available at http://conventions.coe.int last visited 7 September 2011; European Convention for the Protection of Animals Kept for Farming Purposes, Strasbourg, 10 March 1976, European Treaty Series, No. 87, 145 available at http://conventions.coe.int last visited 7 September 2011; European Convention for the Protection of Animals for Slaughter, Strasbourg, 10 May 1979, European Treaty Series, No. 102, available at http://conventions.coe.int last visited 7 September 2011 ; European Convention for the Protection of Vertebrate Animals Used for Experimental and Other Scientific Purposes, Strasbourg, 18 March 1986, European Treaty Series, No. 123, 170 available at http://conventions.coe.int last visited 7 September 2011; European Convention for the Protection of Pet Animals, Strasbourg, 13 November 1987, European Treaty Series, No. 125, available at http://conventions.coe.int last visited 7 September 2011.

[12]   See Agreement on the Application of Sanitary and Phytosanity Measures, WTO Agreement Annex 1A [hereinafter SPS Agreement], Annex A(1), where the definition of the term 'SPS measure' is set out.

animal welfare usually falls within this specialized agreement.[13] We have also chosen not to include labour issues as they involve different considerations, beyond the scope of this Chapter.[14]

C. Roadmap

In section II of this chapter, we will set out the rules on trade in goods, followed by the rules on trade in services in section III and finally, in section IV, we will reflect on the differences between the two. In the course of the analysis, we will also touch upon the issue of why 'mode 2' limitations in trade in services (i.e. limitations on the consumption of services abroad) are not an example of extraterritorial jurisdiction.

II. TRADE IN GOODS

A. Measures Restricting Trade in Goods

Trade measures to address animal welfare or environmental concerns can be divided into two categories: a complete import ban on a particular product, and an import ban on a product made using a particular process or production method (PPM).[15] A good example of a complete ban is the EU prohibition on trade in, and import of, cat and dog fur.[16] That ban was enacted on grounds of animal welfare/public morals in the sense that it was judged to be immoral to use fur from pets for clothing.[17] States may however be in situations in which a total ban is not the optimal solution. This was the case in the two most prominent GATT and WTO cases,

---

[13] But see Panel Report, *European Communities – Measures Affecting the Approval and Marketing of Biotech Products*, WT/DS291/R, WT/DS293/R (29 May 2006), paras 7.196, 7,207, 7,212, that surprisingly included environmental concerns in the scope of this agreement. For further analysis, see Nielsen, above note 5, at 128–32.

[14] But see Frank Emmert, 'Labor, Environmental Standards and World Trade Law', 10 *U. C. Davis J. Int'l L. & Pol'y* 75 (2003).

[15] Strictly speaking PPMs can be divided into two categories: non-product related PPMs and product related PPMs. However all the PPMs discussed in this Chapter are non-product related PPMs. Therefore the term PPM as used here should be read to refer only to non-product related PPMs.

[16] See European Parliament and Council Regulation 1523/2007 of 11 December 2007 banning the placing on the market and the import to, or export from, the Community of cat and dog fur, and products containing such fur.

[17] See ibid.

involving US attempts to protect dolphins and endangered sea turtles.[18] In those cases, the US wished to import both tuna fish and shrimp, but wanted to avoid the incidental taking of, respectively, dolphins and sea turtles. Therefore, the US decided to condition imports of tuna and shrimp on whether the exporters lived up to PPM requirements for 'dolphin-friendly' and 'sea turtle-friendly' fishing methods. The reason for protecting dolphins was purely an animal welfare concern, since dolphins were not endangered. In the dolphin case, the 'Flipper-effect' was enough to spark very high awareness of dolphin deaths in the general public, which the US Congress responded to by enacting a special 'Dolphin Protection Consumer Information Act'.[19] Sea turtles, on the other hand, are an endangered migratory species and the rationale was therefore an environmental one.[20] A third category of trade measure – sanctions – can also be envisaged. In a sanctions scenario, a State would ban imports of all or some products unrelated to the policy purpose pursued by the sanction, solely on the grounds that another State generally treats animals badly or injures the environment. These types of sanctions are, however, beyond the scope of this Chapter as well as being clearly inconsistent with WTO law.[21]

While the bans based on PPMs may appear to be less trade restrictive than total bans because they ban 'only' those products that are produced in a special way, they are nevertheless more problematic. By demanding that imported products be produced in a certain way, the import is con-

---

[18]   See Panel Report, *United States – Restrictions on Imports of Tuna*, DS21/R-39S/155 (3 September 1991), unadopted GATT panel report, [hereinafter *US – Tuna I*] available on LEXIS; Panel Report, *United States – Restrictions on Imports of Tuna*, DS29/R (16 June 1994), unadopted GATT panel report, [hereinafter *US – Tuna II*], available on LEXIS; Appellate Body Report, *United States – Import Prohibition of Certain Shrimp and Shrimp Products, Recourse to Article 21.5 of the DSU by Malaysia*, WT/DS58/AB/RW (22 October 2001) [hereinafter *US – Shrimp 21.5 AB*].

[19]   See 16 U.S.C. § 1385. See also Larry E. Craig and Jade West, Legislative Note from US Senate Republican Policy Committee, S. 39, The International Dolphin Conservation Program Act, 23 July 1997, available at http://www. senate.gov last visited on 7 September 2011 or http://www.senate.gov/~rpc/ releases/1997/32-Tuna.jm.htm last visited on 7 September 2011, which describes how Congress codified the dolphin safe label as initiated by three large producers of tuna. For further analysis and background, see Nielsen, above note 5, at 248–51; Dale D. Murphy, 'The Tuna-Dolphin Wars', 40 *J. World Trade* 597 (2006).

[20]   See Appellate Body Report, *United States – Import Prohibition of Certain Shrimp and Shrimp Products*, WT/DS58/AB/R (12 October 1998), paras. 131–2 [hereinafter *US – Shrimp AB*].

[21]   Trade sanctions that are unrelated to the production of the product itself will not survive the tests in the General Exceptions in GATT Article XX, see Nielsen, above note 5, at 174.

ditioned on activities (PPMs) that are within another State's jurisdiction. This aspect of PPMs has sparked many – often misguided – discussions over the years.[22] It is doubtless true that PPMs are coercive in the sense that an importing State appears to impose on an exporting State a change of PPMs within the exporting State's jurisdiction. However, under general international law, the exporting State is free to export to other States that do not have PPM requirements. Another way to view the issue is that, under general international law, a State is under no obligation to import particular products, since each State has the sovereign right to set its own trade policies and ban whichever products it wishes, or set conditions for their import. This sovereign right over trade policy is, of course, subject to a very important limitation: most States are bound by international treaty obligations with respect to trade, in particular those deriving from their WTO membership. The legality of PPMs therefore boils down in most cases to whether such measures are consistent with WTO law, and it is these limits this Chapter seeks to set out. A further point should be noted. Total bans (that do not involve PPMs) also can serve the purpose of changing undesirable practices inside another State's jurisdiction, if the import market in which the ban operates is large enough to put, for example, cat and dog fur producers out of business.

The legality of trade measures can be evaluated under different Agreements in the WTO. So far, environmental trade measures raised in WTO dispute settlement proceedings are targeted at goods, and have been evaluated under the umbrella agreement covering trade in goods – the General Agreement on Tariffs and Trade (GATT).[23] Should a trade measure be found to violate a GATT provision – for example, it is discriminatory under Article I or Article III, or constitutes a quantitative restriction under Article XI – it may nonetheless be justified under one of the General Exceptions found in Article XX. One apparent difficulty in justifying a trade measure under Article XX has been that the GATT, which was drafted in the 1940s, does not specifically mention 'the environment' or 'animal welfare' in its listing of relevant permissible policy purposes under

---

[22]   See e.g., ibid., at 262–70, that enumerates a range of discussions of extra-territorial, extra-jurisdictional and unilateral issues that have been discussed with more or less success over the years.

[23]   See the General Agreement on Tariffs and Trade, 15 April 1994, WTO Agreement Annex 1A (GATT 1994); the General Agreement on Tariffs and Trade, 30 October 1947, 55 U.N.T.S. 194 (GATT 1947). GATT 1994 incorporates GATT 1947 and GATT 1994 did not alter the Articles at issue in this Chapter (namely GATT Articles I, III, XI and XX) – therefore GATT is used here without specifying whether it is GATT 1947 or GATT 1994.

these exceptions. The Appellate Body has nevertheless interpreted the text of Article XX as covering the environment.[24] The Agreement on Technical Barriers to Trade (TBT Agreement) is, on the other hand, a more modern Agreement having its roots in the Tokyo Round in the 1970s, with updates in the Uruguay Round in the early 1990s.[25] Not surprisingly, the TBT Agreement does mention 'the environment' as a relevant policy purpose, although it still does not speak of 'animal welfare'.[26] This Agreement is *lex specialis* with respect to the more generally applicable GATT,[27] and is used to evaluate trade measures that are 'technical regulations', 'standards' or 'conformity assessment procedures'.[28]

1. GATT substantive obligations

Trade measures based on PPMs, which thus condition import on performance inside another State's jurisdiction, are most likely to violate Articles I, III or XI:1 of the GATT.

Article I establishes 'most favoured nation treatment' (MFN). This requires that 'any advantage' granted to a State with respect to a product be granted 'immediately and unconditionally' to all WTO Members. Article I deals both with *de jure* and *de facto* discrimination.[29] Therefore a PPM-based measure that conditions market access on, for example, special certification of 'sea turtle-friendly' fishing methods for WTO Members that host endangered sea turtles in the waters where the fishermen harvest shrimp will be *de facto* discriminatory because those WTO Members (for example Denmark) that do not host any endangered sea turtles are not subject to the requirement of certification of their production methods, and thus have 'an advantage'.[30]

Article III concerns national treatment, which essentially prohibits

---

[24]   See Claus-Dieter Ehlermann, 'Six Years on the Bench of the "World Trade Court,"' 36 *J. World Trade* 605, 615–16 (2002). See also Nielsen, above note 5, at 157–62, 196.

[25]   See Agreement on Technical Barriers to Trade, WTO Agreement Annex 1A [hereinafter TBT Agreement].

[26]   See TBT Agreement, chapeau, Article 2.2.

[27]   See Panel Report, *European Communities – Trade Description of Sardines*, WT/DS231/R, (29 May 2002) [*EC – Sardines*], where the Panel held that both the TBT Agreement and GATT applied, but that the TBT Agreement dealt 'specifically, and in detail' with technical regulations.

[28]   See TBT Agreement, Annex 1:1, 1:2 and 1:3.

[29]   See Appellate Body Report, *Canada – Certain Measures Affecting the Automotive Industry*, WT/DS139/AB/R, WT/DS142/AB/R (31 May 2000), para. 78.

[30]   This was not the issue in the *US – Shrimp* case, but a hypothetically thought out example.

domestic products from being accorded more favourable treatment than the 'like' imported product. A key to both Articles I and III is to define the 'like' product. [31] In doing so, the Appellate Body evaluates four criteria: physical properties, end-uses, consumers' tastes and habits and tariff classification.[32] Therefore, if a product is 'identical' to another and only distinguished by a PPM, they are most likely to be 'like' products and, if one is discriminated against, either vis-à-vis 'an advantage' granted to another State or vis-à-vis more favourable treatment of the domestic product, these provisions will be violated.

Article XI:1 is a general prohibition against quantitative restrictions with respect to both imported and exported products. A ban, which is a prohibition on all imports of a certain product (whether based on the characteristics of the product itself or on the PPM of the product) would thus violate this provision. Article XI:1 was found, for example, to have been violated in the case of *US – Shrimp*.[33]

2. GATT General Exceptions

We have seen that PPM-based trade measures to protect the environment or animal welfare, because they constitute a quantitative restriction, or treat imported products less favourably than 'like' products from other foreign or domestic sources, will risk violating a substantive obligation under the GATT. If they do violate a provision, then the issue becomes whether the trade measure is justified under one of the General Exceptions in GATT Article XX. Taking a strict textual approach to Article XX, we can see that both animal welfare and the environment may be covered by GATT Article XX(a), (b) or (g):

> Subject to the requirement that such measures are not applied in a manner which would constitute a means of arbitrary or unjustifiable discrimination between countries where the same conditions prevail, or a disguised restriction of international trade, nothing in this Agreement shall be construed to prevent the adoption or enforcement by any contracting party of measures:

---

[31] 'Like' products are to be understood in the same manner in GATT Articles I and III, see Appellate Body Report, *Indonesia – Certain Measures Affecting the Automobile Industry*, WT/DS54/R (2 July 1998), para. 14.141. However, the nature and extent of the competitive relationship required for products to be 'like' differs from provision to provision (the 'accordion' of likeness).

[32] See e.g., Appellate Body Report, *European Communities – Measures Affecting Asbestos and Asbestos-Containing Products*, WT/DS135/AB/R (12 March 2001), para. 110 [hereinafter *EC – Asbestos* AB].

[33] See Panel Report, *United States – Import Prohibition of Certain Shrimp and Shrimp Products*, WT/DS58/R (15 May 1998), para. 7.17.

(a) necessary to protect public morals;
(b) necessary to protect human, animal or plant life or health;

. . .

(g) relating to the conservation of exhaustible natural resources if such measures are made effective in conjunction with restrictions on domestic production
or consumption.

The structure of GATT Article XX requires that a two-step analysis be
undertaken. The measure at issue, already found to be inconsistent with
another provision of the GATT, must first be evaluated to determine
whether it fits within one of the subparagraphs of Article XX listing the
valid policy purposes pursuant to which a measure may been taken. The
measure must then be assessed against the wording of the introductory
clause, commonly known as the 'chapeau'.[34] It has yet to be seen whether
a panel or the Appellate Body will interpret animal welfare as a policy
coming within paragraph (a) 'public morals', or within paragraph (b)
'human, animal or plant life or health' or under paragraph (g) 'conservation of exhaustible natural resources' as the GATT panels did in both
US – Tuna I and *US – Tuna II.* Interestingly, in the two *Tuna* cases,
the measures were *not* environmental, but animal welfare measures (as
mentioned above, dolphins were not endangered).[35] Environmental cases
usually fall within paragraphs (b) or (g), where paragraph (g) was historically preferred because the 'relating to' test was seen as relatively easier
to satisfy than the 'necessary to' test required to justify a measure under
paragraph (b).[36] This appeared quite problematic, as protection of humans
did not fall under paragraph (g), unless, as has been noted with humour,
'mankind is itself an exhaustible natural resource'.[37] Thus measures pursuing this policy goal are subject to the higher threshold of necessity. The

---

[34]   See Appellate Body Report, *United States – Standards for Reformulated and
Conventional Gasoline*, WT/DS2/AB/R (29 April 1996), at pp. 21–2 [hereinafter
US – Gasoline AB].

[35]   See *US – Tuna I*, above note 18, at paras. 5.24–5.25; *US – Tuna II*, above
note 18, at para. 5.30. For further discussion of which subparagraphs that *de sen-
tential ferenda* should apply, see Nielsen, above note 5, at 13–14, 235–41. See also
Steve Charnovitz, 'The Moral Exception in Trade Policy', 38 *Va. J. Int'l L.* 689
(1998); Alan Swinebank, 'Like Products, Animal Welfare and the World Trade
Organization', 40 *J. World Trade* 687 (2006).

[36]   See Appellate Body Report, *Korea – Measures Affecting Imports of Fresh,
Chilled and Frozen Beef*, WT/DS161/AB/R, WT/DS169/AB/R (Dec. 11, 2000), at
para. 161, and accompanying footnote [hereinafter *Korea – Beef* AB]. For a critique of this, see e.g., Nielsen, above note 5, at 190–92, 258–60.

[37]   Arthur E. Appleton, 'Shrimp/Turtle: Untangling the Nets', 2. *J. Int'l Econ.
L.* 477, 483 (1999).

Appellate Body has, however, seemingly sought to cure this problem by modifying the 'necessity' test in its latest ruling on subparagraph (b) in *Brazil – Retreaded Tyres*. The Appellate Body in that case clarified that the 'necessity' test requires that the measure 'materially contribute' to achieve the policy goal in issue, which is closer to the correlating test in paragraph (g) 'relating to', which historically has been understood to require that the measure be 'primarily aimed at' the policy goal in issue:[38]

> In order to justify an import ban under Article XX(b), a panel must be satisfied that it brings about a *material contribution* to the achievement of its objective. Such a demonstration can of course be made by resorting to evidence or data, pertaining to the past or the present, that establish that the import ban at issue makes a *material contribution* to the protection of public health or environmental objectives pursued.[39] (emphasis added)

The factor of material contribution is however only one of a series of factors, which are to be weighed and balanced against each other. The Appellate Body states that the necessity test

> involves in every case a process of weighing and balancing a series of factors which prominently include the contribution made by the compliance measure to the enforcement of the law or regulation at issue, the importance of the common interests or values protected by that law or regulation, and the accompanying impact of the law or regulation on imports or exports.[40]

Another theme closely related to which test is the 'easiest' to meet is whether the different trade tests, the related to and the necessity, are differentiated depending on what 'value' is sought to be protected.[41] Clearly, that would mean that the otherwise historically difficult 'necessity' test would be relaxed if it were applied to a measure taken to pursue a policy of undoubted importance and urgency, such as human health. This approach seems to be suggested by the Appellate Body in *EC – Asbestos*,[42] which refers to a previous holding in *Korea – Beef*, suggesting that a type of

---

[38] See *US – Shrimp* AB, above note 20, at para. 136.

[39] Appellate Body Report, *Brazil – Measures Affecting the Imports of Retreaded Tyres*, WT/DS332/AB/R (3 December 2007), para. 151 [*Brazil – Retreaded Tyres*].

[40] *Korea – Beef* AB, above note 36, at para. 164.

[41] For further discussion, see Nielsen, above note 5, at 239–41.

[42] See *EC – Asbestos* AB, above note 32, at para. 172. Note, however, this is not a holding, but dicta, see Laura Yavitz (Nielsen), 'The World Trade Organization Appellate Body Report, European Communities – Measures Affecting Asbestos and Asbestos-Containing Products, March 12, 2001, WT/DS135/AB/R' 11 *Minn. J. Global Trade* 43, 64, 66–7 (2002).

proportionality test was introduced.[43] The apparent introduction of a proportionality test reaches to the heart of a controversial WTO issue: should measures to be justified under Article XX of the GATT be judged, in part, by assessing the importance of the policy being pursued? Previously, it had been understood that the relative importance of Members' policies within the sub-paragraphs of Article XX was not to be examined, since the importance of a policy purpose was a matter that only the individual Member could assess. Since the apparent adoption of a form of proportionality test in *EC – Asbestos* and *Korea – Beef*, this would appear no longer to be the case.

A measure needs also to be evaluated under the chapeau of Article XX. The chapeau constitutes a last test to ensure that the *application* of the measure does not amount to 'unjustifiable' and/or 'arbitrary' discrimination.[44] With respect to its application, a PPM-based measure will by its very nature raise certification and verification issues, and it is this special feature of the PPM that was greatly clarified in the *Shrimp* cases. Those cases upheld the principle that PPM-based measures could be designed and administered so as to meet the requirements of the chapeau, but the cases did not specify in precise terms how this might be done. Because total bans do not involve any type of certification or verification *inside another State's jurisdiction*, they are far easier to justify under the General Exceptions provisions in GATT Article XX.[45]

In conclusion, WTO Members have a wide range of possibilities for enacting WTO consistent PPM-based measures to protect both the environment and animal welfare, as long as those measures are designed within the limits set out above. The WTO consistency of any particular PPM requirement is difficult to define with a great degree of certainty. It may take further individual cases in the WTO dispute settlement mechanism to provide this clarity.

3. The TBT Agreement

As mentioned earlier, the TBT Agreement is generally applied as a *lex specialis* with respect to the GATT. Therefore, if a trade measure is a 'technical regulation', 'standard' or 'conformity assessment procedure' as laid down in the TBT Agreement, Annex 1, the TBT Agreement applies. In order to be a 'technical regulation', the Appellate Body has held that a measure has to apply to an identifiable group of products, lay down one

---

[43]   See *Korea – Beef* AB, above note 36, at para. 162.
[44]   See *US – Shrimp* AB, above note 20, at paras 161, 177.
[45]   See Nielsen, above note 5, at 275–88.

or more characteristics of a product and compliance must be mandatory.[46] Although private standards, applied by entities such as supermarket chains, are an emerging topic and a highly controversial issue with a great deal of practical relevance, we have chosen not to address the issue as it involves too many – very interesting – issues that are unsettled, pushing us beyond the scope of this chapter.

The TBT Agreement imposes certain obligations on Members with respect to technical regulations that are prepared, adopted or applied by central government bodies. For a start, the agreement requires Members to base their technical regulations on international standards, where these exist, unless they are deemed to be ineffective or inappropriate.[47] More significantly, from the point of view of WTO case law, non-discrimination and necessity obligations. The non-discrimination provision, set out in Article 2.1, combines typical national treatment and MFN obligations with respect to technical regulations. Article 2.2, on the other hand, provides that a technical regulation 'shall not be more trade-restrictive than necessary to fulfil a legitimate objective, taking into account the risks non-fulfillment would create'. A series of 'legitimate objectives' are listed, *inter alia:* national security requirements; the prevention of deceptive practices; protection of human health or safety, animal or plant life or health, or the environment. In assessing such risks, relevant elements of consideration are, *inter alia:* available scientific and technical information, related processing technology or intended end-uses of products.[48] In spite of animal welfare not being directly mentioned in this list, the panel in *US – Tuna II (Mexico)* found that the protection of dolphins was a legitimate objective – as protection of animal life.[49]

Recently, the WTO Appellate Body has analysed three key provisions in the TBT Agreement, each of which has its counterpart in the GATT.[50] As

---

[46] For further analysis of those criteria, see *EC – Asbestos* AB, above note 32, at paras 66–75; Appellate Body Report, *European Communities – Trade Description of Sardines*, WT/DS231/AB/R (26 September 2002), paras 176–95 [hereinafter *EC – Sardines* AB].

[47] See TBT Agreement, Article 2(4), 2(6).

[48] TBT Agreement, Article 2(2).

[49] *See US – Tuna II*, Report by the Panel, WT/DS381/R, paras 7.379–7.407.

[50] See e.g., TBT Agreement, Articles 2(1), 2(2), 2(3), 2(5). These provisions draw on key concepts set out in GATT Articles I, III and XX. The three cases are: *United States – Measures Affecting the Production and Sale of Clove Cigarettes* Report by the Appellate Body, WT/DS406/AB/R; *US – Tuna II (Mexico)* Report by the Appellate Body, WT/DS381/AB/R; and *United States – Certain Country of Origin Labelling (COOL) Requirements* Report by the Appellate Body, WT/DS384,386/AB/R.

mentioned above, one of these cases concerned the protection of dolphins. The focus in *US – Tuna II (Mexico)* was the documentation attached to the US dolphin safe requirements for marketing tuna in the US – and how this differed depending on where the tuna was caught. The Appellate Body found the measure to be discriminatory, in violation of Article 2.1 which reads:

> Members shall ensure that in respect of technical regulations, products imported from the territory of any Member shall be accorded treatment no less favourable than that accorded to like products of national origin and to like products originating in any other country.

The Appellate Body explained that Article 2.1 consists of three elements:

> Article 2.1 of the *TBT Agreement* consists of three elements that must be demonstrated in order to establish an inconsistency with this provision, namely: (i) that the measure at issue constitutes a 'technical regulation' within the meaning of Annex 1.1; (ii) that the imported products must be like the domestic product and the products of other origins; and (iii) that the treatment accorded to imported products must be less favourable than that accorded to like domestic products and like products from other countries.[51] (footnote omitted)

The Appellate Body had to evaluate only the last element of 'treatment no less favourable'. It found that a measure is discriminatory under Article 2.1 only if it is shown to have a 'detrimental impact on imports', and that this impact is not one that 'stems exclusively from a legitimate regulatory distinction'. In a finding that may have major a impact in PPM cases to come, it stated:

> As the Appellate Body has previously explained, when assessing claims brought under Article 2.1 of the *TBT Agreement*, a panel should therefore seek to ascertain whether the technical regulation at issue modifies the conditions of competition in the relevant market to the detriment of the group of imported products *vis-à-vis* the group of like domestic products or like products originating in any other country. The existence of such a detrimental effect is not sufficient to demonstrate less favourable treatment under Article 2.1. Instead, in *US – Clove Cigarettes*, the Appellate Body held that a 'panel must further analyze whether the detrimental impact on imports stems exclusively from a legitimate regulatory distinction rather than reflecting discrimination against the group of imported products.'[52]

Applying these criteria to the US dolphin-safe label, the Appellate Body found that the conditions to qualify, which were more onerous for tuna

---

[51]   *US – Tuna II (Mexico)* Report by the Appellate Body, WT/DS381/AB/R, para. 202.

[52]   *US – Tuna II (Mexico)* AB, at para. 215.

caught in the eastern tropical Pacific, modified the conditions of competition in the US market 'to the detriment' of the imported tuna caught in that particular area. Further, the Appellate Body found that the US had not demonstrated that the detrimental impact on tuna caught in the eastern tropical Pacific stemmed exclusively from a 'legitimate regulatory distinction', and that this was 'even-handed'.[53]

In the same case, the Appellate Body examined the compatibility of the US tuna-safe label conditions with the 'necessity' provision in Article 2.2 of the TBT. This provison states:

> Members shall ensure that technical regulations are not prepared, adopted or applied with a view to or with the effect of creating unnecessary obstacles to international trade. For this purpose, technical regulations shall not be *more trade-restrictive than necessary to fulfil a legitimate objective*, taking account of the risks non-fulfilment would create. Such legitimate objectives are, *inter alia:* national security requirements; the prevention of deceptive practices; protection of human health or safety, animal or plant life or health, or the environment. In assessing such risks, relevant elements of consideration are, *inter alia:* available scientific and technical information, related processing technology or intended end-uses of products. (emphasis added)

In analysing this provision, the Appellate Body drew heavily on its interpretation of the concept of 'necessary' found in the General Exceptions provision in GATT Article XX: As under that GATT provision, the Appellate Body found that three factors needed to be evaluated, combined with an evaluation of possible alternative measures put forward by the complainant:

> . . .
>
> In sum, we consider that an assessment of whether a technical regulation is 'more trade-restrictive than necessary' within the meaning of Article 2.2 of the *TBT Agreement* involves an evaluation of a number of factors. A panel should begin by considering factors that include: (i) the degree of contribution made by the measure to the legitimate objective at issue; (ii) the trade-restrictiveness of the measure; and (iii) the nature of the risks at issue and the gravity of consequences that would arise from non-fulfilment of the objective(s) pursued by the Member through the measure. In most cases, a comparison of the challenged measure and possible alternative measures should be undertaken. In particular, it may be relevant for the purpose of this comparison to consider whether the proposed alternative is less trade restrictive, whether it would make an equivalent contribution to the relevant legitimate objective, taking account of the risks non-fulfilment would create, and whether it is reasonably available.[54]

---

[53] *See US – Tuna II (Mexico)* AB, at para. 298.
[54] *Id.,* at paras 317, 322.

Based on the facts of this case, the Appellate Body found that Mexico had indeed proposed an alternative measure that was less trade restrictive:

> Since under the proposed alternative measure tuna caught in the ETP by setting on dolphins would be eligible for the 'dolphin-safe' label, it would appear, therefore, that the alternative measure proposed by Mexico would contribute to both the consumer information objective and the dolphin protection objective to a lesser degree than the measure at issue, because, overall, it would allow more tuna harvested in conditions that adversely affect dolphins to be labelled 'dolphin-safe'. We disagree therefore with the Panel's findings that the proposed alternative measure would achieve the United States' objectives 'to the same extent' as the existing US 'dolphin-safe' labelling provisions, and that the extent to which consumers would be misled as to the implications of the manner in which tuna was caught 'would not be greater' under the alternative measure proposed by Mexico.[55]

It is interesting to speculate whether the Appellate Body would have reached the same result in the *US – Tuna II (Mexico)* had it analysed the measure solely under the corresponding GATT provisions. It remains to be seen whether the notion of 'legitimate regulatory distinction' introduced by the Appellate Body will serve to widen the circle of technical regulations that are understood to be consistent with Article 2 of the TBT, and that previously were thought to violate the national treatment principle.

III.   TRADE IN SERVICES

A.   Measures Restricting Trade in Services

The scope of services trade covered by the GATS is much broader than the corresponding scope of goods trade covered by the GATT. While both agreements cover 'cross border' trade (a supplier in one country exports a good or a service to a consumer in another country), the GATS covers three other 'modes' of service trade. These extra modes are needed, since the cross-border supply of a service is often inconvenient, or technically or legally impossible because the supplier and consumer of the service need to be proximate, or at least in the same territory. Thus it may be necessary either for a service supplier to be present within the consumer's jurisdiction – surgery, or some types of banking, for example – or for a service consumer to be present in the supplier's jurisdiction – tourism, for

---

[55]   *Id.,* at paras 330–31.

example. So, as well as covering traditional 'cross-border' supply (Mode 1), the GATS also covers 'consumption abroad' (Mode 2) and two types of supplier presence abroad – as a 'commercial presence' (Mode 3), and as the presence of a 'natural person' (Mode 4).

Another way of thinking of the broad coverage of services trade in the GATS is to think of the modes of supply in terms of movement: Mode 1 covers the movement of the *service* into another country (e.g. telecommunications); Mode 2 covers the movement of the *consumer* abroad to consume the service (e.g. tourism); Mode 3 covers the movement abroad of the foreign *supplier* as a 'commercial presence' (e.g. a corporate presence); and Mode 4 covers the movement abroad of the foreign *supplier* as a 'natural person'.[56]

The GATS sets out the definitions of the four modes of supply of trade in services in Article 1:2 as follows:

> For the purposes of this Agreement, trade in services is defined as the supply of a service:
> (a) from the territory of one Member into the territory of any other Member;
> (b) in the territory of one Member to the service consumer of any other Member;
> (c) by a service supplier of one Member, through commercial presence in the territory of any other Member;
> (d) by a service supplier of one Member, through presence of natural persons of a Member in the territory of any other Member.

This chapter focuses only on services trade supplied under 'Mode 2', defined in sub-paragraph (b) as the supply of a service 'in the territory of one Member to the service consumer of any other Member'. Mode 2 supply is also known as 'consumption abroad', and includes consumers who are either physical or natural persons. This mode covers also cases where the consumer does not go abroad, but instead sends property to 'receive' the service. This could involve, for example, sending a ship abroad in order to be repaired. The issue posed in this chapter is how far a State can go, under WTO law, or other obligations in *jus gentium*, in regulating which services persons or companies are allowed to purchase abroad.

The extent to which a State can lawfully limit behaviour abroad is, apart from being a WTO law issue, also an issue of international jurisdiction.

---

[56] This simplified concept based on 'movement' is helpful to understand the concept of modes. However, the GATS legally defines the modes according to somewhat more complex criteria: the movement of the service (Mode 1), the presence of the consumer (Mode 2), and the presence and type of supplier (Modes 3 and 4).

Jurisdictional rules have moved beyond the traditional territorial paradigm in the sense that extra-territorial jurisdiction has become an established principle of international law.[57] Under the notion of 'objective territoriality', conduct occurring outside a State is considered nonetheless to be within its jurisdiction if the conduct has harmful effects inside the territory of that State.[58] In the exceptional case of a person committing a crime violating '*erga omnes*' norm outside a State's territory, it is increasingly accepted that a State may claim 'universal jurisdiction' over the crime, even in the absence of any link with that State.[59] Accordingly, the assertion of jurisdiction over a State's own citizen for actions abroad would appear no longer to be controversial, and could be considered an established principle of international law.[60]

With respect to services trade under the GATS, there arises an intriguing possibility for a WTO Member to reserve the right under WTO law to regulate the behaviour of its natural and legal persons abroad in connection with the consumption of a service by them in another WTO Member. A WTO Member might wish to do this, for example, in relation to consumption abroad by its citizens of entertainment services, such as bull fights, which were considered to be cruel and inconsistent with animal welfare.

How would this work? Under the GATS, a Member is bound to grant MFN treatment (no discrimination between 'like' services or service suppliers of different *foreign* origins) under Article II with respect to *all* services.[61] However, with respect to market access (Article XVI) and national treatment (Article XVII), a WTO Member is free to choose the services and modes of supply to which these commitments apply.[62] Furthermore,

---

[57]   See e.g., Anthony J. Colangelo, 'Constitutional Limits on Extraterritorial Jurisdiction: Terrorism and the Intersection of National and International Law', 48 *Harv. Int'l L. J.* 121, 128–9 (2007).

[58]   See ibid., at 129.

[59]   See ibid., at 130–35.

[60]   See ibid., at 129 and accompanying footnote at n. 60. See also Antonio Cassese, *International Law*, 49 (2005, 2nd ed.).

[61]   GATS Article II. Note, however, that if a Member permits no imports of a particular service, the MFN principle has no application, since no different 'treatment' between services of different foreign origins that can be compared. The principal exceptions to the MFN principle are for a service appearing on a Member's List of MFN Exemptions (Article II), a service supplied between Members of an economic integration area (Article V), a service supplied under government authority (Article I), government procurement (Article XIII), or a service involving air traffic rights (GATS Annex on Air Transport).

[62]   GATS Article XIX.

in the sectors it chooses, a Member is free to inscribe 'limitations' to full market access and national treatment in its GATS Schedule. Therefore, with respect to a market access commitment for a service supplied under Mode 2 ('consumption abroad'), a Member is free to negotiate a valid limitation prohibiting its nationals from purchasing that service abroad – a measure that would otherwise be inconsistent with full market access. Likewise, with respect to a national treatment commitment for a service supplied under Mode 2, a Member could add a limitation burdening its nationals in some way (a tax, or a disallowance of a tax deduction, for example) when they receive that service abroad. Such a measure would otherwise be inconsistent with full national treatment.

With respect to a trade measure prohibiting or limiting in some way the consumption abroad by a Member's nationals of a particular service, one must first determine whether the trade measure is nonetheless consistent with the corresponding commitment assumed by the Member in its GATS Schedule. Unlike for trade in goods the trade measure, even though incompatible with *full* market access or *full* national treatment, might nonetheless be permissible because it falls within a specific limitation negotiated by that Member and inscribed by it in its GATS Schedule, or concerns a service for which the Member has not taken any commitments in its Schedule. If the trade measure turns out to be inconsistent with the Member's commitment (and only in that case), we then proceed with a two-step analysis very similar to that carried out in the trade in goods case. First, does the trade measure fall within the scope of one or more of the sub-paragraphs of GATS Article XIV? Second, if so, is the measure applied in a way that meets the conditions of the chapeau to Article XIV?

Although a number of GATS obligations, notably MFN, are relevant when assessing the GATS consistency of a trade measure, our focus in this Chapter is on the use of *limitations* negotiated by a Member in connection with market access or national treatment commitments taken for the Mode 2 supply of a service. We therefore do not raise MFN issues that could also be present.

1.   Substantive obligations

In order to assess the GATS consistency of a trade measure limiting consumption abroad by its nationals, we need to look in more detail at the scope of the two main GATS obligations that are negotiable by each Member. When a WTO Member chooses to make specific commitments in a particular service sector, it does so with respect to two main obligations: market access (Article XVI) and national treatment (Article XVII). Market access covers quantitative-type limitations on the service or service supplier, whereas national treatment is meant to achieve non-discrimination between foreign and like domestic services and services suppliers by ensuring the equality of competitive conditions between them. Both market access and national treatment obligations cover measures affecting the service and the supplier of the service. By examining the nature of these obligations, we will attempt to discover how far limitations to these obligations entered in a Member's GATS Schedule serve to justify a trade measure that the Member may wish to take in pursuit of the protection of the environment, or to promote animal welfare.

Market access   Article XVI of the GATS defines full market access in terms of the absence of six categories of measures affecting services and service suppliers in the sector. These six categories of measures relate to (1) the number of service suppliers, (2) the quantity of the service, (3) the total number of service transactions, (4) the number of natural persons who may supply the service, (5) the legal form the supplier may take, and (6) restrictions on foreign equity.[63]

For the purposes of this chapter, we need not examine the categories of market access limitations that relate specifically to the number, legal structure, or foreign equity status of the service *supplier*. In the scenario being examined in this chapter, a WTO Member negotiates limitations on market access that directly govern the national as *consumer* of the service (whose actions abroad the Member wishes to restrict when harmful to the environment or animal welfare). Such measures which govern the national

---

[63]   The six categories of limitations that must not be maintained by a Member are stated in Article XVI(2) to be:

(a)   limitations on the number of service suppliers whether in the form of numerical quotas, monopolies, exclusive service suppliers or the requirements of an economic needs test;

(b)   limitations on the total value of service transactions or assets in the form of numerical quotas or the requirement of an economic needs test;

(c)   limitations on the total number of service operations or on the total quantity of service output expressed in terms of designated numerical units in the form of quotas or the requirement of an economic needs test;

(d)   limitations on the total number of natural persons that may be employed in a particular service sector or that a service supplier may employ and who are necessary for, and directly related to, the supply of a specific service in the form of numerical quotas or the requirement of an economic needs test;

(e)   measures which restrict or require specific types of legal entity or joint venture through which a service supplier may supply a service; and

(f)   limitations on the participation of foreign capital in terms of maximum percentage limit on foreign shareholding or the total value of individual or aggregate foreign investment.

as consumer cannot directly affect the number, legal structure or foreign equity status of the service supplier located in another WTO Member, and over whom it has no jurisdiction. Instead, we need to focus only on those market access limitations listed in Article XVI that affect the quantity of the *service*, since a limitation that prohibits the national from purchasing a service abroad will have a clear quantitative effect on the service itself. This is because the existence of each service transaction depends directly on two parties – the consumer and the supplier – and if the national is prohibited by its government from contracting the service abroad, a direct reduction in the quantity of the service will ensue.

From this perspective, we can put aside all but sub-paragraphs (b) and (c) of Article XVI:2, which read:

> (b) limitations on the total *value of service transactions* or assets in the form of numerical quotas or the requirement of an economic needs test;
> (c) limitations on the total *number of service operations* or on the total quantity of service output expressed in terms of designated numerical units in the form of quotas or the requirement of an economic needs test. (emphasis added)

These provisions would indicate that a prohibition by a WTO Member on its nationals from transacting certain committed services abroad that harm the environment or animal welfare could be seen as a measure that limits 'the total value of services transactions' or the 'total number of service operations' in the form of 'quotas'. A possible objection to this interpretation is that the measures in Article XVI are meant to govern only the service supplier, and that the list of measures in Article XVI is closed, and tightly drafted. However, to give weight to this objection one would have to accept that Article XVI has no meaning or application with respect to the supply of a service through Mode 2 (supply abroad), contrary to the Appellate Body's well-known doctrine of *effet utile* in which all the treaty terms must be given a meaning. This objection would run counter to the structure and terms used in GATS schedules of WTO Members, which invariably record in specific terms the absence or presence of limitations on market access for the supply of a service under Mode 2 (supply abroad).

The better view therefore is that a WTO Member that prohibits its nationals from entering into a service transaction abroad that harms the environment or animal welfare may enter this prohibition as a market access limitation under Mode 2 (supply abroad). Thus if a Member prohibits its nationals from purchasing tickets to see a bull fight anywhere (including abroad), it could indicate this as a market access limitation under a commitment it might have made under the relevant section on 'entertainment services' in its GATS Schedule.

Conversely, if the WTO Member were to maintain a trade measure prohibiting its nationals from transacting a particular service abroad for which it had made a full market access commitment without inscribing any limitation in its GATS Schedule, this would constitute a violation of GATS Article XVI. In order to maintain its trade measure, the Member would need to justify it as falling under the General Exceptions provisions of Article XIV.[64]

An interesting further example of this sort of prohibition could arise in animal testing of cosmetics. The EU seemingly attempted to ban the importation of cosmetics tested on animals.[65] The EU could, however, also ban companies from purchasing the service of animal testing abroad. A company might wish to test on animals abroad if, for example, it believed that *in vivo* testing produced better results than *in vitro* testing. After the *in vivo* testing, the company could come out with a new generation of products, and still state that the products had never been tested on animals. This type of deception could not effectively be prevented unless companies were specifically barred from purchasing the service abroad. There might arise an issue as to whether the relevant service was supplied under Mode 1 (cross-border) or Mode 2 (consumption abroad), but the fact that the property of the company (the cosmetic product under test) is sent abroad, would suggest that this would indeed be a service supplied under Mode 2.[66]

National treatment   In Article XVII, the GATS provides full national treatment by ensuring that foreign services and service suppliers are provided treatment no less favourable than that accorded to like domestic ones. The 'less favourable treatment' is specified to mean ensuring that 'conditions of competition' are no less favourable for the like foreign service or service supplier. As in the case of market access under Article XVI, a Member may maintain discriminatory measures by inscribing a corresponding limitation in its GATS schedule. Thus, if a Member wished not to prohibit the consumption of a service abroad that was harmful to the environment or animal welfare, but instead to *burden* the consumption abroad through, for example, the imposition of a tax or a

---

[64]   Or seek to negotiate a withdrawal of the full market access commitment under the provisions of Article XXI.

[65]   See Directive 2003/15/EC of the European Parliament and of the Council of 27 February 2003 amending Council Directive 76/768/EEC on the approximation of the laws of the Member States relating to cosmetic products.

[66]   It generally understood that a customer's property sent abroad for repair (e.g. ships) would be a Mode 2 service.

withdrawal or a tax exemption, this would require the inscription of a limitation under the relevant service sector in the Member's schedule (as long as the same burden was not imposed with respect to the domestic consumption of like service in which case there would clearly be no discrimination). Since a *bona fide* trade measure designed to reduce harm to the environment or animal welfare would presumably *not* create this sort of origin-based discrimination, we do not examine further this scenario.

In conclusion, trade measures taken by a Member in a sector in which it had undertaken GATS commitments would need either to be have been entered in its GATS Schedule, or justified under the General Exceptions of the GATS in Article XIV, to which we now turn.

2.   GATS General Exceptions
In similar fashion to the GATT, the GATS provides a series of General Exceptions that can justify a trade measure that is otherwise inconsistent with its provisions. The General Exceptions are set out in Article XIV of the GATS, which reads in relevant part:

> Subject to the requirement that such measures are not applied in a manner which would constitute a means of arbitrary or unjustifiable discrimination between countries where like conditions prevail, or a disguised restriction on trade in services, nothing in this Agreement shall be construed to prevent the adoption or enforcement by any Member of measures:
> . . .
> (a) necessary to protect public morals or to maintain public order;
> (b) necessary to protect human, animal or plant life or health;
> . . .

Article XIV contains a much shorter list of justifiable policy grounds than does GATT Article XX. In fact the only directly relevant grounds concerning the environment or animal welfare are to be found in paragraphs (a) and (b), which correspond more or less to the same paragraphs in GATT Article XX. What is 'missing' in the GATS is a paragraph corresponding to paragraph (g) of the GATT, on the conservation of exhaustible natural resources, which might possibly affect the range of environmental measures that could be justified under GATS Article XIV. Further, the chapeau is virtually identical in the two agreements.

Article XIV of the GATS has been interpreted only once in WTO case law. In the *US – Gambling* case, the Appellate Body found that the United States was justified in prohibiting foreign firms from supplying online gambling services, contrary to US commitments in its GATS Schedule, on the grounds that this prohibition was necessary to protect 'public morals' (internet gambling by children) under paragraph (a).[67] However, the Appellate Body found that the US had failed to apply the measure consistently with the chapeau, and could not therefore justify its prohibition under Article XIV of the GATS. In applying Article XIV, the Appellate Body used almost exactly the same reasoning – in particular that related to the term 'necessary' – as it had developed under Article XX of the GATT. For that reason, we will not pursue further a separate analysis of the justification of trade measures taken to prevent consumers from consuming services abroad.

IV.   REFLECTIONS

Our analysis has sought to describe the WTO consistency of trade measures taken by States which seek unilaterally to protect the environment or animal welfare. These measures have typically been directed at trade in goods, and are examined for WTO consistency under the GATT or the TBT Agreement. Under the GATT, trade measures that otherwise would violate rules on quantitative restrictions, MFN or national treatment have on several occasions been justified by panels and the Appellate Body under the general exceptions provisions in Article XX. Under the slightly different rules of the TBT Agreement, we still await judicial guidance on the status of trade measures. There have as yet been no WTO judicial decisions on trade measures designed specifically to protect animal welfare.

Measures directed at trade in services could also be used to promote the environment and animal welfare, and this Chapter attempts to show that the much wider coverage of the GATS, in particular consumption abroad under Mode 2, opens up interesting possibilities for a State that is a Member of the WTO to negotiate limitations on the consumption abroad by its nationals of services. The use of limitations – or the exception provisions under Article XIV of the GATS – for committed services covering activities as diverse as bull fighting, hunting endangered species or testing cosmetic products on live animals, could encourage in a WTO consistent manner changes in laws of other States that are WTO Members.

---

[67]   See Appellate Body Report, *United States – Measures Affecting the Cross-Border Supply of Gambling and Betting Services,* WT/DS285/AB/R (7 April 2005).

PART II

HEALTH REGULATION
AND TRADE LAW

8. TRIPs and access to essential medicines
Bryan Mercurio

I. INTRODUCTION

The World Health Organization (WHO) estimates that approximately one-third of the world's population lacks access to essential medicines and adequate medical treatment, with Africa and India making up 53 per cent of those without sufficient access to essential medicines.[1] It is also clear that millions of deaths occur each year from preventable and easily treatable diseases and that these deaths are caused in large part due to the difficulties some countries have in providing their citizens with access to essential medicines.[2] Thus, despite the right to health being enshrined in the International Covenant on Economic, Social and Cultural Rights (ICESCR), a significant portion of the world cannot enjoy this right.[3]

Finding a cause for the lack of access to essential medicines and remedying the situation has proven to be more controversial and illusory.[4] Many commentators and government officials often blame patents, and more specifically the detailed obligations set out in the World Trade Organization (WTO) Agreement on Trade-Related Aspects of Intellectual Property Rights (TRIPs Agreement), for causing or worsening the problem of access to essential medicines in the developing world.[5] Others claim that

---

[1] WHO, *The World Medicines Situation* (2004), 61–63.

[2] See generally WHO, 'World Health Report 2002: Reducing Risks, Promoting Healthy Life' (2002), available at http:// www.who.int/whr/2002/en/whr02_en.pdf (visited on 31 May 2012).

[3] Committee on Economic, Social and Cultural Rights, *The Right to the Highest Attainable Standard of Health*, General Comment 14, 2000. For further information on the right to health in the domestic and international context, see Lisa Forman, 'Trade Rules, Intellectual Property, and the Right to Health' (2007) 21 *Ethics & International Affairs* 337.

[4] See generally, Thomas Pogge, Matt Rimmer and Kim Rubenstein (eds), *Incentives for Global Public Health: Patent Law and Access to Essential Medicines* (Cambridge: Cambridge University Press, 2010).

[5] See, e.g., Panel Discussion, 'AIDS Drugs and the Developing World: The Role of Patents in the Access of Medicines' (2002) 12 *Fordham Intellectual Property, Media and Entertainment Law Journal* 683, 705 (James Love states: 'The WTO agreement is the most important thing').

the TRIPs Agreement exacerbates existing problems and in doing so acts as an impediment to access to essential medicines.

This chapter investigates whether the TRIPs Agreement is actually the cause of the access to essential medicines problem in the developing world, whether it serves as an impediment to access or whether its effects are more neutral. Section II briefly reviews the basics of the TRIPs Agreement as it relates to patents and pharmaceuticals before exploring the flexibilities existing in the Agreement which attempt to provide a balance between owners of intellectual property rights (IPRs) and users/the public interest. The examination reveals that although the TRIPs Agreement sets out numerous obligations which impact upon the issues of access to medicines, the Agreement contains sufficient flexibilities which if properly utilized would counter any negative impact of the Agreement. Section III acknowledges that some countries are experiencing difficulties in implementing the flexibilities existing in the TRIPs Agreement before discussing the emergence of post-TRIPs issues relating to access to essential medicines. Section IV concludes that although the TRIPs Agreement could be improved upon, it is not the cause of the problem of access to medicines nor is it even one of the most important factors in preventing wider access to essential medicines in the developing world.

II.   TRIPS AGREEMENT

A.   Basic Commitments and Obligations

The TRIPs Agreement is comprehensive in coverage and includes seven sectors of IPRs (i.e. copyright and related rights; trademarks; geographical indications; industrial designs; patents; layout-designs of integrated circuits; and protection of undisclosed information).[6] Like other WTO agreements, the basis of the TRIPs Agreement is the non-discrimination principles of most favoured nation (MFN) and national treatment (NT). The TRIPs Agreement also establishes minimum levels of protection and enforcement provisions. In formulating minimum standards, the TRIPs Agreement incorporates the substantive obligations of the WIPO Paris and Berne Conventions and certain provisions of the Treaty on Intellectual

---

[6]   TRIPs also requires Members to provide for the protection of plant varieties, either by patent or an effective sui generis system such as the plant breeder's rights established in the International Union for the Protection of New Varieties of Plants convention.

Property in Respect of Integrated Circuits and the Rome Convention.[7] In addition, the TRIPs Agreement sets standards in areas which were either not addressed in or, according to Members, were not sufficiently covered in the abovementioned WIPO Agreements.

Several provisions in the TRIPs Agreement shifted existing practice in a potentially detrimental manner to public health and access to essential medicines. The reason for this is that prior to the TRIPs Agreement, patent protections in both developed and developing countries varied widely. In essence, the TRIPs Agreement not only harmonizes but also raises protection standards.[8] This can be seen in at least three provisions affecting health and access to medicines.

First, Article 33 of the TRIPs Agreement requires that patent rights must be granted for a period of 20 years from the date a patent application is filed. Prior to the TRIPs Agreement, it was common for countries to provide protection ranging from 15–17 years protection from the date of filing, with some developing countries only granting patent protection for five to seven years.[9] As the entry of generic pharmaceutical manufacturers increases competition with the branded pharmaceutical manufacturer (and patent owner or licensee) the price of most pharmaceuticals dramatically decreases following the expiration of a patent. Thus, any lengthening of the patent period will negatively impact upon the price of medicines in that it will extend the monopoly selling period for the branded pharmaceutical manufacturer.

Second, Article 27.1 of the TRIPs Agreement also requires countries to provide patent protection for both processes and products, in all fields of technology. Prior to the TRIPs Agreement, as many as 50 countries provided patent protection for processes but not products.[10] In essence,

---

[7] See Paris Convention for the Protection of Industrial Property, as last revised at the Stockholm Revision Conference, 14 July 1967, 21 U.S.T. 1583; 828 U.N.T.S. 303; Berne Convention for the Protection of Literary and Artistic Works, 9 September 1886, as last revised at Paris on 24 July 1971, 1161 U.N.T.S. 30; Treaty on Intellectual Property in Respect of Integrated Circuits, opened for signature 26 May 1989, 28 I.L.M. 1477; Rome Convention for the Protection of Performers, Producers of Phonograms and Broadcasting Organisations, 26 October 1961, 496 U.N.T.S. 44.

[8] United Nations Development Programme (UNDP), *Good Practice Guide: Improving Access to Treatment by Utilizing Public Health Flexibilities in the WTO TRIPS Agreement* (2010), p. 4 (calling intellectual property protection 'one of the more significant' factors contributing to the high price of medicines).

[9] WHO, 'WTO and the TRIPs Agreement', available at http://www.who.int/medicines/areas/policy/wto_trips/en/index.html (visited on 31 May 2012).

[10] UNDP, above n 8, 5. See, e.g., the Patents Act, 1970 No. 39, Section 5 (India). Even though the Patents Act allowed for medically-related process patents, such patents offered limited protection (five to seven years) and provided

process patents protect the technology and process or method used to manufacture the product whereas product patents provide more complete protection for the patent holder. The requirement to grant product patents significantly weakened the position of generic pharmaceutical manufacturers, who previously could use 'reverse engineering' to develop a different process or method to create an equivalent product.[11] Thus, the requirement to grant product as well as product patents results in less generic competition during the patent period thereby ensuring that the monopoly selling period for the branded pharmaceutical manufacturer will almost always extend for the entire life the patent.

A third requirement of the TRIPs Agreement relating to medicines is Article 39, which obliges Members to protect undisclosed test data submitted to drug regulatory authorities for the purposes of obtaining marketing approval against 'unfair commercial use'.[12] Although not explicitly limited to pharmaceuticals, there are few other industries which require the submission of test data demonstrating the safety and efficacy of the product prior to receiving approval to market the product. Prior to the implementation of the TRIPs Agreement, the majority of countries allowed a generic manufacturer to simply rely upon the originator test data to approve generic products. In other words, the regulatory authorities in a country could rely upon the test data submitted by the originator company (demonstrating the safety and efficacy of a drug) to approve subsequent applications by generic manufacturers on similar products (which merely had to demonstrate that their drug is chemically identical to the original drug (and in some countries, that their drug is the bioequivalent of the original drug)).[13]

---

for automatic licensing after three years. For these reasons, few companies sought process patents in India. See *ibid* at Section 53(1)(a).

[11]   On the acquired skills of the Indian generic industry, see Sudip Chaudhuri, *The WTO and India's Pharmaceutical Industry: Patent Protection, TRIPs and Developing Countries* (New York: Oxford University Press, 2005), 52. See also Amy Kapczynski, 'Harmonization and its Discontents: A Case Study of TRIPs Implementation in India's Pharmaceutical Sector' (2009) 97 *California Law Review* 1571, 1578 note 33.

[12]   More specifically, TRIPs Article 39.3 provides: 'Members, when requiring, as a condition of approving the marketing of pharmaceutical or of agricultural chemical products which utilize new chemical entities, the submission of undisclosed test or other data, the origination of which involves a considerable effort, shall protect such data against unfair commercial use. In addition, Members shall protect such data against disclosure, except where necessary to protect the public, or unless steps are taken to ensure that the data are protected against unfair commercial use.'

[13]   In addition, some regulatory authorities merely relied on proof of prior approval in another country.

Quite obviously, allowing a generic manufacturer to rely on test data submitted by the originator reduces costs to both the manufacturer and ultimately to consumers (in that the generic manufacturer does not have to repeat costly and time-consuming tests and studies or pass those costs on to the consumer) and facilitates the entry of generic pharmaceuticals into the marketplace.

Some commentators initially feared that Article 39 would be viewed as akin to data exclusivity, which would have granted the originator exclusive rights over its test data and prevented regulatory authorities from relying on the test data to register generic drugs. The result of a data exclusivity approach would have been that prior to gaining marketing approval a generic manufacturer would have had to conduct the costly and time-consuming tests and studies (which raise resource management and ethical issues as the results of the tests and studies would be known prior to conducting them) or simply wait until the expiration of the exclusivity period. Both options would result in higher costs for consumers and thus neither option is in the public interest.[14] Fortunately, most Members interpret Article 39 as allowing for wide discretion and this interpretation has not been challenged in dispute settlement;[15] thus, Members have been essentially free to define 'unfair commercial use' in their domestic legislation as they like.[16] That being the case, as will be discussed below in Part III,

---

[14]   For instance, a prohibition on a generic manufacturer relying on originator test data in order to secure marketing approval would likely prevent the use of compulsory licences unless the originator was deemed to be acting in an anticompetitive manner. See WHO, 'Commission on Public Health, Innovation and Intellectual Property Rights, Public Health. Innovation and Intellectual Property Rights: Report of the Commission on Intellectual Property Rights, Innovation and Public Health' (2006) at 142–5, available at: http:// www.who.int/ intellectualproperty/report/en/index.html (visited on 31 May 2012).

[15]   This is not to suggest that all Members agree with such an interpretation. See, e.g., Communication from the European Communities and their member states, 'The Relationship between the Provisions of the TRIPs Agreement and Access to Medicines' Paper submitted by the EU to the TRIPs Council, for the special discussion on intellectual property and access to medicines, IP/C/W/280 (2001), available at http://www.wto.org/English/tratop_e/trips_e/paper_eu_w280_e.htm (visited on 31 May 2012). See contra, UNCTAD-ICTSD, *Resource Book on TRIPs and Development* (2005), 522–6 (recounting that TRIPs negotiators rejected the option to include stronger 'data exclusivity' provisions, as originally proposed by the US).

[16]   The negotiating history of TRIPs does not indicate that Members intended TRIPs Article 39.3 to entail data exclusivity. See, e.g., Carlos Correa, 'Unfair Competition under the TRIPs Agreement-Protection of Data Submitted for the Registration of Pharmaceuticals' (2002) 3 *Chicago Journal of International Law* 69, 82–4.

recent free trade agreements (FTAs) negotiated by the United States (US), European Union (EU) and other developed countries are including data exclusivity provisions which would prohibit regulatory authorities from relying on originator test data to grant marketing approval to generic manufacturers for a set time period.

B.   Flexibilities

This section will examine several flexibilities existing in the Agreement which counterbalance the obligations explored in the previous section. With regard to pharmaceuticals (and thus its effect on access to essential medicines) this section argues that the substantive and procedural flexibilities available in the TRIPs Agreement, if properly utilized, can counter any negative impact of the obligations.[17] To date, the vast majority of scholarship and policy attention has focused on compulsory licensing.[18] Compulsory licensing no doubt remains an important flexibility, but great potential exists in the further exploration and exploitation of other less prominent flexibilities. This section will canvass the recognized and less well-known flexibilities, including: transitional arrangements; patent protection standards, exhaustion of IPRs and exceptions to owner rights. Throughout this section, repeated reference is made to India; not only is India one of a handful of developing nations with a thriving generic pharmaceutical industry but it is also a nation which has traditionally thrived in part because of its aversion to patent rights in pharmaceuticals[19] and

---

[17]   See also Jerome H. Reichman, 'Intellectual Property in the Twenty-First Century: Will the Developing Countries Lead or Follow?' 46 *Houston Law Review* 1116.

[18]   See, e.g., Frederick M. Abbott, 'The WTO Medicines Decision: World Pharmaceutical Trade and the Protection of Public Health' (2005) 99 *American Journal of International Law* 317; Bryan Mercurio, 'TRIPs, Patents and Access to Life-Saving Drugs in the Developing World' (2004) 8 *Marquette Intellectual Property Law Review* 211.

[19]   This is not to suggest that India's patent laws were solely responsible for the rapid growth of its generic pharmaceutical industry; other laws, such as its requirement that a number of medicines be produced by the public sector or in companies which are at least 60 per cent Indian owned, regulations encouraging local production of active pharmaceutical ingredients, price controls, high tariff rates and other import restrictions also played a significant role in the success of the industry. See generally, Chaudhuri, above n 11, at 133–46, 276–8. Chaudhuri suggests that the market share of locally produced Indian pharmaceuticals rose from just over 20 per cent in 1970 to approximately 80 per cent by 2000. *Ibid* at 18. Agrawal and Saibaba find that the Indian pharmaceutical industry exported over US$1.5 billion dollars of medicines in 2000, a figure which represents 4 per

one that has creatively implemented the TRIPs Agreement so as to maximize available flexibilities.

1.   Transitional arrangements

Some of the most important yet underappreciated flexibilities in the TRIPs Agreement are the transition periods which grant developing and least developed countries (LDCs) an additional period of time to bring national legislation and practices into conformity with the Agreement. More specifically, Part IV of the Agreement provides for three transitional arrangements. The first two transitional arrangements are covered under Article 65 and relate to developing country members.[20] First, Article 65.2 granted developing country Members and Article 65.3 granted Members in transition[21] the right to delay the application of the Agreement (other than Articles 3, 4 and 5) for four years (that is until the year 2000).

Second, Article 65.4 extended the transitional period for an additional five years (that is, until 2005) for developing countries to provide product patent protection in the areas of technology that had not been protected at the time of the TRIPs Agreement coming into force for that Member. Most notably, this extended transitional period includes pharmaceutical and agricultural chemicals. As large generic manufacturing countries did not previously provide product patents on pharmaceuticals, this extended period meant that generic manufacturers in those countries could continue copying and producing drugs which would otherwise have required patent protection by the year 2000. The only caveat to this extended transitional period was that from 1995 countries were obliged to accept patent applications and keep the applications dormant in a patent 'mailbox' until 2005, when the mailbox was unlocked and the applications assessed.[22]

The third transitional arrangement, contained in Article 66 and applying

---

cent of all Indian exports. Pradeep Agrawal and P. Saibaba, 'TRIPs and India's Pharmaceuticals Industry' (2001) 36 *Economic and Political Weekly* 3787, 3787.

[20]   It should be noted that according to TRIPs Article 65.5 any changes Members availing themselves of Article 65 make in their laws, regulations and practice made during the transitional period must not result in a lesser degree of consistency with the provisions of the TRIPs.

[21]   TRIPs Article 65.3 reads: 'Any other Member which is in the process of transformation from a centrally-planned into a market, free-enterprise economy and which is undertaking structural reform of its intellectual property system and facing special problems in the preparation and implementation of intellectual property laws and regulations, may also benefit from a period of delay as foreseen in paragraph 2.'

[22]   Several thousand applications which accumulated in India's 'mailbox' have yet to be assessed and will likely be rejected. See below, Section B.2.

to LDCs, originally allowed such countries until 2006 to implement their obligations. The reason for the additional transitional time was due to 'the special needs and requirements of [LDCs], their economic, financial and administrative constraints, and their need for flexibility to create a viable technological base'.[23] In accordance with the last sentence of Article 66.1,[24] Members agreed in the Doha Declaration on the TRIPs Agreement and Public Health to extend the transitional arrangements for LDCs until 2016 with respect to patents on pharmaceutical products and exclusive marketing rights.[25] Therefore, LDCs are under no obligation to provide for, nor to enforce patents and data protection with respect to pharmaceutical products until 2016.

Even after briefly reviewing the transitional arrangements it should be apparent that patent protection and the TRIPs Agreement could not have been the cause of the problem of access to essential medicines. Not only does lack of access to essential medicines in the developing world pre-date the TRIPs Agreement, but until 2005 any developing country could produce and even export generic versions of any pharmaceutical product. The full implementation of the TRIPs Agreement in developing countries in 2005 curtailed, but did not end, generic production and exportation. Moreover, countries such as Brazil, China and India continue to have thriving generic pharmaceutical industries supplying millions of people across the globe with generic versions of patented pharmaceuticals. Despite these thriving industries, Brazil, China and India fail to fully provide access to essential medicines for their own populations. This dichotomy of providing access to the world yet not being able to adequately provide domestic access clearly illustrates the fact that the problems with access to essential medicines go beyond patents and the TRIPs Agreement. Finally, issues relating to access to essential medicines in LDCs cannot be caused or even greatly exacerbated by the TRIPs Agreement as it (via the extension granted in the Doha Declaration) does not oblige such Members to provide any patent protection until 2016, at the earliest. Thus, LDCs have always been and continue to be freely able

---

[23]   TRIPs Article 66.1.

[24]   The last sentence of TRIPs Article 66.1 reads: 'The Council for TRIPs shall, upon duly motivated request by a least-developed country Member, accord extensions of this period.'

[25]   WTO Ministerial Conference, 'Declaration on the TRIPs Agreement and Public Health', WT/MIN(01)/DEC/2 (20 November 2001), para. 7. The Declaration likewise granted LDCs an extension until 2013 to implement the TRIPs, more generally. This extension remains in force and has now been extended at least until the next Ministerial Conference.

to produce or import any pharmaceutical without violating the TRIPs Agreement. Of course, LDCs do suffer from access problems, which indicate that other deeper issues are involved.

2. Patent protection standards

Article 27.1 of the TRIPs Agreement provides the minimum standards required for obtaining a patent by separating the requirements into four distinct areas:[26] subject matter, novelty, inventive step (non-obviousness) and capacity for industrial application (usefulness).[27] Article 27.1 is drafted in very broad terms:

> [P]atents shall be available for any inventions, whether products or processes, in all fields of technology, provided that they are new, involve an inventive step and are capable of industrial application. ... [P]atents shall be available and patent rights enjoyable without discrimination as to the place of invention, the field of technology and whether products are imported or locally produced.

Such language sets forth stringent standards and requirements for granting patent protection to both products and processes and effectively prohibits Members from excluding pharmaceuticals and chemicals from patentability. Members do however retain some flexibility in tailoring their laws to meet their developmental and/or other needs, such as ensuring that Article 27 does not impede access to essential medicines. This is due to the fact that the Agreement does not define the relevant terms. Moreover, while some direction can be found in the internationally agreed standards contained in the Patent Cooperation Treaty (PCT),[28] the PCT is not incorporated into the TRIPs Agreement nor are all WTO Members signatories. Thus, Members are free to set and apply their own substantive conditions. The remaining portion of this Part will explore these four flexibilities and additional related flexibilities.

Subject matter Article 27.2 of the TRIPs Agreement allows Members to exclude inventions 'necessary to protect *ordre public* or morality, including

---

[26] Other standards exist elsewhere, such as TRIPs Article 29 (enablement).

[27] A footnote to TRIPs Article 27.1 clarifies that the terms 'inventive step' and 'capable of industrial application' may be deemed by a Member to be synonymous with the terms 'non-obvious' and 'useful', respectively. The footnote was seen as necessary due to the fact that 'industrial application' was the standard used in India and most European countries, whereas 'utility' was used in the US and Canada.

[28] Patent Cooperation Treaty, 19 June 1970, 28 U.S.T. 7645; 1160 U.N.T.S. 231; 9 I.L.M. 978 (1970).

to protect human, animal or plant life or health or to avoid serious prejudice to the environment' and Article 27.3 allows exclusions for medical and surgical methods and plants and animals other than microorganisms from patentability. Most nations, both developed and developing, take advantage of these exceptions[29] and several nations further exclude patents on new uses of known substances which do not enhance the efficacy of the substance.[30]

India goes even further in excluding new forms of known substances. For instance, Section 3(d) of India's Patents Act 1970 excludes patents on 'the mere discovery of a new form of a known substance which does not result in the enhancement of the known efficacy of that substance or the mere discovery of any new property or new use for a known substance. . .'.[31] The aim of the limitation is squarely to increase access to medicines by prohibiting the practice of 'evergreening' patents,[32] which are often used to extend patent protection for pharmaceutical products for anti-competitive purposes. Correspondingly, India will only grant patent protection for pharmaceutical derivatives that enhance the efficacy of the known substance.[33]

---

[29]   See Convention on the Grant of European Patents, 5 October 1973, 1065 U.N.T.S. 199, Articles 52–53; The Patent Amendment Act, No. 15 of 2005, Section 3, India Code (2005). India's Patents Act also excludes business methods and algorithms, computer programs from patentability. It seems (although it is untested and perhaps unclear) that Members are free to determine whether, and to what extent, they will protect business methods as patentable subject matter (i.e. the process of conducting an online auction). Currently, the US offers broad protection while the EU and others offer more limited protection and some countries (including Brazil) follow India and offer no protection.

[30]   Since 1989, less than 20 per cent of new drug approvals provide for significant clinical improvement. National Institute for Health Care Management, *Changing Patterns of Pharmaceutical Innovation* (2008), at 3.

[31]   India Patents Act, Section 3(d). An explanatory note further clarifies the restriction: 'For the purposes of this clause, salts, esters, ethers, polymorphs, metabolites, pure form, particle size, isomers, mixtures of isomers, complexes, combinations, and other derivatives of known substance shall be considered to be the same substance, unless they differ significantly in properties with regard to efficacy.' This limitation is almost a word-for-word recitation of Council Directive 2004/27/EC, Amending Council Directive 2001/83/EC on the Community Code Relating to Medicinal Products for Human Use, Article 10(2)(b), 2004 O.J. (L 136) 34, 39. The effect of Section 3(d) is likely to invalidate the vast majority of 'mailbox' claims still pending. See Kapczynski, above n 11, 1594.

[32]   For more information on evergreening, see John R. Thomas, *Patent 'Evergreening' Issues in Innovation and Competition*, Congressional Research Service, 13 November 2009.

[33]   For discussion, see Shamnad Basheer and T. Prashant Reddy, 'The 'Efficacy' of Indian Patent Law: Ironing out the Creases in Section 3(d)' (2008) 5 SCRIPTed

The definition and interpretation of 'efficacy' thus becomes an important element in Section 3(d) of India's Patents Act. The holdings in the recent *Novartis* case indicate that efficacy is to be equated with an improvement to the actual medicinal or healing effect in the body as opposed to merely allowing the medicine to be stored or handled more easily or cheaply.[34] Such an interpretation should significantly limit the number of patents granted to medicines.

Finally, it should be mentioned that countries choosing to allow 'evergreening' still retain flexibilities and the right to regulate, such as by not granting an automatic injunction when an 'evergreening' claim is made for additional patent protection[35] and through legislation penalizing spurious or frivolous patent claims/extensions.[36]

Novelty   The discretion permitted by Article 27.1 has allowed two dis-

---

232. See also Shamnad Basheer and T. Prashant Reddy, 'Ducking TRIPs in India: A Saga involving Novartis and the Legality of Section 3(d)' (2008) 20 *National Law School of India Review* 131.

[34]   *Novartis AG v. Union of India*, Order No. 100/2009 (Intellectual Prop. App. Board, 29 June 2009), available at http://www.i-mak.org/pharma-patent-decisions (visited on 31 May 2012). See also Patent Office (India), Draft Manual of Patent Practice and Procedure, (2008) pp. 57–63 (incorporating the standard set out in *Novartis*). For commentary, see Basheer and Reddy, *Ducking TRIPs*, above n 33. The case was heard in the Indian Supreme Court in March 2012. See also, the recent refusal to register Application No. 4015/DELNP/2006 filed by Warner-Lambert claiming topical formulation of Pfizer's potential potassium channel opener UK-157147 for the treatment of alopecia for, *inter alia*, lack of patentable subject matter under Section 3(d), available at http://www.box.net/shared/d1otfq4n7l (visited on 31 May 2012).

[35]   See contra, the US Drug Price Competition and Patent Term Restoration Act 1984 (better known as the Hatch-Waxman Act), which seeks to make it easier to market generic drugs by creating an 'abbreviated' application process, but allows patent holders to gain an injunction of up to 30 months from generic competition by filing a patent infringement suit. Unsurprisingly, a 2002 report by the US Federal Trade Commission found that evergreening was a major factor in the high price of American drugs and was anti-competitive. The report recommended that manufacturers be limited to only one 'claim' per drug. Federal Trade Commission, *Generic Drug Entry Prior to Patent Expiration: An FTC Study* (2002).

[36]   See, e.g., Australia's Therapeutic Goods Act 1989 (Cth) Sections 26C and 26D, which requires patent holders wishing to claim a patent and institute infringement proceedings to certify that the proceedings are being commenced in good faith, have reasonable prospects of success (as defined in Section 26C(4)) and will be conducted without unreasonable delay. If the certificate is found to be false or misleading, the patent holder can be fined up to $10 million and the Attorney-General may join an action to recoup losses to the Pharmaceutical Benefits Scheme.

tinct concepts of novelty to co-exist – the majority of nations place no geographical limitation on prior art[37] whereas others (most prominently, the US) limit prior art to their own territory. In response to the EC questioning whether the US Patent Act (35 U.S.C. 102(a)), in which only knowledge or use in the US is sufficient for the purposes of defeating novelty is consistent with Article 27.1 of the TRIPs Agreement, the US defended its law by stating:

> There is no definition of the term 'new' in the TRIPs Agreement or in the Paris Convention. In addition, Article 1.1 of the TRIPs Agreement states that 'Members shall be free to determine the appropriate method of implementing the provisions of this Agreement within their own legal system and practice'. In view of these facts, there is no prescription as to how WTO Members define what inventions are to be considered 'new' within their domestic systems.[38]

Members therefore have considerable discretion to tailor the novelty requirement in their domestic laws in a manner which promotes their objectives. Members wishing to prevent Article 27.1 of the TRIPs Agreement from impeding access to essential medicines thus have the ability to draft legislation which ensures that novelty is destroyed through prior art (whether written, oral or publicly available) existing anywhere in the world.[39] Such laws prevent companies, including pharmaceutical companies, from obtaining patent protection based upon knowledge which already exists at the local level.

Inventive step and non-obviousness   Setting a high standard for the determination of an inventive step and obviousness can assist countries in promoting IPRs in a manner conducive to access to medicines rather than as a harmful monopolistic right.[40] Most countries set a standard of inventive-

---

[37]   See, e.g., European Patent Convention Article 54.

[38]   Council for TRIPs, *Review of Legislation in the Fields of Patents, Layout-Designs (Topographies) of Integrated Circuits, Protection of Undisclosed Information and Control of Anti-Competitive Practices in Contractual Licences*, IP/Q3/USA/1, (1 May 1998), p. 4. The EC also questioned whether the US provision was consistent with TRIPs Article 3 and GATT Article III, 'given that [the provision] affords rights with respect to US inventions that it does not afford to others and that these rights overwhelmingly rebound to the benefit of US nationals'.

[39]   In terms of pharmaceutical-related cases, see, e.g., *Norton Healthcare Ltd v. Beecham Group Plc* (BL C/62/95) (India); *SmithKline Beecham Plc's (Paratoxetine Methanesulfonate) Patent* [2006] RPC 10 (India).

[40]   Here again, until recently the US approach differed from world practice in that the US provided priority based on the date of invention whereas the EU and

ness whereby the invention must be 'not obvious to a person skilled in the art'.[41] India again is at the forefront in extending the flexibility available in the TRIPs Agreement in a manner which maximizes access to medicines in that it defines an inventive step as follows:

> a feature of an invention that involves technical advance as compared to the existing knowledge or having economic significance or both and that makes the invention not obvious to a person skilled in the art.[42]

Such a definition enlarges the definition of inventive step to include economic significance of the invention apart from pre-existing criteria for determining inventive step. Thus, economic significance has been given similar standing and importance to technical advancement and both will now have to be interpreted with regard to the knowledge and skill of the person skilled in art. Such enlargement has been called, 'unusual, and perhaps unique'.[43]

The limiting effect of such a definition is as of yet unknown, but it does seem at least theoretically possible for a new form of a known substance which, for example, demonstrates increased efficacy could meet the requirements under Section 3(d) of India's Patents Act but fail to meet the requirements for an inventive step. Finally, it should also be noted that the Indian Patents Office usually treats novelty and inventiveness together, which may limit the above theoretical possibility from becoming reality.[44] Regardless, a strict interpretation of the inventive step requirement could mean that a significant number of pharmaceutical inventions could be refused patent protection.[45]

Useful In order to receive patent protection, an invention must also

---

most other countries provide priority to the inventor that first files an application for a patent. See Leahy-Smith America Invents Act 2011, Public Law 112-29, signed into law on 16 September 2011.

[41] European Patent Treaty Article 56. For case law, see the UK case of *Windsurfing International Inc. v. Tabur Marine* (GB) Ltd. [1985] RPC 59. For the US standard, see 35 U.S.C. 103. For case law, see *Graham et al. v. John Deere Co. of Kansas City et al.*, 383 U.S. 1 (1966).

[42] India Patents Act Section 2(1)(ja).

[43] Kapczynski, above n 11, 1593.

[44] See, e.g., India's recent rejection of Abbott's patent application for Kalentra, an AIDS/HIV medicine. For details on this case, see http://www.i-mak.org/lopinavirritonavir (visited on 31 May 2012).

[45] See 'India rejects Abbott patent on Kaletra' *Online Pharma Times* (5 January 2011), available at http://www.pharmatimes.com/article/11-01-05/India_rejects_Abbott_patent_on_Kaletra.aspx (visited on 31 May 2012).

be useful (that is, have utility or be capable of industrial application). Therefore, if the subject matter is devoid of usefulness/utility/industrial application it would not satisfy the definition of 'invention'. The relevant test is whether the invention will work and whether it will do what the patent applications claimed it can do. The term is often left undefined,[46] but defining or applying usefulness or utility in a manner which promotes access to medicines is possible.

It may also be possible to challenge patentability on the ground that claims made on the basis of *in vitro* test data (without any evidence that the compound is effective *in vivo*) are not useful, since the compound may not work in the same way in humans. Such a challenge would have a reasonable likelihood of success, but the pharmaceutical industry is unlikely to fail to present *in vivo* test data and often include utilities unrelated to human health disorders in order to ensure usefulness. Correspondingly, it may be possible to challenge the effectiveness of compounds tested only in laboratory conditions but not yet field tested. Such challenges would be controversial, and may not even be effective, as laws at present are not drafted in such a way so as to require commercial feasibility or safety prior to being granted a patent.

Other related flexibilities   Other related flexibilities which can also promote access to medicines are also available under the TRIPs Agreement. For instance, Members can ensure that patents of questionable quality are subject to challenge by crafting laws which facilitate easy and fast pre- and post-grant opposition procedures at reasonable cost. Pre-grant opposition procedures are of the utmost importance as they can delay for several years and even potentially avoid any patent monopoly period without the threat of penalty. While most developed countries (except Australia) do not allow pre-grant opposition proceedings, several developing countries (including generic pharmaceutical producing nations such as Brazil and India) allow such proceedings.

Again, India is a leader in maximizing flexibilities in this regard. For instance, not only does India allow 'any person' (not just interested generic manufacturers) to file a pre-grant opposition but Section 25 of India's Patents Act is very expansive in scope and allows pre-grant opposition for a number of reasons, including allegations that the invention does not meet the statutory requirements for novelty and inventive step, that it is not a patentable invention under Section 3(d), that it fails the requirements of specification and that the applicant has not disclosed the status of parallel

---

[46]   See, e.g., India Patents Act Section 2(1)(ac).

applications in other jurisdictions or the geographical origin or source of biological materials used. India also maintains flexible post-grant opposition proceedings for those interested challenging the legitimacy of a patent.[47]

India also maintains some unique requirements aimed at limiting patent protection and increasing access to technology, and correspondingly, access to affordable medicines. For instance, Section 8 of India's Patents Act requires applicants to inform the patent office of any application they have filed with regard to the 'same or substantially the same invention' in another jurisdiction as well as to keep the relevant offices up to date on any 'detailed particulars of such application'. The objective of this law is clearly to inform the Indian patent office of any potential problems with the application identified in foreign jurisdictions.

3. Exhaustion of intellectual property rights

Another area where the TRIPs Agreement provides flexibilities is in the exhaustion of IPRs. Nothing in the TRIPs Agreement prohibits the parallel importation of products; instead, Article 6 allows Members the freedom to incorporate national, international or regional exhaustion of rights – thus agreements and disputes relating to the exhaustion of IPRs are not subject to the WTO dispute settlement system. Paragraph 5(d) of the Doha Declaration on TRIPs and Public Health re-iterates the basic principle: '. . .each Member [is] free to establish its own regime for such exhaustion without challenge.'

Unlike a system of national exhaustion – where IPRs are exhausted only following the first domestic sale – adopting a system of international exhaustion – whereby the first sale of the goods anywhere in the world exhausts IPRs – allows for the parallel importation of goods (so called 'grey market goods').[48] The benefit of international exhaustion is that goods sold in a foreign market may be less expensive than those sold domestically and thus their importation would reduce the price of the goods to consumers.

In the case of medicines, any reduction in price necessarily has a positive effect on access. Thus, parallel importation may have a role to play in reducing the cost of procuring pharmaceuticals and health-related inventions. For this reason, many commentators believe developing countries should adopt the 'widest scope' of flexibilities in this regard.[49] Here again,

---

[47]   *Ibid* at Section 25(2).

[48]   A third system, regional exhaustion, is where IPRs are exhausted following the first sale in the relevant region.

[49]   See, e.g., Sisule F. Musungu and Cecilia Oh, *The Use of Flexibilities in TRIPs by Developing Countries: Can They Promote Access to Medicines Study*

India is considered to be at the forefront of establishing a country-specific approach that fits into a pro-development framework promoting access to medicines.[50]

Importantly, however, countries must, in shaping their laws, be aware of TRIPs-based commitments. At present, it appears that some developing countries only allow for the parallel importation of pharmaceutical products but not of other patented products.[51] This limitation is likely inconsistent with Article 27.1 the TRIPs Agreement, which prevents discrimination as to the field of technology. The inconsistency can be remedied by permitting parallel importation of patented goods in all fields of technology, and not only of pharmaceuticals and health-related inventions.

As grey market goods compete with the goods of the domestic IP rights owner (or licensee), the pharmaceutical industry opposes allowing parallel importation of medicines. Foremost, competition from parallel imported goods distorts differential pricing schemes. While such distortions may mean little when the goods in question are books or DVDs, the pharmaceutical industry relies on differential pricing schemes to both recoup investment from the developed countries as well as to supply medicines and other products to developing countries at a reduced price. Thus, it could be argued that differential pricing ensures that higher income countries pay more for pharmaceuticals than lower income countries.[52] Likewise, it seems unfair for countries such as Brazil to misuse the system and parallel import medicine originally sold into, say, the Guyana market at vastly reduced prices. Foremost, a country such as Brazil already benefits from differential pricing schemes in that it pays significantly lower prices than developed countries. The price it pays has been set according to its developmental level and needs. By parallel importing cheaper drugs

---

4C, Commission on Intellectual Property Rights, Innovation and Health, (August 2005), p. 30. Importantly, safeguards would have to be in place to ensure that donated pharmaceuticals are not diverted from their intended destination.

[50]   For discussion and analysis of, and suggested amendments to, India's legislative framework (Section 107A of the Patents (Amendment) Act, 2005), see Shamnad Basheer and Mrinalini Kochupillai, 'TRIPs, Patents and Parallel Imports: A Proposal for Amendment' (2009) 2 *Indian Journal of Intellectual Property Law* 63.

[51]   See, e.g., South Africa, Medicines and Related Substances Control Act Section 15C.

[52]   See, e.g., Frederic M. Scherer and Jayashree Watal, 'Post-TRIPs Options for Access to Patented Medicines in Developing Nations' (2002) 5 *Journal of International Economic Law* 913; Patricia M. Danzon and Adrian Towse, 'Differential Pricing for Pharmaceuticals: Reconciling Access, R&D and Patents' (2001) 3 *International Journal of Health Care Finance and Economics* 183.

it is undercutting the entire system from which it benefits. As importantly, in parallel importing cheaper medicines originally destined for a poorer (and arguably needier) market, Brazil would be contributing to and exacerbating the problem of access to medicines in the developing world. If such actions occur on a large scale, pharmaceutical companies could end all differential pricing schemes and possibly raise the costs of medicines in some of the poorer markets.

On the other hand, a recent study conducted by Flynn, Hollis and Palmedo indicates that profit-maximizing pricing in the pharmaceutical sector often results in medicines being sold in developing countries at a price affordable only to the few wealthy citizens in a nation rather than selling at a lower price to more people.[53] Allowing for the parallel importation of pharmaceuticals could potentially alleviate such pricing strategies and allow for wider access to such medicines.

Given the differing views and analysis of differential pricing and other current practices, it is puzzling that more developing countries (and especially LDCs) do not instigate a more pro-competition approach to exhaustion, especially with regard to public health and essential medicines.

4.   Exceptions to owner rights

Another flexibility which allows countries to build and maintain an IP system conducive to wider access to essential medicines is the existence of explicit exceptions contained in Articles 30 and 31 of the TRIPs Agreement. In this regard, countries should ensure they retain the capacity to utilize these flexibilities in order to facilitate access to essential medicines by crafting laws which promote the object and purpose of IPRs and TRIPs,[54] including the promotion of the transfer of technology, the prevention of abuse of IPRs and the promotion of public health.

The exceptions to patent rights contained in Article 30 of the TRIPs Agreement are of the utmost importance to countries looking to maximize access to medicines. Article 30 allows for undefined exceptions to patent rights so long as the exceptions meet the three-step test, namely that they (1) are limited; (2) do not unreasonably conflict with the normal exploitation of the patent; and (3) do not unreasonably prejudice the legitimate

---

[53]   Sean Flynn, Aidan Hollis and Mike Palmedo, 'An Economic Justification for Open Access to Essential Medicine Patents in Developing Countries' (2009) 37 *Journal of Law, Medicine and Ethics* 184 (showing that compulsory licences may increase social welfare, increase access and lower costs of essential medicines in developing countries where highly convex demand curves are the norm).

[54]   See TRIPs, Preamble Article 7 ('Objectives') and Article 8 ('Principles').

interests of the patent owner, taking account of the legitimate interests of third parties.[55]

A particularly useful exception in the area of public health and access to affordable medicines is the so-called regulatory exception (also called 'Bolar'[56] and 'early working' exception) which allows generic manufacturers to use and produce test-batches of a patented product prior to the expiry of the patent in order to gain regulatory approval to market the product, thus facilitating the production and sale of the product soon after the expiry of the patent. The legality of the regulatory provision is not in dispute, as the panel in *Canada–Pharmaceuticals* held that it fell within the perimeters of Article 30 of the TRIPs Agreement exception.[57] What is surprising is that the majority of developing countries do not directly provide for such rights in legislation.[58]

Another flexibility which potentially impacts upon access to medicines is that applicable when researchers more broadly utilize patented products or processes for non-commercial experimental purposes. While this exception is narrowly construed in the US, there is scope to widen the applicability of the exception.[59] That being said, careful drafting and implementation is needed in order to remain within the (admittedly contested and legally uncertain) permissible scope of the exception. In this regard, India again can serve as a model as it has drafted a provision which mandates full disclosure and allows for effective study and experimentation in a manner which is likely to be deemed consistent with Article 30

---

[55]   For discussion, see Musungu and Oh, above n 49, 31–6. TRIPs Article 13 provides for an equivalent standard for copyright. The standard was discussed and interpreted in Report of the Panel, *US–Section 110(5) Copyright Act*, WT/DS/160/R (27 July 2000). Academic literature heavily criticizes the panel's interpretation. See, e.g., Jane C. Ginsburg, 'Toward Supranational Copyright Law? The WTO Panel Decision and the "Three Step Test" for Copyright Exemptions' (2001) *Working Paper No. 181 of the Columbia Law School – Revue Internationale du Droit d'Auteur*; Rochelle Cooper Dreyfuss, 'TRIPs – Round II: Should Users Strike Back?' (2004) 71 *University of Chicago Law Review* 21.

[56]   See *Roche Products v. Bolar Pharmaceutical*, 733 F.2d 858 (Fed. Cir. 1984).

[57]   Panel Report, *Canada–Patent Protection of Pharmaceutical Products*, WT/DS114/R (7 April 2000).

[58]   See Phil Thorpe, *Study on the Implementation of the TRIPs Agreement by Developing Countries (undated) Commission on Intellectual Property Rights Study Paper 7*, available at http://www.iprcommission.org/papers/pdfs/study_papers/sp7_thorpe_study.pdf (visited on 31 May 2012). South Africa only adopted such a provision in 2002.

[59]   See Carlos Correa, 'Reforming the Intellectual Property Rights System in Latin America' (2000) 23 *The World Economy* 851.

of the TRIPs Agreement.[60] In so doing, India has provided a pathway to introduce competition into its pharmaceutical marketplace thereby lowering costs and increasing access to medicines.

In terms of pharmaceuticals and access to medicines, Article 31 of the TRIPs Agreement has received considerable attention in the WTO and other international forums. Article 31 allows for the issuance of a compulsory licence subject to certain conditions. Importantly, Article 31 does not limit the grounds upon which a compulsory licence may be granted, but only sets out the (mainly procedural) conditions to be applied when granting a compulsory licence.

Under Article 31, Members are allowed to legislate for 'other use' of a patent without the consent of the rights holder – commonly referred to as the compulsory licensing – as long as the mostly procedural requirements contained in the Article are followed.[61] These requirements are as follows:

(a) authorization of such use shall be considered on its individual merits;
(b) such use may only be permitted if, prior to such use, the proposed user has made efforts to obtain authorization from the right holder on reasonable commercial terms and conditions and that such efforts have not been successful within a reasonable period of time. This requirement may be waived by a Member in the case of a national emergency or other circumstances of extreme urgency or in cases of public non-commercial use. In situations of national emergency or other circumstances of extreme urgency, the right holder shall, nevertheless, be notified as soon as reasonably practicable. In the case of public non-commercial use, where the government or contractor, without making a patent search, knows or has demonstrable grounds to know that a valid patent is or will be used by or for the government, the right holder shall be informed promptly;
(c) the scope and duration of such use shall be limited to the purpose for which it was authorized, and in the case of semi-conductor technology shall only be for public non-commercial use or to remedy a practice determined after judicial or administrative process to be anti-competitive;
(d) such use shall be non-exclusive;
(e) such use shall be non-assignable, except with that part of the enterprise or goodwill which enjoys such use;

---

[60]   See Section 47(3) of the India Patents Act 1970: 'any machine, apparatus or other article in respect of which the patent is granted or any article made by the use of the process in respect of which the patent is granted, may be made or used, and any process in respect of which the patent is granted may be used, by any person, for the purpose merely of experiment or research including the imparting of instructions to pupils.' For discussion and a developing country perspective on the issue, see Shamnad Basheer and Prashant Reddy 'The "Experimental Use Exception" Through a Developmental Lens' (2010) 50 *IDEA – The Intellectual Property Law Review* 831.
[61]   See, e.g., India Patents Act Section 47. See generally, Musungu and Oh, above n 49, 20–27.

(f) any such use shall be authorized predominantly for the supply of the domestic market of the Member authorizing such use; ·

(g) authorization for such use shall be liable, subject to adequate protection of the legitimate interests of the persons so authorized, to be terminated if and when the circumstances which led to it cease to exist and are unlikely to recur. The competent authority shall have the authority to review, upon motivated request, the continued existence of these circumstances;

(h) the right holder shall be paid adequate remuneration in the circumstances of each case, taking into account the economic value of the authorization;

(i) the legal validity of any decision relating to the authorization of such use shall be subject to judicial review or other independent review by a distinct higher authority in that Member;

(j) any decision relating to the remuneration provided in respect of such use shall be subject to judicial review or other independent review by a distinct higher authority in that Member;

(k) Members are not obliged to apply the conditions set forth in subparagraphs (b) and (f) where such use is permitted to remedy a practice determined after judicial or administrative process to be anti-competitive. The need to correct anti-competitive practices may be taken into account in determining the amount of remuneration in such cases. Competent authorities shall have the authority to refuse termination of authorization if and when the conditions which led to such authorization are likely to recur;

(l) where such use is authorized to permit the exploitation of a patent ('the second patent') which cannot be exploited without infringing another patent ('the first patent'), the following additional conditions shall apply:

  (i) the invention claimed in the second patent shall involve an important technical advance of considerable economic significance in relation to the invention claimed in the first patent;

  (ii) the owner of the first patent shall be entitled to a cross-licence on reasonable terms to use the invention claimed in the second patent; and

  (iii) the use authorized in respect of the first patent shall be non-assignable except with the assignment of the second patent.

While compulsory licensing is generally only used in the developed world to combat anti-competitive behaviour, several developing countries use compulsory licences or the threat thereof to provide access to medicines at reasonable cost, etc.). Here again, India's laws on compulsory licensing are broadly drafted and can serve as a model to others: Section 84 of India's Patents Act allows for the issuance of a compulsory licence provided that three years have passed from the grant of the patent and one of the following three criteria is satisfied: (1) failure to satisfy the 'reasonable requirements of the public'; (2) failure to provide the patented invention to the public 'at a reasonably affordable price';[62] and (3)

---

[62]   In addition Section 90 of the India Patents Act provides several situations whereby the reasonable requirements of the public shall be deemed not to have been satisfied.

failure to 'work' the patent in India.[63] In March 2012, India utilized all of these provisions for the first time when it issued a compulsory licence to generic manufacturer Natco to produce and market Nexavar, a drug patented by Bayer Corporation used to treat kidney and liver cancer.[64] Finding the drug to be 'exorbitantly priced and out of reach of most of the people', the Comptroller of Patents (i.e. Indian Patent Office) found Bayer Corporation 'clearly neglected India' and that it had not taken 'adequate or reasonable steps to start the working of the invention in the territory of India on a commercial level and to an adequate extent'.[65] Noting that the drug was only available to approximately 2 per cent of eligible patients,[66] the judgment further stated: 'If the drug is so highly priced that the ordinary public cannot afford it, then it is a fact that the product is not available to the public on reasonable terms . . . such high price becomes a barrier to availability of the drug, which is [the] precise evil the legislation is designed to curb.'[67]

---

[63] In other words, a compulsory licence can be issued not only when the rights owner fails to use the patent (i.e. import the product) but also when they fail to locally produce the product subject to the patent protection. This is allowed by the Paris Convention Article 5A (incorporated into the TRIPs by Article 2), but is arguably a violation of Article 27.1. For discussion on this controversial issue, see Bryan Mercurio and Mitali Tyagi, 'Treaty Interpretation in WTO Dispute Settlement: The Outstanding Question of the Legality of Local Working Requirements' (2010) 19 *Minnesota Journal of International Law* 275.

[64] *Natco Pharma Limited v. Bayer Corporation*, Application for Compulsory Licence under Section 84(1) of the Patents Act 1970 in Respect of Patent No.215758, 9 March 2012, available at http://patentdocs.typepad.com/files/compulsory-license-application.pdf (visited on 1 June 2012). Interestingly, although the Controller of Patents found Natco's attempts to negotiate a voluntary licence not to constitute 'an effort on reasonable terms and conditions' it nevertheless deemed Bayer's response a 'categoric[] refus[al]' to negotiate and thus deemed the requirements of Section 84(4)(iv) to be satisfied. *Ibid* at 9–10.

[65] *Ibid* at 13, 14 and 53. The Controller of Patents pointed out that despite selling the product abroad in 2006 the product was not launched in India until 2009 and further stated: 'If the terms are unreasonable such as high cost of [Rs.280,000], availability is meaningless.' *Ibid* at 15. The Controller of Patents further deemed the alleged infringement of the patent by another manufacturer, Cipla (which is challenging the patent in a case currently pending), who is marketing the product at Rs.30,000 per month as irrelevant to the present dispute. *Ibid* at 15, 20–21. Incidentally, immediately following this decision Cipla announced an 80 per cent reduction in the price of its cancer drugs which make them cheaper than the anticipated sale price of the generic Nexavar produced by Natco. Innovative manufacturer Roche also announced that it would reduce the price of two of its cancer drugs.

[66] *Ibid* at 22.

[67] *Ibid* at 15–16. Such 'conduct', the Controller of Patents stated, 'is not at all justifiable'. *Ibid* at 22–3.

The compulsory licence has been granted until the expiration of the patent in 2020, with Bayer Corporation receiving a 6 per cent royalty on net sales of the drug.[68] Natco is expected to reduce the price by 97 per cent, from Rs.280,428 (US$5,600) per month to Rs.8,800 (US$175) per month.[69] Bayer Corporation has appealed the decision to India's Intellectual Property Appellate Board.[70]

The point of maintaining such flexibilities is not to enable widespread use of compulsory licences. In this regard, compulsory licences should not be viewed as a solution to the access to medicines problem, but rather simply as a tool as part of a broader health and developmental strategy. Moreover, countries wishing to make use of compulsory licences could face economically punishing reprisals. For instance, as a result for issuing a compulsory licence in 2007 for the HIV protease inhibitor *Kaletra* (lopinavir/ritonavir),[71] Thailand suffered at the hands of both the pharmaceutical industry and the US government.[72] Moreover, and unlike FDI

---

[68]   *Ibid* at 58–60.

[69]   *Ibid* at 6.

[70]   Among other arguments, Bayer Corporation is arguing that as a result of Cipla's price reduction, Natco will not be able to meet the 'reasonable requirements of the public' and as a result in two years' time its patent risks revocation under Section 85 of the Indian Patents Act. Of course, at the same time Bayer Corporation is defending its patent against Cipla's challenge and, if the court upholds the patent, stands to benefit from royalties and penalties. More importantly, Cipla would be prohibited from manufacturing and marketing the drug. See Khomba Singh, 'Bayer demands withdrawal of Natco Pharma's compulsory licence', *The Economic Times*, 19 May 2012.

[71]   As noted at footnote 44, India refused to grant patent protection to Kaletra for lack of novelty and non-inventiveness.

[72]   For instance, Abbott announced it would no longer seek approval to market new medicines in Thailand. See Keith Alcorn, 'Abbott to withhold new drugs from Thailand in retaliation for Kaletra compulsory license' NAM aidsmap, 15 March 2007, available at http://www.aidsmap.com/Abbott-to-withhold-new-drugs-from-Thailand-in-retaliation-for-iKaletrai-compulsory-license/page/1426590/ (visited on 31 May 2012). This sparked a call for a global boycott of Abbott products. See http://www.democracynow.org/2007/4/26/aids_activists_call_for_global_boycott (visited on 31 May 2012). Thailand also issued compulsory licences for a cancer and heart medication. For US retaliation, see USTR, *2007 'Special 301' Report Executive Summary*, USTR Reports and Publications (2007), available at http://www.ustr.gov/assets/Document_Library/Reports_Publications/2007/2007_Special_301_Review/asset_upload_file230_11122.pdf (visited on 31 May 2012) (stating: 'In addition to [] longstanding concerns with deficient IPR protection in Thailand, in late 2006 and early 2007, there were further indications of a weakening respect for patents, as the Thai Government announced decisions to issue compulsory licenses for several patented pharmaceutical products. While the United States acknowledges a country's ability to issue such licenses in accordance

which brings with it advanced technologies and managerial and technical know-how, developing countries which issue compulsory licences must possess the capabilities to effectively utilize the licence.[73] Finally, expansive use of compulsory licensing threatens to destroy the differential pricing schemes utilized by pharmaceutical companies which benefit developing countries and LDCs. Thus, it is a worrying development when Brazil so often compares the prices it pays for imported medicines with the prices paid by less developed countries and demands a lower price; it is not only attempting to negotiate a better price for itself but also rebelling against the entire differential pricing system.

5. Test data

As discussed in Section II.A, Article 39.3 of the TRIPs Agreement requires Members to protect against unfair commercial use of confidential test data, but flexibilities exist as to the extent to which countries must protect test data. Thus, scope remains for Members to allow generic manufacturers seeking marketing approval to 'rely on' the test data in order to facilitate the entry of generic products onto the market. In so doing, Members ensure that Article 39.3 does not hamper or negatively affect efforts to enhance access to medicines.

This flexibility is under threat, however, by the addition of test data protections appearing in recent FTAs.[74] Under such FTAs, generic manufacturers wishing to market a generic whilst the period of data exclusivity

---

with WTO rules, the lack of transparency and due process exhibited in Thailand represents a serious concern.'). See also, Press Release, M. Hiebert, Chamber Study Exposes Investor Concerns in Thailand, US Chamber of Commerce Media Center, (March 20 2007), available at http://www.uschamber.com/press/releases/2007/march/07-50.htm (visited on 31 May 2012).

[73] For a useful review of the role of IP in trade, FDI and innovation, see Keith E. Maskus, *Intellectual Property Rights in the Global Economy* (Washington DC: Institute for International Economics, 2000), 186–94.

[74] The US and EU provide data exclusivity domestically for a period of five and ten years, respectively. In 2010, the US also began to provide 12 years of data protection for biologics, an emerging class of drugs derived from living organisms. US FTAs generally seek a five-year period of exclusivity for a new pharmaceutical product (and 10 years for a new agricultural chemical product). For instance, US–Australia FTA (Article 17.10.1(a)); Singapore (Article 16.8.1), Chile (Article 17.10.1), Morocco (Article 15.10.1), CAFTA-DR (Article 15.10.1), Bahrain (Article 14.9.1), Oman (Article 15.9.1) and Korea (Article 18.9.1). Certain agreements contain an additional provision which keeps the data exclusivity period intact even after the expiration of the patent. For instance, US–Australia FTA (Article 17.10.3); Singapore (Article 16.8.1), Morocco (15.10.1, note 11), Oman (Article 15.9.3) and Korea (Article 18.9.4). The EU is now requesting a

is in force must conduct their own clinical trials and generate other data and submit their own findings to the national authority. Such an approach is troublesome, not least because conducting tests and generating clinical data is extremely expensive (sometimes costing into the tens of millions of dollars).[75] The generic industry will find it difficult to implement such onerous requirements, and therefore, from a public health perspective, this requirement is difficult to justify.[76] Even if generic manufacturers were able to generate this data, the cost of the resulting drugs produced would rise considerably and the generics introduction into the marketplace would be delayed as well. Moreover, such duplication of testing could be viewed as unethical, as it simply repeats the testing and clinical trials where safety and efficacy has already been determined.[77]

Even more worrying is that the US is also seeking to include provisions in certain regional FTAs which apply a period of data exclusivity from the approval date in another country even if the manufacturer has not sought to register the drug in that particular country.[78] In such a circumstance, the generic manufacturer would still be prohibited from relying on the data for a certain time period with the end result being that the country does not have access to that particular drug until the expiration of the data exclusivity period.

Several US FTAs also effectively prohibit generic manufacturers from using evidence of registration of the originator drug in another country to prove the safety and efficacy of their version. The only condition that can be imposed on the originator is to require that marketing approval be sought within five years of registering the product in a country other than a member of that particular FTA.[79] Depending on how the originator times its entry into the market, the effect of the provision could result in ten years of test data protection. For example, a pharmaceutical company

---

10-year period of exclusivity for a new pharmaceutical product from its FTA partners, but has faced strong resistance from Colombia, Peru and India.

[75]   Robert Weissman, 'Dying for Drugs: How CAFTA Will Undermine Access to Essential Medicines' *Health Now*, 6 March 2004, at http://www.health-now.org/site/article.php?articleId=75&menuId=13 (visited on 31 May 2012).

[76]   Musungu and Oh, above n 49, 66.

[77]   Rahul Rajkumar, 'The Central American Free Trade Agreement: An End Run Around The Doha Declaration on TRIPs and Public Health' (2005) 15 *Albany Law Journal of Science & Technology* 433, 465.

[78]   See, e.g., Article 15.10 of the CAFTA-DR.

[79]   These provisions are found in US FTAs with Singapore (Article 16.8.2), Australia (Article 17.10.1(c)), Morocco (Article 15.10.1), CAFTA-DR (Article 15.10.1(b)), Bahrain (Article 14.9.1(b)), Oman (Article 15.9.1(b)) and Korea (Article 18.9.1(b)).

could register the original drug in one of the FTA-member countries but wait five years before submitting the market approval application in another FTA-member country. It would then be entitled to a further five years of exclusivity from the latter date.

A period of data exclusivity could be detrimental to countries taking advantage of a compulsory licence. Again, a manufacturer granted authority to produce a generic drug under compulsory licence must still be registered by the national drug regulatory authority and if the generic manufacturer cannot rely on existing data to gain regulatory approval it cannot respond to the compulsory licence and supply the needed drug. Thus, where a medicine is protected by patent, data exclusivity could effectively render the compulsory licence meaningless if the generic manufacturer cannot make effective use of the licence without repeating time-consuming and costly tests to obtain marketing approval for its drug.[80] The US has attempted to counter this argument by contending that 'if circumstances ever arise in which a drug is produced under a compulsory licence, and it is necessary to approve that drug to protect public health or effectively utilize the TRIPs/health solution, the data protection provisions in the FTA would not stand in the way'.[81]

C. Revisiting Access to Medicines: The Doha Declaration on TRIPs and Public Health and Beyond

The previous section illustrates how the flexibilities in the TRIPs Agreement counter most if not all of limitations arising from the Agreement's obligations in relation to access to essential medicines. Yet access to essential medicines continues to be illusory in many countries and the problem shows little sign of abating. This section begins by pointing out the issues facing certain developing country WTO Members in making use of the available flexibilities. The section then briefly describes and evaluates the prevailing international trends which greatly impacts upon the issue of access to essential medicines.

Despite the existence of flexibilities in the TRIPs Agreement, a large number of developing country Members fail to legislate for or otherwise take advantage of these flexibilities. For instance, a study commissioned

---

[80] Some FTAs limit the use of compulsory licensing to emergency situations. In such circumstances, due to time constraints, it will be impossible to conduct the necessary tests and obtain registration of the drug.

[81] Letter from United States Trade Representative General Counsel John K. Veroneau to Congressman Sander M. Levin (in the context of the US–Morocco FTA), 19 July 2004.

by the UK Commission on Intellectual Property Rights (CIPR) found that 27 of the 30 LDCs in Africa provide patent protection for pharmaceutical products despite not having to do so until 2016 (at the earliest).[82] While it could be argued that in reality this concession means very little, as most pharmaceutical companies do not patent their products in LDCs and/or donate or sell their medicines to these countries at cost, the broader issue is simply the loss of flexibility and the failure on the part of the relevant countries to recognize the significance of the loss.

Furthermore, the same CIPR study reported that 30 per cent or less of developing countries and LDCs specifically provide for international exhaustion, include the specific regulatory exception (i.e. Bolar exception) in their legislation or require patent applicants to disclose the source of any biological material used in the invention.[83] Perhaps most significantly, over 60 per cent of the LDCs studied provide patent protection for new uses of known or previously patented subject matter.[84] All studied LDCs do at least provide for compulsory licensing of pharmaceutical and other patents.

Given these statistics, the question must become why LDCs are failing to take advantage of the flexibilities offered by the TRIPs Agreement. There could be numerous answers to this question, but it is apparent that lack of knowledge of these flexibilities is not one of them. The CIPR report states:

> [D]eveloping countries are to a large extent fully aware of the legislative possibilities provided under TRIPs, although only a few appear to have taken advantage of all of the possible flexibilities.[85]

---

[82]   Thorpe, above n 58, 11. The absence of flexibilities is also present in other aspects of patent laws. For instance, despite the fact that TRIPs allows Members to exclude animals and plants from patentability over 75 per cent of developing countries and LDCs in fact grant patent protection for at least some inventions covering plants and animals. *Ibid* at 18. Likewise, only 5 per cent of developing countries and LDCs specifically exclude genetic material from patentability. *Ibid* at 19.

[83]   *Ibid* at 19–23. See also WIPO, *Patent-related Flexibilities in the Multilateral Legal Framework and their Legislative Implementation at the National and Regional Levels* (2010), reporting 26 per cent of the 112 countries surveyed as having international exhaustion and 56 per cent having a specific regulatory exception, with 93 per cent of high-income countries having such an exception and 0 per cent of LDCs having such an exception. These figures differ slightly from those in the Thorpe study.

[84]   *Ibid* at 19.

[85]   *Ibid* at 2. This is not surprising given the amount of free and easily accessible material existing in relation to TRIPs and access to medicines.

Since lack of knowledge can be ruled out, we must turn to other issues and reasons. Here, there are at least three factors which impede the implementation of TRIPs flexibilities. First, many developing countries and LDCs simply lack the monetary and administrative resources necessary to enable them to properly legislate for and implement these flexibilities. Second, several developing countries and in particular LDCs rely (perhaps excessively) on training schemes and other guidance offered by foreign countries and international organizations.[86] While the schemes and guidance are for the most part undoubtedly well-meaning they do portray a developed country view of IPRs and in this regard perhaps underemphasize the role of flexibilities as part of a comprehensive IP regime. Finally, although the potential of unilateral retaliation markedly decreased following the conclusion of the Uruguay Round, the risk did not entirely abate.[87] The omnipresent threat of reduced aid, possible trade sanctions and even merely being named as a country which does not fully respect IPRs still exists and could have serious consequences for the country concerned.[88] Taken together, these three factors at least partly explain the low utilization rates of available TRIPs flexibilities by most developing countries and LDCs.

Beyond the issues involving the implementation and utilization of available flexibilities discussed above, the international IP system has moved beyond the TRIPs Agreement in the slightly more than 15 years since the advent of the TRIPs Agreement. More specifically, three distinct post-TRIPs phases have emerged. In the first phase, what Daniel Gervais calls the 'addition' phase, countries implemented the TRIPs Agreement in a rather uniform manner which sought to protect IPRs around the globe in the hopes of increasing research and development, profits and economic growth.[89] This phase of maximizing IPRs ended around the turn

---

[86]   See generally Carolyn Deere, *The Implementation Game: The TRIPs Agreement and the Global Politics of Intellectual Property Reform in Developing Countries* (Oxford: Oxford University Press, 2009).

[87]   See Fredrick M. Abbott and Jerome H. Reichman, 'The Doha Round's Public Health Legacy: Strategies for the Production and Diffusion of Patented Medicines Under the Amended TRIPs Provisions' (2007) 10 *Journal of International Economic Law* 921, 980–81; Musungu and Oh, above n 49, 43–50.

[88]   Of particular note is the Special 301 provisions of the US Trade Act of 1974, which require the USTR to publish a list of 'priority countries' which 'have the most onerous or egregious acts, policies and practices that (i) deny adequate and effective [IPRs], or (ii) deny fair and equitable market access to United States persons that rely upon [IP] protection'. 19 U.S.C. 2242(b)(1)(A).

[89]   Daniel J. Gervais, Foreword, in *Implementing the WIPO Development Agenda* (Jeremy DeBeer ed.). (Wilfrid Laurier University Press, 2009). Gervais'

of the century when critics seriously questioned the link between trade and IPRs and the issue of the TRIPs Agreement and public health rose to prominence.

In the second phase, which Gervais dubs the 'subtraction' phase, developing countries not only scored public relations victories but also made inroads in pulling back from the maximalist version of IPRs and the TRIPs Agreement. The final sparks leading to the second phase occurred when several drug companies challenged the legality of the South African Medical and Related Substances Control Act of 1997, which allowed for compulsory licensing of patented pharmaceuticals.[90] The lawsuit, filed in the domestic courts of South Africa, brought the issue of access to medicines to the forefront and evoked passionate reactions and extremely unfavourable publicity for the pharmaceutical companies. At the same time, the US not only supported the litigation in South Africa but also filed a WTO complaint challenging the consistency of the compulsory licensing provisions in Brazilian industrial property law, which contained a 'local working' requirement, and the TRIPs Agreement.[91]

With the negative publicity refusing to abate, the pharmaceutical companies relented and dropped their challenge to the South African legislation.[92] The US also backtracked, negotiating a settlement to its WTO dispute settlement complaint whereby Brazil agreed to consult with the US before invoking any domestic compulsory licensing provisions (but did

---

foreword draws from his earlier work on this issue which includes Daniel J. Gervais, 'Intellectual Property, Trade & Development: The State of Play' (2005) 74 *Fordham Law Review* 505; Daniel J. Gervais, 'The Changing Landscape of International Intellectual Property' (2006) 2 *Journal of Intellectual Property Law & Practice* 1; Daniel J. Gervais, 'International Intellectual Property and Development: A Roadmap to Balance?' (2005) 2 *Journal of Generic Medicines* 327.

[90]   See Sarah Boseley, 'At the Mercy of Drug Giants: Millions Struggle with Disease as Pharmaceutical Firms Go to Court to Protect Profits' *The Guardian* (12 February 2001) (reporting that approximately 40 pharmaceutical companies were challenging Article 15c of South Africa's 1997 Medicines Act), available at http://www.guardian.co.uk/Archive/Article/0,4273,4134799,00.html (visited on 31 May 2012).

[91]   *Brazil–Measures Affecting Patent Protection – Request for the Establishment of a Panel by the United States*, WT/DS199/3 (9 January 2001); Article 68 of Brazil's industrial property law (Law No. 9,279 of 14 May 1996; effective May 1997) which was challenged under Article 27.1 of the TRIPs Agreement.

[92]   See Karen DeYoung, 'Makers of AIDS Drugs Drop S. Africa Suit' *Washington Post* (19 April 2001), at A13 (reporting that the pharmaceutical companies were dropping their suit against the South African government due to the 'public relations nightmare'), available at http://www.washingtonpost.com/ac2/wp-dynA34439-2001Aprl18?language=printer (visited on 31 May 2012).

not agree to amend its legislation).[93] Moreover, the US position regarding compulsory licensing became untenable in the wake of the terrorist attacks of September 11 and the subsequent anthrax scares when the government threatened to issue a compulsory licence for Bayer AG Corporation's anti-biotic Cipro (ciprofloxacin) in preparation for any eventual widespread need.[94] This threat placed the US in a difficult position, as it could now not continue requesting developing countries to resist issuing compulsory licences in favour of making medicines more widely available to the masses.[95]

Thus, the time was ripe for developing countries to push developed countries towards shifting their position with regard to access to medicines. The Doha Ministerial Conference became the forum for developing countries to prominently promote public health over IPRs. With public health a global concern and the US unable to continue pressing the issue of compulsory licences, developing countries secured much of what they sought in the final text of the Doha Declaration on TRIPs and Public Health.[96] The Doha Declaration received worldwide notoriety for

---

[93] See Press Release, 'Office of the United States Trade Representative, United States and Brazil Agree to Use Newly Created Consultative Mechanism to Promote Cooperation on HIV/AIDS and Address WTO Patent Dispute', (25 June 2001) (reporting that the US and Brazil mutually agreed to transfer the dispute to a consultative forum and stating that the US government would continue its policy of not raising objections to compulsory licensing provisions in developing countries' laws if they were aimed at addressing HIV/AIDS), available at http:// www.ustr.gov/releases/2001/06/01-46.htm (visited on 31 May 2012).

[94] Canada did actually briefly issue a compulsory licence on Bayer's patent. For background and repository of articles and reports on the US and Canadian threats and actions, see http://www.cptech.org/ip/health/cl/cipro/ (visited on 31 May 2012).

[95] See, e.g., Emma Young, 'US Accused of Double Standard on Drug Patents' *New Scientist* (2 November 2001) (reporting French Trade Secretary Francois Huwart as stating that the US's threats of compulsory licensing with regard to Cipro gave 'developing countries the impression that [a] double standard [was] in place'), available at http://www.newscientist.com/news/news.jsp? id=ns99991512 (visited on 31 May 2012).

[96] See generally Draft Ministerial Declaration, 'Proposal From a Group of Developed Countries' IP/C/W/313 (4 October 2001) (submitted to the TRIPs Council by Australia, Canada, Japan, Switzerland and US); Draft Ministerial Declaration, 'Proposal From a Group of Developing Countries' IP/C/W/312, WT/ GC/W/450 (4 October 2001) (submitted by African Group, Bangladesh, Barbados, Bolivia, Brazil, Cuba, Dominican Republic, Ecuador, Haiti, Honduras, India, Indonesia, Jamaica, Pakistan, Paraguay, Philippines, Peru, Sri Lanka, Thailand and Venezuela).

clarifying the TRIPs Agreement and emphasizing the 'flexibilities' existing in the Agreement.

The Declaration begins by 'recogniz[ing] the gravity of the public health problems afflicting many developing and least-developed countries, especially those resulting from HIV/AIDS, tuberculosis, malaria and other epidemics', before restating the concern over health epidemics and the high cost of medicines in developing countries.[97] At the same time, the Declaration underlines the importance of IPRs in the development of new medicines and reiterates that relaxing protections will not completely eliminate the health problems in the developing world.[98]

Paragraph 4 of the Doha Declaration further provides that the TRIPs Agreement 'does not and should not prevent Members from taking measures to protect public health' and 'affirm[s] that the Agreement can and should be interpreted and implemented in a manner supportive of WTO Members' right to protect public health and, in particular, to promote access to medicines for all'.[99]

Paragraph 5 reaffirms the right of WTO Members to use the provisions in the TRIPs Agreement for the purposes of Paragraph 4, including 'the right to grant compulsory licenses and the freedom to determine the grounds upon which such licenses are granted', 'the right to determine what constitutes a national emergency or other circumstances of extreme urgency' and that 'each Member free to establish its own regime for such exhaustion without challenge'.

Paragraph 6 'recognize[s] that WTO with insufficient or no manufacturing capacities in the pharmaceutical sector could face difficulties in making effective use of compulsory licensing under the TRIPs Agreement', but the paragraph leaves the issue unresolved, instead instructing the Council for TRIPs to find an 'expeditious solution' to the problem and to report to the General Council before the end of 2002.[100] The Decision Implementing Paragraph 6 of the Doha Declaration on the TRIPs Agreement and Public Health, however, was not reached until 30 August 2003.[101] The

---

[97]   Doha Declaration on TRIPs and Public Health paras 1–3.
[98]   Doha Declaration on TRIPs and Public Health paras 2–3.
[99]   Doha Declaration on TRIPs and Public Health para 4.
[100]   Doha Declaration on TRIPs and Public Health para 6. For discussion on Member proposals, see Bryan Mercurio, 'TRIPs, Patents and Access to Life-Saving Drugs in the Developing World' (2004) 8 *Marquette Intellectual Property Law Review* 211, 229–30 (recounting negotiating positions of developed and developing countries over the issue).
[101]   WTO General Council, 'Implementation of paragraph 6 of the Doha Declaration on the TRIPS Agreement and public health'. Decision of the General Council of 30 August 2003, WT/L/540 and Corr.1, 1 September 2003.

Implementation Decision provides a 'waiver' to obligations under Article 31(f) and thus allows any Member to export pharmaceutical products made under compulsory licences to others with insufficient or no manufacturing capabilities within the terms set out in the Decision. The Decision has been criticized for being too cumbersome,[102] and to date has only once been utilized.[103] Despite this, Members have agreed to transform the waiver into the first ever amendment of the TRIPs Agreement.[104] This cannot occur, however, if laws are not in place to allow for compulsory licence. In this regard, it is somewhat surprising that a large percentage of developing countries do not have sufficient legal measures in place to enable both the import and export of drugs under compulsory licence as needed under the waiver (and in future, under the new Article 31 *bis*).[105]

Despite the criticism, the Implementation Decision perhaps marked the watershed of momentum in favour of developing countries on the issue of the TRIPs Agreement and public health. Since that time, developed countries have once again gained the upper hand and through a forum shift to bilateral and regional trade agreements (and to a lesser extent, bilateral investment treaties) are incorporating obligations which build upon the standards existing in the TRIPs Agreement (so called 'TRIPs-plus' provisions). In relation to access to essential medicines, the most notable of these TRIPs-plus provisions include limits on compulsory licensing, the linkage of market approval to patent status, patent term extension, limits on parallel importation and the aforementioned test data protection.[106] All of these provisions have the potential to significantly impede access to essential medicines.

But this shift and resulting attempt to 'ratchet' IP standards upwards does not tell the entire story. The third post-TRIPs phase is one which Gervais deems as informed by 'calibration narratives'. The rising clout of China, India, Brazil and other developing countries, with the corresponding

---

[102] See, e.g., Médecins Sans Frontières, *Neither Expeditious, nor a Solution: the WTO August 30th Decision is unworkable* (2006).

[103] For details, see Matthew Rimmer, 'Race Against Time: The Export of Essential Medicines to Rwanda' (2008) 1(2) *Public Health Ethics* 89; Matthew Rimmer, 'The Jean Chretien Pledge to Africa Act: Patent Law and Humanitarian Aid' (2005) 15 (7) *Expert Opinion on Therapeutic Patents* 889.

[104] WTO General Council, 'Amendment of the TRIPS Agreement' Decision of 6 December 2005, WT/L/641, 8 December 2005.

[105] Numerous developed countries likewise have failed to implement legislation necessary to facilitate the export of drugs under compulsory licence.

[106] See Michael Handler and Bryan Mercurio, 'Intellectual Property' in Simon Lester and Bryan Mercurio (eds) *Bilateral and Regional Trade Agreements: Commentary and Analysis* (Cambridge: Cambridge University Press, 2009) 325–38.

recognition that developing countries do not share developmental needs, priorities or capacities greatly inform this third phase. As important is the recognition that high standards of IPRs alone will not attract FDI or lead to increased research and development or even global profits in countries below certain developmental thresholds. Thus, it is now widely believed that any movement to strengthen IPRs must be accomplished together with other developmental and structural reform and must be cognizant of potential negative impact on welfare.

The World Intellectual Property Organization (WIPO) Development Agenda has become the hope of developing countries in their pull-back from TRIPs-plus standards. Most prominently, the WIPO General Assembly in 2007 adopted 45 recommendations which aim to address the interests and needs of developing countries and ensure that the balance between creators/owners and users/public interest is maintained. The recommendations are distributed in the following clusters: Cluster A: Technical Assistance and Capacity Building; Cluster B: Norm-setting, flexibilities, public policy and public domain; Cluster C: Technology Transfer, Information and Communication Technologies and Access to Knowledge; Cluster D: Assessment, Evaluation and Impact Studies; Cluster E: Institutional Matters including Mandate and Governance; and Cluster F: Other Issues. To date, Members are still in the early process of implementing the WIPO Development Agenda and although they have agreed to some implementation projects, progress has been postponed or stalled on most aspects of implementation.[107]

Finally, it should be noted that reforming patent protection and international IPRs can only do so much to advance access to essential medicines. The vast majority of drugs listed on the WHO's Essential Medicines List are off-patent, and thus freely available to anyone to produce and distribute.[108] Access to essential medicines, however, continues to be problematic. There are numerous reasons why this continues to be the case. Foremost, most developing countries and LDCs give low priority to health. For instance, even though health spending as a percentage of total GDP hovers around 5 per cent in LDCs[109] the WHO reports that low-income countries spend an average of only US$3 per capita per year on

---

[107]   For a recent update, see Jeremy de Beer and Sara Bannerman, 'Foresight into the Future of WIPO's Development Agenda' (2010) 2 *WIPO Journal* 211.

[108]   The list can be viewed at http://www.who.int/medicines/publications/essentialmedicines/en/index.html (visited on 31 May 2012).

[109]   See http://www.tradingeconomics.com/least-developed-countries-un-classification/health-expenditure-total-percent-of-gdp-wb-data.html (visited on 31 May 2012).

medicines. Even with the drastic reduction in prices of essential medicines over the past decade, US$3 per capita per year is far below the necessary level to procure drugs to treat diseases such as HIV/AIDS and malaria.[110] Thus, even though the price of first-line combination antiretroviral therapy has been reduced from over US$10,000 in 2001 to just US$67 in 2010, this price is still out of reach for the vast majority of the populations in low-income countries.[111]

Committing to an improved health framework which includes access to essential medicines is a significant undertaking that involves, *inter alia*, funding issues at all levels, education and retention of health professionals, proper legal and regulatory framework, supply and distribution of health products and services and maintaining the safety and efficacy of pharmaceuticals. Most, if not all, developing countries would need financial assistance to improve their situation, but it is clear that 'some developing countries have aggregate national resources sufficient to meet all the primary healthcare needs of their citizens, yet non-health priorities are . . . given precedence'.[112]

A related barrier is the effects of exogenous factors, such as corruption, crumbling or non-existent infrastructure and civil instability, on public health and access to essential medicines. Another step developing countries and LDCs can take in lowering the costs, and therefore increasing access to, medicines is reducing or eliminating tariffs and taxes on the importation of pharmaceuticals and related products.[113] Tariffs and taxes add millions of dollars to the price of essential medicines and related products and result in delayed access, reduced access, increased counterfeit drugs, increased and worsened health problems and loss of life.[114] Not

---

[110] WHO, *The World Medicines Situation 2011* (2011) at 15, available at http://www.who.int/medicines/areas/policy/world_medicines_situation/en/index.html (visited on 31 May 2012).

[111] United Nations Development Programme, *Good Practice Guide: Improving Access to Treatment by Utilizing Public Health Flexibilities in the WTO TRIPS Agreement* (2010), at 4.

[112] Beryl Leach et al. (eds) *Task Force on HIV/AIDS, Malaria, TB, and Access to Essential Medicines, Prescription for Healthy Development: Increasing Access to Medicines* (2005) at 39, available at http:// www.unmillenniumproject.org/documents/TF5-medicines-Complete.pdf (visited on 31 May 2012).

[113] In 2006, the G-8 advocated the elimination of import tariffs and other non-tariff barriers to the importation of medicines. Group of Eight, Summit 2006, *Fight Against Infectious Diseases* (16 July 2006), available at http://en.g8russia.ru/docs/10.html (visited on 31 May 2012).

[114] See, e.g., Müge Olcay and Richard Laing, *Pharmaceutical Tariffs: What Is Their Effect on Prices, Protection of Local Industry and Revenue Generation?* (paper prepared for the Commission on Intellectual Property Rights, Innovation

only do border delays caused by the facilitation of customs requirements pertaining to tariffs and taxes sometimes result in the medicines expiring during the delays or suffering medicinal degradation due to suboptimal storage facilities (such as heat, cold, humidity or light),[115] but such duties considerably add to the cost of the medicines.

While the average tariff on medicines is 18 per cent, several developing countries and LDCs levy much higher rates on medicines entering their respective countries and the price of imported medicines in certain developing countries can be five times the reported value of the drug.[116] It is sometimes argued that developing countries rely on the revenue tariff rates raise in order to govern, but statistics reveal this to be a fallacy: revenue generated by import tariffs on pharmaceuticals amounts to less than 0.1 per cent of national GDP.[117] Moreover, at least one study has shown that the higher the tariff rate, the less the availability of essential

---

and Public Health, World Health Organization, Geneva, 2005), available at http://www.who.int/intellectualproperty/studies/TariffsOnEssentialMedicines.pdf (visited on 31 May 2012); Richard Laing, *Price, Availability and Affordability of Medicines: International Comparison in 30 Countries* (powerpoint presentation to the WHO, Geneva, 2006), slide 30, available at http://www.dfidhealthrc.org/MeTA/documents/MeTAresearchmtgannex1RL.ppt (visited on 31 May 2012).

[115]   WHO, *Equitable Access to Essential Medicines: A Framework for Collective Action* (2004), at 1, available at http://whqlibdoc.who.int/hq/2004/WHO_EDM_2004.4.pdf. Reducing these delays, in combination with streamlining the supply and distribution of medicines, would reduce human suffering, costs, waste, inefficiencies and opportunities for corruption. On corruption, see Roger Bate et al., *Tariffs, Corruption and Other Impediments to Medicinal Access in Developing Countries: Field Evidence*, AEI Working Paper No. 130 (2006), available at http://www.aei.org/publiccation24749/ (visited on 31 May 2012).

[116]   For instance, India, Sierra Leone, Nigeria and Bolivia also allow for the imposition of significant tariffs on the importation of pharmaceuticals at 55 per cent, 40 per cent, 34 per cent and 32 per cent respectively. The Democratic Republic of Congo and Zimbabwe impose tariff rates of approximately 8 per cent and while pharmaceuticals enter Sri Lanka, Kenya and Armenia duty free, the final mark-up in those countries due to other taxes and the like is 64 per cent, 54.2 per cent and 87.5 per cent, respectively. Countries applying excessive sales tax on medicines include South Africa (14 per cent), Argentina (21 per cent), Bangladesh (15 per cent), the Dominican Republic (28 per cent), India (25 per cent) Greece (15 per cent) and Turkey (18 per cent). Some nations, including Kenya, Morocco and Peru, impose such high levels of duties on imported medications that their actual cost to consumers is higher than in the domestic market of the drugs' manufacture – even with price differentiation. Roger Bate and Kathryn Boateng, *Medicinal Malpractice: Improving Drug Access and Reducing Corruption*, 10 Health Policy Outlook, at 2 (2006), available at http://www.aei.org/publications/pubID25276/pub_detail.asp (visited on 31 May 2012).

[117]   Olcay and Laing, above n 114, 32–3.

medicines.[118] In short, countries which levy significant tariffs on pharmaceuticals simply reveal the low priority that those countries have placed on public health.

Lastly, it must be noted that the flexibilities and the reforms discussed in this Part do nothing to address the issue of the so-called neglected diseases; that is, diseases that affect almost exclusively those in the developing world which receive little research and development. In order to increase research and development into these diseases, it is often suggested that alternatives to the patents regime will need to be developed. Numerous alternatives have been posed and several are currently being trialled.[119]

III. CONCLUDING ANALYSIS

In 2006, the WHO Commission on Innovation, IPR and Public Health (CIIPH) concluded:

> While developing countries (excluding least developed countries) with little technological and innovative capacity are bearing the cost of implementing the TRIPS Agreement, there are no documented cases of positive impact on innovation in the medical field as yet.[120]

The intention of this chapter has been to counter such statements with scientific analysis. More specifically, this chapter introduced the obligations

---

[118]   Kirsten Myhr, Comparing Prices of Essential Drugs between Four Countries in East Africa and with International Prices, available at http://www.msfaccess.org/resources/key-publications/key-publication-detail/?tx_ttnews%5Btt_news%5D=1296&cHash=3aa41e600c (visited on 31 May 2012).

[119]   Alternatives posed include patent pools, patent buy-outs, employer-based payroll taxes, patent auctions and well-funded research centres. See WHO, above n 14, 161–92, Medicines for Malaria Venture, *The New Landscape of Neglected Disease Drug Development* (2005), available at http://mmv.org/IMG/pdf/Chapter_2.pdf; Mattias Ganslandt, Keith E. Maskus and Eina V. Wong, 'Developing and Distributing Essential Medicines to Poor Countries: The DEFEND Proposal' (2001) 24 *World Economy* 779; Michael Kremer, 'Patent Buyouts: A Mechanism for Encouraging Innovation' (1998) 113 *The Quarterly Journal of Economics* 1137; James Love and Tim Hubbard, 'The Big Idea: Prizes to Stimulate R&D for New Medicines' (2007) 82 *Chicago–Kent Law Review* 1519. Two notable developments include the proposal for a 'Health Impact Fund' and the WHO Medicines Patent Pool. See Aidan Hollis and Thomas Pogge, 'The *Health Impact Fund:* Making New Medicines Accessible for All, A Report of Incentives for Global Health', (2008); Medicines Patent Pool, available at http://www.medicinespatentpool.org/ (visited on 31 May 2012).

[120]   Commission on Intellectual Property, Innovation and Public Health (CIPIH), *Public Health, Innovation and Intellectual Property Rights* (2006), at 83.

created by the TRIPs Agreement related to pharmaceuticals before outlining and evaluating the flexibilities in the Agreement. Far from the conclusion of the CIPIH, the actual effect of the TRIPs Agreement on low-income countries and LDCs has been minimal. As documented above, the TRIPs Agreement has not yet obliged LDCs to maintain or increase IP protection in relation to pharmaceuticals to any extent whatsoever, and low-income developing countries have the ability to utilize available flexibilities to minimize or eliminate the negative effect of future obligations.

The same is not entirely true of middle and high income developing countries – most of which it cannot be said suffer from 'little technological and innovative capacity' – as these countries have had to implement their obligations. However, through utilization of available flexibilities, these countries also have the ability to minimize or eliminate any negative effects of the TRIPs Agreement.

This is not to suggest that generic pharmaceutical companies in India, Brazil, China and the like could simply maintain their usual course of business. The TRIPs Agreement has certainly forced the generic industry in developing countries to shift the way it does business, and while most assume that the advent of pharmaceutical product patents has hurt their business, recent research conducted by Amy Kapcynski shows the paradoxical effect of the TRIPs Agreement on generic manufacturers. Focusing on India, Kapcynski demonstrates that the coming of the TRIPs Agreement forced the Indian generic industry to target the developed world. Thus, even though India became a net exporter of medicines in the 1980s, it mainly targeted developing countries and other unregulated pharmaceutical markets. The forthcoming advent of the TRIPs Agreement provided the impetus for the industry to learn more about patents and engage in an export strategy. The TRIPs Agreement also served as a trigger for research and development; the Indian industry realized that it would have to discover and innovate because of the limitations that the obligations of the TRIPs Agreement would impose.[121] The strategy has been an unqualified success, as Indian companies account for 25–50 per cent of all generic applications in the US and the majority of their profit is from exports to the developed world.[122]

Kapcynski cites leading Indian IP guru Gopakumar Nair as stating:

---

[121]   Kapczynski, above n 11, 1583–4. See also Chaudhuri, above n 11, 157–60.

[122]   Kapczynski, above n 11, 1581–6 (prior to TRIPs the Indian industry cited costs and regulations as prohibitively high in the developed country market). See also Chaudhuri, above n 11, 45. Thus, it must be noted that the Indian generic industry does not target developing country or neglected diseases, but rather those prevalent in the developed countries. Kapczynski, above n 11, 1584.

'Indians have now become global players because global standards of intellectual property have come to India'.[123] This does not seem to be the statement of someone lamenting the advent of the TRIPs Agreement. India is perhaps in the unique position of having a thriving generic pharmaceutical industry prior to TRIPs obligations, but the larger point is simply that it has combined sound business strategy with full utilization to ensure the industry continues to succeed.

Thus, while the TRIPs Agreement is often blamed for creating or exacerbating the problems associated with access to essential medicines, the blame is largely misplaced and often times merely serves to disguise the true culprits – national governments, corruption, civil instability and poverty.

---

[123]   Kapczynski, above n 11, 1583.

9. Public perception of food safety risks under WTO law: a normative perspective

Alberto Alemanno*

I. INTRODUCTION

It is almost a truism that in an age of increasing globalisation of the food supply, food safety is no longer a domestic issue alone. As the contemporary interconnectedness of the world makes the globalisation of food supply inevitable, countries around the world are increasingly confronted on a daily basis with decisions concerning risks posed by tradable food products and their manufacturing processes.[1] In response they tend to adopt protective measures that hinder trade in products and often trigger trade disputes. Recent examples of food safety measures include import bans and restrictions on pigs in the aftermath of the appearance of the H1N1 virus, on dairy products following the Chinese melamine scandal, as well as on Japanese feed and food products in the aftermath of the incident at the Fukushima nuclear power station.

While the adoption of those measures may be necessary for the protection of public health, their implementation may also be motivated by a desire to shield domestic industries from food imports. It is indeed tempting for some States to compensate for the reduction in traditional barriers to trade, which has been induced by the GATT/WTO framework, by introducing non-tariff barriers grounded on health concerns.[2]

Hence, the question arises: how to reconcile the inherent tensions between the declared public health goal pursued by these measures and the free trade imperative immanent in our economic system?

To achieve these 'shared, but sometimes competing, interests of promoting international trade and of protecting the life and health of human

*   The author would like to thank Denise Prévost for providing excellent comments on a previous draft and Cliff Wirajendi for his usual patient research assistance.

[1]   Coglianese, Finkel and Zaring (2009).

[2]   For a detailed history of the evolution of GATT rules on domestic regulations, see Sykes (1995) 63–68.

beings',[3] the WTO drafters, recognising the GATT non-discrimination principle as insufficient, decided to develop a new legal instrument: the Sanitary and Phytosanitary Agreement (SPS Agreement). Under this Agreement, science has been chosen as the privileged tool to determine the lawfulness of Members' regulatory autonomy when governing food matters.[4] Yet, as illustrated by several food safety disputes litigated in recent years under this Agreement, occasionally consumers may perceive some kinds of risks that cannot be proven by available scientific knowledge. In particular, consumers may develop fears about some foods developed by new technologies,[5] such as animal cloning, genetic engineering and nanotechnologies, and reject them even though they have been scientifically tested and been proven 'safe', i.e. equivalent to their conventional counterparts.[6]

Public perceptions of risk, by weakening consumer confidence in a given food product, often mature into public concerns which, in turn, inform national risk decision-making and eventually crystallise into regulations.[7] As public perceptions are culturally determined,[8] it is not surprising that the ensuing regulations differ between countries and, as such, result in obstacles to trade. Albeit scientifically unsubstantiated, the resulting regulations do not necessarily imply a protectionist intent or discriminatory effect and reflect what a society fears in a given historical moment.

However, due to the equation between absence of scientific evidence and protectionism built into the SPS Agreement, these restrictive measures

---

[3]   Appellate Body Report, *Measures concerning meat and meat products*, WT/DS26/AB/R, WT/DS48/AB/R adopted on 13 February 1998 (Appellate Body Report, *EC–Hormones*), para. 177.

[4]   Since the 1979 Tokyo Round some countries feared that the lowering of border barriers to trade would be circumvented by disguised protectionist measures in the form of technical regulations, notably sanitary and phytosanitary regulations. For this reason, already on that occasion, a Plurilateral Agreement was adopted on Technical Barriers to Trade, also called the 'Standards Code'. See Trebilcock and Howse (1999) 145.

[5]   Baruch Fischoff, one of the pioneers in risk perception studies, recognises that 'technological risks can evoke the deepest feelings'. Fischoff (1985).

[6]   According to most of the regulatory legal frameworks dealing with these substances, the notion of 'safety' related to their scientific equivalence to the conventional product.

[7]   In international trade law jargon, the term 'public perception of risk', or more generally, 'public opinion', is sometimes used to refer to fears unsupported by scientific evidence and as such are opposed to scientifically based facts or measures. It is in this sense that the terms will be used here. See, e.g., Fraiberg and Trebilcock (1998).

[8]   See, e.g., Douglas, (1985); Weber and Ancker (2010) 480.

are difficult to reconcile with WTO law and tend to be systematically struck down by the dispute settlement judicial bodies.[9] Because of their inherent complexity and multipurpose objectives, they may also give rise to complex and lengthy trade disputes that cannot easily be resolved by the WTO Dispute Settlement System. Indeed, as demonstrated by the *EC – Hormones* and *EC – Biotech* disputes, when public perceptions trigger the adoption of a protective, yet scientifically unsupported regulatory response, not even the threat of retaliation may induce the losing importing country to comply with WTO law.

In view of the above, the exact role that public perception of risks, and more in general public opinion and consumer concerns, may, and ought to, play under the science-based regime described above is one of the most challenging, yet little explored,[10] issues under WTO law, and in particular under the SPS Agreement. This is all the more true if one approaches this question from a broader perspective, outside of the international trade arena. Indeed, the issue of WTO Members' responsiveness to public perception under WTO law evokes, and belongs to, a greater debate existing in the literature on risk regulation about whether decision-makers should prioritise the inputs of the experts over those of the general public in regulatory decision-making.[11] For purposes of understanding this debate, we might distinguish between two approaches: the technocratic and the populist. On the one hand, good technocrats consider public perceptions of risk as 'irrational' and denounce the negative effects that they may have in society because of the high cost incurred by the resulting over-restrictive risk regulations.[12] They argue that, given people's use of mental shortcuts (i.e. cognitive biases) that can distort (risk) judgments,[13] public authorities should 'educate' people through rational risk communication rather than taking into account their expressed concerns.[14] On the other hand, the populists defy this rationalistic view by regarding public perceptions as an

---

[9]   Moreover, as illustrated below, due to the 'regulatory chill' effect generated by the WTO/SPS discipline, Members may sometimes be deterred from adopting trade restrictive measures which, although addressing public perceptions and meeting consumer demands, cannot be substantiated scientifically.

[10]   Notable exceptions are Walker (1998) 307; Scott (2004); Hilson (2005) and Foster (2008).

[11]   See, e.g., Margolis (1996); Rowe and Wright (2001) 341, 356; Douglas and Wildavsky (1983).

[12]   In the risk regulation literature, see, e.g., Breyer (1993) 43–44; Sunstein (2005); Margolis (1996), 35; in the WTO literature, Ju (2010), 19.

[13]   Kanheman, Slovic and Tversky (1982); and more recently, Sunstein and Zeckhauser (2010).

[14]   See above note 12 as well as Eskridge and Ferejohn (2002).

expression of a 'rival rationality' that should enter the regulatory decision-making process on an equal footing with technocratic input.[15] In their view, laypersons may perceive risks more broadly than experts because they take into account factors that tend to be excluded from technical risk assessment.[16]

Where does the WTO stand on this debate? How does the WTO take into account public perceptions and ensuing concerns? What is the place that public perceptions of surrounding risks take in WTO law? How responsive to public perceptions can WTO Members be? Can public perceptions justify regulatory action under the WTO? In the affirmative: are there, as a matter of WTO law, limits upon the extent to which decision-makers may have regard to public perceptions when adopting food regulations?

This chapter aims to address these questions by focusing especially on the extent to which WTO Members' decision-makers are, or ought to be, legitimately entitled to take consumers' perception of food safety risks into account under the SPS Agreement. However it must be recognised from the outset that the normative challenge represented by the issue of public perception of risks within the WTO is somewhat of a different nature than the above described classic 'technocracy vs democracy' debate. As the WTO is not a state itself but rather a mere supervisor of the exercise of regulatory autonomy, its challenge is not to identify the solution (be it expert advice or layman perception) that ensures better risk regulatory outcomes. Rather – in line with its textual mandate – its more humble, yet equally difficult, mission should be to outline the contours of a solution able to circumscribe, in a universal fashion, the conditions under which Members may respond to public perceptions without raising the ghost of protectionism.

Against this backdrop, section II briefly sketches how the WTO governs food safety risks. After illustrating the scientific rationale underpinning the WTO/SPS regime of supervision of risk policies, section III explores whether this discipline allows, at least in principle, Members to accommodate public perceptions of food risks. Section IV systematises the public perception-related case law developed by the WTO Dispute Settlement bodies when reviewing the legality of food safety measures adopted by WTO Members and measures the extent to which these judicial bodies have been willing to take into account public concerns.

---

[15]   Anderson (1993); Heinzerling (1995); Ackerman and Heinzerling (2004); Slovic et al (1985); Winickoff, et al (2005); Slovic (2000), 59; Kahan (2008).
[16]   Margolis (1996).

Section V identifies and discusses the consequences stemming from the SPS Agreement's failure to respond to public perceptions. Finally, section VI takes up the difficult question of how the WTO should take account of public perceptions of food safety risks, by raising questions for further research.

The relevance and salience of this issue will be illustrated throughout this chapter by reference to the regulatory challenges posed by Bisphenol A. This chemical substance, used prominently in food contact material, is facing mounting consumer hostility, as it is increasingly perceived as causing adverse effects on public health. As a result several countries around the world have recently banned its use despite the favourable scientific opinions delivered by the respective food agencies.[17] Similarly, restrictive measures are currently also envisaged vis-à-vis food products deriving from cloned animals and their offspring notwithstanding the lack of scientific evidence suggesting negative health effects stemming from their consumption.

II. THE WTO DISCIPLINES ON FOOD SAFETY RISKS

Due to the globalisation of food supply, food safety has emerged in recent years as a significant global issue with both international trade and public health implications. In particular, today not only new food safety risks can spread among countries, but also old, previously controlled, risks can be re-introduced into countries. Moreover, due to contemporary global inter-connectedness, contaminated food can spread more rapidly and affect wider regions, thus causing illness worldwide. As a result, although public concerns about food safety risks vary across countries and change over time,[18] there is a general sense that consumers, especially in the industrial-ised world, have become increasingly concerned about the risks stemming from food consumption.[19]

Food safety risks may be associated with pests or diseases or arise from the presence of certain substances in food, beverages and feedstuffs. While the former category refers in essence to pathogens (i.e. viruses, illness causing bacteria, parasites, fungi), the latter includes risks from food addi-tives, toxins (i.e. lead and mercury), persistent organic pollutants (dioxins,

---

[17] Alemanno (2010).
[18] See e.g. Wilson (2011).
[19] See e.g. Wildavsky (1979).

DDT, etc) and veterinary drug and pesticides residues. Recently, consumers increasingly identify food safety risks in the application of science to modern agriculture and in innovative food technologies, such as genetic engineering, nanotechnologies, irradiation and animal cloning. Consumer acceptance of these new technologies is the result of a complex assessment of the perceived benefits and risks stemming from the technology itself, whether a product or a process, and its alternatives, mediated by a narrative elaborated by the media around the introduction of the relevant technology.[20]

The increased salience of food safety concerns has been leading governments, in response to the demands of their domestic constituencies, to strengthen existing food regulatory regimes and to enact pre-market approval schemes as well as ad hoc measures aimed at protecting human health. While the adoption of these national measures may be legitimate to protect public health in an increasingly integrated food market, their enactment, as it tends to produce trade restrictive effects, may also be motivated by a desire to protect domestic industries from imports.

To address such a concern, and to strike a balance between the Members' right to protect their citizens from unsafe imported foods and the free trade of food products, at the time of the Uruguay Round paving the way for the creation of the WTO the GATT Contracting Parties adopted two Agreements to prevent technical barriers to trade.[21] Both Agreements, by going beyond the GATT obligation not to discriminate among or against imported products, impose a set of international, both substantive and procedural, rules on national regulations regarding products, their characteristics and production.[22] Yet since sanitary and phytosanitary measures introduce specific concerns for trade in goods, a separate Agreement, the

---

[20]   Henson (1995).

[21]   For a detailed and insightful analysis of the genesis of the SPS Agreement, see Prévost (2009) 451–514.

[22]   The GATT 1994 – like the original GATT of 1947 – does not contain any direct reference to science and leaves countries free to establish whatever public health regulations they wish. The only constraints on the exercise of their legislative autonomy are principally set out in Article III:4 which requires that these regulations be applied in a non-discriminatory way to imported and domestic 'like products', and Article XI prohibiting all restrictions 'instituted or maintained on the importation or exportation of any product'. However, Article XX GATT allows any Contracting Party to depart from GATT obligations by adopting restrictions on imports and exports justified inter alia for the protection of health and life of humans, animals and plants (let. b) or related to conservation of natural exhaustible resources (let. g).

SPS Agreement, was 'carved out' of the TBT Agreement.[23] As a result the two Agreements differ in scope. While the TBT Agreement covers all technical regulations and voluntary standards, and the procedures to ensure that these are met, the SPS Agreement applies to all measures to protect human, animal and plant life and health from specified risks, such as food safety risks and risks from pests/diseases of plants or animals.[24] While both the SPS and the TBT Agreements apply to food, the TBT Agreement is more relevant to labelling requirements than to safety per se.[25]

In particular, the SPS Agreement, by supplementing Article XX(b) GATT,[26] provides Members with a (multilateral) framework to develop their domestic public health policies, such as food safety.[27] Yet this discipline – and this must be highlighted from the outset – unlike those provided for by other international organisations, such as the Food and Agriculture Organization (FAO), the World Health Organization (WHO) and the World Animal Health Organization (OIE), does not pursue among its goals food safety. Its *raison d'être* being free trade, the SPS Agreement is concerned with the trade impact that food safety rules, *rectius* sanitary and phytosanitary measures, may have on international trade rather than on the safety concerns that may support those regulations. Thus, the WTO food trade regime, being exclusively aimed at reducing the negative effects that Members' food safety and quality regulations may have on international food trade, is intended to circumscribe the exercise of Members'

---

[23]   This separation between technical barriers and sanitary and phytosanitary measures has been inspired by the NAFTA Agreement. See NAFTA Chapters 7B and 9, available at http://www.nafta-sec-alena.org (last visited on 20 March 2012).

[24]   It follows that while it is the type of measure which determines whether it is subject to the TBT Agreement, it is the purpose of the measure which is relevant in determining whether a measure is covered by the SPS Agreement.

[25]   The TBT also deals with health risks, and therefore also with safety issues but not those specified in the SPS Agreement. It thus covers safety issues emerging from toxic plastics in toys and asbsestos.

[26]   Article XX(b) reads: 'Subject to the requirement that such measures are not applied in a manner which would constitute a means of arbitrary or unjustifiable discrimination between countries where the same conditions prevail, or a disguised restriction on international trade, nothing in this Agreement shall be construed to prevent the adoption or enforcement by any contracting party of measures: . . .(b) necessary to protect human, animal or plant life or health.'

[27]   Since the 1979 Tokyo Round some countries feared that the lowering of border measures would be circumvented by disguised protectionist measures in the form of technical regulations, notably sanitary and phytosanitary regulations. For this reason, already on that occasion, a Plurilateral Agreement was adopted on Technical Barriers to Trade, also called 'Standards Code'. See Trebilcock and Howse (1999), 145. See also Marceau and Trachtman (2002).

regulatory autonomy 'in negative' – by imposing on them obligations to reduce trade effects – and not 'in positive' by requiring them to ensure a minimum level of safety for consumers.[28]

The purpose of this Agreement is indeed to maintain the sovereign right of any Member to provide the level of health protection it deems appropriate (so called, 'appropriate level of protection' or 'ALOP'),[29] while at the same time ensuring that these sovereign rights are not misused for protectionist purposes and do not result in unnecessary barriers to international trade.

In order to circumscribe the regulatory authority of national governments so as to limit abusive 'scientific claims', the SPS Agreement chose science as the privileged tool enabling the interpreter to determine whether an adopted food safety measure is legitimate (i.e. a genuine food standard) or illegitimate (i.e. a disguised protectionist measure). In particular, the SPS Agreement's scientific discipline builds upon four key science-based provisions.[30]

The primary scientific justification requirement may be found in Article 2.2 of the SPS Agreement. That Article requires that any Member's sanitary and phytosanitary measure be 'based on scientific principles and [. . .] not [be] maintained without sufficient scientific evidence' and be the least-trade restrictive solution available.

Article 5.1 of the SPS Agreement translates this duty into operational terms by dictating that countries should ensure that their measures are 'based on an assessment, as appropriate to the circumstances, of the risks to human, animal or plant life or health'.

Article 5.7, referred to in Article 2.2, authorises a departure from the previous two provisions, permitting the adoption of provisional measures in a situation of insufficient scientific evidence.[31] Finally, under Article

---

[28]   Alemanno (2007) 228–9.

[29]   Annex A, paragraph 5, to the SPS Agreement defines 'Appropriate level of sanitary or phytosanitary protection' as '[t]he level of protection deemed appropriate by the [WTO] Member establishing a sanitary or phytosanitary measure to protect human, animal or plant life or health within its territory'. The footnote attached to this definition states that many WTO Members refer to this concept as the 'acceptable level of risk'. See also the Preamble of the SPS Agreement which stipulates that 'no Member should be prevented from adopting or reinforcing measures necessary to protect human, animal or plant life or health'.

[30]   For a detailed analysis of the scientific discipline established by the SPS Agreement, see, e.g., Prévost (2009) 633–737 ; Gruszczynski (2010) 107–55 ; Scott (2007) 76–138.

[31]   Article 5.7 SPS reads: 'In cases where relevant scientific evidence is insufficient, a Member may provisionally adopt sanitary or phytosanitary measures on

3.1, Members are encouraged to base their standards on international standards, guidelines or recommendations where they exist. Members may introduce or maintain standards which result in a higher level of protection than would be achieved by measures based on such international standards, if there is scientific justification for such increased protection or where the Member has engaged in a process of risk assessment as laid down in Article 5 of the Agreement.

The effect of the SPS Agreement is to mandate a particular approach to decision-making about issues concerning food safety, consumer protection and animal welfare, which amounts to a risk analysis model where the production of authorised knowledge and management of risk is mainly based on scientific evidence.

III. THE SCIENTIFIC RATIONALE OF THE SPS AGREEMENT AND THE CHALLENGES RAISED BY PUBLIC PERCEPTIONS OF RISKS

The increased reliance on science as a benchmark against which to check the legality of regulatory action stems from the belief that, 'by bringing constraints on valid lines of argument being based on data and methods used to estimate risk',[32] science ensures that a given SPS measure, despite its divergence from an international standard, addresses a real, objectively established health risk. Under this view, scientific justification, operating in a denationalised dimension, would be more effective than non-discrimination in spotting protectionist measures and in dismantling sham health measures discovered to be de facto trade barriers.[33] As a result, WTO Members are – at least in principle – free to adopt all measures necessary to protect food safety and they are also given considerable discretion in determining the appropriate level of protection they seek to achieve through their measures.[34] However, any departure from scientific evidence raises

the basis of available pertinent information, including that from the relevant international organizations as well as from sanitary or phytosanitary measures applied by other Members. In such circumstances, Members shall seek to obtain the additional information necessary for a more objective assessment of risk and review the sanitary or phytosanitary measure accordingly within a reasonable period of time.'

[32]   Crawford-Brown, Pauwelyn and Smith (2004), 465.

[33]   For an insightful book on the law and science interface, see Feldman (2009).

[34]   Article 2 SPS provides that: 'Members have the right to take sanitary and phytosanitary measures necessary for the protection of human, animal or plant life or health, provided that such measures are not inconsistent with the provisions of this Agreement.'

the risk that the government may not only pursue a protectionist objective but also serve to 'reinforce popular prejudices about which risks are serious'.[35]

Therefore, to limit the negative effects stemming from the adoption of food-related measures the SPS Agreement encourages decision-makers to make better and more informed decisions by laying down a mandatory evidence-based discipline.

Yet, by imposing such a technocratic approach to risk regulatory decision-making, the text of the SPS Agreement seems to make the adoption of more politically-based decision-making problematic.[36]

To illustrate this point, the current example of the regulatory response to Bisphenol A, also called BPA, can be used.

A. The Case of Bisphenol A

Bisphenol A (BPA) is a chemical building block that is used primarily to make clear polycarbonate plastic and certain epoxy resins of food cans. It is a high-production volume chemical: around 3 billion kilograms of the compound are produced annually, with an estimated value of US$500,000 per hour to the global economy.[37] Virtually every canned food and beverage product on the market today contains some dose, although tiny, of BPA in its can lining.[38] The uses of BPA result in consumer exposure to it via the diet. The two primary dietary sources are through the migration of BPA from the epoxy resins and the migration of BPA from re-usable polycarbonate drinking containers. As a result, over 90 per cent of us excrete BPA metabolites in our urine at any given time.[39] Due to the possible association of BPA with negative health effects, this endocrinally active substance has been the subject of attention worldwide.

Since the late 1990s, a large volume of research has been generated suggesting a possible 'low' dose effect for weakly estrogenic environmental contaminants, such as BPA.[40] Yet virtually all food safety

---

[35] Howse (2000), 2352–3.

[36] Lee (2005), 260.

[37] Environmental Working Group, Bisphenol A: *Toxic Plastics Chemical in Canned Food* (2007), available at http://www.ewg.org/node/20928/print (last visited on 20 March 2012) and A. Lang et al (2008).

[38] National Toxicology Program, US Department of Health & Human Services, NTP-CERHR Expert Panel Report for Bisphenol A (26 November 2007).

[39] Calafat, et al (2005), 391 (reporting on BPA detected in urine samples from 394 randomly selected adults); Vandenberg et al. (2007).

[40] Melnick et al. (2002).

agencies that have been asked to prepare a scientific opinion on BPA have confirmed the existence of safety thresholds allowing its continued use.[41]

Under the pressure of growing public opinion, the EU has recently banned the manufacture, placing on the market and importation of BPA-containing baby bottles in its territory.[42] The EU has adopted this restrictive measure notwithstanding a BPA-favourable opinion of the European Food Safety Authority (EFSA), concluding that 'no new study could be identified, which would call for a revision of the current tolerable daily intake of 0,005 mg/kg bodyweight per day'.[43]

These restrictive measures, although genuinely reflecting public perception of the risks posed by BPA, are not likely to find support in a risk assessment – as required by Article 5.1 of the SPS Agreement[44] – and as such they might be successfully challenged under the SPS Agreement. More critically, given the difficulty in qualifying the existing studies as 'insufficient scientific evidence' (there is indeed a complete scientific opinion by EFSA), also Article 5.7 would be unlikely to accommodate the EU regulatory measure.

Therefore, by favouring techno-scientific decision-making over civically-informed policymaking, the SPS framework seems *prima facie* to prevent Members from legitimately taking into account public perceptions that fail to reflect risk assessments.[45]

This seems critical insofar as – as illustrated by the BPA example – regulations to protect public health, including food safety regulations, reflect public perceptions and necessarily involve social policy choices.[46] Relevant cognitive studies have confirmed that people behave according to percep-

---

[41]   Note that US FDA, although authorising the use of the substance, has never established an acceptable daily intake (ADI) for BPA exposure through food additive use. Only the US Environmental Protection Agency (EPA) has published a reference dose (RfD, 0.05mg/kg/day) for BPA.

[42]   Directive 2011/8/EU amending Directive 2002/72/EC as regards the restriction of use of Bisphenol A in plastic infant feeding bottles OJ L26/11.

[43]   EFSA (2010).

[44]   BPA and other endocrine disruptors present a challenge to traditional toxicology as they do not fit with 'the prevailing paradigm of dosis facit veninum: the dose makes the poison'. See Scott (2008).

[45]   Public perceptions of food risks are the result of a complex function of factors such as baseline food safety risks levels; food safety risks from internationally imported goods; access to and extent and nature of information about food safety and risk levels; trust in the different sources of information; and exposure to major food safety incidents. See, e.g., Buzby (2001).

[46]   Wirth (1994).

tions (not facts) and, inevitably, those perceptions inform decision-making in democratic nations.[47]

B.   Accommodating Public Perceptions in the SPS Agreement

How can the ensuing public perception-based regulations be accommodated within the science-based regime of the SPS Agreement when these fail to reflect risk assessments? In our view, at least two modes of accommodation can, *in abstracto*, be contemplated.[48]

First, certain SPS provisions, being instilled with some sensitivity to the issue of public perception, might accommodate such a dimension when interpreted and applied. In other words, as some provisions are textually open to the acknowledgement of public perceptions, and more generally public opinion, the same provisions may contemplate these factors as legitimate elements in the application of their rules. As will be illustrated below, examples include Article 5.2 (factors to be taken into account within a risk assessment), Article 5.5 SPS (consistency requirement) as well as Article 5.7 (precautionary principle). We call this mode of accommodation 'conform interpretation' to public perception.

Second, public perception could be contemplated as an autonomous defence. WTO Members could justify the adoption of restrictive measures by arguing that they are necessary, regardless of their scientific basis, because the public considers them so. In particular, they could argue that by carrying the potential to reduce consumer anxieties and the ensuing distortions in behaviour, they might produce some social benefits. Although bold and quite extreme, this mode of accommodation is worth exploring and we define it as 'public perception autonomous defence'.

In order to verify the strength of these speculations regarding the ability of WTO Members, in particular under the SPS Agreement, to be responsive to perceived risks associated with potential hazards, it is necessary to examine how the issue has been dealt with in WTO case law. In this space it would be foolhardy to try to examine in an exhaustive manner all the relevant case law developed under the WTO agreements. Instead I will mainly focus on the disputes that have been

---

[47]   Consumer perceptions are the result of a complex function of factors such as baseline food safety risks levels; food safety risks from internationally imported goods; access to and extent and nature of information about food safety and risk levels; trust in the different sources of information; and exposure to major food safety incidents. See Buzby (2001).

[48]   This categorization builds upon Joanne Scott's proposed taxonomy in European Regulation of GMOs: Scott (2004).

litigated under the SPS Agreement since these are more relevant to our purposes.

IV.   PUBLIC PERCEPTIONS OF FOOD SAFETY RISKS IN THE WTO CASE LAW

Although prima facie surprising, the parties in food-related disputes under the SPS Agreement have never raised the issue of public perceptions explicitly. In other words, defendant Members do not try to defend the contested measures on grounds of public perception or public concern. Rather they tend to characterise their regulations as motivated by scientifically sound assessment of health risks, by carefully avoiding suggesting that the underlying regulatory goal is to address public perceptions of risks. This seems also to be the case when the restrictive measure has clearly been enacted to respond to public fears that are disproportionate to the risks as measured by the experts in risks assessments.

Given the obvious preference contained in the SPS Agreement for a rational, evidence-based decision-making process, this outcome is hardly surprising. Why should the defending Member disclose that behind the adoption of the contested food safety measure there are consumer anxieties likely to shed a negative light on the scientific justification of the measure?

In these circumstances, the SPS Agreement seems rather to provide an incentive to the defending WTO Member to hide the real motive, be it public perception of risk or a broader ethical, religious or political ground, of the contested regulation behind scientific clothes.

This is exactly what happened in *EC – Hormones*, 'one of the longest running trade disputes in the modern trading system',[49] litigated between the European Union and the United States and Canada regarding beef treated with growth-hormones.[50] This is also the dispute where the issue of public perception under the SPS Agreement was first raised, although indirectly.

---

[49]   Sykes (2006), 260.
[50]   *EC Measures Concerning Meat and Meat Products (Hormones), Complaint by Canada*, WT/DS48/R/CAN and Complaint by the US WT/DS26/R/USA, adopted 13 February 1998, as modified by Appellate Body Report WT/DS26/AB/R, WT/DS48/AB/R, DSR 1998:II, 235 and 699 (*EC – Hormones*).

A. *EC – Hormones* and Public Perceptions

As is well known, the *EC – Hormones* dispute involved a complaint by the United States and Canada against an EC regulatory regime prohibiting the administration of six growth hormones (such as oestrogen, progesterone and testosterone) to cattle.[51] The EC's concern was the potential for cancer in humans resulting from the consumption of hormone-treated beef. This regulatory regime was adopted by the EC institutions notwithstanding the advice of the Scientific Working Group proving that the outlawed growth-hormones were harmless to human health. Due to its dubious scientific justification, the ban triggered not only the US and Canadian reactions but also some internal resistance.[52]

The EC ban turned out to be motivated by a complex mix of political, social, economic and conflicting scientific factors.[53]

As a result, although both Canada and the US challenged the EU ban on scientific grounds (as not supported by valid scientific evidence),[54] they also argued that this measure was motivated more by the need to address public perception of risks than to tackle genuine food risks. Thus, Canada argued that the EC measures were motivated by 'first, anxiety regarding the danger to human health; second, the pressure of public opinion;

---

[51] See Council Directive 81/602/EEC concerning the prohibition of certain substances having a hormonal action and of any substances having a thyrostatic action (OJ L222 32–3); Council Directive 88/146/EEC prohibiting the use in livestock farming of certain substances having a hormonal action (OJ L70 16–18) and Council Directive 88/299/EEC on trade in animals treated with certain substances having a hormonal action and their meat, as referred to in Article 7 of Directive 88/146/EEC (JO L128 36–8). Other measures relevant to the dispute are contained in Directives 72/462/EEC, 81/602/EEC, 81/851/EEC, 81/852/EEC, 85/358/EEC, referenced in Directive 88/146/EEC; the decisions, control programme and derogations referred to in Article 6(2), Article 6(7) and Article 7, respectively, of Directive 88/146/EEC; and any amendments or modifications, including Directives 96/22/EC and 96/23/EC.

[52] Thus, for instance, an association of pharmaceutical manufacturers sought the annulment of the Directive prohibiting the use of certain hormonal growth promoters for the purpose of fattening cattle. See Case 160/88 *Fedesa v. Council* [1988] ECR 6399. See also Case C-180/96, *United Kingdom v. Commission* [1998] ECR 3903; Case C-157/96, *The Queen v. Ministry of Agriculture, Fisheries and Food, ex parte National Farmers' Union et al.* [1998] ECR I-2211.

[53] To define such a mix of different interests behind regulatory action, Pascal Lamy coined the term 'collective preference'. See Lamy (2004).

[54] Moreover, the United States alleged that the ban stems not from legitimate health concerns but from a desire to protect the Community's domestic cattle industry. This led the US to invoke Article III.4 GATT.

third, the economic consequences of a "sensationalist" campaign'.[55] The US, in its complaint, focused its claim on the lack of scientific grounds supporting the EU ban, by stating that the EU 'had never performed any risk assessment, or relied on any risk assessment, that could serve as a basis for its ban with respect to the six hormones'.[56] Yet it also added that 'the remarkable characteristic of the public debate in the European Communities on these hormones was that the "risk" was usually described in terms of consumer anxieties rather than any observable adverse effect on human health'.[57] In its view, by failing to identify any specific risk to human or animal life or health against which the ban was designed to protect, the EC measure had to be declared incompatible with WTO law.

In sum, these parties claimed the illegality of the contested measure not only because it lacked a scientific basis but also because – in their view – public risk perceptions can never provide a basis for the adoption of a SPS measure under Article 5 of the SPS Agreement. In other words, by assuming that science and public perceptions are separate and mutually exclusive factors behind regulatory action, they suggested that the contested measure, being driven mainly by public perception, could in any event never satisfy the scientific discipline mandated by the SPS Agreement.

In its defence, the EC strongly denied that the purpose of the contested measure was to address consumer anxieties rather than to protect human health. To support its claim, it argued that 'there was nothing in the text of the contested measures, the legislative history or in any other document to suggest that "consumer anxieties" was purpose for which the measures were adopted'.[58] However, the EC also maintained that risk management decisions could include a range of factors, 'such as public health and environmental protection, relevant legislation and legal precedent, application of social, economic and political values and consumer concerns'.[59] As a result, it admitted that it was 'likely that consumer concerns had been taken into consideration during the "risk management" phase, since consumer concerns on potential risks to human health resulting from the use of hormones were very high at that time'.[60] Yet, public anxieties not being

---

[55]   Panel Report, *EC – Hormones, Complaint by Canada*, para. 415.

[56]   Panel Report, *EC – Hormones, Complaint by US*, para. 4.110.

[57]   Ibid., para. 4.110.

[58]   EU reply in Panel Report, *EC – Hormones, Complaint by US*, para. 4.113, '. . . there was nothing in the text of the contested measures, the legislative history or in any other document to suggest that "consumer anxieties" was purpose for which the measures were adopted'.

[59]   Panel Report, *EC – Hormones, Complaint by US*, para. 4.113.

[60]   Panel Report, *EC – Hormones, Complaint by US*, para. 4.113.

the only purpose for which its ban was adopted, the measure should – in its view – be upheld. To downplay the 'public perception' component of its legislation, the EC also added that '[t]here was little question that consumer concerns about safety and other issues also influenced the US agencies' decisions, even where there was arguably little, if any, basis for those concerns'.[61]

Although the Panel recognised, under the factual elements of the dispute, the existence of 'European consumers' concern over the use of hormones for growth promotion purposes in livestock',[62] its analysis remained essentially indifferent to the reasons that led the EC to adopt the contested measure.[63] It found that, by maintaining the ban without a risk assessment as foreseen in Article 5, the EC acted inconsistently with the requirements contained in Article 5.1 of the SPS Agreement. Yet, in its conclusions, the Panel was keen to emphasise that 'none of the parties has argued that factors not listed in Article 5.2, such as consumer preferences, can be taken into account in a risk assessment in accordance with Article 5'. Indeed, the EC, despite its attempt at arguing that consumer perceptions may play a legitimate role in risk management, was careful not to claim that public perceptions should have a place within risk assessment.

On appeal, the issue of public concerns was raised again. This time it occurred in relation to the claim raised under Article 5.5 of the SPS Agreement. This provision, by seeking to achieve consistency in the application of the appropriate level of SPS protection against health risks, provides that WTO Members should avoid arbitrary or unjustifiable distinctions in the levels they consider to be appropriate in different situations, if such distinctions in the level of risk result in discrimination or a disguised restriction on international trade. In other words, when evaluating a particular hazard, Members should adopt similar levels of risk for similar products. While the Panel found a breach of this provision insofar as the '"arbitrary or unjustifiable" difference in the EC levels of protection in respect of the hormones at issue on the one hand and in respect of carbadox and olaquindox on the other resulted in a disguised restriction',[64]

---

[61]   Panel Report, *EC – Hormones, Complaint by US*, para. 4.113.

[62]   Panel Report, *EC – Hormones, Complaint by Canada*, para. 4.183.

[63]   The Panel also acknowledges that such concerns were triggered by the 'illegal use of dethylstilboestrol, commonly known as DES, in veal production in France and incidents, particularly in Italy, where adolescents had been reported to be suffering from hormonal irregularities and veal had come under suspicion as a possible cause'. Panel Report, *EC – Hormones, Complaint by Canada*, para. 4.183.

[64]   The Panel based its finding on: (i) the great difference in the levels of protection, namely, the difference between a 'no residue' level for the five hormones

the Appellate Body reversed this finding. In so doing, the Appellate Body, unlike the Panel, seemed willing to consider this issue under a public perception perspective:

> We do not attribute the same importance as the Panel to the supposed multiple objectives of the European Communities in enacting the EC Directives that set forth the EC measures . . . The documentation that preceded or accompanied the enactment of the prohibition . . . makes clear the depth and extent of the *anxieties experienced within the European Communities* concerning the results of the general scientific studies (showing the carcinogenicity of hormones), the dangers of abuse (highlighted by scandals relating to black-marketing and smuggling of prohibited veterinary drugs in the European Communities) of hormones and other substances used for growth promotion and the *intense concern of consumers* within the European Communities over the quality and drug-free character of the meat available in its internal market. A major problem addressed in the legislative process of the European Communities related to the differences in the internal regulations of various Member States of the European Union (four or five of which permitted, while the rest prohibited, the use for growth promotion of certain hormones), the resulting distortions in competitive conditions in and the existence of barriers to intra-community trade. The necessity for harmonizing the internal regulations of its Member States was a consequence of the European Communities' mandate to establish a common (internal) market in beef . . . We are unable to share the inference that the Panel apparently draws that the import ban on treated meat and the Community-wide prohibition of the use of the hormones here in dispute for growth promotion purposes in the beef sector were not really designed to protect its population from the risk of cancer, but rather to keep out US and Canadian hormone-treated beef and thereby to protect the domestic beef producers in the European Communities.[65]

Therefore the Appellate Body seemed to accept that different levels of protection, although arbitrary or unjustifiable, do not necessarily result in a discrimination or a disguised restriction on international trade should they reflect consumer anxieties. This is because 'governments establish their appropriate levels of protection frequently on an ad hoc basis and over time, as different risks present themselves at different times'.[66] Article 5.5 seems therefore to consider public perception, and more generally public opinion, as a significant element in its application.

---

at issue when used as growth promoters, as opposed to an 'unlimited residue' level for carbadox and olaquindox; (ii) the absence of any plausible justification put forward by the European Communities for this significant difference; and (iii) the nature of the EC measure, i.e., the prohibition of imports, which necessarily restricts international trade.

[65]   Appellate Body Report, *EC – Hormones*, paras 257–8.
[66]   Appellate Body Report, *EC – Hormones*, para. 213.

Lastly, it is in relation to the claim under Article III.4 of the GATT that the issue of public perception, due to the EC's own initiative, arose more prominently in *EC – Hormones*.[67] Under this provision, less favourable treatment of 'like' products is prima facie illegal, whilst if products are not alike, countries do not have to treat them in the same way. With reference to the EC's argument that the perception of European consumers was a relevant factor in determining the 'likeness' of a product, Canada submitted that this factor was irrelevant. In Canada's view:

> the public authorities of WTO Members had a responsibility to educate the public and to make them aware of scientific facts. If the Panel were to allow 'public perception' to become a factor in a 'like product' determination, it would open the door to misapprehensions concerning scientific facts becoming the basis of a justification in the WTO for the adoption of discriminatory measures. Such an interpretation would obviously remove any incentive whatsoever for public authorities in the European Communities to make their populations aware of the scientific facts in respect of the six hormones at issue.[68]

Once more, public perceptions are viewed as scientifically unjustified and as such – according to the complainant – they should not find any room within the WTO. Unfortunately, for reasons of judicial economy, the Panel did not consider the alleged breach of Article III.4 of the GATT, thus it did not examine whether the perception of European consumers could be a relevant factor in determining the 'likeness' of a product under this provision.[69]

Under the classic approach to 'like products', consumer perceptions would not be considered a relevant factor. However, after the Appellate Body Report in *EC – Asbestos* it would seem that non-trade concerns, such as health, may be considered relevant to the question of like products.[70] In

---

[67]   Article III:4 GATT provides: 'The products of the territory of any contracting party imported into the territory of any other contracting party shall be accorded treatment no less favourable than that accorded to like products of national origin in respect of all laws, regulations and requirements affecting their internal sale, offering for sale, purchase, transportation, distribution or use. The provisions of this paragraph shall not prevent the application of differential internal transportation charges which are based exclusively on the economic operation of the means of transport and not on the nationality of the product.'

[68]   Panel Report, *EC – Hormones, Complaint by Canada*, para. 4.348.

[69]   Panel Report, *EC – Hormones, Complaint by Canada*, para. 8.275. ('Since we have found that the EC measures in dispute are inconsistent with the requirements of the SPS Agreement, we see no need to further examine whether the EC measures in dispute are also inconsistent with Articles III or XI of GATT.')

[70]   Appellate Body Report, *EC – Asbestos*, WT/DS135/AB/R, para. 113. ('We are very much of the view that evidence relating to the health risks associated with

particular, the Appellate Body in that case accepted that 'consumer perceptions may similarly influence – modify or even render obsolete – traditional uses of the products'.[71] Thus, not only 'consumer tastes and habits', as expressed in the market, but also consumer perceptions have become a relevant criterion in the analysis of 'likeness'.

Finally, although the Appellate Body in *EC – Hormones* found the EC ban to be a measure unsupported by any risk assessment, and therefore in breach of Article 5.1 of the SPS Agreement, its reasoning regarding Article 5.5 'was based on consumer anxiety about the risk of cancer, not on the risk of cancer itself'.[72] Whilst the EC did not invoke public perceptions as an autonomous defence to justify its restrictive measures, it did not hesitate to mention them within the framework of Article 5.5 (consistency) and, outside of the SPS Agreement, in relation to Article III.4 of the GATT (non discrimination between 'like products').

Overall, the *EC – Hormones* case seems to suggest that WTO Members are extremely wary in invoking public perception as one of the possible grounds that might justify a departure from complying with the SPS science-based regime. This is especially true in relation to Article 5.1 and 5.2 of the SPS Agreement imposing a strict science-based discipline to all measures. Although the Appellate Body recognised that the list of factors to be taken into account in risk assessment under Article 5.2 is not exhaustive, it did not specify what kind of other factors might be relevant.[73] The subsequent case law seems to have interpreted this passage as mainly referring to control problems rather than opening the SPS Agreement to non-scientific factors, such as public perception.[74]

B.   *US – Continued Suspension* and Public Perception[75]

It is generally agreed that other factors, such as public perception, may play a role in the policy decisions taken at the risk management stage of SPS regulation.

This seems to have been recently confirmed in the follow-up to the *EC – Hormones* dispute, in *US – Continued Suspension*. Here the Appellate

---

a product may be pertinent in an examination of "likeness" under Article III:4 of the GATT 1994.')

[71]   Appellate Body Report, *EC – Asbestos*, WT/DS135/AB/R, paras 101–2.

[72]   Walker (1998), 308.

[73]   Appellate Body Report, *EC – Hormones*, para. 187.

[74]   Gruszczynski (2010), 107–55.

[75]   Although this issue was also addressed in *Canada – Continued Suspension* I chose for practical reasons to refer only *US – Continued Suspension*.

Body recognised that the chosen level of protection of a Member may have some bearing on the scope and method of the risk assessment, notably when this level of protection is higher than would be achieved by a measure based on an international standard.[76] Why did the Appellate Body reach this conclusion? This is because 'in such a situation, the fact that the WTO Member has chosen to set a higher level of protection may require it to perform certain research as part of its risk assessment that it is different from the parameters considered and the research carried out in the risk assessment underlying the international standards'. As a result, although the risk assessment should not develop into 'an exercise tailored to and carried out for the purpose of justifying decisions ex post', but remain 'in essence a rigorous and objective process',[77] a risk management consideration such as the ALOP can play a role in determining the scope of the risk assessment requirement.

Yet, as acutely observed, this development 'does not change the overall character of each phase of the risk analysis model' underpinning the SPS Agreement.[78]

The recognition that subjective factors, such the ALOP and the inherent choices in setting this standard of protection, may play a role within risk assessment does not necessarily diminish its scientific integrity. Scientific evidence first, other concerns later if need be.

C. *EC – Biotech* and Public Perceptions

The issue of public perceptions and consumer concerns in relation to food safety risks arose also, even though in a different context, in the *EC – Biotech* dispute. In this dispute, Argentina, Canada and the United States challenged (i) the de facto moratorium on the approval of biotech products in the European Communities; (ii) the failure to approve a number of specific applications for the placing on the market of certain GMOs; and (iii) and the national marketing and import bans on biotech products maintained by some of the EU Member States, despite the products having been given prior approval by the EC.

As is well known, in its addressing the measures set out in (i) and (ii) above, the EC focused its defence on arguing that its GM discipline did not qualify as an SPS measure as 'the issues arising out of the existence

---

[76] Appellate Body Report, *US – Continued Suspension*, WT/DS230/AB, para. 685.

[77] Ibid., para 1413.

[78] Gruszczynski (2010), 129.

of GMOs go far beyond the risks envisaged and regulated by the SPS Agreement'.[79] To prove its claim, the EC argued inter alia that Directive 2001/18 on labelling and traceability requirements was enacted on consumer information grounds rather than on public health grounds. In other words, according to the EC, the underlying goal pursued by the EC legislator with this directive was to address public perception of GM food risks by enabling them to know which products were genetically modified rather than protecting them from their possible adverse effects. Although this specific argument was rejected,[80] the EC was successful in having the Panel conclude that its general moratorium (and the product-specific measures) did not constitute 'SPS measures' within the meaning of Annex A.1 of the SPS Agreement.

D.   Precaution and Public Perceptions

The provision that seems favourably disposed towards public perception-driven regulation is Article 5.7 of the SPS Agreement. It was thoroughly discussed under both the *EC – Hormones* and the *EC – Biotech* disputes. This provision, by allowing Members to adopt 'provisional' SPS measures 'on the basis of available pertinent information' in 'cases where relevant scientific evidence is insufficient', seems to reflect the responses of policy makers to the vicissitudes of public perception of risk.[81] This is because, by allowing the Members, in certain situations that are characterised by insufficient scientific evidence, to adopt measures that are not based on a risk assessment, it enables them – at least in principle – to depart from the

---

[79]   Panel Report, *EC – Biotech*, WT/DS291/R, para. 4.355. ('The issues arising out of the existence of GMOs go far beyond the risks envisaged and regulated by the SPS Agreement. A rigorous interpretation of the definitions in Annex A.1 of the SPS Agreement unequivocally shows that measures addressing issues such as antibiotic resistance or changes in the ecological balance are not among the measures that the SPS Agreement intends to discipline. Since the European Communities, through its actions, aims at the fulfilment of objectives that go beyond the specific situations that determine the applicability of the SPS Agreement, such Agreement does not provide a sufficient legal framework for the examination of the European Communities' behaviour.')

[80]   Panel Report, *EC – Biotech*, para. 6.68. ('In the light of the above elements and considerations, we are not convinced by, and therefore are unable to accept, the European Communities' unsubstantiated assertion in its comments on the old paragraph 7.381 of the interim reports that the relevant labelling requirement in Directive 2001/18 is applied, in part, for the purpose of consumer information.')

[81]   Panel Report, *EC – Biotech*. The Appellate Body in *EC – Hormones* held that this provision does not exhaust the relevance of the precaution in the Agreement and that other provisions of the SPS Agreement may embody this idea.

scientific regime enshrined in Article 5.1 (risk assessment). As such this provision seems the most promising in terms of ability to accommodate risk perceptions failing to satisfy a risk assessment. Although the case law of the WTO judicial bodies is rather confused as to the interpretation of this provision, as it is on the role of precaution in WTO law more generally, the Appellate Body has consistently held that the precautionary principle has not been written into the SPS Agreement as a ground for justifying measures which are otherwise inconsistent with its provisions.[82] In particular, the judicial bodies have interpreted the discipline established by Article 5.7 as derogating from the scientific regime enshrined in Articles 2.2 and 5.1 only when all four conditions to invoke Article 5.7 are satisfied. Under settled case law, these conditions consist of four cumulative requirements: (i) there is *insufficient scientific evidence* for conducting a risk assessment, (ii) an SPS measure is adopted on the basis of *available pertinent information,* (iii) a WTO Member seeks *additional information* for a more objective assessment of risk, and (iv) the adopted SPS measure, being *temporary,* is subject to review within a reasonable period of time.[83]

In particular, according to established case law, 'insufficient scientific evidence' exists when 'a body of available scientific evidence does not allow, in quantitative and qualitative terms, the performance of an adequate assessment of risks as required under Article 5.1 and as defined in Annex A to the SPS Agreement'.[84] This definition of the first requirement enabling the invocation of a precautionary approach under the SPS Agreement has led the WTO judicial bodies to distinguish scientific insufficiency from scientific uncertainty, and to interpret the former concept as much narrower than the latter. To illustrate the consequences stemming from such a restrictive notion of scientific insufficiency, I turn again to the example of BPA. Since the existing scientific studies on this substance have not precluded the European Food Safety Authority from delivering a fully-fledged scientific report, the actual ban against BPA-made bottles would be unlikely to be considered adopted 'in cases where relevant scientific evidence is insufficient', and as such capable of triggering the application of Article 5.7. This outcome would seem to be confirmed by

---

[82] Appellate Body Report, *EC – Hormones*, WT/DS26/R and WT/DS48/R, para. 253; Appellate Body Report, *Japan – Agricultural Products*, WT/DS76/AB/R, paras 81–83.

[83] Appellate Body Report, *Japan – Agricultural Products*, WT/DS76/AB/R, para. 89; Appellate Body Report, *Japan – Apples*, WT/DS76/AB/R, para. 176; Panel Report, *US – Continued Suspension*, WT/DS320/R, para. 7.608.

[84] Appellate Body Report, *Japan – Apples*, WT/DS76/AB/R, para. 179; Panel Report, *US – Continued Suspension*, WT/DS320/R, para. 7.593.

the fact that the only source of uncertainty stemming from EFSA's scientific report consists in a dissenting opinion that, as such, does not seem to have impeded the performance of the risk assessment.[85] This corresponds to the approach followed by the Panel in the *EC – Biotech* dispute when called upon to examine whether the conflicting opinions existing as to the scientific evidence underpinning safeguard measures adopted by inter alia France (vis-à-vis oilseed rape MS1xRF1) and Germany (Maize Bt-176) could be considered as 'insufficient' scientific evidence. The Panel rejected this conclusion by claiming that insofar as the national authorities were able to perform a risk assessment of these products, it was no longer possible for these countries to claim that there was 'insufficiency of scientific evidence'.[86]

V.   ADDRESSING PUBLIC PERCEPTION AS A NORMATIVE CHALLENGE

The analysis of the relevant case law illustrates that neither of the two modes of accommodation of public perception of food safety risks previously sketched out, 'conform-interpretation' and 'autonomous defence', seems happening *in concreto*.

While it is true that some provisions, such as Article 5.5 of the SPS Agreement (internal consistency) or Article III.4 of the GATT (likeness) accommodate public perceptions – as confirmed by the Dispute Settlement Body – by recognising them as relevant criteria in their application, no food safety measure can escape the demanding and specific scientific discipline imposed by Article 5 of the SPS Agreement. Even the adoption of precautionary measures under Article 5.7 – the provision supposed to better reflect the responses of policy makers to the vicissitudes of public perception of risk – has historically been subject to a demanding scientific requirement. This has de facto prevented, and deterred, Members' reliance on this provision in all circumstances where their restrictive measures, having been adopted in the absence of robust scientific evidence, could have benefited from its sensitivity to 'other' factors, such as public perception.

As a result, absent specific scientific evidence of risk, it is not open to a WTO Member to act, regardless of the intensity of the public perception

---

[85]   For a useful taxonomy of the type of uncertainty that may qualify as 'insufficient scientific evidence' see Gruszczynski (2010), 187–91.

[86]   Panel Report, *EC – Biotech*, para 7.3300.

generated by a given risk, to address the perceived hazard. This explains the reticence of WTO Members to try the second, and more direct, mode of accommodation previously envisioned *in abstracto*: public perception as an autonomous defence to a restrictive measure. As public perceptions are regarded as scientifically unjustified and as such perceived outside of the WTO legal framework, they tend to be raised by the complainants as a sword, to delegitimise the scientific authority of the contested measure, rather than as a shield by the defendants.

Therefore, it appears that, under the SPS Agreement as interpreted by the WTO judicial bodies, adequate scientific support is a *sine qua non* for the legality of any public health measure. Only once the restrictive measure has satisfied the tests of scientific validity, Members remain free to be more or less responsive to public perception of risks, on the basis of their own regulatory decision-making procedures. In these circumstances, their responses, notably the determination of the ALOP, may indeed vary with the degree of concern and anxiety among citizens vis-à-vis the relevant food product.

The scientific requirement acts therefore as a bottleneck to the acceptance of risk perception under the SPS Agreement.

The ensuing result is that the WTO judicial bodies could condemn a restrictive measure, such as the current EU ban on BPA-containing baby bottles, which lacks scientific rationality and responds to public perception, despite the absence of protectionist intent. A similar treatment might also be reserved for a regulation restricting the sale of food products derived from cloned animals, such as the one currently discussed by the EU.[87]

This result is troubling for a variety of reasons.

First, the approach to regulatory decision-making mandated by the SPS Agreement, by reducing this process to a scientific exercise, does not do justice to the complexity inherent in any legislative or administrative process leading to the adoption of risk regulations. It is generally

---

[87] Although the EFSA assessments have not suggested that meat or milk from cloned animals and their offspring poses a risk to public health, the EU, notably the EU Parliament, objects to cloning on animal health and welfare grounds. In May 2011 the EU Council Legal Service concluded that all measures under discussion (including bans of food from cloned animals and from their offspring) entail risks as far as their compatibility with the WTO rules is concerned. It went on to consider that only in the case where a WTO panel would decide that food from cloned animals and from their descendants were not 'like' products, the envisaged measures would not amount to a violation of Article III:4 of the GATT or of Article 2.1 of the TBT Agreement.

acknowledged that in democratic societies regulations to protect public health, although largely informed by science, involve social policy choices. Alvin Weinberg has famously expressed this idea in his influential work:

> Attempts to deal with social problems through the procedures of science hang on the answers to questions that can be asked of science and yet which cannot be answered by science. I propose the term trans-scientific for these questions. . . Scientists have no monopoly on wisdom where this kind of trans-science is involved; they shall have to accommodate the will of the public and its representatives.[88]

Therefore, since most regulations are implicitly or explicitly crafted to respond to a particular social, economic or political context, it would not seem possible to infer regulatory outcomes solely on the basis of scientific data. As illustrated by our example, the EU decision to ban BPA-containing baby bottles does not find support in scientific evidence as EFSA concluded the safety of the products, but rather in value judgments largely shaped by public risk perception. There is indeed no doubt that public perception, a collection of notions that individuals or society form on risk sources relative to the information available to them and their basic common sense,[89] rather than science per se was the trigger for the adoption of this restrictive regulatory measure.

In the light of the above, condemning the EU ban would be normatively doubtful.

Second, the failure of the WTO's supervision of risk policies via the SPS Agreement to accommodate public perception compromises the right of a Member to establish its ALOP, although this right is enshrined in the Agreement.[90] Since Members may address risk perception and consumer anxieties only after having satisfied the scientific disciplines, their ability to determine the level of protection that they deem appropriate for society seems undermined. On this point, Vern Walker rhetorically asks 'if . . . consumer anxieties could not be respected, or domestic politics could not be taken into account, what would remain of the sovereignty inherent in risk management decisions?'[91] It has been argued that in the long run, this prioritisation of scientific evidence over the public perception of risk may threaten 'public support' for the international trade regime represented by the WTO.[92]

---

[88]   Weinberg (1972).
[89]   Jaeger et al. (2011).
[90]   Scott (2000), 157.
[91]   Walker (1998), 307.
[92]   Charnovitz (2000), 302.

Third, the current reticence of the regime of the SPS Agreement to account for public perception of risk fails to consider how perception-responsive regulation would fare under economic welfare analysis.[93] This is relevant insofar as, by carrying the potential to reduce consumer anxieties and the resulting distortions in behaviour, these regulations can produce some social benefits. As observed by Robert Howse, 'if citizens believe they need a certain regulation, however, "deluded" such a belief is, their utility will be reduced if they do not get it, in the sense that they will believe themselves exposed to a risk they believe to be significant'.[94] The impact on trade stemming from those fears can be significant, and often higher than the impact generated by the restrictive measures alone.[95] For example, whilst EU consumers fearful of growth hormones may face higher prices stemming from higher production costs, these costs may be smaller than those resulting from the distortions in consumption patterns generated by public perception regarding the safety of meat.

This seems to have been acknowledged even by a supporter of the technocratic approach such as Sunstein, when asserting that 'the reduction of even baseless fear is a social good'.[96] Yet, it remains to be proven that the fear-inspired regulatory response produces relevant distortions capable of justifying the regulation alone.

Fourth, the existing SPS scientific discipline is, in the way it has been normatively construed and judicially interpreted, producing the perverse effect of providing incentives to WTO Members to hide their societies' public perceptions under scientific arguments in order to create (or at least artificially inflate) scientific disagreement on a given phenomenon. As was the case in several SPS disputes litigated so far, this inevitably leads to impasse. Thus, should the EU ban on BPA-containing baby bottles be challenged under the SPS Agreement, it is likely that the EU will try to defend its measure as scientifically-grounded, notwithstanding EFSA's favourable opinion. The EU would also downplay – as it did in *EC – Hormones* – the role played by public perception in the adoption of its restrictive measure. Yet in these circumstances neither Article 5.1 nor 5.7 would accommodate this measure and, by failing to reflect a risk assessment, it will likely be struck down regardless of its non-protectionist objective.

Fifth, given the negative historical record of compliance with rulings

---

[93]   On the role of economic criteria in devising international trade rules, see Lowenfeld (2006) 153–89.

[94]   Howse (2000).

[95]   Chang (2004).

[96]   Sunstein (2001), 104.

disregarding public perception,[97] there is also a risk that 'the credibility of the WTO is also harmed in the complaining state, which observes a legal victory before a panel or the AB, but does not get the benefits of that victory'.[98] Indeed, as demonstrated by the *EC – Hormones* dispute, when public perceptions trigger the adoption of a protective, yet scientifically unsupported, regulatory response, not even the threat of retaliation may induce the losing importing country to comply with WTO law.

Sixth, by dismissing as 'irrational' all food regulations that fail to satisfy a risk assessment, the SPS Agreement may produce a 'regulatory chill' on health regulation, i.e. 'the reluctance of governments to introduce domestic public health laws for fear of inviting trade disputes'.[99] Being aware of the difficult task of defending a risk perception-driven regulation under the SPS Agreement, WTO Members may be deterred from adopting protective regulations even before a formal dispute settlement proceeding is initiated to challenge the regulation. As observed, 'well-resourced companies regularly commission legal opinions from leading domestic and international lawyers that highlight – and have an incentive to overstate – the risks of a successful trade challenge'.[100] This clearly acts as a deterrent to enact regulations that are likely not to be fully substantiated by scientific evidence. In the case of BPA, it is worth observing that all countries concerned by this substance have limited the adoption of their restrictive measures vis-à-vis a tiny niche of the BPA-made products: baby bottles.[101] This is the case even though they have been considering imposing it on all BPA-containing products.

These remarks reveal that the issue of the role of public perception of risk, and more in general public opinion, presents a normative challenge for the WTO. They also illustrate that, although complex, this challenge

---

[97]   While it is true that only the *EC – Biotech* and the *EC – Hormones* rulings have not been complied with, these were the only SPS disputes thus far where public perceptions of highly salient risks were at stake. A similar outcome might be expected in future disputes in relation to, for instance, restrictive measures directed against food coming from cloned animals and their offspring.

[98]   Guzman (2003).

[99]   See on this phenomenon, Liberman and Mitchell (2010), 165; Magnusson (2007), 8. See also, for an analysis on this phenomenon on tobacco control policies: McGrady (2007); and on alcohol control policies, Baumberg and Anderson (2008).

[100]   Liberman and Mitchell (2010), 165.

[101]   Besides Canada, which was the first worldwide mover against BPA, in the US, Connecticut, Minnesota, Washington, Wisconsin, Vermont, Maryland, and New York have passed legislation banning or limiting the use of BPA in products used by infants. In the EU France and Denmark acted before the EU. On 24 December 2012, the French President approved Law no. 2012-1442 (the French BPA Law), banning the manufacture, import, export and placing on the market of all packaging, containers and utensils intended to come into contact with food, if they contain BPA.

should not be avoided. What is at stake is not only the viability of the SPS Agreement but also the social acceptance of the WTO's supervisory role on Members' regulatory autonomy.

This is all the more true and urgent if one considers the significant number of new sources of food risks that, by eliciting public perception, might prompt the adoption of trade restrictive measures which are unlikely to satisfy a risk assessment within the meaning of Article 5.1. Besides the issues linked to the controversial endocrine disruptors, such as BPA, one may think of food deriving from animal cloning, bio-engineering and nanotechnology applications. Although virtually all food safety agencies that have examined the food products deriving from these technologies have excluded that these may pose a risk to public health, mounting consumer hostility suggests that they may soon be subject to restrictive regulatory measures. Their adoption as well as their survival depends largely on how the issue of public perception will be tackled under the WTO.

The next section will focus on this challenge by exploring how the WTO could better accommodate public perception on food risks within the SPS framework.

VI.   WHAT ROLE FOR PUBLIC PERCEPTIONS?

Our previous analysis has shown that while science may be used – conforming to the choice of the SPS drafters – to unveil hidden features of a regulatory measure, be it protectionist intent or economic inefficiency, it can correspondingly prove to be insensitive to public perceptions or social realities. Thus, the SPS science-based regime may condemn a restrictive measure, such the current EU ban on BPA-containing baby bottles, which lacks scientific rationality and responds to public perception, even in the absence of protectionist intent. In so doing, the SPS Agreement's scientific regime proves over-inclusive.

In our view, this outcome is mainly due to the scientific paradigm enshrined in the SPS Agreement that tends to mechanically equate perception-driven regulations with protectionist measures. This is problematic because, as illustrated by the *EC – Hormones* and *EC – Biotech* disputes, there exist regulatory measures that, albeit scientifically unsubstantiated, are not necessarily protectionist (or economically inefficient) and merely reflect public perception of a given risk.

Therefore – in our view – the normative challenge facing the WTO/SPS framework is not to identify an alternative, this being unattainable, to the scientific criterion for filtering out protectionism from genuine health regulations. Rather it is to turn that criterion into a more sensitive tool capable of assuring the survival of genuine perception-motivated regulations notwithstanding their failure to satisfy the requirement of a risk assessment. While facing this challenge the SPS Agreement should not dismiss public perception as irrelevant – as often seems the case – but to define the conditions according to which Members may legitimately take them into account in regulatory decision-making.

In our view, should the SPS Agreement, notably its scientific discipline, be more accommodating of Members' responsiveness to public perceptions, it would be less over inclusive, thus more respectful of Members' ability to regulate risks. In other words, a more sensitive approach towards public perceptions might be able to mitigate the problem of over inclusiveness of science.

Yet as soon as one attempts to turn into practice the above recommendation 'the objections are so numerous and so intense that it may be misconceived to even contemplate traveling down this road'.[102] According to conventional wisdom, broadening the scientific regime to other considerations, such as risk perception, 'may produce even more arbitrariness in the dispute settlement process and probably reduce the predictability of the outcome of potential disputes'.[103]

Although it is evident that the recognition of a generalised right to justify the departure from risk assessment may corrupt the rationale underpinning the science-based regime, our previous analysis reveals that the SPS Agreement cannot longer afford the negative consequences stemming from the over-inclusiveness of its own regime. The risk of jeopardising the predictability of the outcome of potential disputes does not change, but rather strengthens, this conclusion. This is especially true if one considers that such predictability is unidirectional in its outcomes today, as it entails the systematic incompatibility of all perception-driven regulations failing to satisfy a risk assessment regardless of their effects.

The time has come to transcend the intellectual stalemate between those who favour the science-based requirement and those who denounce it as an expression of epistemic imperialism. Therefore, the question is no longer whether to accommodate public perception but how to do that, by identifying in a universal fashion the conditions under which Members may legitimately respond to public perceptions. Laying down these conditions requires reconciling the scientific evidence requirement with the possibility to respond to other non-scientific factors, such as risk perception.

To render the exercise objective and to avoid Members invoking nonexist-

---

[102]   Scott (2007), 26.
[103]   Gruszczynski (2010), 155.

ent fears, the first condition should aim at ensuring that the 'other' information be robust and substantiated as much as possible. The question is therefore how to test the validity claims of this other, competing, information. This, as illustrated by a significant amount of evidence, is not an easy task as 'public opinion is harder to ascertain that it is to manipulate'.[104] Yet – despite this Habermasian note of scepticism,[105] there exist modes to identify, collect and measure public opinion and perceived risks. Public opinion analysis is indeed a well-developed science and as such it might provide surveys confirming the public nature of a given perceived risk.[106] However, given the volatile and fragmented nature of risk perception, a second condition should impose a temporary character on the adopted risk perception-driven measures.

Moreover, an additional condition should be imposed to enable a public perception defence. Whenever a WTO Member deliberately decides to rely on public perception when adopting a restrictive measure, it should be expected to adopt a proactive role vis-à-vis the public. Thus, a third condition might impose a duty to communicate the costs and benefits of the chosen regulatory approach in order to promote an informed debate among the fearful or hostile public.[107] The above conditions may contribute to guard against any abusive claim related to an alleged public perceived risk by filtering legitimate, substantiated public perception, from illegitimate, unrepresentative perceptions.[108]

Although modest and largely speculative, this proposal for a better accommodation of public perceptions under the SPS Agreement nurtures the ambition to initiate a new normative discourse around the issue of public perception of risk. As the issue of how governments should respond to public (mis)perceptions is gaining salience across the word,[109] it is time that the WTO, and in particular its judicial bodies, begin to ponder on this central theme for the politics of global risk regulation.

The significant number of controversial food safety measures looming on the horizon calls for a greater recognition of the challenges raised by public perceptions in the regulation of food safety. Food from cloned animals, nanotechnology applications and other technological advances are likely to trigger disputes which might exhibit once more the inherent limits of the SPS Agreement in tackling unscientific, yet genuine, restrictive measures addressing risk perceptions of food safety risks.

---

[104] Scott (2007), 26.
[105] Habermas (1989).
[106] For a recent contribution to this field, see Saris and Sniderman (2011).
[107] On a similar line of thought, Scott (2007), 28.
[108] Alemanno (2012).
[109] Majone (2012), 295–307.

BIBLIOGRAPHY

Ackerman, F. and L. Heinzerling (2004), *Priceless: On Knowing the Price of Everything and the Value of Nothing*, New York: The New Press.

Alemanno, A. (2007), *Trade in Food – Regulatory and Judicial Approaches in the EC and the WTO*, London: Cameron May.

Alemanno, A. (2010), 'The Fabulous Destiny of Bisphenol A', *European Journal of Risk Regulation*, **1** (4), 397–400.

Alemanno, A. (2012), 'Is there a Role for Cost-benefit Analysis beyond the Nation State? Lessons from International Regulatory Co-operation', in Revesz, R. and M. Livermore (eds), *Global CBA*, Oxford: Oxford University Press.

Anderson, E. (1993), *Value in Ethics and Economics*, Cambridge, MA: Harvard University Press.

Appellate Body Report, *EC – Asbestos*, WT/DS135/AB/R.

Appellate Body Report, *Japan – Agricultural Products*, WT/DS76/AB/R.

Appellate Body Report, *Japan – Apples*, WT/DS76/AB/R.

Appellate Body Report, *Measures concerning meat and meat products*, WT/DS26/AB/R, WT/DS48/AB/R adopted on 13 February 1998 (Appellate Body Report, *EC – Hormones*).

Appellate Body Report, *US – Continued Suspension*, WT/DS230/AB.

Baumberg, B. and P. Anderson (2008), 'Trade and Health: How World Trade Organization (WTO) Law Affects Alcohol and Public Health', *Addiction*, **103**, 1952–1958.

Breyer, S. (1993), *Breaking the Vicious Circle*, Cambridge, MA: Harvard University Press.

Buzby, J.C. (2001), 'Effects of Food Safety Perceptions on Food Demand and Global Trade, Changing Structure of Global Food Consumption and Trade', WRS-01-1, Economic Research Service, USDA.

Calafat, A., Z. Kuklenyik, J. Reidy, S. Caudill, J. Eklong and L. Needham (2005), 'Urinary Concentration of Bisphenol A and 4 nonylphenol in a Human Reference Population', *Environmental Health Perspectives*, **113** (4), 391–395.

Chang, H. (2004), 'Risk Regulation, Endogenous Public Concerns, and the Hormones Dispute: Nothing to Fear but Fear Itself', *Southern California Law Review*, **77**, 8–38.

Charnovitz, S. (2000), 'The Supervision of Health and Biosafety Regulation by World Trade Rules', *Tulane Environmental Law Journal*, **13** (2), 271–302.

Coglianese, C., A. Finkel and D. Zaring (eds) (2009), *Import Safety: Regulatory Governance in the Global Economy*, Philadelphia, PA: University of Pennsylvania Press.

Council Directive 81/602/EEC concerning the prohibition of certain substances having a hormonal action and of any substances having a thyrostatic action (OJ L222 32–33).

Council Directive 88/146/EEC prohibiting the use in livestock farming of certain substances having a hormonal action (OJ L70 16–18).

Council Directive 88/299/EEC on trade in animals treated with certain substances having a hormonal action and their meat, as referred to in Article 7 of Directive 88/146/EEC (JO L128 36–38).

Crawford-Brown, D., J. Pauwelyn and K. Smith (2004), 'Environmenal Risks, Precaution and Scientific Rationality in the context of WTO/NAFTA Trade Rules', *Risk Analysis*, **24** (2), 461–465.

Directive 2011/8/EU amending Directive 2002/72/EC as regards the restriction of use of Bisphenol A in plastic infant feeding bottles OJ L26/11.

Douglas, M. (1985), *Risk Acceptability According to the Social Sciences*, New York: Russell Sage Foundation.

Douglas, M. and A. Wildavsky (1983), *Risk and Culture*, Berkeley, CA: University of California Press.

EFSA (2010), 'Scientific Opinion on Bisphenol A: evaluation of a study investigating its neurodevelopmental toxicity, review of recent scientific literature on its toxicity and advice on the Danish risk assessment of Bisphenol A', *EFSA Journal*, **8** (9), 1829.

Environmental Working Group (2007), 'Bisphenol A: Toxic Plastics Chemical in Canned Food', available at http://www.ewg.org/node/20928/print (accessed 20 March 2012).

Eskridge, W.N. and J. Ferejohn (2002), 'Structuring Lawmaking to Reduce Cognitive Bias: A Critical View', *Cornell Law Review*, **87**, 616–642.

European Court of Justice, Case 160/88, *Fedesa v. Council* [1988] ECR 6399.

European Court of Justice, Case C-157/96, *The Queen v. Ministry of Agriculture, Fisheries and Food, ex parte National Farmers' Union et al.* [1998] ECR I-2211.

European Court of Justice, Case C-180/96, *United Kingdom v. Commission*, [1998] ECR 3903.

Feldman, R. (2009), *The Role of Science in Law*, Oxford: Oxford University Press.

Fischhoff, B. (1985), 'Managing Risk Perceptions', *Issues Science & Technology*, **2**, 83–96.

Foster, C. (2008), 'Public Opinion and the Interpretation of the World Trade Organization's Agreement on Sanitary and Phytosanitary Measures', *Journal of International Economic Law*, **11** (2), 427–458.

Fraiberg, J.D. and M.J. Trebilcock (1998), 'Risk Regulation: Technocratic and Democratic Tools for Regulatory Reform', *McGill Law Journal*, **43**, 836–888.

Gruszczynski, L. (2010), *Regulating Health and Environmental Risks under WTO Law, A Critical Analysis of the SPS Agreement*, Oxford: Oxford University Press.

Guzman, Andrew T., 'WTO Dispute Resolution in Health and Safety Cases', UC Berkeley Public Law Research Paper No. 989371, 231.

Habermas, J. (1989), *The Structural Transformation of the Public Sphere*, Cambridge: Polity.

Heinzerling, L. (1995), 'Justice Breyer's Hard Look', *The Administrative Law Journal*, **8**, 767 et seq.

Henson, S. (1995), 'Demand-side Constraints on the Introduction of New Food Technologies: The Case of Food Irradiation', *Food Policy*, **20** (2), 111–127.

Hilson, C. (2005), 'Beyond Rationality? Judicial Review and Public Concern in the EU and the WTO', *Northern Ireland Legal Quarterly*, **56** (3), 320–341.

Howse, R. (2000), 'Democracy, Science and Free Trade: Risk Regulation on Trial at the World Trade Organisation', *Michigan Law Review*, **98**, 2329–2353.

Jaeger, C., O. Renn, E. Rosa and Th. Webler (2011), *Risk and Rational Action*, London: Earthscan.

Ju, J. (2010), 'Imaginary Risk, Public Health Regulation, and WTO Trade Dispute: A Rational Choice Perspective', *Asian Journal of Law and Economics*, **1** (1).

Kahan, D. (2008), 'Two Conceptions of Emotions in Risk Regulation, *U Pa Law Review*, **156**, 741 et seq.

Kahneman, D., P. Slovic and A. Tversky (eds) (1982), *Judgment under Uncertainty: Heuristics and Biases*, Cambridge: Cambridge University Press.

Lamy, P. (2004), 'The Emergence of Collective Preferences in International Trade: Implications for Regulating Globalisation', available at http://trade.ec.europa.eu/doclib/docs/2004/september/tradoc_118925.pdf (accessed 20 March 2012).

Lang, I., T. Galloway, A. Scarlett, W. Henley, M. Depledge, R. Wallace and D. Melzer (2008), 'Association of Urinary Bisphenol A Concentration with Medical Disorders and Laboratories Abnormalities in Adults', *Journal of the American Medical Association*, **30** (11), 1303–1310.

Lee, M. (2005), *EU Environmental Law, Challenges, Change and Decision Making*, Oxford: Hart Publishing.

Liberman, J. and A. Mitchell (2010), 'In Search of Coherence between Trade and Health: Interinstituional Opportunities', *Maryland Journal of International Law*, **25**, 143–186.

Lowenfeld, A.F. (2006), *International Economics Law*, Oxford: Oxford University Press.

Magnusson, R. (2007), 'Non-communicable Diseases and Global Health Governance', *Globalization and Health*, **3** (2), 1–16.

Majone, G. (2012), 'Strategic issues in risk regulation', in Levi-Faur, D. (ed.), *Handbook on the Politics of Regulation*, Cheltenham: Edward Elgar Publishing.

Marceau, G. and J. Trachtman (2002), 'The Technical Barriers to Trade Agreement, the Sanitary and Phytosanitary Measures Agreement, and the General Agreement on Tariff and Trade, A Map of the World Trade Organization Law of Domestic Regulation of Goods', *Journal of World Trade*, **35** (5), 811–881.

Margolis, H. (1996), *Dealing with Risk: Why the Public and the Experts Disagree on Environmental Issues*, Chicago, IL: University of Chicago Press.

McGrady, B. (2007), 'Trade Liberalisation and Tobacco Control: Moving from a Policy of Exclusion Towards a More Comprehensive Policy', *Tobacco Control*, **16**, 280–283.

Melnick R., G. Lucier, M. Wolfe, R. Hall, G. Stancel, G. Prins, M. Gall, K. Reuhl, SM. Ho, T. Brown, J. Moore, J. Leakey, J. Haseman and M. Kohn, 'Summary of the National Toxicology Program's report of the endocrine disruptors' (2002), available at http://www.ncbi.nlm.nih.gov/pmc/articles/PMC1240807/ (accessed 20 March 2012).

National Toxicology Program (2007), U.S. Department of Health & Human Services, NTP-CERHR Expert Panel Report for Bisphenol A (Nov. 26, 2007).

Prévost, D. (2009), *Balancing Trade and Health in the SPS Agreement – The Development Dimension*, Nijmegen: Wolf Legal Publishers.

Rowe, G. and G. Wright (2001), 'Differences in Expert and Lay Judgments of Risks: Myth or Reality', *Risk Analysis*, **21** (2), 341–356.

Saris, W.E. and P.M. Sniderman (2011), *Studies in Public Opinion: Attitudes, Nonattitudes, Measurement Error, and Change*, Princeton, NJ: Princeton University Press.

Scott, D.N. (2008), 'Confronting Chronic Pollution: A Socio-Legal Analysis of Risk and Precaution', *Osgoode Hall Law Journal*, **46**, 294–319.

Scott, J. (2000), 'On Kith and Kine (and crustaceans): Trade and Environment in the EU and WTO', in Weiler, J.H.H. (ed.), *The EU, WTO and the NAFTA – Towards a Common Law of International Trade*, Oxford: Oxford University Press.

Scott, J. (2004), 'European Regulation of GMOs: Thinking about "Judicial Review" in the WTO', Jean Monnet Working Paper, 04/04, available at http://centers.law.nyu.edu/jean-monnet/archive/papers/04/040401.pdf (accessed 22 March 2012).

Scott, J. (2007), *The WTO Agreement on Sanitary and Phytosanitary Measures*, Oxford: Oxford University Press.

Slovic, P. (2000), *The Perception of Risk*, Sterling, VA: Earthscan.

Slovic, P., B. Fischhoff and S. Lichtenstein (1985), 'Regulation of Risk: A Psychological Perspective', in Nolle, R. (ed.), *Regulatory Policy and the Social Sciences*, Berkeley, CA: University of California.

Sunstein, C. (2001), 'Probability Neglect: Emotions, Worst Cases, and Law', *Yale Law Journal*, **112**, 61–107.

Sunstein, C. (2005), *Laws of Fear: Beyond the Precautionary Principle*, Cambridge: Cambridge University Press.

Sunstein, C. and R. Zeckhauser (2010), 'Dreadful Possibilities, Neglected Probabilities', in Michel-Kerjan, E. and P. Slovic (eds), *The Irrational Economist*, New York: Public Affairs Press.

Sykes, A.O. (1995), *Product Standards for Internationally Integrated Goods Markets*, Washington, DC: Brookings.

Sykes, A.O. (2006), 'Domestic Regulation, Sovereignty and Scientific Evidence Requirements: A Pessimistic View', in Berman, G. and P.C. Mavroidis (eds), *Trade and Human Health and Safety*, Cambridge: Cambridge University Press.

Trebilcock M. and R. Howse (1999), *The Regulations of International Trade*, London: Routledge.

Vandenberg, L.N., R. Hauser, M. Marcus, N. Olea and W.V. Welshons (2007), 'Human Exposure to bisphenol A (BPA)', *Reprod. Toxicol.*, **24** (2), 139–177.

Walker, V.R. (1998), 'Keeping the WTO from Becoming the "Word Trans-Science Organization": Scientific Uncertainty, Science Policy, and Factfinding in the Growth Hormones Dispute', *Cornell International Law Journal*, **31**, 251 et seq.

Weber, E. and J. Ancker (2010), 'Risk Perceptions and Risk Attitudes in the US and Europe', in Wiener, J.B., M.D. Rogers, J.K. Hammitt and P.H. Sand, *Comparing Risk Regulation in the United States and Europe*, London: Earthscan.

Weinberg, A. (1972), 'Science and Trans-Science, *Minerva*, **10**, 209–222.

Wildavsky, A. (1979), 'No Risk is the Highest Risk of All', *American Scientist*, **67** (1), 32–37.
Wilson, M.J. (2011), 'Cultural Understandings of Risk and the Tyranny of the Experts', *Oregon Law Review*, **90**, 113–189.
Winickoff, D.E., S. Jasanoff, L. Bush, R. Grove-White and B. Wynne (2005), 'Adjudicating the GM Food Wars: Science, Risk, and Democracy in World Trade Law', *Yale Journal of International Law*, **30**, 81–123.
Wirth, D. (1994), 'Symposium: The Role of Science in the Uruguay Round and NAFTA Trade Disciplines', *Cornell Int' L.J.*, **27**, 817–833.

10. Pre-market approval systems and the SPS Agreement

Tracey Epps

I. INTRODUCTION

Food safety is a key policy concern for many governments and their citizens and its importance is only heightened by the ever increasing flow of goods across international borders. As countries seek to ensure the safety of their food supply, trade friction may arise where measures are taken to restrict or otherwise control imports of food stuffs. The imposition of trade restrictions to ensure the safety of food and protect public health has long been recognised by international trade rules as a necessary, although qualified, limitation on trade. The General Agreement on Tariffs and Trade (GATT) in Article XX(b) allows Members to enact measures that violate the substantive obligations of the Agreement if they are "necessary to protect human, animal and plant life and health", so long as they are not "applied in a manner which would constitute arbitrary or unjustifiable discrimination between countries where the same conditions prevail, or a disguised restriction on international trade". This provision was negotiated in the 1940s and by the late 1980s, countries recognised that despite the qualifier as to how measures must be applied, there was still room for countries to enact protectionist measures in the name of health. Not only was it perceived that there was room to manouevre around the rules, but many considered that countries were particularly likely to do so in the area of food stuffs where they often face significant domestic political pressure to protect their agricultural sectors. These factors were significant ones in the decision to negotiate the Agreement on the Application of Sanitary and Phytosanitary Measures (SPS Agreement) in the Uruguay Round (1987–1994).

The SPS Agreement goes beyond Article XX(b) of the GATT by establishing a comprehensive set of obligations for Members when they adopt and maintain SPS measures.[1] The SPS Agreement recognises that

---

[1] Denise Prévost and Peter Van den Bossche, "The Agreement on the Application of Sanitary and Phytosanitary Measures", in Patrick F.J. Macrory, Arthur E. Appleton, and Michael G. Plummer, eds, *The World Trade Organization: Legal, Economic and Political Analysis Volume 1* (Springer) 231.

discrimination in trade may be necessary where goods from a particular country pose a greater risk than those from other sources. In its Preamble, the Agreement provides that "no Member should be prevented from adopting or enforcing measures necessary to protect human, animal or plant life or health". The flip side to this, however, is that Members are required to follow the rules set out in the Agreement when they enact SPS measures. In essence, where a Member chooses not to base its measures on an international standard (or where a relevant international standard does not exist), then they must ensure that there is scientific justification for those measures.

This chapter explores the application of the rules in the SPS Agreement to "pre-market approval" measures (also sometimes referred to as "prior market approval"). In basic terms, a pre-market approval system is one that requires the safety of specified products to be assessed before the products are permitted to be marketed and sold to consumers. Such systems are commonly used to ensure the safety of pharmaceuticals and medical devices, and are also seen in the food context, particularly in areas where there are new and emerging risks. The objective of this chapter is to explore whether and how the obligations in the SPS Agreement apply to pre-market approval systems. There have been some doubts raised since the *EC – Biotech* case as to how the obligations apply and this chapter aims to bring greater clarity to this particular application of the SPS Agreement.

Section II describes the key obligations in the SPS Agreement that may be applicable to the use of pre-market approval systems. Section III analyses the only WTO dispute to have considered the application of the SPS Agreement to pre-market approval systems, namely, the *EC – Biotech* dispute. In this case, a WTO disputes panel was called upon to consider the obligations of the European Union (EU) – at the time of the report, still called the European Communities (EC) – in respect of their pre-market approval system for biotechnology products. Section IV considers the application of the SPS Agreement's obligations to pre-market approval systems in the light of the *EC – Biotech* dispute using examples taken from American and Canadian pre-market approval systems. The final section concludes.

II. KEY OBLIGATIONS IN THE SPS AGREEMENT

A. Definition of 'SPS Measure'

The SPS Agreement ties countries to a science-based regime for the regulation of risks to human, animal, and plant life and health. Countries may enact measures to protect against risks, but they are constrained by the rules of the Agreement in how they do so. It is therefore important to be clear as to exactly what kinds of measures are subject to the science-based regime. The SPS Agreement defines a "sanitary or phytosanitary measure" by reference to the type of risks to human, animal, and plant life or health that they seek to address.[2] These risks are set out in subparagraphs (a) to (d) of Annex A(1). In relation to human health, the relevant risks are defined in subparagraph (b) as those arising from additives, contaminants, toxins, or disease causing organisms in foods and beverages; and in subparagraph (c) as those arising from diseases carried by animals, plants or their products. The rules in the SPS Agreement apply to any measure applied by Members to protect against these types of risks (whether these measures take the form of laws, decrees, regulations, requirements, procedures, or otherwise).[3] Annex A(b) also specifies that SPS measures include "inspection, certification and approval procedures".

As will be discussed in detail in section IV, pre-market approval systems (or aspects thereof) fit within the definition of SPS measures to the extent that they constitute measures applied to protect against a risk that falls within the categories set out in subparagraphs (a) to (d). The types of pre-market approval systems discussed in this chapter are focused on human health as provided for in subparagraphs (b) and (c) through ensuring the safety of food, however, similar systems might focus on animal or plant life or health.

B.   Harmonisation

One of the objectives of the SPS Agreement is to further the use of harmonised SPS measures between Members. The idea behind harmonisation is that if all countries have the same health and safety measures, then there will be little room for disruption to trade because a producer who meets standards in their home country will also be able to meet the standards in the destination country. The SPS Agreement encourages Members to harmonise their SPS measures.[4] It does this by saying that Members shall "base" their SPS measures on international standards, guidelines and recommendations, except as otherwise provided for in the Agreement. Relevant international standards, guidelines and recommendations are those developed by the Codex Alimentarius Commission ("Codex"), the

---

[2]   Pursuant to Annex A(1).
[3]   Annex A(1) of the SPS Agreement.
[4]   Article 3.1.

International Office of Epizootics ("OIE"), and international and regional organisations operating within the framework of the International Plant Protection Convention ("IPPC"). However, if a country wanting to enact SPS measures to protect health thinks that these international standards are not rigorous enough to meet their appropriate level of protection (or if there is no international standard) then they may introduce or maintain their own SPS measures that do meet such a level of protection. This right comes with associated obligations however. Most importantly, the country must have a scientific justification for their measures. Articles 2 and 5 of the SPS Agreement set out the key requirements for Members to ensure that their measures are based on science.

C. Scientific Evidence Requirements

Article 2.1 affirms that Members have the right to enact SPS measures necessary for the protection of human, animal, and plant life or health, provided that such measures are consistent with the provisions of the Agreement. Article 2.2 elaborates on what constitutes "consistency" with the Agreement by requiring Members to ensure "that any sanitary or phytosanitary measure is applied only to the extent necessary to protect human, animal or plant life or health, is based on scientific principles and is not maintained without scientific evidence, except as provided for in paragraph 7 of Article 5".

The scientific evidence requirement in Article 2.2 is given effect to in Article 5.1 which states that Members must ensure that their SPS measures are "based on an assessment, as appropriate to the circumstances, of the risks to human, animal or plant life or health, taking into account risk assessment techniques developed by the relevant international organizations".[5] Article 5.2 lists a number of factors that Members *must* take into account in their risk assessments, namely, available scientific evidence; relevant processes and production methods; relevant inspection, sampling and testing methods; prevalence of specific diseases or pests; existence of pest- or disease-free areas; relevant ecological and environmental conditions; and quarantine or other treatment. It is here that the Agreement gives further meaning to Article 2.2 by actually requiring Members to consider, among other factors, available scientific evidence as part of their risk assessment.

Article 5.7 is particularly relevant in the context of new technologies such as genetic engineering, nanotechnology, or synthetic biology. This

---

[5] Codex, the OIE, and the IPPC.

is because it provides for the situation where, due to a lack of scientific evidence, a risk assessment cannot be performed at all. The Article states that in cases where "relevant scientific evidence is insufficient, a Member may provisionally adopt sanitary or phytosanitary measures on the basis of available pertinent information". It goes on to provide that "in such circumstances, Members shall seek to obtain the additional information necessary for a more objective assessment of risk and review the sanitary or phytosanitary measure accordingly within a reasonable period of time". Thus, Article 5.7 provides a safe haven for countries that are concerned about the possible health risks of a certain substance or technology but that do not have sufficient evidence to conduct a risk assessment as required by Article 2.1. It must be noted, however, that scientific uncertainty does not constitute insufficient evidence. So long as sufficient evidence is available to conduct a risk assessment then that is the course that must be followed, regardless of the uncertainties in that evidence.

D.   Risk Management

While the SPS Agreement imposes a set of requirements for how countries are to go about regulating certain types of risks, the Agreement nevertheless aims to respect their regulatory sovereignty regarding one very important aspect of domestic policy, namely, risk tolerance. The Agreement recognises the right of Members to set their appropriate level of protection and to apply measures necessary to achieve that level of protection, so long as scientific evidence has established the presence of a risk. Again, in order to make sure that countries do not abuse this policy space so as to enact trade protectionist measures that protect their own industries, the Agreement does place some parameters around the way in which Members go about enacting and implementing SPS measures. Article 2.3 deals with the situation where countries impose SPS measures on imported goods from one country, but are more lenient on domestic goods or those from another trading partner. Thus, Article 2.3 provides that: "Members shall ensure that their sanitary and phytosanitary measures do not arbitrarily or unjustifiably discriminate between Members where identical or similar conditions prevail, including between their own territory and that of other Members. Sanitary and phytosanitary measures shall not be applied in a manner which would constitute a disguised restriction on international trade."

A related provision, Article 5.5, requires Members to avoid arbitrary or unjustifiable distinctions in the levels they consider to be appropriate in different situations, if such distinctions result in discrimination or a disguised restriction on international trade. Article 5.5 is a recognition that regulatory inconsistencies at the national level could indicate unnecessarily maintained SPS measures, which may constitute disguised trade protection.[6]

Article 5.4 requires Members, when determining the appropriate level of protection, to "take into account the objective of minimizing negative trade effects". In *EC – Hormones*, the Panel stated that this provision does not impose an obligation on Members, rather, it is more of a "best efforts" requirement.[7] Finally, Article 5.6 disciplines Members' risk management decisions by requiring them to ensure that SPS measures are "not more trade-restrictive than required to achieve their appropriate level of sanitary or phytosanitary protection, taking into account technical and economic feasibility". A footnote to this provision says that a measure is more trade restrictive than required if there is another SPS measure which: i) is reasonably available taking into account technical and economic feasibility; ii) achieves the Member's appropriate level of protection; and iii) is significantly less trade restrictive than the SPS measure contested. These elements are cumulative, meaning that a complainant must show that each of them has been met in order for a violation of the Article to be found.[8]

E. Procedures

The SPS Agreement also imposes disciplines on the manner in which countries conduct their control, inspection, and approval procedures. This part of the Agreement requires Members to ensure that their procedures are conducted in a manner that does not restrict trade. This is of great practical importance and supplements the disciplines discussed above. If it were not for these disciplines, a country could undermine market access and the science-based measures by, for example, delaying quarantine inspection of imports. The key disciplines are noted below.

Article 8 requires Members to comply with the obligations set out in Annex C with respect to control, inspection and approval procedures. A footnote to Annex C states that such procedures include, *inter alia*,

---

[6]   Reinhard Quick and Andreas Bluthner, "Has the Appellate Body Erred? An Appraisal and Criticism of the Ruling in the WTO Hormones Case" (1999) 2 J. Int'l Econ. Law 603 at 620.

[7]   *EC – Measures Concerning Meat and Meat Products (Hormones)* Complaint by the United States (1997), WTO Doc. WT/DS322/R, para. 8.166.

[8]   *Australia – Measures Affecting Importation of Salmon* (1998), WTO Doc. WT/DS18/AB/R (Appellate Body Report) at para. 194.

procedures for sampling, testing, and certification.[9] Article 8 emphasises the relevance of the provisions in Annex C for "national systems for approving the use of additives" and "for establishing tolerances for contaminants in foods, beverages or feedstuffs". However, it is not limited to these procedures, and may also encompass other procedures, including pre-market approval systems such as those for approval of novel foods as described in section III. Article 8 applies to measures that countries implement to ensure fulfilment of SPS measures, but not to the substantive measures themselves.[10]

Annex C.1(a) requires Members to undertake and complete procedures to check and ensure the fulfilment of SPS measures without undue delay, and in a no less favourable manner for imported products than for like domestic products.

Annex C.1(b) requires that the standard processing period of each procedure be published, or the anticipated processing period be communicated to the applicant upon request. It also sets out various procedural requirements, including that a competent body receiving an application must promptly examine the completeness of the documentation and inform the applicant of deficiencies; transmit the results of the procedure as soon as possible to the applicant; and proceed as far as practicable with the procedure even where it has deficiencies.

Paragraphs (d), (f), and (g) of Annex C.1 contain non-discrimination provisions with respect to confidentiality of information (treatment of domestic and foreign products has to be "no less favourable"), fees imposed for procedures (these must be equitable as between imported and domestic products), and criteria in the siting of facilities used in the procedures and the selection of samples (the same criteria should be used in procedures for domestic samples as for imported samples).

Paragraphs (c), (e) and (h) of Annex C.1 set out necessity tests. Paragraph (c) says that information requirements are limited to what is necessary for appropriate control, inspection and approval procedures; paragraph (e) says that any requirements for control, inspection and approval of individual specimens of a product are limited to what is reasonable and necessary; while paragraph (h) says that whenever specifications of a product are changed subsequent to its control and inspection in light of the applicable regulations, the procedure for the modified product

---

[9]   Footnote 7 to Annex C. Non-conformity with Article 8 was challenged in *Australia – Salmon*, *EC – Biotech*, *Japan – Agricultural Products*, and *Australia – Apples*.

[10]   *Australia – Salmon (Article 21.5)*, WTO/DS/18/R (Panel Report), paras 7154–7.157.

is limited to what is necessary to determine whether adequate confidence exists that the product still meets the regulations concerned.

Paragraph (i) of Annex C.1 requires each Member to establish a mechanism for reviewing complaints concerning the operation of the procedures that allows them to take corrective action. This mechanism should facilitate the settlement of disagreements at an early stage and may be regarded as a preliminary and specific consultation procedure before reference to consultations under the Dispute Settlement Understanding are made.

Annex C.1 provides that where an importing Member operates a system for the approval of the use of food additives or for the establishment of tolerances for contaminants in food, beverages or feedstuffs which prohibits or restricts access to its domestic markets for products based on the absence of an approval, the importing Member shall consider the use of a relevant international standard as the basis for access until a final determination is made.

Annex C.2 recognises that in some situations, legitimate implementation of an SPS measure may be more easily achieved through measures that require the exporting country to exercise control at the level of production. In such circumstances, the exporting Member is to assist in facilitating such control.

Finally, Annex C.3 states that nothing in the Agreement prevents Members from carrying out reasonable inspection within their own territories.

III.   PRE-MARKET APPROVAL SYSTEMS AND THE SPS AGREEMENT: THE *EC – BIOTECH* DISPUTE

As noted in the Introduction, a pre-market approval system is one that requires the safety of specified products to be assessed before the products are permitted to be marketed and sold to consumers. Such systems are distinguishable from regular SPS approval procedures applied or implemented at the border. Countries regularly inspect imports either prior to shipping or upon arrival at the border to ensure that products do not harbour unwanted pests or diseases. They will also often maintain procedures that only allow certain products to be imported if an assessment has already been made of the risk associated with them. For example, in New Zealand, all fresh fruit and vegetables are prohibited entry unless they are covered by a valid Import Health Standard. An Import Health Standard sets out phytosanitary requirements for all fresh fruit and vegetables that are permitted to be imported into New Zealand. All imports must be accompanied by a completed phytosanitary certificate which contains required information. The focus of the Import Health Standard and the certificate is to ensure that foods are free of listed pests and diseases.[11] This focus on pests and diseases that may pose a risk to New Zealand's biosecurity, and on the act of importation itself, is different in nature from the focus of the type of pre-market approval systems discussed in this chapter. The latter's primary focus is on the health and safety of consumers and therefore approval is being sought to actually place products on the market rather than simply to import. The concern is not a biosecurity one, but rather that the foods or products themselves may inherently be unsafe and present a risk to consumers.

The application of the SPS Agreement to pre-market approval systems has to date only been addressed on one occasion in the WTO dispute settlement system, namely, in the *EC – Biotech* case.[12] This case involved a pre-market approval requirement established in the EU through three separate Directives. Directives 90/220 and 2001/18 both concerned the deliberate release into the environment of genetically modified organisms (GMOs), while Directive 258/97 concerned the placing on the market of products to be used as a novel food or a novel food ingredient.

A.   Directives 90/220 and 2001/18 – Deliberate Release of GMOs into the Environment

Directive 2001/18 is the successor to Directive 90/220, however, the case involved applications covered by both Directives. Both Directives have the objective of avoiding adverse effects on human health and the environment that might arise from the deliberate release into the environment of products consisting of, or containing, GMOs. To this end, the Directives set out administrative procedures for granting consent for the placing on the market of GMOs as or in products.

The first step requires the manufacturer or importer of the product to submit a notification and accompanying dossier to the lead Competent Authority ("lead CA") in the country where they wish to sell the products. These documents must contain certain information including the nature of the GMO, the intended uses of the product, proposals for labelling or for restrictions on use, and an assessment of any risks for human health and the environment related to the GMO.[13]

---

[11]   See Biosecurity New Zealand online at: www.biosecurity.co.nz/files/ihs/152-02.pdf (date accessed: 11 April 2011).

[12]   *EC – Approval and Marketing of Biotech Products* WTO Doc. WT/DS21/292/293 (Panel Report) [referred to hereinafter as *EC – Biotech*].

[13]   Directive 2001/18, Article 6(1) and (2).

Second, the lead CA examines the application for compliance with the Directive and is required to prepare an assessment report within 90 days after receipt of the application.[14] If the assessment report concludes that a GMO should not be placed on the market, the lead CA rejects the application. The application procedure then comes to an end.[15] If, however, the lead CA's assessment report concludes that a GMO may be placed on the market, the procedure moves to the Community level. The lead CA must submit the application together with the assessment report to the European Commission (the "Commission") which in turn forwards it to the competent authorities of all other EU member States. Within 60 days from circulation of the assessment report, a CA of another member State and, in the case of Directive 2001/18, the Commission, may ask for further information, make comments or present reasoned objections to the GMO in question being placed on the market.[16] If there is no reasoned objection from the CA of a member State (or the Commission in the case of Directive 2001/18), the lead CA must give its consent in writing for the product to be placed on the market. Under Directive 2001/18, if the CA of another member State or the Commission raises a reasoned objection, the member States and the Commission may take an additional 45-day period to discuss any outstanding issues with the aim of arriving at an agreement. If outstanding issues are resolved within the prescribed period, the lead CA must give its consent for the product to be placed on the market.[17]

In the absence of such a resolution and where the CA of another member State or the Commission maintains a reasoned objection, the decision on whether to approve the application must be taken at the Community level. This requires the Commission to consult the relevant EU scientific committee regarding the objection. The Commission must prepare a draft measure taking into account the committee's opinion and submit it to the appropriate "Regulatory Committee" (composed of representatives of the member States) for a vote.[18] The Commission must adopt the draft measures if they are in accordance with the opinion of the Regulatory Committee. If they are not (or if no opinion is delivered), the Commission must, without delay, submit to the Council of Ministers

---

[14]   Article 12(1) and (2) of Directive 90/220 and Article 14(1) and (2) of Directive 2001/18.
[15]   Article 12(2)(b) of Directive 90/220 and Articles 14(3)(b) and 15(2) of Directive 2001/18.
[16]   Article 13(2) and (3) of Directive 90/220 and Article 15(1) of Directive 2001/18.
[17]   Articles 15(1) and (3) of Directive 2001/18.
[18]   Article 13(3) of Directive 90/220 and Article 28 of Directive 2001/18.

a proposal relating to the measures to be taken. The Council can either adopt or reject the Commission's draft measure.[19] Where a favourable decision has been taken at the Community level, the lead CA must give consent in writing to the GMO being placed on the market.[20]

B.   Regulation 258/97 – Novel Foods or Novel Food Ingredients

Regulation 258/97 concerned placement on the market of products to be used as a novel food or a novel food ingredient. Such products include foods and food ingredients containing or consisting of GMOs within the meaning of Directives 20/220 and 2001/18. The purpose of Regulation 258/97 is to ensure that the covered novel foods and food ingredients do not present a danger for consumers, do not mislead consumers, and do not differ from foods or food ingredients which they are intended to replace to such an extent that their normal consumption would be nutritionally disadvantageous to consumers.[21]

Where an application involves a product containing or consisting of a GMO, and the product is intended for use as food as well as for feed and for cultivation, the application is assessed under Regulation 258/97 in relation to its use as food and under Directive 90/220 or 2001/18 in relation to its use as feed and in relation to cultivation.[22] The administrative procedures for granting authorisations for the placing on the market of products under Regulation 258/97 are similar to those described above for Directives 90/220 and 2001/18: an application and accompanying dossier must be submitted to the lead CA which is required to prepare an initial assessment report within a period of three months from receipt of the application. The report must determine whether the application complies with the relevant requirements and is in accordance with the Commission's published recommendations.[23] It must also decide whether or not an additional assessment is required. Once the assessment report is complete, the lead CA must forward it to the Commission which in turn forwards it to the other member States. This is followed by the possibility for a member State or the Commission to make comments or present a "reasoned objective" to the marketing of the food concerned.[24] If the lead CA's assessment report determines that no additional assessment

---

[19]   See discussion in *EC – Biotech* at paras 7.115–7.117.
[20]   Article 13(4) of Directive 90/220 and Article 18(2) of Directive 2001/18.
[21]   Article 3 of Regulation 258/97.
[22]   Article 1(2) of Regulation 258/97.
[23]   Article 6(2) and 6(3) of Regulation 258/97.
[24]   Article 6(4) of Regulation 258/97.

is required, and no reasoned objection has been presented by another member State or the Commission, the lead CA must inform the applicant, without delay, that the food may be placed on the market.[25] However, if the lead CA's assessment report concludes that an additional assessment is required, or a reasoned objection has been raised, then an authorisation decision must be taken at the Community level in a similar manner as under Directives 90/200 and 2001/18.[26]

C. The Complaint in *EC – Biotech*

The crux of the complaint by the United States (US), Canada, and Argentina in *EC – Biotech* was that the EU had failed to undertake and complete its approval procedures for biotech products without undue delay, as a result of the adoption and application of a general *de facto* moratorium on approvals. This moratorium arose after five EU member States (Denmark, Greece, France, Italy, and Luxembourg) declared in 1999 that they would "take steps to have any new authorizations for the growing and placing on the market of genetically modified organisms suspended" pending the EU's adoption of rules on labelling and traceability.[27] Together, these five member States had the voting capacity to block the progress of the approval procedures under Directives 90/220, 2001/18, and 258/97.[28] The complainants asserted that this group of five countries had the ability and intention to prevent the final approval of applications between October 1998 and August 2003, and that they succeeded in doing so as there was a suspension of final approvals during this time.[29] They argued that during this time, not a single biotech product was approved (or rejected) under either Directives 90/220 and 2001/18 or under Regulation 258/97. This was despite many applications being pending during the period, a number of which had been favourably assessed by the EU's scientific committees.[30] The Panel exhaustively reviewed the evidence concerning these pending applications, and upheld the complaint that a general moratorium on all applications for approval was in effect between June 1999 and August 2003. The moratorium was a de facto one, in that it had not been applied through a formal EU process, but processing of

---

[25] Article 4(2) of Regulation 258/97.
[26] Directive 258/97 also provided for a simplified procedure for novel foods that are "substantially equivalent" to existing foods.
[27] *EC – Biotech, supra* note 12 at para. 7.474.
[28] *Ibid.* at para. 7.481.
[29] *Ibid.* at para. 7.494.
[30] *Ibid.* at para. 7.496.

applications was in fact suspended due to actions of the Group of Five countries and/or the Commission.[31]

D.   The Panel Report

Having found that the purposes for which the EU maintained its approval procedures fit within the categories in Annex A(1) of the SPS Agreement that qualified them as an SPS measure,[32] the Panel turned to assess the consistency or otherwise of the EU's measures with the obligations under the SPS Agreement. As described in section II, these obligations are both *substantive* (the requirements in Articles 2 and 5 requiring Members to base their measures on scientific evidence) and *procedural* (Article 8 and Annex C(1)).

The complainants argued that the EU's application of a de facto moratorium was in fact a decision to impose an effective marketing ban on all biotech products.[33] However, the Panel rejected this argument, preferring the EU's argument that the complainants' assertions in reality concerned only a delay in the completion of approval procedures, that is, "a failure to act in a timely manner".[34] The Panel concluded that the decision to apply the moratorium was not in itself a substantive decision to reject all applications.[35] Rather, it was a procedural decision to delay and not to make final positive, substantive decisions until certain conditions were satisfied.[36] Regarding the question of whether this decision was really a substantive one, the Panel said that a decision to delay final approval decisions did not cease to be procedural merely because it had a substantive impact. As the Panel noted, procedural decisions virtually always have some substantive impact.[37]

While the EU's decision may have been procedural in nature, this does not automatically mean that it was not subject to the substantive obligations in the SPS Agreement. (The SPS Agreement's substantive obligations do in fact apply to both requirements and procedures.) Nevertheless, the Panel found that the substantive obligations of the SPS Agreement did not apply to the moratorium in this case. This is because while the moratorium did not provide for a "procedure" (it neither created a new procedure

---

[31]   *Ibid.* at paras 7.1268–7.1272.
[32]   *Ibid.* at paras 7.285–7.286, 7.343–7.344, 7.361–7.362, and 7.379–7.380.
[33]   *Ibid.* at paras 7.1344–7.1347.
[34]   *Ibid.* at paras 7.1329–7.1330, 7.1365.
[35]   *Ibid.* at paras 7.1343, 7.1382.
[36]   *Ibid.* at paras 7.1342, 7.1344, and 7.1379.
[37]   *Ibid.* at paras 7.1361–7.1364.

nor amended an existing one). The simple fact that the decision in question related to the application, or operation of, procedures did not, according to the Panel, turn that decision into a procedure for the purposes of Annex A(1).[38]

The Panel did find, however, that the procedural obligations in Annex C applied in this case to the EU's pre-marketing approval procedures more generally. This was because the approval procedures for biotech products were "procedures to check and ensure the fulfilment of SPS measures" as referred to in Annex C(1). This contrasted to the finding that the *de facto* moratorium on the approval of biotech products was not an SPS measure, even although it affected the operation and application of EU approval procedures that were themselves SPS measures.[39]

Regarding the pre-marketing approval procedures themselves, the Panel found that the EU had breached the obligation in Annex C(1)(a) which requires WTO Members to ensure that all procedures to check and ensure the fulfilment of SPS measures are undertaken and completed without undue delay. It also found undue delay in relation to 24 of 27 product-specific approval procedures.[40] The Panel considered the meaning of the obligation in Annex C(1)(a) and stated that "the phrase 'undertake and complete' covers all stages of approval procedures and should be taken as meaning that, once an application has been received, approval procedures must be started and then carried out from beginning to end".[41] In terms of what is meant by the phrase "undue delay", The Panel said that the phrase "undue delay" requires approval procedures to "be under-taken and completed with no unjustifiable loss of time".[42] The Panel stated that it is not the length of the delay that is most important, but whether there is a legitimate reason for the delay.[43] The Panel noted that one indicator of an invalid reason for a delay would be the continuous postpone-ment of a substantive decision for lack of available scientific information. The Panel said that the purpose of Annex C(1) is to prevent a situation where Members avoid the substantive disciplines of Articles 2 and 5 by not reaching a decision on marketing approval. It also noted that the exist-ence of Article 5.7 (which allows Members to adopt provisional measures where there is insufficient scientific evidence to complete a risk assessment) means that Annex C(1) does not prevent the application of a prudent and

---

[38] *Ibid.* at para. 7.1382.
[39] *Ibid.* at paras 7.1386–7.1394.
[40] *Ibid.* at para. 7.2391.
[41] WT/DS291/R, WT/DS292/R, WT/DS293/R, at para. 7.1494.
[42] *Ibid.* at para. 7.1495.
[43] *Ibid.* at para. 7.1496.

precautionary approach to identifying, assessing, and managing risks, but it obliges Members to do so within the bounds of the SPS Agreement.

E. Criticisms of the Panel's Approach

The Panel's approach to pre-marketing approval is an aspect of the decision that has not been subject to a large degree of analysis. However, a helpful critique has been provided by Caroline Foster who argues that the delays caused by the *de facto* moratorium in *EC – Biotech* "called out to be recognized by the Panel as involving non-compliance with the substantive provisions of the SPS Agreement (whether motivated by protectionist or precautionary considerations, or a combination of the two)". She bases her contention on the observation that the moratorium in practice achieved a high level of protection, and in fact functioned as a trade ban, and, further, that the effects included diminution of applicants' market opportunities.[44] Foster emphasises the Panel's recognition that "procedural decisions virtually always have some substantive impact".[45] She notes that at the time of the Uruguay Round negotiations, nearly all developed countries operated prior approval systems for food additives, and that now they do so for GMOs and biotech products. In recognition of this, the concept of procedural delay was agreed upon during the SPS negotiations as the central discipline applicable to the operation of prior approval systems for imports.[46] Taking this negotiating history into account, Foster suggests that it is apparent why the Panel viewed the operation of approval procedures as a matter falling within Annex C(1)(a). However, she questions why the Panel regarded the effects of a moratorium on the operation of such procedures as falling only within Annex C(1)(a). She suggests in this regard that perhaps the Panel wanted to leave the question of the legality of prior approval systems to another day.[47]

While the *EC – Biotech* Panel may not have explicitly addressed the full extent of applicability of the SPS Agreement to pre-approval procedures, it appears to this author that there are in fact many aspects of pre-market approval systems that would be subject to the substantive (and procedural) obligations in the SPS Agreement, but that have not yet been challenged in the WTO's dispute settlement system (including in *EC – Biotech*). For example, the scientific findings of the lead CA with respect to GMOs

---

[44] Caroline Foster, "Prior Approval Systems Under the SPS Agreement" (2008) Journal of World Trade Law 42:6 1203, at 1208–1209 and 1211.

[45] *Ibid.* at 1211.

[46] *Ibid.* at 1213.

[47] *Ibid.*

or novel foods would be open to challenge if they resulted in failure to obtain consent for the product to be placed on the market due to a lack of veracity of the findings. In this case, however, the Panel was faced with an unusual set of circumstances surrounding the de facto moratorium – it was not part of the usual approval process at all.

Foster suggests that pre-market approval systems raise potentially serious questions under the SPS Agreement. She argues that a regulation setting down a pre-market approval system would not necessarily constitute an SPS measure per se, but that it is an act of non-importation under a control, inspection, or approval procedure that should stand to be challenged and should be regarded as constituting an SPS "measure". (It is in this regard that she considers that the EU's moratorium should have been regarded as an SPS measure – because it resulted in the actual non-importation of goods.[48])

This author endorses Foster's contentions that pre-market approval systems have the potential to raise serious trade-related questions, and that an act of non-importation would constitute an SPS measure. However, it is also argued here that a pre-market approval system will potentially also constitute an SPS measure in and of itself, as will its constituent parts, regardless of whether there is an act of non-importation. A pre-market approval system may place onerous requirements on imported products that increase the cost of importing, even if trade is not actually prevented. For example, an onerous evaluation requirement that asks for unnecessary documentation to be provided in respect of foreign products and thereby imposes a burden on importers. In addition, decisions that result from an approval process (i.e., approval to market but subject to conditions) would arguably be a substantive SPS measure and may affect international trade even in the absence of an outright decision to ban importation. It is important to recall in this regard that the obligations in the SPS Agreement apply to "all sanitary and phytosanitary measures which may, directly or indirectly, affect international trade".[49] The Panel in *Australia – Apples* referred to measures falling under the scope of the SPS Agreement where they have an "actual or potential trade effect".[50]

In the next section, I explore further the applicability of the SPS Agreement's core obligations to pre-market approval systems. As I will discuss, the fundamental tenets of pre-market approval systems are embraced

---

[48]   *Ibid.* at 1215.
[49]   SPS Agreement, Article 1.1.
[50]   *Australia – Measures Affecting the Importation of Apples from New Zealand* (WTO Doc. WT/DS367/R, Panel Report, 9 August 2010) at para. 7.172.

by the ordinary application of the SPS Agreement. With the exception of *EC – Biotech*, (a rather unusual case as noted) there has not been a dispute to date dealing directly with a pre-market approval system. This is not surprising as there have only been a handful of SPS cases. Many of the products covered by pre-market approval systems (or at least likely to be subject to controversial decisions) are new ones without established markets. It seems that a situation has not yet arisen where a country feels that its trade interests in products subject to such systems have been compromised to such an extent that resort to WTO dispute resolution is warranted.

IV.   PRE-APPROVAL SYSTEMS AND THE SPS AGREEMENT AFTER *EC – BIOTECH*

An analysis of the applicability of the SPS Agreement to pre-approval systems in the light of the *EC – Biotech* dispute is best done through the lens of specific systems that allow for illustration of the application of the rules through concrete examples. To this end, this chapter considers aspects of pre-approval systems in both the US (food additives) and Canada (novel foods). These systems provide useful examples because they are well-documented and comprehensive systems that provide a good platform for illustrating the ways in which the SPS Agreement disciplines apply to a country's pre-market approval practices.

In determining the applicability of the disciplines in the SPS Agreement to pre-market approval systems in light of the *EC – Biotech* case, it is helpful in the first instance to consider what aspects of those systems actually constitute SPS measures (and if so, whether substantive or procedural), and then whether such measures are subject to the SPS Agreement's substantive obligations, procedural obligations, or a combination of both.[51]

A.   Do Pre-market Approval Systems Involve SPS Measures?

It will be recalled that the SPS Agreement defines the scope of SPS measures by reference to the type of risk that is being regulated. Pre-market approval systems and their constituent parts are likely to fall within the

---

[51]   As discussed in section II, in broad terms, the Agreement's obligations concerning harmonisation, scientific evidence, and risk management, can be considered substantive, while those contained in Annex C(1) (*Control, Inspection and Approval Procedures*) can be considered procedural obligations.

scope of the Agreement due to their emphasis on human health and safety and the nature of the risks against which they are directed. In the first example, food additives in the US are subject to a pre-market approval system managed by the Food and Drug Administration (FDA). A food additive is defined in the Food, Drug and Cosmetic Act (FFDCA) as "any substance the intended use of which results or may reasonably be expected to result, directly or indirectly, in its becoming a component or otherwise affecting the characteristics of any food (including any substance intended for use in producing, manufacturing, packing, processing, preparing, treating, packaging, transporting, or holding food; and including any source of radiation intended for any such use), *if such substance is not generally recognized, among experts qualified by scientific training and experience to evaluate its safety, as having been adequately shown through scientific procedures . . . to be safe under the conditions of its intended use"* (emphasis added).[52]

The second part of this definition of food additive as emphasised is known as the "GRAS exemption" ("generally recognised as safe").[53] If a substance is GRAS, then it will not be considered a food additive. A substance may be GRAS either through scientific procedures or, for a substance used in food before 1958, through experience based on common use in food. The FDA maintains a list of additives known as "Everything Added to Food in the United States" (EAFUS). The EAFUS list contains ingredients added directly to food that the FDA has either approved as food additives or listed or affirmed as GRAS. Any new food additives not already regulated for use in food are presumed to be unsafe for their intended uses unless and until they are proven safe on the basis of science. In order for a food manufacturer or importer to market a new food additive (or before using an additive already approved for one use in another manner not yet approved), a manufacturer or other sponsor must first petition the FDA for its approval. Petitions must provide evidence that the substance is safe for the ways in which it will be used.[54]

---

[52]   Section 201.

[53]   Note that any food additive that is intended to have a technical effect in the food is deemed unsafe unless it conforms either to the terms of a regulation prescribing its use, or to an exemption for investigational use. Otherwise the additive will be deemed unsafe under section 408 of the FFDCA. Also, any substance that is added to food and imparts colour to the food is a colour additive and is deemed unsafe unless its use is permitted by regulation or is exempt by regulation. There is no GRAS exemption for colour additives.

[54]   See online, Food and Drug Administration: www.fda.gov/food/foodingredi entspackaging/ucm094211.htm (date accessed: 2 March 2011).

Where a substance is considered to be a food additive, then a measure to protect against risks associated with that substance squarely falls within paragraph (b) of the definition of SPS measure which talks about risks arising from additives, contaminants, toxins or disease-causing organisms. Such a measure will therefore be subject to the obligations contained in the SPS Agreement. To the extent that the approval system seeks to achieve protection through either the imposition of conditions on marketing of a product, or conditions on marketing, SPS measures may therefore come into being through the US pre-market approval system.

In the second example, all novel foods in Canada are subject to mandatory pre-market notification pursuant to the Food and Drug Regulations.[55] A notification system does not require that products be specifically regulated, however, it is still a process where assessment of a product is required before that product can be marketed. It therefore constitutes a pre-market approval system. Novel foods are defined in the Food and Drug Regulations[56] and encompass: (a) substances that have no history of safe use as a food;[57] (b) food that has been manufactured, prepared, preserved, or packaged by a process that has not previously been applied to food, and that has caused the food to undergo a major change;[58] and (c) food that is derived from a genetically modified plant, animal, or microorganism.

In *EC – Biotech* the Panel found that measures protecting against risks associated with genetically modified organisms did fall within the meaning of SPS measure. The Panel found, inter alia, that measures taken by the EU fell within subparagraphs (b) (risks arising from additives, contaminants, toxins or disease-causing organisms in foods, beverages or feedstuffs; (c) (risks arising from diseases carried by animals, plants or products thereof, or from the entry, establishment or spread of pests); and (d) (other damage from the entry, establishment or spread of pests).

---

[55]   Division 28, Part B. The regulations are made pursuant to the Food and Drug Act (R.S.C., 1985, c. F-27).

[56]   Division 28, Part B.

[57]   E.g., eggs with increased levels of lutein, or purified EPA and DHA oils from fish. See presentation of Health Canada, online at: http://www.ciphi.nl.ca/Novel%20Foods.pdf (date accessed: 5 April 2011).

[58]   Which might include changes in the composition, structure, or nutritional quality of the food or its physiological effects, the manner in which the food is metabolised in the body, or microbiological safety, chemical safety, or the safe use of food. An example is the use of ultraviolet light to treat apple cider. See presentation of Health Canada, online at: http://www.ciphi.nl.ca/Novel%20Foods.pdf (date accessed: 5 April 2011).

B. Application of Obligations to Substantive SPS Measures

The types of pre-market approval systems discussed in the context of the EU, US, and Canada are organised in such a way that products are assessed to determine whether the applicant has successfully demonstrated that allowing them to be marketed and sold would be consistent with a country's desired level of health protection. These systems, in and of themselves, can arguably be considered substantive SPS measures. In *EC – Biotech*, Directives 90/220 and 2001/18 make the granting of marketing approval conditional on a demonstration to the satisfaction of the competent authorities that the GMO to be released into the environment does not pose a risk to human health or the environment. The Panel found that the requirement established by Directives 90/220 and 2001/18 that GMOs released into the environment not pose a risk to human health or the environment was a substantive requirement imposed for the purposes mentioned in Annex A(1).[59] The Panel went on to note that the granting of marketing approval under Regulation 258/97 is conditional, inter alia, on a satisfactory demonstration that the novel food for which approval is sought would not present a danger for the consumer. Again, the Panel found that this requirement is imposed for a purpose mentioned in Annex A(1) and suggested that it is a substantive measure.[60]

Thus, a requirement in the US that an additive that is not GRAS (and therefore assumed to be unsafe) is subject to pre-market approval is an SPS measure – it is a requirement being imposed to protect against risks associated with such additives. Such a requirement may also affect international trade because it places potential limits on market entry of foreign products.

Looking at pre-market approval systems themselves, a measure that is applied as the result of an evaluation or assessment under such a system in order to achieve a country's desired level of protection will be a substantive SPS measure if the risk in question is of the type listed in Annex A(1). In the US system for pre-market approval of food additives, such a measure might be a regulation issued following approval of a petition that sets conditions for how an additive may be used, such as by listing the types of foods in which it can be used, the maximum amounts that can be used, and how it should be identified on food labels. Such regulations are based on a number of factors, including: 1) the composition and properties of the substance; 2) the amount that would typically be consumed; 3)

---

[59] *EC – Biotech, supra* note 12 at para. 7.426.
[60] *Ibid.* at para. 7.427.

immediate and long-term health effects; and 4) various safety factors. The FDA's decision as to whether to approve a new food additive for a particular use depends on whether the anticipated use satisfies the law's safety standard of "reasonable certainty of no harm".[61] Any such regulations must be developed and enacted in accordance with the SPS Agreement's substantive science-based obligations described in section II.

A concrete illustration of regulations that result from the US pre-market approval process involves the food additive azodicarbonamide. This additive is approved for use in food so long as it is used or intended for use (1) as an aging and bleaching ingredient in cereal flour in an amount not to exceed 2.05 grams per 100 pounds of flour (45 parts per million); (2) as a dough conditioner in bread baking in a total amount not to exceed 0.0045 per cent (45 parts per million) by weight of the flour used, including any quantity of azodicarbonamide added to flour. Further, in order to assure safe use of the additive, certain requirements are set out concerning labelling, including that it contain a statement of the concentration or the strength of the additive in any intermediate premixes.[62] These are all substantive requirements put in place to ensure safety for consumers and are subject to the SPS Agreement's obligations. If an importer of flour containing this additive felt that the regulations did not have a sound scientific basis, they could invoke the SPS Agreement's obligations to challenge their imposition. If, for example, there was an international standard as set by Codex for the food additive azodicarbonamide (or any other additive subject to the approval process), then the US would be obliged to "base" their approval conditions on that standard, unless it wished to implement a higher level of protection in which case it would have to comply with the obligations in Articles 2.2 and 5.1. The requirement in Article 5.1 to base SPS measures on a risk assessment would oblige the US to ensure that any evaluation or assessment undertaken in the course of developing the regulations constitutes a risk assessment as defined in Annex A(4). Further, the results of such risk assessment must "sufficiently warrant", or, in other words, "reasonably support", the regulations imposed. There must be a rational relationship between the regulations (i.e., the SPS measure) and the risk assessment.[63] In undertaking its evaluation, the FDA would there-

---

[61]   *Ibid.*

[62]   Electronic Code of Federal Regulations, Title 21: Food and Drugs, Part 172 Food Additives Permitted for Direct Addition to Food for Human Consumption, §172.806 (Azodicarbonamide).

[63]   *EC – Measures Concerning Meat and Meat Products (Hormones)* Complaint by the United States (1997), WTO Doc. WT/DS322/AB/R (Appellate Body Report) at para. 193.

fore have to fulfil the relevant requirements of a risk assessment as defined in Annex A(4) – namely, that it evaluate the potential for adverse effects on human health arising from the presence of additives in food.

A petition under the US system may result in an additive not being approved for use, and this would also likely constitute an SPS measure subject to the Agreement's substantive obligations. Thus the FDA must comply with the obligations to base measures on scientific evidence. Non-approval that was not supported by science would be a violation of the SPS Agreement as it would be a de facto prohibition on importation, imposed in order to protect against the type of risk enunciated in Annex A(1) of the SPS Agreement.

The SPS Agreement's obligations would apply in a similar manner to the approval process for novel foods in Canada. In Canada, a novel food may not be sold or advertised for sale unless the manufacturer or importer of the food has notified the Director in writing of their intention to sell or advertise it for sale, and has received a written notice from the Director under the Regulations.[64] The Novel Foods Section in Health Canada's Food Directorate is responsible for receiving novel foods notifications and submissions of additional information, and for initiating the review process. It distributes the submission material to relevant Food Directorate offices for review.[65] So long as a product is considered novel,[66] evaluators in these offices undertake a scientific assessment of the safety of the foods proposed for sale. They conduct a safety assessment as outlined in the *Guidelines for the Safety Assessment of Novel Foods*.[67] During the evaluation, analysis is conducted of the data submitted and of the protocols used to acquire that data. In completing this evaluation, the various Food Directorate offices would be obliged under the SPS Agreement to ensure that they follow a proper risk assessment process in accordance with Article 5.1.

Similarly to the case of the US system for food additives, where a decision is made that a product is not safe for consumption, the resulting ban would constitute an SPS measure. Likewise, any conditions imposed on

---

[64]   Under para. B.28.003(1)(a) or subsection B.28.003(2).

[65]   These include the Bureau of Chemical Safety for evaluation of chemical and toxicological considerations, the Bureau of Nutritional Sciences for nutritional considerations, and the Bureau of Microbial Hazards for microbial and molecular biological aspects.

[66]   In accordance with Section B.28.001 of the Novel Foods Regulations.

[67]   Food Directorate, Health Products and Food Branch, Health Canada, 2006, online at: http://www.hc-sc.gc.ca/fn-an/legislation/guide-ld/nf-an/guidelines-lignesdirectrices-eng.php (date accessed: 10 April 2011).

the product in question would also likely fall within the definition of an SPS measure and thus would have to be based on scientific evidence in accordance with the Agreement. In the Canadian system, conditions may be placed on the use of a particular product. For example, in 2006, Health Canada notified Ocean Nutrition Canada (the petitioner) that it would take no objection to the addition of microencapsulated fish oil (MFO) when added in such a manner that the food as offered for sale contains not less than 8mg and not more than 100mg eicosapentaenoic fatty acid and docosahexaenoic fatty acid combined per reference amount and per serving of stated size to all foods except for those specified. Further, MFO is not permitted to be added to a food for which a standard exists in the Food and Drug Regulations unless provision is made in the standard for fish oil as an ingredient.[68] This restriction was based upon the human food safety concerns associated with excessive intake of these kinds of fatty acids and Health Canada therefore determined that it was necessary to restrict the amount of fish oil that can be added to foods. This type of condition would be considered an SPS measure within the meaning of Annex A(1) because it is a requirement that is applied to protect human life or health from risks arising from additives in foods. The scientific evidence requirements of the Agreement are therefore applicable.

Another set of substantive provisions applicable to a pre-market approval system such as those of the US or Canada are those that require Members to ensure that their SPS measures do not arbitrarily or unjustifiably discriminate (Articles 2.3 and 5.5), to take into account the objective of minimising negative trade effects (Article 5.4), and to ensure that SPS measures are not more trade-restrictive than required to achieve their appropriate level of protection. In the case of food additives in the US, these provisions would apply to regulations made approving the use of a given additive. Any conditions imposed through the regulations are required to be made in a manner consistent with these obligations. Therefore, the FDA could not for example subject an approval of an additive imported from one of its trading partners to conditions that were particularly onerous and made it a waste of time for the importer to bother using the additive (for example, by only allowing miniscule amounts that would not have the intended effect), while allowing a similar additive that had the same chemical properties to be approved for use by a domestic manufacturer with no conditions.

---

[68]   Health Canada, online at: http://www.hc-sc.gc.ca/fn-an/gmf-agm/appro/nf-an103decdoc-eng.php (date accessed: 10 April 2011).

C. Application of SPS Obligations to Procedural Measures

As discussed, Annex A(1) has been interpreted to have a broad scope and there is no automatic bar to the procedural aspects of pre-market approval measures being considered as SPS measures and therefore subject to the Agreement's disciplines. Scott suggests that the definition of "SPS measure" in Annex A(1) is wide enough to encompass procedural as well as substantive components.[69] In fact, she finds that the definition explicitly contemplates the possibility of a requirement or procedure being an SPS measure.[70]

Procedural measures may be subject to both the substantive obligations around scientific evidence as well as the procedural obligations in Annex C. Regarding Annex C, there is, however, some confusion as to the exact applicability of the obligations. The title of Annex C refers to "control, inspection and approval procedures". However, the chapeau to paragraph (1) (which contains the majority of the procedural obligations) refers to "any procedure to check and ensure the fulfilment of sanitary or phytosanitary measures". A question raised by this wording is whether a pre-market approval system is a "procedure to check and ensure the fulfilment of SPS measures"? A pre-market approval system such as that in place in the US or Canada might be considered in its entirety to be such

---

[69] *Ibid.*

[70] Joanne Scott, *The WTO Agreement on Sanitary and Phytosanitary Measures*, Oxford: Oxford University Press, 2007. After listing the purposes to which a measure must be addressed in order to constitute an SPS measure, Annex A(1) notes that "sanitary or phytosanitary measures include all relevant laws, decrees, regulations, requirements and procedures including, *inter alia*, . . . testing, certification and approval procedures . . ." (emphasis in original). Scott notes that there is some suggestion that Annex C might apply not only to SPS measures, but also to procedures that do not actually qualify as SPS measures under Annex A(1). She refers in this regard to the chapeau of Annex C which she sees as distinguishing procedures on the one hand, and SPS measures on the other, thus implying that an Annex C procedure need not always take the form of an SPS measure. She also refers to the *EC – Biotech* Panel Report which seems to suggest that Annex C applies even in respect of a measure that is not an SPS measure (at p. 219). However, on a second look, Scott suggests that pre-market approval procedures unequivocally constitute SPS measures within the meaning of Annex A(1) and are in fact subject to the disciplines found in Annex C as well as the rest of the Agreement's disciplines. Referring to the Panel Report in *EC – Biotech*, she concludes that the moratorium in that case was viewed neither as a procedure nor as an SPS measure. Rather, it is "simply a fact, the presence of which serves to generate undue delay in the undertaking or completion of approval procedures on at least one occasion; the approval procedures being the subject of attack (at p. 219).

a procedure. This is because such a system exists to ensure the fulfilment of an SPS measure (the SPS measure in this instance being the rule that only products demonstrated to be safe may be given approval for marketing and sale). In *EC – Biotech*, the Panel found that Directives 20/220 and 2001/18, as well as Regulation 258/97, contain procedures to check and ensure the fulfilment of the substantive SPS requirements which are also contained therein.[71] It therefore found the procedures to be "procedures applied to check and ensure the fulfilment of one or more substantive SPS requirements the satisfaction of which is a prerequisite for the approval to place a product on the market".[72]

Individual aspects of such pre-market approval systems might also, individually, constitute procedural SPS measures.[73] An example is the notification and review stages of Canada's procedure for novel foods. In these stages, notifications are reviewed within 45 days from the date of application to determine if the information provided establishes that the food is safe and proponents are advised if additional information is needed to review the product properly. A novel food notification must include specific information, including details of any major change in the food and information about its intended use and directions for its preparation, as well as the text of all labels to be used in connection with the food.[74] Provision is made for the situation where additional information is required to allow a proper safety assessment. This may be the case where an evaluator determines that the data provided with the submission is not sufficient, or if the submission is unclear or incomplete.

In operating these procedures, Canada is obliged to comply with the procedural obligations in the SPS Agreement, for example, by ensuring that processes are not unduly delayed. Each of the procedural obligations contained in Annex C have relevance to the types of pre-market approval systems in place in the US and Canada. Scott notes that these obligations, while many and varied, are actually quite circumscribed in their scope. In particular, there is no generally applicable necessity or reasonableness requirement and no generalised least trade-restrictive means text.[75] Nevertheless, these are not trivial obligations and when looked at in

---

[71]   *EC – Biotech*, para. 7.428.

[72]   *EC – Biotech*, para. 7.429.

[73]   In *Australia – Apples*, the Appellate Body upheld the Panel's characterisation of the 16 measures at issue as constituting SPS measures, both as a whole and individually. *Australia – Apples* WTO Doc. WT/DS367/AB/R (Appellate Body Report) paras 183–184.

[74]   Section B.28.002(2).

[75]   Scott, *supra* note 70 at 210.

context, they do impose a number of quite specific disciplines on the way in which a country designs and conducts pre-market approval procedures.

As noted in section II, Annex C(1)(a) requires Members to come to a decision on an application, with no unjustifiable loss of time, or as soon as possible under the circumstances.[76] The US and Canadian systems described both set out certain timeframes for approval procedures. However, in any pre-market approval system there will undoubtedly be times where an agency has legitimate reasons or justifications for delays, particularly where the promised processing time is short and there is a particularly complex application with large volumes of evidence submitted for review. As the Panel suggested in *EC – Biotech*, it is likely that the issue of whether any given delay may be considered undue will fall to be determined on a case-by-case basis, taking into account all relevant facts and circumstances. The Panel suggested that the key is to determine whether Members reasonably need the time taken in order to determine "with reasonable confidence" whether their WTO-consistent SPS requirements are fulfilled.[77] The Panel acknowledged that Members may take additional time to assess new or additional information that becomes available at a late stage in the approval procedure, and where the information "may appropriately be considered to have a potential impact on a member's determination on whether an application" meets its SPS requirements.[78] Further, the Panel accepted that Members may be justified in actively soliciting further information or clarification, so long as this is "a reflection of genuine caution or prudence" and not "a pretext to delay the completion" of the procedure.[79] This means that in the context of the US and Canadian pre-market approval systems, as well as other similar systems, the approving country must come to a substantive decision, and must do so without undue delay. What is undue will be a question to be decided on a case-by-case basis and in the context of the circumstances. For example, if an applicant in the Canadian system fails to give evaluators additional information that they are seeking, then any delay in the processing of the notification directly resulting from such failure will not be the fault of Health Canada.

Various aspects of the pre-market approval systems described will also be impacted by the obligations set out in Annex C(1) paragraphs (b) to (i). Each system involves a number of steps which include requiring

---

[76] *EC – Biotech, supra* note 12 at paras 7.1494, 7.1496, and 7.1499.
[77] *EC – Biotech*, para. 7.1498.
[78] *EC – Biotech*, para. 7.1498.
[79] *EC – Biotech*, para. 7.1522.

applicants to provide certain information, and each of them state a time period in which decisions will be made. Each of these requirements helps to ensure that a country's pre-market approval system is fair, transparent, and timely. They are important because in the absence of these types of safeguards, these types of systems have the potential to be just as trade restrictive as substantive measures. Administration of approval procedures can essentially be a third line of protectionism that may be targeted at imported products, and imposed in addition to border measures (tariffs and quantitative measures), and regulatory measures. For example, an information requirement placed on applicants (such as the requirements for applications under Canada's novel food notification system to provide certain information) might be considered an SPS measure, as might the requirement for the importing country's authorities to conduct a safety assessment of a particular product. Would these different components of a pre-market approval system fall within the ambit of Annex C(1)? The answer seems to be that one needs to look at the reason for the SPS measure in question. Not all procedural SPS measures will fall under Annex C(1). However, many individual components of a pre-market approval system would likely fall under this paragraph because their ultimate purpose is to ensure that a particular safety standard is met. For example, evaluations or assessments undertaken as part of a pre-market approval system involve decisions as to whether a particular product is safe – they thus ensure fulfilment of an SPS measure (that measure being a ban on sale unless safety is proven and approval is given).

The substantive scientific evidence requirements of the SPS Agreement may also be applicable to procedural measues. Scott justifies the application of the substantive provisions of the SPS Agreement to procedures that are also covered by Annex C by referring to Article 8 which specifically provides that control, inspection, and approval procedures must not be inconsistent with the Agreement. She notes that this reference includes the Agreement's substantive obligations.[80] Thus, Annex C control, inspection, and approval procedures can be seen as a sub-set of the broader category of SPS measures and the discipline imposed by Annex C is additional to that imposed by the Agreement as a whole.[81] Application of the substantive as well as procedural obligations thus exposes a country's pre-market approval systems to the full range of the SPS Agreement's disciplines.

---

[80]   *Ibid.* at 218.
[81]   *Ibid.*

V. CONCLUSION

The above discussion has shown that in pre-market approval systems, there are a combination of substantive and procedural measures. Pre-market approval systems may constitute SPS measures as a whole, and components of them may constitute SPS measures individually. This is consistent with the reality recognised by the SPS Agreement's negotiators that trade-restrictive measures take different forms, and can be both substantive and procedural. The wording of the SPS Agreement suggests that procedural measures are a sub-set of SPS measures and are the only measures subject to the Annex C obligations. However, procedural measures may also be subject to the Agreement's substantive measures. There is nothing in *EC – Biotech* to suggest that this is not the case. The *EC – Biotech* case dealt with an unusual situation in that the *de facto* moratorium meant that the pre-market approval process in the EC was not functioning at all – it had in effect ceased to operate, and in its absence, there was no possibility for biotech products to obtain market approval.

The Panel in *EC– Biotech* found that the SPS Agreement's substantive obligations did not apply to the moratorium, but this was in the context of having found that the moratorium was not an SPS measure. The Panel did not dismiss the possibility of the Agreement's substantive obligations applying to procedural measures that did meet the definition of an SPS measure. Therefore, it can be concluded that the Panel's decision ought not to have any significant systemic implications that would prevent the application of the SPS Agreement's substantive (and procedural) disciplines to pre-market approval systems. Finally, it should be emphasised that the procedural and substantive obligations in the SPS Agreement are equally important. Both sets of obligations exist because countries have the capacity to restrict trade through all kinds of SPS measures, substantive and procedural. This is clear in the case of pre-market approval systems where a myriad of steps and procedures could be used to restrict trade.

11. Scope of application of the SPS Agreement: a post-*Biotech* analysis
Jacqueline Peel*

I. INTRODUCTION

The *Sanitary and Phytosanitary Measures Agreement* (SPS Agreement),[1] which came into being with the World Trade Organization (WTO) in 1995, is one of several novel agreements that focus on non-tariff trade barriers posed by certain forms of domestic regulation. The SPS Agreement formed part of the Uruguay Round's broader negotiations on agriculture and so at its heart is concerned with domestic measures that might restrict trade in agricultural goods, such as overly restrictive quarantine or food safety laws. However, what may be considered a sanitary or phytosanitary (SPS) measure is potentially much broader given the 'deeply ambiguous' definition of SPS measures in Annex A.1 of the SPS Agreement.[2] This potential was realized in the WTO dispute of *Biotech*,[3] in which a WTO panel gave an exceptionally expansive reading to the notion of SPS measures in its consideration of the application of the SPS Agreement to European Union (EU) regulations for genetically modified organisms (GMOs).[4]

---

*   This chapter draws on my article, 'A GMO by Any Other Name . . . Might be an SPS Risk! Implications of Expanding the Scope of the WTO *Sanitary and Phytosanitary Measures Agreement*' published in (2007) 17(5) *European Journal of International Law* 1009–1031.
[1]   *Agreement on the Application of Sanitary and Phytosanitary Measures*, opened for signature 15 April 1994, 1867 UNTS 493 (entered into force 1 January 1995) (SPS Agreement).
[2]   Joanne Scott, *The WTO Agreement on Sanitary and Phytosanitary Measures: A Commentary* (Oxford University Press, Oxford, 2007), 13.
[3]   *European Communities – Measures Affecting the Approval and Marketing of Biotech Products*, Reports of the Panel, WT/DS291/R, WT/DS292/R and WT/DS293/R, 29 September 2006 (*Biotech*).
[4]   These regulations consisted of an EU directive dealing with the environmental release of GMOs, *Directive 2001/18/EC*, [2001] OJ L 106/1 (which replaced the earlier *Directive 90/220/EEC*, [1990] OJ L 117/15), and *Council Regulation 258/97*, [1997] OJ L 43/1 governing the approval of novel foods, including those containing GMOs.

The importance of understanding the scope of application of the SPS Agreement lies in the consequences of designating particular domestic health or environmental risk regulations as SPS measures. If contested regulations, or parts thereof, are *not* SPS measures then they fall to be considered in WTO dispute settlement under the requirements of the *Technical Barriers to Trade Agreement* (TBT Agreement)[5] or those of the *General Agreement on Tariffs and Trade* (GATT).[6] On the other hand, domestic risk regulations classed as SPS measures attract assessment under the more stringent requirements of the SPS Agreement, which focus on the question of the scientific justification for measures, rather than their discriminatory trade effects.[7] In turn, the provisions of the SPS Agreement calling for a firm evidentiary basis for SPS regulations differ from the more broadly oriented, frequently precautionary, requirements of environmental treaties, which might provide an alternative forum for the discussion of disputed regulations.[8] As Joanne Scott notes, 'an expansive reading of the [SPS] agreement amounts in effect to an augmentation of the disciplinary burden implied by the agreement as a whole'.[9] In sum, if the Agreement is capable of applying to a broad range of health and environmental risk concerns this may restrict the scope of domestic regulatory autonomy in these areas where measures could have potential trade impacts.

This chapter examines the scope of application of the SPS Agreement based on the definition of SPS measures in Annex A.1, and its elaboration in recent WTO case law, especially the *Biotech* case. In order to come within the ambit of the SPS Agreement a particular regulation must qualify as a 'measure', have an impact on international trade and deal with one of the risk situations listed in Annex A.1. The chapter focuses particularly on the third of these requirements as the one of most relevance in assessing the scope of domestic health and environmental risk regulation

---

[5]   *Agreement on Technical Barriers to Trade*, opened for signature 15 April 1994, 1868 UNTS 120 (entered into force 1 January 1995) (TBT Agreement).

[6]   *General Agreement on Tariffs and Trade*, opened for signature 15 April 1994, 55 UNTS 194, 1867 UNTS 187 (entered into force 1 January 1995) (GATT).

[7]   Joost Pauwelyn, 'The WTO Agreement on Sanitary and Phytosanitary (SPS) Measures as Applied in the First Three SPS Disputes EC – Hormones, Australia – Salmon and Japan – Varietals' (1999) 2(4) *J. Int'l Economic Law* 641, 644.

[8]   Gilbert R. Winham, 'International Regime Conflict in Trade and Environment: the Biosafety Protocol and the WTO' (2003) 2(2) *World Trade Review* 131. Precautionary regulation is based on the principle that scientific uncertainty should not prevent regulatory action to address serious threats of environmental harm: see chapter 1.

[9]   Scott, above n 2, 17.

potentially caught by the disciplines of the SPS Agreement. Accordingly, the next part of the chapter outlines the concept of an SPS measure in Annex A.1 and considers the arguments that may be put forward in favour of a relatively narrow scope of operation for the SPS Agreement. This is contrasted with the broader health and environmental risks that were the focus of the EU's contested GMO regulations. The chapter then turns to a discussion of the *Biotech* panel findings regarding the nature of SPS measures and the way in which these rulings act to widen the scope of the SPS Agreement. The final section of the chapter examines the implications of a broader scope for the SPS Agreement. It is argued that if the panel's findings in *Biotech* are followed they have the potential to work important changes in the relationship between the SPS Agreement and health and environmental regulatory regimes, both domestic and international. As a result, not only GMO regulations, but also a range of other health and environmental measures with trade impacts, could become subject to SPS oversight, and with it, the institutional rigours of the WTO regime.

II. SCOPE OF APPLICATION OF THE SPS AGREEMENT

A. Definition of SPS Measures

The notion of an SPS measure is defined in Annex A.1 of the SPS Agreement. This definition provides as follows:

> Sanitary or phytosanitary measure – Any measure applied:
> (a) to protect animal or plant life or health within the territory of the Member from risks arising from the entry, establishment or spread of pests, diseases, disease-carrying organisms or disease-causing organisms;
> (b) to protect human or animal life or health within the territory of the Member from risks arising from additives, contaminants, toxins or disease-causing organisms in foods, beverages or feedstuffs;
> (c) to protect human life or health within the territory of the Member from risks arising from diseases carried by animals, plants or products thereof, or from the entry, establishment or spread of pests; or
> (d) to prevent or limit other damage within the territory of the Member from the entry, establishment or spread of pests.
> Sanitary or phytosanitary measures include all relevant laws, decrees, regulations, requirements and procedures including, *inter alia*, end product criteria; processes and production methods; testing, inspection, certification and approval procedures; quarantine treatments including relevant requirements associated with the transport of animals or plants, or with the materials necessary for their survival during transport; provisions on relevant statistical

methods, sampling procedures and methods of risk assessment; and packaging and labelling requirements directly related to food safety.

This definition must be read together with Article 1.1 that limits the application of the SPS Agreement to SPS measures 'which may, directly or indirectly, affect international trade'. In practice this is not a significant hurdle as the requirement for trade impact has been interpreted broadly to include both actual and potential impacts on trade.[10] As the final paragraph of Annex A.1 indicates, the notion of a 'measure' is also expansive. Measures can take a wide range of forms, including laws, decrees, regulations, requirements and procedures of various kinds.[11] Most critical, therefore, in determining whether a regulation is a SPS measure to which the Agreement applies are the four paragraphs (a)–(d) of Annex A.1 that prescribe the necessary 'purpose element' of measures.[12] In summary, four categories of regulatory purpose, or risk situation, are covered by Annex A.1:

(1) *Areas of human health risk regulation*, namely measures to protect human life or health from (i) food safety risks arising from additives, contaminants, toxins or disease-causing organisms in food or beverages; (ii) risks arising from diseases carried by animals, plants or their products; and (iii) risks arising from the entry, establishment or spread of pests.

(2) *Matters of sanitary (i.e. animal health) concern*, namely measures to protect animal life or health from (i) risks arising from the entry, establishment or spread of pests, diseases, disease-carrying organisms or disease-causing organisms; and (ii) risks arising from additives, contaminants, toxins or disease-causing organisms in feedstuffs.

(3) *Matters of phytosanitary (i.e. plant health) concern*, namely measures to protect plant life or health from risks arising from the entry, establishment or spread of pests, diseases, disease-carrying organisms or disease-causing organisms.

---

[10] Lukasz Gruszczynski, *Regulating Health and Environmental Risks under WTO Law: A Critical Analysis of the SPS Agreement* (Oxford, Oxford University Press, 2010), 52.

[11] See *United States – Certain Measures affecting Poultry Imports from China*, Report of the Panel, WT/DS392/R, 29 September 2010, para. 7.100 distinguishing the analysis in *Biotech* on this point. See also *Australia – Measures Affecting the Importation of Apples from New Zealand*, Report of the Appellate Body, WT/DS367/AB/R, 29 November 2010, paras 175–176, 181.

[12] *Biotech*, para. 7.149.

(4) *Pest-related damage*, namely measures to prevent or limit other damage from the entry, establishment or spread of pests.

In each case, measures caught by the SPS Agreement must satisfy a territorial limitation: that is, the measures must be addressed to risks or damage arising within the territory of the member adopting those measures. A footnote to Annex A.1 provides some further clarification as to the coverage of the four listed risk categories. For instance, 'animal' is defined to include fish and wild fauna and the term 'plant' includes forests and wild flora. The term 'pests' includes weeds and 'contaminants' and extends to pesticide and veterinary drug residues and 'extraneous matter'. Even so, many key terms in Annex A.1 remain undefined, including the notions of 'additives', 'diseases', 'toxins' and 'food', as well as the ubiquitous phrase 'risks arising from'. Consequently, if these words are read expansively by WTO dispute settlement panels and the Appellate Body there is the concomitant potential for expanding the scope of application of the SPS Agreement and its disciplines requiring a scientific justification for SPS measures.

B.   Arguments in Favour of a Narrow Scope for the SPS Agreement

A number of arguments can be advanced as to why the SPS Agreement should be construed to have a limited operation, thereby requiring the terms of Annex A.1 to be read down rather than to be interpreted broadly.[13] One set of arguments draws on the negotiating history of the SPS Agreement. In the Uruguay round of trade negotiations that led to the establishment of the WTO, non-tariff trade barriers were one of the topics for which new agreements were proposed in order to supplement the general requirements of the GATT that imported products be 'accorded treatment no less favourable than that accorded to like products of national origin'.[14] Reworking of the Standards Code to produce the TBT Agreement was designed to deal with a broad range of technical product standards and regulations that WTO Members might introduce for public policy reasons, including protection of the environment, human health or consumer safety.[15] On the other hand, documents before the negotiators

---

[13]   However, the language of the SPS Agreement is not without ambiguity and both textual arguments, as well as arguments based on the negotiating history of the Agreement, can be advanced in favour of the position that 'some environmental regulations should be regarded as SPS measures': Gruszczynski, above n 10, 58.

[14]   GATT, article III(4).

[15]   TBT Agreement, Annex 1, para. 1.

suggested that the new SPS Agreement was to be directed to a particular category of non-tariff trade barriers, namely 'sanitary and phytosanitary regulations and barriers' with the potential for adverse effects on trade in agricultural products, such as meat or plant products that are imported into a country but may carry with them pests or diseases.[16] A long-running dispute between the United States (US) and the EU over hormone residues in beef products (that later gave rise to the case of *Hormones*) also cast a 'shadow' over the negotiations, resulting in the inclusion of provisions regarding measures addressed to food safety risks.[17] Analysis of the negotiating history of the SPS and TBT Agreements thus supports the conclusion that 'the SPS Agreement can be seen as a carve-out from TBT', 'intended to deal with a limited set of measures'.[18] In this scheme, any residual non-tariff regulatory measures falling outside the ambit of the SPS and TBT Agreements were left to the provisions of the GATT.

Others have pointed to the distinctive scientific evidence and risk assessment requirements of the SPS Agreement – not replicated in the TBT Agreement or GATT – as evidence in favour of a narrow scope of application for the SPS Agreement.[19] In this respect, it has been maintained that the SPS provisions calling for 'sufficient' supporting scientific evidence[20] and justificatory risk assessments[21] were a response to fears that 'as tariff barriers in agriculture came down, domestic agricultural lobbies would resort to sanitary and phytosanitary measures to keep food and agricultural products out of their markets'.[22] Arguably, these are concerns that are more clearly applicable to quarantine and food safety measures – the measures generally used to impose restrictions or other requirements on imported agricultural products – rather than to broadly targeted health

---

[16]   Ministerial Declaration on the Uruguay Round, MIN.DEC, 20 September 1986, Part I, Section D Agriculture (iii).

[17]   David Victor, 'The Sanitary and Phytosanitary Agreement of the World Trade Organization: An Assessment After Five Years' (2000) 32 *N.Y.U. J. Int'l Law & Politics* 865, 872.

[18]   Doaa Motaal, 'The "Multilateral Scientific Consensus" and the World Trade Organization' (2004) 38(5) *J. World Trade* 855, 856. See also Laurence Boisson de Chazournes and Makane Moïse Mbengue, 'GMOs and Trade: Issues at Stake in the EC Biotech Dispute' (2004) 13(3) *Review of European Community and International Environmental Law* 289, 295.

[19]   Motaal, ibid, 856.

[20]   SPS Agreement, article 2.2.

[21]   SPS Agreement, articles 5.1 and 5.2.

[22]   Andrew Thompson, 'Australia – Salmon and Compliance Issues Surrounding the SPS Agreement: Sovereign Acceptance and Measure Adaptation' (2002) 33 *Law & Pol'y Int'l Bus.* 717, 719.

and environmental regulations with incidental impacts on international trade.

Another line of argument that may be advanced in favour of a narrow scope of application for the SPS Agreement looks to the broader scheme of WTO disciplines concerned with non-tariff trade barriers, and particularly, the inter-relationship between the SPS Agreement, the TBT Agreement and the GATT. The definition of SPS measures in Annex A.1 of the SPS Agreement has particular significance in this regard given that article 1.5 of the TBT Agreement states that its provisions 'do not apply to sanitary and phytosanitary measures as defined in Annex A of the Agreement on the Application of Sanitary and Phytosanitary Measures'. Added to this are the provisions of article 2.4 of the SPS Agreement, which provide that SPS measures conforming to the requirements of the Agreement are 'presumed to be in accordance with the obligations of the Members under the provisions of GATT 1994 which relate to the use of sanitary or phytosanitary measures, in particular the provisions of Article XX(b)'. In the first dispute in which the SPS Agreement was considered, that of *Hormones*, the panel held that the SPS Agreement imposes obligations of a different nature to those under the GATT and its exception for health protective measures in article XX(b). In the panel's view, the SPS Agreement provided 'for specific obligations to be met in order for a Member to enact or maintain specific types of measures, namely sanitary and phytosanitary measures'.[23]

In contrast to the SPS Agreement's apparently narrow concern with measures targeted to sanitary and phytosanitary risks, the provisions of the TBT Agreement and the GATT are more broadly focused, contemplating a wider range of regulatory purposes lying behind domestic measures. The exceptions of the GATT have a particularly extensive ambit, permitting the adoption of trade-restrictive measures,[24] including those 'necessary to protect public morals', 'necessary to protect human, animal or plant life or health', 'necessary to secure compliance with laws or regulations' of a national government, or 'relating to the conservation of exhaustible natural resources'.[25] The TBT Agreement also evidences a concern with a broad range of measures, covering 'technical regulations' directed, inter alia, to the 'prevention of deceptive practices' and the 'pro-

---

[23]   Panel Report, *European Communities – Measures Concerning Meat and Meat Products*, WT/DS26/R and WT/DS48/ R, 12 July 1999 (*Hormones* panel report), para. 8.39.

[24]   The chapeau to GATT, article XX permits discriminatory measures provided the discrimination is not arbitrary or unjustifiable and the measure does not constitute a disguised restriction on international trade.

[25]   GATT, articles XX(a), (b), (d) and (g) respectively.

tection of human health or safety, animal or plant life or health or the environment'.[26] Indeed, given the specific (and exclusive) mention of 'the environment' in the TBT Agreement, it is arguable that environmental risks fall entirely outside the scope of the SPS Agreement, at least to the extent that they do not involve direct injury, through pest or disease-action, to animal or plant life or health.[27]

Questions about the application of the SPS Agreement, vis-à-vis the TBT Agreement and the GATT are particularly difficult in the case of measures addressed to multiple regulatory purposes.[28] Such measures are an increasingly common feature of modern risk regulatory practice given the often-intersecting nature of public concerns regarding health, environmental and consumer safety issues. Sensibly, in *Biotech* the panel ruled that a measure with distinctively different purposes may be assessable under more than one Agreement.[29] However, as frequently occurs in SPS disputes, the panel did not go on to make findings of compatibility under Agreements other than the SPS Agreement on the grounds of the need for judicial economy.[30] Where the SPS Agreement is given a wide ambit of operation and breaches of its provisions are subsequently found, this practice tends to crowd out opportunities for analysis of the potential compatibility of measures under the TBT Agreement or the GATT.

Looking beyond the WTO regime to the sphere of multilateral environmental agreements (MEAs), there are a number of other indications that argue in support of a narrower ambit of operation of the SPS Agreement and its requirements for domestic SPS measures to be based on 'sound science'.[31] In contrast to the SPS regime's call for regulations to bear a 'rational relationship' to scientific evidence and a risk assessment,[32]

---

[26] TBT Agreement, article 2.4.

[27] This was the argument put by the EC in the *EC – Biotech* case although it was ultimately rejected by the Panel. See Panel Report, *Biotech*, paras 7.209–7.211.

[28] For a detailed discussion see Gabrielle Marceau and Joel P. Trachtman, 'The Technical Barriers to Trade Agreement, the Sanitary and Phytosanitary Measures Agreement, and the General Agreement on Tariffs and Trade' (2002) 36(5) *Journal of World Trade* 811, 868–878.

[29] Panel Report, *EC – Biotech*, para. 7.165.

[30] Ibid, paras 7.2505, 7.3422, 7.3429. See also Panel Report, *Hormones*, para. 8.42, observing that this manner of proceeding is 'the most efficient'.

[31] Warren H. Maruyama, 'A New Pillar of the WTO: Sound Science' (1998) 32 *International Lawyer* 651.

[32] These interpretations of the requirements of articles 2.2 and 5.1 of the SPS Agreement were developed principally in *European Communities – Measures Concerning Meat and Meat Products*, Report of the Appellate Body, WT/DS26/AB/R and WT/DS48/AB/R, 16 January 1998 (*Hormones*), para. 193 and *Japan – Measures Affecting Agricultural Products*, Report of the Appellate Body, WT/

environmental regimes invariably couple a requirement for reliance on scientific information with an instruction to act with caution in the face of scientific uncertainty.[33] While the SPS Agreement also allows some scope for precautionary action through its exception for domestic SPS measures adopted in circumstances 'where relevant scientific evidence is insufficient',[34] this is generally considered to be a fairly weak version of the principle of precaution found in international environmental law.[35] The broader scope, under environmental regimes, for precautionary action in conditions of scientific uncertainty (and not just in situations of insufficiency of scientific evidence regarding risks)[36] may in turn reflect states' acknowledgment of the different nature of available scientific knowledge regarding most environmental problems, as opposed to those associated with quarantine pests or diseases, or toxins of concern for human health. Whereas scientific research is frequently extensive and well-developed as

---

DS76/AB/R, 22 February 1999 (*Japan – Varietals*), para. 84, and were affirmed in the Appellate Body's recent decision in *United States – Continued Suspension of Obligations in the EC – Hormones Dispute*, Report of the Appellate Body WT/DS320/AB/R, 16 October 2008 (*Continued Suspension of Obligations*), para. 528.

[33]   See, e.g., *Convention on Biological Diversity*, opened for signature 5 June 1992, (1992) 31 ILM 818 (entered into force 29 December 1993), preamble; *United Nations Framework Convention on Climate Change*, opened for signature 9 May 1992, 1771 UNTS 164 (entered into force 24 March 1994), article 3; *United Nations Agreement Relating to the Conservation and Management of Straddling Fish Stocks and Migratory Fish Stocks*, opened for signature 4 December 1995, (1995) 34 ILM 1542 (entered into force 11 December 2001), articles 5 and 6; *Convention on Persistent Organic Pollutants*, opened for signature 23 May 2001, (2001) 40 ILM 532 (entered into force 17 May 2004) (POPs Convention), article 8(9); *Cartagena Protocol on Biosafety to the Convention on Biological Diversity*, opened for signature 29 January 2000, (2000) 39 ILM 1027 (entered into force 11 September 2003) (Biosafety Protocol), articles 10(6) and 11(8).

[34]   SPS Agreement, article 5.7.

[35]   John Applegate, 'The Taming of the Precautionary Principle' (2002) 27 *William & Mary Envtl L. & Policy Review* 13, 51–55. Article 5.7 of the SPS Agreement permits only provisional measures based on 'available pertinent information' and WTO members adopting such measures are under additional obligations to 'seek to obtain the additional information necessary for a more objective assessment of risk and review the sanitary or phytosanitary measure accordingly within a reasonable period of time'.

[36]   In its decision in *Japan – Measures Affecting the Importation of Apples*, the Appellate Body indicated scientific uncertainty is not the same as an insufficiency of relevant scientific evidence. See Appellate Body Report, *Japan – Measures Affecting the Importation of Apples*, WT/DS245/AB/R, 26 November 2003, (*Japan – Apples*), para. 184. This can be contrasted with the more nuanced understanding of insufficiency of scientific evidence as covering a spectrum of situations in the Appellate Body Report, *Continued Suspension of Obligations*, para. 703.

regards human health (particularly cancer)[37] risks or risks from quarantine pests with the potential to cause serious economic losses to agriculture, knowledge of ecosystem interactions and environmental problems is more often patchy, incomplete and subject to many uncertainties.[38] Moreover, if one accepts that a country agreeing to precautionary provisions in the context of a MEA, while also accepting the science-focused requirements of the WTO SPS Agreement, 'acts as one and the same state (even though it does so in different fora)',[39] one plausible conclusion is that governments intended their SPS commitments to impact little on their broader responsibilities for precautionary health or environmental protection.

C.   GMOs as an SPS Risk?

Prior to the *Biotech* dispute few envisaged that the requirements of the SPS Agreement might be brought to bear on broadly framed environmental regulations with adverse trade impacts. Commentary on the potential for a trans-Atlantic biotechnology dispute in the WTO tended to canvas issues of compatibility under the TBT Agreement and GATT, in addition to the SPS Agreement, reflecting a view that the latter was not comprehensive in its coverage of the health and environmental risk concerns raised with respect to GMOs.[40] In a 2003 article discussing the WTO-compatibility of European GMO laws, Joanne Scott confidently

---

[37]   Occupational health and safety risks, e.g. associated with the use of toxic chemicals in the workplace, also fall into this category of well-researched risks. However, this is not the case for all human health risks, such as the potential risks associated with the use of new technologies such as nanomaterials.

[38]   Robert Costanza and Laura Cornwell, 'The 4P Approach to Dealing with Scientific Uncertainty' (1992) 34(9) *Environment* 12; Daniel Haag and Martin Kaupenjohann, 'Parameters, Prediction, Post-normal Science and the Precautionary Principle – a Roadmap for Modelling for Decision-Making' (2001) 144 *Ecological Modelling* 45. This is not to say that there are not also many uncertainties in health risk assessment (see, e.g. Rory Sullivan and Amanda R. Hunt, 'Risk Assessment: the Myth of Scientific Objectivity' (1999) 16 *Environmental And Planning Law Journal* 522), however, such risks tend to attract more research funding and generate more findings that ecological risks.

[39]   Pauwelyn above n 7, 904.

[40]   Robert Howse and Petros Mavroidis, 'Europe's Evolving Regulatory Strategy for GMOs – The Issue of Consistency with WTO Law: Of Kine and Brine' (2000) 24 *Fordham Int'l L.J.* 317; Joanne Scott, 'European Regulation of GMOs and the WTO' (2003) 9 *Colum. J. Eur. L.* 213; David Morgan and Gavin Goh, 'Genetically Modified Food Labelling and the WTO Agreements' (2004) 13(3) *Review of European Community and International Environmental Law* 306.

declared 'there can be no doubt that the SPS Agreement marks the beginning and not the end, of the WTO story'.[41] Given this general view, there was some force behind criticism of the US strategy in the *Biotech* dispute, launched in 2003, which presented arguments principally on the SPS compatibility of the EU's GMO regulations.[42] This approach required a rather constrained and literal reading of the relevant definitions in Annex A.1 of the SPS Agreement. For instance, it was argued by the complainants that GMO crops escaping from an area of cultivation could be classified as weeds (included within the definition of a pest), which might then out-compete native species or other crop plants, so threatening the health of wild flora (included within the definition of a plant) or causing 'other damage', ranging from impacts on biodiversity, to endangering the continued viability of organic farming practices.[43] By contrast, there seemed to be a readier fit between the EU measures and provisions of the TBT Agreement dealing with technical regulations directed to the prevention of environmental risks, or even those of the GATT Article XX(a) allowing trade-restrictive measures 'necessary to protect public morals' given the strong thread of ethical concern running through public debates over GMOs.[44] Undoubtedly the advantage of a focus on the SPS-compatibility of GMO regulations from the complainants' perspective was the more limited flexibility that the SPS Agreement offered the EU to justify its measures on public policy grounds.

In the *Biotech* case, the response of the EU to the complainants' arguments that the SPS Agreement was of primary relevance in assessing its GMO regulations was that this fundamentally under-estimated the breadth of the risks dealt with in its GMO regulatory regime. The EU also questioned the competence of the WTO dispute settlement system to decide the issues raised by the complainants,[45] contending that its regulatory scheme should instead be judged in light of relevant MEAs, such as the *Cartagena Biosafety Protocol to the Convention on Biological Diversity* (Biosafety

---

[41]   Scott, ibid. 228.

[42]   By contrast, both Canada and Argentina also made arguments under the TBT Agreement and GATT.

[43]   *European Communities – Measures Affecting the Approval and Marketing of Biotech Products*, WTO Docs WT/DS291, WT/DS292, WT/DS293 (2004) (First Submission of the US), paras 78–80.

[44]   Brian Wynne, 'Creating Public Alienation: Expert Cultures of Risk and Ethics on GMOs' (2001) 10(4) *Science as Culture* 445.

[45]   *European Communities – Measures Affecting the Approval and Marketing of Biotech Products*, WT/DS291, WT/DS292, WT/DS293 (2004) (First Written Submission by the EU), para. 10.

Protocol).[46] The rationale behind such arguments is readily apparent on examination of the EU's scheme for the approval of GMO crops and foods, which in terms of both process and coverage is an extremely complex one that has evolved significantly since its initial introduction in 1990. Applications for the approval of GMOs under this scheme proceed through a multi-layered process of Member state and Union level decision-making, informed by scientific assessments and political considerations brought to the process by national authorities and various EU-level committees.[47] The assessments that are carried out are broadly concerned with the potential health and environmental risks relating to the deliberate environmental release of GMOs as crops and the use of GMOs as, or in, foods.

Like an increasing number of domestic regulatory frameworks concerned with GMOs, the EU scheme deals with two different kinds of concerns over GMOs, some of which would seem to extend far beyond harms associated with the spread of pests or the consumption of toxin- or additive-containing food products.[48] The first such category of risk concerns can be described as the direct potential impacts of GMOs on the environment and human health. Included in this suite of risks are the possible allergenic or toxic effects of a GMO for humans or animals if, for instance, a GMO plant is consumed as or in a food, or produces substances which are toxic to insects that eat its pollen, seed or leaves. In an environmental context, the direct impacts of GMOs might also extend to

---

[46] Biosafety Protocol, above n 33. The Biosafety Protocol governs trade in certain categories of GMOs, permitting countries to impose import bans following a risk assessment process.

[47] For a detailed account of the scheme and its evolution over time see Estelle Brosset, 'The Prior Authorisation Procedure Adopted for the Deliberate Release into the Environment of Genetically Modified Organisms: The Complexities of Balancing Community and National Competencies' (2004) 10 *European Law Journal* 555; Theofanis Christoforou, 'Genetically Modified Organisms in European Union Law', in Nicolas de Sadeleer (ed.), *Implementing the Precautionary Principle: Approaches from the Nordic Countries, the EU and USA* (Earthscan, London, 2007), 197; Gregory C. Shaffer and Mark A. Pollack, 'The EU Regulatory System for GMOs', in Michelle Everson and Ellen Vos (eds), *Uncertain Risks Regulated* (Routledge-Cavendish, Abingdon, 2009), 269.

[48] A number of government reports have canvassed issues of GMO risk including concerns over uncertainty, effects on agriculture and ethical issues: see Senate Community Affairs Committee, *A Cautionary Tale: Fish Don't Lay Tomatoes (A Report on the Gene Technology Bill 2000)* (Commonwealth of Australia, Canberra, 2000); Royal Society of Canada, *Elements of Precaution: Recommendations for the Regulation of Food Biotechnology in Canada* (Canadian Government, Ottawa, 2001); National Research Council, *Environmental Effects of Transgenic Plants: the Scope and Adequacy of Regulation* (National Academies Press, Washington D.C., 2002).

potential gene transfer from a GMO plant to non-GMO wild or cultivated plants, leading to the development of so-called superweeds that out-compete other, unmodified, plants. Another possible direct impact of GMO agriculture on the environment relates to the situation where a GMO plant (or its seed) accidentally escapes from an area of cultivation, allowing the GMO to establish in other areas, including areas of native forest.

The other category of GMO risk concerns dealt with by the EU regulatory scheme are best described as indirect impacts of GMO agriculture on human health or the environment. These concerns reflect the way in which the direct impacts of a product on health or the environment are often linked, both temporally and spatially, with a range of other potential harms, many of which extend to issues of social or economic concern rather than pure health or environmental damage. They encompass concerns regarding the risks GMOs pose to biodiversity through altering the dynamics and genetic diversity of species in the receiving environment, risks associated with antibiotic resistance marker genes in GMOs that, if transferred to animal and human gut bacteria, could compromise the clinical effectiveness of medical treatments, and the human and environmental health effects associated with increased insecticide or herbicide use if this becomes necessary to eradicate cross-breed plants that have acquired resistance genes from GMOs.[49]

Characteristic of these types of risk concerns is that they seek to anticipate how a GMO might interact with human health or the environment over time and space, taking account of the ecological and social context in which GMO agriculture takes place. In this conception, not only is potential gene transfer between a GMO and non-GMO plant of concern, but also the long-term effects of such a transfer on the biodiversity of a region, the implications for agricultural practices such as weed management and insecticide use, and the flow-on economic or other damage that may occur to farming areas seeking to preserve scope for non-GMO cropping.[50] In domestic health and environmental regulatory systems it is increasingly considered best practice to adopt a broad approach to conceptualizing possible risk pathways as this helps to map assessment processes to the inter-connected nature of most ecosystems and the reality of complex, multi-faceted risk problems.[51] Yet, applied under an international trade agreement, a similarly broad interpretative approach, covering direct

---

[49]   Panel Report, *Biotech*, paras. 7.190–7.194.

[50]   Les Levidow et al, 'European Biotechnology Regulation: Framing the Risk Assessment of a Herbicide-Tolerant Crop' (1997) 22(4) *Science, Technology and Human Values* 472.

[51]   John Harte, 'Land Use, Biodiversity, and Ecosystem Integrity: The Challenge of Preserving the Earth's Life Support System' (2001) 27 *Ecology Law*

and indirect effects, may have very different consequences. In the case of the SPS Agreement, extending its provisions to an expansive range of trade-restrictive risk regulatory measures may expose the preventative and precautionary structures that address such concerns to scrutiny under the science-based disciplines of the Agreement.[52]

III. SCOPE OF THE SPS AGREEMENT: THE *BIOTECH* PANEL FINDINGS

The WTO panel report in the *Biotech* case, issued in 2006, represented the first (and to date only) comprehensive assessment of the application of the SPS Agreement and the meaning of terms used in the definition of SPS measures in Annex A.1.[53] The dispute centred on allegations made by the three complainants – the US, Canada and Argentina – that the EU had maintained a de facto moratorium on GMO approvals, effectively refusing to implement the decision-making processes specified under its GMO regulatory framework. The complainants also challenged several safeguard measures maintained by Member states of the EU that purported to restrict the growing or sale of particular GMOs or GMO foods in the territories of the Member states concerned.[54] The panel's findings in favour of the complainants, including its rulings concerning the applicability of the SPS Agreement to the EU GMO scheme, were not appealed to the Appellate Body. This leaves the panel's decision in a precedential grey zone and it is not clear to what extent its findings might be followed in subsequent cases. Although the practice of the WTO dispute settlement bodies has been to accord greatest authority to the rulings of the Appellate Body as opposed to panels, the *Biotech* findings are likely to be influential with other panels considering similar regulations in future disputes.[55]

Quarterly 929; Andy Stirling and David Gee, 'Science, Precaution and Practice' (2002) 117(6) *Public Health Reports* 521.

[52] On the notions of harm prevention and precaution that underlie much of environmental regulation see Nicolas de Sadeleer, *Environmental Principles: From Political Slogans to Legal Rules* (Oxford University Press, Oxford, 2002).

[53] Gruszczynski, above note 10, 53.

[54] Safeguard measures may be adopted by individual EU Member states, on a provisional basis, to restrict or prohibit the use and/or sale of a GMO that has received approval under the EU regulations as or in a product on the Member's territory.

[55] Christine Conrad, 'The *EC – Biotech* Dispute and Applicability of the SPS Agreement: are the Panel's Findings Built on Shaky Ground?' 6(2) *World Trade Review* 233, 234.

In most SPS disputes, the issue of whether the SPS Agreement applies has generally been uncontroversial. Cases have either been concerned with quarantine measures adopted for sanitary or phytosanitary purposes,[56] or have addressed food safety concerns associated with the inclusion of contaminants in foodstuffs.[57] By contrast, the question of whether the SPS Agreement adequately captured the complexity of the risk concerns animating the EU GMO regulatory scheme was one that was socially and politically charged.[58] In the panel's *Biotech* report, however, there is little to indicate its awareness of concerns about extending the scope of the SPS Agreement, and the impact that this might have for broader international relationships between trade, health and environmental rules. Instead, looking largely to the 'ordinary meaning' of the terms in Annex A.1 as augmented by the *Oxford English Dictionary*, the *Biotech* panel developed far-reaching interpretations of the nature of SPS risks, bringing within the ambit of the SPS Agreement a wide range of environmental, health, agricultural and economic flow-on effects of GMO use and food production.[59]

A.   Animal and Plant Life and Health

A central plank of the panel's analysis in construing the definitions in Annex A.1 of the SPS Agreement was that the frequently used phrase 'animal or plant life or health' was 'meant to be comprehensive in coverage'.[60] In this regard, the footnote reference in Annex A.1, to animals

---

[56]   See Appellate Body Report, *Australia – Measures Affecting Importation of Salmon*, Report of the WTO Appellate Body, WT/DS18/AB/R, 20 October 1998; Appellate Body Report, *Japan – Measures Affecting Agricultural Products*, Report of the WTO Appellate Body, WT/DS76/AB/R, 22 February 1999; Appellate Body Report, *Japan – Measures Affecting the Importation of Apples*, WT/DS245/AB/R, 26 November 2003; Appellate Body Report, *Australia – Measures Affecting the Importation of Apples from New Zealand*, WT/DS367/AB/R, 29 November 2010.

[57]   Appellate Body Report, *European Communities – Measures Concerning Meat and Meat Products*, WT/DS26/AB/R and WT/DS48/AB/R, 16 January 1998; Appellate Body Reports, *United States – Continued Suspension of Obligations in the EC – Hormones Dispute*, WT/DS320/AB/R, 16 October 2008 (the report issued in DS321 brought by Canada is identical to the US report).

[58]   David Winickoff et al, 'Adjudicating the GM Food Wars: Science, Risk, and Democracy in World Trade Law' (2005) 30 *Yale J. Int'l L.* 81.

[59]   Margaret A. Young, 'The WTO's Use of Relevant Rules of International Law: An Analysis of the *Biotech* Case' (2007) 56 *Int'l Comp. L.Q.* 907, noting the pitfalls of a seductively simple interpretative approach such as one based on determining the 'ordinary meaning' of terms. See also Lukasz Gruszczynski, above note 10, 61 who criticizes the inconsistency of the panel's interpretative approach.

[60]   Panel Report, *Biotech*, para. 7.219.

as including wild fauna and plants as including wild flora, provided the panel with the means to bring broadly-framed environmental concerns within the scope of the risks addressed by the SPS Agreement. According to the panel, risks to animal or plant life or health therefore encompassed concerns relating to the effects of GMO crops on micro-flora and micro-fauna (such as soil organisms), as well as non-target organisms, such as insects that are indirectly affected by the cultivation of an insecticide-producing GMO crop (for example, if they consume the pollen of such plants).[61] In the panel's construction, a possible environmental flow-on risk of GMOs – such as the potential for trans-genes from GMO plants to be introduced into soil and thence, via run-off, into waterways where they could have a detrimental impact on aquatic micro-organisms – was a risk that could be adequately described as one concerned with 'animal or plant life or health'.[62]

This broad understanding of the notion of animal and plant life or health also played into the panel's analysis of the application of the SPS Agreement to the risks to biodiversity posed by GMOs. The EU in its submissions to the panel sought to distinguish between damage to biodiversity and damage to the life or health of particular animals or plants.[63] In effect, its argument was that biodiversity is more than the sum of its individual living parts, a view supported by the ecological science literature.[64] The panel, however, did not accept this approach. Instead, looking to dictionary definitions of biodiversity and the *FAO Glossary of Biotechnology for Food and Agriculture*, it deduced that damage to biodiversity implied damage to living organisms.[65] Thus a measure applied to prevent biodiversity damage could qualify as a measure applied to protect animal or plant life or health from risks of the kind referred to in Annex A.1(a) and (b).[66]

B. Interpretation of Phrase, 'Risks Arising From'

In terms of expanding the scope of the SPS Agreement, of potentially even greater significance was the panel's interpretation of the phrase 'risks arising from', the terminology used in three of the four Annex A.1 definitions. Once again focusing on the text, the panel noted that the phrase 'risks arising from' in the relevant definitions of Annex A.1 is 'broad and

---

[61] Ibid.
[62] Panel Report, *Biotech*, para. 7.220.
[63] Ibid, para. 7.200.
[64] Conrad, above note 55, 242–243.
[65] Panel Report, *Biotech*, para. 7.372.
[66] Ibid.

unqualified'.[67] The panel drew from the omission of qualifications support for applying the phrase to cover both actual and potential risks that arise as a result of a pest, disease, disease-carrying organism or disease-causing organism.[68] Using a similar logic, it also found that '[t]here is nothing in Annex A(1)(a) which indicates that potential risks to animal or plant life or health must necessarily be the direct or immediate result of, e.g., the spread of a pest'.[69] Hence, it held that 'measures taken to protect animal or plant life or health from risks that arise indirectly or in the longer term from pests, diseases, disease-carrying organisms or disease-causing organisms' are not excluded from the scope of the SPS Agreement.[70]

These rulings are significant in that they suggest that the SPS Agreement is not confined simply to risk situations for which there are direct and immediate links between the product at issue, and potential harms to human, animal or plant life or health associated with pests and diseases. Nonetheless, the panel's inclusion of potential indirect risks raises questions as to the nature of the required causal connection between a product restricted by a measure, and one of the risk categories listed in Annex A.1. The panel deployed the concept of a 'rational relationship' to describe the necessary degree of causal connection, but without elaborating what this concept entailed.[71] Christine Conrad suggests that 'minimal hypothetical causality' is all that the panel seemed to require to establish 'rational relationship'. This standard has not been accepted as sufficient in other contexts under the SPS Agreement,[72] for instance, in judging the types of risks that may be evaluated in risk assessment and form the basis of SPS measures.[73] Other commentators, such as Lukasz Gruszczynski, see in the use of the term 'rational' some form of limit that the causal relationship may not be too remote.[74]

Even so, on the panel's broad reading of the phrase 'risks arising from', provided a plausible (rational) chain of causation can be demonstrated or hypothesized to connect a product with a given health or environmental risk it seems a trade restrictive measure directed to mitigating that risk is

---

[67]   Panel Report, *Biotech*, para. 7.225.
[68]   Ibid.
[69]   Ibid, para. 7.226.
[70]   Ibid.
[71]   See ibid, paras 7.258, 7.265, 7.274, 7.284, 7.359, 7.389.
[72]   Conrad, above note 55, 238. See also Gruszczynski, above note 10, 54.
[73]   In *Hormones*, para. 186, the Appellate Body ruled that 'theoretical uncertainty is not the kind of risk which, under Article 5.1, is to be assessed'. Instead, to be of regulatory concern, a SPS risk must be 'an ascertainable risk': ibid.
[74]   Gruszczynski, above note 10, 59.

potentially a SPS measure. In the context of GMOs, this means that both concerns related to their potential for direct adverse effects as pests (for instance, the scenario where GMO crops escape and establish in other areas) and their possible indirect pest effects (for example, through gene transfer to other plants, leading to a reduction in genetic and species diversity) are matters appropriately treated as SPS risks.

C. Pests and Pest-related Damage

In the SPS Agreement, the term pest is undefined, other than via the qualifying footnote stating that pests include weeds.[75] The practice of international organizations concerned with sanitary and phytosanitary matters has generally been to conceive of pests in a narrow fashion. For instance, the International Plant Protection Convention (IPPC) – one of the standard-setting organizations referenced in the SPS Agreement – defines the term 'pest' as '[a]ny species, strain or biotype of plant, animal or pathogenic agent injurious to plants or plant products'.[76] In interpreting the term pest, the *Biotech* panel noted the emphasis in the IPPC definition on the need for injurious effect but ultimately preferred the construction offered by dictionary definitions. This 'ordinary meaning' approach led the panel to find that a pest connoted 'a troublesome, annoying or destructive person, animal, or thing'.[77] In light of the SPS Agreement's reference to matters of health as well as life, and the inclusion of 'other damage' from pests in Annex A.1(d), the panel went on to conclude that 'in the context of the SPS Agreement the term "pest" should be understood as referring to an animal or plant which is destructive, or causes harm to the health of other animals, plants or humans, or other harm, or a troublesome or annoying animal or plant'.[78]

This broad interpretation of the notion of pests had several consequences. Of immediate relevance for GMO regulations such as those of the EU was that a GMO plant could be treated as a pest simply by virtue of the fact that it might be troublesome or annoying by, for example, growing where it was not wanted.[79] On this interpretation, a GMO plant accidentally growing in a field of conventional or organically farmed plants is a

---

[75] SPS Agreement, Annex A, footnote 4.

[76] *International Plant Protection Convention*, New Revised Text, FAO Conference 29th session, November 1192, article II No. 1.

[77] Panel Report, *Biotech*, para. 7.238.

[78] Ibid, paras 7.239–7.240.

[79] Ibid, para. 7.244.

pest.[80] The panel also indicated that the GMO plant itself did not have to be the pest to which risk management measures were addressed.[81] Instead GMO crossbreeds, resulting from gene transfer from a GMO to a non-GMO, might be the relevant pest giving rise to risks (such as the need for increased herbicide use with consequences for human and environmental health) to which domestic risk regulations are targeted.[82] In the context of the possible allergenic effects of GMOs not consumed as food (e.g. those used as biofuels) the panel went even further, finding that a pest need not be a living organism. Consequently, harvested GMO plants might still be considered pests if they cause allergic reactions in humans handling them during harvesting, transport or processing.[83]

Augmenting this broad notion of pests were the panel's rulings on the meaning of the term 'other [pest-related] damage' in Annex A.1(d). An expansive reading of this phrase was used to support findings that the effects of pests extend to a broad range of other harms beyond impacts on agricultural plants and animals. The panel suggested that the phrase 'other damage' could extend to damage to property or infrastructure (such as water intake systems), economic damage (through lost sales), damage to non-biological components of the environment (such as soil nutrient cycles), or adverse effects on the dynamics of species in the broader, receiving environment.[84] By coupling this understanding of pests and the damage they may cause with its earlier ruling as to the inclusion of indirect effects of GMOs within the scope of the SPS Agreement, the panel was readily able to classify a wide-range of potential health and environmental effects of GMOs as SPS matters. These risks included environmental harm suffered if GMOs caused damage to biogeochemical soil cycles of nutrients such as carbon and nitrogen,[85] and damage to the environment (other than to animal or plant life) due to changes in weed control practices associated with the introduction of GMOs.[86]

D.   Coverage of Health Risks

In relation to human health risks, such as those posed by diseases or pests, or deriving from toxins, contaminants or allergens in foods, the *Biotech*

---

[80]   Ibid, para. 7.245.
[81]   Ibid, para. 7.258.
[82]   Ibid, paras 7.273, 7.274.
[83]   Ibid, para. 7.351.
[84]   Ibid, para. 7.370.
[85]   Ibid, para. 7.374.
[86]   Ibid, para. 7.378.

panel's approach was similarly broad to that taken for environmental risks, and also driven by a close analysis of the relevant text. An illustrative example of the panel's general approach is evident in its interpretation of the notion of a food 'additive'. Relying on dictionary definitions once again, the panel concluded that genes, including antibiotic resistance marker genes, 'intentionally added for a technological purpose to GM plants that are eaten or being used as an input into processed foods, can be considered "additives in foods" within the meaning of Annex A(1)(b)'.[87] This interpretation not only represents an artificial understanding of the role of introduced genes like antibiotic resistance marker genes in GMOs,[88] but also departs from relevant international practice (for instance, the term 'additives' where used in Codex Alimentarius standards is restricted to substances added during food manufacture processes).[89] Nonetheless, the panel persisted with a literal approach in its interpretation of other terms in Annex A(1)(b), such as the word 'food'. This led the panel to conclude that possible risks associated with the consumption of GMO pollen or seeds by insects, birds and wild fauna, were properly regarded as food safety risks, despite the overtly environmental nature of these concerns.[90]

In relation to the concept of 'disease', which like the term 'pest', is a central element of several of the risk situations outlined in Annex A.1, the panel again showed a preference for dictionary-based meanings, coupled with selective reliance on international standards. The EU sought to avoid the characterization of GMOs as diseases or disease-causing organisms on the basis that they are not infected or an infection, relying on the definition used by the World Organization for Animal Health.[91] The panel, however,

---

[87]   Ibid, paras 7.301 and 7.303. The panel took a similar approach to the meaning of the terms 'contaminants' (including within the scope of this term substances created or unintentionally expressed in a GMO plant) (see para. 7.314) and 'toxins' (including GMO plants that produce substances that might be poisonous for non-target organisms) (see para. 7.323).

[88]   Such genes are not so much added as integrated into the genetic material of the GMO plant. Moreover, it is not the gene itself, but rather the protein produced if the gene is expressed, that is the substance that may be linked to adverse health effects for consumers. In the case of antibiotic marker resistance genes their purpose is not to confer a specific property on the GMO but rather to allow researchers to detect whether integration of a new gene into a plant has been successful.

[89]   Panel Report, *Biotech*, para. 7.299. The Codex Alimentarius Commission is the international organization designated by the SPS Agreement as the relevant international standard-setting body in the area of food safety.

[90]   Ibid, para. 7.292.

[91]   Ibid, para. 7.276. Along with Codex and the IPPC, this organization is one of the three referenced by the SPS Agreement.

preferred the 'common definition' of disease as a 'disorder' and also referenced the work of the World Health Organization (concerned with human rather than animal or plant health), which defines a disease-carrying organism as a 'vector' and a disease-causing organism as a 'pathogen'. In the panel's view, it was not necessary to determine whether GMOs themselves might be diseases, disease-causing organisms or disease-causing organisms but simply whether their environmental release might give rise to adverse effects covered by Annex A.1. On this broad analysis, the panel saw the EU GMO scheme as seeking to 'prevent GM plants from introducing or spreading diseases, and from altering the susceptibility of animals or plants to pathogens, which might facilitate the introduction or spread of disease-causing organisms (that is, pathogens) or create new disease-carrying organisms (that is, vectors)'.[92] Accordingly, it found the EU directives governing the environmental release of GMOs to be measures applied to protect animal or plant life or health from risks arising from the entry, establishment or spread of diseases, disease-carrying organisms and disease-causing organisms.

E. Summary

In the *Biotech* case, the end result of the panel's analysis, applying its broad understanding of terms in Annex A.1 of the SPS Agreement, was that the entire EU legislative scheme relating to the environmental release of GMO crops, and a substantial portion of its regulations dealing with novel food authorizations, were found to be SPS measures.[93] That such a complex, multi-faceted risk regulatory scheme could be characterized as one directed to protecting against pest, disease and food safety risks illustrates the potential scope of the SPS Agreement where it is interpreted in a literal, de-contextualized fashion. In the field of GMO regulation, there would be few national (or indeed supranational) schemes that would not qualify as SPS-related on this analysis.[94] Moreover, the panel's interpre-

---

[92]   Ibid, para. 7.278.

[93]   The only risk concern found to be potentially outside the SPS Agreement's ambit was that referenced by the novel food regulation directing labelling to prevent the misleading of consumers. Hence, the panel found procedures for the approval of foods and food ingredients set out in Regulation 258/97 were 'in part' SPS measures. See Panel Report, *Biotech*, para. 8.4.

[94]   In fact, the EU scheme is one of the broadest existing GMO regulatory schemes and the model for many other countries introducing biotechnology regulations. For a review of different countries' regulations see Heike Baumüller, 'Domestic Import Regulations for Genetically Modified Organisms and Their

tations of the Annex A.1 definitions – particularly its extension of these provisions to measures dealing with the indirect health and environmental effects of pests, diseases and food additives – suggests the scope for more than just GMO environmental regulations to be caught by the SPS Agreement in the future.

IV. IMPLICATIONS OF EXPANDING THE SCOPE OF APPLICATION OF THE SPS AGREEMENT

If the *Biotech* panel's interpretations of the ambit of SPS measures are followed in subsequent WTO disputes they have the potential to effect a seismic shift in respect of the scope of operation of the SPS Agreement. In the area of biotechnology regulation, it would seem that few schemes are likely, on the panel's approach, to fall outside the scope of SPS review, provided they also have identified impacts on international trade, for example, by banning imports of GMOs or imposing significant regulatory costs on traders attempting to export such products to the market concerned.[95] Although the *Biotech* panel did not rule upon the 'safety' of GMOs or their 'likeness' to non-GMO products,[96] its interpretation of the SPS Agreement has ensured that in any subsequent challenge to GMO regulations, SPS disciplines will be of primary relevance. Questions over GMO safety would therefore need to be substantiated according to the scientific basis for any risk concerns and would stand or fall on the risk assessments that can be produced in support of the potential for detrimental health or environmental impacts. Given the increasingly stringent approach panels and the Appellate Body have adopted in case law construing the scientific evidence requirements of the SPS Agreement,[97] the precautionary tenor of much national and international regulation of biotechnology may make it particularly susceptible to WTO challenge.[98]

While the likely inclusion of GMO regulatory schemes within the ambit

---

Compatibility with WTO Rules' (2004) 6(3) *Asian Biotechnology and Development Review* 33.

[95]   Gruszczynski, above note 10, 56.

[96]   Panel Report, *Biotech*, para. 8.3.

[97]   Jacqueline Peel, *Science and Risk Regulation in International Law* (Cambridge University Press, Cambridge, 2010), chapter 5.

[98]   Precaution has become particularly important in the biotechnology field due to the Biosafety Protocol's operationalization of the principle in decision-making on GMO imports: see Ruth Mackenzie et al, *An Explanatory Guide to the Cartagena Protocol on Biosafety, IUCN Environmental Policy and Law Paper No. 46* (IUCN, Gland, 2003), 14.

of the SPS Agreement is an important consequence of the panel's findings in *Biotech*, this is not the only potential implication of the broad approach taken to construing the scope of SPS measures. A widening area of operation for the SPS Agreement may also have ramifications for other areas of domestic health and environmental risk regulation, as well as international environmental agreements that overlap with the trade regime. At one and the same time this could expose a broader array of national health and environmental measures to SPS, science-based disciplines, while also encouraging international disagreements over such measures to be preferentially discussed and determined in fora of the WTO rather than under the auspices of multilateral environmental institutions and treaties.

A.   Extending the SPS Agreement to Domestic Environmental Regulations

Beyond the GMO context, the panel's interpretations of the SPS Agreement's Annex A.1 definitions in *Biotech* suggest the potential for other domestic health and environmental laws to become subject to SPS scrutiny and challenge in the future. The panel seemed alert to this problem early in its discussion of the scope of Annex A.1, noting:

> a measure to reduce air pollution may be applied to protect the life or health of plants (to the extent that high levels of air pollution could result in certain plant species lacking sufficient sunlight for them to exist and survive), and hence to protect the environment, but it would nonetheless not be a measure applied for one of the purposes enumerated in Annex A(1) of the *SPS Agreement* (in that the measure would not be applied to protect plant life or health from risks arising from the entry, establishment or spread of pests, diseases, disease-carrying organisms or disease-causing organisms, or to prevent other damage from the entry, establishment or spread of pests).[99]

However, this caution was undercut by the panel's later broad interpretations of concepts such as pests and diseases, and the loose designation of required causal relationship between a product and a particular risk in order for risk management measures to fall within the ambit of Annex A.1. Consequently, if an environmental protection purpose, *per se*, is no longer a bar to SPS scrutiny and indirect or long-term risks may be covered, then it is possible to foresee application of the SPS Agreement to a range of environmental risk regulatory measures. For instance, controls on imported products are often put in place to protect against the introduction of species that are likely to become invasive in a country's

---

[99]   *Biotech*, para. 7.210.

environment, threatening biodiversity by out-competing native species.[100] Conceivably there is also scope to take the *Biotech* panel's analysis further if it is accepted that 'measures taken to protect animal or plant life or health from risks that arise indirectly or in the longer-term from pests, diseases, disease-carrying or disease-causing organisms' fall within the ambit of the SPS Agreement.[101] For example, regulations designed to protect bio-diverse marine ecosystems from the adverse effects of pesticide run-off might become, on this analysis, a measure arising indirectly from the introduction of a pest through trade.

If the analytical trends intimated in the panel's *Biotech* rulings are pursued it would take the SPS Agreement into an entirely new territory of health and environmental risk management. The concern here is that this is quite a different field from the Agreement's traditional subject matter of quarantine or food safety risk, and moreover, one where regulatory approaches of a very different hue conventionally apply. In the last few decades, uncertainties regarding the nature and extent of impacts, especially over the longer term, have become a core concern of health and environmental risk regulation in many countries, reflected in the widespread adoption of structures for precautionary action and harm prevention.[102] A capacity for regulators to act in advance of conclusive scientific evidence demonstrating environmental damage is a feature of regulatory systems in place even in those countries that do not subscribe to international notions of the precautionary principle.[103] In addition, contemporary health and environmental regulatory systems in industrialized

---

[100] Sophie Riley, 'Invasive Alien Species and the Protection of Biodiversity: The Role of Quarantine Laws in Resolving Inadequacies in the International Legal Regime' (2005) 17(3) *Journal of Environmental Law* 323.

[101] Panel Report, *Biotech*, para. 7.226.

[102] Elizabeth Fisher, Judith Jones and René von Schomberg (eds), *Implementing the Precautionary Principle* (Edward Elgar, Cheltenham, 2006). See also, Elizabeth Fisher and Ronnie Harding, 'The Precautionary Principle in Australia: From Aspiration to Practice?' in Timothy O'Riordan, James Cameron and Andrew Jordan (eds), *Reinterpreting the Precautionary Principle* (Cameron May, London, 2001) 215; Juli Abouchar, 'The Precautionary Principle in Canada: The First Decade' (2002) 32(2) *Environmental Law Reporter* 11407; Nicolas de Sadeleer, 'The Precautionary Principle in EC Health and Environmental Law' (2006) 12(2) *European Law Journal* 139.

[103] For example, the US, which denies the status of precaution as a principle of general international law, has long allowed precautionary regulatory action under its federal health and environmental legislation: see Jonathon B. Weiner, 'Whose Precaution After All? A Comment on the Comparison and Evolution of Risk Regulatory Systems' (2003) 13 *Duke Journal of Comparative and International Law* 207.

democracies tend to base risk decision-making on broad foundations, which extend beyond science and expert inputs to encompass public participation.[104] Conventional tools of impact assessment in the environmental field are thus not generally limited to science-based risk assessment, but seek to gather wide-ranging, contextualized information on the environmental effects of an activity and any associated socio-economic implications. However, when measured against a SPS benchmark – and particularly the Agreement's requirements for the scientific justification of measures and supporting risk assessments – environmental regulatory measures may be found wanting. Further, the more constrained notions of precaution developed under the SPS Agreement may need to be applied such that the insufficiency of scientific evidence for expert risk assessment becomes the focus, rather than areas of ignorance, problems of indeterminacy or indications of community concern over risk.[105]

At this point, the objection might be raised that the scope of the SPS Agreement is not only determined by a capacity to characterize the concerns addressed by a measure as SPS risks, but also by whether measures are ones which may, directly or indirectly, affect international trade.[106] Are domestic health and environmental regulations, targeted to biodiversity or chemical pollution risks, ones that could be said to affect, directly or indirectly, international trade? At a theoretical level this is certainly possible, especially given the degree of global economic integration brought about by the success of the trade liberalization project to date, and the pressures of global competition that may make even incidental trade effects significant. As David Driesen remarks, 'in a globally integrated world, most regulations . . . might be described as non-tariff trade barriers, since they burden commercial activity, much of which is international'.[107] Nevertheless, at the level of disputes coming before the WTO dispute settlement system it is generally the case that the trade impacts at issue must be substantial enough to attract the concern of groups of exporters with sufficient political clout to lobby their respective governments to initiate

---

[104]   Steve Rayner, 'Democracy in the Age of Assessment: Reflections on the Roles of Expertise and Democracy in Public-Sector Decision Making' (2003) 30(3) *Science and Public Policy* 163.

[105]   For a discussion of such broader sources of uncertainty in risk assessment see Brian Wynne, 'Science and Social Responsibility' in Jake Ansell and Frank Wharton (eds), *Risk: Analysis, Assessment and Management* (John Wiley & Sons Ltd, Chichester, 1992) 137, 141–142.

[106]   SPS Agreement, article 1.1.

[107]   David Driesen, 'What is Free Trade?: The Real Issue Lurking Behind the Trade and Environment Debate' (2001) 41 *Virginia Journal of International Law* 279, 283.

WTO challenges.[108] As Lukasz Gruszczynski points out, the practice of the SPS committee also indicates that SPS notifications generally 'relate to classic SPS risks' rather than 'environmental measures that are only loosely connected with an SPS element'.[109]

A diminished likelihood of WTO disputes under the SPS Agreement being brought in respect of health or environmental regulations that incidentally impact trade is not necessarily the end of the matter. As the *Biotech* case shows, a wider definition of the scope of SPS measures allows the broader elements of domestic regulatory schemes to be targeted in a SPS dispute (which may displace an analysis under the TBT Agreement or GATT); for instance, not just approval processes addressed to the potential for GMO products to act as environmental pests, but also the flow-on effects for natural ecosystems, waterways and so on. In addition, even if not subject to an international trade challenge, the knowledge that environmental regulations could be called to account under the SPS disciplines has the potential to exercise a dampening effect on national regulatory practices considering the introduction, extension or revision of such measures. The review of regulations for their international legal compatibility and trade impacts prior to introduction is a feature of due diligence processes adopted by governments in a globalized regulatory environment.[110] If environmental regulations are treated as SPS measures they would also be subject to the inter-governmental transparency require-ments imposed by the SPS Agreement.[111] Indeed, some governments may see the potential for SPS scrutiny as a bargaining chip in domestic debates over the adoption of science-based versus more precautionary or partici-patory regulatory structures, providing a justification for the extension of processes of scientific justification and risk assessment beyond quarantine and food safety to the broader environmental arena. One further possibil-ity suggested by the *Biotech* panel's expansive definition of SPS measures is that it may strengthen arguments that different categories of environ-mental risks – some quarantine-focused, some biodiversity-focused – are

---

[108] Unlike some regimes for the protection of investors' rights, the WTO dispute settlement system remains one restricted to inter-governmental disputes: see *Marrakesh Agreement Establishing the World Trade Organization*, opened for signature 15 April 1994, 1867 UNTS 3 (entered into force 1 January 1995), annex 2 (*Understanding on Rules and Procedures Governing the Settlement of Disputes*) 1869 UNTS 401.

[109] Gruszczynski, above note 10, 60.

[110] See, e.g., Office of Best Practice Regulation, *Best Practice Regulation Handbook* (Commonwealth of Australia, Canberra, 2010).

[111] SPS Agreement, article 7 and Annex B.

in fact comparable risks of the kind dealt with by article 5.5 of the SPS Agreement. Pursuant to this provision, WTO members, in the interests of regulatory consistency, are to avoid determining different levels of acceptable risk applicable in different risk management situations where this could result in discrimination or a disguised restriction on international trade. By this means, acceptable risk levels determined according to SPS requirements for quarantine risks might also become a benchmark for regulation of other health and environmental risks.[112]

B.   Facilitating Fragmentation of Trade and Environmental Regimes

The implications of a broad ambit of operation for the SPS Agreement potentially extend to effects on international environmental regimes as well as domestic ones. At the global level, environmental risk concerns are increasingly difficult to separate from trade concerns, both because of the growing use of trade measures as a compliance tool in MEAs, and as a result of the amplification of WTO rules regarding non-tariff trade barriers stemming from domestic health or environmental measures.[113] Hence, there now exists significant potential for conflict to arise between the requirements of the WTO regime and those of MEAs. In respect of the GATT (and most likely also the TBT Agreement), concerns over possible conflicts with environmental treaties eased after the WTO Appellate Body's decision in the *Shrimp/Turtle* case, which contained a strong suggestion that trade-restrictive, multilaterally-endorsed environmental measures are unlikely to be found WTO-incompatible if challenged.[114] However, the relationship between the SPS Agreement and MEAs with which it may overlap remains unclear, especially as the Appellate Body has declared that the precautionary principle cannot be relied upon to exempt WTO members from their obligations under the SPS Agreement.[115] Expansion in the sphere of operation of the SPS Agreement thus has the potential to increase competition between the Agreement and relevant

---

[112]   On the problems of comparing different kinds of SPS risks see Jeffery Atik, 'The Weakest Link: Demonstrating the Inconsistency of "Appropriate Levels of Protection" in *Australia – Salmon*' (2004) 24(2) *Risk Analysis* 483.

[113]   Daniel Esty, 'Economic Integration and Environmental Protection' in Regina Axelrod, Stacy Vandeveer and David Downie (eds), *The Global Environment: Institutions, Law, and Policy* (3rd ed, CQ Press, Washington DC, 2011), 155.

[114]   John H. Knox, 'The Judicial Resolution of Conflicts between Trade and the Environment' (2004) 28 *Harvard Environmental Law Review* 1.

[115]   *Hormones*, para. 124.

MEAs, and also to exercise a 'chilling effect' over negotiations for new MEAs or supplementary protocols that might overlap with the (extended) ambit of the SPS Agreement.[116]

Regime competition of this kind can be conceptualized as part of the broader phenomenon of fragmentation in international law.[117] The fear is that such competition will facilitate the development of self-contained regimes, attendant only to their own internal concerns and lacking regard for the broader coherence of international law.[118] In a study undertaken under the auspices of the International Law Commission (ILC), it was argued that treaty interpretation rules provide a 'professional toolbox' for managing global legal fragmentation by requiring decision-makers considering claims under one treaty regime to situate those claims in the wider 'normative environment' of international law.[119] In its report, the ILC study group criticized the *Biotech* panel decision for rejecting the relevance of other treaties, such as the Biosafety Protocol, to the interpretation of provisions of the SPS Agreement. The panel found that it would only be obliged to take into account non-WTO law in interpretation where the rules of international law concerned were ones 'applicable in the relations between the WTO Members', by which it meant *all* WTO members and not just those members party to the dispute.[120] The result of the *Biotech* panel's approach, according to the ILC study group, 'would be the isolation of multilateral agreements as "islands" permitting no references *inter se* in their application', something which it believed to be 'contrary to the legislative ethos behind most of multilateral treaty-making and, presumably, with the intent of treaty-makers'.[121]

Yet even if decision-makers in the WTO regime can be persuaded to adopt principles of 'systemic integration' in their consideration and application of the SPS Agreement,[122] this is unlikely to head off all conflicts between the

---

[116]   Robyn Eckersley, 'The Big Chill: The WTO and Multilateral Environmental Agreements' (2004) 4(2) *Global Environmental Politics* 24.

[117]   Martti Koskenniemi, *Global Legal Pluralism: Multiple Regimes and Multiple Modes of Thought* (Erik Castrén Institute of International Law and Human Rights, University of Helsinki, 2005), 6–7.

[118]   Joost Pauwelyn, 'Bridging Fragmentation and Unity: International Law as a Universe of Inter-connected Islands' (2004) 25 *Michigan J. Int'l Law* 903.

[119]   Martti Koskenniemi, 'Fragmentation of International Law: Difficulties Arising from the Diversification and Expansion of International Law' (A/CN.4/L.682, International Law Commission, 2006).

[120]   Panel Report, *EC – Biotech*, para. 7.68.

[121]   Koskenniemi, n 119 above, 200.

[122]   Such principles are derived particularly from article 31(3)(c) of the *Vienna Convention on the Law of Treaties*, opened for signature 23 May 1969, 1155 UNTS

Agreement and overlapping MEAs. For instance, parties to a particular dispute decided under the SPS Agreement might not all be parties to a competing MEA (as was the case for the Biosafety Protocol in the *Biotech* dispute).[123] Indeed, the WTO Member that has aggressively pursued claims under the SPS Agreement – the US – stands outside a number of major MEAs that address SPS risk-type concerns (a category of agreements that only expands if a broader understanding of the scope of SPS measures is adopted).[124] Further, even where countries have obligations under both trade and environmental regimes, these regimes do not exist on an equal footing in international law. As Robyn Eckersley has observed, compared with the global trade regime, most MEAs 'provide a more fragmented form of governance that lacks the coherence, reach, financial backing and organizational structure of the WTO'.[125] When the compulsory jurisdiction of the WTO dispute settlement system (a feature lacking in the vast majority of MEAs)[126] is added to the mix, powerful incentives are created for disputed health or environmental regulations to be preferentially raised within the institutional structures of the trade regime. These incentives are only enhanced where complainants have a greater opportunity to frame their claims as ones about SPS measures, so attracting the application of the more stringent requirements of the SPS Agreement.

V.   CONCLUSION

While the nature of SPS measures covered by the WTO SPS Agreement is only one small aspect of the very lengthy rulings of the panel in the *Biotech*

---

332 (entered into force 27 January 1980). In the 'Conclusions of the work of the Study Group on the Fragmentation of International Law: Difficulties arising from the Diversification and Expansion of International Law', adopted by the ILC at its 58th session in 2006 (A/61/10, para. 251), article 31(3)(c) of the Vienna Convention was described as giving 'expression to the objective of "systemic integration" according to which, whatever their subject matter, treaties are a creation of the international legal system and their operation is predicated upon that fact' (para. 17). For an explanation of the role of 'systemic integration' in combating international legal fragmentation see Campbell McLachlan, 'The Principle of Systemic Integration and Article 31(3)(c) of the Vienna Convention' (2005) 54 *Int'l Comp. L.Q.* 279.

[123]   Of the parties to the *Biotech* dispute, only the EU is a party to the Biosafety Protocol, although both Argentina and Canada are signatories.

[124]   Eckersley, above n 116, 38–39.

[125]   Ibid, 24.

[126]   Ibid, 36.

case, they are findings which have the potential to leave a significant imprint on health and environmental regulation, both at the domestic and international level. Given the EU's failure to appeal the panel's findings it remains uncertain whether the broad interpretative approach adopted in *Biotech* will be followed in subsequent cases. Faced with controversial issues surrounding interpretation of provisions of the SPS Agreement in the past, the Appellate Body has displayed considerable 'political astuteness',[127] which might see some of the broader aspects of the *Biotech* panel's findings regarding the scope of SPS measures overturned or toned down. Lukasz Gruszczynski for one is confident that the Appellate Body would approach any evaluation of general environmental risk regulations under the SPS Agreement with great care.[128] Nonetheless, the panel's interpretations of the definitions in Annex A.1 of the SPS Agreement – based as they are on adherence to the literal, dictionary-based meaning of terms construed without reference to the wider socio-political context – is not such a radical departure from interpretative practices adopted by the Appellate Body itself, including in other SPS disputes.

In some ways, the notions of SPS risk developed by the panel in *Biotech* could be said to be quite progressive in that there is an increasing trend in the field of health and environmental regulation to consider risk pathways in a holistic fashion, embracing both the direct and indirect impacts of activities. However, applying such broad approach to the risks covered by the SPS Agreement has the potential not only to upset conventional understandings regarding its scope of operation, but also to expose precautionary environmental regulations to the stricter standards of science-based SPS scrutiny. Actual WTO challenges may be reserved for those measures that have the most severe adverse effects on international trade. Yet, even potential SPS coverage of environmental regulations with incidental trade impacts may be enough to discourage use (or expansion) of precautionary regulatory methods in some areas of environmental concern, or to shift issues from discussion and consideration in MEA fora to trade-related ones.

Of course, it may also be that the panel's broad interpretation of the scope of the SPS Agreement in *Biotech* is a symptom, not a cause, of greater emphasis being placed upon the need for firm scientific underpinnings to health and environmental regulation. It was, after all, the EU

---

[127] Victor, above note 17, 936.

[128] Gruszczynski, above note 10, 60. On this basis he suggests that GMO risks may be 'just a special case rather than the first step in the expansive development of the SPS disciplines'.

through its regulatory scheme that constructed GMO concerns primarily as a matter of health and environmental risk, susceptible to objective scientific analysis and risk assessment. This way of framing debates over issues of health and environmental concern is consistent with efforts by western governments more generally to represent technological disputes as issues solely of scientifically assessed risk, rather than recognizing broader questions and concerns.[129] The latter – voiced in different contexts by non-governmental organizations, developing countries and the public – often emphasize the social, economic and ethical dimensions of technological risk, yet are frequently marginalized in regulatory systems that privilege matters of scientific fact over questions of value.[130] Ironically, the panel's decision in *Biotech* may serve to increase the prominence of such alternative discourses on GMO and other health and environmental risks by reason of the fact that they are less able to be subsumed within a wide-ranging, textually focused reading of the WTO SPS Agreement.[131]

---

[129]   Peter Andrée, 'The Cartagena Protocol on Biosafety and Shifts in the Discourse of Precaution' (2005) 5(4) *Global Environmental Politics* 25.

[130]   Les Levidow and Susan Carr, 'How Biotechnology Regulation Sets a Risk/Ethics Boundary' (1997) 14 *Agriculture and Human Values* 29; Aarti Gupta, 'Advanced Informed Agreement: A Shared Basis for Governing Trade in Genetically Modified Organisms' (2001) 9 *Indiana Journal of Global Legal Studies* 265.

[131]   In this respect it is interesting to note recent developments in the EU with regard to its GMO legislation, which contemplate a capacity for Member states to 'opt-out' of GMO cultivation on the basis of grounds other than those covered by EU-level health and environmental risk assessments (e.g. ethical or moral concerns, concerns over the impact of GMOs on conventional or organic agricultural practices). See European Commission, Proposal for a Regulation of the European Parliament and of the Council amending Directive 2001/18/EC as regards the possibility for the Member States to restrict or prohibit the cultivation of GMOs in their territory, COM(2010) 375 final, 13/7/2010.

12. GATS and public health care: reflecting on an uneasy relationship
Panagiotis Delimatsis

I. INTRODUCTION

The foremost objective of the World Trade Organization (WTO) is to liberalize trade through the application of the non-discrimination principle and the implementation of the results of typically multi-year negotiations on a request-and-offer basis. The underlying economic theory of this basically negative integration contract suggests that positive welfare effects for the countries liberalising their trade regime will be generated in the long run, even if such liberalisation occurs unilaterally. However, a multilateral accord allows countries to solve various problems, most notably terms-of-trade externalities.[1] Most of the economic theories justifying trade liberalisation also apply to services.[2] Once considered as non-tradable, services nowadays dominate economic activity in virtually all countries of the world irrespective of their level of development. Thus, market access in foreign services markets becomes quintessential for the expansion strategy of every export-oriented company. This applies with equal force to companies active in the production of goods, as services can be essential inputs for various goods.[3] Therefore, it comes as no surprise that the Uruguay Round single undertaking not only included trade in goods, but also trade in services, as the absence of such rules at the multilateral level would leave unregulated a big part of economic activity.[4]

---

[1] Kyle Bagwell and Robert Staiger, *The Economics of the World Trading System* (Cambridge, MA: MIT Press, 2002).

[2] Brian Hindley and Alasdair Smith, 'Comparative advantage and trade in services', 7(1) *The World Economy* (1984), 369; also Alan Deardorff, 'Comparative advantage and international trade and investment in services' in Robert Stern (ed.), *Trade and Investment in Services: Canada/U.S. Perspectives* (Ontario Economic Council, Toronto), pp. 39–71.

[3] Alan Deardorff, 'International Provision of Trade Services, Trade and Fragmentation', Research Seminar in International Economics, Discussion Paper No 463, 2000.

[4] Panagiotis Delimatsis, *International Trade in Services and Domestic Regulation – Necessity, Transparency, and Regulatory Diversity* (Oxford: Oxford

The General Agreement on Trade in Services (GATS) is the first multi-lateral agreement setting rules for the international provision of services. The scope of the GATS is potentially unlimited, as it covers any possible measure, taken by governments, public authorities at all levels of government or by non-governmental bodies with delegated regulatory powers, which may affect trade in services.[5] According to the Appellate Body, this wording implies a broad scope of application.[6] While its scope is broader than that of the General Agreement on Tariffs and Trade (GATT), the legal framework of the agreement is vested with considerable flexibility. This is made possible also due to the four modes of supplying services: cross-border supply (Mode 1, where only the service moves); consumption abroad (Mode 2, where only the service recipient moves); commercial presence and temporary movement of natural persons (Modes 3 and 4, where only the service supplier moves – in the second case only temporarily). As to the relative importance of modes of supply, over 50 per cent of services trade is conducted through Mode 3, that is, commercial presence.[7]

Interestingly, only few general obligations appear in the GATS. Even the utmost principle and cornerstone of the multilateral trade regime, non-discrimination, is not general, but WTO Members can set qualifications, limitations or even total bans in a WTO-consistent manner. More specifically, in the case of most-favoured nation (MFN), WTO Members could inscribe MFN exceptions in a negative list at the end of the Uruguay Round or upon accession.[8] As to national treatment, it does not apply to any WTO Member unless it decides to open a given services sector. Just to add to this flexibility, Members may decide to open only certain modes of supply within a given sector. For instance, they may liberalize supply of professional services in a remote manner, but still preserve a protectionist policy with regard to the establishment of commercial presence in the domestic market. In addition, in certain sectors, physical proximity

---

University Press, 2007). See also Juan Marchetti and Petros Mavroidis, 'The Genesis of the GATS (General Agreement on Trade in Services)', 22(3) *European Journal of International Law* (2011), 689.

[5]   Art. I GATS.

[6]   Appellate Body Report, *European Communities – Regime for the Importation, Sale and Distribution of Bananas (EC – Bananas III)*, WT/DS27/AB/R, adopted 25 September 1997, DSR 1997:II, 591, para. 220.

[7]   Joscelyn Magdeleine and Andreas Maurer, 'Measuring GATS Mode 4 Trade Flows', WTO Staff Working Paper ERSD-2008-05, October 2008.

[8]   That is, other than these exceptions, WTO Members cannot apply any other exception to the MFN principle. These exceptions are subject to multilateral review and in theory should have lasted no more than ten years – but, in fact, they did.

between supplier and consumer is more important than others. This is notably the case with education and health services. Similar limitations apply to the principle of transparency. For instance, only certain agreements and measures must be notified to the WTO or are subject to objective and reasonable administration or domestic regulation in general.[9]

Thus, WTO Members can, in theory at least, tailor their obligations based on their country-specific needs and capacities. In other words, the GATS applies differently to each WTO Member, depending on the individual commitments undertaken in that Member's Schedule of Commitments. This means that, in theory at least, WTO Members have a wide margin of discretion as to the substantive (which sector?) and temporal (when?) aspects of their liberalizing actions. However, rolling back from liberalization levels reflected in a Member's schedule is subject to compensation pursuant to Article XXI GATS.[10]

The objective of this chapter is to map the controversial interaction of the GATS with public healthcare. The health sector is at the core of those services sectors where governments intervene heavily to pursue legitimate non-economic objectives in the public interest. Arguably, certain activities within the health sector could even be regarded as non-market services, i.e. services which do not constitute a tradable commodity.[11] After discussing various concerns that followed the adoption of the GATS and its admittedly limited impact on global trade in health services, the outdated character of the current GATS classification systems is analyzed. Section IV reviews the relevant legal framework relating to healthcare services and various definitional issues which aim to delimit the scope of the study. The GATS exception of services supplied in the exercise of governmental authority is at the heart of Section V, whereas Section VI focuses on the relevance of the GATS general exceptions provision for our discussion. Section VII concludes.

---

[9]   See Panagiotis Delimatsis, 'Article III GATS (Transparency)', in Rüdiger Wolfrum, Peter-Tobias Stoll and Clemens Feinäugle (eds), *WTO – Trade in Services, Max-Planck Commentaries on World Trade Law* (Leiden: Martinus Nijhoff, 2008).

[10]   In the EU, the CJEU equally held that, once granted, openness is difficult to reverse. See C-141/07, *Commission v Germany* [2008] ECR I-6935, para. 41.

[11]   Cf European Commission, 'Green Paper on Services of General Interest', COM(2003) 270 final. Also Markus Krajewski, 'Commodifying and Embedding Services of General Interest in Transnational Contexts – the Example of Healthcare Liberalization in the EU and the WTO' in Christian Joerges and Josef Falke (eds), *Karl Polanyi – Globalization and the Potential of Law in Transnational Markets* (Oxford: Hart Publishing, 2011).

II.   THE LION SLEEPS TONIGHT: THE LIMITED IMPACT OF THE GATS ON HEALTHCARE SERVICES

Services are positively interrelated with economic growth. This concerns not only bottleneck services such as financial, telecommunications or transport, but also other services such as business services. Education and health services are no exception to this, as they are key inputs and determinants of the stock and growth of human capital.[12] In turn, human capital can be or become a key factor for acquiring comparative advantage. Thus, carefully planned regulatory intervention can divert the necessary resources and efforts towards the empowerment of key inputs through education or healthcare infrastructure. When competition and regulation are managed adequately, trade openness will most likely bolster domestic growth. In that case, institutions play a crucial role, just as institutional adjustment does.

The advent of the GATS was regarded by many as a hostile attempt by the multilateral trading system to put in jeopardy the quality of public health systems and the sovereign ability of WTO Members to continue supplying socially important services such as health or education services in a satisfactory manner. In developed countries, the fear was that the GATS, by bringing about more liberalization and fostering competition in the field of healthcare, will alter for the worse the public nature of health services and increase the costs of preventive and curative treatments particularly through the entry of for-profit companies, thereby menacing social cohesion and solidarity.[13] In part, privatization of public services including health and education but mostly telecommunications or postal services did occur, but not due to the GATS. In the European Union (EU) and the US, the privatization wave in network and communication industries started way before the conclusion of the GATS with a view to reaping the benefits of the respective internal markets.[14] In addition, sophisticated legal frameworks on competition law, e.g. on restrictive arrangements and

---

[12]   See Bernard Hoekman and Aaditya Mattoo, 'Services Trade and Growth' in Juan Marchetti and Martin Roy (eds), *Opening Markets for Trade in Services – Countries and Sectors in Bilateral and WTO Negotiations* (Cambridge: Cambridge University Press, 2008), at 23.

[13]   Cf. Markus Krajewski, 'Public Services and Trade Liberalization : Mapping the Legal Framework', 6(2) *Journal of International Economic Law* (2003), 341.

[14]   Cf. Leigh Hancher and Wolf Sauter, 'One Step Beyond? From *Sodemare* to *DocMorris*: The EU's Freedom of Establishment Case Law Concerning Healthcare', 47 *Common Market Law Review* (2010), 117–146.

abuse of dominance as well as rules on subsidization, contributed to this trend.

For developing countries, the fear was that trade in healthcare services may result in an increase of the existing divide between developed and developing countries as far as the quality of healthcare services is concerned, as it would incentivize profit-seeking healthcare service suppliers to seek access to the more profitable, developed-country markets, thereby deteriorating conditions of health in the developing world and in underserved regions. With respect to the protection of public health in particular, it was suggested that the nature of the GATS is dubious at best and therefore unsuited to promote the development of the health sector globally in the interest of developing countries.[15]

Arguably, the GATS has not been the cause, but rather the *result* of the erosion of the public service *ethos* and ensuing transformations in previously non-marketable services. Such technological, social and political transformations at the domestic level led to the increasing introduction of market values into various public services. The GATS is only the outcome of the desire of various trading powers to multilateralize – and build on – such transformations.

However, such aspirations would materialize only to a certain extent. To start with, WTO Members were unwilling at the end of the Uruguay Round even to lock in the *actual* liberalization levels at the time. This reluctance remains in the current services negotiations, at least with respect to health-related services. In the absence of determined lobbying by health service exporters, the role of the GATS in shaping the current state of health services globally appears to be limited. Thus, concerns for GATS-driven uncontrolled deregulation have rather proven to be unsubstantiated. To date, there is no empirical study attributing to the GATS a key role in major developments in the sector.[16] Rather, the GATS has largely remained outside such an equation.

The current level of liberalization is admittedly low. Major limitations include the non-portability of insurance entitlements;[17] restrictions on

---

[15]   See David Woodward, 'The GATS and trade in health services: implications for health care in developing countries', 12(3) *Review of International Political Economy* (2005), 511.

[16]   Cf WHO and WTO, *WTO Agreements and Public Health – A Joint Study by the WHO and the WTO Secretariat* (Geneva: WTO, 2002), 118.

[17]   Non-portability of insurance schemes under Modes 1 and 2 was identified as one possible restriction to be eliminated. See WTO, Council for Trade in Services (Special Session), 'Report by the Chairman to the Trade Negotiations Committee', TN/S/23, 28 November 2005, p. 18.

commercial establishment of foreign healthcare suppliers, which may even be subject to a discretionary economic needs test,[18] and the absence of any meaningful liberalization regarding mobility of healthcare professionals (e.g. quotas). Additionally, the current round of services negotiations within the framework of the Doha Round does not provide evidence of any attempt on the part of any country to actively advocate more liberalization in the field through aggressive requests or conditional offers. With the exception of health tourism where developing countries are actively seeking increased market share and becoming competitive exporters, both developed and developing countries are rather focused on getting market access in other sectors. Meanwhile, rising incomes and improved information constitute independent variables that enhance mobility of patients. Aware of the impossibility to take control of such movements, Members have adopted a rather liberal policy with regard to Mode 2. As a result, the highest incidence of full bindings (that is, no limitation or 'None' in the Schedule) is to be found in health and social services as well as tourism services.[19]

Attribution of competences and political structures at the domestic level also play a role in the rather mediocre negotiating situation, as the multilateral agenda is mainly determined upon the mandate from the capitals that the negotiators receive. At least for the EU, health policy largely remains a competence for the EU Member States (MS),[20] with social security systems being regulated at the domestic level.[21] After intensive debates, the health sector was excluded from the scope of the notorious Services Directive.[22] Even in MS where a market-based over a solidarity-based provision of health services is preferred, MS retain a considerable scope for manoeuvre, whereas the Court of Justice of the EU (CJEU) will not be as intrusive as in other areas, taking into account the special charac-

---

[18]   Some Members also added criteria for meeting those economic needs such as population density, age structure, or the number of existing facilities.

[19]   WTO, Council for Trade in Services, 'Cross-Border Supply (Modes 1 & 2)', Background Note by the Secretariat, S/C/W/304, 18 September 2009, at 11.

[20]   C-70/95, *Sodemare* [1997] ECR I-3395, para. 27.

[21]   See C-171/07 and 172/07, *Apothekerkammer des Saarlandes and others* [2009] ECR I-4171, para. 19. Article 35 of the Charter of Fundamental Rights of the EU provides that: 'Everyone has the right of access to preventive health care and the right to benefit from medical treatment under the conditions established by national laws and practices. A high level of human health protection shall be ensured in the definition and implementation of all the Union's policies and activities.'

[22]   Directive 2006/123/EC on services in the internal market [2006] OJ L 376/36, Art. 2(f).

ter of these services and the fact that even private companies, when active in this sector, also fulfil a public service or, in any case, their operation in this sector is coupled with strict obligations from the side of the State.[23] Having said this, the Court will be more intrusive when patient rights and mobility within the internal market is at stake. The relevant case-law is now codified in the Patients' Rights Directive.[24]

III.   HEALTH SERVICES IN THE GATS: THE OUTDATED CLASSIFICATION SYSTEM

In the current negotiations, healthcare services are not at the epicentre of the debates. In fact, the health sector is the only major sector in which Members abstained from tabling negotiating proposals or collective request. Nevertheless, one should expect that the rapid growth of the sector will lead to increased lobbying for further openness in the near future. The growth of the sector is mainly due to technological advances, which allowed for e-commerce and telemedicine to flourish. E-health increasingly becomes a trend and it mainly encompasses telemedicine and e-commerce, but also education and training of health professionals through remote means. In addition, e-business in health includes dissemination of practices used and IT for health management and health systems, use and storage of data. Government procurement in particular can benefit from such developments.[25] In addition, easier travel and more relaxed entry regulations at the border have led to higher mobility for patients and health professionals alike, whereas globalization of capital movements has brought about change of ownership and management

---

[23]   See, for instance, C-475/99, *Ambulanz Glöckner* [2001] ECR 2001 I-8089. However, in *Commission v Greece*, the CJEU suggested that restrictions to the public services market shall be justified only for those posts 'which actually involve direct or indirect participation in the exercise of powers conferred by public law and duties designed to safeguard the general interest of the State or other public authorities.' C-290/94, *Commission v Greece* [1996] ECR I-3285.

[24]   Directive 2011/24/EU on the application of patients' rights in cross-border healthcare [2011]OJ L 88/45. Also Wolf Sauter, 'Harmonization in Healthcare: The EU Patients' Rights Directive', TILEC Discussion Paper 2011-030, June 2011.

[25]   See Chantal Blouin, Jens Gobrecht, Jane Lethbridge, Didar Singh, Richard Smith and David Warner, 'Trade in Health Services under the Four Modes of Supply: Review of Current Trends and Policy Issues', in Chantal Blouin, Nick Drager, and Richard Smith (eds), *International Trade in Health Services and the GATS – Current Issues and Debates* (Washington, DC: The World Bank, 2006).

of healthcare facilities.[26] In 2008, the world medical tourism market was estimated to account for about US$60 billion, with estimates that over six million US citizens will soon be seeking medical treatment abroad.[27]

To properly delineate the services at issue, the essential starting point is the Services Sectoral Classification List, which is the Harmonized System counterpart for services.[28] In this List, health-related services are dispersed among various sectors, including business services, financial services, and health-related and social services. The sector entitled 'Health and social services' includes hospital services (that is, health services delivered under the supervision of doctors), other health services (i.e. ambulance services and residential health facilities), social services and 'other' health and social services. Medical and dental services, veterinary services and the services provided by nurses or midwives constitute a sub-category of 'professional services'. This distinction is based on whether the relevant services are associated with a given type of institutional nursing. For instance, medical or dental services are regarded as professional services because they are supplied by out-patient clinics. The above distinction does not apply to veterinary services, which are considered as professional services even if they are supplied in hospitals.[29]

In general, there is no overall coherent classification as far as the health sector is concerned – and this of course undermines the effectiveness of any commitments undertaken and any possible complementarities between them.[30] No cluster approach has ever been adopted when scheduling such commitments, the result being that commitments may be incoherent or undertaken in a fragmented way, as the overwhelming majority of WTO Members followed the WTO Sectoral Classification

---

[26]   See Richard Smith, Chantal Blouin, Nick Drager and David P. Fidler, 'Trade in Health Services and the GATS', in Aaditya Mattoo, Robert M. Stern, and Gianni Zanini (eds), *A Handbook of International Trade in Services* (Oxford: Oxford University Press, 2008), 437.

[27]   Deloitte, 'Medical Tourism : Consumers in Search of Value', Deloitte Center for Health Solutions, 2008.

[28]   GATT, 'Services Sectoral Classification List' MTN.GNS/W/120, 10 July 1991. The List is based on the United Nations' Provisional Central Product Classification (CPC), Statistical Papers, Series M No 77, United Nations, 1991. The CPC has been subsequently revised, but the W/120 remained unchanged.

[29]   WTO, Council for Trade in Services, 'Health and Social Services', Background Note by the Secretariat, S/C/W/50, 18 September 1998, p. 20.

[30]   Cf. David Luff, 'Regulation of Health Services and International Trade Law', in Aaditya Mattoo and Pierre Sauvé (eds), *Domestic Regulation and Service Trade Liberalization* (Washington, DC: World Bank/Oxford University Press, 2003), 191.

List to schedule their commitments.[31] More often than not, schedules depict no coherence, thereby deterring potentially interested parties in the supply of such services. For instance, a given Member may decide to liberalize health insurance, while keeping full control of trade – and thus market access – in healthcare services. The outdated classification adopted in the W/120 more than 20 years ago contrasts sharply the current level of development of the sector. In addition, the fact that all disputes relating to services before the WTO adjudicating bodies related to the interpretation of Schedules points to problematic features of the current classification model under the GATS.

The problematic classification of health services as identified in the GATS still cannot explain the admittedly low level of commitments undertaken in this sector. Less than 40 per cent of WTO Members made commitments in the health sector. Only in education services did Members undertake fewer commitments. In qualitative terms, the 'bite' of the commitments is equally middling. From the commitments inscribed in health-related services, the capital- and skill-intensive services such as medical, dental or hospital services are generally more open than labour-intensive activities such as services supplied by midwives or nurses. There are certain developing countries which have purposely adopted policies to export health services under Mode 2 in order to play a leading role at a regional level (for instance, Thailand, Costa Rica, India, Chile or Jordan) and/or global level (for instance, Cuba).

The same goes for Mode 4, whereby export of doctors or of nurses and other paramedical professionals is becoming increasingly interesting for certain developing countries. India and Philippines are active in this type of market access. Health tourism can help overcome certain domestic constraints with respect to human and infrastructure resources, particularly in developing countries, but it may also lead to price adjustment in developed countries to discourage patients from moving abroad. Movement of medical professionals, on the other hand, is not trivial. It can lead to deteriorating scarcity of medical personnel in developing countries, which may be disadvantageous in financial terms for such professionals, notably the most promising among them. More often than not, in order to improve the quality of a domestic health system, imports rather than exports are necessary. On the other hand, uncontrolled exports can lead to

---

[31]   The GATS allows WTO Members to use their own classification. However, the Appellate Body made clear that in the absence of any explicit reference to the contrary, Members must be deemed to have followed the Services Sectoral Classification List – and, thus, the CPC – when scheduling their commitments. Appellate Body Report, *US – Gambling*, paras 183ff.

a puzzling 'brain drain'.[32] African and Caribbean countries have been particularly affected by the out-migration of physicians. Due to shortages in health personnel, even short-term losses of health professionals may have dramatic consequences. The World Health Organization (WHO), among other organizations, monitors such flows.[33]

The US is the biggest consumer of health services worldwide. Outsourced healthcare in the US alone represents about US$17 billion.[34] However, such consumption does not take place exclusively in developing countries. More generally, developed countries equally compete in the supply side, as cross-border movement of patients thrives. Millions of US citizens have sought medical treatment abroad. In turn, in pursuit of cutting-edge treatment, hundreds of thousands of patients sought treatment in the US.[35] Overall about 35 countries, both developed and developing, welcome more than one million medical tourists annually.[36] Having said this, it remains a challenge for a country's policy to design the sustainability of such flows, as the absence of an adequate strategy may lead to shortages in local supply or low investment returns in a highly competitive global market.

For instance, not the GATS, but well-designed domestic policies can ensure universal access to health services. A well-designed mix of policies can enable cross-subsidization between densely populated areas in which the provision of certain health services is lucrative and areas of low population density where profits are less self-evident. In addition, countries could oblige private, for-profit-seeking health care providers (e.g. private hospitals) to reserve a certain percentage of beds for low-cost treatment for the poor. Such possibilities exist and are GATS-consistent even in sectors where no limitations were inscribed.[37] With respect to trade promotion, public involvement is often essential for successful export pro-

---

[32]   This may be one of the reasons why developing countries do not insist on bolder commitments from developed countries under Mode 4. If access to such markets becomes easier, it would be extremely difficult for low-income countries to incentivize their health professionals so that they stay in their home country.

[33]   Cf WTO, Council for Trade in Services, 'Presence of Natural Persons (Mode 4)', Background Note by the Secretariat, S/C/W/301, 15 September 2009, p. 16.

[34]   NASSCOM, 'Perspective 2020', NASSCOM-McKinsey, April 2009.

[35]   Olivier Cattaneo, 'Trade in Health Services – What's in it for Developing Countries?', World Bank Policy Research Working Paper No 5115, November 2009.

[36]   Ibid.

[37]   Of course, such measures would need to be non-discriminatory, unless limitations under Article XVII GATS were undertaken to this effect.

motion strategies in the health sector.[38] Both developing and developed countries can be attractive to medical tourists and thus incentives for improving healthcare services are substantial, especially as far as quality is concerned.[39]

The outlook of liberalization under Mode 3 also gives the impression of potential remaining largely untapped. Liberalization of commercial presence can be driven by a government's desire to incentivize national providers to improve by exposing them to competition. However, this presupposes the absence of public monopolies or generally providers who are exclusively funded by the governments. Another reason for opening the health market is to use foreign suppliers to meet key shortcomings in the domestic market in terms of capacity and facilities. A third justification can be a government's willingness to offer attractive opportunities to promising health professionals who, absent such opportunities, may look for a better future abroad. Attracting new technologies which would not be available otherwise can also lead to the adoption of a more liberal investment policy.

Opening the domestic health market shall be accompanied by regulations ensuring the quality of the service and rules that allow for synergies among domestic and foreign suppliers, both private and public. Investment in the health sector appears to be occurring independently of the GATS for the most part. Along with other factors, the certain rigidity with regard to reversing commitments can be a reason for not locking in such openness under the GATS. On the other side, foreign investment in the health sector requires significant start-up costs and thus long-term stability may be an important determinant for investments of this type.

The reluctance towards liberalization of health services is also replicated in PTAs. Empirical evidence suggests that PTAs achieve higher levels of liberalization than the GATS. This is true for health services as well. Interestingly, the current level of liberalization of health services largely exceeds the conditional offers that Members have submitted during the current services negotiations. Having said this, the GATS pattern

---

[38]   Olivier Cattaneo, 'Health Without Borders: International Trade for Better Health Systems and Services' in Olivier Cattaneo, Michael Engman, Sebastián Sáez and Robert Stern (eds), *International Trade in Services – New Trends and Opportunities for Developing Countries* (Washington, DC: The World Bank, 2010), at 101.

[39]   Cf Tilman Ehrbeck, Ceani Guevara and Paul Mango, 'Mapping the Market for Medical Travel', McKinsey Quarterly, May 2008.

suggesting that the least meaningful commitments are inscribed in the health sector also appears in the PTAs.[40]

IV. THE GATS LEGAL FRAMEWORK PERTAINING TO HEALTH SERVICES

The GATS contains several provisions that can be relevant for the everyday trade in health services. Some of these provisions are applicable only in case of specific commitments being undertaken in a health-related subsector. These relate in particular to market access and national treatment. As noted earlier, the obligations relating to market access and national treatment are conditional upon commitments made by a given Member. In the GATS, commitments are taken by positively identifying a sector that a Member wants to liberalize (positive listing of sectors) and negatively describing the conditions and limitations of such liberalization (negative listing of limitations and conditions). This means that, once a Member has listed the limitations that it intends to maintain, the level of liberalization reflected in this entry is binding for that Member and can be reversed only through negotiations for compensatory adjustment.

Article XVI GATS on market access outlaws limitations relating to the number of healthcare professionals, total output, or foreign equity participation and legal form of the health service supplier. Thus, subject to the commitments undertaken in the Schedule of a given Member, most quantitative limitations, be they discriminatory or not, are GATS-inconsistent.[41] In the case of national treatment under Article XVII GATS, all discrimination against foreign health service suppliers violates the GATS unless there are commitments inscribed to the contrary. Finally, in sectors where commitments were undertaken, Members are required to administer measures of general application pertaining to services trade in an objective, reasonable and impartial manner. The content of this latter obligation has been clarified in various cases under Article X:3(a) GATT.[42]

The matrix of obligations described above reveals the importance of

---

[40]   See Juan Marchetti and Martin Roy, 'Services Liberalization in the WTO and in PTAs' in Marchetti and Roy (eds), note 12 above, at 90.

[41]   Panagiotis Delimatsis and Martin Molinuevo, 'Article XVI GATS (Market Access)', in Wolfrum, Stoll and Feinäugle (eds), note 9 above, 367.

[42]   Appellate Body Report, *European Communities – Measures Affecting the Importation of Certain Poultry Products (EC – Poultry)*, WT/DS69/AB/R, adopted 23 July 1998, DSR 1998:V, 2031, para. 115; and, in particular, Appellate Body Report, *European Communities – Selected Customs Matters (EC – Customs*

appropriately structuring one's Schedule to reflect the political intentions of the Member concerned, as commitments made constitute guaranteed *minimum* standards of treatment.[43] Thus, with such a little margin for error and in the absence of any GATS provision allowing for the imposition of safeguards, Members rather are liberalization-averse by definition. Having said this, there are measures or practices which fall outside the scope of the GATS and which a government could use. Members are free to discourage their health professionals from going abroad (through taxes, deposit guarantees or other instruments[44]) and to deny any health treatment to foreign patients.[45] In addition, Members could use regulatory instruments to discourage their citizens from seeking medical treatment abroad.

In reality, because of the difficulty in enforcing such rules, Members have in principle liberalized the consumption of health services abroad. Even if a given Member decides subsequently to raise barriers in such movements, it is questionable whether such practices would be consistent with the spirit of the GATS. This is because such practices would nullify the very substance of the commitments previously undertaken and would not live up to the expectations that trading partners have reasonably had. By the same token, issues (and denial) of reimbursement of medical treatment could arguably be viewed under this lens as well.

Other obligations are applicable across the board such as Article III GATS relating to the prompt publication of measures of general application and international agreements relating to trade in services. The same applies to the requirement under Article VI:2 to establish independent review mechanisms of and appropriate remedies for administrative decisions affecting services trade.[46] Typically, such mechanisms are aimed at

---

Matters), WT/DS315/AB/R, adopted 11 December 2006, DSR 2006:IX, 3791, para. 200.

[43] Cf Julia Nielson, 'Ten Steps to Consider Before Making Commitments in Health Services Under the GATS' in Blouin, Drager, and Smith (eds), note 25 above, 204.

[44] See, for instance, the instruments used by Thailand in the late 60s: Suwit Wibulpolprasert, 'International Trade and Migration of Health Care Workers: Thailand's Experience', in Aaditya Mattoo and Antonia Carzaniga (eds), *Moving People to Deliver Services* (Washington, DC: World Bank/Oxford University Press, 2003), at 172.

[45] Only the possibility of a non-violation complaint is available to Members dissatisfied by such policies. However, this action has limited chances of success due to the demanding burden of proof for the complaining party.

[46] Panagiotis Delimatsis, 'Due Process and Good Regulation Embedded in the GATS – Disciplining Regulatory Behaviour in Services through Article VI of the GATS', 10 *Journal of International Economic Law* (2007), 13.

protecting the rights of individual service suppliers from administrative discretion in the host country. It is for each Member to structure such mechanisms in accordance with domestic constitutional and administrative traditions and promulgate the procedures for such review. As to remedies, it is again at the discretion of a given Member to decide as to whether it will allow for compensation or will simply adopt a procedure that allows the replacement of an erroneous administrative decision with a lawful one.[47]

In the following, we will review the most critical provisions which may play a very important role in the future, as health markets will become more open. Most of these provisions are part of the built-in agenda that the GATS foresees: Article VI:4, which calls for the adoption of rules relating to licensing, qualifications and technical standards; Article XIII, which includes a negotiating mandate for the adoption of rules relating to government procurement in services; Article XV, which calls for the adoption of disciplines harnessing unfair subsidization practices in services; and Article X, according to which Members are tasked with the adoption of rules relating to the imposition of emergency safeguards. In addition, the potential benefits of enforcing the possibilities for (mutual or autonomous) recognition of qualifications, licences and standards through Article VII remain largely untapped.

A.   Article VI:4 GATS: Trade-restrictive Regulatory Measures

Article VI:4 GATS requires that Members adopt the necessary disciplines which would ensure that measures of a procedural and substantive nature relating to qualifications, licensing and technical standards are, *inter alia*, (a) based on objective and transparent criteria; (b) not more burdensome than necessary to ensure the quality of the service; and (c) with respect to procedures, not in themselves a restriction on the supply of a given service. Priority was given to professional services and the Working Party on Professional Services (WPPS) was thereby established, which completed its task by developing disciplines on domestic regulation in the accountancy sector in December 1998. In May 1999, the Council for Trade in Services (CTS) established the Working Party on Domestic Regulation (WPDR), which is charged with the development of meaningful and coherent disciplines on domestic regulation which would be applicable across services

---

[47]   Markus Krajewski, 'Article VI GATS (Domestic Regulation)', in Wolfrum, Stoll and Feinäugle (eds), note 9 above, 173–174.

sectors. Members currently negotiate within the WPDR based on a draft text and subsequent revisions prepared by the WPDR Chair.

The forthcoming disciplines add to the required level of transparency and good governance in domestic regulations in procedural and substantive terms alike. There is overall agreement that the forthcoming disciplines will only apply to sectors where commitments are undertaken. However, one of the most controversial aspects remains how to operationalize the part of the mandate incorporated in Article VI:4(b), the so-called necessity test.[48] Members are concerned that such a test would not leave them sufficient flexibility when they pursue public policy objectives, such as those related to education and health, but rather give unfettered discretion to the WTO adjudicating bodies to second-guess the adequacy of political choices at the domestic level.[49]

The main characteristic of measures falling under Article VI:4 that distinguishes them from measures coming under Articles XVI and XVII is that the former are of non-discriminatory nature and aim to ensure the quality of the service. In the absence of discriminatory tariffs at the border hindering services, measures falling under Article VI:4 constitute in reality a significant share of barriers to trade in services. Therefore, the completion of the current negotiations in this area is an important priority for various Members. With regard to health services, three main types of regulation seem to be of relevance here:[50]

(a) A first category would include licensing and qualification requirements for health service suppliers. Ensuring quality and safety are at the core of any domestic regulation governing entry to a health profession. However, identifying objective benchmarks for assessing quality is a daunting task. Only to complicate the task of regulators even further, activities within the health sector may differ largely and thus customized regulatory approaches must be adopted to confront the relevant challenges. Obviously, the margin of discretion for the regulatory authority is virtually unlimited and thus multilateral disciplines intend to ensure that transparency is adhered to, requirements and procedures are clearly defined and pre-established, and review of administrative decisions takes place regularly.

(b) A second category of measures relates to authorization requirements

---

[48] Panagiotis Delimatsis, 'Concluding the WTO Services Negotiations on Domestic Regulation: Hopes and Fears', 9(4) *World Trade Review* (2010), 643.

[49] Cf Rupa Chanda, 'Social Services and the GATS: Key Issues and Concerns', 31(12) *World Development* (2003), 2002.

[50] Cf. WTO, note 29 above.

for legal persons *qua* institutional suppliers such as clinics or hospitals. In such cases, requirements may be leading to a situation which de facto limits the number of service suppliers in the domestic market and thus Article XVI would come into play, as non-discriminatory quantitative restrictions have to be scheduled in committed sectors. This, for instance, would be the case if an economic needs test existed which was based on geographical or population density criteria.

(c)   Finally, a third category includes rules relating to reimbursement under mandatory public or private insurance schemes. Again, such measures can have a restrictive effect on trade in health services, but still not be covered by the market access provision of Article XVI.

B.   Article VII GATS: Recognition Agreements and Regional Initiatives

Pursuant to Article VII GATS, Members can recognize the qualifications of another Member without any obligation to extend this recognition to other Members in derogation from the MFN obligation. Interestingly, the text of Article VII:1 appears to allow recognition arrangements that a given Member may conclude not only with other WTO Members, but also with non-WTO Members, thereby putting into doubt the very essence of a multilateral trade agreement such as the GATS.[51] Such recognition can be granted autonomously or it can be part of a mutual recognition arrangement.[52] The only requirement is that Members signing such recognition agreements also notify the WTO of those agreements and give other interested Members the chance to show that they equally meet the required standards. Mutual recognition can be of paramount importance, as it implies recognition of equivalence of qualifications, education systems and the like. This, for instance, is most likely to affect insurance portability, thereby leading to higher levels of patient mobility.

In terms of personnel, such arrangements can offer additional opportunities for health professionals who can move and work within the geographical area of the Members parties to the arrangement without undertaking additional tests or qualifying again. Such arrangements can be stand-alone, but they can also be part of a more comprehensive package of agreements which, put together, intend to create a free

---

[51]   Cf Markus Krajewski, 'Article VII GATS (Recognition)', in Wolfrum, Stoll and Feinäugle (eds), note 9 above, 201.

[52]   Cf Kalypso Nicolaïdis, 'Non-Discriminatory Mutual Recognition: An Oxymoron in the New WTO Lexicon?' in Thomas Cottier and Petros Mavroidis (eds), *Regulatory Barriers and the Principle of Non-Discrimination in World Trade Law* (University of Michigan Press, 1999), 267.

trade area (FTA). In the latter case, parties to the FTA are arguably not required anymore to offer to other interested Members the possibility to demonstrate the equally high level of education, qualifications or standards with a view to have their systems also recognized as equivalent. They are, however, still obliged to notify such arrangements.[53]

The importance and possible potential of Article VII can be better assessed if one considers interrelated phenomena within the global healthcare market: first, the ever-increasing size of health travel abroad. Interestingly, there is empirical evidence suggesting that medical travel is not exclusively part of North-South trade; rather, medical travel increasingly becomes a lucrative sector among developing countries. Language, availability and costs are factors that determine such movements. In the case of ASEAN, for instance, about 70 per cent of exports in the health sector are regional.[54] By the same token, Chile has become a point of attraction for medical treatment in the region, with patients from Bolivia, Argentina and Peru using the Chilean facilities.[55] Such movements do not preclude trade with developed countries as well. For instance, in Thailand, the biggest exporter of health services in the region, the largest share of foreign patients stems from Japan.[56] There is evidence suggesting that Japanese companies send their employees to Thailand and Singapore for annual physical examinations, as the savings on fees and high-quality medical care are more than satisfactory. With the continuous privatization of medical care and provided that the current cost differentials remain, health tourism can only grow further.[57]

A second phenomenon to be observed is the current, largely unorganized flows of healthcare personnel globally. Informal contractual arrangements may be a welcome development for the health professionals seeking a better future abroad, but when viewed in context such movements, if unmonitored and random, may exacerbate shortages and unwelcome fluctuations in the domestic healthcare labour market.

Recognition arrangements concluded among States may be welcome if

---

[53] The requirement of Article VII:3 may be of particular relevance here in order to identify attempts to circumvent significant GATS obligations.

[54] Cattaneo, note 38 above, p. 117.

[55] Francisco Leon, 'The Case of the Chilean health system, 1983–2000' in Nick Drager and C. Vieira (eds), *Trade in health services: Global, regional and country perspectives* (Washington, DC: PAHO, 2002).

[56] Jutamas Arunanondchai and Carsten Fink, 'Trade in Health Services in the ASEAN Region', World Bank Policy Research Working Paper No 4147, March 2007, 12.

[57] WTO, Council for Trade in Services, 'Tourism Services', Background Note of the Secretariat, S/C/W/298, 8 June 2009, pp. 10–11.

one considers that, in such cases of managed labour mobility of medical and paramedical personnel, the States involved, and notably the home (sending) country, can have a more accurate record of the human capital sent abroad, the prospects of return and the needs of the domestic market. Such streamlined agreements can protect better the labour rights of the natural persons involved in the host country. They can also protect the home country from unexpected shortages in the domestic healthcare market. This is particularly important for those countries where resources of healthcare personnel are already scarce.

In practice, however, foreign hospitals and specialized recruitment agencies recruit directly from a given country's labour market, often without the involvement of domestic authorities, which are unable to control or perceive these rather informal channels. This has been the case, for instance, with Filipino nurses, who combine a high level of education with very good command of English. In this regard, a continuous issue has been how to ensure the adherence to a code of ethics when recruiting through such channels. The International Council of Nurses (ICN), for instance, has done work on this.[58] In addition, while shortages in Philippines are less pronounced (recall that restrictions to labour mobility on the side of the home country may lead to 'brain waste' if human capital abounds), in Indonesia, which is another large exporter of healthcare personnel in South Asia, such movements have caused various challenges in the domestic healthcare system.[59] In other cases, countries opt for bilateral agreements to manage mobility of healthcare personnel. For example, Malaysia concluded bilateral agreements for the supply of nurses with various countries such as Albania, India, Philippines and Vietnam. Philippines also have in force similar agreements with the UK, India and Norway. More generally, bilateral labour agreements for the recruitment of nurses are actually rather common. Finally, FTAs (e.g. the latest EU EPAs with the Caribbean region) may also entail targeted liberalization of Mode 4 movements.

In this respect, an important loophole of Article VII is that agreements among non-governmental bodies appear to be excluded from its scope. This leaves possibly unregulated a great deal of arrangements concluded by self-regulatory bodies at the transnational level. Such a shortcoming can be addressed through the disciplines yet to be developed under Article VI:4, as has been the case with the draft disciplines in the accountancy

---

[58]   See Mike Waghorne, 'Mode 4 and Trade Union Concerns', in Mattoo and Carzaniga (eds), note 44 above, at 206.

[59]   Arunanondchai and Fink, note 56 above.

sector, which also include rules relating to recognition agreements con-cluded between non-governmental bodies. Even if such arrangements are not covered by Article VII, they have the potential of producing sub-stantial effects, as they often entail mutual recognition of diplomas and qualifications among professional associations in different countries. As registration and authorization to practice a profession often depends on the relevant professional association, such agreements may generate con-siderable liberalization and promote mobility.

Another beneficial effect of the culmination of Article VI:4 negotiations is that, in the aftermath of the conclusion of Article VI:4 negotiations, the ensuing managed approximation of laws is expected to generate strong and justified pressures for mutual recognition agreements (MRAs). This is because Members will likely be identifying similarities between their regu-latory systems in certain services sectors. Viewed from this angle, Article VI complements Article VII GATS and is an important, albeit creeping, liberalization vector.

C. The GATS Built-in Agenda – Government Procurement, Subsidies and Safeguards

Government procurement is defined in the GATS as 'the procurement by governmental agencies of services purchased for governmental purposes and not with a view to commercial resale or with a view to use in the supply of services for commercial sale'. However, there is currently no meaningful discipline of such activities. Rather, Article XIII contains a mandate for negotiations in this area, which currently take place under the aegis of the Working Party on GATS Rules (WPGR). This means that, to date, a large bulk of services, ranging from cleaning to essential health services (e.g. nurses and midwives hired by public hospitals) are currently excluded from the scope of the GATS in the case of publicly-run facilities, as they arguably do not fall within the scope of any commitments under-taken under Mode 4.

Just as with government procurement, the GATS only contains a mandate tasking Members with the future development of rules relating to subsidies. The absence of disciplines harnessing subsidies is one of the major weaknesses of the GATS. Until stronger rules are adopted under Article XV, subsidies that are granted to scheduled sectors are subject to the non-discrimination obligation. For this reason, several Members decided to circumvent this obligation by scheduling horizontal limitations to their schedules, typically through statements that limit the granting of subsidies to domestic service suppliers exclusively.

In the case of safeguards, other than the fundamental disaccord between developed and developing countries regarding the necessity of any rules, Members have kept struggling with clarifying concepts such as 'domestic industry', 'serious injury' and 'causal link', which are arguably much more difficult to conceptualize than in the case of goods.[60]

All three areas are very important for the future relevance of the GATS for trade in healthcare services. Much of the current trade in such services would actually be affected by any possible materialization of the respective mandates within the WPGR. Of course, this statement is not unique to healthcare, but applies to all public services as currently supplied in most economies in the world.

D.　Current Loopholes of the WTO Legal Framework

The main legal shortcoming of the GATS is the lack of provisions harnessing restrictive business practices by private parties. Article IX GATS is a rather soft requirement for information and consultation and thus fails to discipline arrangements between private actors such as favourable conditions relating to reimbursement for certain providers but not for others or exclusivity agreements negotiated between insurance companies and hospitals. Such arrangements may lead to unfair market partitioning to the detriment of competition, overall welfare and consumer choice.

V.　THE GOVERNMENTAL EXCEPTION UNDER THE GATS

A.　Health Services in the 'Exercise of Governmental Authority'

Health services being an important public good, asymmetries of information and other market failures very often lead to highly restrictive regulations and/or to the State supplying such services due to the public policy interests involved. Public health being among the core missions of an elected government, public intervention appears to be plausible. A peculiarity of the health sector is that, in various instances, governments supply this type of services free of or below cost, which is made possible through subsidization of the relevant industry. In this case, the State intervenes to ensure an undisrupted and adequate supply of such services both in terms

---

[60]　For a recent account of advances in the negotiations in the three areas, see WTO, 'Annual Report of the Working Party on GATS Rules to the Council for Trade in Services (2011)', S/WPGR/22, 10 November 2011.

of quality and quantity to its populace. Due to the pursuit of legitimate public objectives such as protecting public health, human rights and the safety of the citizens, this type of services is considered as special.

The specificity of the sector is not undermined by the presence of private undertakings in the sector, competing with State health facilities. Indeed, the sector is of a dynamic nature and governments experiment with different concepts and partnerships, which may involve for-profit undertakings, in order to account for budgetary constraints and ensure more productive use of resources while maintaining quality of and equal access to decent health services. The overall pursuit of public interest and control or supervision by a State authority, even if only vague and remote, can ultimately shelter the relevant restrictions out of the scope of any multilateral disciplines, even those of non-discrimination. In CJEU's settled case-law, the pursuit of non-economic objectives has constituted the ultimate litmus test for any measure potentially restricting the free movement rules of the Treaty on the Functioning of the EU (TFEU).

Aware of the importance of a particular set of services which are supplied in the public interest in part or entirely, the GATS drafters exempted from the scope of the GATS any services supplied in the exercise of governmental authority.[61] By virtue of Article I:3(c) GATS, services fall within this category only if they are supplied neither on a commercial basis nor in competition with one or more service suppliers. The two conditions are cumulative in that failure to meet one would lead to the full application of the GATS. For instance, supply of hospital treatment by the State below cost would fall under the exception. On the other hand, private involvement, even if regulations setting qualitative standards and qualifications are present, at prices which are set by the market mechanisms, is less likely to escape the GATS scrutiny. Thus, as one can infer, many public services as provided today would not come under the current, rather narrow definition of governmental authority. Indeed, many of those services are not supplied in the exercise of governmental authority, but are rather of a hybrid nature, being positioned at the confines between public and private law.[62] It bears noting that the initial burden of proof lies with the complaining party, which has to adduce evidence to prove that at least one of the conditions is not met.

With respect to the first condition, it would most likely be met if the service at issue is supplied mainly with a view to making a profit or obtaining a financial gain. Indeed, profit-seeking is a prerequisite for the first

---

[61]   Art. I :3(b) GATS.
[62]   Cf Krajewski, note 13 above.

condition to be met. This is the most plausible meaning of 'commercial basis' that a treaty interpreter would furnish. Additionally, the term 'commercial basis' seems to refer to the supply modalities of the service and not to the operational basis of the service supplier. This means that while many public services can be supplied on a non-profit basis, public service supplies often may offer services on both a commercial and non-commercial basis.[63]

With respect to the second condition, that is, as to whether competition exists with one or more suppliers, one would need to identify whether, in an adequately defined geographical market, service suppliers deliver services that are like or substitutable. Factors to be taken into account would include end-uses, the customer base, price relationships, including cross-price elasticity, and the channels of distribution.[64] For instance, the fact that, even in countries with low-priced public health services, private health service suppliers manage to get a stable market share may suggest that the two services do not compete in the same market and thus they may not be like. Differences in types of treatment offered, quality of service or equipment, and overall infrastructure may be decisive in excluding similar end-uses. Such observations of course cannot be taken to undermine the complexity of such an analysis due to the peculiar nature of services.[65]

It bears noting that the Financial Services Annex to the GATS specifies further the scope of the governmental exception with respect to financial services. More specifically, by virtue of Article 1(d) of the Annex, the general governmental exception of Article I:3(c) GATS does not apply to financial services. Articles 1(b)(ii) and (b)(iii) of the Annex exclude from the scope of the GATS activities forming part of a statutory system of social security or public retirement plans as well as any activity conducted by a public entity for the account or with the guarantee of using the financial resources of the government. However, if a given Member allows its financial service suppliers to provide such services in competition with a public entity or a financial service supplier, then such services are no longer exempted. *E contrario*, the possibility of such services being provided on a commercial basis does not lead to the application of the GATS, as long as no competition with other financial service suppliers exists. This

[63]   Krajewski, note 13 above.

[64]   See Eric Leroux, 'What is a "Service Supplied in the Exercise of Governmental Authority" Under Article I:3(b) and (c) of the General Agreement on Trade in Services?', 40(3) *Journal of World Trade* (2006), 345.

[65]   Cf Rudolf Adlung, 'Public Services and the GATS', 9(2) *Journal of International Economic Law* (2006), 464.

element constitutes a clear derogation from the exception enshrined in Article I:3(c) GATS.

B.   The EU Experience Regarding the 'Governmental Exception'

In practice, a clear distinction between services that come under the scope of the governmental exception and those that do not is not straightforward. Similar challenges for the adjudicator have arisen several times before the CJEU. According to Article 62, when read in conjunction with Article 51 TFEU, the fundamental freedom to provide services does not apply to activities which are connected, even if only occasionally, with the exercise of official authority. Early on, the CJEU ruled that such exceptions must be construed narrowly.[66] In addition, the CJEU has advanced an EU meaning to the term 'official authority'. A first condition for the application of this derogation is that occasional connection would not suffice, but rather a *specific* and *direct* connection would be necessary to benefit from the derogation.[67] Thus, the CJEU has narrowed down the scope of this exception early on in the history of the EU despite the rather straightforward wording of Article 51. An additional condition is the presence of the power of enjoying the prerogatives outside the confines of general law, privileges of official power and powers of coercion over citizens.[68] Furthermore, strict necessity between ends and means is essential.[69] For instance, in a landmark case, the Court found that a nationality requirement in the areas of research, education, public health, transport by land, sea and air, posts and telecommunications, television broadcasting, water, gas and electricity distribution services, and music based on the derogation relating to the exercise of official authority could not stand.[70] More recently, the CJEU found that security services provided by private security undertakings,[71] activities of the private vehicle roadworthiness testing bodies,[72] or the provision of emergency ambulance or qualified

---

[66]   Case 152/73, *Sotgiu* [1979] ECR 153, para. 4

[67]   Case 2/74, *Reyners* [1974] ECR 631, para. 45.

[68]   C-160/08, *Commission v Germany* [2010] ECR I-3713, para. 79.

[69]   C-451/03, *Servizi Ausiliari Dottori Commercialisti* [2006] ECR I-2941, para. 45.

[70]   C-290/94, *Commission v Greece*. That case referred to the free movement of workers and the exception relating to employment in the public service. Thus, even if it appears to be broader than the similar provisions under the freedoms of establishment and services, the CJEU applied an equally narrow standard of review.

[71]   C-114/97, *Commission v Spain* [1998] ECR I-6717; also C-465/05, *Commission v Italy* [2007] ECR I-11091.

[72]   C-438/08, *Commission v Portugal* [2009] ECR I-10219.

patient transport services by private undertakings[73] do not escape the purview of EU law.

By virtue of Article 106(2) TFEU and the relevant case-law, derogations from the EU competition rules is possible in the case of undertakings entrusted with the operation of services of general economic interest if the application of such rules obstructs or jeopardizes the performance in law or in fact of the particular tasks assigned to them and as long as the development of trade has not been affected to such an extent as is incompatible with the interests of the Union.[74] In *Ambulanz Glöckner*, the CJEU found, for example, that emergency transport services are services of general economic interest.[75] In addition, the CJEU also adopted a fairly flexible approach to accommodate the specificities of public services and entities supplying them with respect to the financing of such activities.[76] However, it is questionable as to whether such a justification can also be juxtaposed to the fundamental freedoms. The Court is yet to pronounce on this topic in a definite manner.[77]

VI.   THE GATS PROVISION ON GENERAL EXCEPTIONS

Other than the above-mentioned legal avenues that may, under certain circumstances, shield domestic regulations governing health care services from the scope of the GATS, the Agreement equally contains a general exception provision under Article XIV, which explicitly allows derogations from any obligation under the GATS. Indeed, in the pursuit of non-economic public policy objectives such as the protection of public health, Members are allowed to adopt trade-restrictive measures unilater-

---

[73]   C-160/08, *Commission v Germany*.

[74]   C-266/96, *Corsica Ferries France* [1998] ECR I-3949.

[75]   C-475/99, *Ambulanz Glöckner* [2001] ECR I-8089.

[76]   In the aftermath of the seminal *Altmark* judgment (C-280/00), subsequent cases and work by the Commission led to significant flexibility notably with regard to public procurement. See, more recently, European Commission, 'Services of general interest, including social services of general interest: a new European commitment', COM(2007) 725 final, 20 November 2007. The most recent proposal for reform includes suggestions for a mere adherence to equality of treatment and transparency. See European Commission, 'A Quality Framework for Services of General Interest in Europe', COM(2011) 900 final, 20 December 2011.

[77]   Cf. C-438/05, *Viking Line* [2007] ECR I-10779, para. 53 with C-157/94, *Commission v Netherlands* [1997] ECR I-5699.

ally.[78] In all respects, then, Article XIV GATS follows the model of Article XX GATT. However, because of the inherent flexibility that the GATS depicts, it is expected that Article XIV will be invoked less frequently, as possible disputes will be resolved earlier.[79]

Article XIV being an affirmative defence, it is for the responding party, that is the regulating State, to produce evidence demonstrating that a given measure is necessary to protect public health. For this, the respondent will have to show that the measure is designed and suitable to achieve the ends pursued. The task of the complaining party in this regard is to bring forward possible alternative measures, which were reasonably available to the respondent and could achieve the level of protection that the latter had chosen, while being less trade-restrictive than the measure actually chosen.[80] Once identified, a comparison of alternatives will be made by the WTO adjudicating bodies based on the contribution of the measures to the achievement of the ends pursued; the restrictive impact of the measures on trade and in the light of the relative importance of the interests or values furthered by the impugned measure.[81] Even if the proposed alternative does achieve the level of protection sought, the respondent can still meet its burden of proof by submitting that such an alternative was not reasonably available, for instance, because of shortages in know-how or prohibitive costs associated with its adoption.

In this case, the respondent would also need to prove its compliance with the introductory clause (or 'chapeau') of Article XIV. The focus under the chapeau is on the application or enforcement of the measure at stake. Abuse of the right to derogate from the GATS obligations is avoided through the application of three standards: the application of the measures should not amount to arbitrary or unjustifiable discrimination or disguised trade restriction. The Appellate Body suggested that the three standards entail both substantive and procedural requirements and may actually overlap.

In various cases relating to the protection of public health, the WTO adjudicating bodies demonstrated a high degree of flexibility and sensitivity with respect to certain policies and the ensuing measures adopted by Members which were intended to address specific health policy concerns

---

[78]   Cf. Appellate Body Report, *US – Shrimp*, para. 121.

[79]   See Thomas Cottier, Panagiotis Delimatsis and Nicolas Diebold, 'Article XIV GATS (General Exceptions)' in Wolfrum, Stoll and Feinäugle (eds), note 9 above, 291.

[80]   Appellate Body Report, *Brazil – Retreaded Tyres*, para. 156.

[81]   This is the *Korea – Beef* 'weighting and balancing' test. See Appellate Body Report, *Korea – Beef*, paras 162–164.

at the domestic level. In cases like *US – Gambling*, *Brazil – Tyres*, or *EC – Asbestos*, the Appellate Body upheld Members' fundamental prerogative to protect public health domestically, arguably focusing more on the importance of the value at issue than on the trade-restrictiveness of the challenged measure. Of course, various measures taken in the area of health policy are of economic nature and thus could hardly fit the public health exception under Article XIV. In this case, it is expected that a Member would argue along the lines described under Section V above.

VII.   CONCLUSION

Against this backdrop, a central question seems to remain unanswered: If the GATS is such a flexible regulatory instrument, why there is this aversion *vis-à-vis* the GATS, in particular when it comes to public and/or social services such as education or health? The answer is multifaceted and does not always relate to objective arguments. The changing concept of sovereignty; the eroding nature of public monopolies; the transformation of the role of the State from a positive and a normative point of view; the disconnect between the trade ministry and the other ministries at the domestic level; or the exacerbation of the divide between developed and developing countries are some of the factors that have to be taken into account in this complicated equation. Interdisciplinary research in this area appears apposite, almost 20 years after the adoption of the GATS. Interestingly, even the proliferation of preferential arrangements did not manage to cut the Gordian knot of public services. It is submitted that, in such complicated sectors, where concerns and interests go to every possible direction, a bottom-up approach may prove to be more promising and efficient. In this respect, cooperation and recognition agreements between professional organizations can bring about trade-enhancing outcomes to the benefit of both receiving and sending countries. States have an important, if only subtle, surveillance role to play.

In addition, one should not shy away from recognizing the challenges that global flows of capital and labour engender in the developing world. Not all developments in the sector can contribute to the increasing integration of developing countries in the global economy. Cross-border supply of health services remains dominated by the developed world. This also shows how important it is not to regard individual services sectors in isolation, but rather as interdependent. Underdevelopment of one sector, particularly bottleneck services, can affect entire supply patterns. If the domestic telecommunications network is not trustworthy, how would it ever be possible to deliver services cross-border, including e-health services? If the data protection framework is outdated, how can a developing country remain competitive in health data storage and use? Certain developing countries such as India and Philippines constitute success stories in such respects, whereby medical transcription, health insurance processing, data mining and storage are services that they deliver in a reliable and cost-efficient manner. Nevertheless, such cases appear to constitute the exception rather than the rule. Empirical research shedding light on the question as to whether more regional cooperation can have more advantageous effects more quickly appears to be warranted. Best practices and a better managed mobility of human capital to the benefit of both sending and receiving countries could lead to an eradication of poverty and 'brain gain'.

13. WTO law and risk factors for non-communicable diseases: a complex relationship

*Tania Voon**

I. INTRODUCTION

Non-communicable diseases (NCDs) – principally cardiovascular diseases, cancers, chronic respiratory diseases and diabetes – cause 60 per cent of all deaths in the world, with 80 per cent of deaths due to NCDs occurring in low-income and middle-income countries.[1] The major common risk factors for NCDs are tobacco use, harmful use of alcohol, unhealthy diet and physical inactivity.[2] The World Health Organization (WHO) and other United Nations (UN) bodies are increasingly recognizing NCDs and their associated risk factors as a problem requiring urgent attention. In 2005, the WHO *Framework Convention for Tobacco Control* (FCTC)[3] entered into force; at the time of writing it has 176 parties. In April 2008, the WHO's decision-making body, the World Health Assembly (WHA), adopted a resolution endorsing the *2008–2013 Action Plan for the Global Strategy for the Prevention and Control of Noncommunicable Diseases*.[4] The WHA has also endorsed the *Global Strategy on Diet, Physical Activity*

---

* By way of disclosure: the author has advised governments on the legality under international trade law of tobacco control measures such as standardised tobacco packaging. The author is also conducting research on the implications of international trade and investment law for non-communicable diseases pursuant to grants from the Australian National Preventive Health Agency and the Australian Research Council.

[1] WHO World Health Assembly, *Action Plan for the Global Strategy for the Prevention and Control of Noncommunicable Diseases*, A61/8 (18 April 2008), para. 1.

[2] UN General Assembly, *Resolution Adopted by the General Assembly: Prevention and Control of Non-communicable Diseases*, A/RES/64/265 (20 May 2010), preamble.

[3] 2302 UNTS 166 (adopted 21 May 2003).

[4] WHO World Health Assembly, *Action Plan for the Global Strategy for the Prevention and Control of Noncommunicable Diseases*, A61/8 (18 April 2008).

and Health,[5] the *Global Strategy to Reduce Harmful Use of Alcohol*,[6] and a set of recommendations on the marketing of foods and non-alcoholic beverages to children.[7] In July 2009, the UN Economic and Social Council recognized that NCDs 'impos[e] a heavy burden on society ... with serious social and economic consequences'.[8] In May 2010, the UN General Assembly adopted a resolution highlighting 'the need for concerted action and a coordinated response at the national, regional and global levels in order to adequately address the developmental and other challenges posed by non-communicable diseases', and decided to 'convene a high-level meeting of the General Assembly in September 2011, with the participation of Heads of State and Government, on the prevention and control of non-communicable diseases'.[9] At that meeting, the General Assembly adopted a Political Declaration describing the global burden and threat of NCDs as 'one of the major challenges for development in the twenty-first century'.[10]

In this chapter, I first explore the relevance to NCDs of international trade in general and trade liberalization pursuant to World Trade Organization (WTO) law in particular. The WTO is not a health or development organization, so what does it have to do with NCDs? The answer is that, if unchecked by domestic regulation, trade liberalization has the potential (which has been realized in practice) to increase certain unhealthy consumption habits, leading to a corresponding increase in NCDs. I therefore turn to explain that WTO law does contain generous scope for WTO Members to implement health measures to counter these negative health effects without violating WTO law. Nevertheless, as I expound in the final substantive section of the chapter, the practical effect of a formal or informal complaint in relation to WTO legality may be to

---

[5]   WHO World Health Assembly, *Global Strategy on Diet, Physical Activity and Health*, WHA57.17 (22 May 2004).

[6]   WHO World Health Assembly, *Global Strategy to Reduce the Harmful Use of Alcohol*, WHA63.13 (21 May 2010).

[7]   WHO World Health Assembly, *Marketing of Food and Non-Alcoholic Beverages to Children*, WHA63.14 (21 May 2010).

[8]   UN Economic and Social Council, *Ministerial Declaration – 2009 High-Level Segment: Implementing the International Agreed Goals and Commitments in Regard to Global Public Health* (2009), para. 18.

[9]   UN General Assembly, *Resolution Adopted by the General Assembly: Prevention and Control of Non-communicable Diseases*, A/RES/64/265 (20 May 2010), preamble, para. 1.

[10]   UN General Assembly, *Political Declaration of the High-level Meeting of the General Assembly on the Prevention and Control of Non-communicable Diseases*, A/66/L.1 (16 September 2011).

chill domestic health regulation and, overall, to weaken domestic barriers to trade in and sales of products such as alcohol and tobacco, even in the absence of a legal WTO requirement to do so.

Greater recognition of these competing considerations and of the complexity of the relationship between WTO law and common risk factors for NCDs may assist in supporting individual WTO Members and groups of Members as they pursue novel regulatory strategies to combat those risk factors. The global fight against NCDs would also be strengthened by further scientific, economic and empirical research into the relationship between health measures targeting NCD risk factors and their health objectives, and the health outcomes of specific WTO dispute settlement proceedings.

II.   THE RELEVANCE OF INTERNATIONAL TRADE AND WTO LAW TO NON-COMMUNICABLE DISEASES

Some studies blame international trade for introducing or aggravating burdens on public health such as alcoholism, tobacco addiction and obesity. For example, some commentators contend that trade liberalization as promoted through the WTO agreements has significantly increased tobacco consumption in low-income and middle-income countries.[11] Similarly, trade liberalization is said to have decreased prices and increased the availability and consumption of foodstuffs that may be overrepresented in unhealthy diets, such as vegetable oils, meat and highly processed foods, particularly in developing countries.[12] One alleged reason for increasing obesity rates in the developing world is that energy-dense diets cost less than nutrient-dense diets, and that international trade lowers further 'the

---

[11]   H. Wipfli, D. Bettcher, C. Subramaniam and A. Taylor, 'Confronting the Tobacco Epidemic: Emerging Mechanisms of Global Governance', in M. McKee, P. Garner and R. Stott (eds), *International Co-operation in Health*, (Oxford: Oxford University Press, 2001), 127–149, at 130; World Bank, *Curbing the Epidemic: Governments and the Economics of Tobacco Control* (Washington DC: World Bank 1999) 14–15.

[12]   C. Hawkes, 'The Influence of Trade Liberalisation and Global Dietary Change: The Case of Vegetable Oils, Meat and Highly Processed Foods', in C. Hawkes, C. Blouin, S. Henson, N. Drager and L. Dubé (eds), *Trade, Food, Diet and Health: Perspectives and Policy Options* (West Sussex: Blackwell Publishing, 2010) 35–59, at 40, 49, 53–54.

relative costs of energy-dense foods'.[13] The WHO confirms that 'negative health-related effects of globalization' typically result from 'increased production, promotion and marketing of processed foods and those high in fat, salt and sugar, as well as tobacco and other products with adverse effects on population health status'.[14] Adverse health effects (for example, higher average body mass index and cholesterol levels) also tend to arise indirectly from benefits and trends associated with international trade, globalization and development, such as urbanization, less labour-intensive work, and increased individual and national income.[15]

Accepting that international trade liberalization pursuant to the rules of the WTO lowers prices and increases the availability of given products is not difficult. Indeed, a fundamental objective of and theoretical basis for the WTO is precisely to promote national and global welfare by increasing the quantity, quality and range of products available to consumers throughout the world.[16] In general, WTO rules do not distinguish between 'good' and 'bad' products. Thus, it is unsurprising that legal products that are detrimental to health (such as tobacco) may 'benefit' from trade liberalization alongside products that are detrimental to the environment (such as cars) and products that are beneficial to wellbeing (such as personal exercise equipment). (Whether the producers of these products in any particular country also benefit is another matter.) As discussed further below, individual WTO Members nevertheless have significant scope to regulate and restrict trade in legal and illegal products in accordance with their own domestic policy objectives.

One touted solution to the perceived problem of international trade's negative effects on health is to remove tobacco from the scope of WTO rules, leaving WTO Members free to impose as high tariffs and other barriers on tobacco imports as they wish;[17] the same proposal is sometimes

---

[13] A. Drewnowski, A. Hanks and T. Smith, 'International Trade, Food and Diet Costs, and the Global Obesity Epidemic', in C. Hawkes, C. Blouin, S. Henson, N. Drager and L. Dubé (eds), *Trade, Food, Diet and Health: Perspectives and Policy Options,* (West Sussex: Blackwell Publishing, 2010) 77–90, at 83–84, 88.

[14] World Health Organization, *Preventing Chronic Diseases: A Vital Investment,* (Geneva: World Health Organization, 2005) 51.

[15] *Ibid.*

[16] See generally, e.g., A. Sykes, 'Comparative Advantage and the Normative Economics of International Trade Policy', 1 *Journal of International Economic Law* (1998) 49–82.

[17] See, e.g., C. Callard, H. Chitanondh and R. Weissman, 'Trade and Investment Liberalisation in Tobacco Products Offers no Benefits for Tobacco Control', 10 *Tobacco Control* (2001) 68–70.

394 *Research handbook on environment, health and the WTO*

made regarding alcohol.[18] However, that WTO rules prevent countries from pursuing genuine health objectives with respect to tobacco products is far from clear. Aside from the availability of exceptions and flexibilities in the WTO agreements as discussed below, WTO disciplines themselves may be used to buttress rather than to undermine Members' health policies. To begin with, key WTO disciplines prevent Members from discriminating against imports of all or specific WTO Members, and these disciplines of non-discrimination play an important role in ensuring that Members' measures are properly targeted to achieve their health or other social objectives rather than simply hindering foreign competition.

Take, for example, the United States federal legislation restricting certain 'flavours' in cigarettes,[19] which was successfully challenged by Indonesia in the WTO dispute settlement system.[20] A measure designed to restrict flavours that might tend to initiate smoking or attract smokers or particular groups of smokers certainly seems plausible from a health perspective. However, WTO rules are more likely to censure such measures where they exempt certain products, if the benefit of the exemption is obtained primarily by domestic producers or by producers in particular countries rather than all WTO Members, and in the absence of sound health evidence supporting the exemption. In this case, the United States measure was found inconsistent with Article 2.1 of the WTO's *Agreement on Technical Barriers to Trade* ('TBT Agreement')[21] on the basis that it discriminates against imported products (clove cigarettes, which are largely imported from Indonesia and are subject to the ban) in favour of domestic products (menthol cigarettes, which are largely produced in the United States and are exempt from the ban).[22] However, the measure was found consistent with Article 2.2 of the TBT Agreement because the import ban

---

[18]   See, e.g., D. Zeigler, 'The Alcohol Industry and Trade Agreements: a Preliminary Assessment', 104 (1) *Addiction* (2009) 13–26, at 22.

[19]   *Family Smoking Prevention and Tobacco Control Act 2009* (US).

[20]   Appellate Body Report, *United States – Measures Affecting the Production and Sale of Clove Cigarettes* (*'US – Clove Cigarettes'*), WT/DS406/AB/R (4 April 2012); Panel Report, *US – Clove Cigarettes*, WT/DS406/R (2 September 2011). For further discussion of this dispute, see T. Voon, 'United States – Measures Affecting the Production and Sale of Clove Cigarettes', 106(4) *American Journal of International Law* 824–830 (2012).

[21]   *Marrakesh Agreement Establishing the World Trade Organization*, Annex 1A, 33 *International Legal Materials* 1125 (signed 15 April 1994, entered into force 1 January 1995).

[22]   Appellate Body Report, *US – Clove Cigarettes*, para. 298(a)(v).

on flavoured cigarettes is not more trade-restrictive than necessary to achieve the United States' health objectives.[23]

WTO disciplines on subsidies in general and agricultural subsidies in particular (which would include tobacco subsidies)[24] may also have a role in promoting rather than hindering WTO Members' health objectives. Specifically, obligations imposed on WTO Members under the WTO's *Agreement on Subsidies and Countervailing Measures* and *Agreement on Agriculture*[25] can and have been used to challenge some subsidies on unhealthy foods such as sugar[26] and high fructose corn syrup.[27] Successful enforcement of WTO disciplines in this manner therefore has the potential to combat low and falling prices of certain over-consumed products with minimal nutritional benefits and highly processed products based on them, with positive flow-on effects for global health. Removing tobacco (or any other product) from the scope of the WTO would likely lead to more rather than fewer subsidies and greater consequential distortion of world trade, with particularly harmful results for producers and workers in the poorest regions, such as farmers in Africa.

The importance of multilateral subsidy disciplines for public health measures targeting contributors to poor diet reflects the power of the relevant industries and the utility of international constraints to that power. Removing tobacco from the WTO would do nothing to diminish the power of 'big tobacco'. WTO tariff bindings do impose a ceiling on the tariffs that Members impose on imports of tobacco products from other WTO Members (pursuant to each Member's tariff schedule), and in general terms WTO negotiations are designed to progressively reduce those tariff ceilings. However, although removing WTO rules would allow Members to impose tariffs on tobacco imports above these ceilings (as well as introducing other barriers to trade such as product bans that might otherwise be WTO-inconsistent), this step would not prevent

---

[23] D. Pruzin, 'WTO Panel Ruling Supports U.S. Ban On Flavored Cigarettes From Indonesia' (5 July 2011) *BNA International Trade Daily*.

[24] Tobacco products appear in Chapter 24 of the Harmonized System, which is covered by the *Agreement on Agriculture*, as stated in its Annex 1.

[25] Both agreements are contained in *Marrakesh Agreement Establishing the World Trade Organization*, Annex 1A, 33 *International Legal Materials* 1125 (signed 15 April 1994, entered into force 1 January 1995).

[26] Appellate Body Report, *European Communities – Export Subsidies on Sugar*, WT/DS265/AB/R, WT/DS266/AB/R, WT/DS283/AB/R (circulated 28 April 2005, adopted 19 May 2005).

[27] WTO, *United States – Subsidies and Other Domestic Support for Corn and Other Agricultural Products: Request for the Establishment of a Panel by Canada*, WT/DS357/12 (9 November 2007) and WT/DS357/12/Corr.1 (16 November 2007).

foreign and multinational tobacco companies from imposing pressure on governments to reduce trade barriers. Some counterweight to this pressure might be exerted by local tobacco companies, but this is equally true under the current WTO regime. The balance of power between foreign and local industry (assuming they both existed in any given country) would be unlikely to change as a result of the removal of tobacco from the coverage of WTO law. And for any Members who already apply tariffs on tobacco imports below their bound rate, little reason would exist to increase them. The only difference might be that instead of being lobbied by other WTO Members (who are being lobbied by their own tobacco companies) to reduce tobacco trade barriers, WTO Members would be lobbied directly by tobacco companies throughout the world, although perhaps no more than they already are.

A more practical difficulty with the proposal to remove tobacco from the ambit of the WTO is that it is extremely unlikely to happen, both because very little ever gets done in the way of renegotiation of WTO rules due to the organization's consensus-based decision-making framework[28] (as evidenced by the never-ending Doha Round of negotiations), and because WTO Members are likely to be (rightly, in my view) concerned about the slippery slope represented by this approach. Although tobacco is arguably unique in the sense that no level of consumption is safe and yet it is generally legal, if tobacco is excluded from WTO rules, what next? Do Members also need freedom to regulate alcohol and therefore the ability to impose discriminatory and non-discriminatory trade barriers against international trade in alcohol? Should processed foods high in sugar, fat or salt be excluded from the WTO so that Members can ban their production and importation? What about products or industries with negative effects on the environment or human rights? Could public policy concerns become a means of slowly tearing down the WTO and reversing its achievements in tariff declines and consequential poverty reduction?[29]

This brings us to the proposition that trade measures are generally 'inferior to other forms of government intervention to correct . . . market

---

[28]   *Marrakesh Agreement Establishing the World Trade Organization*, 33 *International Legal Materials* 1125 (signed 15 April 1994, entered into force 1 January 1995), Art. IX:1.

[29]   See, e.g., WTO, *Understanding the WTO*, (Geneva: WTO, 2010) 11–13, 17, 25, 28; A. Winters, N. McCulloch and A. McKay, 'Trade Liberalization and Poverty: The Evidence so Far', 42(1) *Journal of Economic Literature* (2004) 72–115; cf Thomas Hertel and Alan Winters (eds), *Poverty and the WTO: Impacts of the Doha Development Agenda* (Washington DC/Basingstoke: World Bank/Palgrave Macmillan, 2006).

failure'[30] or otherwise achieve a non-economic policy goal – a proposition that arguably holds equally for public health measures addressing tobacco use, alcohol abuse and poor diet as for other social policy measures. From the perspective of a WTO legal academic with a belief in the economic theory of comparative advantage that underlies the WTO but also with concerns about the common risk factors of non-communicable diseases, I therefore proceed in the following sections to assess alternatives to removing tobacco or any other product from the scope of the WTO agreements. In particular, I consider whether the existing flexibilities in the various agreements are sufficient to justify public health measures of the kind needed to target these risk factors, and whether the practical outcome of WTO disputes to date on relevant issues confirms the sufficiency of these flexibilities.

III. FLEXIBILITIES IN WTO LAW FOR PUBLIC HEALTH MEASURES

The structure of WTO law generally provides significant scope for Members to address their own regulatory objectives as they see fit. Most WTO agreements impose largely negative obligations (such as the national treatment obligation *not* to discriminate through internal taxes or regulations against imports from any WTO Members). Members are free to take decisions as fundamental as whether to operate as a democracy, provided that they do not infringe those negative obligations. Moreover, these obligations are subject to significant exceptions, enabling Members in particular circumstances to act contrary to the usual rules. A few WTO agreements do impose extensive positive obligations that encourage or require Members to standardize or harmonize regulations in particular areas, for example the TBT Agreement, the *Agreement on Trade-Related Aspects of Intellectual Property Rights* (TRIPS Agreement),[31] and the *Agreement on the Application of Sanitary and Phytosanitary Measures.*[32]

---

[30] A. Sykes, 'Comparative Advantage and the Normative Economics of International Trade Policy', 1 *Journal of International Economic Law* (1998) 49–82, at 74.

[31] *Marrakesh Agreement Establishing the World Trade Organization*, Annex 1C, 33 *International Legal Materials* 1125 (signed 15 April 1994, entered into force 1 January 1995).

[32] *Marrakesh Agreement Establishing the World Trade Organization*, Annex 1A, 33 *International Legal Materials* 1125 (signed 15 April 1994, entered into force 1 January 1995).

These agreements also contain inherent flexibilities in recognition of the various non-trade policies that Members may wish to pursue.

In a sense, the problem of public health measures designed to address the risk factors of non-communicable diseases is nothing new. The drafters of the WTO agreements were fully aware of the potential for Members' health objectives to conflict with WTO rules and incorporated mechanisms into the agreements to deal with such conflicts. The scope and strength of the existing exceptions and flexibilities in the different agreements can be illustrated with respect to public health measures using the current example of plain packaging of cigarettes and other tobacco products.

On 1 December 2012, Australia's world-first legislation mandating the so-called 'plain' packaging of cigarettes was fully implemented. All tobacco products sold in Australia must now be contained in standardised packaging of the same colour ('drab dark brown'), largely taken up by graphic and textual warnings, and with brand names reduced to the same font and size. Tobacco companies have unsuccessfully challenged the legislation within the High Court of Australia (Australia's highest court) on constitutional grounds.[33] Philip Morris Asia Limited has also launched an investment arbitration against Australia[34] pursuant to the Hong Kong – Australia Bilateral Investment Treaty[35] (mirroring an ongoing claim against Uruguay).[36] Within the WTO, Ukraine, Honduras and the Dominican Republic have requested the establishment of panels to hear their claims[37] about the

---

[33]   *JT International SA v Commonwealth; British American Tobacco Australasia Limited v Commonwealth* [2012] HCA 43 (5 October 2012).

[34]   *Philip Morris Asia Ltd and Commonwealth of Australia* (Notice of Arbitration, 21 November 2011); Philip Morris Limited, *News Release: Philip Morris Asia Initiates Legal Action Against the Australian Government Over Plain Packaging* (27 June 2011). See also A. Mitchell and S. Wurzberger, 'Boxed in? Assessing Australia's Tobacco Plain Packaging Initiative under International Investment Law', 27(4) *Arbitration International* (2011) 623–651.

[35]   *Agreement between the Government of Hong Kong and the Government of Australia for the Promotion and Protection of Investments*, 1748 UNTS 385 (signed and entered into force 15 September 1993).

[36]   *FTR Holding SA et al v Oriental Republic of Uruguay*, ICSID Case ARB/10/7. See also WHO, *Report on the Global Tobacco Epidemic 2011: Warning about the Dangers of Tobacco* (WHO, 2011) 58.

[37]   Request for the Establishment of a Panel by Ukraine, *Australia – Certain Measures Concerning Trademarks and Other Plain Packaging Requirements Applicable to Tobacco Products and Packaging*, WT/DS434/11 (17 August 2012); Request for the Establishment of a Panel by Honduras, *Australia – Certain Measures Concerning Trademarks, Geographical Indications and Other Plain Packaging Requirements Applicable to Tobacco Products and Packaging*, WT/DS435/16 (17 October 2012); Request for the Establishment of a Panel by the

measure pursuant to the TBT Agreement, the TRIPS Agreement, and the *General Agreement on Tariffs and Trade 1994* (GATT 1994).[38]

Under the TRIPS Agreement, the strongest argument that can be made against the scheme is that it violates Article 20, which provides that '[t]he use of a trademark in the course of trade shall not be *unjustifiably encumbered* by special requirements, such as . . . use in a special form or use in a manner detrimental to its capability to distinguish the goods or services of one undertaking from those of other undertakings'.[39] Some commentators query whether plain packaging requirements such as those proposed by Australia constitute an encumbrance within the meaning of Article 20.[40] However, assuming that it is a relevant encumbrance, this would be inconsistent with Article 20 only if the encumbrance is *unjustifiable*. In assessing what might make it justifiable to encumber a trademark, Articles 7 and 8 of the TRIPS Agreement may be relevant as context and purpose[41] for the interpretation of Article 20. The 'Objectives' in Article 7 point out that the 'protection and enforcement of intellectual property rights' should take place 'in a manner conducive to social and economic welfare', while the 'Principles' in Article 8 make clear that Members may adopt TRIPS-consistent measures that are 'necessary to protect public health'. These factors strengthen the argument that a measure such as plain packaging may justifiably hinder the use of trademarks for public health reasons without contravening Article 20.

The words 'necessary to protect public health' call to mind Article XX(b) of the GATT 1994 which provides a general exception from GATT rules for measures that are 'necessary to protect human, animal or plant life or health', subject to certain stringent requirements in the 'chapeau' to Article XX. Article XX(b) of the GATT 1994 and Article 20 of the TRIPS Agreement are part of a single treaty, meaning that the former

---

Dominican Republic, *Australia – Certain Measures Concerning Trademarks, Geographical Indications and Other Plain Packaging Requirements Applicable to Tobacco Products and Packaging*, WT/DS441/15 (14 November 2012).

[38] *General Agreement on Tariffs and Trade*, 55 UNTS 194 (signed 30 October 1947), as amended and incorporated into *Marrakesh Agreement Establishing the World Trade Organization*, Annex 1A, 33 *International Legal Materials* 1125 (signed 15 April 1994, entered into force 1 January 1995).

[39] Emphasis added.

[40] See, e.g., B. McGrady, 'TRIPs and Trademarks: the Case of Tobacco', 3(1) *World Trade Review* (2004) 53–82, at 61, 63–64; cf A. Mitchell, 'Australia's Move to the Plain Packaging of Cigarettes and its WTO Compatibility', 5 *Asian Journal of WTO & International Health Law & Policy* (2010) 405–425, at 418.

[41] *Vienna Convention on the Law of Treaties*, 1155 UNTS 133 (adopted 22 May 1969), Art. 31(1).

provision may be regarded as relevant context in interpreting the latter, and the approach of the WTO Appellate Body in applying Article XX(b) may provide useful guidance as to how it might approach a health measure challenged under Article 20.[42] Thus, relevant considerations could include the trade-restrictiveness of the measure (and, potentially, in the context of TRIPS Article 20, the degree to which it encumbers the use of a trademark), the extent to which the measure contributes to its health objective, the importance of that objective, and whether reasonably available alternative measures exist that would make an equivalent contribution to the Member's objective while restricting trade (or encumbering the use of a trademark) to a lesser extent.[43]

Applying these considerations to Australia's plain packaging measure, the measure is likely to have only a limited impact on trade because it applies equally to all tobacco products sold in Australia (most of which are manufactured domestically) and it does not preclude importation of any products. The extent to which it encumbers the use of a trademark is debatable, but on one view it is a significant encumbrance in that it may prevent particular trademarks from being used at all (e.g. logos, pictures, colours) and requires word marks to appear in a specified font and size. The extent to which the measure will contribute to its health objectives (of reducing smoking initiation, maintenance, relapse etc.) is also contentious and difficult to verify given that Australia is the first country in the world to implement such a scheme. Nevertheless, numerous studies indicate that packaging plays a vital role in brand marketing and recognition for tobacco products and that plain packaging has the potential to make a significant impact on smoking rates and consequently on associated illness.[44]

---

[42]   See Appellate Body Report, *United States – Section 211 Omnibus Appropriations Act of 1998,* WT/DS176/AB/R (circulated 2 January 2002, adopted 1 February 2002), para. 242, where the Appellate Body referred to the utility of its jurisprudence on Article III:4 of the GATT 1994 in interpreting the similarly-worded national treatment obligation in Article 3.1 of the TRIPS Agreement.

[43]   Cf Appellate Body Report, *Brazil – Measures Affecting Imports of Retreaded Tyres,* WT/DS332/AB/R (circulated 3 December 2007, adopted 17 December 2007), paras 156, 178 (outlining a test for assessing necessity pursuant to Article XX(b) of the GATT 1994).

[44]   See, e.g., National Preventative Health Taskforce, *Australia: The Healthiest Country by 2020 – Technical Report 2,* (Canberra: Commonwealth of Australia, 2009) 20–21; US Department of Health & Human Services, *Preventing Tobacco Use Among Youth and Young Adults: A Report of the Surgeon General* (2012) 530–535; Public Health Research Consortium, UK, *Plain Tobacco Packaging: A Systematic Review* (2012).

This view is supported by guidelines adopted by the Conference of the Parties to the WHO FCTC (to which Australia is a party), which suggest that parties consider adopting plain packaging measures.[45] As regards the importance of the objective pursued by plain packaging, the Appellate Body has previously recognized the value of 'preserv[ing] human life and health' as 'both vital and important in the highest degree' in the context of Article XX(b).[46] Finally, the universe of reasonably available alternative measures is limited by the fact that Australia's approach to tobacco control is already among the most stringent in the world, including significant excise taxes (raised by 25 per cent in 2010), bans on cigarette displays at the point of sale pursuant to legislation in several States/territories, and generous funding of social marketing and educational campaigns. The Appellate Body has already recognized that an existing element of a 'comprehensive strategy' of a Member to deal with a given problem cannot constitute an *alternative* measure in the context of GATT Article XX(b).[47]

All in all, then, the text of Article 20 of the TRIPS Agreement and the surrounding context and approach of the Appellate Body to health measures under GATT Article XX(b) suggest ample scope for a Member such as Australia to defend a health measure to combat a risk factor for NCDs such as plain packaging. Similar considerations would also be relevant and are likely to combine to prevent plain packaging from breaching Article 2.2 of the TBT Agreement, which requires that WTO Members' 'technical regulations . . . not be more trade-restrictive than necessary to fulfil a legitimate objective' including 'protection of human health'.[48] Thus, the legal architecture of WTO law does seem to provide Members with sufficient flexibility to construct targeted, country-specific health measures to combat the perceived contribution of international trade and trade liberalization to the global proliferation of unhealthy habits and associated NCDs. However, is this enough to allay fears for public health? In the next section I consider the practical impact of WTO-level regulation and activ-

---

[45] WHO, *Guidelines for Implementation of Article 11 of the WHO Framework Convention on Tobacco Control* (2009); WHO, *Guidelines for Implementation of Article 13 of the WHO Framework Convention on Tobacco Control* (2009).

[46] Appellate Body Report, *European Communities – Measures Affecting Asbestos and Asbestos-Containing Products*, WT/DS135/AB/R (circulated 12 March 2001, adopted 5 April 2001), para. 172.

[47] Appellate Body Report, *Brazil – Measures Affecting Imports of Retreaded Tyres*, WT/DS332/AB/R (circulated 3 December 2007, adopted 17 December 2007), para. 172.

[48] Analysis under this provision will require examination of the three Appellate Body reports circulated in 2012 on the TBT Agreement, including Appellate Body Report, *US – Clove Cigarettes*.

ities on domestic health measures, which suggests some cause for concern despite the adequacy of existing exceptions and recognitions in the WTO agreements. This problematic impact is best demonstrated through an examination of the apparent effects to date of WTO law on alcohol and tobacco control measures.

IV.   EFFECTS OF WTO LAW ON DOMESTIC REGULATIONS CONCERNING ALCOHOL AND TOBACCO

Commentators have recognized that WTO law may have a chilling effect on regulation, including health regulation in particular,[49] even if a proper application of that law would permit the proposed regulation. The same applies to domestic and other forms of international law. For example, the financial and resource costs of defending simultaneous legal challenges at the domestic and international levels (as is the case of plain packaging in Australia) may also test the limits of a given government even if the claims are likely to fail. Countries with few resources or little expertise in the field of WTO law would likely find this situation difficult to deal with while maintaining health as a priority.

Regulatory chill may also arise even if no formal dispute settlement proceedings are commenced within the WTO or other domestic or international fora to challenge a given measure. Informal complaints or media statements by particular countries or companies may be enough to prevent a WTO Member from pursuing a proposed health measure, particularly but not only if it is a measure that other WTO Members are yet to adopt. The threat or risk of litigation or other forms of international or domestic conflict may have implications for financial and other government resources that are too great to be ignored. This is so even if the government in question is reasonably certain that its proposed actions are WTO-consistent and that it would win a WTO dispute on the matter.

WTO Members (informed by their affected industries) may also impose pressure on governments proposing bold health measures by raising complaints in WTO contexts short of bringing a WTO dispute. In particular, the WTO's Committee on Technical Barriers to Trade has in recent months and years become a frequent battle ground in relation to various tobacco

---

[49]   See, e.g., J. Liberman and A. Mitchell, 'In Search of Coherence Between Trade and Health: Inter-Institutional Opportunities', 25 *Maryland Journal of International Law* (2010) 143–186, at 165.

and alcohol control measures of different Members. As an example, Canada has faced numerous complaints from many other WTO Members in the TBT Committee[50] in relation to its legislation restricting tobacco flavouring,[51] which is similar to the United States legislation discussed above. Members have also complained within the TBT Committee about large pictorial health warnings to be introduced for alcoholic beverages in Thailand; in that context, the United States also raised concerns about the negative impact of the labelling requirements on trademarks.[52] More recently, several Members raised concerns about draft regulations introduced by Brazil limiting the amounts of tar, nicotine and carbon monoxide and prohibiting other additives in tobacco products.[53] These examples show how comments of other WTO Members in the international forum of the WTO may influence and potentially restrict progressive health regulation in connection with the common risk factors for NCDs, even in the absence of a formal dispute settlement complaint (which might not be pursued because an actual violation of WTO law is unlikely).

Where a successful WTO dispute settlement complaint is brought against a regulatory measure concerning alcohol or tobacco, this may also have a negative impact on health regulation, even if the measure is not specifically or solely directed at a public health objective (but rather, for instance, to raise revenue) and even if bringing the measure into conformity with WTO rules does not of itself necessitate any modification to or relaxing of health objectives. Some have noted in the context of alcohol control that, due to 'the political dynamics following such decisions, the result is usually a lowering of the net tax rate on the affected group of beverages'.[54] Similar observations have been made in the context of bilateral and regional relationships such as the European Union and Canada/

---

[50]   See, e.g., WTO Committee on Technical Barriers to Trade, *Minutes of the Meeting of 5–6 November 2009: Note by the Secretariat*, G/TBT/M/49 (22 December 2009), paras 8–16; WTO Committee on Technical Barriers to Trade, *Minutes of the Meeting of 23–24 June 2010: Note by the Secretariat*, G/TBT/M/51 (1 October 2010), paras 181–216.

[51]   *Cracking Down on Tobacco Marketing Aimed at Youth Act 2009* (Canada).

[52]   WTO Committee on Technical Barriers to Trade, *Minutes of the Meeting of 23–24 June 2010: Note by the Secretariat*, G/TBT/M/51 (1 October 2010), paras 237–251.

[53]   WTO, *News item: Members concerned about public health* (24–25 March 2011).

[54]   T. Babor et al, *Alcohol: No Ordinary Commodity – Research and Public Policy* (Oxford: Oxford University Press, 2nd ed., 2010) 90.

United States.[55] A lowering of taxes might be expected in circumstances where, for example, the WTO violation arises from tax discrimination against imports, because domestic alcohol producers and distributors are likely to object to a raising of taxes on their products and so instead tax rates are equalized by lowering the taxes on imports. If taxes on domestic products were raised to the level imposed on imports, not only would the products now compete on an equal playing field (to the detriment of domestic producers, who were previously partially protected from such competition), but also consumers would now have to pay more for domestic products, placing them out of some consumers' reach or causing consumers to use their money to purchase something else (including an entirely unrelated product) given the change in relative prices. The resulting hypothesis that adverse WTO rulings against alcohol regulations are likely to lead to lower taxes (and consequently lower prices, increased consumption[56] and more NCDs) can be tested by considering the ultimate outcome of the WTO cases to date concerning regulatory measures on alcohol that have been found WTO-inconsistent.

The expected response of a Member forced to bring its alcohol regulations into conformity with WTO rules is borne out by the dispute in *Chile – Alcoholic Beverages*. In that case, the Appellate Body found that Chile was acting inconsistently with the national treatment obligation in GATT Article III:2, second sentence, by imposing regulations that had the effect of taxing most imported alcoholic beverages at a rate of 47 per cent *ad valorem* and most directly competitive or substitutable domestic alcoholic beverages at a rate of 27 per cent *ad valorem*, so as to afford protection to domestic production.[57] Chile complied with this adverse ruling by enacting 'legislation providing for the progressive reduction of taxes to a single rate for all alcoholic beverages of 27 per cent'.[58] Thus, alcoholic bev-

---

[55]   See, e.g., P. Mäkela and E. Österberg, 'Weakening of One More Alcohol Control Pillar: a review of the effects of the alcohol tax cuts in Finland in 2004', 104 *Addiction* (2009) 554–563; R. Room, N. Giesbrecht and G. Stoduto, 'Trade Agreements and Disputes', in N. Giesbrecht et al (eds), *Sober Reflections: Commerce, Public Health and the Evolution of Alcohol Policy in Canada, 1980–2000* (McGill-Queen's University Press: Quebec, 2006) 74–96.

[56]   See World Bank, *Public Policy and the Challenge of Chronic Noncommunicable Diseases*, (Washington DC: World Bank, 2007) 86.

[57]   Appellate Body Report, *Chile – Taxes on Alcoholic Beverages*, WT/DS87/AB/R, WT/DS110/AB/R (circulated 13 December 1999, adopted 12 January 2000), paras 53–55, 76.

[58]   WTO, *Chile – Taxes on Alcoholic Beverages: Status Report by Chile*, WT/DS87/17/Add.2, WT/DS110/16/Add.2 (27 February 2001).

erages became cheaper for consumers, which would generally be regarded as a negative result from the perspective of public health.

However, the impact of an adverse WTO dispute settlement ruling is not as clear cut in the other two alcohol disputes. In *Korea – Alcoholic Beverages*, the Appellate Body upheld the Panel's determination that Korea was taxing imported beverages such as whisky, brandy and gin in excess of the directly competitive or substitutable traditional Korean beverage soju in a manner contrary to the second sentence of Article III:2 of the GATT 1994.[59] Korea brought the WTO-inconsistent measures into conformity by imposing flat tax rates on all alcoholic beverages. However, in this instance not all modified tax rates fell. Although the liquor tax rate on whiskies and brandies dropped from 100 per cent to 72 per cent and on general distilled alcoholic beverages from 80 per cent to 72 per cent, the liquor tax on soju jumped from 35–50 per cent to 72 per cent and on liqueurs from 50 per cent to 72 per cent.[60] Thus, the path that may have been preferred by local producers of alcoholic beverages (simply lowering the taxes on imported beverages and maintaining existing tax rates on soju) was not followed, and the outcome did not necessarily have an overall impact of reducing prices on alcoholic beverages.

Finally, in the first alcohol case before the WTO, *Japan – Alcoholic Beverages II*, the Appellate Body found that Japan had acted inconsistently with the first and second sentences of GATT Article III:2 by taxing the predominantly domestic product shochu in excess of the predominantly imported like product vodka and by failing to tax shochu similarly to other directly competitive or substitutable imported distilled spirits and liqueurs in a manner so as to afford protection to domestic production.[61] Following this ruling, Japan reached settlements with Canada, the European Union (then the European Communities) and the United States. Under these settlements, Japan revised its tax rates in a manner that increased the rates for shochu and decreased the rates for some typically imported spirits such as whiskies.[62] This demonstrates that, despite

---

[59] Appellate Body Report, *Korea – Taxes on Alcoholic Beverages*, WT/DS75/AB/R, WT/DS84/AB/R (circulated 18 January 1999, adopted 17 February 1999), paras 2, 169.

[60] WTO, *Korea – Taxes on Alcoholic Beverages: Status Report by Korea*, WT/DS75/18, WT/DS84/16 (17 January 2000) p. 2.

[61] Appellate Body Report, *Japan – Taxes on Alcoholic Beverages*, WT/DS8/AB/R, WT/DS10/AB/R, WT/DS11/AB/R (circulated 4 October 1996, adopted 1 November 1996) p. 32.

[62] WTO, *Japan – Taxes on Alcoholic Beverages: Mutually Acceptable Solution on Modalities for Implementation – Addendum*, WT/DS8/17/Add.1, WT/DS10/17/Add.1, WT/DS11/15/Add.1 (12 January 1998), annex A (European Communities);

possible political difficulties, Japan was able to remedy its laws in a way that increased the burden on domestic alcohol producers compared to the situation before the dispute. Although a concern with alcohol's contribution to NCDs might indicate that a preferable result would have been to increase all tax rates to the level originally imposed on imported spirits, this middle ground of raising taxes on shochu and decreasing taxes on whisky was at least less likely to promote alcohol consumption than the solution adopted in Chile's case.

However, also pursuant to the settlements in *Japan – Alcoholic Beverages II*, Japan progressively eliminated import tariffs on several common beverages such as brandy, whisky, rum, gin and vodka.[63] The tariff eliminations would have had to extend, pursuant to the WTO's most-favoured nation rule,[64] to imports of the relevant products from all WTO Members. This change would again have disadvantaged domestic producers of alcoholic beverages compared to the pre-dispute situation, while also lowering the price of the relevant imported beverages, with the likely result of increasing consumption of alcoholic beverages. These progressive tariff reductions were not legally required as a direct result of the WTO dispute settlement decision; rather, they represented a concession to the complainants in the dispute in view of the fact that Japan had failed to comply with the decision before the expiry of the 'reasonable period of time' for doing so.[65] Nevertheless, that Japan eliminated tariffs on alcoholic beverages, with potential negative health consequences, was a practical effect of the dispute.

WTO, *Japan – Taxes on Alcoholic Beverages: Mutually Acceptable Solution on Modalities for Implementation*, WT/DS8/19, WT/DS10/19, WT/DS11/17 (12 January 1998), annex A (United States); WTO, *Japan – Taxes on Alcoholic Beverages: Mutually Acceptable Solution on Modalities for Implementation*, WT/DS8/20, WT/DS10/20, WT/DS11/18 (12 January 1998), annex 1 (Canada).

[63]   WTO, *Japan – Taxes on Alcoholic Beverages: Mutually Acceptable Solution on Modalities for Implementation – Addendum*, WT/DS8/17/Add.1, WT/DS10/17/Add.1, WT/DS11/15/Add.1 (12 January 1998), annex B (European Communities); WTO, *Japan – Taxes on Alcoholic Beverages: Mutually Acceptable Solution on Modalities for Implementation*, WT/DS8/19, WT/DS10/19, WT/DS11/17 (12 January 1998), annex B (United States); WTO, *Japan – Taxes on Alcoholic Beverages: Mutually Acceptable Solution on Modalities for Implementation*, WT/DS8/20, WT/DS10/20, WT/DS11/18 (12 January 1998), annex 1–2 (Canada).

[64]   GATT 1994, Art. I:1.

[65]   *Understanding on Rules and Procedures Governing the Settlement of Disputes* ('DSU'), Art. 21.3: *Marrakesh Agreement Establishing the World Trade Organization*, Annex 2, 33 *International Legal Materials* 1125 (signed 15 April 1994, entered into force 1 January 1995).

Although extensive empirical and economic analysis would be required to attempt to determine the health impact of these three WTO disputes on alcoholic beverages, the above survey suggests that dispute settlement findings of WTO violations cannot be said to lead typically to either lower or higher overall prices for alcoholic beverages in the respondent Members. At a minimum, it does seem possible for countries to find feasible and politically acceptable ways of raising taxes on domestic alcoholic beverages in some circumstances and to some extent. On the other hand, a WTO Member that finds itself facing complaints by other Members about its alcohol regulation, backed by a WTO dispute settlement determination that it is breaching WTO rules, may experience pressure to lower barriers to trade in alcoholic beverages (whether sales taxes or tariffs) even beyond the changes required by the legal determination.

V.   CONCLUSION

This chapter highlights the growing public health problem posed by NCDs and the crucial role of the WTO in supporting international efforts to combat that problem. The legal provisions of the WTO agreements, as interpreted by WTO Panels and the Appellate Body in a substantial body of jurisprudence, do contain significant exceptions and other forms of flexibility to enable WTO Members to implement genuine health measures even where they may have negative effects on international trade. Nevertheless, certainty of outcomes under WTO dispute settlement, including predictable regulatory freedom, could be further enhanced by the generation of additional scientific evidence concerning the impact of the many available regulatory measures on the risk factors for NCDs of tobacco consumption, alcohol abuse and poor diet, and their consequential health implications. This evidence should, to the extent possible, be generalizable from one country to another, allowing less well-resourced countries to benefit from studies conducted in regulatory leaders and better-resourced economies. International cooperation towards preferred regulatory approaches to these risk factors, for example through treaties, decisions or guidelines developed under the auspices of the WHO FCTC or the WHO more generally, may also assist in ensuring that WTO Members' health measures targeting NCD risk factors are able to withstand a challenge in the WTO dispute settlement system.

In addition to the details of WTO law and its operation in WTO dispute settlement, a holistic understanding of the complex relationship between international trade and NCD risk factors requires a consideration of extra-legal factors associated with the WTO. In particular, the WTO Secretariat, WTO Member delegates, and practitioners and academics in this field need to recognize the legitimate concerns of public health officials and advocates regarding the contribution of trade liberalization and international trade law to rising rates of smoking, alcohol abuse and obesity, particularly in the developing world. Increased awareness of these connections might temper Members' apparent enthusiasm for making complaints about others' health measures in the TBT Committee, WTO dispute settlement system or elsewhere.

Greater research would also be worthwhile into the practical effects of adverse WTO rulings on health measures (including taxes and tariffs) and consequentially public health in respondent Members. This research could include an examination of the political strategies used to achieve modifications to existing laws and regulations in order to achieve compliance with WTO law. The results of this kind of research could assist WTO Members and other countries in adopting domestic regulatory processes and structures that reduce the likelihood of capture by special interest groups, including industries whose products represent risk factors for NCDs. Improving national approaches in this way will be increasingly important, since the factor of poor diet is much more wide-ranging and variable than the factors of tobacco consumption and alcohol abuse.[66] The WTO and WTO law must certainly remain receptive to non-trade concerns including health. However, the natural effects of trade liberalization do impose increased responsibility on domestic governance, requiring Members to adopt more sophisticated techniques to combat NCDs and their associated risk factors than simply blocking or discriminating against imports.

---

[66]   On the range of possible legal responses to poor nutrition and obesity, see R. Magnusson, 'What's Law Got to Do With it? Part 2: Legal strategies for healthier nutrition and obesity prevention', 5(11) *Australia and New Zealand Health Policy* (2008) 1–17.

PART III

ENVIRONMENTAL REGULATION AND TRADE LAW

Section 1

Climate Change Mitigation

14. International trade and climate change
Thomas Cottier and Nashina Shariff

I. INTRODUCTION

Climatic changes over time have been a major factor influencing human history and civilization. From the fall of the Mayan Empire to the collapse of the Mesopotamians, changing patterns of temperature and precipitation have influenced the fate of regions and kingdoms.[1] Perhaps more than we know, the history of international trade has been influenced by climatic changes, inducing the rise and fall of global trading centers throughout the history of mankind. International trading regimes from barter trade to mercantilism and the ideals of free trade all had to cope with such changes in nature. In modern times the exploitation of fossil fuels that enabled the industrial revolution and has fueled economic growth thereafter has led humanity to a juncture where societies are not only affected by but also have effects on the climate. The result is that the intersection of trade rules and climate change will be of increasing importance in the years to come. They not only need to cope with natural climatic changes, but also to address man-made causes of climate change and its repercussions.

The warming of the climate is unequivocal and this warming is very likely a result of increasing anthropogenic concentrations of greenhouse gases.[2] Continued and increased patterns of consumption will likely lead to increases in global temperatures, projected to be between 1.1 and 6.4 degrees Celsius in the next 100 years.[3] These increases in temperature will in turn lead to rising sea levels and shrinking sea ice as well as increased severity of storms, heat waves, areas affected by droughts and resulting

---

[1] de Menocal, P. (2001), 'Cultural Responses to Climate Change During the Late Holocene', *Science, ***292** (5517), 667–673.
[2] IPCC (2007), *Climate Change 2007: Synthesis Report. Contribution of Working Groups I, II and III to the Fourth Assessment Report of the Intergovernmental Panel on Climate Change,* Geneva, Switzerland: IPCC. See pp. 2 and 5, available at http://www.ipcc.ch/pdf/assessment-report/ar4/syr/ar4_syr_spm.pdf (accessed 21 April 2011).
[3] Ibid., p. 8.

increases in health impacts.[4] The impacts from climate change will be felt disproportionately by those that have the least capacity to adapt to them, including least developed countries and small island states.

In 1992 the United Nations Framework Convention on Climate Change (UNFCCC) was established with the goal of ensuring the 'stabilization of greenhouse gas concentrations in the atmosphere at a level that would prevent dangerous anthropogenic interference with the climate system'.[5] In 2005 the Kyoto Protocol entered into force.[6] It aimed to reduce global greenhouse gas emissions to 5 percent below 1990 levels over the 2008–2012 period.[7] The Protocol and the Convention are based on the principle of common but differentiated responsibilities, recognizing that because developed countries are responsible for the bulk of the historic emissions that have caused the climate change problem they have the responsibility to take the lead in finding the solution.[8] As a result the Kyoto Protocol sets out specific emissions reduction targets for developed nations and includes provisions to enable the transfer of low-emitting technology to developing countries as well as assistance to help developing countries adapt to the impacts of climate change.

In 2009 in Copenhagen a general consensus began to emerge that temperatures should be limited to within 2 degrees Celsius above pre-industrial levels.[9] The main achievement of that conference was that all countries, industrialized and developing, agreed to a dialogue, recognizing the need for common responsibilities. This in turn led to the Cancun Agreement

---

[4]   Ibid., pp. 8 and 10.

[5]   (1992) ILM 31, 849.

[6]   United Nations Framework Convention on Climate Change, 'Status of Ratification of the Kyoto Protocol', http://unfccc.int/kyoto_protocol/items/2830.php (accessed 21 April 2011).

[7]   (1997) ILM 37, 22.

[8]   United Nations Framework Convention on Climate Change (1992), Article 3.1 and preamble.

[9]   In 2009 the Conference of the Parties, the governing body of the UNFCCC took note of the Copenhagen Accord in which nations agreed '. . . that deep cuts in global emissions are required according to science, and as documented by the IPCC Fourth Assessment Report with a view to reduce global emissions so as to hold the increase in global temperature below 2 degrees Celsius, and take action to meet this objective consistent with science and on the basis of equity. . .'. See UNFCCC (2010), *Report of the Conference of the Parties on its fifteenth session, held in Copenhagen from 7 to 19 December 2009 Addendum Part Two: Action taken by the Conference of the Parties at its fifteenth session*, FCCC/CP/2009/11/Add.1, Bonn. See decision 2/CP.15, para. 1, available at http://unfccc.int/resource/docs/2009/cop15/eng/11a01.pdf#page=4 (accessed 21 April 2011).

where parties further recognized the 2-degrees limit.[10] Developed countries committed to mobilize up to $100 billion a year by 2020 to help developing countries address the issues associated with climate change,[11] and the precedent-setting Green Climate Fund was established.[12] However, despite this progress, there is no consensus as to how the goals should be achieved, what the appropriate policy instruments might be, and to what extent they should be addressed commonly in international law or shaped by countries in their own right. There is also a lack of consensus on how to operationalize the principle of common but differentiated responsibility. While historic responsibility for carbon dioxide (CO_2) concentrations lies in the hands of industrialized countries, the severity of the problem requires commitments by today's emerging economies and industrialized countries alike. Diverging economic interests, the need to secure adequate access to energy sources and the desire to ensure their industries remain competitive in an increasingly cut-throat global economy have kept countries from agreeing on a comprehensive framework in international environmental law. Prosperity and power is at stake. It is hoped that progress can be made in agreeing on principles and instruments in the coming years and trade rules will likely be of importance in moving this issue forward.

Patterns of energy consumption translate into the production and consumption of goods and services – the very subjects of international trade regulation. While goals and policies remain unsettled in environmental law, trade rules are firmly in place, both within the multilateral framework of the World Trade Organization (WTO) and within an increasing number of regional and preferential agreements. Rules such as those regarding the provision of subsidies, the imposition of tariffs, the rules pertaining to product and process standards, to the protection of intellectual property rights and to professional, educational, financial, engineering and energy related services are of paramount importance to the climate debate. In the absence of an internationally agreed upon framework on the interface between trade rules and climate change mitigation and adaptation measures, compliance of domestic policies with the trade system has to be taken into account in policy making and may be assessed on a case by case basis

---

[10]   UNFCCC (2011), *Report of the Conference of the Parties on its sixteenth session, held in Cancun from 29 November to 10 December 2010 Addendum Part Two: Action taken by the Conference of the Parties at its sixteenth session,* FCCC/CP/2010/7/Add.1, Bonn. See decision 1/CP.16, para. 4, available at http://unfccc.int/resource/docs/2010/cop16/eng/07a01.pdf#page=2 (accessed 21 April 2011).

[11]   Ibid., para. 98.

[12]   Ibid., para. 102.

in dispute settlement. The first cases were filed in 2010 and 2011.[13] These determinations may shape the future of both the availability of trade compliant domestic policies and the future role of the trade system in any emerging climate change framework.

Contemporary trade rules emerging after World War II were shaped at a time when energy and minerals were available in abundance. The primary goals of the trading system – growth, welfare, full employment and the alleviation of poverty – were premised on the assumption that an ample supply of energy would remain available to facilitate the achievement of these objectives. Emerging environmental concerns have fundamentally changed this view and while these concerns are beginning to be reflected in the trade system, as demonstrated by the preamble of the agreement to establish the WTO, which recognizes the objective of sustainable development,[14] much work still needs to be done. The importance of the impending impacts of climate change has made it imperative that further work ensures that trade liberalization and efforts to address the critical issue of climate change work in a mutually beneficial and not a conflicting manner.

This chapter provides a general assessment of the role of trade regulation in the climate debate which, in international law, also bears upon environmental law, human rights and investment protection.[15] It addresses the current state of play of climate and trade policies, explores the interaction with climate change laws and policies and discusses regulatory challenges which may need to be addressed within the multilateral and preferential trade agreements.

II.   INTERDEPENDENCIES BETWEEN CLIMATE CHANGE AND TRADE

Climate change and trade have many interdependencies with trade impacting on the level of greenhouse gas emissions as well as playing a role in making countries less vulnerable to the impacts of climate change. In addition climate change is likely to impact future patterns of trade as well as the reliability of trade routes.

An often used framework for understanding the effects of liberalized

---

[13]   See below, note 58.
[14]   (1994) ILM 37, 1144.
[15]   See generally, Aerni, P. et al. (2010), 'Climate Change and International Law: Exploring the Linkages between Human Rights, Environment, Trade and Investment: Exploring the Linkages Between Human Rights, Environment, Trade and Investment', **53** *German Yearbook of International Law*, 139–188.

trade on the environment breaks down these effects into three categories, the scale, composition and technique effects.[16] The net impact of trade on greenhouse gas emissions will depend on the strength of each of these effects.

- *The scale effect* is the increased emissions that result from increased economic activity as a result of liberalized trade.
- *The composition effect* is the change in emissions that results from countries specializing in particular industries: countries can either see an increase or decrease in emissions depending on which industries they specialize in.
- *The technique effect* is the decrease in emissions that results from increased access to low emitting technologies that comes with liberalized trade as well as from increasing demand for environmental regulations that arise from populations earning higher incomes as a consequence of trade liberalization.

It is well understood that the liberalization of trade leads to increased economic output. As increases in production are driven primarily by fossil fuels, the consequence may be a resultant increase in greenhouse gas emissions. This effect has important implications for the general goal of increasing levels of trade.

The composition effect will depend on factors that influence which countries have a comparative advantage after the liberalization of trade. The 'pollution haven' hypothesis reasons that liberalized trade in goods may cause pollution intensive production to migrate to countries with less stringent environmental regulations in place.[17] This implies that carbon policies can result in carbon leakage – carbon reductions from the imposition of regulations being diluted by increased production in more carbon intensive countries.[18] As a result of these concerns a number of countries have contemplated policies to minimize so-called 'carbon leakage' and ensure pollution havens do not arise.

The technique effect is the most positive aspect of increased international

---

[16] This methodology was first used by Grossman, G.M. and A.B. Krueger (1993), 'Environmental Impacts of a North American Free Trade Agreement', in P.M. Garber (ed.), *The US-Mexico Free Trade Agreement*, Cambridge, MA: MIT Press, 13–56, pp. 13–14.

[17] Taylor, M.S. (2004), 'The Pollution Haven Hypothesis – Unbundling the Pollution Haven Hypothesis', *Advances in Economic Analysis & Policy*, **4** (2), 1–26, p. 3.

[18] Ibid.

trade on climate change. Increased trade leads to technology and knowledge spillovers.[19] This increased access to clean technology can offset emissions increases that result from the scale effect. However policies to improve access can at times come into conflict with international trade rules.

The income effects of trade liberalization can in theory also result in increased levels of environmental protection. The environmental Kuznets curve hypothesizes that as incomes increase, environmental degradation increases initially. However, once incomes rise above some threshold, the increase in incomes leads to greater concern for environmental quality which in turn results in decreases in environmental damage.[20] Evidence that the environmental Kuznets curve does in fact exist for greenhouse gas emissions is mixed.[21] Nonetheless increased incomes can result in certain behavioral changes such as increased demand for labeling of the environmental impacts of goods, which has trade related ramifications.

On balance evidence indicates that overall trade liberalization is likely to increase greenhouse gas emissions as the scale effect dominates the technique effect.[22] The relationship of these effects depends upon the shape of trade rules, and future trade regulation will need to take this into account.

In addition to its impacts on emissions, trade can also help mitigate economic vulnerability caused by climate change. The impacts of climate change can include decreased food supply in particular regions. Liberalized trade can help countries manage this vulnerability in food security by providing increased access to imports of food products countries can no longer produce themselves.[23] An intuitive move towards higher self-reliance in agriculture and food production in light of climatic

---

[19]   Grossman, G.M. and E. Helpman (1991), *Innovation and Growth in the Global Economy*, Cambridge, MA: MIT Press, pp. 237–257.

[20]   See for example Tamiotti, L. et al. (2009) *Trade and Climate Change – A report by the United Nations Environment Programme and the World Trade Organization*, Geneva, Switzerland: World Trade Organization, at p. 55 for an overview of literature related to the environmental Kuznets curve and greenhouse gas emissions. For an example of empirical reviews of the existence of the environmental Kuznets curve for greenhouse gases see Huang, W.M. et al. (2008), 'GHG Emissions, GDP Growth and the Kyoto Protocol: A Revisit of Environmental Kuznets Curve Hypothesis', *Energy Policy*, **36** (1), 239–247.

[21]   Ibid.

[22]   See Tamiotti et al., above note 20, p. 53.

[23]   See Tamiotti et al., above note 20, p. 62. See also Karapinar, B. and C. Häberli (eds.) (2010), *Food Crises and the WTO*, Cambridge: Cambridge University Press.

challenges is a double edged sword that may result in shortages in the absence of open borders and well developed trade in agricultural products.

Finally, climate change can also have an impact on trade. There are two means by which this might occur. First climate change may change the patterns of trade by changing the comparative advantages of nations. For example agriculture may be impacted by climate change, leading some countries to decrease exports of particular goods, and potentially some countries to increase exports of particular goods.[24] In addition some countries rely upon tourist attractions, for example skiing or beach destinations that may be negatively impacted by climate change. The second major way in which climate change may impact trade is through the disruption of transportation services that are necessary to facilitate trade.[25]

The physical and economic interdependencies between trade and climate change are thus significant. These interdependencies in many ways give rise to the legal and policy issues around trade and climate change which are the subject of much debate and require careful consideration.

III.   KEY CLIMATE CHANGE POLICIES

Climate change policies fall into two main categories, policies aimed at mitigating greenhouse gas emissions and policies aimed at adapting to the impacts of climate change. These policies can be domestic in nature or they can be designed and applied at the international level. The current international system for managing greenhouse gas emissions under the Kyoto Protocol expects that for the most part domestic policies will be used to achieve a set of internationally agreed emissions reduction targets. Looking towards the future, failing the development of a much more detailed international regime to address the impacts of climate change, the policies used to mitigate these effects are likely to continue to be predominantly domestic in nature. However, there are some international policies arising out of the current international system that are likely to persist.

Requirements under the UNFCCC and Kyoto Protocol for developed countries to assist developing countries through adaptation funding and

---

[24]   See Tamiotti et al., above note 20, p. 62.
[25]   See for example IPCC (2007) *Climate Change 2007: Impacts, Adaptation and Vulnerability. Contribution of Working Group II to the Fourth Assessment Report of the Intergovernmental Panel on Climate Change*, Cambridge, UK: Cambridge University Press. See p. 368, available at http://www.ipcc.ch/publications_and_data/publications_ipcc_fourth_assessment_report_wg2_report_impacts_adaptation_and_vulnerability.htm (accessed 21 April 2011).

technology transfer are critical elements of the international climate management system. The UNFCCC requires that '. . . developed country Parties . . . support the development and enhancement of endogenous capacities and technologies of developing country Parties'.[26] To this end the Bali Action Plan recommends a number of actions to address the technology transfer needs of developing countries including, assessing technology needs, information sharing, capacity building, and mechanisms for financing.[27] The annex also encourages parties '. . . to avoid trade and intellectual property rights policies, or lack thereof, restricting transfer of technology'.[28] This plan was further strengthened by the creation of a Technology Mechanism including a Technology Executive Committee and a Climate Technology Centre and Network under the Cancun Agreements.[29]

The UNFCCC also requires that developed countries assist the developing countries '. . . that are particularly vulnerable to the adverse effects of climate change in meeting costs of adaptation to those adverse effects. . . '.[30] To this end the Adaptation fund has been created which is funded through a 2 percent share of the proceeds on all credits purchased through the clean development mechanism.[31] Adaptation measures are also funded through other funds under the UNFCCC's Global Environmental Facility[32] as well as through the newly created Green Climate Fund.

The Kyoto Protocol enables international emissions trading through three mechanisms: the trade of assigned amount units, which allows the trade of emissions permits between countries with binding emissions reduction commitments under the Protocol; joint implementation,

---

[26] United Nations Framework Convention on Climate Change (1992), Article 4.5.

[27] UNFCCC (2008), *Report of the Conference of the Parties on its thirteenth session, held in Bali from 3 to 15 December 2007 Addendum Part Two: Action taken by the Conference of the Parties at its thirteenth session,* FCCC/CP/2007/6/Add.1, Bonn. Decision 3/CP.13 available at http://unfccc.int/resource/docs/2007/cop13/eng/06a01.pdf#page=12 (accessed 23 April 2011).

[28] Ibid. Annex I to Decision 3/CP.13 para. 12.b.

[29] See UNFCCC, above note 10, para. 117.

[30] United Nations Framework Convention on Climate Change (1992), Article 4.4.

[31] UNFCCC (2011), 'Adaptation Fund', http://unfccc.int/cooperation_and_support/financial_mechanism/adaptation_fund/items/3659.php (accessed 9 May 2011).

[32] See for example information on the Special Climate Change Fund and the Least Developed Countries Fund. UNFCCC (2011), 'Financial Mechanisms', http://unfccc.int/cooperation_and_support/financial_mechanism/items/2807.php (accessed 9 May 2011).

which allows these countries to cooperate on projects; and the Clean Development Mechanism (CDM), an international mechanism through which developed countries can purchase emissions reductions created in developing countries to contribute towards meeting their emissions reduction commitments under the Protocol.[33] The CDM is perhaps the most important of the Kyoto mechanisms to facilitate international emissions trading. It offers an incentive and potential for transfer of technology to developing countries which, however, has not sufficiently materialized and calls for further work on the mechanism.[34]

Given the lack of agreement at the international level on a uniform international mechanism for reducing emissions, a range of domestic policies have been, and are likely to continue to be, put in place, some with important ramifications for trade policies. The most common are emissions pricing systems. Emissions pricing systems can take the form of emissions taxes or emissions trading systems. In an emissions trading system an emissions target is set and emitters trade permits to achieve this limit. In the case of an emissions tax, emitters pursue emissions reductions in response to a set price. The best known emissions trading system is the European Union Emissions Trading System. However, a number of other schemes are planned or in place around the world.[35]

A second important domestic policy is the subsidization of renewable energy and other low carbon technologies. These technologies, which can be effective at reducing a nation's emissions, are subsidized to increase deployment while their prices remain uncompetitive with traditional technologies. These policies can take a number of different forms, such as production subsidies, tax rebates, or feed in tariffs. In addition substantial investment in research and development of renewable energy and low-carbon technologies is occurring globally.[36]

Other potentially important domestic policies include energy efficiency

---

[33]   UNFCCC, 'Mechanisms under the Kyoto Protocol: Emissions Trading, Joint Implementation and the Clean Development Mechanism', http://unfccc.int/kyoto_protocol/mechanisms/items/1673.php (accessed 9 May 2011).

[34]   de Sépibus, J. (2009), *Reforming the Clean Development Mechanism to Accelerate Technology Transfer,* NCCR Trade Working Paper No. 2009/42. Available at http://phase1.nccr-trade.org/images/stories/publications/IP6/upload CDM%20and%20technology%20transfer%2020%20october%20finalfinal.pdf (accessed 9 May 2011).

[35]   Hood, C. (2010), *Reviewing Existing and Proposed Emissions Trading Systems,* Paris, France: International Energy Agency. Available at http://www.iea.org/papers/2010/ets_paper2010.pdf (accessed 9 May 2011).

[36]   For a review of renewable energy support see IEA (2011), *Clean Energy Progress Report IEA Input to the Clean Energy Ministerial,* Paris, France:

standards, aimed at increasing the efficiency of goods used in a country and eco-labeling schemes aimed at educating consumers about the carbon footprints of the goods they consume.

IV.   THE STATE OF PLAY IN TRADE REGULATION

WTO law and climate change policies have not been well integrated to date. While trade rules do have the ability to meet the needs of environmental policy, they may also pose some barriers to the implementation of these policies, indicating a need for frameworks that seek to harmonize the relationship between the issues.

WTO law, in its current form, is blind to the energy related inputs into goods and services that are traded internationally and therefore may make achieving emissions reductions more difficult. The system essentially aims to create a level playing field for all competing products.[37] For example, tariff rates are uniform for products, irrespective of their impact on the production of greenhouse gases. Similarly, national treatment rules that apply to goods and services do not distinguish between those which employ exhaustible and renewable energy.[38] The standard analysis of likeness does not consider how emissions intensive the production process to create a product is.[39] The rules on subsidies in principle do not distinguish

---

International Energy Agency. Available at http://www.iea.org/papers/2011/CEM_Progress_Report.pdf (accessed 9 May 2011).

[37]   The preamble to the General Agreement on Tariffs and Trade (1947) indicates that the system is directed towards '. . . the elimination of discriminatory treatment in international commerce. . .'. See generally Cottier, T. and M. Oesch (2005), *International Trade Regulation: Law and Policy in the WTO, the European Union and Switzerland,* Bern and London: Staempfli and Cameron May.

[38]   Article 1 of the General Agreement on Tariffs and Trade (1947) states that '. . .any advantage, favour, privilege or immunity granted by any contracting party to any product originating in or destined for any other country shall be accorded immediately and unconditionally to the like product originating in or destined for the territories of all other contracting parties'.

[39]   While it is recognized that 'likeness' must be determined on a case by case basis, the WTO Appellate body has in general employed '. . . four categories of "characteristics" that the products involved might share: (i) the physical properties of the products; (ii) the extent to which the products are capable of serving the same or similar end-uses; (iii) the extent to which consumers perceive and treat the products as alternative means of performing particular functions in order to satisfy a particular want or demand; and (iv) the international classification of the products for tariff purposes'. These criteria restrict the term likeness such that it does not include the methods used to produce the goods but rather the character-

between the greenhouse gas intensity of products and means of production.[40] The same is true for agricultural products under the Agreement on Agriculture. The energy intensity of farming practices, including the use of fertilizers, is not a relevant factor in shaping trade rules.[41] Intellectual property rules create another similar barrier, in this case the same rules apply to all fields of technology, irrespective of the impact of a technology on the environment. The increased transfer of technology from developed countries to developing countries as envisioned under the UNFCCC may be hampered by the fact that intellectual property rights must in general be applied in a uniform, non-discriminatory manner.[42]

Despite these potential obstacles to climate change policies, the long-standing process of interfacing trade and the environment over recent decades, shows a more nuanced and complex picture. While WTO law in principle is blind to specific technologies, important policy exemptions relating to human and animal health and the environment opened the door to wider policy spaces for Members.[43] Whether or not non-product related process and production methods (PPMs) can be taken into account

---

istics of the goods themselves. WTO (2001), Appellate Body Report, *European Communities – Measures Affecting Asbestos & Products Containing Asbestos,* WT/DS135/AB/R. See generally, Cottier, T. and P. Mavroidis (eds) (2000), *Regulatory Barriers and the Principle of Non-discrimination in World Trade Law*, Ann Arbor: University of Michigan Press.

[40]　There is no existing exception for environment related subsidies under the Agreement on Subsidies and Countervailing Measures; for a discussion see Bigdeli, S.Z. (2009), 'Incentive Schemes to Promote Renewables and the WTO Law of Subsidies', in T. Cottier et al. (eds.), *International Trade Regulation and the Mitigation of Climate Change*, Cambridge: Cambridge University Press

[41]　Similar to other trade rules the '. . . long-term objective [of the Agreement on Agriculture] is to provide for substantial progressive reductions in agricultural support and protection sustained over an agreed period of time, resulting in correcting and preventing restrictions and distortions in world agricultural markets'. Preamble to the Agreement on Agriculture available at http://www.wto.org/english/docs_e/legal_e/14-ag_01_e.htm (accessed 9 May 2011). It does not explicitly recognize that in some areas, such as the protection of the environment, distortions may be desirable.

[42]　For a discussion of some of these issues see for example, Littleton, M. (2009), 'The TRIPS Agreement and Transfer of Climate-change-related Technologies to Developing Countries', *Natural Resources Forum*, **33** (3), 233–244.

[43]　The General Agreement on Tariffs and Trade (1947) Articles XX(b) and (g) allow exceptions to ordinary trade rules for measures necessary to protect human, animal or plant life or health and relating to the conservation of exhaustible natural resources. For a discussion see e.g. Cottier, T. and M. Oesch (2005), *International Trade Regulation: Law and Policy in the WTO, the European Union and Switzerland*, Bern and London: Staempfli and Cameron May, pp. 428–466.

in the analysis of like products, for both goods and services, is a matter of controversy.[44] It is, however, well established that distinctions may be drawn on the basis of PPMs under the general exceptions of the General Agreement on Tariffs and Trade (GATT) Article XX(g).[45] Jurisprudence under the Agreement on the Application of Sanitary and Phytosanitary Measures (SPS Agreement) and the Agreement on Technical Barriers to Trade (TBT Agreement) also takes into consideration health and environmental concerns.[46] The case law of panels and the Appellate Body of the WTO endeavors to balance competing interests and allows the consideration of environmental concerns on an equal footing with other interests, giving equal weight to science and consumer preferences in a particular jurisdiction. The jurisprudence of panels and the Appellate Body today is characterized by a methodology which no longer privileges market access in a manner that was typical under the functionalist approach and interpretation that was applied in the past.[47] However, this methodology still requires a case by case assessment of environmental policies, a situation that does

---

[44]   The standard test of likeness described in note 39 above does not explicitly allow for the consideration of non-product related PPMs, however there have been other tests suggested such as the aims and effects test that would allow these factors to be taken into account. For a review of the application of the likeness test to the case of border adjustments see Holzer, K. (2010), 'Proposals on Carbon-Related Border Adjustments: Prospects for WTO Compliance', *Carbon and Climate Law Review*, **4** (1), 51–64. For a review of the history of the aims and effects test see Hudec, R. (1998), 'GATT/WTO Constraints on National Regulation: Requiem for an "Aims and Effects" Test', *International Lawyer*, **32** (3), 619–649, see Regan, D.H. (2009), 'How to Think about PPMs (and Climate Change)', in T. Cottier et al. (eds), *International Trade Regulation and the Mitigation of Climate Change*, Cambridge: Cambridge University Press for a general discussion on the basis for PPM related considerations.

[45]   For example the Appellate Body found in the *US–Shrimp/Turtle* cases that a US requirement for the use of Turtle Excluding Devices when harvesting shrimp was permissible, although it did reject the US law because it was applied in a discriminatory manner. WTO (2001), Appellate Body Report, *United States – Import Prohibition of Certain Shrimp and Shrimp Products,* WT/DS58/AB/R. See also Appellate Body Report, *United States – Standards for Reformulated and Conventional Gasoline,* WT/DS2/AB/R, 29 April 1996.

[46]   See in particular Appellate Body Report, *EC – Measures Concerning Meat and Meat Products (Hormones),* WT/DS26/AB/R, WT/DS28/AB/R, 16 January 1998; Appellate Body Report, *United States – Continued Suspension of Obligations on the EC – Hormones Dispute,* WT/DS320/AB/R, 16 October 2008; cf. also Panel Report, *EC – European Communities – Measures affecting the Approval and Marketing of Biotech Products,* WT/DS291/R, 29 September 2006.

[47]   See in particular the 1991 Panel Report *United States – Restrictions on Imports of Tuna* (unadopted) requiring that measures relating to exhaustible natural resources be taken 'in conjunction with restrictions on domestic produc-

offer incremental progress but does not yield certainty to the relationship between trade and environmental rules moving into the future.

A resolution to this issue may arise through continued negotiations on trade and environment that further attempt to align these concerns. Conceptual progress, albeit limited, has been made. In agriculture, the shift from production subsidies to de-coupled and direct payments allows members to take into account environmental concerns.[48] Tariff reductions relating to environmental goods and services (EGS) seek to bring about enhanced access to energy efficient products and technology. The main problem with this approach is that tariff reductions in most of the advanced and relevant products may primarily benefit industrialized countries. The approach may need to focus more on particular sectors and goals, in particular technologies that will help address climate change while being mindful of development goals, and be included as part of the general equation of sectoral negotiations to improve market access to non-agriculture sector markets.[49]

The relationship between measures to improve access to low emitting technologies and their possible impacts on developing countries is a critical issue in the current system. These measures tend to restrict market access for products originating in developing countries and therefore may face opposition from these countries. A pertinent example of this type of occurrence is the opposition by developing countries to the categorization of subsidies for research and development as non-actionable subsidies under the Agreement on Subsidies and Countervailing Measures (ASCM). Developing countries were concerned that this would provide an unfair advantage to developed countries.[50] This category of subsidies, which

---

tion or consumption', GATT (1995), *Analytical Index: Guide to GATT Law and Practice*, Geneva: World Trade Organization, Vol. I, 584–585.

[48] For example the OECD finds that production based subsidies in agriculture are relatively more harmful than other types of subsidies, see OECD (2006), 'Synthesis Report on Environmentally Harmful Subsidies', in OECD, *Environmentally Harmful Subsidies: Challenges for Reform*, Paris, France: OECD Publishing, p. 39, available at http://www.oecd-ilibrary.org/agriculture-and-food/environmentally-harmful-subsidies/synthesis-report-on-environmentally-harmful-subsidies_9789264012059-3-en;jsessionid=1w0txof2wbciu.delta (accessed 9 May 2011).

[49] See Cottier, T. and D. Baracol (2009), 'Environmental Goods and Services: The Environmental Area Initiative Approach and Climate Change', in T. Cottier et al. (eds), *International Trade Regulation and the Mitigation of Climate Change*, Cambridge: Cambridge University Press, 395–419.

[50] For example in its submission to the WTO in preparation for the 1999 Ministerial conference, India indicated its view that: 'The subsidies commonly used by developing countries for their industrialization and development have

expired at the end of 1999, has not been renewed.[51] This situation is indicative of the tension between developmental and environmental concerns that currently exists at the WTO.

Overall, WTO law offers a complex and nuanced picture which requires in-depth analysis on a case by case basis. While 'colour blind' to the environmental impacts of various products in principle, it allows some concerns relating to action on climate change to be taken into account.

V.   THE DIALECTICAL RELATIONSHIP TO ENVIRONMENTAL LAW AND POLICY

The United Nations Framework Convention on Climate Change and the Kyoto Protocol created a framework under international law to address climate change concerns based on the principles of shared but differentiated responsibility for the climate as a common concern of mankind. However, efforts to bring about binding targets and instruments which decisively define commitments are still largely lacking for the post-2012 period. Currently under the Kyoto Protocol the emissions reductions required under international obligations are to be met primarily through national measures.[52] In the discussions concerning a post-2012 regime, important emitters, in particular the US[53] and China,[54]

---

been included in the actionable or prohibited category, while those used by developed countries are in the non-actionable category.' Communication from India (1999), *Preparations for the 1999 Ministerial Conference – Proposals Regarding the Agreement on Subsidies and Countervailing Measures in terms of Paragraph 9(a) (i) of the Geneva Ministerial Declaration,* WT/GC/W/201. Available at http://com merce.nic.in/trade/international_trade_general_council_39.asp (accessed 9 May 2011).

[51]   See WTO, 'Understanding the WTO, Subsidies and countervailing measures', http://www.wto.org/english/thewto_e/whatis_e/tif_e/agrm8_e.htm#subsidies (accessed 9 May 2011).

[52]   (1997) ILM 37, 22.

[53]   The United States in its submission for consideration at the Copenhagen meeting indicated that 'the United States is committed to reaching a strong international agreement in Copenhagen ... that will be embodied in US domestic law...'. UNFCCC (2009), *Draft implementing agreement under the Convention prepared by the Government of the United States of America for adoption at the fifteenth session of the Conference of the Parties,* FCCC/CP/2009/7. Available at http://unfccc.int/resource/docs/2009/cop15/eng/07.pdf (accessed 9 May 2011).

[54]   China has specified in its submissions to the UNFCCC concerning the Copenhagen Accord that its '... autonomous domestic mitigation actions are voluntary in nature ...' . See Letter from the Department of Climate Change,

show a clear preference for avoiding extensive international rules and maintaining their sovereignty in defining appropriate policies. Efforts by the EU to bring about a global network of linked emissions trading systems have so far been unsuccessful[55] – although the EU seeks to link its own system to others. Similarly, efforts to implement a global carbon tax which, according to many economists, would be the most efficient tool[56] have also been unsuccessful and are unlikely to find support in the future. While it is still possible that a field of climate change law is emerging, it lacks the substance and enforcement of international trade regulation.

The absence of a single international policy to manage global greenhouse gas emissions does not mean that countries remain idle on climate policy. Many enact measures autonomously. In fact, experience indicates that climate change mitigation is likely to be built bottom-up, with a variety of different policy measures applied in domestic law commensurate with domestic needs and interests.[57] This constellation implies a high likelihood that the trade related aspects of such measures, not supported by international environmental law per se, will be measured against the yardstick of WTO law and disciplines. Initial cases have reached the stage of consultations at the WTO and are likely to be assessed by panels and the Appellate Body.[58] As a result, the room to maneuver is already being defined by trade rules, rather than the UNFCCC framework.

It is understandable that the Director-General of the WTO, Pascal Lamy opined before the Copenhagen summit in 2010 that environmental

---

National Development and Reform Commission of China to the UNFCCC Secretariat, Bonn, Germany, available at http://unfccc.int/files/meetings/cop_15/copenhagen_accord/application/pdf/chinacphaccord_app2.pdf (accessed 9 May 2011).

[55] European Commission Climate Action (2010), 'Linking the EU ETS to other Emissions Trading Systems and incentives for international credits'. Available at http://ec.europa.eu/clima/policies/ets/linking_en.htm (accessed 9 May 2011).

[56] For example see Cooper, R.N. (2008), *The Case for Charges on Greenhouse Gas Emissions*, Harvard Kennedy School, John F. Kennedy School of Government. Available at http://belfercenter.ksg.harvard.edu/files/CooperWeb4.pdf (accessed 9 May 2011).

[57] Some go so far as to advocate that a bottom up approach is likely to be more successful. For example see Ostrom (2009), *A Polycentric Approach for Coping with Climate Change*, World Bank Policy Research Working Paper 5095.

[58] See *Canada – Certain Measures affecting the Renewable Energy Generation Sector*, Request for Consultations by Japan, WT/DS412, 16 September 2010; *China – Measures concerning Wind Power Equipment*, Request for Consultations by the United States, WT/DS419, 6 January 2011.

rules should come first,[59] with trade rules to follow. In reality the relationship is likely to be the reverse. Trade rules may well define the scope of action left to states, based upon which international environmental law will emerge. The findings of panels and the Appellate Body will be of importance in shaping future climate change policies. These may be in line with WTO rules, but they may also challenge them to the extent that important and commonly shared goals cannot be reached. It is also possible that climate change negotiations can learn from areas of international economic law which use a bottom-up approach, building on sectoral agreements that are based on creating a critical mass of support to bring about results. Progress within the UNFCCC, in return, may also stimulate further developments both in the WTO and in regional fora and preferential trade and investment agreements.

This process shows a need for common debate and discourse. It requires both fora to develop appropriate institutional sensitivity for concerns of other areas in order for legitimate goals to be pursued in either forum.[60] In this dialectical process, traditions of institutional divide and fragmentation need to be overcome and overall coherence must be sought.[61] This is not only a matter of substance, but also of procedures. It is by way of procedures and common debate among the different constituencies that progress can and will be made.

Governance and international law, unfortunately, are not well prepared to take up these challenges. The relationship between different regimes remains one of separation, rather than integration. In domestic policy making, climate change mitigation and adaptation largely remains a specialized area under the responsibility of environmental agencies. Policy coordination with trade is not often conducted in an integrated and proactive manner. This is not only true at the domestic but also at the international level. International organizations continue to operate primarily within their mandate, and cooperation in negotiations is difficult to bring about.

This situation arises both for climate change and at the trade level. In

---

[59]   WTO, 'WTO News, Speeches – DG Pascal Lamy, 2 November 2009, "Lamy underscores the urgency of responding to the climate crisis"'. Available at http://www.wto.org/english/news_e/sppl_e/sppl140_e.htm (accessed 9 May 2011).

[60]   Foltea, M. (2010), *International Organizations in the WTO Dispute Settlement: How much Institutional Sensitivity?* (PhD, University of Bern (publication forthcoming, on file with authors).

[61]   See generally Cottier, T. and P. Delimatsis (eds) (2011), *The Prospects of International Trade Regulation: From Fragmentation to Coherence*, Cambridge: Cambridge University Press.

the field of climate change the institutional organization is relatively young and less developed than in the area of trade. The UNFCCC does recognize the need for coherence with trade rules, noting that '. . . measures taken to combat climate change, including unilateral ones, should not constitute a means of arbitrary or unjustifiable discrimination or a disguised restriction on international trade . . .'.[62] The UNFCCC secretariat has also made efforts in the past to increase communication with the WTO,[63] however substantive efforts to coordinate policies between the organizations have not yet been made. The UNFCCC does have a compliance committee under the Kyoto Protocol. However, its purpose is restricted to assessing non-compliance with emissions reduction obligations under the Kyoto Protocol.[64] The consequence for non-compliance with these commitments is limited to suspension of the ability to use international emissions credits and increased emissions reduction obligations in any subsequent commitment periods.[65]

In international trade law, comparable difficulties with interfacing with different regimes also exist. WTO panels and the Appellate Body do not have jurisdiction to make rulings on breaches of any rules save WTO rules.[66] They may take into account other norms of international law under the general rules of treaty interpretation as expressed in Article

---

[62]   United Nations Framework Convention on Climate Change (1992), Article 3.5.

[63]   UNFCCC (2003), *Cooperation with relevant International Organizations*, Bonn, UNFCCC. FCCC/SBSTA/2003/INF.7. Available at http://unfccc.int/resource/docs/2003/sbsta/inf07.pdf (accessed 9 May 2011).

[64]   Kyoto Protocol to the United Nations Framework Convention on Climate Change (1998), Article 18.

[65]   UNFCCC (2006), *Report of the Conference of the Parties serving as the meeting of the Parties to the Kyoto Protocol on its first session, held at Montreal from 28 November to 10 December 2005 – Addendum Part Two: Action taken by the Conference of the Parties serving as the meeting of the Parties to the Kyoto Protocol at its first session. Decisions adopted by the Conference of the Parties serving as the meeting of the Parties to the Kyoto Protocol*, Bonn: UNFCCC, FCCC/KP/CMP/2005/8/Add.3. See decision 27/ CMP.1. Available at http://unfccc.int/resource/docs/2005/cmp1/eng/08a03.pdf#page=92 (accessed 9 May 2011).

[66]   The WTO's Dispute Settlement Understanding, Article 1 indicates that 'The rules and procedures of this Understanding shall apply to disputes brought pursuant to the consultation and dispute settlement provisions of the agreements listed in Appendix 1 to this Understanding (referred to in this Understanding as the "covered agreements").' The agreements listed in the appendix are limited to the Agreement establishing the World Trade Organization, and the Multilateral and Plurilateral Trade agreements listed. For discussion and a wider understanding see Pauwelyn, J. (2001), 'The Role of Public International Law in the WTO: How Far Can We Go', *American Journal of International Law*, **95** (3), 535–578.

31 of the Vienna Convention on the Law of Treaties.[67] However panels and the Appellate Body, so far, have refrained from doing so in an extensive manner: for example, in the recent *EU-Biotech* case the Panel held that other agreements may only be taken into account in resolving a dispute if all WTO members are signatories of the agreement.[68] As a result, important instruments, such as the European Energy Charter, the Convention on Biodiversity and related instruments remain outside the purview of the WTO. The law of treaties does not prescribe such a narrow reading of the context. It certainly is possible to take into account an agreement to which the parties to the disputes are signatories. It is also possible to take into account other sources of international law in the process of interpretation of WTO law. These sources may apply as much to human rights as to future prescriptions available in environmental law. In addition, panels and the Appellate Body can take into account concerns expressed in the form of non-binding soft law which nevertheless expresses the shared concerns of the international community.[69]

Finally, the relationship between preferential agreements and climate change is largely unexplored. Countries may address shared concerns in bilateral agreements, including shared standards and rules which they pledge to respect. The same is true for investment protection which largely lacks a dimension of climate change beyond established environmental concerns.

---

[67]   The Vienna Convention on the Law of Treaties (1968), Article 31.3 (c) states: 'There shall be taken into account, together with the context: ... any relevant rules of international law applicable in the relations between the parties.'

[68]   In interpreting Article 31.3 (c) of the Vienna Convention on the Law of Treaties (1968), the Panel has indicated that '. . . the rules of international law to be taken into account in interpreting the WTO agreements at issue in this dispute are those which are applicable in the relations between the WTO Members'. WTO (2006), Panel Report, *European Communities – Measures Affecting the Approval and Marketing of Biotech Products*, WT/DS291/R, WT/DS292/R, WT/DS293/R, Add.1 to Add.9, and Corr.1, adopted 21 November 2006, DSR 2006:III-VIII, para. 7.68.

[69]   For example Pauwelyn provides a substantive analysis of the issue and concludes that non-WTO rules may be considered provided they '. . . can reasonably be considered to express the common intentions or understanding of all members as to the meaning of the WTO term concerned'. See Pauwelyn, above note 66, 576.

VI. THE FUTURE AGENDA OF INTERNATIONAL TRADE REGULATION

Climate change offers major challenges to WTO law. To some extent, these challenges may be addressed through litigation. Panels and the Appellate Body may find answers within the existing framework, developing appropriate institutional sensitivity to the concern of climate change. However, these challenges will also likely require negotiations and amendments in a post-Doha Agenda, or within other international fora addressing trade and environmental concerns. Some of these challenges will be dealt with in more detail by separate chapters in this volume.[70] This section seeks to provide a brief survey of agenda items which either need to be addressed and solved in litigation or in future negotiations within the WTO or elsewhere. We examine these issues as they pertain to climate change mitigation, adaptation and communication and transparency.

Before doing so, we suggest that there exists a need for further studies on the principle of common concern. While mentioned in the UNFCCC, its shape, contours and relationship to instruments of international economic law remains relatively unexplored.[71] This emerging principle may offer the potential to bridge the gap between environmental concerns, trade and extraterritorial jurisdiction and liability in a manner that can assist in shaping the responsibilities of States and future trading rules. Emerging duties to protect in the field of human rights and with regard to the responsibility to protect (R2P) may further assist in clarifying these intersections. The principle of common concern may guide future rights and obligations relating to non-product related PPMs, the transfer of technology, and the funding of extraterritorial activities as well as helping to define where liability and responsibility for omission lie, which, in the case of climate change and the production of global public goods, can no longer stop at the borders of countries. The contours of common concern may be influenced by general considerations. It will be equally informed by policy measures in the areas of climate change mitigation, adaptation and communication and transparency.[72]

---

[70] See chapters in Part III of this volume.

[71] See Cottier, T. and S. Matteotti-Berkutova (2009), 'International Environmental Law and the Evolving Concept of Common Concern of Mankind', in T. Cottier et al. (eds) *International Trade Regulation and the Mitigation of Climate Change*, Cambridge: Cambridge University Press.

[72] See ibid., pp. 21–47.

A.   Climate Change Mitigation

To mitigate greenhouse gas emissions, the appropriate incentives for clean technologies and for products which rely on them in the consumption or production of goods and services must be created. Such technologies are geared towards either minimizing the use of exhaustible resources or deploying renewable resources and thus are able to contribute to the abatement of CO_2 emissions. Exhaustible resources include for example, coal, oil and natural gas. Renewable resources include solar energy, wind energy, and biomass (second and third generation). Other technologies such as large hydro or nuclear power plants also reduce greenhouse gas emissions but are arguably undesirable due to other environmental and safety concerns. In order to create the appropriate incentives for the research, development and deployment of appropriate technologies, trade rules may need to take into account the energy sources and the amount of energy consumed by or for a trade product. Trade rules equally need to take into account the energy used in the transportation of goods and related to services.

1.   Encouraging low carbon technology: product standards, PPMs and the transfer of technology
A number of policies will be needed to encourage the deployment of low carbon technology including product standards and potentially tariffs. The energy efficiency of a product is a characteristic on which differential treatment may be based for regulatory purposes. Product standards that restrict low efficiency products may not run into difficulties arising from rules requiring non-discriminatory treatment of like products although there is some risk that these standards could be considered to be technical barriers to trade and face resistance under the TBT Agreement.[73]

In the future nations may also wish to limit the imports of products produced using emission-intensive production methods through tariff or

---

[73]   Technical barriers to trade such as product standards are permissible if they fulfill a legitimate purpose such as the protection of the environment, however any such '. . . regulations shall not be more trade-restrictive than necessary to fulfil a legitimate objective. . .'. As a result standards must be carefully designed to ensure they do not contravene the TBT Agreement. See Agreement on Technical Barriers to Trade, Article 2.2. See for example Waide, P. and N. Bernasconi-Osterwalder (2008), *Standards, Labelling and Certification*, Trade and Climate Change Seminar, 18–20 June 2008, Copenhagen, GMF/IISD, Background Paper. Available at http://www.iisd.org/pdf/2008/cph_trade_climate_standards.pdf (accessed 15 May 2011).

non-tariff measures. As a result, the extension of product differentiation based on non-product related PPMs (i.e characteristics which are related to the production process and not the product itself) is of key importance in the realization of climate change mitigation. Whether such measures are justified within the analysis of like products or based upon exemptions is the subject of much debate.[74] However, the bigger question is how such measures will impact market access for developing country products and how monitoring and enforcement of PPMs can be accomplished in an effective manner.

One solution is for negotiations to address these problems by linking the PPM issue to funding and transfer of technology. The use of PPMs to distinguish between products, while meaningful from an environmental point of view, amounts to trade barriers which could be neutralized by combining PPM requirements with incentives and support for the introduction of state-of-the-art technologies. The acceptance of PPM requirements on the part of developing countries is inherently linked to enhanced transfer of technology. The Agreement on Trade-Related Aspects of Intellectual Property Rights (TRIPS) obliges developed countries to support the transfer of technology to developing countries by industries.[75] The implementation of this provision to date has been limited to information provision, and advanced tools to enable technology transfer have not yet been developed.[76] Tax breaks are one means of implementing this provision and should be seriously explored as a means to support transfer of knowledge and technology to developing countries. In addition, to ensure PPMs do not act as a barrier to trade for developing countries, restrictions on export subsidies may also need to be relaxed in certain circumstances as these could compensate for the additional costs that would result from the imposition of PPMs.

If such measures could be taken to address the PPM issue, they could also act to help fulfill UNFCCC commitments on technology transfer. In addition negotiations could establish linkages with the CDM to help alleviate PPM issues by directing CDM projects in a manner that ensures that they occur in areas where they might counteract the impacts of the use of PPMs to distinguish between products.

---

[74] See above, notes 39 and 44.

[75] Agreement on the Trade-Related aspects of Intellectual Property Rights, Article 66.2.

[76] For an overview of action taken to date in implementing this provision, see WTO, 'TRIPS Issues', http://www.wto.org/english/tratop_e/trips_e/techtransfer_e.htm (accessed 9 May 2011).

2.   Encouraging low carbon technology-subsidies

To stimulate the use of low carbon technologies it will be necessary to support research, development and deployment of these technologies. Under the ASCM subsidies can include direct payments as well as fore-gone government revenue from, for example, tax breaks.[77] WTO law does not distinguish between the provision of government assistance to renew-able and non-renewable energy or to other low carbon technologies[78] and treats all such subsidies as actionable provided they meet the necessary criteria.[79] It also bans all export subsidies, which include tax breaks for the transfer of clean technology.[80] Future negotiations need to address these issues and clarify whether a distinction between fossil fuels and renewable energy should be made and export subsidies for transfer of technology to developing countries should be allowed. Negotiations should also revisit the category of non-actionable subsidies.[81] At the same time, it will be important to distinguish between research and development and produc-tion subsidies. Production subsidies for clean technology may result in the same distortions and risks creating effects on competition which WTO law is aimed at addressing. By contrast research and development subsidies may have far less impact in this regard.

The subsidization of fossil fuel is another contentious area that may need to be addressed by the WTO. Studies show that reductions in green-house gas emissions in the order of 1.1 percent by 2010 to 18 percent by 2050 could result from the removal of existing subsidies from fossil fuel industries. At the same time this could raise GDP by 0.1 percent in 2010 to 0.7 percent in 2050 globally.[82] Given the WTO's commitment to reducing

---

[77]   Agreement on Subsidies and Countervailing Measures, Article 1.

[78]   An exception is agricultural subsidies where some subsidies not tied to pro-duction are permissible, see Agreement on Agriculture, Article 6.5.

[79]   Subsidies are actionable if they create adverse effects which include injury to the domestic industry of another member, nullification or impairment of benefits conferred by the GATT or serious prejudice to the interests of another member. Agreement on Subsidies and Countervailing Measures, Article 5. See Bigdeli, above note 40, for a detailed discussion on the compliance of renewable energy subsidies with WTO law.

[80]   Agreement on Subsidies and Countervailing Measures, Article 3.1 (a).

[81]   As noted in note 49 above, this category has expired but included subsidies to research and development as well as subsidies put in place for the implement-ation of environmental regulations.

[82]   IISD (2010), *Untold Billions: Fossil Fuel Subsidies, Their Impacts and the Path to Reform – Summary of Key Findings*, Geneva, Switzerland: The International Institute for Sustainable Development. Available at http://www.globalsubsidies. org/files/assets/synthesis_ffs.pdf (accessed 9 May 2011).

trade barriers, addressing this issue is an area where the WTO can make a substantial contribution towards mitigating greenhouse gas emissions.[83]

3.   Carbon policies – carbon tariffs and border tax adjustments

Carbon tariffs and border tax adjustments (BTAs) have in recent times gained prominence as trade related policies. There are a number of reasons for their rise in importance. These include a desire to level the playing field between domestic producers subject to stringent domestic carbon policies and foreign producers that are not subject to such policies to address competitiveness concerns; a desire to price emissions related to goods that are consumed locally but produced in foreign countries; and a means to entice foreign countries to adopt carbon policies as part of an international effort to address climate change.

Primary concerns that surround the use of unilateral domestic policy measures to combat climate change are carbon leakage and the competitiveness impacts of such policies. As some countries move to put in place stringent carbon policies there is a risk that industries in these countries will be put at a competitive disadvantage and may even migrate to those countries with less stringent or no mitigation policies in place.[84] Means of addressing these concerns include, among others such as the free allocation of allowances in emissions trading systems, the imposition of carbon tariffs or border tax adjustments to mitigate these impacts. [85]

---

[83]   The WTO has begun discussing the possibility of this work. See WTO, 'WTO: 2010 NEWS ITEMS, 14 October 2010, Deputy-Directors General, DDG Singh: "Fossil fuel subsidy reform is an important tool in fight against climate change"'. Available at http://www.wto.org/english/news_e/news10_e/ddg_14oct10_e.htm (accessed 9 May 2011).

[84]   See e.g. Parker, L. and J. Blodgett (2008), *'Carbon Leakage' and Trade: Issues and Approaches*, Congressional Research Services Report for Congress. For a discussion of competitiveness concerns in the context of US carbon policies.

[85]   A number of countries explicitly consider measures to address competitiveness and carbon leakage concerns in their proposed domestic systems. For example the European Union's Emissions Trading System intends to allocate allowances for free to facilities at risk of 'carbon leakage'. The proposed US and Australian schemes consider the allocation of allowances on the basis of output to trade exposed emissions intensive sectors. The proposed Canadian scheme is based on the output based allocation of allowances. See Environment Canada, 'News Release – Government Delivers Details of Greenhouse Gas Regulatory Framework, Ottawa, March 10, 2008'. Available at http://www.ec.gc.ca/default.asp?lang=En&n=714D9AAE-1&news=B2B42466-B768-424C-9A5B-6D59C2AE1C36 (accessed 9 May 2011), *H.R. 2454 – American Clean Energy and Security Act of 2009*, Section 763. Available at http://thomas.loc.gov/cgi-bin/query/D?c111:4:./temp/~c111t5xdS0:: (accessed 9 May 2011), and Australian

A second concern with the imposition of unilateral measures on production is that these policies price carbon from products produced in the nation, but leave the carbon emissions of products produced abroad but consumed locally unaffected. These emissions can be significant, for example, studies have shown that in the US 7.3 percent of emissions are related to imports, for Germany this value is 16.6 percent and for Switzerland it is as high as 122.9 percent.[86] Countries thus may show a clean record but in fact substantially contribute to carbon emissions through imported consumables. The imposition of carbon tariffs or border tax adjustments can tax products as they are imported into the country, ensuring that all emissions associated with the products consumed are priced and that consumers in these countries pay the full costs of their consumption.

The final reason for imposing such measures is as a means to provide an incentive for countries without carbon policies to put in place commensurate measures domestically. By imposing carbon tariffs or border tax adjustments the emissions from countries without carbon policies are taxed in the country with the carbon policy in place. The result is that the funds from these taxes are collected by the country imposing the tariff or the BTA and they therefore have the ability to spend that money as they wish. Many proposals for BTAs or carbon tariffs include exemptions from the tariff for countries that have commensurate policies in place domestically, for example, the proposal to require the submission of allowances by importers of certain goods included in the recently proposed American Clean Energy and Security Act of 2009 was designed in this manner.[87] In theory, once such a carbon tariff or BTA is in place, it is in an exporting nation's best interest to put commensurate policies in place domestically as they would then collect the funds from that policy at home and have the ability to spend those funds as they choose. Therefore BTAs and carbon tariffs provide a powerful incentive to countries without carbon policies in place to adopt these policies and avoid taxation of their goods by a

---

Government (2008), *Carbon Pollution Reduction Scheme White Paper Australia's Low Pollution Future.* See p. 12-2 available at http://www.climatechange.gov.au/en/government/initiatives/cprs/~/media/publications/white-paper/V2012Chapter-pdf.ashx (accessed 9 May 2011).

[86]   Peters G.P. and E.G. Hertwich (2008), 'CO$_2$ Embodied in International Trade with Implications for Global Climate Policy', *Environmental Science and Technology*, **42** (5), 1401–1407.

[87]   *H.R. 2454 – American Clean Energy and Security Act of 2009,* Section 767 c.) and 768. Available at http://thomas.loc.gov/cgi-bin/query/D?c111:4:./temp/~c111t5xdS0::

foreign nation.[88] However, while these measures may be legal, they have the potential to create unintended negative political consequences.[89]

The introduction of higher tariffs on CO_2 intensive industrial products, such as steel, cement, and aluminum is one means of addressing all of the aims noted. WTO law does not prevent Members from consolidating tariffs provided that appropriate consultation is undertaken and compensation is offered.[90] High tariffs on incoming products mean domestic producers will not be at a competitive disadvantage compared to their foreign counterparts. It also means consumers will feel price increases on imported as well as domestic goods. Finally, analysis has shown that this could be a powerful tool to encourage countries to adopt the appropriate measures – for example a recent analysis found that a 1 percent increase in the simple average tariff rate on a number of carbon intensive industrial products resulted in decreased imports in developed countries of between 25 percent and 86 percent depending on the country.[91] This type of impact on the economies of countries without carbon policies in place would provide a strong incentive for those countries to adopt such policies and dodge the tariff. In order for this type of measure to prove acceptable, dispute settlement may need to settle the issue of the extent to which tariff differentiation of like products can be based on non-product related PPMs, either within Article II or within Article XX(g) GATT. Negotiations may bring about clarification of these issues and acceptance of such policies. As discussed, any such measures would need to be appropriately linked to the transfer of technology in order to ensure they do not place an undue economic burden on developing countries.

---

[88]   The use of trade related measures to compel compliance with environmental regulation arose first under the Montreal Protocol and has been considered in many forms since then. See for example Barrett, S. and R. Stavins (2003), 'Increasing Participation and Compliance in International Climate Change Agreements', *International Environmental Agreements: Politics, Law and Economics*, **3**(4), 364–366.

[89]   See for example Bhagwati, J. and P. Mavroidis (2007), 'Is Action against US Exports for Failure to Sign Kyoto Protocol WTO-legal?', *World Trade Review*, **6** (2), 299–310.

[90]   General Agreement on Tariffs and Trade (1994), Article XXVIII.

[91]   The analysis indicates that a 1 percent increase in tariffs on paper, rubber, glass, plastics, iron and steel and basic chemicals on products from selected exporting countries including Argentina, Brazil, Chile, China, India, Indonesia, Israel, Mexico, the Philippines, Russia, South Africa, South Korea, Thailand, Turkey and the USA, resulted in decreased imports by 25 percent in Australia, 50 percent in Canada, 32 percent in the EU, 86 percent in Japan and 43 percent in the USA. Cottier, T. et al. (2011), *Potential of Tariff Policies for Climate Change Mitigation*, NCCR Working Paper, http://www.nccr-climate.unibe.ch/conferences/climate_economics_law/papers/Shingal_Anirudh.pdf.

A second useful tool for managing competitiveness impacts, encouraging countries to adopt stringent climate policies and pricing the emissions of imports is border tax adjustments. Traded goods are generally taxed according to the destination principle, i.e. goods are taxed in the jurisdiction in which they are consumed: as a result border tax adjustments are needed to take exports out of the system and bring imports into the system.[92] That is, border tax adjustments relieve exported products of a domestic tax and impose such a tax on imported products.[93] It is a tool that is often used to manage the effects of taxes directly levied on products, for example value added and sales taxes, and in these cases border tax adjustments are for the most part considered consistent with WTO rules.[94] In the context of climate change, border tax adjustments or other border adjustment measures have been considered as a means of imposing emissions prices from a domestic emissions pricing system on imported goods and rebating these costs to exporters. These measures would then alleviate competitiveness concerns of local industry, serve to price emissions from products consumed in the importing country and could act as a 'stick' to encourage countries to put in place commensurate climate policies. However there is no clear answer as to whether these measures would be consistent with trade rules, and this consistency may depend largely on the design and implementation of such systems.

The legal question of whether a border measure is consistent with trade rules is complicated by the fact that there is no single border tax adjustment provision within the GATT, rather border measures would have to prove consistent with a number of different provisions.[95] Depending

---

[92]   Keen, M. and S. Lahir (1998), 'The Comparison between Destination and Origin Principles under Imperfect Competition' *Journal of International Economics*, **45** (2), 323–350.

[93]   Specifically, the OECD Working Party in 1970 defined border tax adjustments as 'any fiscal measures which put into effect, in whole or in part, the destination principle (i.e. which enable exported products to be relieved of some or all of the tax charged in the exporting country in respect of similar domestic products sold to consumers on the home market and which enable imported products sold to consumers to be charged with some or all of the tax charged in the importing country in respect of similar domestic products)'. See *Report of the Working Party on Border Tax Adjustments*, 2 December 1970, GATT Doc. L/3464, para. 4.

[94]   The OECD Working Party '. . . concluded that there was convergence of views to the effect that taxes directly levied on products were eligible for tax adjustment. Examples of such taxes comprised specific excise duties, sales taxes and cascade taxes and the tax on value added.' Ibid., para. 14.

[95]   For a summary of relevant provisions see Holzer, K. (2010), 'Proposals on Carbon-related Border Adjustments: Prospects for WTO Compliance', *The Carbon and Climate Law Review*, **4** (1), 51–64, pp. 53–54.

on the design and implementation of the measures they could run afoul of trade rules in a number of areas. For example, a border measure that places differing obligations on two products that are alike in all ways save their greenhouse gas emissions profile may constitute a violation of like product rules. Similarly, whether a border measure that requires the remission of emissions allowances rather than the payment of a charge can be considered an allowable border adjustment, is another significant legal question.[96] Finally, even if the border measures can be designed in a manner that meets the legal tests imposed by trade laws, if measures are not based on non-product PPMs they will not price all carbon from emitters and as a result, while these measures would address competitiveness issues posed by domestic industry, they would not result in the full pricing of imported emissions and for this reason may not be as effective as might be desired.[97] In addition to legal concerns, other issues with border tax adjustments are that they pose the same difficulties as tariffs in that they may place burdens on developing countries that will need to be addressed through, for example, improved technology transfer.

It is generally feared that tariff increases and border tax adjustments will lead to the dismantling of the tariff reductions and elimination of tariff barriers that have been achieved by the international trading system in the last 50 years. These options, however, could be used to encourage countries to join an international system of shared goals and rules on climate change, to price consumption emissions and to address competitiveness and carbon leakage concerns associated with such systems. Carbon tariffs and border tax adjustment offer major incentives to bring about a common and shared system of climate change mitigation in international law. This type of system is a good example of the dialectical process operating between trade regulation and environmental law in this field.

4. Environmental goods and services (EGS)

Negotiations on environmental goods and services can be targeted to serve the purposes of climate change mitigation more specifically than is expected under the approaches currently being negotiated under the Doha

---

[96]   For a review of legal considerations related to border adjustments see Holzer (2010), ibid., pp. 57–58.

[97]   Because developing countries tend to have higher emission-intensive production than developed countries border tax adjustment not based on an assessment of emissions released during the production of individual goods may not result in pricing all of the targeted emissions in the country to which they are applied.

Development Agenda.[98] A sector specific approach should define over-arching goals in the context of climate change and include appropriate clean products and services, as well as a reduction in the technical barriers to trade with a view to promoting the trade of such goods and services.[99]

5. Supply of clean energy, transit and access to grids

Shifts to clean energy, in particular wind and solar energy, will require production to occur in suitable locations. These locations, for large scale operations, will be different from areas of consumption and may be different from the areas where traditional power generation is located. While electricity has not traditionally been traded across international borders (with the exception of trade within the EU and between Canada and the US), ongoing changes in electricity market structures from regulated monopolies to the unbundling of electricity generation, transmission, grid operation and generation, as well as the creation of future and option markets for energy and the creation of new instruments such as renewable energy certificates implies that international trade law may play an increasing role in issues around trade in electricity.[100]

Some issues surrounding electricity trade and WTO law include determinations as to whether electricity qualifies as a good or service under trade law; the applicability of WTO rules to renewable energy certificates; barriers to access to grids; and the ability of the WTO to ensure equitable access for renewable energy.[101]

International law therefore needs to address access to grids and transit rights in order to offer better legal security than can be found today in

---

[98] The current agenda of the Doha Round of negotiations includes negotiations on the reduction or elimination of tariff and non-tariff barriers to environmental goods and services, WTO, 'Trade and environment, New negotiations'. Available at http://www.wto.org/english/tratop_e/dda_e/dohaexplained_e. htm#environment (accessed 9 May 2011).

[99] For further discussion see Cottier, T. and D.S. Baracol Pinhao (2009), *WTO Negotiations on Environmental Goods and Services: A Potential Contribution to the Millennium Development Goals*, New York and Geneva: UNCTAD; Cottier, T. and D.S. Baracol Pinhao (2009), 'Environmental Goods and Services: The Environmental Area Initiative Approach and Climate Change', in T. Cottier, O. Nartova and S. Z. Bigdeli (eds), *International Trade Regulation and the Mitigation of Climate Change*, Cambridge: Cambridge University Press, 395–419.

[100] Howse, R. (2006), 'World Trade Law and Renewable Energy: The Case of Non-Tariff Measures Focus: Renewable Energy Sources', *Journal for European Environmental & Planning Law*, **3** (6), 500–518.

[101] Howse, R. (2009), *World Trade Law and Renewable Energy: The Case of Non-Tariff Measures*, Geneva and New York: United Nations. Executive Summary.

Article V GATT, a provision that has largely arisen as a result of national security considerations. Access to grids will also require the development of appropriate frameworks on competition and a means of reviewing state trading and existing legal and factual monopolies. In addition, controls on exports as well as rules surrounding energy related services need to be developed. Since all forms of energy are subject to WTO law in terms of their substance and the modes of delivery, trade rules will need to address these issues in future negotiations. The Energy Charter Treaty may well provide a first step towards such an agreement.[102]

6.   Intellectual property rights

An important issue that has been raised at the UNFCCC is the relationship between TRIPS and technology transfer. Some argue that TRIPS acts as a barrier to technology transfer by limiting access to low cost clean technology while others argue that the protection of patent rights is necessary to enable the continued development of such technology.[103] In either case, this issue is an important area where the WTO could play a role in advancing discussions. Recognizing the need for empirical evidence, data and transparency, the United Nations Environment Programme (UNEP), the European Patent Office (EPO) and the International Centre for Trade and Sustainable Development (ICTSD) have conducted a joint project on the role of patents in the transfer of climate change mitigation technologies that has resulted in the publication of a report.[104] It positively contributes towards transparency,[105] and thus also towards access to (technological) information, a first step in the freedom to be informed of research findings.[106] It has also been observed that for developing countries to get

---

[102]   The Energy Charter Treaty has taken a first step towards developing an agreement on freedom of transit of energy, by requiring that: 'Each Contracting Party shall take the necessary measures to facilitate the Transit of Energy Materials and Products consistent with the principle of freedom of transit and without distinction as to the origin, destination or ownership of such Energy Materials and Products or discrimination as to pricing on the basis of such distinctions, and without imposing any unreasonable delays, restrictions or charges.' See Article 7.1 Energy Charter Treaty, (1995) ILM 34, 360.

[103]   See Littleton, M., above note 42.

[104]   Karachalios K., et al. (eds) (2010), *Patents and Clean Energy: Bridging the Gap Between Evidence And Policy,* UNEP/EPO/ICTSD. Available at http://ictsd.org/i/publications/85887/ (accessed 14 May 2010).

[105]   Among the findings in this paper are the observations that indicate that India, Brazil and Mexico feature among the top claimant countries for specific (solar PV, hydro/marine) technology sectors (as judged by patenting activity).

[106]   Note that the freedom to be informed of research findings is not fully satisfied with access to patent information, thus this is considered a first step that is

access to climate change technologies, they will have to create parts of it themselves, claim it as intellectual property and find ways to treat their intellectual capital as an economic asset.[107] One of the main areas where progress in access to technology relating to climate change can be made is in the potential to improve the Clean Development Mechanism in the Kyoto Protocol. This is the primary area where incentives for industrialized countries to engage in transfer of technology (including knowledge) to developing countries currently exist. Appropriate tools combining the CDM and IPRs need to be designed and negotiated.

7. Towards an agreement on energy

The complexity of the problem shows that the traditional divide between goods and services as well as intellectual property rights is no longer sufficient to meet these challenges. It may be appropriate to examine the feasibility and potential for a sectoral agreement on energy in WTO law which combines all the relevant aspects and appropriate linkages to other fora relevant in this field. Such an agreement would seek to establish disciplines on carbon related tariffs, border tax adjustment, subsidies for renewable and non-renewable energies, transit and access to grids, disciplines on competition and on export restrictions.[108] Reviewing classifications of energy services is key to bringing about enhanced competition and more efficient use of energy supplies around the globe.[109]

B. Climate Change Adaptation

Climate change adaptation is the second mainstay to be addressed in trade regulation. The effects of climate change are very likely to be seen in the coming decades, even if mitigation is successful and able to stabilize and reduce global CO_2 emissions. One of the prime areas that requires adaptation to climate change is agriculture and this effect necessitates a review of current agricultural policies within the WTO and in individual countries.

---

relevant for economic development and trade as it is limited to inventions with the potential for commercial application.

[107] Cannady, C. (2009), *Access to Climate Change Technology by Developing Countries: A Practical Survey*, ICTSD's Programme on IPRs and Sustainable Development, Issue Paper No. 25.

[108] For a more detailed outline see Cottier, T., et al. (2011), 'Energy in WTO law and policy', in Cottier, T. and P. Delimatsis (eds) *The Prospects of International Trade Regulation – From Fragmentation to Coherence*, Cambridge: Cambridge University Press, 211–244.

[109] See Nartova, O. (2010), Energy Services and Competition Policies under WTO Law, PhD thesis University of Bern, Infra M: Moscow.

1. Food security

Climate change is likely to increase unstable conditions for agricultural production. Since all regions may be affected, albeit not at the same time, it is of paramount importance to operate in an open trading system which allows food supplies to flow without stringent restrictions and reach areas beyond food aid. WTO law will play an important role in bringing about such a global regime. Climate change adaptation calls for a review of predominant patterns of agricultural policies, in particular policies in Europe, Japan and the US. The need to adapt to the impacts of climate change makes a strong case for enhanced trade liberalization and the reduction of export restrictions in order to offset shortages in times of climatic problems affecting regions of the world.[110] It is doubtful whether current rules on agriculture in international trade will be able to cope with these challenges. As a result new instruments need to be developed and explored.

Climate change adaptation will also require reviewing predominant views on biotechnology and genetic engineering, in particular in Europe. Climate change requires enhanced adaptability which, both for plants and animals, may be greatly aided by the use of genetic engineering.[111] Negotiations on genetic engineering, in particular in the context of intellectual property protection and in the field of food safety will need to take these considerations into account.[112]

Climate change will require reviewing established principles of investment protection, both within and outside the WTO. The phenomenon of land grabbing by means of foreign direct investment in other regions of the world, in particular in Africa[113] raises new problems in the context of climate change adaptation. While these investments can be seen as a

---

[110] Hertel, T. and T. Randhir (2000), 'Trade Liberalization as a Vehicle for Adapting to Global Warming', *Agriculture and Resource Economics Review* **29** (2), 1–14. For example, the authors find that once subsidies in agriculture are eliminated the trading system contributes positively to economic adaptation under climate change.

[111] See for example Karapinar, B. and Temmerman, M. (2007), 'Benefiting from Biotechnology: Pro-poor IPRs and Public-Private Partnerships', *Biotechnology Law Report* **27** (3), 189–202 for a review of how biotechnology can address stresses on crops.

[112] Ibid.

[113] There has been a large scale rise of land acquisitions in recent times. A recent study found that there have been 2,492,684 ha. of approved land allocations since 2004 in five African countries: the drivers for such investments include food security concerns in the investing country. Cotula, L. et al. (2009), *Land Grab or Development Opportunity? Agricultural Investment and International Land Deals in Africa,* London/Rome: IIED/FAO/IFAD.

means to secure food supplies in the investor state, they may destroy traditional forms of livelihood and accelerate the risk of famine and shortages for local populations. International law as it stands is helpless to address this point and calls for enhanced protection of property rights of those affected by such investment.[114] It also calls for reviewing the ban on the local content requirements in the TRIMs Agreement[115] and the exploration of additional disciplines.

2.   Trade in water

Water supplies will play a critical role in adapting to future climate changes, both for agriculture and for life in general. Water is predominantly used in agriculture, at times at the expense of consumption by humans in need. Climate change adaptation will need to examine issues related to trade in water. Currently, water is a commodity without legal status. It may be necessary to define rights and obligations in providing access to water beyond traditional foundations in public international law. Bulk trade in water may become relevant to drought stricken areas.[116] However, bulk water trade is also a subject that has raised concerns among some nations and as a result requires further discussion.[117] Trade in virtual or 'embedded' water, the idea that the water used in the production of agricultural products which are subsequently traded must be considered in relation to water available in a region, is an increasingly important issue and may lead to new disciplines in food supplies and international trade.[118]

---

[114]   Cotula et al. (above, note 113) note: 'Many countries do not have in place legal or procedural mechanisms to protect local rights and take account of local interests, livelihoods and welfare.' As a result there may be an increasing need for international organizations to play a role in ensuring these rights are protected.

[115]   See Agreement on Trade Related Investment Measures, Annex. Available at http://www.wto.org/english/docs_e/legal_e/18-trims_e.htm (accessed 9 May 2011).

[116]   Luo, B. et al. (2003), 'Adaption to Climate Change through Water Trading under Uncertainty – An Inexact Two-Stage Nonlinear Programming Approach', *Journal of Environmental Informatics*, 2 (2), 58–68, found that '. . . water trading is a suitable method for adaptation to climate change impacts under water scarcity. . .'.

[117]   See for example Johansen, D. (2002), *Bulk Water Removals, Water Exports and the NAFTA*. Available at http://dsp-psd.pwgsc.gc.ca/Collection-R/LoPBdP/BP/prb0041-e.htm (accessed 9 May 2011), detailing the controversy on this matter in Canada.

[118]   For an overview of major issues on this topic see for example Hoekstra, A.Y. (2010), *The Relation between International Trade and Freshwater Scarcity*, World Trade Organization Economic Research and Statistics Division, Staff Working Paper ERSD-2010-05.

C.   Climate Change Communication and Transparency

Climate change policies depend on effective communication and information to the public. The problem has not had much attention paid to it. It relates to freedom of information and freedom of expression which is not universally secured. While freedom of information and expression are largely beyond the scope of WTO law, transparency is an important contribution to be further explored and strengthened. Consumers are increasingly aware of policies relating to climate change mitigation and adaptation and seek appropriate product information. This will in the future also entail information about energy sources used to produce the goods and services at hand. Labeling requirements therefore can make a major contribution towards increasing transparency. Similar to fair trade labels, climate change related labels are likely to increase. Energy efficiency labels are already common and are largely accepted under trade rules. However, the legal position of labels that indicate the level of greenhouse gases emitted in the production of a good is currently unclear under WTO law.[119] They need to be addressed by proper disciplines achieving a balance between the provision of information and the need to avoid protectionist side effects. Again, it is a matter of combining these efforts with transfer of knowledge and technology in order to enable exporters in developing countries to comply with future labeling requirements introduced under the umbrella of climate policies.

International trade agreements can result in increases in emissions through expanded economic growth and increased transportation. While these emissions may be able to be offset, to some extent, by improved access to clean technologies, assessments of the emissions impacts of trade agreements could help allow the WTO to be viewed as a transparent organization that is mindful of sustainable development goals. Currently some countries do perform environmental assessments of trade

---

[119]   Under the TBT Agreement carbon emissions would be considered to be non-product-related processes and production methods (NPR-PPMs), i.e. carbon emissions associated with a product's production or transport that are indiscernible in the final product, and therefore may or may not fit the definition pertaining to labels in the TBT Agreement which is limited to 'a product, process or production method'. See Nartova, O. (2009), *Carbon Labelling: Moral, Economic and Legal Implications in a World Trade Environment*, Swiss National Centre for Competence in Research, Working Paper No 2009/5, pp. 7–16 for a discussion of the role of carbon labels in the WTO.

agreements,[120] however an increased effort in this regard could improve communication about the impacts of trade on climate change.

VII.   CONCLUSIONS

The relationship between climate change and international trade regulation raises a host of complex issues. The challenge of taking into account energy efficiency and energy sources in the production and distribution of goods and services raises many new problems. Climate change is an environmental issue. Yet there is much more to be done than simply accommodating and interfacing it with existing trade rules. Climate change is bound fundamentally to alter the multilateral trading system in the coming negotiations if the goals of climate change mitigation and the challenge of adaptation as well as communication and transparency are taken seriously. The regulation of energy, so far at the margins of WTO law, is at the heart of the matter. Incentives need to be created to stimulate increased efficiency and the use of renewable energy in the production of goods and services. Trade policy tools to this effect are partly available, but highly controversial, and they may have the tendency to create disadvantages for developing countries. They may, however, also be used to bring about a multilateral system of climate change policy goals and instruments and trade restrictions should not apply to those participating in such a system. Moreover, members of the system should further benefit from effective transfers of knowledge and technology to which trading rules need to lend more active support. There is an important dialectical relationship between climate change policies and international trade rules which needs to be fleshed out and examined in detail. The experience of trade and international economic law may stimulate new approaches in climate change talks, taking recourse to club models, bottom-up approaches and critical mass to build consensus. In fact, it may be beneficial to look at a smaller negotiating forum than that currently in place at the UNFCCC, including for example only the ten major polluting countries around the world, to develop an effective international framework to mitigate the impacts of climate change. At the same time, an entirely different constituency is

---

[120]   For a list of environmental reviews see WTO, 'Committee on Trade and Environment, List of Environmental Reviews'. Available at http://www.wto.org/english/tratop_e/envir_e/reviews_e.htm (accessed 9 May 2011), document WT/CTE/W/245/Add.1.

required to address climate change adaptation. It is here that those most affected by climate change need to be fully included.

While existing WTO law offers an important yardstick to gauge climate change policies, the overall goals of climate change will create a need to revisit existing WTO rules and those of regional and preferential agreements. Existing patterns and rules that secure equal conditions of competition may need to take into account methods of production, in particular the sources of energy used in the production of goods and services. Clearly, the issue of non-product related PPMs is at the heart of the matter, but the debate is not limited to this one issue. In exploring foundations, the principle of common concern may create a bridge between trade and environmental concerns in state responsibility and liability, and this principle should be further assessed and developed. Energy is bound to play a major role in a rules based system. Largely ignored up to now, it will lead to the increased integration of rules related to goods and services, perhaps altering the basic structure of the current WTO. It calls for an integrated approach which may be provided in a framework agreement on energy. Since many of its aspects fall into the domain of international trade law, such an agreement, to a large extent, may form the backbone of a new generation of trade agreements in the age of actively combating global warming with appropriate incentives, rules and disciplines in international law.

15. Carbon leakage measures and border tax adjustments under WTO law
Joost Pauwelyn

I. INTRODUCTION[1]

One of the major obstacles toward the adoption of mandatory limits on greenhouse gas emissions is the impact of such limits on the international competitiveness of domestic firms. Limits on greenhouse gas emissions – be they in the form of regulation, a carbon tax or a cap-and-trade system[2] – may impose extra costs on domestic industries. Where foreign firms do not bear similar costs, domestic firms may lose their competitive edge. In particular, with a domestic climate policy in place, imports from countries *without* mandatory carbon restrictions may gain a price advantage over domestic goods. It is exactly this asymmetry that led the US Senate[3] to

---

[1]   This chapter updates earlier research published as a working paper. For the original working paper, see Joost Pauwelyn, *U.S. Federal Climate Policy and Competitiveness Concerns: The Limits and Options of International Trade Law* (Durham: Nicholas Institute for Environmental Policy Solutions, Duke University, 2007).

[2]   This chapter only addresses government intervention that restricts greenhouse gas emissions, not subsidies that promote alternative energy sources (although such subsidies raise questions of WTO consistency of their own). In terms of ranking these different policy instruments, *The Economist* put it bluntly: 'Governments can try to reduce emissions in three ways: subsidise alternatives, impose standards on products and processes, and price the greenhouse gases that cause the damage. The first is almost always a bad idea; the second should generally be avoided; the third is the way to go' (*What price carbon?* The Economist, 17 March 2007, 15).

[3]   For a contextual background, see the Byrd-Hagel Resolution (S.RES. 98, 105th Congress, 1997), determining that 'the United States should not be a signatory to any protocol . . . which would . . . mandate new commitments to limit or reduce greenhouse gas emission for the Annex I Parties, unless the protocol . . . also mandates new specific scheduled commitments to limit or reduce greenhouse gas emissions for Developing Country Parties within the same compliance period. . .'. See also President George W. Bush, *President Bush's Speech on Global Climate Change*, 11 June 2001.

reject the Kyoto Protocol,[4] an international agreement that did not require emission cuts from developing countries.[5] The competitiveness impact of climate change policy may play out both at home (on the domestic market) and abroad (on world markets). It can be particularly acute for energy-intensive manufacturers such as the iron and steel, aluminium, cement, glass, chemicals and pulp and paper industries.

This chapter examines the extent to which domestic climate policy could alleviate this competitiveness concern. More particularly, the chapter assesses the limits imposed by World Trade Organization ('WTO') agreements on possible competitiveness provisions in climate legislation. Such competitiveness provisions would essentially aim at levelling the playing field by imposing the same or similar costs on *imports*, as domestic climate policy imposes on *domestic* production. To level the playing field on world markets, *exports* could also be exempted from domestic climate restrictions.[6] As WTO Members are internationally bound by WTO law, any competitiveness provision that violates WTO agreements risks a challenge by trading partners before the WTO dispute settlement body. If competitiveness provisions were to be used as a sweetener to enable the adoption of domestic climate legislation, the WTO consistency of such provisions is, therefore, crucial.

Section II briefly examines the policy reasons for and against competitiveness provisions in climate legislation and discusses recent initiatives to this effect. Section III explains how competitiveness provisions can

---

[4] Kyoto Protocol to the United Nations Framework Convention on Climate Change (Kyoto Protocol), Kyoto, 10 December 1997, in force 16 February 2005, 37 *International Legal Materials* (1998) 22. The Kyoto Protocol came into force on 16 February 2005, when Parties accounting for at least 55 per cent of total carbon dioxide emissions for 1990 had deposited their ratification (see Article 25.1 of the Protocol). Currently, the Kyoto Protocol includes 193 Parties (192 States and one regional economic integration organization), accounting for a total percentage of Annex I Parties emissions of 63.7 per cent.

[5] The Kyoto Protocol required commitments (see Article 3) from parties included in Annex I to the United Nations Framework Convention on Climate Change, adopted in 1992 (Annex I only includes developed countries). See also Nicholas Stern, *The Economics of Climate Change: The Stern Review* (Cambridge: Cambridge University Press, 2007), 478. For a study on carbon-intensiveness of certain developing countries, see Giles Atkinson, Kirk Hamilton, Giovanni Ruta, Dominique Van Der Mensbrugghe, 'Trade in "Virtual Carbon": Empirical Results and Implications for Policy', *Policy Research Working Paper 5194, Background paper to the 2010 World Development Report*, The World Bank, 2010.

[6] For *tax* rebates on export see note 74 below (explicitly permitted). For non-application to exports of domestic *regulations*, see note 94 below (not explicitly addressed in the SCM Agreement).

take the form of trade measures, but that non-trade alternatives are also available. Section IV elaborates on the types of trade restrictions that would most likely *not* pass WTO muster (import bans, punitive tariffs, anti-dumping duties and countervailing (anti-subsidy) duties). Finally, Sections V and VI provide alternatives that the WTO would most likely accept. *First*, a carbon tax or emission allowance requirement on imports could be framed as WTO permissible 'border adjustment' of a domestic carbon tax or cap-and-trade system (Section V). Crucially, if such 'border adjustment' does not discriminate imports as against domestic products (national treatment), and does not discriminate some imports as against others (most-favoured nation treatment), this type of competitiveness provision could pass WTO scrutiny *without* any reference to the environmental exceptions in Article XX of the General Agreement on Tariffs and Trade ('GATT'). *Second*, even if 'border adjustment' would *not* be permitted for process-based measures such as a domestic carbon tax, regulation or cap-and-trade system imposed on producers, and/or such 'border adjustment' would be found to be discriminatory, the resulting GATT violation may still be justified by the environmental exceptions in GATT Article XX (Section VI). Such justification would then most likely centre on whether, under the introductory phrase of GATT Article XX, a carbon tax, emission allowance requirement or other regulation on imports is applied on a variable scale that takes account of local conditions in foreign countries, including their own efforts to fight global warming and the level of economic development in developing countries.

II.   POLICY REASONS FOR AND AGAINST COMPETITIVENESS PROVISIONS IN CLIMATE LEGISLATION

A.   The Benefits of a Competitiveness Provision

The immediate demand for competitiveness provisions is economic in nature. As a matter of arms-length competition, affected industries want to level the playing field by imposing the same costs on imports as climate legislation would impose on their own production. This economic *rationale* for competitiveness provisions – although it matters under the principle of 'national treatment' discussed in Section V.D – is not likely to carry much weight in the WTO system for environmental exceptions (addressed in Section VI). There, our attention should focus on the non-economic, environmental reasons for competitiveness provisions. There are at least four such reasons:

- *Internalizing the social cost of carbon*: As the 2006 Stern Report points out, climate change 'is the greatest and widest-ranging market failure ever seen'.[7] In particular, carbon emissions cause harm or social costs that are not calculated into the actual price of goods. To internalize this social cost of carbon – assessed in the Stern Report at \$85 per tonne of CO_2[8] – government intervention is needed. However, science tells us that emissions cause their negative effect on our planet irrespective of where they arise. Hence, one government alone cannot resolve the matter. Climate change is, in other words, a collective action problem. International cooperation is needed. Where such cooperation fails or is insufficient, as remains the case today especially after the Copenhagen Summit,[9] a government can either resign itself to the problem or do something about it without the support of others. Unilateral action, albeit second or third best, could then include a competitiveness provision forcing at least all those goods that enter the domestic market of the legislating country to internalize the social cost of carbon.[10]

- *Carbon leakage or 'emission migration'*: In a scenario where not all countries cut emissions – that is, some countries are free-riders – certain countries may decide to cut their own emissions anyhow. Doing so may, however, shift market shares from (capped or 'cleaner') domestic sources to (uncapped and 'dirtier') imports. It may even lead some domestic companies to relocate to free-riding

---

[7] Stern, note 5 above, Executive Summary. On price and market mechanism to internalize environmental costs of GHG emissions, see WTO-UNEP Report, *Trade and Climate Change: a Report by the United Nations Environment Programme and the World Trade Organization*, 2009, 90–110; and Ludivine Tamiotti and Vesile Kulaçoğlu, 'National Climate Change Mitigation Measures and their Implications for the Multilateral Trading System', *Journal of World Trade* 43, No. 5, 2009.

[8] Stern, note 5 above, xvi.

[9] The 2009 United Nations Climate Change Conference, also known as the Copenhagen Summit, was held between 7 and 18 December 2009 and included the 15th Conference of the Parties (COP 15) to the United Nations Framework Convention on Climate Change, and the 5th Meeting of the Parties (MOP 5) to the Kyoto Protocol. The Copenhagen Summit resulted only in nonbinding commitments.

[10] For a full explanation of the economic case for a competitiveness provision, in particular, border tax adjustment on carbon-intensive imports, see Roland Ismer and Karsten Neuhoff, *Border Tax Adjustments: A Feasible Way to Address Nonparticipation in Emission Trading*, Cambridge: CMI Working Paper 36, January 2004, 4–8, available at http://ideas.repec.org/p/cam/camdae/0409.html, last visited October 2011.

countries altogether. This would not only cost jobs and tax money in the legislating country, but could also increase carbon emissions elsewhere: Rather than reducing emissions under a new domestic climate regime, relocated supplies or firms may then actually emit more in countries with no carbon restrictions. A competitiveness provision would avoid market shifts to 'dirtier' imports to the extent that even relocated firms would, in any event, have to pay the cost of carbon when they re-export their products back to the home market.

- *Enabling wider and deeper emission cuts within the regulating country*: Competitiveness provisions are likely to reduce domestic business opposition against emission cuts. With a competitiveness provision in place, especially energy-intensive domestic industries may agree to be covered by the climate policy. Without such provision, in order to gain support for the adoption of climate policies, policy makers may end up having to exclude a number of industries altogether, impose lower overall cuts and/or be pressured into handing out emission allowances for free (instead of auctioning them off; a system that is generally regarded as more effective).[11]

- *Offer an incentive for other countries to join international efforts to cut emissions*: Competitiveness provisions would force imports to pay the social cost of carbon. This would offer an incentive to foreign companies to reduce their emissions. Foreign governments would also be given an incentive to impose their own emission cuts, or to agree to emission cuts under an international agreement: Doing so may exclude them from import taxes or other regulations under a competitiveness provision when exporting to a country with carbon restrictions. Indeed, even if the enactment of a competitiveness provision never materializes, it must be kept in mind that the mere threat of its enactment may push certain countries, particularly those highly dependent on foreign trade, to cut emissions or otherwise engage in coordinated efforts to tackle climate change.[12]

---

[11]   The first phase of the European scheme, for example, covered only 46 per cent of the EU's total CO_2 emissions and caps 'only' 13,000 installations. The waste, chemicals, aluminium and transport sectors are excluded from the scheme. See Javier de Cendra, 'Can Emissions Trading Schemes be Coupled with Border Tax Adjustments? An Analysis vis-à-vis WTO Law', 15 *Review of European Community & International Environmental Law* 2006, 131, 133.

[12]   Some reports indicated, for example, that China was planning to impose an export tax of 5 to 15 per cent on energy-intensive exports such as iron and steel, cement, aluminium and certain chemicals. *After the Stern Review: Reflections and Responses, Building an Effective International Response to Climate Change*, February 2007, 18, available at http://www.hm-treasury.gov.uk/media/B71/79/

B.   The Costs of a Competitiveness Provision

As noted by the 2006 Stern Review, unilateral trade barriers 'are clearly second best to implementing a similar carbon price across the global economy' through international agreements.[13] One must, therefore, remain acutely aware of the costs and risks of competitiveness provisions, five of which are summarized below.

- *Barriers to trade are inefficient*: Trade restrictions skew the optimal allocation of the world's resources and the principle of comparative advantage. They are also costly especially for domestic consumers and domestic industries that depend on imported inputs (such as an automobile industry using imported steel).
- *Competitiveness impact can be exaggerated or abused*: Even where trade barriers may be needed as second or third best solutions, competitiveness provisions risk being abused by importing-competing domestic industries for purely protectionist purposes unrelated to global warming. In this respect, the competitiveness impact of climate policy is often exaggerated. The Stern Review estimates that the cost of combating climate change now, would only be 1 per cent of global GDP, 'this is equivalent to price changes of an order

---

paper_c.pdf. This strategy is also present in China's National Climate Change Programme, where it is stated that China would 'deepen institutional reform of foreign trade in controlling export of energy-intensive, pollution-intensive and resource-intensive products, so as to formulate an import and export structure favourable to promote a cleaner and optimal energy mix'. National Development and Reform Commission, *China's National Climate Change Programme* (2007), 31, available at http://www.ccchina.gov.cn/WebSite/CCChina/UpFile/File188. pdf. See also, National Development and Reform Commission, *China's Policies and Actions for Addressing Climate Change – The Progress Report* (2009), 75 available at http://www.ccchina.gov.cn/WebSite/CCChina/UpFile/File571.pdf ('The government has . . . revoked the tax rebate on the export of energy-, pollution- and resource-intensive products, and heightened the efforts to phase out of the backward production capacities in the power, iron and steel, building materials, . . . coal, and flat glass industries.'); Chinese Ministry of Finance and the State Administration of Taxation, Circular Caishui (2010) No. 57 of 22 June 2010, revoking export VAT refund for 406 items, covering amongst others steel products, nonferrous metal products, chemical products, and plastic, rubber and glass products. For major adjustments to China's export VAT refund rates of energy-intensive products (2004–2010), see Xin Xang, Ji Feng Li and Ya Xiong Zhang, 'Can export tax be genuine climate policy? An analysis on China's export tax and export VAT refund rebate policies', 8 *Idées pour le débat, IDDRI Sciences Po* (2010), Table A2, 15–17.

[13]   Stern, note 5 above, 487.

that we are used to dealing with all the time, through, for example, changes in exchange rates'.[14] In the Report's opinion, even in energy intensive sectors, 'the impacts are not very high' and since the bulk of trade in many of these industries is limited to within regional blocs (such as the European Union ('EU')), '[a]pplication of greenhouse gas policies within these blocs is likely to reduce competitive impacts dramatically'.[15] Equally, the risk of relocation and carbon leakage can be exaggerated. Much will depend on how carbon-intensive products are and the extent to which domestic firms are able to pass on the cost of carbon into higher consumer prices: if pass on is not possible (due to, for example, high levels of openness to trade and low entry barriers), the market share of (uncapped) imports will increase and assuming imports are 'dirtier', carbon leakage is more likely. One OECD study, for example, showed that if the price of one tonne of CO_2 were 15 Euros, the loss of production of the cement industry in the EU would have been 7.5 per cent in 2010 and that, as a result, production and emissions in the rest of the world would have increased. In other words, in this instance, there would be carbon leakage (for cement, passing on the full price of carbon into cement prices is difficult, given high levels of import competition and energy-intensity).[16] In contrast, the introduction of mandatory emission cuts in Europe did lead to a significant increase in the price of electricity (where passing on price increases is easier). Since there is no competition from outside the EU, European utilities simply reflected the price of emission allowances into higher electricity prices, affecting not only end-consumers but also EU industry.[17]

- *Future cooperation*: Competitiveness provisions, and the unilateral action that comes with them, may undermine the trust necessary for future international cooperation and agreement on emission reductions. This is the potential flip-side of one of the hoped for benefits of a competitiveness provision. On the one hand, such provision may incentivize free-riders to join an international scheme. On the

---

[14]   *After the Stern Review*, see note 12 above, 18.

[15]   *Ibid.*

[16]   Damien Demailly and Philippe Quirion, *The Competitiveness Impact of CO_2 Emissions Reduction in the Cement Sector,* COM/ENV/EPOC/CTPA/CFA (2004) final, November 2005.

[17]   See, for instance, Christian Egenhofer, Noriko Fujiwara and Kyriakos Gialoglou, *Business Consequences of the EU Emission Trading Scheme* (CEPS Report: 2005), 23.

other hand, it may distance them even further and make it more difficult to find consensus.

- *Cost and complexity of implementation*: The administration of competitiveness provisions may be complicated. If, for example, a carbon tax or other restriction were imposed on imports, customs authorities would need to set up a system to collect information and decide on the carbon footprint of foreign countries and/or producers. If not only primary products (such as cement or steel) but also processed goods (such as cars or mobile phones) would be covered, and taxes or restrictions would target the actual carbon footprints of products (rather than country or product averages or benchmarks) more practical difficulties would arise. Similarly, if import restrictions would require justification under GATT Article XX (discussed in Section VI), a scheme would need to be set up that varies the tax or import restriction depending, for example, on climate legislation already in place in the country of origin of, say, the imported steel. These costs and practical difficulties must be weighed against the benefits that can be expected from a competitiveness provision.
- *Risk of a WTO challenge*: Any competitiveness provision with a serious trade impact is likely to trigger a WTO complaint.[18] Given the ambiguity of WTO law explained below, the WTO may either uphold or strike down the provision. Importantly, even if parts of a climate change measure were found to violate WTO law, the only formal remedy currently offered by the WTO dispute settlement system is that the WTO Member would then have to change its legislation as to the future (or suffer retaliation if it fails to do so

---

[18]   See, for example, Patrick Low, Gabrielle Marceau, Julia Reinaud, 'The Interface Between the Trade and Climate Change Regimes: Scoping the Issues', *Staff Working Paper ERSD-2011-1* (WTO, Economic Research and Statistics Division, 2011); Gary Clyde Hufbauer, Jisun Kim, *The World Trade Organization and Climate Change: challenges and options*, Working Paper Series WP09-9 (Washington: Peterson Institute of International Economics, 2009); Aaron Cosbey, *Border Carbon Adjustment: Questions and Answers (but more of the former)*, background paper, International Institute for Sustainable Development, 2009; Matthew Genasci, 'Border Tax Adjustments and Emissions Trading: the Implications of International Trade Law for Policy Design', 33 *Carbon & Climate Law Review,* 2008; Timothy E. Deal, 'WTO Rules and Procedures and their Implication for the Kyoto Protocol', *United States Council for International Business* 2008; and Ernst-Ulrich Petersmann, 'International Trade Law and International Environmental Law: Environmental Taxes and Border Tax Adjustment in WTO Law and EC Law', *Environmental Law, the Economy and Sustainable Development: the United States, the European Union and the International Community* (Cambridge: Cambridge University Press, 2000), 127–155.

within a reasonable period of time). No damages for past harm are due. Hence, a competitiveness provision could be included as part of a good faith effort to tackle climate change, pursuant to a good faith interpretation of relevant WTO rules. If the effort fails, and the WTO strikes down the provision or particular implementing details, the legislating country gets a second chance to correct its measure so as to bring it in line with WTO recommendations. It would get the chance to do so within a reasonable period of time, without any sanction or obligation to pay compensation.

C.   Recent Initiatives Toward the Enactment of Competitiveness Provisions

The above list of costs and risks related to competitiveness provisions may well explain why they have so far not been implemented, at a general scale, by any country (although in defeated US climate change proposals they played a prominent role).[19] The first phase of the EU emissions trading scheme did include the possibility for EU member States to adapt their

---

[19]   See, for example, Larry Parker, John Blodgett, Brent D. Yacobucci, 'U.S. Global Climate Change Policy: Evolving Views on Cost, Competitiveness, and Comprehensiveness', *CRS Report for Congress*, RL30024, Congressional Research Service, 24 February 2011; Larry Parker, Jeanne J. Grimmet, 'Climate Change: EU and Proposed U.S. Approaches to Carbon Leakage and WTO Implications', *CRS Report for Congress*, R40914, Congressional Research Service, 12 April 2010; and Trevor Houser, Rob Bradley, Britt Childs, Jacob Werksman, Robert Heilmayr, *Leveling the Carbon Playing Field: International Competition and US Climate Policy Design* (Washington: Peterson Institute for International Economics, World Resources Institute, 2008), 10–12. See also, Julia Reinaud, *Issues Behind Competitiveness and Carbon Leakage: Focus on Heavy Industry* (Paris: International Energy Agency – IEA Information Paper, 2008); *International Trade and Climate Change: Economic, Legal and Institutional Perspective* (Washington: The World Bank, 2008), chapter 2: 'Climate Change Policies and International Trade: Challenges and Opportunities', 19–43; Ben Lockwood, John Whalley, 'Carbon Motivated Border Tax Adjustments: Old Wine in Green Bottles?', *The World Economy*, 2010; John Stephenson, Simon Upton, *Competitiveness, Leakage, and Border Adjustment: Climate Policy Distractions?*, OECD, SG/SD/ RT(2009) 3; Mark Kenber, Oliver Haugen, Madeleine Cobb, 'The Effects of EU Climate Legislation on Business Competitiveness: a Survey and Analysis', *Climate & Energy Paper Series 09* (The Climate Group, Washington: The German Marshall Fund of the United States, 2009); Gilbert E. Metcalf, David Weisbach, 'The Design of a Carbon Tax', 33 *Harvard Environmental Law Review* 2009; and Victoria Alexeeva-Talebi, Andreas Löschel, Tim Mennel, *Competitiveness in Unilateral Climate Policy: Border Tax Adjustments or Integrated Emission Trading?* (Mannheim: Centre for European Economic Research, 2008).

national allocation plan to take account of 'the existence of competition from countries or entities outside the Union'.[20] Yet, this criterion was not applied by a single member State in the first stage of EU emission cuts (ending in 2007).[21] The second phase of the EU scheme (2008–2012) also foresaw that for '[e]nergy-intensive industries which are determined to be exposed to a significant risk of carbon leakage . . . an effective carbon equalisation system could be introduced with a view to putting install-ations from the Community which are at significant risk of carbon leakage and those from third countries on a comparable footing'.[22] Yet, no such 'carbon equalization system' has been put in place to date (instead, energy-intensive industries based within the EU have received large amounts of free allowances). Australia's recently enacted Clean Energy Act (2011) imposes a carbon tax of 23 Australian dollars (as of July 2012), increas-ing over time, and planned to be replaced by a carbon trading scheme in 2015.[23] However, at this stage, it only imposes this tax on carbon emitted within Australia (and only on the 500 biggest polluters), not on the foreign carbon footprint of imported products (instead, as is the case in the EU, free carbon units are issued to certain energy-intensive, trade exposed pro-ducers). Australia's Productivity Commission, under a newly set up Jobs

---

[20]   Annex III of the Directive 2003/87/EC of the European Parliament and of the Council of 13 October 2003 establishing a scheme for greenhouse gas emission allowance trading within the Community and amending Council Directive 96/61/EC.

[21]   de Cendra, note 11 above, 133. On proposals based on the EU ETS, see Javier de Cendra de Larragán, 'From the EU ETS to a Global Carbon Market: an Analysis and Suggestions for the Way Forward', *European Energy and Environmental Law Review* 2010; and Daniel Gros, Christian Egenhofer, *Climate Change and Trade: Taxing Carbon at the Border?* (Brussels: Centre for European Policy Studies, 2010).

[22]   Directive 2009/29/EC of the European Parliament and of the Council of 23 April 2009 amending Directive 2003/87/EC so as to improve and extend the green-house gas emission allowance trading scheme of the Community, Preambular paragraph 25 ('Such a system could apply requirements to importers that would be no less favourable than those applicable to installations within the Community, for example by requiring the surrender of allowances. Any action taken would need to be in conformity with the principles of the UNFCCC, in particular the principle of common but differentiated responsibilities and respective capabilities, taking into account the particular situation of least developed countries (LDCs). It would also need to be in conformity with the international obligations of the Community, including the obligations under the WTO agreement') and referred to in Article 10b(1)(b).

[23]   See Clean Energy Act 2011, available at http://www.comlaw.gov.au/Details/C2011A00131/Html/Text#_Toc308513393.

and Competitiveness Program, must keep an eye open on whether such border tax adjustment may be necessary in the future.

Similarly, prominent voices – such as Nobel prize winner Joseph Stiglitz,[24] former French President Chirac and former Prime Minister de Villepin,[25] former EU Commissioner Verheugen,[26] French President Sarkozy,[27] and Michael Morris, CEO of American Electric Power[28] – have called for a carbon tax or trade measures against countries not cutting carbon emissions. Yet, in response, former EU Trade Commissioner Mandelson,[29] German Chancellor Merkel,[30] and former US Secretary of State Rice[31] have all been quick to reject the idea.

The question remains whether domestic pressures for adjustments on

---

[24]   Joseph Stiglitz, *A New Agenda for Global Warming*, Economists' Voice, July 2006, available at http://www.bepress.com/cgi/viewcontent.cgi?article=1210& context=ev.

[25]   *M. de Villepin Propose une Taxe sur le CO_2 des Produits Importés*, Le Monde, 14 November 2006.

[26]   *Letter by G. Verheugen to Commission President Barroso*, 21 November 2006.

[27]   France says EU nations would back CO_2 border tax, Bloomberg Businessweek, 26 March 2010, available at http://www.businessweek.com/ap/ financialnews/D9EMBHBG1.htm ('I'm sure there would be a big majority to demand the end of Europe's naivety . . . Can we impose environmental standards on EU steel-makers and at the same time import steel from China that would be produced without environmental specification? . . . It would mean we accept production of all steel products shifting to China, or India or another country . . . In terms of unemployment, Europe would be penalized. We have to realize that . . .')

[28]   Michael Morris & Edwin Hill, *Trade is the Key to Climate Change*, Energy Daily, 20 February 2007, available at http://www.ujae.org/globalwarming/hill%20 morris%20article%20in%20energy%20daily% 20feb% 2020%2007.pdf.

[29]   *Trade and Climate Change*, Speech by EU Trade Commissioner Peter Mandelson, Brussels, 18 December 2006, available at http://ec.europa.eu/commis sion_barroso/mandelson/speeches_articles/ sppm136_en.htm ('There is one trade policy response to climate change about which I have serious doubts. That is the idea of a specific "climate" tariff on countries that have not ratified Kyoto. This would be highly problematic under current WTO rules and almost impossible to implement in practice. I also suspect it would not be good politics').

[30]   *Europe's Green Summit is Seeking to Bury the Carbon Past*, Financial Times, 8 March 2007, at 9 ('Ms. Merkel has dismissed – at this stage – a French idea that Europe should impose a "Kyoto tax" on countries that undercut European producers at the expense of the environment').

[31]   *US Pours Scorn on International Greenhouse Tax Proposal*, The Sidney Morning Herald, 20 November 2006 available at http://www.smh.com.au/news/ world/us-pours-scorn-on-international-greenhouse-tax-proposal/2006/11/19/1163 871272165.html. Australian Prime Minister Howard called the idea of a carbon tax 'silly'.

imports or other competitiveness provisions can be prevented once free allowances dry up and/or the price of carbon reaches substantial levels (in November 2011, the EU market price for one tonne of carbon was below 10 Euros, a far cry from the Stern review's estimate of $85 per tonne[32]). Limited border adjustments have already been enacted in the EU, firstly, in the area of biofuels where both EU *and* imported biofuels are subject to emission reduction and land use requirements[33] (taking account of the entire life cycle of the fuel, including emissions outside the EU) and, secondly, in the aviation sector where, as of 1 January 2012, all planes, both EU *and* foreign, landing in or leaving from the EU will need to present or buy emission allowances.[34] A December 2011 judgment by the European Court of Justice confirmed the validity of this scheme, finding that it violates neither customary international law (rules on extra-territoriality) nor the Air Transport Agreement between the EC and the United States (the so-called Open Skies Agreement which, *inter alia*, exempts fuel load from any taxes, duties, fees and charges).[35] That said, both the United States

---

[32] See note 5 above. The first phase of the EU scheme was not a success: In 2007, prices for allowances for the first phase collapsed with permits trading in March 2007 at about 1 Euro or less per tonne, down from a high of over 30 Euros, because more allowances were issued than were needed to cover companies' emissions in the first phase (*Energy Chief Wants Sharp Rise in Carbon Permit*, Financial Times, 8 March 2007, 2). As for phase two, it was expected that emissions would be reduced by 2.4 per cent in 2010, as compared to expected emissions without the cap (Ben Jones, Michael Keen, John Norregaard, Jon Strand, 'Appendix 1.2: Climate Change: Economic Impact and Policy Responses', *Chapter 1: Global Prospects and Policies, World Economic Outlook* (Washington: International Monetary Fund, 64). Even in Europe, therefore, genuine internalization of the social cost of carbon is still at an early stage. For an overview of the carbon market, see Alexandre Kossoy and Philippe Ambrosi, *State and Trends of the Carbon Market* (Washington: Carbon Finance, The World Bank, 2010).

[33] Directive 2009/28/EC of the European Parliament and of the Council of 23 April 2009 on the promotion of the use of energy from renewable sources and amending and subsequently repealing Directives 2001/77/EC and 2003/30/EC, Article 17.1 ('Irrespective of whether the raw materials were cultivated inside or outside the territory of the Community, energy from biofuels and bioliquids shall be taken into account for the purposes referred to in points (a), (b) and (c) only if they fulfil the sustainability criteria set out in paragraphs 2 to 6').

[34] See Lorand Bartels, The Inclusion of Aviation in the EU ETS, WTO Law Considerations, November 2011, available at http://papers.ssrn.com/sol3/papers. cfm?abstract_id=1959981.

[35] *Air Transport Association of America et al. v. Secretary of State for Energy and Climate Change*, Case C-366/10, 21 December 2011, finding, for example at para. 127: 'It is only if the operator of such an aircraft has chosen to operate a commercial air route arriving at or departing from an aerodrome situated in the

and China, are vehemently opposed to the idea that their airline operators would have to pay the carbon price of entire flights whenever they take off or land in the EU (and this including parts flown *outside* EU territory). In both countries initiatives are under way that would prohibit operators from paying the applicable fees.[36]

Within the United States, the state of California has enacted climate change legislation, including a Low Carbon Fuel Standard (LCFS) Program.[37] California's LCFS applies to transportation fuels sourced within California and those sourced outside California (be it in another US state or imported from a foreign country). The standard relates to the total amount of carbon emitted during the entire life cycle of the fuel (including its extraction, refinement and production process as well as transportation to California). Fuel providers are required to calculate the carbon intensity of each fuel component to determine their score. If this score is below a statewide average carbon intensity level (which decreases over time), the provider gets credits; if the score is above that average, credits must be purchased. Interestingly, however, a US federal district judge recently issued a preliminary injunction against the LCFS finding that it violates the Dormant Commerce Clause in the US Constitution by discriminating against out-of-state fuels as compared to California fuels.[38] The EU is currently considering a similar measure, to be enacted pursuant to Directive 2009/30/EC on fuel quality. It would also allocate carbon intensity scores and default values to transportation fuels, based on emissions during the entire life cycle of the fuel. As a result, oil from tar sands in Canada, for example, whose extraction generates far more GHG

---

territory of a Member State that the operator, because its aircraft is in the territory of that Member State, will be subject to the allowance trading scheme'.

[36] See *China Bans Airlines from Complying with EU ETS*, Flightglobal, 6 February 2011, available at http://www.flightglobal.com/news/articles/china-bans-airlines-from-complying-with-eu-ets-367796/.

[37] Information available at http://www.arb.ca.gov/fuels/lcfs/lcfs.htm, in particular, the Low Carbon Fuel Standard Regulation of April 2010. Cal. Code Regs. tit. 17, §§95480-95490.

[38] *Rocky Mountain Farmers Union et al. v. James N. Goldstene, Executive Officer of the California Air Resources Board*, Order on Summary Adjudication Motion, Case No. CV-F-09-2234 LJO DLB, US District Court for the Eastern District of California (Judge O'Neill), 29 December 2011 (concluding that the LCFS 'discriminates against out-of state corn-derived ethanol while favoring in-state corn ethanol and impermissibly regulates extraterritorial conduct. In addition, Defendants have failed to establish that there are no alternative methods to advance its goals of reducing GHG emissions to combat global warming').

emissions than conventional oil would have a much harder time meeting EU fuel standards.[39]

III.   POLICY OPTIONS TO ADDRESS COMPETITIVENESS CONCERNS

A.   Competitiveness Provisions other than Trade Measures

The focus of this chapter is trade measures, such as a carbon tax or other border restriction on carbon-intensive imports. Competitiveness concerns can, however, also be addressed by policies other than trade instruments. Below are six such alternatives.

- *Flexibility mechanisms*: such as emissions trading, making abatement less costly by letting companies who can abate at the lowest cost do so, and sell their extra reductions to other companies whose abatement costs are higher (the latter companies can then 'buy off' their reduction limits); additional flexibility can be offered where the legislation would permit the handing out of carbon credits to domestic firms for their carbon abating investments in developing countries, similar to the existing Clean Development Mechanism under the Kyoto Protocol.[40] Similar carbon credits could be provided for so-called carbon sinks such as forestry or agricultural projects or activities which reduce or transform carbon emissions.
- *Grandfather current emission levels – free allowances*: that is, hand out free permits to emitting industries up to current emission levels,

---

[39]   See EU Commission Consultation Paper under Article 7(a) of Directive 2009/30/EC, available at http://ec.europa.eu/environment/air/transport/fuel.htm.

[40]   Lessons should then, however, be learned from the current Kyoto mechanism which covers not only CO_2 but also certain other gases such as HFC23, a heat-trapping gas 11,700 times stronger than CO_2. Under Kyoto's Clean Development Mechanism, a reduction by, for example, Chinese chemical companies in HFC23 emissions can be bought by, for example, a European electricity company that cannot meet its carbon targets. However, to reduce HFC23 emissions is extremely cheap compared to the price of a CO_2 emission credit. Some accounts speak of 0.5 Euros/t of HFC23 in return of 8 Euros/t of carbon. Put differently, Europe can continue to emit, that is, for example, to expand its electricity sector, by paying a subsidy to China. See Jean-Pierre Hauet, *Vers une Taxe Compensatoire sur le Carbone Importé*, Power Point Presentation, 15, available at http://www.kbintelligence.com/fileadmin/pdf/TCCI_JPHdec06.pdf, last visited on October 2011.

thereby not imposing any immediate emission cuts and only requiring companies to buy allowances if they increase their emissions; if companies lower their emissions, they can sell the permits that they received for 'free' in the market. Such grandfathering of current emission levels would, however, have the drawback of rewarding the biggest emitters, i.e., those domestic companies that have so far not done anything to cut their emissions. It would also make it more difficult for new companies to enter the market (thereby potentially stifling competition). Solutions to this are to hand out free allowances based on emission averages or best available technologies (so that the most polluting firms get fewer allowances) and to reserve a number of free allowances for new entrants.

- *Industry carve-outs*: to alleviate competitiveness concerns, the legislation can exclude certain energy-intensive industries from any emission reductions;[41] the country's overall carbon target could then still be met by reductions elsewhere.
- *Cross-subsidization*: revenues raised by a carbon tax or auctioning emission permits could be used to lower other costs on domestic firms such as taxes on labour or capital, or technology development and application costs.
- *Safety-valves*: a climate policy could impose a maximum price or safety-valve above which emission permits cannot be traded; this safety-valve could also be coupled to periodic review of whether trading partners address climate change appropriately; if trading partners fail to act, in order to alleviate resulting competitiveness concerns, the safety-valve or ceiling price of domestic emission permits could then be lowered.[42]
- *Promise extra emission cuts in case other countries join*: Another way to attract participation from other countries in the reduction of greenhouse gas emissions is to promise additional cuts in case other countries impose emission cuts of their own; this carrot (rather than stick) approach is exactly what Europe decided to do at the March 2007 Summit: the EU–27 made a pre-commitment of a 20 per cent cut by 2020 compared with 1990 levels, with a promise to move to 30 per cent if other industrialized countries follow suit.[43]

---

[41]   See note 11 above.

[42]   See, for example in the United States, the Bingaman Bill at Section 1521 and the Udall-Petri Bill at Section 5.

[43]   *EU Seizes Leadership of Climate Fight,* Financial Times, 10–11 March 2007, 2.

B. Trade Restrictions in Respect of 'Locally-emitted' Carbon versus 'Foreign-emitted' Carbon

Notwithstanding the above alternative, or complementary, policies to address competitiveness concerns, this chapter focuses on trade instruments. Trade policy can be used in the fight against climate change not only as a stick but also as a carrot (for example, by linking trade benefits to a country's efforts in fighting climate change[44]). The concern of this chapter is, however: When and how can a country use its trade policy as a stick against high-carbon imports? There are generally two types of trade measures that could be used against imports in the fight against climate change:

(1) *Import restrictions in respect of 'locally-emitted' carbon*: that is, trade restrictions such as taxes, energy efficiency standards or other emission regulations in respect of the carbon emitted by imported products *while they are used or consumed on the territory of the importing country*; a good example is the recently adopted European rule requiring that cars sold in Europe will have to cut emissions to 130g/km by 2012, or the rule that biofuels will have to make up 10 per cent of the fuel mix;[45] emission standards for fuels (domestic or imported) combusted in the regulating country is another example.

(2) *Import restrictions in respect of 'foreign-emitted' carbon*: that is, trade restrictions such as tariffs, taxes or emission regulations in respect of carbon emitted by imported products *in their country (or countries) of production and/or during international transportation outside the importing country*; good examples are Joseph Stiglitz's proposal for Japan, Europe and other Kyoto parties to impose anti-dumping or

---

[44] Examples of how trade can be used as a carrot to convince other countries to make emission cuts or join an international agreement on climate change are: (1) the reported deal between the EU and Russia whereby the EU agreed to Russia's accession to the WTO in exchange for Russia ratifying the Kyoto Protocol (see, for example, Jeffrey Frankel, 'Climate Change and Trade, Links between the Kyoto Protocol and WTO', 47 *Environment* 2005 8, 12); (2) European tariff preferences for goods coming from developing countries who have ratified and implemented, among other agreements, the Kyoto Protocol (Council Regulation (EC) No 980/2005 of 27 June 2005 applying a scheme of generalized tariff preferences, Annex III, Part B, item 23, available at http://eur-lex.europa.eu/LexUriServ/LexUriServ.do?uri=CONSLEG:2005R0980:20080301:EN:PDF, last visited on October 2011).

[45] *Europe's Green Summit*, see note 30 above. But for an economic ranking of possible government interventions see note 2 above.

anti-subsidy duties on imports from the United States, the French proposal to impose a carbon tax on imports from all countries that refuse to cooperate in a new post-Kyoto regime as of 2012, or the suggestion by Michael Morris that emission credits accompany exports from major emitting nations that have not joined a post-Kyoto global cap-and-trade framework or otherwise capped their emissions.[46] The EU's biofuels directive and California's low carbon fuel standard, discussed in the previous section, also include foreign-emitted carbon into their calculations.

Restrictions in respect of locally-emitted carbon simply bring imported products into the fold of domestic regulations on climate change, targeting the carbon they emit *within* the importing country. For as long as such restrictions do not discriminate imports as against domestic products, nor between imports of different origins,[47] these restrictions are generally accepted under WTO rules. At the same time, since restrictions on locally-emitted carbon only aim at meeting *internal* (domestic/national) targets of emission reductions, such restrictions only very partially address the competitiveness concerns of climate policy. They make, for example, Brazilian cars or Chinese refrigerators subject to carbon-restricting regulations of the importing country on energy efficiency; they do not at all address the competitive edge that steel from China or cement from Brazil may have because of the absence of emission cuts in China or Brazil. Import restrictions in respect of foreign-emitted carbon do address those concerns. Yet, because they have an extraterritorial element – they concern carbon emitted outside the territory of the importing country – such restrictions are far more controversial.

These offshore-carbon restrictions are the focus of the remainder of this chapter. The next section (Section IV) sums up import restrictions that would most likely violate WTO rules (import bans; punitive tariffs; anti-dumping duties and countervailing (anti-subsidy) duties). Section V provides alternatives that stand a better chance of surviving WTO

---

[46]   Note also the alternative of export duties on carbon-intensive exports from, say, China. That is apparently what China introduced to alleviate US and, in particular, European competitiveness concerns, see notes 12 above and 150 below.

[47]   Discussed below in Sections V.D and E. Even if there is discrimination, it can still be justified under the environmental exception of GATT Article XX, discussed in Section VI. For a short comparison between different policies, see Carolyn Fisher, Alan K. Fox, 'Comparing Policies to Combat Emissions Leakage: Border Tax Adjustments Versus Rebates', Discussion Paper, Washington: Resources for the Future (RFF DP 09-02), 2009.

scrutiny, namely: adjustment at the border of a domestic carbon tax, cap-and-trade system or other carbon regulation. Section VI, finally, explains how even import restrictions that violate basic WTO rules can, nonetheless, still be justified under the environmental exceptions of GATT Article XX. Note, however, that once border adjustment of domestic climate legislation is permitted and is applied on a non-discriminatory basis, there would not even be a need to go to the exceptions of GATT Article XX.

IV. IMPORT RESTRICTIONS IN RESPECT OF 'FOREIGN-EMITTED' CARBON THAT WOULD MOST LIKELY VIOLATE WTO RULES

Although in economic terms trade restrictions to address offshore-carbon may be little or no different depending on the form they take, in legal terms, the choice of instrument is crucial. Depending on whether a country were to impose a tariff on imports or rather frames the adjustment in the form of a tax, anti-dumping duty, technical regulation or carbon label, the WTO consistency of competitiveness provisions can vary dramatically. This Section sums up import restrictions in respect of foreign-emitted carbon that would have no, or very little, chance of survival if they were challenged before the WTO (subject to the exceptions discussed in *Section VI* below).

A. An Import Ban or Punitive Tariffs on Imports from Free-riding Countries

One can only assume that a complete ban on imports from countries that do not have carbon restrictions in place is not on the table. If such a ban, or any other quantitative restriction on imports (say, China can only export 100,000 tonnes of steel made with coal into the United States), were nonetheless imposed, it would violate the prohibition in Article XI of the GATT which imposes the general elimination of all quantitative restrictions.[48] Unless such violation could be justified under the environmental exceptions in GATT Article XX (see *Section VI* below), any such scheme would violate WTO rules.

Besides a ban, the most obvious way to sanction imports from free-riding

---

[48]   For the line between GATT Article XI border measures and GATT Article III internal measures, see below Section V.B.

countries is to make them subject to additional or punitive import tariffs. This not only risks a violation of the most-favoured-nation (MFN) principle discussed in Section V.E (in that imports from some countries, say, China would be discriminated as against imports from other countries who do have emission cuts in place, say, Europe). It also risks a violation of maximum tariff levels WTO Members committed to. Under Article II of the GATT, each WTO Member bound itself to a certain maximum ceiling of tariffs, on a product by product basis, in exchange for similar tariff reductions by its trading partners. Most of the tariffs that, for example, the United States currently applies are at, or very close to, that maximum ceiling. Especially developed country WTO Members have no or little leeway to add tariffs on imports for reasons related to climate change (developing countries, in contrast, often have a wider scope of manoeuvring in that their currently applied rates tend to be much lower than their maximum bound ceilings).[49] Unless such violation could be justified under the environmental exceptions in GATT Article XX (see *Section VI* below), any punitive 'carbon tariff' would violate WTO rules.

B.   Anti-dumping Duties Against 'Environmental Dumping'

Rather than outright punitive tariffs, a more subtle alternative could be to frame the additional customs duties on imports from countries that do not have carbon restrictions in place, as duties to offset dumping, more specifically, 'environmental dumping'. In his proposal for a carbon tax, French Prime Minister de Villepin explicitly referred to 'environmental dumping' as a justification for the tax.[50] On this view, since the price of imports from, for example, China, India or Brazil would not include the social cost of the carbon emitted during the production process of the imports – given that none of these countries impose binding carbon cuts – the imports are 'dumped' on the domestic market. According to this argument, an importing country that adopts binding carbon cuts should then have the right to impose anti-dumping duties, that is, extra tariffs to offset the dumping up to the margin of dumping that would include the amount of the social cost of the carbon. Doing so would correct the failure of, for example, the

---

[49]   Tariff commitments can be renegotiated pursuant to GATT Article XXVIII but this is subject to consent by other WTO Members or, in the absence thereof, a reciprocal withdrawal of tariff concessions by other WTO Members. Moreover, even with a higher tariff ceiling for, say, steel imports, the question of most-favoured-nation violation remains.

[50]   See note 25 above.

Indian government which did not force its producers to internalize the full cost of carbon-intensive products.

Although anti-dumping duties take the form of tariffs, they are explicitly permitted under WTO rules even if the resulting tariff exceeds a country's maximum ceiling discussed earlier.[51] However, this right to impose anti-dumping duties is strictly limited. The basic question is: When is an import considered to be 'dumped' on the domestic market? What is the benchmark or 'normal value' against which we must compare the price of the import? The answer is simple: The benchmark is *not* domestic prices which would fully incorporate the cost of carbon. Rather, the benchmark is 'normal prices' in China, Brazil or India, that is, the market of the exporting country. In other words, the WTO defines dumping as sales of, for example, exported Indian steel in the United States at a price below that asked for the same steel *in India*.[52] Hence, the United States can only impose anti-dumping duties on products from India when export prices are below *Indian* prices. In addition, the price comparison thus made looks at sales 'made at the same level of trade, normally at the ex-factory level'[53] and must make abstraction of 'differences' between local sales (in India) and export sales (in the United States) 'which affect price comparability, including differences in conditions and terms of sale, taxation ... and any other differences which are also demonstrated to affect price comparability'. As result, in our hypothetical (which assumes that the United States does, but India does not, impose a cost on carbon), a calculation of dumping would *not* include the cost of carbon, neither on the 'export price' side (price of the Indian steel as it reaches the United States *before* paying any carbon tax) nor on the 'normal value' side (price of Indian steel sold in India where no cost on carbon is imposed). Consequently, differences in the price of carbon in India as opposed to the United States would not add to a finding of 'dumping'. In sum, for dumping purposes, export prices are not compared to carbon-restricted domestic prices or to an ideal market price that internalizes the social cost of carbon. They are compared to normal prices in the country of export itself.

The WTO's Anti-Dumping (AD) Agreement does, however, foresee situations where home country (Indian) prices may be disregarded as a

---

[51]   See GATT Article II:2(b).

[52]   Pursuant to Article 2.1 of the AD Agreement, 'a product is to be considered as being dumped, i.e. introduced into the commerce of another country at less than its normal value, if the export price of the product exported from one country to another is less than the comparable price, in the ordinary course of trade, for the like product when destined for consumption in the exporting country'.

[53]   Article 2.4 of the WTO's Anti-Dumping (AD) Agreement.

basis for the determination of 'normal value'. This includes situations 'when, because of the *particular market situation* . . . such sales [on the Indian market] do not permit a proper comparison'.[54] A WTO Member could, therefore, consider that the non-application of binding carbon restrictions (in India) constitutes a 'particular market situation' (a market failure?) that does not permit a 'proper comparison'.[55] Yet, even assuming that the investigating authority could disregard Indian prices on this or other grounds referred to in AD Article 2.2, even in those cases 'normal value' must still be determined with reference to the regulatory context of the exporting country (India), that is, either with reference to the export price of *Indian steel* to an 'appropriate third country' (say, Brazil) or a so-called 'constructed' normal value based on 'the cost of production *in the country of origin* [India] plus a reasonable amount for administrative, selling and general costs and for profits'.[56] In other words, the export price from India to an 'appropriate third country' (Brazil) would also not internalize the social cost of carbon. It would also seem difficult to internalize such cost through the constructed normal value, since AD Article 2.2 refers to cost of production 'in the country of origin' (India) although AD Article 2.2.1.1 adds that 'costs shall normally be calculated on the basis of records kept by the exporter or producer under investigation, provided that such records . . . *reasonably reflect the costs associated with the production and sale of the product under consideration*'. One could argue that not factoring in the cost of carbon in a constructed normal value does not '*reasonably* reflect the costs associated with the production and sale of the product [steel] under consideration' and on that ground include within the constructed normal value the carbon cost associated with steel production in India even if such cost is not imposed by India itself. Doing so would increase 'normal value' as compared to 'export prices' and (assuming one does not also add the cost of carbon to export prices) make a finding of dumping more likely. It is, however, doubtful that a WTO panel would follow this interpretation as it would go beyond the regulatory context of the exporting country (by including a production cost not imposed in India).

   Another scenario where local prices may be disregarded in the determination of 'normal value' is defined by the Ad Note to GATT Article VI:1. This provision clarifies that 'special difficulties may exist' in determining

---

[54]   Article 2.2 of the AD Agreement.

[55]   The expression 'particular market situation' is neither defined by the AD Agreement, nor has WTO jurisprudence clarified its meaning.

[56]   AD Article 2.2. See Article 2.2.2 of the AD Agreement for the calculation of the amounts for 'administrative, selling and general cost and for profits'.

'normal value' in the case of imports from a country 'which has a complete or substantially complete monopoly of its trade and where all domestic prices are fixed by the State', often referred to as non-market economies. Section 15(a) of the Protocol on the Accession of China has similar language when it states that '[i]n determining price comparability under Article VI of the GATT 1994 and the Anti-Dumping Agreement, the importing WTO Member shall use either Chinese prices or costs for the industry under investigation or *a methodology that is not based on a strict comparison with domestic prices or costs in China. . .'.*[57] In this scenario, importing countries may disregard 'a strict comparison with' Chinese 'prices or costs' and could decide to determine 'normal value' based on an analogue, third country (say, Australia). Regardless of whether such normal value is then calculated based on the *price* in the ordinary course of trade in the analogue country or whether it is a constructed normal value based on *costs* in the analogue country, if such analogue country imposes carbon restrictions, particularly in the form of producer taxes (rather than product taxes),[58] one could consider that such costs would be incorporated in (and thereby increase) 'normal value'. Assuming that export prices (from, say, China to the United States) would not include this carbon cost, finding dumping in respect of imports from non-market economy producers would then be facilitated. In that case, however, the issue for the (US) investigating authority would be to justify the selection of an analogue country (such as Australia) which, unlike the investigated country, does incorporate the cost of carbon.

In sum, using anti-dumping as an instrument to level the carbon playing field is unlikely to pass WTO muster except perhaps in very limited circumstances such as those involving imports from non-market economies and acceptable analogue countries that do internalize the price of carbon.

---

[57]   Note that Section 15(d) of the Protocol on the Accession of China establishes conditions upon which Section 15, or part thereof, would be terminated.

[58]   If carbon restrictions are imposed in the form of a carbon tax on products, the carbon cost would not normally be reflected in the 'normal value' at the ex-factory level (or, in case of a constructed normal value, the carbon tax would not normally be part of the production cost in the analogue country). As such, the amount corresponding to a carbon tax applicable to products (and not producers) would then be adjusted (i.e. not be added to normal value) due to (tax) differences affecting price comparability as referred to in AD Article 24. Note that when it comes to 'border adjustment' under GATT Article III, the situation is the reverse: imposing the cost of carbon also on imports is easier when the domestic tax or regulation is imposed on products (as opposed to producers), see Section V.A and B below.

C.   Countervailing Duties to Offset the 'Subsidy' of not Imposing Carbon Restrictions

Another alternative that also takes the form of additional tariffs on imports would be to impose so-called countervailing duties to offset subsidization of the imports in their country of origin. Joseph Stiglitz's proposal for a carbon duty is premised on this idea of 'unfair subsidies'. In his words, and applied to the absence of energy taxes and emission cuts in the United States as opposed to Europe:

> subsidy means that a firm does not pay the full costs of production. Not paying the cost of damage to the environment is a subsidy, just as not paying the full costs of workers would be . . . other countries should prohibit the importation of American goods produced using energy intensive technologies, or, at the very least, impose a high tax on them, to offset the subsidy that those goods currently are receiving.[59]

As with anti-dumping, the WTO explicitly permits the imposition of extra tariffs to offset a foreign subsidy, even if the resulting tariff exceeds a country's maximum ceiling discussed earlier. However, this right to impose countervailing duties is strictly limited. The basic question is: When is an import considered to be 'subsidized'? In our example, what is the benchmark against which the absence of emission cuts or a carbon tax in, for example, China – or, in Stiglitz's case, the United States – must be compared?

For government policy to qualify as a subsidy under WTO rules there must be a 'financial contribution' by the government (say, interest free loans) or other 'income or price support' which, in either case, confers a 'benefit'.[60] In our example, the problem is not that the Chinese government is paying Chinese producers or is otherwise transferring funds. Rather, the problem is that the government *fails to act*, that is, it fails to impose and collect a carbon tax or to otherwise force Chinese producers to internalize the full cost of carbon emitted in China.

One type of financial contribution recognized by the WTO that might, at first sight, cover this failure to act, is: 'government revenue that is

---

[59]   Above note 24 above, 2.

[60]   Article 1.1 of the *Agreement on Subsidies and Countervailing Measures* ('SCM Agreement'). In this chapter, only the right to impose countervailing duties is examined. In response to subsidies which cause certain adverse effects, WTO Members can also file a direct complaint at the WTO against so-called actionable subsidies identified in Part III of the SCM Agreement.

otherwise due is foregone or not collected'.[61] However, the question under this provision is: What is the benchmark for what is 'otherwise due'? The WTO Appellate Body has interpreted this provision as requiring a comparison between the measure (or failure to act) in question, on the one hand, and a prevailing *domestic* standard, on the other hand. In other words, the benchmark of what is 'otherwise due' is the normal or standard policy within the country in question (say, China). It is not the policy of the European Union or some other internationally agreed intervention to cut emissions or to impose a carbon tax.[62] Hence, for as long as, for

---

[61]   Article 1.1(a)(ii) of the SCM Agreement.

[62]   Appellate Body Report on *US – FSC* (Appellate Body Report, *United States – Tax Treatment for 'Foreign Sales Corporations'*, WT/DS108/AB/R, adopted 20 March 2000, DSR 2000:III, 1619), para. 90 (underlining added):

> the basis of comparison must be the tax rules applied by the Member in question [e.g. China]. To accept the argument of the United States that the comparator in determining what is 'otherwise due' should be something other than *the prevailing domestic standard* of the Member in question would be to imply that WTO obligations somehow compel Members to choose a particular kind of tax system; this is not so. A Member, in principle, has the sovereign authority to tax any particular categories of revenue it wishes. *It is also free **not** to tax any particular categories of revenues* . . . What is 'otherwise due', therefore, depends on the rules of taxation that each Member, by its own choice, establishes for itself.

In a subsequent proceeding, the Appellate Body further explained that:

> . . . a 'financial contribution' does not arise simply because a government does not raise revenue which it could have raised. It is true that, from a *fiscal* perspective, where a government chooses not to tax certain income, no revenue is 'due' on that income. However, although a government might, in a sense, be said to 'forego' revenue in this situation, this alone gives no indication as to whether the revenue foregone was 'otherwise due'. In other words, the mere fact that revenues are not 'due' from a fiscal perspective does not determine that the revenues are or are not 'otherwise due' . . . .

> . . . the treaty phrase 'otherwise due' implies a comparison with a 'defined, normative benchmark'. The purpose of this comparison is to distinguish between situations where revenue foregone *is* 'otherwise due' and situations where such revenue is *not* 'otherwise due'. . . . Such a comparison enables panels and the Appellate Body to reach an objective conclusion, *on the basis of the rules of taxation established by a Member, by its own choice*, as to whether the contested measure involves the foregoing of revenue that would be due in some other situation or, in the words of the *SCM Agreement*, 'otherwise due'.

Appellate Body Report, *United States – Tax Treatment for 'Foreign Sales Corporations' – Recourse to Article 21.5 of the DSU by the European Communities*, WT/DS108/AB/RW, adopted 29 January 2002, DSR 2002:I, 55, paras 88–89 (emphasis added).

example, China does not have a general policy of restricting carbon emissions within China, for Chinese exports not to internalize the social cost of carbon cannot normally be called a subsidy.[63] An alternative in this respect is to argue that not imposing the cost of carbon, especially where other countries do so, is a 'form of income or price support'[64] to domestic (Chinese) producers which compete with foreign producers that must pay this cost. No WTO jurisprudence exists, however, that clarifies this rather broad residual category of WTO 'subsidies' in the shape of 'any form of income or price support' (other than a 'financial contribution' by the government). However, even if 'income or price support' would be found, for there to be a 'subsidy' such support must also confer a 'benefit' (SCM Article 1.1(b)). Yet, 'benefit' in the WTO has been interpreted to mean a situation that is better than the prevailing market situation, that is, in normal circumstances with reference to in-country prices[65] (e.g., in our example, prices within China). If China would not impose a carbon price in the first place, the 'income or price support' offered to Chinese producers by not taxing carbon would not put these producers in a better situation as compared to the normal market situation in China since, in that market, no one must pay the cost of carbon.

In any event, even if the failure to impose a carbon tax or to otherwise force producers to internalize the cost of carbon were to qualify as a 'subsidy', under WTO rules countervailing duties to offset subsidies by foreign governments can only be levied in case the subsidy is *specific* to 'an enterprise or industry or group of enterprises or industries'.[66] Not imposing a carbon tax or other emission cuts is a country-wide policy and not likely to meet the specificity requirement. In addition, carbon emissions and other environmental considerations could be seen as 'objective criteria or conditions' governing the eligibility for, and the amount of, a subsidy,

---

[63]   *But* see China's programme for export taxes on carbon-intensive exports, notes 12 above and 150 below. Arguably, an export tax rebate could be seen as a financial contribution within the meaning of Article 1.1(a)(1)(ii) of the SCM Agreement.

[64]   SCM Article 1.1(a)(2).

[65]   In some situations, however, the Appellate Body has accepted the use of external, out-of-country benchmarks ('an investigating authority may reject in-country private prices if it reaches the conclusion that these are too distorted due to the predominant participation of the government as a supplier in the market, thus rendering the comparison required under Article 14(d) of the *SCM Agreement* circular', Appellate Body Report, *United States – Definitive Anti-Dumping and Countervailing Duties on Certain Products from China*, WT/DS379/AB/R, adopted 25 March 2011, para. 446).

[66]   Article 1.2 and Article 2 of the SCM Agreement.

within the meaning of Article 2.1(b) of the SCM Agreement. In this case, specificity shall not exist, 'provided that the eligibility is automatic and that such criteria and conditions are strictly adhered to'.[67] If so, there is no right to impose countervailing duties.

Although export subsidies are deemed to be specific,[68] not imposing a carbon tax at all is not likely to be qualified as a subsidy contingent on export performance:[69] Even if goods are not exported (i.e. consumed within China), they would not pay a carbon tax. That said, *de facto* export contingency could be found 'when the subsidy [assuming that not internalizing the cost of carbon could be seen as a subsidy] is granted so as to provide an incentive to the recipient to export in a way that is not simply reflective of the conditions of supply and demand in the domestic and export markets undistorted by the granting of the subsidy'.[70] Hence, not imposing a carbon tax is most likely neither a specific subsidy nor an export subsidy.

In sum, even though in economic terms not internalizing the full cost of carbon could be seen as 'dumping' or a 'subsidy', in legal-WTO terms, the failure of a government to impose a carbon tax or to otherwise force producers to internalize the full price of carbon, does not normally give other WTO members the right to impose offsetting duties on imports.

V. IMPORT RESTRICTIONS IN RESPECT OF 'FOREIGN-EMITTED' CARBON THAT STAND A BETTER CHANCE TO SURVIVE WTO SCRUTINY

Rather than imposing a ban, quantitative restriction or extra tariff on *imports only*, a better way to frame a competitiveness provision would be to portray the trade measure on imports as simply the import-equivalent of *domestic* climate policy. For WTO purposes, any measure that applies only to imports is suspect, as it can be presumed to be protectionist (it

---

[67]   Article 2.1(b) of the SCM Agreement. Footnote 2 of the SCM Agreement determines that '[o]bjective criteria or conditions, as used herein, mean criteria or conditions which are neutral, which do not favour certain enterprises over others, and which are economic in natural and horizontal in application, such as number of employees or size of enterprise'.

[68]   Article 2.3 the SCM Agreement.

[69]   As required under Article 3.1 of the SCM Agreement for a subsidy to be a prohibited export subsidy.

[70]   Appellate Body Report, *European Communities and Certain Member States – Measures Affecting Trade in Large Civil Aircraft*, WT/DS316/AB/R, adopted 1 June 2011, para. 1045.

applies only to foreign goods; not to domestic products). That explains the outright prohibitions in GATT Article II (as discussed above, tariffs above a particular ceiling are prohibited) and GATT Article XI (quantitative restrictions on imports are generally prohibited). In contrast, a measure that applies to both imports *and* domestic products is fully accepted as long as it does not discriminate against imports (the obligation of 'national treatment' discussed in Section D) or against imports from particular countries (the obligation of 'most-favoured-nation treatment' discussed in Section E).

The main challenge is, however, to convince the WTO that a competitiveness provision is only the extension of domestic climate policy, applied on an equal footing to imports. Section A addresses this challenge assuming that climate policy takes the form of a carbon tax or other price-based measure. Section B extends the analysis to carbon regulations (such as carbon intensity standards or labels). A particularly thorny question in this respect is whether a cap-and-trade scheme is best qualified as a charge or regulation (addressed in Section C).

A.   'Border Tax Adjustment' for Imports based on a Domestic Carbon 'Tax'

If a competitiveness provision were to take the form of a price-based measure such as a duty, charge or tax on carbon-intensive imports, equivalent to the tax or duty imposed on domestic products, the first question that would arise is whether this duty on imports is either (i) a *border* duty 'on importation' (prohibited under GATT Article II if it goes beyond scheduled tariff bindings) or (ii) an *internal* tax or charge (permitted under GATT Article III:2 for as long as it is not discriminatory). This distinction was recently clarified by the WTO Appellate Body in *China – Auto Parts*. Duties on imports are *border* duties (subject to GATT Article II) when they 'accrue . . . *by virtue of the event of importation*'.[71] Duties on imports are *internal* taxes or charges (subject to GATT Article III:2) when 'the obligation to pay them is triggered by an "internal" factor, something that takes place *within* the customs territory'.[72] In that case, the Appellate Body found that Chinese duties on auto parts were 'internal' charges (not customs duties) as they accrued and were triggered or set by an internal

---

[71]   Appellate Body Report, *China – Measures Affecting Imports of Automobile Parts*, WT/DS339,340,342/AB/R, adopted 12 January 2009, para. 158 (emphasis added).
[72]   Ibid., para. 161.

factor (not by virtue of the event of importation), namely their internal assembly within China (if this assembly included a sufficient number of local, Chinese car parts, the duty was lower). In the present case, the question would be whether the carbon tax or charge on, for example, imported steel accrues or is triggered by an internal factor, such as internal sale or offering for sale of the steel (in which case it would be an internal tax or charge) or whether it accrues by virtue of the event of importation (in which case it would be a border duty). To attract the more permissive GATT Article III, carbon taxes or charges on imports should, therefore, be designed in such a way that they are triggered not by importation as such, but by the sale, offering for sale, distribution or use of imported products once these products have cleared customs. Importantly, this internal trigger does not prevent a WTO member from actually *collecting* or *enforcing* the duty at the time or moment of importation (as long as the substantive trigger for the duty remains internal). With reference to the Ad Note to GATT Article III, the Appellate Body in *China – Auto Parts* confirmed that 'the moment at which a charge is *collected* or *paid* is not determinative of whether it is an ordinary customs duty or an internal charge'.[73]

Importantly, even if the carbon tax or duty on imported steel were seen as a *border* duty, that is, triggered 'by virtue of the event of importation' (rather than an *internal* duty triggered by an internal factor or activity) it could still be carved out or permitted pursuant to GATT Article II:2(a). This provision explicitly allows WTO Members to impose

> on the importation of any product . . . *a charge equivalent to an internal tax . . . in respect of the like domestic product* or in respect of an article from which the imported product has been manufactured or produced in whole or in part.

Such border charge (on e.g. steel imports) equivalent to an internal (carbon) tax on domestic steel ('like domestic product') must then, however, not discriminate against imports (in line with GATT Article III:2, discussed below in Section D).

The right to thus impose a domestic tax also on imports – be it in the form of an *internal* tax extended to imports or a *border* duty on imports referred to in GATT Article II:2(a) – is also referred to as 'border tax adjustment'. This raises the second core question: do WTO rules permit 'border tax adjustment' for something like carbon taxes? Under 'border tax adjustment', the flip-side of the right to impose a domestic tax also on imports is the right to rebate the same tax on domestic products that get exported (thereby levelling the playing field not only on the domestic

---

[73] Ibid., para. 158.

market but also on the world market, assuming no carbon cost is imposed there). Under WTO rules, such rebates are not considered to be prohibited export subsidies.[74]

Indeed, not every internal tax can be 'adjusted' and also be imposed on imports: The tax must, as pointed out earlier, be one 'in respect of . . . *product[s]*' or '*article[s]*' used to manufacture or produce *products* (GATT Article II:2(a)). As GATT Article III:2 puts it, it must be an 'internal tax or other internal charge of any kind . . . applied, directly or indirectly, to . . .*products*'.[75] Put differently, generally speaking, US *product* taxes can be adjusted and applied to imports, not US *producer* taxes.[76] Adjustable product taxes are also referred to as 'indirect taxes' such as sales, value-added and excise taxes. We find it quite normal, for example, that when Chinese TVs or French cigarettes are sold in the United States they pay the same sales or excise tax as US-made TVs or cigarettes. Such product or indirect taxes can be applied also to imports. In contrast, producer taxes or 'direct taxes' such as payroll or income taxes, social security charges or taxes on profits or interests cannot be adjusted or imposed on imported products. We find it quite normal, for example, that imports from Monaco or Lichtenstein are not subject to an import tax to make up for the fact that Monaco and Lichtenstein impose much lower income taxes than the United States does. Such producer or direct taxes cannot be applied to imports.

The reason behind this distinction between, on the one hand, adjustable product or indirect taxes and, on the other hand, non-adjustable producer or direct taxes is the so-called 'destination principle' according to which products themselves should only be taxed in the country of consumption (in other words: exports get a rebate; imports get taxed). On this view, if prod-

---

[74]   GATT Article VI:4 and *Ad Note* to GATT Article XVI. See also footnote 1 and paragraphs (g) and (h) of Annex I to the SCM Agreement. The *Working Party on Border Tax Adjustments* (below note 76, at para. 10) found that rules on rebates for exports and taxes on imports are equivalent: 'it was agreed that GATT provisions on tax adjustment applied the principle of destination identically to imports and exports'.

[75]   GATT Article III:2. On the export side, rebates are permitted for 'duties or taxes *borne by . . . product[s]*' (see GATT Article VI:4, *Ad Note* to GATT Article XVI and footnote 1 to the SCM Agreement). Paragraphs (g) and (h) of Annex I to the SCM Agreement refer more broadly to permissible rebates for indirect taxes 'in respect of the *production* and *distribution* of exported products'.

[76]   *Report of the Working Party on Border Tax Adjustments*, L/3464, 20 November 1970, at para. 14 ('The Working Party concluded that there was convergence of views to the effect that taxes directly levied on products were eligible for tax adjustment . . . Furthermore, the Working Party concluded that there was convergence of views to the effect that certain taxes that were not directly levied on products were not eligible for tax adjustment').

ucts are only taxed in their place of consumption, countries preserve the right to choose their own level of taxation *and* trade neutrality is maintained as all products in a given market compete on the same competitive terms (without either double taxation or advantages from a more favourable tax regime in their country of origin).[77] The distinction also finds some support in the economic theory that generally *product* taxes (say, a 10 per cent VAT or sales tax on an iPhone) are shifted forward into consumer prices (the tax simply gets added to my invoice for the iPhone), whereas *producer* taxes (say, a 30 per cent income tax on Apple) are generally not passed on into the price of a product. Thus, on this view, producer taxes, as they do not influence product prices, do not affect the competitiveness of products and there is, therefore, no need to make adjustments for imports so as to level the economic playing field. However, it is acknowledged today that even producer taxes are to a certain degree reflected in the price of a product (high taxes on Apple may, in the end, increase the price of an iPhone; this will depend, amongst other things, on the elasticity of supply and demand of the particular product and the competition in the market place).[78]

So, assuming (for now) that the climate policy for domestic businesses takes the form of a carbon tax, would such domestic carbon tax be regarded as an adjustable product tax that can be imposed also on imports for carbon produced abroad? Or would the WTO classify it as a producer (or direct) tax which cannot be adjusted at the border for imports? In case the carbon tax is imposed *on products* at the time of, for example, distribution or sale within the regulating country (much like a VAT or sales tax), the answer is straightforward. In that scenario, there can be no doubt that the tax is 'applied, directly . . . to . . . products' (say, when buying one tonne of cement, a carbon tax of 20 Euros is added). As a result, the tax *can* be adjusted on imports (subject to national treatment discussed in Section D below).

---

[77] Paul Demaret and Raoul Stewardson, 'Border Tax Adjustments under GATT and EC Law and General Implications for Environmental Taxes', 29 *Journal of World Trade* 1994, 5, at 6.

[78] See Christian Pitschas, 'GATT/WTO Rules for Border Tax Adjustment and the Proposed European Directive Introducing a Tax on Carbon Dioxide Emissions and Energy', 24 *Ga. J. Int'l &Comp. L.* 1994–1995, 479 at 485. Be that as it may, calculating how much of a producer or direct tax shifts forward into consumer prices is extremely difficult and any corresponding border adjustment is open to abuse. As one study concluded, '[w]hile a blanket prohibition [on adjustment for producer or direct taxes] may not reflect economic reality . . . it reduces the possibility of serious trade disputes arising due to arbitrary impositions . . . [hence] for practical reasons, there is no real prospect of the distinction being abandoned' (Demaret and Stewardson, above note 77 at 16).

Where the carbon tax or charge is imposed not directly on the product as such but on its producer, based, for example, on the carbon emissions measured at a production installation (for practical purposes it is easier to check carbon emissions at the production site), the situation is more complicated.[79] On the one hand, following the definitions of 'direct' versus 'indirect' taxes in the SCM Agreement, a carbon tax (even one imposed on *producers*) would seem to be classified as an 'indirect tax' and thus, in principle, be adjustable.[80] On the other hand, it remains unclear whether a tax on inputs (such as energy) which are *not* physically incorporated into the final product (such as a tax on carbon emitted in, say, China but not, of course, physically present in the steel imported into the United States) can be adjusted at the border. These so-called 'hidden taxes' (or *taxes occultes*) target not the physical features of the imported product itself, but rather the process or production method of the product abroad, that is, the fact that when producing, say, steel in China, carbon was emitted *in China*.

The 1970 *GATT Working Party Report on Border Tax Adjustments* left the question, of whether hidden or process taxes can be adjusted at the border, unanswered.[81] A 1987 GATT panel report in the *US – Superfund* dispute, however, did permit the United States to impose a domestic tax

---

[79]   Given the discussion below it is, however, surprising how on the WTO website the following categorical statement could, until recently, be found: 'Under existing GATT rules and jurisprudence, "product" taxes and charges can be adjusted at the border, but "process" taxes and charges by and large cannot. For example, a domestic tax on fuel can be applied perfectly legitimately to imported fuel, but a tax on the energy consumed in producing a ton of steel cannot be applied to imported steel' (available until December 2006 at http://www.wto.org/english/tratop_e/envir_backgrnd_e/c3s3_e.htm).

[80]   Footnote 58 of the SCM Agreement states: 'The term "*direct taxes*" shall mean taxes on wages, profits, interests, rents, royalties, and all other forms of income, and taxes on the ownership of real property'. In contrast, '[t]he term "*indirect taxes*" shall mean sales, excise, turnover, value added, franchise, stamp, transfer, inventory and equipment taxes, border taxes and *all taxes other than direct taxes* and import charges'. A carbon tax imposed on products is arguably a specific excise tax and thus explicitly covered as an adjustable indirect tax. A carbon tax imposed on producers does not fall under any of the types listed under 'direct taxes'; hence, even a carbon tax on producers would seem to be an 'indirect tax' as it is 'other than direct taxes'. The question remains, however, to what extent these definitions in the SCM Agreement on border adjustment for exports can be used also for purposes of interpreting GATT provisions on border adjustment for imports. In support of import-export equivalence see above note 74.

[81]   Above note 76 at para. 15: 'It was generally felt that while this area of taxation was unclear, its importance – as indicated by the scarcity of complaints reported in connection with adjustment of *taxes occultes* – was not such as to justify further examination.'

on certain chemicals and also on imports that had used the same chemicals 'as materials in the manufacture or production' of these imports.[82] Importantly, the panel did not specify whether these chemicals still had to be physically present in the imported product. Even more to the point, the United States introduced a tax on ozone depleting chemicals and applied this tax also to imports of such chemicals or products containing or produced with such chemicals. No GATT or WTO decision was ever rendered on this tax, but like border adjustment for a carbon tax, this tax on ozone depleting chemicals is process-related, not related to the physical characteristics of the final imported product.[83]

The relevant question is, ultimately, how broadly the WTO Appellate Body would interpret the words 'internal taxes . . . applied . . . *indirectly, to . . . products*' in GATT Article III:2[84] and corresponding provisions in the SCM Agreement.[85] The very idea of a carbon tax (even where it

---

[82]   Panel Report on *United States – Taxes on Petroleum and Certain Imported Substances*, GATT, BISD 34S/136 (17 June 1987), at para. 2.5 and para. 5.2.4.

[83]   See Frank Biermann and Rainer Brohm, 'Implementing the Kyoto Protocol without the USA: The Strategic Role of Energy Tax Adjustments at the Border', 4 *Climate Policy* 2005 289, at 294. It is also interesting to recall that when the US House of Representatives passed an energy tax on all fuels based on the heat content (or Btu, British Thermal Unit) of the particular fuel, it included a provision for a border tax adjustment, which was then criticized by the EC as a GATT violation. See Steve Charnovitz, 'Trade and Climate: Potential Conflicts and Synergies', in *Beyond Kyoto: Advancing the International Effort Against Climate Change*, 141 at 147, http://www.c2es.org/docUploads/Trade%20and%20Climate.pdf.

[84]   The corresponding provision in GATT Article II:2(a) refers to internal taxes 'in respect of an *article* from which the imported product has been *manufactured or produced*'. Such 'article' could be interpreted as including the energy (and resulting carbon) used to produce the product. However, the equally authentic French text refers to '*une merchandise qui a été incorporée dans l'article importé*' which some have interpreted as requiring that the input must be physically incorporated into the imported product. The (equally authentic) Spanish version, however, refers again more broadly to '*una mercancía que haya servido, en todo o en parte, para fabricar el producto importado*' without any reference to (physical) incorporation.

[85]   The corresponding provision for border rebates upon exportation is even broader. Paragraph (g) of Annex I to the SCM Agreement permits border tax adjustment for exports more broadly for indirect taxes 'in respect of the *production* and *distribution* of exported products'. This could arguably cover process or production-related taxes such as a carbon tax on producers. Paragraph (h) of Annex I, in turn, explicitly permits border tax adjustment upon exportation for a certain type of indirect taxes (namely, prior-stage cumulative indirect taxes) even when such taxes are 'levied on inputs that are consumed in the production of the exported product' including not only 'inputs physically incorporated' but also '*energy, fuels and oil used in the production process*' (Footnote 61). Yet, specific environmental taxes such as a carbon tax are not normally 'cumulative' indirect

is imposed on *producers*) is to internalize the social cost of carbon in the ultimate price of products so as to give an incentive to both producers and consumers to limit the use of carbon-intensive products and to shift to greener energy. From that perspective, a carbon tax is a tax applied at least 'indirectly' to products. As the very reason for the tax is to make carbon-intensive products more expensive, the tax does (or should) shift forward to consumers (depending, again, on factors such as market competition and elasticity of supply and demand) and therefore could be said to be adjustable at the border. The tax will, in other words, change the terms of competition, and to ensure trade neutrality the tax of the country of consumption should apply; hence, border tax adjustment could, in principle, be permitted. Put differently, under a carbon tax, the 'nexus' between the tax and the products concerned (say, steel or cement) appears to be tight enough so as to allow adjustment (this 'nexus' is, in any event, tighter than under many other process taxes such as social security and wage taxes).[86] Therefore, even if technically the carbon tax or charge were levied on producers based on emissions at the production site, rather than directly on products at the point of sale, such tax or charge could still be regarded as 'applied . . . indirectly . . . to . . . products'.

B. 'Border Adjustment' for Imports based on a Domestic Carbon 'Regulation'

In the previous section we have assumed that both the domestic climate policy and the competitiveness provision on imports would take the form

---

taxes and would thus normally not be covered by paragraph (h); as a result, they would fall under the more general provision of paragraph (g). See J. Andrew Hoerner and Frank Muller, *Carbon Taxes for Climate Protection in a Competitive World*, A Paper Prepared for the Swiss Federal Office for Foreign Economic Affairs, June 1996, at 33–34.

[86] A WTO panel report (Panel Report, *Mexico – Tax Measures on Soft Drinks and Other Beverages*, WT/DS308/R, adopted 24 March 2006, as modified by Appellate Body Report WT/DS308/AB/R, DSR 2006:I, 43, paras 8.42–8.45) elaborates on the required 'nexus' between the tax and the products it affects. The panel found that GATT Article III:2 'requires some connection, even if indirect, between the respective taxes or other internal charges, on the one hand, and the taxed product, on the other'. It found that a tax on soft drinks containing sweeteners other than cane sugar is a tax applied 'indirectly' to beet sugar, among other reasons, because 'the burden of the tax can be expected to fall, at least in part, on the products containing the sweetener, and thereby to fall on the sweetener'. Even a distribution tax on soft drinks containing certain sweeteners was found to be a tax applied 'indirectly' to beet sugar, although the panel admitted that, in that instance, 'the degree of connection between the tax and the relevant products is more remote'.

of a price-based measure such as a tax or other charge. If so, WTO rules on border tax adjustment permit imposition also on imports as long as (i) the tax or duty on imports can be construed as an *internal* measure (or border measure *equivalent* to an internal tax) and (ii) the tax or duty on domestic production is sufficiently related or applied to *products*. What now if a country's climate policy would take the form of a trade restrictive *regulation*? One could imagine, for example, that the United States imposes maximum carbon intensity standards (tons of carbon equivalent emitted per ton of product produced) for energy-intensive products sold on the US market regardless of origin. A less trade restrictive type of carbon regulation would, for example, be to label all energy-intensive products as 'harmful to our climate'.[87]

In this case, the line between generally prohibited quantitative restrictions (GATT Article XI) and generally permitted domestic regulation (GATT Article III:4) is set out in an *Ad Note* to GATT Article III. This provision explains that

> any law, regulation or requirement . . . which applies to an imported product *and* to the like domestic product and is collected or enforced in the case of the imported product at the time or point of importation, is nevertheless to be regarded as . . . a law, regulation or requirement . . . subject to the provisions of Article III.

In other words, even if US climate legislation were to restrict imports at the border, if it is applied also domestically in respect of US products, it should, in principle, fall under the more flexible GATT Article III (permitting regulations for as long as they are not discriminatory) rather than the more stringent GATT Article XI (generally prohibiting quantitative import restrictions).[88]

Yet, as is the case for taxes and permissible border tax adjustment, not all domestic regulations can be applied to imports at the border. The *Ad Note* limits border adjustable regulations to 'any law, regulation or requirement of the kind referred to in paragraph 1 [of Article III]'. GATT

---

[87]   On carbon labelling, see Paul Breton, Gareth Edwards-Jones, Michael Friis Jensen, 'Carbon Labelling and Low-income Country Exports: a Review of the Development Issues', 27 *Development Policy Review* 3 2009, 243–267; and James MacGregor, *Carbon Concerns: how standards and labelling initiatives must not limit agricultural trade from developing countries*, Issue Brief No. 3, ICTSD-IPC Platform on Climate Change, Agriculture and Trade, 2010.

[88]   Discussed earlier when referring to a complete ban or other quantitative restriction on imports from countries without emissions cuts in place, above note 48.

Article III:1, in turn, is limited to 'laws, regulations and requirements *affecting* the *internal* sale, offering for sale, purchase, transportation, distribution or use of *products*'.

As was the case for possible border tax adjustment in respect of carbon taxes, the first question is whether the carbon regulation 'affects' – i.e., targets, regulates or addresses – an *internal* activity or act such as sale or use of products once these products have been imported within the regulating country (rather than the act or event of importation as such).[89] Where the carbon regulation is a labelling requirement or carbon intensity standard affecting or addressing the internal *sale* of energy-intensive products once these products have cleared customs, there can be little doubt that the measure is an *internal* regulation (subject to GATT Article III:4) rather than a border measure (subject to GATT Article XI). Pursuant to the *Ad Note* to GATT Article III, the fact that this internal regulation would, as it applies to imports, be 'enforced at the time or point of importation' would not detract from this characterization.

Assuming the measure is, indeed, an *internal* one, the second question is whether a carbon regulation which, after all, targets the process or production method of, say, imported steel – not the physical characteristics of the steel itself – can be classified as a regulation 'affecting . . . *products*'. Put differently, is border adjustment for regulations limited to 'product' measures or does it extend also to 'process' measures? Two unadopted GATT panel reports found that 'process' measures fall outside the scope of GATT Article III and must, instead, be presumed to be prohibited under GATT Article XI. These reports were issued – though never formally adopted by GATT parties – in the famous *Tuna – Dolphin* dispute where a US ban on certain tuna captured in a way that risks killing dolphin was found to violate GATT Article XI and not justified under the environmental exceptions in GATT Article XX (discussed below in Section VI).

The first *Tuna – Dolphin* panel explained the exclusion of 'process' measures – such as carbon regulations – from the scope of permissible border adjustment under GATT Article III as follows:

> under the national treatment principle of Article III, contracting parties may apply border *tax* adjustments with regard to those taxes that are *borne by products*, but not for domestic taxes not directly levied on products (such as corporate income taxes). Consequently, the Note Ad Article III covers only internal taxes that are borne by products. The Panel considered that it would be inconsistent to limit the application of this Note to taxes that are borne

---

[89]   See the discussion above, text at footnote 71 ff. referring, *inter alia*, to the Appellate Body Report on *China – Auto Parts*.

by products while permitting its application to regulations not *applied to the product as such*.[90]

Put differently, according to this panel, as is the case for taxes, regulations as well can only be adjusted at the border if they 'apply to the product as such'; not if they regulate the producer. As the US domestic restriction on tuna harvesting 'did not regulate tuna products as such ... Nor did it prescribe fishing techniques that could have an effect on tuna as a product',[91] the GATT panel found that the regulation could *not* be adjusted at the border for imported tuna. Hence, the US tuna ban was not covered by GATT Article III, but instead fell under (and automatically violated) GATT Article XI.

Although the *Tuna – Dolphin* panels would almost certainly have decided against border adjustment for carbon regulations, the fact remains that these panels were never adopted and that WTO thinking on the issue of border adjustment has evolved, as discussed in Section A above. Indeed, if the argument is that there must be broad equivalence between border adjustment for taxes and border adjustment for regulations (as the first *Tuna – Dolphin* panel itself found), then many of the arguments discussed in Section A above in support of permitting border adjustment for carbon *taxes* also support border adjustment for carbon *regulations*. Ultimately, the question is, once more, how broadly the WTO Appellate Body would interpret the words 'regulations ... *affecting* ... *products*' in GATT Article III:1 and 4. As with border tax adjustment, some line must be drawn between purely producer regulations that cannot be adjusted at the border, and product-related regulations that can be adjusted at the border. However, this does not necessarily mean that all process regulations are by definition not adjustable. If they sufficiently 'affect' the 'product' they could be found to be subject to GATT Article III. From that perspective, the 'nexus' between a carbon label or intensity standard and the products affected by it (say, carbon-intensive steel or cement) could be found to be tight enough so as to permit a finding that the carbon regulation is one 'affecting ... products' in the sense of GATT Article III:4 and, therefore, adjustable at the border.[92] A recent WTO panel addressing US 'dolphin-safe' labelling requirements for the sale of tuna (with reference to where and how this tuna was caught) did confirm that such process-

---

[90] GATT Panel Report on *United States – Restrictions on Imports of Tuna*, DS21/R, 3 September 1991, BISD 39S/155, at para. 5.13.

[91] *Ibid.*, para. 5.10.

[92] For a panel report interpreting this 'nexus' relatively broadly, see *Mexico – Soft Drinks*, discussed above note 86.

based labelling requirements are 'labelling requirements as they apply to a product', *in casu*, tuna. That was sufficient for the label to be a technical regulation of tuna.[93] The same reasoning could apply to a carbon label or carbon intensity standard. Since such labels or standards apply to products (e.g. carbon-intensive steel or cement) they are 'requirements affecting [a product's] . . . internal sale' and can therefore be imposed on both domestic and imported products pursuant to GATT Article III:4. From this perspective, the reason or purpose of the regulation does not matter (i.e. whether it regulates something physically in the product or how the product was produced). What matters is whether the regulation applies to or 'affects' the internal sale of a 'product' (here, steel or cement sold in the regulating market; in *Tuna Label*, tuna and how tuna can be labelled for sale within the United States).[94]

Note, finally, that carbon regulations (as opposed to carbon taxes) could also fall under the WTO *Agreement on Technical Barriers to Trade* (TBT). This agreement applies to both technical regulations 'which lay down product characteristics', that is, features of the product itself, 'and their related *processes and production methods*'.[95] Although this might be read as including only process regulations that leave a trace in the end product itself (as the process and production method must be '*related to*' the product characteristics), the carbon footprint of a product could still

---

[93]   Panel Report, *United States – Measures Concerning the Importation, Marketing and Sale of Tuna and Tuna Products*, WT/DS381/R, circulated 15 September 2011 (on appeal at the time of writing), para. 7.78.

[94]   Note, however, that for process regulations – as opposed to process taxes – we do not have the above explained flexibilities set out in the SCM Agreement (discussed in note 85 above). Indeed, the SCM Agreement only refers to (and explicitly permits) adjustment upon exportation (i.e. rebates) for *taxes* or *duties*, not for *regulations* (although it remains unclear whether non-application of regulation to exports could be seen as a 'financial contribution' or 'subsidy' in the first place). Therefore, the broad definition of 'indirect' taxes; the reference to taxes 'in respect of the production' of exported products; and the inclusion of certain energy taxes, do not broaden the adjustability of process *regulations*. Moreover, the mere fact that a regulation increases the price of a product cannot, in and of itself, be sufficient for the regulation to be adjustable at the border (if not, a higher minimum wage in the United States as opposed to China, which arguably increases some US product prices, might also become adjustable). To avoid such slippery slope a closer 'nexus' between the regulation and the product affected by it must be demonstrated. In the end, it may, therefore, be easier to adjust taxes at the border as compared to regulations, something that would not be illogical given the preference that trade law (and economics) holds for tariffs or price-based measures over regulations on the ground that the former are generally more transparent and efficient than the latter.

[95]   *Agreement on Technical Barriers to Trade*, Annex I, paragraph 1.

be found to be a 'product characteristic' or 'related' process or production method. Nothing in the text of the definition of 'technical regulation' requires that product characteristics or their related process or production methods must be intrinsic or physically incorporated in the end product.[96] In any event, regulations that address 'terminology, symbols, packaging, marking or labelling requirements' would be covered by the *Agreement on Technical Barriers to Trade*, as such requirements are covered as soon as they apply to '*a product, process or production method*' without the 'related to' *caveat*.[97] In other words, a carbon label for energy-intensive products including imports would seem to fall under the *Agreement on Technical Barriers to Trade*.[98] It is more doubtful, however, whether, for example, a maximum carbon intensity standard would be so covered, as such standard is not limited to 'marking or labelling' but actually prohibits certain high-carbon products to be marketed in the first place. That said, the carbon intensity on which this prohibition would then be based (say, a ban on steel with a carbon footprint above a certain level) could still be said to relate to the 'product characteristics' of the steel (and/or its related process or production method) and, therefore, be classified as a technical regulation subject to the TBT Agreement.

Once covered by the *TBT Agreement* a carbon label or regulation on imports must be non-discriminatory (see Sections D and E) and 'not more trade-restrictive than necessary to fulfil a legitimate objective ... *inter alia:* protection of the environment'.[99] The latter requirement will involve an analysis similar to that under GATT Article XX discussed in Section VI. Where 'relevant international standards exist' WTO Members must 'use them ... as a basis for their technical regulations' (TBT Article 2.4). In case a country's technical regulation, adopted to protect the environment, 'is in accordance with relevant international standards' it shall be

---

[96]   In *EC – Measures Affecting Asbestos and Asbestos-Containing Products* (Appellate Body Report, *European Communities – Measures Affecting Asbestos and Asbestos-Containing Products*, WT/DS135/AB/R, adopted 5 April 2001, DSR 2001:VII, 3243, para. 67), the Appellate Body clarified that 'the "characteristics" of a product include, in our view, any *objectively definable* "features", "qualities", "attributes", or other "distinguishing mark" of a product. Such "characteristics" might relate, *inter alia*, to a product's composition, size, shape, colour, texture, hardness, tensile strength, flammability, conductivity, density, or viscosity.' However, it went on to state that 'product characteristics include, *not only features and qualities intrinsic to the product itself*, but also related "characteristics", such as the means of identification, the presentation and the appearance of a product'.

[97]   *Ibid.*

[98]   In support, see the Panel Report on *US – Tuna Label*, above note 93.

[99]   *Agreement on Technical Barriers to Trade*, Article 2.2.

'rebuttably presumed not to create an unnecessary obstacle to international trade'. That said, where a relevant international standard is 'ineffective or inappropriate' to fulfil a country's environmental objectives, TBT Article 2.4 allows WTO Members to deviate from the standard. It remains unclear which climate change standards could be regarded as 'international standards' for TBT purposes. One recent WTO panel defined an 'international standard' as a 'standard that is adopted by an international standardizing/standards organization and made available to the public'.[100]

C.   'Border Adjustment' for Imports based on a Domestic 'Cap-and-Trade' System

In many countries, climate change policy takes the form not of an outright carbon tax or a clear carbon regulation, but rather of a cap-and-trade regime. Political and other reasons may prevent policy makers from calling climate legislation a form of 'tax'. Raising taxes is, for example, not particularly palatable for many US politicians. In a cap-and-trade regime, producers must normally hold emission credits or allowances up to the level of carbon they emit at their production installations. In the context of the debate above on permissible 'border adjustment', the question is whether such obligation to hold emission allowances can be qualified as an 'internal *tax* or other internal *charge* of any kind' (in the sense of GATT Article III:2, discussed in Section A above) or is rather part of 'laws, *regulations* and requirements affecting [a product's] . . . internal sale . . .' (in the sense of GATT Article III:4, discussed in Section B above).

The general definition of a tax is a compulsory contribution imposed by the government for which taxpayers receive nothing identifiable in return.[101] The need to hold a permit for emitting CO_2 almost exclusively serves the interests of the wider community; companies subject to the obligation do not receive anything specific or identifiable in return (as compared to, for example, a highway fee, where in return for the fee a

---

[100]   Panel Report on *US – Tuna Label*, above note 93, para. 7.663. The Panel added that it must constitute a 'document, established by consensus and approved by a recognized body, that provides, for common and repeated use, rules, guidelines or characteristics for activities or their results, aimed at the achievement of the optimum degree of order in a given context' (paras. 7.666–7.672, 6.36–6.38) and be 'open on a non-discriminatory basis to the relevant bodies of at least all WTO Members in accordance with the principle of openness as described in the TBT Committee Decision' (paras. 7.687–7.691).

[101]   Ismer and Neuhoff, note 10 above, 11, referring to an OECD definition.

driver gets to use the highway). From this perspective, the cost of having to present an emission credit could qualify as a 'tax'.[102] In contrast, the obligation to hold an emission allowance could also be qualified as a 'regulation'. In a recent case before the European Court of Justice, for example, Advocate General Kokott rejected the notion that the obligation to buy emission allowances is a tax or charge and construed it rather as a special type of regulation.[103] The ECJ implicitly confirmed this view when holding that the requirement imposed on aircraft operators to buy emission allowances is not a tax or charge on fuel load (prohibited by Article 11 of the Open Skies Agreement): 'in contrast to the defining feature of obligatory levies on the possession and consumption of fuel, there is no direct and inseverable link between the quantity of fuel held or consumed by an aircraft and the pecuniary burden on the aircraft's operator ... actual cost ... depends, inasmuch as a market-based measure is involved ... on the number of allowances initially allocated to the operator and their market price when the purchase of additional allowances proves necessary ... Nor can it be ruled out that an aircraft operator, despite having held or consumed fuel, will bear no pecuniary burden ... or will even make a profit by assigning its surplus allowances for consideration'.[104]

As a regulation, the question could then arise whether not only GATT but also the TBT Agreement applies to an allowance requirement. The criteria discussed in Section B above apply. Be that as it may, as argued above, in both cases, 'border adjustment' would be permitted in case (i) the carbon measure imposed on imports can be classified as an *internal* measure, that is, a *tax or charge* triggered by an 'internal factor' (e.g. sale

---

[102] In support: Ismer and Neuhoff, note 10 above, 10 and de Cendra, note 11 above, 135–136.

[103] Advocate General's Opinion, 6 October 2011, The Air Transport Association of America and Others, Case C-366/10, available at http://eur-lex.europa.eu/LexUriServ/LexUriServ.do?uri=CELEX:62010CC0366:EN:NOT: '216. It would be unusual, to put it mildly, to describe as a charge or tax the purchase price paid for an emission allowance, which is based on supply and demand according to free market forces, notwithstanding the fact that the Member States do have a certain discretion regarding the use to be made of revenues generated . . . .'

[104] *Air Transport Association of America et al. v. Secretary of State for Energy and Climate Change*, Case C-366/10, 21 December 2011, para. 142, adding in para. 143: 'It follows that, unlike a duty, tax, fee or charge on fuel consumption, the scheme . . . apart from the fact that it is not intended to generate revenue for the public authorities, does not in any way enable the establishment, applying a basis of assessment and a rate defined in advance, of an amount that must be payable per tonne of fuel consumed for all the flights carried out in a calendar year.'

or consumption within the regulating country) or 'equivalent' to an internal tax (pursuant to GATT Article II:2(a)), or a *regulation* addressing or affecting an 'internal act' such as internal sale or use (even if, for imports, the tax or regulation is 'collected or enforced . . . at the time or point of importation' and (ii) the carbon measure on domestic production sufficiently applies to or affects *products* (although the obligation to present carbon allowances is normally imposed on *producers*, such obligation may still sufficiently apply to or affect the price or sale of *products*, thereby allowing adjustment at the border). As applied to imports, such border adjustment of a domestic cap-and-trade regime could then take the form of an obligation, imposed on importers, to submit, upon sale in the regulating market, a number of emission allowances that corresponds to the amount of carbon emitted abroad in the production of the import (to simplify matters, one could also use sector averages or default values based on particular production methods). That is, for example, what Michael Morris, CEO of American Electric Power proposed, namely that *emission credits* accompany imports from major emitting nations that have not joined a post-Kyoto global cap-and-trade framework or otherwise capped their emissions.[105]

D.   National Treatment: No Discrimination of Imports as Against Like Domestic Products

Even if border adjustment on imports were permitted for domestic carbon taxes and/or carbon regulations, that is not the end of the story. Once found to be covered by GATT Article III, the carbon tax or regulation must also meet the substantive test in that provision.[106] This test essentially requires that *imported products* are not treated less favourably than *like domestic products*. A crucial question in this respect is which products can thus be compared? The answer is: Only imports and domestic products that

---

[105]   This proposal does, however, raise the question of where importers could buy these allowances? Presumably on the US market. However, if that would be the case, the total amount of allowances (or cap) would have to be increased (or a separate pool of allowances for imports created) so as to take account of carbon emitted by imports; if not, the price for allowances handed out with only internal US emissions in mind, would sky-rocket.

[106]   The carve-out in GATT Article II:2(a) for 'charges equivalent to an internal tax', is only a carve-out for the tariff discipline in GATT Article II; not for the national treatment discipline in GATT Article III, compliance with which is explicitly required in GATT Article II:2(a) itself.

are 'like'.[107] Assuming that US climate legislation would apply equally to imports as opposed to domestic products (that is, US steel made with coal would be subject to the same restrictions as imported, Chinese steel made with coal), for our purposes, the issue is primarily whether, for example, steel from China *made with coal* (subject to a *high* carbon tax or regulation) is 'like' domestically produced US steel *using natural gas* (subject to a *lower* carbon tax or regulation, as steel made with natural gas emits less carbon). In other words, one would not expect that US climate legislation will explicitly (or *de jure*) distinguish based on national origin. However, the question remains whether, by taxing one type of steel differently than the other, US legislation distinguishes, in effect (or *de facto*), based on nationality.

On the one hand, it would be rather odd for the WTO to intervene in this question of differentiating between types of steel depending on their carbon footprint, once the WTO has earlier accepted that carbon taxes or regulations can be adjusted at the border.[108] In the *US – Superfund* case, for example, the panel found that 'the tax on certain chemicals, being a tax directly imposed on products, was eligible for border tax adjustment independent of the purpose it served'.[109] In addition, under the substantive test of GATT Article III itself, the panel never questioned whether (taxed) imports *produced with* the chemicals were 'like' US products *not produced with* the chemicals. Once it found that the tax was adjustable at the border, the panel simply 'did not examine whether the tax on chemicals served environmental purposes and, if so, whether a border tax adjustment would be consistent with these purposes'.[110] If this approach were followed by the WTO Appellate Body, then the distinction made by a carbon tax between high-carbon and low-carbon steel could be equally taken for granted so that it could at least be *presumed* that these different types of steel are *not* like (and a WTO member can, as a result, validly distinguish between them without violating its 'national treatment' obligation).

On the other hand, a series of WTO disputes did revolve around perfectly 'border adjustable' excise taxes on alcoholic beverages which were nonetheless found to be *de facto* discriminatory because the tax system

---

[107] For tax measures both 'like' products and products that are 'directly competitive or substitutable' can be compared (*Ad Note* to GATT Article III:2, second sentence).

[108] Remember, in case no border adjustment would be permitted, then GATT Article III would not apply in the first place and, instead, a violation of GATT Article XI would be found.

[109] Above note 82 at para. 5.2.4.

[110] *Ibid.*

taxed one type of alcoholic beverage (say, predominantly imported vodka) higher than another *like* (or directly competitive) alcoholic beverage that was predominantly domestically produced (say, shochu, predominantly made within Japan). If the WTO were to apply the test it thus adopted to determine likeness of products covered (or not covered) by a carbon tax or regulation, there is little doubt that, for example, steel made with coal and steel made with natural gas would, indeed, be found to be like (or at least directly competitive). According to the WTO Appellate Body,

> a determination of 'likeness' . . . is, fundamentally, a determination about the nature and extent of a competitive relationship between and amongst products.[111]

As explained earlier in this chapter, the very reason to introduce a competitiveness provision – that is, to apply a US carbon tax or regulation also to imports – is that otherwise imports (say, Chinese steel made with coal that was not subject to emission cuts) would gain an unfair competitive advantage as opposed to domestic products (say, more expensive US steel made with carbon limits in place and, as a result, produced, for example, with natural gas). In other words, if the United States argues that it needs adjustment at the border because of competitiveness concerns, it cannot turn around later under a 'likeness' examination and say that high-carbon and low-carbon products do not compete in the first place.

That said, even if imports covered by US climate legislation (say, a limited list of carbon-intensive raw materials like steel and glass) and imports *not* so covered (say, less carbon-intensive raw materials or finished products like cars)[112] – or one type of product compared to another based

---

[111]   Appellate Body Report on *EC –Asbestos*, note 96 above. For taxes, also 'directly substitutable or competitive' products can be compared, see above note 107. WTO jurisprudence has used the following four criteria to determine comparability: (1) physical characteristics of the products; (2) end-use; (3) consumer tastes and habits; (4) tariff classification (*ibid.*, para. 101). Under all of these criteria, different types of steel depending on the energy used to produce the steel are most likely to be found comparable (they are physically the same; used for the same end-use; and not normally classified differently for import tariff purposes). Only the third criterion of 'consumer tastes and habits' could arguably make them different if one could demonstrate that US consumers really do make a difference between types of steel in their consumption patterns based on climate change concerns; however, if this were the case, then there would be no need for competitiveness provisions in the first place as consumers themselves would already turn to, and be willing to pay a premium for, low-carbon products without any need for the government to intervene.

[112]   One could imagine, for example, that to make any scheme of border adjustment manageable, it could be limited to a certain number of raw materials that

on the energy with which it was produced – were all found to be 'like', this does not by itself mean that the legislation discriminates *based on national origin*. As the Appellate Body found:

> even if two products are 'like', that does not mean that a measure [violates national treatment] . . . a [WTO] Member may draw distinctions between products which have been found to be 'like', without, for this reason alone, according to the *group of 'like' **imported** products* 'less favourable treatment' than that accorded to the *group of 'like' **domestic** products.*[113]

In other words, for a competitiveness provision in US climate legislation to be found to violate national treatment it must also be demonstrated that somehow the overall group of imported like products into the United States (e.g., all types of imported steel) is affected more heavily than the overall group of like domestic, US production (e.g., all types of US steel). This would require, for example, that US production is inherently or historically predominantly low-carbon; whereas imports are predominantly high-carbon. In a more recent case, the Appellate Body required even more before it could find a national treatment violation. In that case, it was willing to accept a 'detrimental effect on a given imported product' for as long as it could be 'explained by factors or circumstances *unrelated to the foreign origin of the product*'.[114] If that finding were applied in an examination of a carbon tax or regulation under GATT Article III, then the environmental reasons summarized earlier could be used to explain why the tax or regulation relates to environmental concerns of climate

---

are particularly energy intensive. One study, premised on a carbon tax of 32 Swiss Francs (26 US$) per ton of CO_2, concludes, for example, that 'only a handful of carbon-intensive raw materials industries will see price increases . . . that are large enough to pose a meaningful threat to competitiveness. [Import adjustments] on bulk transfer of ten to twenty basic materials – unfabricated metals, bulk glass and paper, fertilizer and a few chemicals – should suffice to offset nearly all discernible impacts' (see Hoerner and Muller, above note 85 at 21).

[113]   *EC – Asbestos*, note 96 above, para. 100 (italics in original, underlining added). In respect of a tax that differentiates between 'directly competitive or substitutable products' (see above note 107), it must be proven that the tax is 'applied so as to afford protection to domestic production' (Appellate Body Report, *Japan – Taxes on Alcoholic Beverages*, WT/DS8/AB/R, WT/DS10/AB/R, WT/DS11/AB/R, adopted 1 November 1996, DSR 1996:I, 97, 27–31).

[114]   Appellate Body Report, *Dominican Republic – Measures Affecting the Importation and Internal Sale of Cigarettes*, WT/DS302/AB/R, adopted 19 May 2005, DSR 2005:XV, 7367, para. 96 (emphasis added). See also Panel Report, *European Communities – Measures Affecting the Approval and Marketing of Biotech Products*, WT/DS291/R, WT/DS292/R, WT/DS293/R, Add.1 to Add.9, and Corr.1, adopted 21 November 2006, DSR 2006:III-VIII, 847, para. 7.2514.

change, not to 'the foreign origin of the product'. If that explanation were accepted, a violation of GATT Article III could be avoided, and there would be no need to go into the intricate requirements of the GATT Article XX justification (discussed in Section VI). As one recent WTO panel found, under the national treatment test of the TBT Agreement,

> it is possible that a technical regulation [say, a carbon intensity standard], by setting out certain requirements that must be complied with, would affect different operators on the market differently [say, US steel producers may find it easier to comply than Chinese steel producers], depending on a range of factors such as their geographical circumstances, their existing practices or their technical capacities. Such factors may have an impact on how easily products of various origins will or will not be able to meet the requirements at issue. However, the existence of such differences does not necessarily imply, in our view, that the measures at issue discriminate against products of certain origins ... This is especially the case, in our view, where the differential impact of the measures on products of different origins is the result of *external factors other than the origin of the products itself* [e.g. the carbon footprint of the steel; not its national origin as such].[115]

Finally, if US climate legislation were to apply to imports, how could US customs figure out the carbon content of specific imports without discriminating against those imports? The carbon is not physically in the steel or cement; hence, one would have to rely on supporting documents provided by the foreign manufacturer. What happens if such voluntary reporting is not complied with? An alternative basis for calculation of the carbon tax (or amount of emission credits to be provided) could then be the amount of carbon that would have been emitted had the imported product been produced in the United States using the US *predominant method of production*.[116] This is exactly the system that was adopted in the *Superfund* legislation for the tax on imports produced with certain chemicals. The

---

[115] Panel Report, *United States – Measures Concerning the Importation, Marketing and Sale of Tuna and Tuna Products*, WT/DS381/R, circulated 15 September 2011 (subject to appeal), para. 7.345. See also Panel Report, *United States – Measures Affecting the Production and Sale of Clove Cigarettes*, WT/DS406/R, circulated 2 September 2011 (subject to appeal), paras 7.268–7.269 ('it is not sufficient to find inconsistency with Article III:4 solely on the basis that the measure at issue adversely affects the conditions of competition for an imported product. The complainant must also show that those adverse effects are related to the foreign origin of the product at issue ... a panel is required to consider whether the detrimental effect(s) can be explained by factors or circumstances *unrelated to the foreign origin of the product*', in our case, the carbon footprint of the product rather than its national origin).

[116] In support, see Hoerner and Muller, above note 85 at 35–36.

GATT panel in this dispute did not find fault with this mechanism.[117] The WTO Appellate Body Report in *US – Gasoline* did, however, find that if domestic gasoline refiners get an individual baseline – representing the quality of gasoline produced by that refiner – as a starting point for cleaner standards on gasoline, then not to give the same opportunity to importers (which, instead, had to follow a statutory baseline) is discriminatory.[118] The Appellate Body rejected US arguments that verification on foreign soil and enforcement problems related to tracking the exact refinery or origin of specific gasoline made individual baselines, based on information provided by the foreign refiners themselves, an unrealistic option (especially not if compared to similar problems faced in respect of domestic gasoline). Yet, the Appellate Body did agree that statutory baselines – or, in our case, the fall-back of the US *predominant method of production* – could be used 'when the source of imported gasoline could not be determined or a baseline could not be established because of an absence of data'.[119] An alternative method of calculation that has been suggested, largely to avoid any semblance of discrimination, is to calculate a carbon tax or emission allowance requirement on imports based on the carbon emitted using the *best available technology*.[120] This would mean that, for example, Chinese steel made with coal would only have to pay the price of carbon emitted for the same steel produced in the United States with the least polluting technology, say, natural gas. This would, of course, seriously reduce the amount of adjustment that can be imposed on imports and may not be sufficient to address competitiveness concerns. Yet, it would avoid claims of discrimination as all 'like' products – for example, all steel – would then be taxed the same.

E.   Most-Favoured-Nation Treatment: No Discrimination Between Like Products from Different Countries

Climate legislation must not only avoid discrimination of imports *versus* domestic products ('national treatment' under GATT Article III). It must also avoid discrimination between imports from different countries. That

---

[117]   The same mechanism – voluntary reporting and backup imputation based on the US predominant method of production – was adopted also in the US ozone-depleting chemicals tax as well as the proposed BTU tax legislation of 1993. See above note 83.

[118]   Appellate Body Report, *United States – Standards for Reformulated and Conventional Gasoline*, WT/DS2/AB/R, adopted 20 May 1996, DSR 1996:I, 3.

[119]   *Ibid.*, 27.

[120]   See Ismer and Neuhoff, note 10 above, 15.

is the requirement under the so-called 'most-favoured-nation' obligation of GATT Article I. This provision requires, more specifically, that

> any advantage . . . granted by any Member to any product originating in . . . any other country shall be accorded *immediately and unconditionally* to the *like* product originating in . . . all other [WTO] Members.

In this respect, at least two problems may arise. First, the United States may decide to apply a carbon tax or regulation only on imports from countries that do not have emission cuts in place. In that event, the United States would be granting an 'advantage' to, for example, European imports (which are subject to emission cuts in Europe) which it does not 'immediately and unconditionally' accord to, for example, China, Brazil or India (which do not have emission cuts in place). The question remains, however, whether European steel produced subject to an emission tax (or emission allowances) is 'like' Chinese steel produced *without* such domestic restrictions. As explained earlier, WTO jurisprudence has interpreted 'likeness' as a question of competitiveness so that the two types of steel are most likely to be found 'alike'.[121] Moreover, the distinction thus made between types of steel that are 'like' can be said to be based on national origin: Chinese steel pays the tax; not European steel.[122] Hence, in all likelihood, US climate legislation that excludes from its scope imports from countries that have emission cuts in place would violate GATT Article I.[123] Crucially, however, this violation can still be justified under the environmental exception in GATT Article XX as explained in Section VI.

A second question that may arise is what would happen if US climate legislation applies to all imports across the board, including imports from countries that have their own emission cuts in place. One could imagine that, for example, Europe would then challenge such legislation, arguing that its producers must, thereby, pay the price of carbon twice: once under domestic EU legislation; and a second time at US customs. From that perspective, Chinese imports, for example, are granted an 'advantage' (i.e., only taxed once) not accorded to European imports. One possible

---

[121]   See above note 111.

[122]   *But* see recent cases referred to above notes 113 and 114 which, if applied to GATT Article I, might require additional evidence that the distinction was really made based on national origin rather than environmental concerns.

[123]   A similar violation of GATT Article I (MFN) would be found in case a US competitiveness provision would exclude, or apply differently to, developing countries depending on their stage of economic development. Yet, as discussed below in Section VI, this differentiation could be justified (or even required) under GATT Article XX (and/or the *Enabling Clause*, see below note 154).

response, at least when the US legislation takes the form of a carbon *tax* on imports, is that Europe can avoid this 'double taxation' by rebating any tax or costs borne by European products upon exportation. That is, after all, the other side of border tax adjustment: European goods get a rebate upon exportation but, according to the destination principle, pay the US carbon tax when imported into the United States. Thus, if European exports get taxed twice it is not because the US imposes an import tax, but because the EU failed to rebate exports.[124]

In sum, for a competitiveness provision to target only countries with no emission cuts in place would most likely violate MFN (the United States would then be treating 'like' products differently based on their origin); for a competitiveness provision to apply to all countries – including those that have their own emission cuts in place such as Europe – is less likely to raise an MFN problem (the United States can then be said to be treating all 'like' products in the same way). For a country to treat imports differently based on their carbon footprint (say, more carbon allowances required for Chinese steel imports as compared to Swiss steel imports) may imply differential treatment of 'like products'. However, for there to be an MFN violation one would, in addition, have to demonstrate that this differential treatment is linked to the national origin of the products rather than 'factors or circumstances *unrelated to the foreign origin of the product*' such as the objectively determined carbon footprint of the product or its producer.[125]

---

[124]   If border adjustment takes the form of a *regulation*, 'rebating' a regulation upon export is not an option (under the SCM Agreement it could even be regarded as a prohibited export subsidy, see above notes 85 and 94). In that case, the argument that European imports are discriminated against (because they are covered by a US carbon regulation applied to imports as much as Chinese imports) becomes stronger. On this view, discrimination could then be argued to exist not only when like products are treated differently (say, Chinese steel is taxed; not European steel); but also when different products are treated alike (say, Chinese steel with no emission cuts in place is taxed as much as European steel with emissions cuts). Yet, for Europe to convince the WTO that products become different or 'unlike' based on whether they were produced with or without emission cuts in place would be hard, given the WTO's competitiveness test for likeness explained earlier (see above note 111). Thus, even a carbon regulation that applies to all countries across the board would not likely violate MFN.

[125]   See above note 114, albeit under GATT Article III, rather than GATT Article I. To achieve the same approach, the term 'unconditionally' in GATT Article I could then be interpreted as limited to conditions addressed to *countries*, such as whether or not they adopted a certain regulatory system or ratified a treaty; not 'conditions' (or other burdens) addressed to individuals (such as a producer's or product's carbon footprint). See Lorand Bartels, above note 34, at 11

VI.   ENVIRONMENTAL EXCEPTIONS IN GATT ARTICLE XX

As indicated in the introduction to this chapter, and hinted at throughout the analysis of the substantive rules of the WTO, any violation of the GATT may still be justified under the environmental exceptions of GATT Article XX as a measure

> relating to the *conservation of exhaustible natural resources* if such measures are made effective in conjunction with restrictions on domestic production or consumption.[126]

In other words, a punitive tariff or quantitative restriction on carbon-intensive imports (discussed in Section IV.A above) might still be justified under GATT Article XX. Equally, even if the WTO would *not* accept that a domestic carbon tax, cap-and-trade system or other carbon regulation (such as a maximum carbon intensity standard or carbon label) is subject to 'border adjustment' (as discussed in Section V.A to C above), a domestic carbon tax or emission credit requirement or other regulation on imports can still be justified under GATT Article XX. Finally, even if domestic climate legislation were found to be discriminatory (for example, because it favours domestic steel over imported steel; or only imposes duties or an emission credits requirement on steel from countries that do not have emission cuts in place, as discussed in Section V.D and E), GATT Article XX might justify such discrimination.[127]

---

and, in support, Stephan Schill, *The Multilateralization of International Investment Law* (Cambridge: Cambridge University Press, 2009), 129–139 and Panel Report, *Canada – Automobiles,* WT/DS139/R, adopted as modified by the Appellate Body Report, 19 June 2000, para. 10.25 (referring to 'conditions that entailed different treatment of imported products depending upon their origin').

[126]   GATT Article XX(g) (emphasis added). Alternatively, climate legislation might also be justified as a measure under GATT Article XX(b), namely: 'necessary to protect human, animal or plant life or health'. Yet, since the qualifier 'necessary' (in Article XX(b)) is generally perceived as more difficult to meet than that of 'relating to' (in Article XX(g)) this chapter focuses on Article XX(g).

[127]   Most observers take the view that violations of the AD Agreement and SCM Agreement cannot be justified under GATT Article XX. Hence, in the case of a carbon 'tariff' (rather than a carbon tax or regulation), it may be better to call and structure the measure as just an 'ordinary customs duty' so that the charge would be seen as falling under GATT Article II and thereby justifiable under GATT Article XX, rather than a violation of the AD Agreement or SCM Agreement that would not normally be justifiable under the environmental exceptions of GATT Article XX. In this regard, and qualifying the argument that Article XX does not apply to the AD and SCM Agreements, note the Appellate Body's understand-

Whereas pre-1995 GATT panels never found that a measure met the exceptions in GATT Article XX;[128] post-1995 WTO jurisprudence has proven to be much more flexible and 'greener'. In 2001, the WTO Appellate Body accepted a French ban on imports of asbestos as qualifying under the exception of GATT Article XX(b) for health protection;[129] later that year, it also found that a modified US ban on shrimp based on how these shrimp were caught *abroad* – that is, a pure process measure, similar to a carbon tax or regulation – was justified under GATT Article XX(g) as a conservation measure for endangered turtles.[130]

A.   The Conditions under Paragraph (g) of GATT Article XX

For a carbon tax or regulation on imports to meet the GATT Article XX(g) exception, three cumulative conditions must be met:

- *Is the planet's atmosphere an 'exhaustible natural resource'?*: In previous cases, stocks of fish that were not even endangered (herring,

---

ing in *China – Publications and Audiovisual Products* regarding the relationship between China's Accession Protocol and GATT Article XX ('we find that China may rely upon the introductory clause of paragraph 5.1 of its Accession Protocol and seek to justify these provisions as necessary to protect public morals in China, within the meaning of Article XX(a) of the GATT 1994') (*China – Measures Affecting Trading Rights and Distribution Services for Certain Publications and Audiovisual Entertainment Products*, WT/DS363/AB/R, adopted 19 January 2010, para. 233); and the recent Panel Report on *China – Raw Materials* ('the wording and the context of Paragraph 11.3 precludes the possibility for China to invoke the defence of Article XX of the GATT 1994 for violations of the obligations contained in Paragraph 11.3 of China's Accession Protocol') (Panel Reports, *China – Measures Related to the Exportation of Various Raw Materials*, WT/DS394/R and Corr.1, WT/DS395/R and Corr.1, WT/DS398/R and Corr.1, circulated to WTO Members 5 July 2011 (currently under appeal), para. 7.158).

[128]   The first *Tuna – Dolphin* panel (above note 90) found that the United States ban on tuna to protect dolphin abroad was not justified under GATT Article XX(b) as, according to the panel, this provision is 'focused on the use of . . . measures to safeguard . . . animals or plants within the jurisdiction of the importing country' (para. 5.26). In addition, the panel found that if the United States were permitted to ban imports based on unilaterally determined US standards on dolphin protection, then the GATT 'would provide legal security only in respect of trade between a limited number of contracting parties with identical internal regulations' (para. 5.27). Note that, for present purposes, a carbon tax or regulation would not impose a full ban, but rather an extra tax or charge.

[129]   See note 96 above.

[130]   Appellate Body Report, *United States – Import Prohibition of Certain Shrimp and Shrimp Products – Recourse to Article 21.5 of the DSU by Malaysia*, WT/DS58/AB/RW, adopted 21 November 2001, DSR 2001:XIII, 6481.

salmon and dolphin), clean air and endangered sea turtles were found to be 'exhaustible natural resources'.[131] Considering the international importance given today to the problem of climate change[132] – and the catastrophic consequences that are linked to it for all forms of life on earth – it would be surprising if the WTO would not accept that the planet's atmosphere (that is, the layer of gases around the earth that regulates the planet's climate) is an 'exhaustible natural resource'. The fact that a carbon tax or regulation on imports would address carbon emitted *abroad* should not impose a jurisdictional limitation on a regulation from a carbon-restricting country. What is required is 'a sufficient nexus'[133] between carbon emissions in, for example, China and the climate change consequences that such carbon emissions can have for such a carbon-restricting country. In *US – Shrimp*, the United States was permitted to protect turtle in India based on the fact that (1) the turtle are an endangered species; and (2) the turtle are highly migratory animals which are known to occur in US waters. If the United States was permitted to protect turtle in India that may at some point cross US waters, it is hard to imagine why a country would not be permitted to protect against carbon emitted in India that certainly crosses territorial borders and is known by science to be as dangerous for climate change as carbon emitted within that carbon-restricting country itself. The world's atmosphere is, after all, a global commons; and carbon emissions are, because of their global impact, a collective action problem.[134]

- *Does domestic climate legislation 'relate to the conservation of' the planet's atmosphere?*: Importantly, what needs to be examined under this test is not the actual trade restriction or discrimination found earlier under other GATT provisions, but rather the domestic

---

[131]   See the Appellate Body in *US – Gasoline* (see note 118 above), considering clean air to be an exhaustible natural resource, and the Appellate Body in *US – Shrimp*, finding that sea turtles at issue also constituted exhaustible natural resources (see Appellate Body Report, *United States – Import Prohibition of Certain Shrimp and Shrimp Products*, WT/DS58/AB/R, adopted 6 November 1998, DSR 1998:VII, 2755, paras 127–134).

[132]   In its assessment of what constitutes 'exhaustible natural resources', the Appellate Body has, indeed, referred to the 'contemporary concerns of the community of nations about the protection and the conservation of the environment' as well as the preamble to the *WTO Agreement* which refers to 'the objective of sustainable development' (Appellate Body Report, *US – Shrimp*, see note 131 above, para. 129).

[133]   *Ibid.*, para. 133.

[134]   See Stern, note 5 above.

legislation *as a whole*.[135] The 'related to' test requires that there be
a 'substantial relationship' between the domestic climate legislation
and the conservation of the planet's atmosphere and related climate.
This relationship must be 'a close and genuine relationship of ends
and means'.[136] For example, the legislation must not be 'disproportionately wide in its scope and reach in relation to the policy
objective of protection and conservation' of the planet's climate.[137]
This test must be applied to the legislation as such and its general
design; not so much to its specific details. As a result, in two WTO
cases (*US – Gasoline* and *US – Shrimp*) this test was easily met.[138]

---

[135] Appellate Body Report, *US – Gasoline*, see note 118 above, 14–16 ('The
chapeau of Article XX makes it clear that it is the "measures" which are to be
examined under Article XX(g), and not the legal finding of "less favourable treatment.'). In apparent contrast with the Appellate Body Report on *US – Gasoline*,
see however the Appellate Body Report on *Thailand – Cigarettes (Philippines)*,
where the Appellate Body, referring to the 'necessity test' in GATT Article XX(d)
stated that 'when Article XX(d) is invoked to justify an inconsistency with Article
III:4, what must be shown to be "necessary" is the treatment giving rise to the
finding of less favourable treatment. Thus, when less favourable treatment is found
based on differences in the regulation of imports and of like domestic products,
the analysis of an Article XX(d) defence should focus on whether those regulatory
differences are "necessary" to secure compliance with "laws or regulations" that
are not GATT-inconsistent.' (Appellate Body Report, *Thailand – Customs and
Fiscal Measures on Cigarettes from the Philippines*, WT/DS371/AB/R, adopted
15 July 2011, para. 177). It is not clear whether this Appellate Body understanding would influence the 'relating to' test in GATT Article XX(g), and whether
the Appellate Body is hereby reverting to previous GATT panels' understanding
on this matter (see GATT Panel Report, *United States – Taxes on Automobiles*,
DS31/R, 11 October 1994, unadopted, para. 5.64 ('It also recalled that it was not
the CAFE scheme as a whole but the specific measure inconsistent with Article
III:4 that required justification and which, under Article XX(g), needed to be primarily aimed at the conservation of exhaustible natural resources. . .'); and GATT
Panel Report, *United States Section 337 of the Tariff Act of 1930*, L/6439, adopted
7 November 1989, BISD 36S/345, para. 5.27 ('In the view of the Panel, what has to
be justified as "necessary" under Article XX(d) is each of the inconsistencies with
another GATT Article found to exist . . .')).
[136] Appellate Body Report, *US – Shrimp*, see note 131 above, para. 136.
[137] *Ibid.*, at para. 141. This reference to 'scope and reach' may justify a possible
limitation of a carbon tax or other regulation on imports that is limited to a certain
class of energy-intensive raw materials (as suggested in note 112 above) even if
such limited list might otherwise violate national treatment or MFN.
[138] See, however, the recent Panel Report on *China – Raw Materials* (see note
127 above, paras. 7.434–7.435), where the panel found that China had not met its
burden of proving that its measures, an export quota on refractory-grade bauxite
and an export duty on fluorspar 'relate to the conservation' of these raw materials
– considered to be 'exhaustible natural resources' ('For the Panel, measures that

Unless there are blatant inconsistencies or protectionist features in the domestic legislation, climate change legislation should normally pass this 'related to' test. For environmental reasons in support of a competitiveness provision, see Section II.A above.

- *Is the domestic climate legislation on imports 'made effective in conjunction with restrictions on domestic production and consumption'?*: As long as the domestic legislation imposes broadly similar restrictions also on domestic businesses, this clause will be met. In *US – Gasoline*, the Appellate Body confirmed that this is only a 'requirement of *even-handedness* in the imposition of restrictions . . . [there is] no textual basis for requiring identical treatment of domestic and imported products'.[139] More specifically, even if the legislation in some of its details were to discriminate imports as opposed to domestic products, the legislation or measure as a whole can still be found to meet this test (as was the case in *US – Gasoline*).[140] This third test under GATT Article XX(g) should therefore not be difficult to meet.

B.   The Conditions Under the Introductory Phrase of GATT Article XX

Finally, even if all three conditions under the specific paragraph of GATT Article XX(g) were met, the domestic climate legislation that was found to violate any other GATT provision would also have to fulfil the introductory phrase of GATT Article XX. This phrase requires that

> measures are not *applied* in a manner which would constitute a means of *arbitrary or unjustifiable discrimination* between countries where *the same conditions prevail*, or a *disguised restriction* on international trade.[141]

The Appellate Body has given great importance to the introductory phrase of GATT Article XX exception. For present purposes as well, this phrase

---

increase the costs of refractory-grade bauxite and fluorspar to foreign consumers but decrease their costs to domestic users are difficult to reconcile with the goal of conserving refractory-grade bauxite and fluorspar.').

[139]   Appellate Body Report, *US – Gasoline*, see note 118 above, 21.

[140]   As the Appellate Body in *US – Gasoline* (see note 118 above, 21) explains, if the exception in GATT Article XX(g) required 'identity of treatment . . . it is difficult to see how inconsistency with Article III:4 [i.e. a national treatment violation] would have arisen in the first place'.

[141]   Chapeau of GATT Article XX (emphasis added). Article 3.5 of the *UN Framework Convention on Climate Change* provides similarly that '[m]easures taken to combat climate change, including unilateral ones, should not constitute a means of arbitrary or unjustifiable discrimination or a disguised restriction on international trade'.

may well be the most important provision in the entire GATT agreement. The introductory phrase of GATT Article XX is not about the climate legislation as such, but about its 'detailed operating provisions' and how it is 'actually applied'.[142] As importantly, under this phrase, according to the Appellate Body in *US – Shrimp*, the environmental policy goal no longer matters; the legitimacy of the policy goal and how the legislation relates to it must be examined under the paragraph, not the introductory phrase.[143] Finally, the discrimination to be avoided under the introductory phrase of Article XX ('arbitrary or unjustifiable discrimination between countries where the same conditions prevail') is different from the discrimination referred to earlier under national treatment (GATT Article III) and MFN (GATT Article I). Under Articles I and III, the discrimination is focused on 'like *products*'; under Article XX it is focused on '*countries* where the same conditions prevail'. Moreover, and quite logically, the discrimination under the exception in Article XX must be different in 'nature and quality'[144] or 'go beyond'[145] the discrimination under the rule in Article I or III. Indeed, if the discrimination in Article XX were the same as that in, say, Article I on MFN, then as soon as one finds MFN discrimination, one would not, by definition, be able to justify it under Article XX.[146] At the same time, discrimination under the introductory phrase of Article XX covers both discrimination between different foreign countries exporting to the carbon-restricting country (MFN-type discrimination as was found to be the case in *US – Shrimp*) and discrimination between foreign countries and the carbon-restricting country (national treatment-type discrimination as was found to be the case in *US – Gasoline*).

With this general background in mind, when examining whether a

---

[142]   Appellate Body Report, *US – Shrimp*, see note 131 above, para. 160.

[143]   Appellate Body Report, *US – Shrimp*, see note 131 above, para. 149. But see Appellate Body Report, *Brazil – Measures Affecting Imports of Retreaded Tyres*, WT/DS332/AB/R, adopted 17 December 2007, para. 227 which does refer back to the objectives of the measure (under the paragraphs of Article XX) to check discrimination under the chapeau ('there is arbitrary or unjustifiable discrimination when a measure provisionally justified under a paragraph of Article XX is applied in a discriminatory manner "between countries where the same conditions prevail", and when the reasons given for this discrimination bear no rational connection to the objective falling within the purview of a paragraph of Article XX, or would go against that objective. The assessment of whether discrimination is arbitrary or unjustifiable should be made in the light of the objective of the measure').

[144]   Appellate Body Report, *US – Shrimp*, see note 131 above, para. 150.

[145]   Appellate Body Report, *US – Gasoline,* see note 118 above, 28.

[146]   If not, '[t]o proceed down that path would be both to empty the [introductory phrase] of its contents and to deprive the exceptions ... of meaning' (Appellate Body Report, *US – Gasoline*, see note 118 above, 23).

competitiveness provision within a carbon-restricting policy amounts to 'arbitrary or unjustifiable *discrimination* between countries where the *same conditions* prevail', the Appellate Body, based on its decisions in previous environmental disputes, is likely to refer to at least the following three elements:

- *Does the domestic climate legislation take account of local conditions in foreign countries or does it essentially require that foreign countries adopt domestic policies?* In *US – Shrimp*, the original US ban was faulted because of its 'intended and actual coercive effect on the specific policy decisions made by foreign governments'; more specifically, it required that all other countries 'adopt essentially the same policy' as the United States does; '[o]ther specific policies and measures that an exporting country may have adopted for the protection and conservation of sea turtles are not taken into account'.[147] When, in response, the United States no longer required the 'adoption of essentially the same program' but conditioned market access for imported shrimp on 'the adoption of a program *comparable in effectiveness*' to that of the US program, the Appellate Body found that such 'allows for sufficient flexibility in the application of the measure so as to avoid "arbitrary or unjustifiable discrimination"'.[148] This would seem to require that any carbon tax or regulation on imports is sufficiently flexible and takes 'into consideration different conditions which may occur' in different foreign countries. This requirement has two important consequences for any competitiveness provision:

  Firstly, it may force the carbon-restricting country to consider whether a foreign country already imposes emission cuts or otherwise addresses climate change. This, in turn, may oblige (or at least enable) the carbon-restricting country to impose lower (or no) import taxes or emission allowance requirements on imports from countries that have their own climate policies in place.[149] In other words, even if excluding European countries would violate MFN (as suggested earlier), such violation would seem to be justified under the introductory phrase of GATT Article XX. Note, however,

---

[147]   Appellate Body Report, *US – Shrimp*, see note 131 above, paras 161 and 163.

[148]   Appellate Body Report, *US – Shrimp (Implementation under Article 21.5)*, note 130 above, para. 144.

[149]   The Kyoto Protocol, for example, leaves it open as to how countries meet their targets, be it through taxes, regulations or a cap-and-trade system.

that the same reasoning would then apply to, for example, Chinese efforts to combat climate change (China has, for example, introduced a domestic target to improve energy intensity and imposed an export tax on energy-intensive exports such as iron and steel, cement, aluminium and certain chemicals).[150]

Secondly, the requirement to take 'into consideration different conditions which may occur'[151] in different foreign countries, may force the carbon-restricting country to consider whether developing countries should, for historical reasons, carry the same burden as other countries. Under the UN Framework Convention on Climate Change (ratified by the United States), for example, protection of the climate system must be pursued 'on the basis of equity and in accordance with [the parties'] common but differentiated responsibilities and respective capabilities'.[152] This, in turn, may oblige (or at least enable) the carbon-restricting country to impose a graduated import tax or regulation depending on the stage of economic development of the foreign country in question.[153] In other words, the introductory phrase of Article XX may force the

---

[150] See note 12 above. See also follow-up to the *Stern Review*, note 12 above, 20 ('This compares well to the cost imposed by the EU ETS [emissions-trading scheme] on firms in these sectors. At allowance prices of €20/t CO_2, the impact is estimated at 1% for integrated steel and 4% for aluminum, based on the increase in electricity prices. Current prices for EU ETS allowances are €2 to €5 euros, implying far smaller impacts'). India as well has made 'changes to energy subsidies, plans for more efficient coal-fired power plant[s] and further development of innovative new technologies for renewable energy' (*ibid.*, 4).

[151] See note 147 above.

[152] Article 3.1 of the UN Framework Convention on Climate Change. See also Article 3.4 of the Convention: 'Policies and measures to protect the climate system against human-induced change should be appropriate for the specific conditions of each Party and should be integrated with national development programmes, taking into account that economic development is essential for adopting measures to address climate change'.

[153] Recall that under the Kyoto Protocol, developing countries did not have to commit to any emission reductions. Yet, since the United States did not ratify the Kyoto Protocol it cannot be held by this concession that developing countries should not cut emissions at all (but see the UN Framework Convention on Climate Change, note 141 above, which the United States did ratify). If the EU were to impose a carbon tax on imports, however, the fact that it ratified the Kyoto Protocol could force the EU to exclude those developing countries from its carbon tax. That the WTO may, and should, in certain cases refer to other treaties, such as the Kyoto Protocol, as long as both disputing parties are bound by such other treaty, see Joost Pauwelyn, 'How to Win a WTO Dispute based on non-WTO law: Questions of Jurisdiction and Merits', *Journal Of World Trade* 2003, 997.

carbon-restricting country to have lower or even no carbon restrictions on imports from developing countries, especially the very
poor ones.[154] In contrast, if the climate legislation would be found
to comply with GATT rules and there would, therefore, be no need
to revert to the environmental exception in GATT Article XX, such
graduation or even exclusion of (i) countries with their own climate
policies in place, and (ii) developing countries, could be avoided.
That largely explains why it is, after all, useful to try to justify future
climate legislation as it applies to imports as, for example, 'border
tax adjustment' rather than justify the measure directly under the
exceptions in GATT Article XX.

- *Before imposing the 'unilateral' carbon tax or regulation on imports,
did the carbon-restricting country engage in 'serious, across-the-board
negotiations with the objective of concluding bilateral or multilateral
agreements' to address climate change?*[155] This does not require the
actual conclusion of agreements with, say, China, Brazil or India,[156]
but at the very least good faith efforts by the carbon-restricting
country to bring these countries into the fold of an international
effort to combat climate change before making a move to the
second or third best option of unilateral border adjustments. Such
negotiations must also occur on a non-discriminatory basis with all
countries affected.[157] Note, however, that unlike the absolute ban in

---

[154] Imposing a more lenient carbon tariff or tax on developing countries, especially the poorest ones, could not only be justified because 'the same conditions' do
not prevail in those countries (under GATT Article XX); but also with reference to
the 1979 *Enabling Clause* which permits developed countries to give *tariff* preferences to developing countries that they do not need to extend to developed nations.
See above note 44 for how Europe gives tariff preferences to developing countries
that have signed the Kyoto Protocol. Making a distinction between developing countries based on whether they have ratified Kyoto or have other climate
change policies in place, could then be justified with reference to the 'development,
financial and trade needs of developing countries' as permitted by the Appellate
Body Report on *EC – Tariff Preferences* (Appellate Body Report, *European
Communities – Conditions for the Granting of Tariff Preferences to Developing
Countries*, WT/DS246/AB/R, adopted 20 April 2004, DSR 2004:III, 925). See
also, Daniel Gros, 'A Border Tax to Protect the Global Environment?', *CEPS
Commentary*, Centre For European Policy Studies, 2009. The *Enabling Clause* also
permits extra preferential treatment in this context for least developed countries.

[155] Appellate Body Report, *US – Shrimp*, see note 131 above, para. 166.

[156] Appellate Body Report, *US – Shrimp (Implementation under Article 21.5)*,
note 130 above, para. 124.

[157] Appellate Body Report, *US – Shrimp*, see note 131 above, paras 169–172
(where the United States was found to have discriminated in favour of five coun-

> *US – Shrimp*, a carbon tax or regulation on imports would not ban imports, but only make them pay the social cost of carbon. In that sense, the unilateral action would be less trade restrictive than in *US – Shrimp*.

- *Does the implementation and administration of the climate legislation respect 'basic fairness and due process'?*[158] If there would, for example, be certification or rebates for domestic efforts to fight climate change or developing countries, is the process transparent and predictable; are parties heard and is the system non-discriminatory in its procedures?

VII. CONCLUSION

Concerns of economic competitiveness are a core explanation for why there are, to date, relatively few mandatory limits on greenhouse gas emissions, be it under domestic climate legislation or international treaties (Section I). This chapter examined the advantages and disadvantages of including a competitiveness provision in domestic climate policy (Section II). Although such competitiveness provision could take different forms, one of the options is to enlist trade policy in the fight against global warming (Section III). Most controversial by far would be the imposition of trade restrictions on imports based on the carbon or other greenhouse gases that were emitted in their production *abroad* (so-called trade restrictions in respect of 'foreign-emitted' or 'offshore' carbon). Although there are certain options to be avoided as they would most likely violate WTO law (e.g. anti-dumping duties and countervailing (anti-subsidy) duties, discussed in Section IV), the broader WTO consistency or authorization of such process-based restrictions is unclear and remains to be tested. When carefully designing carbon restrictions on imports as the extension or 'border adjustment' of *internal* carbon measures (that is, a tax, charge or regulation on imports triggered by an 'internal factor' or affecting an 'internal act' such as sale or consumption within the regulating country) and ensuring that the carbon measure on domestic production sufficiently applies to or affects *products*, carbon restrictions on imports can pass WTO muster on condition that they avoid origin-based discrimination. Moreover, certain discriminations

---

tries by concluding the Inter-American Convention for the protection and conservation of sea turtles, without negotiating with other countries).

[158] Appellate Body Report, *US – Shrimp*, see note 131 above, para. 181.

or other WTO violations could also be justified under environmental exceptions (GATT Article XX). Carbon leakage measures and border tax adjustments can therefore be WTO consistent. The devil will be in the details.

16. Challenges for technology transfer in the climate change arena: what interactions with the TRIPS Agreement?
Dalindyebo Shabalala

I. INTRODUCTION

According to the relatively conservative 2007 Fourth Assessment Report by the Intergovernmental Panel on Climate Change (IPCC AR4), the Earth continues to experience record-breaking temperatures caused by increased atmospheric concentrations of carbon dioxide (CO_2) and other greenhouse gases (GHGs).[1] The transfer of technology, from industrialized to developing countries (as well as between industrialized countries) is a key pillar of the international framework for addressing global climate change. Addressing climate change requires a radical shift in economy-wide investment, production and consumption patterns in each country. The development and diffusion of technologies is a necessary element in ensuring that standards of living are maintained and poverty continues to be reduced as global warming is mitigated and weather impacts are minimized.

Climate change is also a fundamental development challenge. The United Nations Framework Convention on Climate Change (UNFCCC)[2] and its Kyoto Protocol[3] were built on a political bargain directly involving technology transfer. On one side, industrialized countries would take the first steps to reduce GHG emissions while transferring technology to enable developing countries to make progress on carbon efficiency.

---

[1] IPCC *Climate Change 2007: Synthesis Report – Intergovernmental Panel on Climate Change Fourth Assessment Report,* (Cambridge: Cambridge University Press, 2007), 30. Available at http://www.ipcc.ch/pdf/assessment-report/ar4/syr/ar4_syr.pdf (last visited 7 March 2012).

[2] United Nations Framework Convention on Climate Change (UNFCCC), New York, 9 May 1992, in force 21 March 1994, 1771 *United Nations Treaty Series* (1994) 107.

[3] Kyoto Protocol to the United Nations Framework Convention on Climate Change (Kyoto Protocol), Kyoto, 10 December 1997, in force 16 February 2005, 37 *International Legal Materials* (1998) 22.

The technologies developed and demonstrated to enable success would ensure that developing countries would be in a position to act to reduce their emissions once the initial first steps had been taken by industrialized countries.

However, developing countries have argued that commitments on technology transfer have not been met and that industrialized countries have largely failed to provide effective transfer of environmentally sound, climate-related technologies. This failure was the primary bone of contention during the Bali Conference of the Parties (COP) in December 2007, and is a significant contributing factor to the difficulties in negotiating a new post-Kyoto protocol framework beyond 2012.

Analyses vary as to the causes for the perceived failure of industrialized countries to deliver on technology transfer. Factors that contribute to this perceived failure include: the absence of political will; lack of agreement on definitions and methodologies for what constitutes technology transfer; the lack of institutional capacity in both developing and industrialized countries to enable, measure and verify technology transfer; and *ad hoc* and unreliable processes for financing technology transfer. One area where all these arguments come together is disagreements about the role of intellectual property (IP) as a barrier to developing and disseminating climate-related technologies in developing countries. In a nutshell, developing countries have argued that too restrictive and high intellectual property protection constrains their ability to access products and knowledge to enable them to address climate change and develop. The argument on intellectual property is two-fold: intellectual property policies in industrialized countries serve to promote and protect their own knowledge industries and prevent participation by enterprises in developing countries; the international framework on intellectual property, embodied by the WTO Agreement on Trade Related Aspects of Intellectual Property Rights[4] (TRIPS Agreement), denies developing countries the policy space that they require to try and ensure that technology transfer takes place. Developing countries argue that they need such policy space in light of the failure of industrialized countries to deliver on their technology transfer commitments.

The framing of the issue by developing countries suggests that there is a conflict between the goals and aims of the UNFCCC and those of the

---

[4]   Agreement on Trade-related Aspects of Intellectual Property (TRIPS), Annex 1C to the Marrakesh Agreement establishing the World Trade Organization, Marrakesh, 15 April 1994, in force 1 January 1995, 1867 *United Nations Treaty Series* (1995) 4.

TRIPS Agreement. Thus action to address climate change is constrained by the fear that such actions may be considered to be out of compliance with the obligations of the TRIPS Agreement. As a consequence, developing countries argue that the UNFCCC negotiations must address intellectual property. They have generally been opposed by industrialized countries who argue that the UNFCCC is an inappropriate forum for addressing intellectual property and in any case, TRIPS poses no such barrier. This chapter will try to address two main issues raised by the UNFCCC debate on the need to address IP: what constraints does the TRIPS Agreement place on unilateral action by developing countries; what constraints does WTO and TRIPS jurisprudence place on the UNFCCC's ability to justify IP measures. In addressing these questions, this chapter will begin with an overview of the UNFCCC legal obligations on technology transfer before outlining some of the basic principles underlying the structure of the IP mechanisms and how they relate to climate change and potential actions to address climate change.

II. THE UNFCCC STRUCTURE FOR TECHNOLOGY TRANSFER[5]

The UNFCCC was concluded at the 1992 Rio Earth Summit to achieve the stabilization of greenhouse gas concentrations in the atmosphere at a low enough level to prevent dangerous anthropogenic interference with the climate system. The UNFCCC and the Kyoto Protocol establish a legal framework of technology transfer, including some of the clearest and most strongly articulated provisions on the role of technology transfer in Multilateral Environmental Agreements (MEAs).

Technology transfer is addressed in Article 4 of the UNFCCC. This provision covers a range of issues, including financing, transfer and commitments. Notably, Article 4.7 links the ability of developing country Parties to fulfil their commitments under the UNFCCC to the effective implementation by industrialized country Parties of their commitments, particularly on financial resources and technology transfer.

---

[5] This section is partly based on a forthcoming CIEL Discussion Paper by D. Shabalala and C. Twiss 'The State of Play on Technology Transfer in the UNFCCC' Centre for International Environmental Law, 2012, material which also appears in the CIEL/ICHRP Working Paper 'Technology Transfer in the UNFCCC and other International Legal Regimes: the Challenge of System Integration' 2010, available at: http://www.ichrp.org/files/papers/181/138_technol ogy_transfer_UNFCCC.pdf (last visited 7 March 2012).

Further, while the Convention provides for the diffusion of technologies amongst all Parties, the key provision for transfer of technology from industrialized countries (Annex II Parties) to developing countries is Article 4.5:

> The industrialized country Parties and other industrialized Parties included in Annex II shall take all practicable steps to promote, facilitate and finance, as appropriate, the transfer of, or access to, environmentally sound technologies and know-how to other Parties, particularly developing country Parties, to enable them to implement the provisions of the Convention. In this process, the industrialized country Parties shall support the development and enhancement of endogenous capacities and technologies of developing country Parties. Other Parties and organizations in a position to do so may also assist in facilitating the transfer of such technologies.

Finally, Article 4.3 addresses the financing of technologies, requiring industrialized country Parties to 'provide new and additional financial resources' for the transfer of technologies to developing countries

The UNFCCC has no official definition of technology transfer and this has been generally part of the debate between industrialized and developing countries. The International Panel on Climate Change (IPCC) has suggested a definition that it has used in carrying out a study on methodological issues in technology transfer.[6] However, that definition has not yet been adopted by the Conference of the Parties or the UNFCCC Secretariat. The IPCC defined technology transfer as:

> a broad set of processes covering the flows of know-how, experience and equipment for mitigating and adapting to climate change amongst different stakeholders such as governments, private sector entities, financial institutions, NGOs and research/education institutions. [. . .] The broad and inclusive term 'transfer' encompasses diffusion of technologies and technology co-operation across and within countries. It covers technology transfer processes between developed countries, developing countries and countries with economies in transition. It comprises the process of learning to understand, utilise and replicate the technology, including the capacity to choose and adapt to local conditions and integrate it with indigenous technologies.[7]

For the purposes of this chapter, we will adopt the broad definition proposed by the IPCC.

---

[6]   Bert Metz et al. (eds) *Methodological and Technological Issues in Technology Transfer*, A Special Report of the Intergovernmental Panel on Climate Change, (Cambridge: Cambridge University Press, 2000), available at: http://www.ipcc.ch/ipccreports/sres/tectran/index.htm (last visited 7 March 2012).

[7]   *Id.*, Section 1.2.

The UNFCCC structure for negotiating and discussing technology transfer consists of the following:

- *The Conference of the Parties (COP)* is the authoritative body of the Convention. Annual meetings function to 'review the implementation of the convention, adopt decisions to further develop the Convention's rules, and negotiate new commitments'.[8] On technology transfer, two subsidiary bodies support the work of the COP:
- *the Subsidiary Body for Scientific and Technological Advice (SBSTA),* which supports the work of the COP on 'matters of science, technology, and methodology, including guidelines for improving standards of national communications and emission inventories';[9] and
- *the Subsidiary Body for Implementation (SBI),* which supports the COP in assessing and reviewing implementation, 'for instance by analyzing national communications submitted by Parties. It also deals with financial and administrative matters.'[10] It also had responsibility for monitoring the Expert Group on Technology Transfer (EGTT) until it was phased out in 2011 with the establishment of a new technology mechanism in the Cancun Accords.

Bodies that exist independently from the UNFCCC are retained to provide important assistance to the Parties to the convention. These include the following:

- the *Intergovernmental Panel on Climate Change (IPCC)* provides information via reports at the request of the COP or the SBSTA. The most relevant of these is to conduct studies and assessments of the scientific evidence for climate change and evaluations of the actions taken to address climate change mitigation and adaptation. With respect to technology transfer, the most relevant is a study on 'Methodological and Technological Issues in Technology Transfer, A Special Report of the Intergovernmental Panel on Climate Change' IPCC, July 2000.

---

[8] United Nations Framework Convention on Climate Change (UNFCCC), 'Uniting on Climate: A Guide to the Climate Change Convention and the Kyoto Protocol', November 2007, 16, available at: http://unfccc.int/resource/docs/publi cations/unitingonclimate_eng.pdf (last visited 7 March 2012).
[9] *Id.*
[10] *Id.*

- the *Global Environment Facility (GEF)* operates the Convention's general financing mechanism,[11] including channelling grant or loan funds to developing countries for actions to address climate change mitigation and adaptation. The GEF has played a significant role in funding technology transfer, both explicitly and implicitly as part of its role as the financing mechanism.

There is no mention of intellectual property in the legal obligations under the UNFCCC and the Kyoto Protocol. UNFCCC Article 4.3 specifies that industrialized countries must cover 'the agreed full incremental costs of implementing measures that are covered by paragraph 1 of this Article and that are agreed between a developing country Party and the international entity or entities referred to in Article 11, in accordance with that Article'. However, there is some debate as to whether the agreed full costs of Article 4.3 also cover payment for licensing of technologies covered by intellectual property. In contrast, the Montreal Protocol Multilateral Fund[12] explicitly covers such payments in its operations. While the UNFCCC clearly establishes that costs of action should be borne by developed countries, it is less clear whether or not the costs are envisioned to cover such issues as the costs of accessing licences for IP.

The international framework is crucial to understanding why developing countries feel a need to act, especially on intellectual property and technology transfer. However, it is crucial to clearly define the *type* of problem that intellectual property protection can pose for technology transfer to address climate change. This next section tries to provide some basic introduction to the kinds of IP implicated by the climate change debate and the kinds of IP-related actions that states are considering.

---

[11] The GEF is also a finance mechanism for: The Convention on Biological Diversity; The United Nations Framework Convention on Climate Change; The United Nations Convention to Combat Desertification; The Stockholm Convention on Persistent Organic Pollutants. For more information visit http://www.gefweb.org/ (last visited 7 March 2012).

[12] The Montreal Protocol on Substances that Deplete the Ozone Layer is a protocol to the Vienna Convention for the Protection of the Ozone layer. In ways similar to the Kyoto Protocol, the Montreal Protocol establishes quantified commitments on the parts of industrialized countries and provides for technology transfer to developing countries. In addition, the Montreal Protocol explicitly set up a fund to accomplish technology transfer and financial support to developing countries.

III.　UNDERSTANDING THE IP MECHANISM

Intellectual property rights (IPRs) can be a positive force, facilitating licensing which allows the transfer of knowledge to occur securely and predictably. In the case of climate change, we are primarily concerned with patents, as the primary form of IP that implicates technology transfer. At the core, patents are designed as an incentive system to encourage the production and dissemination of new knowledge and information. The primary incentive is to encourage the translation of research into technological products, and to have the methods of producing those products, and the products themselves diffused. To do so, it has proven necessary to provide limited periods of exclusivity to inventors so that, rather than keep their inventions secret, they are willing to produce and share them through commercial activities such as sales and licensing. The patent system has several built-in safety valves to ensure that appropriate patents are given (requiring patent applications to meet basic criteria such as novelty, inventive step, and industrial applicability) and that others can test and learn from the invention (providing research exceptions and requiring disclosure), encouraging follow-on innovation, and preventing wasteful duplication of efforts. In addition, there is a whole exogenous system of control over the behaviour of patent owners that exists in the realm of competition law.

However, patents may sometimes have negative effects. For example, patents can create a type of monopoly control through the exclusive rights they confer on the owners of patented technology or knowledge. In this sense they may reduce competition, maintaining high product prices above marginal cost of production as the patent owner has no incentive to lower the price of the technology or make it more competitive. Thus, intellectual property is a trade off between present (static) anti-competitive costs and the generation of future technologies (dynamic cost).

A.　The Patent Mechanism and Technology Transfer

It is crucial for the purposes of discussing technology transfer to distinguish between the price of a product embodying knowledge/technology and the price of the knowledge/technology itself. Generally, as a function of normal pricing, the price paid for goods will include the price paid by the producer/seller for the access to the knowledge/technology. The concerns and goals will be very different depending on whether the primary concern is access to the products embodying the knowledge/technology or the knowledge/technology itself.

When speaking about technology transfer, the discourse tends to conflate two issues: namely access to the goods embodying the knowledge/technology or access to the knowledge/technology itself.

Where the issue is access to goods there are two levels of concern. The first is ensuring the normal flow of goods by making certain that prices of products are not set so high that it is too expensive for the relevant economic actors to afford. The second level, which applies to climate change the most, is ensuring that prices of products are not set so high that they make it too uneconomical to adopt 'climate-friendly' technologies.

Where the issue is access to the knowledge there are multiple concerns, primarily related to those situations where there is a need to change production processes themselves as the source of the problem. In such cases, where access to technologies is required to change the nature of a production process some of the most difficult problems to overcome are refusals to license, the high cost of licensing, and patent owners maintaining a monopoly on the knowledge so as to prevent competition. The final element is particularly undesirable as without it, countries or firms can produce competing products, thus more efficiently achieving widespread dissemination of the knowledge and products. The knowledge and/or technology may then be used and adapted or particularized to local market conditions.

B.   Intervening to Address IP Barriers and Potential Effects on Incentives and Dissemination

All these concerns prompt responses from governments to address supply problems. Actions taken to reduce monopolies and force sharing of knowledge or to enforce lowering of prices of goods may affect incentives to produce future technologies. The extent and effect of that lowering are in dispute but it is clear that at least some economic stakeholders will act as if they believe this to be the case. In addition, the patent is a market-based mechanism. Where no group of purchasers with consumer power exists there is zero incentive to research and develop technologies for that market, or to produce and distribute technologies that serve the needs of that market.

Intervention, then, need only occur when there is a market failure – based on the principle that intervention is justified where there is insufficient distribution of products embodying a technology in the national market to meet demand at a price that is affordable. This justification may be even stronger in a situation of emergency, threats to survival, the environment, health, human rights and other fundamental needs that economic policies such as intellectual property are designed to achieve. Clearly, there are interventions beyond the intellectual property sphere that could be carried out. There are a variety of ways this may be achieved. Industrialized countries could assist through direct aid, purchasing the goods for transfer to developing countries. They could also offer tax incentives and subsidies for exporting companies. Developing countries could put public procurement programs in place and offer lower import tariffs on environmentally sustainable technologies. However, where these place the burden and cost of action on developing countries, such options contravene the letter and spirit of the UNFCCC framework, hence the search for unilateral options that shift the cost to actors from industrialized countries and do not place the costs of accessing technology on developing country actors.

In the absence of financial or other support from industrialized countries, developing countries then have to seek out unilateral options. The kinds of IP interventions that are sometimes proposed to address the production and access to goods problem include:

- *compulsory licences*, which are licences normally issued by the government, without the consent of the right holder, to another economic actor to use the patent;
- *working requirements*, where a right holder is required to 'work', i.e. produce, the product in the domestic market in order to continue to receive patent protection. Failure to do so may result in revocation or the issuance of a compulsory licence;
- *exceptions and limitations* to patent rights, which would involve the introduction of legislation to allow specific acts or actors to engage in and use the patent for stated public policy purposes without being considered to have infringed the patent e.g. a research exception;
- *patent exclusions*, namely excluding from patentability certain technology sectors deemed to be necessary and crucial to achieving specific public policy goals; and
- *parallel imports*, i.e. importing goods produced and put on the market in another country, with the consent of the right holder or because the technology is not patent protected.

Addressing the access to goods problem is somewhat different from that of access to the technologies. In an emergency, the priority is the production of more goods at a cheaper price in as short a period of time as possible. Thus access to the goods is a priority, and concerns regarding the generation of future technologies fade into the background. We can see that this is the case in the case of vaccine production for swine flu, for example. In the climate change arena, this is most applicable to climate change adaptation, especially to address climate vulnerabilities in food security and health.

However, if the concern is for long term sustainable action, access to the knowledge or technology also needs to be ensured. This requires a more complex policy response, one that measures the gains from enforcing, or otherwise providing better technology transfer, versus reducing the incentives available to innovators. This is most relevant to the situation of mitigation technologies, where the goal is to ensure sufficient dissemination to enable appropriate action in the near term while ensuring sufficient incentives to create a knowledge market in green technologies that will serve to sustain GHG reduction through 2050 and beyond. This means that, for those countries with sufficient manufacturing and absorptive capacity, levels of IP protection that provide a strong enough market signal to outside companies to ensure voluntary licensing and FDI are a vital part of the policy mix.[13] However, there is a point beyond which the level of protection may provide diminishing returns and it is necessary for each country to find the optimal balance for itself and its specific market. Of note is that what empirical data exists suggests that, in comparison to other technology sectors, patents do not play a large role in providing incentives for research and development for environmentally sustainable technologies, although they may play a greater role in determining targets for flows of FDI and licensing for middle income countries.[14] However, there is clearly a point beyond which patents and other IP protection may inhibit the kinds of positive technology spillovers which are the public policy aim of FDI measures aimed at encouraging technology transfer in the first place.

An added complication in the arena of climate technologies is that there may be significant elements of technologies that are maintained as trade secrets which fall outside the realm of patents as an incentive system and form part of a broader system of protection against unfair competition. Access to such trade secrets, or undisclosed information, may be necessary to ensure effective availability and transfer of knowledge.

As previously noted, for the access to goods problem, there may indeed be options that lie outside the IP arena but the ones of most use to developing countries are those that fall within the 'common but differentiated responsibilities' framework of the UNFCCC. Of course, industrialized countries could publicly fund research and development, leading to publicly owned knowledge. This knowledge could be transferred between

---

[13]   Keith Maskus, 'Differentiated Intellectual Property Regimes for Environmental and Climate Technologies' OECD Environment Working Papers, No. 17, OECD Publishing 2010, 15.

[14]   *Id.*, 17.

governments or between governments and firms. They could also provide subsidies for those firms who lower the cost of licences offered to firms in developing countries. Developing countries could implement environmental standards and enforcement (regulatory structuring) and tax incentives for companies which used environmentally sustainable knowledge. However, where financial and other support from industrialized countries is not forthcoming, developing countries will seek other unilateral options aimed at ensuring access to knowledge and technology. These include some of those described above:

- working requirements;
- technology transfer and other performance requirements to qualify for foreign direct investment;
- compulsory licences;
- research and other patent exceptions;
- patent exclusions;
- and the application of competition law.

In considering these unilateral IP interventions developing countries are required to comply with the existing international framework for the protection of intellectual property, the TRIPS Agreement. It is precisely the issue of whether such interventions are available and in conformity with the TRIPS Agreement that drives developing country critiques of the international system and the argument for amending or restructuring the international IP framework.

IV. INTERPRETING TRIPS AND THE LIMITS ON UNILATERAL ACTION

A. Introduction

Addressing climate change will require a major shift in production and consumption patterns across the majority of sectors in most economies. Developing countries have the added complication of ensuring greater access to energy and energy services as they work to reduce emissions. This suggests that any international solution to address the policy space needs of developing countries cannot be limited to a specific sector but must be sufficiently flexible to cover *all* the relevant sectors identified under the UNFCCC and Kyoto Protocol. In this sense, the climate change problem is fundamentally distinct from that addressed by the Montreal Protocol, which covered primarily a single sector with a limited set of technologies.

In addition, account must be taken of the special role that emerging economies play as targets for technology transfer but also as a vector for enabling technology transfer to other developing countries. China, Brazil and India are beginning to compete well on production and dissemination of clean technologies. They are also the countries in which there may be clearest evidence of significant patenting of clean technologies in developing countries.[15] However, they are also the most likely developing countries to be able to afford to pay reasonable market rates for licensing of technologies. The problems that they face are ones of accessing licences for existing technologies from potential competitors in industrialized countries thus dealing with such issues as refusals to license, above market rates for technology or restrictive licensing practices. They also urgently want to participate in new and innovative research on clean technology and generate leading companies that are IP holders themselves. Their most urgent need is for the creation of a transparent and equal playing field for licensing of technologies, as they generally have sufficient domestic production capacity. However, emerging economies are also the most likely to have to take on quantified emissions reductions obligations in some form in the new post-Kyoto framework and thus have a fundamental need for access to existing technologies to help them make the transition out of technologies in which they have significant sunk costs.

Least developed countries (LDCs) and other developing countries have an urgent need for access to existing products at low prices that will maintain and increase energy access. In general, these countries have little capacity for production and innovation of complex clean technologies, nor do they have the funds to purchase goods in quantities necessary. They are also the ones in least need of mitigation technologies, to the extent that they have no GHG emission reduction obligations and they have comparatively low levels of fossil fuel energy consumption. Their mitigation technology need is largely related to access to existing technology products, and the adaptation of low level technologies to local conditions. The evidence suggests that most mitigation technologies are not patented or otherwise IP protected in these countries.[16] However, the countries

---

[15]   Copenhagen Economics and the IPR Company 'Are IPR a Barrier to the transfer of Climate Change Technology?' Study Commissioned by European Commission DG Trade, January 2009, 18. Available at: http://trade.ec.europa.eu/doclib/docs/2009/february/tradoc_142371.pdf (last visited 7 March 2012).

[16]   Copenhagen Economics and the IPR Company 'Are IPR a Barrier to the transfer of Climate Change Technology?' Study Commissioned by European Commission DG Trade, January 2009. Available at: http://trade.ec.europa.eu/doclib/docs/2009/february/tradoc_142371.pdf (last visited 7 March 2012) and

from which LDCs and other developing countries tend to purchase low cost technology products, especially China, may be increasingly unable to provide these if they are unable to access licences for technologies that allow them to export to other developing countries. China, Brazil and India tend to be best placed to provide low cost mitigation technologies to other developing countries because their companies are better placed and more willing to establish production centres and distribution systems in economies that are less interesting, or too risky for companies from industrialized countries. The emerging economies can fill that gap but only if they can become production and distribution centres themselves and that will need to occur through access to licensing.

Any legal and regulatory assessment of the limits that TRIPS places on unilateral action by developing countries will have to take into account: the breadth of sectors and technologies that it will be necessary to address; and the special role played by emerging economies as intermediaries for technology production and distribution for other developing countries. The next two sections will carry out an assessment of the potential limitations that TRIPS may place on developing countries by first examining the specific provisions within the TRIPS Agreement itself, and then examining the ways in which the UNFCCC may play a role in shifting the boundaries of any TRIPS limitations.

B. TRIPs-specific Limitations on Unilateral Action

Developing countries have identified the TRIPS Agreement as the primary barrier to unilateral action. From a purely legal standpoint, the concern is that unilateral actions taken to address climate change will subject them to complaints by other countries under the WTO Dispute Settlement Understanding. There remains significant debate within climate change and IP circles as to whether the TRIPS Agreement truly poses such a barrier, and if there is a theoretical possibility that it does, whether such unilateral actions are even necessary in the first place. This section addresses both questions, as 'necessity' is a fundamental element of WTO provisions such at GATT Article XX, and which rears its head in several of the WTO covered agreements. The interpretation and jurisprudence

---

John Barton, 'New Trends in Technology Transfer: Implications for National and International Policy', Intellectual Property and Sustainable Development Series, Issue Paper No. 1, ICTSD February 2007. Available at: http://www.iprsonline.org/ resources/docs/Barton%20-%20New%20Trends%20Technology%20Transfer%20 0207.pdf (last visited 7 March 2012).

related to these necessity provisions may have an impact on how limiting the TRIPS Agreement is.

1. The broader WTO jurisprudence

There have been no WTO disputes regarding how actions to address environmental concerns should be treated under the TRIPS Agreement. However, the broader WTO jurisprudence on exceptions may have a strong influence on the interpretation of the TRIPS Agreement. The General Exceptions clause under the GATS, for example, has been interpreted in ways similar to those under Article XX of the GATT and the jurisprudence on the 'necessity' test may be useful in this context.[17]

The GATT exceptions are generally the last stop in a series of analytical steps looking at like products and discrimination. It is in the context of these exceptions that the public policy aim of a measure is directly addressed. In this context, analyses are divided into two steps: the chapeau and the applicable sub-articles. For the purposes of this chapter we will focus primarily on the jurisprudence on Article XX(b) which embodies the 'necessity' requirement regarding measures to protect plant, animal and human health, with only a short overview of other issues.

The first case which addressed Article XX, in particular Article XX(b), was *Tuna – Dolphin II.*[18] The GATT Panel used an extremely narrow interpretation of Article XX on the basis that environmental measures would threaten international trade in goods and the exception should therefore be read extremely narrowly.[19]

In the post-GATT period since *Tuna – Dolphin II*, WTO Panels and the Appellate Body have moved towards a broader approach to Article XX. In examining environmental measures under Article XX(b) and XX(g), WTO jurisprudence places some limitations, while also exercising some deference. We can note:

1. The kinds of measures considered to be covered by Article XX(b) and XX(g) are very broad.[20]

---

[17]   Nathalie Bernasconi-Osterwalder et al., *Environment and Trade: A Guide to WTO Jurisprudence,* (London: Earthscan, 2006), 77.

[18]   GATT Panel Report, *United States – Restrictions on Imports of Tuna,* DS29/R, 16 June 1994, unadopted (*US – Tuna (EEC) also known as Tuna-Dolphin II*).

[19]   Nathalie Bernasconi-Osterwalder et al., note 17 above, 76.

[20]   Appellate Body Report, *United States – Standards for Reformulated and Conventional Gasoline*, WT/DS2/AB/R, adopted 20 May 1996, DSR 1996:I, 3 (*US – Gasoline*), Section III.A.

2. Under Article XX(g), the term 'exhaustible natural resources' is also interpreted very broadly.[21]
3. In examining the 'relating to' obligation under XX(g), the Appellate body does not require that the policy be primarily aimed at environmental aims, but only that there be a 'relationship between the measure at stake and the legitimate policy of conserving exhaustible natural resources'.[22]

The 'necessity' requirement of Article XX(b) is at the core of how the WTO relates to regulations to protect human, animal and plant life and health. The exact scope of this requirement remains unclear, although it has been addressed by several WTO Panels and the Appellate Body.[23] Initial decisions suggested that a measure would qualify only if there were no other available GATT-consistent measures.[24] Otherwise the least-inconsistent and reasonably available measure would have to be applied.[25] Further cases also suggested that necessity did not imply that the measure should be indispensable, but should make a contribution to achieving its policy objective. In other words, the measure does not need to be sufficient, in and of itself, to meet the policy goal.[26]

In July 2011, a panel report applied these standards, especially for Article XX(b) in *China – Raw Materials*.[27] Brought primarily by the US and Europe, the case challenged China's export restrictions (duties and quotas) on primary products and raw materials such as bauxite, coke, fluorspar, magnesium, manganese, silicon metal and zinc, and the re-use of scraps from primary production of these raw materials.

In considering the argument relating to export duties, under which, in any case, the panel found that China could not invoke Article XX to

---

[21]   Panel Report, *United States – Standards for Reformulated and Conventional Gasoline*, WT/DS2/R, adopted 20 May 1996, as modified by Appellate Body Report WT/DS2/AB/R, DSR 1996:I, 29, para. 6.37; Appellate Body Report *US – Shrimp*, para. 129 and para. 134.

[22]   Appellate Body Report, *US – Shrimp*, para. 135.

[23]   Nathalie Bernasconi-Osterwalder et al., note 17 above, 149.

[24]   *Id.*

[25]   *Id.*

[26]   Appellate Body Report, *Korea – Measures Affecting Imports of Fresh, Chilled and Frozen Beef*, WT/DS161/AB/R, WT/DS169/AB/R, adopted 10 January 2001, DSR 2001:I, 5, (*Korea – Various Measures on Beef*), para. 161.

[27]   Panel Reports, *China – Measures Related to the Exportation of Various Raw Materials*, WT/DS394/R and Corr.1/WT/DS395/R and Corr.1/WT/DS398/R and Corr.1, circulated to WTO Members 5 July 2011 (*China – Raw Materials*).

defend measures in violation of its accession protocol, there are some significant clarifications of how the standard of necessity would be applied. I primarily address the Article XX(b) analysis of the panel with respect to China's export duties and quotas on coke and silicon carbide, and looking broadly at primary product exports (EPRs). The Chinese argument on XX(b) related to the necessity of using duties and quotas to create a preference for recycling of scrap rather than primary extraction and production of raw materials.[28] The panel notes China's citation of the Appellate Body interpretation in *Brazil – Retreaded Tyres*[29] in support of its contention that a measure should '(i) bring about a material contribution to the achievement of its objective; and, (ii) be apt to produce a material contribution to the objective pursued, even if the contribution is not "immediately observable."'[30] China argued that while the materiality of a contribution can be examined by a panel, this cannot extend to an assessment of whether the right level of protection was chosen, again citing the Appellate Body in *Brazil – Retreaded Tyres*.[31] In general the panel did not go beyond the bounds of interpretation set up in *Brazil – Retreaded Tyres*. In its examination of the evidence the panel suggests that the measures must, in their formulation or justification, state the environmental justification. Otherwise this may be evidence of post-hoc justifications for the measures.[32] They appear to require more than just general relationships to environmental policy but specific and internally consistent justifications such that the measure is clear as to what its policy goal is. This begins to almost suggest a 'primarily' aimed at test such as that in XX(g). We note that the panel cites the inclusion of other aims in China's supporting documents such as 'energy, transport, the economy and economic development' to suggest that the primary aim is not environmental.[33] The panel seems to require that an explicit link must be made between the specific measure and environmental protection and that such measures cannot concurrently have other goals beyond the environmental.[34] The panel creates a standard that requires not only a statement of environmental purpose but how the measure will achieve the goals to be explicitly

---

[28]   *Id.,* para 7.471.

[29]   Appellate Body Report, *Brazil – Measures Affecting Imports of Retreaded Tyres*, WT/DS332/AB/R, adopted 17 December 2007, DSR 2007:IV, 1527 (*Brazil – Retreaded Tyres*).

[30]   Panel Reports, *China – Raw Materials*, para. 7.475.

[31]   Panel Reports, *China – Raw Materials*, para. 7.479.

[32]   *Id.,* para. 7.501.

[33]   *Id.,* para. 7.505.

[34]   *Id.*

stated in the legislation or the law.[35] Such a measure must then also be carried out in the context of a specific and comprehensive framework for protecting the environment and not be deduced from an accumulation of the multiplicity of related measures and goals.[36] The member must show how it contributes, but apparently this must be done in the legislation or rule establishing the measure itself.

In addressing the issue of least trade-restrictive measures, the panel examines the availability of alternative measures, and notes that since China argued that it had already taken the measures proposed by the complainant, it had negated any argument that they are not 'reasonably available'. The panel also finds that China's evidence of the implementation of such measures is weak, and concludes that these have not been exhausted to such an extent that they are not sufficient alternatives to export duties and quotas.[37] In essence, the panel requires that the alternative measure be fully utilized and exhausted before it will accept that they are not reasonably available and effective in materially contributing to the desired outcome, requiring the 'necessity' of export restrictions. The panel's evaluation concludes that while these measures appear to be reasonably available, China has not actually shown that it is implementing many of these measures and that there is therefore sufficient room for action to achieve its goals by implementing such actions rather than by using export restrictions.

One cannot escape the conclusion that while the standards established by the Appellate Body appear to leave some room in XX(b) for application of environmental measures that may restrict trade, the panel's evidentiary standard is so high that it is less likely that such measures would survive. Of particular concern is the argument by the panel that alternative measures that have been applied must be used to their full capacity before a trade-restrictive measure will be found to be justified, rather than focusing on the ability to make a material contribution, in concert with other measures. Clearly, export restrictions are viewed by the panel as one step short of the most restrictive kind of action that could have been taken i.e. a ban on trade, but the panel's analysis also suggests that the burden for meeting the Article XX(b) standard is quite high, requiring not just specific legislation but (i) implementation of the legislation in a way that specifically address the individual measures at hand; (ii) within a broader environmental regulatory framework, that states exactly how those meas-

---

[35] *Id.*, para. 7.507.
[36] *Id.*, para. 7.510.
[37] Panel Reports, *China – Raw Materials*, paras 7.569–7.570.

ures fit into the broader framework; and (iii) with a clear showing that other WTO-consistent measures have been exhausted, before the claimed measure is adopted. In its appeal,[38] China did not address the issue of Article XX(b) and thus the panel's analysis stands for the moment as the most recent application of the Appellate Body's articulation of the necessity test under the GATT 1994.

The necessity test also raises its head in other WTO Agreements including the Agreement on Sanitary and Phytosanitary Measures (SPS Agreement), in Articles 2.1 and 5.6; the Agreement on Technical Barriers to Trade (TBT Agreement) in Article 2.2; and the General Agreement on Trade in Services (GATS) in Article 14. While there are some differences, such as the burden of proof under the SPS Agreement, these Agreements also require, to varying extents, that the least trade-restrictive option be taken, where no alternative consistent measure can be found, rather than lay down a standard that focuses on the most effective environmental outcome. In September 2011, a panel report addressed the necessity issue in the TBT Agreement in *US – Tuna (Mexico)*.[39] The case was the third iteration of a long-running dispute between Mexico and the US regarding its 'Dolphin-Safe' tuna labelling scheme. In this case, the new issue related to the fact that a regional agreement (AIDPC) had established a dolphin-safe certification scheme for the Eastern Tropical Pacific (ETP) ocean region, which allowed for flexibility in national implementation, but provided a specific definition of 'dolphin-safe', referring to mortality and injury of dolphins, unlike the US definition which refers primarily to the mode of fishing i.e. chase and encirclement of dolphins. The regional agreement allows flexibility in implementation of the procedures under the agreement especially to address where the national law of the state may conflict with the standard established by the agreement.[40] Mexico argued that the US standard is inconsistent with Article 2.2 because 'its objective is not legitimate or, in the alternative, it is more trade-restrictive than *necessary* [emphasis added] to fulfil a legitimate objective taking account of the risks non-fulfilment would create'.[41] Article 2.2 defines legitimate objectives as

---

[38]　Appellate Body Reports, *China – Measures Related to the Exportation of Various Raw Materials*, WT/DS394/AB and Corr.1/WT/DS395/AB and Corr.1/WT/DS398/AB and Corr.1, circulated to WTO Members 30 January 2012 (*China – Raw Materials*).

[39]　Panel Report, *United States – Measures Concerning the Importation, Marketing and Sale of Tuna and Tuna Products* WT/DS381/R, circulated 15 September 2011, appealed 20 January 2012 (*US – Tuna II(Mexico)*).

[40]　*US – Tuna II (Mexico)* para. 2.41.

[41]　*US – Tuna II (Mexico)* para. 4.55.

those aimed at addressing 'national security requirements; the prevention of deceptive practices; protection of human health or safety, animal or plant life or health, or the environment'. However, unlike Article XX(b) of the GATT which is an exception to positive obligations and thus functions as a defence, the panel characterizes Article 2.2 of the TBT agreement as a positive obligation laying the burden on the complainant to show that the requirements of the article have not been met. This is a crucial difference in how necessity is measured because the burden of evidence and showing failure to comply lies with the complainant.

The panel adopts a two-step approach: first to determine whether the measures pursue a legitimate objective and then whether the measure is more trade-restrictive than necessary to achieve that objective.[42] In addressing the legitimacy of the objectives, the panel finds that it as long as the claimed measures falls within those described by Article 2.2, they 'need not be directed exclusively to endangered or depleted species or populations, to be legitimate'.[43] Unlike in *China – Raw Materials,* the panel in this case finds that having other objectives does not break the link between ends and means that the measure addresses. The panel also established that potentially adverse environmental effects in other areas do not necessarily affect the legitimacy of the claimed measure.[44] The panel easily found that the measures were legitimate. In determining 'necessity', the panel notes that some degree of trade-restrictiveness is clearly envisioned by Article 2.2 and that the necessity therefore is measured against possible alternative measures that would be less trade-restrictive.[45] Thus unlike GATT Article XX(b), the panel argues that necessity in TBT Article 2.2 is measured primarily against trade-restrictiveness rather than against the necessity for the achievement of the objective.[46] The panel finds more support in footnote 3 to Article 5.6 of the SPS Agreement, which also focuses on measuring necessity against the availability of less restrictive-trade measures. In that case footnote 3 requires the measure not just to be less trade-restrictive but significantly less trade-restrictive, which the panel uses as indicative but not dispositive.[47] The trade-restrictiveness analysis is modified by a consideration that any less restrictive-measure must not pose a greater risk of non-fulfilment of the legitimate objective.[48]

---

[42] *Id.*, para. 7.388.
[43] *Id.*, para. 7.437.
[44] *Id.*, para. 7.440.
[45] *US – Tuna II (Mexico)* para. 7.458.
[46] *Id.*, para. 7.460.
[47] *Id.*, para. 7.464.
[48] *Id.*, para. 7.467.

The panel's standard therefore involves a deep examination of exactly how the measure functions, so as to determine whether it actually functions to achieve the legitimate objective in the way claimed. This then allows the panel to compare it to the complainant's proposed alternative(s). In assessing the comparability of the measures, regarding consumer information in achieving the actual level of protection achieved by the challenged measure, the panel finds that the use in conjunction of the standards in the regional agreement with those of the US would indeed be less trade-restrictive. The panel found that the use of such standards is reasonably available and that the standards are equally capable of meeting the *actual* level of protection provided by the challenged measures, at least as far as the consumer information objective is concerned.[49] With respect to the objective of protecting animal health and the environment, the panel also finds that the US measures are only truly effective in the ETP fisheries region and cannot be considered to actually extend protection of dolphins outside of the region. The issue is therefore whether allowing Mexico to use the regional agreement standard would accomplish the same level of protection in terms of the dolphin populations aimed at by the US measures.[50] The panel finds that it does.

The *US – Tuna II (Mexico)* panel takes a very similar approach to that taken to cases under the SPS Agreement in analysing necessity. Driving that similarity is that these are positive obligations in which the burden lies with the complainant. In addition, the primary assessment lies in the trade-restrictiveness of the measure in relation to other methods. However, where the SPS Agreement requires a significant difference in trade-restrictiveness for the alternative measure to be accepted, the panel in *US – Tuna II (Mexico)* adopts a less stringent standard only requiring that the alternative be less trade-restrictive while still enabling the achievement of the legitimate objective at the level chosen by the respondent. This is supposedly in contrast to GATT XX(b) analyses which are meant to measure necessity against the capacity to contribute materially to the aim of protecting human, animal or plant life or health. However, the 2011 *China – Raw Materials* panel report suggests that even in such cases, the trade-restrictiveness of the measure is the primary measure of necessity even where there is a showing that the challenged measure contributes or is apt to contribute to the achievement of the objective.

The WTO jurisprudence suggests that the necessity test is still assessed very narrowly and may not be as useful a principle in enabling broad

---

[49]   *Id.*, paras 7.577–7.578.
[50]   *US – Tuna II (Mexico)* para. 7.612.

IP-related measures to ensure technology transfer to address climate change as it first seems. In particular, it is not clear that the measures would constitute the least restrictive measures. As noted in Section III, the issue with technology transfer is not that options are not available but that the options most in conformity with the UNFCCC are those that do not impose the burden on developing countries. The narrowness of the jurisprudence on necessity has implications for how the similar term is interpreted in the TRIPS Agreement, which I will elaborate on below.

2. TRIPS provisions and jurisprudence

The 'necessity' requirement is also used in Article 8.1 of the TRIPS Agreement, which states that:

> Members may, in formulating or amending their laws and regulations, adopt measures *necessary* to protect public health and nutrition, and to promote the public interest in sectors of vital importance to their socio-economic and technological development, provided that such measures are consistent with the provisions of this Agreement. (emphasis added)

There is similarity with respect to the legitimate objectives analyses conducted under the TBT and SPS agreements. TRIPS Article 8.1 specifically mentions 'public health and nutrition' as subject matter areas, but also the more general goal 'to promote the public interest', which is broader than the language in Article XX(b) of the GATT 1994, as well as that in Article 5.6 of the SPS Agreement and Article 2.2 of the TBT.

Crucially, the wording of Article 8.1 may also be construed as a positive obligation of the kind established in Article 5.6 of the SPS Agreement and in Article 2.2 of the TBT Agreement. Thus the burden of proof of non-compliance with Article 8.1 would lie on the complaining party to show that such measures were not necessary. This issue remains unaddressed in the jurisprudence described below, in part because the only panel that has addressed the issue appears to have simply treated Article 8.1 as synonymous with the limitations and exceptions enumerated in Articles 30, 31 and 40.

The issue of the burden of proof is complicated by the fact that, unlike GATT Article XX exceptions which are premised on the idea that the measures in question are not in conformity with the other requirements of the GATT, in the case of Article 8.1 of the TRIPS Agreement, the test already states that such provisions must be in conformity with the TRIPS Agreement before they are tested. The key part of the provision that enables this is the final element of the sentence: 'provided that such measures are consistent with the provisions of this agreement'. The task for any person seeking to create some analogy or symmetry with Article 2.2 of the

TBT Agreement, Article 5.6 of the SPS Agreement and Article XX(b) of the GATT 1994, is to determine the exact effect of that last sentence of Article 8.1.

As an initial premise, we must establish that Article 8 has to be given full effect and cannot simply be left as a statement devoid of any specific content. It cannot be that Article 8 is entirely subsumed by Articles 30 and 31 and other limitations and exceptions.[51] The first part of Article 8.1 must be given content separate from that of other articles on limitations and exceptions and on balancing rights and obligations. Whereas Article 30 (on exceptions) and 31 (on compulsory licences) can be considered specific sub-sets of situations under Article 8, the article itself recognizes a broad right which in and of itself constitutes an additional scope beyond those of the 'exceptions' in the TRIPS Agreement.

In addition, Article 8 has to be seen as a reiteration of the basic principle of state sovereignty and rights to make policy in these crucial areas. As such, restrictions on that broad right must function as exceptions and should be construed narrowly, even where those rights are restricted by being submitted to regulation under an international treaty. The burden for non-compliance with Article 8 should be on those claiming that the discretion under the broad right established by Article 8.1 has been abused.

However, that burden may be shifted by the last sentence of Article 8.1. We are therefore tasked with answering the question of what is meant by 'consistent with the provisions of this agreement'. By definition this must of course include *all* the TRIPS articles. Thus Article 7[52] is one of the measures of consistency with the agreement, just as much as Articles 27, 30, or 31. The phrase may also have the consequence of shifting the burden of proof that would normally be the case in a positive obligation such as this one. In this case, we understand that the burden of showing that a measure is not in compliance with the provisions of the TRIPS Agreement lies with the complainant. The question is whether such a finding is final and dispositive regarding the TRIPS Agreement. Is it the

---

[51]   For a slightly contrary view, see Daniel Gervais, *The Trips Agreement: Drafting History and Analysis 2nd ed.*, (London: Sweet and Maxwell, 2003), 121, who views Article 8 as primarily a statement of the policy embodied on Articles 30, 31 and 40.

[52]   This requires that the 'protection and enforcement of intellectual property rights should contribute to the promotion of technological innovation and to the transfer and dissemination of technology, to the mutual advantage of producers and users of technological knowledge and in a manner conducive to social and economic welfare, and to a balance of rights and obligations'.

case that where a measure is found to be in violation of one of the rights established by Article 28,[53] that Article 8 cannot be used as an independent defence? That appears to be the case if the language is taken literally. This appears to be the same outcome even where a violation of Article 28 is found, *and* it is not excused under Article 30.[54] Thus, given the literal content of the last part of Article 8.1, it does not appear possible to access or give content to the first part of Article 8.1 where a measure is already found to be inconsistent with the any of the provisions of the TRIPS Agreement. Does that mean that the first part of Article 8.1 has no content?

The formulation in Article 8.1 is unique and not found in any of the other WTO covered agreements. For there to be an article that appears to allow flexibility to address key issues but conditions that flexibility on compliance is an unusual but, it appears, deliberate approach. Some sense of the meaning of the provision can be found in looking at the legislative history of the two related provisions, Article 7 and Article 8 of the TRIPS Agreement, in the Uruguay Round negotiations.

The main body of the Anell text[55] included a draft on 'Principles':[56]

---

[53]   Article 28 states:

1. A patent shall confer on its owner the following exclusive rights:
(a) where the subject matter of a patent is a product, to prevent third parties not having the owner's consent from the acts of: making, using, offering for sale, selling, or importing(6) for these purposes that product;
(b) where the subject matter of a patent is a process, to prevent third parties not having the owner's consent from the act of using the process, and from the acts of: using, offering for sale, selling, or importing for these purposes at least the product obtained directly by that process.
2. Patent owners shall also have the right to assign, or transfer by succession, the patent and to conclude licensing contracts.

[54]   Article 30 states: 'Members may provide limited exceptions to the exclusive rights conferred by a patent, provided that such exceptions do not unreasonably conflict with a normal exploitation of the patent and do not unreasonably prejudice the legitimate interests of the patent owner, taking account of the legitimate interests of third parties.'

[55]   This was a draft titled 'Chair's Draft' produced by the Chair of the TRIPS Negotiating Group Mr Lars Anell in June 1990, on his own responsibility and then later adopted as a formal negotiating document. The text was 'Chairman's report to the Group of Negotiation on Goods, document MTN.GNG/NG11/W/76, dated July 23, 199 cited by Daniel Gervais, 'The TRIPS Agreement: Interpretation and Implementation' *EIPR* 1999, 21(3), 156–162, 157.

[56]   ICTSD/UNCTAD, *Resource Book on TRIPS and Development,* (Cambridge: Cambridge University Press, 2005). See p. 122, available at: http://www.iprsonline.org/unctadictsd/ResourceBookIndex.htm (last visited 7 March 2012).

8. Principles

8B.1 PARTIES recognize that intellectual property rights are granted not only in acknowledgement of the contributions of inventors and creators, but also to assist in the diffusion of technological knowledge and its dissemination to those who could benefit from it in a manner conducive to social and economic welfare and agree that this balance of rights and obligations inherent in all systems of intellectual property rights should be observed.

8B.2 In formulating or amending their national laws and regulations on IPRs, PARTIES have the right to adopt appropriate measures to protect public morality, national security, public health and nutrition, or to promote public interest in sectors of vital importance to their socio-economic and technological development.

8B.3 PARTIES agree that the protection and enforcement of intellectual property rights should contribute to the promotion of technological innovation and enhance the international transfer of technology to the mutual advantage of producers and users of technological knowledge.

With respect to Article 8.1, the later Brussels Draft[57] stated:

1. Provided that PARTIES do not derogate from the obligations arising under this Agreement, they may, in formulating or amending their national laws and regulations, adopt measures necessary to protect public health and nutrition, and to promote the public interest in sectors of vital importance to their socio-economic and technological development.

The constraint in Article 8.1, as it was finally adopted, is that the measures they adopt should not violate the terms of the agreement. The UNCTAD IPRs Resource Book suggests that 'measures adopted by Members to address public health, nutrition and matters of vital socio-economic importance should be presumed to be consistent with TRIPS, and that any Member seeking to challenge the exercise of discretion should bear the burden of proving inconsistency'.[58] In that sense, this comports with approaches from the TBT and SPS Agreements. This approach presumes that the sequence of examination begins with whether the measures are of the kind envisioned, and if they are, then it goes on to address the issue of whether they are inconsistent. Again, this comports with the approach taken under the SPS and TBT Agreements. Under such an approach, there therefore exists a difference in scope between Article 30, and Article 8. Thus, where a measure is aimed specifically to 'protect public health and nutrition, and to promote the public interest in sectors of vital importance

---

[57]   This draft was produced six months later at the Brussels Conference in December 1990. See Daniel Gervais, 'The TRIPS Agreement: Interpretation and Implementation' *EIPR* 1999, 21(3), 156–162, p. 157.

[58]   See ICTSD/UNCTAD, note 56 above, 127.

to their socio-economic and technological development' then Article 8 would create a presumption that the measure is consistent, which must be rebutted by the complainant. This would comport with the structure of Article 30 which requires no subject matter limitation on exceptions, or Article 31 which places no subject matter restriction on why compulsory licences can be granted. Article 8 would thus shift the burden for public interest measures whereas all other measures would be directly addressed by Articles 30 and 31. This would require that a claim be structured in the following way: the complainant would assert that a measure either does not fall under those contemplated by Article 8.1, and even if it did, the measure was not consistent with the provisions of the TRIPS Agreement. The burden of showing inconsistency would then lie with the complainant which can be crucial in the weighing of evidence. This approach however only allows Article 8.1 to have a burden shifting role in certain situations. This approach, however, does not negate the fact that compliance with Article 8.1 would remain dependent on either not violating a right granted by a provision or by coming within the boundaries of an exception or limitation enumerated elsewhere in the TRIPS Agreement. There would still be no substantive effect to the first half of Article 8.1

An alternative approach to that advocated by the authors of the UNCTAD IPRs Resource Book would be to take the approach that measures *must* be consistent with the TRIPS Agreement before they will be covered by the terms of Article 8.1 In that case, an examination of consistency takes place first and if the measures are found to be inconsistent, Article 8.1 plays the role of a thumb on the scale to move measures that fall under its coverage back into consistency. This would not necessarily be in literal line with the wording of the article but not doing so leaves the first part of Article 8 devoid of content. The negotiating history, as well as the broader context in which the TRIPS Agreement stands suggests that *literal* consistency with the TRIPS Agreement cannot be the limit of the effect of the provision. Why is the 'necessity' language in there if the consistency requirement has to be met? Article 8.1 cannot simply be co-terminous with the sum of the exceptions and limitations in the agreement. If that is the case why have Article 8.1 in the first place? Thus there must already be a sense in which the measures contemplated by Article 8 go beyond the strict limits of consistency. Necessity therefore could be seen as controlling how far outside the limits of consistency they may go and that it may not allow the provisions of the agreement to be entirely null and void. It may be possible to refer back to the broader jurisprudence on 'necessity' from the SPS and TBT Agreements and argue that the necessity test standard of 'least-inconsistent and reasonably available measure' should be applied here.

In addition, Article 8.1 is supported by Article 7, which Members must also comply with in their implementation of the TRIPS Agreement.[59] Authors such as Derclaye[60] and Correa[61] argue that Article 7 establishes that intellectual property rights clearly must be in service of broader social values. Where the provision of rights contradicts or conflicts with broader public welfare goals, the article provides a means by which IPR protection can be modified, diminished or removed. Correa also argues that while Article 8 contains the limitations on 'consistency', Article 7 does not and thus, one of the provisions with which Article 8 must be consistent is Article 7, as well as the preambles.[62] Thus, as an overriding principle, interpreters are bound to ensure that Article 7 is given as much effect as any other provisions of the agreement and cannot be considered only hortatory.

Article 7 provides guidance for the interpreter of the TRIPS Agreement, emphasizing that it is designed to strike a balance among desirable objectives. As Article 7 makes clear, TRIPS negotiators did not mean to abandon a balanced perspective on the role of intellectual property in society. However, given the structure of Article 8.1 the approach that seems to have won out over others is that any attempt to justify measures to protect health and nutrition and to promote the public interest in sectors of vital importance to socio-economic and technological development cannot rely solely on Articles 7 and 8 but must enter first through other provisions in the TRIPS Agreement and then, in the course of applying these articles, use the weight of Articles 7 and 8.1 to tip the scales in favour of justifiable policy actions. This has ostensibly been the approach that has been taken in the context of the interpretation of TRIPS provisions relating to exceptions and limitations. The next few sections address the extent to which this issue has been addressed by panels with respect to patents, and whether Article 8.1 has truly been given content, such that Members are actually able to take measures to protect human health and nutrition and to promote the public interest in sectors of vital importance to socio-economic and technological

---

[59]   Article 7 states: 'The protection and enforcement of intellectual property rights should contribute to the promotion of technological innovation and to the transfer and dissemination of technology, to the mutual advantage of producers and users of technological knowledge and in a manner conducive to social and economic welfare, and to a balance of rights and obligations.'

[60]   Estelle Derclaye, 'Intellectual Property Rights and Global Warming' 12 *John Marshall Review of Intellectual Property Law* 263 (2008), 270. Available at SSRN: http://ssrn.com/abstract=1016864

[61]   Carlos M. Correa, *Trade Related Aspects of Intellectual Property Rights: A Commentary to The TRIPS Agreement,* (Oxford: Oxford University Press, 2007), 99–101.

[62]   *Id.*, 107.

development. As a preliminary matter, we can note that the Appellate Body itself has found that Article 7 and 8 have yet to be interpreted in a way that provides guidance to their applicability in future cases.[63]

TRIPS exceptions The TRIPS Agreement contains no General Exceptions article such as that embodied by GATT Article XX, but for each specific category of rights, it establishes a standard exception (for copyright in Article 13, for trademarks in Article 17, for patents in Article 30). In the context of the discussion on transfer of technology, the area of most concern is patent law, as well as any technology transfer provisions. In that context we can point not just to Article 8.1, but also to Article 30.[64]

Article 30 was interpreted in the *Canada – Pharmaceutical Patents*[65] case. In this case, Canada defended the stockpiling of medicines prior to the expiration of a patent as well as allowing generic competitors to produce samples of the product for the purposes of regulatory approval. Canada based its entire case on the assertion that the measures fell within the Article 30 exceptions. The panel divides the Article 30 test into three cumulative steps. The measure:

(i)   must be 'limited';
(ii) must not 'unreasonably conflict with normal exploitation of the patent'; and
(iii) must not 'unreasonably prejudice the legitimate interests of the patent owner, taking account of the legitimate interests of third parties'.[66]

The examination carried out by the panel is sequential and cumulative. *All* three steps had to be met in sequence, if the measure was to be found consistent with Article 30.[67]

---

[63]   Appellate Body Report, *Canada – Term of Patent Protection*, WT/DS170/AB/R, adopted 12 October 2000, DSR 2000:X, 5093 (*Canada – Patent Term*), para. 101.

[64]   Article 30 states: 'Members may provide limited exceptions to the exclusive rights conferred by a patent, provided that such exceptions do not unreasonably conflict with a normal exploitation of the patent and do not unreasonably prejudice the legitimate interests of the patent owner, taking account of the legitimate interests of third parties.'

[65]   Panel Report, *Canada – Patent Protection of Pharmaceutical Products*, WT/DS114/R, adopted 7 April 2000, DSR 2000:V, 2289 (*Canada – Pharmaceutical Patents*).

[66]   Panel Report, *Canada – Pharmaceutical Patents*, para. 7.20.

[67]   *Id.*

As an initial issue the panel had to first determine the role that Article 8.1 should play: whether it constituted an independent defence; if not, what role it had in the interpretation of Article 30 with respect to burden of proof or the interpretation of the terms in Article 30.

The panel placed the burden of proof on the party claiming justification under the exceptions. As noted above in discussing the role of Article 8.1, it is not obvious that this would be the case given the approach in the TBT Agreement and the SPS Agreement. Reading Article 30 and Article 8.1 together, it is equally plausible that since Article 30 contemplates measures which are in conflict with other rights provided by the TRIPS Agreement and since the right to take such measures is acknowledged and embedded in Article 8.1, the burden for showing that the measures do not comply with TRIPS Article 30 should lie with the complainant. In contrast, the panel argued that Article 30 functioned as an exception in the same way that Article XX(b) did in the GATT 1994.[68] The article only applies where a measure has already been found non-compliant with other positive obligations in the TRIPS Agreement, in this case Article 28. Thus as a defence that has to be asserted, the burden lies on the respondent who asserts it and thus should have the burden of showing it. As noted above, this approach to the burden of proof is also in part a function of the structure of the claim. The European Communities did not claim that Canada was in violation of Article 8.1, but that it was in violation of Articles 27.1, 28.1 and 33, and thus was in violation until it could justify it through some other TRIPS provision. In its defence, Canada did not argue for a restructuring of the claim through Article 8.1 but asserted only that it should have interpretive weight in applying Article 30. Thus, no panel has addressed what would occur in the circumstances under which a respondent argued that a claim challenging the application of a measure to protect health and nutrition and to promote the public interest in sectors of vital importance to socio-economic and technological development is more properly made under Article 8.1.

Canada first asserted that Article 30 should be read in light of the objectives and purposes of the TRIPS Agreement, in particular Article 8.1. The panel acknowledged that Article 8.1 had some interpretive force, but viewed the existence of Article 30, and the way it was narrowly constructed, as a significant indicator that Article 30 should not be read to alter the 'negotiated' balance exhibited by the TRIPS Agreement.[69] The panel stated: 'Obviously, the exact scope of Article 30's authority will

---

[68]   *Id.*, para. 7.16.
[69]   Panel Report, *Canada – Pharmaceutical Patents*, para. 7.26.

depend on the specific meaning given to its limiting conditions. The words of those conditions must be examined with particular care on this point. Both the goals and the limitations stated in Articles 7 and 8.1 must obviously be borne in mind when doing so as well as those of other provisions of the TRIPS Agreement which indicate its object and purposes.'

Thus it appears that the panel would at least consider the goals stated in Article 8.1 in interpreting the provisions of the three-step test. However, when examining the actual reasoning of the panel, the influence of Article 8.1 is difficult to discern.

In examining the panel's interpretation of the first step, i.e. the 'limited' nature of the measure, there appears to be no way for the Article 7 or Article 8.1 public interest elements to enter into what may be considered 'limited'. In the first instance the panel adopts the position that the term 'limited' must be read in conjunction with the term 'exception', so that 'limited' is read as narrow, rather than as 'definite' or defined in scope, as argued by Canada. The panel argued that by definition, an exception is already meant to be a curtailment of rights, and thus the use of the term 'limited' in this context must modify that curtailment so that it becomes a narrow curtailment.

In the second instance, regarding whether a measure is indeed 'limited' the panel's reasoning means that this is assessed purely against the extent to which the patent right is affected.[70] Therefore, the test is fundamentally one that requires that the measure have a small qualitative and quantitative effect on the rights of the patent holder. If a measure does not meet this test, its public policy purpose(s) need never be examined or taken into account. No matter how dire a need the measure is attempting to address, if the measure is not limited, then it fails the test.[71] Thus the stockpiling exception failed at the first hurdle because it allowed unlimited production in the six months prior to expiry of the patent, while the regulatory exception passed because it was limited to levels of production solely for the purposes of meeting the goal of regulatory approval. At no point in the analysis does the panel address Article 7 or Article 8.1 in determining how to address the interpretation of the term 'limited'.

One can contrast this approach with the way in which an examination of 'least-restrictive trade' measure embodied in GATT Article XX(b), Article 5.6 of the SPS Agreement and Article 2.2 of the TBT Agreement might take place. In those provisions, the 'limited' nature of a measure, i.e. its effect on trade, is assessed against the reasonable availability of other

---

[70]   Panel Report, *Canada – Pharmaceutical Patents,* para. 7.31.
[71]   *Id.*, paras 7.30–7.38.

measures which would achieve its goal. In the approach to Article 30, there is no way to balance the 'restrictiveness' or level of violation of the measure against other less restrictive or less violating measures that would achieve the same goal. Because the panel approaches the test cumulatively and fails to use Article 8.1 to influence the interpretation of whether a measure is limited, it is possible to never address the public interest goal of a measure in assessing Article 30. This would seem to render Article 8.1 devoid of any content with respect to Article 30. Whether such an approach would be sustained by the Appellate Body is an open question as the panel decision in this case was never appealed. Thus while the panel's decision is therefore not required to be carried over into future panel decisions on similar issues, this approach will continue to influence the interpretation of Article 30, unless a respondent makes the point of raising an Article 8.1 argument in this context.

In examining the regulatory approval exceptions conformity with the second and third steps, the panel continues to fail to apply Articles 7 and 8.1. In interpreting the second step, the panel first defined 'normal exploitation' as 'to exclude all forms of competition that could detract significantly from the economic returns anticipated from a patent's grant of market exclusivity'.[72] They sought support for this from a dictionary definition of 'normal', which did not address the normative aspects of the definition but focused on the elements referring to 'regular, usual, typical, ordinary, conventional'.[73] However, finding that the measure in question (i.e. production for regulatory approval) did not conflict with normal exploitation, the panel did not find it necessary to decide whether the conflict was unreasonable. What is key is that the panel worked on the presumption that a patent holder had the right to expect income from *all* forms of exploitation. At no point is a normative element included that details certain kinds of markets from which a right holder should not be expected to receive income or be able to exploit nor certain kinds of measures that a state has a right to take as articulated by Article 8.1. Thus public interest justifications play no part in this portion of the analysis either. The panel made no reference to any influence that Article 8.1 or Article 7 might have on their understanding on what constituted normal exploitation which would have been modified by the assertion in Article 8.1 that states may take actions to protect human health and nutrition and to promote the public interest in sectors of vital importance to socio-economic and technological development. It is possible that the panel

---

[72]   Panel Report, *Canada – Pharmaceutical Patents,* para. 7.55.
[73]   *Id.,* para. 7.54 citing the New Shorter Oxford Dictionary, 1940.

would have referred to Article 8.1 in determining the unreasonableness of the conflict, but since that was not addressed, it remains an open question. If in fact Article 8.1 is not addressed in determining whether or not a conflict exists, the only way in which Article 8.1 can have an influence on the interpretation of the second step is through an assessment of the reasonableness of the conflict. Applying Article 8.1, those measures that passed the first step, conflicted with the normal exploitation of the right but were of the kind covered by Article 8.1 would therefore be presumed to pass the second step. Any other outcome would, again, seem to rob Article 8.1 of any content with respect to Article 30.

The panel then moved to the third step, describing what the 'legitimate interests' of the right holder and third parties might be. The panel noted that '[t]o make sense of the term "legitimate interests" in this context, that term must be defined in the way that it is often used in legal discourse – as a *normative* [emphasis added] claim calling for protection of interests that are "justifiable" in the sense that they are supported by relevant public policies or other social norms'.[74] This would appear to have been an ideal place to insert the measures contemplated by Article 8.1 into the assessment, as a way of deciding the extent of the legitimate interests of the right holder and what were the legitimate interests of third parties. However, while examining what were 'legitimate interests' of the patent holder, the panel provided no further indication of what might be encompassed by the legitimate interests of third parties, as it found that there was no legitimate interest of the patent holder at play in the regulatory approval process. Thus, as far as patent law goes, there is no indication of how future panels or the Appellate Body might view: what would constitute prejudice to the legitimate interests of the right holder; what would constitute unreasonable prejudice; what would be defined as the legitimate interests of third parties. Again, an approach that would be consistent with Article 8.1 would take measures that fell within the scope of the article as presumptively of the kind that lay outside the legitimate interests of the right holder given that Article 8.1 is a clear statement of WTO Members' right to balance the interests of the right holder against others as it deems appropriate in addressing public health and nutrition and promoting the public interest in sectors of vital importance to socio-economic and technological development. For exceptions that do not fall within the scope of the measures contemplated in Article 8.1, the unreasonableness of the prejudice to the legitimate interests could still be tested, including the interests of third parties that are not covered by Article 8.1.

---

[74]   Panel Report, *Canada – Pharmaceutical Patents*, para. 7.69.

In looking at the entire analytical approach by the panel in the *Canada – Pharmaceutical Patents* case, there still seems to be room in the approach for the application of Article 8.1 in the second and third steps. However, if the panel's approach to the application of the first step of Article 30 continues to be the standard, and the burden of proof remains as stated by the panel, then the key hurdle that any measures to address climate change face may be that of being appropriately limited. As such, measures can be found invalid long before any justification can be considered.

The interplay between Article 8.1 and Article 30 is crucial when we consider what room Article 30 leaves for the creation of exceptions to address access to and transfer of climate technologies for adaptation and mitigation. The first question to be answered is whether the proposed measures would technically fall under Article 30 as an exception. For example, a working requirement for patents would be difficult to categorize as an exception in that it functions as an additional burden placed on the right holder to carry out certain activities in order not to lose the patent right. This would be similar to what the patent holder has to do in paying renewal fees at intervals during the life of the patent. In contrast, an exception allows third parties to carry out certain acts that would nominally be disallowed by the existence of the patent and either justifies a specific category of activities related to the patent (e.g. non-commercial research) or allows a specific category of actors to carry out activities related to the patent (e.g. exceptions to use or adaptation for students or blind people). Given the structure of the TRIPS Agreement, compulsory licences are also not classified as exceptions and the standards for their application are also very different, as will be addressed below. In addition, actions to exclude certain categories of technologies from patents would also not function as exceptions, as these again, relate to the conditions for grants of patents rather than directly enabling third parties to act while a patent is still in force.

Article 8.1 of TRIPS clearly envisions measures capable of addressing broad sectoral issues. It allows Members to take actions to promote the public interest in *sectors* of vital importance to socio-economic and technological development. Applying that standard to the area of climate change it can be argued that addressing climate change mitigation and adaptation is in the public interest of countries signatory to the UNFCCC. It can also be argued that certain specifically identified sectors, (e.g. drought-resistant agriculture, or fuel-efficient motor vehicles) constitute sectors of vital importance to socio-economic and technological development. This would justify exceptions that are sufficiently broad to have an effect on a whole sector. However, the framework for the creation of exceptions under TRIPS as outlined by the panel in *Canada – Pharmaceutical Patents* does not include Article 8.1 in determining whether an exception is limited. Only in the second and third steps of the Article 30 analysis can the justification in Article 8.1 potentially be considered. Thus, the key design limitation may be in ensuring that an exception is sufficiently limited. Given the scope of the climate change challenge, is it possible to envision exceptions that would meet this standard? If the aim is to fundamentally alter the direction and use of climate technologies by producers and consumers, the exception clearly cannot exclude commercial activities. It is precisely these commercial activities that an exception would aim to address through research, development, and distribution of climate mitigation and adaptation technologies. For climate change purposes, an exception that was targeted at a limited set of actors may not be very effective as it would limit the kind of broad sectoral participation that climate change measures require. However, there may be circumstances, such as a clearly identified bottleneck, where such an exception targeted at a limited set of actors might be possible. The type of exception could relate perhaps to size of business enterprise, or to a category of actors such as students. For climate change, perhaps the size of the business enterprise could be relevant, but probably only when also limited to a specific product or set of products. This may be especially appropriate in an economic sector where many of the actors engage in small informal commerce. For example, such an exception could be applied to allow farmers with an agricultural holding below a certain size, and/or engaged in at least 50 per cent subsistence farming to save, sow, reuse, exchange and sell climate adapted seeds from their own crops, so as to encourage widespread use and adoption of drought resistant seeds for those farmers most in need of the ability to adapt to changing climates to ensure food security. Such an exception would still leave large scale commercial farmers of largely cash crops to still serve as the key market for the right holder.

The other approach to exceptions that may be more viable for designing climate change measures, would be to look at a specific set of especially desirable activities and exempt those from liability. The classic type of patent exception in such cases is the research exception. Usually limited to noncommercial activities, the research exception can, however, be made broader to include research and development that could lead or is meant to lead to a commercial product. In the case of the 'regulatory approval' exception in the *Canada – Pharmaceutical Patents* case, research and development on the patented drug is allowed to enable third parties to learn how to produce generic versions of the drug *AND* production is allowed to the extent that such production is used only for the purposes of showing regulators that the generic version is equivalent to the patented product. However, the product cannot be stockpiled or sold until after the expiration of the patent. A climate research and development exception could then be limited in several dimensions: it would be limited to research and development on patented technologies with the aim of addressing climate change mitigation and adaptation; it could be used only for the development of improved, adapted or entirely new products or processes; it would be limited to research up to the point of prototyping but disallowing any activity related to marketing, licensing or sales of the new product or process. Such a research exception would be of benefit to stakeholders in emerging economies who already have such research capacity, such as in Brazil, India and China, which could then produce and distribute those products in countries were the patent was not protected (many developing countries).

As much as the previous set of suggestions seems to argue for the fact that designing TRIPS-compliant exceptions is a real possibility, this is modified by two caveats. The first is that, for such exceptions to be possible, TRIPS jurisprudence must take a different approach to the application of Articles 7 and 8.1 which must be included in at least the second and third steps of the Article 30, three-step test. The second is that exceptions are by definition a limited tool and can never go so far as to fundamentally alter the balance of power away from the right holder. The question that arises is how many exceptions can be created and how large can their cumulative effect be before they run afoul of the broader obligation to provide effective patent protection.

The use of exceptions as a policy tool would have to be part of a broader concerted effort that will have interactions with other patent limitations and TRIPS flexibilities. Using exceptions to manage sectoral development will require a concerted effort to identify bottlenecks where exceptions may be appropriately given to categories of actors, but will also require action across a broad set of sectors, requiring the exemption of certain categories of action. Multiple sets of individual exceptions addressed to specific issues and problems may each be limited but, taken as a whole, may have a broad effect. While not a haven, those exceptions that are based on or are extensions of exceptions historically practised by most states are less likely to be challenged. Despite the narrow reading provided by the *Canada – Pharmaceutical Patents* panel, there is an understanding that certain kinds of exceptions such as private use, research, educational and experimental uses, as well as other exceptions existing at the time of the TRIPS Agreement and common in most countries' patent laws would likely fall within the scope of Article 30.[75] These, such as the regulatory

---

[75] Christopher Garrison 'Exceptions to Patent Rights in Developing Countries' Issue Paper No. 17, UNCTAD-ICTSD Project on IPRs and Sustainable

approval exception, could then be extended and designed to specifically address climate change mitigation and adaptation technologies.

Compulsory licences In addition to Article 30, public policy concerns beyond simple IP protection find their way into the TRIPS Agreement with provisions on compulsory licensing (Article 31 on 'Other Use without Authorization of the Right Holder'). States may use a compulsory licence to take the patent rights held by another party and either exercise the rights themselves, or license the rights to third parties to help the state exercise such rights. There has been no WTO dispute related to compulsory licensing under the TRIPS Agreement to date.

There are generally two categories of compulsory licence that can be taken into account. To the extent that compulsory licences are issued in the course of addressing anti-competitive practices and abuses of patents, countries remain free to determine when and how such licences should be issued under Article 31(k) and Article 40.[76] There is no requirement that there be remuneration to the right holder in such cases. In the US, such licences are issued by judges on a frequent basis for software, merger reviews, and other anti-competition remedies.[77] These kinds of licences are also primarily concerned with ensuring that the system operates the way that it is meant to: ensuring enough competitive room for innovation in the near and long-term.

The kind of licences that have caused the most difficulty and have been the basis of significant controversy are compulsory licences for reasons other than addressing competitive practices, including such examples as public health emergencies etc. In such cases, the behaviour of the state is regulated by TRIPS Article 31(b) which foresees the use of such compulsory licences as a way to address significant shortages, distribution problems and pricing issues addressed at either meeting short-term demand for goods and products or at enabling public (government) non-commercial use for any reason. It is important to note that the TRIPS Agreement

Development, October 2006, Geneva, Section 2. Available at: http://www.unctad. org/en/docs/iteipc200612_en.pdf (last visited 7 March 2012)

[76] Article 40.2 states: 'Nothing in this Agreement shall prevent Members from specifying in their legislation licensing practices or conditions that may in particular cases constitute an abuse of intellectual property rights having an adverse effect on competition in the relevant market. As provided above, a Member may adopt, consistently with the other provisions of this Agreement, appropriate measures to prevent or control such practices, which may include for example exclusive grant-back conditions, conditions preventing challenges to validity and coercive package licensing, in the light of the relevant laws and regulations of that Member.'

[77] For more examples see: http://keionline.org/content/view/41/1.

actually places no limitations on the grounds for issuance of compulsory licences but only regulates the process by which such licences are to be granted. In all the instances of compulsory licences for non-competition purposes, adequate remuneration based on local market conditions is required. Generally, good faith negotiation with patent holders is required, except if there is national emergency or other situation of extreme urgency, in which case government may proceed without first carrying out good faith negotiations. In the case of public non-commercial use, there is never a requirement to negotiate with the patent holder. There has been no case testing the application of such compulsory licences.

In terms of addressing climate change, Article 31 places no restriction on the domain and sectors in which compulsory licences can be applied. This is also true for compulsory licences to address anti-competitive behaviour. At the very least, Article 8.1 and Article 8.2 can be seen as requiring a broad interpretation of Article 31, provided that the basic procedural requirements of Article 31 are met and the substantive elements of Article 8.2 are met.[78] A proof of concept can be found in the US Clean Air Act codified in 42 U.S.C. § 7608. It provides the possibility of compulsory licences for those required to meet a rule or standard set up under the Clean Air Act, where the technology to meet such a standard is held by a patent holder and lack of access may place such a stakeholder at a competitive disadvantage.[79] As Derclaye points out, the provision has never been the subject of WTO dispute settlement[80] but its existence and lack of objection from other states suggests that such provisions can clearly be established in the context of other countries' actions to address climate change. Compulsory licences are ideal tools for market restructuring where sectoral development suffers from lack of production, or further research and development, due to the existence of a patent.

However, for patents that do not address anti-competitive practices, TRIPS establishes constraints that may be so limiting as to make such licences ineffective as tools to address production and dissemination of

---

[78]　Estelle Derclaye, 'Intellectual Property Rights and Global Warming', 12 *John Marshall Review of Intellectual Property Law* 263 (2008), 281. Available at SSRN: http://ssrn.com/abstract=1016864

[79]　Derclaye also points to this as an example of compulsory licence provision in the public interest. See p. 669, Estelle Derclaye, 'Not Only Innovation but also Collaboration, Funding, Goodwill and Commitment: Which Role for Patent Laws in Post-Copenhagen Climate Change Action' 9 *John Marshall Review of Intellectual Property Law* 657 (2010). She also notes that the system has never been used in the entire time the Clean Air Act has existed, although she points to the incentive to cooperate that it establishes.

[80]　*Id.*, 270.

climate change mitigation and adaptation technologies. A key limitation is the one requiring that patents be addressed on a case by case basis.[81] This limits the granting on public interest licences to an evaluation for each and every patent that must meet the rest of the requirements of Article 31. Where the technologies to be addressed are complex technologies that constitute not just a single patent but a 'family' of patents, the application of compulsory licences can become a slow and cumbersome process as each patent in the family will require a separate compulsory licence. Such complex technologies include windmills, fuel cells, and agricultural bio-technologies for biofuels, as well as for seeds.

A second limitation is that such a licence must be granted primarily for supply of the domestic market.[82] While this clearly contemplates that some portion of the supply will be exported, the wording suggests that a significant majority of the production should still go to the domestic market. If we consider the role that countries such as China, India and Brazil must play in ensuring dissemination of climate technologies to other developing countries that do not have as much R&D and production capacity, this limitation ensures that these countries will not be able to use compulsory licensing effectively to achieve that goal. This points to the largest problem with Article 31, which is that, for those countries with limited or no production capacity, compulsory licensing is not an option, since there will be no domestic actors to whom such licences could be granted and who could thus produce for the domestic market. Article 31 does not contemplate that a member could grant a compulsory licence to an actor outside its territory for the purposes of that actor exclusively producing for supply of that country's domestic market. Patent rights are territorial and can only be exercised on the territory of the patent-granting state. Thus limitations and exceptions to patents created by a state can only be exercised on the territory of the patent-granting state. In principle, if the state presents a sufficiently large market, this should encourage outside companies to locate production in these states to take advantage of the possibility of being granted a compulsory licence for production to meet domestic needs. However, in the absence of a guarantee that such a licence would be issued, most companies are unlikely to take the investment risk. In addition, many developing countries, assessed individually, do not present sufficiently large markets to justify establishment of production facilities on their territory primarily to supply their domestic market, regardless of the lack of patents. Even where patents exist, such small markets are of little

---

[81] TRIPS Article 31(a).
[82] TRIPS Article 31(f).

interest to originator/right holder companies and they present an additional barrier to investment by generic or other non-originator/imitator companies. The ability to provide compulsory licences does not add to the attractiveness of the investment. Where patents do not exist, these markets remain too small to be of interest for investors to establish facilities. With respect to governments themselves establishing such facilities, this requires an assessment of whether it would be more cost-effective to import the drugs from elsewhere or to expend significant amounts of money to import the expertise, facilities etc. to enable domestic production. Such an analysis nearly always falls in favour of directly paying for the importation of drugs, even from markets that are extremely expensive. This is especially true for the relatively short time frames in which shortages or other needs arise and at which Article 31 appears primarily aimed. The Doha Declaration on the TRIPS Agreement and Public Health[83] sought to address this issue with respect to pharmaceuticals which were seen as a particularly crucial sector for small developing countries. Paragraph 6 of the Declaration recognized that the use of compulsory licences was a problem for those countries with insufficient or no manufacturing capacity in the pharmaceutical industry and instructed the TRIPS Council to find a solution. The solution proposed by the TRIPS Council was adopted as a General Council Decision in August 2003 (The August 2003 Waiver).[84] This decision waived the requirements of Article 31(f) and of Article 31(h) (requiring adequate remuneration) for those countries with insufficient manufacturing capacities. It allows WTO Members with production capacity to export to those Members lacking such capacity, where a compulsory licence has been issued for that purpose in the importing country, or if there is no patent in the importing member, where the exporting country has issued a compulsory licence for that purpose in conjunction with a request from an eligible importing member. The decision also contains several other requirements related to the packaging, timing, size, and that the entirety of the production must be exported to the specific member. The requirement that adequate remuneration be paid is waived for the importing member but not for the exporting member. Of particular interest for technology transfer and intellectual property issues related to climate change is paragraph 7 of the August 2003

---

[83]   Declaration on the TRIPS Agreement and Public Health, WT/MIN(01)/DEC/2, adopted on 14 November 2001.

[84]   'Decision on the Implementation of Paragraph 6 of the Doha Declaration on the TRIPS Agreement and Public Health' WT/L/540 and Corr.1 adopted 30 August 2003.

Waiver[85] which notes that the system should be implemented in such a way as to increase technology transfer and capacity in eligible importing Members.

Paragraph 11 of the August 2003 Waiver ensures that it remains in force until such time as an amendment to the TRIPS Agreement implementing the waiver enters into force for each member that ratifies it. This led in 2005 to the adoption of an amendment (Article 31*bis*) to the TRIPS Agreement in the form of a protocol attached to a General Council Decision.[86] The text essentially restated the conditions outlined in the waiver, as well as the paragraph 7 provision on technology transfer. The amendment enters into force after two-thirds of WTO Members have ratified it and replaces the August 2003 Waiver for those countries that have ratified it. The Waiver remains in force for all others until they have also ratified the amendment. The success of the Waiver system and the amendment is difficult to measure. By one measure, i.e. use of the system, the waiver system has been a failure. Since the Waiver was made effective in August 2003, only one importing member (Rwanda) has used it to access drugs from Canada. Despite the fact that the product in question was not actually patented in Canada, the process proved so cumbersome that the company that was granted the exporting licence under Canadian law declared that the system was economically unsustainable.[87] By the same measure, it may be considered unnecessary or superfluous as apparently only a fraction of developing countries have felt the need to utilize the system. Support for this could be found in the fact that only a relatively small number of developing

---

[85] 'Members recognize the desirability of promoting the transfer of technology and capacity building in the pharmaceutical sector in order to overcome the problem identified in paragraph 6 of the Declaration. To this end, eligible importing Members and exporting Members are encouraged to use the system set out in this Decision in a way which would promote this objective. Members undertake to cooperate in paying special attention to the transfer of technology and capacity building in the pharmaceutical sector in the work to be undertaken pursuant to Article 66.2 of the TRIPS Agreement, paragraph 7 of the Declaration and any other relevant work of the Council for TRIPS.'

[86] Amendment of the TRIPS Agreement, WT/L/641, adopted 6 December 2005. Available at: http://www.wto.org/english/tratop_e/trips_e/wtl641_e.htm (last visited 7 March 12).

[87] Apotex Inc. 'Submission to the Standing Committee on Industry, Science and Technology Bill C-393. An Act to amend the Patent Act (drugs for international humanitarian purposes) and to make a consequential amendment to another Act' (26 October 2010). Available at: http://www.apotex.com/global/docs/submission_order_en.pdf (last visited 7 March 2012).

countries have ratified the amendment.[88] However, this is modified by two issues: the waiver remains in force and available so there is little incentive so far for developing countries to move over to ratifying the amendment; use of the system requires implementing legislation, especially in exporting countries as they bear the larger administrative burden under both the Waiver and the Amendment. The most recent data shows that relatively very few countries (13 plus the European Union 25) have actually notified such implementing legislation.[89] It is difficult to escape the impression that the system may not be as effective as once thought at enabling access to compulsory licensing for small developing countries and economies with little or no manufacturing capacity.

The Waiver and the Amendment apply only to pharmaceuticals and, while it is tempting to view it as a model for access to climate technologies, the complexity of the system suggests that expanding it to a broader set of products and processes may not work. In addition, unlike the pharmaceutical industry, it is not clear that most markets for climate technologies have large generic manufacturers who can easily replicate the products at a very low cost, making reliance on generic supply a key pillar of policies on access. In the case of agriculture and health this may be the case, but in many energy production and efficiency fields, the 'generic' industry does not really exist in the same way as in the pharmaceutical industry. This suggests that compulsory licensing as restricted by TRIPS as a means of managing shortages through reliance on generic producers is probably not applicable to the climate arena for economies with little or no manufacturing capacity. Even with the application of a paragraph 6-like system, this situation seems unlikely to improve. Only if licences are more easily available for export, as part of a broader commercial process might this become an effective option.

Compulsory licences also come with other limitations under the TRIPS Agreement. There remains a requirement under Article 31(h) for adequate remuneration to be paid by taking into account the economic value of the authorization. This must clearly be below the level of that which would

---

[88]   As of 5 January 2012, (the last date at which official WTO data are available) only 23 developing countries had notified their acceptance of the Amendment. See Members accepting amendment of the TRIPS Agreement. Available at: http://www.wto.org/english/tratop_e/trips_e/amendment_e.htm(last visited 7 March 2012).

[89]   As of 28 February 2011, the most recent date on which WTO official data is available only the European Union, Canada, Norway, India, Hong Kong, Switzerland, the Philippines, Singapore, Albania, Croatia, China, South Korea and Japan, had implementing legislation and/or regulations.

be acceptable to the right holder under a normal voluntary licence but it remains unclear as to what the threshold of 'adequate' remuneration would be. In the case of climate change, it may be possible to justify a relatively low amount by including considerations of whether and how much the licence contributes to the full incremental cost of accessing the technology.[90] Nevertheless, such remuneration is left to the authorities of the issuing state.

While the forgoing discussion suggests that there are significant limitations to compulsory licensing in ensuring or enabling production of technologies and technology transfer to developing countries with insufficient or no manufacturing capacity, it remains an effective option for those countries with significant manufacturing capacity. The kinds of compulsory licences that go beyond addressing supply issues and seek to restructure the market so that it is more competitively efficient are those that are targeted at anti-competitive practices and abuses of patents. Article 31(k) exempts such compulsory licences from the requirements of: Article 31(b) (on the need for prior negotiations with the right holder); Article 31(f) (limiting production primarily for supply of the domestic market. It also modifies the obligation on remuneration in Article 31(h) to allow for providing little or no remuneration. These specific kinds of compulsory licences and their potential for addressing climate change are addressed in the next sub-section.

A final note on this section is that it clearly also falls under the kinds of measures contemplated by Article 8.1. As such, where the compulsory licence is issued in particular to address issues to address health, nutrition or to promote the development of vital economic sectors, this must have an influence on the interpretation of provisions relating to remuneration (Article 31(h)), and level of production for domestic supply (Article 31(f)).

Compulsory licences and other action to address anti-competitive practices Other provisions which may relate to climate policy purposes are Articles 8.2[91] and 40 of the TRIPS Agreement, which address competition policy and abuses of patent rights. Parties can adopt any measures, including compulsory licences to address the following issues that are explicitly laid out:

---

[90]   UNFCCC Article 4.5.

[91]   Article 8.2 states: 'Appropriate measures, provided that they are consistent with the provisions of this Agreement, may be needed to prevent the abuse of intellectual property rights by right holders or the resort to practices which unreasonably restrain trade or adversely affect the international transfer of technology.'

- preventing the abuse of intellectual property rights by right holders (Article 8.2);
- preventing the resort to practices which unreasonably restrain trade (Article 8.2);
- preventing the resort to practices that adversely affect the international transfer of technology (Article 8.2).

Specific examples of such practices cited in the TRIPS Agreement include:

- exclusive grantback conditions;
- conditions preventing challenges to validity;
- coercive package licensing.

Article 40.1, as does Article 8.2, recognizes that some IP-related practices that restrain competition may have a negative effect on trade and technology transfer.[92] In pursuance of measures to address this, Article 40.2 ensures that nothing in the TRIPS Agreement shall limit the freedom of states to determine the nature, kind and scope of practices that constitute 'an abuse of intellectual property rights having an adverse effect on competition in the relevant market'.[93]

For transfer of technologies for climate change mitigation and adaptation it is important to note that included in the ambit of restrictive practices are practices that adversely affect international transfer of technology[94] and practices that impede the transfer and dissemination of technology.[95] This means that, by definition, where a WTO member finds that technology transfer of climate change technologies is being adversely affected by the licensing (or lack thereof) of a patented technology, action to address this can be presumptively justified. In addition, such measures

---

[92] Members agree that some licensing practices or conditions pertaining to intellectual property rights which restrain competition may have adverse effects on trade and may impede the transfer and dissemination of technology.

[93] Article 40.2 states in full: 'Nothing in this Agreement shall prevent Members from specifying in their legislation licensing practices or conditions that may in particular cases constitute an abuse of intellectual property rights having an adverse effect on competition in the relevant market. As provided above, a Member may adopt, consistently with the other provisions of this Agreement, appropriate measures to prevent or control such practices, which may include for example exclusive grantback conditions, conditions preventing challenges to validity and coercive package licensing, in the light of the relevant laws and regulations of that Member.'

[94] TRIPS Article 8.2.

[95] TRIPS Article 40.1.

can be taken pre-emptively so as not only to address a problem once it has arisen but also to prevent a problem from arising in the first place. Thus a member can pre-emptively put legislation and regulations in place to structure the market is such a way as to enable and encourage technology transfer into the relevant markets. Crucially, Article 40 also has an international dimension in that it requires consultations and sympathetic consideration of requests for information and enforcement regarding their domestic enterprises from other Members seeking to investigate and/or address anti-competitive behaviour by those enterprises in their own market.[96] This encourages cooperation and recognizes that a significant amount of the restrictive practices that Articles 8.2 and 40 cover occurs across borders and that Members have a right to legislate and to seek cooperation from other Members to address such cross-border behaviour.

However, both Article 8.2 and Article 40.2 come with the caveat that any measures taken to address restrictive practices must be consistent with the provisions of the TRIPS Agreement. Since the most common measures to address anti-competitive practices are compulsory licences, or other involuntary measures, this includes Articles 30 and 31. Focusing first on Article 31, licences to address anti-competitive practices must still comply with all provisions except: Article 31(k), which exempts such compulsory licences from the requirements of Article 31(b) (on the need for prior negotiations with the right holder); Article 31(f) (limiting production primarily for supply of the domestic market; Article 31(h), modifying the obligation on remuneration to allow for providing little or no remuneration. As noted, the use of such licences remains a powerful market restructuring tool, especially because, outside of the Paris Convention and the TRIPS Agreement, there exist no international restrictions on the criteria, nature

---

[96]   TRIPS Article 40.3: 'Each Member shall enter, upon request, into consultations with any other Member which has cause to believe that an intellectual property right owner that is a national or domiciliary of the Member to which the request for consultations has been addressed is undertaking practices in violation of the requesting Member's laws and regulations on the subject matter of this Section, and which wishes to secure compliance with such legislation, without prejudice to any action under the law and to the full freedom of an ultimate decision of either Member. The Member addressed shall accord full and sympathetic consideration to, and shall afford adequate opportunity for, consultations with the requesting Member, and shall cooperate through supply of publicly available non-confidential information of relevance to the matter in question and of other information available to the Member, subject to domestic law and to the conclusion of mutually satisfactory agreements concerning the safeguarding of its confidentiality by the requesting Member.'

and scope of such licences. Nevertheless, the requirement for case by case assessment may mean that such licences are complex to assess and manage.

Patent exclusions and special treatment for climate technologies   One approach that has been proposed in the climate change negotiations is the exclusion of patents on climate technologies. The legal basis for that exclusion in the TRIPS Agreement is, however, extremely difficult to discern.

Article 27 of the TRIPS Agreement has some provisions allowing for patent exclusions but also requires that patents be available for all fields of technology, both products and processes. The problem with Article 27.2 is that it ostensibly allows the exclusion of patents on particular products or processes for purposes of *ordre public* or public morals, but that also means that the purpose of such exclusions aims to stop the commercial exploitation of such products and processes. This runs counter to the aim of technology transfer, which is to expand the commercialization and adoption of the relevant technologies. Article 27.2 therefore does not provide a viable pathway to excluding patents on relevant climate technologies so as to allow common and public access.

However, looking at Article 27.1, some have argued that there may still be a possibility to discriminate among fields of technology. The panel in the *Canada – Pharmaceutical Patents* case argued that establishing special systems for particular product sectors was acceptable as long as these were supported by justifiable and specific policy purposes.[97] Thus, in that case, a special regime allowing an exception for use of a patent for meeting pharmaceutical regulatory requirements was allowed. The panel saw this as a bona fide differentiation. However, the panel also noted that the point at which differentiation began to shade into discrimination was if a policy appeared to be deliberately targeted at a sector where foreign right holders dominated.[98]

Article 27.3 also allows exclusions from patentability of very specific areas of technology without the requirement that they also be excluded from commercialization. These are:

1. diagnostic and therapeutic methods for treating animals and people; and
2. plants and animals other than micro-organisms; essentially biological process for the production of animals and plants other than non-biological and microbiological processes.

---

[97]   Panel Report, *Canada – Pharmaceutical Patents*.
[98]   *Id.*, para. 7.92.

For addressing adaptation needs in the agricultural arena, the prohibition on patenting of plants and animals is crucial. This allows free access to new and adapted products for adaptation. However, the limitations also require protection of micro-organisms, possibly limiting access, for example, to new bacteria that can be used to create biofuels from cellulosic plants.

Countries are also still required to protect non-biological and micro-biological processes. Thus processes that use bacteria to produce biofuels may also be covered for example, as well as possibly processes for genetic manipulation of plants and plant genes.

In addition, there is the additional requirement that countries provide protection to plant varieties through some *sui generis* regime. However, as the *sui generis* regime is not defined, any method that they use to provide effective protection will pass muster. This could arguably be a liability regime that ensures not only access for third parties but also remuneration for the right holder, without requiring lengthy negotiations or permitting processes. There is no term requirement or criteria for grant so countries are free to design whatever system they feel is appropriate.

Parallel importation TRIPS Article 6 on exhaustion[99] of IP rights is very clear. Nothing in the Agreement shall be deemed to address the issue of exhaustion, so Members are free to determine when and how products that have been legitimately placed on the market in other countries can be imported without the consent of the patent holder. This is called parallel importation and it is fundamental to ensuring that access to goods is enabled. This would allow products produced legitimately in other countries to be imported.

However, the key question here is what constitutes 'legitimate'? The traditional test is that such products have been placed on foreign markets with the consent of the right holder. Thus goods that are infringing IP rights in those foreign markets where they are produced would not be subject to the exhaustion principle. Goods produced under a compulsory

---

[99] Exhaustion applies primarily to product patents and the extent to which a right holders' right to control the 'sale' and distribution of such products ends after the first sale. The principle states that, once a patented product has been placed on the market by the right holder through a sale or distribution, the right holder has 'exhausted' the right of sale, having benefitted from the first sale. The right holder cannot prevent the onward sale or expect to benefit from such follow-on sales of the exact same product. However, the right holder retains all the other rights granted by the patent. The principle of exhaustion is most significant when it interacts with the right of importation of the patented product.

licence would be another matter. It can be argued that such goods, while not produced with the consent of the right holder, have been lawfully placed on the market in the foreign country where the product has been made and can therefore lawfully be imported. Article 107A(b) of the Indian Patent Act directly addresses this issue by ensuring that rights are exhausted when the products are placed on the market by an 'authorised person', whether by the right holder or a compulsory licensee. While it could be argued that such an approach clashes with the TRIPS Article 31 requirement that compulsory licences be issued primarily for domestic supply, at the very least some portion of products produced under a compulsory licence can be expected to be sold, directly across borders, even if the licence is primarily for domestic production. In addition, once products have been placed on the market, Article 31(f) would not function as a limitation on onward sales by others besides the compulsory licensee, especially where the right holder had already received adequate compensation. Thus direct sales by the producer may be limited but those by others would not be. More importantly, with respect to the right of importation, a country that applies such a regime of exhaustion cannot be brought before a WTO panel as, according to Article 6 of the TRIPS Agreement, the issue is entirely non-justiciable under the WTO.

C.   Limits on the Role of other Multilateral Regimes

In addition to limits on unilateral action within the TRIPS Agreement, there are some perceived limits to the role that other multilateral obligations can play in expanding the limits on action imposed by the TRIPS Agreement. In the case of climate change, the argument would be that the UNFCCC imposes obligations on states that WTO panels must take into account in TRIPS-related disputes that challenge Members' implementation of their UNFCCC obligations. Such an approach requires two conditions to succeed: first, that there are obligations within the UNFCCC and COP decisions that impose obligations to take action that may affect rights and obligation under the TRIPS Agreement; and second, that there is a mechanism, or interpretive approach, within the WTO for taking into account the rights and obligations imposed by other multilateral treaties. This section will explore whether both elements are present, and what solutions may be proposed, if they are not.

1.   The UNFCCC and its legal relationship to the TRIPS Agreement and other fora
There is little indication within the UNFCCC of what the relationship to the broader environmental regime and to the WTO should be. Within the

Convention itself, there are few mentions of how to relate to other regimes. The preamble affirms 'that responses to climate change should be coordinated with social and economic development in an integrated manner with a view to avoiding adverse impacts on the latter, taking into full account the legitimate priority needs of developing countries for the achievement of sustained economic growth and the eradication of poverty'.

Article 3.5 on principles notes:

> The Parties should cooperate to promote a supportive and open international economic system that would lead to sustainable economic growth and development in all Parties, particularly developing country Parties, thus enabling them better to address the problems of climate change. Measures taken to combat climate change, including unilateral ones, should not constitute a means of arbitrary or unjustifiable discrimination or a disguised restriction on international trade.

This provision suggests that the UNFCCC asks Parties to act in this manner in other fora relevant to the international economic system. The test that they impose here is one that imports language from the chapeau of Article XX of the GATT, which as discussed above embodies the General Exceptions clause. To the extent that measures affecting trade in goods are used to address climate change, this principle provides interpretive guidance from the UNFCCC as to the how the UNFCCC views the relationship between actions aimed at achieving climate aims and those actions as they relate to rules on trade in goods. The language does not, however, translate well into the TRIPS arena. As noted before, TRIPS provisions on exceptions and limitations to patents are primarily to be viewed through the lens of Articles 7 and 8, 30 and 31. The only UNFCCC equivalent to the TRIPS Agreement may be the UNFCCC Article 3.5 language pointing to arbitrary or unjustifiable discrimination (implicating TRIPS Article 27). Within the TRIPS Agreement there is no analogous 'disguised restriction on international trade' language or principle.

UNFCCC Article 4.5 commits Parties to:

> Take climate change considerations into account, to the extent feasible, in their relevant social, economic and environmental policies and actions, and employ appropriate methods, for example impact assessments, formulated and determined nationally, with a view to minimizing adverse effects on the economy, on public health and on the quality of the environment, of projects or measures undertaken by them to mitigate or adapt to climate change.

This provision, however, seems more aimed at not interfering with economic issues, while also suggesting some degree of balancing and consideration of climate change policies in other fora. It is not clear that this translates into a commitment also to act in pursuance of climate change mitigation objectives in other international fora.

In the Kyoto Protocol there is also little, if any, direction to states on how the Protocol relates to other regimes.

There is no language in the UNFCCC specifically addressing intellectual property, although the clear language on who should bear the costs of action suggests that the costs of paying for IP licences should be financially supported by industrialized countries, in the absence of other measures to ensure that technology transfer takes place. It is the issue of costs that points to a key missing element: that the technology transfer and financial support obligations of the UNFCCC fall squarely on the shoulders of industrialized countries. Developing countries wishing to take unilateral action to enable technology transfer cannot rely on those obligations to justify their actions in a TRIPS dispute. This suggests that other avenues are necessary. One possibility emerges as the most likely: that developing countries point to their own obligations in Article 4 of the UNFCCC to take action both individually and jointly with other UNFCCC Members to mitigate GHG emissions and address climate change adaptation. Developing countries could point to Article 4.1(b) which requires all parties to formulate and implement measures to mitigate climate change.[100] The counter to that would be that this is not a true obligation in that developing country parties are not required to take action where the full incremental costs of implementing measures are not covered by industrialized countries.[101] Article 4.4 addresses the same issue with respect to adaptation. To the extent that the

---

[100]   1. All Parties, taking into account their common but differentiated responsibilities and their specific national and regional development priorities, objectives and circumstances, shall:

[. . .]

(b) Formulate, implement, publish and regularly update national and, where appropriate, regional programmes containing measures to mitigate climate change by addressing anthropogenic emissions by sources and removals by sinks of all greenhouse gases not controlled by the Montreal Protocol, and measures to facilitate adequate adaptation to climate change.

[101]   UNFCCC Article 4.3: 'The developed country Parties and other developed Parties included in Annex II shall provide new and additional financial resources to meet the agreed full costs incurred by developing country Parties in complying with their obligations under Article 12, paragraph 1. They shall also provide such financial resources, including for the transfer of technology, needed by the developing country Parties to meet the agreed full incremental costs of implementing measures that are covered by paragraph 1 of this Article and that are agreed between a developing country Party and the international entity or entities referred to in Article 11, in accordance with that Article. The implementation of these commitments shall take into account the need for adequacy and predictability in

measures taken are ones that should nominally be supported under Article 4.3 or 4.4, Article 4.1 would be interpreted as not imposing a requirement of action on developing country parties. This is borne out by the statement in UNFCCC Article 4.7 that:

> The extent to which developing country Parties will effectively implement their commitments under the Convention will depend on the effective implement-ation by developed country Parties of their commitments under the Convention related to financial resources and transfer of technology . . . .

Thus developing countries are not truly in the position of having obliga-tions as yet, unless and until such obligations are embedded in a new post-2012 treaty that actually imposes a non-dependent obligation of action on developing countries. By definition, the obligation or benefits that would accrue to developing countries under the UNFCCC are conditional. The retaliation is already built-in: if developed countries do not provide tech-nology transfer and financial support, then developing countries have no obligations to mitigate climate change. However, in the situation where there is a commons problem, such that the effects of failure to mitigate climate change fall primarily on developing countries, the right of with-drawal of privileges or even retaliation may be triggered, since this affects not just rights but benefits that would have accrued under the treaty had it not been for the lack of action by industrialized countries.

The lack of clarity, especially with respect to IP issues, suggests a real need for an understanding of how to address these issues within the UNFCCC in a way that is legally consistent but that provides clarity to states on how they should act unilaterally; provides direction to negotia-tors on the boundaries of what can be negotiated; and provides guidance to dispute settlement bodies, in whatever forum, on how they should address climate change and IP issues, if and when they arise.

2. The WTO and its legal relationship to other treaties and regimes

The usefulness of statements in the UNFCCC or approaches to establish-ing obligations in the UNFCCC relies on one other key issue: whether and how the WTO jurisprudence makes space for considering these oblig-ations. There is an enormous literature on the relationship between trade and environment and several of the analytical frameworks developed in this discussion are covered in other chapters in this volume. These frame-works are generally addressed at three potential access points: jurisdiction,

---

the flow of funds and the importance of appropriate burden sharing among the developed country Parties.'

in which a WTO panel decides whether the dispute or claimed violation falls within the scope of rights and obligations of the covered agreements; applicable law, which is the sources of law which determine the scope and nature of the rights and obligations over which the panel has jurisdiction; and interpretive weight, addressing the evidentiary weight to be given to various sources in determining the meaning of specific terms and provisions of a covered agreement. In practice, where environmental issues are concerned this has meant that a panel has to determine whether an environmental measure is within its jurisdiction to address; whether the environmental treaty or regime which governs that environmental measure should be applicable law in a WTO dispute; and failing that, whether the meaning ascribed to a term or provision in an environmental treaty/ regime, should inform (either by expanding or narrowing) or have the same meaning as a similar or identical term in a WTO covered agreement. These questions have been addressed with respect to trade in goods and in the context of the SPS Agreement and the TBT Agreement.

Clearly, the role of measures pursued in the implementation of multilateral environmental agreements (MEAs) would be one of the best indicators of how the WTO jurisprudence views its relationship to international environmental law. However, there have been no cases directly addressing measures taken in order to comply with an obligation in an MEA. Nevertheless, the Appellate Body has stated a preference for international cooperation, suggesting that measures taken outside of efforts to cooperate would receive far stricter scrutiny.[102] The Appellate Body has noted that measures do not need to be based on an agreement, and that good faith attempts to participate and engage in cooperation or multilateral agreements are enough to satisfy the needs of the chapeau.[103]

It is not the intent of this chapter to go over issues that are much more effectively covered in other chapters in this volume but the aim is to explore how these principles would apply in the context of a TRIPS dispute that addressed unilateral measures on technology transfer. Drawing from the jurisprudence we find that:

- In applying Article 31(3)(c) of the Vienna Convention on the Law of Treaties, all sources of law can be considered as applicable law including customary law, principles of international law as well as treaties. However, as applicable law in the context of a dispute between WTO Members, only those rules that are applicable

---

[102] Nathalie Bernasconi-Osterwalder et al., note 17 above, 83.
[103] Appellate Body Report, *US – Shrimp*, para. 153(b).

between the parties to the WTO can be considered meaning that only treaties to which *all* WTO Members are party can be considered applicable law in a WTO dispute.[104]

- Other rules of international law may nevertheless play a role in providing evidence of the ordinary meaning of a term or provision in a WTO covered agreement, but a panel is not required to use such evidence where it does not consider it necessary or relevant.[105]

Significant controversy has attended the panel approach in *EC – Approval and Marketing of Biotech Products* that the applicable law referred to by Article 31(3)(c) VCLT was limited only to those treaties to which all WTO Members were parties at the time of the dispute. The International Law Commission's report on the Fragmentation on International Law went so far as to suggest that the panel made a fundamental error, arguing that this would make it impossible for any treaty to have the role of applicable law in a WTO dispute as none could have the exact same scope of membership as the WTO,[106] or even be one to which the membership of the WTO is a subset.

The effect of this approach in the technology transfer, climate change and TRIPS discussion is clear. If one presumes that the panel's approach in *EC – Approval and Marketing of Biotech Products* remains applicable, then, absent any other statement from within the institutions of the WTO, the UNFCCC cannot be used as applicable law between the parties to a dispute at the WTO that challenges a unilateral measure that has an effect of a TRIPS-related right or obligation. However, this does not preclude the use of UNFCCC terms and provisions in informing the meaning and scope of similar or identical terms in the TRIPS Agreement. Since these could not be used to actually alter or justify a measure that is TRIPS-inconsistent, this would have to enter through the traditional interpretive route of exceptions and limitations covered in the previous section.

As a general matter therefore, there appears to be a very limited set

---

[104] Panel Report, *European Communities – Measures Affecting the Approval and Marketing of Biotech Products*, WT/DS291/R, WT/DS292/R, WT/DS293/R, Add.1 to Add.9, and Corr.1, adopted 21 November 2006, DSR 2006:III-VIII, 847 (*EC – Approval and Marketing of Biotech Products*), 334.

[105] *Id.*, 341,

[106] Martti Koskenniemi et al. 'Fragmentation of International Law: Difficulties Arising from the Diversification and Expansion of International Law', Report of the Study Group of the International Law Commission, A/CN.4/L.682, April 2006, 227 and 237.

of ways in which WTO panels must or can take into account other international treaties. Combined with the fact that technology transfer obligations do not fall on developing countries in the UNFCCC, this suggests that there is little room for the UNFCCC, in and of itself, to play a role in justifying IP-related actions, unless those justifications can be found within the TRIPS Agreement itself.

V.   IMPLICATIONS OF THIS IP ANALYSIS FOR ACTION ON CLIMATE CHANGE

The climate challenge is a global emergency. The TRIPS Agreement seems to be a useful tool for some situations, as its exceptions on public health and the environment, as well as the use of compulsory licences, suggests that legally, countries should be free to exercise the broadest use of exceptions to reduce greenhouse gas emissions. However, the jurisprudence under the TRIPS Agreement and the uncertainty surrounding much that remains to be interpreted suggest otherwise. There are few options that do not rely on some of form of compulsory licensing. In the absence of a solution that allows for cross-border production and implementation of licences, the vast majority of developing countries will not be in a position to benefit from the use of such compulsory licences.

Exceptions to patent rights appear to be quite severely constrained by the approach taken by the panel in *Canada – Pharmaceutical Patents*. Any solution that will meet the needs of developing countries will have to address the need for cross-border supply by those countries with domestic production and knowledge capacity as well as provide a platform for appropriate climate-friendly interpretation of existing TRIPS obligations, especially to enable the kinds of measures envisaged under TRIPS Articles 7 and 8.1.

Nevertheless, there clearly do remain some flexibilities under the TRIPS Agreement for those countries with sufficient domestic capacity, including the ability to ensure that anti-competitive behaviour by patent holders is addressed. Given a rigorous process for identifying relevant technologies and a proper analysis showing market failure, the exercise of all exceptions and compulsory licences can be justified by these countries.

In addition, countries should develop and make full use of their law on anti-competitive practices to address not just failure to license or work patents, but also failures to license or share trade secrets and undisclosed information. This is especially important as compulsory licences to address anti-competitive behaviour need not be subject to the requirement for adequate compensation.

The unavoidable conclusion, however, is that, at present, there appears to be insufficient flexibility in the TRIPS Agreement to enable unilateral action by the majority of developing countries, which have little or no domestic manufacturing capacity. In addition, while the UNFCCC provides obligations on transfer of technology, and financial support to enable GHG mitigation and adaptation, the failure to explicitly address intellectual property and the barriers it may pose leave little leverage for UNFCCC provisions and terms to enter into interpretation of the TRIPS Agreement.

With respect to access to existing technologies in the near term, especially to address adaptation and mitigation issues, it is clear that a special regime of technology transfer and/or use of compulsory licences may be necessary. This must enable emerging economies to supply necessary technological products to developing countries, but without the burdens that Article 31 of the TRIPS Agreement presently imposes. This will be especially necessary in the health and agricultural sectors. It is apparent that addressing the issue of IP at the international level in the UNFCCC negotiations is not only desirable but necessary.

The Cancun Agreements that came out of the December 2010 UNFCCC Conference of the Parties, however, did not contain any text on intellectual property.[107] The COP decisions primarily focused on institutional and financial mechanisms for enabling technology transfer. Underlying the lack of mention of intellectual property was the idea that sufficient financing and technology cooperation will obviate the need for developing countries to have options for unilateral IP actions. However, it is also clear that unless the new technology transfer mechanism explicitly includes support for payment for licences, including licences that enable export to other developing countries, it will not meet the needs of developing countries. In addition, even if the mechanism would provide for such support, it is not clear how it would deal with issues such as unreasonable pricing and refusals to license, which are a real concern for emerging economies. Thus far, the negotiations on the technology transfer mechanism have failed to address this issue of financing of licences.

The absence of any reference to intellectual property was continued in the Durban Platform that was agreed in December 2011 and which elaborated draft modalities for the Technology Executive Committee agreed to

---

[107] UNFCCC 'The Cancun Agreements: Outcome of the work of the Ad Hoc Working Group on Long-term Cooperative Action under the Convention' Decision 1/CP.1 (FCCC/CP/2010/7/Add.1) Available at: http://unfccc.int/resource/docs/2010/cop16/eng/07a01.pdf#page=2

in Cancun.[108] The decision establishing the Climate Technology Centre and Network (CTC) is likewise silent on intellectual property.[109] Nevertheless, several of the CTC's tasks will clearly require processes for managing intellectual property issues that arise.[110]

It appears that the issue of intellectual property has faded from the foreground in the UNFCCC negotiations. It no longer forms an explicit part of the existing content of decisions and may have been relegated to a sub-element of the discussion on financing. However, the agreement to establish the Ad Hoc Working Group on the Durban Platform for Enhanced Action Durban to negotiate a post-Kyoto treaty may still present an opportunity to re-address the issue of technology transfer and intellectual property in the UNFCCC.[111] Paragraph 5 includes technology development and transfer within the mandate of the working group. The issue of intellectual property is likely to remain a significant part of the negotiations of the post-Kyoto framework and some workable proposals for how to deal with intellectual property barriers and issues will be needed in the UNFCCC and perhaps in the WTO as well.

---

[108]   UNFCCC 'Technology Executive Committee – modalities and procedures' Decision 4/CP.17. Available at: http://unfccc.int/files/meetings/durban_nov_2011/decisions/application/pdf/cop17_tec.pdf (last visited 7 March 2012).

[109]   UNFCCC 'Outcome of the work of the Ad Hoc Working Group on Long-term Cooperative Action under the Convention' Decision 2/CP.17 http://unfccc.int/files/meetings/durban_nov_2011/decisions/application/pdf/cop17_lcaoutcome.pdf#page=23 (last visited 7 March 2012).

[110]   *Id.*, para. 135.

[111]   UNFCCC 'Establishment of an Ad Hoc Working Group on the Durban Platform for Enhanced Action' Draft Decision/ CP.17, http://unfccc.int/files/meetings/durban_nov_2011/decisions/application/pdf/cop17_durbanplatform.pdf (last visited 7 March 2012).

17. Subsidies for emissions mitigation under WTO law[1]

Luca Rubini

I. INTRODUCTION

Since almost two-thirds of greenhouse gasses (GHGs) are energy related,[2] any strategy to mitigate GHGs emissions needs to focus on energy production and use. Policy action should take various and simultaneous directions. On the one hand, the dependency of modern society on heavily polluting, and subsidized, fossil fuels should be tackled.[3] It is thus commonly noted how the phase-out of fossil fuel subsidies is one of

---

[1] This chapter develops L. Rubini, 'Ain't Wasting Time No More: Subsidies For Renewable Energy, the SCM Agreement, Policy Space, and Law Reform', *Journal of International Economic Law* (2012), 525–579, and L. Rubini and I. Jegou, 'Who'll Stop the Rain? Allocating Emission Allowances for Free: Environmental Policy, Economics, and WTO Subsidy Law', 1(2) *Transnational Environmental Law* (2012), 325–354 (forthcoming). For various discussions on the topic and comments of previous drafts of this chapter I would like to thank Sadeq Bigdeli, Thomas Cottier, Denny Ellerman, Petros Mavroidis, Richard Newfarmer, Ron Steenblik, Geert Van Calster. Any error remains mine.

[2] In its *World Energy Outlook 2011* report (210), the International Energy Agency (IEA) notes that in 2009 energy-related CO_2 emissions contributed 61 percent to total GHGs.

[3] Fossil-fuel consumption subsidies worldwide have been estimated at US $409 billion in 2010, $300 billion in 2009, $558 billion in 2008 and $342 billion in 2007, with changes in international fuel prices being chiefly responsible for differences from year to year (IEA, *World Energy Outlook 2011*, 508). For the first time, in October 2011, the OECD compiled a partial inventory of over 250 measures in support of fossil fuel production and consumption in 24 industrialized countries. Support was estimated at between US $45 and 75 billion per year in the 2005–2010 period, with production support amounting to about one-fifth to one-quarter of the total in most years (see OECD, *Inventory of Estimated Budgetary Support and Tax Expenditure for Fossil Fuels*, available at http://www.oecd.org/dataoecd/40/35/48805150.pdf, last access 20 October 2011). Making allowance for different methodologies, a very superficial comparison between these figures seem to indicate that non-OECD countries subsidize more (at least with respect to the consumption side).

the best steps towards GHGs emissions mitigation.[4] On the other hand, the possibility of reducing and eventually replacing this dependency relies on increasing energy efficiency[5] and renewable energy production and use.[6] Other supplementary emission abatement options, like carbon capture and storage (CCS), should also be explored.[7] Any effective and rational energy and environmental strategy, with the aim to mitigate climate change, is thus centered around a more efficient use of low-carbon energy.

To achieve this objective, various forms of disincentives and incentives can be deployed.[8] A tax can be imposed on the use of energy (energy tax) or on the emissions caused by this use (carbon tax). The disincentive to emit, and hence the incentive to be more efficient and invest in more cost-effective green technologies, can also be achieved through market-based instruments like cap-and-trade systems where a price is put on emissions and linked to tradable permits. Alternatively, economic resources can be transferred through subsidies to firms or consumers and support R&D, production or consumption. Governments thus use grants and loan schemes, tax incentives and regulation to achieve their aims.

This chapter attempts to answer various questions. It starts by asking whether energy efficiency and renewable energy, which play a crucial role in the mitigation of climate change, are in need of public support, and, if so, what guidelines should be followed to ensure their effectiveness in relation to its goals. Assuming that certain climate change subsidies may be 'good', the central question, which occupies much of the analysis, is

---

[4]   B. Sovacool, 'The Importance of Comprehensiveness in Renewable Electricity and Energy-efficiency Policy', 37 *Energy Policy* (2009), 1529.

[5]   Energy efficiency relies on all technologies and behavior aimed at reducing the amount of energy required to provide goods and services.

[6]   Renewable energy comes from renewable natural sources, encompassing bio-energy, direct solar energy, geothermal energy, ocean energy and wind energy.

[7]   CCS (which refers to the technologies *preventing* large quantities of carbon emissions from being released into the atmosphere in the power generation and other industries) has an emission reduction potential of 18 percent (IEA, *World Energy Outlook 2011*).

[8]   The IEA has, for example, estimated that global renewable energy subsidies increased from $39 billion in 2007 to $66 billion in 2010, in line with rising production of biofuels and electricity from renewable sources. In the New Policies Scenario (in which recent government policy commitments are assumed to be implemented in a cautious manner) subsidies to renewables reach almost $250 billion in 2035 (*World Energy Outlook 2011*, 508). It is clear that, although important, any parallel between these figures and those on fossil fuel support cited in n. 3 above should be made with extra care. Comparisons should not be done only on the basis of gross values but considering per unit of energy supplied.

whether the current WTO regulatory framework does recognize appropriate autonomy to domestic measures of support.

II. ARE CLIMATE CHANGE SUBSIDIES GOOD OR BAD? ECONOMICS, INDUSTRIAL POLICY, POLITICAL ECONOMY

While support for energy saving and energy efficiency is readily endorsed by energy and environmental experts,[9] the issue of whether renewable energy needs support is much more controversial.

Economic theory posits that public intervention may be warranted whenever the market fails to provide desirable public goods or to tackle externalities. Climate change has been dubbed the 'greatest and widest-ranging market failure ever seen'.[10] More specifically, renewable energy faces various barriers related to the financial markets, infrastructure, regulation and, information[11] which may, at least in principle, justify the use of subsidies. In truth, '[i]n theory from an efficiency viewpoint, the ideal approach for encouraging clean energy would be the elimination of distortions in terms of support for conventional energy plus a charge on pollution at a socially optimum level'.[12] The implementation of these actions would allegedly put alternative energy on an equal competitive footing with competing (and often under-priced) conventional sources making public support unnecessary. The problem is, however, that these actions are difficult to be fully implemented: 'even in the most environmentally friendly countries in the world, there might be a level of existing distortion or regulatory bias in favor of conventional energy and the level of carbon taxes are not nearly optimal'.[13] Further, as Howse recently noted,

> [y]et even if all these measures [supporting fossil fuel] were removed at once [. . .] the market distortions and consequent environmental harm flowing from

---

[9]   S.Z. Bidgeli, 'Resurrecting the Dead? The Expired Non-Actionable Subsidies and the Lingering Question of "green space"', *Manchester Journal of International Economic Law* (2011), 2, 27.

[10]   N. Stern, *The Economics of Climate Change: Stern Review* (Cambridge: Cambridge University Press, 2007), executive summary, i.

[11]   See, e.g., C. Beaton and T. Moernhout, 'A Literature Review on Subsidies to Electricity from Renewable Energy Sources' (2011) NCCR Working Paper 2011/63, 7, 8–10; see also Sovacool, n. 4 above, 1530–1531; M. Mendonça, D. Jacobs and B. Sovacool, *Powering the Green Economy – The Feed-in Tariff Handbook* (London: Earthscan 2010), chapter 8.

[12]   Bigdeli, n. 9 above, 28.

[13]   Ibid.

past investment decisions and established patterns of producer and consumer behaviour based on these decisions could hardly be eliminated in the short term. Thus, there is a clear need for proactive interventions to correct market failures, such as subsidies that *favour* the use of alternative energy sources.[14]

In addition to these level playing field considerations, what makes the case for (even imperfect) subsidies in support of renewable energy stronger is the dramatic action needed to tackle the massive and urgent challenge of reducing GHGs emissions substantially – 80 percent by 2050 if the target of preventing a temperature rise of 2 degrees Celsius is to be achieved.

That said, however, it is on numerous occasions noted that, rather than correcting distortions, purportedly 'green' subsidies have often introduced them, have encouraged inefficiency, rent-seeking and protection; when introduced have been difficult to remove; and may ultimately have been ineffective towards their stated aims, or, more simply, may have not been needed in presence of altruistic and environmental friendly behavior.[15] Practical examples where one or more of these circumstances would be present would abound.[16] If the arguments above may in some cases lead to the rejection of the subsidy option, nevertheless, when the decision to grant subsidies is taken, the same concerns should always force policy-makers to design the subsidies properly in relation to their objectives so that the desired incentive effect is maximized and their costs and distortions are kept to the minimum.

Whether public support for green energy is needed is often motivated by a mix of policy objectives: environmental, social and economic goals (such as job creation and industry support), energy security. As will be seen, this variety of goals is important in the context of the legal assessment of subsidies. The question of the desirability and effectiveness of public support is increasingly framed as one of *green industrial policy*.[17] While recent research seems to indicate that 'soft' industrial policy (e.g.

---

[14]   R. Howse, 'Climate Change Mitigation Subsidies and the WTO Legal Framework: A Policy Analysis' (International Institute for Sustainable Development, 2010), 6.

[15]   For a literature review see Bidgeli, n. 9 above.

[16]   For an account of feed-in tariffs (FITs) in the solar PV sector see M. Scott, 'Subsidy cut puts heat on solar panel installers', *The Financial Times*, 27 November 2011. To be sure, the definitive assessment of specific cases of support is quite often difficult to make. The interesting debate spurred by the recent collapse of the US solar-panel maker Solyndra, which had received a $535 million worth of loan guarantees, is a good example in point. See, e.g., B. Plumer, 'Five Myths about the Solyndra collapse', *The Washington Post*, 15 September 2011.

[17]   See, e.g., A. Cosbey, 'Renewable energy subsidies and the WTO: The wrong law and the wrong venue', *Subsidy Watch*, Issue 44, June 2011, 1.

standards, infrastructure and export promotion) has a higher success rate than 'hard' industrial policy (e.g. tariffs, subsidies, tax breaks, domestic content requirements),[18] contemporary industrial policy discourse in the trade-and-environment circles has been influenced by recent disputes on renewable energy support that concern subsidies with local content requirements[19] (i.e. where the grant is subject to the use of local inputs). Some note that the obligation to source certain inputs locally is clearly protectionist and cannot really be justified on environmental grounds. Any beneficial green impact deriving from domestic industry support would be compensated by a detrimental green impact for the competing industries of other countries. At best, it would be a 'green vs green' conflict, with no obvious decider in favor of domestic support. Others, by contrast, suggest that import substitution would not only create competitive domestic players in the sector but, ultimately, if it meant 'more agents of innovation' internationally, it would increase competition globally, and this 'at a time when innovation in renewable energy technology is a critically important global public good'.[20]

In the light of these considerations, it is clear that the issue of whether subsidies are needed is not a 'black-and-white' one, and that the answer is necessarily nuanced. The key question is whether public support is *cost-effective in relation to the goals pursued* by public action.[21] In the presence of scarce resources and competing priorities, a proper methodology which analyzes and compares benefits and costs in relation to the intended goals is crucial. The quest for better policy is continuous. The effectiveness of a particular measure of support ultimately depends on the specifics of the case,

---

[18] A.E. Harrison and A. Rodriguez-Clare, 'Trade, Foreign Investment, and Industrial Policy for Developing Countries', in D. Rodrik and M. Rosenzweig (eds), *Handbook of Development Economics*, Volume 5 (North Holland: 2010), 4039–4214.

[19] *China – Measures Concerning Wind Power Equipment* (DS 419); *Canada – Certain Measures Affecting the Renewable Energy Sector* (DS 412); *Canada – Measures Relating to the Feed-In Tariff Program* (DS 426).

[20] Cosbey, n. 17 above, 2.

[21] Beaton and Moernhout, n. 11 above, have recently highlighted how most studies analyze the cost-effectiveness of renewable energy subsidies with respect to deployment, as opposed to their ultimate objectives, which does not seem to be fully appropriate. See also R. Bridle and C. Beaton, *The Cost-effectiveness of Solar PV Deployment Subsidies* (2011) NCCR Working Paper 2011/31; C. Beaton and T. Moerenhout, *Assessing the Cost-Effectiveness of Renewable Energy Deployment Subsidies: Biomass in the United Kingdom and Germany* (2011) NCCR Working Paper 2011/73; T. Moerenhout, T. Liebert and C. Beaton, *Assessing the Cost-Effectiveness of Renewable Energy Deployment Subsidies: Wind Power in Germany and China* (2012) NCCR Working Paper 2012/03.

and, crucially, on the design of the measure and its synergy with other policies.[22] Furthermore, subsidies can operate at different stages and have different targets. Governments may decide to subsidize consumers or instead firms, supporting, for example, their R&D or production. Depending on the circumstances, the effects of these subsidies are different. The competitive position of domestic and foreign producers is not necessarily affected unless, in law or in fact, the incentive discriminates in favour of domestic production, preference which may well be a policy decision.[23]

A common policy prescription is that subsidies should be as targeted as possible, with a preference for activities rather than sectors.[24] Further principles for a 'smart' industrial policy, which are applicable to subsidies, include the following: policy, institutional and cost elements in the value chain, limiting production and export, should be removed; the measure should be as transparent as possible; the goals pursued should be spelled out with clear criteria for success and failure; incentives should be provided only for 'new' activities; the impairing of competition should be avoided; the project should entail private risks commensurate to public risks; the governmental agency administering the policy should have demonstrated competence, with clear political oversight and accountability; the project should be subject to regular external valuations.[25] It is also suggested that, since market failures (and hence the policies to target them) may be difficult to identify and quantify, private and public sectors should cooperate in a 'discovery process – one where firms and the government learn about underlying costs and opportunities and engage in strategic coordination'.[26] This continuous – necessary but certainly difficult – process should assist in attuning the subsidy to the changing needs and removing it when it becomes unnecessary. Further, to avoid opportunistic behavior, unnecessary distortions and excessive spending, subsidies should be granted only insofar as they are necessary to produce the incentive effect and only until the obstacle justifying them is present. It is in this respect even noted that, as a general rule, subsidies should only be temporary and subject to a sunset clause.

---

[22]   *IPCC Special Report on Renewable Energy Sources (SRRES)*, May 2011, Summary for Policy-makers, 24. See also Sovacool, n. 4 above, 1537–1539.

[23]   The possible justification and status of discriminatory subsidies are analyzed at length below.

[24]   D. Rodrik, *Industrial Policy for the XXIst century* (Cambridge MA: Harvard John F. Kennedy School of Government: 2004).

[25]   From the '10 principles for smart industrial policy' outlined by Richard Newfarmer in his paper at the IISD Conference, 18 October 2011.

[26]   Rodrik, n. 24 above, 3–4.

Two final remarks may shed some light on the political economy of subsidy decisions.

First, if properly designed, carbon taxes or market-based mechanisms seem to be more cost-effective in terms of GHGs offset. Why then do governments find it so difficult to implement these options and instead resort to the second-best of subsidies? The answer is predominantly a political economy one. Subsidies are often easier to implement because, rather than imposing a cost on emissions and on the polluting activity, they confer an economic advantage.

Second, it is worth noting that, even if the previous guidelines are followed, it does not follow that the subsidy does not cause any distortion, including trade ones. From a policy-making angle however, trade distortion is not necessarily the ultimate baseline. If it is accepted that public support is needed to complement the market and that certain subsidies are cost-effective in achieving the desired goal, certain distortions can be accepted. What underlies any policy decision and any legal compromise is a trade-off. Economic distortions are accepted if, in consideration of the preferences and choices of the granting government, it is expected that the benefits will be greater. There is no precision or inevitability in where the line is drawn. The main difficulty however comes when negative and positive effects are produced in different countries since it is not easy to make and gain acceptance for transnational trade-offs. In these cases, the policy discourse clearly transcends the domestic and local level to reach the international and global one. Complex issues of settlement of conflicts of interests and multilevel regulation enter into play.

III.   OVERVIEW OF THE KEY LEGAL QUESTIONS

The key legal questions posed are the following: What type of public action that may contribute to the mitigation of climate change is covered by WTO rules applicable to subsidies? How does the regulatory framework cope with the distorted nature of energy markets, on the one hand, and with the novelty of many of the policy tools used, on the other? Are the guidelines coming from the regulatory framework in line with the policy prescriptions? Is the legal framework coherent? Is it sufficiently or appropriately friendly towards the use of subsidies to mitigate climate change? Is law reform needed?

To answer these questions it is necessary to navigate between various rules and WTO covered agreements, notably the Agreement on Subsidies and Countervailing Measures (SCM Agreement), the General Agreement on Tariffs and Trade (GATT), the Agreement on Agriculture (AoA) and the General Agreement on Trade in Services (GATS).

It is worth at this point sketching how the SCM Agreement, the main set of rules applicable to subsidies, operates. Under the definition of SCM Article 1, a subsidy shall be deemed to exist if there is a 'financial contribution' by the government or 'any form of income or price support' and, as a result, a 'benefit' is conferred. The subsidy must then be 'specific' to certain enterprises or industries. Once it has been established that the measure constitutes a specific subsidy, it is necessary to determine whether it causes 'adverse effects' to the interests of one Member or 'material injury' to the domestic industry of a Member.[27] If this is the case, the subsidy will be actionable before WTO dispute settlement (and should be withdrawn or its effects removed) or countervailable in the affected domestic jurisdiction. Subsidies that are contingent on exportation or on the use of domestic inputs (called local-content or import-substitution subsidies) are simply prohibited.[28]

IV.   WHAT DO THE RULES INTEND TO COVER?

The first legal question is to determine what is actually covered by the relevant disciplines.

A.   Goods, Services and Agriculture

What may not be clear in the first place is the nature of what can be benefited by the subsidy. For example, is energy a good or a service? This classification is important because different WTO covered agreements may apply. While the SCM Agreement features a comprehensive subsidy regulation for the goods sector, the GATS, which regulates trade in services, does not have any meaningful set of rules on subsidies,[29] except for

---

[27]   The SCM Agreement identifies three types of adverse effects: injury, serious prejudice (arising in case of various forms of displacement and price effects in various markets, or in the case of an effect on world market shares) and nullification and impairment of benefits, in particular tariff concessions.

[28]   Unless prohibited subsidies are subject to countervailing duty action, there is no need to prove specificity or negative effects. If granted, the only alternative is withdrawal.

[29]   Article XV GATS calls for negotiations 'to develop the necessary multilateral disciplines' to avoid the distortive effects of subsidies, and for consultations between the Member which considers that it is adversely affected by a subsidy of

the possible application of the obligation of national treatment.[30] The issue is not settled. Despite the debate continuing, it looks like what matters is indeed the aspect of the measure at issue and the perspective taken. Energy can thus be regarded both as a good *and* a service.[31] It is, for example, increasingly accepted that the generation of electrical energy is covered by the goods discipline, while its transmission and distribution by the GATS.[32]

The distinction between goods and services comes into play also when we consider the nature of 'emission allowances'[33] whose allocation can confer an economic benefit. Allowances can be considered goods.[34] They have economic value because they can be traded in a market.[35] Their transfer can therefore be regulated by the WTO discipline on goods. At the same time, however, since they are traded in the market as securities, they can aptly be regarded as financial instruments, and thus trigger the application of the discipline on services. As with the definition of energy, the issue of the proper classification of emission allowances is still open but, again, the answer may well be that, depending on the perspective, they are both a good *and* a service. For the purposes of subsidy rules, the characterization of emission allowances does not seem to be crucial since their (free) allocation would be considered a financial contribution in the form of a 'provision of goods *or* services' and subject to the SCM Agreement in both cases.[36]

---

another Member and that granting Member. 'Such requests' – Article XV reads – 'shall be accorded sympathetic consideration'.

[30]   According to Article XVII, the obligation to accord to foreign services 'treatment no less favourable' than that accorded to domestic services – which may put into question a subsidy granted only to the domestic 'energy-service' industry – does apply only 'in the sectors inscribed in its Schedule, and subject to any conditions and qualifications set out therein'.

[31]   See, e.g., Appellate Body Report, *European Communities – Regime for the Importation, Sale and Distribution of Bananas*, WT/DS27/AB/R, adopted 25 September 1997, para. 221.

[32]   For a discussion see S. Bigdeli, 'Incentive Schemes to Promote Renewables and the WTO Law of Subsidies' in S. Bigdeli, T. Cottier, and O. Nartova (eds), *International Trade Regulation and the Mitigation of Climate Change* (Cambridge: Cambridge University Press, 2009), 166.

[33]   See E. Vranes, 'Climate Change and the WTO: EU Emission Trading and the WTO Disciplines on Trade in Goods, Services and Investment Protection', *Journal of World Trade* (2009), 151–720, 707.

[34]   Howse, n. 14 above, 12–13.

[35]   It could even be asked whether the permission to exploit the atmosphere, which is in essence what emissions allowances bestow, amounts to the provision of a good, a natural resource that can be used and subjected to economic transactions. For this line of argument see Rubini and Jegou, n. 1 above, 13.

[36]   See discussion below under IV.C. below.

Another important definitional issue regards the classification of bio-fuels. Are they industrial or agricultural goods? The issue is important because the AoA applies only to those products that are listed in Annex 1. To identify the agricultural products covered, this list follows the Harmonized System (HS) of Tariff Classification of the World Customs Organization (WCO). Biodiesel and ethanol are two of the most important biofuels. Biodiesel is expressly classified under Chapter 38 of the HS (on the basis of its composition, production process and end-use as fuel). Ethanol, by contrast, does not have a specific classification, and is thus classified – with reference to its chemical composition only – under the more general categorization of undenatured or denatured alcohol, both covered in Chapter 22 of the HS. Now, the said Annex 1 to the AoA defines its scope to cover products classified under HS Chapters 1–24. Hence, while biodiesel is clearly excluded from the scope of the agriculture discipline, fuel ethanol could be covered. While the preceding analysis reflects a common reading of the AoA, the issue is not fully settled, and some room of maneuver may actually be present.[37]

The classification of biofuels as agricultural or industrial goods may have significant legal consequences. As we are about to see, while subsidies to industrial goods are regulated only by the SCM Agreement, subsidies to agricultural goods can in principle be regulated by both the AoA and the SCM Agreement. The implications for policy space may be dramatic.

B. Minimum Quantitative and Pricing Requirements

What *type* of public subsidies contributing to the mitigation of climate change do the WTO subsidy disciplines intend to address?

Regulatory incentives are particularly common in the green energy sector. For example, governments use mandates, containing quantity- or price-based minimum requirements, to raise the demand for, or the price of, renewable energy.[38] Can these mandates amount to subsidies?

The issue of whether regulatory measures can give rise to subsidies has always been very controversial, representing a true 'elusive frontier' of subsidy law and policy.[39] This is one of the cases where legal discourse is

---

[37]   Bigdeli, n. 32 above, for example, reports that the US notifies its biofuels subsidies under Article 25 of the SCM under the heading 'energy and fuels' rather than under the AoA.

[38]   Notable examples are respectively renewable portfolio standards or blending requirements or feed-in tariffs (FITs).

[39]   For an analysis of EU law see L. Rubini, 'The Elusive Frontier: Regulation under EC State Aid Law', *European State Aid Law Quarterly* (2009), 277.

most clearly affected by broader constitutional and policy considerations. Regulation is often linked to the inner prerogatives of countries to define their domestic policies according to societal choices and preferences. This explains why international trade law tries to avoid interference with governmental regulatory-making powers unless there are elements of discrimination that would impair competition. This notion of deference also explains why, in the context of subsidy laws, the possibility of including certain types of regulation in the definition of 'subsidy' is rejected based on legal arguments of seemingly technical nature – for example the given language of subsidy definition – which are however, in our view, largely based on justifications of policy or even principle.

The need to answer the question, 'Where and how should we draw the line with regulation?' shows the divide between economic and legal analyses. From an economic perspective, regulatory measures are instruments of subsidization if they produce similar effects to subsidies, i.e. interfere with costs and prices, reallocating resources from one sector to another. The legal notion of subsidy, however, is usually less inclusive and is the result of the balancing of various rationales – economic, systemic and policy ones – ultimately based on the *telos* of subsidy discipline within the broader *teloi* of the trade system.

According to Article 1 of the SCM Agreement, a subsidy exists if, apart from conferring a benefit, there is a financial contribution by the government. This contribution may come about through the purchase of goods or services by the government itself or by a third party entrusted or directed by it.[40] In the latter case, item (iv) hastens to add that the 'function' of purchasing goods or services should be one 'which would normally be vested in the government and the practice, in no real sense, differs from practices normally followed by governments'. As an alternative to the notion of 'financial contribution', Article 1.1(b) provides that a subsidy is present if there is 'any form of income or price support'.

As regards the concept of financial contribution, there has been some discussion on the meaning of 'entrust' and 'direct', with a progressively more liberal approach prevailing.[41] It is however the construction of the two largely elliptical sentences that require that 'function' and 'practice' should correspond to 'normal' governmental conduct that ultimately determines whether certain regulatory measures are apt to qualify as subsidy under

---

[40] Under the combined application of letters (ii) and (iv) of Article 1.1(a)(1).

[41] See WTO Appellate Body, *Japan – Countervailing Duties on Dynamic Random Access Memories from Korea*, WT/DS336/AB/R, adopted 17 December 2007.

WTO law. Now, it is argued, the crux of the problem is that the interpretation of these two provisos is decisively influenced by broader policy – we could say teleological – considerations which revolve around the question: 'Is it appropriate that regulation, or this type of regulation, be caught?'

It is in this light that Howse's suggestion that a feed-in tariff (FIT) for renewable energy should not constitute a subsidy can be appreciated. He noted that the minimum price purchase requirements of a FIT (in the instant case the German laws discussed in the EU *PreussenElektra* case)

> do not represent a delegation of a governmental function to any private body; rather they represent a *regulation* of the electricity market, and their directive character goes to regulating market behavior and transactions, not imposing a governmental function on a private body.[42]

If we look for a moment at the economic consequences of FIT schemes, however, it is not difficult to see that these measures may produce similar if not identical effects to more traditional forms of subsidies and in that sense are comparable to them. Although appealing, Howse's abstract distinction between 'delegation of function' and 'market regulation' is not an easy legal test to apply in order to classify public conduct under subsidy laws. Its value is more in its ability to describe rather than to prescribe. What is, for example, the element, or the elements, telling us that a FIT scheme is 'market regulation' rather than 'delegation of function'? In the common version of FIT schemes, the fixing of the price is often combined with a purchase obligation. In the context of the legal analysis of subsidy, it is this mandate to buy energy that comes into play as a candidate for the financial contribution.[43] But – crucially – what distinguishes this mandate to buy from any other mandate to buy?

---

[42]   R. Howse, 'Post-Hearing Submission to the International Trade Commission: World Trade Law and Renewable Energy: The Case of Non-Tariff Measures', 5 May 2005, Renewable Energy and International Law Project, 22.

With an even clearer policy-informed language it was concluded that FIT's pricing law could not constitute 'price support' either: 'In my view, price regulation by government, in the context of utilities as well as network industries more generally, ought not to be considered price support under Article 1.1(a)(2). Because such utilities are often characterized by elements of monopoly provision, and price regulation reflects a variety of public policy goals, including universal service and incentives for appropriate investment in infrastructure, it would be difficult and very intrusive into the operation of the democratic regulatory state for the WTO dispute settlement organs to assess whether, against some hypothetical model of a perfect market, the tariffs in question constitute price support.' Howse, n. 14 above, footnote 6.

[43]   The fixing of the tariff is only relevant in so far as it confers an economic benefit to the sellers. An additional element of advantage may derive from the support of demand through the purchase obligation.

If it is true that the legal definition of subsidy does not rest only on the economic effects of the measure and does not encompass *any* type of conduct liable to produce similar effects,[44] too restrictive and formalistic an interpretation would appear unreasonably to distinguish like measures, as well as offer an easy incentive to circumvent the law. Although it is not easy to draw the line, it could be suggested that measures that constitute *equally direct* and *immediate forms of support* – like FITs and purchase mandates – should be covered by a legal definition of subsidy.[45]

Although, ultimately, the subsidy status of FITs, and more generally regulation, is a policy issue, it is clear that from a legal standpoint a positive finding must find some textual basis in Article 1 of the SCM Agreement.

In the context of the financial contribution, what eventually determines whether a mandate is a subsidy is the possibility of classifying the mandated purchase of goods or services as 'normal' governmental function or practice.[46] The notion of *normality* is however an uncertain criterion which may be interpreted in various ways. In a brief paragraph, the Appellate Body has recently shed some light on its reading of the two final sentences of letter (iv) by referring to 'what would ordinarily be considered part of governmental practice in the legal order of the relevant Member' and 'within WTO Members generally'.[47] This seems to apparently dispose of more abstract or philosophical approaches about what government is or should be in favor of a more factual one. Crucial issues remain open though. How does one define 'ordinarily'? What is the relevant baseline? Is there a minimum recurrence or a certain pattern that makes something 'ordinary'? Furthermore, moving to the interpretation of 'practices normally followed by governments', how do we define what 'WTO Members generally' do? Does this mean 'what most governments do'? If so, is there

---

[44] This is the main point of the fundamental report of the Panel Report, *United States – Measures Treating Export Restraints as Subsidies*, WT/DS194/R, adopted 23 August 2001.

[45] See L. Rubini, *The Definition of Subsidy and State Aid – WTO Law and EC Law in Comparative Perspective* (Oxford: Oxford University Press, 2009), 121. This reading would, in our view, explain why tariffs and export restraints, and in general other border measures, are not considered subsidies. Ibid., 95.

[46] See A. Reich, 'Privately Subsidized Recycling Schemes and their Potential Harm to the Environment of Developing Countries: Does International Trade Law Have a Solution?', Bar Ilan University Public Law Working Paper No. 2–5, 4 March 2004, 12–13.

[47] See Appellate Body Report, *United States – Definitive Anti-Dumping and Countervailing Duties on Certain Products from China*, WT/DS379/AB/R, adopted 25 March 2011, para. 297.

a minimum number of governments that is required to satisfy the evidential burden? In our view, the open-ended nature of these questions shows the inherent flexibility of the concept of 'normality' that cannot rest on a simple examination of legal systems or on empirical surveys. A qualitative judgment is eventually called for, one that is (more) prone to conclusions based (also) on policy preferences.[48]

Against the uncertainties of the concept of normality, the easiest technical route for including regulation in the definition of subsidy is the notion of 'any price support' whose language is broad and unqualified.[49] In the context of the definition of subsidy, this limb has a clear extensive function going beyond what may amount to a financial contribution. The Appellate Body expressly confirmed that this provision should regulate measures *different* from, and in particular *additional to*, those considered as financial contribution when, after outlining the various forms of governmental action disciplined therein, it noted that the 'range of government measures capable of providing subsidies is *broadened still further* by the concept of "income or price support" in paragraph (2) of Article 1.1(a)'.[50] A FIT seems to be readily covered by the notion of 'price support' which the *China – GOES* Panel has recently found to involve the government 'setting and maintaining' a fixed price level.[51]

The pending *Canada – Renewable Energy* and *Canada – Feed-In Tariff Program* disputes may provide an answer to these crucial issues. Although the element challenged in these cases is the local content requirement, the success of the case under the SCM Agreement initially depends on the determination that the FIT is a subsidy. Hence, unless the parties are in agreement on the existence of a subsidy, the Panel will have to first estab-

---

[48]   What is arguably clear, however, is that the two final sentences of letter (iv) cannot be equated to the exercise of the prerogatives of taxation and expenditure, since this construction would by necessity imply that a financial contribution always requires a cost to government which has been rejected by the Appellate Body (*Canada – Aircraft*, para. 161). See Rubini, n. 45 above 144–145.

[49]   S. Bigdeli, n. 32 above, 171–172. *Contra* R. Howse, n. 14 above, footnote 6. For an analysis of this notion see Rubini, n. 45 above, 123–125.

[50]   Appellate Body Report, *United States – Final Countervailing Duty Determination with Respect to Certain Softwood Lumber from Canada*, WT/DS257/AB/R, adopted 17 February 2004, para. 52 (emphasis added).

[51]   Panel Report, *China – Countervailing and Antidumping Duties on Grain Oriented Flat-Rolled Electrical Steel from the United States*, WT/DS414/R, adopted 16 November 2012, para. 7.86. The Panel was careful in noting that, while the concept of 'price support' would involve the direct 'setting and maintaining' of price, it would not cover 'a random change [in price] merely being a side-effect of any form of government measure'.

lish whether the FIT is a subsidy and then determine whether it is prohibited because it is contingent on the use of local inputs.[52]

In the previous exposition, we have tested the scope of the concept of 'financial contribution' and 'price support' using the example of FITs for renewables. Broadly similar considerations apply also to quantity purchase mandates, like renewable portfolio standards or fuel blending requirements, whereby green producers are ensured that all or part of their production will be purchased. A mandate to buy is also a crucial element of FIT schemes and is a key element for the legal analysis. As before, the key issues would be whether the mandate to purchase does represent the 'entrustment' or 'direction' on private parties to 'purchase goods' and, crucially, whether this would be a 'normal' governmental practice. The same difficulties outlined above would appear here. Alternatively, the mandate to buy energy, or indeed technology, could be more easily construed as a form of 'income support' (as opposed to the 'price support' of pricing requirements) inasmuch as its intended goal is to ensure a market for the relevant goods.

C. Cap-and-Trade Systems and Allocation of Emission Allowances

Cap-and-trade systems, also known as emissions trading schemes, are a common regulatory measure intended to reduce emissions in a cost-effective manner. The cost-effectiveness relates to the incentives purposely created to cash in one's own efficiency in reducing emissions by trading the relevant permits.[53]

We continue our analysis by asking how extensive the coverage of WTO subsidy law can be. An interesting question is whether the participation in a cap-and-trade system can confer a subsidy. More specifically, the most raised issue is whether the allocation of tradable allowances, the characterizing element of this market-based mechanism, can be caught.

The allocation of allowances free of charge may be a case of foregoing of governmental revenue 'otherwise due' under SCM Article 1.1(a)(1)(ii). As we are about to see in the next section, the counterfactual analysis of the 'otherwise due' test is particularly challenging. The crux of the problem is the identification of the 'otherwise' applicable benchmark.

There is no international norm that expressly requires that allowances

---

[52] For an initial assessment of the case see M. Wilke, *Feed-in Tariffs for Renewable Energy and WTO Subsidy Rules: An Initial Legal Review* (ICTSD Programme on Trade and Environment; Trade and Sustainable Energy Series; Issue Paper No. 4; ICTSD, Geneva, Switzerland).

[53] Industries with low emissions abatement costs can save allowances and sell them to those industries with less favorable abatement opportunities.

be paid. Neither the UNFCCC nor any other international agreement provides an obligation to introduce an emissions trading scheme. More importantly, they do not touch upon whether, in the context of such a scheme, allowances should be auctioned or sold. The possibility to derive a normative benchmark from the polluter pays principle (PPP) is highly disputed, and, in any event, may have some relevance only for the EU (countries) and maybe the OECD countries.[54]

The central point of reference for a benchmark should therefore more likely be found in the domestic legal system of the cap-and-trade mechanism, and more specifically in the legal framework of the scheme itself. Thus, the general norm in domestic law with respect to allowances allocation is what needs to be identified. At the current nascent stage, existing emissions trading schemes allocate virtually all allowances for free. However, the fact that at least some allowances are auctioned could possibly confirm the existence of an 'otherwise due' scenario and offer a possible baseline. Further, the regulatory framework may provide that, at a certain point in time in the future, a larger share of allowances will be auctioned or otherwise distributed with a charge. This progressive phasing out of free allocation could help establish that the current scenario of free allocation is exceptional and the charge or price would be otherwise due.

Alternatively, the allocation of allowances may be considered as a form of 'provision of goods or services',[55] language which has been analyzed above. What is worth repeating is that the actual classification of emission allowances as goods or services is irrelevant in this respect since the SCM Agreement discipline covers the transfer of both. The interesting point to underline is that the coverage of the 'provision of goods or services' is particularly ample also because it would be apt to cover the allocation of allowances itself – irrespective of whether it is for free or for a price. As noted in section VI below, it could be argued that, in certain conditions, the participation in a cap-and-trade system itself can confer various forms of economic advantages.

Finally, it could be argued that the free allocation of allowances is a form of income support, particularly in the form of an increase in wealth of the recipient undertakings, which may produce an impact on trade.[56] As noted in section IV.B, the limb of the definition of subsidy focusing on 'any income or price support' in Article 1.1(a)(2) of the SCM is relatively unexplored but is increasingly attracting attention.

---

[54]   For a full analysis see Rubini and Jegou, n. 1 above.
[55]   Ibid.
[56]   See Rubini and Jegou, n. 1 above, 338.

V.   THE PUZZLES OF ENERGY AND ENVIRONMENTAL TAXATION

The subsidy status of tax incentives[57] is perplexing. The following analysis first outlines a few conceptual matters, which may be useful as a framework for analysis, and then applies this framework to real and hypothetical cases of environmental, energy and carbon taxation (using also, for their significance, a couple of examples of emission trading systems).

A.   The Inherent Instability of the 'Otherwise Due' Determination

According to item (ii) of Article 1.1(a)(1) of the SCM Agreement, the determination of whether a tax incentive constitutes a form of financial contribution depends on a positive finding that the measure involves the foregoing of government revenue that would otherwise be due. As shown by the *US – FSC* litigation, this determination is inherently unstable because of the difficulties of the 'otherwise due' language.[58] To determine what is 'otherwise due' requires a complex counterfactual analysis that ultimately rests on whether the measure under examination is a derogation from the otherwise applicable benchmark norm.[59]

But how can we identify the relevant norm in the field? How can we determine what is general and what is an exception? Taxation, in particular, is notorious for targeted interventions and a fast-changing pace. Complexity is pervasive, coherency rarely reached. The search for the general tax rule is therefore often difficult.[60]

If mechanical approaches and formalistic tests are to be avoided,[61] what

---

[57]   While tax exemptions involve a dispensation from tax liability, tax credits operate as offsets against tax owed.

[58]   The panels and the Appellate Body used no less than four different tests to approach this language. See Rubini, n. 45 above, 263–274.

[59]   For an analysis of this 'derogation test', see Rubini, n. 45 above, Chapter 9.

[60]   For an excellent conceptual analysis of all these issues, see L.B. Murphy and T. Nagel, *The Myth of Ownership: Taxes and Justice* (Oxford: Oxford University Press, 2002). See also E.J. McCaffery, 'The Holy Grail of Tax Simplification', 66 *Wisconsin Law Review* (1990), 1267.

[61]   The Appellate Body warned that, apart from the possibility of giving wrong results, a formalistic test like the 'but for' test may be easy to circumvent. See Appellate Body Report, *United States – Tax Treatment for 'Foreign Sales Corporations'*, WT/DS108/AB/RW, adopted 20 March 2000, para. 91; Appellate Body Report, *United States – Tax Treatment for 'Foreign Sales Corporations' – Recourse to Article 21.5 of the DSU by the European Communities*, WT/DS108/AB/RW, adopted 29 January 2002, para. 91.

should be looked at is the *substance*. Only a substantive analysis can show whether the tax incentive under examination is in line with the relevant general tax norm or in fact constitutes a deviation from it. But, and this is the crucial point, to look at the substance of (tax) rules means to consider their *objectives* and evaluate how they actually relate to the (tax) measure at issue and to the broader (tax) system. If a tax incentive is designed and applied in such a way that it is fully in line with and implements, without exceeding, the objectives of the relevant general tax norm, there is no financial contribution. There are no 'otherwise' applicable alternative scenarios which have not been considered or have been deviated from. This is the kind of analysis that, in our view, the Appellate Body report in *US – Boeing* naturally drives at. To require a Panel to examine 'the *structure of the domestic tax regime* and its *organizing principles*',[62] is nothing but asking to entertain with the objectives informing the tax system and consequently the tax measure at issue.

The reference to the objectives of the domestic measure when it comes to assess whether a certain provision has been breached is not new. It can be found in provisions that establish obligations, such as non-discrimination, and in justification provisions.[63] The controversy surrounding the ill-fated 'aims-and-effects' doctrine under Article III of the GATT is known.[64] The understandable fear of the critics of this approach is that *any* allegation based on the legitimacy of the public policy goals of the tax (and regulatory) measure could pass muster with the risk of excluding protectionist conduct from the scope of a crucial GATT obligation. Despite being aware of this danger, the Appellate Body has not, however, rejected that objectives can play a useful role in the analysis of the differential treatment under Article III of the GATT. This is the message famously conveyed in the early *Japan – Alcohol II* dispute: '[w]e believe it is possible to examine objectively the underlying criteria used in a particular tax measure, its structure, and its overall application to ascertain whether it is applied in a way that affords protection to domestic

---

[62] Appellate Body, *United States – Measures Affecting Trade in Large Civil Aircraft (Second Complaint)*, WT/DS353/AB/R, adopted 23 March 2012, para. 815 (emphasis added).

[63] A recent insight into the role of the objectives of the measure under the national treatment obligation of Article 2.1 of the TBT Agreement can be found in the recent *United States – Measures Affecting the Production and Sale of Glove Cigarettes* (DS 406), Panel Report, paras 7.80 ff; Appellate Body Report, paras 155 ff. (both reports were adopted 24 April 2012).

[64] See e.g. R. Hudec, 'GATT/WTO Constraints on National Regulation: Requiem for an "Aims and Effects Test"', *International Lawyer* (1998), 619.

products'.[65] What the Appellate Body is doing is simply to ring-fence such analysis and to deny that each and every argument based on any objective could be relevant. The key is distinguishing among objectives, taking into account only those that relate inherently to the general norm (e.g. the 'polluter pays principle') underlying the measure, and assessing the relation between those objectives and the same measure. These remarks can be safely transposed to the context of subsidy rules. The objectives are thus a useful indicator of whether differential taxation is in fact justified.

At the time of writing, there is no WTO case-law on the role played by objectives in the subsidy analysis of tax measures (as noted, the recent Appellate Body report in *US – Boeing* may have taken this path). It can however be safely expected that future litigation will have to focus on this issue. Since analysis of the 'otherwise due' jargon unveils tests and issues that are essential when it comes to establish whether a tax incentive is a tax subsidy, a foretaste of what we can expect can be found in the rich EU case-law and practice in the State aid field.

B. Examples from the EU Case-law on the 'Logic of the System'

Since the seminal *Italy* v *Commission* case of the European Court of Justice of 1974, the same tension in the GATT 'aims-and-effect' debate can be found in the case-law on the definition of State aid (which is the EU law jargon for 'subsidy'). On the one hand, it is consistently repeated that the notion of State aid is objective. In order to define a State aid one does not need to look at aims or causes but only at the effects. On the other hand, and often at the same time, the analysis seems more subjective, being substantially focused on the rationality of a measure in terms of its goals. A finding of differential treatment does not necessarily lead to a State aid determination if it can be explained by the 'logic of the system'. This language significantly echoes that recently used by the Appellate Body when talking of the 'structure of the domestic tax regime and its organizing principles'.[66] The Court of Justice noted that to conclude that a State aid exists, we have to establish whether a State measure favors certain undertakings 'in comparison with other undertakings that are in a

---

[65] Appellate Body Report, *Japan – Taxes on Alcoholic Bevarages*, WT/DS8/AB/R, WT/DS10/AB/R, WT/DS11/AB/R, adopted 1 November 1996, p. 29. See also Appellate Body Report, *Chile – Taxes on Alcoholic Beverages*, WT/DS87/AB/R, WT/DS110/AB/R, adopted 12 January 2000, para. 62.

[66] Appellate Body, *United States – Measures Affecting Trade in Large Civil Aircraft (Second Complaint)*, WT/DS353/AB/R, adopted 23 March 2012, para. 815.

legal and factual situation that is comparable in the light of the objective pursued by the measure in question'.[67] This is the same application of the principle of equality that was followed also by the Appellate Body in the *US – FSC* case when it concluded that, in order to determine whether a tax measure involves the foregoing of revenue otherwise due, it is necessary 'to compare the fiscal treatment of legitimately comparable income'.[68]

The EU jurisprudence highlights two points. First, only those objectives that are *inherent* in the type of measure at issue, their true justification, matter in this assessment. By contrast, the objectives that are not directly connected to the first and natural purpose of the tax but rather pursue different policy goals are not taken into account.[69] Second, the assessment of the objective at the level of the definition of State aid involves what is essentially a *proportionality* test. The regulation must be designed in true pursuit of that objective and any distinction should be capable of being objectively explained in its light.

We can illustrate these principles with the analysis of few cases which focus on environmental taxation and emission trading systems.

In *Adria-Wien* the European Court of Justice concluded that an exemption from an energy tax in favor of undertakings of the manufacturing sector (and excluding those in the service sector) was not justified by the alleged environmental goal of the tax.[70] Service undertakings may, just like undertakings manufacturing goods, be major consumers of energy, and energy consumption, whatever its origin, is damaging to the environment. The fundamental distinction of the tax was thus not tenable – from an environmental perspective.[71]

Two more recent cases show the tension between a very deferential and a more rigorous approach. The core issue is the same and revolves around the definition of the material scope of the state measures under review – an environmental tax in one case, a cap-and-trade system in the other. The *British Aggregates* case concerned a UK environmental levy on aggregates with the aim of reducing and rationalizing the extraction of

---

[67]   Case C-143/99, *Adria-Wien* [2001] ECR I-8365, para. 41.

[68]   Appellate Body Report, *United States – Tax Treatment for 'Foreign Sales Corporations' – Recourse to Article 21.5 of the DSU by the European Communities*, WT/DS108/AB/RW, adopted 29 January 2002, para. 91.

[69]   The distinction between 'internal' and 'external' objectives can be found in the Commission Notice on the application of the State aid rules to measures relating to direct business taxation, OJ C384, 10.12.1998, 3.

[70]   Case C-143/99, *Adria-Wien* [2001] ECR I-8365, paras 50 and 52.

[71]   In fact what emerged from the statement of reasons for the bill was that the advantageous treatment of manufacturing firms was intended to preserve their competitiveness.

minerals commonly used as aggregates. To incentivize the replacement of virgin materials, an exemption was ostensibly granted to recycled products or by-products or waste products from other processes. Furthermore, the tax did not apply to the same minerals if they were not used as aggregates. The first exemption was allegedly justified by the contribution of the use of those materials to the environmental rationalization of the sector, the second by the sectoral approach of the tax (motivated by the desire to maintain the international competitiveness of other extractive sectors). In the *Dutch NO$_x$* case the issue was whether the Dutch emission trading system for nitrogen oxides (NO$_x$) constituted State aid. In particular, the key question was whether the installations with total thermal capacity of more than 20 thermal megawatts (MWth), to which the emission trading system was applicable, were comparable with those with lower thermal capacity, which were excluded.

In the two appeal decisions, the European Court of Justice heavily criticized the General Court for concluding that the relevant measures did not confer State aid.[72] The thrust of the criticism is that the General Court had essentially approved the measures loosely on the basis of their stated environmental objective, without scrutinizing whether the coverage of the tax exemptions in one case and the cap-and-trade system in the other were properly structured around and justified by that objective. Once a certain objective is chosen, for example the prevention of a certain type of environmental damage, a degree of rationality is required, and this should first of all be reflected in the *scope* of the measure. It may, for example, look dubious to consider relevant for the application of the environmental tax the use of certain minerals as aggregates rather than their extraction. It is the latter, not the former, that has an impact on the environment. Equally, any differentiation between installations that produce emissions in the design of cap-and-trade systems requires a legitimate justification. The simple fact that the system covers only those installations that produce 'substantial' NO$_x$ emissions is not as such enough to justify the exclusion of other installations.

The question of coverage is key for policy space and the proper design of tax incentives under subsidy laws. How far shall a tax go in covering comparable situations? What differentiations can be reasonably introduced without defeating the generality of the measure? On what basis? The case-law has not clearly answered these key questions yet.[73] Arguably,

---

[72] C-487/06P, *British Aggregates v Commission* [2008] ECR I-10515; Case C-279/08P, *Netherlands v Commission*, Judgment of 8 September 2011, not yet reported.

[73] A good example is the recent remand decision in *British Aggregates*. The General Court did not really discuss the UK prerogative to limit the scope of

without conferring an arbitrary discretion, a selective, sectoral or progressive approach may be justifiable in light of *objective* considerations such as the nature or source of damage, the type or degree of risk, or even practical considerations such as the novelty of the scheme or the difficulty of its application. Despite these limitations the measure could still be considered general, self-contained and balanced.[74]

C. Two Hypothetical Applications: The US 'Black Liquor' Tax Credit and the Swiss Climate Cent Tax Biofuel Exemption

The application of the conceptual analysis above to two examples concerning an energy tax and a carbon tax, which have not been subject to litigation, can further illustrate the intricacies of the subsidy status of tax incentives.

The US 'black liquor' tax credit. The 2005 US Federal Highway Bill introduced a fuel tax credit to promote the use of ethanol and other biofuels in vehicles. Companies were eligible for a US\$ 0.50 tax credit for every gallon (3.7854 litres) of gasoline or diesel they used if they blended an alternative fuel with it. In 2007 the coverage of the tax credit was expanded to include non-mobile uses of liquid alternative fuel derived from biomass. For more than 30 years the US pulp industry has been using a carbon-rich by-product of the wood pulping process (known as 'black liquor') as fuel to power its mills. In a 2008 ruling the Internal Revenue Service concluded that black liquor was an alternative fuel eligible under the Highway Bill tax credit and that, to qualify for the tax credit, alternative fuels only needed to contain 0.1 percent of a taxable fuel. The economic impact of this extension was massive in a period of crisis for the paper industry.[75]

---

the environmental levy to the aggregate sector only, simply calling for the latter's coherent definition. See T-202/02 RENV, *British Aggregates v Commission*, Judgment of 7 March 2012.

[74] It is interesting to read the analysis of the Court of Justice in Case C-127/07, *Arcelor* [2008] ECR I-09895, where the issue was whether the step-by-step approach of the EU emission trading system under Directive 2003/87/EC, which excluded the chemical and the non-ferrous metal sectors from its application, breached the general principle of equal treatment or could be justified by the objectives, complexity and novelty of the mechanism.

[75] 'Papermakers dig deep in Highway Bill to hit gold', *The Washington Post*, 28 March 2009, available at http://www.washingtonpost.com/wp-dyn/content/article/2009/03/27/AR2009032703116.html (last access 15 September 2011). Since this tax credit is refundable, money-losing companies could qualify for direct payments from the US Treasury. A little gloss here. Although tax credits are expressly named as one example of a tax incentive under Article 1.1(a)(1)(ii) of the SCM

In 2009 alone, the US pulp industry received billions of US dollars from this tax credit (estimates indicate benefits of up to US$ 8 billion), more than any other industry apart from the auto sector. One company alone, International Paper, received as much as US$ 3.7 billion. The frequent assimilation of 'black liquor' with 'gold' can thus be understood.[76]

This is an example of how, whether due to sloppiness of legal drafting, political pressure and/or unwarranted administrative interpretation, the broadening of the eligibility for a tax credit resulted in a paradoxical result which clearly went beyond, indeed *against the purpose* of the tax incentive. The original goal of the Highway Bill tax credit was to boost the use of bio-fuels in the transport sector, and this was later extended to cover non-mobile uses. The tax credit operated to create the incentive to do this by requiring companies to blend biofuels with their fossil fuels. By using their own kind of biofuel – the 'black liquor' – for decades, pulp companies did not need any incentive to replace fossil fuels, even partially. Not only was the subsidy not necessary, it even created a perverse incentive to use fossil fuels. To qualify for the tax credit paper manufacturers had to add some fossil fuel, even in a negligible quantity (0.1 percent), to their alternative fuel. They were there-fore induced to alter their behavior but in exactly the opposite direction than that envisaged by the logic of the tax incentive and stated goal of the subsidy. Ultimately, the perverse effect of the extension of the Highway Bill tax credit to black liquor meant that a *more polluting conduct was rewarded.*

While the Highway Bill alternative fuel tax credit may well not have constituted a subsidy, particularly if it could be considered an integral part

---

Agreement, if a payment is involved they could be likened to a direct transfer of funds under letter (i) with the consequence that the 'otherwise due' counterfactual analysis would not apply.

[76]   One further element can show the financial dimension of this 'black liquor' tax credit. The eligibility of the pulp industry to the Highway Bill tax credit expired on 31 December 2009, thus helping to cover the costs of the Healthcare law of January 2010. This was not the end of support, however, since the pulp industry could inter alia benefit from a different tax credit for cellulosic biofuel for tran-sportation for which it was eligible according to another ruling of the Internal Revenue Service. See 'Paper industry pushed further into the black by 'black liquor' tax credits', *The Washington Post*, 27 April 2011, available at http://www.washingtonpost.com/business/economy/paper-industry-pushed-further-into-the-black-by-black-liquor-tax-credits/2011/04/19/AFdkrMtE_story.html (last access 15 September 2011).

The 'black liquor' subsidy not only caused controversy within the US but prom-pted Canada to grant $882 million to their domestic paper industry. See 'The Black Liquor War', *The Wall Street Journal*, 30 June 2009, available at http://online.wsj.com/article/SB124623488607866601.html#articleTabs%3Darticle (last access 15 September 2011).

of a general scheme to promote biofuels, the extension of the incentive to the pulp industry was clearly contrary to the purpose of the scheme. It could not easily escape the determination that it deviated from the logic of the scheme and that, by granting it, the US government was 'foregoing or not collecting' revenue otherwise due under Article 1.1.(a)(1) of the SCM Agreement. It did not therefore come as a surprise that a joint letter from Canada, the EU, Brazil and Chile demanded the US to end the tax incentive threatening to commence a dispute before the WTO because '[f]rom a legal perspective, it is clear that these credits amount to actionable subsidies and that any adverse effects caused by them could be subject to remedies in the WTO or through domestic countervailing duty investigations'.[77]

The Swiss Climate Cent tax biofuel exemption. Carbon taxes are one way to put a cost on GHG emissions. Quite often the tax liability is limited through tax exemptions which specifically recognize that certain goods or activities do not emit or emit less. The use of exemptions reinforces the incentive to use those desirable goods or activities or, from another perspective, the disincentive to use other more polluting goods. As the review of EU case-law shows, this is indeed a common technique in environmental taxation. However, 'a fully fledged carbon taxation system need not entail a tax exemption. In such a system, any emitter would pay a consistent rate of carbon tax according to the amount of CO_2 they emit'.[78] In other words, a carbon tax properly designed should already reflect the different impact on the environment of goods or activities by providing a different tax liability.

But different liability does not mean no liability. It is indeed difficult to identify goods or activities that do not produce CO_2 or other GHGs emissions at all over their life cycles. Consequently, strictly speaking, no goods or activity should be exempt from the tax.

This is why tax exemptions are troublesome from a subsidy perspective.[79] The marked differential treatment of a full exemption cannot be easily justified. Inasmuch as the mischief of the carbon tax – carbon pollu-

---

[77] Communication reported in 'Black Liquor', Schott's Vocab, *The New York Times*, 11 June 2009, available at http://schott.blogs.nytimes.com/2009/06/11/black-liquor/ (last access 15 September 2011). As regards the alleged adverse effects, it was noted that the tax credit encouraged US companies to overproduce in a depressed market.

[78] Bigdeli, n. 32 above, 166.

[79] Policy-wise, it may be desirable to increase the incentive (or disincentive) effect of an environmental tax by resorting to blunt techniques like exemptions. Furthermore, other reasons of a pragmatic or political nature, not strictly linked to the environmental discourse may justify a differential approach and contribute to the effectiveness and acceptability of the measure. But the legal framework may

tion – is present, irrespective of its extent, an explicit and complete carve-out would clearly constitute a derogation from the underlying norm that 'the polluter must pay'. Bigdeli analyzed the case of the Swiss Climate Cent tax where CHF 0.0015 per litre were paid on gasoline and diesel with a full exemption for biofuels, and made comments along the previous lines.[80] If we consider the emissions generated during the life cycle of biofuels, the Swiss tax exemption led to a contradictory result.[81] If the exemption is a subsidy, this would be greater for biofuels with a bigger life cycle and hence more polluting.

D. Conclusion

The subsidy status of tax incentives is inherently uncertain. This does not depend on how the relevant applicable rules are drafted. The laconic wording of the WTO 'otherwise due' test is the simple and pure reproduction of the logical test that underlies any subsidy determination, and which in essence calls for an analysis of the measure's rationality in light of its objectives. If it is difficult to conceive a better formulation,[82] it is clear that legal uncertainty is inherently inimical to policy space.

VI.   BENEFIT ANALYSIS IN A DISTORTED MARKET: BENCHMARKING CONDUCT, CORRECTING FAILURES

To qualify as a subsidy under the SCM Agreement, a financial contribution or a measure of income/price support has to confer a benefit. This requires establishing that the recipient is 'better off' than it would have been absent the alleged measure of support.[83]

In some cases the benefit analysis is straightforward. It is, for example, almost intuitive that if the government is foregoing government revenue

---

not be so responsive, at least at the level of the definition of what is and what is not subsidy.

[80]   Bigdeli, n. 32 above, 166–167.

[81]   Like in the 'Black Liquor' tax credit saga.

[82]   EU State aid law has progressed on a much more laconic textual language which forbids 'any aid granted in any form whatsoever'. The test used by the Commission and the Community Courts has however been the same.

[83]   Appellate Body Report, *Canada – Measures Affecting the Export of Civilian Aircraft*, WT/DS70/AB/R, adopted 20 August 1999, para. 157.

which, under normal conditions, the recipient should have paid, this, by nature, confers a benefit.

In other cases, however, if the government is acting in the market, the determination of whether this conduct is conferring a benefit may not be easy. The Appellate Body has repeated various times that the benchmark in this case is the 'marketplace'.[84] This benchmarking process may, however, face difficulties in the case of energy markets which have been heavily distorted by various forms of government intervention with the result that price and other market signals are not fully reliable. Howse recently noted:

> The 'market' into which subsidies to address climate change are intervening is one that has historically been pervasively distorted by subsidies, including fiscal advantages, provided to producers and consumers of (greenhouse gas-emitting) fossil fuels. It is also a market in which existing networks for the distribution and retailing of energy – whether electricity grids or chains of service stations – have been largely designed to favour fossil fuels. In addition, subsidies schemes and tax systems have often, apart from distorting choices among energy sources, led to a reduction in incentives for energy efficiency in that they relieve users from paying the full marginal cost of an additional unit of energy.[85]

If the 'market' is significantly distorted, the identification and determination of the actual benchmark to test the advantage allegedly conferred by the subsidy may thus be elusive.[86]

While a crucial objective of subsidy discipline is to determine whether the subsidy confers a competitive benefit, the benefit analysis at this stage is more limited. Its goal is to ascertain whether, by virtue of the governmental action, the recipient of the subsidy finds itself in a more advantageous position than before the subsidy. This assessment should emerge

---

[84]   Ibid.; Appellate Body Report, *Japan – Countervailing Duties on Dynamic Random Access Memories from Korea*, WT/DS336/AB/R, adopted 17 December 2007, para. 172; *European Communities – Measures Affecting Trade in Large Civil Aircraft*, WT/DS 316/AB/R, adopted 1 June 2011, paras 974–976.

[85]   Howse, n. 14 above, 6.

[86]   The Appellate Body has addressed difficulties of this nature in those cases where the heavy public intervention in the economy made the benefit analysis difficult. The solution was the use of other proxies, like costs. See Appellate Body Report, *Canada – Measures Affecting the Importation of Milk and the Exportation of Dairy Products – Recourse to Article 21.5 of the DSU by New Zealand and the United States*, WT/DS103/AB/RW, WT/DS113/AB/RW, adopted 18 December 2001, and, more controversially, Appellate Body Report, *United States – Final Countervailing Duty Determination with Respect to Certain Softwood Lumber from Canada*, WT/DS257/AB/R, adopted 17 February 2004. See Rubini, n. 45 above, 226–233.

from what is merely a preliminary and limited (and, possibly, using Sykes' words, 'myopic')[87] counterfactual analysis which refers to a positive alteration of the *status quo*. Whether the subsidy ultimately affects the competitive position of the recipient and its relation with competitors is analyzed subsequently and separately when the actual effects of the subsidy on trade are determined. If the subsidy is not really conferring a competitive advantage but is just compensating a disadvantage faced by the recipient, e.g. a renewable energy producer or a provider of energy efficiency technology,[88] in all likelihood this will result in a no-negative-effects determination. Any residual negative effect may be taken into account, and discounted for, when the positive impact of the subsidy is considered, and balanced with, at the justification level.[89]

Far than being a deficiency of the legal framework, this simplification is necessary to avoid an otherwise daunting assessment.[90] As energy markets demonstrate, a simplified benefit determination may already be difficult for the identification and application of the appropriate baseline. To charge it with too complex an analytical framework, potentially encompassing *any* action, or indeed omission, that might affect the matrix of positive and negative effects for the subsidy recipient, would mean unpracticability (where do we stop?) and potentially – a dooming effect for subsidy control – a possible sequence of invariably negative (no-benefit) determinations.[91]

For these reasons, any type of compensatory or corrective logic at the level of the benefit analysis is ultimately unwarranted.[92] A common temptation is to distinguish between scenarios. In some cases the exclusion of a benefit would immediately emerge from a situation where we have the

---

[87]   A.O. Sykes, 'The Questionable Case for Subsidies Regulation: A Comparative Perspective', *Journal of Legal Analysis* (2010), 473, 502.

[88]   It is also obvious that a crucial and preliminary issue for any subsidy discipline is to determine what kind of disadvantages should be relevant for the analysis, which is eminently a policy choice.

[89]   The existence of justification provisions already covering these considerations may be an additional argument to support the rejection of a too comprehensive benefit analysis. Its lack, however, cannot be used as argument to include a compensation logic in the benefit determination. It may simply highlight a lacuna in the system.

[90]   The different notions of 'benefit' in economic and legal analysis are a good example of the different operation of the two disciplines.

[91]   *Contra* Sykes, n. 87 above, 502–503, who crucially questions 'the utility of any system of disciplines that ignores the myriad of potentially offsetting government measures'.

[92]   The various versions of this logic are extensively analyzed in Bigdeli, n. 9 above, 28–30.

clear and simple compensation of a cost, burden or disadvantage.[93] For the reasons noted above, this temptation should be resisted.[94]

This brief exposition suggests a significant degree of complexity for many cases of benefit determinations in the energy field. There is one interesting case though where the benefit analysis would not be linked to complex market benchmarking and the conclusion that a benefit has been conferred might be more easy to reach.

In the *Dutch NO_x* case the European Court of Justice made interesting remarks on the advantages of participating in a cap-and-trade system (emission trading system, in the EU jargon). While, in general, *every* Dutch firm the operations of which produce NO_x emissions had to comply with obligations regarding the limitation or reduction of those emissions, *only* the large firms covered by the scheme, and subject to its emission reduction standard, did however

> enjoy the advantage of being able to monetise the economic value of the emission reductions they achieve, by converting them into tradable emission allowances or, as the case may be, avoiding the risk of having to pay fines when they exceed the NO_x emission limit per unit of energy laid down by the national authorities by buying such emission allowance from other undertakings falling within the measure in question.[95]

In a nutshell, the suggestion coming from this case-law is that the participation in a cap-and-trade system may be advantageous in itelf, if the

---

[93]　Howse (n. 14 above, 13) offers a good example of this argumentation: 'Measures that merely defray the cost of businesses acquiring renewable energy systems or that compensate enterprises for providing renewable energy in remote locations do not necessarily, for instance, confer a benefit on the recipient enterprise. They simply reimburse or compensate the enterprise for taking some action that it would otherwise not take, and the enterprise has not necessarily acquired any competitive advantage over other enterprises that neither take the subsidy nor have to perform these actions.'

[94]　This is the approach followed in the EU, the only exception being the compensation of the costs of a public service obligation. After fluctuations, the European Court of Justice accepted in the *Altmark* decision (Case C-280/00, *Altmark Trans GmbH, Regierungspräsidium Magdeburg v Nahverkehrsgesellschaft Altmark GmbH* [2003] ECR I-7747) that, in the presence of certain conditions of transparency and strict proportionality, there should be no advantage and hence no State aid. For an early commentary see A. Biondi and L. Rubini, 'Aims, Effects and Justifications: EC State Aid Law and its Impact on National Social Policies', in M. Dougan and E. Spaventa (eds), *Social Welfare and EU Law* (Oxford: Hart Publishing, 2005), 79.

[95]　Case C-279/08P, *Netherlands v Commission*, Judgment of 8 September 2011, not yet reported, para. 63.

starting point is one where all undertakings are in any case subject to emission reduction commitments. In other words, if the prevailing regulatory framework already imposes a 'cap', the only new element introduced – and the one which would confer a benefit – is the possibility to cash in on one's own efficiency by 'trading' emissions and, if the case may be, to escape penalties for inefficient over-pollution.

VII. THE PARADOX OF SPECIFICITY AND ADVERSE EFFECTS: POLICY AND LAW AT VARIANCE?

Unless we are dealing with a prohibited subsidy, the next steps of the legal analysis require a determination of whether the subsidy is specific and whether it causes certain negative trade effects. Although separate, these two steps are examined together because they share the same paradox.

A. Specificity

According to Article 2 of the SCM Agreement, a subsidy must be specific to certain enterprises or industries. This provision encompasses multiple tests which can be used in a determination, in a way that is flexible, unclear and, in the end, expansionist.[96] Apart from the relatively easy cases where the granting authority or the legislation explicitly limits access to a subsidy to certain enterprises (in law or *de jure* specificity), the outcome of the analysis depends on a comprehensive examination of the factual scenario relating to the criteria of eligibility of the subsidy and its actual impact.

Under Article 2.1(b) of the SCM Agreement, the subsidy cannot be specific if the eligibility of the subsidy depends on 'objective criteria or conditions', that is 'criteria or conditions which are neutral, which do not favour certain enterprises over others, and which are economic in nature and horizontal in application, such as number of employees or size of enterprises'. Bigdeli has recently suggested that these criteria could offer some policy space, particularly if the subsidy is *designed* following them as guidelines of neutrality and non-discrimination.[97] As examples he referred to energy-saving subsidies or subsidies for consumers of renewable energy. Both these subsidies would be non-specific inasmuch as they would be

---

[96] Rubini, n. 45 above, Chapter 13.
[97] Bigdeli, n. 9 above, 23–27.

technology-neutral, horizontal and non-discriminatory (i.e. not favouring domestically produced green energy or technology over imported ones).

There are two obstacles here, one policy-based and one legal.

Assuming a climate change subsidy could be designed to comply with the said guidelines, a paradox would emerge. If, as noted in section II, sound economic and environmental policy requires the measure to be as targeted as possible in order to be effective, this means that there is clearly a preference for precise, probably non-neutral and, perhaps in some cases, even discriminatory (read: favoring domestic producers or products) measures of support. This would mean that the policy prescription and the legal requirements are at variance with each other. In so far as this conflict cannot be reconciled, the room for policy space would be seriously compromised.

From a legal perspective, despite the formal adherence to the principles of neutrality and non-discrimination of Article 2.1(b), the subsidy may still be found to be specific under Article 2.1(c) if it can be shown that, in fact, the subsidy mainly benefits certain enterprises.[98] What should be proven is not 'a rigid quantitative definition' but that the subsidy is 'sufficiently limited', or, with a negative formulation, that it is not 'sufficiently broadly available throughout the economy'.[99] It is clear from the case-law that the large number of the undertakings or even sectors affected is not sufficient to conclude that the subsidy is general and not specific.[100] Consequently, the specificity test may be very easy to fulfill in the case of subsidies in support of renewable energy or energy efficiency, and, in this regard, the design and breadth of the measure do not seem really relevant. Whether the subsidy targets only a certain technology (e.g. wind or solar, or fluorescent lighting) or certain uses (e.g. transport, electricity, heat, insulation), or is rather more generally available across the broad spectrum of renew-

---

[98] The factors to consider are 'use of a subsidy programme by a limited number of certain enterprises, predominant use by certain enterprises, the granting of disproportionately large amounts of subsidy to certain enterprises, and the manner in which discretion has been exercised by the granting authority in the decision to grant a subsidy'.

[99] Panel Report, *United States – Subsidies on Upland Cotton*, WT/DS267/R, adopted 21 March 2005, para. 7.1142.

[100] See Panel Report, *United States – Final Countervailing Duty Determination with Respect to Certain Softwood Lumber from Canada*, WT/DS257/R, adopted 17 February 2004, paras 7.115–7.122. The Panel Report, *United States – Measures Affecting Trade in Large Civil Aircraft (Second Complaint)*, WT/DS353/R, adopted 23 March 2012, noted that the Panel in *US – Cotton* even indicated that 'something less than universal availability can lead to a finding of non-specificity' (para. 7.762).

able energy sources and applications, or energy efficiency technologies; whether it focuses on investment or R&D; whether it operates at the levels of supply or demand of clean energy, the fact remains that the 'clean energy' industry is still a small, albeit increasingly significant, player in the energy market. Further, even if it were to expand and become the dominant or even the exclusive actor in the energy field, it would still be one industry in the broader economy.

What is crucial for the purposes of our analysis is the relationship between this test of *de facto* specificity and its factors on the one hand, and the previous 'objectivity criteria' on the other. Although the Appellate Body has recently underlined that the principles outlined in paragraphs (a), (b) and (c) should be applied concurrently,[101] the language of Article 2 seems to give ultimate significance to *de facto* specificity.[102] This means that the possibility of designing certain climate change subsidies in a neutral and non-discriminatory way may not be enough to escape a finding of specificity.

B.   Adverse Effects

Specific subsidies may be actionable only if they cause adverse effects to the interests of other countries. This, on its face, seems to recognize a reasonable leeway to governments granting subsidies. On the one hand, this is a notoriously difficult legal hurdle for the complainants to prove. On the other, if the granting government could reduce or even eliminate the negative effects of the subsidy, the measure of support would be safe. On a closer scrutiny, however, the same paradox of the specificity test emerges.

The various tests of adverse effects can be found in Articles 5 and 6 of the SCM Agreement: (i) injury to the domestic industry,[103] (ii) nullification and impairment of benefits, i.e. tariff concessions, and (iii) serious prejudice in various forms mainly of displacement and price effects in various markets. Subsidies can thus cause harm in different ways that

---

[101]   Appellate Body Report, *United States – Definitive Anti-Dumping and Countervailing Duties on Certain Products from China*, WT/DS379/AB/R, adopted 25 March 2011, paras 363 ff.

[102]   'If, notwithstanding any appearance of non specificity resulting from the application of the principles laid down in subparagraphs (a) and (b), there are reasons to believe that the subsidy may in fact be specific, other factors may be considered. Such factors are: . . .'. See Appellate Body Report, *United States – Measures Affecting Trade in Large Civil Aircraft (Second Complaint)*, WT/DS353/AB/R, para. 796.

[103]   Subsidized imports causing material injury to the domestic industry of another country may also be subject to countervailing duty actions.

substantially reflect the impact of the benefit of the subsidy on competitors. Subsidy laws are not concerned with simple financial benefits but with competitive benefits.[104]

Clearly, any assessment of the adverse impact on trade must be based on each actual scenario and take into account the various elements of the various legal tests. Since each measure differs from another, generalizations are not easy. It is therefore necessary to look at the terms and effects of each one individually. That said, it is clear that some predictions are possible, in particular with respect to the impact of subsidy design on the likelihood of a finding of adverse effects. Thus, for example, subsidies that do not discriminate against imported renewable energy and technology or energy saving technology, like consumption subsidies and purchase obligations with no discrimination as to the origin of energy or technology, are less likely to cause adverse effects. Furthermore, unless they are fully technology neutral, adverse effects may be claimed by any competitor, irrespective of whether he deals with conventional or renewable energy, energy saving or non-energy saving technologies. The likelihood of adverse effects can also significantly depend on trade patterns, which seem to show more trade with respect to technology or fuel rather than actual electricity.[105] A general difficulty in determining and attributing adverse effects may derive from the already noted heavy regulation of energy markets and from the significant subsidization of fossil fuels.

From a policy perspective, even assuming a subsidy could be adapted – in its design phase or during litigation compliance – so as to minimize its adverse effects, the fact remains that, if this means that a distinct policy benefit has to be renounced to comply with subsidy guidelines, the constraint on policy space may be significant.

To conclude, with remarks which are equally valid for the specificity and adverse effects tests, the guidelines of trade law, which are informed by the fundamental principles of neutrality and non-discrimination, are not fully consistent with the guidelines that come out from best economic and environmental policy practice. The most effective measures of support of green energy should be targeted, specific and encompass a differential

---

[104]   See R. Diamond, 'Privatization and the Definition of Subsidy: A Critical Study of Appellate Body Texturalism', *Journal of International Economic Law* (2008), 649.

[105]   Thus the focus of current trade litigation is on renewable energy inputs, like wind turbines, or biofuels, and much less on electricity. One therefore wonders whether scenarios like those of the EU *PreussenElektra* case (Case C-279/98, *PreussenElektra AG v Schleswag AG* [2001] ECR I-2099) are likely to be controversial in a WTO trade context. For an analysis, see sections VIII and IX.E below.

– in some cases possibly even a discriminatory (i.e. one favouring domestically produced energy or equipment) – approach.

VIII. DISCRIMINATORY SUBSIDIES: PROHIBITED OR PERMITTED?

In this section we address one puzzle. One would expect that measures that produce the same or similar effects are assessed in the same or similar way. This is not what happens with various types of discriminatory subsidies that are a very common and broad category – substantially encompassing any subsidy that directly or indirectly favors domestic producers or products.

The most recent disputes on renewable energy support – *China – Wind* (DS 419), *Canada – Renewable Energy* (DS 412), *Canada – Feed-In Tariff Program* (DS 419) – concern *local-content subsidies*. Local-content requirements are often considered as a very effective tool of industrial policy, particularly in certain settings, inasmuch as they can ensure the steady and fast development of a crucial domestic industry.[106] The green energy sector is one of those, with China being a notable example.[107] Cosbey crucially noted how, in the cases above, '[t]he disputed measures are clearly designed to pursue both *environmental* objectives (reducing the environmental impact of generating electricity) and *industrial* policy objectives (fostering a competitive domestic renewables sector), and they will either succeed or fail on both objectives in tandem'.[108] If they succeed

in creating competitive domestic players in the sector, there are obvious domestic economic benefits, direct and indirect, in terms of jobs and foreign exchange.

---

[106] See, e.g., D. Rodrik, *One Economics, Many Recipes – Globalization, Institutions, and Economic Growth* (Princeton: Princeton University Press, 2008); H.J. Chang, *Kicking Away the Ladder – Development Strategy in Historical Perspective* (London: Anthem Press, 2003).

[107] It is interesting to note that the *China – Measures Concerning Wind Power Equipment* dispute has been settled during the consultation phase. Although it looks like the subsidy has been withdrawn, the reason why China decided to withdraw the subsidy seems to depend on the fact that support was simply no longer needed, and not on the recognition of the clear illegality of domestic content. See 'US Proclaims Victory in Wind Power Case: China Ends Challenged Subsidies' in *Bridges Weekly Trade News Digest*, Volume 15, Number 21, 8 June 2011. On the effectiveness of China's local content policies of support of wind energy sector, particularly in terms of establishing a manufacturing base, see T. Moerenhout, T. Liebert and C. Beaton, n. 21 above, 9–10.

[108] Cosbey, n. 17 above, 2.

Environmentally, a viable new player means more competition in the sector, which inevitably speeds up dissemination. From a global perspective, it may also mean more agents of innovation, at a time when innovation in renewable energy technology is a critically important global public good.[109]

More generally, discriminatory subsidies, including local-content subsidies, may have a role in winning domestic resistance against enhancing environmental standards and may indeed constitute the only political way to do so.[110]

The appraisal of local-content subsidies has changed over time, together with that of import substitution industrialization (tellingly, local-content subsidies are also known as import-substitution subsidies). In legal terms, in the GATT, they were subject to action only in presence of negative effects, like any other domestic subsidy.[111] The scenario changed during the Uruguay Round as a sign of the more pronounced free trade credo of the new times. Local-content subsidies were likened to export subsidies and subject *in all circumstances* to a harsher discipline. According to Article 3 of the SCM Agreement, if a subsidy is 'contingent, whether solely or as one of several other conditions, upon the use of domestic over imported goods', it is simply prohibited, without there being any need to prove a specific impact and adverse effects.[112]

Another type of subsidy which is common in the support of renewable energy is *production subsidies*.[113] As other measures of domestic support, these are generally permitted unless they cause adverse effects, in which case they are actionable.

If we now consider local-content and production subsidies together a

---

[109]   Ibid. If this is certainly a plausible scenario, it is not an unqualified endorsement of import substitution subsidization. It cannot be excluded that aggressive subsidization may generate a subsidy race, leading to over-supply, cut-rate prices, collapse of all but a handful of companies and, in the longer run, consolidation.

[110]   Bidgeli, n. 9 above, 29.

[111]   A different discipline was however already present with respect to the national treatment obligation. See n. 115 below.

[112]   There is still a need to prove material injury to the domestic industry in order to apply countervailing duties.

[113]   Subsidies that support demand for technology and energy, at both distribution and final consumption level, or their price, can in effect support production. See R. Steenblik, 'Subsidies in the Traditional Energy Sector', in J. Pauwelyn (ed), *Global Challenges at the Intersection of Trade, Energy and the Environment* (Geneva: Centre for Trade and Economic Integration, 2010), 186, who uses a broad concept of production subsidies, broad enough to cover most of the measures of support currently used.

significant inconsistency emerges. From an economic perspective, they *may be* exactly the same, they *may* produce the same effects. Sykes notes:

> a per unit subsidy to *all domestic buyers* of a good can be completely equivalent in its effects to an equal per unit subsidy to *all domestic sellers* – net output of domestic producers, net imports, and the net price to buyers will be exactly the same under competitive conditions.[114]

Assuming there is an equivalence in economic effects, this is not reflected in the legal treatment. As seen, while production subsidies are permitted, unless a negative impact is proved, local-content subsidies are just prohibited.[115] The implications for countries' policy space is noticeable. Should, once again, a different legal treatment depend on how the measure of support is designed? Is it reasonable to attach a completely different, indeed opposite, legal status to measures on the basis of what seems to be a mere formal consideration? Or – rather – is there any justification for this different regulatory treatment? Could it be that there is in fact some distinction in economic terms? For example, by expressly tying a subsidy to industry A to support industry B, the protectionist impact of the measure seems to be more marked, particularly because two domestic constituencies could end up being benefited as a result of one single measure. It could further be argued that the stifling effect on imports of the requirement to source locally is more defined than that of a production subsidy to the same local industry. Assuming this is correct, can this be enough to justify the strictest sanction of prohibition in any case and without qualifications? Is this the best regulatory arrangement to enable, at the same time and in a balanced way, industry development, environmental protection and trade? Or, from a law reform perspective, should subsidies with local-content requirements be re-classed as actionable, maybe recognizing their

---

[114] A.O. Sykes, 'The Economics of WTO Rules on Subsidies and Countervailing Measures', Chicago. John M. Olin Law and Economics Working Paper No. 186 (2nd Series) May 2003, 19. In fact the percentage production subsidy (expressed, say, as a payment per unit produced) that is equivalent to a local-content obligation will differ both according to the percentage local-content and the current market circumstances.

[115] Quite similarly, Article III of the GATT distinguishes subsidies to domestic producers, which are not subject to the obligation of national treatment (paragraph 8:(b)), and regulation which require that a 'specified amount or proportion of any product . . . must be supplied from domestic sources', which is prohibited. Along this line the early GATT *Italy – Agricultural Machinery* Panel (L/833, adopted 23 October 1958, BISD 7S/60) found that, unlike producer subsidies, purchasers subsidies were prohibited. For commentary see Sykes, n. 87 above, 518–519.

higher danger (if there is such a danger) with the use of a simple rebuttable presumption of adverse effects?[116]

The analysis of the relation between economic effects and legal consequences, and their impact on policy options, can be extended even further to consider *FITs.*

The fixed tariff is just the pricing element of the FIT incentive. These schemes include other terms either to reinforce their incentive effect or to impact on other related markets.[117] The obligation to buy all renewable energy produced nearby the grid is a very common, even essential, element of FITs because it provides investment security. Inasmuch as this purchase obligation affords a privileged access on locally sourced electricity, it is equivalent in economic effects to a local content requirement. It certainly operates differently since the obligation is not on the (first) recipient of the subsidy but on a third-party (the distributor) but the effect – from the producer's end – is the same. One implies that you must buy all or a certain proportion of renewable energy produced in your area, the other that you must buy inputs or other goods necessary for renewable energy deployment in your country.

Both of these requirements are discriminatory in the sense that they favor domestic production but – and this is the second inconsistency – their assessment seems to be different.

FITs are widely praised as one of the most, if not the most, cost-effective tools to support renewable energy.[118] This praise extends to the purchase obligation, with seemingly no real effort in distinguishing those with a discriminatory effect from those with a neutral impact.[119] Frequent reference is, for example, made to the German system, which includes a purchase obligation on locally sourced energy, as a good example of well-designed FIT that significantly contributed to the German success in deploying renewable energy.[120] By contrast, local-content requirements attached to FITs are more controversial and, as the pending *Canada – Renewable Energy* and *Canada – Feed-In Tariff Program* disputes show, are being challenged.

What do we make of this discrepancy in judgment? One good explanation could be that, at least with respect to energy, the two obligations

---

[116]   Similar to those of the now expired Article 6.1 of the SCM Agreement.

[117]   The 'local content' requirement at issue in *Canada – Certain Measures Affecting the Renewable Energy Sector* (DS 412) and *Canada – Measures Relating to the Feed-In Tariff Program* (DS 426) is an example of the latter.

[118]   See, e.g., Beaton and Moernhout, n. 11 above, 27.

[119]   See, e.g., M. Mendonça, D. Jacobs and B. Sovacool, n. 11 above, 30.

[120]   Ibid.

apply to different economic products and markets (technology vs energy), for which we still have a different degree of international competition and trade. This depends on technical reasons or on the difficulty of tracing the origin of electricity in the absence of an established and widespread system of certification. But these circumstances may change and with them trade patterns, making the availability of cross-border energy easier and more common. If so, what will be the legal implication of the equivalence in effects between local-content and FITs' purchase obligation? Can the (discriminatory) purchase obligation of FITs be legally assimilated to a local-content subsidy and be objected to as prohibited subsidy under Article 3 of the SCM Agreement?[121] If so, can it be justified?[122]

This section has attempted to show that the legal analysis of subsidies supporting *production* is not fully coherent or definite. The focus has been on the first level of analysis where the determination is on whether there is a breach of subsidy rules. The framework within which policy-makers have to operate offers contradictory or still uncertain indications. It remains to be seen whether the analysis at the justification level can offer the opportunity for resolution and clarity.

IX.   ARTICLE XX OF THE GATT: A CREDIBLE BUT TROUBLESOME POSSIBILITY

The previous analysis has shown that, with all their uncertainties, current subsidy rules can offer only limited shelter to climate change subsidies. Dispute settlement interpretations may provide some clarification and relief in this regard, but the vagaries and piecemeal nature of the case-law make this a sub-optimal solution. The most promising route would be the use of legal justifications. In this respect, the possibility to justify an otherwise objectionable subsidy by resorting to general exceptions provisions available in the broader legal system, like GATT Article XX, is an important hypothesis to test. Although this would also happen in a litigation scenario, the recognition of domestic autonomy that could result is potentially significant. If the conclusion is that this is not a viable path,

---

[121]   Andrew Lang, LSE, called my attention to the fact that there might be an even stronger case in investment law. Suppose you have a FIT in one region of the country only and a foreign RE power company sets up in another region and cannot benefit from the the purchase obligation. Is this a national treatment claim under a possible investment treaty?

[122]   This important question is analyzed in section IX.E below.

the only remaining option is law reform – i.e. the introduction of a specific legal shelter for certain subsidies.

A.   Article XX of the GATT: Content and Significance

Article XX of the GATT includes two 'exceptions' with environmental relevance, paragraphs (b) and (g). Paragraph (b) concerns measures that are 'necessary to protect human, animal or plant life or health'. This covers not only public health policy measures but also 'environmental' ones. The Appellate Body has already found in *Brazil – Tyres* that paragraph (b) could also cover climate change.[123] Paragraph (g), on the other hand, refers to 'measures relating to the conservation of exhaustible natural resources'.[124] Importantly, the Appellate Body in *US – Gasoline* has concluded that clean air can be protected under this exception.[125]

The key terms are 'necessary to' in paragraph (b) and 'relating to' in paragraph (g), which invoke different tests, the former being stricter than the latter.[126] The current interpretation of the 'necessity' test is that of a 'weighing and balancing exercise' where a considerable degree of deference is given to Members particularly with respect to the level of protection decided. The 'relating to' test is admittedly lower than the 'necessity' test, but this does not exclude the need to establish a 'real and close' relationship between 'means and end'. Crucially, the Appellate Body has acknowledged that the contribution of certain environmental measures, like climate change measures that often operate within a comprehensive

---

[123]   Appellate Body Report, *Brazil – Measures Affecting Imports of Retreaded Tyres*, WT/DS332/AB/R, adopted 17 December 2007, para. 151.

[124]   Although partly overlapping, the focus of the two exceptions differs slightly. Due to its language, reliance on paragraph (b) in order to justify climate change measures is likely to require evidence of the contribution of the measures to the protection of human, animal or plant life or health specifically. See Panel Report, *Brazil – Measures Affecting Imports of Retreaded Tyres*, WT/DS332/R, adopted 17 December 2007, para. 7.46 where it is noted that a party invoking an environmental justification under Article XX(b) of the GATT 'has to establish the existence not just of risks to "the environment" generally, but specifically of risks to animal or plant life or health'.

[125]   Appellate Body Report, *United States – Standards for Reformulated and Conventional Gasoline*, WT/DS2/AB/R, adopted on 20 May 1996, p. 18.

[126]   See Appellate Body Report, *Brazil – Measures Affecting Imports of Retreaded Tyres*, WT/DS332/AB/R, adopted 17 December 2007, para. 178 for a good formulation of the 'necessity' test, and Appellate Body Report, *United States – Import Prohibition of Shrimp and Certain Shrimp Products*, WT/DS58/AB/R, adopted 6 November 1998, para. 141 for the 'relating to' language.

set of policy actions, cannot be evaluated in the short term, but only with the 'benefit of time'.[127]

In *US – Gasoline* the Appellate Body presented the two-tiered approach that should be used under Article XX of the GATT.[128] According to this test, first, the existence of a provisional justification of the measure at issue will have to be determined under one of the subparagraphs of Article XX. Secondly, if such a provisional justification is established, the application of the measure will have to be considered under the chapeau. While the first step would analyze the measure itself, in the second step it is the application of this same measure that is under scrutiny. More specifically, the chapeau of Article XX requires that the measure is 'not *applied in a manner which would constitute a means of arbitrary or unjustifiable discrimination* between *countries where the same conditions prevail*, or a *disguised restriction on international trade*'.[129]

The Appellate Body established that the purpose and object of the chapeau is 'the prevention of abuse of the exceptions' of Article XX.[130] What is then proscribed is the *arbitrary* and *unjustifiable* discrimination with regard to how the measure is applied, not discrimination *per se*.[131] The *chapeau* thus requires an analysis – and justification – of the 'causes and the rationale of the discrimination'.[132] This ultimately turns on the final and comprehensive assessment of the legitimacy of the objective of the measure.[133]

Article XX is a crucial provision for the functioning of the GATT with a distinct *normative value*. Since its inception in 1947, it provides the express recognition of other-than-trade concerns and the possibility for these to trump trade under certain circumstances. Indeed, '[t]hese exceptions

---

[127] Appellate Body Report, *Brazil – Measures Affecting Imports of Retreaded Tyres*, WT/DS332/AB/R, adopted 17 December 2007, para. 151.

[128] Appellate Body Report, *United States – Standards for Reformulated and Conventional Gasoline*, WT/DS2/AB/R, adopted on 20 May 1996, p. 20.

[129] Emphasis added. J. Pauwelyn, 'US Federal Climate Policy and Competitiveness Concerns: The Limits and Options of International Trade', (2007) Nicholas Institute Working Paper NI-WP 07/02, Duke University, defined the chapeau as 'the most important provision in the entire GATT agreement'.

[130] Appellate Body Report, *United States – Standards for Reformulated and Conventional Gasoline*, WT/DS2/AB/R, adopted on 20 May 1996, p. 20.

[131] The requirement that the measure should not be applied so as to arbitrarily and unjustifiably discriminate cannot be equalled to the test of inconsistency of the most-favored-nation and national treatment provisions. They must and do have a different meaning.

[132] Appellate Body Report, *Brazil – Measures Affecting Imports of Retreaded Tyres*, WT/DS332/AB/R, adopted 17 December 2007, para. 225.

[133] After this has been initially considered in the first step of the 'relating to' or 'necessity' analysis of the exceptions.

clearly allow Members, under specific conditions, to give *priority* to certain societal values and interests over trade liberalization'.[134] These values prominently feature the environment, thus giving full significance and practical shape, in the WTO context, to the reference of the preamble of the WTO Agreement to 'sustainable development'.

There is therefore a double significance for policy space. On the one hand, there is an express recognition of Members' autonomy (subject to certain conditions of necessity and unjustified discrimination). On the other hand, this express recognition means that, when we move to Article XX, the trade-only perspective of provisions like subsidy rules, which protect market access and competition, makes room for a more comprehensive trade-and-environment, trade-and-health etc. perspective.[135] This entails a significant shift of setting and framework of analysis, so that the interests and expectations of consumers and citizens are engaged and matter as much as, in fact even more than, those of producers.[136]

It is arguably for this special role that, despite the name of 'general exceptions', the justifications of Article XX have consistently and increasingly been interpreted broadly, rather than like 'exceptions'.[137] The Appellate Body already showed in its early case law that Article XX is about balancing the 'general rule' that is breached and the 'exception' that is invoked as defence.[138] There truly is a 'weighing and balancing exercise' of different values central to the operation of this provision in each of its steps.[139] Ultimately, this is the typical hermeneutic process of general

---

[134]   P. Van den Bossche, *The Law and Policy of the World Trade Organization: Text, Cases and Materials* (Cambridge: Cambridge University Press, 2008), 616.

[135]   If, as has been seen above, non-trade objectives (like environmental protection) are important to establish the existence of a subsidy, this is limited to the question of whether there is an exceptional or discriminatory treatment. By contrast, as we will see soon, the operation of GATT Article XX assumes the latter's presence. What has to be determined is whether this exceptional or discriminatory treatment can be nonetheless justified in the light of the objectives pursued by the measure.

[136]   On the current and potential focus of WTO regulation see P.C. Mavroidis, 'Come Together? Producer Welfare, Consumer Welfare, and WTO Rules', in E.U. Petersmann and J. Harrison (eds), *Reforming the World Trading System – Legitimacy, Efficiency and Democratic Governance* (Oxford: Oxford University Press, 2003), 277; J. Pauwelyn, 'New Trade Politics After the Doha Round', Center for Trade and Economic Integration, Working Paper 1/2008.

[137]   Van den Bossche, n. 134 above, 618.

[138]   Appellate Body Report, *United States – Standards for Reformulated and Conventional Gasoline*, WT/DS2/AB/R, adopted on 20 May 1996, pp. 16–17.

[139]   P. Eeckhout, 'The Scales of Trade – Reflections on the Growth and Functions of the WTO Adjudicative Branch', *Journal of International Economic Law* (2010), 3.

clauses where the protection of different values has to be assessed on a case-by-case basis.[140]

B. The Applicability of GATT Article XX beyond the GATT: the SCM Agreement

Over the recent years a lively discussion on the applicability of Article XX to WTO agreements other than the GATT has emerged. Thus far, neither law nor jurisprudence provide a final answer. The relevance for environmental protection measures is, however, clear with numerous scenarios where the availability of the broad exceptions of Article XX would make a difference.[141]

1. The arguments in favour and against applicability

With respect to the case of the applicability to the SCM Agreement, it may be useful to briefly outline the arguments put forward by the opposing camps. Views dramatically differ. On the one hand, we have those, quite numerous, that fiercely object to beyond-the-GATT applicability of Article XX. The core of the argument is that this applicability would undermine the 'inner balance of the rights and obligations' of the SCM Agreement which already had a category of (also environmental) justifications – non-actionable subsidies – that is now expired. A finding that Article XX can apply to the SCM Agreement would alter this balance – against the intention of the Members – and could potentially have broader negative systemic implications, opening such claims of applicability for all other covered agreements and ultimately significantly undermining market access. When Members wanted a justification to be available they made this clear. Contrary to the SCM Agreement, other agreements, like SPS, do refer to GATT Article XX. Finally, the wording of the chapeau, whereby '*nothing in this Agreement* shall be construed to prevent the

---

[140] This process does not necessarily require a precise cost-benefit analysis, but what is, in substance, a proportionality assessment. An informative taxonomy of 'trade-off' adjudicative 'devices' can be found in J. Trachtmann, *The Economic Structure of International Law* (Harvard University Press, 2008), 222–223.

[141] For example: Can Article XX of the GATT justify such measures that are imposed in breach of the Anti-Dumping Agreement (ADA) or SCM Agreement? What about technical regulations, standards or sanitary or phytosanitary measures that are not fully in line with respectively the provisions of the Agreement on Technical Barriers to Trade or the Agreement on Sanitary and Phytosanitary Measures? In absence of specific provisions on legitimate environmental subsidies, can Article XX of the GATT provide protection for subsidies to mitigate climate change, support renewable energy or energy efficiency?

adoption or enforcement by any contracting party of measures ...',[142] would clearly limit its scope of application.

On the other hand, there are those, less numerous, who are more positive about Article XX of the GATT justifying breaches of other-than-the-GATT covered agreements. They put forward various arguments.

First, the applicability of Article XX beyond the GATT cannot be excluded altogether, almost as a matter of principle. It is an issue that has to be assessed case-by-case, instrument-by-instrument and provision-by-provision. The systemic concerns outlined above cannot hide the fact that what is at issue is always the application of a specific legal provision in a specific case. The spirit of this approach is that Article XX does have a natural expansiveness because of its central position in the GATT, its general and broad wording, and its policy (one would even be tempted to say 'constitutional') value. Its applicability to other WTO provisions is accordingly a serious hermeneutic hypothesis. In this respect, although obvious, it is recalled that GATT Article XX does not offer a carte blanche to protectionism. As the following analysis will show, there are various requirements that need to be satisfied before a measure restricting trade can be finally justified.

Second, the foundational legal argument supporting this hypothesis is that the WTO is a single undertaking and that the GATT is clearly developed in various covered agreements. This comes out from the General Interpretative Note to Annex 1A of the WTO Agreement and from the language or subject matter of various provisions scattered in the covered agreements on trade in goods.[143] In this regard, it is undisputed that the SCM Agreement develops the GATT with respect to subsidies to industrial goods.[144]

Third, the rise and fall of the fairly limited category of non-actionable subsidies can provide arguments either way, but certainly not a clear-cut legal obstacle.[145] To be sure, the absence of an extension of these rules

---

[142]   Emphasis added.

[143]   Analysing the 'double-remedy' issue in the *United States – Definitive Anti-Dumping and Countervailing Duties on Certain Products from China* (DS379) dispute, the Appellate Body recently reminded the fact that the WTO is one single legal system and consequently the covered agreements cannot be read in clinical isolation.

[144]   See Appellate Body Report, *Brazil – Measures Affecting Desiccated Coconut*, WT/DS22/AB/R, adopted 20 March 1997, paras 11–14, on the different normative framework between GATT and WTO, and on the relationship between GATT and SCM provisions on subsidies.

[145]   Up to the end of 1999 there were specific provisions (Articles 8 and 9 of the SCM Agreement) recognizing that certain subsidies, including certain environmental subsidies, were overall beneficial and hence were non-actionable as well as sheltered from countervailing duty action. According to Article 31 of the

could be seen as a sign of lack of willingness that exceptions should exist to the subsidy obligations and prohibitions under the SCM Agreement. That being said, however, the narrow scope of these past exceptions is also read as confirmation of the ongoing authority of GATT XX – an influence untouched by the *lex specialis* principle of the General Interpretative Note mentioned above. In other words, it could be contended that, even when Article 8 was in force, there was not really a common purpose and subject matter between the broad 'environmental exceptions' of Article XX and the confined remit of Article 8,[146] with the result that Article XX could in principle have applied to subsidies not specifically permissible under the SCM Agreement. In other words, while it is clear that the SCM Agreement develops Articles VI and XVI of the GATT, it is not fully clear that Article 8 of the SCM Agreement was developing Article XX of the GATT in the context of subsidy discipline.[147]

In fact, the expiry of Articles 8 and 9 would reinforce the legal and policy argument in favour of applying Article XX of the GATT to subsidies that are clearly contributing to tackling climate change. It is clear that, in the absence of law reform, the application of Article XX of the GATT may constitute the only alternative to tackle an undesirable lacuna in the system.[148] The urgency of the situation would be confirmed by recent developments in litigation which are seeing a surge in cases concerning measures of 'green' support.[149]

SCM Agreement, Articles 8 and 9 were in force only for five years and, absent any determination of the Committee on Subsidies to extend their application, in the original or modified form, they would lapse. On the history and prospects of non-actionability see the detailed analysis S. Bigdeli, 'Resurrecting the Dead? The Expired Non-Actionable Subsidies and the Lingering Question of "Green Space"', *Manchester Journal of International Economic Law* (2011), 3.

[146]   And hence no possibility of conflict as provided by the Interpretative Note to Annex 1A of the WTO Agreement.

[147]   Drawing a parallel, we do not, therefore, see the same kind of elaboration-relationship found by the Panel Report, *United States – Certain Measures Affecting Imports of Poultry from China*, WT/DS392/R, adopted 25 October 2010, for the SPS Agreement and Article XX(b) of the GATT.

[148]   In this regard, it would be incoherent if certain measures restricting trade would be justifiable while others would not, and this differential treatment would depend on an arbitrary distinction of the type of measure chosen. Howse highlighted this incoherency with respect to climate change subsidies, noting that, from a narrow trade perspective, it would be paradoxical if Article XX of the GATT is not applicable to subsidies but is applicable to other arguably more trade-distorting measures like quotas. See Howse, n. 14 above, 17.

[149]   See *Canada – Certain Measures Affecting the Renewable Energy Sector* (DS 412) and *Canada – Measures Relating to the Feed-In Tariff Program* (DS 426).

Fourth, there are no major textual barriers. The language of the chapeau of Article XX ('nothing in this Agreement shall be construed to prevent the adoption or enforcement by any contracting party of measures . . .') cannot be read to imply more than what it expressly says: there are no obstacles *in the GATT* to the application of Article XX exceptions. This, it could be argued, refers to any measure in contravention of GATT obligations or of those arising out of any covered agreement developing GATT disciplines.

This conclusion, of course, is not determinative of *what other applicable agreements* (the existence of which was not even contemplated at the time GATT 1947 was drafted) provide, or what general principles of interpretation indicate. In this respect, there does not seem to be any language in the SCM Agreement (or elsewhere) directly interfering with the application of GATT Article XX to subsidies.[150]

Fifth, if no textual obstacles can be found, conversely and as a matter of general interpretation, there is no need for an express reference to give way to the application of a provision,[151] particularly if this has a general nature.[152]

Sixth, the negotiating history does not offer clear indications that non-actionable categories were supposed to be the only avenue of justification of certain 'good' subsidies, and that GATT XX either could or should not apply to subsidies.

In conclusion, according to this front, there would be no major technical obstacles to the applicability of GATT XX to subsidies, the issue thus being eminently of *policy* (do we have a gap in the system?) or *political*

---

[150]   As a final point, it is interesting, even ironic, to note that the historical meaning of the language of the chapeau of GATT Article XX dates back to the willingness to guarantee a 'universal' application of the 'general' exceptions to breaches of any GATT provision. See J.H. Jackson, *World Trade and the Law of the GATT* (Bobbs-Merrill, 1969), 743–744; D.A. Irwin, P.C. Mavroidis and A.O. Sykes, *The Genesis of the GATT* (Cambridge: Cambridge University Press, 2009), 164.

[151]   Others, however, have argued the opposite in the special context of the SCM Agreement, mainly because the SCM Agreement makes an explicit reference to the WTO Agreement on Agriculture to define their respective applicability and because other WTO agreements such as the Agreement on Sanitary and Phytosanitary Measures (SPS Agreement) make an express reference to Article XX of the GATT to indicate their relationship with the latter. See F. Pierola, 'The Availability of a GATT Article XX Defence with Respect to a non-GATT Claim: Changing the Rules of the Game?', 5(4) *Global Trade and Customs Journal* (2010), 172–175.

[152]   The *lex specialis – lex generalis* relationship has to be determined on a case-by-case basis, as required by the General Interpretative Note to Annex 1A of the WTO Agreement.

(where do Members stand on this issue?) nature. This political dimension is also clearly present in the position of those that reject the applicability. To alter the 'balance of the rights and obligations' of the SCM Agreement is in legal jargon what to 'breach the WTO bargain' is in political discourse.

2. What does the case-law say?

The issue of the applicability of Article XX of the GATT to other WTO agreements is appearing more frequently before the WTO dispute settlement system. However, the indications of the case-law are unclear so far. We have *obiter dicta*, which do not represent more than slips of the pen (Panel, *Colombia – Ports of Entry*),[153] *arguendo analysis* where the issue is substantially avoided (Appellate Body, *US – Shrimp/Customs Bond*), and special cases whose significance beyond their specific context is not fully clear (Appellate Body, *China – Periodicals*; *China – Raw Materials*).

Two recent decisions merit closer scrutiny. The decision in *China – Periodicals* seems to offer ammunition to the pro-applicability camp because the Appellate Body concluded that Article XX of the GATT could apply to China's Accession Protocol.[154] It could, however, be argued that, although providing the first example of beyond-the-GATT application, this finding's significance is limited to the specific legal circumstances of the case, particularly the language of Article 5.1 of the Protocol recognizing 'China's right to regulate trade in a manner consistent with the WTO Agreement'.[155] There are, however, good arguments that the significance of this report goes beyond the case-specific circumstances of the dispute. Firstly, the Appellate Body shows a positive attitude towards the need to consider the hypothesis that GATT XX is applicable beyond the GATT. This comes out for example in the resolute rejection of the *arguendo analysis* used by the Panel (and, significantly, by the Appellate Body

---

[153] This was confirmed by a private conversation with one of the panelists.

[154] On the important Appellate Body decision in *China – Periodicals* (Appellate Body Report, *China – Certain Measures Affecting Trading Rights and Distribution Services for Certain Publications and Audiovisual Entertainment Products*, WT/DS363/AB/R, adopted 19 January 2010) see J. Pauwelyn, 'Squaring Free Trade in Culture with Chinese Censorship: The WTO Appellate Body Report on "China – Audiovisuals"', *Melbourne Journal of International Law* (2010), 119; J. Qin, 'Pushing the Limits of Global Governance: Trading Rights, Censorship and WTO Jurisprudence – A Commentary on the *China – Publications* case', 10(2) *Chinese Journal of International Law* (2011), 271–322, particularly 292–295.

[155] The linking factor here was the expression 'consistent with the WTO Agreement', representing a clear gateway to the GATT.

itself in previous decisions).[156] Secondly, we find a sweeping recognition of the Members' power to regulate:

> we see the 'right to regulate', in the abstract, as an *inherent power* enjoyed by a Member's government, rather than a right bestowed by international treaties such as the WTO Agreement.[157]

Furthermore:

> With respect to trade, the WTO Agreement and its Annexes instead operate to, among other things, *discipline the exercise* of each Member's inherent power to regulate by requiring WTO Members to comply with the obligations that they have assumed thereunder.[158]

The framework of analysis is clear. The 'power to regulate' is 'inherent' and, as such, does not – cannot – find its origin in treaty language that rather merely acts as a 'discipline' to its 'exercise'. Clearly, these general statements reach beyond the language of the Protocol. It remains to be seen, however, whether the recognition of the 'abstract right to regulate' can constitute the future normative foundation for the applicability of GATT Article XX to other WTO Agreements, particularly by embedding the mindset where the power to regulate is inherent and treaty language can only operate to constrain this built-in prerogative and, arguably, must do so in a clear fashion. An ancillary effect of this ruling could be the rooting of another hermeneutic attitude, that of a two-step analysis where following a breach determination there should always be a serious enquiry of a possibility of justification.[159]

What these findings certainly represent, more simply but no less importantly, is the Appellate Body's intellectual disposition to consider attentively any such claim in the future.

This can perhaps be contrasted with the recent (Panel and Appellate Body) reports in the *China – Raw Materials* case which, if they were taken

---

[156] Appellate Body Report, *China – Certain Measures Affecting Trading Rights and Distribution Services for Certain Publications and Audiovisual Entertainment Products*, WT/DS363/AB/R, adopted 19 January 2010, paras 213–215.

[157] Para. 222 (emphasis added).

[158] Ibid (emphasis added).

[159] The Appellate Body noted, in this regard, that a Member may be compliant with WTO law not only by not contravening it but also when it is justified under an applicable exception (see para. 223). The Geneva-based body then went on to elaborate on the justification alternative, noting that its availability 'may also depend on whether the measure has a clearly discernible, objective link to the regulation of trade in the goods at issue' (para. 230).

to suggest that 'express language' referring to, or in any case connecting to, GATT Article XX would be necessary for its applicability beyond the GATT,[160] would be unduly restrictive and, most importantly, clearly wrong under general principles of interpretation.[161] The application of rules does not depend (only) on their express *renvoi* – unless one wishes to consider the WTO legal system unique in this respect. That being said, it has recently been suggested that a significant textual connection between the GATT and the SCM Agreement could be found. In the *China – Periodical* decision, the gateway for the applicability of GATT Article XX to the Protocol of Accession of China was the phrase 'in conformity with the WTO Agreement' in the Protocol's Article 5.1. Article 32.1 of the SCM Agreement would similarly provide a strong link when reading that '[n]o specific action against a subsidy of another Member can be taken except *in accordance with the provisions of GATT 1994, as interpreted by this [i.e. the SCM] Agreement*' (emphasis added).[162]

The issue of whether GATT Article XX could apply beyond the GATT, and in particular to measures that were breaching the Sanitary and Phytosanitary Measures (SPS) Agreement, was also recently addressed in *US – Poultry*.[163] The panel concluded that a measure already found to be inconsistent with various provisions of the SPS Agreement, which expressly elaborates Article XX (b) of the GATT, could not be justified by then having direct recourse to that general exception. This conclusion is a natural consequence of the fact that the SPS Agreement develops Article XX (b) of the GATT exhaustively.[164]

---

[160]   Panel Report, *China – Measures Related to the Exportation of Various Raw Materials,* WT/DS394/R, WT/DS395/R, WT/DS398/R, adopted 22 February 2012, para. 7.154 notes that, were GATT Article XX intended to apply the China's Accession Protocol (and particularly to para. 11.3), 'language would have been inserted to suggest this relationship'. Along the same lines see the Appellate Body Report, WT/DS394/AB/R, WT/DS395/AB/R, WT/DS398/AB/R, adopted 22 February 2012, para. 303.

[161]   This is not to say that the finding of no applicability of GATT Article XX to para. 11.3 of China's Accession Protocol was not correct. The latter provision seems indeed to be quite specific with respect to the available exceptions to its obligation, thus seemingly excluding other more general avenues of justification.

[162]   Appellate Body Report, *China – Measures Related to the Exportation of Various Raw Materials,* WorldTradeLaw.net Dispute Settlement Commentary, 6 February 2012, p. 17.

[163]   Panel Report, *United States – Certain Measures Affecting Imports of Poultry from China,* WT/DS392/R, adopted 25 October 2010.

[164]   But only Article XX (b). It may well be that a defence could be raised under another Article XX exception, such as the one on public morals (paragraph (a)). See Pauwelyn, n. 129 above, 137, drawing this argument from Panel

C.   The Justification of Climate Subsidies

Assuming GATT Article XX is applicable to the SCM Agreement, we can briefly analyze the issues that would arise from its application to energy efficiency and renewable energy subsidies.

The key argument would be that the subsidy that supports cleaner energy and technology does contribute to the objective of reducing GHGs emissions and hence to fighting climate change. Although the issue is clearly one of evidence and has to be assessed on a case-by-case basis, arguably, no great difficulties can be thought of in this respect.

On the one hand, while the beneficial impact of energy saving measures is self-evident, renewable energy has also a less negative environmental impact in terms of emissions than conventional sources. On the other hand, the necessity test of paragraph (b) requires balancing the environmental objective pursued and the contribution of the measure to that objective with the restrictions on trade. Climate change is certainly an important objective, which would lower the standard of proof. Furthermore, as noted above, the Appellate Body crucially acknowledged that the evaluation of the contribution of climate change measures can be made only with the 'benefit of time'.[165] Finally, the existence of less trade-restrictive alternatives to achieve the same aim can negate the necessity only if these are 'reasonably available', a qualification that adds to the deference to the country adopting the measure. Broadly analogous considerations can be made if the exception of paragraph (g) is considered.

The application of the chapeau does raise interesting issues with respect to the broad category of discriminatory subsidies (see IX,E below).

D.   The Justification of Free Emissions Allowances

There are two possible lines of defense for the allocation of allowances free of charge under Article XX and both revolve around the alleged environmental merits of free allocation. The first argument would rely on the *contribution of free allocation to the reduction of GHG emissions*. Economic analysis seems, however, to reject this possibility.[166] At best, free allowances are as efficient as paid allowances when regarded as opportunity

---

Report, *European Communities – Measures Affecting the Approval and Marketing of Biotech Products*, WT/DS291/R, WT?DS292/R, WT/DS293/R, adopted 21 November 2006.

[165]   Appellate Body Report, *Brazil – Measures Affecting Imports of Retreaded Tyres*, WT/DS332/AB/R, adopted 17 December 2007, para. 151.

[166]   See Rubini and Jegou, n. 1 above.

costs. At worst, they may reduce the incentives to reduce emissions, thus going squarely against the proposed aim of emissions trading schemes. The second argument would rely on the prevention of *carbon leakage* as a justification. Even here economic analysis seems to show that there is no strong evidence supporting carbon leakage claims or suggesting that free allowances would be effective in reducing leakage (at least in the short term).[167] That being said, the latter seems, however, to be the most logical line of defense and will therefore be analyzed for its merits below.

Even assuming that the country at issue aims for a very high level of environmental protection, it is clear that both the case of carbon leakage and the contribution of free allowances to addressing it should be properly substantiated. Assuming that the existence of one of the exceptions under letters (b) of (g) of Article XX can be established, it is however under the chapeau that the most interesting questions arise.

The requirement that the measure should not be applied so as to arbitrarily and unjustifiably discriminate cannot be equalled to the test of inconsistency of the most-favoured-nation and national treatment provisions, and substantially implies that discrimination can be justified, and this should be done in relation to the policy objectives of the measure. Further, this discrimination should be established 'between countries where the same conditions prevail', not only between different exporting countries but also between importing and exporting countries.

Case-law offers more concrete criteria to assess whether the application of a measure is in line with the chapeau. Three important 'groups' of such criteria will be discussed here. Firstly, the Appellate Body has stressed the importance of applying a measure that allows for an inquiry into its appropriateness regarding the conditions prevailing in exporting countries.[168] As such, it is crucial that a measure provides flexibility, by accepting *comparable* measures abroad as a basis for exempting countries from the application of the trade-restrictive measure.[169] Secondly, the requirements of 'due process' and fairness have been taken into account under the chapeau.[170] It is important that, in the application of the measure,

---

[167] Ibid.

[168] Appellate Body Report, *United States – Import Prohibition of Shrimp and Certain Shrimp Products*, WT/DS58/AB/R, adopted 6 November 1998, para. 165.

[169] Appellate Body Report, *United States – Import Prohibition of Shrimp and Certain Shrimp Products – Recourse to Article 21.5 DSU by Malaysia*, WT/DS58/AB/RW, adopted 21 November 2001, para. 144.

[170] See for example Appellate Body Report, *United States – Import Prohibition of Shrimp and Certain Shrimp Products*, WT/DS58/AB/R, adopted 6 November 1998, paras 180–181.

decisions are taken with the use of objective and transparent criteria.[171] Thirdly, to comply with the chapeau, it is vital that the means of international cooperation are adequately explored and good faith efforts have been made to negotiate an international agreement.[172]

The phrase 'between countries where the same conditions prevail' can be of great importance in the context of climate change measures, as shown by the following two examples. Firstly, there is a question of whether the notion of 'prevailing' conditions is in conflict with the UNFCCC[173] principle of common but differentiated responsibilities that allows different reduction commitments, and thus different treatments on the basis of historical – not prevailing – conditions. The second example relates to the need to provide flexibility in the application of a measure, as established by case-law. In the application of the measure, it is important to ensure that it is not 'closed' but instead 'open' to comparable policy measures of other countries, one of the main lessons of the *US – Shrimp* litigation.[174] In the case of emissions trading schemes, it is key to ensure a transparent, non-discriminatory and well-designed 'linking' with other schemes, or, in their absence, with other policy measures that aim to achieve the same objective of emissions reduction. The legality of various national climate policy measures may eventually depend on this. The practical difficulties in determining and comparing the effectiveness of different regulatory systems and tools may indeed be considerable, but attempts towards this end need to be made. Good faith efforts and practical cooperation between countries in this respect may also constitute an additional factual element helping to ensure the WTO consistency of the measure, and, more

---

[171] Panel, *European Communities – Conditions for the Granting of Tariff Preferences to Developing Countries*, WT/DS246/R, adopted on 20 April 2004, paras 7.228–7.229.

[172] See Appellate Body Report, *United States – Standards for Reformulated and Conventional Gasoline*, WT/DS2/AB/R, adopted on 20 May 1996, p. 29 and Appellate Body Report, *United States – Import Prohibition of Shrimp and Certain Shrimp Products – Recourse to Article 21.5 DSU by Malaysia*, WT/DS58/AB/RW, adopted 21 November 2001, paras 132–134.

[173] New York, NY (US), 9 May 1992, in force 21 March 1994, available at http://unfccc.int.

[174] It has been noted that this introduces in the chapeau of GATT Article XX 'an "embryonic" and "soft" requirement on Members to recognize the equivalence of foreign measures comparable in effectiveness'. See Van den Bossche, n. 134 above, 645; G. Marceau and J.P. Trachmann, 'A Map of the WTO Law of Domestic Regulations of Goods', in G.A. Bermann and P.C. Mavroidis (eds), *Trade and Human Health and Safety* (Cambridge: Cambridge University Press, 2006), 42.

radically, may contribute to creating a positive international environment for ongoing efforts to respond to the climate change challenge.

Thus, for example, the fact that the EU-ETS legislation limits the possibility of concluding linking agreements with countries listed in Annex B of the Kyoto Protocol that have ratified the Protocol[175] could prevent a justification under GATT Article XX. The chapeau clearly requires equal treatment in the application of the measure to countries 'where the same conditions prevail'. On the other hand, failure to ratify the Kyoto Protocol, the most important international climate change agreement, is a significant legal, political and environmental condition that could ultimately allow a difference in treatment. The limitation, which excludes those countries that have not ratified the Kyoto Protocol, is intended to exercise political pressure on them to do so.[176] Bhagwati and Mavroidis have noted the possible relevance of the principle established by the Appellate Body in *EC – Tariff Preferences*,[177] though this did not concern the chapeau discussion directly.[178]

In this case, the granting by the EU (then European Communities – EC) of preferences to developing countries was conditioned on the adoption of anti-drug production policies. The Appellate Body concluded that discriminatory preferences are WTO consistent if they are based on 'objective criteria'. Applying this argument in the context of climate change, the signing of the Kyoto Protocol may well be considered an objective criterion to discriminate between countries. At the same time, however, simple reliance on the signing of an international agreement – without considering the policy measures adopted at the domestic level – may be unreasonable. If there is an emissions trading scheme that could be linked to the EU-ETS, then this other country *is*, irrespective of any international commitment, undertaking climate change measures. Excluding such a country from the EU-ETS would not seem to be justifiable.[179] This would

---

[175]   Article 25 of EC Directive 2003/87/EC.

[176]   R. Howse and A.L. Eliason, 'Domestic and International Strategies to Address Climate Change: an Overview of the WTO Legal Issues', in T. Cottier, O. Nartova and S.Z. Bigdeli (eds), *International Trade Regulation and the Mitigation of Climate Change* (Cambridge University Press, 2009), 49–93, at 58.

[177]   Appellate Body Report, *European Communities – Conditions for the Granting of Tariff Preferences to Developing Countries*, WT/DS246/AB/R, adopted on 20 April 2004.

[178]   J. Bhagwati and P.C. Mavroidis, 'Is Action Against US Exports for Failure to Sign Kyoto Protocol WTO-legal?', *World Trade Review* (2007), 306–307.

[179]   This seems indeed the rationale of the newly introduced Article 25.1a in the Directive 2003/87/EC, which allows for agreements on the recognition of allowances of 'compatible mandatory greenhouse gas emissions trading systems

not make any environmental sense; neither, under the chapeau of Article XX of the GATT, would it make sense from a trade law perspective.

Even though linking an emissions trading scheme is indeed a way of recognizing foreign climate change mitigation efforts, the important question remains whether the free allocation of allowances specifically also takes into account foreign mitigation efforts. The problem is that free allowances can only be allocated to those installations participating in the emission trading scheme. Consideration of comparable efforts is further restricted by the fact that, in contrast to border measures (which can selectively target the exports from highly emitting economies and sectors), it would be more difficult to shield firms in foreign countries from the effects of subsidies like free allowances on the basis of their mitigation efforts and resulting carbon prices. In this sense, it could be very difficult for a country to bring the allocation of free allowances in line with the chapeau of Article XX.

Additionally, in order for a validation under the chapeau to be possible, it is important that allowances are not allocated for free without an inquiry into other ways of tackling carbon leakage through the means of international negotiations and cooperation. In other words, automatically resorting to free allocation without showing any attention to the broader picture of international policy and discussions with trading partners on the issue may lead to the conclusion that the differential treatment inherent in subsidization is arbitrary and not justified. Lastly, it would be important that the criteria used to determine the beneficiaries of the free allocation of allowances, and those used to determine the amount of allowances allocated free of charge, are transparent and objectively applied.

Finally, even if grounded, competitiveness concerns cannot find any shelter under any of the exceptions of Article XX of the GATT. If this is the main or exclusive reason underlying the free allocation, then the only avenue is law reform.

E.   The Justification of Discriminatory Subsidies

One key question is whether those forms of discriminatory subsidies analyzed above, that is, those subsidies that directly or indirectly support domestic producers or products, could pass muster with both the 'necessity' test and the criteria of lack of 'unjust or arbitrary discrimination' in

---

with absolute emissions caps established in any other country or in sub-federal or regional entities'. What remains to be seen is whether this amendment eliminates possible claims of bias. One factor that could lead to controversy is the limitation of the linking to ETSs with absolute caps only.

the chapeau. Although the Appellate Body neatly distinguished the two levels of analysis in *US – Gasoline,* there is a significant overlap between them since they both closely scrutinize the objective of the measure. They are therefore treated together here.

In section VIII it has been seen that measures of support with differential – often discriminatory – impact are indeed common in the renewable energy sector, and are also, quite often, particularly effective because of their targeting. We have also seen how their treatment is not fully consistent, with production subsidies being permitted (unless they cause adverse effects) and local content subsidies being prohibited. With respect to local-content subsidies, it has been suggested that it may be difficult for them to be justified, mainly at the stage of proportionality.[180] The assessment would be somewhat more favorable for production subsidies.[181] Although local content requirements and production subsidies may have the same effects from an economic standpoint, we have speculated on whether a subsidy *including* a local content requirement could produce more markedly negative effects. If this is correct, this may well have an impact at the level of the necessity test.

That said, there is no subsidy that, at least in principle, is not capable of being justified. Talking of the *China – Wind* case at a recent conference at Columbia University,[182] Howse, for example, suggested that China might have had 'a plausible argument', based on environmental grounds, justifying their local content subsidies under GATT Article XX. He noted in particular that the local content obligation could have been found 'necessary' for three reasons: limited possibility of technology transfer, exceptionally great demands for alternative energy, and the 'life and death' environmental situation behind those needs.

A key point of the necessity analysis is the determination of whether there are less trade restrictive alternatives available to achieve the same aim. It could thus be counter-argued that, if a measure less trade restrictive than a local-content requirement, quite possibly achieving the same result, could be envisaged, the previous analysis would become mere academic speculation.

A few comments can be made. First, it should be reiterated that the

---

[180] Bigdeli, n. 9 above, 32.

[181] Ibid.

[182] 'Climate Change, China and the WTO', 30 March 2011, Panel Discussion with Joseph Stiglitz, Rob Howse and Andrew Shoyer. A blog discussion, with comments of Rob Howse, following the Panel is available at http://worldtradelaw. typepad.com/ielpblog/2011/04/article-xx-domestic-production-of-environmental-goods.html (last access 4 July 2011).

fact that local content subsidies are prohibited is not conclusive of their final legal assessment. GATT Article XX justifies 'any measure' within its scope, including those, like quotas, that are prohibited and, most significantly, are more distorting than subsidies. Even assuming that a local-content requirement would have a more distinct impact on imports than a simple production subsidy to a competing product, it would still be less distorting than an outright ban. Second, the assessment turns on the specifics of the case. Howse's comments on the plausibility of a Chinese defense to local content requirements in the *China – Wind* case is a good example in point. It will be the specific factual and legal circumstances and conditions of the scenario prevailing in the granting country that establish or not the 'necessity' and the 'justification' of the discriminatory subsidy, and the local content element in particular.[183] Furthermore, the existence of alternative less trade restrictive measures should not be assessed in the abstract but should be 'reasonably available' to the granting country.[184] This qualification, which calls for a comprehensive assessment of various conditions,[185] adds to the deference of the country adopting the measure.

Finally, the fact that measures of support for renewable energy, and of the green economy more in general, pursue a combination of objectives should not be determinative. Howse recently noted:

> simply excluding subsidies from WTO compatibility because they have indus-trial policy as well as environmental goals is unrealistic, especially in the current economic and financial crisis, where support for climate measures may be inadequate unless such measures also serve economic recovery or reconstruc-tion goals.[186]

Far from giving the green light to any kind of measure, whatever its justification, this comment calls for a circumstantial and pragmatic resolution of the balancing of the various objectives that typically underlie green subsidies. More radically, as was highlighted above for some cases

---

[183]   What is subject to analysis under GATT Article XX is the justification of the violative aspect of a measure, in the instant case the discriminatory impact of the subsidy caused by the local content obligation, naturally set within its broader factual and legal context. Cf Appellate Body Report, *Thailand – Customs and Fiscal Measures on Cigarettes from the Philippines*, WT/DS371/AB/R, adopted 15 July 2011, para. 177.

[184]   Appellate Body Report, *Brazil – Measures Affecting Imports of Retreaded Tyres*, WT/DS332/AB/R, adopted 17 December 2007, para. 156. See Eeckhout, n. 139 above, 18.

[185]   Which are arguably not limited to the 'technical' or 'financial' consider-ations the Appellate Body use as examples.

[186]   Howse, n. 14 above, 17.

of support to renewable energy, the objectives of environmental and industrial policy may be in line with and reinforce each other.[187] Finally, other – less targeted or discriminatory – measures might be chosen but there is then the question of whether they would be (equally) effective in relation to the proposed goals, which has been analyzed extensively above.[188]

Assuming now that the assessment of a simple production subsidy would be more positive than that of a local-content subsidy, we cannot escape two alternatives. If, beside both being discriminatory, production and local content subsidies may be, as Sykes suggests, economically the same, their legal treatment should accordingly be the same, at least at the justification level where the analysis seems to be more focused on substance and effects. By contrast, if, as we tentatively suggested, local content subsidies are more dangerous because they would have a clearer impact on trade and would in substance amount to a 'double' measure of support (i.e., one favoring two different recipients), and may have a clearer detrimental impact on trade, the question is again a matter of context surrounding the measure. But logic requires coherency. Would the assessment be different if we formally had two separate production subsidies rather than a subsidy-with-local-content tie? In principle, it should not.

Some food for thought is offered by the famous EU *PreussenElektra* case which concerned a discriminatory subsidy.[189] What is known in WTO circles is that the European Court of Justice concluded that a German FIT law – which combined a pricing requirement with the obligation to buy all renewable energy electricity produced in the area – was not a State aid because there was no cost to government. What is less known is that the Court analyzed the purchase obligation also from another perspective and concluded quite easily that this obligation amounted to a measure equivalent to a quota because it restricted, potentially, the market access for renewable energy electricity coming from outside Germany. Like in the GATT, EU law prohibits quotas and equivalent measures. Even these measures can be justified, however, using a provision (Article 36 TFEU) which was introduced in the 1957 Treaty of Rome using as its model GATT Article XX. To cut matters short, the Court concluded that the German purchase obligation was justified because it was in line with the protection of the environment and because of the nature of the electricity market in the EU (the certification of origin of renewable energy electricity

---

[187] See Cosbey, n. 17 above.
[188] See sections II and VII.
[189] C-379/98, *PreussenElektra v Schleswag* [2001] ECR I-2099.

was under-developed). One is left to wonder whether, in the future, we will enjoy an alignment of WTO and EU jurisprudence in this regard.

F.   Conclusions of the Justification Promise of GATT Article XX

Article XX of the GATT can potentially offer a significant answer to the request for policy space. Its application is, however, politically trouble-some for the same reasons that support its invocation. It is flexible and its potential reach cannot be fully predicted. The strain put on the WTO dispute settlement system may be significant, as it would have to deal with uncertain language and perform difficult and sensitive balancing acts. That said, the applicability of Article XX to climate change or renewable subsidies is both a credible argument and a significant possibility. The protection of the environment and the fight against climate change are crucial objectives and various policy measures, including subsidies, may be adopted to pursue them. As repeatedly noted above, it would be incoher-ent if certain measures restricting trade would be justifiable while others would not, this differential treatment depending on an arbitrary distinc-tion of the type of measure chosen. Further, in the governmental policy arsenal, subsidies are certainly not the most trade distortive measures. If the perception of a lacuna in the system intensifies and inaction in climate and trade negotiations persists, the Appellate Body may be persuaded of the need to take the lead.

In the presence of the various uncertainties raised by the application of a general justification provision, however, law reform is the first-best scenario since it would allow WTO members to negotiate new language to tailor the exceptions to the needs of justification and accommodate the required policy space in the most appropriate way. A blueprint for law reform is briefly analyzed in section XI.

X.   BIOFUEL SUBSIDIES BETWEEN AOA AND SCM: NAVIGATING IN THE SYSTEM

The starting point, which has been analyzed above in section IV.A, is that biofuels can be classified differently, either as agricultural or industrial goods. If biofuel production is subsidized this difference in classification can have an impact on the applicable rules. In a nutshell, while subsidies to industrial goods are regulated by the SCM Agreement alone, subsidies to agricultural goods can, at least in principle, be regulated by both the AoA and the SCM Agreement.

The rules of the SCM Agreement have been extensively examined above. We now outline the special rules on agriculture support.

A. The Regulatory Framework of Agriculture Support and Biofuel Subsidies

The long-term objective of the special disciplines on agriculture is to establish a fair and market-oriented agricultural trading system. This is mainly done through progressive negotiated reductions in agricultural support.

The key distinction of the disciplines of agriculture support of the AoA is between domestic support and export subsidies. In both cases, the disciplines are not general but can only be defined in relation to the commitments Members have entered into in their schedules.

With respect to export subsidies, for those that are *listed* among the six categories of Article 9.1 of the AoA, Members are allowed to provide them but a) *only* to the agricultural products specified in the schedule, and b) *not in excess of* the budgetary outlay and quantity commitment levels specified therein.[190] Those export subsidies *not listed* in Article 9.1 cannot be applied in a manner which results in, or which threatens to lead to, circumvention of export subsidy commitments.[191] Domestic support, i.e. domestic subsidies, is mainly expressed with the single figure of the Aggregate Measurement of Support (AMS) which refers to the annual aggregate level of support in monetary terms which is subject to reduction commitments (so-called 'amber box').[192] Members can thus provide support in favor of domestic producers *but not in excess of* the AMS level.

Crucially, not all domestic support is subject to reduction commitments. In particular, apart from more lenient disciplines for subsidies in developing countries[193] and *de minimis* subsidies,[194] the AoA exempts certain direct payments under production-limiting programmes (so-called 'blue box' subsidies)[195] and various types of subsidies with no or minimal trade-distorting effects or effects on production (so-called 'green box' subsidies).[196]

---

[190] Article 3.
[191] Article 10.
[192] Article 6 and Annex 3.
[193] Articles 6.2 and 15.
[194] Article 6.4.
[195] Article 6.5.
[196] Article 7 and Annex 2. For a comprehensive analysis of the 'green box' see R. Meléndez-Ortiz, C. Bellmann and J. Hepburn (eds), *Agricultural Subsidies in the WTO Green Box – Ensuring Coherence with Sustainable Development Goals* (Cambridge: Cambridge University Press, 2009).

Now, what is the impact of this complex regulation on biofuel subsidies?[197] Although the relevance of the export subsidy rules cannot be excluded, the main focus should be on the domestic support regulation since most of biofuel subsidies target domestic production. In this respect, the first consideration is that, if subsidies supporting – directly and indirectly (e.g. in favor of feedstock) – biofuels are included in the AMS reduction commitment, this ceiling may be easily reached and even pierced, which explains the temptation to classify ethanol as an industrial rather than agricultural product.[198]

The key factor is that, as a consequence of how the regulation of support in the AoA is designed, most of the subsidies are – irrespective of their effects on trade – *constrained* inasmuch as they are subject to reduction commitments. If it is true that the scheduling or 'positive approach' of the AoA seems to give deference to the autonomous negotiating choices of Members, it is also true that, once a commitment has been entered into, this operates as an objective and automatic constraint – without any need to show that adverse effects on trade have been produced or the possibility to rebut the occurrence of these effects. In this sense, if we compare for a minute the subsidy disciplines of the AoA with those of the SCM Agreement, while the AoA regulation on export subsidies is in general more lenient than that of the SCM Agreement, the regulation of domestic subsidies, which is probably more relevant in the biofuel sector, is harsher. Support under the SCM Agreement is not constrained by fixed ceilings, and, whereas export subsidies are prohibited, domestic subsidies are substantially permitted unless adverse effects are proved.

At the same time, however, if certain conditions are fulfiled, some agriculture subsidies are expressly permitted, an option which is not available – as the previous analysis has shown – for industrial subsidies. The key question in this regard then concerns the impact of the exceptions. How much policy space do these carve-outs, and especially the 'green box', offer?

---

[197]   For a comprehensive analysis see IPC and REIL, 'WTO Disciplines and Biofuels: Opportunities and Constraints in the Creation of a Global Marketplace', IPC Discussion Paper, October 2006, and T. Harmer, *Biofuel Subsidies and the Law of the WTO*, ICTSD Issue Paper No. 20, June 2009.

[198]   It should further be noted that 'upstream' subsidies may contribute to the AMS figure. Furthermore, subsidies granted to feedstock used to produce biofuels, whether they are part of general programmes of agricultural support or are rather targeted to a phase of the production of biofuels, may well confer a competitive advantage on 'downstream' biofuels. Of course, this effect cannot be presumed but has to be proved on a case-by-case basis. See, e.g., Panel Report, *United States – Subsidies on Upland Cotton*, WT/DS267/R, adopted 21 March 2005.

The general conditions governing the availability of 'green box' exceptions should be considered first. According to Article 1 of Annex 1, public support should have no or minimal trade-distorting effects or effects on production. Furthermore, it should satisfy two basic criteria: a) it should be provided through a publicly-funded government programme (including government revenue foregone) not involving transfers from consumers, and b) it should not operate as price support to producers. It can be immediately observed how these conditions can seriously constrain support to biofuels.

To benefit from the shelter of the 'green box', the measure should also satisfy the policy-specific criteria and conditions of the applicable categories. Among the numerous categories of exceptions, four are particularly relevant for biofuel subsidies. First, public support in relation to 'programmes which provide services or benefits to agriculture or the rural community', including in particular research.[199] Crucially, this support should 'not involve direct payments to producers or processors'. Second, structural adjustment assistance through resource retirement programmes.[200] In other words, only payments conditional on the 'retirement of land from marketable agricultural production (for a minimum of three years)' are eligible. The big question, which seems to have a positive answer, is whether feedstock used to produce biofuels is a 'marketable agricultural product'. This was certainly true for first generation feedstock, like corn or sugar. The question of marketability, which is mainly a factual one and can change over time, is less clear with respect to second generation feedstock. Third, payments under environmental programmes.[201] These should be 'part of a clearly-defined government environmental or conservation programme' and should be 'limited to the extra costs or loss of income' for complying with the programme. The requirement that the compensation should be limited to the compliance costs may be difficult to satisfy in practice, also in terms of the evidential burden of the relationship between payments and costs. Fourth, decoupled income support. A biofuel subsidy, completely unrelated to production, would be permissible. This is, again, a difficult test to meet.

If, as noted above, particularly considering the reduction commitment mechanism of domestic support, the AoA seems to be more onerous than the SCM Agreement, the interesting question is whether this regulatory balance is somewhat positively altered by the green box shelter. The

---

[199] Article 2(a) of Annex 2.
[200] Article 10 of Annex 2.
[201] Article 12 of Annex 2.

answer, at least with respect to biofuel subsidies, seems to be negative. Both the general and specific conditions of the applicable exceptions are such that the ability to support biofuels seems to be significantly constrained.

B.   The Cumulative Application of SCM Agreement and AoA: a Real Risk?

Two legal provisions are particularly important to define the relation between AoA and SCM Agreement.

Article 21.1 of the AoA highlights the special nature of the AoA: 'The provisions of GATT 1994 and of other Multilateral Trade Agreements in Annex 1A to the WTO Agreement shall apply *subject to* the provisions of this Agreement'.[202]

Article 13 of the AoA, entitled 'due restraint' and dubbed 'peace-clause', more specifically defines the relationship with the SCM Agreement, establishing that subsidies conforming with the agriculture disciplines were either exempt from action under the SCM Agreement or the latter should have been subject to 'due restraint'.[203] During the implementation period: a) domestic support within the green box was non-actionable (no countervailing duties, no multilateral disciplines, no nullification or impairment), b) countervailing duty investigations in relation to domestic support in line with reduction commitments and export subsidies were subject to due restraint, and both domestic and export support was exempt from multilateral disciplines and nullification and impairment claims.

With the expiry of the implementation period on 1 January 2004, the shelter variously provided by the 'peace clause' lapsed. There is no legal obstacle now that precludes a biofuel subsidy which is in line with the requirements of the AoA to be nonetheless challenged under the SCM Agreement.

Two comments here. First, the existence itself of the 'peace clause', which presupposes that a measure which complies with the AoA might nonetheless fall foul of the SCM Agreement, confirms that if the AoA might overall be *more onerous* than the SCM Agreement, particularly because of the general limit of its AMS reduction commitments, it is not, strictly speaking, necessarily *stricter* in terms of legal requirements. Individually taken, a measure sheltered by the AMS ceiling may be trade-distortive and objected to under the SCM Agreement. For example,

---

[202]   Emphasis added.
[203]   Various provisions of the SCM Agreement (Articles 3.1, 5, 6.9, 7) do refer to and give precedence to Article 13 AoA. Article 10 generally refers to the AoA.

biofuel subsidies which include local content requirements may be prohibited under the SCM Agreement.

At the same time, however, if a government managed to have its agricultural subsidies covered by the (this time) strict conditions of the green box, the likelihood of a challenge under the SCM Agreement is significantly diminished. One of the general conditions of green box eligibility is that the measure does not cause distortions to trade or production. If this happens, it is unlikely that a case under the general subsidy disciplines, which require evidence of negative trade impact, could be sustained.

XI. IS THERE REALLY A POLICY SPACE PROBLEM?

The previous analysis has shown that, at the level of plain legal analysis, the current WTO subsidy disciplines are not on balance favourable to governmental autonomy to adopt and design subsidies for emissions mitigation that may be desirable.[204] Whether because of legal uncertainty (deriving from the complexity of support measures, like tax incentives, or lack of clarity of the legal text, for regulatory measures), or because of the typical, but not always consistent, trade law prescription of neutrality and non-discrimination (with respect to the specificity and adverse effects tests, and discriminatory subsidies), or because of the limit of reduction commitments or the strictures of exceptions (for biofuel subsidies), policy space with respect to certain measures of support that can be assumed to be desirable may end up being significantly impaired.

There is one important argument though, which would dispel any sort of anxiety. Irrespective of the legal question of whether some measures of support of green energy amount to a subsidy objectionable under WTO rules, what really matters is whether somebody is going to file a complaint. Who is going to challenge these measures if, as has been seen, they are so widespread? If the answer is that nobody does or will do this, then, pragmatically, we may fairly conclude that there is no real problem with policy space.

We have had many and important subsidy disputes in the WTO making the SCM Agreement one of the most litigated covered instruments before

---

[204] The determination of the actual impact and proportions of the policy contraints emerged from the legal analysis can however only become fully clear through empirical analysis. It may well be, for example, that, due to the minimal size of the support, certain measures are 'below the radar' of WTO subsidies discipline.

WTO dispute settlement. Equally, countervailing duties are among the most used tools of the domestic trade remedies toolbox, and are also subject to significant review in WTO disputes.

That said, energy subsidies in general (which include both subsidies to fossil fuels and to renewable energy) are laconically absent from the register of cases or administrative proceedings. We have a typical 'glasshouse' situation here. Who is going to throw stones that could eventually damage the thrower too? Everybody gives subsidies in support of energy. Nobody has an interest in raising a claim and risking a highly probable counter-claim.[205]

Subsidization of energy is tolerated, the only exceptions largely being those cases where we have more obvious breaches (like export subsidies or subsidy measures with local content requirements). Furthermore, even in these cases, the strategic element inherent in litigation is particularly marked. The strong impression is that negative statements and official complaints escalate to the level of formal disputes only when litigation is necessary to reassert the 'rules of engagement' and the tacit agreement that public support for energy be allowed, provided that the most overt protectionist tendencies are kept at bay.

The existence of substantial real or expected trade interests is the main catalyzer of trade litigation. For example, renewable energy production and trade are increasingly significant. The magnitude of the economic and political interests is high and on the rise. The technology of renewable energy (e.g. wind turbines, solar PV cells) is developing fast and, far from being merely limited to satisfying domestic needs, is exported. There are several examples. The annual turnover of Germany's renewable energy industry amounts to €30 billion, of which a large part is due to exports of goods. Renewable energy itself is increasingly traded too. Brazil is the second biggest producer of fuel ethanol (the first being the USA) and the world's largest exporter. These technological and commercial successes are often owing to various forms of sustained, present or past, public support. This is known and accepted. When the stakes of international intra-industry competition become high, however, policies that interfere too defiantly with the trade process may not be accepted.

It may be useful to consider the recent litigation on renewable energy

---

[205]   The risk-aversion described in the text is substantially the same which explains why, during its five years of application, the discipline of non-actionable subsidies of the SCT Agreement was never used. There are many reasons for this, including the limited scope of these exceptions. To a large extent, however, this is a second indication of silent acquiescence. On the history of the rules on non-actionable subsidies see Bigdeli, n. 9 above, 4–10.

support. In September 2010, Japan, immediately joined by the EU and US, entered into consultations with Canada, challenging the local content requirement of Ontario's FIT system (*Canada – RE*, DS 412). Interestingly, according to practictioners active in the field, this legal action, still pending, has been perceived in the trade circles as a 'mistake', somewhat altering the previous equilibrium. Whether this is correct or not, in August 2011, the EU decided to initiate a separate litigation (DS 426). Again in September 2010, the US Steelworkers Union filed a petition with the United States Trade Representative (USTR) claiming that various measures of support of the Chinese green technology sector were WTO illegal. What is interesting is that the complaint was lodged in the context of a 'section 301' procedure[206] which, strategically, opens up a wide range of possibilities for the USTR, including the filing of a dispute at the WTO.[207] In October 2011, while the EU was initiating a countervailing duty investigation on imports of bioethanol from the US,[208] Solarworld Inc., a solar cell and panel manufacturer (and the US-based arm of the German company Solarworld AG), filed a petition with the US Department of Commerce (DOC) asking for the imposition of anti-dumping and countervailing duties on solar cells and panels imported from China.[209] In late March 2012 the US DOC preliminarily found that the Chinese imports had been subsidized and that countervailing duties could be imposed at rates of between 2.9 to 4.73 percent.[210] If not the amount of the duties imposed, what makes this case interesting is that, for the first time, what is challenged are not local-content requirements but

---

[206]   US Trade Act of 1974. After a petition is filed, the USTR – who can also act ex officio – has 45 days to decide whether to initiate an investigation. The investigation is intended to establish whether any foreign government practice breaches or jeopardizes US benefits under a trade agreement. In case of positive determination, various types of unilateral action are possible. For an analysis of section 301 see J.H. Jackson, W.J. Davey and A.O. Sykes, *Legal Problems of International Economic Relations – Cases, Materials, Texts* (West Publishing Co, 2008), Chapter 7.

[207]   This is indeed what happened with the *China – Measures Concerning Wind Power Equipment* (DS 419) dispute, filed in December 2010 and, as noted above, recently settled.

[208]   Notice of initiation of an anti-subsidy proceeding concerning imports of bioethanol originating in the United States of America OJ (2011/C 345/05), 25.11.2011.

[209]   A. Beattie and E. Crooks, 'Call for US tariffs on solar panel imports', *The Financial Times*, 19 October 2011.

[210]   Interestingly, for the first time the US DOC made a 'critical circumstances' finding resulting in the retroactive application of duties (90 days before the determination, i.e., in the instant case, since December 2011).

domestic subsidies, like cash grants and subsidized loans.[211] Definitely more significant is the amount of the duties the US DOC imposed in the concurrent anti-dumping investigation in May 2012 which range from 31 percent up to 250 percent.[212] Crucially, in late July 2012, Germany's Solarworld also launched a complaint against Chinese support for the solar panel industry in Brussels asking the EU Commission to impose anti-dumping duties.[213]

The big question is whether, in a few years, with hindsight, these few disputes will just be viewed as skirmishes that served to reinstate the international 'rules of engagement' of public support for renewable energy. Or whether they will pave the way for a dramatic readjustment of these rules with a substantial lowering of the tolerance level.[214] Various factors may contribute to this change of balance. The obstacles to renewable energy and market failures may disappear or in any event diminish. At the same time, if current trends continue, production and trade in renewable energy will increase. The markets will become larger, competition greater and the distortions caused by subsidies more evident. Complaints from aggrieved industries to act and action by governments, in the form of trade remedies and WTO litigation, will thus increase. A good case in point of these dynamics is the solar panels market.[215]

We now reach a conundrum. If there are no challenges, then although the rules do not provide enough policy space, such space is *de facto* ensured by the tolerance governments show. The justification for supporting the renewable energy industry is recognized in practical terms, albeit not in formal normative terms. It can thus be reasonably argued that there is no issue to fix. When challenges become more frequent, because the market has been substantially freed from hindrances and distortions, and the technology and commercial practices are mature, the justification

---

[211] According to press reports, following the US DOC investigation, the Chinese solar panel industry was seeking legal advice on filing its own anti-dumping and anti-subsidy case against the US, with respect to American exports of polysilicon, the main material used in making conventional solar panels, to China. K. Bradsher, *China Bends to US Complaint on Solar Panels but Plans Retaliation*, *New York Times*, 21 November 2011.

[212] E. Crooks, 'Trade War Fears Over US Solar Duties', *The Financial Times*, 18 May 2012.

[213] J. Shaffin, 'EU Solar Groups Seek China Probe', *The Financial Times*, 23 July 2012.

[214] It is interesting in this regard to note the more general trend in WTO subsidy litigation which seems to be followed in the renewable energy sector as well. In the first disputes, only prohibited support and import substitution were challenged. This soon enlarged to encompass more complex litigation on domestic subsidies.

[215] See Scott, n. 16 above. See also Beattie and Crooks, n. 209 above.

for supporting the industry is far less evident. It can therefore equally be argued that the legal framework, which offers the possibility to challenge these measures of support, is still appropriate and no change is needed.

While this conclusion is sound – undesirable subsidies should be restrained – the first account – one of tacit agreement and equilibrium – is not necessarily accurate. Another narrative is possible. The possibility cannot be excluded that the substantial acquiescence to subsidies observed so far might turn into a more aggressive stance even before the market has become – if it will ever be – fully competitive. The magnitude of public support used to ensure the steady deployment of renewable energy is already large, and on the rise. Governments may want to ensure – or challenge – first-mover advantages. It is exactly when market conditions are more difficult that the fight to emerge is fierce. Moreover, the vagaries of litigation cannot be fully predicted since unexpected exogenous factors can take place and spark trade rows.

The equilibrium may be less stable than it appears. If this is correct, (by definition volatile) tacit tolerance does not suffice to ensure legal certainty. In other words, in unstable conditions, the lack of a formal and positive recognition that some forms of support for renewable energy are justifiable and should be legitimate would cause problems for international relations and the business community alike. Legal certainty must be reinstated, possibly in new ways.

XII. THE INEVITABLE QUEST FOR BALANCE: A FEW NOTES ON LAW REFORM

The original setting of the SCM Agreement did provide that, in the presence of certain substantive and procedural conditions, certain regional, environmental and R&D subsidies were non-actionable and were sheltered from countervailing duty action.[216] The introduction of an express shelter for certain subsidies was however very much controversial,[217] with the result that the exception of non-actionability was only provisional and without the necessary support to maintain it, even in amended form, it expired at the end of 1999.[218]

Albeit not perfect, the original scheme of the SCM Agreement was

---

[216] Articles 8 and 9 of the SCM Agreement.

[217] For a detailed account see Bidgeli, n. 9 above, 4–8.

[218] Furthermore, the discipline of non-actionable subsidies was never used. In note 205 above we explain this as further indication of the tacit acquiescence of members to a widespread scenario of subsidization.

certainly *balanced*. On the one hand, it shed some light on what consti-tuted a subsidy. On the other hand, depending on their real or perceived effects, subsidies were divided according to a tripartite taxonomy: prohib-ited, (permitted but) actionable, and (permitted and) non-actionable.

The idea of reviving a shelter for certain 'good' subsidies is increasingly aired,[219] and the most likely candidate is certainly climate change sub-sidies. What follows is a blueprint for a possible law reform.[220]

First, the prerequisite and cornerstone of any subsidy discipline is *trans-parency*. Collins-Williams and Wolfe recently noted:

> The most general observation is that transparency mechanisms too often seem to have been an afterthought in the negotiations. Transparency is a fundamen-tal WTO norm, but few agreements are designed from the ground up to make significant use of transparency as a tool. Transparency does not work as a tool if it is thought to be merely an elegant appendage to third-party 'enforcement'. It does not work if negotiators do not think carefully about the government behaviour they wish to modify using transparency.[221]

Notification and transparency are key elements for both tracks of the gov-ernance approach suggested below, and should offer a clear picture of the measures of support.[222] The current WTO system is deficient in this respect. Many Members do not notify, or do so inconsistently.[223] To be effective,

---

[219]   See, e.g., R. Howse, 'Do the World Trade Organization Disciplines on Domestic Subsidies Make Sense? The Case for Legalizing some Subsidies', in K.W. Bagwell, G.A. Bermann, and P.C.Mavroidis (eds), *Law and Economics of Contingent Protection in International Trade* (Cambridge: Cambridge University Press, 2009); Howse, n. 14 above; Bigdeli, n. 9 above; G. Horlick and P. Clarke, 'WTO Subsidies Disciplines During and After the Crisis', *Journal of International Economic Law* (2010), 859; P. Aerni et al, 'Climate Change, Human Rights and International Economic Law: Exploring the Linkages between Human Rights, Trade and Investment', 53 *German Yearbook of International Law*, (2010), 139; Rubini, n. 45 above, Chapter 2; D. Steger, 'The Subsidies and Countervailing Measures Agreement: Ahead of its Time or Time for Reform?', *Journal of World Trade* (2010), 779.

[220]   These are the initial thoughts of a broader project on the future regulation of climate change subsidies in the WTO. The gist of these suggestions can also be applied to the reform of agriculture support.

[221]   T. Collins-Williams and R. Wolfe, 'Transparency as a Trade Policy Tool: the WTO's Cloudy Windows', *World Trade Review* (2010), 551, 573.

[222]   A good analysis of the importance of monitoring subsidies is Steenblik, n. 113 above, 190–191. See also Collins-Williams and Wolfe, n. 221 above, 575.

[223]   Writing in 2001, but with conclusions still valid today, see G.N. Horlick, 'Subsidies Discipline under WTO and US Rules', in C.D. Ehlermann and M. Everson (eds), *European Competition Law Annual 1999: Selected Issues in the Field of State Aids* (Oxford: Hart Publishing, 2001), 593, 601. See also

the system should be designed with the proper *incentives* to notify, coupled with appropriate sanctions for non-compliance.[224] The issues and options are various. We just name a few here. A crucial element is the definition of a useful template of subsidies notification.[225] The use of presumptions and standstill obligations could represent a powerful device to improve compliance. The benefit of non-actionability could, for example, be subject to the complete notification of the subsidy measure (as occurred under the now expired SCM Article 8). More generally, it could even be provided that the subsidy cannot be implemented if not duly notified.[226] If granted, it should be withdrawn (retroactively) or, at least, the interest accrued on the sums granted be paid back. Recourse to counter- and third-party notifications, from other international organizations and NGOs, and perhaps even affected private parties, and subject to verification, should be considered too.[227] The system of transparency should also be open at its 'output' end with both 'raw' and 'processed' information made available to the wider public that could then exert control and influence governments.[228]

WTO, *World Trade Report 2006*, Geneva, 111. The Committee on Subsidies and Countervailing Measures, meeting on 26–27 October 2011 and on 26 April 2012, focused on improving the timeliness and completeness of notifications (see http://www.wto.org/english/news_e/news11_e/scm_26oct11_e.htm; http://www.wto.org/english/news_e/news12_e/scm_26apr12_e.htm).

[224] During the current Doha Round of negotiations the EC proposed 'to explore the possibility of penalising partial or non-notifications'. It further suggested to 'devise a mechanism through which the quality and scope of notifications could be scrutinized and if failings were found or suspected a review procedure could be generated through an expedited WTO dispute settlement procedure similar to the one envisaged for spurious initiations or by referring the matter to an empowered Permanent Group of Experts', (TN/RL/W/30, 21 November 2002, para. 4).

[225] For a proposal of a new template for subsidies notification see R. Steenblik and J. Simón, *A New Template for Notifying Subsidies to the WTO* (Geneva: IISD, 2011). Clearly, the most important – but at the same time most controversial – information concerns the trade impact of the subsidy. This may be considered as sensitive information, apt to constitute some form of 'self-incrimination', and thus attract litigation.

[226] Following a proposal of the EC during the Uruguay Round. See Horlick, n. 223 above, 603.

[227] Along these lines, Collins-Williams and Wolfe, n. 221 above, 575–576. At Article 25.10, the SCM Agreement provides for counter-notifications, i.e. Members can notify subsidies granted by other Members. This power has never been used until very recently when, in October 2011, the US acted on its basis, notifying 200 programmes implemented by China and 50 by India.

[228] Collins-Williams and Wolfe, n. 221 above, 576. This should be set in the context of the more general discussion on the governance of subsidies, briefly examined in the next recommendation.

Second, a renewed discipline on subsidies should be based on a system of governance with *two interconnected tracks*.

On the one hand, we would have the usual set of detailed conditions outlining what is permitted and what is not permitted – the *legal positive* side. This should be implemented through a more effective institutional and procedural system, and become more entrenched and internalized through litigation and discussions within the Committee of Subsidies and Countervailing Measures.

In parallel and in close interaction with this 'hard law' track, a soft governance track should be introduced (or, better, reinforced). This is the place where information on subsidies is exchanged and evaluated (with no prejudice to legal assessment), thus representing the *knowledge-enhancing* side of the system.[229] This forum would ultimately contribute to create a positive climate helping to embed open discussion, to generate, share, test and develop ideas and values, 'symbols' and 'legal images' on what constitutes normal and legitimate governmental practice and what does not.[230] This process may reinforce mutual trust and trust in the system, reducing tensions and conflict and, eventually and crucially, improving the effectiveness of the 'hard law' track of the system (via interpretation or amendment).

The institutional settings for this double-track system can be various, can involve a re-design of current bodies like the (heavily-used) Secretariat or the (never-used) Group of Experts, or the creation of ad hoc bodies. More generally, the possibility of resorting to external 'experts', maybe also based in other international organizations with jurisdiction on public subsidization, should be considered and designed in order to render their participation particularly effective as input to the political side of the discussion.[231] A crucial issue to define is the relation and interplay of the Committee on Subsidies and Countervailing Measures – where the representatives of the Members convene – with such other bodies. What should certainly be implemented is a sense of regularity and continuity in the

---

[229]   When we write these notes we clearly have in mind the positive experience of the SPS and TBT Commitees, and also the Committee on Trade and Environment.

[230]   This process has been recently and effectively analyzed by A. Lang in *World Trade Law after Neo-Liberalism: Reimagining the Global Economic Order* (Oxford: Oxford University Press, 2011).

[231]   The possibility of entrusting to an independent body the role of evaluation and analysis of the information and data on subsidies, in terms of cost-effectiveness and best practice in relation to the stated objectives, could be a plausible option. The results of this independent review could then feed back to a revamped, and more frequent, Trade Policy Review Mechanism, and constitute additional material for governments to share and discuss in the Committee on Subsidies and Countervailing Measures.

meetings and exchange between the various actors, in order to make the whole process productive.

Third, the glue keeping the whole system together should be an entrenched *'sense of community'*.[232] This refers to the real or perceived presence of shared interests and goals, to the belief and confidence in the system as a shared resource towards the attainment of public goods.[233]

The sense of community is the determining factor in giving shape to the system and maintaining it, in deciding how ambitious – or more simply effective – it is and in making it acceptable and valuable to its participants. Arguably, the main ingredients of this narrative have nothing novel or revolutionary but belong to the core of the rule of law ethos and good governance (transparency, accountability, fairness, inclusiveness, effectiveness) which inform the other two guidelines we have just suggested. This community understanding should inform every step of the life of the system of subsidy control – from its negotiation and design up to its various levels of operation. From an operational perspective, it is *good norm and regime design*, with the creation of the right incentives to co-operate, that can foster this sense of Community.

The narrative of community plays a crucial role also for the acceptability of the GATT Article XX defense. The main finding of the analysis was that the issue of the applicability of this crucial provision is not technical. The more we leave a *contractual* approach and shift towards a *community* one,[234] the easier the acceptability of trade-with-non-trade balances, with the possible outcome that trade interests do not indeed prevail, becomes acceptable. This process, it is argued, is inevitable. The increasing pressure of the various challenges of the current era[235] make a mere contractual approach insufficient to solve issues and disputes that, although inextricably linked to the trade discourse, go beyond it.[236]

---

[232]   This sociological concept has been applied to the WTO context by Sungjoon Cho in his work. See S. Cho, 'The WTO's *Gemeinschaft*', *Alabama Law Review* (2004), 483; id, 'Reconstructing an International Organization: A Paradigm Shift in the World Trade Organization', SSRN, draft of 26 April 2011.

[233]   Rubini, n. 45 above, 33–37.

[234]   This is a progressive movement, through stages. It is also more than likely that elements of both approaches do coexist. For a description of contractual and community approaches see Cho, 'Reconstructing an International Organization' n. 232 above.

[235]   T. Cottier, 'Challenges Ahead in International Economic Law', *Journal of International Economic Law* (2009), 3.

[236]   The step to what a few years ago was dubbed 'constitutionalism in a modest sense' is short. See T. Cottier, 'Limits to International Trade: The Constitutional Challenge', *American Society of International Law Proceedings* (2000), 220, 221.

Fourth, when designing new rules on legitimate subsidies, the first principle is that the guidelines coming from *economic and policy analysis* should be adhered to as much as possible (see section II above). This also means that the *political economy* implications of subsidy decisions should be duly accounted for. Thus, for example, if free emissions allowances are questionable from both an environmental and economic perspective, pending a multilateral solution to tackle climate change, they may still be a useful bargaining chip to win the consensus of reluctant industries in the adoption of an ETS (being one of the less troublesome unilateral actions to mitigate climate change) and, thus, accommodate any real or alleged competitiveness risk. That being said, however, their questionable economic and environmental merit indicates that, should the path of law reform be followed, attempts to structure a legal shelter for acceptable forms of free allowances should be narrowly constrained and temporary.[237]

Fifth, the existence of a system of justifications to draw direction from is also useful. In this regard the *EU system of State aid control* can offer valuable inspiration in terms of rule and regime design.[238] In particular, from the perspective of someone seeking inspiration or guidance on subsidy governance, the EU system of State aid does not represent a 'single package'. Some elements, notably those related to the case-by-case scrutiny and authorization of a supranational adjudicatory body, are not easily transposable beyond the EU.[239] What the EU experience can, however, certainly offer is good reference for the substantive design of the justification,[240] for

---

[237]   See Rubini and Jegou, n. 1 above.

[238]   The European model of State aid justifications already played an important part in the design of the category of non-actionable subsidies.

[239]   For example, the balancing test cannot be imported at the global level for the simple reason that it needs to be administered and applied on a case-by-case basis. In the WTO, the necessity-proportionality assessment would need to be 'pre-made', embodied in precise rules subject to clear and automatic application. In this context it is notable that a mechanism whereby subsidies could not be considered 'non-actionable' until approved by the SCM Committee was deleted at the very last minute of the Uruguay Negotiations. See P.A. Clarke, J. Bourgeois and G. Horlick, 'WTO Dispute Settlement Practice Relating to Subsidies and Countervailing Measures', in F. Ortino and E.U. Petermann (eds), *The WTO Dispute Settlement System* (The Hague: Kluwer, 2004) 353, 378.

[240]   The EU permits aid intensities much further than the 20 percent of Article 8.2(c) of the SCM Agreement. Further, while under the chapeau of Article 8.2(c) of the SCM Agreement, only 'existing facilities' can benefit from the exemption, under the EU regulation aid can be granted for investment in renewable energy production. Another example of the difference refers to the possibility for EU State aid to cover operating costs, which is excluded in the SCM Agreement.

the mechanisms to enforce transparency,[241] and, if necessary, the adjustment of the rules[242] or the measure.[243]

EU law has a very sophisticated system of justifications for State aid, including environmental and energy subsidies. These justifications find their textual basis in the very broad language of few clauses introduced in 1957 in the Treaty of Rome. Over time, the normative development has been robust, passing from the interpretation of general treaty clauses to policy definition and consolidation, often tested before the EU Courts, to reach the more recent stage of secondary legislation. Individual decisions have built up a practice which was first codified into 'soft' law to eventually become, in virtually all State aid areas, 'hard' law. Procedurally, the system is based on two cornerstones which aim to guarantee the effective control by the EU Commission in Brussels, which has the exclusive power to authorize planned State aid. Members must notify all planned State aid in advance and refrain from implementing it before authorization.[244]

A crucial development took place in 2008 with the introduction of the 'General Block Exemption Regulation' (GBER).[245] The underlying concept is that State aid measures pursuing horizontal – not sectoral – objectives which satisfy the precise conditions of the regulation are automatically permissible, without any need of prior authorization.[246] The benefit of the exemption applies only if certain conditions, mainly referring to cost-eligibility, aid intensity, transparency and incentive effect, are present. The GBER covers numerous types of State aid including several

---

[241] The procedural obligations of notification and 'standstill' before a positive authorization are strictly enforced in the EU, mainly through the remedy of retroactive repayment.

[242] The fast development of both EU State aid soft and hard law, often following public consultations, is very instructive.

[243] In this regard, the 'safety-valve' of Article 9 of the SCM Agreement, whereby non-actionable subsidies would be subject to closer scrutiny if causing 'serious adverse effects', with the possibility of removing the negative effects, should be revived. This device would operate in a similar way to what happens in the EU where – at the stage of the assessment of the compatibility with the common market – the Commission has the power to require various forms of changes to the planned aid in order to reduce the negative distorting effects of the measures.

[244] National courts of the EU Member States have ensured the respect of these obligations with far-reaching powers, including most notably that to order the repayment of any aid granted in contravention of these two procedural obligations.

[245] Commission Regulation (EC) No. 800/2008 of 6 August 2008 declaring certain categories of aid compatible with the common market in application of Articles 87 and 88 of the Treaty, OJ L214, 9.8.2008, 3.

[246] There are still however reporting and monitoring provisions.

instances of environmental aid.[247] One of these is aid for the production of fuels, heat or electricity derived from renewable-energy sources.[248]

If the conditions of the GBER are not satisfied, the planned measure of support is subject to the individual scrutiny and authorization by the Commission. In the environmental area, the Commission applies the principles of the 2008 Guidelines on State aid for Environmental Protection ('Guidelines').[249] In general, although the normative framework is very similar to the GBER, the Guidelines are more generous with higher levels of aid intensity permitted.[250] This can happen because it is ultimately for the Commission, which enjoys wide discretion in this regard, to decide whether the State aid measure should eventually be permitted or not. The process through which this decision is reached involves the execution of a flexible balancing test largely centered on a proportionality assessment.[251]

If we now compare the normative approach of the GBER and the Guidelines with that of the GATT/WTO, strikingly, we see a similar development. At the beginning there were only general clauses (see Treaty of Rome) or statements (see Article 11 of the Tokyo Round Subsidies Code). With time, however, the general recognition that certain subsidies

---

[247] These refer to i) investment aid for environmental protection beyond Community standards; ii) aid for the acquisition of transport vehicles beyond Community standards; iii) aid for early adaptation to future Community standards for SMEs; iv) aid for investment in energy saving; v) aid for investment in high efficiency cogeneration; vi) aid for investments to exploit renewable energy sources; vii) aid for environmental studies; and viii) aid in the form of tax reductions.

[248] In this regard the eligible costs are the additional costs compared with production from conventional power plant or heating systems with equivalent capacity. The maximum aid intensity is 45 percent for large enterprises, 55 percent for medium-sized enterprises and 65 percent for small enterprises.

[249] OJ C82 of 01.04.2008, 1.

[250] For investment in renewable energy, for example, we have 60 percent for large enterprises, 70 percent for medium-sized enterprises, 80 percent for small enterprises. If the aid is granted through a competitive bidding process on non-discriminatory criteria the intensity can reach even 100 percent.

[251] The three steps are as follows: i) is the aid aimed at a well-defined objective of common interest, for example environmental protection?; ii) is the aid well designed to achieve that objective (i.e. is the aid appropriate, does it produce an incentive effect, is it proportional)?; iii) are the distortions on competition and effect on intra-EU trade limited, so that the overall balance is positive? See K. Bacon, *European Community Law of State Aid* (Oxford: Oxford University Press, 2009), Chapter 3, para. 3.28. For an analysis, see also H.W. Friederiszick, L.H. Röller and V. Verouden, 'European State Aid Control: An Economic Framework', in P. Bucirossi (ed.), *Handbook of Antitrust Economics* (Cambridge MA: MIT Press, 2008), 625.

may be legitimate has generated, through practice and experience, a more detailed discipline.[252]

This trend *from general to specific* is quite significant. In the politically sensitive area of public subsidies, the anti-abuse goal is clear. It is in this light that we therefore have some misgivings with the suggestion that a 'much simpler, principle-based approach' would be needed, whereby a climate change subsidy would *simply* not be actionable if included in one of the policies of the Kyoto Protocol, contribute to its goals (like technology transfer and equitable allocation of responsibilities) and, to the extent possible, respects fundamental principles of the WTO like non-discrimination and transparency.[253] While the reference to an important multilateral instrument has clear advantages, particularly by ensuring coherency of action, the problem with this approach is the same as a GATT Article XX option. The guidelines of the Kyoto Protocol (notably Article 2.1(a)) are too general and too little prescriptive. Detailed rules are certainly less flexible, liable to be over- or under-inclusive and more prone to 'micro-management'. And, clearly, they seem to constrain policy space. This is not necessarily the case, however, if the terms and conditions of these clauses are properly negotiated and drafted, and, if necessary, are subsequently reconsidered (a beneficial by-product of the soft governance process outlined above). In our view, the noticeable benefit of precision is the capability of reducing the potential for abuse which has been one of the main criticisms towards subsidies, and improve the acceptability of the idea itself of a 'resurrection' of non-actionability. On the centrality of transparency we have commented above. As for respect for the principle of non-discrimination, although this is certainly important as a general tenet of the system, the possibility of introducing appropriate carve-outs for those limited cases where a discriminatory approach may be warranted should be considered.

How do the conditions of the EU regulation embodied in the GBER/Guidelines compare with the previous criteria of non-actionability?

From an initial assessment,[254] it emerges that, not only do they share the same general approach, but they also 'follow the same logic' based on what has been called the 'polluter *shares* principle' of cost allocation. To be sure, there are significant differences which show a more generous scope for justification under EU rules. This depends on the complexity and

---

[252] In a sense, we could even say that the first substantial global and multilateral discipline on subsidies (the SCM Agreement) started from the point of arrival of the more established EU system.
[253] Howse, n. 14 above, 21.
[254] See Bidgeli, n. 9 above, 12–17.

comprehensiveness of the EU system which combines stricter pre-defined rules of justification with a flexible individual scrutiny by the Commission.

XIII. CONCLUSIONS

The previous analysis has shown that the general scenario with respect to the status of subsidies for emissions mitigation under WTO subsidy disciplines is one of significant legal uncertainty and even conflict between legal requirements and policy prescriptions. This situation, in itself, produces a constraint on policy space. The possibility that some issues may be clarified through litigation, through friendly interpretation of the current rules and justifications, does not improve the situation since disputes are subject to many vagaries and may offer, at best, a piecemeal and partial solution. The pressure put on the judiciary should also not be underestimated. The analysis of the possible application of GATT Article XX to subsidies is the best example in point.

The unsatisfactory nature of the scenario is more than merely hypothetical. As the market is getting larger and competition fiercer, the stability of the tacit agreement not to challenge one another's subsidies is put into question. The various trade disputes on the support to renewable energy that have recently been filed at both the WTO and national level are evidence of this.

Now, an inadequate legal framework, and increasing litigiousness, support the case for a legal shelter that defines what types of government interventions are legitimate and what are not in a clear and positive way. The first-best solution is new rules that would expressly permit certain subsidies for emissions mitigation. Only law reform would enable the new rules to be tailored to the need for justification and to accommodate the required policy space in the most appropriate way.

In a nutshell, the answer to the problem is better regulation which does not necessarily mean less regulation.

We do not share the view that *laissez-faire* is the answer to the deficiencies of subsidy disciplines.[255] The way to achieve rationality and policy space is not through a substantial downgrade of the current rules and the reliance on the non-violation nullification and impairment remedy to tackle subsidies frustrating negotiated market access. Subsidy rules

---

[255]　As suggested by Sykes, n. 87 above. The following notes are just the first reaction to Sykes' comprehensive criticism which certainly deserves a more developed response.

undoubtedly present incoherencies and difficulties but, to be honest, this is the case in many regulatory areas, in trade and beyond.[256] They certainly feature, indeed require, a good amount of simplification and approximation too but, again, this is not new.

The bottom line is that a better international regulation of subsidies can be a valuable asset. Particularly when it can simultaneously act as a control of the negative spillovers of many subsidies, as a transparency-enhancing mechanism and as a forum for the discussion and advancement of a shared knowledge on the question of what is and what is not a legitimate government intervention. All this can – this is the hope – result in better practice, better regulation and, ultimately, better subsidization. This would indeed represent a good result for the governance of subsidies generally, and of subsidies for emissions mitigation in particular.[257]

---

[256] Key trade law provisions rely on the determination of whether a certain conduct is discriminatory, protectionist or otherwise, which are notoriously difficult questions. Similarly, complex economic determinations are pervasive in antitrust laws and crucial questions, like the assessment of unilateral conduct, are still subject to great uncertainty and dramatic fluctuations. Most significantly, even the route of non-violation nullification and impairment, which is suggested as a desirable remedy to rely on, is fraught with several uncertainties, which probably explains the scarcity of its use.

[257] Other suggested options for policy space have been advanced. Some are alternative to a new discipline of justifications, others can indeed be applied in conjunction with or as a preliminary step towards a new WTO discipline. It has for example been suggested that a temporary truce or waiver with respect to action to fight climate change be introduced, conditional on various transparency obligations and on the respect of fundamental WTO principles like non-discrimination. Another possibility is a plurilateral solution, either within or outside the WTO, whose attractiveness would be alleged capacity to garner consensus among the willing countries. This alternative may indeed constitute the starting point for a future multilateral solution. A 'negotiation' sectoral approach has also been suggested which would be based on the method of operation of the Agreeement on Agriculture (with negotiated reduction commitments) or on the EGS liberalization, and in particular in the commitment to remove fossil fuel subsidies as non-tariff barriers to renewable energy goods and services, possibly coupled with the scheduling of permitted measures of support of renewable energy. For discussion of these options see G. Hufbauer, S. Charnovitz and J. Kim, *Global Warming and the World Trading System* (Peterson Institute of International Economics, 2009); Howse, n. 14 above; Aerni, n. 219 above, Sykes n. 87 above; A. Ghosh and G. Himani, *Governing Clean Energy Subsidies: What, Why and How Legal?* (Geneva: Geneva, 2012).

18. Emission trading schemes and WTO law: a typology of interactions
Javier de Cendra de Larragán

I. INTRODUCTION

The relationship between Emission Trading Schemes (ETS) and WTO law has been intensively analyzed in the literature in recent years.[1] For quite some time, analysis was either limited to rather theoretical studies or to examining the European Union Emissions Trading System (EU ETS).[2] Moreover, the literature has generally focused on the relationship by looking at one particular ETS and one particular WTO agreement.[3] This is changing, due to the increasing number of ETS that are being proposed or adopted.[4] Moreover, this trend has led to the realization that ETS can in practice look very different indeed from each other, and certainly from the 'textbook' ETS. This should not come as a surprise, given that domestic legislators have to try and accommodate many different and sometimes opposing interests and concerns when designing an ETS. In doing so,

---

[1]   One of the first to do so was Werksman, J. (1999). 'Greenhouse Gas Emissions Trading and the WTO'.

[2]   Directive 2003/87/EC of the European Parliament and of the Council of 13 October 2003 establishing a scheme for greenhouse gas emission allowance trading within the Community and amending Council Directive 96/61/EC, OJ L 275, 25.10.2003, as amended.

[3]   Most scholarship reviews the compatibility with the WTO, and in particular the GATT and SCM Agreements, of provisions that address carbon leakage or losses of competitiveness. As a recent example, see Genasci, M. (2008). 'Border Tax Adjustments and Emissions Trading'; Voigt, C. (2008), 'WTO Law and International Emissions Trading: Is there Potential for Conflict?'. Others have focused on the relation between allocation methodologies and the SCM Agreement. See for instance Windon, J. (2009). 'The Allocation of Free Emissions Units and the WTO Subsidies Agreement'. . . See also Redmond, D. and K. Kendall (2010). 'Emissions Trading Schemes, Domestic Policy and the WTO'. Yet others have focused on the relations between the EU ETS and the GATS; see Martin, M. (2007). 'Trade Law Implications of Restricting Participation in the European Union Emissions Trading Scheme'.

[4]   For an overview and information on those schemes, see the website of the International Energy Agency, climate change policies and measures database, http://www.iea.org/textbase/pm/?mode=cc. Last visited 10 March 2012.

they will face constraints (political or otherwise) that may limit the available range of design choices that would seem to be WTO compatible.[5] Moreover, ensuring its compatibility with WTO is just one (albeit important) variable in the policy debate, which might be trumped in practice by other seemingly more urgent domestic imperatives. Indeed, the realization that, as more jurisdictions consider implementing ETS, the chances of an actual clash with WTO law increase, has led many to consider avenues to reduce the likelihood of clashes.[6]

This chapter however does not aim at contributing to that literature. Rather, and in keeping with the nature of this volume, it modestly seeks to provide a bird's eye view of possible interactions between ETS and WTO law. The premise is that, as more and more domestic ETS are being proposed and implemented[7] and studied[8] the need for a synthesis grows. Whilst such exercise will not take us very far in terms of deciding the compatibility or otherwise of a specific ETS with a specific provision of WTO law, it can nevertheless serve to form a broad impression of the extent of the problem and to facilitate the consideration of possible systemic solutions. The chapter is structured as follows: first, I recap the theory behind ETS. Second, I briefly examine the main architectural choices that could be made when designing an ETS. Third, I identify from the existing literature the relevant WTO agreements that will be engaged by (different types of) ETS, and the nature of the interaction. Fourth, I briefly canvass the literature considering possible solutions to avoid a clash. Concluding remarks will follow.

---

[5]   For an analysis of the relation between political constraints and design choices that would seem to be prima facie consistent with WTO (GATT), see Veel, P.-E. (2009). 'Carbon Tariffs and the WTO: An Evaluation of Feasible Policies'.

[6]   See, Messerlin, P. A. (2010). 'Climate Change and Trade Policy: From Mutual Destruction to Mutual Support'.

[7]   For an assessment of existing and proposed emission trading systems, see for instance Hood, C. (2010). 'Reviewing Existing and Proposed Emissions Trading Systems'.

[8]   For an analysis of proposed federal schemes in the US, see for instance Veel, P.-E. (2009). 'Carbon Tariffs and the WTO: An Evaluation of Feasible Policies'. For an analysis of the compatibility of the Australian Carbon Pollution Reduction Scheme with the SCM Agreement, see Redmond, D. and K. Kendall (2010). 'Emissions Trading Schemes, Domestic Policy and the WTO'.

II.   ETS IN THEORY AND LINKAGES WITH WTO LAW

A.   ETS: The Theory

ETS are tools of environmental policy that seek to harness the power of markets to achieve environmental goals in a cost-effective and economically efficient manner.[9] The core goal of ETS is, by attaching a price to pollution, to force economic actors to internalize in their production and consumption decisions the social costs created by pollution. ETS do this in practice by: (i) setting some limits on the total amount of legitimate pollution (thus creating scarcity regarding how much economic units may emit); (ii) creating units (in this chapter the term 'allowance' will be used throughout for consistency) each representing a specific amount of pollution; (iii) imposing upon economic actors a legal obligation to surrender periodically enough allowances to cover their pollution; and (iv) allowing actors covered by the scheme to trade allowances with each other in order to achieve efficiency and cost-effectiveness. The price of the allowances will depend on a number of variables, the most important of which is their relative scarcity.[10]

It is clear therefore that ETS are markets entirely created by governmental intervention, often through law. Moreover, because ETS deal with emissions generated by products and services, they are superimposed upon existing markets in goods and services, thereby having necessarily a variety of impacts upon them. From the perspective of the analysis of ETS vis-à-vis WTO law, this means that ETS can engage WTO law both directly and indirectly. As a newly created market in allowances, they could potentially engage WTO law directly, provided that trade in that new market would be subject to WTO law in the first place. Moreover, because they will have an impact upon trade in existing goods and services – by changing their terms of trade – they can also engage WTO law indirectly. These two modes of engagement will be analyzed in more detail below.

---

[9]   See for instance Article 1 of the EU ETS describing the goals of the scheme. The literature on ETS is very voluminous. A good bibliography with the fundamental literature can be found at http://www.colby.edu/~thtieten/. Last accessed 30 March 2011.

[10]   For an analysis of the variables affecting the price of the allowances in the EU ETS (known as European allowances), see for instance Convery, F. J. and L. Redmond (2007). 'Market and Price Developments in the European Union Emissions Trading Scheme'.

B. Main Architectural Choices in Designing ETS that can be Relevant for WTO Law

Regulators seeking to introduce an ETS need to make choices in relation to each of the main architectural elements of the ETS, and some of these choices will engage WTO law. As mentioned above, specific choices may well owe more to domestic political opportunities and constraints than to legal considerations coming from international law,[11] including WTO law, so a detailed assessment is always necessary.[12]

1. The coverage

The first choice to make is at which level of the production chain the ETS will be introduced. If the ETS covers only carbon dioxide, then it could be introduced upstream at the point of extraction of the fossil fuels used in the production process, so that extractors of fossil fuels would face the need to hold allowances representing the carbon contained in those fuels. Alternatively, the ETS could be introduced at the point of processing or sale, whereby sellers of energy products would be required to hold allowances at the point of delivery or sale. Or it could be introduced at the point where the fossil fuels are combusted, thereby generating emissions. Or it could be introduced completely downstream at the level of final consumers of energy and energy products, so that consumers would face the obligation of having to support their energy consumption or purchase of energy-using products with allowances.

A second, related choice concerns the width of coverage. An ETS could be designed to cover just one economic sector or indeed the entire economy. Reasons behind this choice include the availability of emissions data, the costs and benefits of including certain sectors and sources (e.g. small ones), the desire to focus only on sectors with great abatement potential and capacity to respond to price signals, the existence of other policy instruments for climate change mitigation and the coherence of the policy mix, the political acceptability of including certain sectors, and so forth.

Another issue is which greenhouse gases (GHG) to introduce. Coverage can range from just one GHG (normally carbon dioxide), to all six GHGs covered by the Kyoto Protocol, or to even more GHGs.

---

[11] As will be shown below, ETS can attract international law other than WTO law, including international environmental law, aviation law, maritime shipping law, etc.

[12] This section builds partially on the analysis performed in Hood, C. (2010). 'Reviewing Existing and Proposed Emissions Trading Systems'.

2.   The setting of the cap

The term cap refers to the volume of emissions that is allowed within the boundaries of the ETS. A cap can be absolute – representing a maximum volume of emissions that can be emitted – or relative, representing a standard applicable to installations covered by the scheme and governing the emissions intensity of their production processes. The latter does not impose an absolute cap on emissions. Aside from the choice of imposing an absolute or relative cap there is the choice of the stringency or environmental ambition of the cap. Reasons for imposing an absolute or a relative cap – and for setting the stringency of the cap, may include the desire to balance the environmental benefits of the scheme with economic realities and political acceptability – particularly in its early stages. The cap can further be shaped by measures that seek to increase flexibility to promote cost-effectiveness and by rules put in place to manage price uncertainty and volatility (see below). The effect of these rules is that at any point in time the actual stringency of an ETS might be less than originally anticipated.

3.   The choice of allocation methodologies

Actors covered by an ETS need to surrender allowances periodically to cover their emissions. There are several ways in which they could theoretically get hold of these allowances. Essentially, the regulator can decide to give allowances for free, sell them through auctions, or use both approaches in combination. This could take place in a stable environment or in the context of a transition towards full auctioning (as foreseen in the EU ETS, where by 2027 all allowances will be auctioned). Further, participants may always purchase allowances on the market. They could be limited to purchase them from other participants on the market, or they may be authorized to purchase them from actors outside the boundaries of the ETS, for instance from other ETS or from the flexible mechanisms of the Kyoto Protocol (Clean Development Mechanism (CDM), and Joint Implementation (JI)).

Primary legislation governing ETS usually establishes rules governing the criteria according to which free allocation will take place (based either on historical or future emissions or production levels), as well as the particular circumstances of some participants (new entrants, closures, transfers of activities). Also, auctioning allowances is by no means a straightforward matter, and regulations may need to be very detailed to cover adequately all the elements of the auction process.[13]

---

[13]   See for instance the EU ETS's example. See Commission Regulation 1031/2010 on the timing, administration and other aspects of auctioning of green-

4. Use of revenues from auctioning allowances

The auction of allowances generates revenues that can then be used in a variety of manners. They could either go to the general public purse, or be earmarked for a number of purposes, including to reduce impacts on consumers, to reduce negative impacts on the competitiveness of some industrial sectors, to fund climate change policies and measures (including promotion of renewable energy sources, technologies such as carbon capture and storage, and energy efficiency), or to meet international climate financing obligations.

5. Measures to deal with concerns regarding potential impacts on competitiveness

Although ETS might have limited economic impacts on average, some industries will be more strongly affected. Hence an oft-heard argument against ETS is that they might lead to loss of competitiveness vis-à-vis producers that do not face similar production constraints, which would lead to loss of investments, production and jobs in the covered industries. An additional argument revolves around the idea of leakage, a situation whereby, as a result of the introduction of an ETS, global emissions increase rather than decrease because some production will be relocated to jurisdictions with lower or no emissions controls.[14] To decide on the credibility and seriousness of these arguments, regulators are confronted with a large number of complex questions demanding answers as precise as possible. Is the risk of loss of competitiveness real, and is it created by the ETS? If so, how large is it? Is it likely to disappear if and when other jurisdictions adopt broadly comparable climate change policies and measures? Is it legitimate, in the light of the goals and responsibilities of governments – including economic, development and environmental policies – to compensate industries for the loss of competitiveness? And if so, how should they be compensated and to what extent? How will compensation affect the environmental (static and dynamic) effectiveness of the ETS?

---

house gas emission allowances, OJ L302/1. The regulations are in the process of being amended to determine the volume of allowances that will be auctioned. See Commission Regulation No. 1210/2011 of 23 November amending Regulation (EU) No. 1031/2010 in particular to determine the volume of greenhouse gas emission allowances to be auctioned prior to 2013, OJ L308, 24.11.2011.

[14] Carbon leakage can take place in two ways: first, through loss of production market share or new investment to jurisdictions with no or weaker climate policies; second, through a price effect on fossil fuels as a result of developed countries' climate policies, which can lead to increased consumption in other countries, leading to higher global emissions.

This question arises because protecting existing industries may detract from the stringency of the ETS and may also use up revenues that could otherwise be used to finance the transition to a low carbon economy. Further, is the risk of carbon leakage a real one and if so how serious is it? Is there a need to deal with it, and if so what would be the best way to do so?

While it is clear that many of these questions demand political choices, the way in which they are phrased (or not phrased) and particularly the way in which they are answered may have various legal implications, including in the context of WTO law, as will be seen below. If legislators decide to address these issues through regulatory measures, there are a variety of manners in which they could do so, including grandfathering all or part of the allowances, using other allocation mechanisms whilst carving out exemptions for particularly affected sectors, giving compensation through various means to those sectors, and/or coupling them with border measures of various sorts to level the playing field between local and foreign emitters.

6. Measures to increase cost-effectiveness

ETS will lead to increases in prices of energy and energy products, which will in turn lead to economic impacts. While modeling work done within the decision making process accompanying existing and proposed ETS generally shows that impacts on economic growth (expressed in units of GDP) tend to be small, they nevertheless are considered sufficiently important to warrant some mitigating measures. The type of measures that have been adopted in several ETS include multi-year compliance periods, provisions for banking and borrowing allowances, allowing the use of credits from offsets (either international or domestic), and linking directly ETS. So far the only existing links are indirect – that is, two domestic ETS are indirectly linked when both allow the use of offset credits from the same mechanisms (as the CDM), but most ETS foresee the possibility of future direct links and mention the requirements that other ETS need to fulfil for linkage to take place.[15] Currently there is no consensus in the literature as to which minimum conditions two ETS need to fulfil to be linkable, and in any case different ETS impose different conditions, so linking in practice

---

[15] For analysis of linking ETS, see for instance Haites, E. and M. Mehling (2009). 'Linking Existing and Proposed GHG Emissions Trading in North America'. Tuerk, A. and M. Mehling (2009). 'Linking Carbon Markets: Concepts, Case Studies, and Pathways'. For a legal analysis of linking the EU ETS to other domestic ETS, see for instance de Cendra, J. (2010). 'From the EU ETS to a Global Carbon Market: An Analysis and Suggestions for the Way Forward'.

might be very challenging, particularly if a global blueprint for an ETS is not agreed upon at international level. Some of the measures that seek to increase flexibility and therefore cost-effectiveness (borrowing, allowing the use of credits from offsets), work to reduce the stringency of the cap. Since such a trade-off might be approached differently across jurisdictions, the overall burden imposed by otherwise similar ETS might be very different indeed and not easy to determine.

7.   Measures to manage price uncertainty and volatility

On top of measures to increase flexibility and therefore cost-effectiveness, many existing ETS have incorporated additional mechanisms to manage uncertainty and volatility in the price of allowances. Uncertainty and volatility regarding prices is mainly due to the fact that ETS are entirely artificial markets, and, in case of having absolute caps, have a fixed supply. As a result, changes in demand do not affect the supply, which can lead to volatility. Moreover, uncertainty in the volume of demand for allowances compounds the potential for volatility. Indeed, supply can be set structurally above or below demand, and moreover demand can change in a very dynamic fashion in ways that might not be fully foreseeable. All this generates uncertainty about the long-term evolution of carbon prices, and might deter new investments in low-carbon technologies. The key question for policy makers is whether market participants have sufficient tools to manage uncertainty and volatility or whether additional regulatory intervention is needed. Those that think that more regulatory intervention is necessary often argue for introducing caps and floors on prices. Those against such solutions argue that they do not only undermine the only certainty that an ETS can create – an absolute cap leading to environmental certainty – but can actually generate further uncertainty if regulators are able to tamper with the ceilings and floors further down the line. There are many ways in which such cost containment measures can be introduced, including by releasing an unlimited number of allowances when the price reaches a certain level, by keeping reserve allowances within the cap that can be released to temporarily control price spikes, or by laying down financial penalties for not surrendering sufficient allowances that have the effect of releasing operators from having to surrender those allowances, effectively transforming the ETS into a tax. In general, it is thought that price ceilings and floors pursue essentially different aims; while a ceiling aims at limiting negative impacts from an ETS, price floors aim at providing long-term certainty to investors in low-carbon technologies. Hence, even if both can be coupled with what is essentially an environmental measure (an ETS), they could lead to different results when assessed for compatibility with WTO law.

8.   Rules on monitoring, reporting and verification and on market oversight

For an ETS to function properly, complete, consistent, transparent and accurate monitoring and reporting of greenhouse gas emissions is essential.[16] So important is this architectural element that it is widely considered that two ETS cannot be linked unless their monitoring, reporting and verification (MRV) regimes are very similar in terms of reliability and accuracy. Moreover, the international carbon market is very new but is already worth around US $100 billion, therefore it can generate substantial incentives for fraud. Hence strong regulations are necessary to prevent and minimize the impact on the market of fraudulent activities.[17]

9.   Rules regulating the secondary market in derivatives

So far this chapter has listed and briefly described the main architectural elements of ETS. But the aim at the end of the day is to create a functioning market, which will attract not only those legally obliged to participate in it by virtue of their emissions of greenhouse gases, but also other market participants that can deliver services necessary for the market to work, such as intermediary services, banking, insurance, and management and trade of derivative instruments. Legislation setting up an ETS may wish to regulate participation in these markets – for instance by restricting participation to domestically situated actors, which may have relevant legal implications, including within WTO law.[18]

C.   Points of Engagement between ETS and WTO Law

There is a large degree of ambiguity in the relationship between trade and environmental protection and sustainable development. This ambiguity is as much a matter of facts as of norms and values.[19] As a result, measures

---

[16]   See Commission Decision of 18 July 2007 establishing guidelines for the monitoring and reporting of greenhouse gas emissions pursuant to Directive 2003/87/EC of the European Parliament and of the Council, OJ L 229/1.

[17]   This was proven by the scandals that affected the EU ETS in 2010, which forced the Commission to react swiftly and forcefully. See Communication from the Commission to the European Parliament and the Council, towards an enhanced market oversight framework for the EU Emissions Trading Scheme, COM(2010)796 Final.

[18]   For an analysis of the way in which this issue has been dealt with in the EU ETS and its potential implications vis-à-vis WTO law, see Martin, M. (2007). 'Trade Law Implications of Restricting Participation in the European Union Emissions Trading Scheme'.

[19]   UNEP/IISD (2005). *Environment and Trade – A Handbook.*

that seek to protect the environment often conflict with the WTO core goal of essentially undistorted and ever-expanding trade.[20] ETS create a new market where a new currency is traded, with the explicit aim of increasing allocative efficiency within the coverage of the scheme. This suggests that ETS are in principle in full harmony with WTO goals. Indeed, the international emissions trading mechanism incorporated in Article 17 of the Kyoto Protocol has been seen by many as the core of a global carbon market with common rules. However, the years that have passed since the adoption of the Kyoto Protocol have not seen the development of a global carbon market. On the contrary, as we noted above, we have seen a progressive implementation of very different domestic ETS across the world, which are creating a patchy landscape of unconnected schemes, largely designed to satisfy national needs and interests, with limited capacity for inter-scheme trading and with noticeable potential for increasing barriers to trade in products and services underpinning the markets in allowances. Thus, reality indicates that the potential for a good marriage between ETS as a theoretical instrument and WTO law remains largely unfulfilled, and numerous points of conflict can arise. Indeed, the breadth of WTO law means that the forms of engagement can be multiple.[21] ETS can engage WTO law directly or indirectly. Directly, in that the rules applicable to trade in allowances among private parties provide allowances that may be considered either goods under the GATT, services under the GATS, or subsidies under the SCM Agreement.

An ETS could engage with WTO law indirectly through a number of avenues as illustrated in Table 18.1 below:

The next section will describe each of these issues and assess its WTO relevance.

---

[21]   Low and Marceau have identified the WTO rules that could engage climate change policies, including ETS: the General Agreement on Tariffs and Trade (GATT), the General Agreement on Trade in Services (GATS), the Agreement on Technical Barriers to Trade (TBT Agreement), the Agreement on Subsidies and Countervailing Measures (SCM Agreement), the Agreement on Rules of Origin, the Government Procurement Agreement, the Agreement on Implementation of Article VII GATT (customs valuation), the Agreement on Implementation of Article VI GATT (antidumping), the Agreement on Trade-Related Investment Measures (TRIMS Agreement), and the Agreement on Trade-Related Aspects of Intellectual Property Rights (TRIPS Agreement. Low, P., G. Marceau, et al. (2011). 'The Interface between the Trade and Climate Change Regimes'.

Table 18.1

ETS architectural rules	WTO Agreements potentially engaged
Coverage	GATT, TBT, GATS
Cap	SCM Agreement
Allocation methodologies	SCM Agreement
Use of revenues	SCM Agreement
Competitiveness concerns	GATT
Cost-effectiveness	GATT, GATS
Management uncertainty and volatility	GATT
MRV	GATT
Regulation of services	GATS

III.   ETS FROM THE PERSPECTIVE OF RELEVANT WTO LAW

A.   Direct Engagement

For an ETS to be affected directly by WTO law, three cumulative conditions need to hold. If they do not, then WTO law can still become relevant indirectly:

First, trading must take place among private parties. If the trading partners are sovereign states, then the acquisition and transfer of allowances among them does not create a 'market' in either goods or services, and the transfer of allowances is not covered by WTO agreements. As Werksman notes, this type of ETS should be better categorized as a dynamic renegotiation of burden-sharing obligations among sovereign states, akin to those that have taken place under Article 4 of the Kyoto Protocol.[22]

Second, the ETS needs to have an impact on international trade in allowances. If an ETS is of a purely domestic measure, then it cannot engage WTO law directly – which is focused on regulating and managing international trade, though it can engage it indirectly (by generating impacts upon existing markets in products and services). However, a purely and totally isolated ETS is, in practice, a very unlikely proposition for the following reasons: first, at international level, Article 17 of the Kyoto Protocol has laid the basis of international emissions trading. Although that provision refers exclusively to states, it is reasonably clear

---

[22]   Werksman, J. (1999). 'Greenhouse Gas Emissions Trading and the WTO'.

that parties intended from the outset to agree upon rules, mechanisms and procedures to enable private parties to participate in the market. The Marrakech Agreements indeed laid down those rules, according to which private parties can participate in international emissions trading under the responsibility of the host country, in order to purchase and sell 'allowances' (in that context, allowances receive different names depending on the provision under which they have been created); second, existing, domestic ETS incorporate generally a provision regulating on the one hand access to units coming from the UNFCCC regime (Assigned Amount Units (AAUs), Certified Emission Reductions (CERs), Emission Reduction Units (ERUs), Removal Units (RMUs), and on the other hand the conditions for establishing linkages with other domestic ETS. By so doing, trade in allowances gains an international dimension and therefore could be directly covered by WTO law.

Third, the new currency – the allowance – needs to fall within the definition of a good under the GATT, a service under the GATS, or constitute a subsidy under the SCM Agreement. If that is not the case, then the WTO does not have any direct bearing on the market for allowances. This is the most controversial of the three conditions, as becomes clear from the literature, and yet constitutes a key threshold question.

1. Can allowances be considered to be products under WTO law?
There are in the literature two essentially different and incompatible propositions: (1) that allowances are not products; and (2) that allowances could be considered to be products of a particular kind.

Werksman has noted that 'it can be concluded with some confidence that internationally traded emissions allowances are themselves neither goods nor services under WTO law'.[23] They would be instead licences or permits issued by a government authority and entitling, under specified conditions, the holder to carry out a regulated activity within its territory. However, he cautions that, since international trade in emissions allowances has never been carried out on such scale, precedents to classify these instruments are lacking. This conclusion is reached as follows: he notes that the term product is a legal one that takes a specific meaning in the context of the GATT in the light of the object and purpose of the agreement, and thus cannot simply include anything that is tradable and has economic value. The GATT does not provide a definition of product, which should be built therefore on the basis of WTO sources of law. And guidance as to what WTO Members understand to be products can be

---

[23]   Ibid.

taken from the tariff schedules in which Members include the products they have agreed will be subject to bindings, as well as from the internationally agreed rules on customs classification. Those lists of products suggest that WTO Members understand products to be 'tangible' goods. Moreover, Werksman notes that there is no evidence that WTO Members have or will expand their understanding of the meaning of product. In support of this last point, he notes that many forms of financial instruments, including currency, have been traded internationally for decades, but none have been considered to be 'products' for GATT purposes, and in so doing he refers to the findings of the Panel in *Canada – Measures Affecting the Sale of Gold Coins*.[24] In stark contrast to that position, Vranes has argued precisely the opposite,[25] namely that allowances themselves might have to be classified as products, and has based its conclusion partially on the same evidence relied upon by Werksman. Vranes in particular considers that, while the concept of product has to be interpreted in the light of the object and purpose of the GATT, 'its system and *telos* may nonetheless call for a wide definition of this term',[26] and goes on to mention the case law of the European Court of Justice in the field of the free movement of goods, which has classified electricity as a product.[27] The second argument used by Vranes to support its conclusion is the findings of the GATT Panel in *Canada – Measures Affecting the Sale of Gold Coins*. There, the Panel held that gold coins used as legal tender function not merely as means of payment but can also constitute products in terms of Article III GATT if they are normally purchased as investment goods. While Vranes notes that the notion of investment implies a longer-term commitment of assets, he concludes that this suffices to support the view that allowances within an ETS might have to be classified as products.

It is argued here that the reason both authors defend apparently incompatible positions is testimony to the rather undeveloped state of the law as much as to the (different) starting points of the authors. To start with, Werksman adopts a historical approach to the understanding

---

[24]   Werksman refers to the unadopted GATT Panel Report, *Canada – Measures Affecting the Sale of Gold Coins*, L/5863, para. 51. He notes that unadopted GATT Panel Reports 'have no legal status in the GATT or WTO system since they have not been endorsed through decisions by the contracting parties to GATT or WTO Members. However, 'a [WTO] panel could nevertheless find useful guidance in the reasoning of an unadopted panel report that it considered to be relevant'. *Japan – Taxes on Alcoholic Beverages*, WT/DS10/AB/R, 4 October 1996, p. 17.

[25]   Vranes, E. (2009a). 'Climate Change and the WTO: EU Emission Trading and the WTO Disciplines on Trade in Goods, Services and Investment Protection'.

[26]   Ibid.

[27]   Case C-393/92, *Almelo* [1994] ECR I-1447, para. 28.

of the concept of product within the GATT, while Vranes adopts a teleological approach. Further, neither GATT panels nor the WTO Dispute Settlement System (DSS) have had the chance to elaborate on the definition of the term product in the same way as the ECJ has, given the volume of cases reaching it. Moreover, ETS are a very novel instrument, and WTO Members have not yet had to consider whether to treat allowances as goods in the context of the GATT. But the more developed ETS become, and the larger the volume of global trade in allowances, the more pressing the need will be to consider explicitly the legal nature of allowances. It is already clear that allowances can be classified legally in a number of ways, depending on the object and purpose of each regime. So allowances widely used for investment purposes might render the conclusion of the GATT Panel in *Canada – Gold Coins* relevant.

2. Can allowances be considered to be services under WTO law?
If allowances are services, then they are directly regulated by the GATS. However, the GATS does not provide a definition of services, and there is disagreement in the literature regarding this point. Werksman summarily dismisses the possibility by observing that since allowances are government-issued licences, they cannot be services.[28] Vranes looks to the Annex on Financial Services to determine whether allowances could fit under any of the particular services mentioned therein. He dismisses the idea that they could be considered to be derivative products or transferable securities because both are based on a contractual relationship, while allowances document the grant of a right by the state. However, he asks whether allowances could constitute financial assets in the sense of Article 5(x)(F) of the Annex. All depends on the definition of financial asset that one considers. If one adopts a definition based on financial accounting, financial assets are seen as anything tangible or intangible that is capable of being owned or controlled to produce value and that is held to have positive economic value. An allowance could fall within that definition, since it can be traded on the market by anyone, irrespective of whether one holds an emission permit.[29] If this approach is not accepted, then the GATS does not cover allowances, although it would certainly cover contractual instruments based on them – including futures and options.

Provided the three above-mentioned conditions concur, the primary market for trading in allowances will be directly covered by WTO law,

---

[28] Werksman, J. (1999). 'Greenhouse Gas Emissions Trading and the WTO'.
[29] Vranes, E. (2009a). 'Climate Change and the WTO: EU Emission Trading and the WTO Disciplines on Trade in Goods, Services and Investment Protection'.

in particular by the GATT and the GATS. This would mean that many measures that states have taken or might consider taking to restrict such trade would be subject to the WTO principles of Most Favoured Nation, National Treatment and prohibition of quantitative restrictions, and therefore could be considered to be in breach of the GATT and GATS unless they can be held compatible with the general exceptions contained in Article XX GATT or Article XIV GATS. Examples of such measures would include quantitative restrictions on allowances imported in order to comply with the principle of supplementarity as provided for by the Kyoto Protocol and the Marrakech Accords (or within domestic law), qualitative restrictions to ban or reduce the import of allowances coming from particular project-types, restrictions on exports to comply with obligations of international climate law such as the commitment period reserve within the Kyoto Protocol, and restrictions on mutual recognition of allowances from one domestic ETS into another domestic ETS.[30]

B.   Indirect Engagement

Even if trade in allowances between states and primary trade in allowances between private parties are not covered by WTO law, ETS might engage WTO law through a number of their design features, as shown in Table 18.1 above. These issues will be reviewed in turn.

1.   Point of regulation and WTO implications
A crucial question in the design of an ETS, certainly from the perspective of WTO law, relates to its extraterritorial implications. If it covers emissions associated with products (indirect emissions), a further choice is whether indirect emissions generated abroad will be covered, and if so, whether emissions not embodied in the product will be covered. If the ETS covers stationary sources (direct emissions), it is clear that, under international law, it can only cover sources placed within the limits of the jurisdiction. By seeking to regulate emissions from production processes abroad, it would raise concerns about extraterritoriality. Finally, an ETS could cover mobile sources crossing domestic borders. These choices will be reviewed in turn.

Coverage of indirect emissions at the point of extraction or import   Imposing upon producers of energy the obligation to surrender allowances as a

---

[30]   For an analysis of some of the issues that could arise vis-à-vis WTO law, see ibid.

condition to import their products onto the domestic market could be interpreted, in case the ETS has an absolute cap, as akin to a quantitative restriction on the trade of those products, which would be a violation of Article XI GATT. In this case, the measure would need to be assessed under Article XX GATT. Moreover, as Werksman notes, if the delivery of energy services can be construed as falling within an importer's market access commitments as set out in its services schedule under the GATS, limiting the delivery of energy services at the border might violate GATS.[31] No ETS has chosen this point of regulation so far.

A related possibility would be to establish an ETS covering emissions associated with energy-using products. If importers would need to hold allowances in order to import their products, and if there is an absolute cap in place, then there is a risk that Article XI GATT would be breached.

Regulation of indirect emissions at the point of sale   Another possibility would be to allow energy and energy-using products to be imported into the country, but to require that the sellers, in order to be able to sell their products, hold a sufficient number of allowances to cover the associated emissions. The key issue here is whether this option could be made to comply with the obligations imposed by Articles I and III:4 GATT, and Articles II:1 and XVII GATS.

There are at least some issues that would raise difficulties from the perspective of GATT and GATS:

First, to comply with GATT, the allocation rules of the ETS should not discriminate between domestic and foreign products. Of course, different products will have different carbon content, which will therefore be differently affected by the ETS, but as long as the allocation rules do not discriminate against foreign products, National Treatment would be respected.

Second, new entrants cannot be put at a disadvantage vis-à-vis incumbents, but that might be difficult if there is an absolute cap in place. For instance, the EU ETS has set in place an elaborate procedure to ensure that new entrants have access to allowances from a new entrant reserve.[32] Nevertheless, the European Commission has argued that in a deep and liquid market, new entrants can always purchase allowances in the market and therefore are not placed at a disadvantage vis-à-vis incumbents. The problem from the perspective of WTO law is that, as a WTO Panel has

---

[31]   Werksman, J. (1999). 'Greenhouse Gas Emissions Trading and the WTO'.
[32]   See Article 10(a)7 Directive 2003/87/EC as amended by Directive 2009/29/EC.

ruled, imported products must be treated in a manner equivalent to the best treatment afforded to a like domestic product.[33] This might prove difficult if the new entrants reserve is exhausted and sellers of imported products need to purchase allowances in the market.

Third, if the allocation method is based on the emissions generated during the production process of products, and not on the emissions embodied within the product (for instance on the basis of the carbon intensity of products), then the question is whether this would stand the test of likeness included in Articles I and III GATT. This issue will be considered again in section III.B.4 below.

Fourth, as Werksman notes, there is the question of what would happen if a country sets export restrictions on electricity in order to make sure that imports from other countries do not inflate the total emissions of the country where the electricity is being generated. An alternative would be to allow exports of electricity only to countries that can provide sufficient allowances in exchange for that electricity. But if the allowances generated within the importing country are not acceptable to the exporting country for whatever reason, and as a result the allowances need to be purchased in the exporting country, then an export restriction may also be present. If allowances would come from importing countries, then the exporting country could violate Article XIII GATT requiring that quantitative restrictions be administered on a non-discriminatory basis.

Regulation of direct emissions from stationary sources   Domestic sources would be the only ones participating in the ETS in this situation. They would hold allowances and have the obligation to surrender them periodically to the competent public authority to cover their emissions. In this case, the ETS has purely domestic effects. The challenges that could arise from the perspective of WTO law would be of four types: (1) allocation methodologies designed to have a larger negative impact upon sources with majority of foreign ownership could fall foul of GATS obligations regarding national treatment of foreign suppliers; (2) allocation volumes could, if larger than real or expected emissions, be deemed to be actionable subsidies under the SCM Agreement; (3) rules put in place to protect the competitiveness of domestic sources, either in the form of border tax adjustments or requirements for importers to hold allowances could violate GATT; (4) rules restricting access of foreign participants to the secondary market in allowances could fall foul of the National Treatment

---

[33]   *United States – Standards for Reformulated Gasoline,* Report of the Panel, WT/DS2/R, 29 January 1996, paras 6.11–6.12.

obligation under Article XVII GATS, Most Favoured Nation treatment obligation under Article II.1 GATS, and Market Access rules under Article XVI GATS.[34]

Regulation of direct emissions from mobile sources In recent years, there have been ongoing discussions under the auspices of international organizations such as the International Civil Aviation Organization and the International Maritime Organization on the desirability of using market-based mechanisms – in particular ETS – to reign in the continuously increasing contribution of the transport sector to climate change. These measures have the potential to breach GATT-related obligations, for instance if they discriminate among imported goods coming from different countries, or if they discriminate between goods shipped by EU operators and by foreign operators/vessels. In addition, an ETS could breach GATS if it can be shown that a measure that prohibits vessels from third countries to come into port due to their GHG emissions or failure to meet technical specifications is a restriction on trade in services. Whilst the applicability of GATT is not controversial, that of GATS is less so.[35]

The EU has already adopted legislation to bring aviation into the EU ETS,[36] and is currently considering whether emissions trading would be a good instrument to regulate emissions from shipping.

In the case of aviation, some countries have threatened to take the Aviation Directive to the WTO DSS, but this has not happened so far.[37] At the same time, the Air Transport Association of America and several US airlines have challenged the legality of the Aviation Directive vis-à-vis international law before the High Court of Justice (Queen's Bench Division) in the UK, which has led in turn to a preliminary ruling from the CJEU. The CJEU ruled in December 2011 that the Aviation Directive

---

[34]   See Martin, M. (2007). 'Trade Law Implications of Restricting Participation in the European Union Emissions Trading Scheme'.

[35]   For a detailed analysis, see Meltzer, J. (2012). 'Climate Change and Trade – the EU Aviation Directive and the WTO'.

[36]   Directive 2008/101/EC amending Directive 2003/87/EC so as to include aviation activities in the scheme for greenhouse gas emission allowance trading within the Community, OJ L8/3, 13.1.2009.

[37]   When the EU announced its intention to bring aviation into the EU ETS, C. Boyden Gray, then US ambassador to the EU, declared that in his view a legal challenge in the WTO would be unavoidable. See International Centre for Sustainable Development, Bridges Trade BioRes, 7(17), 5 October. Available at http://ictsd.org/i/news/biores/9134/. Last visited 25 March 2012.

is consistent with international law and the Chicago Convention.[38] But of course this ruling does not preempt members to the WTO to challenge the legality of the directive vis-à-vis the applicable WTO rules (GATT and likely the GATS).[39]

In relation to emissions trading for maritime shipping, Article V(3) GATT could be of application:

> [S]uch traffic coming from or going to the territory of other contracting parties shall not be subject to any unnecessary delays or restrictions and shall be exempt from customs duties and from all transit duties or other charges imposed in respect of transit, except charges for transportation or those commensurate with administrative expenses entailed by transit or with the cost of services rendered.

As Tim Bäuerle et al. have noted, there are so far no decisions of the WTO DSS on this provision, but some have argued that the introduction of an ETS regime for transit traffic is a charge imposed in respect of transit and therefore not in line with GATT. This is especially the case if the ETS regime would provide for a ban on vessels not participating in any ETS regime.[40] However, even if the ETS would be in breach of Article V, it could possibly be justified under Article XX GATT.[41]

Regulation of indirect emissions at the level of final consumers   A downstream ETS would apply at the level of final consumers of energy and energy-using products, including household consumers. Traditionally it has been considered that implementing a purely downstream scheme presents almost insurmountable technical difficulties and dubious cost-effectiveness. For instance, the European Commission briefly considered including transport in the EU ETS in its Green Paper on emissions trading, and quickly dismissed the idea for those reasons. However, the concept of downstream ETS has been increasingly gaining attention in academic and policy circles particularly within the United Kingdom, which has led to the review and amendment of some of the early assump-

---

[38]   Judgment of the Court of Justice of the European Union, *Air Transport Association of America and others v Secretary of State for Energy and Climate Change*, C-366/10, 21 December 2011.

[39]   For an analysis of the relationship between the Aviation Directive and the WTO, see Meltzer, J., supra n. 35, pp. 12 *et seq.*

[40]   Bäuerle, T., J. Graichen, et al. (2010). 'Integration of Marine Transport into the European Emissions Trading System' at 92.

[41]   Ibid., at 93.

tions.[42] At the moment, only one pilot scheme has been implemented (in Norfolk Island, off the coast of Australia[43]), but its proponents have declared that their ultimate goal would be to extend and export the idea to other countries over the next years. Personal trading schemes, or Personal Carbon Trading (PCT)[44] as the concept is often denominated, have one major rationale: to engage consumers directly in climate change mitigation – a presently daunting and largely unaddressed challenge in climate policy – by making them active carbon managers. Moreover, certain versions of PCT, such as the Tradable Energy Quotas recently discussed in the UK,[45] seek also to reduce energy consumption per capita in order to deal with concerns about energy insecurity.

While currently PCT is advocated to address emissions from the built environment (which includes emissions generated through the use of electronic appliances and heating) and transport sectors, it is not unimaginable that at some point in the future it could be extended to also cover emissions embodied in all products purchased by consumers.

Regardless of the practical feasibility of such a scheme, its introduction would certainly engage WTO law because its implementation would require that all energy and energy-using products covered display accurate information about their carbon intensity (whether embedded in the product or as a result of its use), and this would require that they are labeled. Such labeling scheme would moreover need to be mandatory, hence engaging the GATT and TBT Agreements. The single most crucial issue from the perspective of WTO law is whether the scheme is concerned only with emissions generated by the use of the products, or also with emissions caused by production processes. If it concerns the latter, then mandatory labeling would be concerned with Non Product Related-Process and Production Methods (NPR-PPM), which raises the question of their status under WTO law. There is disagreement in the literature about the legality of these labeling schemes within WTO law. In a recent examination of the issue, Vranes has concluded, against the view of other commentators, that such a scheme would fall under the purview of

---

[42]   For a review of the literature and arguments pro and against personal carbon trading, see special issue published in *Climate Policy*, 10(4), pp. 329–486.

[43]   http://www.niche.nlk.nf/. Last visited 5 April 2011.

[44]   PCT works as follows: allowances would be allocated to individuals on an equal per capita basis (or some other criterion); every time they consume fossil fuel generated energy, they would have to surrender allowances to cover those emissions. There would be a market for allowances where consumers can purchase and sell them, at a price determined by the market.

[45]   Fleming, D. and S. Chamberlain (2010). 'Tradable Energy Quotas'.

Articles III:4 and I:1 GATT, while not necessarily constituting a violation of them, and under Article 1 and Annex I TBT Agreement, which again would not necessarily be breached by such a labeling scheme.[46] Everything would then depend on the particulars of the proposed scheme.

2.   Allocation methodologies and volumes

Allowances can be allocated for free or against a payment (normally by means of an auction). Given the existence of a market for allowances, and provided there is scarcity in the market, the allowances will have a market price and thus a value. The relevant question is whether a state, by allocating allowances for free or below market price, is conferring a subsidy in the sense of the SCM Agreement. In order to ascertain whether a subsidy has been granted through the allocation methodology the following method has to be followed:

1. Is there a subsidy as defined in Article 1 SCM Agreement? In the context of ETS, the most relevant types of subsidies are in Article 1.1(a)(1)(i), namely direct transfers of funds from a public organism of a party, and Article 1.1(a)(1)(ii), namely government revenue that is otherwise due which is foregone or not collected.
2. Is a benefit thereby conferred? (Article 1.1(b)).

If there is a subsidy, then it is only caught by the SCM Agreement if it is specific (Article 1.2). Specificity is defined in Article 2. If a subsidy is specific, then the next question is whether it is prohibited or actionable. If the subsidy is found to be actionable, then the affected state can decide to enter into consultations with the subsidizing state and, if those consultations fail, can refer the matter to the DSB for the establishment of a panel (Article 7.4). Provided the complainant state wins the case before the panel, and if appealed, before the Appellate Body, the other state must take appropriate steps to remove the adverse effects or withdraw the subsidy. In case it fails to do so after six months, and in the absence of agreement on compensation, the DSB will grant to the complaining state authorization to take commensurate countermeasures. The determination of whether there is an specific subsidy and if so whether it is actionable can become very complex indeed in the context of an ETS for a number of reasons. While this chapter cannot start to analyze all the permutations regarding allocation within existing and proposed ETS, it can nevertheless set out a number of general considerations.

---

[46] Vranes, E. (2009b). *Trade and the Environment: Fundamental Issues in International Law, WTO Law.*

First, it is necessary to clarify whether and how an ETS could become a subsidy. An ETS could become a subsidy either through the choice of cap or through the choice of allocation methodology. An ETS is a regulatory measure that seeks to implement the polluter pays principle. But the choice of not implementing in national law the polluter pays principle is not per se a violation of the SCM Agreement. In other words, lack of internalization of environmental damages through laws is not deemed a subsidy under the SCM Agreement. Now, when an ETS is introduced, such internalization is sought. The choice of allocation methodology – whether for free or through auctioning – is a separate element from the setting of the cap and the internalization flows from the cap, not from the choice of allocation methodology.

Can setting a cap be a subsidy? And if so, can it be considered to be specific? If an absolute cap is set at a level above real or expected emissions, or if a very weak relative cap is set, then an ETS will fail to implement the polluter pays principle, and allowances will be worth zero or close to zero. But allocating allowances worth zero for free is obviously not a subsidy, because there is no direct transfer in any meaningful sense. The problem may arise when other states have introduced meaningful ETS and a posteriori another country establishes an environmentally meaningless ETS to provide competitive advantage to its domestic industry. Is this lack of internalization a subsidy? The answer would depend on whether states have an obligation under international law to introduce an ETS domestically. If that is not the case, then the answer would be probably negative, so there would not be a need to continue the enquiry.

Coming to the question whether the choice of allocation methodology and its design could lead to a subsidy in the sense of the SCM Agreement, the same methodology needs to be considered: is there a subsidy, and if so, is it specific? In relation to the first question, the findings of the Appellate Body when interpreting Article 1.1(a)(1)(ii) in *United States – Tax Treatment for Foreign Sales Corporations*[47] are of relevance. There, the Appellate Body stated that in order to determine whether otherwise due revenue has been foregone, a normative benchmark needs to be defined against which a comparison can be made between the revenue actually raised and the revenue that would have been raised otherwise. The Appellate Body notes that 'what is otherwise due, therefore, depends on the rules of taxation that each Member, by its own choice, establishes

---

[47] Appellate Body Report, *United States – Tax Treatment for Foreign Sales Corporations,* WT/DS108/AB/R, (24 February 2000).

for itself'.[48] And it is a very extended practice that states, when putting in place environmental taxes or regulations, consistently exempt industries that are energy intensive and open to international competition. An ETS that would do the same would therefore probably not lead to the conclusion that it leads to foregoing of revenue otherwise due, because it is in the very nature of the ETS to treat certain sectors differently. Moreover, even if it could be determined that there is indeed a subsidy, it is not clear that it confers any benefit, because installations receive allowances in order to comply with an emission reduction obligation imposed by the same instrument. So the allocation of allowances does not in principle confer any benefit, unless those allowances are tradable between different domestic ETS and allocation rules are different among those ETS so that installations within one of them have an advantage over installations covered by others. But it would seem strange that domestic ETS can become linked if allocation methodologies are such that industry within one of those ETS clearly benefits vis-à-vis industry within the other(s) ETS.

Second, as a matter of fact, all existing and proposed ETS afford special treatment to energy intensive industries subject to global competition, so the chances that any one of them would be challenged on the basis of granting a prohibited subsidy seems remote. To conclude, it is highly unlikely that an ETS will ever be challenged on the charge of violating the SCM Agreement, notwithstanding the conclusions that one can reach by performing a purely legal analysis.[49]

Third, as a matter of fact, a much more urgent and crucial (political) issue than the potential breach of the SCM Agreement by ETS is the widespread state practice of giving subsidies to polluting sources of energy. It has been noted that globally, subsidies for carbon-based fuels reach $500 billion. The Intergovernmental Panel on Climate Change has noted that removing those subsidies would reduce global emissions by 10 per cent while allowing the money to be used for other societal ends. The G20 at its meeting in Pittsburgh took up this issue and issued a resolution to completely phase out subsidies for fossil fuels.

As a possible way forward, a number of ideas have been suggested to prepare the WTO do deal with climate change related subsidies, which, as mentioned, is a broader concept than allowances in ETS: for example, in order to promote transparency, a notifiable subsidies template might be

---

[48]   Ibid., para. 90.

[49]   For an analysis of ETS vis-à-vis the SCM Agreement that concludes that a breach of the SCM Agreement through allocation methodologies is likely, see Redmond, D. and K. Kendall (2010). 'Emissions Trading Schemes, Domestic Policy and the WTO'.

prepared and a subsidy review mechanism could be considered. Of course, some have suggested that the WTO itself has not been very effective in disciplining subsidies. The fundamental constraint on subsidies is of a political nature: given that they are the 'currency' of politics, it is inherent in the nature of subsidies not to seek the spotlight. As a result, work done by, for example, the OECD on subsidies has achieved very little coverage. Hence, the key work to solve the subsidies issue lies outside the remit of the WTO. The WTO could help in this by making fossil fuels subsidies illegal under the SCM Agreement – depending on their characteristics, instead of making that dependent on whether the conditions set out in Article 3.1 are fulfilled.[50]

Allocation methodologies and GATS   While a finding that an ETS has violated the SCM Agreement is unlikely, an allocation methodology that is in some way skewed against installations owned by foreign corporations could breach the GATS. It is difficult to imagine how this could happen, unless the allocation rules make explicit mention to issues of ownership. However, rules that are prima facie neutral could nevertheless have a more negative impact upon foreign owned installations.

3.   Use of revenues

In this context, it is worthwhile remembering that according to Article 8 SCM Agreement, subsidies consisting in 'assistance to promote adaptation of existing facilities to new environmental requirements imposed by law and/or regulations which result in greater constraints and financial burden on firms' were, provided some conditions were satisfied, non-actionable until 31 December 1999, when this provision expired. The use of auction revenues could lead to straightforward cases of breach of the SCM Agreement, if it can be characterized as falling within the category of actionable subsidies. Of particular relevance are provisions that foresee the earmarking of revenues, for instance so that they remain within certain companies covered by the ETS. Here, we could likely have an actionable subsidy.

4.   Competitiveness and environmental concerns

A background   Most of the focus in the literature analyzing the inter-relations between ETS and WTO law has focused on this specific issue.[51] The question generally considered in this regard is whether solutions that

---

[50]   Ciuriak, D. (2009). 'Climate Change and the Trading System', at p. 6.
[51]   See references included in footnote 3 above.

seek to address either carbon leakage and/or competitiveness concerns of domestic industry by 'levelling the playing field' such as border tax adjustments, carbon tariffs or carbon conditional measures are either compatible with Articles I:1 and III:4 GATT or could be justified under Article XX GATT.

Given the complexity of the topic and the nature of this Chapter, we should frame the discussion by making a few initial specifications, regarding both form and substance:

First, as a matter of fact, it seems to be in the nature of proposed and adopted ETS (and more generally environmental policies) to include provisions that deal explicitly with the concerns of carbon leakage and loss of competitiveness. These concerns look likely to subsist until either one of two possible futures becomes a reality: (1) a global carbon market is in place covering all products or installations worldwide, whether established top-down (as part of an international climate change agreement) or bottom-up (through linkages among domestic ETS); or (2) all countries relevant for the purposes of international competitiveness have in place regulatory measures that, while not being identical, tend to generate a (carbon) level playing field. In the light of current progress both in the international climate change negotiations and in countries such as the US, China and India, the concerns may continue for a long time. In fact, the problem may intensify if comparability is rendered very difficult or impossible in the context of the new 'outlook' of the international negotiations, whereby a set of patterns is emerging that is very different from the one laid down by the Kyoto Protocol: (1) a focus on self-determined targets; and (2) a focus on non-legally binding yet robust MRV.

Second, and given the practical relevance of competitiveness and carbon leakage, it is necessary to clarify their meaning. An analysis of the literature suggests that competitiveness at the sectoral level has two aspects: (i) ability to sell; and (ii) ability to earn.[52] This means that companies subjected to a carbon price will need to increase the prices of their products and therefore will lose market share; alternatively, they may decide not to increase their prices so as to maintain their market share, but lose earnings as a result.[53] Two main consequences will follow: job losses and an increase of greenhouse gas emissions in countries where a carbon price does not exist (carbon leakage). Carbon leakage can be of two types:

---

[52]   Alexeeva-Talebi, V., C. Bohringer and U. Moslener, (2007). 'Climate and Competitiveness: an Economic Impact Assessment of EU Leadership in Emission Control Policies'.

[53]   Monjon, S. and P. Quirion (2010). 'How to Design a Border Adjustment for the European Union Emissions Trading System?'.

industry-based leakage (as just described), and energy leakage (climate policies reduce energy consumption, which lead to lower energy prices worldwide which in turn lead to more energy consumption in countries without climate policies in place). Industry-based leakage has two components: operational and investment leakage. Operational leakage means short-term relocation of production, while investment leakage refers to long-term relocation of investments. So far, there is very little empirical evidence of leakage of either of these types.

Third, and as hinted at above, it is necessary to make precise distinctions between the different types of measures proposed in the literature to deal with concerns about competitiveness and leakage. A distinction can be made between: (i) border tax adjustments; (ii) carbon tariffs; and (iii) carbon conditional measures. Each one represents an archetype within which many sub-options are possible.[54] The main differences between the three instruments is as follows: border tax adjustments seek to apply the destination principle in respect of indirect taxes; carbon tariffs seek to 'punish' imports from countries identified as not having in place 'comparable' carbon policies or on imports from countries that are not part of a global agreement to cut carbon emissions. Finally, carbon conditional measures tend to focus on products instead of on countries, and seek to apply the disciplines of Articles VI and XIX GATT allowing antidumping, anti-subsidy and safeguard measures to eliminate unfair practices or to bring relief in case of imports surges. Clearly, the legal analysis of the compatibility of each of these instruments with WTO law if they were to be coupled with an ETS is different, and it is not possible to go into detail here. Nevertheless, there is some agreement that of the three, border tax adjustments are the option with the most chance of being compatible with WTO law.[55] Hence, some authors have suggested that, for example, in order to make the solution more WTO compatible, it would be more appropriate to use two-way border tax adjustments in relation to allowances. On the import side, there would be a requirement to surrender allowances rather than to pay a tax. The amount of allowances could be

---

[54] For instance, a border tax adjustment could be defined in three ways: The first option is based on the specific carbon tax of the *importing* country combined with the carbon content of the *exporting* country. The second option is based on the *specific* carbon tax and carbon content of the *importing* country. The third option is based on the *ad valorem* equivalent of the specific carbon tax of the *importing* country, and this *ad valorem* equivalent is applied on the price of the imported widget. See Messerlin, P. A. (2010). 'Climate Change and Trade Policy: From Mutual Destruction to Mutual Support'.

[55] Ibid., at p. 16 et seq.

determined by using sectoral benchmarks, and they should be requested upon importation and not at the end of the year. On the export side, there could be a rebate on the amount of allowances a domestic emitter has to surrender, on the basis of product-specific benchmarks rather than specific plant or firm emissions. It should nevertheless be clear from this brief description that even this solution raises serious questions regarding its legality vis-à-vis WTO law.

Fourth, and related to the previous point, the literature cannot reach clear conclusions on the compatibility or otherwise of this type of measure with the GATT, even if some options would seem to stand a better chance than others if they were subjected to a legal challenge.

Fifth, no state has yet lodged a case before the WTO dispute settlement system claiming that one of those measures arguably violates WTO law, and therefore neither a panel nor obviously the Appellate Body has had the chance of examining one of these measures and clarifying its relationship with WTO law.

The next paragraphs will provide the contours of the legal analysis without going into depth. The point of departure is a rather obvious one: existing WTO rules were not drafted with climate change and other environmental problems in mind. Hence, the entire legal analysis is unavoidably characterized by a certain degree of awkwardness, which has given rise to a rather circumvoluted literature which does not lead to generally agreed conclusions. Low and Marceau provide two relevant examples of such awkwardness.[56]

First, according to Low and Marceau, the GATT National Treatment principle applies to the treatment of imported versus domestic products and prohibits distinctions based on process and production methods that are not embodied in the final product. However, many climate change mitigation policies target industrial installations, and focus precisely on NPR-PPMs. So the introduction of a measure that targets foreign products in order to compensate for the impacts on competitiveness caused by a measure tackling domestic processes and production methods would seem unavoidably to treat imported and domestic products differently. Second the GATT allows governments to rebate or remit domestic taxes imposed on exported products (indirect taxes), but prohibits doing the same in relation to taxes on firms or industries (direct taxes) producing for export. And since an ETS coupled with full auctioning of allowances is similar to a tax imposed upon firms or industries – rather than on products

---

[56]   Low, P., G. Marceau, et al. (2011). 'The Interface between the Trade and Climate Change Regimes'.

– it might be argued that granting a rebate of costs imposed by the ETS at the border could be in breach of WTO law. Of course these are just two examples among many others, but point to two key sources of uncertainty in the decision whether to couple an ETS with measures to address competitiveness concerns and carbon leakage.

The product/process distinction and border tax adjustments   This distinction is of course one of the most controversial issues within the literature on trade and the environment, and remains largely unresolved, both in general and in relation to border tax adjustments. After an examination of the literature, Vranes concludes that 'while it is clear that taxes that are directly levied on final products are adjustable vis-à-vis like imported products, doubts persist as to whether taxes on non-incorporated inputs to the production process can be adjusted on importation'.[57] Therefore many authors have examined whether these measures could be saved under Article XX GATT.[58]

The legality of border tax adjustments, carbon tariffs and carbon conditional measures coupled with ETS vis-à-vis the GATT and the SCM Agreement   In the context of this chapter, the question is whether border tax adjustments on non-incorporated inputs could be coupled with an ETS, and if so, which requirements would need to be fulfilled. If they cannot, an alternative solution could be to introduce a carbon equalization system by asking importers to surrender allowances and by enabling exporters to have their obligation to surrender allowances reduced?[59] A separate analysis would have to be made as well regarding the compatibility of carbon tariffs (as defined above) with Articles III:4, I:1, and XX GATT.

Given the level of uncertainty about the acceptability of measures, the measure of choice so far has been the allocation of allowances for free. This would seem the safest approach from the perspective of WTO law, though as seen above some consider that it could lead to a breach of the SCM Agreement.

It is generally understood that these measures might breach either the GATT or SCM Agreement, and in the case of GATT might require justification under Article XX GATT. One policy related question is whether

---

[57]   Vranes, E. (2009b). *Trade and the Environment: Fundamental Issues in International Law, WTO Law*.

[58]   See for instance de Cendra, J., (2006). 'Can Emissions Trading Schemes be Coupled with Border Tax Adjustments? An Analysis vis-à-vis WTO Law'.

[59]   See Veel, P.-E. (2009). 'Carbon Tariffs and the WTO: An Evaluation of Feasible Policies', at pp. 770 et seq.

this solution is satisfactory. A number of observations are warranted before aiming at reaching any (tentative) conclusion:

On the one hand, it is possible to argue that Article XX GATT constitutes – in the absence of a comprehensive international climate change agreement – a second best solution, for a number of reasons:[60]

First, the scope of Article XX has been progressively expanded over time to justify public (environmental) policies that would otherwise be inconsistent with the GATT/WTO, and as a result states have some leeway to take measures that prevent carbon leakage.

Second, some have suggested that Article XX GATT could offer a harbour against violations of the SCM Agreement, since the latter can be understood as interpreting and implementing Articles VI and XVI GATT.[61] If this would be the case, it could be crucial for states that opt to allocate free allowances as a solution to protect industry from losing competitiveness vis-à-vis international competitors in case free allocation was determined to be in breach of the SCM Agreement.

Third, the analytical test under Article XX developed by the Appellate Body in the *Shrimp/Turtle* case puts a premium on negotiated solutions, which provides an extra incentive to find commonly agreed solutions to the crucial issue of comparability of domestic efforts along widely recognized variables, regardless of specific choices made domestically. This would not necessarily require reaching agreement on an international climate change treaty setting legally binding mitigation targets for all countries including developed and developing ones, which might not come any time soon, but rather requires a serious attempt to achieve one. For instance, some

---

[60]   Low, P., G. Marceau, et al. (2011). 'The Interface between the Trade and Climate Change Regimes', at p. 21.

[61]   Ibid., at p. 21. The authors refer to two rulings from the Appellate Body where the use of Article XX GATT outside the GATT has been mentioned. First, in *China Audiovisual Services,* the Appellate Body ruled that Article XX was available as a defence to claims under paragraph 5.1 of China's Accession Protocol. See Appellate Body Report, *China – Measures Affecting Trading Rights and Distribution Services for Certain Publications and Audiovisual Entertainment Products ('China – Audiovisual Services'),* WT/DS363/AB/R, adopted 12 December 2009, paras 205–233. Moreover, In *US-Shrimp Anti-Dumping from Thailand and India* it was submitted *'in arguendo'* that such Article XX justifications could be used against allegations of violation of the Antidumping Agreement and the Appellate Body entertained the argumentation. See Appellate Body Report, *United States – Measures Relating to Shrimp from Thailand ('US-Shrimp (Thailand)'),* WT/DS343/AB/R, adopted 16 July 2008, paras 308–310, 319, and Appellate Body Report, *United States – Customs Bond Directive for Merchandise Subject to Anti-Dumping/Countervailing Duties ('US-Customs Bond Directive'),* WT/DS345/AB/R, adopted 16 July 2008, pp. 117 et seq.

have suggested the possibility of adopting a future international climate change agreement superseding the Kyoto Protocol that would incorporate guidelines on how to impose measures against countries that are not implementing climate policies, and by making sure that determinations on questions of fact are made by experts, and not by politicians.[62] Whether this is a realistic prospect is open to question.

On the other hand, it has to be noted that Article XX does not include, within the legitimate goals that would justify trade restrictive measures, competitiveness concerns. So a key question is whether a border tax adjustment can be related to the exceptions mentioned in subparagraphs (a) and (b) of Article XX. One could argue on the one hand that a BTA or a similar measure is essential for the acceptability of an ETS, and that without such a measure, an ETS will either not be adopted or will be adopted in a very much watered-down form that will make it environmentally ineffective. However, there are reasons to be skeptical of such an approach, particularly if it is put forward in abstract manner without analyzing in detail the structure and reach of the measure. Doing this could show that the measure is not actually seeking to protect the environment but rather to protect domestic firms from international competition. In that case, it would risk not being justifiable under the exemptions listed in Article XX. An illustration is the methodology used by the European Commission to determine which sectors face a significant risk of leakage. While the methodology was used to determine the allocation methodology to be applied (essentially free allocation versus auctioning), it clearly shows how the regulatory process was 'captured' by industry. Indeed, the methodology led the Commission to declare that no less than 164 sectors were exposed to a significant risk of carbon leakage. A closer look at the definitions used to arrive at that number and at the sectors that were finally included in the list reveals two things: first, that 117 sectors were included because they have a large trade intensity – which has nothing to do with climate change concerns but rather with protectionist interests; second, many of those sectors have very little impact on climate change, for instance the wine industry, watches and clocks, bicycles, and underwear.[63] And the onus is placed on the state introducing those measures to justify their environmental nature. Economists trying to establish theoretically and empirically evidence of carbon leakage have

---

[62] See Frankel, J. A. (2008). 'Addressing the Leakage/Competitiveness Issue in Climate Change'.

[63] Taken from the NACE list of industries with a 'significant risk of carbon leakage', quoted in Messerlin, P. A. (2010). 'Climate Change and Trade Policy: From Mutual Destruction to Mutual Support'.

found precious little indeed, and always associated to very few sectors.[64] It could then be argued that these address legitimate concerns within otherwise primarily environmental measures, and by so doing make them possible.

Nevertheless, it is critical not to lose sight of the fact that, as states continue experimenting with domestic ETS and with measures to avoid carbon leakage and avoid losses of competitiveness, they might not be interested in challenging the solutions found by other states at the time when they themselves struggle to find acceptable solutions. This suggests that states might be well advised to put their efforts into designing and implementing domestic ETS that are 'linkable' with each other. And one of the conditions for links to be established is that they achieve a similar level of environmental effectiveness.[65] Hence, negotiations on how to establish mechanisms that enable states to measure the degree of comparability of efforts across climate policies in different countries is one way of reducing the tensions arising from competitiveness concerns.

5. Measures to improve cost-effectiveness and to manage price uncertainty and volatility

The relevance of these types of measures from the perspective of WTO law is that they might benefit only domestic producers, for instance if importers of foreign products need to purchase allowances in order to be able to import products or sellers in order to be able to sell them – and in doing so cannot enjoy the flexibility granted by those provisions. However, it should not be difficult to ensure that this incompatibility does not materialize, for instance by allowing importers to open accounts where they can hold allowances, by only obliging them to surrender allowances at the same time as domestic producers, and by ensuring that they can make use of the same flexibilities – for example banking and borrowing.

6. Measures regulating services in the carbon market

As already mentioned, while allowances are possibly neither products nor services, and therefore governments are not constrained by WTO rules in deciding how to allocate them or in deciding whether to place

---

[64]   See for instance Reinaud, J. (2009). 'Trade, Competitiveness and Carbon Leakage: Challenges and Opportunities'.

[65]   On conditions for linking ETS, see for instance Tuerk, A. and M. Mehling (2009). 'Linking Carbon Markets: Concepts, Case Studies, and Pathways'.

restrictions on the import and export of allowances and if so, which, the creation of a market on which allowances can be bought and sold means that a range of services can be provided within that market. And those services, including financial and brokering services, would be covered by the GATS. It follows that provisions that restrict the participation in the market of foreign financial service providers might violate the GATS.[66]

IV. PROGRESS IN THE LITERATURE

The literature, particularly the economic literature, has started to move beyond the discussion on the potential points of tension between climate change policies (including ETS) and WTO law towards finding possible ways to reduce the chances of a 'clash', which could occur because climate change policies are developing at multiple levels of governance and often in uncoordinated ways. These include:[67]

1. letting the WTO dispute settlement system decide on particular cases as they arise; the cons are that the outcome may take many years to materialize and it is likely that it will generate even more resentment on the part of the losing party;
2. negotiating a new code as a plurilateral agreement under Annex 4 of the WTO Agreement, which would create ample space for climate change measures that are broadly consistent with core WTO principles – while tolerating minor breaches;
3. if option 2 proves impossible, then negotiating a code outside the WTO among like-minded countries that would regulate the types of trade-restrictive measures that they consider acceptable. This could be agreed for instance among countries with broadly comparable climate policies;
4. establishing an arbitration forum for private firms under WTO rules, whereby firms could ask for advisory opinions on the WTO-compatibility of national and sub-national climate policies.

---

[66] For a detailed analysis of the (in)compatibility of the EU ETS with the GATS in this respect, see Martin, M. (2007). 'Trade Law Implications of Restricting Participation in the European Union Emissions Trading Scheme'.

[67] These solutions are proposed and further explained in Hufbauer, G. C. and J. Kim (2009). 'Climate Change and Trade: Searching for ways to avoid a train wreck'.

V.   CONCLUDING REMARKS

From the foregoing, it is possible to reach three conclusions: first, although ETS have a very considerable potential to be WTO-compatible, they are very complex instruments and thus create room for tensions, particularly when domestic policy makers are not particularly concerned with WTO law (which might well be the case when ETS are adopted at sub-national level); second, one should probably not overplay the risk that such tensions will actually lead to legal challenges under WTO law, given the state of flux of carbon governance across the world, with so many states experimenting with new approaches to climate policies and what that might imply for the appetite of states for challenging each other before the WTO dispute settlement system; third, given the ambiguity of WTO law to discipline climate policies, the literature is moving towards imaginative – and ambitious – solutions that can avoid a 'clash'. The next years will show whether this is a success story.

BIBLIOGRAPHY

Alexeeva-Talebi, V., C. Bohringer and U. Moslener (2007). 'Climate and Competitiveness: an Economic Impact Assessment of EU Leadership in Emission Control Policies', *Centre for European Economic Research (ZEW)*, Mannheim.

Bäuerle, T., J. Graichen, et al. (2010). Integration of Marine Transport into the European Emissions Trading System Environmental, economic and legal analysis of different options. Dessau-Roßlau, German Federal Environment Agency: 171.

Bossche, P. v. d. (2008). *The Law and Policy of the World Trade Organization: Texts, Cases and Materials*. Cambridge, Cambridge University Press.

Cendra, J. d. (2006). 'Can Emissions Trading Schemes be Coupled with Border Tax Adjustments? An Analysis vis-à-vis WTO Law'. *Review of European Community and International Environmental Law* 15(2): 131–145.

Cendra, J. d. (2010), 'From the EU ETS to a Global Carbon Market: An Analysis and Suggestions for the Way Forward', *European Energy and Environmental Law Review* 19(1): 2–17.

Ciuriak, D. (2009). Climate Change and the Trading System: Report of a meeting organized by the Centre for International Governance Innovation and the Canadian International Council. Toronto, Canadian International Council 8.

Convery, F. J. and L. Redmond (2007). 'Market and Price Developments in the European Union Emissions Trading Scheme'. *Review of Environmental Economics and Policy* 1(1): 88–11.

Fleming, D. and S. Chamberlain (2010). Tradable Energy Quotas: A Policy Framework for Peak Oil and Climate Change. London, All Party Parliamentary Group on Peak Oil & The Lean Economy Connection, House of Commons: 60.

Frankel, J. A. (2008). Addressing the Leakage/Competitiveness Issue in Climate Change Policy Proposals, Brookings Global Economy and Development: 19.

Genasci, M. (2008). 'Border Tax Adjustments and Emissions Trading: The Implications of International Trade Law for Policy Design'. *Carbon and Climate Law Review* 2(1): 33–42.

Haites, E. and M. Mehling (2009). 'Linking Existing and Proposed GHG Emissions Trading Schemes in North America'. *Climate Policy* 9(4): 373–388.

Hood, C. (2010). Reviewing existing and proposed emissions trading systems. Information Paper. Paris, International Energy Agency: 110.

Hufbauer, G. C. and J. Kim (2009). Climate Change and Trade: Searching for ways to avoid a train wreck. Geneva, Centre for Trade and Economic Integration: 38.

Larragán, J. d. C. d. (2010). 'From the EU ETS to a Global Carbon Market: An Analysis and Suggestions for the Way Forward'. *European Energy and Environmental Law Review* **19**(1): 2–17.

Low, P., G. Marceau, et al. (2011). The Interface between the Trade and Climate Change Regimes: Scoping the Issues. WTO Staff Working Papers. Geneva, World Trade Organization: 45.

Martin, M. (2007). 'Trade Law Implications of Restricting Participation in the European Union Emissions Trading Scheme'. *Georgetown International Environmental Law Review* **19**: 437–474.

Meltzer, J. (2012). 'Climate Change and Trade – the EU Aviation Directive and the WTO', *Journal of International Economic Law*, published online.

Messerlin, P. A. (2010). Climate Change and Trade Policy: From Mutual Destruction to Mutual Support. World Bank Policy Research Working Papers. Washington, World Bank: 35.

Monjon, S. and P. Quirion (2010). 'How to Design a Border Adjustment for the European Union Emissions Trading System?' *Energy Policy* **38**(9): 5199–5207.

Redmond, D. and K. Kendall (2010). 'Emissions Trading Schemes, Domestic Policy and the WTO'. *Macquarie Journal of Business Law* **7**: 15–31.

Reinaud, J. (2009). Trade, Competitiveness and Carbon Leakage: Challenges and Opportunities. Energy, Environment and Development Programme Papers. London, Chatham House: 25.

Tuerk, A. and M. Mehling (2009). 'Linking Carbon Markets: Concepts, Case Studies, and Pathways'. *Climate Policy* **9**(4): 341–357.

UNEP/IISD (2005). *Environment and Trade – A Handbook*. Winnipeg, International Institute for Sustainable Development.

Veel, P.-E. (2009). 'Carbon Tariffs and the WTO: An Evaluation of Feasible Policies'. *Journal of International Economic Law* **12**(3): 749–792.

Voigt, C. (2008). 'WTO Law and International Emissions Trading: Is there Potential for Conflict?' *Carbon Climate Law Review* **2**: 54–66.

Vranes, E. (2009a). 'Climate Change and the WTO: EU Emission Trading and the WTO Disciplines on Trade in Goods, Services and Investment Protection'. *Journal of World Trade* **43**(4): 707–735.

Vranes, E. (2009b). *Trade and the Environment: Fundamental Issues in International Law, WTO Law, and Legal Theory*. Oxford, Oxford University Press.

Werksman, J. (1999). 'Greenhouse Gas Emissions Trading and the WTO'. *Review of European Community and International Environmental Law* **8**(3): 251–264.

Windon, J. (2009). 'The Allocation of Free Emissions Units and the WTO Subsidies Agreement'. *Georgetown Journal of International Law* **41**(1): 189–222.

Section 2

Other Than Climate Change

19. Trade in environmental goods, with focus on climate-friendly goods and technologies[1]
ZhongXiang Zhang

I. INTRODUCTION

The global market for environmental goods and services (EGS) is huge and has been growing rapidly. Depending on the definitions and coverage, its size is estimated to be at least about US$ 700 billion in 2006 by Environmental Business International (Japan Ministry of the Environment, 2008) and as much as £3.046 trillion in 2007/08 by the UK Department for Business Enterprise and Regulatory Reform (2009). This high end of the estimated market size accounted for about 10 percent of global GDP. Negotiations on 'the reduction or, as appropriate, elimination of tariff and non-tariff barriers to environmental goods and services' mandated under Paragraph 31(iii) of the Doha Ministerial Declaration (DMD) are to promote further market development of global environmental goods and services, by expanding current supply and technological upgrades of goods and services and making them affordable to consumers. Given the growing consensus that climate change has the potential to seriously damage our natural environment and affect the global economy, this mandate offers a good opportunity to put climate-friendly goods and services on a fast track to liberalization to address one of the world's most pressing long-term threats to future prosperity and security. As the Director-General of the World Trade Organization (WTO) puts it, an agreement on this paragraph would represent one immediate contribution that the WTO can make to fight against climate change (Lamy, 2008).

---

[1]   This chapter expands upon a short contribution (Zhang, 2010a) in *Trade and Environment Review 2009/2010*, a flagship publication of the United Nations Conference on Trade and Development (UNCTAD) every three years. It has benefited from helpful comments by Ulrich Hoffmann and Darlan F. Martí and work in this area from International Centre for Trade and Sustainable Development (ICTSD). That said, the views expressed here are those of the author, and do not reflect the positions of the UNCTAD and ICTSD. The author bears sole responsibility for any errors and omissions that may remain.

Climate-friendly technologies (or goods) refer to those the production or utilization of which reduce climate risks to a greater extent than alternative technologies for producing the same product (or alternative products that serve the same purpose). Climate-friendly technologies include those aimed at improving energy efficiency or increasing energy generation from new and renewable sources and goods. Liberalizing such climate-friendly technologies, goods and services contributes not only to increasing the choices available for importing countries, but also to lowering the costs of those choices for those countries to either comply with existing and future greenhouse gas (GHG) emission commitments or to limit the growth of GHG emissions. The resulting market expansion from trade liberalization will put a downward pressure on prices in home country markets and increase competition between imported and domestic goods, thus further lowering the compliance costs. By increasing the dissemination of climate-friendly goods and technologies at a lower cost, trade liberalization will make it less difficult to set stringent GHG emission targets beyond 2012, given that the world's GHG emissions should be reduced at least by half by 2050, which the IPCC (2007) argues is necessary in order to avoid dangerous climate change consequences.

This chapter will focus on environmental goods (EGs), as that is the area in which negotiations within WTO have to date been more active. This by no means undermines the importance of environmental services in preserving the environment and mitigating climate change. Indeed, many services directly address climate change mitigation. In its discussion and analysis, the chapter makes use of official WTO documents, which include submissions by Members, and their synthesis by the WTO Secretariat and minutes of meetings, to illustrate the divergent negotiating positions of Members on an issue that still remains very much open. These divergent negotiating positions not only exemplify challenges ahead and uncertainty about negotiations on the desired degree and level of trade liberalization on EGs, and more importantly suggest the need for a high degree of flexibility to accommodate different situations and stakes in the liberalization of trade in EGs.

The chapter is structured as follows. Section II discusses a variety of approaches in the current negotiations on the liberalization of trade in EGs. Section III explores options to move such negotiations forward. Section IV presents key findings and conclusions.

II.   APPROACHES TO THE EG NEGOTIATIONS: WHAT PRODUCTS TO LIBERALIZE AND HOW?

A.   Negative Approach versus Positive Approach

To identify which goods and services to ban or promote, a basic distinction can be drawn between negative and positive approaches. A negative approach would be to identify specific goods and services that countries should be required to ban from trade. The Montreal Protocol on Substances that Deplete the Ozone Layer, which was signed in 1987 and has since been amended and strengthened (UNEP Ozone Secretariat, 2000), takes this approach. The Montreal Protocol uses trade measures as one enforcement mechanism among several policy instruments for achieving its aim of protecting the ozone layer. Parties to the convention are required to ban trade with non-parties in ozone-depleting substances (ODS), such as chlorofluorocarbons (CFCs), in products containing them (e.g. refrigerators), and potentially in products made with but not containing CFCs, such as electronic components. This latter provision has not yet been implemented primarily because of problems of detection, and also because of the small volumes of CFCs involved. These trade measures have been extended gradually to all the categories of ozone-depleting substances covered by the Montreal Protocol (Brack, 1996; Zhang, 1998). Accompanied with finance and technology transfer mechanisms, this approach has been effective in phasing out ODS and contributing to the recovery of the ozone layer (Zhang, 2009).

It is clear which products must be banned under product-specific agreements such as the Montreal Protocol, but it is less straightforward to identify products that should be banned in relation to carbon abatement and climate change mitigation. Every product or technology causes environmental harm or affects the climate to some degree. A climate-friendly product or technology is just a concept of relative environmental performance. Such a product or technology tends to be sector- and country-specific, and is subject to change over time. For example, natural gas is less carbon-polluting than coal. Shifting to natural gas has been indentified as part of the solution for climate change mitigation. This has been the main reason why Qatar (2003), in its submission to the WTO, has proposed liberalizing natural gas and natural gas-related technologies as a way to reduce GHG emissions. But natural gas is more carbon-polluting than wind power that emits zero carbon emissions when operating. A coal-fired power plant is more carbon-polluting than one which uses natural gas, but if coupled with carbon capture and storage (CCS) technology, it is more climate-friendly than a natural gas-fired power plant without CCS.

Besides, a country's choice of fuels and technologies depends to a large extent on its resource endowments and their relative prices. The fact that countries like China and India use more coal is not because they prefer it, but because of their abundant supplies of coal and its relatively lower price compared with its more environmentally friendly substitutes. Thus, while some countries or regional agreements (e.g. the North American Free Trade Agreement) may have a negative list of services or investments in certain technologies which are restricted, it is most unlikely that countries will broadly agree on a list of goods that need to be banned. Moreover, arguably, for the purpose of meeting a climate change mitigation objective, any likely ban or restriction would tend to be on goods that emit high levels of GHGs. This will face resistance from Members that object to the use of trade restrictions based on non-product related process and production methods (PPMs), partly because it is difficult for customs officials to distinguish between high and low GHG-emitting products unless Members would be able to establish an acceptable labeling regime – which would in turn rely on those Members that are not in favor of such non-product related PPM distinctions anyway. In addition, there is uncertainty about the WTO compatibility of distinguishing a product based on the way that product is produced, rather than on the final product's characteristics. There is also controversy over whether WTO jurisprudence has moved beyond the PPM concept (Zhang, 2004; Zhang and Assunção, 2004; Howse and Van Bork, 2006; Zhang, 2010c).[2] Thus a negative approach will not necessarily work in a post-2012 climate regime.

By contrast, a positive approach, which seeks to identify certain goods and services for enhanced market access, holds some promise. Establishing a list of goods, technologies and services in which trade is encouraged has its own problems, but is easier than having a common list of goods, technologies and services that need to be banned.

---

   [2]   Some analysts (e.g., Howse and Van Bork, 2006) have argued that WTO jurisprudence has moved beyond the PPM concept. The *Shrimp/Turtle* dispute settlement reasoning, if sustained, would permit WTO Members to invoke the GATT (General Agreement on Tariffs and Trade) Article XX exemptions to regulate imports on the basis of non-product related PPMs to accomplish environmental objectives both outside their jurisdiction and in the global commons – and perhaps to achieve other social objectives (Morici, 2002). Moreover, an OECD study by Steenblik et al. (2005) has suggested that developing countries have substantial export potential, particularly when PPMs are included. It should be pointed out, though, that there is no universally accepted interpretation of the Appellate Body decision (Zhang, 2004). Other analysts (e.g., Jackson, 2000) argue that such a conclusion that PPMs no longer violate WTO by their very nature is premature legally or has been insufficiently debated and tested in the scientific literature.

B.   List, Project, Integrated and Request-Offer Approaches

Under the negotiating structure by the Trade Negotiations Committee in February 2002, negotiations on EGs have been taking place in the Committee on Trade and Environment in Special Session (CTE-SS) (Steenblik, 2005; Harashima, 2008). Such negotiations aim to create a WTO-agreed list of such goods that would then be turned over to the Negotiating Group on Non-Agricultural Market Access (NAMA) to negotiate tariff reductions and/or elimination. The question then is which EGs should be encouraged. Identifying them depends on their definition. Given their conceptual complexities and a lack of consensus on their definition, WTO Members have persistently disagreed over how to identify which EGs should be subject to trade liberalization. Four approaches, namely list, project, integrated and request-offer approaches, have been proposed to define EGs in the WTO negotiations (WTO, 2005; Argentina and Brazil, 2010). Because all other three approaches originate from the list approach, we start with the list approach. And our discussions on this approach are more elaborate than discussions on the other three approaches.

1.   List approach
The list approach proposes the establishment of a multilaterally agreed list of environmental goods. The Organization for Economic Cooperation and Development (OECD) advocates a list-based approach, whereby goods and services on an agreed list will gain enhanced market access through the elimination or reduction of bound tariffs and non-tariff barriers (NTBs) permanently and on a most-favored-nation (MFN) basis. Such lists have been produced by the OECD and by the Asia-Pacific Economic Cooperation (APEC) group. While the two lists were developed for purposes other than the WTO negotiations, some WTO Members, in the development of their lists, have used as 'reference points' the OECD and/ or APEC definitions (WTO, 2005).

There are 164 goods on the OECD list at the Harmonized Commodity Description and Coding System (HS) six-digit level, compared with 109 on the APEC list (WTO, 2002). The OECD list appears to be about 50 percent longer than the APEC list. This difference in the number of goods results largely from the differing objectives of and procedures for generating the two lists (Steenblik, 2005). The OECD list was the result of an exercise intended to illustrate, primarily for analytical purposes, the scope of the environmental industry. It was created deductively, starting from general categories based on classifications in the environmental industry manual (OECD and Eurostat, 1999), and adding more specific examples, where available, in order to produce an estimate of average tariffs on a previously undefined class of goods. By contrast, the APEC approach started with nominations. This yielded a list of goods, which was then arranged according to an agreed classification system. Given that the aim of the APEC list was to obtain more favorable tariff treatment for environmental goods, APEC economies limited themselves to specific goods that could be readily distinguished by customs agents and treated differently for tariff purposes (Steenblik, 2005). The two lists have 54 goods in common, accounting for 27 percent of the goods in the combined lists. However, 50 goods on the APEC list do not appear on the OECD list, while 68 goods on the OECD list do not appear on the APEC list. The main difference between the two lists is that only the OECD list contains minerals and chemicals for water/waste treatment, while the APEC list includes a relatively more extensive set of goods needed for environmental monitoring and assessment. The OECD list also contains a large number of environmentally preferable products (Steenblik, 2005). Taking the OECD or APEC lists of EGs as reference points, the so-called 'Friends of Environmental Goods' group of countries, comprising Canada, the EU, Japan, the Republic of Korea, New Zealand, Norway, Switzerland, Chinese Taipei, and the United States proposed in April 2007 a list of 153 products. Just prior to the United Nations Climate Change Conference in Bali in December 2007, the EU and the United States submitted a joint proposal at the WTO calling for trade liberalization of 43 climate-friendly goods that were identified by the World Bank (2007) from a list of the Friends' 153 products. This proposal aims to secure a zero tariff for these climate-friendly goods by 2013 in developed and emerging economy Members. Least developed countries are excluded from the proposal as a response to developing counties' criticism of an across-the-board elimination.

Many developing countries have consistently expressed concerns about the use of the two lists of environmental goods slated for expedited liberalization, noting that a number of products on the two lists are primarily of export interest to industrialized countries, thus compromising the development dimension.[3] As stated by Cuba (2005) in its submission, the use of the APEC and OECD lists as reference for preparing a potential

---

[3]   The United States Trade Representative rejected complaints that the EU-United States list consisted only of products of export interest to industrialized countries, pointing out that in 2006 the United States was in fact a net importer of the 43 products, with US$18 billion in imports of such products, surpassing exports by US$3 billion, and citing China and Mexico as the two top sources for those products (ICTSD, 2007c).

multilateral list has failed to serve the interests of developing countries in that it benefits developed country export products and services. In the case of the goods included in APEC list, for example, the developed countries make up 79 percent of environmental goods exports, the developing countries about 20 percent and the least developed countries less than 1 percent (Bora and Teh, 2004). The Indian Ambassador was quoted as saying that this EU-United States proposal was 'a disguised effort at getting market access through other means and does not satisfy the mandate for environment' (ICTSD, 2007a).

China has suggested creating two lists of different sets of commitments. Taking into consideration the needs of developing countries' development and the vulnerability of their domestic industries in the area of environmental goods, China (2004) in its submission has proposed the establishment of a development list to better reflect the development dimension of trade liberalization. Such a list is selected by developing countries from a common list that includes specific product lines, on which there is consensus that they constitute environmental goods. These selected products would be exempted from or subject to a lower level of reduction commitments.[4]

2. Project approach

Another sticking point is related to the issue of dual use, in that many product categories proposed on an EGs list include, at the HS six-digit level, other products that have non-environmental uses in addition to environmental uses. In response, India (2005a,b) has advocated a project-based approach, whereby each WTO Member would designate a national authority to select environmental projects based upon criteria developed by the Special Session of the Committee on Trade and Environment and whose domestic implementation would be subject to WTO dispute settlement. The EGSs required for a selected environmental project would temporarily enjoy preferred market access for the duration of the project.

---

[4]   The practical use of China's proposal is open to debate. Singh (2005) argues that China's proposal for preparing separate common and developmental lists to protect infant industries may actually not be the most pragmatic way to reflect special and differential treatment. From the point of view of the negotiations, a development list approach could actually bring more complexities. Given that the economic development level of each of the WTO Members is different and so are their priorities for protection of domestic industries, it is quite possible that with this approach most items that appear in the common list might also appear in the development list, as different countries would want exemptions for different products. Put simply, it would be quite a difficult task to capture all developing countries' special protection needs in one such list.

India has argued that the project approach would ensure that the approved EGSs are used for environmental purposes, thus addressing dual-use issues associated with a list-based approach, and would bring positive measures like capacity building and technology transfer. India's proposal, aimed at finding a reasonable balance between environmentally meaning-ful commitments and the broad application of EGSs across Members is conceptually innovative, and may be appealing, in particular to WTO Members that lack much negotiating leverage to solve access problems caused by regulation or subsidization in major markets. However, the devil is in the details. This approach is more difficult and requires more resources to operate in practice than a list-based approach. It is also criti-cized by the 'Friends of Environmental Goods' group for failing to offer predictable and permanent liberalization, a criticism that also holds true for the integrated approach.

3.   Integrated approach

Argentina (2005) has proposed an integrated approach that aims to bridge the gap between the list approach and project approach. It resembles the project approach but with multilaterally agreed pre-identified categories of goods used in the approved projects. Given the World Bank's sugges-tion to grant priority to products, technologies and services imported for Clean Development Mechanism (CDM) projects (World Bank, 2007) and the WTO Director-General's statement that trade barriers stand in the way of the CDM (Lamy, 2009), Argentina (2009) emphasizes the link between trade liberalization and CDM projects, providing a specific example of the implementation of this approach to CDM projects. Argentina has argued that linking the integrated approach with CDM projects would encourage the direct use of goods, the environmental objectives of which are climate change mitigation and adaptation, thus preventing dual or multiple usage and ensuring that liberalization effectively contributes to climatic improvement and sustainable development. At the same time it would help to reduce the costs of setting up CDM projects and promote the transfer of technologies to developing countries, thus facilitating the development of domestic capacity in the sector.

4.   Request-offer approach

Brazil has suggested a request-offer approach, whereby countries would request specific liberalization commitments from each other on products of interest to them and then extend tariff cuts deemed appropriate equally to all WTO Members on an MFN basis. Brazil's proposal would not limit environmental goods to industrial goods, but would include agricultural products, such as biofuels, in the EGS negotiations as well. Brazil has argued that this approach follows along the lines of previous GATT/WTO negotiations and takes into account developing country interests more adequately than the common list put forward by the EU-United States submission (ICTSD, 2007a,b). An analysis of the Friends' 153 EGs list by Jha (2008) indicates that a handful of developing countries are among the top 10 importers and exporters in various categories of EGs relevant to climate change mitigation. Based on these findings, she suggests that these countries could usefully engage in a request-offer approach to ensure trade gains. In this way, while the benefits of trade liberalization may be multilateralized, the cost would be borne by only a few players. These would be the very players that have a lot more to gain through liberalization.

All these different arguments clearly suggest that some WTO Members have yet to be convinced of the climate change mitigation credentials of some of the products that the EU and the United States have proposed. Moreover, advancing technologies will inevitably eclipse the continuing merits of some existing products. According to an estimate by the OECD (2005), half of existing EGs will be replaced within 15 years. Thus, an exclusive focus on the liberalization of these existing products raises the risk of being locked into current patterns of international trade in technologically advanced climate change mitigation products (i.e. producers of technology and importers of that technology). To better reflect the reality of the evolution of environmental goods and technological change and encourage technological innovation in a field where evolution in technologies is the key to successfully addressing environmental challenges, New Zealand, the Commission of the European Communities, and Switzerland have suggested that an agreed list of environmental goods should be considered a 'living list' and that a review process of product coverage should be set up to update and expand the list (WTO, 2005). Indeed, issues related to the advancement of technology are not confined to EGs. Sectoral agreements like the 1996 Information Technology Agreement and the Agreement on Trade in Pharmaceutical Products under the Uruguay Round have a mandate to review and update their product coverage on a regular basis (see Kim (2007) for discussions on the review process of these agreements). Furthermore, the developing world is in search of both an economic and an environmental gain through these negotiations under the Doha Round – and rightly so (Lamy, 2008). Even though these negotiations are on environmental issues, they must nevertheless deliver a trade gain if they are being conducted through the Doha Round of the WTO.

III.   POTENTIAL WAYS TO MOVE THE EG NEGOTIATIONS FORWARD

A.   Amending HS Codes and Creating Ex-headings to Clarify Product Coverage and Descriptions

It is important to note that the mandate under Paragraph 16 of the DMD is applicable to environmental goods as well. Paragraph 16 of the DMD guides NAMA negotiations and mandates special attention to 'products of export interest to developing countries' as well as requires the 'special needs and interests of developing and least developed country participants', to be taken into account. UNCTAD (1995) proposes environmentally preferable products (EPPs) as a trade opportunity for developing countries. EPPs are defined as products that, from a life-cycle perspective, cause significantly less 'environmental harm' than alternative products that serve the same purpose, or products the production and sale of which contribute significantly to the preservation of the environment (UNCTAD, 1995). UNCTAD (2005) has further compiled a core list of EPPs. According to this UNCTAD study, there are significant export opportunities for developing countries in a large number of low-tech EGs in its core list of EPPs. The inclusion of EPPs in the EGS negotiations raises the concerns about processes and production methods. The majority of WTO Members have argued against the use of criteria based on non-product-related PPMs to select products for the negotiations. Eco-labeled products and others made with environmentally friendly processes, as well as organic products, are clear cases of the use of PPM criteria and hence are beyond the scope of the negotiations (Singh, 2005). Moreover, such EGs also happen to be dual-use products (Hamwey, 2005).

However, most developing countries are hesitant to liberalize bound tariffs on dual-use products due to concerns about the adverse impact of such broader liberalization on their established domestic industries and jobs and, in some cases, on their tariff revenues that continue to represent a large portion of government revenue[5] (ICTSD, 2008; World Bank, 2007). They insist on applying a single end-use parameter in screening EGs, and only those indentified EGs based on this parameter would then be taken up for tariff reduction negotiations (Howse and Van Bork, 2006).

Isolating products of single environmental use requires assigning clearer HS codes or product descriptions for environmental goods. The HS allows

---

[5]   According to the WCO (2003), customs collects over 50 percent of all government revenues in many developing countries.

countries to track trade volumes and tariff levels. The more digits there are in a code, the more specific is the description of the product. Currently, HS numbers for products are only harmonized across WTO Members up to the six-digit level. However, there are only a very few cases in which there is an (almost) perfect match between a single-use EG and a HS code at the six-digit level. HS 841011 and HS 841012 (hydraulic turbines) and HS 850231 (wind powered electricity generating sets) are among a few cases that can pass the single-use test (Vossenaar, 2010; Vikhlyaev, 2010). In most cases, however, HS product categories at the six-digit level contain products that have both non-environmental uses and environmental uses. In these cases, a single-use EG may represent only a very small portion, if any, of trade of all products included in a specific six-digit HS code. Take a windmill pump as a case in point. A windmill pump is clearly identified as a single-use EG. It is part of HS 841381, which includes other pumps. The Harmonized Tariff Schedule of the United States breaks down HS 841381 into various sub-positions, including 8413.81.00.30 (household water systems, self-contained; and windmill pumps). During the 2007–2009 period, imports of pumps under the provisions of this 10-digit code accounted for just 1 percent of the value of US imports of pumps included in HS 841381, and windmill pumps were only an unknown part of this 1 percent (USITC, 2009; Vossenaar, 2010). This exemplifies that fast-tracking pumps of multiple use in a specific six-digit HS code under the EGS mandate would be difficult to justify.

Clearly, identifying the so-called 'ex-outs' of single environmental use, which, in the language of trade negotiations, refer to those goods that are not separately identified at the six-digit level of the HS code and have to be identified in national tariff schedules at the eight- or 10-digit level, needs to go beyond the six-digit level. However, no uniform code exists beyond this level. So, as product descriptions get more specific, different WTO Members use different codes and descriptions. To identify and liberalize specific goods of single environmental use, including those climate mitigation goods, WTO Members need to harmonize at least the ex-out product descriptions across countries. However, harmonizing HS codes beyond the six-digit level will be time-consuming and would not be viable, given the short time horizon for a possible conclusion of the Doha Round and the timing of review cycles of the World Customs Organization, which considers HS amendments once every five years, with the latest amendment in June 2004 and entered into force on January 1, 2007. It is not evident that the desire to enable better targeted and deeper tariff reduction for EGs would be deemed sufficiently important to introduce sub-divisions.

Another option to operationalize the use of 'ex-outs' is to create ex-headings in national customs nomenclatures. Given that each country has different sub-headings within its national customs nomenclatures, if this option is to be considered, countries should agree to a process to ensure the consistency of the product descriptions and encoding of ex-heading goods across countries, so that including ex-heading goods would not cause classification problems at the border (Kim, 2007).

B.   Alternative Options to Accelerate Negotiations on Liberalization of Trade in EGs

What are the other options that need to be explored to accelerate liberalization of trade in EGs? Arguably, countries are likely to agree upon a narrow choice of climate-friendly products that would be acceptable to a broader range of countries rather than a broader range of products that would be acceptable to only a few countries. It would be most efficient to start by identifying a single list of specific goods that all Members can agree on as a basis for further negotiations. One way forward along this line is to focus initially on specific EGs sectors in which the interests of both developed and developing countries coincide in fostering trade liberalization. Increasing energy efficiency is widely considered the most effective and lowest cost means of cutting GHG emissions, and trade in renewable energy equipment in developing countries appears sensitive to tariff reductions (Jha, 2008). Moreover, industrialized countries are set to take on higher proportions of renewable energies in their energy mix, either in order to comply with their GHG emission targets or with the aim of reducing their dependence on foreign oil, or both. Thus the initial round of liberalization should include renewable energy products and energy-efficient technologies. The World Bank (2007) estimates that the removal of tariffs for four basic clean energy technologies (clean coal, energy-efficient lighting, solar and wind energy) covering 12 specific EGs in the 18 largest GHG-emitting developing countries would result in a trade gain of up to 7.2 percent. The trade gain could be boosted by as much as 13.5 percent if non-tariff barriers to those technologies were also removed (see Table 19.1). These gains, which were calculated based on a static trade analysis, were considerably underestimated because they failed to take into account the dynamics of these EGs (i.e. trends in growth of their export levels and the size of their world export market). In addition to the trade gains, using these more climate-friendly technologies and products to replace those that are more GHG-polluting will translate into a significant reduction in GHG emissions. Therefore, clearly, liberalizing trade in low-carbon goods and technologies would serve both trade and climate mitigation interests, not to mention its contribution to reductions in conventional pollutants and the resulting health risks.

Table 19.1 *Estimated benefits of removal of tariffs and non-tariffs barriers to four select clean energy technologies covering 12 environmental goods*

Technologies (HS codes)	Increases in trade volumes (%)	
	Removal of tariffs	Removal of tariffs and non-tariffs barriers
Clean coal (HS codes 840510, 840619, 841181, 841182, 841199)	3.6	4.6
Wind (HS codes 848340, 848360, 850230)	12.6	22.6
Solar photovoltaic (HS codes 850720, 853710, 854140)	6.4	13.5
Energy-efficient lighting (HS code 853931)	15.4	63.6
Total	7.2	13.5

Source: World Bank (2007).

A 'procedural' area of accelerated liberalization relates to products, technologies and services used in small-scale CDM projects (e.g. micro-hydro projects, efficient cooking and efficient lighting) and programmatic CDM.[6] The CDM has been partially successful (Zhang, 2008): the global number of CDM projects registered and in the pipeline by September 1, 2011 totaled 6,724 (UNEP Risoe Center, 2011) – well above what was envisioned by countries when they negotiated, designed and launched this mechanism. However, the lion's share of these CDM projects has gone to a handful of major developing countries like China and India, whereas many countries, especially those in sub-Saharan Africa, have been left out (see Table 19.2).[7] One of the main reasons is that the transaction costs associated with the CDM project cycle have seriously hampered

---

[6] Van der Gaast and Begg (2009) argue that programmatic CDM is highly suited to energy efficiency improvement projects in households (e.g. cooking, lighting) and industry (e.g. one technology applied within an industrial sector at different locations but under similar circumstances).

[7] The established truth that Africa and the least developed countries (LDCs) have been lagging behind in CDM project hosting is based simply on an analysis of the numbers of projects per country. Lütken (2011) suggests, however, that if more relative indicators are used, such as the size of an economy, the level of carbon

small-scale CDM projects in these countries. Although registration fees are set considerably lower for small-scale CDM projects, and simplified methodologies and procedures are also set for those projects, many other transaction costs are independent of project size and will thus have a bigger relative impact on small-scale CDM projects. Programmatic CDM, which bundles together small-scale CDM projects or a program of activities, makes a better contribution to sustainable development and communality empowerment than a single CDM project, but it entails high transaction costs (Zhang and Maruyama, 2001; Paulsson, 2009). Thus, liberalizing products, technologies and services in this area could reduce equipment costs and contribute to lowering transaction costs for potential investors. This would facilitate capitalizing on the untapped potential of programmatic CDM and extend the mechanism's reach in terms of both project type and geographical spread.[8]

Even in these two areas, developing country concerns about the possible impacts of liberalization on their domestic industries would need to be addressed before a deal could be hammered out. This applies particularly to environmental goods and technologies that developing countries are not competitive in producing. The question then is whether it is better for home countries to import such goods and technologies at lower costs to foster greater domestic environmental improvements or to keep a certain level of protection to build up domestic capacities, which could then be reduced over time to provide an incentive to manufacturers to reduce costs and eventually become globally competitive. There is no one-size-fits-all strategy for tariff liberalization for all countries and for all EGs. Some developing countries take the first course, reducing tariffs on finished products for some time to meet nationally set clean energy targets while domestic manufacturing capacities are developing. For example, South Africa has set a target to install more than three million solar water heating (SWH) systems over the five years until 2013. The government's policy is to develop local industry, but due to the lack of local production

---

emissions and CDM project development, the conclusion would have to be that Africa and the LDCs are no longer the lost world in CDM terms.

[8]   In liberalizing trade in EGS, priority should be given to products, technologies and services used in small-scale CDM projects and programmatic CDM. In other words, such products, technologies and services should be included in any list of EGSs for accelerated liberalization. While the motivation would be to facilitate small-scale CDM projects and programmatic CDM, any agreed tariff reduction or elimination would apply to all these EGSs, irrespective of whether these are used for CDM projects. This makes it conceptually different from the Indian proposal for a project-approach that ties the liberalization of any EGS to specific projects.

Table 19.2   Pipeline of CDM projects at the validation stage or beyond (as of September 1, 2011)

Region	CDM projects at validation or beyond		Projected certified emission reductions by 2012	
	Number	%	Million tons CO_2	%
Latin America	948	14.1	375.6	13.8
Asia and Pacific	5453	81.1	2174.2	79.7
China	2813	41.8	1496.0	54.8
India	1735	25.8	418.3	15.3
Europe and Central Asia	72	1.1	40.2	1.5
Africa	178	2.6	97.9	3.6
Middle-East	73	1.1	40.5	1.5
Total	6724	100.0	2728.3	100.0

Source: UNEP Risoe Center (2011).

capacity, SWH systems must be imported in the short- to medium-terms to ensure that target is met (Tudor-Jones, 2009).

By contrast, some countries, in particular those countries with a sufficiently large domestic market to develop domestic manufacturing capacities across the supply chain would prefer to take the latter course. Taking that course may have short-term economic and environmental costs, but if successful, may pay off in the longer run (Wooders, 2009). For example, with regard to wind turbines, India has imposed very high tariffs with the aim of encouraging domestic production and jobs, China has put in place a local content requirement (Box 19.1) (Alavi, 2007; Zhang, 2008), and the Ukraine developed a domestic wind sector. These policies act as barriers to foreign suppliers of wind turbines, and are seen as beneficial for local wind turbine makers. However, such policies hurt home countries in financial terms. In the case of China's local content requirement, while being less costly, domestic wind turbines in China break down more often (even collapse in the worst cases (China Environment News, 2010)) and their overall capacity factors are several percentage points lower than those of foreign models. Such a few percentage points difference might not seem significant, but could well make a difference between a wind farm that is economically viable and one that is not (Zhang, 2010b). Nevertheless, such protection helped China build up its wind turbine manufacturing capacities, and has made its domestically made wind turbines

BOX 19.1   LOCAL CONTENT REQUIREMENT FOR WIND POWER PROJECTS

While China sets itself on a course of rapid development of wind power, its technology and manufacturing capacity can hardly match its demand. China has to rely on foreign turbine manufacturers. Generally speaking, huge orders of turbines from China help to expand these manufacturers' scale of production and thus reduces their cost and price of wind turbines. However, one needs to take account of the so-called 'China factor'. When China needs something, prices go up; when China sells something, prices go down. The monopoly behaviors of foreign turbine manufacturers keep the prices of turbines rising as China's order size is growing. China has indeed viewed itself subsidizing foreign manufacturers. A 'China factor' may be acceptable for increasing oil prices associated with China's increasing demand, as oil is an exhaustible natural resource. However it is less acceptable for wind turbines. Consequently, top Chinese policymakers added a 70 percent local content requirement, meaning that wind power projects must have over 70 percent of their turbine components locally made, and that the wind turbine generator must be assembled in China. The aim is to encourage technology and manufacturing industry for wind turbines in China. This requirement was originally proposed in relation to wind concession farms in China, but was extended to include ordinary wind farm projects as well in 2005. The bidding mechanism, coupled with the 70 percent local content requirement, speeds up the localization of wind turbines. Local wind turbine makers account for an increasing share of total new installations. Now, Sinovel Wind, Goldwind Science and Technology, and Dongfang Electric, the three largest local wind turbine makers together supply over 55 percent of a market dominated by foreign firms until 2008. With domestic turbine makers now dominating the wind power market, China abolished the local content requirement in November 2009.

Sources: Zhang (2010b and 2011).

globally competitive. However, not all instances of countries taking the latter course have a happy ending. In the Ukraine projects ended up being saddled with installation costs two to three times the world average, and a near complete lack of foreign private investment in the sector despite otherwise favorable conditions (Point Carbon, 2008). The Ukraine is not an exception. A study by the WTO (2004) shows that most countries open to trade adopt cleaner technologies more quickly, and increased real income is often associated with greater demand for environmental quality.

These examples suggest the need for a high degree of flexibility to accommodate different situations and stakes in the liberalization of trade in EGS. They accordingly exemplify the challenges ahead and the uncertainty about whether a deal can be concluded on a desired degree and level of such trade liberalization. Needless to say, the objective of having an agreement on EGs or a subset of EGs – such as climate-friendly goods – under the WTO should be pursued as the best choice. However, should WTO Members fail to reach such an agreement, then alternative options, ideally still under the Doha Round,[9] need to be explored, although business groups have even suggested removing EGs from the Doha agenda.[10]

An agreement similar to the Information Technology Agreement (ITA) is one option to consider.[11] However, it would require a certain number of Members representing a minimum percentage of trade in climate-friendly goods and services to join[12] in order for it to come into effect (World Bank,

---

[9] In view of the latest developments in the Doha negotiations this would become increasingly difficult, but not impossible. Veteran trade negotiators suggest that several smaller agreements could be salvaged from the existing negotiations, with an agreement on EGS identified as one of the four areas (Schwab, 2011).

[10] In a letter to United States President Barack Obama on August 3, 2009, the National Foreign Trade Council and eight other United States business groups urged his Administration to 'use all possible channels' to pursue an agreement on reducing barriers to trade in EGSs, even if that meant going outside the Doha Round (Palmer, 2009).

[11] The problem of ensuring a consistent interpretation of customs classifications under the ITA has led to disagreements among trade negotiators as well as between customs authorities and traders, to the point that some analysts are questioning the relevance of this Agreement (Vikhlyaev, 2010).

[12] It would make more sense in the context of climate change mitigation to define critical mass as a share of emissions rather as a share of trade. After all, any agreement on climate-friendly goods aims to cut GHG emissions by providing more choices at lower costs. However, this approach depends on how such climate-friendly goods are produced and what goods they would replace. However, it is much more difficult to calculate emissions than to calculate trade value/volume, and it is an area unfamiliar to WTO negotiators. Taken together, while the

2007). Such an agreement would be open to voluntary participation, and once in effect, the benefits of trade liberalization in climate-friendly goods and technologies would extend to all WTO Members on an MFN basis. The ITA has incorporated a mechanism for review of product coverage every three years. This may have tempered the disappointment of many countries with the initial exclusion of certain products. Given that developing countries are currently not significant suppliers of climate-friendly goods and technologies, priority should be given to additional products being submitted by developing countries for inclusion in a future review. However, the downside of this ITA mechanism is that no new products have been added since 1997. Thus developing countries may be suspicious of this offer for review, and feel reluctant to join.

Another option is a plurilateral agreement in this area, similar to the WTO Agreement on Government Procurement. WTO Members could opt to sign up to such an agreement or not, but the benefits of trade liberalization would extend only to participating Members on an MFN basis, unlike the aforementioned ITA-type Agreement which would extend MFN treatment to non-signatory WTO Members as well. While such a plurilateral agreement would not be ideal, it would still have value, particularly if the key trading parties were involved. Such an agreement could eventually be made multilateral once a certain number of Members representing a minimum percentage of trade in climate-friendly goods and services joined.

Other options for this sort of agreement may be within the context of regional or bilateral trade agreements. Such agreements aim to liberalize substantially all goods at the HS six-digit level. As a result, product classification and the dual-use problems associated with WTO negotiations on EGs and services may be less of a concern. These agreements would liberalize EGs fully. However, the downside of the regional or bilateral trade agreement approach is that trade may be diverted from countries that are most efficient at producing certain EGs but are excluded from those agreements. Moreover, by entailing generally the zero rating of all products, this approach would remove any tariff differential between EGs and their non-preferable like products. Whether such an elimination of tariffs in EGs would be enough to encourage their larger utilization in a competitive environment with other non-EGs would depend on their relative prices and the stringency of environmental policy in the home countries. Even if the prices of energy-efficient EGs were higher than those

---

approach sounds very appealing theoretically, these complications would make it hard to implement, in practice.

of their non-preferable like products, this would not necessarily put those EGs at a disadvantage. Provided energy subsidies are removed and costs are attached to emissions reductions, any higher initial costs of energy-efficient EGs may well be compensated by cost savings through energy savings over their lifetimes. The demonstration of new EGs (technologies) that a country is not yet familiar with but has a high potential to replicate plays a role in this context as well: it is the first but crucial step in showing the effectiveness of these new EGs in cutting pollution and supporting its spin-off to the rest of the economy.

C. Market Creation versus Market Access

This chapter focuses on liberalizing environmental goods and technologies through the reduction or elimination of tariffs. Undoubtedly, the results of such a tariff reduction or elimination would be positive, but would not be significant for increased uptake of these goods and technologies in developing countries. Many African countries already have very low tariffs on many environmental goods, but import few, if any, of them because of a lack of purchasing power and technical assistance. For many developing countries where there are simply not enough environmental markets or these markets are weak, what is the point of having opportunities if there are no capabilities? Clearly, creating markets for EGS is far more important than just improving market-access conditions for associated EGS (UNCTAD, 2010; Vossenaar, 2010; Vikhlyaev, 2010). Put another way, market creation should take precedence over market access.

There are indications that a growing number of developing countries have established some kind of policy targets for renewable energy and are taking measures aimed at creating domestic markets for associated products and technologies. By 2010, at least 96 countries including all major economies, up from 45 countries in 2005, had set renewable energy targets in renewable energy portfolio standards or specific percentage goals of electricity production, total primary or final energy supply from renewables (REN21, 2011). Supportive policies are crucial for the widespread deployment of green energy technologies to meet that target. The development of wind power in China shows that a policy does make a difference. With policies favorable for the development of wind power, wind power capacity in China doubled over the five consecutive years until 2009 (Zhang 2010b and 2011). Moreover, as the development of Solar PV in Germany has shown, developing countries need more use of subsidies to create demand for EGs and enhance domestic manufacturing capacities. In the German case, while Germany has unfavorable solar radiation conditions compared with its Southern European countries, with its feed-in tariffs, it leads the world in both accumulated installations and new PV additions, with its cumulative PV installations through 2009 amounting to more than the sum of the next nine ranked countries combined (Kazmerski, 2011).

With respect to market access, as tariffs in developed countries are already very low – generally less than 3 percent for EGs on the OECD list (Vikhlyaev, 2003) – and as not all EGs are sensitive to tariff reductions,[13] the access of developing countries to developed-country markets would depend more on reduction or removal of trade restrictions in the form of NTBs.

NTBs include technical standards and certification requirements, local content requirements, labeling requirements, public procurement policies in favor of domestic products, and tied-aid that requires the receipt to grant tariff preference for a donor country's goods and services, as well as tax and subsidy measures and other incentives. In some cases, subsidies and incentives have been instrumental in creating demand for single-use EGs, including those imported from developing countries. Most of the increase in developing-country exports of PV devices was triggered by increased EU imports, which in turn was the result of increased demand driven by incentives, in particular feed-in tariffs. In 2008, EU imports accounted for more than half the value of world imports, three quarters of which originated in developing countries. In the case of wind turbines, US imports accounted for almost two thirds of the increase in world trade in the period 2004–2008 (Vossenaar, 2010). In many cases, however, NTBs are considered significant impediments to developing countries' access to developed country markets. They might be implemented in such a way as to favor domestic producers over foreign ones. Such differential treatment could occur in governing eligibility for, and the amount of, a subsidy, in establishing energy efficiency standards, in determining the category of eco-labeled products and the procedures for establishing eco-labels, and in specifying criteria for tenders and conditions for participating in government procurement bids such as 'Buy American' type of provisions which create biases for US home-made goods under the US stimulus package (Zhang and Assunção, 2004). Developing countries constantly refer to intellectual property rights as a barrier to access to much-needed and advanced low-carbon technologies, in addition to their high licensing fees or royalty payments. All this suggests that high tariffs are only

---

[13]   An analysis by Jha (2008) of 84 energy supply products in the Friends' 153 EGS list reveals that only 30 percent of those products are sensitive to a tariff reduction.

one of the factors that determine access to and affordability of climate-friendly goods and technologies, and thus that action beyond tariff reduction or elimination is also needed to achieve the desired effect. However, Members' submissions on NTBs related to environmental goods have thus far been quite general. They simply indicate sectors where there could be potential NTBs. A lot of work is still required in this area to identify measures with any real degree of specificity, with one suggestion along this line being Mauritius's submission to include NTBs in the category-by-category exercise (ICTSD, 2011).

IV. CONCLUSIONS

Paragraph 31(iii) of the DMD mandates the liberalization of environmental goods and services. This mandate offers a good opportunity to put climate-friendly goods and services on a fast track to liberalization. Agreement on this paragraph should represent one immediate contribution that the WTO can make to fight against climate change, one of the world's most pressing long-term threats to future prosperity and security.

Under current negotiations on the liberalization of trade in EGs in the CTE-SS, the approach to defining the universe of EGs covered still remains open, with options ranging from adopting an agreed set of EGs, undertaking a request-offer process to reduce tariffs to these products, or providing concessions for goods used in environmental projects, for instance under the Clean Development Mechanism. Some WTO Members have submitted lists of environmental goods with a view to creating a WTO-agreed list of such goods that would then be turned over to the NAMA negotiating group to negotiate tariff reduction and/or elimination. While significant progress has been achieved, much work remains on environmental goods. Members still disagree over how to decide which EGs should be subject to trade liberalization. As a potential way forward, countries would need to examine the possibility of a hybrid approach combining aspects of the different approaches that have thus far been proposed. A list of products would be coupled with project-specific liberalization for goods that may not have qualified for the list but are being used in an environmental project under the Clean Development Mechanism. This could be complemented by a request-offer process for products where there is no agreement (ICTSD, 2011). Whatever the approaches to the EG negotiations, it will be important to have accuracy of HS classification and descriptions and clear ex-outs. This issue is crucial to clarify product coverage and descriptions, but is still unresolved.

Moreover, under the negotiating structure of the Trade Negotiations

Committee, the negotiations on EGs are pursued in parallel tracks. As a result, the pace of these negotiations continues to be tied to progress in other negotiating groups, in particular to the NAMA negotiations whose progress remains sluggish. Clearly, progress in the NAMA negotiations will boost negotiations on EGs. However, if progress in the NAMA negotiations remains slow, the question then arises in this context: should negotiations on EGs continue to take place in the Negotiating Group on NAMA? Progress in negotiations on tariff reductions and/or elimination for an agreed list of EGs might move faster if they were separated from the broader talks on NAMA. However, moving in this desirable direction would face a significant challenge, given the fact that the Doha Round mandates a single undertaking, which implies that nothing is considered agreed until everything is agreed.[14]

Talks on WTO EGSs need a boost from other areas as well. Effective technology transfer and financial mechanisms are widely believed to have played a decisive role in making the Montreal Protocol work effectively (Brack, 1996; Zhang, 2009). Given that the scope of economic activities affected by a climate regime is several orders of magnitude larger than those covered by the Montreal Protocol, technology transfer and deployment, financing and capacity-building are considered to be even more essential components of any post-2012 climate change agreement that developing countries would agree upon to succeed the Kyoto Protocol. Moreover, the Joint Working Party on Trade and the Environment at the OECD (2009) stresses a lack of appreciation of how large the stakes are in the EGS negotiations as the obstacle to obtaining an agreement on the liberalization of trade in EGS, which is attributed to a lack of more stringent climate commitments of broader scope. If and when such a post-2012 climate change deal is reached, it would significantly enhance the possibilities of a breakthrough in reaching an EGSs deal under the WTO. As aforementioned, most of the increase in developing country exports of PV devices and wind turbines between 2004 and 2008 was largely driven by regulations that mandate specific shares of renewable energy in the total energy supply, favorable feed-in tariffs and other incentives in developed countries. If history provides any indication, a post-2012 climate change deal, once reached, will create the urgent need for low-cost climate-friendly goods and services and thus drive their market development at a

---

[14]   This rule was designed to encourage countries to make tough calls in one sector knowing that they would be able to show gains in other sectors. However, in the context of the Doha Round, the rule has enabled individual countries to play the spoiler and seek the lowest common denominator outcomes or to free ride on others' concessions (Schwab, 2011).

pace and on a scale unprecedented with the existing regulations and incentives in developed countries.

Discussions throughout the chapter illustrate that there is no one-size-fits-all strategy for tariff liberalization for all countries and for all EGs. This suggests the need for a high degree of flexibility to accommodate different situations and stakes in the liberalization of trade in EGs, and accordingly exemplifies the challenges ahead and the uncertainty about the negotiations on the desired degree and level of such trade liberalization. Needless to say, the objective of having an agreement on EGs or a subset of EGs – such as climate-friendly goods – under the WTO should be pursued as the best choice. However, should WTO Members fail to reach such an agreement, alternative options, ideally still under the Doha Round although in view of the latest developments in the Doha negotiations this would become increasingly difficult, need to be explored. An agreement similar to the Information Technology Agreement is one option to consider. Another option is a plurilateral agreement similar to the WTO Agreement on Government Procurement. Other options may be within the context of regional or bilateral trade agreements. Such agreements aim to liberalize substantially all goods at the HS six-digit level. As a result, product classification and the dual-use problems associated with WTO negotiations on EGs and services may be less of a concern.

Finally, it should be emphasized that tariff reduction or elimination alone for EGS will have little effect on their use if it is not implemented as an integral part of broader policies and strategies. This is simply because there are not enough environmental markets or these markets are weak in many developing countries. Therefore, creating markets for EGS in developing countries is far more important than just improving market-access conditions for associated EGS. There is a positive sign that a growing number of developing countries have established some kind of policy targets for renewable energy and are taking measures aimed at creating domestic markets for associated products and technologies. Given that the access of developing countries to developed country markets would depend more on reduction or removal of trade restrictions in the form of NTBs, there is a need to consider other efforts rather than adopting an exclusive focus on tariff reduction or elimination in order to serve the best interests of developing countries and enable them to access both climate-friendly goods and technologies at an affordable price and developed country markets. Special and differential treatment provisions will also be essential to take into account the concerns of developing countries. These include less than full reciprocity in terms of an exemption from or a lower level of reduction commitments, as suggested for a development list in China's submission, and flexibility in terms of longer implementation periods – or both – for developing countries, and optional participation for least developed countries. In addition, a package of technical and financial assistance is badly needed to ensure that all developing countries are able to benefit from the rapidly growing world market for climate-friendly goods and technologies. At least one WTO developed country Member – Canada – in its submission has recognized the importance of such assistance and has pledged to provide it (Canada, 2005). All these aforementioned initiatives should be made part of the EGs package for it to work.

REFERENCES

Alavi, R. (2007), 'An overview of key markets, tariffs and non-tariff measures on Asian exports of select environmental goods', ICTSD Trade and Environment Series Issue Paper No.4, International Centre for Trade and Sustainable Development (ICTSD), Geneva.

Argentina (2005), 'Integrated proposal on environmental goods for development', Submission to the World Trade Organization, TN/TE/W/62, October.

Argentina (2009), 'The Doha Round and climate change', Submission to the World Trade Organization – Paragraph 31(iii), TN/TE/W/74, November.

Argentina and Brazil (2010), 'Environmental goods and services paragraph 31(iii) – special and differential treatment, communication from Argentina and Brazil', Submission to the World Trade Organization, TN/TE/W/76, June.

Bora, B. and R. Teh (2004), 'Tariffs and trade in environmental goods', Presented at the Workshop on Environmental Goods, organized by WTO Secretariat, Geneva, October 11.

Brack, D. (1996), *International Trade and the Montreal Protocol*, London: The Royal Institute of International Affairs and Earthscan.

Brazil (2007), 'Committee on Trade and Environment (Special Session), submission by Brazil – Paragraph 31(iii)', JOB(07)/146, October.

Canada (2005), 'Canada's initial list of environmental goods', Submission to the World Trade Organization, TN/TE/W/55, July.

China (2004), 'Statement on environmental goods at the CTESS meeting of 22 June 2004, Geneva', Submission to the World Trade Organization, TN/TE/W/42, July.

China Environment News (2010), 'National Energy Administration initiates a thorough investigation into the equipment quality reacting to frequent collapses of domestic wind turbines', *Sina Net*, December 6, available at: http://finance.sina.com.cn/chanjing/cyxw/20101206/09319059835.shtml.

Cuba (2005), 'Environmental goods', Submission to the World Trade Organization, TN/TE/W/50, June.

Hamwey, R. (2005), 'Environmental goods: where do dynamic trade opportunities for developing countries lie?', Working Paper, Centre for Economic and Ecological Studies, Geneva.

Harashima, Y. (2008), 'Trade and environment negotiations in the WTO: Asian perspectives', *International Environmental Agreements: Politics, Law and Economics*, **8** (1), 17–34.

Howse, R. and P. van Bork (2006), 'Options for liberalizing trade in environmental goods in the Doha Round', Trade and Environment Series Issue Paper No.2, International Centre for Trade and Sustainable Development, Geneva.

ICTSD (2007a), 'EU, US call for eliminating trade barriers to climate-friendly goods and services', International Centre for Trade and Sustainable Development (ICTSD), Geneva, December 18, available at: http://ictsd.net/i/news/biores/9151/.

ICTSD (2007b), 'Brazil Peru discuss new ideas on environmental goods liberalisation',

International Centre for Trade and Sustainable Development (ICTSD), Geneva, November 16, available at: http://ictsd.net/i/news/biores/9144/.

ICTSD (2007c), 'Bali Climate Conference: the next two years will tell', International Centre for Trade and Sustainable Development (ICTSD), Geneva, November, available at: http://ictsd.net/i/news/bridges/3159/.

ICTSD (2008), 'Liberalization of trade in environmental goods for climate change mitigation: the sustainable development context', International Centre for Trade and Sustainable Development (ICTSD), Geneva.

ICTSD (2011), 'WTO environmental goods talks find way forward', *Bridges Weekly Trade News Digest*, **15** (1), 6–7.

India (2005a), 'An alternative approach for negotiations under paragraph 31(iii)', Submission to the World Trade Organization, TN/TE/W/51, June.

India (2005b), 'Structural dimensions of the environmental project approach', Submission to the World Trade Organization, TN/TE/W/54, July.

Intergovernmental Panel on Climate Change (IPCC) (2007), *Climate Change 2007: Mitigation of Climate Change*, Working Group III Contribution to the Fourth Assessment Report, Cambridge, UK: Cambridge University Press.

Jackson, J.H. (2000), 'Comments on shrimp/turtle and the production/process distinction', *European Journal of International Law*, **11** (2), 303–307.

Japan Ministry of the Environment (2008), 'White paper on the environment', Tokyo.

Jha, V. (2008), 'Environmental priorities and trade policies for environmental goods: a reality check', Trade and Environment Series Issue Paper No.7, International Centre for Trade and Sustainable Development, Geneva.

Kazmerski, L.L. (2011), 'Solar photovoltaics: no longer an outlier', in F. Fesharaki, N.Y. Kim, Y.H. Kim and Z.X. Zhang (eds), *Global Dynamics in the Green Energy Industry: A New Engine of Growth*, Seoul: Korean Energy Economics Institute Press, pp. 48–80.

Kim, J.A. (2007), 'Issues of dual use and reviewing product coverage of environmental goods', Trade and Environment Working Papers No. 2007/1, Organization for Economic Cooperation and Development, Paris.

Lamy, P. (2008), 'A consensual international accord on climate change is needed', Presented to the Temporary Committee on Climate Change, The European Parliament, Brussels, May 29, available at: http://www.wto.org/english/news_e/sppl_e/sppl91_e.htm.

Lamy, P. (2009), 'Climate first, trade second – GATTzilla is long gone', Keynote Address at the Carleton University, November 2, Ottawa, Canada, available at: http://www.wto.org/english/news_e/sppl_e/sppl140_e.htm.

Lütken, S. (2011), 'Indexing CDM distribution: leveling the playing field', Capacity Development for the Clean Development Mechanism CD4CDM Working Paper Series No. 10, May, available at: http://www.cd4cdm.org/Publications/IndexingCDMdistribution.pdf.

Morici, P. (2002), *Reconciling Trade and the Environment in the WTO*, Washington, DC: Economic Strategy Institute.

OECD (2005), 'The environmental goods and services industry', Organization for Economic Cooperation and Development (OECD), Paris.

OECD (2009), 'Report on the Global Forum on Trade and Climate Change of 9–19 June 2009, Paris', Joint Working Party on Trade and the Environment, Organization for Economic Cooperation and Development (OECD), Paris.

OECD and Eurostat (1999), 'The environmental goods and services industry: manual on data collection and analysis', Organization for Economic Cooperation and Development (OECD), Paris.

Palmer, D. (2009), 'Remove environmental goods talks from Doha: U.S. groups', *Reuters*, August 4, available at: http://www.reuters.com/article/GCA-GreenBusiness/idUSTRE5725Z520090804.

Paulsson, E. (2009), 'A review of the CDM literature: from fine-tuning to critical scrutiny?', *International Environmental Agreements: Politics, Law and Economics*, **9** (1), 63–80.

Point Carbon (2008), 'Clean energy investment in the former Soviet Union region (Ukraine and Kazakhstan): the domestic context', International Institute for Sustainable Development, Winnipeg, Canada, available at: http://www.iisd.org/pdf/2008/cei_ukraine_kazakhstan.pdf.

Qatar (2003), 'Negotiations on environmental goods: efficient, lower-carbon and pollutant-emitting fuels and technologies', Submission to the World Trade Organization, TN/TE/W/19, January.

Renewable Energy Policy Network for the 21st Century (REN21, 2011), *Renewables 2011 Global Status Report*, Paris.

Schwab, S.C. (2011), 'After Doha: why the negotiations are doomed and what we should do about it', *Foreign Affairs*, **90** (3), 104–117.

Singh, S. (2005), 'Environmental goods negotiations: issues and options for ensuring win-win outcomes', International Institute for Sustainable Development, Winnipeg, Canada, June.

Steenblik, R. (2005), 'Environmental goods: a comparison of the APEC and OECD lists', The OECD Joint Working Party on Trade and Environment, COM/ENV/TD(2003)10/FINAL, Organization for Economic Cooperation and Development, Paris, available at: http://www.oecd.org/dataoecd/44/3/35837840.pdf.

Steenblik, R., D. Drouet and G. Stubbs (2005), 'Synergies between trade in environmental services and trade in environmental goods', The OECD Joint Working Party on Trade and Environment, COM/ENV/TD(2004)23/FINAL, Organization for Economic Cooperation and Development, Paris, available at: http://www.oecd.org/dataoecd/21/48/35161237.pdf.

Tudor-Jones, D. (2009), 'Solar', presented at the WTO Workshop on Environmental Goods and Services, Geneva, September 23–25, available at: http://www.wto.org/english/tratop_e/envir_e/wksp_goods_sept09_e/tudorjones_e.pdf.

UK Department for Business Enterprise and Regulatory Reform (2009), *Low Carbon and Environmental Goods and Services: An Industry Analysis*.

UNCTAD (1995), 'Environmentally preferable products (EPPs) as a trade opportunity for developing countries', UNCTAD/COM/70, United Nations Conference on Trade and Development (UNCTAD), Geneva.

UNCTAD (2005), 'Environmental goods: identifying items of export interest to developing countries', CBTF Briefing Note, United Nations Conference on Trade and Development (UNCTAD), Geneva.

UNCTAD (2010), *The Green Economy: Trade and Sustainable Development Implications*, UNCTAD/DITC/TED/2010/2, Geneva: United Nations Conference on Trade and Development (UNCTAD).

UNEP Ozone Secretariat (2000), 'The Montreal Protocol on Substances that Deplete the Ozone Layer', United Nations Environment Programme (UNEP), Nairobi, Kenya, available at: http://ozone.unep.org/pdfs/Montreal-Protocol2000.pdf.

UNEP Risoe Center (2011), 'CDM and JI pipelines by September 1', Denmark, available at: http://www.cdmpipeline.org/publications/CDMpipeline.xlsx.

USITC (2009), 'Wind turbines, industry and trade summary', United States International Trade Commission (USITC), Office of Industries, Publication ITS-02, Washington DC, June.

Van der Gaast, W. and K. Begg (2009), 'Enhancing the role of the CDM in accelerating low-carbon technology transfers to developing countries', *Carbon and Climate Law Review*, **3** (1), 58–68.

Vikhlyaev, A. (2003), 'Environmental goods and services: defining negotiations or negotiating definitions', in United Nations Conference on Trade and Development, *Trade and Environment Review 2003*, Geneva, pp. 33–60.

Vikhlyaev, A. (2010), 'WTO negotiations on environmental goods and services: the case of renewables', in United Nations, *Trade and Environment Review 2009/2010: Promoting Poles of Clean Growth to Foster the Transition to a More Sustainable Economy*, UNCTAD/DITC/TED/2009/2, Geneva, Switzerland: United Nations Conference on Trade and Development, pp. 184–193.

Vossenaar, R. (2010), 'Climate-related single-use environmental goods', ICTSD Programme on Trade and Environment Issue Paper No. 13, International Centre for Trade and Sustainable Development (ICTSD), Geneva, September.

WCO (2003), 'Annual survey to determine the percentage of government revenue provided customs duties', Document No. NC0655, World Customs Organization (WCO), Brussels.

Wooders, P. (2009), 'Greenhouse gas emissions impacts of liberalizing trade in environmental goods and services', International Institute for Sustainable Development, Winnipeg, Canada, October.

World Bank (2007), *International Trade and Climate Change: Economic, Legal and Institutional Perspectives*, Washington, DC: World Bank.

WTO (2002), 'List of environmental goods – paragraph 31(iii)', Note by the Secretariat, TN/TE/W/18, World Trade Organization (WTO), Geneva, November 20.

WTO (2004), 'Trade and environment at the WTO', background paper, World Trade Organization (WTO), Geneva.

WTO (2005), 'Synthesis of submissions on environmental goods', Informal Note by the Secretariat, Committee on Trade and Environment Special Session, TN/TE/W/63, World Trade Organization (WTO), Geneva, available at: http://www.jmcti.org/2000round/com/doha/tn/te/tn_te_w_063.pdf.

Zhang, Z.X. (1998), 'Greenhouse gas emissions trading and the world trading system', *Journal of World Trade*, **32** (5), 219–239.

Zhang, Z.X. (2004), 'Open trade with the U.S. without compromising Canada's ability to comply with its Kyoto Target', *Journal of World Trade*, **38** (1), 155–182.

Zhang, Z.X. (2008), 'Asian energy and environmental policy: promoting growth while preserving the environment', *Energy Policy*, **36**, 3905–3924.

Zhang, Z.X. (2009), 'Multilateral trade measures in a post-2012 climate change regime?: What can be taken from the Montreal Protocol and the WTO?', *Energy Policy*, **37**, 5105–5112.

Zhang, Z.X. (2010a), 'Liberalizing climate-friendly goods and technologies in the WTO: product coverage, modalities, challenges and the way forward', in United Nations, *Trade and Environment Review 2009/2010: Promoting Poles of Clean Growth to Foster the Transition to a More Sustainable Economy*, UNCTAD/DITC/TED/2009/2, Geneva, Switzerland: United Nations Conference on Trade and Development, pp. 178–183.

Zhang, Z.X. (2010b), 'China in the transition to a low-carbon economy', *Energy Policy*, **38**, 6638–6653.

Zhang, Z.X. (2010c), 'The U.S. proposed carbon tariffs, WTO scrutiny and China's responses', *International Economics and Economic Policy*, **7** (2–3), 203–225.

Zhang, Z.X. (2011), *Energy and Environmental Policy in China: Towards a Low-Carbon Economy*, New Horizons in Environmental Economics Series, Cheltenham, UK and Northampton, MA, USA: Edward Elgar.

Zhang, Z.X. and L. Assunção (2004), 'Domestic climate policy and the WTO', *The World Economy*, **27** (3), 359–386.

Zhang, Z.X. and A. Maruyama (2001), 'Towards a private-public synergy in financing climate change mitigation projects', *Energy Policy*, **29**, 1363–1378.

20. Emerging technologies and the WTO: comparing biotechnology and nanotechnology regulations in the EU and the US

Heike Baumüller

I. INTRODUCTION

Technologies are developing at breath-taking pace. Computers have shrunk from the size of a room to fit into a mobile phone, we can recreate animals from a single cell and household appliances can clean themselves with the help of miniscule silver particles. Regulators continuously struggle to keep up with these developments. Not only do they have to ensure that the new technologies do not harm their populations and the environment, they also have to take into account the interests of their trading partners and their differing perceptions of risk and need for oversight, as well as obligations under multilateral trade rules that influence the development and implementation of domestic legislation.

Tensions over trade in genetically modified organisms (GMOs) and the evolving (though as yet less controversial) regulatory regime for nanotechnology products highlight some of the challenges in striking this balance. Indeed, comparisons between the two technology sectors are frequently made. Questions have been raised about whether nanotechnology regulations can avoid the antagonism that the GMO regulatory regime created within the European Union (EU) and between the EU and its GMO-producing trading partners, such as the US, Canada and Argentina. Will we see a repeat of divergences in regulatory responses in the EU and US? How likely are tensions over nanotechnology to arise in the World Trade Organization (WTO) similar to what was witnessed with regard to GMOs?

The approaches taken by the European and US authorities to regulate the two technologies have to be seen against a backdrop of political, economic and societal dynamics at national level. This chapter briefly assesses these dynamics in the EU and the US where public opinion and commercial and political interests have shaped policy making in both technology areas. It then compares the regulatory responses in the two jurisdictions. The chapter concludes with an evaluation of possible WTO issues that may arise, or in the case of GMOs have already arisen, with regard to each field of technology.

II. BIOTECHNOLOGY AND NANOTECHNOLOGY – A BRIEF OVERVIEW

A. Modern Biotechnology

Biotechnology is any technology that uses biological systems or living organisms to make or modify products or processes for a specific use. The focus of this chapter is on 'modern biotechnology' – i.e. the application of *in vitro* nucleic acid techniques (including recombinant DNA and direct injection of nucleic acid into cells or organelles) or fusion of cells beyond the taxonomic family[1] – and in particular its application in the agriculture sector. Modern biotechnology is more commonly (though not universally) referred to as genetic modification or genetic engineering.

The area cultivated with GM crops has expanded rapidly from 1.7 million ha in the mid-1990s to 148 million ha in 2010 in 29 countries.[2] The US is by far the largest producer, accounting for almost half of the global area, followed by Brazil (18 per cent) and Argentina (26 per cent) as well as India, Canada, China, Paraguay, Pakistan, South Africa and Uruguay (>1 million ha each). The most commonly cultivated GM crops are soy, maize, cotton and canola, genetically engineered to be herbicide tolerant or pest-resistant. In the EU biotech crops are grown in eight countries, including pest-resistant maize and the recently approved Amflora, a starch potato for industrial use.[3]

The underlying difference between the EU and US approaches to regulating biotechnology products relates to differing opinions on whether GMOs constitute a fundamentally new product or just another form of plant breeding or technological manipulation of food. The EU takes the former approach, defining GMOs as 'an organism, with the exception of human beings, in which the genetic material has been altered in a way that does not occur naturally by mating and/or natural recombination'.[4]

By contrast, the United States Food and Drug Administration defines

---

[1]   Codex (2003).

[2]   ISAAA (2010), p. 2.

[3]   ISAAA (2010), p. 7.

[4]   Directive 2001/18/EC of the European Parliament and of the Council of 12 March 2001 on the deliberate release into the environment of genetically modified organisms and repealing Council Directive 90/220/EEC, Article 2(2).

genetic modification much more widely as 'the alteration of the genotype of a plant using any technique, new or traditional', arguing that almost all cultivated food crops have undergone some form of genetic modification.[5] Instead of GM food, the FDA refers to 'bioengineered foods', i.e. 'foods derived from a plant that is developed using the introduction into an organism of genetic material that has been manipulated in vitro'.[6]

B. Nanotechnology

Broadly speaking, nanotechnology involves the manipulation of matter or creation of structures at the molecular level (typically at a scale of approximately 100 nanometres or less, a nanometre being one-billionth of a metre).[7]

The Project on Emerging Nanotechnologies (PEN) at the Woodrow Wilson International Center of Scholars lists over 1,300 nanotechnology consumer products that are currently on the market in 30 countries (as of March 2011) – a more than five-fold increase from 212 products since the inventory was first released in 2006.[8] The largest number of products (738) is found in the Health and Fitness category, including for instance cosmetics, sunscreens and clothing. Food and beverages account for a relatively small share of products in the inventory (105). The US and EU are the largest markets (587 and 367 products respectively), but the reach into East Asian markets is also sizable (261). Silver is by far the most common material mentioned in the product descriptions, followed by carbon, titanium, silicon, zinc and gold. Projections put the market for applications of nanotechnology at somewhere between US$1 trillion and US$3.1 trillion by 2015.[9]

While initial definitions are starting to be developed at the EU and US government levels as well as at international level by the International Organization for Standardization (ISO), it is too early to assess their implication for the still evolving regulatory frameworks. In the first European regulation explicitly referring to nanomaterials (in cosmetic products), the EU defines nanomaterial as 'an insoluble or biopersistant and intentionally manufactured material with one or more external dimensions, or an

---

[5]   USFDA (1992).
[6]   USFDA (2001).
[7]   Breggin et al. (2009), p. 1.
[8]   PEN (2011a).
[9]   Roco and Bainbridge (2001) and Lux Research (2008), cited in Breggin et al. (2009), p. 10.

internal structure, on the scale from 1 to 100 nm'.[10] The regulation also notes, however, that this definition can be adapted to technical and scientific progress and to definitions subsequently agreed at international level.

In the context of the on-going review of the EU's Novel Food Regulation (as elaborated below), the European Parliament and the Council of the European Union have both suggested defining 'engineered nanomaterials' as:

> any intentionally produced material that has one or more dimensions of the order of 100 nm or less or is composed of discrete functional parts, either internally or at the surface, many of which have one or more dimensions of the order of 100 nm or less, including structures, agglomerates or aggregates, which may have a size above the order of 100 nm but retain properties that are characteristic to the nanoscale.[11]

Under this proposed definition, nanomaterials would no longer exclude soluble or biodegradable nanoparticles, as demanded by organisations such as the European Consumer Organisation (BEUC).[12] It would also extend the definition to include materials that may be larger than 100 nm, but have nanoscale-characteristic properties, which the Parliament and the Council propose to define as:

(i)   those related to the large specific surface area of the materials considered and/or

(ii)   specific physico-chemical properties that are different from those of the non-nanoform of the same material.[13]

On 18 October 2011, the European Commission put forward its own definition of nanomaterials which would introduce a threshold of 50 per cent for the presence of particles smaller than 100 nm. Specifically, the Commissions has suggested to define nanomaterials as:

> A natural, incidental or manufactured material containing particles, in an unbound state or as an aggregate or as an agglomerate and where, for 50 % or more of the particles in the number size distribution, one or more external dimensions is in the size range 1 nm–100 nm.
>
> In specific cases and where warranted by concerns for the environment,

---

[10]   Regulation (EC) No 1223/2009 on cosmetics, Article 2(k).

[11]   European Parliament (2009), p. 19; Council of the European Union (2009), p. 18.

[12]   Bowman et al. (2010), pp. 115–122, p. 118.

[13]   European Parliament (2009), p. 20; Council of the European Union (2009), p. 18.

health, safety or competitiveness the number size distribution threshold of 50 % may be replaced by a threshold between 1 and 50%.[14]

In the US, the FDA's Draft Guidance for Industry issued in June 2011 does not explicitly define nanomaterials, but notes that when considering whether 'an FDA-regulated product contains nanomaterials or otherwise involves the application of nanotechnology, FDA will ask:

- Whether an engineered material or end product has at least one dimension in the nanoscale range (approximately 1 nm to 100 nm); or
- Whether an engineered material or end product exhibits properties or phenomena, including physical or chemical properties or biological effects, that are attributable to its dimension(s), even if these dimensions fall outside the nanoscale range, up to one micrometer.[15]

Thus, similar to the proposed definition of nanomaterials in the European food regulation, the FDA not only takes into account the size of the materials, but also their properties.

III. DYNAMICS SHAPING REGULATORY APPROACHES TO BIOTECHNOLOGY AND NANOTECHNOLOGY IN THE EU AND US

Regulatory developments are influenced by various constituents and their interests, including consumer (and hence voter) attitudes, campaigns by non-governmental organisations (NGOs), political interests by different political players (such as EU Member States or US states) and private sector lobbies.

A.   Public Attitudes on Biotech and Nanotech in the EU and US

The introduction of GM foods and crops met with little resistance in the US. Since the launch of the Flav Savr tomato in 1994, genetically engineered for longer shelf life, GM foods have become widely available in US supermarkets while GM crops are grown all over the country. If asked in public opinion surveys, more Americans tend to support biotechnology,

---

[14]   *Commission Recommendation of 18 October 2011 on the definition of nanomaterial*, 2011/696/EU, Articles 2.
[15]   USFDA (2011).

though not overwhelmingly so (45 per cent compared to 40 per cent who oppose it according to a 2005 Gallup poll).[16] The US public also tends to be less concerned about possible health impacts (33 per cent)[17] compared to Europeans (59 per cent)[18] (see also Figure 20.1).

In the EU, on the other hand, the introduction of GM products was marred by controversies and strong rejection among many consumers. Rather than being driven by civil society campaigns, NGOs in fact 'found themselves in a position of responding to the intensity of wider public unease'.[19] Many reacted angrily to the seeming disregard for consumer concerns when biotech companies (notably Monsanto) sought to introduce GM crops into Europe in the mid-1990s.[20] Close to two thirds of the European public feel uneasy about GM food and believe that it should not be encouraged, while just over half fear environmental and personal harm (see Figure 20.1). Public opposition was further fanned by negative media reports evoking visions of 'frankenfoods' and 'genetic monsters'.

Opposition is mainly directed at the application of modern biotechnology to food, which the majority of European consumers regard as 'fundamentally unnatural' (70 per cent in 2010, see Figure 20.1). At times likening genetic modification to 'playing God', their concerns go beyond the application of modern technology to food as such, which has become a central element of the modern food processing industry.[21] Consumers also tend to perceive limited benefits for themselves that would justify bearing the potential risks, as the most widely used traits – pest resistance and herbicide tolerance – respond mainly to the needs of farmers.[22] However, their ambivalence about possible benefits for developing countries suggests that even among the people wary of GM food, some can envisage potentially useful alternative applications of the technology (see Figure 20.1).

Nanotechnology, at least so far, has not grabbed public attention in the EU in the same way as GMOs. Awareness of nanotechnology is generally low. Only around half of the people surveyed by Eurobarometer had heard of the technology, with wide variations in awareness among EU Member States (ranging from 21 per cent in Portugal to 78 per cent in Norway).[23] Overall, European consumers appear to have adopted a wait-

---

[16]   Gallup (2011).
[17]   Gallup (2011).
[18]   Eurobarometer (2010), p. 18.
[19]   Macnaghtan (2008).
[20]   Charles (2001).
[21]   Thompson (2008), p. 134.
[22]   Thompson (2008), p. 141.
[23]   Eurobarometer (2010), p. 33.

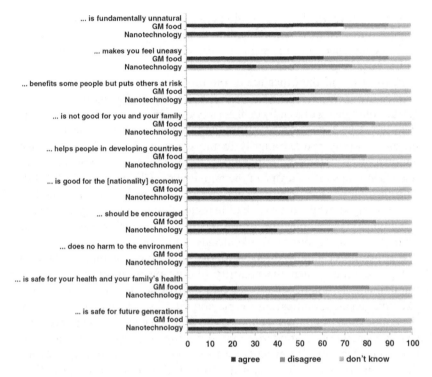

Figure 20.1   Public opinion about biotechnology and nanotechnology in the EU

and-see attitude. In contrast to GM food, a small majority of those aware of the technology believe that it should be encouraged (40 per cent), but an almost equal number did not have an opinion either way. A similar response pattern can be observed when asked how nanotechnology would affect their way of life in the next 20 years (41 per cent positive, 10 per cent negative, 9 per cent no effect and 40 per cent did not know).[24] In general,

---

24   Eurobarometer (2010), p. 9.

the prevalence of 'don't know' responses in the Eurobarometer opinion survey is noticeable (see Figure 20.1).

The fact that the uncertainty over possible risks and benefits has not translated into negative opinions about nanotechnology suggests that people do not necessarily reject the technology on principle as was the case in the early days of genetic modification. This attitude can probably in part be attributed to concerted efforts at the EU level to facilitate debates and educate the public.[25] Interestingly, the European countries most supportive of nanotechnology (e.g. Denmark, Luxembourg and Sweden) are nevertheless opposed to agri-biotechnology, suggesting that opinions are more differentiated than simply rejection of modern technologies.[26]

Similar to biotechnology, US consumers are generally more open than Europeans to the adoption and development of nanotechnology. A comparison of attitudes to the technology in the US and EU found an inverse trend, i.e. around half of US respondents expected nanotechnology to improve their life and just over a third did not know, while the reverse is true in Europe.[27] This trend has also been found in a number of other public opinion surveys.[28] They generally confirm that in the US, the benefits of nanotechnology are expected to outweigh the risks in the longer term.[29]

B. The Role of NGOs in Framing Public Opinion

Widespread opposition to modern biotechnology among European NGOs has also driven GMO regulation in the EU. European NGOs strongly lobbied against the introduction of GMOs, some on principle, others because they did not feel that environmental and health safety was sufficiently assured. Environmental groups such as Greenpeace and Friends of the Earth have been at the forefront of these protests. In some countries, such as the UK and France, strong opposition even led to the destruction of GMO trial fields. Widely publicised stories, such as Monsanto's court case against a Canadian farmer over alleged violations of its GM canola patent or the suspension of a UK scientist who claimed to have found negative impacts of GM potatoes on the immune system of rats,[30] helped to reinforce their case against GMOs.

---

[25] Sandler and Kay (2006), p. 59.
[26] Gaskell et al. (2005), p. 84.
[27] Gaskell et al. (2005), pp. 83–84.
[28] For an overview, see Currall (2009).
[29] FAO/WHO (2010), p. 51.
[30] Baumüller et al. (2006), pp. 15, 23.

The anti-GMO lobby brought together a diverse range of interest groups, including environmental groups, consumer groups, anti-globalisation movements and small farmers in developed and developing countries. They objected to the corporate control of the food system dominated by a few of the major seed companies (dubbed 'genes giants' by the ETC Group), accused companies and governments of quashing scientific dissent (such as alleged impacts of GM potatoes on the immune system of rats) and warned of food security impacts of GMO patents that do not allow small farmers in developing countries to save and re-plant seeds.[31]

In the US, civil society engagement on biotechnology has been less antagonistic. A number of public interest groups are leading a continued campaign, focusing in particular on labelling, but they have generally not expressed the same fundamental opposition as found in Europe.[32] Media coverage of GMOs has also been much more limited compared to the EU where at the peak of the controversy in the late 1990s newspapers would carry almost daily stories about GM crops.

In the case of nanotechnology, NGO reactions have been comparatively subdued and largely constructive in both the EU and the US. Fewer NGOs have taken up the cause. Among the most prominent campaigners are the environmental groups, in particular those that also deal with genetic modification and organic farming, as well as consumer organisations such as UK-based Which? or the BEUC.[33] The ETC Group – also one of the main lobbyists against modern biotechnology – was one of the first to highlight potential health and environmental risks, warning of 'Grey Goo', i.e. the 'obliteration of life that could result from the accidental and uncontrollable spread of self-replicating assemblers'[34] and the 'Green Goo Revolution' where living materials are used to mimic machinery. Several groups initially called for a moratorium on nanotechnology to allow time for further research on possible risks.[35]

C.   Political Interests Influencing Regulatory Approaches in the EU and US

Deep divisions among EU Member States over the potential risks and benefits have also contributed to the stringent regulatory regime for GM products, as well as delays in the development and application of related

---

[31]   Baumüller and Tansey (2008), pp. 174–184.
[32]   Osgood (2001), p. 98.
[33]   FAO/WHO (2010), p. 55.
[34]   ETC Group (2003), p. 30.
[35]   FAO/WHO (2010), p. 55.

legislation. Approvals of new GM products for the European market remain extremely slow – not because EU Member States reject the applications, but because they have repeatedly failed to reach a qualified (two thirds) majority in favour or against, thus leaving the final decision up to the European Commission. This situation continues despite the 2006 ruling by the WTO panel that found that delays in the approval process for most GM products contravened multilateral trade rules. The panel also ruled against bans imposed by Austria, France, Germany, Greece, Italy and Luxembourg on marketing certain GM products, but attempts by the European Commission to overturn these bans are repeatedly defeated in the Council of Ministers.[36]

Since the WTO panel ruling, the Commission approved a small number of GM products, but they are limited to a few food products and one GM crop – the 'Amflora' potato used in industrial production, which was the first GM crop authorised for planting in the EU in 13 years.[37] Much of the opposition stems from concern over possible environmental impacts and risks of cross-fertilisation when GM crops are released into the environment. Several Member States and regions have imposed moratoria on GM cultivation.[38] To overcome the deadlock that has prevented implementation of the WTO ruling, the Commission has recently sought to delink GM commodity imports from planting of GM crops with new legislative proposals that would allow Member States to restrict or ban the cultivation of GMOs on part or all of their territory (see below).

In the area of nanotechnology, such deep divisions between EU Member States have not emerged. Instead, political pressure is mainly exerted by the European Parliament which has been calling for new risk assessment

---

[36] The bans have come under scrutiny again following a judgment by the European Court of Justice In September 2011 assessing the French ban on the cultivation of the GM maize Mon 810. The Court concluded that emergency measures, such as the Mon 810 ban, could only be invoked if the situation 'is likely to constitute a clear and serious risk to human health, animal health or the environment' and that such measures must be based on a risk assessment. Two months later, the French Conseil d'État (where Monsanto and a number of seed producers had brought the case against the French ban in 2007) ruled against the ban on MON 810. The French government, however, has renewed the ban and has submitted a revised justification to the EU. Court of Justice of the European Union (2011). The Court rules on the conditions under which the French authorities could introduce a provisional prohibition on the cultivation of MON 810 maize. Press Release No 86/11, Luxembourg: Luxembourg. Le Monde (2012). Le maïs transgénique MON810 reste interdit en France. *Le Monde*, 13 January.

[37] ICTSD (2010).

[38] See http://www.gmo-free-regions.org/gmo-free-regions.html.

procedures and labelling of nanotech products. Overall, however, there seems to be little disagreement that nanotechnology can be regulated by amending existing legislation rather than developing a new regulatory regime.

In the US political tensions over the introduction of GMOs and the need and nature of biotech regulation have been limited. Fourteen States are debating the introduction of mandatory labelling requirements for GM foods (or in some cases only GM fish), but none of these have yet been adopted. Concerns have been raised in particular about the introduction of GM salmon which has yet to receive FDA approval. Proponents of such initiatives claim widespread support among their constituents. Nevertheless, compared to the EU, these initiatives remain much less visible and have come rather late, given that GM foods have been consumed in the US for nearly two decades. Political reactions to nanotechnology have been even more muted, and every US State now hosts organisations involved in nanotech research and development.[39]

D.   Private Sector Lobbies in the Biotech and Nanotech Industries

Private sector interest groups also have significant influence on policy making, although perhaps less publicly so than consumers or civil society groups. In the US, farmers have been quick to adopt the new technology while American biotech companies are global market leaders in this field. Their lobbies exert strong pressure on their State and federal government representatives to limit the extent of regulatory requirements for GMOs.

In the EU, on the other hand, the pro-GM camps have been less vocal. Farmers recognised that there is little value in fighting for a crop for which there is no market. It has also been suggested that European farm groups may in fact find it in their interest to lobby for stringent GM regulations, given that they are unlikely to reap the same benefits from GM crops as their large-scale counterparts in the US due to the comparatively small size of their farms.[40] Even biotech companies such as Monsanto, DuPont, Bayer Cropscience and Syngenta, conceded that there was little value in continuing field trials that may be destroyed by NGO activists. At the same time, the anti-GM movement found strong support among the supermarkets and food retailers, such as Sainsbury, Tesco, Marks & Spencer, Burger King and McDonalds, who saw a market advantage in banning GMOs from their shelves and products and advocated for GMO labelling.[41]

---

[39]   PEN (2011b).
[40]   Anderson et al. (2004), p. 18.
[41]   Runge et al. (2001), p. 227; Falkner (2009), p. 235.

Private sector groups have not been as visible in their position for or against nanotechnology nor as organised as the biotech lobby due to the diversity of sectors using nanotechnology, such as health care, food, cosmetics, chemicals, energy and information technology. The rapid expansion in patent applications along with the growing number of nanotech products on the market highlight significant commercial interests in both the US and EU which have emerged as industry leaders in this field. Public investments into research and development are also significant; the US government invested close to US$12 billion in its National Nanotechnology Initiative between 2001 and 2010 while the EU allocated €3.5 billion between 2007 and 2013 under its Seventh Framework Programme.[42] On the other side, there is currently limited commercial interest among retailers and processors to avoid nanotech products given limited consumer concerns. Having said that, this attitude may change as labelling requirements for cosmetics and possibly food come into effect in the EU. Processors may also be less inclined to apply nanotechnologies in food production on a larger scale – compared to, for instance, packaging – to avoid a possible consumer backlash.

IV. BIOTECHNOLOGY AND NANOTECHNOLOGY REGULATIONS IN THE EU AND US

In the area of biotechnology, regulatory responses in the US and EU have diverged considerably. The US follows a product-based regulatory approach based on existing legislation. The EU, on the other hand, has increasingly moved towards process-based legislation, developing a comprehensive set of regulatory texts specifically focused on GMOs. Due to the relatively recent emergence of nanotechnology, it is still too early for a direct comparison of regulatory regimes. For now, it appears that the US will again pursue a case-by-case approach while the EU has started to adapt its regulations to reflect special considerations for nanomaterials.

With regard to labelling of nanotech products, transatlantic arguments resemble those put forward in the case of modern biotechnology. US authorities tend to argue that labelling of entire product classes, for which risks have not been scientifically established, should be avoided. The EU sees labelling – already in place for biotech and under development for various nanotech products – as a useful tool to allow for consumer choice and trace back possible environmental or health impacts.

---

[42] USNNI, n.d., p. 1; Breggin et al. (2009), p. 11.

A.   Biotechnology: Product versus Process-based Regulations

The US took a lenient approach to regulating biotech products, relying on existing legislation, approval procedures and institutions, based on the assumption that the process of genetic modification does not result in a different product *per se*. Bioengineered products are assessed on a case-by-case basis by comparing them to their conventional counterparts and assessing the identified differences (if any). Risk assessments are undertaken by the companies. Regulatory oversight is divided between the Department of Agriculture, the Environmental Protection Agency and the Food and Drug Administration.

European biotech legislation has evolved significantly over the past two decades. GMO-specific legalisation – Directive 90/220[43] – was already adopted in 1990. The Directive was revised in 2001[44] and elaborated on in 2003 with Regulation 1829/2003.[45] Labelling of foods and food ingredients, which contain or consist of a GMO has been mandatory since 1997 under Regulation 258/97 on novel foods and novel food ingredients ('Novel Foods Regulation').[46] More extensive labelling and traceability requirements were adopted in 2003 through Regulation 1830/2003.[47] An overview of the main features of these legislative texts is provided in Table 20.1.

Under the 1990 Directive, approval could be granted by Member States and if no objections were raised by other Member States, the product could be marketed throughout the EU. Under the revised Directive, a qualified majority of EU Member States is required for a GM product to be placed on the European market. If Member States fail to reach a majority, the European Commission is authorised to take a decision. Risk assessments are undertaken by EU authorities, initially by the Scientific Committees on Plants or Food and since the early 2000s by the newly

---

[43]   Council Directive 90/220/EEC of 23 April 1990 on the deliberate release into the environment of genetically modified organisms.

[44]   Directive 2001/18/EC of the European Parliament and of the Council of 12 March 2001 on the deliberate release into the environment of genetically modified organisms and repealing Council Directive 90/220/EEC.

[45]   Regulation (EC) No 1829/2003 of the European Parliament and of the Council of 22 September 2003 on genetically modified food and feed.

[46]   Regulation (EC) No 258/97 of the European Parliament and of the Council of 27 January 1997 concerning novel foods and novel food ingredients.

[47]   Regulation (EC) No 1830/2003 of the European Parliament and of the Council of 22 September 2003 concerning the traceability and labelling of genetically modified organisms and the traceability of food and feed products produced from genetically modified organisms and amending Directive 2001/18/EC.

established European Food Safety Authority. The approval process was simplified by only requiring a single risk assessment and a single application to obtain approval for the deliberate release of GMOs into the environment and for use in food or feed.

The main change resulting from the legal revisions relates to the treatment of products derived from but no longer containing GMOs. Such products – provided they are 'substantially equivalent' to existing foods – initially only had to be notified, but did not have to undergo the full authorisation procedure nor did they need to be labelled. Under current regulations, the same authorisation and labelling requirements apply, irrespective of whether the GM material can still be detected in the final product. Thus, the EU over time has increasingly moved towards a centralised, entirely process-based regulatory approach.

To overcome the current deadlock in the approval process, the European Commission has suggested devolving some decision-making powers back to the Member States and (to some extent) delinking decisions on environmental release and food and feed use. Under a proposal put forward in 2010, risk assessment and EU-wide approval would still be undertaken at the Community level, but national governments would have the freedom to restrict or ban the cultivation of GMOs 'on grounds other than those related to the assessment of the adverse effect on health and environment'.[48] To alleviate possible concerns of the EU's trading partners, the proposal explicitly states that Member States would not be allowed to prohibit, restrict or impede the free circulation of approved GMOs. The proposal has met with some resistance from the European Parliament which would like to see the grounds for prohibition be expanded to include environmental concerns, while on the other side France, Britain and Germany have raised concerns over possible violation of WTO rules.[49]

B.   Nanotechnology: An Evolving Regime

Similar to GMOs, there are no moves in the US towards specific regulations for nanomaterials as a class. Rather, products are assessed on a case-by-case basis under existing regulatory processes, without specifically referencing nanomaterials or nanotechnologies. The government thereby follows 'historical precedent for other emerging technologies as well as its

---

[48]   European Commission (2010), Article 26b.
[49]   Dunmore, C. (2011). EU lawmakers vote to widen proposed GM crop bans. *Reuters*, 12 April.

standing practice for review of products that contain natural (as opposed to engineered) nanoscale materials'.[50]

Nevertheless, in its 2007 Task Force report the US Food and Drug Administration (FDA) acknowledged that 'there may be general differences in properties relevant to evaluation of safety and effectiveness (as applicable) of products using nanoscale materials compared to products using other materials. For example, size, shape, and charge of a nanoscale material can affect disposition or toxicity in the body in ways that differ from molecular forms of materials and that may be generalizable across different particle or other material types.'[51] The Task Force therefore recommended requesting submission of information regarding the effects on product safety of nanoscale materials, irrespective of whether they are subject to pre-market authorisation.

The FDA sees no need for labelling all products containing nanoscale materials, arguing that current science does not suggest that such materials *per se* present greater safety concerns than other products. Instead, labelling should be addressed on a case-by-case basis. Voluntary labelling would be possible provided that it is not misleading, and producers are encouraged to consult with the FDA in this regard.

In a 2008 regulatory review, the European Commission also concluded that 'risks [in relation to nanomaterials] can be dealt with under the current legislative framework'.[52] However, in contrast to the US approach, the EU is starting to introduce amendments to existing regulations targeted specifically at nanomaterials. So far, regulatory amendments have been largely material- rather than process-based, i.e. products are regulated differently if they contain nanomaterials, not if they were produced using nanotechnology. As elaborated below, labelling requirements for nanomaterials have been introduced for cosmetics and proposed for foods.

Due to the diversity of nanotech applications, many EU and US regulations are relevant. A detailed assessment of these regulations is provided in a 2009 report by the London School of Economics and Political Science, Chatham House, the Environmental Law Institute and the Project on Emerging Nanotechnologies.[53] This chapter focuses on EU regulations which already refer to or are being revised to deal specifically with nanomaterials: Regulation 1333/2008 ('Food Additives Regulation'),[54] the 1997

---

[50]   Breggin et al. (2009), p. 64.
[51]   USFDA (2007), p. 15.
[52]   European Commission (2008), p. 3.
[53]   Breggin et al. (2009).
[54]   Regulation (EC) No 1333/2008 of the European Parliament and of the Council of 16 December 2008 on food additives.

Novel Foods Regulation currently under review and the recently adopted Regulation 1223/2009 ('Cosmetics Regulation').[55]

1. Food regulation

The Food Additives Regulation was the first EU regulation to explicitly mention nanotechnology (although nanotechnology is not defined therein). Article 12 on 'Changes in the production process or starting material of a food additive already included in a Community list' states:

> When a food additive is already included in a Community list and there is a significant change in its production methods or in the starting materials used, or *there is a change in particle size, for example through nanotechnology,* the food additive prepared by those new methods or materials shall be considered as a different additive and a new entry in the Community list or a change in the specifications shall be required before it can be placed on the market.[56] (emphasis added)

More far-reaching requirements for nanotech products are expected to emerge out of the ongoing review of the 1997 Novel Foods Regulation, underway since 2008.[57] In its regulatory review, the European Commission concluded: 'Novel food should [include] foods modified by new production processes, such as nanotechnology and nanoscience, which might have an impact on food.'

In their respective proposals for a revision of the Novel Food Regulation, the European Parliament and the Council of the European Union agree that the definition of novel foods should include 'food containing or consisting of engineered nanomaterials'[58] as well as food produced with new production processes not used before 1997 that lead to 'significant changes in the composition or structure of the food which affect its nutritional value, metabolism or level of undesirable substances'.[59]

Both the European Parliament and the Council feel that current risk assessment methods are not adequate for assessing the risks associated with nanomaterials and that new methods should be developed.

---

[55] Regulation (EC) No 1223/2009 of the European Parliament and of the Council of 30 November 2009 on cosmetic products.

[56] A reference to changes in particle size is also included in Regulation EC 1332/2008 on food enzymes, but without explicit mention of nanotechnology.

[57] The revision has been stalled due to disagreements between the European Parliament and the Council over how to deal with meat of cloned animals on the European market.

[58] European Parliament (2009), p. 18; Council of the European Union (2009), p. 17.

[59] European Parliament (2009), p. 18; Council of the European Union (2009), p. 17.

Parliamentarians go one step further, however, demanding that food produced using nanotechnologies should not be authorised for sale 'until such specific methods have been approved for use, and an adequate safety assessment on the basis of those methods has shown that the use of the respective foods is safe'. The European Parliament has also called for all ingredients present in the form of nanomaterials to be indicated in the list of ingredients, followed by the word 'nano' in brackets.

2.   Cosmetics regulation

The Cosmetics Regulation, adopted in 2009 and set to enter into force in July 2013, is the first piece of EU legislation to define and require labelling of nanomaterials (see Table 20.1). It offers a first definition, although

Table 20.1   EU regulations on GMOs and nanomaterials in cosmetics

	Genetically modified organisms	Nanomaterials in cosmetics
EU regulatory framework	Directive 2001/18/EC (deliberate release into the environment of GMOs) Regulation (EC) No 1829/2003 (genetically modified food and feed) Regulation (EC) No 1830/2003 (traceability and labelling)	Regulation (EC) No 1223/2009 (cosmetics)
Scope	Deliberate release, the placing on the market and labelling of GMOs. GMO: an organism, with the exception of human beings, in which the genetic material has been altered in a way that does not occur naturally by mating and/or natural recombination.	Rules applied to any cosmetic product made available on the market, including those containing nanomaterials. Nanomaterial: an insoluble or biopersistant and intentionally manufactured material with one or more external dimensions, or an internal structure, on the scale from 1 to 100 nm (definition to be adapted to technical and scientific progress and to definitions subsequently agreed at international level).

Table 20.1   (continued)

	Genetically modified organisms	Nanomaterials in cosmetics
Risk assessment	Risk assessment carried out by the European Food Safety Authority. One risk assessment for cultivation, importation, processing into food/feed or industrial products.	Safety assessment carried out by producer prior to placing on the market (all products).
Approval	EC proposes approval or refusal of authorisation to the Member States Decision by the Standing Committee on the Food Chain and Animal Health by qualified majority. If no or negative opinion, decision passed on to the Council of Ministers. If no qualified majority achieved, EC can adopt the decision.	No formal approval, but submission of certain information to the Commission prior to placing on the market, including the presence of substances in the form of nanomaterials. Producer must also notify cosmetic products containing nanomaterials to the Commission, incl. safety data of the nanomaterial and 'reasonably foreseeable exposure conditions' EC can request an opinion from Scientific Committee for Consumer Safety and, in case of risk or insufficient data, prohibit the cosmetic product in question.
Labelling and traceability	Mandatory labelling and traceability of food and feed containing or produced from GMOs (regardless of whether the GMO is still detectable in the final product). Exemption for conventional products unintentionally containing < 0.9% of GMOs.	All ingredients present in the form of nanomaterials should be indicated in the list of ingredients and names of such ingredients should be followed by the word 'nano' in brackets.

leaving it open for amendment. While no particular approval process or safety assessment is required, producers need to inform the Commission of the presence of nanomaterials, including safety data of the nanomaterial and 'reasonably foreseeable exposure conditions' (among other information). The Commission reserves the right to request an opinion about the product from the Scientific Committee for Consumer Safety and, if deemed necessary, to ban the product from the European market. The regulation also for the first time requires labelling, stipulating that nanomaterials are included in the list of ingredients with the word 'nano' in brackets.

V.   WTO IMPLICATIONS

Exporters of GM commodities have repeatedly used the threat of a WTO challenge to lobby for more lenient biotech regulations. In 2003, the first (and so far only) case was launched at the WTO where the US, Canada and Argentina challenged the EU's application of its approval procedures for biotech products and the safeguard measures applied by certain EU Member States (see Box 20.1). In its ruling in favour of the complainants, the panel successfully skirted the issue of product safety, focusing instead on procedural questions. Nevertheless, the panel report, along with other past WTO cases, provides some useful lessons for current and future regulations of nanotech products. It is important to stress, however, that nanotechnology regulations have to date not evoked similar transatlantic trade tensions and EU-US engagement on this issue has been much more conciliatory and constructive than in the case of GMOs.

A.   *De Facto* Moratorium on New Approvals

The proposal by the European Parliament to suspend marketing authorization for novel foods containing nanomaterials until new risk assessment methods have been approved raises possible parallels with the *de facto* moratorium imposed on GMO approvals. The panel in the *EC – Biotech case* ruled that the moratorium had led to 'undue delay' and therefore violated WTO rules. In this context, the panel rejected the EU's justification that the *de facto* moratorium had been imposed pending finalisation of new legislation, arguing that objections by some Member States and segments of public opinion to the granting of approvals under the old Directive was not a sufficient reason to justify the delay. The panel also noted that the Commission could have implemented alternative measures to address the inadequacies of the legislation in the meantime, such as voluntary commitments from applicants or conditional approval of

---

BOX 20.1   EC – BIOTECH CASE

In 2003, the US, Canada and Argentina launched a dispute against the EU. Specifically, the three countries claimed that the EU had contravened WTO rules with its *de facto* moratorium on approvals on new GMOs in place since 1998, its failure to approve a number of specific biotech products and national-level bans imposed by France, Germany, Greece, Austria, Italy and Luxembourg on the marketing of certain EU-approved GM products. After almost 42 months of deliberations, the WTO panel finally released its much-anticipated report in September 2006.[i]

In a nutshell, the panel sided with the complaining countries on all three counts. The panel concluded that the general *de facto* moratorium and most of the product-specific measures had led to 'undue delay' in the completion of the EU's approval procedures for biotech products, thereby breaching the EU's obligations under the SPS Agreement. The panel also rejected the national bans as precautionary measures, but left it open for Member States to either lift the bans or provide a risk assessment to justify their measures. The EU did not appeal the decision.

Note: [i] *European Communities – Measures Affecting the Approval and Marketing of Biotech Products – Reports of the Panel.* WT/DS291/R, WT/DS292/R and WT/DS293/R. 29 September 2006. For a detailed analysis of the ruling, see Baumüller and Oliva (2006).

---

applications. A similar conclusion could conceivably apply to a *de facto* moratorium on nano food approvals.

Two additional points are worth noting. The panel concluded that the length of time was not necessarily the deciding factor for judging a delay to be undue, but rather the reason for the delay which needed to be assessed on a case-by-case basis. Moreover, the panel did not regard the *de facto* moratorium itself as a sanitary or phytosanitary (SPS) measure – and therefore not subject to the SPS Agreement's requirements for scientific evidence and risk assessment – but rather as an application of an SPS measure (i.e. the EU's GMO approval procedures). As a result, the panel focused its analysis on procedural issues. Thus, should a *de facto* moratorium be placed on the approval of nano foods, the process would likely also be investigated individually for each product to assess whether there had been an 'undue delay'.

B.   Like Product Discrimination

A question that is often raised with regard to GMOs is whether biotech products should be regarded as 'like' their conventional counterparts. Both the General Agreement on Tariffs and Trade 1994 (GATT, Article III.4) and the Agreement on Technical Barriers to Trade (TBT Agreement, Article 2.1) require WTO Members to accord treatment to imported products no less favourable than that accorded to like products of national origin. As noted above, the US regards bioengineered products as simply another form of genetic modification which should therefore not be treated as a separate product category. With its move towards process-based regulations, the EU clearly regards products involving genetic modification as distinct.

Similar to its position in the case of GMOs, the US argues that products containing nanomaterials are not a distinct class of products and existing regulations and safety assessments for specific products are deemed sufficient. In the evolving European regime, the approach is less clearly articulated. So far, regulatory amendments and proposals have focused on products containing nanomaterials rather than produced using nanotechnology, no matter whether nanomaterials are still present in the final product. While the regulations may still undergo the same evolution as the GMO regime, this seems unlikely given the difficulties in adopting a unified regulatory regime that can deal with the diversity of nanotechnologies, the overlap in definitional proposals by the Parliament and Council and the application of labelling requirements only to nano-ingredients.

To date, no precise definition of what constitutes a 'like product' has been adopted in the WTO and assessments are made on a case-by-case basis. Nevertheless, four criteria have been used in WTO jurisprudence to analyse 'likeness', i.e. (1) the physical properties of the products; (2) the extent to which the products are capable of serving the same or similar end-uses; (3) the extent to which consumers perceive and treat the products as alternative means of performing particular functions in order to satisfy a particular want or demand; and (4) the international classification of the products for tariff purposes.[60] Each of these criteria should be assessed

---

[60]   E.g. *Japan – Taxes on Alcoholic Beverages – Report of the Appellate Body.* WT/DS8/AB/R, WT/DS10/AB/R and WT/DS11/AB/R, 4 October 1996, pp.19–21; *European Communities – Measures Affecting Asbestos and Asbestos-Containing Products – Report of the Appellate Body.* WT/DS135/AB/R, 12 March 2001, paras 101–103; *Thailand – Customs and Fiscal Measures on Cigarettes from the Philippines – Report of the Panel.* WT/DS371/R, 15 November 2010, paras 7.432–

along with other evidence to arrive at an overall determination regarding the 'likeness' of two products.[61] WTO panels have also examined internal regulations to assess whether a Member regards different products as similar.[62]

The *EC – Biotech* case provides little guidance on this issue, as the panel did not address the question whether biotech and non-biotech products should be seen as 'like'. One point worth noting, however, relates to the panel's focus on the foreign origin of the product as the motivation for the discrimination between biotech and non-biotech products. Thus, the panel concluded that Argentina had failed to show that imported biotech products had been treated less favourably as a result of their foreign origin rather than, for instance, perceived difference in safety of biotech and non-biotech products.

Noteworthy in this context is a recent panel ruling in the *US – Clove Cigarette* case.[63] Indonesia had challenged a US ban on cigarettes containing certain additives, arguing that the exclusion of menthol cigarettes from the ban amounted to *de facto* discrimination against clove cigarettes imported from Indonesia. While previous disputes had assessed likeness under GATT Article III.4, the *US – Clove Cigarette* case for the first time ruled on this issue under the TBT Agreement. Importantly, the panel concluded that likeness needed to be assessed bearing in mind the objective of the technical regulation at issue (rather than focusing primarily on the competitive relationship between products as was generally the case in GATT-related jurisprudence). Thus, products 'may be considered "like" in certain contexts but not in others' (para. 7.226). In this case, the objective, i.e. to reduce youth smoking, informed the comparison of the products' physical characteristics, the choice of relevant consumers and the scope of substitutability of products. Should a technical regulation affecting nano-products be subject to a dispute under the TBT Agreement,

---

7.451; *Philippines – Taxes on Distilled Spirits – Reports of the Panel.* WT/DS396/R and WT/DS403/R, 15 August 2011, paras 7.30–7.90; *United States – Measures Affecting the Production and Sale of Clove Cigarettes – Report of the Panel.* WT/DS406/R, 2 September 2011, paras 7.70–7.248; *United States – Measures concerning the Importation, Marketing and Sale of Tuna and Tuna Products – Report of the Panel.* WT/DS381/R, 15 September 2011, paras 7.213–7.251.

[61] *European Communities – Measures Affecting Asbestos and Asbestos-Containing Products – Report of the Appellate Body.* WT/DS135/AB/R, 12 March 2001, para. 109.

[62] E.g. *Philippines – Taxes on Distilled Spirits – Reports of the Panel.* WT/DS396/R and WT/DS403/R, 15 August 2011, paras 7.72–7.74

[63] *United States – Measures Affecting the Production and Sale of Clove Cigarettes – Report of the Panel.* WT/DS406/R, 2 September 2011, paras 7.70–7.248.

the aim of the regulation would likely play an equally important role in the analysis of likeness.

C.   Safeguard Clauses for EU Member States

The leeway for EU Member States to implement safeguard measures such as the banning of EU-wide approved GM products was one of the central questions in the *EC – Biotech* case. The national bans had been imposed despite a favourable assessment by the competent authority of the Member State where the application for the marketing of the product had been made. Under European legislation, Member States are explicitly allowed to invoke such safeguards if new or additional information has become available that affects the environmental risk assessment or the reassessment of existing information.[64] No such clause exists with regard to nanotechnology products, but a similar situation could conceivably occur if EU Member States decide to ban a nanotech product from their market that has been approved at the EU level.

While the panel in the *EC – Biotech* case rejected the EU's argument that the national bans had been imposed as a precautionary measure, it did not rule against the bans on principle. Rather, it argued that the studies and documents provided by the countries to justify the bans did not constitute adequate risk assessments in line with requirements under the SPS Agreement. Also, the panel conceded that a national government may at times follow a divergent scientific view, but such divergent views should have been reflected in the original risk assessment undertaken before approving the GMOs. The bans could continue if WTO-compliant risk assessments could be produced that would be deemed a valid basis for the bans.

How a panel would judge the new Commission proposal to allow bans on cultivation of GM crops within Member States' territories is difficult to predict. First of all, the panel would have to decide whether the bans would fall under its jurisdiction, given that they would not necessarily restrict the movement of GM seeds, but only their planting. If judged to be a WTO-related measure, the panel would also need to assess (among other issues) whether there was sufficient justification for the bans. Thus, whether bans can be imposed only on grounds other than environmental and health impacts as proposed by Commission or also on environmen-

---

[64]   Directive 2001/18/EC, Article 23; Regulation (EC) No 258/97, Article 12. See also above note 36 on the recent judgement of the European Court of Justice clarifying the conditions under which such emergency measures can be invoked.

tal grounds as demanded by the Parliament could influence the decision under which agreement to evaluate the measures and consequently which requirements they would need to fulfil. Bans imposed for reasons that are not related to environmental and health impacts would not fall under the scope of the SPS Agreement and would therefore not be subject to the Agreement's requirements for scientific justification.

D.   International Standards

Countries tend to stand a higher chance of having their national measures accepted as WTO compliant if they are based on international standards. Indeed, both the TBT and SPS Agreements explicitly encourage the use of such standards. The SPS Agreement cites the Codex Alimentarius Commission (CAC), the Office International de Epizooties (OIE; World Organization for Animal Health) and the Secretariat of the International Plant Protection Convention (IPPC) as international standard-setting bodies whose standards are presumed to be consistent with the SPS Agreement. According to existing WTO jurisprudence under the exceptions to the GATT 1994, the effort made to find a multilateral solution before imposing a unilateral measure is also relevant, even if no agreement was actually concluded.[65]

Various standards and agreements already exist in the area of biotechnology. Among them, the Codex Alimentarius Commission has adopted several guidelines for foods derived from modern biotechnology, although discussions on biotech labelling remain stalled. In 2003, the Cartagena Protocol on Biosafety entered into force, which regulates the transboundary movement, transit, handling and use of living modified organisms.

While the US is a member of Codex, it has not signed or ratified the Cartagena Protocol and is unlikely to do so anytime soon. This raises the question to what extent international agreements are relevant in a dispute if some parties to the dispute are not signatories. The panel in the *EC – Biotech* case did not feel that it was obliged to take international treaties into account in the interpretation of WTO rules if not, at least, all parties to the dispute have ratified these treaties (although it agreed that it had the discretion to do so to examine the ordinary meaning of terms).

International discussions on nanotechnology are still at an early stage

---

[65]   E.g. *United States – Import Prohibition Of Certain Shrimp And Shrimp Products – Report of the Appellate Body*. WT/DS58/AB/R, 12 October 1998, paras 166–172.

and to date no proposal to develop a multilateral agreement similar to the Cartagena Protocol has been put forward. Similarly, no new standards on nanotechnology or amendments to existing standards have so far been adopted by the CAC, the OIE or the IPPC. The *International Organization for Standardization (ISO) Technical Committee 229 on Nanotechnologies* set up in 2005 has published 12 standards (as of June 2011) dealing with issues such as terminology and definitions and protocols for toxicity testing and environmental impact studies.[66] To what extent these would qualify as 'international standards' in the context of the WTO is unclear.

Moreover, the OECD has set up two working parties to deal with nanotechnology, including:

- The *Working Party on Manufactured Nanomaterials* as a subsidiary to the Chemicals Committee to assess the implications of the use of nanomaterials for human health and environment safety, focussing on testing and assessment methods; and
- The *Working Party on Nanotechnology* as a subsidiary to the Committee for Scientific and Technological Policy to provide advice on emerging policy issues of science, technology and innovation related to the responsible development of nanotechnology.

Given the restricted membership of the OECD, it seems unlikely that any resulting standards or agreements would be judged to be 'international' for purposes of the SPS or TBT Agreements.

Also noteworthy are discussions at the *International Conference on Chemicals Management* of the United Nations Environment Programme, which at its second meeting adopted a resolution on nanotechnologies and manufactured nanomaterials, that calls on governments and industry to safeguard human health and the environment, and requests that governments and other stakeholders facilitate access to relevant information and develop a report on this issue for its next meeting in July 2012.

VI. FINAL REMARKS

This comparative analysis suggests that European rejection of GMOs does not necessarily stem from a general distrust of new and emerging

---

[66]   The standards are available at http://www.iso.org/iso/iso_technical_committee?commid=381983. Breggin et al. (2009), p. 25.

technologies. While many European consumers may indeed be more cautious in their support for scientific progress – combined with a certain level of cynicism regarding the ability and willingness of companies to regulate themselves – the more open attitude towards nanotechnologies among both consumers and NGOs in the EU indicates that more complex considerations are at play. Similarly, European regulations of emerging technologies do not necessarily follow predetermined paths, but need to be anticipated and judged against a multi-faceted backdrop of interests and concerns that will influence regulations of different technologies in different ways. At the same time, US authorities do not blindly accept any emerging technologies as simply a continuation of the past, but are open to assess new risks that these technologies may pose and that might require a regulatory response.

As a result, general conclusions about the likely WTO implications of emerging technology regulations need to be drawn with caution. Some of the same questions are likely to resurface as legislation adapts to technological change. In particular the flexibility of governments under WTO rules to respond to the preferences of their constituents remains a recurring theme, as countries seek to balance trade obligations with demands from consumers, civil society, industry and political actors. The nanotechnology experience shows that continuous dialogue within countries and with regulators in key trading partners can provide a good basis for early coordination to head off tensions before regulatory responses are set. It remains to be seen whether this constructive engagement can continue, or whether the transatlantic relationship will descend into the same level of antagonism as in the case of GMOs.

BIBLIOGRAPHY

Anderson, K., Damania, R. & Jackson, L.A. (2004). *Trade, Standards, and the Political Economy of Genetically Modified Food.* Washington D.C.: The World Bank.

Baumüller, H. & Oliva, M.J. (2006). WTO/EC Biotech Panel Report: Key Issues and Implications. *Environmental Policy and Law Journal*, 36(6), pp. 257–264.

Baumüller, H. & Tansey, G. (2008). Responding to Change. In G. Tansey & T. Rajotte (eds) *The Future Control of Food: A Guide to International Negotiations and Rules on Intellectual Property, Biodiversity and Food Security.* London: Earthscan, pp. 171–196.

Baumüller, H., Oliva, M.J. & Mohan, S. (2006). *Biotechnology: Addressing Key Trade and Sustainability Issues.* Geneva: International Centre for Trade and Sustainable Development.

Bowman, D.M., D'Silva, J. & van Calster, G. (2010). Defining Nanomaterials for the Purpose of Regulation within the European Union. *European Journal of Risk Regulation*, 1(2), pp. 115–122.

Breggin, L., Falkner, R., Jaspers, N., Pendergrass, J. & Porters, R. (2009). *Securing the Promise of Nanotechnologies: Towards Transatlantic Regulatory Cooperation.* London and

Washington D.C.: London School of Economics and Political Science, Chatham House, the Environmental Law Institute and the Project on Emerging Nanotechnologies at the Woodrow Wilson International Center for Scholars.

Charles, D. (2001). *Lords of the Harvest: Biotech, Big Money, and the Future of Food.* Jackson: Basic Books.

Codex (2003). *Principles for the Risk Analysis of Foods derived from Modern Biotechnology.* Rome: Codex Alimentarius Commission.

Council of the European Union (2009). *Proposal for a Regulation of the European Parliament and of the Council on novel foods and amending Regulation (EC) No XXX/XXXX.* Brussels: Council of the European Union.

Currall, S.C. (2009). Nanotechnology and Society: New Insights into Public Perceptions. *Nature Nanotechnology*, 4(2), pp. 79–80.

Dunmore, C. (2011). EU lawmakers vote to widen proposed GM crop bans. *Reuters*, 12 April.

ETC Group, 2003. *The Big Down: From Genomes to Atoms.* Winnipeg: ETC Group.

Eurobarometer (2010). Biotechnology Report, Brussels: Directorate-General for Communication. Brussels: European Commission.

European Commission (2008). *Communication from the Commission to the European Parliament, the Council and the European Economic and Social Committee – Regulatory Aspects of Nanomaterials, COM(2008) 366 final.* Brussels: European Commission.

European Commission (2010). *Proposal for a Regulation of the European Parliament and of the Council amending Directive 2001/18/EC as regards the possibility for the Member States to restrict or prohibit the cultivation of GMOs in their territory, COM(2010) 375 final.* Brussels: European Commission.

Court of Justice of the European Union (2011). *The Court rules on the conditions under which the French authorities could introduce a provisional prohibition on the cultivation of MON 810 maize.* Press Release No 86/11, Luxembourg: Luxembourg.

European Parliament (2009). *European Parliament legislative resolution of 25 March 2009 on the proposal for a regulation of the European Parliament and of the Council on novel foods and amending Regulation (EC) No XXX/XXXX [common procedure] (COM(2007)0872 – C6-0027/2008 – 2008/0002(COD)).* Brussels: European Parliament.

Falkner, R. (2009). The Troubled Birth of the 'Biotech Century': Global Corporate Power and Its Limits. In J. Clapp & D. Fuchs (eds) *Corporate Power in Global Agrifood Governance.* Cambridge, MA: MIT Press, pp. 225–252.

FAO/WHO (2010). *FAO/WHO Expert meeting on the application of nanotechnologies in the food and agriculture sectors: potential food safety implications – Meeting report.* Rome and New York: Food and Agriculture Organization of the United Nations and World Health Organization.

Gallup (2011). Nutrition and Food. Available at: http://www.gallup.com/poll/6424/nutrition-food.aspx [Accessed June 18, 2011].

Gaskell, G., Eyck, T.T., Jackson, J. & Veltri, G. (2005). Imagining Nanotechnology: Cultural Support for Technological Innovation in Europe and the United States. *Public Understanding of Science*, 14(1), pp. 81–90.

ICTSD (2010). Amflora: Europe's New Hot Potato. *Bridges*, 14(2), p. 16.

ISAAA (2010). *Global Status of Commercialized Biotech/GM Crops: 2010.* New York: International Service for the Acquisition of Agri-biotech Applications.

Macnaghtan, P. (2008). From Bio to Nano: Learning the Lessons, Interrogating the Comparisons. In K. David & P.B. Thompson (eds) *What Can Nanotechnology Learn From Biotechnology? Social and Ethical Lessons for Nanoscience from the Debate over Agrifood Biotechnology and GMOs.* Maryland Heights: Academic Press, pp. 107–123.

Osgood, D. (2001). Dig It Up: Global Civil Society's Responses to Plant Biotechnology. In H. Anheier, M. Glasius & M. Kaldor (eds) *Global Civil Society 2001.* London: Centre for the Study of Global Governance, London School of Economics, pp. 79–107.

PEN (2011a). *Nanotech-enabled Consumer Products Continue to Rise*, Washington D.C.: Project On Emerging Nanotechnologies, The Woodrow Wilson International Center

For Scholars. Available at http://www.nanotechproject.org/news/archive/9231 [Accessed October 26, 2011].

PEN (2011b). *Nanotechnology Map*, Washington D.C.: Project On Emerging Nanotechnologies, The Woodrow Wilson International Center For Scholars. Available at http://www.nanotechproject.org/inventories/map/ [Accessed October 26, 2011].

Press Release No 86/11 (2012). Le maïs transgénique MON810 reste interdit en France. *Le Monde*, January 13. Luxembourg.

Runge, C.F., Bagnara, G.L. & Jackson, L.A. (2001). Differing U.S. and European Perspectives on GMOs: Political, Economic and Cultural Issues. *Estey Centre Journal of International Law and Trade Policy*, 2(2), pp. 221–234.

Sandler, R. & Kay, W.D. (2006). The GMO-Nanotech (Dis)Analogy? *Bulletin of Science, Technology & Society*, 26(1), pp. 57–62.

Satterfield, T., Kandlikar, M., Beaudrie, C.E.H., Conti, J. & Herr Harthorn, B. (2009). Anticipating the Perceived Risk of Nanotechnologies. *Nature Nanotechnology*, 4(11), pp. 752–758.

Thompson, P.B. (2008). Nano and Bio: How are they Alike? How are they Different? In K. David & P.B. Thompson (eds) *What Can Nanotechnology Learn From Biotechnology? Social and Ethical Lessons for Nanoscience from the Debate over Agrifood Biotechnology and GMOs*. Maryland Heights: Academic Press, pp. 125–155.

USFDA (1992). *Statement of Policy – Foods Derived from New Plant Varieties*. Washington D.C.: United States Food and Drug Administration.

USFDA (2001). *Premarket Notice Concerning Bioengineered Foods*. Washington D.C.: United States Food and Drug Administration.

USFDA (2007). *Nanotechnology: A Report of the U.S. Food and Drug Administration Nanotechnology Task Force*. Washington D.C.: United States Food and Drug Administration.

USFDA (2011). *Guidance for Industry: Considering Whether an FDA-Regulated Product Involves the Application of Nanotechnology*. Washington D.C.: United States Food and Drug Administration.

USNNI (n.d.). *National Nanotechnology Initiative: Investments by Agency FY 2001–2010*. Washington D.C.: United States National Nanotechnology Initiative.

PART IV

DISPUTE SETTLEMENT ISSUES

21. Standard of review of health and environmental regulations by WTO panels*
Lukasz Gruszczynski

I. INTRODUCTION

The issue of the applicable standard of review in health and environment-related trade disputes has recently become prominent in scholarly discussions. While earlier research tended to concentrate on specific substantive requirements of WTO law,[1] more recent scholarship has turned its attention to this specific procedural question. This shift is most probably a result of developments in WTO case law. The applicable standard of review had a direct impact on the outcome of the *EC – Biotech Products*[2] dispute. It was also one of the major issues in the Appellate Body ruling in *US/Canada – Continued Suspension*[3] and in the more recent *Australia – Apples* case.[4] The latter report demonstrated that the standard of review, at least in the context of the WTO Agreement on the Application of Sanitary and Phytosanitary Measures (SPS Agreement),[5] remains ambiguous and will most probably generate further controversies in future WTO disputes.

---

* Some parts of this chapter draw on my earlier article: (2011), 'How deeply we should go? In a search of appropriate standard of review in the SPS cases', *European Journal of Risk Regulation*, 2(1), 111–114.

[1] There are important exceptions, *cf. e.g.*, Christoforou, 1999–2000; Button, 2004.

[2] Panel Report, *European Communities – Measures Affecting the Approval and Marketing of Biotech Products*, WT/DS291/R, WT/DS292/R, WT/DS293/R, Add.1 to Add.9, and Corr.1, adopted 21 November 2006, DSR 2006:III–VIII, 847.

[3] Appellate Body Report, *United States – Continued Suspension of Obligations in the EC – Hormones Dispute*, WT/DS320/AB/R, adopted 14 November 2008, DSR 2008:X, 3507 and Appellate Body Report, *Canada – Continued Suspension of Obligations in the EC – Hormones Dispute*, WT/DS321/AB/R, adopted 14 November 2008.

[4] Appellate Body Report, *Australia – Measures Affecting the Importation of Apples from New Zealand*, WT/DS367/AB/R, adopted 17 December 2010.

[5] Agreement on the Application of Sanitary and Phytosanitary Measures, 1867 UNTS 493, signed on 15 April 1994.

This chapter analyses the existing WTO case law in order to determine the basic parameters that characterize the applicable standard of review in health and environment-related trade disputes. This should allow a critical assessment of the current practice, identifying both its advantages and disadvantages. The analysis presented here is, however, restricted in two ways. First, the chapter is primarily interested in the standard of review applicable to domestic factual determinations rather than to the legal interpretation advanced by the WTO Members or degree of scrutiny exercised by the Appellate Body over panels' findings. Second, the analysis is limited to the SPS Agreement, and specifically to those provisions which require the review of scientific evidence. While other WTO agreements, such the General Agreement on Tariffs and Trade 1994 (GATT 1994) or the Agreement on Technical Barriers to Trade (TBT Agreement), may be relevant when assessing national health and environmental measures, the problem of applicable standard of review under those agreements remains either a secondary or an abstract issue. The relevant case law under the GATT 1994 (e.g. *EC – Measures Affecting Asbestos and Asbestos-Containing Products* or *Brazil – Measures Affecting Imports of Retreaded Tyres*) did not require panels to make really complex factual determinations. The existence of risk related to the use of asbestos products was rather uncontroversial and supported by significant scientific evidence. The same was true for risks of mosquito-borne diseases (e.g. dengue or yellow fever) connected with accumulation of waste tyres.[6] On the other hand, any discussion on the standard of review applied to scientific evidence under the TBT Agreement remains theoretical, as until now no case has been decided which would be directly relevant to the issues addressed here.

This chapter is organized as follows: The first part introduces the concept of standard of review and discusses its different meanings. The second part focuses on the SPS Agreement, briefly describing its basic disciplines and analysing in some detail the applicable standard of review in the early SPS case law. The third part addresses the two most recent rulings (i.e. *US/Canada – Continued Suspension* and *Australia – Apples*), both of which extensively elaborated on the applicable standard of review. The chapter concludes that the WTO dispute settlement bodies have failed to articulate a clear and operable model, and their jurisprudence remains ambiguous or sometimes even contradictory.

---

[6]   Note also that none of the parties in those disputes argued that any specific standard of review should have been applied by the WTO panel.

II. THE STANDARD OF REVIEW IN WTO DISPUTE SETTLEMENT PRACTICE

Standard of review is conventionally understood as the level of scrutiny that is applied by a superior body (a court or a higher administrative authority) over a decision taken by a lower body that is subject to review. Depending on the one's perspective, the standard of review can be therefore defined as 'the degree of deference or discretion that the court accords to legislator or regulator' or 'degree of intrusiveness or invasiveness into the legislator's or regulator's decision-making process'.[7] Consequently, standard of review determines the extent of discretionary powers enjoyed by a lower body (i.e. lower court or administrative authority) in making certain determinations. In theory, the standard of review may range from *de novo* review to full deference. Under *de novo* review, a superior body is able to review all the determinations made by an inferior body and substitute them with its own. A fully deferential standard restricts the reviewing powers of a superior body to procedural compliance (i.e. whether prescribed procedure was followed) and bars review of the substance. Between these two extremes there are a number of less or more deferential/ *de novo* types of review. In practice they appear under different names, such as the 'arbitrary and capricious' standard, 'clearly erroneous' standard, or 'reasonable deference'.[8]

The concept of standard of review is common to many national jurisdictions, including all major continental and Anglo-Saxon systems. In a national legal context, it serves as a mechanism for allocating the power between different branches of government (i.e. executive and judicial). A deferential standard favours the body that takes an initial decision (e.g. executive) while *de novo* review introduces additional checks by another body (e.g. judicial). Just as there is no optimal and one-size-fits-all model for the distribution of powers within a state, so too there is also no ideal and universal standard of review. The level of intrusiveness varies from jurisdiction to jurisdiction, reflecting local particularities or current preferences of society – e.g. a need to guarantee a greater oversight by courts over activities of administrative agencies.[9]

On the international level, the standard of review fulfils a similar function. It determines, alongside the substantive obligations, the distribution

---

[7] Bohanes and Lockhart, 2009, p. 379.

[8] For an overview of the approaches in US courts see: Strauss, Rakoff and Farina, 2003, p. 902.

[9] Bohanes and Lockhart, 2009, p. 380.

of powers between national governments and international bodies. *De novo* review transfers a power to international level at the expense of prerogatives of domestic governments. A deferential standard of review has the opposite effect, empowering national bodies and limiting the competences of international authorities. As noted by one scholar in the context of WTO rules: 'granting greater deference to the decisions of the state is equivalent to increasing the substantive power of the state to impact trade.'[10] For example, if a WTO panel has only limited competence to re-evaluate scientific evidence which constitutes a basis for a national SPS measure (e.g. whether growth promotion hormones in cattle increase the risk of cancer for humans consuming beef), national authorities gain a wider regulatory freedom. They may evaluate and assess scientific data in a rather unconstrained way, reflecting local preferences and particularities. On the other hand, if the scientific support for a municipal trade measure is reviewed afresh, such measure may be regarded as unjustified if a panel comes to different conclusions than a national government. This aspect (i.e. distribution of powers) was clearly recognized by the Appellate Body in *EC – Hormones*, when it stated: 'the standard of review (. . .) must reflect the balance established [in WTO law] between the jurisdictional competences conceded by the Members to the WTO and the jurisdictional competences retained by the Members for themselves.'[11]

Before going further, one should also conceptually distinguish between the standard of review applied to factual determinations, and that applied to legal determinations. The first category relates to the review of factual findings made by a body whose decision is subject to review (i.e. factual determinations underlying a regulatory decision of a WTO Member), and will be discussed in more detail below. The second category is concerned with the legal interpretations advanced by such a body. It is enough to mention that in the context of the WTO, both the Appellate Body and panels enjoy a wide margin of discretion when interpreting WTO provisions and are not obliged to follow the interpretations advanced by the parties to the dispute.[12] This may be labelled as an intrusive standard of review and it is conventionally justified by the need to maintain consistency in the interpretation of WTO provisions.[13]

---

[10]   Guzman, 2008, p. 4.
[11]   Appellate Body Report, *EC Measures Concerning Meat and Meat Products (Hormones)*, WT/DS26/AB/R, WT/DS48/AB/R, adopted 13 February 1998, DSR 1998:I, 135, para. 115.
[12]   Oesch, 2003, p. 18.
[13]   Ehlermann and Lockhart, 2004, p. 498. In particular, Ehlermann and Lockhart noted that deferring to the WTO Members' interpretations would lead

In addition, one may also speak about the standard of review applied by a higher reviewing body to determinations made by a lower body (if a review system is based on two instances). In the context of the WTO, this type of review determines the extent of scrutiny of the Appellate Body of a panel's findings (both legal and factual). According to Article 17.6 of the Dispute Settlement Understanding (DSU),[14] such a review is limited to issues of law covered in a panel report and legal interpretations developed by a panel. This in principle excludes any review of factual determinations made by a panel. However, the standard of review applied by a panel when examining evidence put forward by the parties to a dispute falls within the purview of the Appellate Body's review. The same is true for 'consistency or inconsistency of a given fact or set of facts with the requirements of a given treaty provision', which is clearly a legal issue.[15]

In principle, WTO law does not provide any explicit standard of review to be followed by panels when evaluating and assessing the factual elements of a dispute. The only exception is the Anti-Dumping Agreement,[16] which stipulates in Article 17.6 (i) that:

> in its assessment of the facts of the matter, the panel shall determine whether the authorities' establishment of the facts was proper and whether their evaluation of those facts was unbiased and objective. If the establishment of the facts was proper and the evaluation was unbiased and objective, even though the panel might have reached a different conclusion, the evaluation shall not be overturned.

The above standard is conventionally described as a deferential one as it mainly concentrates on procedural rather than substantive compliance (i.e. unbiased and objective evaluation). Consequently, it gives a considerable margin of discretion to national authorities when making factual determinations during the course of an anti-dumping proceeding.

None of the other WTO agreements, including the SPS Agreement, contain any comparable provision. As a consequence, it was for the WTO dispute settlement bodies to identify the applicable standard of review (either as a general standard to be applied across different agreements

---

to the 'Tower of Legal Babel'; this would mean that 'the obligations assumed by WTO Members, and the rights acquired, would differ from Member to Member, undermining the core objectives of the rule-based system'.

[14] Understanding on Rules and Procedures Governing the Settlement of Disputes, 1869 UNTS 401, signed on 15 April 1994.

[15] Appellate Body, *EC – Hormones*, para. 132.

[16] Agreement on Implementation of Article VI of the General Agreement on Tariffs and Trade 1994, 1868 UNTS 201, signed on 15 April 1994.

or a specific variation that would be applicable in the context of a particular agreement). At least on its face, the Appellate Body opted for the first option and identified Article 11 of the DSU as a rule determining the applicable standard of review for the entire WTO system (except for the Anti-Dumping Agreement). According to the Appellate Body in *EC – Hormones*, Article 11 'articulates with great succinctness but with sufficient clarity the appropriate standard of review for panels in respect of both the ascertainment of facts and the legal characterization of such facts under the relevant agreement'.[17] On that basis, the Appellate Body vaguely characterized the applicable standard as 'neither *de novo* review as such, nor "total deference", but rather the "objective assessment of the facts"'.[18] The Appellate Body also added that:

> many panels have in the past refused to undertake de novo review, wisely, since under current practice and systems, they are in any case poorly suited to engage in such a review. On the other hand, 'total deference to the findings of the national authorities', it has been well said, could not ensure an 'objective assessment' as foreseen by Article 11 of the DSU.[19]

A closer look at the statement of the Appellate Body reveals, however, its deficiencies. The Appellate Body, by merely describing an applicable standard of review as objective, missed the opportunity to provide future panels with more precise interpretative guidelines. In particular, it was noted that 'this broad formulation does not assist in defining an operable standard of review because any assessment of the facts, whether highly deferential, marginally deferential, or not deferential at all, can be "objective"'.[20] Although, this observation is probably overstated (at the end of the day the Appellate Body at least identified what types of review are excluded in WTO law), it highlights the vagueness inherent in the statement. Even if one eliminates the extremes (*de novo* review and total deference) the remaining range of options remains quite broad.

One may also have some doubts about the choice of Article 11 of the DSU as the appropriate legal basis for determining the applicable standard of review.[21] The expression 'objective' seems to be more concerned

---

[17]   Appellate Body, *EC – Hormones*, para. 116.
[18]   *Ibid.*, para. 117.
[19]   *Ibid.*
[20]   Bohanes and Lockhart, 2009, p. 389.
[21]   Croley and Jackson once suggested that Article 3.2 DSU would be a more appropriate provision. In the relevant part it provides: '[r]ecommendations and rulings of the DSB cannot add to or diminish the rights and obligations provided in the covered agreements' (Croley and Jackson, 1996, p. 199).

with guarantees, in the context of WTO law, of due process rights (i.e. fairness and impartiality of a panel, neutrality in assessment of presented evidence) rather than with determination of the applicable standard of review.[22] In fact, the Appellate Body expressly recognized this aspect of Article 11, when it held that:

> [t]he duty to make an objective assessment of the facts is, among other things, an obligation to consider the evidence presented to a panel and to make factual findings on the basis of that evidence. The deliberate disregard of, or refusal to consider, the evidence submitted to a panel is incompatible with a panel's duty to make an objective assessment of the facts.[23]

Nevertheless, the holding of the Appellate Body in *EC – Hormones* has become a point of reference for WTO dispute settlement bodies and since then Article 11 has been cited as a rule that elucidates the required level of scrutiny. Thus, Article 11 may be regarded as having a dual function: a provision that determines (very imperfectly) the applicable standard of review, and a rule which establishes due process rights for the parties to a dispute.

Although the objective standard of review was introduced as a general rule applicable across various WTO agreements, a substantive analysis of the various panel reports shows that in practice different agreements attract different types of review.[24] As discussed in section III.C below, this is also true for various requirements contained in one agreement.

III. STANDARD OF REVIEW AND THE SPS AGREEMENT

A. SPS Agreement and its Disciplines

The SPS Agreement is particularly important for the settlement of health and environment-related trade disputes. The major aim of agreement is to limit the impact on international trade[25] of national SPS measures (i.e. measures which aim at protection of human, animal and plant life and

---

[22] Guzman, 2008, p. 4.

[23] Appellate Body, *EC – Hormones*, para. 133.

[24] Ehlermann and Lockhart, 2004, pp. 503–521.

[25] As noted in the literature, domestic health and environmental measures 'can often be manipulated or exploited to protect domestic industry from international competition' (Trebilcock and Soloway, 2002, p. 537).

health against some specifically enumerated risks).[26] At the same time, the agreement intends to guarantee to WTO Members a wide margin of regulatory discretion in the SPS area. Consequently, while WTO Members are expected to observe certain requirements when introducing and implementing their SPS measures, they remain in principle free to establish whatever level of protection they deem appropriate. In WTO nomenclature this right is conventionally referred to as the right to establish the appropriate level of protection (ALOP) and indicates the maximum SPS risk that a particular WTO Member is ready to tolerate.

This discretion is reflected in Article 3 of the SPS Agreement. As a general rule WTO Members are obliged to base their SPS measures on international standards, guidelines, and recommendations (Article 3.1),[27] however under certain conditions they may also deviate therefrom (Article 3.3). This option becomes available if there is sufficient scientific evidence to support a domestic measure, i.e. a deviating measure needs to be based on scientific principles and cannot be maintained without sufficient scientific evidence.[28] This general instruction is translated into the specific requirement of scientific risk assessment. Thus, Article 5.1 stipulates that Members have to ensure that their SPS measures are based on an assessment, as appropriate to the circumstances, of the risks to human, animal or plant life health. The agreement also enumerates elements that need to be included in such assessment (Articles 5.2–5.3). These cover not only available scientific evidence, but also other relevant elements such as processes and production methods, ecological and environmental conditions, and economic factors (but only for quarantine risks). WTO Members may also act if the available scientific evidence is insufficient to perform an adequate risk assessment. A provisional measure, based on available pertinent information, is then a permissible option. In such a case, a Member should seek to obtain the additional information necessary for more objective assessment of risk and review of its SPS measure within a reasonable period of time (Article 5.7).

Therefore, under the SPS Agreement, science operates as a criterion

---

[26]   The relevant risks include risks arising from additives, contaminants, toxins or disease-causing organisms in foods, beverages or feedstuffs. On more detailed discussion on the applicability of the SPS Agreement see Chapter 11 of this book.

[27]   The category of relevant international organizations includes: the Codex Alimentarius Commission, the World Organization for Animal Health and the International Plant Protection Convention. SPS measures, which conform to such international standards, are presumed to be in compliance with the SPS Agreement.

[28]   Article 2.2 of the SPS Agreement.

which allows one to distinguish between permissible and prohibited measures. It may be seen either as a proxy (although imperfect) for detection of protectionist measures taken in the guise of health and environmental regulations, or as a method of improving market access by introducing a certain technical rationality (at the end of the day a measure is condemned irrespective of whether it has a protectionist character or not).[29] Such a mechanism requires panels, as sole fact-finders in the WTO dispute settlement process, to assess and evaluate scientific claims made by the parties to the dispute. This obviously raises the question of the appropriate standard of review over scientific determinations made on a national level.

A separate set of SPS obligations is imposed on the risk management phase of the national regulatory process. As noted above, WTO Members may in principle adopt any ALOP. At least in theory this also encompasses a zero risk level, even if potential costs to international trade clearly exceed expected health/environmental benefits.[30] On the other hand, the Agreement introduces in Article 5.5 the idea of consistency in ALOP for domestic risk-related regulations and requires a certain level of uniformity in different but comparable risk situations (e.g. regulatory response with respect to the same or similar pathogen or disease). This obligation is, however, not absolute as Members may still differentiate in their regulatory reactions if they are able to provide persuasive justification or show that there is no arbitrariness. Members also need to ensure that their SPS measures are not more trade-restrictive than necessary to achieve their ALOP, taking into account technical and economic feasibility (Article 5.6). In this context, the SPS Agreement identifies two concepts that may help in ensuring least-trade restrictiveness: regionalization (i.e. adapting domestic SPS measures to the specific conditions prevailing in the place of the origin and import destination) and equivalence (i.e. accepting measures of other Members as equivalent to domestic ones, if they guarantee the same level of protection). In addition, measures have to be applied only to the extent necessary to protect human, animal or plant life or health (Article 2.2) and cannot arbitrarily or unjustifiably discriminate between Members where identical or similar conditions prevail, including between the territory of the regulating Member and that of other Members (Article 2.3).

---

[29] On the role of science in the SPS Agreement see Gruszczynski, 2010, pp. 147–155 and literature cited there.

[30] The Agreement imposes in this regard a soft obligation that only requires Members, when determining the appropriate level of SPS protection, to take into account the objective of minimizing negative trade effects (Article 5.3).

B.   Standard of Review under the SPS Agreement – Initial Developments

The SPS Agreement is silent about applicable standard of review. In the first SPS case (*EC – Hormones*), the EC argued on appeal that the panel was obliged to apply a deferential reasonableness standard, or the standard of review that is provided by Article 17.6(i) of the Anti-Dumping Agreement. According to the EC, such a standard would be applicable to 'all highly complex factual situations, including the assessment of the risks to human health arising from toxins and contaminants'.[31] In practical terms, this would mean a concentration on procedural rather than substantive compliance (i.e. whether a procedure prescribed by SPS Agreement was followed, without going into the substance of a national SPS measure).[32] The Appellate Body disagreed. It found no indication in the SPS Agreement that Members wanted to incorporate the standard set out in Article 17.6(i) of the Anti-Dumping Agreement. Instead, as was already mentioned, the Appellate Body identified Article 11 of the DSU as providing the applicable standard of review.

Article 11 calls for an objective standard of review which, according to the Appellate Body, is neither *de novo* review nor total deference. The analysis of the *EC – Hormones* report shows that in practice the Appellate Body opted for a rather deferential approach.[33] Under this standard, a panel, although entitled to examine the underlying science and scientific evidence, has to grant a WTO Member a relatively broad degree of deference. In particular, the Appellate Body recognized that Members are entitled to base their SPS measure not only on the mainstream (i.e. the best available) science, but could also rely on minority scientific opinions.[34] This obviously limits the discretion of panels with regard to the re-assessment of scientific evidence. As a consequence, a panel is not allowed to condemn a national measure based on a finding that a majority of scientists hold a different view from the one supporting a domestic measure. Second, risks that need to be evaluated under Article 5.1 are not only those which are 'ascertainable in a science laboratory operating under strictly controlled conditions' but also real world risks that take into account enforcement problems, human errors etc.[35] Again this gives Members an opportunity to take into account different factors and to contextualize risk in a specific national setting. Third, the required connection between risk

---

[31]   Appellate Body Report, *EC – Hormones*, para. 112.
[32]   EC appellant submission in *EC – Hormones*, para. 126.
[33]   *Cf.* Thomas, 1999, p. 507, Bloche, 2002, p. 837.
[34]   Appellate Body Report, *EC – Hormones*, para. 194.
[35]   *Ibid.*, para. 187.

assessment (scientific evidence) and the SPS measure was characterized as merely a reasonable one, as opposed to the more demanding standard of strict conformity. Fourth, the Appellate Body instructed the panel to 'bear in mind that responsible, representative governments commonly act from perspectives of prudence and precaution where risks of irreversible . . . damage to human health are concerned'.[36] This implies that an additional margin of discretion needs to be granted to national governments when evaluating those measures aimed at eliminating irreversible risks to human health and life.

The subsequent case law, however, gradually engaged in a more and more intrusive assessment of the scientific data provided as a justification for domestic SPS measures. Such a standard of review allowed WTO panels to assess the quality, persuasive force, and correctness of scientific determinations made on national levels and to substitute them with their own. In practice this came very close to *de novo* review. In *Australia – Salmon*, the Appellate Body made clear that the panel was not required to 'accord to factual evidence of the parties the same meaning and weight as do the parties'.[37] In a similar fashion in *Japan – Apples* the Appellate Body explained that the panel did not need to favour Japan's approach to risk and scientific evidence over the views of its own experts.[38] Consequently, the panel had a considerable margin of discretion in assessing the value of the evidence and the weight to be ascribed to such evidence. As explained by the Appellate Body 'requiring panels (. . .) to give precedence to the importing Member's evaluation of scientific evidence and risk is not compatible with this well-established principle [of objective review]'.[39] Indeed, the analysis of the report in *Japan – Apples* shows that the panel did replace the factual determinations of national authorities (i.e. Japanese) with its own.[40] On the other hand, one may still find traces of the earlier more deferential approach. The panels consistently emphasized that they could not engage in *de novo* review of scientific determinations made by WTO Members. For example, the panel in *Japan – Agricultural Products* explained that its duty was not to conduct a new risk assessment, but

---

[36]   *Ibid.*, para. 181.
[37]   Appellate Body Report, *Australia – Measures Affecting Importation of Salmon*, WT/DS18/AB/R, adopted 6 November 1998, DSR 1998:VIII, 3327, para. 267.
[38]   Appellate Body Report, *Japan – Measures Affecting the Importation of Apples*, WT/DS245/AB/R, adopted 10 December 2003, DSR 2003:IX, 4391, para. 165.
[39]   *Ibid.*, para. 167.
[40]   *Cf.* Prévost, 2005, p. 11.

rather to assess the quality of the national evaluation.[41] The SPS case law, at least on its face, also confirmed that Members could base their measures on minority scientific opinions.

The idea of engaging in a rather aggressive examination of scientific evidence was followed and developed further by the panel in the *EC – Biotech Products* case.[42] The panel conducted a detailed and intrusive analysis of the scientific evidence that was put forward as a justification for the EC measures. It chose between competing scientific claims articulated by its experts, preferring some over others. The panel's analysis of the scientific materials submitted by the EC under Article 5.7 may serve as a good example of this approach. The aim of panel's examination was to determine whether the evidence was insufficient, and therefore justified the defendant's recourse to the disciplines of Article 5.7. In this context, the panel was required to evaluate a range of scientific data relied on by the competent authorities in several EU Member States (e.g. the opinion of the French Biomolecular Engineering Committee) as well as more recent scientific materials. The panel also consulted six independent experts on some specific scientific issues. In line with the *Japan – Apples* ruling, the panel did not see its task as limited (i.e. to whether evidence relied on by the EC reasonably supported the conclusion of the existence of insufficiency) but rather adopted the role of final arbiter. Thus when assessing the evidence on oilseed rape MS1xRF1, it arbitrarily disregarded not only the view expressed by the Biomolecular Engineering Committee, but also the opinions of some of its own experts who seemed to support the position of the EC.[43] What the panel considered important was the fact that the Scientific Committee on Plants (a body responsible for evaluation of risk at the EU level) was able to perform relevant risk assessment. The panel did not explain why it did not pay attention to other evidence.[44]

The panel in the *US/Canada – Continued Suspension* disputes took essentially the same approach.[45] It confirmed that it enjoyed a broad

[41]   Panel Report, *Japan – Measures Affecting Agricultural Products*, WT/DS76/R, adopted 19 March 1999, as modified by Appellate Body Report WT/DS76/AB/R, DSR 1999:I, 315, para. 8.32.

[42]   Panel Report, *European Communities – Measures Affecting the Approval and Marketing of Biotech Products*, WT/DS291/R, WT/DS292/R, WT/DS293/R, Add.1 to Add.9, and Corr.1, adopted 21 November 2006, DSR 2006:III–VIII, 847.

[43]   *See generally*, Gruszczynski, 2010, pp. 194–195.

[44]   Panel Report, *EC – Biotech Products*, para. 7.3300.

[45]   Panel Report, *United States – Continued Suspension of Obligations in the EC – Hormones Dispute*, WT/DS320/R, adopted 14 November 2008, as modified by Appellate Body Report WT/DS320/AB/R and Panel Report, *Canada – Continued*

discretion as to the choice of evidence when making factual findings. It also added that it was not 'expected to refer to all statements made by [its] experts and should be allowed a substantial margin of discretion as to which statements are useful to refer to explicitly as long as [it does] not deliberately disregard or distort evidence'.[46] The panel admitted that under the SPS Agreement, it was not asked to carry out its own risk assessment, but it also explained that in fact its position was similar to that of a national body producing such an assessment. This meant that the panel wanted to receive the full spectrum of expert views to form an opinion as to the correctness of the risk assessment.[47] Although the *Suspension* panel confirmed that a measure could be based on minority scientific opinions, in practice it adopted the role of an ultimate arbiter as to what could be considered scientific and what not. The following passage from the panel report precisely summarizes its approach:

> while, on some occasions, we followed the majority of experts expressing concurrent views, in some others the divergence of views were such that we could not follow that approach and decided to accept the position(s) which appeared, in our view, to be the most specific in relation to the question at issue and to be best supported by arguments and evidence.[48]

Overall, this approach may be described as a '*quasi de novo*' standard of review.

The direction of the SPS case law, which favours a rather intrusive inquiry into national scientific determinations, is problematic in many respects. From the pragmatic point of view, panels seem to lack sufficient scientific competence to make a judgement over complex technical and scientific issues. Although they are assisted by experts, it is still 'very difficult for them to be sure that they are focusing on the most relevant statements'[49] or that they correctly appreciate the value and relevance of specific scientific claims. Panellists also need to decide how to interpret the opinions of their experts, how to assess and choose between conflicting views, or what kind of inferences to make therefrom. This is rarely an easy

---

Suspension of Obligations in the EC – Hormones Dispute, WT/DS321/R, adopted 14 November 2008, as modified by Appellate Body Report WT/DS321/AB/R. I refer only to the *US – Continued Suspension* case hereafter, as the findings in both reports are almost identical.

[46]   *Ibid.*, para. 7.416.
[47]   *Ibid.*, para. 7.418.
[48]   *Ibid.*, para. 7.420.
[49]   Epps, 2011, p. 16.

task. Note that the answers of experts are frequently formulated in conditional language to reflect the uncertainties inherent in scientific research. This qualified character of the scientific discourse relating to identification and assessment of health and environmental risks is well captured by the group of eminent scholars who noted that:

> the complete description of particular risks usually looks as follows: 'exposure to [X] carries with it a probability of adverse effect that varies from person to person, but is generally in the range of (for example) one in a million to ten in a million; this range is subject to uncertainty and so the true range may be from one in a million to a hundred in a million or may be even zero.'[50]

Unless a panel grants the WTO Members a considerable degree of discretion, there is the risk that some legitimate measures will be condemned not because they lack scientific basis, but because of subjective differences in assessment of the scientific evidence between a particular national government and a panel. This, in turn, will bring the right of WTO Members to adopt SPS measures that achieve their ALOP into question.

Even if there is no qualification, replies may fail to provide straightforward yes or no answers. In such a case, a panel will either need to conduct an additional investigation into a particular scientific problem, or simply decide the issue on the basis of the received answers (e.g. by choosing those answers which appear to it as more direct or pertinent). This option may be tempting for a panel – at least on its face it makes the task of a panel easier and speeds up the whole fact-finding process. However, it also creates a risk of misunderstanding and simplification, or at least some arbitrariness in selecting evidence. The discussion on genotoxicity in *US/Canada – Continued Suspension* illustrates this problem. There was a fundamental disagreement between the parties to the dispute as to the existence of a threshold for substances having genotoxic potential (in this case for oestradiol-17β). The EC claimed that no threshold could be identified, meaning that there was no level below which intakes from hormone residues should have been considered safe. This also meant that the size of doses used in the growth promotion process was of no relevance (at least as far as the existence of risk was concerned, not its extent). Both Canada and the US maintained that the threshold for oestradiol-17β could be determined. In this context, the panel asked its experts a very specific question: whether the scientific evidence referred to by the EC supported its position. The answer of Dr Boisseau was straightforward. He confirmed that the scientific evidence referred to by the EC did not demonstrate a

---

[50]   Crawford-Brown, Pauwelyn and Smith, 2004, p. 463.

no-threshold mechanism for oestradiol-17β.[51] Dr Cogliano was of different opinion and explained that 'the EC's statement that a threshold cannot be identified reflects their view of genotoxic mechanisms, just as the contrary statement that there is a threshold and that this threshold is above the levels found in meat residues reflects how Canada and the US view genotoxic mechanisms'.[52] He also clarified that none of the statements was scientifically demonstrated, and that both positions could be considered as simply based on different assumptions used in the interpretation of the available evidence.[53] Dr Guttenplan, the third expert answering this question, was the most ambiguous. He noted at the beginning that there was no reason to expect a threshold to exist for a genotoxic chemical. However, he explained that the statement that 'the fact that doses used in growth promotion are low is not of relevance [was] not necessarily true'.[54] In this context, he clarified that a dose always determined the risk (i.e. low exposure produces low risk). Finally, he added that 'at very low levels of genotoxic carcinogens the decrease in risk [was] more than proportional than the decrease in applied dose'.[55] On the basis of the above answers one may ask what is the relevance of the observation made by Dr Cogliano? To what extent did the EU's reliance on a non-scientific assumption affect its overall position? What does the expression 'not necessarily true' used by Dr Guttenplan mean? Does it indicate a genuine disagreement between scientists, or it is simply an expression of diligence and precaution in making definitive scientific statements? Unfortunately, the report does not provide the answers to these questions. The panel apparently accepted the answer of Dr Boisseau as being the most straightforward (and therefore correct) and simply disregarded the others. As a consequence, it found that the EC did not submit evidence which would indicate that there is no threshold for oestradiol-17β.[56]

The risk of failing to properly appreciate the scientific value and importance of specific claims and evidence is aggravated by the institutional infrastructure that the panels rely on and the time constraints built into the dispute settlement system. The WTO is an international organization which possesses specialized knowledge (and one arguably superior to that of its Members) in matters relating to international trade, but not

---

[51]   Panel Report, *US – Continued Suspension, Annex D, 'Replies of the Scientific Experts to Questions Posed by the Panel'*, para. 182.
[52]   *Ibid.*, para. 186.
[53]   *Ibid.*
[54]   *Ibid.*, para. 187.
[55]   *Ibid.*
[56]   Panel Report, *US – Continued Suspension*, para. 7.572.

with respect to scientific issues relating to protection of health and life of humans, animals and plants. To put it differently, the WTO lacks the capacity to 'undertake its own inquiry into the science'.[57] If one combines this fact with tight time constraints imposed on panels by the DSU, an in-depth examination of the scientific evidence put forward by the parties hardly seems to be an advisable option.

Lack of expertise is, however, not the only problem faced by the dispute settlement bodies when evaluating scientific evidence. As recognized in the literature, assessment of risk is not a purely scientific task, and depends on the specific socio-cultural conditions of a particular country.[58] Such assessment inevitably involves the subjective judgements of assessors and reflects their attitudes toward particular risks, values of the relevant community in which the experts are acting, and other normative elements such as required level of protection or approach to uncertainties. Consequently, the same set of scientific data may produce entirely different risk estimates in various jurisdictions. The panel seems to be worse placed to make such judgements than the WTO Member that conducted research and evaluated scientific evidence in the context of its specific risk frames and concerns.[59] If a panel ends up imposing on the WTO Members its own vision of science, these normative and context-dependent elements will be lost, and the ultimate determination may fail to produce a correct result. Although, the *de novo* standard of review allows for avoiding what are conventionally referred to as Type 2 errors (i.e. allowing protectionist or 'unnecessary' measures to escape scrutiny from WTO obligations), it may also produce so-called Type 1 errors (i.e. condemning a measure that actually protects health and safety). Is it worth losing one statistical life to achieve some additional trade liberalization? How does one compare the damage to environment caused by the invasion of foreign species with the potential gains generated by an increase in trade? These are difficult decisions that should be addressed rather at the national than international level.

These questions bring us to yet another issue, which seems to be particularly important in the context of health and environment-related trade disputes. The potential costs of a mistake on the side of the WTO dispute settlement bodies appear to be considerably higher in SPS disputes, as compared to other trade disagreements. A loss of statistical life as a consequence of removing a trade barrier is arguably more costly (as a matter of principle and not in terms of specific monetary value) than any damage

---

[57]   Guzman, 2007, p. 229
[58]   See generally, Winickoff *et al*, 2005.
[59]   *Cf.*, Button, 2004, p. 181.

to international trade. Some additional costs may also be generated by problems in compliance. In particular, it is noted that national health and safety measures regulate very sensitive areas which were always considered within the core of national sovereignty. Due to the high values at stake, it may be simply politically impossible (arguably more frequently than under other WTO agreements) to comply with a WTO ruling. Potential costs here relate not only to additional distortions of international trade resulting from the suspension of a concession in response to non-compliance, but also to the harm that is caused to the credibility of the WTO as such. If Members do not comply with rulings, the whole dispute settlement system is called into question.[60]

Another factor which speaks against *de novo* review is the impact that such a standard has on the length of the dispute settlement process. Note that one of the functions of the WTO is the efficient settlement of disputes. In particular, Article 3.3. DSU provides that:

> the prompt settlement of situations in which a Member considers that any benefits accruing to it (. . .) under the covered agreements are being impaired by measures taken by another Member is essential to the effective functioning of the WTO and the maintenance of a proper balance between the rights and obligations of Members.

Elaborating on this rule, Article 12.9 DSU stipulates that as a general rule a panel is required to issue its report within six months. An extension is possible but it should not exceed nine months.[61] *De novo* review, which requires a detailed examination of complex scientific evidence, prolongs that process considerably as compared to disputes decided under the other agreements. The *EC – Biotech* and *US/Canada – Continued Suspension* cases are good examples here. Both of them lasted for years (three and almost four respectively). The same is true for the latest *Australia – Apples* dispute, where the publication of the panel report was postponed several times and the whole procedure continued for almost three years. One may legitimately ask whether such period of time meets the requirement of prompt settlement of a dispute provided for by the DSU. A more deferential standard under which a panel would concentrate on methodological rather than substantive issues has the potential to considerably shorten that process.

The above concerns provoked a group of scholars to argue that WTO panels should not function as adjudicatory bodies reviewing the

---

[60] Guzman, 2007, p. 230.
[61] In practice a panel proceeding takes on average about 12 months.

substantive scientific details of domestic risk assessments, but rather as administrative bodies that only supervise transparency and procedural aspects of the national regulatory process.[62] Another author proposed the limitation of a panel's review to the assessment whether a measure is arbitrary/unjustifiably discriminatory, constitutes the least trade restrictive alternative, or complies with the transparency requirements of Annex B of the SPS Agreement. According to him, any scrutiny into the scientific value of a measure, national preferences for risk or the relationship between risk assessment and a measure, should be very restricted, with a panel concentrating on procedural rather than substantive issues (whether a government took scientific evidence into account, not whether such evidence supports a measure under the examination).[63] This would amount to very deferential standard of review.

The problem with such proposals is that they seem go against the text of the SPS Agreement, which requires some form of substantive scrutiny of both risk assessment and scientific evidence. Article 3.3 allows deviation from international standards when there is scientific justification (and not merely when a Member complies with some procedural rules). Both Article 2.2 and 5.1 require a scientific basis for an SPS measure. This implies at least some kind of enquiry (more or less deferential) into the substance of evidence supporting a measure. This language arguably cannot be reduced to a simple procedural review. Similarly, the definition of risk assessment relies on substantive rather than procedural factors (e.g. it refers to examination of probability/possibility and not to the risk assessment process as such). This is also true for other provisions of the SPS Agreement, which in most cases are of a substantive character – e.g. Article 5.7 and its obligation to base a measure on pertinent information.[64] The procedural requirements of the SPS Agreement remain general and relatively underdeveloped. Consequently, they can hardly be regarded as benchmarks against which national measures can be effectively tested and assessed. Moreover, without denying the advantages of procedural checks (i.e. increased transparency of decision-making processes, which may help to detect instances when a measure is adopted due to pressure from rent-seeking groups), such a model will be most probably under-inclusive, with many measures escaping the scrutiny of WTO dispute settlement bodies. As noted by Trebilcock and Soloway 'if too wide a degree of deference is afforded to the Member's regulation, and any remotely plausible explana-

[62]   Winickoff *et al*, 2004, p. 109.
[63]   Guzman, 2007, p. 231.
[64]   *Cf.* Goh, 2006, pp. 667–668.

tion can be offered as a rationale for trade-restrictive health and safety standards, the world trading system risks being seriously undermined with attendant global and domestic welfare losses in gains from trade'.[65] This might suggest that although adopting a fully deferential standard of review in the context of the SPS Agreement is not an advisable option, a considerable degree of deference is still called for.

C.   Standard of Review under the SPS Agreement – Some Recent Developments

The 2008 Appellate Body's report in the *US/Canada – Continued Suspension* cases may be seen as a response to the above concerns. At the time of its adoption, it appeared to be a revolutionary shift in WTO jurisprudence, with the Appellate Body opting for a more deferential approach which would grant an additional margin of discretion to national governments in the SPS area.

One of the issues contested by the EC in the appeal was the standard of review applied by the panel to factual determinations, including scientific evidence. The Appellate Body first observed, rather uncontroversially, that it was the task of each Member State to perform a risk assessment, while a panel was only expected to review it. This meant to the Appellate Body that it was not for the panel to determine whether a risk assessment was correct but only whether it was supported by coherent reasoning and respectable scientific evidence.[66] The Appellate Body went on to identify four specific steps that should have been taken by the panel when performing this limited task. Thus, a panel must:

a)   identify the scientific basis underlying an SPS measure;
b)   verify that the scientific basis comes from a respected and qualified source – this should be relatively easy for mainstream scientific claims, whereas for minority scientific opinions some more detailed examination will be required;
c)   assess whether the reasoning articulated on the basis of the scientific evidence is objective and coherent – in other words, the panel needs to assess whether a conclusion reached by a WTO Member finds sufficient support in scientific evidence relied upon; and
d)   determine whether the results of the risk assessment sufficiently warrant the SPS measure at issue.[67]

---

[65]   Trebilcock and Soloway, 2002, p. 541.
[66]   Appellate Body Report, *US – Continued Suspension*, para. 590.
[67]   *Ibid.*, para. 591.

The Appellate Body again confirmed that both mainstream science as well as minority scientific opinions could serve as a basis for a measure. What is important is epistemic value of a particular claim. As explained by the Appellate Body, 'evidence must have necessary scientific and methodological rigour to be considered reputable science'.[68] This aspect is to be assessed using the methodological parameters of the relevant scientific community. Note again that the question here is not whether in the opinion of a particular scientist the evidence is correct, but rather whether specific information is defensible as a scientific claim.

Once a scientific basis is established and its epistemic status verified, a panel would need to examine the coherence and objectivity in the interpretation of these raw data. Although the Appellate Body did not elaborate on this particular point, one could legitimately expect that a task of a panel would also be limited here. This would mean that conclusions drawn by a WTO Member on the basis of scientific evidence are only to be checked against scientific logic (i.e. whether a specific interference is justified in the light of a particular methodology that may be described as scientific, and whether an interference is objective or biased). However, as will be discussed below, the subsequent case law decided that panel's scrutiny is actually more intrusive when evaluating coherence and objectivity of reasoning (as compared to scientific evidence as such).

Finally, a panel needs to inquire into the relationship between the conclusions of a risk assessment and an SPS measure. This is the second point where the Appellate Body was rather enigmatic. It remains unclear what level of compatibility between those two elements is required. One may assume, in line with the logic of the existing case law, that scientific findings may support a whole range of different SPS measures. As noted elsewhere by the panel in *EC – Biotech*:

> there may conceivably be cases where a Member (. . .) would be justified in applying (i) an SPS measure even though another Member might not decide to apply any SPS measure on the basis of the same risk assessment, or (ii) an SPS measure which is stricter than the SPS measure applied by another Member to address the same risk.[69]

In any case, some additional guidance for assessing the existence of a sufficient relationship between the conclusions of risk assessment and an SPS measure seems to be desirable.

The new methodology proposed by the Appellate Body also has an

---

[68]   *Ibid.*
[69]   Panel Report, *EC – Biotech Products*, para. 7.3065.

impact on the consultation process that takes place between a panel and its experts. In particular, a panel may seek the assistance of experts in order to examine the individual steps described above (e.g. to identify the scientific basis of an SPS measure, determine whether it constitutes a defensible scientific claim, or review whether it is objective and coherent). In this context, the Appellate Body warned that the panel should not attempt to test whether its experts would have done a risk assessment in the same way as a particular WTO Member. Their task is limited, as they should only review an assessment in terms of its scientific value (i.e. whether it is defensible).[70] This obviously determines the extent of scientific advice that may be sought by a panel – e.g. what questions are appropriate and what kind of answers are to be considered relevant when deciding a particular issue.

The above approach differs considerably from the approach taken in the previous case law. It explicitly prohibits a panel from inquiring into the correctness of evidence and instructs it to concentrate on methodological issues in order to assess epistemic value and the coherence of scientific findings. A panel may equally check (in order to verify the objectivity of a process) whether municipal authorities have collected and considered all relevant evidence and whether the evaluation of this evidence was unbiased. This standard leaves WTO Members with a greater degree of discretion as to how to assess scientific data and what kind of interferences to make on their basis. It also greatly reduces the need for a panel to engage in a detailed examination of scientific evidence and decide which scientific view is better. In theory, once it is established that a particular claim is scientifically defensible, even if improbable, the task of the panel ends.

The initial reactions from academic circles to the report of the Appellate Body were rather positive. Some even claimed that the Appellate Body had decided to adopt a predominantly deferential approach, under which the main focus would be on the process of risk assessment rather than its outcome. In this context, a parallel was draw between the approach of the Appellate Body and that of the US Supreme Court in the Chevron case.[71] Others, however, were more sceptical. For example, Peel, although labelling the approach of the Appellate Body as procedural in nature, also recognized that it 'still contains a substantial emphasis on scientific factors'.[72] Indeed the tests provided by the Appellate Body appear to go beyond a

---

[70] Appellate Body Report, *US – Continued Suspension*, para. 592.

[71] *Cf.* Robert Howse on the International Economic Law and Policy Blog (http://worldtradelaw.net).

[72] Peel, 2010, p. 218.

merely procedural approach that concentrates only on formal compliance. Arguably points (c) and (d) (i.e. whether the reasoning articulated on the basis of the scientific evidence is objective and coherent and whether the results of the risk assessment sufficiently warrant the SPS measure at issue) require the performance of a substantive analysis (albeit a deferential one). Moreover, an inquiry into underlying methodology (in order to verify that a specific claim is regarded as reputable science) can be also connected with different levels of scrutiny. As will be elaborated further below, a detailed methodological assessment may in practice come quite close to *de novo* review. Nevertheless, the overall impression that one gets is that the Appellate Body 'open[ed] the door a little wider to recognition of a greater diversity of risk assessment approaches in the SPS context'.[73] The holding that the proper task of the panel is not to assess the correctness of domestic scientific determinations but rather their overall coherence and objectivity is important. It suggests a rather deferential approach that considerably differs from the previous practice. Having said that, it is also true that the Appellate Body left many important interpretative questions open.

Australia – Apples was the first case to elaborate on this new approach. The applicable standard of review actually turned out to be one of the major issues in the appeal lodged by Australia. Although the Appellate Body provided rather extensive legal analysis, the report leaves a reader disappointed and perplexed. Its tone is very different from the spirit of the *US/Canada – Continued Suspension* report and indicates that the investigation of the WTO panel remains relatively intrusive.

The dispute arose in the context of an Australian import prohibition applicable to New Zealand apples on phytosanitary grounds. At least in theory, Australia was concerned with the risks posed by two pests (i.e. European canker and apple leafcurling midge) and one disease (i.e. fire blight), which were absent on its territory but had been reported for New Zealand. The Australian risk assessment, which was completed in 2006, recognized New Zealand apples as a potential transmission vector. It listed a number of specific conditions that had to be met before any export could take place. New Zealand contested the measure in the WTO dispute settlement system and the panel found in its favour. On appeal, Australia contested a number of different issues, including the standard of review that was applied by the panel in its assessment of scientific determinations. In essence, Australia argued that the panel, following the instruction of the Appellate Body in *US/Canada – Continued Suspension*, was obliged to adopt a relatively deferential approach.

---

[73]   *Ibid.*

The Appellate Body, however, rejected Australia's assertion that the panel had exceeded its mandate. The Appellate Body started its analysis with its traditional statement that the applicable standard of review was neither *de novo* review nor full deference. It also recalled that the panel was expected to review a contested risk assessment and not to carry out such assessment on its own.[74] Apparently, the Appellate Body used two different standards of review to be applied in the context of Article 5.1 (and arguably also under Article 2.2). The first one relates to the evaluation of the scientific basis as such (steps (a) and (b) of the *Continued Suspension* test) and is rather deferential. This was correctly justified by the epistemic superiority of a domestic risk assessor ('a panel is not well suited to conduct scientific research and assessments itself and should not substitute its judgement for that of a risk assessor'[75]).

The second type is concerned with the review of reasoning articulated on the basis of scientific evidence, which is a step (c) in the *Continued Suspension* test (i.e. whether the scientific evidence supports the conclusions of the risk assessment to a sufficient degree).[76] Although the Appellate Body did not identify the applicable standard of review for deciding whether the results of the risk assessment sufficiently warrant the SPS measure (step (d)), one may expect the same level of scrutiny here. Contrary to the first type, this standard of review involves a relatively intrusive examination.

On the basis of this distinction, the Appellate Body rejected Australia's claim that the panel should have only evaluated whether 'intermediate conclusions were "within a range that could be considered legitimate" according to the standards of the scientific community'.[77] Since conclusions (both immediate and ultimate) constitute a part of reasoning and they are subject to more intense scrutiny. The Appellate Body also disagreed with Australia that the panel's review should be limited to the ultimate conclusion reached in a municipal risk assessment. The mandate of the panel covered examination of the reasoning, which also included intermediate conclusions in a risk assessment. The same was true for expert judgements used in a risk assessment to compensate for missing scientific data or to address scientific uncertainties. In this context, the Appellate Body concurred with the panel that Australia was obliged to show that the exercise of such expert judgements was sufficiently documented, transparent,

---

[74] Appellate Body Report, *Australia – Apples*, paras 212–213.
[75] *Ibid.*, para. 225.
[76] *Ibid.*, para. 215.
[77] *Ibid.*, para. 231.

and based on the relevant reliable scientific information.[78] The Appellate Body believed that the documentation and transparency requirement was 'instrumental in the determination of whether the overall risk assessment, even when it is conducted in the face of some scientific uncertainty, relies on the available scientific evidence'.[79] Nor did the Appellate Body accept Australia's assertion that the panel's role was limited to determining whether alleged flaws in the reasoning of risk assessment were sufficiently serious to undermine 'reasonable confidence' in the assessment as a whole. This threshold was considered to be too low.[80]

As noted at the outset, the overall approach of the Appellate Body to the applicable standard of review remains ambiguous. On one hand, some elements in its analysis indicate that it opted for quasi-deferential standard that follows the test articulated in the *Continued Suspension* report. The Appellate Body stressed that the panel's role is limited when 'reviewing whether the scientific basis constitutes legitimate science'[81] (steps (a) and (b) of the test). A panel is only expected to determine that a specific claim can be regarded as 'legitimate' science (i.e. whether it holds a minimum epistemic value and not whether it is correct). It also accepted the panel's approach to concentrate on the methodology used in Australia's risk assessment rather than its ultimate outcome. This is a characteristic feature of deferential types of review.[82] Similarly, the documentation and transparency requirements (i.e. how risk assessors reached specific expert judgments), which were introduced by the panel and subsequently upheld by the Appellate Body, may be also regarded as a tool for deferential review, as it concentrates on the process of risk assessment and not its substance.

On the other hand, the Appellate Body rejected Australia's argument that the panel's task, when reviewing intermediate conclusions in its risk assessment, should consist in deciding whether they 'fall within a range that could be considered legitimate by the scientific community'. One may also assume that the same approach would be taken for expert judgements, which also constitute a part of reasoning articulated on the basis of scientific evidence. Although the report did not specify the precise level of this more intrusive review, its finding may be seen as an invitation for future panels to assess the correctness of such reasoning rather than its reasonableness. It is not clear why the Appellate Body decided that a

---

[78]   *Ibid.*, para. 248.
[79]   *Ibid.*, para. 244.
[80]   *Ibid.*, paras 259–260.
[81]   *Ibid.*, para. 215.
[82]   *Ibid.*, paras 258–259.

separate and more demanding standard of review was applicable to the reasoning of risk assessors. In support of its conclusion, the Appellate Body referred to the *Continued Suspension* report and explained that in this case it 'considered that the manner of scrutinizing the underlying scientific evidence differs from the manner of scrutinizing the reasoning of the risk assessor'. However, an examination of the relevant paragraphs shows that no such distinction was made in the *Continued Suspension* case. To the contrary, the deferential standard of review identified there appeared to be a uniform concept that is applicable to different steps of the risk assessment process. What seem to be even more problematic are the reasons which could justify such a distinction. The Appellate Body, when introducing a deferential standard of review for scientific evidence, was primarily concerned with the limited epistemic competence of a panel in scientific matters. However, a panel is in no way better equipped to decide on the correctness of intermediate conclusions in a risk assessment or expert judgements used to compensate for uncertainties (or more generally – the reasoning in a risk assessment). Both aspects are highly complex and require the involvement of experts to advise a panel. In this sense, the challenge that is faced by a panel when evaluating reasoning is not so different from that of scrutinizing scientific evidence as such. This fact was indirectly recognized by the Appellate Body in *US/Canada – Continued Suspension,* when it observed:

> The panel may seek the experts' assistance in order to identify the scientific basis of the SPS measure and to verify that this scientific basis comes from a qualified and respected source (. . .). It may also rely on the experts to review whether the reasoning (. . .) is objective and coherent, and whether the particular conclusions drawn by the Member (. . .) find sufficient support in the evidence. The experts may also be consulted on the relationship between the risk assessment and the SPS measure in order to assist the panel in determining whether the risk assessment 'sufficiently warrants' the SPS measure.[83]

In the same paragraph, the Appellate Body also warned the panel that it should not seek to determine 'whether the experts would have done a risk assessment in the same way and *would have reached the same conclusions* as the risk assessor' (emphasis added).[84]

This brings us to the second issue. The Appellate Body accepted that the investigation into the underlying methodology could be quite intrusive. However, as correctly observed in the literature, if a reviewing body examines the details of underlying methodology, its task is not so different

---

[83] Appellate Body, *US – Continued Suspension,* para. 592.
[84] *Ibid.*

from a body that reviews the substance of evidence. The only difference will be that such a body would concentrate on methodological rather than substantive issues.[85] The complexity of the required examination (and thus the epistemic inferiority of a panel), as well as the need to rely on specialized expert knowledge, could actually be similar in both cases. A panel may, therefore, end up deciding which methodology is better, which would constitute a situation close to *de novo* review. Consequently an inquiry into methodological aspects does not in itself determine whether we are dealing with a deferential or *de novo* review. If examination is intrusive all concerns raised above with regard to substantive examination of scientific evidence will also apply here.

IV. CONCLUSIONS

The standard of review applicable to complex factual determinations remains ambiguous under the SPS Agreement. The early SPS case law adopted a rather deferential approach that gave a considerable degree of deference to WTO Members. Subsequent jurisprudence opted, however, for a more intrusive examination into the scientific data provided as a justification for national measures. The change in the Appellate Body report in *US/Canada – Continued Suspension* was truly unexpected and had potentially far-reaching implications. Under the new standard, a panel was not expected to determine whether a risk assessment is correct but rather examine its reasonableness. *Australia – Apples* was the first case to elaborate on this new approach. Some of the findings in the Appellate Body report may, however, be disappointing for those who expected to see fairly deferential language. Although the applicable standard of review under the SPS Agreement (and in particular under Articles 2.2 and 5.1) is not *de novo*, the investigation of the WTO panel remains intrusive when assessing the objectivity and coherence of the reasoning included in a contested risk assessment. The same is true with respect to the permissible inquiry into underlying methodology. This may indicate that WTO dispute settlement bodies are unwilling to resign their investigative prerogatives when adjudicating on national SPS measures. This conclusion is not affected by the fact that the standard of review applicable to scientific evidence as such continues to be fairly deferential.

Consequently, one may consider *US/Canada – Continued Suspension* as an anomaly in an otherwise rather consistent line of cases that subscribed

---

[85]   Button, 2004, p. 186.

to a fairly intrusive standard of review. The *Australia – Apples* report generally followed this trend, however, with one important change relating to the assessment of scientific evidence as such. It was clearly recognized that a panel's task is limited and consists of determining a minimal epistemic status of such evidence. Since the position of the Appellate Body is quite clear on this issue, one may expect to see the same approach in future panel reports.

Another explanation that could reconcile these two different approaches is that the Appellate Body intends to distinguish between cases on the basis of the risk in question. This would mean that the Appellate Body is willing to apply a more deferential standard of review to trade disputes involving human health issues. *US/Canada – Continued Suspension* is a perfect example of such case with potential risks for human life and health resulting from the consumption of meat from hormone-treated animals. On the other hand, *Australia – Apples* is a traditional phytosanitary case where the values at stake are much lower (namely plant health as opposed to human health). This may justify, in the view of the Appellate Body, a more intrusive examination of a relevant risk assessment. Future reports will most probably shed some more light on the relevance of this distinction. This should allow the more precise identification of future trends in SPS jurisprudence.

BIBLIOGRAPHY

Bloche, M. Gregg (2002), 'WTO deference to national health policy: Toward an interpretative principle', *Journal of International Economic Law*, 5(4), 825–848.

Bohanes, Jan and Nicolas Lockhart (2009), 'Standard of review in WTO law', in Daniel Bethlehem, Donald McRae, Rodney Neufeld and Issabelle van Damme (eds), *The Oxford Handbook of International Trade Law*, Oxford: Oxford University Press.

Button, Catherine (2004), *Power to Protect. Trade, Health and World Trade Organization*, Hart Publishing: Oxford and Portland.

Christoforou, Theofanis (1999–2000), 'Settlement of science-based disputes in the WTO: A critical review of the developing case law in the face of scientific uncertainty', *New York University Environmental Law Journal*, 8(3), 622–648.

Crawford-Brown, Douglas, Joost Pauwelyn and Kelly Smith (2004), 'Environmental risk, precaution, and scientific rationality in the context of WTO/NAFTA trade rules', *Risk Analysis*, 24(2), 461–469.

Croley, Steven P. and John H. Jackson (1996), 'WTO procedures, standard of review, and deference to national governments', *American Journal of International Law*, 90(2), 193–213.

Ehlermann, Claus-Dieter and Nicolas Lockhart (2004), 'Standard of review in WTO law', *Journal of International Economic Law*, 7(3), 491–521.

Epps, Tracey (2011), 'Recent Developments in WTO Jurisprudence: Has the Appellate Body resolved the issue of an appropriate standard of review in SPS cases?', unpublished manuscript, on file with the author.

Goh, Gavin (2006), 'Tipping the apple cart: the limits of science and law in the SPS Agreement after Japan – Apples', *Journal of World Trade*, 40(2), 655–686.

Gruszczynski, Lukasz (2010), *Regulating Health and Environmental Risks under WTO Law: A Critical Analysis of the SPS Agreement*, Oxford: Oxford University Press.
Guzman, Andrew (2007), 'Dispute resolution in SPS Cases', in Dan Horovitz, Daniel Moulis and Debora Steger (eds), *Ten Years of WTO Dispute Settlement*, London: International Bar Association, pp. 215–233.
Guzman, Andrew (2008), 'Determining the appropriate standard of review in WTO disputes', paper available at: http://ssrn.com/abstract=1270894
Oesch, Matthias (2003), *Standards of Review in WTO Dispute Resolution*, Oxford: Oxford University Press.
Peel, Jacqueline (2010), *Science and Risk Regulation in International Law*, Cambridge: Cambridge University Press.
Prévost, Denise (2005), 'What role for the precautionary principle in WTO law after Japan – Apples?', *Economic Journal of Trade and Environment Studies*, 2(4), 1–14.
Strauss, Peter L., Todd D. Rakoff and Cynthia R. Farina (2003), *Administrative Law: Cases and Comments*, Westbury: Foundation Press.
Thomas, Ryan D., (1999), 'Where is the beef? Mad cows and the blight of the SPS Agreement', *Vanderbilt Journal of Transnational Law*, 32(2), 487–517.
Trebilcock, Michael and Julie Soloway (2002), 'International trade policy and domestic food safety regulation: the case for substantial deference by the WTO Dispute Settlement Body under the SPS Agreement', in Daniel Kennedy and James Southwick (eds), *The Political Economy of International Trade Law*, Cambridge: Cambridge University Press, pp. 537–574.
Winickoff, David, Sheila Jasanoff, Lawrence Busch, Robin Grove-White and Brian Wynne (2005), 'Adjudicating the GM food wars: science, risk, and democracy in world trade law', *Yale Journal of International Law*, 30, 81–123.

PART V

EMERGING ECONOMIES AND HEALTH/ ENVIRONMENTAL BARRIERS TO TRADE

22. The impact of sanitary and phytosanitary measures on India's exports and the challenges/opportunities of the SPS Agreement
Kasturi Das

I. INTRODUCTION

Over the recent past, sanitary and phytosanitary (SPS) issues have assumed an increasing significance in the context of international trade. This may be attributable to several factors. On the one hand, there has been a significant increase in trade in fresh, semi-processed and ready-to-eat food since the 1990s, led by the demand in developed countries.[1] On the other, enhanced scientific understanding, coupled with growing public awareness and concern about food safety and health has resulted in an ever-increasing preference for safe and hygienic food, particularly in the developed countries. While these countries have responded to such preferences by putting in place ever stricter SPS regulations and standards, these requirements have often acted as significant market access barriers for exports from developing countries. In fact, SPS requirements are widely considered by developing countries as one of the greatest impediments confronting their exports of agricultural and food products, particularly to the developed countries. This may be attributable, in large measure, to the fact that developed countries typically apply stricter SPS measures than developing countries and that SPS controls in many developing countries are weak and overly fragmented.[2] The problems that the developing countries confront in complying with SPS requirements reflect their wider resource and infrastructure constraints. These limit not only their ability to comply with SPS requirements, but also their ability to demonstrate compliance.[3] A particularly critical problem emanates from the lack of appropriate scientific and technical expertise. In many developing countries, knowledge of SPS issues is poor, both within government and in the food supply chain,

---

[1]   Sawhney (2005), 329.
[2]   DFID (2000), 1.
[3]   *Ibid.*

and the skills required to assess SPS requirements imposed by developed countries are lacking.[4] Furthermore, SPS requirements applied by developed countries may sometimes be incompatible with prevailing systems of production and marketing in developing countries.[5] For instance, while the food processing industry is highly mechanised in the developed countries, the food sector in developing countries is largely scattered and labour-intensive in nature.[6] Complying with the SPS requirements in such cases may call for fundamental structural and organisational overhaul in the developing countries, the cost implications of which may often be deleterious for many of these poor countries. In such cases, the costs of compliance often act as an absolute barrier to trade. Moreover, there is no guarantee that once suitable changes in the production processes are made, the goods would get continued or enhanced market access, as buyers do not give any such guarantee upfront. A concomitant problem is that of shifting standards. By the time exporters/producers are prepared to meet a particular standard, developed countries might move to a different standard, which may be only slightly different from the previous one. However, adjusting once again to the new standard can involve huge costs for the exporters/producers.[7] Not surprisingly, therefore, SPS issues have emerged as one of the most contested areas of international trade over the past few decades.

The World Trade Organisation (WTO) Agreement on the Application of Sanitary and Phytosanitary Measures (SPS Agreement) came into being against this backdrop, with the aim of putting in place an array of multilateral rules that would, on the one hand, recognise the legitimate right of WTO Members to adopt SPS measures that they deem necessary to protect human, animal or plant life or health, and on the other, enshrine certain checks and balances to address the possibility of these measures emerging as non-tariff barriers (NTBs) to trade.

However, the existence of this agreement notwithstanding, SPS measures seem to have continued to act as a major form of NTB, particularly for the developing countries. This was indicated in the submissions made by the developing countries under the notification process established by the Negotiating Group on Market Access (NGMA) as a part of the Non-agricultural Market Access (NAMA) negotiations of the Doha Round of trade talks. Under this process, WTO Members were invited to submit

---

4   *Ibid.*
5   *Ibid.*
6   *Ibid.,* 14.
7   UNCTAD (2006), 51.

notification on NTBs that directly affected their exports according to the NAMA Inventory of Non-tariff Measures, which provided for a broad and comprehensive coverage of NTBs.[8] Between March 2003 and October 2004, 21 non-Organisation for Economic Co-operation and Development (OECD) countries[9] made a total of 1200 notifications.[10] Notably, the set of 21 countries could be regarded as fairly representative of the perceptions of developing countries about NTBs, given that it comprised a geographically and economically diverse and balanced sample of developing countries.[11] As per the incidence of notifications, SPS measures (with 137 entries) turned out to be the third most frequently reported barriers for developing countries, after technical barriers to trade (TBT) (with 530 entries) and customs and administrative procedures (380 entries). It was widely reported by developing countries that certain countries were imposing onerous standards without first conducting a comprehensive risk assessment. These measures included chemical residue limits, the requirement of freedom from disease, and specified product treatments, among others (74 per cent of SPS entries). Approximately 17 per cent of complaints in this area pertained specifically to testing, certification and other conformity assessment related to SPS requirements.[12] The product group that was found to be the worst victim of NTBs was 'live animals and products' (309 notifications) and SPS measures turned out to be

---

[8]   The Inventory of Non-tariff Measures groups barriers into seven broad categories. For this inventory, see, WTO (2003d).

[9]   The sample of developing countries used in this analysis is non-OECD countries that submitted notifications as of 1 November 2004. These are from Africa and the Middle East: Egypt, Jordan, Kenya, and Senegal; from Asia and the Pacific: Bangladesh, China, Hong Kong, India, Macao, Malaysia, Pakistan, Philippines, Chinese Taipei, Singapore, and Thailand; from Latin America and the Caribbean: Argentina, Trinidad and Tobago, Uruguay, and Venezuela; and from Eastern Europe: Bulgaria and Croatia. Countries from Asia and the Pacific are the most represented (87.7 per cent of NTB notifications), with Latin America and the Caribbean and Africa and the Middle East following in the number of barriers reported (OECD (2005), 16).

[10]   *Ibid.*, 15.

[11]   In terms of income level as per the World Bank classification, 19 per cent of these countries are high-income economies; 28 per cent upper-middle income; 28 per cent lower-middle income; and 24 per cent low-income (of the latter, one country – Bangladesh – is a least developed country (LDC) according to the UN classification). In 2002, the total value of merchandise exports from these 21 countries was US$ 1,132,567 million, representing approximately 57 per cent of total DC exports and 18 per cent of total global exports (*Ibid.*, 16).

[12]   *Ibid.*, 17–19.

the primary concern in this product category (114 notifications).[13] As for India, in its notification, the country exemplified in some detail how various restrictive standards and burdensome regulations and procedures in the areas of both SPS and TBT were acting as barriers significantly affecting its capacity to trade with several countries. In fact these formed the first entry in India's notification, clearly reflecting their importance vis-à-vis other NTBs.[14]

The experiences of developing countries with SPS requirements[15] imposed in particular by developed countries tend to indicate that the SPS Agreement has thus far not been fully effective in addressing the possibility of these measures emerging as NTBs to trade. This may largely be attributable to the fact that the Agreement has left considerable wiggle room for WTO Members, thereby leaving the door ajar to use SPS measures for protectionist purposes on grounds of their legitimate concerns about protection of human, animal or plant life or health. This leeway seems to have been further reinforced by the mode of interpretation of the provisions of the Agreement by the WTO Dispute Settlement System (DSS). Written against this backdrop, the present Chapter brings to the fore some of the key SPS challenges confronting developing countries by taking India as a case in point. It should, however, be stated upfront that by no means is India considered as a representative for all developing countries here. In fact, as an 'emerging economy' it is in a rather different position to many other developing countries. In view of the significant diversities among developing countries, any attempt to generalise India's experience for all other developing countries may not be appropriate. While no such generalisations are attempted in this chapter either, it is indeed intriguing to note the multi-pronged SPS challenges that India is still confronted with, notwithstanding its so-called 'emerging economy' status.

The chapter is organised as follows. Section II begins with a brief overview of the SPS Agreement. Section III exemplifies certain product-specific SPS concerns of India, while Section IV goes on to discuss certain more general SPS-related concerns of the country vis-à-vis two of its major trading partners, the EU and US. Section V analyses some of the key provisions of the SPS Agreement and the case law pertaining to them with the aim of exploring the extent of wiggle room available to WTO Members to adopt these measures. Section VI proposes a few strategies that India

---

[13]   *Ibid.*, 20–21.
[14]   For further details, refer to WTO (2003a), 31–41.
[15]   See, for instance, the experience of the South Asian countries in Das (2009).

could consider under the aegis of the WTO and beyond, towards coping with the multi-faced SPS challenges it is confronted with in a more effective manner. Section VII concludes the chapter.

II. THE GENESIS OF THE SPS AGREEMENT AND ITS KEY FEATURES

The SPS Agreement was not the maiden initiative at the multilateral level to deal with trade-related SPS issues. Article XX (b)[16] of the General Agreement on Tariffs and Trade (GATT) 1947 allowed Contracting Parties to deviate from their obligations under the Agreement when 'necessary to protect human, animal or plant life or health'.[17] This flexibility, however, was subject to compliance with the *chapeau* of Article XX,[18] which required that in order to be justified under one of the paragraphs of Article XX, a measure must not be 'applied in a manner which would constitute a means of arbitrary or unjustifiable discrimination between countries where the same conditions prevail, or a disguised restriction on

---

[16] Article XX (b) of the GATT (with the *Chapeau)* reads as follows:

Subject to the requirement that such measures are not applied in a manner which would constitute a means of arbitrary or unjustifiable discrimination between countries where the same conditions prevail, or a disguised restriction on international trade, nothing in this Agreement shall be construed to prevent the adoption or enforcement by any contracting party of measures:

. . .

(b) necessary to protect human, animal or plant life or health;

[17] The 'General Exceptions' provisions of the GATT contained in its Article XX allow a WTO Member to deviate from its GATT obligations in order to serve certain legitimate policy objectives, provided the conditions included in the *chapeau* (i.e. the introductory part) of Article XX are met.

[18] In *US – Gasoline*, the Appellate Body presented a two-tiered test under Article XX, as follows:

In order that the justifying protection of Article XX may be extended to it, the measure at issue must not only come under one or another of the particular exceptions – paragraphs (a) to (j) – listed under Article XX; it must also satisfy the requirements imposed by the opening clauses of Article XX. The analysis is, in other words, two-tiered: first, provisional justification by reason of characterization of the measure under [one of the exceptions]; second, further appraisal of the same measure under the introductory clauses of Article XX. (Appellate Body Report, *United States – Standards for Reformulated and Conventional Gasoline* (henceforth *US – Gasoline*), WT/DS2/AB/R, adopted 20 May 1996, DSR 1996:I, 3, 20–21).

international trade'.[19] Thus, while Article XX created room for the GATT Contracting Parties to pursue certain legitimate policy objectives (like protection of human, animal or plant life or health, among others), it also attempted to ensure that such measures were not applied for protectionist purposes. The latter attempt was quite in keeping with the stated objective of the GATT to substantially reduce tariffs and other barriers to trade and to eliminate discriminatory treatment in international commerce.[20]

Notwithstanding such assertion on reduction of NTBs, the process of trade liberalisation that was embarked on under the aegis of the GATT became almost synonymous with the lowering of tariffs, while the critical issue of non-tariff barriers remained on the margins. Moreover, despite the existence of a range of non-tariff barriers, much of the efforts in the initial years of the GATT were devoted to elimination of quantitative restrictions – the most prevalent form of non-tariff barrier during that time. The Kennedy Round of negotiations (1963–69) under the GATT considered the issue of quantitative restrictions, both agricultural and non-agricultural. Although these discussions could not make much headway, an important initiative was undertaken during this period to develop an Inventory of non-tariff measures (NTMs) under the aegis of the Committee on Trade in Industrial Products. The GATT work programme on non-tariff measures underwent significant expansion during the Tokyo Round of negotiations (1973–79), when six multilateral instruments on Non-tariff Measures were negotiated.[21] These included, among others, the Agreement on Technical Barriers to Trade, generally referred to as the 'Standards Code'. This plurilateral agreement was negotiated with the aim of ensuring non-discrimination in the preparation, adoption and application of technical regulations and standards, and transparency

---

[19]   The Appellate Body, in *Shrimp-Turtle Article 21.5* stated that:

There are three standards contained in the chapeau: first, arbitrary discrimination between countries where the same conditions prevail; second, unjustifiable discrimination between countries where the same conditions prevail; and third, a disguised restriction on international trade (Appellate Body Report, *United States – Import Prohibition of Certain Shrimp and Shrimp Products – Recourse to Article 21.5 of the DSU by Malaysia (Shrimp-Turtle Article 21.5),* WT/DS58/AB/RW, adopted 21 November 2001, DSR 2001:XIII, 6481, para 118.).

In order for the measure not to be entitled to the justifying protection of Article XX, the existence of only one of these three standards would have to be proven.

[20]   Preamble to GATT 1947.

[21]   Dhar and Kallummal (2007), 140–41.

of such technical measures. The Standards Code covered the technical aspects of trade in both food and non-food products.

Finally, the decision to negotiate a stand-alone agreement on the application of SPS measures was taken during the Uruguay Round (1986–94) of negotiations that were launched in Punta del Este and culminated in the formation of the WTO, subsuming the GATT 1947 into it. The Punta del Este Declaration (of 20 September 1986) called for increased disciplines in three areas pertaining to agriculture: market access, subsidies, and SPS regulations.[22] The need for a separate agreement dealing exclusively with SPS measures was felt due to the perceived shortcomings in the then-existing legal instruments dealing with SPS, namely Article XX of the GATT and the 1979 Standards Code.[23] A view had emerged that these two instruments had failed to prevent disruptions in trade caused by ever-increasing technical restrictions, including those related to SPS issues. Moreover, some countries were apprehensive that the proposed elimination of agriculture-specific tariffs and non-tariff measures under the Uruguay Round would be circumvented by disguised protectionist measures in the form of SPS requirements. This perception reinforced the need for negotiating a separate agreement, which, among other things, would seek to establish a multilateral framework that would allow simplification and harmonisation of SPS measures and would eliminate all restrictions lacking any scientific basis.[24]

From a political standpoint, there were two streams of advocacies involved in the Uruguay Round negotiation: one that wanted to adhere to the GATT Article XX *chapeau* benchmark and allow only the 'least trade restrictive' SPS measures, and another that wanted to protect the right of

---

[22]   The Punta del Este Declaration states:

. . . Negotiations shall aim to achieve greater liberalization of trade in agriculture and bring all measures affecting import access and export competition under strengthened and more operationally effective GATT rules and disciplines, taking into account the general principles governing the negotiations by: (i) improving market access through, inter alia, the reduction of import barriers; (ii) improving the competitive environment by increasing discipline on the use of all direct and indirect subsidies and other measures affecting directly or indirectly agricultural trade, including the phased reduction of their negative effects and dealing with their causes; (iii) minimizing the adverse effects that sanitary and phytosanitary regulations and barriers can have on trade in agriculture, taking into account the relevant international agreements . . . (GATT (1986), General Agreement on Tariffs and Trade (GATT) Punta Del Este Declaration, Ministerial Declaration of 20 September).

[23]   For further details on shortcomings, see Ratna (2005), 74.
[24]   *Ibid.*, 74–75.

countries to decide on the 'appropriate level of SPS protection' (ALOP) relevant for their society based on consumer preference, in addition to SPS concerns. The agreement that finally emerged in 1994 and became operational with effect from 1 January 1995 under the aegis of the WTO, set in place an array of multilateral trade rules that on the one hand, recognised the legitimate right of WTO Members to adopt SPS measures necessary to protect human, animal or plant life or health, and on the other, enshrined certain checks and balances to address the possibility of these measures emerging as non-tariff barriers.

Under the SPS Agreement, WTO Members have the right to take SPS measures 'necessary for the protection of human, animal or plant life or health', provided such measures are consistent with the provisions of this Agreement (Article 2.1). However, Members are required to ensure that any SPS measure is applied only to the extent necessary to protect human, animal or plant life or health. Such measures are, in general, required to be based on scientific principles and are not to be maintained without sufficient scientific evidence (Article 2.2). Moreover, as per Article 5.1 of the SPS Agreement, WTO Members are obliged to base their SPS measures on a risk-assessment, taking into account risk assessment techniques developed by the relevant international organisations. Other provisions under Article 5 of the SPS Agreement contain the requirements that WTO Members are to comply with for assessment of risk and for determination of the ALOP for their territories. Article 5.6 requires WTO Members to ensure that their SPS measures are not more trade-restrictive than necessary to achieve their ALOP, taking into account technical and economic feasibility. While 'sufficient scientific evidence' (Article 2.2) is the general requirement of the SPS Agreement, in case, relevant scientific evidence is insufficient, the SPS Agreement allows a Member to 'provisionally' adopt SPS measures on the basis of available pertinent information. However, since such measures may be applied on a provisional basis only, Members must seek to obtain the additional information necessary for a more objective assessment of risk and review the SPS measure accordingly, within a reasonable period of time. Members are required to ensure that their SPS measures do not arbitrarily or unjustifiably discriminate between countries where identical or similar conditions prevail, and are not applied in a manner, which would constitute a disguised restriction on international trade (Article 2.3). With the aim of achieving harmonisation, the Agreement urges WTO Members to base their SPS measures on international standards, wherever they exist (Article 3.1) and to participate (subject to their resource constraints) in the standardisation processes of relevant international organisations, such as the Codex Alimentarius Commission (CAC), the International Office of Epizootics (OIE), and

International Plant Protection Convention (IPPC) (Article 3.4). Members, however, are allowed to introduce or maintain SPS measures, which result in a higher level of SPS protection than would be achieved by measures based on the relevant international standards, guidelines or recommendations, if there is a scientific justification, or if it is determined to be appropriate by the Member in accordance with the relevant provisions of Article 5. Such higher level of SPS measures, however, must not be inconsistent with any other provision of this Agreement (Article 3.3). The Agreement (Article 4) encourages Members to recognise the concept of 'equivalence' and enter into consultations with other Members with the aim of achieving bilateral and multilateral agreements on recognition of the equivalence of specified SPS measures. It also urges them to recognise the concepts of pest- or disease-free areas or regions and accordingly adapt their SPS requirements for products originating from such areas or regions (Article 6). The SPS Agreement acknowledges the need to provide technical assistance to the developing countries (Article 9) and also includes certain special and differential treatment (S&DT) provisions for them (Article 10).

III. SELECTED PRODUCT-SPECIFIC SPS CHALLENGES FACED BY INDIA

Even though manufactured exports constitute the bulk of the merchandise exports from India, agricultural and allied products, particularly food items, continue to play an important role in India's global export basket.[25] Agriculture and allied activities remain critical for a broad based, inclusive and sustained growth of the Indian economy as well as food and livelihood security, since about 58 per cent of the population is still dependent on agriculture.[26] The principal food products exported by India include rice, tea, spices, meat, fruits and vegetables, among others. Over the past several years, Indian exporters of agricultural and allied products have encountered various SPS-related problems in various export destinations including the European Union (EU), United States (US), Japan, South East Asia, Russia, and the Middle East, among others.[27] According to the Government of India, the rising incidence of non-tariff barriers, in the form of SPS (and TBT) measures has emerged as a major trade concern

---

[25] Sawhney (2005), 332.
[26] WTO (2011a), 7.
[27] Divvaakar, Agarwal and Bhatia (2006), 241–42.

for the country.[28] This section of the Chapter dwells on some of the product-specific SPS problems experienced by India.[29]

A.   Marine Products

SPS-related problems have always remained a major cause of concern for Indian marine exports to the EU, which has very stringent regulations in the field of marine products. In August 1997, the EU banned seafood imports from India on grounds of health hazard and substandard processing units. The ban was imposed after a European Commission team inspected Indian seafood processing units in June 1997. Although the ban was subsequently lifted, the compliance with the stringent EU requirements involved substantial investment in infrastructure and equipment, apart from higher running costs. Roughly estimated, the upgrading of production facilities involved an expenditure of about US$250,000 to US$500,000 (per production unit) as a fixed cost. The Seafood Exporters Association of India claimed to have spent US$25 million on upgrading facilities to meet the EU requirements. In addition, substantial expenses had to be incurred for appropriate training of the personnel involved in various stages of production and processing.[30]

More recently, Indian marine exports have faced several detentions/rejections in the EU, on grounds of use of antibiotics and bacterial inhibitors. There is a view among the Indian exporters that the justification of the EU complaints in this area is often questionable. For instance, there are nearly 250 bacterial inhibitors, of which fewer than 10 are banned substances. However, it has been observed that in some cases, complaints are filed by the EU authorities on grounds of the mere presence of any of these 250 inhibitors, even if these are not specifically banned substances.[31] Moreover, detentions by different EU Member States have often been on different grounds for the same or similar consignments. A view has also emerged among the Indian exporters that these detention/rejection patterns coincide with the high season in the Mediterranean catch, leading to

---

[28]   WTO (2011a), 22.

[29]   While the list of sectors included here and the SPS issues pertaining to each of them is in no way exhaustive, the discussion is aimed at exemplifying the nature of the SPS challenges confronting the country in some of its major export destinations.

[30]   For further details, see Kaushik and Saqib (2001).

[31]   Divvaakar, Agarwal and Bhatia (2006), 264–265.

a drop in domestic prices in some of the EU Member States, such as Italy and Spain.[32]

India's shrimp exports have also encountered SPS problems in Japan. While mouldy smell[33] has turned out to be the foremost problem, other periodic quality problems include lack of freshness and inclusion of foreign materials (metal, plastics), among others.[34]

B.   Meat and Meat Products

India's exports of meat and meat products have encountered diverse SPS problems, particularly in the EU. The EU barred import of Indian buffalo meat on grounds of the prevalence of foot and mouth diseases (FMD) in Indian cattle. India argued that the EU standards in this area were more stringent than the international standards and urged the EU to be guided by the OIE stipulations for trade in livestock products. The EU, however, argued that four of its Member States hit by the FMD epidemic in 2001 had to spend a total of 12 billion Euro on eradication measures. In order to preserve these huge investments, the EU applied SPS measures follow-ing the scientific advice provided by the European Food Safety Authority (EFSA), which, according to the EU, was in compliance with the OIE and WTO law.[35]

Another problem pertained to the risk assessment process followed by the EU for geographical bovine spongiform encephalopathy (BSE) or 'mad cow disease'.[36] The Scientific Standing Committee of the EU categorised India as a country of GBR[37] level-II, i.e. 'BSE is unlikely but not excluded that domestic cattle are infected with BSE agent'. Such

---

[32]   Notably, both Italy and Spain, where detentions are the highest, have large domestic fisheries sectors, which depend on this catch for the tourist seasons.

[33]   The mouldy smell originates from the chemicals Geosmin and 2-Methyl-Iso-Borneol, which are produced by some types of algae that grow in turbid water. It occurs mostly in shrimp from the Bimavaram area of Andhara Pradesh (a state in Southern India), where a substantial proportion of shrimp farming of India is located. According to biologists, phyto-plankton that causes this smell thrives in water with low salinity, caused, for example, by the flow of fresh water into the culture ponds during the monsoon season; or in super-nutritious water, caused by insufficient cleaning of ponds or by overcrowded culture (Jonker, Ito and Fujishima (2005), 30).

[34]   *Ibid.*

[35]   WTO (2007a), 439.

[36]   Bovine spongiform encephalopathy (BSE), commonly known as mad-cow disease, is a fatal, neurodegenerative disease in cattle that causes a spongy degen-eration in the brain and spinal cord.

[37]   GBR stands for 'Geographical BSE-Risk'.

categorisation could potentially disrupt India's beef trade not only with the EU Member States but also with other trading partners. According to India, the assumptions made by the EU while conducting the risk assessment needed to be reconsidered, as BSE had never been reported in Indian cattle and buffalos.[38]

Another recent concern of India pertains to the EU requirements (vide EC Regulation No. 1099/2009 dated 24 September 2009) regarding the humane treatment of animals at the time of slaughter, which is scheduled to enter into force on 1 January 2013. According to this regulation, the import of meat from third countries must be supplemented by a health certificate indicating that requirements at least equivalent to those established under this regulation had been met. India is of the view that the EU regulation contained animal welfare requirements beyond those that had been in place since 1993, that these requirements would be trade restrictive, and as the slaughter of animals is a sanitary issue, this measure should be notified to the WTO.[39]

C.   Mango and Mango Pulp

Indian exports of mango and mango pulp have been affected by SPS-related problems in various export destinations including the US, Japan, the EU, Australia and New Zealand. Even though India is the largest mango producer in the world, accounting for roughly 50 per cent of the global mango production, with the highest number of varieties, exports of mango and mango pulp from India have not really been significant.[40] Issues related to pesticide residues on Indian mangoes and other SPS requirements are some of the key reasons underlying this poor performance on the export front.

Way back in the late 1980s, Japan banned the import of Indian mango on health grounds. The process of vapour heat treatment had to be put in place to comply with Japan's SPS requirements before mango exports could resume in 2007.

Until April 2007, India was not allowed to export mango to the US on

---

[38]   WTO (2007b).

[39]   For further details, see WTO (2012d), 35–37.

[40]   India produces around 15 million tonnes of mangoes that accounts for over 50 per cent of the world production. Other major producers of mangoes in the world are Pakistan, Brazil, Mexico, South Africa, Australia and Philippines etc. India exports less than half a per cent of its total production. Available at: <http://www.khaleejtimes.com/DisplayArticle.asp?xfile=data/business/2011/June/business_June524.xml&section=business&col> (last visited 31 May 2012).

SPS grounds. India had been pursuing the matter for several years with the US and finally the Agricultural and Processed Food Products Export Development Authority (APEDA) of India formulated a protocol for market access of mango to the US. With the aim of exporting 100 per cent pest and disease-free mangoes, an operations work plan (OWP) was agreed upon between the quarantine authorities of the two countries. Satisfied by the results of the work plan, the US agreed to import treated mangoes and the export of Indian mango finally began in April 2007. However, a major cause of concern has turned out to be the exorbitant cost of certification. According to the requirements, the entire cost of travel and stay of the United States Department of Agriculture (USDA) inspector in India at the irradiation facility as well as the officials of USDA located at different places and involved in the process, will have to be borne by India. This has raised critical questions about the commercial viability of mango exports to the US. It is felt by the APEDA that a mutually acceptable solution needs to be found for bringing down the transaction cost. Recognition of India's conformity assessment procedure by the US, for instance, may reduce the transaction costs significantly, according to the APEDA.[41]

D. Rice

India's exports of rice face SPS-related problems in countries such as the EU, the US, Japan, the Middle East and Russia. In June 2007, Russia banned imports of rice (along with sesame seeds and groundnuts) from India on grounds of detection of pests in rice consignments.[42] The problems in the EU and Japan largely relate to pesticide residues, frequent changes in standards and lack of clarity on the scientific justification of the standards. The difficulties of exporting to the Middle East arise primarily from a lack of clarity in the specification of standards and the extensive documentation requirements.[43] In the US, there are problems pertaining to delays in clearing consignments, repeated tests and bidding down of prices, among others.[44]

Recently exports of Indian Basmati rice has confronted problems relating to pesticide residues in the US. In August 2011, the US FDA issued an import alert because of the presence of the fungicide Tricyclazole in a shipment of Basmati rice. Tricyclazole is a fungicide used for treatment of

---

[41]   APEDA (2008), 13.
[42]   Available at: <http://oryza.com/Europe/Russia-Market/russian-imports-india-ban.html> (last visited 31 May 2012).
[43]   Jha (2002), 27.
[44]   *Ibid.*

blast in rice. The shipment concerned and all subsequent consignments of Basmati rice by that exporter were detained without physical examination. It is claimed that these detentions and the imposition of testing charges had resulted in huge losses to the Indian exporter. India argued that the measures were contrary to several core principles of the SPS Agreement. In particular, there appeared to be no scientific justification. This particular incidence is attributable to the US Food, Drug, and Cosmetic Act, according to which a food is deemed adulterated if it contains a pesticide for which there is no US Environmental Protection Agency (EPA)-established tolerance or exemption, and food that is found to be adulterated according to this rule is not admitted into the US. The Indian consignments were detained since no tolerances for the use of Tricyclazole as a pesticide in rice had been established by US EPA. The US has suggested India use one of the alternative fungicides for which the EPA had established tolerance limit.[45]

E.   Red Chilli Powder

On grounds that Sudan Red[46] – an azo dye – is potentially carcinogenic, the EU banned its use in processed foods. In October 2003, the EU stipulated the requirement of Sudan Red-free certificates for all spices, including red chilli powder and notified the appropriate agencies in India (the Spices Board and the Export Inspection Council (EIC)) after finding traces of Sudan Red in some export consignments of red chilli powder from India. The Spices Board of India was of the view that the harmful effects of Sudan Red could occur only at intake levels of red chilli powder that were substantially higher than even in countries like India, where chilli formed a key ingredient in daily diets. Such high intake levels were unforeseeable in the European countries. Hence, this was perceived by the Indian authorities as a case of over-stringent requirements based on unrealistic apprehensions. Notably, other large markets for red chilli powder like Africa, South East Asia and the Middle East did not impose such requirements, and allowed Indian red chilli powder to be exported without Sudan Red-free certificates. Sudan Red tests would cost INR 2,000 (US$ 40, approximately, with 1 US$ = INR 50) per sample, and several samples would be required to be drawn from a container load. The cost of inspection was very high for a low value product like red chilli powder. It was

---

[45]   WTO (2012d), 72–73.

[46]   The red dyes Sudan I, II, III and IV are oil soluble, azo dyes.

estimated to be around 3 per cent of the Cost, Insurance and Freight (CIF) value.[47]

F. Milk Products

India is the world's largest producer of milk accounting for around 14 per cent of the world milk production. However, presently, Indian milk products are not allowed to be exported to the EU. This is the case notwithstanding the fact that the EIC of India is operating a food safety management system based certification for export of milk products to ensure that the quality of the products exported meets the requirements of the importing countries. A major problem emanates from the fact that much of the milk production in India is by smallholders, who milk by hand and are members of cooperatives that collect milk for processing and further distribution. There are relatively few large-scale producers with mechanised milking facilities. The EU, however, requires that dairy products be manufactured from milk derived from cows that have been kept on farms and which have been mechanically milked. Given the predominance of hand milking in India, this effectively precludes smallholder producers and much of India's milk output from export to the EU.[48]

G. Tea

India is the world's largest producer and consumer of tea. However, pesticide residues in Indian tea have been a major cause of concern for India with respect to market access in various export destinations, particularly in the EU. For example, Germany complained about high residue levels of ethion in Darjeeling tea; and high levels of bicofol in Assam, Terai and Dooars tea. The justifications for some of these complaints, however, have been questioned by major tea exporting countries like India and China.[49]

---

[47] For further details, see, Divvaakar, Agarwal and Bhatia (2006), 263–264.

[48] DFID (2000), 15.

[49] For instance, in 1995, the residue limits of 0.01 mg of tetradifon and 2 mg of ethion per kg of tea, were allegedly imposed by Germany somewhat arbitrarily because of lack of data from India on its pesticide safety limits for tea. Later, the Teekanne Darjeeling Gold brand of tea was rejected because it contained 0.24 mg of tetrafidon per kg, which was 24 times the limit set by Germany. The rejection was soon followed by a report by the German Institute of Environment Analytics, Messzelle, branding it as unsafe. However, there were no rejections from the UK, another European market. This raised questions among the Indian stakeholders as to whether the German ban was based on protectionist intent.

H.   Flowers

Indian floriculture consignments have faced various market access problems in the EU, particularly in the Netherlands. Indian floricultural products were subjected to 50 per cent checks at entry points in the Netherlands. This was despite the fact that most entities involved in floriculture exports from India had stringent pest control management systems in place, which adhered to international standards. Most of them had also adopted Good Agricultural Practices (GAPs). The 50 per cent check was a time consuming process and resulted in unwanted delays in clearances, processing and delivery of the consignments to the end clients. Such delays caused loss of quality and reputation, particularly because floricultural products are very delicate with a short shelf-life. Notably, this practice has been maintained notwithstanding the fact that rejection rates have been negligible for years. India has proposed that the EU should reduce checks on Indian floriculture consignments to a reasonable level of say, 3–5 per cent so as to avoid unnecessary delays leading to heavy losses in the ornamental quality of flowers.[50] A key problem in addressing this issue at the EU level is that it is the prerogative of the Member States to decide on the level of checks.[51]

Floricultural exports from India have also confronted barriers in Japan due to stringent plant quarantine procedures, including zero tolerance for the insects and pests which already exist in Japan. Consignments were fumigated even when the fumigation had been done by the exporters and phytosanitary certificates accompanied the consignments.[52]

I.   Grapes

Import of grapes from India was banned by Japan on grounds of the presence of a variety of fruit fly called *Bactrocera dorsalis*. The Japanese authorities quoted one reference of 1960 stating that grapes in Pakistan were infested with oriental fruit fly. However it was far from clear how this reference was relevant for India. Notably, surveys conducted by two leading research institutes in India (namely, National Research Centre for Grapes, Pune and Indian Institute of Horticulture Research, Bangalore) on the presence of fruit flies on Indian grapes produced in the Western and

---

[50]   WTO (2007a), 439–440.
[51]   APEDA (2008), 5.
[52]   *Ibid.*, 12.

Southern regions did not find any infestation of *Bactrocera dorsalis* fruit fly on Indian grapes.[53]

IV.   SELECT DESTINATION-SPECIFIC SPS CONCERNS OF INDIA

Having exemplified select product-specific SPS-challenges confronting India, this section puts forward some of the more general SPS-related concerns of the country vis-à-vis two important trading partners, the EU and US.

A.   European Union

It is evident from the product-specific experiences enumerated in the previous section that the EU has consistently been a major source of SPS-related problems confronting India. This is not unexpected given that the EU is generally known to have one of the strictest SPS regulations in the world. Developing countries at large have been severely affected due to its non-acceptance of established international standards and the application of its own higher standards on grounds of observance of higher safety norms. The EU does not always provide sufficient evidence to justify those stricter requirements. In many cases, the scientific justification of the EU requirements has also been called into question.[54]

Indian exports of various food products including spices, peanuts, groundnuts, cereals and various other processed foods have confronted problems in the EU markets on grounds of the presence of aflatoxins[55] beyond the maximum residue levels (MRLs) permitted by the bloc. According to the EU requirements, the MRLs should be respected on arrival of the consignment at the ports of the EU Member States. India considered this approach to be impractical, because aflatoxins could come up at any stage after drawing of samples for testing and the voyage provided an optimum environment for growth of aflatoxins. Moreover, the

---

[53]   *Ibid.*, 12–13.

[54]   Jha (2002), 22.

[55]   Aflatoxins are toxic metabolites produced by certain fungi in/on foods and feeds. They are mycotoxins that have been associated with various diseases, such as aflatoxicosis, in livestock, domestic animals and humans throughout the world. The occurence of aflatoxins is influenced by certain environmental factors. <http://www.ansci.cornell.edu/plants/toxicagents/aflatoxin/aflatoxin.html> (last visited 9 June 2012).

sampling procedure for testing for the presence of aflatoxin is so complex and expensive that it is often very difficult for exporters from developing countries to undergo.

The EU requirements regarding MRLs of certain pesticides have been another cause of concern over the recent past. This pertains to the EU legislation on pesticide residues that has been in place since 1 September 2008, which, according to India, has set the MRLs for a number of chemicals at the 'limit of detection' (LOD). The LOD is the limit below which residues could not be detected by using sophisticated analytical methods. According to India, the setting of MRLs at the LOD had impacted its exports of agricultural products to the EU. Moreover, it alleged that no scientific evidence had been provided by the EU to justify the setting of the MRLs at the LOD, especially for imported products. Furthermore, different climatic conditions in India required different use of pesticides in agricultural production. According to the EU, an LOD was set when there was a safety concern for consumers from the use of a pesticide at high levels or when there was no authorised use on a specific crop within the EU or third countries. Nevertheless, the EU allows trading partners to apply for getting import tolerances set for higher MRLs in specific cases, by providing scientific evidence. Although India has attempted to use this window of opportunity to have the MRLs set at higher levels for certain products, it has alleged that the EU procedure for this purpose is lengthy, costly and burdensome. India has urged the EU to replace the measures concerned with 'more predictable and science-based ones'.[56]

While the EU as a whole has often deviated from international standards in defiance of the harmonisation principle of the SPS Agreement, lack of harmonisation among the Member States of this bloc with regard to SPS requirements and their implementation has turned out to be another major cause of concern for the trade partners of the bloc like India. A special characteristic of EU integration is that even Member States are allowed to maintain their own internal regulations and standards on a range of subjects. It has been observed that often food products entering into the EU are subject to inspections under the common EU standards at the first point of entry to the EU, and once again at the point of entry into the final destination country. Due to the independent jurisdiction of Member States, there is no uniformity in EU standards for risk management, detentions, and disposal at the point of entry. This causes enormous uncertainty in the resolution of issues relating to SPS matters. The absence of a common and harmonised regulatory environment in the EU is the

---

[56]   WTO (2012d), 29–31.

underlying cause for a majority of rejections encountered by many exporters, including those from India.[57] Other key issues include the absence of clearly laid out procedures for detention and disposal of consignments and inadequate coordination among Member States' agencies in the notification and de-notification of suppliers placed under alerts, following detentions.[58]

The EU system of 'rapid alert' is worth a special mention in this context.[59] Rapid alert is a border control mechanism for monitoring and ensuring the quality of imported food products by issuing a notification in case of detection of contaminated imports or of products not meeting the required standards. The notification is made to all EU Member States as well as to the exporter. As a result of such alert, a predetermined number of subsequent export consignments of that particular exporter face 100 per cent inspection at the border of every port of the EU Member States. However, this 'predetermined number' varies by Member State. While termination of the alert requires the same procedures to be followed by the authorities as its institution, it does not take place as promptly, thereby continuing to hinder trade.

Another damaging procedure followed by the EU is the system of destruction of rejected food consignments[60] on account of lack of conformity with standards, without even informing the consignors, let alone returning the consignments. This is particularly frequent in France and Italy. The destruction is carried out on grounds that consignments declared unfit for human consumption should not be salvaged. This is different from the practices followed by India and several other countries. It has been alleged that the EU system results in destruction of good cargos along with the bad ones, all at the cost of the exporters, thereby resulting in huge losses for them. It is reasonable to expect that the exporter should have the first right to a rejected consignment and should have the option to either take it back or to divert the consignment to another country where it may be acceptable according to its SPS requirements. This may help in curtailing the financial losses for the exporters – particularly for food items with a sufficiently long shelf life. However, exporters are not able to explore such alternatives owing to the EU system of destruction of rejected food consignments.

---

[57] Divvaakar, Agarwal and Bhatia (2006), 225–226.

[58] *Ibid.*, 242–243.

[59] The discussion on 'rapid alert' draws heavily on Divvaakar, Agarwal and Bhatia (2006), 265.

[60] *Ibid.*, 266.

B.   United States

Food and health safety-related requirements in the US have impacted India significantly. Imports into the US are regulated under the Federal regulations. They require that the purchaser/importer of the products be able to demonstrate to the authorities that the products have been produced in a safe and acceptable manner i.e. they are in compliance with quality assurance system that incorporates hazard analysis critical control point (HACCP), Standard Sanitary Operating Procedures (SSOP) and Good Manufacturing Practices (GMP). Compliance with so many sanitary procedures act as NTBs. India has urged the US to take steps to streamline these requirements.[61] Other SPS concerns of India vis-à-vis the US include, among others, generally strict and burdensome SPS requirements; delays at labs testing processed food imports; longstanding ban on uncooked meat products even from disease-free regions; fresh dairy products (e.g. yogurt) banned due to Grade A certification difficulties.[62]

The 'Public Health Security and Bioterrorism Preparedness and Response Act of 2002', or the Bioterrorism Act, which came into being after the September 11 terrorist attacks has been a major cause of concern for India.[63] Title III of this Act deals with *'Protecting Safety and Security of Food and Drug Supply'*. It requires, among other things, that domestic and foreign facilities that manufacture, process, pack and hold food for consumption in the US register with the US Food and Drug Administration (FDA); the FDA receives notice prior to the entry of food that is imported or offered for import into the US; and the persons involved in the manufacture, distribution and receipt of food in the US establish and maintain records that identify the immediate previous sources and immediate subsequent recipient of that food. The Bioterrorism Act has also given the FDA the authority to administratively detain any food for which there is credible evidence or information that the food presents a threat of serious adverse health consequences or death to humans or animals.

Despite a general recognition that greater bioterrorism protection is needed, concerns have widely been raised about the potential trade-restrictive implications of Title III. It has been pointed out that Title III discriminates between domestic and foreign food manufacturers by imposing increased transaction costs and procedural burdens solely on

---

[61]   WTO (2006a), 32.
[62]   Becker (2006), 24.
[63]   *Ibid.*, 6–7.

foreign facilities, thereby creating NTBs.[64] The foreign agent requirement for exporters and the problems associated with implementation of the prior notice requirements for imports are some of the potential sources of such NTBs, as discussed below.

Under the registration process, exporters of the products covered under this Act must designate a US agent at the time of registration. The agent is required to live or maintain a place of business in the US and be physically present there. For the developing country exporters, to find a US agent is not only difficult, but also costly.[65]

Under the prior notice requirement of the Act, all food imports must be notified to the FDA.[66] There are time limits for sending the notice of food imports to the FDA, based on the mode of transportation used: eight hours for food arriving by water, four hours by air or rail, and two hours by road. The exporter or her US agent can file this information with the FDA. The problem arises because the exact arrival details of vessels are not easily disclosed to exporters by shipping lines or their agents, especially in the case of trans-shipment vessels. This makes it difficult to honour the deadlines stipulated. Moreover, these deadlines are often alleged to be based on the FDA's administrative convenience and not on security concerns. Some Indian exporters have expressed the view that the compulsory Advance Cargo Declaration requirements for US ports also provide nearly the same information, and hence there should not be any need for filing pre-arrival declarations with the FDA separately.[67]

Another recent cause of concern has been the US Food Safety Modernization Act (FSMA), which was formally adopted in January 2011. According to India, FSMA introduced an elaborate multi-layered scheme of checks within the food supply chain to minimise the possibility of food contamination, putting extra burden on exporters and leading to higher transaction costs. India's key concerns relate to the registration of Foreign Food Facilities, the Voluntary Qualified Importer Program, Certification and Audit and the Foreign Supplier Verification Program. India is of the view that several provisions of FSMA did not reflect the

---

[64]   Boisen (2007), 670–71.

[65]   Some export organisations of India, such as the Cashew Export Promotion Council, have collectively appointed US agents and share the costs through a pool account or through membership service charges (Divvaakar, Agarwal and Bhatia (2006), 222).

[66]   http://www.fda.gov/Food/FoodDefense/Bioterrorism/PriorNotice/default. htm (last visited 9 June 2012).

[67]   Divvaakar, Agarwal and Bhatia (2006), 222.

core principles of equivalence and harmonisation of the SPS Agreement. The country has urged the United States to ensure that FSMA was in line with the SPS Agreement, and the Codex principles and guidelines for the design, operation, assessment and accreditation of food import and export inspection and certification systems.[68]

V.   SPS REQUIREMENTS AND THE WTO JURISPRUDENCE[69]

The experience of India, as exemplified in the aforesaid discussion, tends to indicate that it is still an open question as to what extent the SPS Agreement has been effective in preventing the SPS measures from emerging as NTBs. This raises the question as to what extent this could be attributable to legal loopholes embedded in the Agreement itself. This Section explores this issue in the light of some of the key provisions of the SPS Agreement and related case law.

It may be noted at this juncture that a recurring and delicate issue in the GATT/WTO dispute settlement processes, in general, and SPS-related disputes, in particular, is whether, and to what extent, WTO panels and the Appellate Body (AB) should defer to national government decisions.[70] The point up to which WTO panels should respect national government determinations has been a widely debated issue that has sometimes been labelled the 'standard of review'.[71] In other words, standard of review marks the boundary of a Member State's discretion, and determines the power of WTO panels to investigate, evaluate and judge the acts of a Member State against its legal obligations.[72] Thus while it is fundamentally a legal question, the issue of the standard of review relates to the allocation of power between Member States and the WTO.[73]

A close look at the mode of interpretation of some of the key provisions of the SPS Agreement put forward by the WTO panels and the Appellate Body indeed indicates a tendency to bestow upon WTO Members a large measure of autonomy and flexibility in imposing SPS requirements,

---

[68]   WTO (2012d), 69–72.
[69]   This section draws partly on Das (2008), 982–96.
[70]   For a detailed discussion, see Oesch (2003).
[71]   Croley and Jackson (1996), 194.
[72]   Cass (2001), 58.
[73]   Du, (2010), 441.

thereby leaving the scope for these measures emerging as NTBs, as elaborated upon in this Section.[74]

As mentioned before, the Agreement requires the SPS measures, in general, to be based on sufficient scientific evidence (Article 2.2[75]) and risk assessment (Article 5.1[76]). In *Japan – Agricultural Products II*, the WTO Appellate Body observed that '*the obligation in Article 2.2 that an SPS measure not be maintained without sufficient scientific evidence requires that there be a* rational or objective relationship *between the SPS measure and the scientific evidence*' (emphasis added).[77]

In *EC – Hormones*, the Appellate Body clarified that Articles 2.2 and 5.1 should '*constantly be read together*' and pointed out that: Article 2.2 informs Article 5.1; the elements that define the basic obligation set out in Article 2.2 impart meaning to Article 5.1.[78]

Importantly, the Appellate Body, in the same case, referred to the requirement of 'sufficient scientific evidence' as part of a 'balance' contained in the SPS Agreement. It stated that '[t]he requirements of a risk assessment under Article 5.1, as well as of "sufficient scientific evidence"

---

[74] It may be noted here that while strictly speaking the doctrine of precedent is not a part of the WTO dispute settlement system, in practice the previous reports of panels and the Appellate Body receive due consideration in subsequent disputes and therefore form an important part of the WTO *acquis*. The Appellate Body in *US – Stainless Steel (Mexico)* ruled that 'the legal interpretation embodied in adopted panel and Appellate Body reports becomes part and parcel of the *acquis* of the WTO dispute settlement system. Ensuring "security and predictability" in the dispute settlement system, as contemplated in Article 3.2 of the DSU, implies that, absent cogent reasons, an adjudicatory body will resolve the same legal question in the same way in a subsequent case' (Appellate Body Report, *United States – Final Anti-Dumping Measures on Stainless Steel from Mexico* [henceforth *US-Stainless Steel (Mexico)*], WT/DS344/AB/R, adopted 20 May 2008, DSR 2008:II, 513, para. 160].

[75] Article 2.2: 'Members shall ensure that any sanitary or phytosanitary measure is applied only to the extent necessary to protect human, animal or plant life or health, is based on scientific principles and is not maintained without sufficient scientific evidence, except as provided for in paragraph 7 of Article 5.'

[76] Article 5.1: 'Members shall ensure that their sanitary or phytosanitary measures are based on an assessment, as appropriate to the circumstances, of the risks to human, animal or plant life or health, taking into account risk assessment techniques developed by the relevant international organizations.'

[77] Appellate Body Report, *Japan – Measures Affecting Agricultural Products* (henceforth *Japan – Agricultural Products II*), WT/DS76/AB/R, adopted 19 March 1999, para. 84.

[78] Appellate Body Report, *EC Measures Concerning Meat and Meat Products (Hormones)* (henceforth *EC – Hormones*), WT/DS26/AB/R, WT/DS48/AB/R, adopted 13 February 1998, para. 180.

under Article 2.2, are essential for the maintenance of the delicate and carefully negotiated balance in the SPS Agreement between the shared, but sometimes competing, interests of promoting international trade and of protecting the life and health of human beings'.[79]

However, the interpretations of these two provisions (Articles 2.2 and 5.1) alongside other related provisions of SPS Agreement seem to have tilted the 'balance' in favour of the latter interest to a great extent, as discussed below.

Regarding the first definition of 'risk assessment' as enshrined in Paragraph 4 of Annex A of the SPS Agreement,[80] the Appellate Body in *Australia – Salmon* observed that 'the first type of risk assessment demands an evaluation of the likelihood of entry, establishment or spread of a disease, and of the associated potential biological and economic consequences'.[81] However, it pointed out that '*the SPS Agreement does not require that the evaluation of the likelihood needs to be done quantitatively. The likelihood may be expressed either quantitatively or qualitatively*' (emphasis added).[82] It furthermore clarified, citing its findings in the *EC – Hormones* that '*there is no requirement for a risk assessment to establish* a certain magnitude or threshold level of degree of risk' (emphasis added).[83]

As for the second definition of 'risk assessment' in Paragraph 4 of Annex A, the Appellate Body in *Australia – Salmon* observed that it 'requires only the evaluation of the potential for adverse effects on human or animal health'.[84]

The Appellate Body in *EC – Hormones* also pointed out, in the course of commenting on the Panel's interpretation of 'risk assessment', that:

---

[79]   *Ibid.*, para. 177.

[80]   Para 4 of Annex A reads as follows:

Risk assessment – The evaluation of the likelihood of entry, establishment or spread of a pest or disease within the territory of an importing Member according to the sanitary or phytosanitary measures which might be applied, and of the associated potential biological and economic consequences; or the evaluation of the potential for adverse effects on human or animal health arising from the presence of additives, contaminants, toxins or disease-causing organisms in food, beverages or feedstuffs.

[81]   Appellate Body Report, *Australia – Measures Affecting Importation of Salmon* (henceforth *Australia – Salmon*), WT/DS18/AB/R, adopted 6 November 1998, DSR 1998:VIII, 3327, fn. 69.

[82]   *Ibid.*, para. 124.

[83]   *Ibid.*

[84]   *Ibid.*, fn. 69.

[t]o the extent that the Panel purported to require a risk assessment to establish a minimum magnitude of risk, we must note that imposition of such a quantitative requirement finds no basis in the SPS Agreement. A panel is authorised only to determine whether a given SPS measure is 'based on' a risk assessment. As will be elaborated below, this means that a panel has to determine whether an SPS measure is sufficiently supported or reasonably warranted by the risk assessment.[85]

The lack of requirements to undertake a quantitative evaluation of risk and to establish a minimum magnitude or threshold level of degree of risk seem to dilute the stringency of the obligation under Article 5.1 to a large extent.

Moreover, on the question of whether a WTO Member is required to carry out a 'risk assessment' by itself, the Appellate Body in EC – Hormones observed that 'Article 5.1 does not insist that a Member that adopts a sanitary measure shall have carried out its own risk assessment . . . The SPS measure might well find its objective justification in a risk assessment carried out by another Member, or an international organization.'[86] This is another flexibility available to the WTO Members, which, however, may be beneficial for Members that lack scientific capacity to carry out their own risk assessments.

In another significant pronouncement, the Appellate Body in *EC – Hormones* ruled that reliance on a non-majority opinion in the scientific community does not, by itself, 'necessarily signal the absence of a reasonable relationship between the SPS measure and the risk assessment, especially where the risk involved is life-threatening in character and is perceived to constitute a clear and imminent threat to public health and safety'.[87] It noted that '[t]he risk assessment could set out both the prevailing view representing the "mainstream" of scientific opinion, as well as the opinions of scientists taking a divergent view. Article 5.1 does not require that the risk assessment must necessarily embody only the view of a majority of the relevant scientific community.'[88]

While this interpretation creates flexibility for regulators in cases of scientific controversy,[89] the Appellate Body has also mentioned that divergent or minority views have to be coming from a qualified and respected source.[90] The Appellate Body in *US – Continued Suspension* further ruled that:

---

[85]   Appellate Body Report, *EC – Hormones*, para. 186.
[86]   *Ibid.*, para. 190.
[87]   *Ibid.*, para. 194.
[88]   *Ibid.*, para. 194.
[89]   Prévost (2005), 5.
[90]   Appellate Body Report, *EC – Hormones*, para. 194.

(a)lthough the scientific basis need not represent the majority view within the scientific community, it must nevertheless have the necessary scientific and methodological rigour to be considered reputable science. In other words, while the correctness of the views need not have been accepted by the broader scientific community, the views must be considered to be legitimate science according to the standards of the relevant scientific community.[91]

According to the Appellate Body, a panel should also assess whether the reasoning articulated on the basis of the scientific evidence is objective and coherent and then determine whether the results of the risk assessment 'sufficiently warrant' the SPS measure at issue. However, '[h]ere, again, the scientific basis cited as warranting the SPS measure need not reflect the majority view of the scientific community provided that it comes from a qualified and respected source'.[92]

Several findings of the Appellate Body in *US – Continued Suspension* indicate that the Appellate Body imposed a new requirement on the panel to provide reasoned and adequate explanation as to why it did not consider divergent opinions.[93] As observed by some commentators, after *US – Continued Suspension*, 'WTO panels will need to address divergent opinions more fully, explain clearly why they decide not to accept these divergent opinions, and the AB will be more willing to intervene in this regard'.[94]

Regarding the factors to be taken into account in assessment of risk as per Article 5.2[95] of SPS Agreement, the Appellate Body in *EC – Hormones* apparently depicted its 'willingness to descend into the real social world',[96] by observing that:

---

[91]   Appellate Body Report, *United States – Continued Suspension of Obligations in the EC – Hormones Dispute* (henceforth *US – Continued Suspension*), WT/DS320/AB/R, adopted 14 November 2008, DSR 2008:X, 3507, para. 591.

[92]   *Ibid.*

[93]   The Appellate Body stated that 'given that the European Communities was entitled to rely on minority views, the panel was required to explain why it did not consider that Dr. Guttenplan's testimony supported the European Communities' position' (*Ibid.*, para 613). The Appellate Body also criticised the panel for not giving any reasons why it did not consider certain other studies in this respect as relevant (*Ibid.*, para. 605).

[94]   Du, (2010), 454.

[95]   Article 5.2 of SPS Agreement: 'In the assessment of risks, Members shall take into account available scientific evidence; relevant processes and production methods; relevant inspection, sampling and testing methods; prevalence of specific diseases or pests; existence of pest- or disease-free areas; relevant ecological and environmental conditions; and quarantine or other treatment.'

[96]   Chimni (2000), 1758.

> [i]t is essential to bear in mind that the risk that is to be evaluated in a risk assessment under Article 5.1 is not only risk ascertainable in a science laboratory operating under strictly controlled conditions, but also risk in human societies as they actually exist, in other words, the actual potential for adverse effects on human health in the real world where people live and work and die. (emphasis added)[97]

The Appellate Body further noted the 'depth and extent of the anxieties experienced'[98] and 'the intense concern of consumers'[99] within the European Communities (EC). As observed by some commentators, the Appellate Body report reveals 'surprising sensitivity to public anxieties regarding ecological risks, and adopts a broad concept of risk'.[100] It thus creates a legal link between the level of public anxiety and conformity to WTO rules, endowing the civil society with the power to confer legitimacy on governmental regulatory measures.[101] Some commentators have sounded caution that '[t]he WTO DSS has to be alert to the fact that this legal link between the democratic sentiment and trade measures can be mobilised in future by the forces of protection to curtail free trade'.[102]

An exception to the obligation of Members to base SPS measures on scientific principles is provided in Article 5.7,[103] which allows them to adopt provisional measures on the basis of available pertinent information, in cases where relevant scientific evidence is insufficient. However, the Member applying such a provisional measure must seek to obtain the necessary additional information for a more objective risk assessment and review the measure accordingly within a reasonable period of time.

The relationship between the precautionary principle and the SPS Agreement was first raised in the *EC – Hormones* case in the context of Article 5.7. Although the Appellate Body in *EC – Hormones* observed that

---

97 Appellate Body Report, *EC – Hormones*, para. 187.
98 *Ibid.*, para. 245.
99 *Ibid.*
100 Perez (1998), 563.
101 *Ibid.*, 572.
102 Chimni (2000), 1758.
103 Article 5.7 of SPS Agreement:

In cases where relevant scientific evidence is insufficient, a Member may provisionally adopt sanitary or phytosanitary measures on the basis of available pertinent information, including that from the relevant international organizations as well as from sanitary or phytosanitary measures applied by other Members. In such circumstances, Members shall seek to obtain the additional information necessary for a more objective assessment of risk and review the sanitary or phytosanitary measure accordingly within a reasonable period of time.

the precautionary principle has not been written into the SPS Agreement as a ground for justifying SPS measures that are otherwise inconsistent with the obligations of Members, nevertheless it pointed out that 'the precautionary principle indeed finds reflection in Article 5.7 of the SPS Agreement'. The Appellate Body also found that Article 5.7 did not exhaust the relevance of a precautionary principle and that the principle was also reflected in the sixth paragraph of the preamble and in Article 3.3 of the SPS Agreement.[104] It furthermore suggested that:

> a panel charged with determining, for instance, whether 'sufficient scientific evidence' exists to warrant the maintenance by a Member of a particular SPS measure may, of course, and should, bear in mind that *responsible, representative governments commonly act from perspectives of prudence and precaution where risks of irreversible, e.g. life-terminating, damage to human health are concerned* (emphasis added).[105]

The aforesaid pronouncement seems to depict significant deference towards the judgment of the representative governments imposing SPS measures (which in that particular case happened to be the EC).

However, the findings of the panels and Appellate Body in certain subsequent cases do seem to reduce somewhat the room available to Members for application of Article 5.7 and the precautionary principle.

In *Japan – Agricultural Products II*, the Appellate Body identified four requirements that must be met cumulatively in order to adopt and maintain a provisional SPS measure under Article 5.7. Under the first sentence, 'a Member may provisionally adopt an SPS measure if this measure is: (1) imposed in respect of a situation where "relevant scientific information is insufficient"; and (2) adopted "on the basis of available pertinent information"'.[106]

Under the second sentence, such a provisional measure cannot be maintained unless the Member concerned '(1) "seek[s] to obtain the additional information necessary for a more objective assessment of risk"; and (2) "review[s] the . . . measure accordingly within a reasonable period of time"'.[107]

The Appellate Body clearly stated that '[w]henever one of these four requirements is not met, the measure at issue is inconsistent with Article 5.7'. Thus the adoption and maintenance of any provisional measure

---

[104]   Appellate Body Report, *EC – Hormones*, para. 124.
[105]   *Ibid.*, para. 124.
[106]   Appellate Body Report, *Japan – Agricultural Products II*, para. 89.
[107]   *Ibid.*

under Article 5.7 is possible only when all the four requirements enumerated above are complied with.

Subsequently, in *Japan – Apples*, the panel and the Appellate Body addressed the first requirement of Article 5.7, namely that the situation is one where 'relevant scientific evidence is insufficient'. Japan in this case argued that should the panel find the scientific evidence insufficient to support Japan's measure under Article 2.2, the measure could be considered to be a provisional measure in the context of Article 5.7. The panel found that the fact that a particular measure was maintained 'without sufficient scientific evidence' under Article 2.2 did not necessarily mean that 'relevant scientific evidence is insufficient', which the panel regarded as a separate question.[108] Thus, a clear distinction was made between the concepts of sufficiency in Article 2.2 and that in Article 5.7. Whereas the *sufficiency* requirement under Article 2.2 requires that the evidence supporting the SPS measure in question be sufficient,[109] the body of material that might be considered with regard to the *insufficiency* of the 'relevant scientific evidence' under Article 5.7 includes not only the evidence supporting the position of the Member imposing the measure, but also evidence supporting other views.[110] Thus, 'all available information must be insufficient before a Member can rely on Article 5.7'.[111] While upholding the panel's findings, the Appellate Body in *Japan – Apples* found a link or relationship between the first requirement under Article 5.7 and the obligation to perform a risk assessment under Article 5.1. It ruled that 'relevant scientific evidence' will be 'insufficient' within the meaning of Article 5.7 'if the body of available scientific evidence does not allow, in quantitative or qualitative terms, the performance of an adequate assessment of risks . . .'.[112] The Appellate Body further pointed out, while upholding the panel's finding that Article 5.7 was 'triggered not by the existence of scientific uncertainty, but rather by the insufficiency of scientific evidence'.[113] Thus the findings of *Japan – Apples* clarified that Article 5.7 cannot be invoked to justify an SPS measure that is adopted in disregard of existing scientific evidence; nor can it be used in situations of scientific controversy,

---

[108] Panel Report, *Japan – Measures Affecting the Importation of Apples* (henceforth *Japan – Apples*), WT/DS245/R, adopted 10 December 2003, upheld by Appellate Body Report, WT/DS245/AB/R, DSR 2003:IX, 4481, para. 8.215.

[109] Prévost (2005), 8.

[110] Panel Report, *Japan – Apples*, para 8.216.

[111] Prévost (2005), 8.

[112] Appellate Body Report, *Japan – Apples*, WT/DS245/AB/R, adopted 10 December 2003, DSR 2003:IX, 4391, para. 179.

[113] *Ibid.*, para. 184.

where proper risk assessments have been conducted, but are in conflict with each other.[114]

According to some analysts, the findings in *Japan – Apples* 'establish the fact that the precautionary principle, as embodied in Article 5.7, does not create a broad loophole in the scientific disciplines of the SPS Agreement through which protectionist measures can slip. Rather, it creates a limited exception for cases where there is a true lack of relevant and reliable scientific evidence on the risk at issue'.[115]

As regards the third requirement for application of Article 5.7, i.e. the requirement that a Member applying a provisional measure under this Article must seek to obtain the necessary additional information for a more objective risk assessment, in *Japan – Agricultural Products II*, the Appellate Body clarified that the obligation in this respect is only to 'seek to obtain' additional information. There are no 'explicit prerequisites regarding the additional information to be collected or a specific collection procedure'. Nor is there any requirement as to what actual results must be achieved. However, the Appellate Body observed that since the additional information was to be sought in order to enable the Member concerned to conduct a more objective risk assessment, so the information sought must be germane to conducting such a risk assessment.[116] The Appellate Body in *US – Continued Suspension* further clarified that a Member is merely required to seek to obtain additional information but is not expected to guarantee specific results. 'Nor is it expected to predict the actual results of its efforts to collect additional information at the time when it adopts the SPS measure.'[117] In other words the obligation is in the nature of endeavour, rather than achievement of actual results, which would have made the obligation more stringent.

As for the fourth requirement for application of Article 5.7, i.e. the requirement for the Member applying the provisional measure to review the measure within 'a reasonable period of time', the moot question of what constitutes a 'reasonable period of time' was addressed by the Appellate Body in *Japan – Agricultural Products II*. The Appellate Body ruled that it has to be established on a 'case-by-case basis' and depends on the specific circumstances of each case, including the difficulty of obtaining the additional information necessary for the review and the characteristics of the provisional SPS measure.[118] In view of this pronouncement, there seems to

---

[114]   Prévost (2005), 9.
[115]   *Ibid.*, 10.
[116]   Appellate Body Report, *Japan – Agricultural Products II*, para. 92.
[117]   Appellate Body Report, *US – Continued Suspension*, para. 679.
[118]   Appellate Body Report, *Japan – Agricultural Products II*, para. 93.

be enough room for taking into account the state of scientific knowledge and the time needed for this knowledge to develop.[119] Thus, a provisional measure under Article 5.7 may be maintained for a long time, if it turns out to be 'reasonable period of time' for the particular case in point and all other requirements of Article 5.7 are satisfied cumulatively.

Although promotion of harmonisation of SPS measures across countries through adherence to international standards is purportedly a key objective of SPS Agreement, the interpretations of the relevant provisions under Article 3 leave sufficient room for WTO Members to deviate from international standards, even where they exist. The Appellate Body in *EC – Hormones* observed that:

> [i]n generalized terms, the object and purpose of Article 3 is to promote the harmonization of the SPS measures of Members on as wide a basis as possible, while recognizing and safeguarding, at the same time, *the right and duty of Members to protect the life and health of their people.* The ultimate goal of the harmonization of SPS measures is to prevent the use of such measures for arbitrary or unjustifiable discrimination between Members or as a disguised restriction on international trade, *without preventing Members from adopting or enforcing measures which are both 'necessary to protect' human life or health and 'based on scientific principles', and without requiring them to change their appropriate level of protection.*[120] (emphasis added)

Regarding the obligation to base SPS measures on international standards as included in Article 3.1,[121] the Appellate Body in *EC – Hormones* stated that '[u]nder Article 3.1 of the SPS Agreement, a Member may choose to establish an SPS measure that is based on the existing relevant international standard, guideline or recommendation'. However, it clearly mentioned that '(s)uch a measure may adopt some, not necessarily all, of the elements of the international standard',[122] thereby leaving adequate room for WTO Members to deviate partly from the international standard in question.

Moreover, Article 3.3[123] explicitly allows WTO Members to diverge

---

[119]   Prévost (2005), 7.
[120]   Appellate Body Report, *EC – Hormones*, para. 177.
[121]   Article 3.1 of SPS Agreement: 'To harmonize sanitary and phytosanitary measures on as wide a basis as possible, Members shall base their sanitary or phytosanitary measures on international standards, guidelines or recommendations, where they exist, except as otherwise provided for in this Agreement, and in particular in paragraph 3.'
[122]   Appellate Body Report, *EC – Hormones*, para. 171.
[123]   Article 3.3 of SPS Agreement:

> Members may introduce or maintain sanitary or phytosanitary measures which result in a higher level of sanitary or phytosanitary protection than would be

from international standards under certain conditions. In *EC – Hormones*, the Appellate Body observed that:

> [u]nder Article 3.3 of the *SPS Agreement*, a Member may decide to set for itself a level of protection different from that implicit in the international standard, and to implement or embody that level of protection in a measure not 'based on' the international standard. The Member's appropriate level of protection may be higher than that implied in the international standard. The right of a Member to determine its own appropriate level of sanitary protection is an important right.[124]

The Appellate Body furthermore clarified that the 'right of a Member to establish its own level of sanitary protection under Article 3.3 of the SPS Agreement is an autonomous right and not an "exception" from a "general obligation" under Article 3.1'.[125] The determination of the Appellate Body that it is the autonomous right of a state to adopt a higher than international standard offers states greater latitude in the adoption of SPS measures than if it had deemed it an exception.[126]

The Appellate Body, in *Australia – Salmon*, further stressed that an explicit statement by a Member about its level of protection could not be questioned by a panel or the Appellate Body. It stated that '[t]he determination of the appropriate level of protection, a notion defined in paragraph 5 of Annex A, as "the level of protection deemed appropriate

---

> achieved by measures based on the relevant international standards, guidelines or recommendations, if there is a scientific justification, or as a consequence of the level of sanitary or phytosanitary protection a Member determines to be appropriate in accordance with the relevant provisions of paragraphs 1 through 8 of Article 5 (footnote omitted). Notwithstanding the above, all measures which result in a level of sanitary or phytosanitary protection different from that which would be achieved by measures based on international standards, guidelines or recommendations shall not be inconsistent with any other provision of this Agreement.

The footnote added to this provision reads as follows:

> For the purposes of paragraph 3 of Article 3, there is a scientific justification if, on the basis of an examination and evaluation of available scientific information in conformity with the relevant provisions of this Agreement, a Member determines that the relevant international standards, guidelines or recommendations are not sufficient to achieve its appropriate level of sanitary or phytosanitary protection.

[124]   Appellate Body Report, *EC – Hormones*, para. 172.
[125]   *Ibid.*
[126]   Chimni (2000), 1758.

by the Member establishing a sanitary . . . measure", is a prerogative of the Member concerned and not of a panel or of the Appellate Body'.[127]

While distinguishing between risk assessment under Article 5.1 and the determination, by a Member, of its own ALOP, the Appellate Body in *Australia – Salmon* further clarified that the 'risk' evaluated in a risk assessment must be an ascertainable risk; theoretical uncertainty is not the kind of risk, which is to be assessed under Article 5.1. However, it pointed out that this does not mean that a Member cannot determine its own appropriate level of protection to be 'zero risk'.[128]

Article 5.4 of SPS Agreement states that '[m]embers should, when determining the appropriate level of sanitary or phytosanitary protection, take into account the objective of minimizing negative trade effects'. However, the mode of interpretation of this and other provisions of SPS Agreement pertaining to trade effects of SPS measures (e.g. Articles 5.5 and 5.6), as put forward by the WTO DSS, seems to make it quite difficult to effectively address this issue. For instance, the panel in *EC – Hormones*, in a finding not reviewed by the Appellate Body, held that Article 5.4[129] was of a hortatory nature. It observed that '[g]uided by the wording of Article 5.4, in particular the words "should" (not "shall") and "objective", we consider that this provision of the SPS Agreement does not impose an obligation. However, this objective of minimizing negative trade effects has nonetheless to be taken into account in the interpretation of other provisions of the SPS Agreement.'[130]

In *EC – Hormones*, the Appellate Body considered the three elements of Article 5.5[131] and held that these elements were cumulative in nature. It stated that:

---

[127] Appellate Body Report, *Australia – Salmon*, para. 199.

[128] *Ibid.*, para. 125.

[129] Article 5.4 of SPS Agreement: 'Members should, when determining the appropriate level of sanitary or phytosanitary protection, take into account the objective of minimizing negative trade effects.'

[130] Panel Report, *EC Measures Concerning Meat and Meat Products (Hormones), Complaint by Canada (EC – Hormones (Canada))*, WT/DS48/R/CAN, adopted 13 February 1998, modified by Appellate Body Report, WT/DS26/AB/R, WT/DS48/AB/R, para. 8.169; and Panel Report, *EC Measures Concerning Meat and Meat Products (Hormones), Complaint by the United States (EC – Hormones (US))*, WT/DS26/R/USA, adopted 13 February 1998, modified by Appellate Body Report, WT/DS26/AB/R, WT/DS48/AB/R, para. 8.166.

[131] Article 5.5 of SPS Agreement:

With the objective of achieving consistency in the application of the concept of appropriate level of sanitary or phytosanitary protection against risks to human life or health, or to animal and plant life or health, each Member shall

[t]he first element is that the Member imposing the measure complained of has adopted its own appropriate levels of sanitary protection against risks to human life or health in several different situations. The second element to be shown is that those *levels of protection* exhibit arbitrary or unjustifiable differences ("distinctions" in the language of Article 5.5) in their treatment of different situations. The last element requires that the arbitrary or unjustifiable differences result in discrimination or a disguised restriction of international trade. We understand the last element to be referring to the *measure* embodying or implementing a particular level of protection as resulting, in its application, in discrimination or a disguised restriction on international trade . . . We consider the above three elements of Article 5.5 to be cumulative in nature; all of them must be demonstrated to be present if violation of Article 5.5 is to be found. In particular, both the second and third elements must be found. The second element alone would not suffice. The third element must also be demonstrably present: the implementing measure must be shown to be applied in such a manner as to result in discrimination or a disguised restriction on international trade.[132]

As noted by some commentators, '[t]he interpretations of the Appellate Body make it relatively more difficult to strike down protectionist measures. Thus, a mere demonstration that levels of protection exhibit arbitrary or unjustifiable differences in their treatment of different situations will not suffice. It must further be shown that it constitutes a disguised restriction in international trade.'[133]

As for Article 5.6,[134] the Appellate Body in *Australia – Salmon* identified

---

avoid arbitrary or unjustifiable distinctions in the levels it considers to be appropriate in different situations, if such distinctions result in discrimination or a disguised restriction on international trade. Members shall cooperate in the Committee, in accordance with paragraphs 1, 2 and 3 of Article 12, to develop guidelines to further the practical implementation of this provision. In developing the guidelines, the Committee shall take into account all relevant factors, including the exceptional character of human health risks to which people voluntarily expose themselves.

[132] Appellate Body Report, *EC – Hormones*, paras 214–215.
[133] Chimni (2000), 1759.
[134] Article 5.6 of SPS Agreement:

Without prejudice to paragraph 2 of Article 3, when establishing or maintaining sanitary or phytosanitary measures to achieve the appropriate level of sanitary or phytosanitary protection, Members shall ensure that such measures are not more trade-restrictive than required to achieve their appropriate level of sanitary or phytosanitary protection, taking into account technical and economic feasibility. (footnote omitted)

The footnote to this provision reads as follows:

three separate elements and found that these elements applied cumulatively. It stated that:

> Article 5.6 and, in particular, the footnote to this provision clearly provides a three-pronged test to establish a violation of Article 5.6. As already noted, the three elements of this test under Article 5.6 are that there is an SPS measure which:
> (1) is reasonably available taking into account technical and economic feasibility;
> (2) achieves the Member's appropriate level of sanitary or phytosanitary protection; and
> (3) is significantly less restrictive to trade than the SPS measure contested.
> These three elements are cumulative in the sense that, to establish inconsistency with Article 5.6, all of them have to be met. If any of these elements is not fulfilled, the measure in dispute would be consistent with Article 5.6. Thus, if there is no alternative measure available, taking into account technical and economic feasibility, *or* if the alternative measure does not achieve the Member's appropriate level of sanitary or phytosanitary protection, *or* if it is not significantly less trade-restrictive, the measure in dispute would be consistent with Article 5.6.[135]

This three-pronged test seems to make it extremely difficult to make a case for violation of Article 5.6.

The significance of the difficulty of making a case needs to be judged in the light of the distribution of the burden of proof in any SPS-related dispute at the WTO. As pointed out by the Appellate Body in *EC – Hormones*, the initial burden lies on the complaining party, which must establish a *prima facie* case of inconsistency with a particular provision of the SPS Agreement on the part of the defending party, or more precisely, of its SPS measure or measures complained about. When that *prima facie* case is made, the burden of proof moves to the defending party, which must in turn counter or refute the claimed inconsistency.[136] Rejecting an argument put forward by the panel in *EC – Hormones*, the Appellate Body further ruled that the burden of proof to make a *prima facie* case of inconsistency was on the complainant even when the measure at issue resulted

---

For purposes of paragraph 6 of Article 5, a measure is not more trade-restrictive than required unless there is another measure, reasonably available taking into account technical and economic feasibility, that achieves the appropriate level of sanitary or phytosanitary protection and is significantly less restrictive to trade.

[135] Appellate Body Report, *Australia – Salmon*, para. 194.
[136] Appellate Body Report, *EC – Hormones*, para. 98.

in a higher level of protection than would be achieved by measures based on relevant international standards.[137]

It may be noted that 'a *prima facie* case is one which, in the absence of effective refutation by the defending party, requires a panel, as a matter of law, to rule in favour of the complaining party presenting the *prima facie* case'.[138] Thus a *prima facie* case is not made out unless there is such strong and compelling evidence that it cannot be ruled against in the absence of contrary evidence.[139] Besides, there are issues as to 'how and when to decide that a *prima facie* case has been established by the complaining party and, as the case may be, that this *prima facie* case has been rebutted by the defendant party'.[140] Some commentators have argued that there is a risk that the indeterminacies, which characterise the meaning of a *prima facie* case and its rebuttal can be used to arrive at rulings which favour the use of SPS measures.[141]

The problems of the developing countries have been further exacerbated by the lack of teeth in many S&DT provisions of the SPS Agreement[142] and their interpretations by the WTO DSS. In *EC – Biotech*, for instance, the panel gave a very weak interpretation of the S&DT provision enshrined in Article 10 of SPS Agreement. It observed that:

> the obligation laid down in Article 10.1 is for the importing Member to 'take account' of developing country Members' needs. The dictionary defines the expression 'take account of' as 'consider along with other factors before reaching a decision'. (footnote omitted) Consistent with this, *Article 10.1 does not prescribe a specific result to be achieved. Notably, Article 10.1 does not provide that the importing Member must invariably accord special and differential treat-

---

[137]   The Appellate Body noted:

Under Article 3.1 of the SPS Agreement, a Member may choose to establish an SPS measure that is based on the existing relevant international standard, guideline or recommendation. Such a measure may adopt some, not necessarily all, of the elements of the international standard. The Member imposing this measure does not benefit from the presumption of consistency set up in Article 3.2; but, as earlier observed, the Member is not penalized by exemption of a complaining Member from the normal burden of showing a prima facie case of inconsistency with Article 3.1 or any other relevant Article of the SPS Agreement or of the GATT 1994. (*Ibid.*, para. 171).

[138]   *Ibid.*, para. 104.
[139]   Chimni (2000), 1759.
[140]   Pauwelyn (1998), 258.
[141]   Chimni (2000), 1758.
[142]   For further details, refer to Ratna (2005), 81–84.

ment in a case where a measure has led, or may lead, to a decrease, or a slower increase, in developing country exports (emphasis added).[143]

The panel further noted that:

> [w]hile the European Communities must take account of the interests of developing country Members in applying its approval legislation, the European Communities may at the same time take account of *other legitimate interests, including those of its own consumers, its environment, etc. There is nothing in Article 10.1 to suggest that in weighing and balancing the various interests at stake, the European Communities must necessarily give priority to the needs of Argentina as a developing country* (emphasis added).[144]

The discussion in this section indicates that the SPS Agreement and the mode of interpretation of its provisions by the WTO Dispute Settlement System has provided sufficient leeway for WTO Member countries to impose SPS measures according to their own preferences and priorities, in the process increasing to a large extent the risk of these measures being used for protectionist purposes.

VI.   ADDRESSING SPS CHALLENGES IN INDIA

It is evident from the discussions in the foregoing sections that SPS requirements have acted as a major market access barrier for India, particularly in the developed country markets. India has also suffered significant export losses from time to time on account of its inability to respond to such SPS requirements adequately. The worst affected in the whole process are the small players, who are often technically ill-equipped and financially hard-pressed to be able to comply with SPS requirements. The small firms find implementation of the stringent SPS measures expensive or sometimes even economically unfeasible because installation of certain facilities required for compliance often becomes cost-effective only at a certain minimum scale of operation. Therefore, SPS requirements often have the effect of pushing small players out of business, thereby putting their livelihoods at stake. While this phenomenon is not unique to a developing country like India, it is certainly more acute for these countries, where small-scale operators are more prevalent than in developed

---

[143]   Panel Report, *European Communities – Measures Affecting the Approval and Marketing of Biotech Products* (*EC – Biotech*), WT/DS291/R, WT/DS292/R, WT/DS293/R, adopted 21 November 2006, para. 7.1620.

[144]   *Ibid.*, para. 7.1621.

Table 22.1   Issues raised against India in SPS Committee Meetings between 1995 and 2011

Specific trade concern number	Description of measure	Member(s) raising the issue	Status	Year
61	Import restrictions on bovine semen	Canada, European Union	PR	1999
62	Restrictions on imports of horses	European Union	NR	1999
185	Restrictions due to avian influenza	European Union	NR	2004
186	Phytosanitary import restrictions	United States, European Union	PR	2004
192	Non-notification of various SPS measures	United States	NR	2004
200	Ban on food grade wax	United States	NR	2004
240	Biotech labelling and import approval process regulations	United States	NR	2006
253	Export certification requirements for dairy products	United States	NR	2007

Notes: NR= Not Reported, P = Partially Resolved, R= Resolved.
Source: WTO (2012d), 4–19.

countries. Hence, coping with SPS challenges assumes enormous significance for developing countries like India as well as for the livelihoods of the people concerned.

Notwithstanding the difficulties faced by India on the SPS front, it may be noted that in several instances, questions have also been raised against SPS requirements imposed by India. As shown in Table 22.1, eight concerns were raised against India in the SPS committee meetings between 1995 and 2011, all by developed countries.

India also had to confront several SPS-related questions from various WTO Members including the EU, US, Canada, Australia and New Zealand, among others, during its latest Trade Policy Review carried out by the WTO in 2011.[145]

---

[145]   See, WTO (2011b). Also see WTO (2011c).

One category of measures that has generated a long-drawn debate over the past several years is the restrictions imposed by India on grounds of Avian Influenza (see Box 22.1 for further details). The issue was first raised in the SPS Committee meeting in June 2004 by the EU. Since then this issue has repeatedly been discussed in the SPS Committee meetings and the US, Canada and China have subsequently joined forces to oppose

---

BOX 22.1   RESTRICTIONS IMPOSED BY INDIA ON GROUNDS OF AVIAN INFLUENZA: A BRIEF OVERVIEW

In the SPS Committee meeting of June 2004 the EU first expressed its concern (issue no. 185 in Table 1) regarding India's alleged ban on a range of poultry products, including live birds, fresh meat and fresh meat products from several countries allegedly in response to highly pathenogenic avian influenza (HPAI), since February 2004. The EU alleged that these blanket import bans were disproportionate to the risk and should be confined to imports from regions affected by the disease in accordance with OIE recommendations, which did not include the EU. Since then this issue has repeatedly been discussed in the SPS Committee meetings. In fact this was the only issue against India that was discussed in these meetings in 2011.

In June 2007, the US joined forces with the EU on grounds that since February 2007 India was banning poultry, swine and other products in response to the detection of low pathogenic avian influenza (AI) in wild birds in some parts of the US. According to the US, these restrictions far exceeded the standards developed by the OIE for the control of AI. Subsequently Australia, Canada and China also joined the EU and US in opposing these measures in the SPS Committee meetings.

Apart from the lack of adherence to international standards, another key allegation raised against India during the course of these debates in the SPS Committee meetings and beyond was that the measures imposed by India were not scientifically justified. India responded that measures prohibiting poultry and poultry products had been implemented as temporary measures. It argued that the prevalence of the family-based poultry industry and the significant numbers involved in the industry would make it impossible to control the disease if it spread to India. India stressed the dangers related to AI and how widespread the virus had been. It was pointed out that following the 2006 HPAI outbreak in India, the country was extremely cautious to safeguard its animal and human health, particularly in view of the family run poultry industry in India and because AI was known to reoccur in countries where outbreaks had previously taken place. On these grounds, India restricted imports from countries reporting AI. With respect to the OIE guidelines, India argued that it had already voted against a resolution in the OIE, which proposed that low pathogenic AI was not a concern for international trade. India subsequently lifted its ban on certain products, but continued to apply a ban on certain other items.

As for scientific basis, India, upon repeated requests by the EU and US, provided its risk analysis in October 2010. However, according to the EU and US the risk analysis provided by India was not complete and did not evaluate the likelihood of entry, establishment or spread of the disease, and the associated potential biological and economic consequences. It was alleged that the risk analysis was also not consistent with international standards for conducting a risk analysis and did not contain sufficient scientific evidence to support India's ban either. The expert opinion provided by the OIE also indicated that the scope and purpose of the risk assessment was not clearly defined, and that the assessment was poorly supported by references to the relevant scientific literature. The OIE experts concluded that the document did not meet the definition of an import risk analysis as set out in Chapter 2.1 of the OIE Terrestrial Animal Health Code. In response, India clarified that the risk assessment it provided in October 2010 was only a summary document and not a full risk assessment. It pointed out that the final one would take some time.

The US has recently moved the WTO DSS on the issue. On 6 March 2012, the United States requested consultations with India.* According to the US, India appears to have acted inconsistently with its WTO obligations in this case. In particular, India's ban does not appear to be supported by scientific evidence or a valid risk assessment. The US Trade Representative (USTR) has argued that 'India's ban on U.S. poultry is clearly a case of disguising trade restrictions by invoking unjustified animal health concerns'.# On 15 March 2012, Colombia requested to join the consultations. On 11 May 2012, the US requested the establishment of a panel. At its meeting on 24 May 2012, the DSB deferred the establishment of a panel. India, reportedly blocked the US request to establish a panel.@

Notes:
* http://www.wto.org/english/tratop_e/dispu_e/cases_e/ds430_e.htm (last visited 8 June 2012).
#http://www.ustr.gov/about-us/press-office/press-releases/2012/march/ us-trade-representative-kirk-enforces-rights-us-farm (last visited 8 June 2012).
@ wtonewsstand.com/Inside-US-Trade/Inside-U.../menu-id-445.html (last visited 8 June 2012).

India's measures. In fact, this was the only issue against India that was discussed in these meetings in 2011.[146] The key concerns regarding the measures at issue are that the import bans imposed by India are disproportionate to the risk concerned; that the measures far exceed the international standards developed by the OIE; and that the measures are not scientifically justified – they are not backed by appropriate risk assessment as per international standards.

The US has recently moved the WTO DSS on the issue.[147] According to the US, India's ban does not appear to be supported by scientific evidence or a valid risk assessment. While the establishment of the dispute panel has apparently been blocked by India for now, it remains to be seen what happens subsequently, particularly whether India succeeds in justifying its measures on the basis of scientific evidence.

A close look at the Indian scenario seems to indicate that India needs to traverse a long way both at the domestic as well as international fronts before the country can address the multi-pronged SPS challenges confronting it in an effective manner. Rather than merely reacting to problems that may occur from time to time, India needs to undertake a more proactive approach to SPS management, focusing on development of a

---

[146] For details of the debate on this issue in the SPS Committee meetings over the years, see WTO (2012c), 37–49.

[147] This is the third time the WTO DSS has been moved against SPS measures imposed by India among the 38 cases that cite the SPS Agreement in the request for consultations. The earlier two cases against India were moved by the EU. See <http://www.wto.org/english/tratop_e/dispu_e/dispu_agreements_index_e.htm?id =A19#selected_agreement> (last visited 8 June 2012).

well-knit and comprehensive action plan for the medium to long term. The rest of this Section dwells on some strategies that the country could adopt under the aegis of the SPS Agreement and beyond towards this end, while Box 22.2 summarises the key policy recommendations for India emanating from this discussion.

A. Voicing SPS Concerns at the WTO

The SPS Committee meetings, held every three to six months, provide a forum where WTO Members may discuss various issues and concerns around implementation of the SPS Agreement; bring their SPS-related difficulties to the attention of other countries; and challenge specific SPS measures proposed or applied by other WTO Members. Notwithstanding the range of SPS concerns of India, particularly vis-à-vis developed countries, India has so far made very limited use of this window of opportunity. Among the 328 specific trade concerns raised by all WTO Members in the SPS committee meetings between 1995 and 2011, only nine were raised by India (Table 22.2). Among them, four were against the EU, two each against the US and Japan; and the remaining one was against China. However, it may be noted that while during the first 11 years, India raised only three concerns, the remaining six were raised between 2010 and 2011 only. This may arguably signal more proactive participation by India in the SPS Committee meetings over the past couple of years. It is important for India to participate in SPS Committee meetings regularly and flag its concerns proactively.

B. Utilizing the Trade Facilitation Negotiations

A significant point that emerges from India's experiences with SPS requirements is that there is often a substantial overlap between issues that come under the purview of the SPS Agreement and those that may very well be covered under the Doha Round negotiations on trade facilitation.[148] Interestingly, India has been trying to make use of this window

---

[148] It may be noted here that as part of its 2012 Work Plan, the STDF will initiate the preparation of a global level event on SPS and trade facilitation, to be held in 2013. Possible objectives of this STDF work could be to raise awareness about the synergies between SPS and trade facilitation and identify lessons learned and good practices to strengthen future work and technical cooperation focused on SPS and trade facilitation. The work would be based on examples of trade facilitation in the SPS area, which may include activities focused on the simplification, standardization and harmonization of SPS procedures and information systems to

Table 22.2   *Issues raised by India in SPS Committee Meetings between 1995 and 2011*

Specific trade concern number	Description of measure	Member(s) maintaining the measure	Member(s) raising the issue	Year	Status
39	Maximum levels for certain contaminants (aflatoxins) in foodstuffs	European Union	Argentina, Australia, Plurinational State of Bolivia, Brazil, Gambia, India, Indonesia, Malaysia, Philippines, Senegal, Thailand	1998	R
96	Geographical BSE risk assessment	European Union	Canada, Chile, India	2001	R
223	Import requirements for Indian mangoes	Japan	India	2005	NR
299	US 2009 Food Safety Enhancement Act	United States	China, India	2010	NR
300	EC Regulation No. 1099/2009	European Union	India	2010	NR
306	Maximum residue levels of pesticides	European Union	India	2010	NR
307	Prohibition of certain food additives	Japan	India	2010	NR

facilitate compliance with SPS requirements and trade, management collaboration between SPS agencies and customs to harmonise and improve SPS border management, and/or the impact of large trade facilitation projects on the national SPS situation (WTO (2012b), 3).

Table 22.2   (continued)

Specific trade concern number	Description of measure	Member(s) maintaining the measure	Member(s) raising the issue	Year	Status
324	China's requirement for registration and supervision of foreign enterprises	China	India	2011	NR
328	US default MRLs limits of determination or limits of quantification on basmati rice	United States	India	2011	NR

Notes: NR= Not Reported, R= Resolved.

Source: WTO (2012d), 4–19.

of opportunity to address some such overlapping issues. These include, (i) lack of harmonised rules and regulations among the EU Member States; (ii) destruction of rejected consignments by the EU; (iii) the EU system of 'rapid alert'; and (iv) information on detained consignments, among others. India has also submitted textual proposals for this purpose.[149]

There has been substantial refinement of the proposals on the table during the course of negotiations on trade facilitation leading to presentation of draft negotiating texts. Currently, negotiators are discussing the compilation of these draft negotiating texts, with the aim of arriving at the final shape of the agreement.[150] The latest such compilation was released in May 2012.[151] The frequency of square brackets in this text, however, clearly indicates that a consensus text is still eluding the WTO Members. Notably, this draft text does include most of the textual proposals submitted by India, though often within square brackets. The country must

---

[149]   For details, see WTO (2006c); and WTO (2006d).
[150]   Dominic, et al. (2012), 86–87.
[151]   WTO (2012c).

try and ensure that these proposals form part of the final outcome of the negotiations on trade facilitation.

C.   Transparency Issues

In India, the National Enquiry Points (NEPs), responsible for responding to SPS-related queries, and the National Notification Authority (NNA), responsible for all procedures associated with notification of new or amended SPS measures, established under the transparency provisions of SPS Agreement, are housed in separate agencies. While NEPs for food-safety-related issues is under the Ministry of Health and Family Welfare; NEPs for animal health- and plant health-related issues are with two separate departments of the Ministry of Agriculture. NNA, on the other hand is based at the Ministry of Commerce and Industry. The experience of several WTO Members that have combined these two functions in the same agency reveals that this helps in ensuring better coordination.[152] On the other hand, the lack of effective communication among SPS-related institutions has been identified as a key factor contributing to a country's failure to notify, send comments and reply to questions.[153]

Effective functioning of NEPs and the NNA is not only necessary for the foreign countries to get information, it is equally important for the domestic exporters to get access to information on SPS-related matters in other countries. However, in India, access to relevant information is a major problem for the domestic industries and exporters. NEPs and the NNA of the country need to be strengthened for this purpose.

Given the large volume of SPS notifications being circulated, it is essential to have well-qualified, technically-skilled and experienced staff in NEPs to undertake the preliminary screening of the notifications to determine the relative importance of a notification for domestic exporters, to disseminate them among appropriate domestic stakeholders, and so on.

Although the Geneva Mission of India might get information from SPS notifications by other WTO Members, due to the enormity of the number of such notifications, the information often takes a long time to reach the appropriate agencies or organisations back home, which have the technical expertise to comment on a notification. In the process, a substantial proportion of the comment period (usually 60 days) might get wasted making it difficult or often impossible to comment on a notification within the stipulated time limit. Thus India often ends up losing the opportunity

---

[152]   WTO (2004).
[153]   WTO (2003c).

to raise its concerns before the notified measure comes into effect. A possible way to deal with this problem could be to develop a mechanism to dispatch any new notification directly to the relevant agencies in the country, thereby saving the time that otherwise gets wasted.

If a notification and/or detailed rules and regulations issued by a developed country is in languages other than English then it may be proposed that the onus would be on the developed country to ensure that authentic English translations of such notification and/or rules and regulations are dispatched to the relevant agencies in India.[154] Otherwise getting the documents translated in English would also waste substantial time (thereby curtailing the time available for comment) and resources.

Regarding comments on notifications, Annex B of the SPS Agreement states that comments from other Members should be taken into account and the recommended procedures adopted by the SPS Committee indicate that a period of at least 60 days should be provided for the submission of comments. However, an analysis of the SPS notifications submitted during 2002 undertaken by China[155] revealed that majority of WTO Members who made routine notifications in that year allowed for a comment period of less than 60 days, or they did not specify a final date for receiving comments. Furthermore, it was found that some Members did not provide an interval for considering comments. Adequate time period for comments is crucial for developing countries. Given the lack of technical capacity to analyse risk assessments and other technical information available from the notifying Member, preparation of substantive comments within the short comment period becomes a challenging task for these countries.

According to China's analysis, during 2002, most notifying Members did not indicate the date of adoption or the date of entry into force of the SPS measure notified and of those Members that did mention this, most indicated an interval that was less than six months from the date of publication. However, Paragraph 2, Annex B of SPS Agreement, states that:

> [e]xcept in urgent circumstances, Members shall allow a reasonable interval between the publication of a sanitary or phytosanitary regulation and its entry into force in order to allow time for producers in exporting Members, and particularly in developing country Members, to adapt their products and methods of production to the requirements of the importing Member.

---

[154]   It may be noted that para. 8 of Annex B of the SPS Agreement states that 'Developed country Members shall, if requested by other Members, provide copies of the documents or, in case of voluminous documents, summaries of the documents covered by a specific notification in English, French or Spanish'.

[155]   WTO (2003b).

Article 3.2 of the Doha Ministerial Declaration defined the 'reasonable interval' as a period of normally not less than six months, except in urgent circumstances. Sufficient interval between publication of an SPS measure and its coming into force are crucial for developing countries like India in order to get prepared.

India should be proactive in voicing its concerns in the SPS Committee meetings as well as bilaterally in the instances of any such lack of adherence to the stipulated time intervals by other WTO Members.

Back home, it is also essential for the country to involve experts, industry and other relevant stakeholders to formulate comments on SPS measures notified by other Members.

D.   Participation in International Standard Setting

In view of the harmonisation provision of the SPS Agreement (discussed earlier), it is important for India to ensure that its views and concerns are taken on board in the course of developing international standards. This requires effective participation in the standard setting processes of the key international standard setting bodies, in particular, the three bodies explicitly mentioned in SPS Agreement: the CAC, OIE, and the international and regional organisations operating within the framework of the IPPC. The track record of India, however, indicates that like most other developing countries, its participation in the proceedings of the international standard-setting bodies is very poor, both in quantitative and qualitative terms.[156] The lack of an effective participation by developing countries implies that international standards generally get set in accordance with the wishes of the developed countries, by default or often with a slender majority vote.

India should try to increase its participation in the standard setting processes both in quantitative and qualitative terms. Given that a major constraint in this regard is financial, it should try to get as much funding support from donor agencies for this purpose as possible. As far as enhancing participation in the CAC is concerned, funding support is available from the Codex Trust Fund (CTF). Launched in 2003, the main objective of CTF is to help developing countries and economies in transition to enhance their levels of effective participation in the development of global food safety and quality standards by the CAC. India has benefited from the CTF funding to some extent. However, given the large number of developing countries eligible to apply for the CFT support and the

---

[156]   Jha (2002), 43–44.

inadequacy of donor support made available to the CTF, it is obvious that each country would have to wait for its turn to get such support. Hence, there is a need to tap alternative funding sources. In case participation in all international standardisation exercises turns out to be difficult, given its resource constraints, India may prioritise by identifying the sectors in which it has major export interests or potential and accordingly try to ensure participation in standardisation exercises relevant for these sectors.

It needs to be underscored here that physical presence is not enough to effectively participate in an outright technical exercise like standard setting. Numbers may not adequately reflect the quality of participation or the degree to which the country benefits from participation in international standard setting.[157] In order to contribute effectively the representatives of India need to be technically skilled too.

Efforts should also be made by the country to involve the relevant industries or industry chambers alongside experts in the process. The governments may develop strategies to work together with business communities towards achieving effective participation in the standardisation process.

India should also try and develop its own national SPS standards in more and more areas in line with international standards.

E.   Engaging in Equivalence and Mutual Recognition Agreements

As mentioned before, the SPS Agreement (Article 4.1[158]) encourages WTO Members to accept the SPS measures of other Members as equivalent, even if these measures differ from their own or from those used by other countries, provided the exporting Member objectively demonstrates to the importing Member that its measures achieve the importing Member's ALOP. The Agreement (Article 4.2[159]) further encourages Members to enter into consultations with other Members with the aim of achieving

---

[157]   WTO (2001b).

[158]   Article 4.1: 'Members shall accept the sanitary or phytosanitary measures of other Members as equivalent, even if these measures differ from their own or from those used by other Members trading in the same product, if the exporting Member objectively demonstrates to the importing Member that its measures achieve the importing Member's appropriate level of sanitary or phytosanitary protection. For this purpose, reasonable access shall be given, upon request, to the importing Member for inspection, testing and other relevant procedures.'

[159]   Article 4.2: 'Members shall, upon request, enter into consultations with the aim of achieving bilateral and multilateral agreements on recognition of the equivalence of specified sanitary or phytosanitary measures.'

bilateral and multilateral agreements in recognition of the equivalence of specified SPS measures.

The concept of equivalence in the SPS context is based on the principle that different measures can achieve the same level of SPS protection and therefore countries can enjoy flexibility about the kind of measures to adopt to ensure adequate SPS protection.[160] Recognition of equivalence could be done unilaterally, or through Mutual Recognition Agreements (MRAs).

Equivalence is the best option when harmonisation of standards is not desirable or when international standards are lacking or are inappropriate.[161] Harmonisation and equivalence are both methods for bringing about regulatory convergence or uniformity. While harmonization takes two (or more) differing standards or procedures and converts them into one, equivalence allows two differing standards or procedures to remain intact but treats them as if they were the same, because in theory they produce the same or similar results.[162] For developing countries like India recognition of equivalence could go a long way in enhancing market access, particularly in developed countries.

As far as Mutual Recognition Agreements (MRAs) are concerned, these could involve two or more parties and could take several forms.[163] MRAs could, for instance, (a) be limited to testing methods only; (b) cover conformity assessment certificates; or (c) be full-fledged – including the standards themselves. While the coverage of the MRAs of the first type is rather limited, these could still play an important role in building up confidence between laboratories in different countries and usually represent a necessary step towards the conclusion of broader MRAs. MRAs of the second type help in improving market access by avoiding duplicative testing and the related costs, by reducing possible discrimination against foreign products and by eliminating delays. Moreover, this type of MRAs could provide the much needed learning experience, since they imply an intensive exchange of information and close contacts between relevant authorities. MRAs of the third type, i.e. full-fledged MRAs, require that parties consider their domestic requirements as equivalent, which implies that a good which can be legally sold in one country may be legally sold in the other(s) as well.

In an MRA, two or more parties agree to recognise and accept each other's testing methods, conformity assessment certificates, product standards, etc., because they are harmonised or judged to be equivalent, or

---

[160]   Zarrilli (1999), 17.
[161]   *Ibid.*
[162]   Doherty (2010), 15.
[163]   This discussion on MRAs draws on Zarrilli (1999), 19.

because they satisfy other agreed-upon external criteria, such as adherence to international standards.[164]

The WTO SPS Committee has over the years discussed the implementation of Article 4 on equivalence. These deliberations resulted in the 'Decision on the Implementation of Article 4 of the Agreement on Application of Sanitary and Phytosanitary Measures', adopted by the SPS Committee in 2001 and revised several times subsequently. In July 2004, the SPS Committee completed its work on guidelines on the implementation of Article 4 in response to concerns raised by developing countries. The Decision on Equivalence adopted by the SPS Committee notes, *inter alia*, the work on recognition of equivalence undertaken in the CAC, OIE and IPPC, and requests for further elaboration of specific guidance by these organisations to ensure that such recognition is maintained. Equivalence still remains a standing agenda item of the Committee.[165]

However, the implementation of Article 4 has so far been rather limited owing to several practical difficulties and high transaction costs involved. In practice, the procedure to reach recognition of equivalence is rather complicated and consists of several steps.[166] First, the importing country has to explain the objective of the sanitary measure for which recognition of equivalence is sought and identify its ALOP. Then the exporting country has to demonstrate that its SPS measures achieve the importing country's ALOP. For this purpose, the exporting country must provide robust technical information to support its application for an importing country to recognise alternative SPS measures as providing protection against risks equivalent to that achieved by the prescribed import requirements.[167] The evidence that the exporting country may be requested to provide for this purpose includes its domestic legislation regarding standards, procedures, policies, infrastructure, enforcement and control; the efficacy of its enforcement and control programme; and the powers of its regulatory authority, among others. On the basis of the evidence provided by the exporting country, the importing country then decides whether the exporting country's measures achieve its ALOP, and, therefore, can be regarded as equivalent. Since negotiations are highly demanding in terms of resources and time, formal equivalence agreements or MRAs are rare even between developed countries. A US submission to the WTO observes that:

---

[164]   Doherty (2010), 15.
[165]   Codex (2007).
[166]   The discussion on these steps draws heavily on Zarrilli (1999), 18.
[167]   WTO (2001a), 3.

[e]quivalence determinations require a significant investment of technical and trade experts to address and resolve safety issues. Even in instances where ALOPs and governmental institutions of two WTO Members may appear to be similar, determinations of equivalence have taken several years of negotiations and a great deal of the time of technical and trade experts and have not resulted in immediate new trade opportunities.[168]

According to the US, there are several practical problems that could limit the use of Article 4. These include, among others, the following issues: (i) whether the request for equivalence would be pursued where no trade barrier exists; (ii) whether the actual trade benefits justify the administrative burden of making a determination of equivalence and/or negotiating an agreement; (iii) the inherent difficulty of linking numerous and disparate measures to a country's ALOP; and (iv) stakeholder acceptance of equivalence determinations and negotiated equivalence agreements.[169]

The EU also pointed out clear limitations with regard to applying both equivalence agreements and MRAs. According to the EU, such comprehensive agreements are often costly to negotiate and maintain and they normally necessitate some prior harmonisation before negotiations can start. Although the EU has generally entered into negotiations with partners having a comparable level of development, the agreements have turned out to be very difficult to implement in practice. Both the EU and the US seem to agree on the view that the costs sometimes exceed the benefits of such agreements.[170]

The concept of equivalence presumes difference, not *sameness*. However, developing countries have reported that in several instances importing countries are looking for *sameness*, instead of equivalence, of measures.[171]

India has already entered into a few equivalence and mutual recognition agreements on SPS-related and other matters. India's experience in this respect reveals that most developed countries take many years to reach a decision on equivalence. For instance, the US took three years to decide on the equivalence of organic standards, Japan took as long as 20 years on market access to mango, and so on.[172] Nonetheless, India should try to get into more and more equivalence and mutual recognition agreements with its major trading partners, particularly developed countries.[173] The initial

---

[168] WTO (2000), 4.
[169] *Ibid.*, 3.
[170] Veggeland (2006), 48–50.
[171] Zarrilli (1999), 17.
[172] Planning Commission (2007), 225–26.
[173] India is trying hard to create room for such arrangements in its negotiations on the Trade and Investment Agreement with the EU.

hitches and costs notwithstanding, these avenues are worth pursuing since once done, they could greatly facilitate market access for Indian products in the countries concerned.

F.   Capacity Constraints and Technical Assistance

Various capacity constraints act as barriers to India's ability to comply with SPS requirements in export markets. Many of these constraints emanate from and persist due to the inadequate financial and technical resources available. Some of the key constraints confronting India, among others, are enumerated below:[174]

- Insufficient awareness and preparedness on the part of various stakeholders, particularly, small and medium enterprises (SMEs), to effectively tackle SPS challenges;
- Lack of an effective mechanism for dissemination of SPS-related information among the stakeholders;
- Inadequate access to appropriate technology and adequate finance among various stakeholders, particularly SMEs;
- Infrastructural constraints, such as lack of well-equipped and state of the art laboratories; inadequate accreditation and certification bodies, among others;
- Dearth of technically-skilled people in national enquiry points, laboratories, accreditation bodies and inspection agencies;
- Insufficient know-how for carrying out risk analysis/assessments;
- Inadequacy of state of the art ports and time-consuming customs procedures.

Technical assistance by developed countries and donor agencies is of great significance to assist India to better cope with such capacity constraints. It is also important to underscore that compliance with the SPS requirements predominantly imposed by the developed countries significantly increases the cost of production for the developing country exporters, but often does not result in price premiums in return. This implies that the developing countries are required to bear the burden of the high levels of food safety preferences of the developed country consumers. This is not justifiable. In order to shift the burden from the less wealthy to the wealthier, there is thus a case for redistribution through SPS-related technical assistance.

---

[174]   The capacity constraints enlisted here are largely based on personal communication with the Ministry of Commerce and Industry, Government of India.

However, the provisions on technical assistance as enshrined in Article 9[175] of the SPS Agreement are in the nature of 'best endeavour' clauses only. Hence they do not impose any legal obligation on the developed countries to provide technical assistance to developing countries. Way back in 1998, India and certain other developing countries proposed to the WTO to convert the Article 9 provisions into specific obligations. However, no concrete progress is visible in that direction so far. Although the Doha Ministerial Conference (2001) discussed the issue, the outcome was merely a renewed call for financial and technical assistance, including for LDCs, without any legal obligation whatsoever. The soft approach is clearly evident from the relevant provisions of the Doha Declaration that:

(i) *urges* Members to provide, *to the extent possible*, the financial and technical assistance necessary to enable least-developed countries to respond adequately to the introduction of any new SPS measures which may have significant negative effects on their trade; and

(ii) *urges* Members to ensure that technical assistance is provided to least developed countries with a view to responding to the special problems faced by them in implementing the Agreement on the Application of Sanitary and Phytosanitary Measures. (emphasis added)[176]

Given the existing legal status of the provisions of the SPS Agreement on technical assistance, such assistance has always remained grossly inadequate when judged in terms of the needs of the developing countries. This is despite the fact that a number of agencies are engaged in providing SPS-related technical assistance.[177] The Standards and Trade Development

---

[175] Article 9.1 of SPS Agreement mentions that: 'Members agree to facilitate the provision of technical assistance to other Members, especially developing country Members, either bilaterally or through the appropriate international organizations.'

Article 9.2 further states that:

Where substantial investments are required in order for an exporting developing country Member to fulfil the sanitary or phytosanitary requirements of an importing Member, the latter shall consider providing such technical assistance as will permit the developing country Member to maintain and expand its market access opportunities for the product involved (emphasis added).

[176] WTO (2001e), para 3.6.

[177] These include, among others, the WTO; Food and Agriculture Organisation (FAO); International Trade Centre (ITC); the Joint Integrated Technical Assistance Programme (JITAP); the Commonwealth Secretariat; the European Commission; the Inter-American Institute for Agricultural Cooperation (IICA); the German Corporation for International Cooperation (GTZ); the Swedish International Development Corporation Agency (SIDA); the UK Department for

Facility (STDF) is worth a particular mention here. The STDF is both a financing and a coordination mechanism that was established in August 2002 with three years of seed funding from the World Bank Development Grant Facility (DGF). It aims to support developing countries in building their capacity to implement international SPS standards, guidelines and recommendations as a means to improve their human, animal and plant health status and ability to gain and maintain market access. The partner agencies of the STDF are: the Food and Agricultural Organisation (FAO), OIE, the World Bank, the World Health Organisation (WHO) and the WTO. The WTO is the administrator of the STDF and provides the secretariat. Grant financing from STDF is available for private and public organisations in developing countries seeking to comply with international SPS requirements and hence gain or maintain market access. The STDF provides funds for two types of grants: project grants and project preparation grants (PPGs).

In March 2012, the WTO Secretariat issued a note regarding SPS technical assistance and training activities undertaken by the Secretariat from 1 September 1994 to 31 December 2011. The main objective of these SPS technical assistance and training activities is to increase participants' awareness about Members' rights and obligations under the SPS Agreement and its implications for national policymaking. Altogether, 242 SPS training activities have been undertaken by the WTO Secretariat during the aforesaid period.[178] This is certainly way below the immense requirement of the large number of developing country Members, particularly the LDCs that are fraught with a range of capacity constraints in the field of SPS. Inadequate financial support from developed countries and donor agencies seems to be a key reason underlying the lack of technical assistance and training activities.

An independent evaluation of the operation of the STDF carried out in December 2005 revealed the inadequacy of available funding for technical assistance. Till that time, only nine WTO Members had made contributions to the STDF. Of these nine donors, two had entered into formal multi-annual commitments. Thus while the STDF was found to be relatively successful in attracting short term financing, raising funds for a longer period proved more challenging. In contrast, the demand for SPS-related technical assistance has shown an upward trend. The records of the STDF show, for instance, that the number of applications increased four-

International Development (DFID); the US Department of Agriculture (USDA); and the US Agency for International Development (USAID).

[178]   WTO (2012a), 1.

fold in 2005 compared to 2003. The ratio of the number of project applications to projects approved for funding stood at 3:1 in 2005.[179] The picture did not change much by the time the next round of independent evaluation of the STDF was completed in November 2008. It was found even in this evaluation that the STDF was facing serious funding constraints and was unable to fund all the projects it had already approved. Between January 2006 and November 2008, STDF funding had been requested for a total of 80 projects and 31 PPGs, all together amounting to over US$ 35 million. Approval was, however, granted for only 29 projects and 18 PPGs to a total cost of just over US$ 8 million. The report observed that the donor base was quite narrow, being concentrated mainly in Europe (especially Northern Europe) and North America. It recommended widening of the donor base and stressed the need for multi-annual contributions from the donors.[180] As of now, multi-annual Contribution Agreements have been concluded with Canada (2010–14), the European Union (2010–15), the Netherlands (2008–11) and Sweden (2009–13).[181]

To effectively improve the access of the developing countries to developed country markets, technical assistance ought to address the major SPS-related impediments that the former face in the latter. Since the funds available for technical assistance are limited, it is also important that the funding agencies focus on building capacities in areas where they are needed the most and where they can make some concrete contribution in terms of improving the export performance of developing countries. Effective technical assistance thus requires a systematic analysis before funds are actually allocated. Experience, however, reveals that technical assistance provided by the WTO more often than not takes the form of courses and seminars on SPS rules and their implications.[182] Technical assistance in more concrete areas is generally found to be rather rare. Moreover, a review of the allocation decisions of some major providers of technical assistance has revealed that allocation decisions are made in an unsystematic manner, with little emphasis on the expected effect of technical assistance.[183]

It may be noted here that technical assistance is made available on

---

[179] WTO (2006b), Update on the Operation of the Standards and Trade Development Facility, Note by the Secretariat, Committee on Sanitary and Phytosanitary Measures, G/SPS/GEN/648 of 24 March.

[180] WTO (2009), 22.

[181] < http://www.standardsfacility.org/en/AUDonorSupport.htm> (last visited 6 June 2012).

[182] WTO (2001d).

[183] Wiig and Kolstad (2003).

request from developing countries. Hence, a basic principle of allocation is how vocal countries are in expressing their needs. So, it is important that India puts forward concrete demands for technical assistance in areas where it needs it. However, given the constraints in the availability of funds for technical assistance, it is obvious that the assistance available for a single country would be very limited. Hence, it is important for the country to prioritise its needs for technical assistance. For instance, it may rank various sectors of export interest and map out the technical assistance needs in each of those sectors, giving the most important area of assistance-need the greatest priority and so on. This approach may be helpful in maximising benefits, given the constraints on availability of technical assistance.

G.   Domestic Efforts on Awareness Building and Support Services

The general level of awareness about SPS issues is very low among the stakeholders in India, particularly the SMEs. Organisation of workshops and training programmes for entrepreneurs, managers, workers etc. may help in increasing awareness. However, to solve practical problems faced by the exporters, it may be helpful to have appropriate consultancy services. Given resource constraints, it may not always be possible for the government to provide such services by experts free of cost. However, government or semi-government agencies could open consultancy wings where such services could be provided to exporters at a price commensurate with their financial conditions and size of business, thereby taking into account the resource constraints confronting the SMEs. The general awareness level among consumers about SPS matters also needs to be improved.

H.   Better Coordination

It is essential for a vast country with a federal structure like India to ensure effective coordination among various relevant national and sub-national agencies dealing with SPS issues. There is also a need for increased collaboration among research organisations, government departments, standard-setting agencies, and industry.

Importantly, with a view to streamline the food sector that has thus far been governed by a multiplicity of laws and ministries, often resulting in overlapping jurisdictions, lack of coordination and concomitant problems of standard setting and implementation, India has enacted the Food Safety and Standards Act (FSS Act), 2006 under the aegis of the union Ministry of Health and Family Welfare, subsuming the existing food-related laws at the national level.[184] The Food Safety and Standards Authority of India (FSSAI) has been established under this Act as a statutory body for laying down science-based standards for food products and regulating manufacturing, processing, distribution, sale and import of food so as to ensure safe and wholesome food for human consumption. It is also supposed to enforce standards specifications for ingredients, contaminants, pesticide residues, biological hazards and labels. Food Safety and Standards Rules 2011 and Food Safety and Standards Regulation, 2011 were notified in May 2011 and August 2011, respectively, by the Government of India and the FSS Act came into effect from 5 August 2011.[185] Under the FSS Act, the FSSAI has a mandate of also ensuring safety of food items imported into the country. The FSSAI has developed a draft 'Food Safety and Standards (Food Import) Regulations, 2011' in terms of provisions under FSS Act to ensure the safety of imported food.[186] Special provisions are proposed to be made in these regulations to facilitate fast clearance of perishable food items.[187]

While the establishment of FSSAI may be regarded as an important step forward in streamlining food safety-related issues in India, implementation is likely to become a significant challenge at least as far as regulation of the domestic food market is concerned. While there are large players, the vast majority are small players operating in unorganised sectors that have by and large remained unregulated thus far. Various provisions of this legislation, in fact, have attracted significant criticism, particularly from the point of view of their possible implications for the unorganised sector in India.[188]

---

[184] The eight laws are: The Prevention of Food Adulteration Act, 1954 (37 of 1954), The Fruit Products Order, 1955. The Meat Food Products Order, 1973, The Vegetable Oil Products (Control) Order, 1947, The Edible Oils Packaging (Regulation) Order, 1998, The Solvent Extracted Oil, De oiled Meal, and Edible Flour (Control) Order, 1967, The Milk and Milk Products Order, 1992 and any other order issued under the Essential Commodities Act, 1955 (10 of 1955) relating to food.

[185] WTO (2011b), 10.

[186] This draft was put up for comments on the website of FSSAI on 7 July 2011 and the comment period ended on 8 August 2011. http://fssai.gov.in/Outreach/DraftforConsultations.aspx

[187] *Ibid.*, 142.

[188] See, for instance, Sharma, (2005). Madhavan and Sanyal (2006). Also see, FICCI (2007).

BOX 22.2   KEY POLICY RECOMMENDATIONS FOR INDIA

(i)   Adoption of a proactive rather than defensive approach to SPS management on the basis of an all-encompassing strategy;

(ii)   More proactive participation at the WTO on SPS issues;

(iii)   Voicing concerns in the SPS Committee meetings as well as bilaterally towards ensuring adequate time period for comments on SPS notifications; and for allowing sufficient time interval between publication of an SPS measure by a WTO member and its coming into force;

(iv)   Development of an appropriate mechanism to ensure effective and timely comments on SPS notifications made by other WTO Members;

(v)   Ensuring that the textual proposals submitted by India under the Doha Round negotiations on Trade Facilitation are incorporated in the final outcome of these negotiations;

(vi)   Concentration of technical assistance requests in select areas of export interests, identified in a systematic manner;

(vii)   More frequent and effective participation in the standard setting exercises of key global agencies, like the CAC, IOE, and IPPC;

(viii)   Making concerted efforts, in association with other like-minded developing countries, towards ensuring adequate technical and financial support from developed countries and donor agencies for enhanced participation in the standard setting processes of the key international bodies;

(ix)   Ensuring effective functioning of National Enquiry Points and National Notification Authorities on SPS;

(x)   Making concerted efforts towards negotiating equivalence and mutual recognition agreements (MRAs) with key trading partners, particularly developed countries;

(xi)   Bringing in appropriate institutional reforms on the domestic front with a view to tackling the SPS challenges more effectively;

(xii)   Bringing national SPS standards in more and more areas into line with international standards and strengthening accreditation and certification systems;

(xiii)   Investment in physical infrastructure for building capacity for compliance, including testing activities, risk analysis and assessment, among others;

(xiv)   Awareness building among the domestic stakeholders, including small and medium enterprises and consumers about SPS matters;

(xv)   Adequate and timely dissemination of information among the domestic stakeholders; and if required, provision of SPS-related consultancy services on a payment basis by government and semi-government agencies for the exporters;

(xvi)   Enhanced coordination among various relevant government bodies/agencies at the central and sub-national levels;

(xvii) Increasing collaboration and coordination among government agencies dealing with SPS issues, research organizations and industry;

(xviii) Provision for supporting small and medium enterprises to better cope with SPS challenges, given their capacity constraints.

VII. CONCLUDING REMARKS

The WTO SPS Agreement was negotiated with the dual objective of recognising the legitimate right of Members to adopt SPS measures necessary to protect human, animal or plant life or health, while at the same time setting in place certain checks and balances to address the possibility of these measures emerging as NTBs. However, the experience of India, as exemplified in this Chapter, tends to indicate that it is still an open question as to what extent the SPS Agreement has been effective in preventing these measures from emerging as NTBs. Indeed, a close look at some of the key provisions of the SPS Agreement seems to indicate that its dual objective notwithstanding, the SPS Agreement has left ample room for the discretion of Member countries. This leeway seems to have been further reinforced by the WTO DSS, which in various rulings has demonstrated a clear tendency to bestow upon Member countries a large measure of autonomy and flexibility in imposing SPS measures, thereby leaving the door ajar for using these measures for protectionist purposes.

Importantly, despite the fact that SPS measures were identified by the developing countries at large as the third-most important category of NTB under the notification mechanism established under the Doha Round, SPS did not form part of the negotiating mandate of this Round. This is notwithstanding the fact that enhanced market access for developing countries was identified by the Doha Ministerial Declaration as one of the fundamental objectives of the Doha Round.[189] The fact remains that unless and until such NTBs are effectively disciplined, they will continue to limit real market access for the developing countries to a great extent. Hence, it is imperative for the developing countries, including India, to work towards disciplining SPS-related NTBs under the aegis of the WTO.

Although India, on many occasions, has succeeded in complying with SPS requirements imposed by its trading partners, these success stories have largely been induced by immediate market access problems. India needs to undertake a more proactive approach to SPS management, focusing on development of a well-knit and comprehensive strategy for the medium to long term to cope with its SPS challenges in a more effective manner, both at the domestic and international levels. This would call for tackling the multi-pronged capacity constraints at the domestic level, coupled with appropriate reforms in the institutional structure, among others. At the WTO, the country must try and use all the windows of opportunity towards addressing its SPS concerns. It must also enhance its participation in international standard setting exercises both in quantitative and qualitative terms (see Box 22.2 for key policy recommendations for India).

BIBLIOGRAPHY

APEDA (2008), *Non-Tariff Barriers Faced by Indian Agricultural Products*. Available at: <http://www.apeda.gov.in/apedawebsite/Databank/NTBs_July_08.pdf> (last visited 30 May 2012).

Becker, G. S. (2006), *Sanitary and Phytosanitary (SPS) Concerns in Agricultural Trade*, Congressional Research Service Report for Congress. Available at: <http://www.hsdl. org/?view&did=464440> (last visited 2 June 2012).

Boisen, C. S. (2007), 'Title III of the Bioterrorism Act: Sacrificing U.S. Trade Relations in the Name of Food Security', *American University Law Review*, 56 (3), 667–718.

Cass, D. Z. (2001), 'The "Constitutionalization" of International Trade Law: Judicial Norm-Generation as the Engine of Constitutional Development in International Trade', *European Journal of International Law*, 12 (1), 39–75.

Chimni, B. S. (2000), 'WTO and Environment: Shrimp-Turtle and EC-Hormones Cases', *Economic and Political Weekly*, 13 May, 1752–1761.

Codex (2007), Activities of the SPS Committee and Other Relevant WTO Activities From 2006 to the Present, Joint FAO/WHO Food Standard Programme, CAC/30 INF/5, Codex Alimentarius Commission.

---

[189]   WTO (2001c), para. 2.

Croley, S. P. and J. H. Jackson (1996), 'WTO Dispute Procedures, Standard of Review, and Deference to National Governments', *The American Journal of International Law*, 90 (2), 193–213.

Das, K. (2008), 'Coping with SPS Challenges in India: WTO and Beyond', *Journal of International Economic Law*, 11 (4), 971–1019.

Das, K. (2009), 'Coping with SPS Challenges in South Asia', Chapter 4 in Chimni, B. S. *et al.* (eds), *South Asian Yearbook of Trade and Development – Harnessing Gains from Trade: Domestic Challenges & Beyond* (New Delhi: Academic Foundation), 105–170.

DFID (2000), Impact of Sanitary and Phytosanitary Measures on Developing Countries, UK Department for International Development (DFID). Available at: <http://webar chive.nationalarchives.gov.uk/+/http://www.dfid.gov.uk/AboutDFID/files/itd/spsdc.pdf> (last visited 30 May 2012).

Dhar, B. and M. Kallummal (2007), 'Taming the Non-tariff Barriers: Can the World Trade Organization Find a Solution?', Chapter V in *Future Trade Research Areas That Matter To Developing Country Policymakers – A Regional Perspective on the Doha Development Agenda and Beyond – Studies in Trade and Investment*, No. 61, Economic and Social Commission for Asia and the Pacific (ESCAP) (New York: United Nations), 131–180.

Divvaakar, S.V., P. Agarwal and R. K. S. Bhatia (2006), 'Trade Facilitation Problems of Indian Exporters A Survey', Chapter 4, in V. Jha (ed.) *India and the Doha Work Programme: Opportunities and Challenges* (New Delhi: UNCTAD and MacMillan India Ltd.), 220–306.

Doherty, M. (2010), *The Importance of Sanitary and Phytosanitary Measures to Fisheries Negotiations in Economic Partnership Agreements*, ICTSD Series on Fisheries, Trade and Sustainable Development, Issue Paper No. 7, International Centre for Trade and Sustainable Development, Geneva.

Dominic, J., S. Priya and P. Agrawal (2012), Trade Facilitation Gap Analysis for Border Clearance Procedures in India, Centre for WTO Studies, Indian Institute of Foreign Trade, New Delhi.

Du, M. M. (2010), 'Standard of Review under the SPS Agreement after *EC – Hormones II*', *International and Comparative Law Quarterly*, 59, 441–459.

FICCI (2007), *FICCI study on Implementation of Food Safety and Standards Act: An Industry Perspective,* Federation of Indian Chamber of Commerce and Industry, New Delhi.

GATT (1986), General Agreement on Tariffs and Trade (GATT) Punta Del Este Declaration, Ministerial Declaration of 20 September.

Jha, V. (2002), 'Strengthening Developing Countries' Capacities to Respond to Health, Sanitary and Environmental Requirements: A Scoping Paper for South Asia', United Nations Conference on Trade and Development (UNCTAD), Geneva.

Jonker, T. H., H. Ito and H. Fujishima (2005), *Food Safety and Quality Standards in Japan: Compliance of Suppliers from Developing Countries*, The International Bank for Reconstruction and Development, The World Bank, Washington, DC.

Kaushik, A. and M. Saqib (2001), 'Environmental Requirements and India's Exports: An Impact Analysis', *RGICS Working Paper Series No. 25*, Rajiv Gandhi Foundation, New Delhi.

Madhavan, M. R. and K. Sanyal (2006), 'PRS Legislative Brief: Food Safety and Standards Bill, 2005'. Available at: <http://www.indiatogether.org/2006/feb/law-foodsafe.htm> (last visited 30 May 2012).

OECD (2005), 'Analysis of Non-Tariff Barriers of Concern to Developing Countries', *OECD Trade Policy Working Papers*, No. 16, Organisation for Economic Co-operation and Development, OECD Publishing, Paris.

Oesch, M. (2003), *Standards of Review in WTO Dispute Resolution* (Oxford: Oxford University Press).

Pauwelyn, J. (1998), 'Evidence, Proof and Persuasion in WTO Dispute Settlement: Who Bears the Burden?', *Journal of International Economic Law*, 1, 227–258.

Perez, O. (1998), 'Reconstructing Science: The *Hormone* Conflict between the EU and the United States', *European Foreign Affairs Review*, 1 (4), 563–582.

Planning Commission (2007), *Report Of The Working Group On Agricultural Marketing Infrastructure And Policy Required For Internal And External Trade For The XI Five Year Plan 2007–12*, Agriculture Division Planning Commission, Government of India, January.

Prévost, D. (2005), 'What Role for the Precautionary Principle in WTO Law after *Japan – Apples?*', *Journal of Trade & Environment Studies*, 2 (4), 1–14.

Ratna, R. S. (2005), 'The SPS Agreement: Indian Perspective', Chapter 5, in R. Mehta and J. Jeorge (eds) *Food Safety Regulation Concerns and Trade* (New Delhi: McMillan India), 73–98.

Sawhney, A. (2005), 'Quality Measures in Food Trade: The Indian Experience', *The World Economy*, 28 (3), 329–348.

Sharma, D. (2005), 'Food safety bill may hurt hawkers'. Available at: <http://www.indiato gether.org/2005/feb/dsh-safefood.htm> (last visited 10 December 2007).

UNCTAD (2006), *Trade and Environment Review 2006*, United Nations Conference on Trade and Development, United Nations, New York and Geneva.

Veggeland, F. (2006), *Trade Facilitation through Equivalence and Mutual Recognition: The EU Model* (Oslo: Norwegian Agricultural Research Institute).

Wiig, A. and I. Kolstad (2003), 'Lowering Barriers to Agricultural Exports through Technical Assistance', *Working Paper 2003:8*, Chr. Michelsen Institute, Norway.

WTO (2000), Equivalence, Submission from the United States, G/SPS/GEN/212, 7 November.

WTO (2001a), Experiences in Recognizing Equivalence of Phytosanitary Measures, Submission by New Zealand, Committee on Sanitary and Phytosanitary Measures, G/SPS/GEN/232, 28 February.

WTO (2001b), Summary Report of the Workshop on the International Standard-Setting Organizations: Process and Participation, 13 March, Note by the Secretariat, Committee on Sanitary and Phytosanitary Measures, G/SPS/GEN/250, 14 May.

WTO (2001c), Ministerial Declaration, Adopted on 14 November 2001, Ministerial Conference, Fourth Session, Doha, 9–14 November, WT/MIN(01)/DEC/1, 20 November.

WTO (2001d), Technical Assistance to Developing Countries, Statement by the European Communities at the Meeting of 14–15 March, Committee on Sanitary and Phytosanitary Measures, G/SPS/GEN/244, 27 April.

WTO (2001e), Implementation-Related Issues and Concerns, Decision of 14 November 2001, Ministerial Conference, Fourth Session, Doha, 9–14 November.

WTO (2003a), Non-Tariff Barrier Notification, Negotiating Group on Market Access, TN/MA/W/25, 28 March.

WTO (2003b), Report of the Analysis on SPS Notifications in 2002, Submission by China, Committee on Sanitary and Phytosanitary Measures, G/SPS/GEN/378, 31 March.

WTO (2003c), IICA's Experience in Implementing the WTO Agreement on the Application of Sanitary And Phytosanitary Measures (SPS Agreement), Information Presented by the Inter-American Institute for Cooperation on Agriculture (IICA), G/SPS/GEN/427, 13 October.

WTO (2003d), Table of Contents of the Inventory of Non-Tariff Measures, Note by the Secretariat, Revision, Negotiating Group on Market Access, TN/MA/S/5/Rev.1, 28 November.

WTO (2004), Special Meeting of the SPS Committee on the Operation of Enquiry Points Held on 31 October 2003, Note by the Secretariat, Committee on Sanitary and Phytosanitary Measures, G/SPS/R/32, 6 February.

WTO (2006a), Trade Policy Review: United States, Minutes of Meeting, Addendum, WT/TPR/M/160/Add.1, 27 September.

WTO (2006b), Update on the Operation of the Standards and Trade Development Facility, Note by the Secretariat, Committee on Sanitary and Phytosanitary Measures, G/SPS/GEN/648, 24 March.

WTO (2006c), Communication from India, Proposal on GATT Article VIII, TN/TF/W/121, 4 July.

WTO (2006d), Communication from India, Proposal on GATT Article X, TN/TF/W/122, 4 July.

WTO (2007a), Trade Policy Review: European Communities, Minutes of Meeting, Addendum, WT/TPR/M/177/Add.1, 30 April.

WTO (2007b), Specific Trade Concerns, Note by the Secretariat, Addendum, Issues Not Considered In 2006, Committee on Sanitary and Phytosanitary Measures, G/SPS/GEN/204/Rev.7/Add.2, 7 February.

WTO (2009), Evaluation of the Standards and Trade Development Facility (STDF), Note by the Secretariat, Committee on Sanitary and Phytosanitary Measures, G/SPS/GEN/899, 2 February.

WTO (2011a), Trade Policy Review, Report by India, Trade Policy Review Body, WT/TPR/G/249, 10 August.

WTO (2011b), Trade Policy Review, India, Record of the Meeting, Addendum, Trade Policy Review Body, 14 and 16 September, WT/TPR/M/249/Add.1, 14 October.

WTO (2011c), Trade Policy Review, India, Record of the Meeting, Addendum, Trade Policy Review Body, 14 and 16 September, WT/TPR/M/249/Add.2, 28 October.

WTO (2012a), SPS Technical Assistance and Training Activities, 1 September 1994 to 31 December 2011, Note by the Secretariat, Revision, Committee On Sanitary And Phytosanitary Measures, G/SPS/GEN/521/Rev.7, 5 March.

WTO (2012b), Update on the Operation of the Standards and Trade Development Facility, Note by the Secretariat, Committee on Sanitary and Phytosanitary Measures, G/SPS/GEN/648, 19 March.

WTO (2012c), Draft Consolidated Negotiating Text, Revision, Negotiating Group on Trade Facilitation, TN/TF/W/165/Rev.12, 8 May.

WTO (2012d), Specific Trade Concerns, Note by the Secretariat, Revision, Committee on Sanitary and Phytosanitary Measures, G/SPS/GEN/204/Rev.12, 2 March.

Zarrilli, S. (1999), *WTO Sanitary* and *Phytosanitary Agreement: Issues* for *Developing Countries*, T.R.A.D.E. Working Paper 3, South Centre.

Index